Sommario

Nomenclatura delle località citate e carta della regione
Alphabetisches Ortsverzeichnis und Übersichtskarte

Inhaltsverzeichnis

3

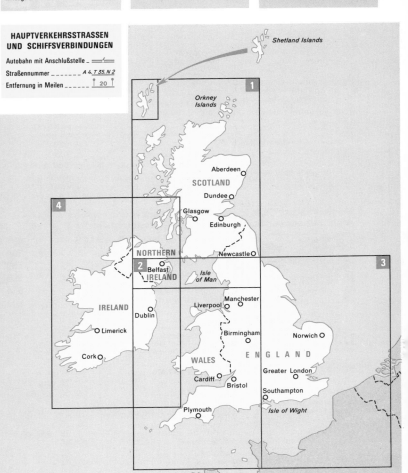

1
SHETLAND ISLANDS
Unst
Yell
Whalsay
Mainland
Scalloway
Lerwick
Kirkwall
Aberdeen
ORKNEY ISLANDS
Westray
Sanday
Rousay
Stronsay
Mainland
Stromness
Kirkwall
Hoy
Scalloway
Thurso
Wick
A 836
A 882
A 9
16
39
58
Brora
Loch Shin
130
Stornoway
Lewis
NORTH MINCH
Tarbert
Ullapool
31
A 835
89
Garve
North Uist
Lochmaddy
Uig
Skye
Portree
57
Kyle of Lochalsh
South Uist
Lochboisdale
Sea of the Hebrides
Armadale
Rhum
Mallaig
Castlebay
Elgin
35
Banff
Fraserburgh
Nairn
39
21
A 98
28
17
Keith
70
Inverness
43
A 82
A 9
A 95
64
A 96
51
Loch Ness
50
40
A 87
Spey
Lerwick
ABERDEEN
Invergarry
Kingussie
25
Dee
A 86
52
A 92
46
Stonehaven
A 830
Fort William
A 9
72
67
A 94
68
Coll
SCOTLAND
Tiree
Mull
46
A 82
52
Loch Tay
A 92
NORTH SEA
Craignure
Oban
41
A 85
DUNDEE
22
A 849
53
A 85
Perth
A 85
17
Lochearnhead
77
St.Andrews
38
49
33
29
A 816
A 83
A 84
A 9
A 91
51
Tarbet
43
M 90
A 915
Colonsay
Stirling
41
Lochgilphead
Kirkcaldy
Dunfermline
Falkirk
Greenock
29
13
Port Askaig
Jura
Tarbert
Skelmorlie
69
39
GLASGOW
EDINBURGH
56
8
M 8
39
Rothesay
Largs
Motherwell
Berwick upon Tweed
Islay
Millport
34
41
A 7
34
Port Ellen
31
A 721
Peebles
Brodick
Ardrossan
M 74
A 702
A 83
63
Galashiels
A 72
45
Arran
51
A 77
Ayr
Abington
17
NORTH CHANNEL
A 698
Hawick
Campbeltown
A 713
A 1
63
60
62
51
35
46
A 702
A 701
43
A 7
A 696
A 77
39
New Galloway
Dumfries
A 74
Esbjerg
Cairnryan
44
14
18
34
A 75
A 69
59
Tynemouth
55
A 75
8
Stranraer
CARLISLE
NEWCASTLE
12
SUNDERLAND
A 2
31
Coleraine
A 26
25
Waterfoot
90
A 6
Ballymena
Larne
70
28
A 8
Liverpool
34
A 596
20
Penrith
43
Lough Neagh
Bangor
Workington
38
49
BELFAST
42
A 66
Keswick
A 66
Darlington
Ballygawley
M 1
Strangford Lough
Whitehaven
A 595
M 6
53
M 1
57
17
A 3
Armagh
Banbridge
ENGLAND
37
52
A 25
Isle of Man
55
Kendal
34
Monaghan
32
N 2
A 1
Newcastle
21
A 1
2
13
A 2
Douglas
Barrow in Furness
A 65
5
Dundalk
12
17
Lancaster
59
Heysham

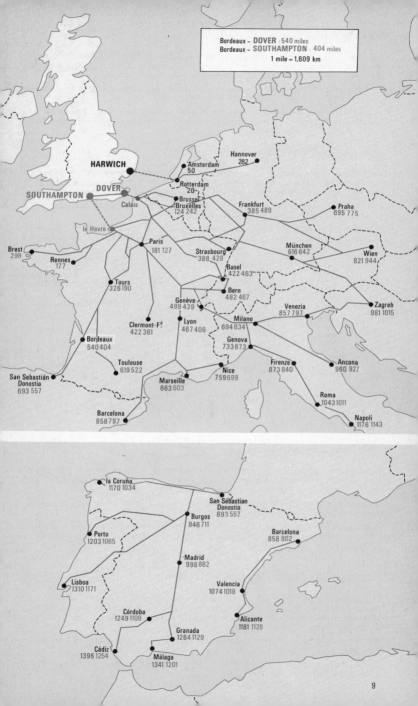

DISTANCES

All distances in this edition are quoted in miles. The distance is given from each town to its neighbours and to the capital of each region as grouped in the guide. Towns appearing in the charts are preceded by a lozenge ◆ in text.

To avoid excessive repetition some distances have only been quoted once — you may therefore have to look under both town headings.

The mileages quoted are not necessarily the lowest but have been based on the roads which afford the best driving conditions and are therefore the most practical.

DISTANCES EN MILES

Pour chaque région traitée, vous trouverez au texte de chacune des localités sa distance par rapport à la capitale et aux villes environnantes. Lorsque ces villes sont celles des tableaux, leur nom est précédé d'un losange noir ◆.

La distance d'une localité à une autre n'est pas toujours répétée aux deux villes intéressées : voyez au texte de l'une ou de l'autre.

Ces distances ne sont pas nécessairement comptées par la route la plus courte mais par la plus pratique, c'est-à-dire celle offrant les meilleures conditions de roulage.

Belfast
250	Cork										
103	154	Dublin							**133 Miles**
50	200	53	Dundalk						Dublin - Sligo
196	122	135	153	Galway					
273	54	189	223	133	Killarney				
204	58	120	154	64	69	Limerick			
70	281	146	98	176	300	231	Londonderry		
68	247	112	64	148	266	197	34	Omagh	
126	200	133	106	90	216	147	86	69	Sligo
132	118	60	82	82	141	72	163	129	95	Tullamore
197	73	96	147	141	112	77	242	208	176	81	Waterford

DISTANZE IN MIGLIA

Per ciascuna delle regioni trattate, troverete nel testo di ogni località la sua distanza dalla capitale e dalle città circostanti. Quando queste città sono comprese nelle tabelle, il loro nome è preceduto da una losanga ◆.

La distanza da una località all'altra non è sempre ripetuta nelle due città interessate : vedere nel testo dell'una o dell'altra.

Le distanze non sono necessariamente calcolate seguendo il percorso più breve, ma vengono stabilite secondo l'itinerario più pratico, che offre cioè le migliori condizioni di viaggio.

ENTFERNUNGSANGABEN IN MEILEN

Die Entfernungen der einzelnen Orte zur Landeshauptstadt und zu den nächstgrößeren Städten in der Umgebung sind im allgemeinen Ortstext angegeben. Die Namen der Städte in der Umgebung, die auf der Tabelle zu finden sind, sind durch eine Raute ◆ gekennzeichnet.

Die Entfernung zweier Städte voneinander können Sie aus den Angaben im Ortstext der einen oder der anderen Stadt ersehen.

Die Entfernungsangaben gelten nicht immer für den kürzesten, sondern für den günstigsten Weg.

DISTANCES BETWEEN MAJOR TOWNS

DISTANCES ENTRE PRINCIPALES VILLES

DISTANZE TRA LE PRINCIPALI CITTÀ

ENTFERNUNGEN ZWISCHEN DEN GRÖSSEREN STÄDTEN

442 Miles

Example	Esempio
Exemple	Beispiel
Edinburgh – Southampton	

Cities (diagonal labels):

Aberdeen · Ayr · Birmingham · Blackpool · Brighton · Bristol · Cambridge · Cardiff · Carlisle · Coventry · Dover · Dumfries · Dundee · Edinburgh · Glasgow · Inverness · Ipswich · Kingston upon Hull · Leeds · Leicester · Liverpool · London · Manchester · Middlesbrough · Newcastle · Norwich · Nottingham · Oban · Oxford · Plymouth · Portsmouth · Sheffield · Southampton · Stoke on Trent · Swansea · Wick

Distance chart (miles) — triangular table; each row lists distances from that city to the cities listed before it:

City	Aberdeen	Ayr	Birmingham	Blackpool	Brighton	Bristol	Cambridge	Cardiff	Carlisle	Coventry	Dover	Dumfries	Dundee	Edinburgh	Glasgow	Inverness	Ipswich	Kingston upon Hull	Leeds	Leicester	Liverpool	London	Manchester	Middlesbrough	Newcastle	Norwich	Nottingham	Oban	Oxford	Plymouth	Portsmouth	Sheffield	Southampton	Stoke on Trent	Swansea
Ayr	196																																		
Birmingham	442	293																																	
Blackpool	336	187	130																																
Brighton	616	467	180	304																															
Bristol	526	377	91	214	157																														
Cambridge	545	396	110	221	166	200																													
Cardiff	242	93	201	117	88	158	259																												
Carlisle	461	148	201	18	158	148	233	219																											
Coventry	221	311	117	84	199	96	120	179	252																										
Dover	67	488	325	408	318	292	337	34	396	179																									
Dumfries	130	59	234	128	59	84	233	127	101	175	394																								
Dundee	107	129	375	269	549	433	173	478	100	319	34	154																							
Edinburgh	553	81	475	385	385	404	277	101	56	121	208	173	63																						
Glasgow	397	35	300	194	474	358	123	403	100	318	127	127	79	46																					
Inverness	366	207	488	362	642	552	319	571	268	487	247	247	134	156	172																				
Ipswich	470	219	274	123	203	54	237	312	90	141	123	160	388	411	579	247																			
Kingston upon Hull	368	56	277	121	208	173	155	141	178	100	301	299	231	254	423	190	126																		
Leeds	558	409	53	121	246	155	317	208	55	317	100	350	157	200	330	486	262	61																	
Leicester	363	214	86	51	260	163	189	122	105	76	188	350	299	223	392	188	96	101	35																
Liverpool	331	182	177	123	319	267	200	286	90	178	354	157	200	327	496	261	95	75	141	130	202														
London	235	150	206	150	208	349	297	208	59	208	173	261	293	392	394	231	61	204	131	107	246	219													
Manchester	527	377	161	248	193	170	225	259	285	149	318	283	200	327	496	188	105	235	117	66	188	159	130												
Middlesbrough	432	282	50	143	149	161	170	190	52	214	173	126	157	276	394	174	174	109	72	95	170	107	227	132											
Newcastle	180	127	193	149	484	248	190	52	43	223	318	43	384	553	289	117	235	26	188	235	132	256	161	41											
Norwich	509	360	63	197	105	88	166	503	148	146	301	460	365	289	458	105	235	109	135	174	109	120	289	258	485										
Nottingham	641	492	206	329	222	236	244	326	116	442	442	273	266	93	326	74	235	135	59	55	120	256	258	326	485	120									
Oban	604	455	329	222	124	287	161	161	65	574	574	475	368	118	63	367	289	153	224	170	254	485	153	326	390	390	467								
Oxford	418	268	148	89	100	92	232	162	149	537	537	116	188	289	324	175	255	44	149	149	52	85	105	412	485	264	199	98							
Plymouth	583	434	232	105	232	79	342	87	177	463	463	475	350	444	462	175	253	41	105	44	376	182	254	412	541	190	177	264	194						
Portsmouth	397	248	180	127	180	128	342	64	246	516	516	189	375	441	609	251	263	87	162	162	188	137	320	346	541	190	177	599	85	161					
Sheffield	542	392	227	130	227	133	156	85	271	189	330	186	256	423	568	255	95	58	41	41	105	162	41	177	355	192	192	562	182	245	53	233			
Southampton	233	333	82	133	82	40	149	113	208	192	475	399	295	186	399	192	184	189	59	57	135	215	350	342	500	192	177	187	64	208	21	187			
Stoke on Trent	233																																233		
Swansea	542	392	229	236	158	40	300	65	227	537	537	475	400	568	568	275	158	143	179	197	197	225	295	342	500	192	192	187	158	225	158	158	175		
Wick	233	333	594	488	768	678	652	697	613	789	789	260	282	126	549	298	705	518	710	622	710	515	483	387	584	679	584	467	793	756	735	679	549	694	

Discover
the guide...

To make the most of the guide know how to use it. The Michelin Guide offers in addition to the selection of hotels and restaurants a wide range of information to help you on your travels.

The key to the guide

...is the explanatory chapters which follow.
Remember that the same symbol and character whether in red or black or in bold or light type, have different meanings.

The selection of hotels and restaurants

This book is not an exhaustive list of all hotels but a selection which has been limited on purpose. The final choice is based on regular on the spot enquiries and visits. These visits are the occasion for examining attentively the comments and opinions of our readers.

Town plans

These indicate with precision pedestrian and shopping streets ; major through routes in built up areas ; exact location of hotels whether they be on main or side streets ; post offices ; tourist information centres ; the principal historic buildings and other tourist sights.

For your car

In the text of many towns is to be found a list of agents for the main car manufacturers with their addresses and telephone numbers. Therefore even while travelling you can have your car serviced or repaired.

Your views or comments concerning the above subjects or any others, are always welcome. Your letter will be answered.

Thank you in advance.

Michelin Tyre Public Limited Company
Tourism Department
Davy House, Lyon Road, HARROW
Middlesex HA1 2DQ

Bibendum wishes you a pleasant journey.

Choosing your hotel or restaurant

We have classified the hotels and restaurants with the travelling motorist in mind. In each category they have been listed in order of preference.

CLASS, STANDARD OF COMFORT

🏨🏨🏨	Luxury in the traditional style	XXXXX
🏨🏨	Top class comfort	XXXX
🏨🏨	Very comfortable	XXX
🏨	Good average	XX
🏨	Quite comfortable	X
☆	Modest comfort	
↑	Other recommended accommodation, at moderate prices	
without rest.	The hotel has no restaurant	
	The restaurant has bedrooms	with rm

HOTEL FACILITIES

Hotels in categories 🏨🏨🏨, 🏨🏨, 🏨🏨, usually have every comfort and exchange facilities ; details are not repeated under each hotel.

In other categories, we indicate the facilities available, however, they may not be found in each room.

30 rm	Number of rooms
🛗	Lift (elevator)
▤	Air conditioning
TV	Television in room
🛏wc 🛏	Private bathroom with toilet, private bathroom without toilet
🚿wc 🚿	Private shower with toilet, private shower without toilet
☏	Telephone in room : outside calls connected by the operator
☎	Telephone in room : direct dialling for outside calls
♿	Rooms accessible to the physically handicapped
⤵ 🏊	Outdoor or indoor swimming pool
🌴	Garden
🎾	Hotel tennis court
🏌	Golf course and number of holes
🎣	Fishing available to hotel guests. A charge may be made
🏛	Equipped conference hall (minimum seating : 25)
🚗	Garage available (usually charged for)
Ⓟ	Car park
🐕	Dogs are not allowed
	Where dogs are allowed, they are generally accepted only in bedrooms
May-October	Dates when open, as indicated by the hotelier
season	Probably open for the season - precise dates not available
	Where no date or season is shown, establishments are open all year round
LL35 0SB	Postal code
(T.H.F.)	Hotel Group *(See list at end of the Guide)*

13

AMENITY

Your stay in certain hotels will be sometimes particularly agreeable or restful.

Such a quality may derive from the hotel's fortunate setting, its decor, welcoming atmosphere and service.

Such establishments are distinguished in the guide by the symbols shown below.

🏨🏨🏨 ... 🏠	Pleasant hotels
XXXXX ... X	Pleasant restaurants
« Park »	Particularly attractive feature
🕭	Very quiet or quiet, secluded hotel
🕭	Quiet hotel
≤ sea	Exceptional view
≤	Interesting or extensive view

By consulting the maps preceding each geographical area you will find it easier to locate them.

We do not claim to have indicated all the pleasant, very quiet or quiet, secluded hotels which exist.

Our enquiries continue. You can help us by letting us know your opinions and discoveries.

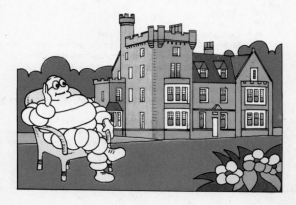

CUISINE

The stars for good cooking

We indicate by ❀, ❀❀ or ❀❀❀, establishments where the standard of cooking, whether particular to the country or foreign, deserves to be brought especially to the attention of our readers (see list p. 48 and the maps preceding each geographical area).

In the text of these establishments we show some of the dishes typical of their style of cooking.

❀ **An especially good restaurant in its class**

The star indicates a good place to stop on your journey.

But beware of comparing the star given to a " de luxe " establishment with accordingly high prices, with that of a simpler one, where for a lesser sum one can still eat a meal of quality.

❀❀ **Excellent cooking, worth a detour**

Specialities and wines of first class quality... Do not expect such meals to be cheap.

❀❀❀ **Some of the best cuisine, worth a journey**

Superb food, fine wines, faultless service, elegant surroundings... One will pay accordingly !

M **The red « M »**

Whilst appreciating the quality of the cooking in restaurants with a star, you may, however, wish to find some serving a perhaps less elaborate but nonetheless always carefully prepared meal.

Certain restaurants seem to us to answer this requirement. We bring them to your attention by marking them with a red « M » in the text of the Guide.

Alcoholic beverages-conditions of sale

The sale of alcoholic drinks is governed in Great Britain and Ireland by licensing laws which vary greatly from country to country.

Allowing for local variances, hotel bars and public houses close during the afternoon and after 11 pm. Hotel residents, however, may buy drinks outside the permitted hours at the discretion of the hotelier.

Children under the age of 14 are not allowed in bars.

Choosing your hotel or restaurant

PRICES

Valid for late 1986, the rates shown may be revised if the cost of living changes to any great extent. They are given in the currency of the country. In any event they should be regarded as basic charges.

Your recommendation is self-evident if you always walk into a hotel guide in hand.

Hotels and restaurants whose names appear in bold type have supplied us with their charges in detail and undertaken, on their own responsability, to abide by them, wherever possible, if the traveller is in possession of this year's guide.

If you think you have been overcharged, let us know. Where no rates are shown it is best to enquire about terms in advance.

Prices are given in £ sterling, except for the Republic of Ireland (Punts)

Where no mention s., t. or st. is shown, prices are subject to the addition of service charge, V.A.T., or both (V.A.T. does not apply in the Channel Islands).

Meals

M 9.00/12.00	**Set meals** — Lunch 9.00, dinner 12.00 — including cover charge, where applicable
M 13.00/15.00	See page 15
s. t.	Service only included. — V.A.T. included
st.	Service and V.A.T. included
🍾 5.00	Price of 1/2 bottle or carafe of ordinary wine
M a la carte 14.00/18.00	**A la carte meals** — The prices represent the range of charges for a plain to an elaborate 3 course meal and include a cover charge where applicable
⊆ 5.00	Charge for full cooked breakfast (i.e. not included in the room rate) Continental breakfast may be available at a lower rate

Rooms

rm 25.00/45.00	Lowest price 25.00 for a comfortable single and highest price 45.00 for the best double room (including bathroom when applicable)
rm ⊆ 30.00/50.00	Full cooked breakfast is included the price of the room
suites 100.00/200.00	Lowest and highest prices for a suite comprising bedroom, bathroom and sitting room

Short Breaks (see p. 17)

SB 50.00/60.00	Prices indicated are lowest and highest per person for two nights
◰ AE Ⓞ VISA	Principal **credit cards** accepted by establishments : Access — American Express — Diners Club — Visa (Barclaycard)

16

Choosing your hotel or restaurant

A FEW USEFUL DETAILS

Meals

Ask for menus including set meals and a la carte menus with the prices clearly marked if they are not produced automatically.

Hotels

Breakfast is often included in the price of the room, even if it is not required.

Special Rate for "Short Breaks"

Many hotels now offer a special rate for a stay of two nights which includes dinner, room and breakfast usually for a minimum of two people.
It is always advisable to agree terms in advance with the hotelier.

Reservations

Hotels : Reserving in advance, when possible, is advised. Ask the hotelier to provide you, in his letter of confirmation, with all terms and conditions applicable to your reservation.

In seaside resorts especially, reservations usually begin and end on Saturdays.

Certain hoteliers require the payment of a deposit. This constitutes a mutual guarantee of good faith. Deposits, except in special cases, may amount to 10 % of the estimated hotel account.

Restaurants : it is strongly recommended always to book your table well ahead in order to avoid the disappointment of a refusal.

Animals

It is forbidden to bring domestic animals (dogs, cats...) into Great Britain and Ireland.

CAR, TYRES

In the text of many towns are to be found the names of garages or motor agents many of which offer a breakdown service.

The wearing of seat belts is obligatory for drivers and front seat passengers in Great Britain and Ireland.

Motoring organisations

The major motoring organisations in Great Britain are the Automobile Association and the Royal Automobile Club. Each provides services in varying degrees for non-resident members of affiliated clubs.

AUTOMOBILE ASSOCIATION
Fanum House
BASINGSTOKE, Hants., RG21 2EA
☎ (0256) 20123

ROYAL AUTOMOBILE CLUB
RAC House, Lansdowne Rd,
CROYDON, Surrey CR9 2JA
☎ (01) 686 2525

Seeing a town and its surroundings

SIGHTS

Star-rating

★★★	Worth a journey
★★	Worth a detour
★	Interesting
AC	Admission charge

Finding the sights

See	Sights in town
Envir.	On the outskirts
Exc.	In the surrounding area
N, S, E, W	The sight lies north, south, east or west of the town
A 22	Go by road A 22, indicated by the same symbol on the Guide map
2 m.	Mileage

TOWNS

✉ York	Post office serving the town
☎ 0225 Bath	STD dialling code (name of exchange indicated only when different from name of the town). Omit 0 when dialling from abroad
401 M 27, ⑩	Michelin map and co-ordinates or fold
West Country G.	See the Michelin Green Guide England : The West Country
pop. 1,057	Population
ECD : Wednesday	Early closing day (shops close at midday)
BX **A**	Letters giving the location of a place on the town map
🏌️18	Golf course and number of holes (visitors unrestricted)
☀,	Panoramic view, viewpoint
✈️	Airport
🚗 ☎ 218	Place with a motorail connection ; further information from telephone number listed
⚓	Shipping line
⛴	Passenger transport only *see list of companies at the end of the Guide*
🛈	Tourist Information Centre

Standard Time

In winter standard time throughout the British Isles is Greenwich Mean Time (G.M.T.). In summer British clocks are advanced by one hour to give British Summer Time (B.S.T.). The actual dates are announced annually but always occur over weekends in March and October.

Seeing a town and its surroundings

TOWN PLANS

Roads

Motorway, dual carriageway
   Interchange : complete, limited, number
Major through route
One-way street - Unsuitable for traffic
Pedestrian street
Pasteur   P Shopping street - Car park
Gateway - Street passing under arch - Tunnel
Low headroom (16'6" max.) on major through routes
Station and railway
Car ferry - Lever bridge

Sights — Hotels — Restaurants

Place of interest and its main entrance
Interesting place of worship :
   Cathedral, church or chapel
Windmill - Other sights
Castle - Ruins
B Reference letter locating a sight
Hotel, restaurant with reference letter

Various signs

Tourist Information Centre - Michelin Branch
Hospital - Mosque - Synagogue
Garden, park, wood - Cemetery - Cross
Stadium - Golf course
View - Panorama
Airport - Racecourse
Funicular - Cable-car
Monument, statue - Fountain
Pleasure boat harbour - Lighthouse
Ferry services : passengers and cars
Public buildings located by letter :
   County Council Offices
H M T   Town Hall - Museum - Theatre
POL.   Police (in large towns police headquarters)
U   University, colleges
Main post office with poste restante, telephone
Golf course (with restrictions for visitors)
Communications tower or mast
Underground station

London

BRENT   SOHO Borough - Area
Borough boundary - Area boundary

19

Découvrez
le guide...

et sachez l'utiliser pour en tirer le meilleur profit. Le Guide Michelin n'est pas seulement une liste de bonnes tables ou d'hôtels, c'est aussi une multitude d'informations pour faciliter vos voyages.

La clé du Guide

Elle vous est donnée par les pages explicatives qui suivent.

Sachez qu'un même symbole, qu'un même caractère, en rouge ou en noir, en maigre ou en gras, n'a pas tout à fait la même signification.

La sélection des hôtels et des restaurants

Ce Guide n'est pas un répertoire complet des ressources hôtelières, il en présente seulement une sélection volontairement limitée. Cette sélection est établie après visites et enquêtes effectuées régulièrement sur place. C'est lors de ces visites que les avis et observations de nos lecteurs sont examinés.

Les plans de ville

Ils indiquent avec précision : les rues piétonnes et commerçantes, comment traverser ou contourner l'agglomération, où se situent les hôtels (sur de grandes artères ou à l'écart), où se trouvent la poste, l'office de tourisme, les grands monuments, les principaux sites, etc.

Pour votre véhicule

Au texte de la plupart des localités figure une liste de représentants des grandes marques automobiles avec leur adresse et leur numéro d'appel téléphonique. En route, vous pouvez ainsi faire entretenir ou dépanner votre voiture, si nécessaire.

Sur tous ces points et aussi sur beaucoup d'autres, nous souhaitons vivement connaître votre avis. N'hésitez pas à nous écrire, nous vous répondrons.

Merci par avance.

Services de Tourisme Michelin
46, avenue de Breteuil, 75341 PARIS CEDEX 07

Bibendum vous souhaite d'agréables voyages.

Le choix d'un hôtel, d'un restaurant

Notre classement est établi à l'usage de l'automobiliste de passage. Dans chaque catégorie les établissements sont cités par ordre de préférence.

CLASSE ET CONFORT

🏨	Grand luxe et tradition	XXXXX
🏨	Grand confort	XXXX
🏨	Très confortable	XXX
🏨	De bon confort	XX
🏠	Assez confortable	X
⌂	Simple mais convenable	
⌂	Autre ressource hôtelière conseillée, à prix modérés	
without rest.	L'hôtel n'a pas de restaurant	
	Le restaurant possède des chambres	with rm

L'INSTALLATION

Les hôtels des catégories 🏨, 🏨, 🏨, possèdent tout le confort et assurent en général le change, les symboles de détail n'apparaissent donc pas au texte de ces hôtels.

Dans les autres catégories, les éléments de confort indiqués n'existent le plus souvent que dans certaines chambres.

30 rm	Nombre de chambres
🛗	Ascenseur
🟦	Air conditionné
📺	Télévision dans la chambre
🛁wc🛁	Salle de bains et wc privés, Salle de bains privée sans wc
🚿wc🚿	Douche et wc privés, Douche privée sans wc
📞	Téléphone dans la chambre relié par standard
☎	Téléphone dans la chambre, direct avec l'extérieur (cadran)
♿	Chambres accessibles aux handicapés physiques
🏊 🏊	Piscine : de plein air ou couverte
🌳	Jardin de repos
✂	Tennis à l'hôtel
⛳18	Golf et nombre de trous
🎣	Pêche ouverte aux clients de l'hôtel (éventuellement payant)
🏛	Salles de conférences (25 places minimum)
🚗	Garage
🅿	Parc à voitures
🐕❌	Accès interdit aux chiens
	Lorsque les chiens sont acceptés, ils ne le sont que dans les chambres.
May-October	Période d'ouverture communiquée par l'hôtelier
season	Ouverture probable en saison mais dates non précisées
	Les établissements ouverts toute l'année sont ceux pour lesquels aucune mention n'est indiquée.
LL35 OSB	Code postal de l'établissement
(T.H.F.)	Chaîne hôtelière (voir liste en fin de guide)

L'AGRÉMENT

Le séjour dans certains hôtels se révèle parfois particulièrement agréable ou reposant.

Cela peut tenir d'une part au caractère de l'édifice, au décor original, au site, à l'accueil et aux services qui sont proposés, d'autre part à la tranquillité des lieux.

De tels établissements se distinguent dans le guide par les symboles rouges indiqués ci-après.

🏰 ... 🏠	Hôtels agréables
XXXXX ... X	Restaurants agréables
« Park »	Élément particulièrement agréable
🐝	Hôtel très tranquille ou isolé et tranquille
🐝	Hôtel tranquille
≤ sea	Vue exceptionnelle
≤	Vue intéressante ou étendue

Consultez les cartes placées au début de chacune des régions traitées dans ce guide, elles faciliteront vos recherches.

Nous ne prétendons pas avoir signalé tous les hôtels agréables, ni tous ceux qui sont tranquilles ou isolés et tranquilles.

Nos enquêtes continuent. Vous pouvez les faciliter en nous faisant connaître vos observations et vos découvertes.

LA TABLE

Les étoiles :

Nous marquons par ✿, ✿✿ ou ✿✿✿ les établissements dont la qualité de la table nous a paru mériter d'être signalée spécialement à l'attention de nos lecteurs, qu'il s'agisse de cuisines propres au pays ou étrangères (voir liste p. 48).

Au texte de ces établissements nous indiquons quelques plats caractéristiques du genre de cuisine de la maison.

✿ **Une très bonne table dans sa catégorie**

L'étoile marque une bonne étape sur votre itinéraire.

Mais ne comparez pas l'étoile d'un établissement de luxe à prix élevés avec celle d'une petite maison où à prix raisonnables, on sert également une cuisine de qualité.

✿✿ **Table excellente, mérite un détour**

Spécialités et vins de choix, attendez-vous à une dépense en rapport.

✿✿✿ **Une des meilleures tables, vaut le voyage**

Table merveilleuse, grands vins, service impeccable, cadre élégant... Prix en conséquence.

M **Le « M » rouge**

Tout en appréciant les tables à « étoiles », on peut souhaiter trouver sur sa route un repas plus simple mais toujours de préparation soignée. Certaines maisons nous ont paru répondre à cette préoccupation.

Un « M » rouge les signale à votre attention dans le texte de ce guide.

La vente de boissons alcoolisées

En Grande-Bretagne et en Irlande, la vente de boissons alcoolisées est soumise à des lois pouvant varier d'une région à l'autre.

D'une façon générale, les bars situés dans les hôtels ainsi que les pubs ferment l'après-midi et après 23 heures, les horaires d'ouverture pouvant varier localement.

Néanmoins, l'hôtelier a toujours la possibilité de servir, à sa clientèle, des boissons alcoolisées en dehors des heures légales.

Les enfants au-dessous de 14 ans n'ont pas accès aux bars.

LES PRIX

Les prix que nous indiquons dans ce guide ont été établis en fin d'année 1986. Ils sont susceptibles d'être modifiés si le coût de la vie subit des variations importantes. Ils doivent, en tout cas, être considérés comme des prix de base.

Entrez à l'hôtel le Guide à la main, vous montrerez ainsi qu'il vous conduit là en confiance.

Les hôtels et restaurants figurent en gros caractères lorsque les hôteliers nous ont donné tous leurs prix et se sont engagés, sous leur propre responsabilité, à les appliquer aux touristes de passage porteurs de notre guide.

Prévenez-nous de toute majoration paraissant injustifiée. Si aucun prix n'est indiqué, nous vous conseillons de demander les conditions.

Les prix sont indiqués en livres sterling (1 L = 100 pence), sauf en République d'Irlande (Punts).

Lorsque les mentions s.t., ou st. ne figurent pas, les prix indiqués peuvent être majorés d'un pourcentage pour le service, la T.V.A. ou les deux. (La T.V.A. n'est pas appliquée dans les Channel Islands).

Repas

M 9.00/12.00	**Repas à prix fixe** — Déjeuner 9.00, dîner 12.00 y compris le couvert éventuellement
M 13.00/15.00	Voir page 23
s. t.	Service compris — T.V.A. comprise
st.	Service et T.V.A. compris (prix nets)
▯ 5.00	Prix de la 1/2 bouteille ou carafe de vin ordinaire
M a la carte 14.00/18.00	**Repas à la carte** — Le 1er prix correspond à un repas simple mais soigné, comprenant : petite entrée, plat du jour garni, dessert. Le 2e prix concerne un repas plus complet, comprenant : hors-d'œuvre, plat principal, fromage ou dessert. Ces prix s'entendent couvert compris
⊆ 5.00	Prix du petit déjeuner à l'anglaise, s'il n'est pas compris dans celui de la chambre. Un petit déjeuner continental peut être obtenu à moindre prix

Chambres

rm 25.00/45.00	Prix minimum 25.00 d'une chambre pour une personne et prix maximum 45.00 de la plus belle chambre occupée par deux personnes
rm ⊆ 30.00/50.00	Le prix du petit déjeuner à l'anglaise est inclus dans le prix de la chambre
suites 100.00/200.00	Prix minimum et maximum d'un appartement comprenant chambre, salle de bains et salon

"Short Breaks" (voir p. 25)

SB 50.00/60.00	Prix minimum et maximum par personne pour un séjour de deux nuits
▨ ▨ ▨ ▨	Principales **cartes de crédit** acceptées par l'établissement : Access (Eurocard) — American Express — Diners Club — Visa (Carte Bleue)

QUELQUES PRÉCISIONS UTILES

Au restaurant

Réclamez les menus à prix fixes et la carte chiffrée s'ils ne vous sont pas présentés spontanément.

A l'hôtel

Le prix du petit déjeuner, même s'il n'est pas consommé, est souvent inclus dans le prix de la chambre.

Conditions spéciales pour "Short Breaks"

De nombreux hôtels proposent des conditions avantageuses pour un séjour de deux nuits ou "Short Break". Ce forfait comprend la chambre, le dîner et le petit déjeuner, en général pour un minimum de deux personnes.

Réservations

Hôtels : Chaque fois que possible, la réservation préalable est souhaitable. Demandez à l'hôtelier de vous fournir dans sa lettre d'accord toutes précisions utiles sur la réservation et les conditions de séjour. Dans les stations balnéaires en particulier, les réservations s'appliquent généralement à des séjours partant d'un samedi à l'autre.

A toute demande écrite il est conseillé de joindre un coupon-réponse international.

Certains hôteliers demandent parfois le versement d'arrhes. Il s'agit d'un dépôt-garantie qui engage l'hôtelier comme le client. Sauf accord spécial le montant des arrhes peut être fixé à 10 % du montant total estimé.

Restaurants : il est vivement recommandé de réserver sa table aussi longtemps que possible à l'avance, de façon à éviter le désagrément d'un refus.

Animaux

L'introduction d'animaux domestiques (chiens, chats…) est interdite en Grande Bretagne et en Irlande.

LA VOITURE, LES PNEUS

Au texte de la plupart des localités figure une liste des garagistes ou concessionnaires automobiles pouvant, éventuellement, vous aider en cas de panne.

En Grande Bretagne et en Irlande, le port de la ceinture de sécurité est obligatoire pour le conducteur et le passager avant.

Automobile Clubs

Les principales organisations de secours automobile dans le pays sont l'Automobile Association et le Royal Automobile Club, toutes deux offrant certains de leurs services aux membres de clubs affiliés.

AUTOMOBILE ASSOCIATION
Fanum House
BASINGSTOKE, Hants., RG21 2EA
✆ (0256) 20123

ROYAL AUTOMOBILE CLUB
RAC House, Lansdowne RD
CROYDON, Surrey CR9 2JA
✆ (01) 686 2525

Pour visiter une ville et ses environs

LES CURIOSITÉS

Intérêt

★★★	Vaut le voyage
★★	Mérite un détour
★	Intéressant
AC	Entrée payante

Situation

See	Dans la ville
Envir.	Aux environs de la ville
Exc.	Excursions dans la région
N, S, E, W	La curiosité est située : au Nord, au Sud, à l'Est, à l'Ouest
A 22	On s'y rend par la route A 22, repérée par le même signe sur le plan du Guide
2 m.	Distance en miles

LES VILLES

⊠ York	Bureau de poste desssservant la localité
✿ 0225 Bath	Indicatif téléphonique interurbain suivi, si nécessaire, de la localité de rattachement (De l'étranger, ne pas composer le 0)
401 M 27, ⑩	Numéro des cartes Michelin et carroyage ou numéro du pli
West Country G.	Voir le guide vert Michelin England : The West Country
pop. 1,057	Population
ECD : Wednesday	Jour de fermeture des magasins (après-midi seulement)
BX **A**	Lettres repérant un emplacement sur le plan
🏌18	Golf et nombre de trous
✳, ≼	Panorama, point de vue
✈	Aéroport
🚗 ☏ 218	Localité desservie par train-auto. Renseignements au numéro de téléphone indiqué
⚓	Transports maritimes
⚓	Transports maritimes (pour passagers seulement) *Voir liste des compagnies en fin de guide*
🛈	Information touristique

Heure légale

Les visiteurs devront tenir compte de l'heure officielle en Grande Bretagne : une heure de retard sur l'heure française.

LES PLANS

Voirie

Autoroute, route à chaussées séparées
　　échangeur : complet, partiel, numéro
Grande voie de circulation
Sens unique - Rue impraticable
Rue piétonne
Pasteur　P　Rue commerçante - Parc de stationnement
Porte - Passage sous voûte - Tunnel
Passage bas (inférieur à 16'6'') sur les grandes voies de circulation
Gare et voie ferrée
F B　Bac pour autos - Pont mobile

Curiosités — Hôtels Restaurants

Bâtiment intéressant et entrée principale
Édifice religieux intéressant :
　　Cathédrale, église ou chapelle
Moulin à vent - Curiosités diverses
Château - Ruines
B　Lettre identifiant une curiosité
Hôtel, restaurant. Lettre les identifiant

Signes divers

AGENCE MICHELIN　Information touristique - Agence Michelin
Hôpital - Mosquée - Synagogue
Jardin, parc, bois - Cimetière - Calvaire
Stade - Golf
Aéroport - Hippodrome - Vue - Panorama
Funiculaire - Téléphérique, télécabine
Monument, statue - Fontaine - Port de plaisance - Phare
Transport par bateau :
　　passagers et voitures
Bâtiment public repéré par une lettre :
C　　Bureau de l'Administration du comté
H　M　T　Hôtel de ville - Musée - Théâtre
POL.　U　Police (commissariat central) - Université, grande école
Bureau principal de poste restante, téléphone
Golf (réservé)
Tour ou pylône de télécommunications
Station de métro

Londres

BRENT　SOHO　Nom d'arrondissement (borough) - de quartier (area)
Limite de « borough » - d' « area »

Scoprite la guida...

e sappiatela utilizzare per trarre il miglior vantaggio. La Guida Michelin è un elenco dei migliori alberghi e ristoranti, naturalmente. Ma anche una serie di utili informazioni per i Vostri viaggi !

La " chiave "

Leggete le pagine che seguono e comprenderete !
Sapete che uno stesso simbolo o una stessa parola in rosso o in nero, in carattere magro o grasso, non ha lo stesso significato ?

La selezione degli alberghi e ristoranti

Attenzione ! La guida non elenca tutte le risorse alberghiere. E' il risultato di una selezione, volontariamente limitata, stabilita in seguito a visite ed inchieste effettuate sul posto. E, durante queste visite, amici lettori, vengono tenute in evidenza le Vs. critiche ed i Vs. apprezzamenti !

Le piante di città

Indicano con precisione : strade pedonali e commerciali, il modo migliore per attraversare od aggirare il centro, l'esatta ubicazione degli alberghi e ristoranti citati, della posta centrale, dell'ufficio informazioni turistiche, dei monumenti più importanti e poi altre e altre ancora utili informazioni per Voi !

Per la Vs. automobile

Nel testo di molte località sono elencati gli indirizzi delle principali marche automobilistiche. Così, in caso di necessità, saprete dove trovare il « medico » per la Vs. vettura.

Su tutti questi punti e su altri ancora, gradiremmo conoscere il Vs. parere. Scriveteci e non mancheremo di risponderVi !

Michelin Tyre Public Limited Company
Tourism Department
Davy House, Lyon Road, HARROW
Middlesex HA1 2DQ

Grazie e buon viaggio.

La scelta di un albergo, di un ristorante

La nostra classificazione è stabilita ad uso dell'automobilista di passaggio. In ogni categoria, gli esercizi vengono citati in ordine di preferenza.

CLASSE E CONFORT

🏨🏨	Gran lusso e tradizione	XXXXX
🏨🏨	Gran confort	XXXX
🏛🏛	Molto confortevole	XXX
🏛🏛	Di buon confort	XX
🏛	Abbastanza confortevole	X
⚘	Semplice ma conveniente	
⌂	Altra risorsa, consigliata per prezzi contenuti	
without rest.	L'albergo non ha ristorante	
	Il ristorante dispone di camere	with rm

INSTALLAZIONI

I 🏨🏨, 🏨🏨, 🏛🏛 offrono ogni confort ed effettuano generalmente il cambio di valute ; per questi alberghi non specifichiamo quindi il dettaglio delle installazioni.

Nelle altre categorie indichiamo gli elementi di confort esistenti, alcune camere possono talvolta esserne sprovviste.

30 rm	Numero di camere
🛗	Ascensore
▤	Aria condizionata
TV	Televisione in camera
🛁wc 🛁	Bagno e wc privati, bagno privato senza wc
🚿wc 🚿	Doccia e wc privati, doccia privata senza wc
☏	Telefono in camera collegato con il centralino
☎	Telefono in camera comunicante direttamente con l'esterno
🚹	Camere d'agevole accesso per i minorati fisici
🏊 🏊	Piscina : all'aperto, coperta
🌿	Giardino da riposo
🎾	Tennis appartenente all'albergo
🏌18	Golf e numero di buche
🎣	Pesca aperta ai clienti dell'albergo (eventualmente a pagamento)
🏛	Sale per conferenze (minimo 25 posti)
🚗	Garage
P	Parcheggio
🐕	E' vietato l'accesso ai cani
	Se i cani sono accetati, lo sono soltanto nelle camere.
May-October	Periodo di apertura comunicato dall'albergatore
season	Possibile apertura in stagione, ma periodo non precisato.
	Gli esercizi senza tali indicazioni sono aperti tutto l'anno.
LL35 0SB	Codice postale dell'esercizio
(T.H.F.)	Catena alberghiera (Vedere la lista alla fine della Guida)

AMENITÀ

Il soggiorno in alcuni alberghi si rivela talvolta particolarmente ameno o riposante.

Ciò può dipendere sia dalle caratteristiche dell'edificio, dalle decorazioni non comuni, dalla sua posizione, dall'accoglienza e dai servizi offerti, sia dalla tranquillità dei luoghi.

Questi esercizi sono così contraddistinti :

🏠🏠🏠 ... 🏠	Alberghi ameni
XXXXX ... X	Ristoranti ameni
« Park »	Un particolare piacevole
🦢	Albergo molto tranquillo o isolato e tranquillo
🦢	Albergo tranquillo
⩽ sea	Vista eccezionale
⩽	Vista interessante o estesa

Consultate le carte che precedono ciascuna delle regioni trattate nella guida : sarete facilitati nelle vostre ricerche.

Non abbiamo la pretesa di aver segnalato tutti gli alberghi ameni, nè tutti quelli molto tranquilli o isolati e tranquilli.

Le nostre ricerche continuano. Le potrete agevolare facendoci conoscere le vostre osservazioni e le vostre scoperte.

LA TAVOLA

Le stelle di ottima tavola

Abbiamo contraddistinto con ❀, ❀❀ o ❀❀❀ quegli esercizi che, a nostro parere, meritano di essere segnalati alla vostra attenzione per la qualità della cucina, che può essere tipicamente nazionale o d'importazione (vedere p. 48).

Nel testo di questi esercizi indichiamo alcuni piatti tipici della cucina della casa.

❀   **Un'ottima tavola nella sua categoria.**

La stella indica una tappa gastronomica sul vostro itinerario.

Non mettete però a confronto la stella di un esercizio di lusso, dai prezzi elevati, con quella di un piccolo esercizio dove, a prezzi ragionevoli, viene offerta una cucina di qualità.

❀❀   **Tavola eccellente : merita una deviazione.**

Specialità e vini scelti... Aspettatevi una spesa in proporzione.

❀❀❀   **Una delle migliori tavole : vale il viaggio.**

Tavola meravigliosa, grandi vini, servizio impeccabile, ambientazione accurata... Prezzi conformi.

M   **La « M » rossa**

Pur apprezzando le tavole a « stella », si desidera alle volte consumare un pasto più semplice ma sempre accuratamente preparato.

Alcuni esercizi ci son parsi rispondenti a tale esigenza e sono contraddistinti nella guida da una « M » in rosso.

La vendita di bevande alcoliche

In Gran Bretagna e Irlanda la vendita di bevande alcoliche è soggetta a leggi che possono variare da una regione all'altra.

Generalmente i bar degli alberghi, così come i pubs, chiudono il pomeriggio e dopo le ore 23.00 ; gli orari d'apertura possono variare di località in località.

L'albergatore ha tuttavia la possibilità di servire alla clientela bevande alcoliche anche oltre le ore legali.

Ai ragazzi inferiori ai 14 anni è vietato l'accesso ai bar.

La scelta di un albergo, di un ristorante

I PREZZI

Questi prezzi, redatti alla fine dell'anno 1986, possono venire modificati qualora il costo della vita subisca notevoli variazioni. Essi debbono comunque essere considerati come prezzi base.

Entrate nell'albergo o nel ristorante con la Guida alla mano, dimostrando in tal modo la fiducia in chi vi ha indirizzato.

Gli alberghi e ristoranti figurano in carattere grassetto quando gli albergatori ci hanno comunicato tutti i loro prezzi e si sono impegnati, sotto la propria responsabilità, ad applicarli ai turisti di passaggio in possesso della nostra pubblicazione.

Segnalateci eventuali maggiorazioni che vi sembrino ingiustificate. Quando i prezzi non sono indicati, vi consigliamo di chiedere preventivamente le condizioni.

I prezzi sono indicati in lire sterline (1 £ = 100 pence) ad eccezione per la Repubblica d'Irlanda (Punts).

Quando non figurano le lettere **s.**, **t.**, o **st.** i prezzi indicati possono essere maggiorati per il servizio o per l'I.V.A. o per entrambi. (L'I.V.A. non viene applicata nelle Channel Islands).

Pasti

M 9.00/12.00	**Prezzo fisso** — Pranzo 9.00, cena 12.00 compreso il coperto se del caso
Ⅿ 13.00/15.00	Vedere p. 31
s. t.	Servizio compreso. — I.V.A. compresa
st.	Servizio ed I.V.A. compresi (prezzi netti)
🍶 5.00	Prezzo della mezza bottiglia o di una caraffa di vino
M a la carte 14.00/18.00	**Alla carta** — Il 1° prezzo corrisponde ad un pasto semplice comprendente : primo piatto, piatto del giorno con contorno, dessert. Il 2° prezzo corrisponde ad un pasto più completo comprendente : antipasto, piatto principale, formaggio e dessert Questi prezzi comprendono, se del caso, il coperto
⌑ 5.00	Prezzo della prima colazione inglese se non è compreso nel prezzo della camera Una prima colazione continentale può essere ottenuta a minor prezzo

Camere

rm 25.00/45.00	Prezzo minimo 25.00 per una camera singola e prezzo massimo 45.00 per la camera più bella per due persone
rm ⌑ 30.00/50.00	Il prezzo della prima colazione inglese è compreso nel prezzo della camera
suites 100.00/200.00	Prezzo minimo e massimo per un appartamento comprendente camera, bagno e salone

"Short Breaks" (vedere p. 33)

SB 50.00/60.00	Prezzo minimo e massimo per persona per un soggiorno di due notti
🔲 AE ⦿ VISA	Principali **carte di credito** accettate da un albergo o ristorante : Access (MasterCard) — American Express — Diners Club — Visa (BankAmericard)

QUALCHE CHIARIMENTO UTILE

Al ristorante

Chiedete i menu a prezzo fisso e la carta coi relativi prezzi se non vi vengono spontaneamente presentati.

All'albergo

Il prezzo della prima colazione, anche se non viene consumata, è spesso compreso nel prezzo della camera.

Condizioni speciali per "Short Breaks"

Numerosi alberghi propongono delle condizioni vantaggiose per un soggiorno di due notti o "Short Break". Questo forfait comprende la camera, la cena e la colazione del mattino generalmente per un minimo di due persone.

Le prenotazioni

Alberghi : appena possibile, la prenotazione è consigliabile ; chiedete all'albergatore di fornirvi, nella sua lettera di conferma, ogni dettaglio sulla prenotazione e sulle condizioni di soggiorno. Nelle stazioni balneari in particolar modo, le prenotazioni si applicano generalmente a soggiorni che vanno da un sabato all'altro.

Si consiglia di allegare sempre alle richieste scritte di prenotazione un tagliando risposta internazionale.

Alle volte alcuni albergatori chiedono il versamento di una caparra. E' un deposito-garanzia che impegna tanto l'albergatore che il cliente. Salvo accordi speciali, l'ammontare della caparra può venire fissato nella misura del 10 % dell'ammontare totale previsto.

Ristoranti : è sempre consigliabile prenotare con un certo anticipo per evitare uno spiacevole rifiuto all'ultimo momento.

Animali

Non possono accedere in Gran Bretagna e Irlanda animali domestici (cani, gatti...)

L'AUTOMOBILE, I PNEUMATICI

Nel testo di molte località abbiamo elencato gli indirizzi di garage o concessionari in grado di effettuare, eventualmente, il traino o le riparazioni.

In Gran Bretagna e in Irlanda, l'uso della cintura di sicurezza e' obbligatorio per il guidatore e il passeggero che gli siede accanto.

Soccorso automobilistico

Le principali organizzazioni di soccorso automobilistico sono l'Automobile Association ed il Royal Automobile Club : entrambe offrono alcuni loro servizi ai membri dei club affiliati

AUTOMOBILE ASSOCIATION
Fanum House
BASINGSTOKE, Hants, RG21 2EA
℘ (0256) 20123

ROYAL AUTOMOBILE CLUB
RAC House, Lansdowne Rd,
CROYDON, Surrey CR9 2JA
℘ (01) 686 2525

LE CURIOSITÀ

Grado d'interesse

★★★	Vale il viaggio
★★	Merita una deviazione
★	Interessante
AC	Entrata a pagamento

Situazione

See	Nella città
Envir.	Nei dintorni della città
Exc.	Nella regione
N, S, E, W	La curiosità è situata : a Nord, a Sud, a Est, a Ovest
A 22	Ci si va per la strada A 22 indicata con lo stesso segno sulla pianta
2 m.	Distanza in miglia

LE CITTÀ

⊠ York	Sede dell'ufficio postale
✆ 0225 Bath	Prefisso telefonico interurbano (nome del centralino indicato solo quando differisce dal nome della località). Dall'estero non formare lo 0
401 M 27, ⑩	Numero della carta Michelin e del riquadro o numero della piega
West Country G.	Vedere la Guida Verde Michelin England : The West Country.
pop. 1,057	Popolazione
ECD : Wednesday	Giorno di chiusura settimanale dei negozi (solo pomeriggio)
BX **A**	Lettere indicanti l'ubicazione sulla pianta
⌐₁₈	Golf e numero di buche (accesso consentito a tutti)
☀, ⟨	Panorama, punto di vista
✈	Aeroporto
🚗 ✆ 218	Località con servizio auto su treno. Informarsi al numero di telefono indicato
⛴	Trasporti marittimi
⛴	Trasporti marittimi (solo passeggeri) *Vedere la lista delle compagnie alla fine della Guida*
🛈	Ufficio informazioni turistiche

Ora legale

I visitatori dovranno tenere in considerazione l'ora ufficiale in Gran bretagna : un' ora di ritardo sull'ora italiana.

Per visitare una città ed i suoi dintorni

LE PIANTE

Viabilità

Autostrada, strada a carreggiate separate

   svincolo : completo, parziale, numero

Grande via di circolazione

Senso unico - Via impraticabile - Via pedonale

Pasteur   P   Via commerciale - Parcheggio

Porta - Sottopassaggio - Galleria

Sottopassaggio (altezza inferiore a 16'6") sulle grandi vie di circolazione

Stazione e ferrovia

F B   Battello per auto - Ponte mobile

Curiosità — Alberghi — Ristoranti

Edificio interessante ed entrata principale

Costruzione religiosa interessante :

   Cattedrale, chiesa o cappella

Mulino a vento - Curiosità varie

Castello - Ruderi

B   Lettera che identifica una curiosità

Albergo, Ristorante. Lettera di riferimento che li identifica sulla pianta

Simboli vari

AGENCE MICHELIN   Centro di distribuzione Michelin

Ufficio informazioni turistiche

Moschea - Sinagoga - Ospedale

Giardino, parco, bosco - Cimitero - Calvario

Stadio - Golf

Vista - Panorama

Aeroporto - Ippodromo

Funicolare - Funivia, Cabinovia

Monumento, statua - Fontana

Porto per imbarcazioni da diporto - Faro

Trasporto con traghetto : passeggeri ed autovetture

Edificio pubblico indicato con lettera :

    C   Sede dell' Amministrazione di Contea

    H   M   T   Municipio - Museo - Teatro

    POL.   Polizia (Questura, nelle grandi città)

    U   Università, grande scuola

Ufficio centrale di fermo posta, telefono

Golf riservato - Stazione della Metropolitana

Torre o pilone per telecomunicazione

Londra

BRENT   SOHO   Nome del distretto amministrativo (borough) - del quartiere (area)

Limite del « borough » - di « area »

35

Der
Michelin-Führer...

Er ist nicht nur ein Verzeichnis guter Restaurants und Hotels, sondern gibt zusätzlich eine Fülle nützlicher Tips für die Reise. Nutzen Sie die zahlreichen Informationen, die er bietet.

Zum Gebrauch dieses Führers

Die Erläuterungen stehen auf den folgenden Seiten.

Beachten Sie dabei, daß das gleiche Zeichen, rot oder schwarz, fett oder dünn gedruckt, verschiedene Bedeutungen hat.

Zur Auswahl der Hotels und Restaurants

Der Rote Michelin-Führer ist kein vollständiges Verzeichnis aller Hotels und Restaurants. Er bringt nur eine bewußt getroffene, begrenzte Auswahl. Diese basiert auf regelmäßigen Überprüfungen durch unsere Inspektoren an Ort und Stelle. Bei der Beurteilung werden auch die zahlreichen Hinweise unserer Leser berücksichtigt.

Zu den Stadtplänen

Sie informieren über Fußgänger- und Geschäftsstraßen, Durchgangs- oder Umgehungsstraßen, Lage von Hotels und Restaurants (an Hauptverkehrsstraßen oder in ruhiger Gegend), wo sich die Post, das Verkehrsamt, die wichtigsten öffentlichen Gebäude und Sehenswürdigkeiten u. dgl. befinden.

Hinweise für den Autofahrer

Bei den meisten Orten geben wir Adresse und Telefonnummer der Vertragshändler der großen Automobilfirmen an. So können Sie Ihren Wagen im Bedarfsfall unterwegs warten oder reparieren lassen.

Ihre Meinung zu den Angaben des Führers, Ihre Kritik, Ihre Verbesserungsvorschläge interessieren uns sehr. Zögern Sie daher nicht, uns diese mitzuteilen... wir antworten bestimmt.

**Michelin Tyre Public Limited Company
Tourism Department
Davy House, Lyon Road, HARROW
Middlesex HA1 2DQ**

Vielen Dank im voraus und angenehme Reise !

Wahl eines Hotels, eines Restaurants

Unsere Auswahl ist für Durchreisende gedacht. In jeder Kategorie drückt die Reihenfolge der Betriebe eine weitere Rangordnung aus.

KLASSENEINTEILUNG UND KOMFORT

🏨	Großer Luxus und Tradition	XXXXX
🏨	Großer Komfort	XXXX
🏨	Sehr komfortabel	XXX
🏨	Mit gutem Komfort	XX
🏨	Mit ausreichendem Komfort	X
⌂	Bürgerlich	
⌂	Preiswerte, empfehlenswerte Gasthäuser und Pensionen	
without rest.	Hotel ohne Restaurant	
	Restaurant vermietet auch Zimmer	with rm

EINRICHTUNG

Für die 🏨, 🏨, 🏨 geben wir keine Einzelheiten über die Einrichtung an, da diese Hotels im allgemeinen jeden Komfort besitzen. Außerdem besteht die Möglichkeit, Geld zu wechseln.

In den Häusern der übrigen Kategorien nennen wir die vorhandenen Einrichtungen, diese können in einigen Zimmern fehlen.

30 rm	Anzahl der Zimmer
🛗	Fahrstuhl
🗔	Klimaanlage
📺	Fernsehen im Zimmer
🛁wc 🛁	Privatbad mit wc, Privatbad ohne wc
🚿wc 🚿	Privatdusche mit wc, Privatdusche ohne wc
☎	Zimmertelefon mit Außenverbindung über Telefonzentrale
☎	Zimmertelefon mit direkter Außenverbindung
♿	Für Körperbehinderte leicht zugängliche Zimmer
🏊 🏊	Freibad, Hallenbad
⚘	Liegewiese, Garten
🎾	Hoteleigener Tennisplatz
⛳	Golfplatz und Lochzahl
🎣	Angelmöglichkeit für Hotelgäste, evtl. gegen Gebühr
🏛	Konferenzräume (mind. 25 Plätze)
🚗	Garage
🅿	Parkplatz
🐕	Das Mitführen von Hunden ist im ganzen Haus unerwünscht
	Falls Hunde dennoch geduldet werden, dann nur in den Zimmern.
May-October	Öffnungszeit, vom Hotelier mitgeteilt
season	Unbestimmte Öffnungszeit eines Saisonhotels
	Die Häuser, für die wir keine Schließungszeiten angeben, sind ganzjährig geöffnet.
LL35 0SB	Angabe des Postbezirks (hinter der Hoteladresse)
(T.H.F.)	Hotelkette *(Liste am Ende des Führers)*

ANNEHMLICHKEITEN

In manchen Hotels ist der Aufenthalt wegen der schönen, ruhigen Lage, der nicht alltäglichen Einrichtung und Atmosphäre und dem gebotenen Service besonders angenehm und erholsam.

Solche Häuser und ihre besonderen Annehmlichkeiten sind im Führer durch folgende Symbole gekennzeichnet :

⚑ … 🏠	Angenehme Hotels
XXXXX … X	Angenehme Restaurants
« Park »	Besondere Annehmlichkeit
🐿	Sehr ruhiges, oder abgelegenes und ruhiges Hotel
🐿	Ruhiges Hotel
⩽ sea	Reizvolle Aussicht
⩽	Interessante oder weite Sicht

Die Karten in der Einleitung zu den einzelnen Landesteilen geben Ihnen einen Überblick über die Orte, in denen sich mindestens ein angenehmes, sehr ruhiges Haus befindet.

Wir wissen, daß diese Auswahl noch nicht vollständig ist, sind aber laufend bemüht, weitere solche Häuser für Sie zu entdecken ; dabei sind uns Ihre Erfahrungen und Hinweise eine wertvolle Hilfe.

KÜCHE

Die Sterne für gute Küche

Mit ❀, ❀❀ oder ❀❀❀ kennzeichnen wir die Häuser mit landesüblicher oder ausländischer Küche, deren Qualität wir der Aufmerksamkeit der Leser besonders empfehlen möchten (siehe S. 48).

Für diese Häuser geben wir im Text einige typische Gerichte bürgerlicher Küche an.

❀ **Eine sehr gute Küche : verdient Ihre besondere Beachtung**

Der Stern bedeutet eine angenehme Unterbrechung Ihrer Reise. Vergleichen Sie aber bitte nicht den Stern eines teuren Luxusrestaurants mit dem Stern eines kleinen oder mittleren Hauses, wo man Ihnen zu einem annehmbaren Preis eine ebenfalls vorzügliche Mahlzeit reicht.

❀❀ **Eine hervorragende Küche : verdient einen Umweg**

Ausgesuchte Spezialitäten und Weine... angemessene Preise.

❀❀❀ **Eine der besten Küchen : eine Reise wert**

Ein denkwürdiges Essen, edle Weine, tadelloser Service, gepflegte Atmosphäre... entsprechende Preise.

M **Das rote « M »**

Wir glauben, daß Sie neben den Häusern mit Stern auch solche Adressen interessieren werden, die einfache, aber sorgfältig zubereitete Mahlzeiten anbieten.

Auf solche Häuser weisen wir im Text durch das rote « M » hin.

Ausschank alkoholischer Getränke

In Großbritannien und Irland unterliegt der Ausschank alkoholischer Getränke gesetzlichen Bestimmungen, die in den einzelnen Gegenden verschieden sind.

Im allgemeinen schließen die Hotelbars und Pubs nachmittags sowie nach 23 Uhr ; die genauen Öffnungszeiten sind jedoch örtlich verschieden.

Hotelgästen können alkoholische Getränke jedoch auch außerhalb der Ausschankzeiten serviert werden.

Kindern unter 14 Jahren ist der Zutritt zu den Bars untersagt.

PREISE

Die in diesem Führer genannten Preise wurden uns Ende 1986 angegeben. Sie können sich 1987 erhöhen, wenn die allgemeinen Lebenshaltungskosten steigen. Sie können aber in diesem Fall als Richtpreise angesehen werden.

Halten Sie beim Betreten des Hotels den Führer in der Hand. Sie zeigen damit, daß Sie aufgrund dieser Empfehlung gekommen sind.

Die Namen der Hotels und Restaurants, die ihre Preise genannt haben, sind fett gedruckt. Gleichzeitig haben sich diese Häuser verpflichtet, die von den Hoteliers selbst angegebenen Preise den Benutzern des Michelin-Führers zu berechnen.

Informieren Sie uns bitte über jede unangemessen erscheinende Preiserhöhung. Wenn keine Preise angegeben sind, raten wir Ihnen, sich beim Hotelier danach zu erkundigen.

Die Preise sind in Pfund Sterling angegeben (1 £ = 100 pence) mit Ausnahme der Republik Irland (Punts).

Wenn die Buchstaben s., t., oder st. nicht hinter den angegebenen Preisen aufgeführt sind, können sich diese um den Zuschlag für Bedienung und/oder MWSt erhöhen (keine MWSt auf den Channel Islands).

Mahlzeiten

M 9.00/12.00	**Feste Menupreise** — Mittagessen 9.00, Abendessen 12.00 (inklusive Couvert)
M 13.00/15.00	Siehe Seite 39
s. t.	Bedienung inbegriffen - MWSt inbegriffen
st.	Bedienung und MWSt inbegriffen (Inklusivpreise)
⌢ 5.00	Preis für 1/2 Flasche oder eine Karaffe Tafelwein
M a la carte 14.00/18.00	**Mahlzeiten « à la carte »** — Der erste Preis entspricht einer einfachen aber sorgfältig zubereiteten Mahlzeit, bestehend aus kleiner Vorspeise, Tagesgericht mit Beilage und Nachtisch Der zweite Preis entspricht einer reichlicheren Mahlzeit mit Vorspeise, Hauptgericht, Käse oder Nachtisch (« couvert » ist in den Preisen enthalten)
⌸ 5.00	Preis des englischen Frühstücks, wenn dieser nicht im Übernachtungspreis enthalten ist Einfaches, billigeres Frühstück (Continental breakfast) erhältlich

Zimmer

rm 25.00/45.00	Mindestpreis 25.00 für ein Einzelzimmer und Höchstpreis 45.00 für das schönste Doppelzimmer
rm ⌸ 30.00/50.00	Übernachtung mit englischem Frühstück
suites 100.00/200.00	Mindest- und Höchstpreis für ein Appartement bestehend aus Wohnzimmer, Schlafzimmer und Bad

"Short Breaks" (Siehe Seite 41)

SB 50.00/60.00	Mindest- und Höchstpreis pro Person bei einem Aufenthalt von 2 Nächten
⬛ AE ◐ VISA	Von Hotels und Restaurants angenommene **Kreditkarten :** Access (MasterCard) — American Express — Diners Club — Visa (BankAmericard)

NÜTZLICHE HINWEISE

Im Restaurant

Verlangen Sie die Karte der Tagesmenus zu Festpreisen und die Speisekarte, wenn sie Ihnen nicht von selbst vorgelegt werden.

Im Hotel

Im allgemeinen ist das Frühstück (auch wenn es nicht eingenommen wird) im Zimmerpreis enthalten.

Pauschale für "Short Breaks"

Zahlreiche Hotels bieten Vorzugspreise bei einem Aufenthalt von 2 Nächten ("Short Break"). Diese Pauschalpreise (für mindestens 2 Personen) umfassen Zimmer, Abendessen und Frühstück.

Zimmerreservierung

Hotels : Es ist ratsam, wenn irgend möglich, die Zimmer reservieren zu lassen. Bitten Sie den Hotelier, daß er Ihnen in seinem Bestätigungsschreiben alle seine Bedingungen mitteilt.

Besonders in Seebädern wird Vollpension im allgemeinen nur wochenweise, von Samstag zu Samstag, gewährt.

Bei schriftlichen Zimmerbestellungen empfiehlt es sich, einen Freiumschlag oder einen internationalen Antwortschein beizufügen.

Einige Hoteliers verlangen eine Anzahlung (etwa 10 % wenn nichts anderes vereinbart wird) auf den voraussichtlichen Endpreis. Sie ist als Garantie für beide Seiten anzusehen.

Restaurant : Es empfiehlt sich, Tische immer und so früh wie möglich vorzubestellen.

Tiere

Das Mitführen von Haustieren (Hunde, Katzen u. dgl.) bei der Einreise in Großbritannien und Irland ist untersagt.

DAS AUTO, DIE REIFEN

Bei den meisten Orten geben wir Adressen von Kfz-Vertragswerkstätten an ; viele davon haben einen Abschlepp- bzw. Reparaturdienst.

In Großbritannien und Irland besteht Gurtanlegepflicht für Fahrer und Beifahrer auf den Vordersitzen.

Automobilclubs

Die wichtigsten Automobilclubs des Landes sind die Automobile Association und der Royal Automobile Club, die den Mitgliedern der der FIA angeschlossenen Automobilclubs Pannenhilfe leisten und einige ihrer Dienstleistungen anbieten.

AUTOMOBILE ASSOCIATION
Fanum House
BASINGSTOKE, Hants., RG21 2EA
✆ (0256) 20123

ROYAL AUTOMOBILE CLUB
RAC House, Lansdowne Rd
CROYDON, Surrey CR9 2JA
✆ (01) 686 2525

HAUPTSEHENSWÜRDIGKEITEN

Bewertung

★★★   Eine Reise wert
★★   Verdient einen Umweg
★   Sehenswert
AC   Eintritt (gegen Gebühr)

Lage

See   In der Stadt
Envir. In der Umgebung der Stadt
Exc.   Ausflugsziele
N, S, E, W Im Norden (N), Süden (S), Osten (E), Westen (W) der Stadt.
A 22   Zu erreichen über die Straße A 22.
2 m.   Entfernung in Meilen

STÄDTE

✉ York   Zuständiges Postamt
✆ 0225 Bath   Vorwahlnummer und evtl. zuständiges Fernsprechamt (bei Gesprächen vom Ausland aus wird die erste Null weggelassen)
🔢 M 27, ⑩   Nummer der Michelin-Karte und Koordinaten des Gratfeldes oder Faltseite
West Country G. Siehe auch den grünen Michelinführer "England : The West Country"
pop. 1,057   Einwohnerzahl
ECD : Wednesday   Tag, an dem die Läden nachmittags geschlossen sind
BX **A**   Markierung auf dem Stadtplan
⛳₁₈   Öffentlicher Golfplatz und Lochzahl
☀, ≼   Rundblick, Aussichtspunkt
✈   Flughafen
🚗 ✆ 218   Ladestelle für Autoreisezüge - Nähere Auskünfte unter der angegebenen Telefonnummer
⛴   Autofähre
⛴   Personenfähre
                    Liste der Schiffahrtsgesellschaften am Ende des Führers
ℹ   Informationsstelle

Uhrzeit

In Großbritannien ist eine Zeitverschiebung zu beachten und die Uhr gegenüber der deutschen Zeit um 1 Stunde zurückzustellen.

STADTPLÄNE

Straßen

Autobahn, Straße mit getrennten Fahrbahnen

0   0   Anschlußstelle : Autobahneinfahrt und/oder -ausfahrt, Nummer

Hauptverkehrsstraße

Einbahnstraße - nicht befahrbare Straße

Fußgängerzone

Pasteur   **P**   Einkaufsstraße - Parkplatz

Tor - Passage - Tunnel

Unterführung (Höhe angegeben bis 16'6'') auf Hauptverkehrsstraßen

Bahnhof und Bahnlinie

F B   Autofähre - Bewegliche Brücke

Sehenswürdigkeiten — Hotels — Restaurants

Sehenswertes Gebäude mit Haupteingang

Sehenswerter Sakralbau :

   Kathedrale, Kirche oder Kapelle

Windmühle - Sonstige Sehenswürdigkeiten

Schloß - Ruine

B   Referenzbuchstabe einer Sehenswürdigkeit

Hotel, Restaurant - Referenzbuchstabe

Sonstige Zeichen

AGENCE MICHELIN   Informationsstelle - Michelin-Niederlassung

Krankenhaus - Moschee - Synagoge

Garten, Park, Wäldchen - Friedhof - Bildstock

Stadion - Golfplatz

Flughafen - Pferderennbahn - Aussicht - Rundblick

Standseilbahn - Seilschwebebahn

Denkmal, Statue - Brunnen - Jachthafen - Leuchtturm

Schiffsverbindungen : Autofähre

Öffentliches Gebäude, durch einen Buchstaben gekennzeichnet :

C   Sitz der Grafschaftsverwaltung

H   M   T   Rathaus - Museum - Theater

POL.   Polizei (in größeren Städten Polizeipräsidium)

U   Universität, Hochschule

Hauptpostamt (postlagernde Sendungen), Telefon

Golfplatz (Zutritt bedingt erlaubt)

Funk-, Fernsehturm - U-Bahnstation

London

BRENT   SOHO   Name des Verwaltungsbezirks (borough) - des Stadtteils (area)

Grenze des „ borough '' - des „ area ''

43

Location	Town	Hotel
M 1		
Scratchwood Service Area	Hendon (L.B. of Barnet)	🏨 TraveLodge
Junction 5 — S : ½ m. on A 41	Watford	🏨 Ladbroke
Junction 6 — NE : 1 m. on A 405 (this hotel also under M 10)	St. Albans	🏨 Noke Thistle
Junction 8 — W : ½ m. on A 4147	Hemel Hempstead	🏨 Post House
Junction 9 — NW : 1 m. on A 5	Flamstead	🏨 Hertfordshire Moat House
Junction 11 — E : ¾ m. on A 505	Luton	🏨 Chiltern
Junction 11 — on A 505	Luton	🏨 Crest
Junction 11 — E : 1 ½ m. on A 505	Luton	🏛 Humberstone
Newport Pagnell Service Area 3	Newport Pagnell	🏨 TraveLodge
Junction 13 — W : 1 ½ m.	Aspley Guise	🏨 Holt
Junction 15 — NE : 3 m. by A 428 on A 45	Northampton	🏨 Swallow
Junction 18 — E : 1 m. on A 428	Rugby (at Crick)	🏨 Post House
Junction 21/21A — NE : 2 ½ m. on A 46	Leicester (at Braunstone)	🏨 Post House
Junction 25 — W : ¼ m. on A 52	Nottingham (at Sandiacre)	🏨 Post House
Junction 25 — S : ½ m. on B 6002	Nottingham (at Long Eaton)	🏨 Novotel Nottingham
Junction 28 — on A 38	South Normanton	🏨 Swallow
Junction 30 — NW : 1 ½ m. on A 616	Renishaw	🏨 Sitwell Arms
Junction 39 — W : ¼ m. on A 636	Wakefield	🏨 Cedar Court
Junction 40 — E : ½ m. on A 638	Wakefield	🏨 Post House
A 1 (M)		
Junction 1, A 638 — N : 2 ½ m. on A 1	Wentbridge (at Barnsdale Bar)	🏠 Doncaster TraveLodge
A 1 (M) via A 66 (M) — E : 2 m. on A 66	Darlington	🏨 Blackwell Grange Moat House
A 1 (M) via A 167 — S : ¾ m. by A 167	Darlington (at Coatham Mundeville)	🏨 Hall Garth Country House
A 1 (M) Junction with A 195 — E : ½ m. by A 1231	Washington	🏨 Post House
A 1 (M) Junction A 6 and M 25 (this hotel also under M 25)	South Mimms	🏨 Crest
M 2		
Junction 1 — W : 1 ½ m. on A 2	Shorne	🏨 Inn on the Lake
Junction 3 — N : 1 m. on A 229	Rochester	🏨 Crest
M 3		
Junction 3 — N : 1 m. on A 30	Bagshot	🏠 Cricketer's
Junction 6 — N : 1 m. at Blackdam roundabout	Basingstoke	🏨 Ladbroke Lodge
Junction 6 — SW : 1 ½ m. at junction A 30 and A 339	Basingstoke	🏨 Crest

M 4

Junction 3 — N : 1 ½ m. off A 312	Heathrow Airport (L.B. of Hillingdon)	Arlington
Junction 4 — S : ½ m. on B 379	Heathrow Airport	Post House
Junction 4 — N : ½ m. on B 379	Heathrow Airport	Holiday Inn
Junction 5 — NW : 1 m. by A 287 and 2 m. by A 30	Basingstoke (at Rotherwick)	Tylney Hall
Junction 5 — NW : ¼ m. on A 4	Slough	Holiday Inn
Junction 8-9 — SE : 3 m. by A 308 (M) and A 308	Windsor	Oakley Court
Junction 9 A — NE : ½ m. on Shoppenhangers Rd	Maidenhead	Crest
Junction 11 — N : ½ m. on A 33	Reading	Post House
Junction 15 — N : 2 m. by A 419 on A 4259	Swindon	Post House
Junction 19 — SW : 2 ½ m. by M 32 on A 4174 (this hotel also under M 32)	Bristol (at Hambrook)	Crest
Junction 24 — S : ½ m. on A 48	Newport (Gwent)	Celtic Manor
Junction 24 — E : 1 ½ m. on A 48	Newport (Gwent) (at Langstone)	New Inn Motel
Junction 24 — S : ¼ m. on A 48	Newport (Gwent)	Ladbroke
Junction 34 — N : 1 ¾ m. by A 4119 (Groes Faen road)	Miskin	Miskin Manor
Junction 38 (A 48 m) — NW : 1 m. on A 48	Port Talbot	Twelve Knights

M 5

Junction 1 — W : 1 m. by A 41	Birmingham (at West Bromwich)	West Bromwich Moat House
Junction 5 — SW : 1 m. on A 38	Droitwich	Château Impney
Junction 11 — E : 1 m. on A 40	Cheltenham	Golden Valley Thistle
Junction 13 — SE : 1 ¾ m. on A 419	Stroud (at Stonehouse)	Stonehouse Court
Junction 14 — SW : 1 ½ m. by A 4509 on A 38	Falfield	Park
Junction 22 — N : 1 m. on A 38	Brent Knoll	Battleborough Grange
Junction 29 — N : 1 ½ m. by Moor Lane	Exeter (at Pinhoe)	Gipsy Hill
Junction 31 — S : 2 ½ m. at junction of A 379 and B 3182	Exeter	Exeter Moat House

M 6

Junction 2 — S : 1 m. on A 46	Coventry (at Walsgrave-on-Sowe)	Crest
Junction 3 — SE : 1 m. on A 444	Coventry (at Longford)	Novotel Coventry
Junction 7 — N : ¼ m. on A 34	Birmingham (at Great Barr)	Post House
Junction 7 — N : 2 ½ m. on A 34	Walsall	Crest
Junction 12 — E : 2 m. on A 5	Cannock	Roman Way
Junction 13 — N : 1 m. on A 449	Stafford	Garth
Junction 14 — SE : ½ m. on A 5013	Stafford	Tillington Hall
Junction 15 — N : ¼ m. on A 519	Newcastle-under-Lyme	Post House
Junction 15 — N : ¾ m. on A 519	Newcastle-under-Lyme	Clayton Lodge
Junction 15 — NE : 1 ½ m. on A 34	Stoke on Trent	White House
Charnock Richard Service Area	Charnock Richard	TraveLodge
Junction 19 — NE : 2 ½ m. on A 556 (this hotel also under M 56)	Knutsford (at Bucklow Hill)	Swan Inn
Junction 23 — N : ½ m. on A 49	Haydock	Post House
Junction 28 — W : ¼ m. on B 5256	Leyland	Ladbroke
Junction 29 — SE : ¼ m. by A 6	Preston	Novotel
Junction 31 — W : ¼ m. on A 59	Preston (at Samlesbury)	Tickled Trout
Junction 34 — SW : ¼ m. on A 683	Lancaster	Post House
Junction 40 — S : 1 m.	Penrith	North Lakes Gateway
Junction 44 — N : ¼ m. on A 7	Carlisle (at Kingstown)	Crest
at Tebay West service area	Tebay, Cumbria	Tebay Mountain Lodge

M 8

Junction 3 — SE : 2 ½ m. by A 899	Livingston	Ladbroke
Junction 11 — E : 1 ¾ m. by M 898 and on A 726	Erskine	Crest
Junction 27 — N : ¼ m. on A 741	Renfrew	Glynhill
Junction 27 — S : ½ m. on A 741	Paisley	Rockfield
Junction with M 9 — E : 1 m. on A 8	Edinburgh	Norton House

45

M 9

Junction 6 − NW : ¼ m. on A 905	Falkirk (at Grangemouth)	🏨	Grange Manor
Junction with M 8 − E : 1 m. on A 8	Edinburgh	🏨	Norton House

M 10

Junction 1 − SW : 1 m. on A 405 (this hotel also under M 1)	St. Albans	🏨	Noke Thistle

M 11

Junction 10 − SE : 1 ½ m. by A 505	Cambridge (at Duxford)	🏨	Duxford Lodge
Junction 14 with A 604 − NW : 1 ¾ m. on A 604	Cambridge (at Bar Hill)	🏨	Cambridgeshire Moat House

M 20

Junction 2 A	Wrotham Heath	🏨	Post House

M 23

Junction 9 − in Gatwick Airport	Gatwick	🏨	Gatwick Hilton International
Junction 9 − W : 1 m. on A 23	Gatwick	🏨	Gatwick Penta
Junction 9 − W : 1 m. on A 23	Gatwick	🏨	Post House
Junction 9 − W : 1 m. on A 23	Gatwick	🏨	Gatwick Moat House

M 25

Junction 8 − S : ½ m. on A 217	Reigate	🏨	Bridge House
Junction 10 − N : 1 ¼ m. by A 3 and A 245	Cobham	🏨	Ladbroke Seven Hills
Junction 13 − S : 1 m. by A 30 on A 308	Egham	🏨	Runnymede
Junction 26 − S : 4 m. on B 1393 and A 121	Epping	🏨	Post House
Junction 28 − NE : ¾ m. on A 1023	Brentwood	🏨	Brentwood Moat House
Junction 28 − NE : ¼ m. on A 1023	Brentwood	🏨	Post House
Junction A 6 and A 1 (M) (this hotel also under A 1 (M))	South Mimms	🏨	Crest

M 26

Junction 2 A	Wrotham Heath	🏨	Post House

M 27

Junction 1 − on A 337 at Junction of A 31 and A 336	Cadnam	🏨	Bartley Lodge
Junction 12 − N : at junction of A 3 and A 27	Portsmouth & Southsea (at Cosham)	🏨	Holiday Inn

M 32

Junction 1 − W : ½ m. on A 4174 (this hotel also under M 4)	Bristol (at Hambrook)	🏨	Crest

M 40

Junction 2 − E : 1 ¾ m. by A 355 on A 40	Beaconsfield	🏨	Bellhouse
Junction 4 − on Crest Road	High Wycombe	🏨	Crest
Junction 7 − W : 2 m. by A 329	Oxford (at Great Milton)	XXXX	with rm Le Manoir aux Quat Saisons

M 45

Junction 1 − E : 1 ¼ m. on A 45	Dunchurch	🏨	Dun Cow

M 54

Junction 5 − SW : ½ m.	Telford	🏨	Telford Moat House
Junction 7 − N : ½ m.	Telford	🏨	Falcon
Junction 7 − S : 1 m.	Telford	🏨	Buckatree Hall

M 55

Junction 1 − N : ¾ m.	Preston	🏨	Broughton Park

M 56

Junction 5 — on Airport Approach Road	Manchester (at Airport)		Excelsior
Junction 6 — N : ¼ m. on A 538	Altrincham		Four Seasons
Junction 6 — S : 2 m. on A 538	Wilmslow		Valley Lodge
Junction 7/8 — SW : 2 m. on A 556 (this hotel also under M 6)	Knutsford (at Bucklow Hill)		Swan Inn
Junction 11 — N : ¼ m. on A 56	Daresbury		Lord Daresbury
Junction 12 — SE : ½ m. by A 557	Runcorn		Crest

M 57

Junction 2 — E : ½ m.	Kirkby		Crest

M 61

Junction 5 — NE : 1 m. on A 58	Bolton		Crest

M 62

Junction 24 — SE : 1 ½ m. on A 629	Huddersfield		Ladbroke
Junction 30 — N : 1 m. on A 639	Leeds (at Oulton)		Crest

M 63

Junction 9 — by approach Rd	Manchester (at Northenden)		Post House

M 69

Junction with M 1 — NE : 2 ½ m. on A 46	Leicester (at Braunstone)		Post House
Junction 1 — NW : 1 m. by A 447	Hinckley		Sketchley Grange

M 606

Junction 1 — E : ¼ m.	Bradford		Novotel

TOWNS WITH ESTABLISHMENTS AWARDED ✿✿✿, ✿✿, ✿, M

Localités possédant des établissements à ✿✿✿, ✿✿, ✿, M
Località che possiedono esercizi con ✿✿✿, ✿✿, ✿, M
In folgenden Orten finden sie Häuser mit ✿✿✿, ✿✿, ✿, M

✿✿✿

England and Wales
Bray-on-Thames   Waterside Inn   London   pages bordered in red

✿✿

England and Wales
London   pages bordered in red   Oxford   Le Manoir aux Quat'Saisons

✿

England and Wales

Bournemouth	Provence	Royal Leamington Spa	Mallory Court
Bristol	Les Semailles	Taunton	Castle
Canterbury	Seventy-Four	Tetbury	Calcot Manor
Chagford	Gidleigh Park	Wymondham	Adlard's
Dartmouth	Carved Angel		
Great Malvern	Croque-en-Bouche	**Scotland**	
Ilkley	Box Tree	Fort William	Inverlochy Castle
London	pages bordered in red	Peat Inn	Peat Inn
New Milton	Chewton Glen		
Oakham	Hambleton Hall	**Republic of Ireland**	
Plymouth	Chez Nous	Cork	Arbutus Lodge
Reading	L'Ortolan	Kenmare	Park
		Navan	Dunderry Lodge

England and Wales

Abergavenny	Walnut Tree Inn	Pateley Bridge	Sportsman's Arms
		Pool-in-Wharfedale	Pool Court
Bakewell	Fischers	Shipdham	Shipdham Place
Bath	Homewood Park	Storrington	Manley's
Bath	Hunstrete House	Sturminster Newton	Plumber Manor
Bath	The Priory	Tetbury	Gibbons
Birmingham	Henry Wong	Thornbury	Thornbury Castle
Broadway	Buckland Manor	Ullswater	Sharrow Bay
Brockenhurst	Le Poussin		Country House
Bromsgrove	Grafton Manor	Warwick	Westgate Arms
Bury St. Edmonds	Bradley's	Waterhouses	Old Beams
		Williton	White House
Cheltenham	Redmond's	Windermere	Miller Howe
Chesterton	Woods	Worcester	Brown's
Chichester	White Horse	Yattendon	Royal Oak
Clanfield	Plough		
Dartmouth	Bistro 33	**Scotland**	
Earl Stonham	Mr Underhill's	Arisaig	Arisaig House
Eastbourne	Hungry Monk	Auchtermuchty	Hollies
Flitwick	Flitwick Manor	Gullane	La Potinière
Fowey	Food for Thought	Perth	Balcraig House
Fressingfield	Fox and Goose	Port Appin	Airds
Grasmere	Michael's Nook	Ullapool	Altnaharrie Inn
	Country House		
Grasmere	White Moss House	**Northern Ireland**	
Grayshott	Woods	Portrush	Ramore
Great Dunmow	Starr		
Grimsthorpe	Black Horse Inn	**Republic of Ireland**	
Helford	Riverside	Bunratty	McCloskey's
Horton	French Partridge	Dingle	Doyle's Seafood Bar
Ledbury	Hope End Country House	Gorey	Marlfield House
London	pages bordered in red	Mallow	Longueville House
Melksham	Beechfield House	Moycullen	Drimcong House
Northallerton	McCoys at the Tontine	Shanagarry	Ballymaloe House
Padstow	Seafood		

48

England
and Wales

ENGLAND

Avon	Avon	Kent	Kent
Bedfordshire	Beds.	Lancashire	Lancs.
Berkshire	Berks.	Leicestershire	Leics.
Buckinghamshire	Bucks.	Lincolnshire	Lincs.
Cambridgeshire	Cambs.	Merseyside	Merseyside
Cheshire	Cheshire	Norfolk	Norfolk
Cleveland	Cleveland	Northamptonshire	Northants.
Cornwall	Cornwall	Northumberland	Northumb.
Cumbria	Cumbria	North Yorkshire	North Yorks.
Derbyshire	Derbs.	Nottinghamshire	Notts.
Devon	Devon	Oxfordshire	Oxon.
Dorset	Dorset	Shropshire	Salop
Durham	Durham	Somerset	Somerset
East Sussex	East Sussex	South Yorkshire	South Yorks.
Essex	Essex	Staffordshire	Staffs.
Gloucestershire	Glos.	Suffolk	Suffolk
Greater Manchester	Greater Manchester	Surrey	Surrey
Hampshire	Hants.	Tyne and Wear	Tyne and Wear
Hereford and Worcester	Heref. and Worc.	Warwickshire	Warw.
Hertfordshire	Herts.	West Midlands	West Midlands
Humberside	Humberside	West Sussex	West Sussex
Isle of Wight	I. O. W.	West Yorkshire	West Yorks.
		Wiltshire	Wilts.

WALES

Clwyd	Clwyd	Mid Glamorgan	Mid Glam.
Dyfed	Dyfed	Powys	Powys
Gwent	Gwent	South Glamorgan	South Glam.
Gwynedd	Gwynedd	West Glamorgan	West Glam.

49

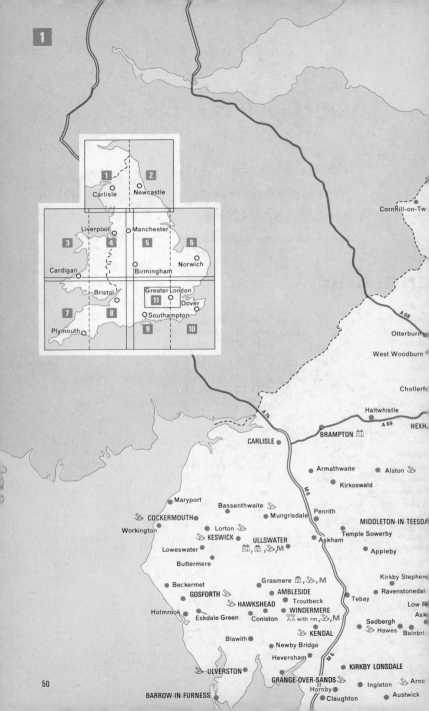

1

Carlisle ○ Newcastle ○ **2**

Cornhill-on-Tw

Liverpool ○ Manchester ○
3 **4** **5** **6**

Cardigan ○ Birmingham ○ Norwich ○

A 68

Otterburn ●

Bristol ○ Greater London ○
7 **8** **11** Dover ○

West Woodburn ●

Southampton ○
Plymouth ○ **9** **10**

Chollerf

Haltwhistle ●

BRAMPTON ⌂ A 69 HEXH.

CARLISLE ●

Armathwaite ● Alston ⌂

Kirkoswald ●

Maryport ●

Bassenthwaite ⌂ Penrith ●

⌂ **COCKERMOUTH** ● Mungrisdale ● **MIDDLETON-IN-TEESDA**

Workington ● Lorton ⌂ Temple Sowerby ●

⌂ **KESWICK** ● **ULLSWATER** Askham ●

Loweswater ● ⌂ 益 , ⌂ ,M Appleby ●

Buttermere ●

Kirkby Stephen

Beckermet ● Grasmere 益 , ⌂ ,M Ravenstonedal

GOSFORTH ⌂ **AMBLESIDE** Low R

⌂ **HAWKSHEAD** Troutbeck Tebay ● Ask

Holmrook ● **WINDERMERE** Sedbergh ●

Eskdale Green ● Coniston ● ⌂⌂ with rm. ⌂ ,M ⌂ Hawes Bainbri

KENDAL

Blawith ● Newby Bridge ●

Heversham ● **KIRKBY LONSDALE**

⌂ **ULVERSTON** ● **GRANGE-OVER-SANDS** ⌂ Ingleton ● ⌂ Arnc

50 Hornby ● Austwick ●

BARROW-IN-FURNESS ● Claughton ●

Place with at least :

one hotel or restaurant	● Ripon
one pleasant hotel	🏠 , ✗ with rm
one quiet, secluded hotel	🌡
one restaurant with	✿, ✿✿, ✿✿✿, M
See this town for establishments located in its vicinity	MORPETH

Localité offrant au moins :

une ressource hôtelière	● Ripon
un hôtel agréable	🏠 , ✗ with rm
un hôtel très tranquille, isolé	🌡
une bonne table à	✿, ✿✿, ✿✿✿, M
Localité groupant dans le texte les ressources de ses environs	MORPETH

La località possiede come minimo :

una risorsa alberghiera	● Ripon
un albergo ameno	🏠 , ✗ with rm
un albergo molto tranquillo, isolato	🌡
un'ottima tavola con	✿, ✿✿, ✿✿✿, M
La località raggruppa nel suo testo le risorse dei dintorni	MORPETH

Ort mit mindestens :

einem Hotel oder Restaurant	● Ripon
einem angenehmen Hotel	🏠 , ✗ with rm
einem sehr ruhigen und abgelegenen Hotel	🌡
einem Restaurant mit	✿, ✿✿, ✿✿✿, M
Ort mit Angaben über Hotels und Restaurants in seiner Umgebung	MORPETH

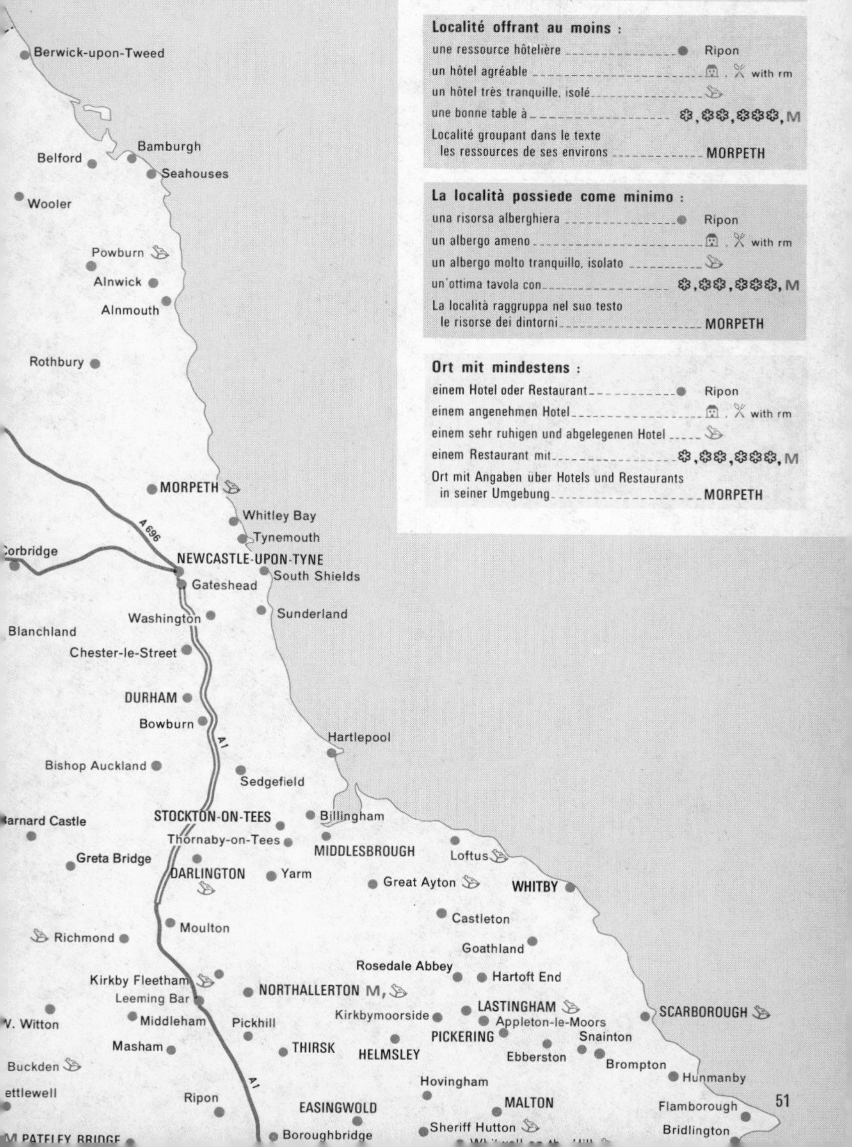

Berwick-upon-Tweed

Bamburgh
Belford
Seahouses
Wooler

Powburn
Alnwick
Alnmouth

Rothbury

MORPETH
Whitley Bay
Tynemouth
Corbridge
NEWCASTLE-UPON-TYNE
Gateshead
South Shields
Washington
Sunderland
Blanchland
Chester-le-Street

DURHAM
Bowburn
Hartlepool
Bishop Auckland
Sedgefield

Barnard Castle
STOCKTON-ON-TEES
Billingham
Greta Bridge
Thornaby-on-Tees
MIDDLESBROUGH
Loftus
DARLINGTON
Yarm
Great Ayton
WHITBY
Richmond
Moulton
Castleton
Goathland
Rosedale Abbey
Kirkby Fleetham
Hartoft End
Leeming Bar
NORTHALLERTON M,
LASTINGHAM
SCARBOROUGH
W. Witton
Middleham
Pickhill
Kirkbymoorside
Appleton-le-Moors
Masham
THIRSK
PICKERING
Snainton
Buckden
HELMSLEY
Ebberston
Brompton
Hunmanby
Hovingham
MALTON
Flamborough
ettlewell
Ripon
EASINGWOLD
Sheriff Hutton
Bridlington
M PATELEY BRIDGE
Boroughbridge

51

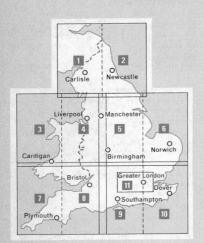

3

Carlisle
Newcastle

1
2

Liverpool
Manchester

3
4
5
6

Cardigan
Birmingham
Norwich

Bristol
Greater London

7
8
11
Dover

Southampton

Plymouth
9
10

Benllech

Beaumaris

A 5

PORT DINORWIC
Bango

Caernarfon

Llanberis

Beddgelert

Nefyn
PORTHMADOC

Criccieth

Tudweiliog

ABERSOCH
HARLECH

Llanbedr

Barmouth

Aberdovey

ABERYSTWYTH

New Quay
ABERAERON

Aberporth

Lampeter

Pontshaen

CARDIGAN

FISHGUARD
NEWPORT
Newcastle-Emlyn

Boncath

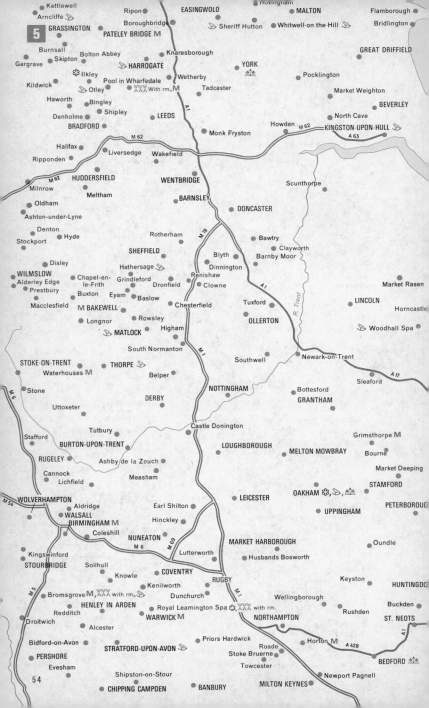

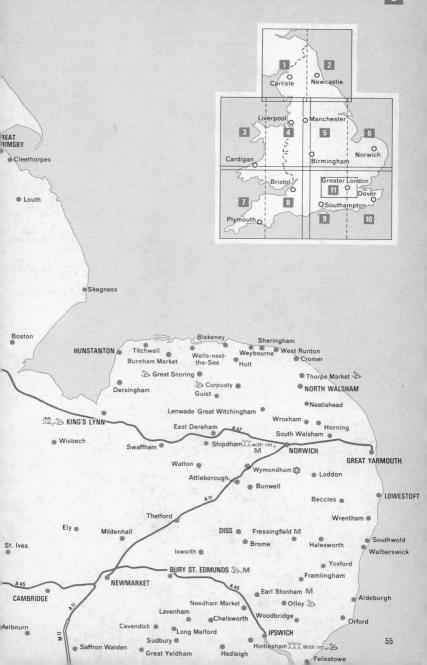

1 Carlisle 2 Newcastle

Liverpool ○ Manchester
3 4 5 6
Cardigan Birmingham Norwich
Bristol
Greater London
11 Dover
7 8 Southampton
Plymouth 9 10

GREAT GRIMSBY
● Cleethorpes

● Louth

● Skegness

● Boston

HUNSTANTON
Titchwell Blakeney Sheringham
Wells-next- Weybourne West Runton
Burnham Market the-Sea Cromer
Great Snoring Holt
🍴 Corpusty Thorpe Market 🍴
Dersingham Guist NORTH WALSHAM
Lenwade Great Witchingham ● Neatishead
🏛,🍴 KING'S LYNN East Dereham A47 Wroxham
● Wisbech Swaffham Shipdham ⚔ with rm.🍴 Horning
  M South Walsham
Watton ● NORWICH
Attleborough Wymondham ✿ GREAT YARMOUTH
  Bunwell ● Loddon
A11 LOWESTOFT
Thetford Beccles ●
Ely ● Wrentham ●
Mildenhall Southwold
St. Ives DISS ● Fressingfield M Walberswick
  Brome ● Halesworth ●
Ixworth ● Yoxford ●
BURY ST. EDMUNDS 🍴,M Framlingham
A45 Earl Stonham M Aldeburgh
NEWMARKET Needham Market Otley 🍴
Lavenham Woodbridge 🍴 Orford
CAMBRIDGE Chelsworth IPSWICH
Melbourn ● Cavendish ● Long Melford Hintlesham ⚔ With rm.🍴 Felixstowe
Saffron Walden Sudbury 55
Great Yeldham Hadleigh

7

NEWPORT · Newcastle-Emlyn

FISHGUARD · Boncath · Brechfa

Welsh Hook · Wolf's Castle

St. David's

Carmarthen · A 40

Whitland · Pont-ar-G

Haverfordwest · St. Clears · A 48

Narberth

Little Haven · Llanel

Milford Haven · Saundersfoot

PEMBROKE · Tenby

MANORBIER · Mumble

ISLE OF LUNDY

ILFRACOMBE · Combe Ma

WOOLACOMBE

Croyde · Putsborough

Saunton · BRAUNTO

BARNSTAPLE

Westward Ho! · Appledore

BIDEFORD

Umberleigh

Horns Cross

Bradworthy · HATHERLEIC

Milton Damerel

Bude · OKEHAMPT

Clawton · South Ze

Crackington Haven

Boscastle · Lewdown

Tintagel · Lifton

Port Isaac · TAVISTOCK

Trebetherick · Pendoggett

M PADSTOW · Rock · Gunnislake · Calstock

Mawgan Porth · Yelverto

ST. COLUMB MAJOR · BODMIN · LISKEARD

Watergate Bay · Pillaton

NEWQUAY · A 30 · Lostwithiel · PLYMOUTH

ST. AUSTELL XX with rm · Lanreath

Polkerris · LOOE · Cawsand

ST. AGNES · M FOWEY · Polperro · NEWTON FERRE

TRURO · Mevagissey

ST. IVES · REDRUTH · VERYAN · Portloe

PENZANCE · MARAZION · Portscatho

ST. JUST · Mousehole · Rosudgeon · FALMOUTH · ST. MAWES

Sennen · Praa Sands · Helston

Lamorna Cove · HELFORD M, XX With rm,

Mawgan

Mullion

Lizard

ISLES OF SCILLY

Bryher · Tresco

St.Mary's

1 Carlisle · 2 Newcastle

3 Liverpool · 4 · 5 Manchester · 6 Norwich

Cardigan · Birmingham

Bristol

7 · 8 · 11 Greater London · Dover

Plymouth · Southampton

9 · 10

56

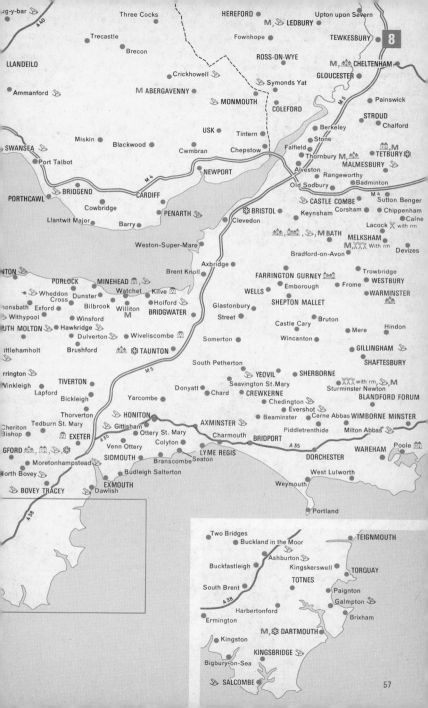

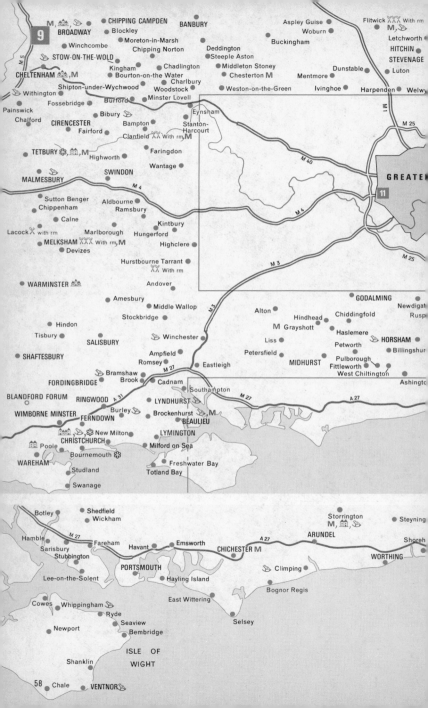

Sudbury
Hadleigh
IPSWICH
Hintlesham ✕✕✕ With rm
Saffron Walden
Great Yeldham
East Bergholt
Felixstowe
Baldock
Dedham
Manningtree
Harwich and Dovercourt
Clavering
THAXTED
Great Bardfield
Colchester
Bishop's Stortford
Braintree
Coggeshall
Frinton-on-Sea
Great Dunmow M
Felsted
Clacton-on-Sea
Witham
West Mersea
CHELMSFORD
M 25
Maldon
South Woodham Ferrers
Burnham-on-Crouch
Rochford
Basildon
LONDON ✿✿✿
Southend-on-Sea
North Stifford
Sheerness
Gravesend
A 2
Shorne
Rochester
Broadstairs
Herne Bay
Sittingbourne
RAMSGATE
M 2
Whitstable
Faversham
Sandwich
CANTERBURY
MAIDSTONE
Hadlow
WYE
A 2
Horley
Penshurst
Pluckley
DOVER
Gatwick Airport
ROYAL TUNBRIDGE WELLS
ASHFORD
Biddenden
Folkestone
EAST GRINSTEAD
Goudhurst
AWLEY
Wadhurst
Cranbrook
Hythe
FOREST ROW
Crowborough
Hawkhurst
Tenterden
Dymchurch
Cuckfield
Mayfield
Robertsbridge
Northiam
New Romney
A 259
UCKFIELD
Dallington
Sedlescombe
RYE
Halland
Rushlake Green
Battle
Icklesham
HERSTMONCEUX
Lewes
A 27
Hailsham
Bexhill
Selmeston
HASTINGS AND ST. LEONARDS
GHTON AND HOVE
Alfriston
tingdean
Seaford
EASTBOURNE M

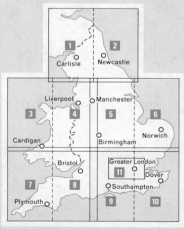

1 Carlisle
2 Newcastle
Liverpool
Manchester
3
4
5
6 Norwich
Cardigan
Birmingham
Bristol
Greater London
11 Dover
7
8
9 Southampton
10
Plymouth

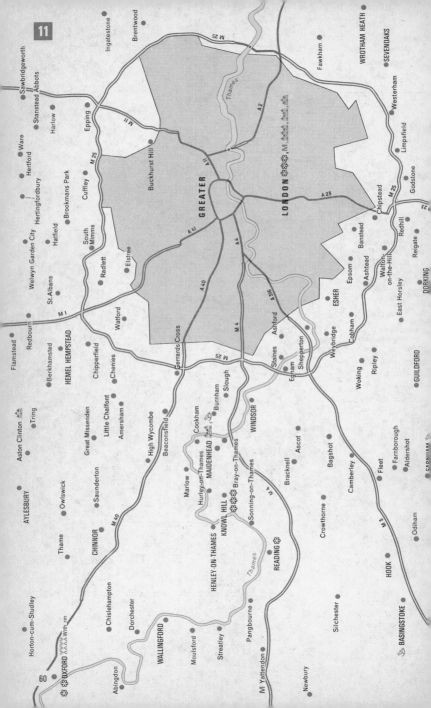

ENGLAND and WALES

Towns

ABBERLEY Heref. and Worc. **408** **404** M 27 – pop. 604 – ECD : Wednesday – ⊠ Worcester – ✆ 029 921 Great Witley.
♦ London 137 – ♦Birmingham 27 – Worcester 13.

🏨 **The Elms** ⍕ , WR6 6AT, W : 2 m. on A 443 ℰ 666, Telex 337105, ≼, 🏕, park, 🍽 – 📺 ☎ 🅿. 🏧 🖭 AE ⓪ VISA ⌘
M 10.95/17.00 **st.** and a la carte 22.25/27.50 **st.** ▲ 4.50 – **27 rm** ⌚ 46.00/69.00 **st.**, **1 suite** 91.00/97.00 **st.** – SB 93.00 **st.**

ABERAERON Dyfed **408** H 27 – pop. 1 445 – ECD : Thursday – ✆ 0545.
Envir. : New Quay (site★) SW : 8 m.
🛈 The Quay ℰ 570602 (summer only).
♦ London 237 – Carmarthen 36 – Fishguard 42 – ♦ Swansea 64.

🏠 **Feathers Royal,** SA46 0AQ, ℰ 570214, 🖳 – 📺 ⌨wc ⋔wc 🅿. 🏧 🖭 VISA
M 2.90/5.90 **st.** and a la carte ▲ 4.25 – **13 rm** ⌚ 19.50/29.50 **st.**

at Penant E : 4 m. by A 487 on B 4577 – ⊠ Llanon – ✆ 097 46 Nebo :

↟ **Bikerehyd Farm** ⍕ , SY23 5PB, NE : ½ m. ℰ 365, « Farmhouse and 14C converted cottages », 🏕 – 📺 ⋔wc 🅿
closed December and January – **6 rm** ⌚ –/17.00 **st.**

FORD, VOLVO Alban Sq ℰ 570312

ABERDAUGLEDDAU = Milford Haven.

ABERDOVEY (ABERDYFI) Gwynedd **408** H 26 – pop. 778 – ECD : Wednesday – ✆ 065 472.
See : Afon Dovey's mouth (site★★).
Envir. : Llanegryn (church★) N : 8 m. – Dolgoch Falls★ NE : 10 m.
🛈 Snowdonia National Park Centre, The Wharf ℰ 321 (summer only).
♦ London 230 – Dolgellau 25 – Shrewsbury 66.

🏨 **Plas Penhelig** ⍕ , LL35 0NA, E : 1 m. by A 493 ℰ 676, ≼, « Terraced gardens », park, 🍽 – ⌨wc ☎ 🅿. 🏧 AE ⓪ VISA ⌘
closed January-mid March – **M** (bar lunch Monday to Saturday)/dinner 11.25 **t.** – **11 rm** ⌚ 19.00/36.00 **t.** – SB (October-April) 57.00 **st.**

🏨 **Trefeddian,** Tywyn Rd, LL35 0SB, W : 1 m. on A 493 ℰ 213, ≼ golf course and sea, 🖳, 🏕, park, 🍽 – 🛗 📺 ⌨wc ⋔wc ♿ ⟷ 🅿. 🖾
Mid .March-mid November – **M** 6.00/10.00 **t.** ▲ 3.00 – **46 rm** ⌚ 19.30/55.00 **t.** – SB 48.00/64.00 **st.**

🏠 **Penhelig Arms,** Terrace Rd, LL35 0LT, ℰ 215, Telex 338751, ≼ – 📺 ⌨wc ⋔wc 🅿. 🏧 AE ⓪ VISA ⌘
M (bar lunch)/dinner 9.00 **t.** ▲ 2.50 – **11 rm** ⌚ 16.50/46.00 **t.** – SB (October-May) 50.00 **st.**

🏡 **Harbour,** 17 Glandovey Terr., LL35 0EB, ℰ 250, ≼ – ⋔wc. 🏧 VISA
April-October – **M** 7.50/10.00 **t.** and a la carte ▲ 2.75 – **6 rm** ⌚ 12.50/30.00 **t.**

🏡 **Bodfor,** Bodfor Terr., LL35 0EA, ℰ 475, ≼ – ⋔wc. 🏧 VISA
M (bar lunch Monday to Saturday)/dinner 8.00 **t.** and a la carte ▲ 2.50 – **15 rm** ⌚ 12.50/29.00 **t.** – SB 37.00/45.00 **st.**

✕ **Maybank** with rm, LL35 0PT, E : 1 m. on A 493 ℰ 500, ≼ – 📺 ⋔wc. AE VISA
closed February and November – **M** (booking essential)(bar lunch)/dinner 10.00 **t.** – **5 rm** ⌚ 17.00/34.00 **t.** – SB 48.00/53.00 **st.**

4

ABERGAVENNY (Y-FENNI) Gwent **403** L 28 – pop. 9 427 – ECD : Thursday – ✪ 0873.
Envir. : Llanthony Priory★ N : 10 m. – Bwlch (≼★ of the Usk Valley), NW : 9 ½ m.
🏠 Llanfoist, ✆ 3171, S : 2 m.
🗓 Brecon Beacons National Park Centre, 2 Lower Monk St. ✆ 3254 (summer only) – at Brecon : Brecon Beacons National Park, Watton Mount ✆ 0874 (Brecon) 4437 (summer only) – Market Car Park ✆ 0874 (Brecon) 2485 or 5692 (summer only).
♦ London 163 – Gloucester 43 – Newport 19 – ♦Swansea 49.

🏨 **Angel** (T.H.F.), 15 Cross St., NP7 5EW, ✆ 7121 – 📺 ⇌wc ☎ 🅿. 🍴. 🔼 🆎 ⓞ 𝘝𝘐𝘚𝘈
M 6.45/8.95 **st.** and a la carte ⌀ 3.40 – ☲ 5.65 – **29 rm** 41.00/51.00 **st.**

🏠 **Park,** 36 Hereford Rd, NP7 5RA, ✆ 3715 – 🅿
7 rm ☲ 10.00/20.00 **st.**

🏠 **Halidon House,** 63 Monmouth Rd, NP7 5HR, ✆ 77855, 🔟, 🌳 – 🅿. 🌂
4 rm ☲ 10.00/20.00 **st.**

at Llandewi Skirrid NE : 3 ½ m. by A 465 on B 4521 – ✉ ✪ 0873 Abergavenny :

✕ **Walnut Tree Inn,** NP7 8AW, ✆ 2797 – 🅿
closed lunch Monday and Bank Holidays, Sunday, 12 to 26 February and 4 days at Christmas –
M (bar lunch and Monday dinner)/dinner a la carte 14.35/19.85 **t.** ⌀ 3.50.

at Llanwenarth NW : 3 m. on A 40 – ✉ Abergavenny – ✪ 0873 Crickhowell :

🏨 **Llanwenarth Arms,** Brecon Rd, NP8 1EP, ✆ 810550, ≼, 🔥 – 📺 ⇌wc ☎ 🅿. 🔼 🆎 ⓞ
𝘝𝘐𝘚𝘈. 🌂
M a la carte 9.50/16.00 **st.** ⌀ 3.00 – **18 rm** ☲ 38.00/43.00 **st.**

AUSTIN-ROVER, FORD Brecon Rd ✆ 2126   RENAULT 9 Monmouth Rd ✆ 2323
PEUGEOT, TALBOT Penpergwm, Gobion ✆
0873 840287

ABERGWAUN = Fishguard.

ABERGWESYN Powys **403** I 27 – see Llanwrtyd Wells.

ABERGYNOLWYN Gwynedd **402 403** I 26 – ✉ Twywn – ✪ 065 477.
♦London 228 – Dolgellau 12 – Shrewsbury 63.

🏠 **Dolgoch Falls,** SW : 2 ½ m. on B 4405 ✆ 258, ≼, 🌳 – 🅿. 𝘝𝘐𝘚𝘈
March-October – **6 rm** ☲ 12.00/24.00 **st.**

ABERHONDDU = Brecon.

ABERLLYNFI = Three Cocks.

ABERMAW = Barmouth.

ABERMULE (ABER-MIWL) Powys **403** K 26 – see Newtown.

ABERPORTH Dyfed **403** G 27 – pop. 1 614 – ECD : Wednesday – ✪ 0239.
See : Site★ – **Envir. :** Llangranog (cliffs★) NE : 4 m.
♦ London 249 – Carmarthen 29 – Fishguard 26.

🏨 **Penrallt,** SA43 2BS, SW : 1 m. by B 4333 ✆ 810227, 🔟 heated, 🌳, 🍴 – 📺 ⇌wc 🏮wc ☎
🅿. 🔼 🆎 ⓞ 𝘝𝘐𝘚𝘈. 🌂
closed 25 to 31 December – **M** (bar lunch)/dinner 10.00 **st.** and a la carte – **17 rm**
☲ 30.00/44.00 **st.** – SB (October-May) 70.00 **st.**

🏨 **Highcliffe,** SA43 2DA, ✆ 810534 – 📺 ⇌wc 🅿. 🔼 🆎 𝘝𝘐𝘚𝘈
M (bar lunch)/dinner 12.00 **st.** and a la carte – **12 rm** ☲ 19.00/48.00 **st.** – SB (except July and August) 38.00/42.00 **st.**

🏨 **Morlan Motel,** SA43 2EN, ✆ 810611 – 📺 ⇌wc 🅿. 🔼 🆎 ⓞ 𝘝𝘐𝘚𝘈
April-October – **M** (bar lunch Monday to Saturday)/dinner a la carte 6.50/11.00 **st.** ⌀ 1.70 –
16 rm ☲ 17.50/29.50 **st.** – SB (weekends only) 32.00/40.00 **st.**

ABERSOCH Gwynedd **402 403** G 25 – ECD : Wednesday – ✉ Pwllheli – ✪ 075 881.
Envir. : Llanengan (church★ : twin aisles rood screen) W : 2 m. – Hell's Mouth★ W : 3 m. – Aberdaron (site★) W : 10 m. – Braich y Pwll (≼★★ from 2nd car park) W : 12 m.
🏠 Golf Rd, Pwllheli, ✆ 0758 (Pwllheli) 612520, NE : 7 m. – 🏠 Pwllheli, ✆ 2622.
♦ London 265 – Caernarfon 28 – Shrewsbury 101.

🏨 **Riverside,** LL53 7HW, ✆ 2419, ≼, 🔼 – 📺 ⇌wc 🏮wc 🅿. 🔼 𝘝𝘐𝘚𝘈. 🌂
March-October – **M** (bar lunch)/dinner 16.50 **t.** ⌀ 3.40 – **12 rm** ☲ 20.00/50.00 **t.** – SB (except summer) 85.00/90.00 **st.**

🏨 **Abersoch Harbour** (Best Western), Long Engan, LL53 7HR, ✆ 2406, ≼ – 📺 ⇌wc 🏮wc
🅿. 🔼 🆎 ⓞ 𝘝𝘐𝘚𝘈
March-October – **M** 10.00 **t.** (dinner) and a la carte ⌀ 2.85 – **14 rm** ☲ 20.00/52.00 **t.** – SB 52.00/60.00 **st.**

↑ **Llysfor,** Lôn Garmon, LL53 7AL, ℰ 2248, ⋨ – 🅿
Easter-October – **8 rm** ⚏ 10.00/24.00 **st.**

✗✗ **Bronheulog** ⤳ with rm, Lôn Garmon, LL53 7UL, NW : ¾ m. ℰ 2177, ⋨ – 🚽wc 🅿 ⋨
closed Sunday to Thursday November-March – **M** *(closed Sunday to non-residents)* (dinner only)(booking essential) 9.00 **st.** and a la carte ⚱ 2.80 – **4 rm** ⚏ 12.50/25.00 **st.**

at Bwlchtocyn S : 2 m. – ✉ Pwllheli – ☎ 075 881 Abersoch :

🏛 **Porth Tocyn** ⤳, LL53 7BU, ℰ 2966, ≼ Cardigan Bay and mountains, « Country house atmosphere », ⛢ heated, ⋨, ✗ – 📺 🚽wc ☎ 🅿 ⤳
Easter-early November – **M** (buffet lunch)/dinner 15.00 **t.** ⚱ 2.75 – **17 rm** ⚏ 25.00/58.00 **t.**

ABERTAWE = Swansea.

ABERTEIFI = Cardigan.

ABERYSTWYTH Dyfed �403 H 26 – pop. 8 636 – ECD : Wednesday – ☎ 0970.
See : ≼★ from the National Library.
Envir. : Vale of Rheidol★ SE : 6 m.
🐎 Bryn-y-mor Rd, ℰ 615104, N : ½ m.
🛈 Eastgate ℰ 612125 and 617911.
♦ London 238 – Chester 98 – Fishguard 58 – Shrewsbury 74.

🏛 **The Groves,** 44-46 North Par., SY23 2NF, ℰ 617623 – 📺 🚽wc 🍴wc 🅿 ⤳ AE ⑩ VISA ✨
closed 23 December-3 January – **M** (bar lunch)/dinner 8.25 **t.** ⚱ 2.90 – **12 rm** ⚏ 21.50/39.00 **t.** – SB (except Bank Holidays) 51.00 **st.**

🏛 **Four Seasons,** 50-54 Portland St., SY23 2DX, ℰ 612120 – 📺 🚽wc 🅿 ⤳ VISA
closed 25 December-3 January – **M** (bar lunch Monday to Saturday)/dinner 10.60 **st.** ⚱ 2.50 – **15 rm** ⚏ 17.00/38.00 **st.** – SB (weekends only) 40.00/48.00 **st.**

at Chancery (Rhydgaled) S : 4 m. on A 487 – ✉ ☎ 0970 Aberystwyth :

🏛 **Conrah Country** ⤳, SY23 4DF, ℰ 617941, ≼, « 18C country house », ⛢, ⋨, park – 🛏 📺 🚽wc 🍴wc 🚲 ⚑ 🅿 ⤳ AE ⑩ VISA ✨
closed 1 week at Christmas – **M** 7.75/12.75 **t.** and a la carte ⚱ 3.00 – **22 rm** ⚏ 35.00/62.00 **t.** – SB (October-June)(weekends only) 64.00/70.00 **st.**

AUSTIN-ROVER-JAGUAR Park Av. ℰ 4841   FORD North Parade ℰ 4171
FIAT Llanfarian ℰ 612311

ABINGDON Oxon. �403 �404 Q 28 – pop. 29 130 – ECD : Thursday – ☎ 0235.
🛈 8 Market Pl. ℰ 22711.
♦ London 64 – ♦Oxford 6 – Reading 25.

🏛 **Upper Reaches** (T.H.F.), Thames St., OX14 3JA, ℰ 22311 – 📺 🚽wc ☎ 🅿 🔧 ⤳ AE ⑩ VISA
M 6.95/10.95 **st.** and a la carte ⚱ 3.40 – ⚏ 5.65 – **26 rm** 50.50/62.00 **st.**

AUSTIN-ROVER Drayton Rd ℰ 22822

ACOCKS GREEN West Midlands �403 �404 ② – see Birmingham.

ADLINGTON Lancs. �402 �404 M 23 – see Chorley.

AIGBURTH Merseyside – see Liverpool.

ALBRIGHTON Salop �402 �403 L 25 – see Shrewsbury.

ALCESTER Warw. �403 �404 O 27 – pop. 5 207 – ECD : Thursday – ☎ 0789.
Envir. : Ragley Hall★★ (17C) AC, SW : 2 m.
♦London 104 – ♦Birmingham 20 – ♦Coventry 28 – Gloucester 34.

✗ **Rossini,** 50 Birmingham Rd, B49 5EG, on A 435 ℰ 762764, Italian rest. – 🅿 ⤳ AE ⑩ VISA
closed Sunday and 4 weeks in summer – **M** 7.50 **t.** (lunch) and a la carte 8.40/13.70 **t.** ⚱ 2.80.

AUSTIN-ROVER Station Rd ℰ 764146   RENAULT Stratford Rd ℰ 762191

ALDBOURNE Wilts. �403 �404 P 29 – pop. 1 479 – ☎ 0672 Marlborough.
♦London 77 – ♦Oxford 36 – ♦Southampton 53 – Swindon 9.

✗ **Raffles,** 1 The Green, SN8 2BW, ℰ 40700 – ⤳ AE ⑩ VISA
closed lunch Monday and Saturday, Sunday, last 2 weeks August, 25 to 30 December and Bank Holidays – **M** 12.50 **t.** and a la carte 9.10/16.55 **t.** ⚱ 5.25.

ALDEBURGH Suffolk **404** Y 27 – pop. 2 711 – ECD : Wednesday – ☎ 072 885.

☒ at Thorpeness ♟ 2176, N : 2 ½ m.

🆔 Foundation Office, High St. ♟ 3637 (summer only).

◆ London 97 – ◆Ipswich 24 – ◆Norwich 41.

🏨 **Wentworth**, Wentworth Rd, IP15 5BD, ♟ 2312, ≤ – 📺 ➟wc �🛏wc 🅿. AE ⓞ
closed first 2 weeks January – **M** 8.50/10.50 t. and a la carte ⬧ 2.50 – **33 rm**.

🏨 **Brudenell** (T.H.F.), The Parade, IP15 5BU, ♟ 2071, ≤ – 📶 📺 ➟wc 🐾 🅿. 🏌 🕭 AE ⓞ
VISA
M 6.50/9.50 **st.** and a la carte ⬧ 3.40 – ☲ 5.65 – **47 rm** 38.00/51.00 **st.**

🏨 **Uplands**, Victoria Rd, IP15 5DX, ♟ 2420, 🌿 – 📺 ➟wc ⅙ 🅿. 🕭 AE ⓞ **VISA** 🕺
M (dinner only and Sunday lunch)/8.00 **t.** (dinner) and a la carte 10.00/14.25 **t.** – **20 rm**
☲ 19.15/40.80 **t.** – SB (winter only) 45.00/50.00 **st.**

ALDERLEY EDGE Cheshire **402 403 404** N 24 – pop. 4 272 – ECD : Wednesday – ☎ 0625.

Envir. : Capesthorne Hall★ (18C) *AC*, S : 4 ½ m.

◆ London 187 – Chester 34 – ◆Manchester 14 – ◆Stoke-on-Trent 25.

🏨 **De Trafford Arms** (De Vere), Congleton Rd, SK9 7AA, ♟ 583881 – 📶 📺 ➟wc 🐾 🅿. 🕭
AE ⓞ **VISA**
M 4.50/8.75 **st.** and a la carte ⬧ 4.25 – **36 rm** ☲ 44.00/56.00 **st.** – SB (weekends only)
52.00/55.00 **st.**

XX **Mandarin**, 2-3 The Parade, SK9 7JX, ♟ 584434, Chinese rest. – AE
closed Monday and 25-26 December – **M** 3.50/12.50 **t.** and a la carte ⬧ 2.90.

X **Octobers**, 47 London Rd, SK9 7JT, ♟ 583942, Bistro – 🕭 **VISA**
closed Sunday – **M** (dinner only) 8.50 **t.** and a la carte 8.85/12.75 **t.** ⬧ 3.30.

X **Wizard Country**, Macclesfield Rd, Nether Alderley, SK10 4UB, SE : 1½ m. on B 5087
♟ 584000 – 🅿. 🕭 AE ⓞ **VISA**
closed Sunday dinner and Monday – **M** (dinner only and Sunday lunch)/dinner 10.00 **t.**
and a la carte 9.15/12.90 **t.** ⬧ 3.25.

AUSTIN-ROVER-JAGUAR London Rd ♟ 582218   VOLVO 77 London Rd ♟ 583912
VAUXHALL-OPEL 34 Knutsford Rd ♟ 582691

ALDERSHOT Hants. **404** R 30 – pop. 53 665 – ECD : Wednesday – ☎ 0252.

◆London 43 – Guildford 9 – ◆Southampton 43.

⌂ **Glencoe**, Eggars Hill, ♟ 20801, 🌿 – ➟wc 🅿
12 rm.

ALDRIDGE West Midlands **402 403 404** O 26 – pop. 17 549 – ECD : Thursday – ✉ Walsall –
☎ 0922.

◆London 130 – ◆Birmingham 12 – Derby 32 – ◆Leicester 40 – ◆Stoke-on-Trent 38.

🏨 **Fairlawns**, 178 Little Aston Rd, WS9 0NU, E : 1 m. on A 454 ♟ 55122, Telex 339873 – ▤ rest
📺 ➟wc ⅏wc 🕾 🅿. 🏌 🕭 AE ⓞ **VISA**
M (closed to non-residents Sunday and Bank Holidays) 12.50/10.00 **st.** and a la carte ⬧ 3.00 –
30 rm ☲ 38.00/45.00 **st.**

FORD Northgate ♟ 54031

ALFRISTON East Sussex **404** U 31 – pop. 811 – ECD : Wednesday – ✉ Polegate – ☎ 0323.

◆ London 66 – Eastbourne 9 – Lewes 10 – Newhaven 8.

🏨 **Star** (T.H.F.), High St., BN26 5TA, ♟ 870495 – 📺 ➟wc 🐾 🅿. 🕭 AE ⓞ **VISA**
M 9.65/9.95 **st.** and a la carte ⬧ 3.40 – ☲ 5.65 – **32 rm** 42.00/57.00 **st.**

🏨 **Deans Place**, Polegate, BN26 5TW, ♟ 870248, ≤, ⩫ heated, 🌿, park, 🕺 – ➟wc 🕾 🅿.
🕭 AE **VISA** 🕺
closed 29 December-mid February – **M** 6.00/10.50 **t.** and a la carte – **43 rm** ☲ 30.00/70.00 **t.**

🏨 **White Lodge Country House**, Sloe Lane, BN26 5UR, ♟ 870265, ≤, «Ornate decor», 🌿,
🕺 – 📺 ➟wc 🐾 🅿. 🕭 AE **VISA** 🕺
M 7.40/10.75 **t.** and a la carte ⬧ 2.90 – **10 rm** ☲ 32.50/60.00 **t.** – SB (October-April)
55.00/60.00 **st.**

XX **Moonrakers**, High St., BN26 5TD, ♟ 870472
closed Sunday, Monday and 5 January-13 February – **M** (dinner only) 13.50 **t.** ⬧ 3.00.

ALLESLEY West Midlands **403 404** P 26 – see Coventry.

ALNMOUTH Northumb. **401 402** P 17 – pop. 605 – ECD : Wednesday – ☎ 0665.

◆London 314 – ◆Edinburgh 90 – ◆Newcastle-upon-Tyne 37.

⌂ **Marine House**, 1 Marine Rd, NE66 2RW, ♟ 830349, ≤, 🌿 – ⅏wc
8 rm ☲ –/30.00 **t.**

ALNWICK Northumb. **401** **402** O 17 – pop. 6 972 – ECD : Wednesday – ✆ 0665.

See : Castle★★ (Norman) AC.

Envir. : Dunstanburgh Castle 14C-15C (ruins, coastal setting★) AC, 1 ¼ m. walk from Craster, no cars, NE : 7 ½ m. – Warkworth (castle★ 12C) AC, SE : 7 m. – Rothbury (Cragside gardens★ : rhododendrons) AC, SW : 12 m.

🏌 Foxton Hall,Alnmouth ✆ 0665 (Alnmouth) 830368, SE : 5 m. – 🏌 Swansfield Park, Alnwick ✆ 602632 – 🏌 Alnmouth Village, Marine Rd, Alnmouth ✆ 0665 (Alnmouth) 830370, SE : 5 m.

🛈 The Shambles ✆ 603129 (summer only).

♦ London 320 – ♦Edinburgh 86 – ♦Newcastle-upon-Tyne 34.

   🏨 **White Swan** (Swallow), Bondgate Within, NE66 1TD, ✆ 602109, Group Telex 53168 – 📺 🚾 ⇌ 📶 🛥 ⚫ VISA
     M 6.50/10.50 **st.** and a la carte ≬ 3.95 – **41 rm** ⚌ 35.00/55.00 **st.** – SB 60.00/70.00 **st.**

   🏛 **Hotspur,** Bondgate Without, NE66 1PR, ✆ 602924 – 📺 🚾 ☎ 🛥 VISA
     M (bar lunch)/dinner a la carte 7.25/11.35 **t.** ≬ 2.95 – **26 rm** ⚌ 20.00/43.00 **t.** – SB 50.00/56.00 **st.**

   ↑ **Bondgate House,** Bondgate Without, NE66 2QQ, ✆ 602025 – 📺
     8 rm ⚌ 10.00/22.00 **st.**

FORD Lagny St. ✆ 602294

ALRESFORD Hants. **403** **404** Q 30 – see New Alresford.

ALSAGER Cheshire **402** **403** **404** N 24 – pop. 12 944 – ✉ Stoke-on-Trent – ✆ 093 63.

♦ London 180 – Chester 36 – ♦ Liverpool 49 – ♦ Manchester 32 – ♦ Stoke-on-Trent 11.

   🏨 **Manor House,** Audley Rd, ST7 2QQ, SE : ½ m. ✆ 78013 – 📺 📶 🚾 ☎ ⚫ 🛥 🛥 AE ⚫ VISA ✦
     M (buffet lunch Saturday) 7.95 **st.** (lunch)and a la carte 12.10/18.10 **t.** ≬ 3.25 – **28 rm** ⚌ 37.00/50.00 **st.**

AUSTIN-ROVER Lawton Rd ✆ 2146   FORD 52 Sandbach Rd South ✆ 3241
CITROEN Rode Heath ✆ 6226

ALSTON Cumbria **401** **402** M 19 – pop. 1 968 – ECD : Tuesday – ✆ 0498.

🛈 Railway Station ✆ 81696.

♦ London 309 – ♦Carlisle 28 – ♦Newcastle-upon-Tyne 45.

   🏨 **Lovelady Shield Country House** ⏳, Nenthead Rd, CA9 3LF, E : 2 ½ m. on A 689 ✆ 81203, ≤, 🌲, ✦ – 📺 🚾 📶 🚾 ⚫ AE ⚫ ✦
     March-November – **M** (dinner only and Sunday lunch)/dinner 13.00 **t.** ≬ 3.50 – **12 rm** ⚌ 22.00/50.00 **t.** – SB (December-Easter) 44.00 **st.**

   🏛 **Lowbyer Manor,** Hexham Rd, CA9 3JX, ✆ 81230, 🌲 – ⇌🚾 📶🚾 ⚫ 🛥 AE ⚫ VISA ✦
     M a la carte 5.20/8.60 **t.** – **12 rm** ⚌ 26.00/37.50 **t.** – SB (November-April) 45.00 **st.**

   🏛 **High Fell Old Farmhouse** ⏳, CA9 3BP, S : 1 ¾ m. on A 686 ✆ 81597, ≤ – ⚫. ✦
     M (booking essential) a la carte 13.40/21.40 **st.** ≬ 3.50 – **5 rm** ⚌ 18.50/42.00 **st.**

☞ *By January 1988 this guide will be out of date.*
   Get the new edition.

ALTON Hants. **404** R 30 – pop. 14 163 – ECD : Wednesday – ✆ 0420.

🏌 Old Odiham Rd ✆ 82042, N : 2 m.

♦ London 53 – Reading 24 – ♦Southampton 29 – Winchester 18.

   🏨 **Swan,** High St., GU34 1AT, ✆ 83777, Group Telex 858875 – 📺 ⇌🚾 📶🚾 ☎ ⚫ 🛥 🛥 AE ⚫ VISA
     M (carving rest.) 8.00 **t.** (lunch) and a la carte 9.80/13.60 **t.** ≬ 3.35 – **38 rm** ⚌ 43.00/54.00 **t.** – SB (weekends only) 57.00/59.00 **st.**

   🏛 **Grange,** 17 London Rd, Holybourne, GU34 4EG, ✆ 86565, 🌲 – 📺 ⇌🚾 📶🚾 ☎ ⚫
     13 rm.

AUSTIN-ROVER, VAUXHALL Butts Rd ✆ 84141   PEUGEOT, TALBOT Four Marks ✆ 62354
FORD Ackender Rd ✆ 83993

ALTRINCHAM Greater Manchester **402** **403** **404** N 23 – pop. 39 528 – ECD : Wednesday – ✆ 061 Manchester.

🏌 Stockport Rd, Timperley ✆ 928 0761, E : 1 m. on A 160 – 🏌 Dunham Forest, Oldfield Lane ✆ 928 2605, W : 1 m.

♦ London 191 – Chester 30 – ♦Liverpool 30 – ♦Manchester 8.

   🏨 **Cresta Court** (Best Western), Church St., WA14 4DP, on A 56 ✆ 928 8017, Telex 667242 – 📶
     📺 ⇌🚾 ⚫ 🛥 🛥 VISA
     M a la carte 6.10/9.00 **t.** – **139 rm** ⚌ 38.50/48.75 **st.** – SB (weekends only) 52.00 **st.**

   🏨 **George and Dragon** (Greenall Whitley), 22 Manchester Rd, WA14 4PH, on A 56 ✆ 928 9933
     – 📶 📺 ⇌🚾 📶🚾 ⚫ 🛥 🛥 VISA ✦
     M *(closed Sunday dinner)* (bar lunch Monday to Saturday)/dinner a la carte 11.60/15.15 **st.**
     ≬ 3.75 – **47 rm** ⚌ 21.50/53.00 **st.**

🏨 **Pelican** (Greenall Whitley), Manchester Rd, West Timperley, WA14 5NH, N : 2 m. on A 56
  ℘ 962 7414 – 📺 🛏wc ☜ 🅿. ⚡
  50 rm.

⌂ **Bollin,** 58 Manchester Rd, WA14 4PJ, on A 56 *℘* 928 2390 – 🅿
  10 rm ⊠ 13.80/23.00 **st.**

at Timperley NE : 2 m. by A 560 on B 5165 – ✉ Altrincham – ✆ 061 Manchester :

XXX **Le Bon Viveur** (at Hare and Hounds H.), Wood Lane, WA15 7LY, on A 560 *℘* 904 0266,
  French rest. – 🅿 🔼 AE ① VISA
  closed Sunday and Bank Holidays – **M** 7.95/19.50 **t.** and a la carte 12.05/18.95 **t.** 🍷 3.50.

at Hale SE : 1 m. on B 5163 – ✉ Altrincham – ✆ 061 Manchester :

🏨 **Ashley** (De Vere), Ashley Rd, WA15 9SF, *℘* 928 3794, Group Telex 669406 – 🛗 📺 🛏wc ☜.
  🔼. 🔼 AE ① VISA
  M 6.50/8.50 **st.** and a la carte 🍷 4.00 – **49 rm** ⊠ 48.00/57.00 **st.**

XX **Evergreen,** 169-171 Ashley Rd, WA15 9SD, *℘* 928 1222, Chinese-Cantonese rest. – 🔼 AE
  VISA
  M (dinner only) 8.75 **t.** and a la carte 6.15/10.95 **t.**

at Halebarns SE : 3 m. on A 538 – ✉ Altrincham – ✆ 061 Manchester :

🏰 **Four Seasons,** Hale Rd, WA15 8XW, *℘* 904 0301, Telex 665492 – 🛗 📺 🛏wc ☎ 🅿. 🔼. 🔼
  AE ① VISA
  M (bar lunch Saturday)/dinner a la carte 10.40/21.50 **t.** – **48 rm** ⊠ 33.00/80.00 **t.**

at Bowdon SW : 1 m. – ✉ Altrincham – ✆ 061 Manchester :

🏨 **Bowdon,** Langham Rd, WA14 2HT, *℘* 928 7121, Telex 668208 – 📺 🛏wc ☎ 🅿. 🔼. 🔼 🔼
  ① VISA
  closed 26 December – **M** 9.00 **st.** and a la carte 10.45/17.65 **st.** 🍷 2.75 – **41 rm** ⊠ 24.00/51.00 **st.**
  – SB (weekends only) 48.00 **st.**

🏰 **Bowdon Croft** ⌂, Green Walk, WA14 2SN, *℘* 928 1718, ≼, « Tastefully furnished 19C
  house », ☞ – 🛏wc 🅿. 🔼 VISA. ⚡
  M *(closed lunch to non-residents)* (booking essential) 8.50/11.00 **s.** 🍷 3.50 – **8 rm**
  ⊠ 36.00/52.00 **s.**

ALFA-ROMEO Money Ash Rd, Hale Bridge *℘*
928 5980
AUSTIN-ROVER-DAIMLER-JAGUAR Victoria Rd *℘*
928 7124
FORD 44 Hale Rd Bridge *℘* 928 2275
HONDA, SAAB Bancroft Rd, Hale *℘* 980 8004

RENAULT-HYUNDAI Manchester Rd *℘* 973 3021
SAAB Bancroft Rd, Hale *℘* 980 8004
TOYOTA Mobberley Rd, Ashley *℘* 928 3112
VAUXHALL-OPEL 276-280 Stockport Rd, Timperley
℘ 980 3212
VOLVO Manchester Rd *℘* 928 2384

ALVESTON Avon ⁴⁰³ ⁴⁰⁴ M 29 – pop. 3 154 – ECD : Wednesday – ✉ Bristol – ✆ 0454 Thornbury.

♦London 127 – ♦Bristol 11 – Gloucester 23 – Swindon 42.

🏰 **Post House** (T.H.F.), Thornbury Rd, BS12 2LL, on A 38 *℘* 412521, Telex 444753, ⊠ heated,
  ☞ – 📺 🛏wc 🅿. 🔼. 🔼 AE ① VISA
  M 7.50/9.75 **st.** and a la carte 🍷 3.40 – ⊠ 5.65 – **75 rm** 51.00/60.00 **st.**

🏰 **Alveston House,** BS12 2LJ, on A 38 *℘* 415050, Telex 449212, ☞ – 📺 🛏wc 🛏wc ☎ 🅿.
  🔼. 🔼 VISA. 🍷
  M 12.25 **st.** and a la carte 12.95/17.75 **st.** 🍷 3.55 – **30 rm** ⊠ 42.50/54.50 **st.** – SB (weekends
  only) 63.00 **st.**

AMBERLEY Glos. – see Stroud.

AMBLESIDE Cumbria ⁴⁰² L 20 – pop. 2 689 – ECD : Thursday – ✆ 0966.

Envir. : Tarn Hows⋆⋆ (lake) SW : 6 m. by A 593 AY – Langdale Valley⋆⋆ W : 7 m. by B 5343 AY.

🅱 Old Courthouse, Church St. *℘* 32582 (summer only).

♦London 278 – ♦Carlisle 47 – Kendal 14.

Plan opposite

🏰 **Kirkstone Foot Country House** ⌂, Kirkstone Pass Rd, LA22 9EH, NE : ¼ m. *℘* 32232, ☞
  – 📺 🛏wc 🛏wc 🅿. 🔼 AE ① VISA. ⚡   AZ **c**
  closed 21 December-28 February – **M** (bar lunch Monday to Saturday, residents only)/dinner
  12.00 **t.** 🍷 3.75 – **15 rm** ⊠ (dinner included) 29.50/65.00 **t.** – SB 45.00/65.00 **st.**

🏠 **Rothay Garth,** Rothay Rd, LA22 0EE, *℘* 32217, ☞ – 📺 🛏wc 🛏wc 🅿. 🔼 AE ① VISA. ⚡
  M (bar lunch)/dinner 9.25 **st.** 🍷 3.00 – **15 rm** ⊠ 20.50/49.00 **st.** – SB (except summer)
  45.00/57.00 **st.**   AZ **e**

⌂ **Elder Grove,** Lake Rd, LA22 0DB, *℘* 32504 – 📺 🛏wc 🅿. 🔼 VISA   AZ **a**
  March-October – **14 rm** ⊠ 14.00/35.00 **t.**

⌂ **Chapel House,** Kirkstone Rd, LA22 9DZ, *℘* 33143 – 🛏wc. ⚡   AZ **n**
  closed 1 January-26 February – **9 rm** ⊠ 18.50/40.00 **st.**

⌂ Smallwood House, Compston Rd, LA22 9DJ, *℘* 32330 – 🛏wc 🅿   AZ **x**
  14 rm.

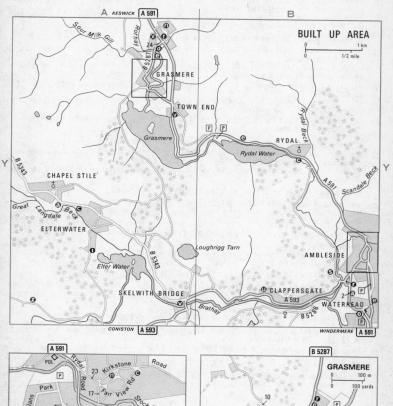

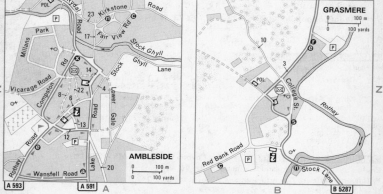

Town plans : roads most used by traffic and those on which guide listed hotels and restaurants stand are fully drawn ; the beginning only of lesser roads is indicated.

at Waterhead S : 1 m. on A 591 – ✉ ☏ 0966 Ambleside :

⌂⌂⌂ **Regent,** LA22 0ES, ✆ 32254, 🏊 – 📺 🛁wc 🚿wc ☎ 🅿. ▣ VISA — BY **e**
M (dinner only and Sunday lunch)/dinner 15.00 **st.** and a la carte 🍷 3.00 – **20 rm** ☕ 35.00/60.00 **st.** – SB (winter and spring only) 55.00/75.00 **st.**

⌂⌂ **Wateredge,** Borrans Rd, LA22 0EP, ✆ 32332, <, « Part 17C Fishermans cottages, lakeside setting », 🌳 – 🛁wc 🚿wc 🅿. ▣ VISA — BY **o**
closed December and January – **M** (bar lunch)/dinner 13.90 **t.** – **20 rm** ☕ (dinner included) 26.00/80.00 **t.** – SB (November-mid May) 56.00/68.00 **st.**

at Rothay Bridge S : ½ m. on A 593 – ✉ ☏ 0966 Ambleside :

⌂⌂⌂ **Rothay Manor,** LA22 0EH, ✆ 33605, <, « Elegant Regency interior », 🌳 – 📺 🛁wc ☎ ♿ 🅿. ▣ AE ⓓ VISA. ⊘ — BY **r**
closed 4 January-12 February – **M** (buffet lunch Monday to Saturday)/dinner 18.00 **t.** 🍷 3.00 – **16 rm** ☕ 49.00/78.00 **t.**, **2 suites** 96.00 **t.** – SB (November-March) 72.00/96.00 **st.**

⌂⌂ **Riverside H. and Lodge** ☾, Under Loughrigg, LA22 9LJ, ✆ 32395, 🌳 – 📺 🛁wc 🚿wc 🅿. ▣ VISA. ⊘ — BY **s**
closed December and January – **M** (bar lunch)/dinner 15.00 **t.** 🍷 3.75 – **15 rm** ☕ (dinner included) 35.00/60.00 **t.** – SB (except summer) 26.00/60.00 **st.**

⌂⌂ Borrans Park, Borrans Rd, LA22 0EN, ✆ 33454, 🌳 – 📺 🛁wc 🚿wc ♿ 🅿. ▣ ⓓ VISA. ⊘
13 rm ☕ 24.00/38.00 **st.** — BY **a**

at Clappersgate W : 1 m. on A 593 – ✉ ☏ 0966 Ambleside :

⌂⌂⌂ **Nanny Brow Country House** ☾, LA23 9NF, ✆ 32036, < Brathay Valley and Langdale, « Landscaped gardens », 🎾 – 📺 🛁wc 🚿wc ☎ 🅿. ▣ VISA — BY **u**
M (dinner only) 12.50 **st.** 🍷 2.50 – **19 rm** ☕ 22.50/45.00 **st.**, **3 suites** 55.00/65.00 **st.** – SB 45.00/79.00 **st.**

at Skelwith Bridge W : 2 ½ m. on A 593 – ✉ ☏ 0966 Ambleside :

⌂⌂ **Skelwith Bridge,** LA22 9NJ, ✆ 32115, <, 🌳 – 🛁wc 🅿. ▣ VISA — AY **v**
M (bar lunch Monday to Saturday)/dinner 9.95 **t.** 🍷 3.10 – **24 rm** ☕ 18.00/48.00 **t.** – SB (except September and October) 40.00/62.00 **st.**

at Little Langdale W : 4 ½ m. by A 593 – ✉ ☏ 096 67 Langdale :

⌂ **Three Shires Inn** ☾, LA22 9NZ, ✆ 215, <, 🌳 – 🅿. ⊘ — AY **z**
accomodation closed midweek December and January – **M** (bar lunch)/dinner 11.25 **st.** and a la carte 🍷 3.20 – **10 rm** ☕ 16.50/33.00 **st.**

at Elterwater W : 4 ½ m. by B 5343 – ✉ Ambleside – ☏ 09667 Langdale :

⌂⌂ **Eltermere Country House** ☾, LA22 9HY, ✆ 207, <, 🌳 – 📺 🛁wc 🚿wc 🅿. ▣ VISA. ⊘
closed 25 and 26 December – **M** (bar lunch by arrangement)/dinner 10.50 **t.** 🍷 3.00 – **16 rm** ☕ 20.00/40.00 **t.** – SB 52.00/58.00 **st.** — AY **i**

at Chapel Stile W : 5 m. on B 5343 – ✉ Chapel Stile – ☏ 096 67 Langdale :

⌂⌂⌂⌂ Pillar ☾, Great Langdale, LA22 9JB, ✆ 302, Telex 65188, 🏊, 🎾, park, squash – ▤ rest 📺 ☎ 🅿. ⛺ – **36 rm**, **18 suites**. — AY **c**

⌂⌂ Langdales ☾, Great Langdale, LA22 9JF, ✆ 253, 🎾, 🌳 – 🛁wc 🚿wc 🅿 – **20 rm**. — AY **a**

at Rydal NW : 1 ½ m. on A 591 – ✉ ☏ 0966 Ambleside :

⌂ **Rydal Lodge,** LA22 9LR, ✆ 33208, 🌳 – 🅿. ▣ ⓓ VISA — BY **c**
closed January – **8 rm** ☕ 17.00/42.00 **t.**

FORD Millans Park ✆ 33033

AMERSHAM (Old Town) Bucks. **404** S 28 – pop. 21 326 – ECD : Thursday – ☏ 024 03.

◆London 29 – Aylesbury 16 – ◆Oxford 33.

⌂⌂ **Crown** (T.H.F.), High St., HP7 0DH, ✆ 21541, 🌳 – 📺 🛁wc ☎ 🅿. ▣ AE ⓓ VISA
M 5.00/10.50 **st.** and a la carte 🍷 3.40 – ☕ 5.65 – **25 rm** 48.00/58.00 **st.**, **2 suites**.

XX **King's Arms,** High St., HP7 0DJ, ✆ 6333 – 🅿. ▣ AE ⓓ VISA
closed Sunday dinner and Monday – **M** 15.00 **t.** (dinner) and a la carte 11.05/15.25 **t.** 🍷 3.15.

AUSTIN-ROVER London Rd ✆ 5911
DAIMLER JAGUAR London Rd ✆ 28013
PEUGEOT TALBOT 4-8 White Lion Rd ✆ 024 04 (Little Chalfont) 4666
RENAULT The Broadway ✆ 4656

AMESBURY Wilts. **403** **404** O 30 The West Country G. – pop. 5 519 – ECD : Monday – ☏ 0980.

Envir. : Stonehenge (Megalithic Monument)★★★ *AC*, W : 2 m.

⛳18 Tidworth Garrison, Tidworth, Hants. ✆ 0980 (Stonehenge) 42301 N : 7 m.

ℹ Redworth House, Flower Lane ✆ 22833 and 23255.

◆London 88 – ◆Bristol 52 – ◆Southampton 31 – Taunton 61.

⌂⌂⌂ **Antrobus Arms,** 15 Church St., SP4 7EY, ✆ 23163, 🌳 – 📺 🛁wc ☎ 🅿. ▣ AE ⓓ VISA
M (carving lunch)/dinner 8.50 **t.** and a la carte 🍷 3.00 – **20 rm** ☕ 22.00/42.00 **t.**

RENAULT High St. ✆ 22525

AMMANFORD (RHYDAMAN) Dyfed 408 I 28 – pop. 5 708 – ECD : Thursday – ⊠ ✆ 0269 Llandybie.

◆London 208 – Carmarthen 22 – ◆Swansea 19.

　🏛 **Mill at Glynhir** ⟍, SA18 2TE, NE : 3 ¼ m. by A 483 and Glynhir Rd ✆ 850672, ⟍, ⛭ – 📺 ⇌wc �🛁wc ℗
　closed Christmas – **M** 6.50/10.50 t. and a la carte ⌀ 2.50 – **10 rm** � 23.00/46.00 t. – SB (except summer)(weekends only) 48.00/58.00 st.

AMOTHERBY North Yorks. 402 R 21 – see Malton.

AMPFIELD Hants. 408 404 P 30 – pop. 1 675 – ECD : Wednesday – ⊠ Romsey – ✆ 0794 Braishfield.

◆London 79 – Bournemouth 31 – Salisbury 19 – ◆Southampton 11 – Winchester 7.

　🏛 **Potters Heron** (Whitbread), Winchester Rd, SO51 9ZF, on A 31 ✆ 042 15 (Chandlers Ford) 66611 – 📺 ⇌wc ℗. 🛂. ⟍ AE ⓞ VISA ⚘
　M 8.00/12.00 t. and a la carte ⌀ 3.00 – **60 rm** ⊒ 45.00/65.00 t. – SB (weekends only) 50.00/60.00 st.

　✕✕ **Keats,** SO51 9BQ, on A 31 ✆ 68252, Italian rest. –
　closed Sunday dinner and Monday – **M** 5.90/15.00 t. and a la carte 11.15/15.25 t. ⌀ 2.75.

ANDOVER Hants. 408 404 P 30 – pop. 30 632 – ECD : Wednesday – ✆ 0264.

🛈 Town Mill car park, Bridge St. ✆ 24320 (summer only).

◆London 74 – Bath 53 – Salisbury 17 – Winchester 11.

　🏛 **Danebury,** High St., SP10 1NX, ✆ 23332 – 📺 ⇌wc ☎. 🛂. ⟍ AE ⓞ VISA ⚘
　M 4.95 st. and a la carte ⌀ 3.20 – **24 rm** ⊒ 40.00/48.00 st. – SB (weekends only) 25.00/28.00 st.

　🏛 **White Hart,** Bridge St., SP10 1BH, ✆ 52266 – 📺 ⇌wc �🛁wc ⚘ ℗. 🛂. ⟍ AE ⓞ VISA
　M (buffet lunch)/dinner a la carte 7.65/16.95 t. ⌀ 3.50 – **21 rm** ⊒ 30.00/51.00 t. – SB (weekends only) 54.00/60.00 st.

ALFA-ROMEO, FIAT, LANCIA Salisbury Rd ✆ 61166　　FORD West St. ✆ 51811
AUDI, VW 50 London St. ✆ 252839　　VAUXHALL Newbury Rd ✆ 24233
AUSTIN-ROVER 278 Weyhill Rd ✆ 23781

ANDOVERSFORD Glos. 408 404 O 28 – see Cheltenham.

APPLEBY Cumbria 402 M 20 – pop. 2 344 – ECD : Thursday – ✆ 07683.

🛆 ✆ 51432, S : 2 m.

🛈 Moot Hall, Boroughgate ✆ 51177.

◆London 285 – ◆Carlisle 33 – Kendal 24 – ◆Middlesbrough 58.

　🏛 **Appleby Manor** (Best Western), Roman Rd, CA16 6JD, E : ½ m. by B 6542 via Station Rd ✆ 51571, ≤, ⛭ – 📺 ⇌wc ℗. ⟍ VISA ⚘
　M 10.50 st. and a la carte 12.35/15.50 st. ⌀ 3.60 – **19 rm** ⊒ 30.50/49.00 st. – SB 58.00/78.00 st.

　🏠 **Tufton Arms,** 10 Boroughgate, Market Sq., CA16 6XA, ✆ 51593 – ⇌wc ℗. ⟍ ⓞ VISA
　M (buffet lunch)/dinner 9.00 t. and a la carte ⌀ 3.00 – **16 rm** ⊒ 20.00/38.00 t. – SB 35.00

　🏠 **Royal Oak Inn,** Bongate, CA16 6UN, ✆ 51463 – 📺 �🛁wc ℗. ⟍ AE ⓞ VISA
　closed Christmas Day – **M** a la carte 4.55/10.50 t. ⌀ 3.00 – **7 rm** ⊒ 14.50/36.00 t.

FORD The Sands ✆ 51133　　　　PEUGEOT-TALBOT ✆ 61435

APPLEDORE Devon 408 H 30 **The West Country G.** – pop. 2 180 – ECD : Wednesday – ⊠ ✆ 023 72 Bideford.

See : Site★.

◆London 235 – Bideford 4 – Exeter 47 – ◆Plymouth 62.

　🏠 **Seagate,** The Quay, EX39 1QS, ✆ 72589 – 📺 ⇌wc ℗. ⟍ AE ⓞ VISA
　M (bar lunch)/dinner 15.00 t. and a la carte ⌀ 3.00 – **9 rm** ⊒ 20.00/35.00 t.

APPLETON-LE-MOORS North Yorks. 402 R 21 – pop. 166 – ✆ 075 15 Lastingham.

◆London 245 – ◆Middlesbrough 37 – ◆Scarborough 27 – York 33.

　🏠 **Dweldapilton Hall** ⟍, YO6 6TF, ✆ 227, ⛭ – 🚿 📺 ⇌wc �🛁wc ℗. ⟍ ⓞ VISA
　closed January and February – **M** (bar lunch)/dinner 10.50 t. and a la carte ⌀ 3.10 – **12 rm** ⊒ 24.50/49.00 t. – SB (except summer) 54.00 st.

ARBERTH = Narberth.

ARDSLEY South Yorks. – see Barnsley.

ARMATHWAITE Cumbria 401 402 L 19 – ⊠ Carlisle – ✆ 069 92.

◆London 305 – ◆Carlisle 10 – Penrith 12.

　🏠 **Fox and Pheasant,** CA4 9PY, ✆ 400, ≤ – 📺 ⇌wc ℗. ⚘
　M 8.25 t. – **6 rm** ⊒ 12.50/30.00 t.

69

ARMITAGE Staffs. **402 403 404** O 25 – see Rugeley.

ARNCLIFFE North Yorks. **402** N 21 – pop. 67 – ⊠ Skipton – ✆ 075 677.

◆London 232 – Kendal 41 – ◆Leeds 41 – Preston 50 – York 52.

🏠 **Amerdale House** ≫, BD23 5QE, ℰ 250, ≤, 絵 – 氚wc ℗. 🔼 VISA
Easter–December – **M** (bar lunch)/dinner 12.00 **st.** ◊ 2.50 – **9 rm** ⊐ 22.00/44.00 **st.** – SB 52.00/58.00 **st.**

ARUNDEL West Sussex **404** S 31 – pop. 2 595 – ECD : Wednesday – ✆ 0903.

See : Castle★ (keep 12C, ≤★ 119 steps, State apartments★) AC – St. Nicholas' Church (chancel or Fitzalan chapel★ 14C).

Envir. : Bignor (Roman Villa : mosaics★★ AC) NW : 7 m.

🖪 61 High St. ℰ 882268.

◆London 58 – ◆Brighton 21 – ◆Southampton 41 – Worthing 9.

🏨 **Norfolk Arms,** 22 High St., BN18 9AD, ℰ 882101 – 📺 ⇌wc ☎ ℗. 🔼. 🔼 AE ① VISA
M 7.95/11.95 **t.** ◊ 4.25 – **34 rm** ⊐ 32.00/46.00 **t.** – SB 59.00/63.00 **st.**

🏠 **White Swan Inn,** Chichester Rd, BN18 0AD, W : 1 m. on A 27 ℰ 882677 – 📺 ⇌wc ℗. 🔼 AE VISA. ℅
M a la carte 9.90/13.80 **st.** – **16 rm** ⊐ 35.00/40.00 **st.**

🏤 **Swan,** 29 High St., BN18 9AD, ℰ 882314 – 📺 ⇌wc 氚wc. 🔼 AE ① VISA. ℅
M 6.00 **t.** (dinner)and a la carte ◊ 2.75 – **10 rm** ⊐ 25.00/30.00 **t.** – SB (November–April except Bank Holidays) 30.00/37.00 **st.**

🏠 **Portreeves Acre,** The Causeway, BN18 9JJ, ℰ 883277, 絵 – 📺 ⇌wc ℗. ℅
5 rm ⊐ 20.00/32.00 **t.**

at Burpham NE : 3 m. by A 27 – ⊠ ✆ 0903 Arundel :

🏠 **Burpham Country** ≫, Old Down, BN18 9RJ, ℰ 882160, ≤, 絵 – 📺 ⇌wc ℗. 🔼 ℅
M 7.00/9.00 **st.** – **8 rm** ⊐ 17.00/45.00 **t.**

at Crossbush E : 1 m. on A 27 – ⊠ ✆ 0903 Arundel :

🏠 **Howards,** BN18 9PQ, ℰ 882655 – 📺 ⇌wc ℗. 🔼 AE ① VISA. ℅
M *(closed Christmas Day)* 6.80/7.80 **t.** and a la carte ◊ 2.40 – **9 rm** ⊐ 34.00/44.00 **st.** – SB (weekends only) 53.00 **st.**

at Walberton W : 3 m. by A 27 on B 2132 – ⊠ Arundel – ✆ 0243 Yapton :

🏨 **Avisford Park,** Yapton Lane, BN18 0LS, ℰ 551215, Group Telex 86137, ≤, 🔼 heated, 🔼, Ⓡ, 絵, park, ℅, squash – 📺 ☎ ℗. 絵. 🔼 AE VISA
M (buffet lunch)/dinner 16.75 **st.** and a la carte – **86 rm** ⊐ 44.00/80.00 **st.**, **3 suites** 88.00 **st.** – SB (weekends only) 75.00/93.50 **st.**

ASCOT Berks. **404** R 29 – pop. 17 930 (inc Sunningdale) – ECD : Wednesday – ✆ 0990.

🖪 Downshire, Easthampstead Park ℰ 0344 (Bracknell) 424066, W : 4 m. – 🖪 Lavender Park, Swinley Rd ℰ 0344(Bracknell) 884074, SW : 3 ½ m. on A 332.

◆London 36 – Reading 15.

🏨 **Royal Berkshire** (Ladbroke) ≫, London Rd, Sunninghill, SL5 0PP, NE : 2 m. on A 322 ℰ 23322, Telex 847280, 絵, park, ℅, squash – 📺 ☎ ℗. 絵. 🔼 AE ① VISA
M 26.50/35.70 **t.** and a la carte – ◊ 8.50 – **40 rm** 60.50/137.50 **st.**, **1 suite** 192.50/302.50 **st.** – SB (weekends only) 93.50 **st.**

🏨 **Berystede** (T.H.F.), Bagshot Rd, Sunninghill, SL5 9JH, S : 1 ¼ m. on A 330 ℰ 23311, Telex 847707, 🔼 heated, 絵 – 📺 ☎ ℗. 絵. 🔼 AE ① VISA
M 10.25/14.50 **st.** and a la carte ◊ 3.75 – ⊐ 6.50 – **92 rm** 56.00/68.00 **st.**

✗ **Grooms,** 6 Hermitage Par., High St., SL5 7HE, ℰ 22285 – 🔼 AE ① VISA
closed Saturday lunch, Sunday and Bank Holidays – **M** a la carte 11.85/16.95 **t.**

AUSTIN-ROVER Ascot Motor Works ℰ 20324   CITROEN Lyndhurst Rd, South Ascot ℰ 22257

ASHBURTON Devon **403** I 32 The West Country G. – pop. 3 610 – ECD : Wednesday – ✆ 0364.

◆London 220 – Exeter 20 – ◆Plymouth 23.

🏠 **Holne Chase** ≫, Two Bridges Rd, TQ13 7NS, NW : 3 m. on B 3357 ℰ 036 43 (Pounds-gate) 471, ≤, « Country house atmosphere », ≫, 絵, park – 📺 ⇌wc 氚wc 🖑 ᕱ ℗. 🔼 AE ① VISA
M 7.75/12.00 **t.** ◊ 2.40 – **16 rm** ⊐ 15.00/49.00 **st.** – SB 54.00/64.00 **st.**

🏠 **Dartmoor Motel,** Peartree Cross, TQ13 7JW, W : ½ m. ℰ 52232 – 📺 ⇌wc ℗. 🔼 AE ① VISA
closed 25 and 26 December – **M** 5.00/6.00 **t.** and a la carte ◊ 2.40 – **22 rm** ⊐ 27.85/50.85 **t.** – SB (October–June) 44.85/48.85 **st.**

🏠 **Gages Mill,** Buckfastleigh Rd, TQ13 7JW, S : ½ m. on A 38 ℰ 52391, 絵 – 氚wc ℗. ℅
March–November – **8 rm** ⊐ 16.00/25.00 **st.**

✗✗✗ **Country Garden,** 22 East St., TQ13 7AZ, ℰ 53431, « Ornate decor », 絵
M (dinner only)(booking essential).

COLT 6 East St. ℰ 52215   PEUGEOT North St. ℰ 52588

ASHBY DE LA ZOUCH Leics. 402 403 404 P 25 — pop. 9 987 — ECD : Wednesday — 🕿 0530.

🛈 13-15 Lower Church St. 🍽 415603 (summer only).

♦London 119 — ♦Birmingham 29 — ♦Leicester 18 — ♦Nottingham 22.

🏛 **Royal,** Station Rd, LE6 5GP, 🍽 412833, 🚳 — 📺 ⌷wc 🚿wc 🕿 ☎ 🅿 🛋 🛦 AE ① VISA
   M (bar lunch Saturday) 12.75/13.50 **t.** and a la carte — **31 rm** ⌷ 41.00/51.50 **t.** — SB (weekends only) 64.00/68.00 **st.**

AUSTIN-ROVER, SHERPA Bath St. 🍽 412770

ASHFORD Kent 404 W 30 — pop. 45 198 — ECD : Wednesday — 🕿 0233.

Envir. : Hothfield (St. Margaret's Church : memorial tomb★ 17C) NW : 3 m. — Lenham (St. Mary's Church : woodwork★) NW : 9 ½ m.

🛈 Information Kiosk, High St. 🍽 37311 ext 316.

♦London 56 — Canterbury 14 — ♦Dover 24 — Hastings 30 — Maidstone 19.

🏛 **Eastwell Manor** 🌤, Eastwell Park, TN25 4HR, N : 3 m. by A 28 on A 251 🍽 35751, Telex 966281, ≤, « Reconstructed period mansion in formal gardens », 🎿, park, 🎾 — 🛗 📺 ☎ 🛦
   🅿 🛋 🛦 AE ① VISA 🎿
   M 12.50/18.00 **st.** and a la carte 🛈 4.50 — **24 rm** ⌷ 60.00/95.00 **st.**, **3 suites** 135.00/153.00 **st.** — SB 105.00 **st.**

   at Kennington NE : 2 m. on A 28 — ✉ 🕿 0233 Ashford :

🏛 **Spearpoint** (Best Western), Canterbury Rd, TN24 9QR, 🍽 36863, 🚳 — 📺 ⌷wc 🚿wc ☎
   🅿 🛋 🛦 AE ① VISA
   M 9.50 **t.** and a la carte 🛈 2.40 — **36 rm** ⌷ 44.00/58.00 **st.** — SB (weekends only) 48.00/54.00 **st.**

🏠 **Downsview,** Willesborough Rd, TN24 9QP, 🍽 21953, 🚳 — 📺 ⌷wc 🚿wc 🅿
   M (dinner only) 6.80 **st.** and a la carte — **16 rm** ⌷ 16.00/32.40 **st.** — SB 36.20/42.20 **st.**

   at Mersham SE : 3 m. by A 292 off A 20 — ✉ Ashford — 🕿 023 372 Aldington :

XX **Stone Green Hall** 🌤 with rm, TN25 7HE, S : 1 m. via Church Rd 🍽 418, « Tastefully decorated Queen Anne house », 🚳, park — 📺 ⌷wc 🅿 🛋 🛦 AE ① VISA 🎿
   closed mid February-March — **M** (dinner only and Sunday lunch) 14.00/16.00 **t.** — **4 rm** ⌷ 35.00/75.00 **st.**

AUSTIN-ROVER 20-46 New St. 🍽 20334
FORD Station Rd 🍽 23451
NISSAN Maidstone Rd 🍽 34177

SKODA, FIAT Chart Rd 🍽 20624
VOLVO Chart Rd 🍽 35661

ASHFORD Surrey 404 S 29 — ECD : Wednesday — 🕿 078 42.

♦London 21 — Reading 27.

XX **Terrazza,** 45 Church Rd, TW15 2TY, 🍽 44887, Italian rest. — 🍽 🛋 🛦 AE ① VISA
   closed Saturday lunch, Sunday and Bank Holidays — **M** 12.75 **t.** and a la carte 17.40/24.45 **t.**

AUSTIN-ROVER 445 Staines Rd West 🍽 43591
CITROEN 594 London Rd 🍽 52125

VAUXHALL Staines Rd 🍽 41901
VW-AUDI 554 London Rd 🍽 50051

ASHFORD-IN-THE-WATER Derbs — see Bakewell.

ASHINGTON West Sussex 404 S 31 — pop. 1 728 — ECD : Wednesday — ✉ Pulborough — 🕿 0903.

♦London 50 — ♦Brighton 20 — Worthing 9.

🏠 **Mill House** 🌤, Mill Lane, RH10 3BZ, 🍽 892426, 🚳 — 📺 ⌷wc 🚿wc ☎ 🅿 🛋 🛦 ① VISA
   M (dinner only and Sunday lunch) 7.50/8.50 **t.** and a la carte 🛈 2.75 — ⌷ 4.50 — **10 rm** 20.00/44.00 **t.** — SB (weekends only) 50.00/55.00 **st.**

ASHTEAD Surrey 404 T 30 — 🕿 037 22.

♦London 19 — Guildford 15.

X **Snooty Fox,** 21 The Street, KT21 1AA, 🍽 76606 — 🛋 🛦 ① VISA
   closed Sunday, 1 week August, January and Bank Holidays — **M** 8.50/10.95 **t.** and a la carte 10.05/14.30 **t.** 🛈 4.00.

ASHTON-UNDER-LYNE Greater Manchester 402 403 404 N 23 — pop. 43 605 — ECD : Tuesday — 🕿 061 Manchester.

♦London 209 — ♦Leeds 40 — ♦Manchester 7 — ♦Sheffield 34.

🏛 **York House,** York Pl., off Richmond St., OL6 7TT, 🍽 330 5899 — 📺 ⌷wc 🚿wc ☎ 🅿 🛋 🛦 ① VISA
   closed 26 December and 1 January — **M** a la carte 7.70/15.20 **st.** 🛈 2.50 — **24 rm** ⌷ 29.00/44.00 **st.** — SB (weekends only) 50.00/70.00 **st.**

FORD Manchester Rd 🍽 330 0121
PEUGEOT TALBOT Hill St 🍽 330 6711

VAUXHALL 185 Katherine St 🍽 330 2222

ASKHAM Cumbria 401 402 L 20 – pop. 387 – ECD : Thursday – ⊠ Penrith – ☎ 093 12 Hackthorpe.

See : Lowther (Wildlife Park★) *AC*.

◆London 288 – ◆Carlisle 23 – Kendal 28.

- ☎ **Queen's Head Inn,** CA10 2PF, ℰ 225, « Miniature model railway » – **Ⓟ**
  M (bar lunch)/dinner 13.50 **t.** ⓵ 3.50 – **6 rm** ⌖ 17.50/35.00 **st.**

ASKRIGG North Yorks. 402 N 21 – pop. 404 – ⊠ Leyburn – ☎ 0969 Wensleydale.

◆London 251 – Kendal 32 – ◆Leeds 70 – York 63.

- ☎ **King's Arms,** Market Sq., DL8 3HQ, ℰ 50258 – 📺 ⇔wc ⋔wc. 📶 ⑩ 𝘝𝘐𝘚𝘈
  M (bar lunch)/dinner 9.75 **st.** ⓵ 2.95 – **10 rm** ⌖ 23.50/39.50 **t.** – SB 40.00/50.00 **st.**
- ✕ Rowan Tree, DL8 3HT, ℰ 50536.

ASPLEY GUISE Beds. 404 S 27 – pop. 2 296 – ⊠ ☎ 0908 Milton Keynes.

◆London 50 – Bedford 12 – Luton 15 – Northampton 22.

- 🏛 **Holt,** The Square, MK17 8DW, ℰ 583652, � – 📺 ⇔wc ⋔wc ☎ **Ⓟ** 📶 𝘝𝘐𝘚𝘈
  M (closed lunch Saturday, Sunday and Monday) a la carte 10.45/16.00 **t.** ⓵ 3.30 – **16 rm**
  ⌖ 35.00/65.00 **st.** – SB (weekends only) 50.00/60.00 **st.**

ASTON CLINTON Bucks. 404 R 28 – pop. 3 671 – ECD : Wednesday – ⊠ ☎ 0296 Aylesbury.

◆London 42 – Aylesbury 4 – ◆Oxford 26.

- 🏛🏛 **Bell Inn,** HP22 5HP, ℰ 630252, Telex 83252, « Courtyard and gardens » – ▤ rest 📺 ☎ **Ⓟ**
  📶 📶 𝘝𝘐𝘚𝘈. ✀
  M (closed Sunday dinner and Monday to non-residents) 14.00 **st.** (lunch) and a la carte
  27.95/43.00 **st.** ⓵ 3.20 – **21 rm** 55.00/97.00 **st.**, **6 suites** 96.75/112.50 **st.**

ATTLEBOROUGH Norfolk 404 X 26 – pop. 6 322 – ECD : Wednesday – ☎ 0953.

◆London 94 – ◆Cambridge 47 – ◆Norwich 15.

- 🏛 **Sherbourne,** Norwich Rd, NR17 2JX, NE : ½ m. ℰ 452129, � – 📺 ⇔wc ⋔ **Ⓟ** 📶 𝘈𝘌 𝘝𝘐𝘚𝘈.
  M (closed Sunday dinner and Monday except Bank Holidays) 8.95/12.95 **t.** and a la carte ⓵ 3.00
  – **5 rm** ⌖ 14.00/42.00 **t.** – SB 35.00/45.00 **st.**
- ☎ **Griffin,** Church St., NR17 2AH, ℰ 452149 – 📺 **Ⓟ**. ✀
  M (closed Sunday dinner) (bar lunch)/dinner 6.50 **t.** and a la carte ⓵ 2.75 – **7 rm** ⌖ 16.00/25.00 **t.**

FORD High St. ℰ 452274   RENAULT Station Rd ℰ 452223

AUSTWICK North Yorks. 402 M 21 – pop. 478 – ⊠ Lancaster (Lancs.) – ☎ 046 85 Clapham.

◆London 237 – Kendal 26 – Lancaster 23 – ◆Leeds 47.

- 🏛 **Traddock** ✎, LA2 8BY, ℰ 224, � – ⇔wc ⋔wc **Ⓟ**. ✀
  Easter-October – **M** (dinner only) (booking essential) 9.50 **t.** ⓵ 2.50 – **12 rm** ⌖ 16.00/31.00 **t.**

AVENING Glos. 403 404 N 28 – see Tetbury.

AVON Hants. – see Ringwood.

AXBRIDGE Somerset 403 L 30 The West Country G. – pop. 1 724 – ECD : Wednesday – ☎ 0934.

See : Site★★ – King John's Hunting Lodge★*AC* – St. John the Baptist Church★.

Envir. : The Cheddar Gorge★★ (The Gorge★★ - Jacob's Ladder≼★*AC* - The Caves★★*AC*)
– St. Andrews Church★, SE : 1 ½ m.

◆London 142 – ◆Bristol 17 – Taunton 31 – Weston-Super-Mare 10.

- ✕✕ **Oak House** with rm, The Square, BS26 2AP, ℰ 732444 – 📺 ⇔wc. 📶 𝘈𝘌 ⑩ 𝘝𝘐𝘚𝘈. ✀
  M (closed Sunday dinner to non-residents) 8.95/14.95 **t.** and a la carte 12.45/16.85 **t.** ⓵ 3.80 –
  11 rm ⌖ 29.50/45.00 **t.** – SB (weekends only) 65.00 **st.**

AXMINSTER Devon 403 L 31 – pop. 4 457 – ECD : Wednesday – ☎ 0297.

🄴 Old Court House, Church St. ℰ 34386 (summer only).

◆London 156 – Exeter 27 – Lyme Regis 5.5 – Taunton 22 – Yeovil 24.

- 🏛 **Woodbury Park Country House** ✎, Woodbury Cross, EX13 5TL, SE :1½ m. on A 35
  ℰ 33010, ≼, ⌑ heated, �, park – ⇔wc ⋔wc **Ⓟ**. 📶 𝘈𝘌 ⑩ 𝘝𝘐𝘚𝘈. ✀
  M (bar lunch)/dinner 10.00 **t.** – **7 rm** ⌖ 22.00/34.00 **t.** – SB (winter only) 30.00/34.00 **st.**

  at Hawkchurch NE : 4 ½ m. by A 35 off B 3165 – ⊠ Axminster – ☎ 029 77 Hawkchurch :

- 🏛🏛 **Fairwater Head** ✎, EX13 5TX, S : ¾ m. ℰ 349, ≼ Axe Vale, � – 📺 ⇔wc ☎ **Ⓟ** 📶 ⑩
  𝘝𝘐𝘚𝘈. ✀
  closed January and February – **M** (bar lunch)/dinner 10.50 **st.** and a la carte ⓵ 3.00 – **18 rm**
  ⌖ 29.00/54.00 **st.**

AYLESBURY Bucks. **404** R 28 – pop. 51 999 – ECD : Thursday – 🕿 0296.

Envir. : Waddesdon Manor (Rothschild Collection★★★) *AC*, NW : 5 ½ m. – Ascott House★★ (Rothschild Collection★★) and gardens★ *AC*, NE : 8 ½ m. – Stewkley (St. Michael's Church★ 12C) NE : 12 m.

🛧 Weston Turville, New Rd 🖉 24084, SE : 2 ½ m.

🏢 County Hall, Walton St. 🖉 5000 ext 308.

◆London 46 – ◆Birmingham 72 – Northampton 37 – ◆Oxford 22.

🏨 **Bell** (T.H.F.), Market Sq., HP20 1TX, 🖉 82141 – 📺 ➪wc ☎. 🖾 AE ⑩ VISA
M 5.25/8.95 **st.** and a la carte ⓘ 3.40 – ⊋ 5.65 – **17 rm** 40.00/50.00 **st.**

✗✗ **Pebbles,** 1 Pebble Lane, HP20 2JH, 🖉 86622 – 🖾 AE ⑩ VISA
closed Saturday lunch, Sunday dinner, Monday, 3 weeks August and 1 week Christmas – **M** 12.00/22.50 **st.** and a la carte 12.95/16.65 **st.** ⓘ 2.95.

at Weston Turville SE : 3 ½ m. by A 413 on B 4544 – ⊠ Aylesbury – 🕿 029 661 Stoke Mandeville :

🏨 **Five Bells,** 40 Main St., HP22 5RW, 🖉 3131 – 📺 ➪wc ☎ 🅿. 🖾 AE ⑩ VISA
M 8.50 **st.** and a la carte ⓘ 3.50 – **17 rm** ⊋ 30.00/45.00 **st.** – SB (weekends only) 42.00 **st.**

at Stoke Mandeville S : 3 ¼ m. by A 413 on A 4010 – ⊠ Aylesbury – 🕿 029 661 Stoke Mandeville :

🏨 **Belmore,** Risborough Rd, HP22 5UT, 🖉 2022, ⅀ heated, ✿ – 📺 ➪wc ➪wc ➪ ⅍ 🅿. 🖾 AE ⑩ VISA. ✖
closed 5 days at Christmas – **M** (dinner only) 7.80 **st.** ⓘ 3.00 – ⊋ 3.60 – **16 rm** 25.50/42.00 **st.** – SB (weekends only) 52.00/62.00 **st.**

AUSTIN-ROVER-DAIMLER-JAGUAR Buckingham Rd 🖉 84071
MERCEDES-BENZ Bicester Rd 🖉 81641
RENAULT Little Kimble 🖉 029 661 (Stoke Mandeville) 2239

VAUXHALL-OPEL 143 Cambridge St. 🖉 82321
VOLVO Stocklake 🖉 35331

BABBACOMBE Devon **403** J 32 – see Torquay.

BACKFORD CROSS Cheshire **402 403** L 24 – see Chester.

BADMINTON Avon **403 404** N 29 The West Country G. – pop. 283 – 🕿 045 423 Didmarton.
See : Badminton House★ *AC*.

◆London 114 – ◆Bristol 19 – Gloucester 26 – Swindon 33.

🏨 **Petty France,** GL9 1AF, NW : 3 m. on A 46 🖉 361, ✿ – 📺 ➪wc ➪wc ☎ 🅿. 🖾 AE ⑩ VISA. ✖
M 11.95 **t.** and a la carte ⓘ 3.50 – ⊋ 3.95 – **20 rm** 27.50/43.00 **st.** – SB (except Christmas)(weekends only) 65.00 **st.**

BAE COLWYN = Colwyn Bay.

BAGSHOT Surrey **404** R 29 – pop. 4 239 – ECD : Wednesday – 🕿 0276.

◆London 37 – Reading 17 – ◆Southampton 49.

🏨 **Pennyhill Park** ⌖, College Ride, GU19 5ET, off A 30 🖉 71774, ≤, ⅀ heated, 🛧, ⅀, ✿, park, ✖ – 📺 ☎ 🅿. 🕮. 🖾 AE ⑩ VISA. ✖
M 16.50/24.00 **t.** and a la carte ⓘ 3.75 – ⊋ 6.50 – **50 rm** 68.00 **t.**, **3 suites** 120.00/130.00 **st.** – SB (weekends only) 125.00 **st.**

🏨 **Cricketer's,** London Rd, GU19 5HR, N : ½ m. on A 30 🖉 73196, ✿ – 📺 ➪wc ➪wc ☎ 🅿
M (grill rest. only) – **14 rm**.

AUSTIN-ROVER London Rd, Windlesham, Nr Bagshot 🖉 73561

FORD 9 High St 🖉 63222

BAINBRIDGE North Yorks. **402** N 21 – pop. 474 – ECD : Wednesday – ⊠ Leyburn – 🕿 0969 Wensleydale.

◆London 249 – Kendal 31 – ◆Leeds 68 – York 61.

🏨 **Rose and Crown,** DL8 3EE, 🖉 50225 – 📺 ➪wc ➪wc 🅿. 🖾 VISA. ✖
M 5.00/11.00 **t.** and a la carte ⓘ 2.95 – **13 rm** ⊋ 16.50/40.00 **st.** – SB (November-April)(except Christmas) 40.00/46.00 **st.**

BAKEWELL Derbs. **402 403 404** O 24 – pop. 3 839 – ECD : Thursday – 🕿 062 981.

Envir. : Chatsworth★★★ : site★★, house★★★ (Renaissance) garden★★★ *AC*, NE : 2 ½ m. – Haddon Hall★★ (14C-16C) *AC*, SE : 3 m.

🛧 Station Rd 🖉 2307.

🏢 Old Market Hall, Bridge St. 🖉 3227.

◆London 160 – Derby 26 – ◆Manchester 37 – ◆Nottingham 33 – ◆Sheffield 17.

🏛 **Rutland Arms,** The Square, DE4 1BT, ☎ 2812 – 📺 ⌷wc 🅿 🔲 AE ⓪ VISA
M 6.25 st. (lunch) and a la carte 8.50/14.15 st. ⏴ 2.40 – ⌷ 2.25 – **36 rm** 33.00/43.00 st.

⌂ **Milford House,** Mill St., DE4 1DA, ☎ 2130, 🖼 – ⌷wc 🅿 ⌘
April-October and weekends in March and November – **11 rm** ⌷ 19.00/40.00 t.

XX **Fischer's,** Bath St., DE4 1BX, ☎ 2687 – 🔲 AE ⓪ VISA ⌘
closed Saturday lunch, Sunday dinner, Monday, 25 August-9 September and 23 December-
5 January – M (restricted lunch) 9.50 t. and a la carte 13.45/19.50 t. ⏴ 3.00.

at Hassop N : 3 ½ m. by A 619 on B 6001 – ✉ Bakewell – 🕿 062 987 Great Longstone :

🏛 **Hassop Hall** ⌘, DE4 1NS, ☎ 488, ≤, « Part 16C hall », 🖼, park, ⌘ – ⇥ 📺 🅿 🔲 AE ⓪
VISA ⌘
closed 3 days at Christmas – M (closed Monday lunch and Sunday dinner) 8.50/14.95 st.
⏴ 3.95 – ⌷ 5.45 – **12 rm** 40.00/60.00 st., **1 suite** 145.00 st. – SB (November-March)
118.00/138.00 st.

at Ashford-in-the-Water NW : 1 ¾ m. by A 6 and A 6020 on B 6465 – ✉ 🕿 062 981 Bakewell :

XX **Riverside Country House** with rm, Fennel St., DE4 1QF, ☎ 4275, 🖼 – 📺 ⌷wc ⌷wc 🅿.
🔲 AE VISA ⌘
M (closed Sunday dinner to non-residents) (dinner only and Sunday lunch)/dinner 17.00 t.
⏴ 4.60 – **4 rm** ⌷ 45.00/55.00 t. – SB (except Bank Holidays) 85.00/90.00 st.

BALA Gwynedd 402 403 J 25 – pop. 1 852 – ECD : Wednesday – 🕿 0678.
See : Site★ – Envir. : SW : Road ★ from Pandy to Dinas Mawddwy.
🟊 Penlan ☎ 520359.
🛈 Snowdonia National Park Visitor Centre, High St. ☎ 520367 (summer only).
◆London 216 – Chester 46 – Dolgellau 18 – Shrewsbury 52.

🏛 **Palé Hall** ⌘, Llandderfel, LL23 7PS, E : 4 ¾ m. by A 494 on B 4401 ☎ 067 83 (Llandderfel) 285,
≤, « Ornate decor », 🖼, 🖼, park – ⇥ 📺 🅿 🔲 AE ⓪ VISA ⌘
M 8.50/15.00 t. and a la carte – **17 rm** 📺 55.00/70.00 t., **2 suites** 55.00/105.00 t. – SB (except
summer) 75.00/100.00 st.

🏛 **White Lion Royal** (Greenall Whitley), 66 High St., LL23 7AE, ☎ 520314 – ⌷wc 🅾 🅿 –
22 rm.

🏛 **Bala Lake** ⌘, LL23 7YF, SW : 1 ¼ m. by B 4391 on B 4403 ☎ 520344, ≤, ⊿, 🟊 – 📺 ⌷wc 🅿.
🔲 ⓪ VISA
M 7.00/8.00 st. ⏴ 3.20 – **13 rm** ⌷ 23.00/38.00 st., **1 suite** 35.00/42.00 st. – SB (except July and
August) 46.00/48.00 st.

🏯 **Plas Coch,** High St., LL23 7AB, ☎ 520309 – ⌷wc 🔧 🅿 🔲 AE ⓪ VISA
closed Christmas Day – M (bar lunch)/dinner 7.00 st. ⏴ 2.00 – **10 rm** ⌷ 22.00/35.00 st. – SB
44.00 st.

⌂ **Plas Teg,** 45 Tegid St., LL23 7EN, ☎ 520268, 🖼 – 🅿
6 rm ⌷ 9.25/18.50 s.

X **Tyddyn Llan Country House** ⌘ with rm, LL21 0ST, E : 7¾ m. by A 494 on B 4401
☎ 049 084 (Llandrillo) 264, 🖼 – ⌷wc 🔧 wc 🅿. 🔲 VISA
M (closed Monday and Tuesday October-March to non-residents) (bar lunch Monday to
Saturday)/dinner 10.50 st. ⏴ 2.50 – **9 rm** ⌷ 22.50/39.00 st. – SB (October-June except Bank
Holidays) 53.00 st.

VOLVO High St. ☎ 520210

BALDOCK Herts. 404 T 28 – pop. 6 703 – ECD : Thursday – 🕿 0462.
Envir. : Ashwell (St. Mary's Church★ 14C : Medieval graffiti) NE : 4 ½ m.
◆London 42 – Bedford 20 – ◆Cambridge 21 – Luton 15.

🏛 **Butterfield House,** 4 Hitchin St., SG7 6AE, ☎ 892701, 🖼 – 📺 ⌷wc ☎ & 🅿. 🔲 AE VISA
⌘
M (dinner only Monday to Thursday)(weekends by arrangement) 7.50 s. and a la carte ⏴ 2.50 –
⌷ 1.75 – **13 rm** ⌷ 24.50/33.00 s.

COLT High St. ☎ 893305

BALSALL COMMON West Midlands – see Coventry.

BAMBER BRIDGE Lancs. 402 M 22 – see Preston.

BAMBURGH Northumb. 401 402 O 17 – pop. 567 – ECD : Wednesday – 🕿 066 84.
See : Castle★★ (12C-18C) AC – 🟊 Bamburgh Castle ☎ 378.
◆London 337 – ◆Edinburgh 77 – ◆Newcastle-upon-Tyne 51.

🏛 **Lord Crewe Arms,** Front St., NE69 7BL, ☎ 243 – 📺 ⌷wc 🅿
April-early November – M (bar lunch)/dinner 11.50 t. ⏴ 3.25 – **25 rm** ⌷ 21.00/44.00 t. – SB
45.00/50.00 st.

⌂ **Sunningdale,** 21-23 Lucker Rd, NE69 7BS, ☎ 334 – ⌷wc 🅿
March-October – **18 rm** ⌷ 12.00/28.50.

BAMPTON Oxon. 403 404 P 28 – pop. 1 948 – ✪ 0993 Bampton Castle.
♦London 75 – ♦Oxford 18 – Swindon 18.

 ☺ **Farmhouse,** University Farm, Lew, OX8 2AU, NE : 2 m. on A 4095 ♒ 850297, « Working
 farm », ☞ – ⊡ ⇔wc ♿ ❹ ⬦
 closed Christmas, New Year and first 3 weeks January – **M** (dinner only)(Sunday, residents
 only) 10.50 **t.** ⓐ 3.55 – **6 rm** ⊑ 20.00/30.00 **t.**

BANBURY Oxon. 403 404 P 27 – pop. 37 463 – ECD : Tuesday – ✪ 0295.
Envir. : Upton House (pictures★★★, porcelain★★) *AC*, NW : 7 m. – East Adderbury (St. Mary's
Church : corbels★) SE : 3 ½ m. – Broughton Castle (great hall★, white room : 1599 plaster ceiling★★)
and St. Mary's Church (memorial tombs★) *AC*, SW : 3 ½ m. – Wroxton (thatched cottages★)
NW : 3 m. – Farnborough Hall (interior plasterwork★) *AC*, NW : 6 m.
 ⬠ Cherwell Edge, Chacombe ♒ 711591, NE : 4 m.
 ⬢ 8 Horsefair ♒ 59855.
♦London 76 – ♦Birmingham 40 – ♦Coventry 25 – ♦Oxford 23.

 ⬢ **Whately Hall** (T.H.F.), Horsefair, by Banbury Cross, OX16 0AN, ♒ 3451, Telex 837149, « Part
 17C hall », ☞ – ▥ ⊡ ❹ ⬤ ⬛ ⒶⒺ ⓄⅥ𝖲𝖠
 M 7.50/10.75 **st.** and a la carte ⓐ 3.40 – ⊑ 5.65 – **74 rm** 46.00/55.00 st., **5 suites.**

 ⬢ **Banbury Moat House** (Q.M.H.), 24-29 Oxford Rd, OX16 9AH, ♒ 59361 – ⊡ ⇔wc ☎ ❹.
 ⬛ ⬛ ⒶⒺ Ⓞ Ⅴ𝖲𝖠
 M 11.50/12.50 **st.** and a la carte ⓐ 3.00 – **32 rm** ⊑ 40.00/52.00 **st.** – SB 59.00 **st.**

 ⬢ **Lismore,** 61 Oxford Rd, OX16 9AJ, ♒ 67661 – ▥ ⇔wc ☎ ❹. ⬛ Ⅴ𝖲𝖠
 closed 25 December-5 January – **M** (dinner only) 9.00 **t.** and a la carte ⓐ 3.60 – **14 rm**
 ⊑ 14.00/40.00 **t.** – SB (weekends only) 45.00/55.00 **st.**

 ⬢ **White Lion,** 64 High St., OX16 8JW, ♒ 4358 – ⊡ ⇔wc ☎ ❹. ⬛ ⒶⒺ ⓄⅤ𝖲𝖠
 M a la carte 9.25/11.25 **t.** – **27 rm** ⊑ 30.00/85.00 **st.** – SB (weekends only) 48.50 **st.**

 ⬢ **Cromwell Lodge,** North Bar, OX16 0TB, ♒ 59781, ☞ – ⊡ ⇔wc ⬚wc ☎ ❹. ⬛ ⒶⒺ ⓄⅤ𝖲𝖠
 M (buffet lunch)/dinner 16.95 **t.** ⓐ 3.60 – **32 rm** ⊑ 39.00/49.00 **t.** – SB (weekends only)
 55.00/58.00 **st.**

 ⬠ **Tredis,** 15 Broughton Rd, OX16 9QB, ♒ 4632, ☞ – ⊡
 6 rm ⊑ 9.00/18.00 **st.**

 at Thorpe Mandeville (Northants.) NE : 5 ½ m. by A 422 and B 4525 – ⊠ ✪ 0295 Banbury :

 ✗ **Three Conies,** OX17 2EX, ♒ 711025 – ❹. ⬛ Ⅴ𝖲𝖠
 closed dinner Sunday and Monday – **M** a la carte 8.65/15.45 **t.** ⓐ 2.95.

 at Bloxham SW : 4 ¼ m. on A 361 – ⊠ ✪ 0295 Banbury :

 ⬢ **Olde School,** Church St., OX15 4ET, ♒ 720369 – ⊡ ⇔wc ⬚wc ⊛ ❹. ⬛ ⒶⒺ ⓄⅤ𝖲𝖠
 ⫸
 M 7.50/10.25 **t.** and a la carte ⓐ 2.80 – ⊑ 4.50 – **16 rm** 32.00/49.00 **t.** – SB (weekends only)
 48.00/56.00 **st.**

 at Wroxton NW : 3 m. by A 41 on A 422 – ⊠ Banbury – ✪ 029 573 Wroxton St. Mary :

 ⬢ Wroxton House, Silver St., OX15 6QB, ♒ 482, ☞ – ⊡ ⇔wc ⬚wc ☎ ❹
 15 rm.

AUSTIN-ROVER Southam Rd ♒ 51551
DAIHATSU Hook Norton ♒ 0608 (Hook Norton)
737641
FIAT, SAAB 21-27 Broad St. ♒ 50733
FORD 98 Warwick Rd ♒ 67711
PEUGEOT, TALBOT Thorpe Rd, Middleton Cheney
♒ 710325

PEUGEOT-TALBOT Southam Rd ♒ 53511
VAUXHALL-OPEL 8 Middleton Rd ♒ 3551
VOLVO Main Rd, Middleton Cheney ♒ 710233
VW-AUDI 9-16 Southam Rd ♒ 50141

BANGOR Gwynedd 402 403 H 24 – pop. 12 126 – ECD : Wednesday – ✪ 0248.
Envir. : Bethesda (slate quarries★) SE : 5 m. – Nant Francon Pass★★ SE : 9 m.
 ⬠ St. Deiniol ♒ 353098.
 ⬢ Texaco Service Station, Beach Rd ♒ 352786 – Town Hall ♒ 352786 (Easter-September).
♦London 247 – Birkenhead 68 – Holyhead 23 – Shrewsbury 83.

 ⬢ **Ty-Uchaf,** Tal-y-Bont, LL57 3UR, SE : 2 m. by A 5122 ♒ 352219 – ⊡ ⇔wc ⬚wc ⊛ ❹. ⬛
 Ⅴ𝖲𝖠. ⫸
 closed first 2 weeks January – **M** (bar lunch)/dinner 9.50 **t.** and a la carte ⓐ 3.00 – **9 rm**
 ⊑ 16.50/30.00 **t.**

BANSTEAD Surrey 404 T 30 – pop. 35 360 (inc. Tadworth) – ECD : Wednesday – ⊠ Tadworth
– ✪ 073 73 Burgh Heath.
 ⬠ Sandy Lane, Kingswood, Tadworth ♒ 0737 (Mogador) 832188, S : 3 m.
♦London 17 – ♦Brighton 39.

 ⬢ **Heathside** (Best Western), Brighton Rd, Burgh Heath, KT20 6BW, S : 1 ½ m. on A 217
 ♒ 53355, Telex 929908 – ⊡ ⇔wc ☎ ❹. ⬛ ⬛ ⒶⒺ ⓄⅤ𝖲𝖠
 M 12.00 **t.** (dinner) and a la carte 4.60/8.80 **t.** ⓐ 2.80 – ⊑ 3.80 – **44 rm** 39.00/60.00 **t.**

BARFORD Warw. 403 404 P 27 – see Warwick.

BAR HILL Cambs. 404 U 27 – see Cambridge.

BARKSTON Lincs. 402 404 S 25 – see Grantham.

BARMOUTH (ABERMAW) Gwynedd 402 403 H 25 – pop. 2 142 – ECD : Wednesday – ☎ 0341.
See : Site★★ – Panorama walk★★.
The Old Library ✆ 280787 (summer only).
♦London 231 – Chester 74 – Dolgellau 10 – Shrewsbury 67.

- **Ty'r Craig Castle,** Llanaber Rd, LL42 1YN, on A 496 ✆ 280470, ← – TV wc wc P. VISA.
  April-October – **M** (bar lunch)/dinner 8.00 **t.** 3.00 – **12 rm** 18.50/36.00 **t.** – SB (except summer) 40.00 **st.**
- **Bryn Melyn**, Panorama Rd, LL42 1DQ, ✆ 280556, ← Mawddach estuary and mountains – wc P.
  March-mid November – **9 rm** 18.00/29.00 **t.**
- **Coesfaen,** Clock House, LL42 1TE, E : ½ m. on A 496 ✆ 280355, ← Mawddach estuary and mountains – wc P. AE.
  6 rm 15.00/35.00 **st.**

AUSTIN-ROVER, DAIMLER-JAGUAR Park Rd ✆ 280449
COLT Smithy Garage ✆ 034 17 (Dyffryn) 279

BARNARD CASTLE Durham 402 O 20 – pop. 6 075 – ECD : Thursday – ☎ 0833 Teesdale.
See : Bowes Museum★★ *AC* – Castle★ (ruins 12C-14C).
Envir. : Raby Castle★ (14C) *AC*, NE : 6 m.
18 Harmire Rd ✆ 37237 – 18 Manwood ✆ 38355, N : ¾ m. on B 6278.
43 Galgate ✆ 38481.
♦London 258 – ♦Carlisle 63 – ♦Leeds 68 – ♦Middlesbrough 31 – ♦Newcastle-upon-Tyne 39.

- Kings Head, 14 Market Pl., DL12 8ND, ✆ 38356 – TV wc ☎ P.
  20 rm, 1 suite.
- **Blagraves House,** 34-36 The Bank, DL12 8PH, ✆ 37668, « 15C town house » – AE VISA
  closed Sunday, Monday and first 2 weeks February – **M** (restricted lunch) 8.00/18.00 **t.** 3.50.

FORD, AUSTIN-ROVER 19 Galgate ✆ 37129
VAUXHALL Newgate ✆ 38352

BARNBY MOOR Notts. 402 403 404 Q 23 – pop. 268 – ECD : Wednesday – ✉ ☎ 0777 Retford.
♦London 151 – ♦Leeds 44 – Lincoln 27 – ♦Nottingham 31.

- **Ye Olde Bell** (T.H.F.), DN22 8QS, ✆ 705121, « 16C coaching inn », – TV wc ☎ P. AE VISA
  M 7.95/12.00 **st.** and a la carte 3.50 – 5.65 – **55 rm** 42.00/50.00 **st.**

BARNSDALE BAR West Yorks. 402 404 Q 23 – see Wentbridge.

BARNSLEY South Yorks. 402 404 P 23 – pop. 76 783 – ECD : Thursday – ☎ 0226.
18 Wakefield Rd, Staincross ✆ 382856, N : 4 m.
Civic Hall, Eldon St. ✆ 206757.
♦London 177 – ♦Leeds 21 – ♦Manchester 36 – ♦Sheffield 15.

- **Queens,** Regent St., S70 2HQ, ✆ 248047, Telex 547348 – TV wc ☎. AE VISA
  M 6.00/10.50 **st.** and a la carte 3.00 – **36 rm** 37.50/47.50 **st.** – SB (weekends only) 45.00/55.00 **st.**
- **Royal,** Church St., S70 2AD, ✆ 203658 – TV P. AE VISA
  M 4.00/5.90 **t.** – **17 rm** 22.50/37.50.

at Ardsley E : 2 ½ m. on A 635 – ✉ ☎ 0226 Barnsley :

- **Ardsley Moat House** (Q.M.H.), Doncaster Rd, S71 5EH, ✆ 289401, Telex 547762, – TV ☎ P. AE VISA
  M *(closed Saturday lunch)* 8.00/10.00 **t.** 3.00 – 6.00 – **62 rm** 40.00/50.00 **t.** – SB (weekends only) 58.00 **st.**

AUSTIN-ROVER Claycliff Rd, Barkgreen ✆ 299891
CITROEN The Cross, Silkstone ✆ 790636
FORD Dodworth Rd ✆ 205741
HONDA Doncaster Rd ✆ 287417
RENAULT Doncaster Rd ✆ 291554
TALBOT, FIAT, PEUGEOT Stairfoot ✆ 206675
VAUXHALL-OPEL New St. ✆ 289181
VW, AUDI Huddersfield Rd ✆ 299494

BARNSTAPLE Devon 403 H 30 **The West Country G.** – pop. 24 490 – ECD : Wednesday – ☎ 0271.
See : Site★★ – The Long Bridge★.
Envir. : Arlington Court★★ *AC* The Carriage Collection★, NE : 8 m. on A 39.
Holland St. ✆ 72742.
♦London 222 – Exeter 40 – Taunton 51.

🏛 **Imperial** (T.H.F.), Taw Vale Par., EX32 8NB, ℰ 45861 – 📶 📺 🛏wc 🅿️ 🅿️ 🛋 🔼 🔺 ⓪ 𝘝𝘐𝘚𝘈
M 8.70/9.75 st. and a la carte ⌂ 3.40 – ⌂ 5.65 – **56 rm** 39.00/50.00 st.

🏛 **North Devon Motel,** Taw Vale, EX32 9AD, ℰ 72166, Group Telex 42551 – 📺 🛏wc ☎ 🅿️
🔼 🔺 ⓪ 𝘝𝘐𝘚𝘈
M 4.75/7.50 t. and a la carte – **26 rm** ⌂ 26.45/39.10 t. – SB 44.85/60.95 st.

✕✕ **Lynwood House,** Bishops Tawton Rd, EX32 9DZ, on A 377 ℰ 43695, Seafood – 🅿️ 🔼 🔺
⓪ 𝘝𝘐𝘚𝘈
closed Saturday lunch, Sunday and Bank Holidays – **M** a la carte 9.30/17.25 t. ⌂ 2.95.

at Bishop's Tawton S : 2 m. on A 377 – ✉ 🟢 0271 Barnstaple :

🏛 **Downrew House** 🏖, EX32 0DY, SE : 1 ½ m. on Chittlehampton Rd ℰ 42497, ≼, « Country
house atmosphere », 🏊 heated, 🐎, park, 🎾 – 📺 🛏wc ☎ 🅿️. 🎾
late March-29 December – **M** (bar lunch)(residents only)/dinner 14.50 ⌂ 2.95 – **14 rm**
⌂ 37.50/78.00 – SB 71.30/74.50 st.

AUSTIN-ROVER-DAIMLER-JAGUAR Boutport St. ℰ 73232
DAIHATSU Newport Rd ℰ 45363
FIAT, TOYOTA, VOLVO Pottington Industrial Estate, Pillandway ℰ 76551

FORD New Rd ℰ 74173
VAUXHALL-OPEL 42 Boutport St. ℰ 74366

BARROW-IN-FURNESS Cumbria **402** K 21 – pop. 50 174 – 🟢 0229.

🏌 Barrow Rakesmoore, Hawcoat ℰ 25444, N : 2 m. off A 590.

🅹 Civic Hall, 28 Duke St. ℰ 25795.

♦London 295 – Kendal 34 – Lancaster 47.

🏛 **Victoria Park** (Whitbread), Victoria Rd, LA14 5JX, ℰ 21159 – 📺 🛏wc 🎵wc ☎ 🅿️ 🛋 🔼
🔺 ⓪ 𝘝𝘐𝘚𝘈
M 6.00/9.50 st. and a la carte ⌂ 2.50 – **40 rm** ⌂ 30.00/47.00 st. – SB (weekends only)
40.00/48.00 st.

at Rampside S : 5 m. by A 5087 – ✉ 🟢 0229 Barrow-in-Furness :

🏨 **Clarkes Arms** (Whitbread), LA13 0PX, ℰ 20303 – 📺 🎵wc 🅿️. 🔼 🔺 𝘝𝘐𝘚𝘈
M 9.00 t. (dinner) and a la carte ⌂ 3.00 – **10 rm** ⌂ 28.00/36.00 t. – SB (weekends only)
66.00 st.

BARRY (BARRI) South Glam. **403** K 29 – pop. 44 443 – ECD : Wednesday – 🟢 0446.

🅹 Barry Island ℰ 747171 (summer only).

♦London 167 – ♦Cardiff 10 – ♦Swansea 39.

🏛 **Mount Sorrel,** Porthkerry Rd, CF6 8AY, ℰ 740069 – 📺 🛏wc 🎵wc ☎ 🅿️ 🔼 🔺 ⓪ 𝘝𝘐𝘚𝘈
closed 25 and 26 December – **M** 9.50 t. (dinner) and a la carte ⌂ 3.10 – **37 rm** ⌂ 30.00/40.00 t.
– SB (weekends only) 40.00/46.00 st.

AUSTIN-ROVER Brook St. ℰ 734365

BARTON Lancs. **402** L 22 – see Preston.

BARWICK Somerset **403 404** M 31 – see Yeovil.

BASFORD Staffs. – see Stoke-on-Trent.

BASILDON Essex **404** V 29 – pop. 94 800 – ECD : Wednesday – 🟢 0268.

🏌 Kingswood ℰ 3297 – 🏌 Pipps Hill Country Club, Cranes Farm Rd ℰ 27278, N : off A 127.

♦London 30 – Chelmsford 17 – Southend-on-Sea 13.

🏛 **Crest** (Crest), Cranes Farm Rd, SS14 3DG, NW : 2 ¼ m. by A 176 off A 1235 ℰ 3955, Telex
995141, 🐎 – 📶 📺 🛏wc ☎ 🅿️. 🛋 🔼 🔺 ⓪ 𝘝𝘐𝘚𝘈
M 8.50/11.50 st. and a la carte ⌂ 3.85 – ⌂ 5.85 – **116 rm** 48.00/58.00 st. – SB (weekends only)
65.00 st.

AUSTIN-ROVER Southern Hay ℰ 22661
BEDFORD Service House, West Mayne, Laindon

FORD Cherrydown ℰ 22741
NISSAN Nethermayne ℰ 22261

BASINGSTOKE Hants. **403 404** Q 30 – pop. 73 027 – 🟢 0256.

🏌 Bishopswood, Bishopswood Lane ℰ 073 56 (Tadley) 5213, N : 6 m. off A 340 Z.

♦London 55 – Reading 17 – ♦Southampton 31 – Winchester 18.

Plan on next page

🏛 Ladbroke Lodge (Ladbroke), Old Common Rd, Black Dam, RG21 3PR, ℰ 460460, Telex 859038,
🔄 – 📶 📺 🛏wc ☎ 🅿️ 🛋 🔼 🔺 ⓪ 𝘝𝘐𝘚𝘈   Z i
M (closed Saturday) (carving rest.) – ⌂ 5.50 – **114 rm** 50.50/58.00 st.. **6 suites** 90.00 st. – SB
(weekends only) 64.00 st.

🏛 Ladbroke (Ladbroke), Aldermaston Roundabout, Ringway North, RG24 9NV, N : 2 m. junction
A 339 and A 340 ℰ 20212, Telex 858223 – 📶 📺 🛏wc ☎ 🅿️ 🛋 🔼 🔺 ⓪ 𝘝𝘐𝘚𝘈   Z a
M (carving rest.) – ⌂ 5.50 – **108 rm** 50.50/58.00 st. – SB (weekends only) 63.00 st.

77

BASINGSTOKE

North is at the top on
all town plans.

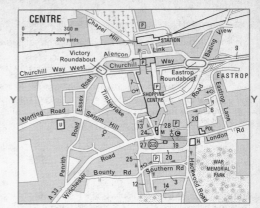

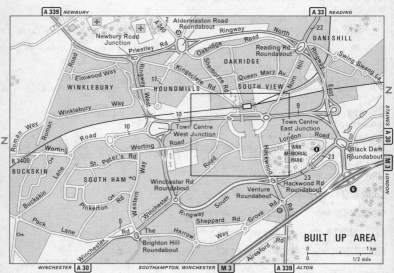

🏨 **Crest** (Crest), Grove Rd, RG21 3EE, SW : 1 m. junction A 339 and A 30 📞 468181, Telex 858501 – 📺 🍴wc ♟ & Ⓟ 📱 AE ① VISA
    Z e
    M (bar lunch Saturday) 7.50/11.50 **t**. and a la carte – ⊒ 5.85 – **86 rm** 51.00/60.00 **st**. – SB (weekends only) 54.00 **st**.

🏨 **Red Lion** 24 London St., RG21 1NY, 📞 28525, Telex 859504 – 📶 📺 🍴wc 🛁wc ♟ Ⓟ 📱 AE ① VISA
    Y c
    M (carving rest.) a la carte approx 10.35 **t**. – **63 rm** ⊒ 47.00/57.00 **t**. – SB (weekends only) 54.00/60.00 **st**.

at Rotherwick E : 6 ¾ m. by Black Dam roundabout, A 30 and Rotherwick road – ⊠ Basingstoke – ☎ 025 672 Hook :

🏰 **Tylney Hall** 🛏, RG27 9AJ, W : 1 m. 📞 4881, Telex 859864, « 19C mansion in extensive gardens », park, ⚔ – 📶 📺 ☎ Ⓟ 📱 AE ① VISA 🌹
    M 13.00/19.00 **st**. and a la carte § 5.00 – **37 rm** ⊒ 61.00/110.00 **st**.. **8 suites** 154.00/210.00 **st**. – SB (weekends only) 97.00/150.00 **st**.

at Oakley W : 5 m. on B 3400 –Z– ⊠ ☎ 0256 Basingstoke :

🏩 **Beach Arms,** Andover Rd, RG23 7EP, on B 3400 📞 780210, 🛏 – 📺 🍴wc ☎ Ⓟ AE VISA
    M *(closed Saturday lunch)* 8.00 **st**. and a la carte § 2.75 – **17 rm** ⊒ 42.00/52.00 **st**. – SB (weekends only) 44.00 **st**.

AUDI, VW London Rd *&* 24444
AUSTIN-ROVER-JAGUAR New Rd *&* 24561
BEDFORD, VAUXHALL-OPEL West Ham *&* 62551
FIAT, LANCIA London Rd *&* 55221

FORD Lower Wote St. *&* 3561
PEUGEOT-TALBOT Houndmills *&* 465991
RENAULT Eastdrop Roundabout *&* 65454
VOLVO London Rd *&* 466111

BASLOW Derbs. **402 403 404** P 24 – pop. 1 205 – ECD : Wednesday – ✉ Bakewell – ☎ 024 688.
♦London 161 – Derby 27 – ♦Manchester 35 – ♦Sheffield 13.

Cavendish, DE4 1SP, on A 619 *&* 2311, Telex 547150, ≤, « Tasteful decor », ✎, ✍ – 📺 ☎
🅿 🆎 ⓞ 𝗩𝗜𝗦𝗔 ⅏
M a la carte 15.50/24.75 **t.** ⌕ 3.80 – � 6.10 – **23 rm**.

BASSENTHWAITE Cumbria **401 402** K 19 – pop. 533 – ☎ 059 681 Bassenthwaite Lake.
♦London 300 – ♦Carlisle 24 – Keswick 7.

Armathwaite Hall ⌕, CA12 4RE, W : 1 ½ m. on B 5291 ✉ Keswick *&* 551, ≤ Bassenthwaite
Lake, « Part 18C mansion in extensive grounds », ⬚, ✎, ✍, park, ✖, squash – ⬥ 📺 ☎
⟿ 🅿 🔼 🆎 ⓞ 𝗩𝗜𝗦𝗔
M a la carte 13.25/19.85 **t.** – **40 rm** ⊇ 40.00/80.00 **t.** – SB (weekends only) 78.00/88.00 **st.**

Pheasant Inn, CA13 9YE, SW : 3 ¼ m. by B 5291 off A 66 ✉ Cockermouth *&* 234, « 16C
inn », ✍ – ⌂wc 🅿. ⅏
closed Christmas Day – **M** 6.80/11.50 **st.** and a la carte ⌕ 2.50 – **20 rm** ⊇ 28.00/54.00 **st.** – SB
(mid November-mid March) 54.00/66.00 **st.**

Overwater Hall ⌕, CA5 1HH, NE : 2 ¼ m. on Uldale Rd ✉ Ireby *&* 566, ≤, ✍, park – 📺
⌂wc 🅿. 🔼 𝗩𝗜𝗦𝗔
closed January-20 February – **M** (dinner only) 11.50 **t.** ⌕ 2.90 – **13 rm** ⊇ 21.00/36.00 **t.** – SB
(October-June) 46.00/50.00 **st.**

BATH Avon **403 404** M 29 **The West Country** G. – pop. 84 283 – ECD : Monday and Thursday –
☎ 0225.

See : Site★★★ : Royal Crescent★★★ (N° 1 Royal Crescent★★*AC*) V – Circus★★★ V – Museum of
costume★★★*AC* V M2 – Royal Photographic Society National Centre of Photography★★*AC* V M3 –
Roman Baths★★*AC* (Pump Room★*AC*) X D – Holburne of Menstrie Museum★★*AC* V M1 – Pulteney
Bridge★ X – Assembly Rooms★*AC* V M2 – Bath Abbey★ X B – Camden Works Museum★*AC* V M4
– Bath Carriage Museum★*AC* V M5.

Envir. : Lansdown Crescent★★ (Somerset Place★) Y – at Claverton, E : 2 ½ m. by A36 Y American
Museum★★*AC* - Claverton Pump★*AC* – Camden Crescent★ V – Beckford Tower and Museum *AC*
(prospect★) Y M6 – Dyrham Park★*AC*, N : 8 m. by A 46 Y.

🏌, 🏌 Tracy Park, Bath Rd, Wick *&* 027 582 (Abson) 2251, N : 5 m. by Lansdown Rd Y – 🏌 Lansdown
& 22138, NW : 3 m. by Lansdown Rd Y.

🏛 Abbey Churchyard *&* 62831.

♦London 119 – ♦Bristol 13 – ♦Southampton 63 – Taunton 49.

Plan on next page

Royal Crescent, 16 Royal Crescent, BA1 2LS, *&* 319090, Telex 444251, ≤, « Tastefully
restored Georgian town houses », ✍ – ⬥ ▤ rest 📺 ☎ ⟿, ♨ 🔼 🆎 ⓞ 𝗩𝗜𝗦𝗔 ✖   V **u**
M 21.00/27.00 **st.** ⌕ 10.05 – ⊇ 8.00 – **45 rm** 68.00/125.00 **st.,** **12 suites** 180.00/275.00 **st.** – SB
(except winter)(weekdays only) 115.00/160.00 **st.**

The Priory, Weston Rd, BA1 2XT, *&* 331922, Telex 44612, ≤, ⬚ heated, ✍ – 📺 ☎ 🅿. 🔼
🆎 ⓞ 𝗩𝗜𝗦𝗔 ✖   Y **c**
M 12.50 **s.** (lunch) and a la carte 17.50/22.50 **s.** ⌕ 3.50 – ⊇ 5.00 – **21 rm** 42.00/95.00 **s.** – SB
(November-May) 108.10/133.40 **st.**

Lansdown Grove (Best Western), Lansdown Rd, BA1 5EH, *&* 315891, Group Telex 444850,
✍ – ⬥ 📺 ☎ 🅿. ♨ 🔼 🆎 ⓞ 𝗩𝗜𝗦𝗔   Y **o**
M (buffet lunch)/dinner 12.00 **t.** and a la carte ⌕ 2.95 – **41 rm** ⊇ 38.50/68.00 **t.** – SB (weekends
only) 68.00/76.00 **st.**

Francis (T.H.F.), Queen Sq., BA1 2HH, *&* 24257, Telex 449162 – ⬥ 📺 ☎ 🅿. ♨ 🔼 🆎 ⓞ
𝗩𝗜𝗦𝗔   X **o**
M 9.60/12.50 **st.** and a la carte ⌕ 3.50 – ⊇ 6.00 – **94 rm** 53.00/66.50 **st.,** **1 suite**.

Six Kings Circus without rest, 6 The Circus, BA1 2EW, *&* 28288, « Georgian town house »,
✍ – ☎. 𝗩𝗜𝗦𝗔. ✖   V **n**
closed first 2 weeks January – **6 rm** ⊇ 55.00/99.00 **t.**

Ladbroke Beaufort (Ladbroke), Walcot St., BA1 5BJ, *&* 63411, Telex 449519 – ⬥ 📺 ☎ 🅿.
♨ 🔼 🆎 ⓞ 𝗩𝗜𝗦𝗔 ✖   V **i**
⊇ 5.50 – **124 rm** 49.50/67.50 **st.** – SB (weekends only) 70.50 **st.**

Number Nine, 9 Miles Building, George St., BA1 2QS, *&* 25462, ✍ – 📺 ⌂wc ⊪wc ☎. 🔼
🆎 ⓞ 𝗩𝗜𝗦𝗔 ✖   V **a**
closed first 2 weeks January – **M** (closed Sunday and Monday) (dinner only) 25.00 **st.** ⌕ 2.50 –
9 rm ⊇ 40.00/80.00 **st.,** **1 suite** 70.00 **st.**

Redcar, 27 Henrietta St., BA2 6LR, *&* 69151, Telex 444842 – ▤ rest 📺 ⌂wc ☎ 🅿. ♨ 🔼
🆎 ⓞ 𝗩𝗜𝗦𝗔   V **a**
M 9.95/10.95 **t.** and a la carte ⌕ 3.50 – ⊇ 6.00 – **31 rm** 32.50/51.00 **t.** – SB (weekends only)
68.00/72.00 **st.**

BATH

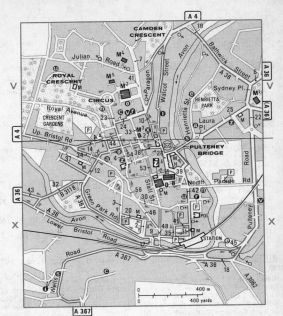

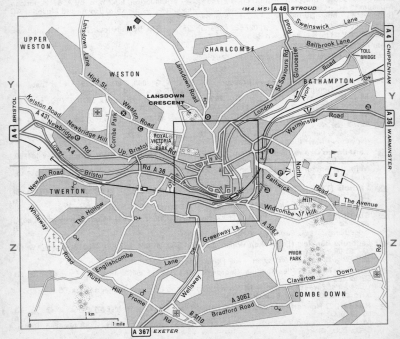

🏨 **Pratt's,** South Par., BA2 4AB, ✆ 60441, Group Telex 444827 – |$| TV ⌂wc ☎. 🅐. ▣ AE ① VISA X **r**
M (bar lunch Monday to Saturday)/dinner a la carte 8.95/11.95 **t.** – **45 rm** ☕ 36.00/48.00 **t.** – SB 63.00 **st.**

🏨 **Apsley House,** 141 Newbridge Hill, BA1 3PT, ✆ 336966, ≤, 🌳 – TV ⌂wc ☎ Ⓟ. ▣ AE ① VISA. ✗ Y **e**
M (bar lunch)/dinner a la carte approx. 15.95 **st.** 🍷 3.25 – **7 rm** ☕ 55.00/85.00 **st.** – SB (November-March) 75.00/85.00 **st.**

🏨 **Bath** (Best Western), Widcombe Basin, BA2 4JP, ✆ 338855, Telex 445876 – |$| TV ⌂wc ☎ Ⓟ. 🅐. ▣ AE ① VISA X **e**
M 8.50/9.50 **st.** – ☕ 4.95 – **96 rm** 48.00/75.00 **st.** – SB (weekends only) 76.00 **st.**

🏨 **Dukes,** Great Pulteney St., BA2 4DN, ✆ 63512 – TV ⌂wc ⌂wc ☎. ▣ AE VISA V **z**
M 6.00/8.00 **t.** and a la carte 🍷 4.50 – **22 rm** 25.00/60.00 **t.** – SB 55.00/65.00 **st.**

🏠 **Sydney Gardens** without rest., Sydney Rd, BA2 6NT, ✆ 64818, ≤, no smoking, 🌳 – TV ⌂wc Ⓟ. ▣ VISA. ✗ Y **i**
closed Christmas and New Year – **7 rm** ☕ 20.00/45.00 **st.**

🏠 **Paradise House** 🐦 without rest., 86-88 Holloway, BA2 4PX, ✆ 317723, ≤, 🌳 – TV ⌂wc. ▣ VISA. ✗ X **c**
closed 15 December-20 January – **8 rm** ☕ 22.00/42.00 **st.**

🏠 **Somerset House,** 35 Bathwick Hill, BA2 6LD, ✆ 66451, ≤, 🌳 – ⌂wc ☎ Ⓟ. ▣ VISA. ✗
closed 4 January-4 February – **M** *(closed lunch Monday, Tuesday, Thursday and Saturday)* (no smoking) 6.85/10.85 **st.** 🍷 2.50 – **9 rm** ☕ (dinner included) 29.50/59.00 **st.** – SB (November-March)(weekdays only) 49.50 **st.** Z **e**

🏠 **Gainsborough,** Weston Lane, BA1 4AB, ✆ 311380, 🌳 – TV ⌂wc ⌂wc ☎ Ⓟ. ▣ AE VISA. ✗ Y **x**
closed Christmas and first 2 weeks January – **M** (dinner only) 7.95 **st.** – **16 rm** ☕ 18.00/44.00 **t.** – SB 51.00/53.00 **st.**

🏠 **North Parade,** 10 North Par., BA2 4AL, ✆ 63384 – TV ⌂wc ⌂wc ☎. ▣ AE ① VISA X **n**
M (dinner only) 6.75 **t.** 🍷 2.50 – **17 rm** ☕ 18.00/45.00 **t.** – SB (except summer) 44.00/54.00 **st.**

🏠 **Villa Magdala** without rest., Henrietta Rd, BA2 6LX, ✆ 66329, 🌳 – TV ⌂wc ⌂wc Ⓟ. ✗ V **e**
closed January – **17 rm** ☕ 20.00/42.00 **st.**

🏠 **Oldfields** without rest., 102 Wells Rd, BA2 3AL, ✆ 317984, 🌳 – TV ⌂wc Ⓟ. ▣ VISA. ✗ X **s**
closed mid December-mid January – **14 rm** ☕ 20.00/38.00 **st.**

⌂ **Oakleigh,** 19 Upper Oldfield Park, BA2 3JX, ✆ 315698 – TV ⌂wc ⌂wc Ⓟ. ▣ VISA. ✗ X **i**
4 rm ☕ 25.00/30.00 **st.**

⌂ **Charnwood House,** 51 Upper Oldfield Park, BA2 3LB, ✆ 334937 – TV ⌂wc Ⓟ. VISA. ✗ X **i**
8 rm ☕ 18.00/40.00 **st.**

⌂ **Lynwood,** 6-7 Pulteney Gdns., BA2 4HG, ✆ 26410 – TV ⌂. ▣ AE ① VISA. ✗ X **v**
closed Christmas – **14 rm** ☕ 14.50/25.00 **t.**

⌂ **Holly Villa,** 14 Pulteney Gdns, BA2 4HG, ✆ 310331, 🌳 – ✗ Z **a**
5 rm ☕ 12.00/22.00 **st.**

XXX **Popjoy's,** Beau Nash's House, Sawclose, BA1 1EU, ✆ 60494, English rest., « Former residence of Beau Nash » – ▣ VISA X **z**
closed Sunday, Monday and 3 weeks after Christmas – **M** (dinner only) a la carte approx. 15.50 **t.** 🍷 3.25.

XX **Woods,** 9-13 Alfred St., BA1 2QX, ✆ 314812 – ▣ VISA V **o**
closed Sunday and 1 week Christmas – **M** a la carte 8.90/11.90 **t.** 🍷 3.50.

XX **The Hole in the Wall** with rm, 16 George St., BA1 2EN, ✆ 25242, « Converted Georgian kitchen and coal hole » – TV ⌂wc ☎. ▣ AE ① VISA. ✗ V **v**
closed 2 weeks after Christmas – **M** *(closed Sunday lunch)* 22.00 **st.** and a la carte 14.50/22.00 **t.** 🍷 3.75 – **8 rm** ☕ 50.00/80.00 **t.** – SB 83.00/119.00 **st.**

XX **Clos du Roy,** 7 Edgar Buildings, George St., BA1 2EE, ✆ 64356, French rest. – ▣ AE ① VISA V **r**
closed Sunday, Monday and 2 weeks January-February – **M** 9.50/21.50 **t.** and a la carte 🍷 4.50.

XX **Rajpoot,** 4 Argyle St., BA2 4BE, ✆ 66833, Indian rest. – ▣ AE ① VISA VX **s**
closed 25 and 26 December – **M** 10.50 **t.** and a la carte 7.20/9.25 **t.**

X **Flowers,** 27 Monmouth St, BA1 2AP, ✆ 313774 – ▣ AE ① VISA X **a**
closed Sunday and 10 days Christmas-New Year – **M** 8.50/15.50 **t.** 🍷 3.50.

X **Ainslie's,** 12 Pierrepont St., BA1 1LA, ✆ 61745, Bistro – ▣ AE ① VISA X **u**
closed 25 and 26 December – **M** (bar lunch)/dinner a la carte 12.05/13.90 **t.** 🍷 2.80.

X **Moon and Sixpence,** 6a Broad St., BA1 5LJ, ✆ 60962, Bistro – ▣ AE VISA V **x**
closed 25-26 December and 1 January – **M** (restricted lunch) 9.00/16.50 **t.** and a la carte 13.80/16.50 **t.** 🍷 3.50.

at Bathampton E : 2 ½ m. on A 36 – ✉ ☎ 0225 Bath :

🏠 **Orchard House,** Warminster Rd, BA2 6XG, ✆ 66115 – TV ⌂wc Ⓟ. ▣ AE ① VISA Y **a**
M (dinner only) 9.00 **st.** 🍷 3.00 – **12 rm** ☕ 25.00/42.00 **st.** – SB (November-April) 46.50 **st.**

at Bathford E : 3 ½ m. by A 4 off A 363 − Y − ⊠ ✪ 0225 Bath :

🏛 **Eagle House** 🍴 without rest., Church St., BA1 7RS, 𝒫 859946, ⩽, « Georgian house », 🌳 − 🔟 ⌁wc 🅿
closed 23 December-1 January − ⌷ 1.80 − **6 rm** 19.00/36.00 **st.**

at Monkton Combe S : 6 m. by A 36 − Y − ⊠ Bath − ✪ 022 122 Limpley Stoke :

♙ **Wheelwrights Arms**, BA2 7HD, 𝒫 2287 − 🔟 ⌁wc 🅿 🔊 🔳 VISA ✂
M (bar lunch)/dinner 13.50 **st.** and a la carte ⏅ 2.95 − **8 rm** ⌷ 24.00/38.00 **st.** − SB (October-March) 46.00 **st.**

at Freshford S : 7 ½ m. on A 36 − Y − ⊠ Bath − ✪ 022 122 Limpley Stoke :

🏛🏛 **Homewood Park** 🍴, Hinton Charterhouse, BA3 6BB, S : 1 ½ m. on A 36 𝒫 3731, Telex 444937, ⩽, « Tastefully converted country house », 🌳, park, ✗ − 🔟 🔊 🅿 🔳 🏛 🔳 AE ⓞ VISA ✂
closed 24 December-13 January − **M** 16.50/22.50 **st.** ⏅ 5.00 − ⌷ 5.50 − **15 rm** 40.00/95.00 − SB (weekdays only)(April-October) 95.00 **st.**

at Woolverton (Somerset) S : 10 m. on A 36 − Y − ⊠ Bath − ✪ 0373 Frome :

🏛 **Woolverton House**, BA3 6QS, 𝒫 830415, 🌳 − 🔟 ⌁wc 🅿 🔳 ⓞ VISA
M a la carte 14.20 **t.** ⏅ 2.25 − **14 rm** ⌷ 29.50/40.00 **t.** − SB (November-March) 45.00 **st.**

at Hunstrete W : 8 ½ m. by A 4 − Y − and A 39 off A 368 − ⊠ Pensford − ✪ 076 18 Compton Dando :

🏛🏛 **Hunstrete House** 🍴, BS18 4NS, 𝒫 578, Telex 449540, ⩽, « Country house atmosphere and gardens », ⏆ heated, park, ✗ − 🔟 🔊 ⅙ 🅿 🔳 🔳 AE ⓞ VISA ✂
M (restricted lunch in summer) 21.00/28.00 **s.** ⏅ 3.50 − ⌷ 4.00 − **21 rm** 60.00/125.00 **s.**, **1 suite** 105.00/145.00 **s.**

AUSTIN-ROVER Newbridge Rd 𝒫 312774
BMW Wellsway 𝒫 29187
CITROEN, DAIHATSU Prior Park Rd 𝒫 29552
FIAT, ALFA ROMEO Margarets Buildings, Circus Pl. 𝒫 27328
FORD 5-10 James St. West 𝒫 61636

NISSAN Lower Bristol Rd 𝒫 25864
VAUXHALL, BEDFORD Rush Hill 𝒫 833338
VAUXHALL-OPEL, BEDFORD Upper Bristol Rd 𝒫 22131
VOLVO Bathwick Hill 𝒫 65814

BATTISBOROUGH CROSS Devon − see Newton Ferrers.

BATTLE East Sussex 𝟜𝟘𝟜 V 31 − pop. 4 662 − ✪ 042 46.

See : Abbey★ (11C-14C) *AC* (site of the Battle of Hastings 1066).

🎫 88 High St. 𝒫 3721.

◆London 55 − ◆Brighton 34 − Folkestone 43 − Maidstone 30.

🏛 **Netherfield Place** 🍴, TN33 9PP, NW : 1 ¾ m. by A 2100 on Netherfield Rd 𝒫 4455, Telex 95284, ⩽, « Gardens », park − 🔟 ⌁wc 🔊 🅿 🔳 🔳 AE ⓞ VISA ✂
closed first week January − **M** (buffet lunch Sunday) 12.95/15.00 **t.** and a la carte ⏅ 3.50 − **11 rm** ⌷ 35.00/90.00 **t.** − SB (October-March) 80.00/100.00 **st.**

🏛 **George**, 23 High St., TN33 0EA, 𝒫 4466 − 🔟 ⌁wc 🔊 🅿 🔳 AE ⓞ VISA
closed Christmas − **M** 9.50 **t.** (dinner)and a la carte 8.35/10.50 **t.** ⏅ 2.75 − ⌷ 2.00 − **21 rm** 22.50/40.00 **st.**

↑ **Little Hemingfold Farmhouse** 🍴, Telham, TN33 0TT, SE : 1 ¾ m. on A 2100 𝒫 2910, ⩽, « Lakeside setting », 🐎, 🌳, park, ✗ − 🔟 ⌁wc 🅿 🔳 AE VISA ✂
12 rm ⌷ 18.00/40.00 **st.**

XX **Bayeux**, 31 Mount St., TN33 0EG, 𝒫 2132 − 🅿 🔳 AE ⓞ VISA
closed Monday lunch and Sunday − **M** a la carte 11.65/17.15 **st.**

X **Blacksmiths**, 43 High St., TN33 0EE, 𝒫 3200 − 🔳 VISA
closed Monday and first 2 weeks September − **M** 7.90/10.90 **t.** and a la carte ⏅ 3.25.

AUSTIN-ROVER High St. 𝒫 2425
CITROEN Ninfield 𝒫 0424 (Ninfield) 892278
CITROEN Whatlington 𝒫 042 487 (Sedlescombe) 307

FORD Upper Lake 𝒫 3155
RELIANT, SKODA 𝒫 0424 (Ninfield) 892286
VAUXHALL-OPEL Battle Hill 𝒫 2286

BAWTRY South Yorks. 𝟜𝟘𝟚 𝟜𝟘𝟛 𝟜𝟘𝟜 Q 23 − pop. 2 677 − ⊠ ✪ 0302 Doncaster.

🎫 Hoveringham, Austerfield Park, Cross Lane 𝒫 710841, NE : 2 m. off A 614.

◆London 158 − ◆Leeds 39 − Lincoln 32 − ◆Nottingham 36 − ◆Sheffield 22.

🏛 Crown (Anchor), High St., DN10 6JW, 𝒫 710341, Telex 547089, 🌳 − 🔟 ⌁wc 📞 🅿 🔳
57 rm.

BAYCLIFF Cumbria 𝟜𝟘𝟚 K 21 − see Ulverston.

BEACONSFIELD Bucks. 404 S 29 – pop. 13 397 – ECD : Wednesday and Saturday – ☎ 049 46.
♦London 26 – Aylesbury 19 – ♦Oxford 32.

🏨 **Bellhouse** (De Vere), Oxford Rd, HP9 2XE, E : 1 ¾ m. on A 40 ℘ 0753 (Gerrard'sCross) 887211, Telex 848719 – 🕴 📺 ᐁwc ☎ 🅿 🏊 🔼 🄰🄴 ⓞ 𝘝𝘐𝘚𝘈
M 8.75/9.75 **st.** and a la carte ⚬ 3.65 – **118 rm** ⚬ 61.00/79.00 **st.**, **2 suites** 94.00/112.00 **st.** – SB (weekends only) 59.50 **st.**

🏨 **White Hart**, Aylesbury End, HP9 1LW, ℘ 71211, Telex 837882 – 📺 ᐁwc ☎ 🅿
38 rm.

XX **Wheeler's**, 14 London End, HP9 2JH, ℘ 77077, Seafood – 🔼 🄰🄴 ⓞ 𝘝𝘐𝘚𝘈
M a la carte 12.50/20.25 **t.** ⚬ 3.15.

XX **La Lanterna**, 57 Wycombe End, HP9 1LX, ℘ 5210, Italian rest. – 🄰🄴 ⓞ 𝘝𝘐𝘚𝘈
closed Sunday – **M** 7.70 **t.** (lunch) and a la carte 8.75/17.15 **t.** ⚬ 3.00.

XX **Santella**, 43 Aylesbury End, HP9 1LV, ℘ 6806, Italian rest. – 🔼 🄰🄴 ⓞ 𝘝𝘐𝘚𝘈
closed Sunday – **M** 7.00/15.00 **t.** and a la carte 13.00/20.25 **t.** ⚬ 3.00.

MERCEDES-BENZ, TOYOTA 55 Station Rd ℘ 2141   VAUXHALL-OPEL Penn Rd, Knotty Green ℘ 3730

BEAMINSTER Dorset 403 L 31 The West Country G. – pop. 2 338 – ECD : Wednesday – ☎ 0308.
♦London 149 – Dorchester 19 – Exeter 40 – Taunton 31.

X **Nevitt's Eating House**, 57 Hogshill St., DT8 3AG, ℘ 862600 – 𝘝𝘐𝘚𝘈
M (dinner only and Sunday lunch)/dinner 12.00 **t.** ⚬ 4.00.

BEARSTED Kent 404 V 30 – see Maidstone.

BEAULIEU Hants. 403 404 P 31 – pop. 1 027 – ECD : Tuesday and Saturday – ✉ Brockenhurst – ☎ 0590.
See : Beaulieu Abbey★ (ruins 13C) : Palace House★ 14C, National Motor Museum★★, Buckler's Hard Maritime Museum AC.
🛈 John Montagu Building ℘ 612345.
♦London 102 – Bournemouth 24 – ♦Southampton 13 – Winchester 23.

🏨 **Montagu Arms**, Palace Lane, SO42 7ZL, ℘ 612324, Telex 47276, « Part 18C inn », 🐎 – 📺
☎ 🅿 🔼 🄰🄴 ⓞ 𝘝𝘐𝘚𝘈
M 11.25/17.50 **t.** and a la carte ⚬ 4.50 – **26 rm** ⚏ 46.50/84.50 **t.** – SB (except summer) 74.50/82.75 **st.**

at Bucklers Hard S : 2 ½ m. – ✉ Brockenhurst – ☎ 059 063 Bucklers Hard :

🏨 **Master Builder's House**, SO4 7XB, ℘ 253, ≤, 🐎 – 📺 ᐁwc ☎ 🅿 🔼 🄰🄴 ⓞ
𝘝𝘐𝘚𝘈
M a la carte 10.85/14.65 **t.** ⚬ 3.10 – **23 rm** ⚏ 30.00/49.00 **st.** – SB 65.00 **st.**

BEAUMARIS Gwynedd 402 403 H 24 – pop. 1 413 – ECD : Wednesday – ☎ 0248.
See : Castle★ (13C) AC.
Envir. : Menai Strait★ (Channel), Menai Suspension Bridge ≤★ SW : 4 ½ m. – Bryn Celli Du (burial chamber★) SW : 8 m.
🛈 Baron Hill ℘ 810231, NW : 1 m.
♦London 253 – Birkenhead 74 – Holyhead 25.

🏨 **Bulkeley Arms**, 19 Castle St., LL58 8AW, ℘ 810415, ≤ Menai Strait, 🐎 – 🕴 📺 ᐁwc
🔥wc ☎ 🅿 🔼 🄰🄴 ⓞ 𝘝𝘐𝘚𝘈 🍴
M 7.95/8.75 **t.** ⚬ 2.95 – **41 rm** ⚏ 21.95/44.95 **t.**, **2 suites** 48.95/51.95 **t.** – SB 51.95/61.95 **st.**

🏨 **Liverpool Arms** without rest., Castle St., LL58 8BA, ℘ 810362 – 📺 ᐁwc 🔥wc 🅿 🔼 𝘝𝘐𝘚𝘈
🍴
10 rm ⚏ 26.00/44.00 **t.**

🏨 **Bishopsgate House**, 54 Castle St., LL58 8AB, ℘ 810302 – 📺 🔥wc 🅿 🔼 𝘝𝘐𝘚𝘈
April-December – **M** 5.95/8.95 **t.** and a la carte ⚬ 2.50 – **10 rm** ⚏ 17.00/40.00 **t.** – SB (except Bank Holidays) 55.00/60.00 **st.**

BECCLES Suffolk 404 Y 26 – pop. 10 677 – ECD : Wednesday – ☎ 0502.
🛈 The Quay, Fen Lane ℘ 713196 (summer only).
♦London 113 – Great Yarmouth 15 – ♦Ipswich 40 – ♦Norwich 18.

🏨 **Waveney House** 🌫, Puddingmoor, NR34 9PL, ℘ 712270 – 📺 ᐁwc 🔥wc 🍴 🅿
13 rm.

AUSTIN-ROVER,LAND-ROVER,RANGE-ROVER   VAUXHALL-OPEL Station Rd ℘ 717023
Beccles Rd, Barnby ℘ 050 276 (Barnby) 204

BECKERMET Cumbria 402 J 20 – ECD : Tuesday and Thursday – ✉ ☎ 094 684.
♦London 326 – ♦Carlisle 45 – Kendal 62 – Workington 17.

🏨 **Royal Oak** without rest., CA21 2XB, ℘ 551 – 📺 ᐁwc ☎ 🅿
8 rm ⚏ 22.00/44.00 **st.**

83

BEDDGELERT Gwynedd 402 403 H 24 – pop. 646 – ECD : Wednesday – ✆ 076 686.

Envir. : NE : Llyn Dinas valley★★ – Llyn Gwynant valley★.

Exc. : Blaenau Ffestiniog (site : slate quarries★) E : 14 m. by Penrhyndeudraeth.

♦London 249 – Caernarfon 13 – Chester 73.

🏨 **Royal Goat,** LL55 4YE, ℰ 224, ◥, – ⫼◻️wc ℗ ◪ AE ⑩ VISA
M 8.00/12.00 **st.** and a la carte ⫼ 3.50 – **22 rm** ⊑ 22.00/43.00 **t.** – SB (except summer) 49.00/56.00 **st.**

🏠 **Tanronen,** LL55 4YB, ℰ 347 – ℗. ◪ VISA
M (bar lunch Monday to Saturday)/dinner 9.50 **t.** ⫼ 2.50 – **9 rm** ⊑ 13.50/27.00 **t.** – SB 41.00 **st.**

BEDFORD Beds. 404 S 27 – pop. 75 632 – ECD : Thursday – ✆ 0234.

See : Embankment★ – Cecil Higgins Art Gallery (porcelain★ 18C).

Envir. : Elstow (Abbey Church★ 11C, Moot Hall : John Bunyan Museum AC) S : 1 ¼ m. – Ampthill (Houghton House : site★, ≼★) S : 5 m. – Old Warden (St. Leonard's Church : woodwork★ – Aeroplane Museum, near Biggleswade Aerodrome : the Shuttleworth collection★ AC) SE : 7 ½ m.

🛇 Bedford and County, Green Lane, Clapham ℰ 52617, N : 2 m. on A 6 – 🛇 Bedfordshire, Biddenham ℰ 53241, NE : 1 m. on A 428 – 🛇🛇 Beadlow Manor, Shefford ℰ 0525 (Silsoe) 60800, S : 9 m.

🖪 10 St. Paul's Sq. ℰ 215226.

♦London 59 – ♦Cambridge 31 – Colchester 70 – ♦Leicester 51 – Lincoln 95 – Luton 20 – ♦Oxford 52 – Southend-on-Sea 85.

🏨 **Bedford Swan,** The Embankment, MK40 1RW, ℰ 46565 – TV ⫼◻️wc ℗ ◪ 🛄 ◪ AE ⑩ VISA
M 7.85 **st.** and a la carte ⫼ 3.45 – **85 rm** ⊑ 39.00/49.00 **st.**, **1 suite** 85.00 **st.** – SB (weekends only) 44.00 **st.**

🏠 **Shakespeare,** 27 Shakespeare Rd, MK40 2DX, ℰ 213147, ⟪ – TV ⫼◻️wc ⫼wc ℗ ◪ AE VISA ⫼
M (closed Saturday lunch, Sunday dinner and Bank Holidays) 8.00 **t.** and a la carte – **18 rm** ⊑ 32.50/40.00 **t.** – SB (weekends only) 42.00 **t.**

🏠 **De Parys,** 41-45 de Parys Av., MK40 2UA, ℰ 52121, ⟪ – TV ⫼◻️wc ⫼wc ℗ ◪ 🛄 ◪ AE VISA ⫼
closed 1 week at Christmas – M (bar lunch Monday to Saturday)/dinner 8.00 **st.** and a la carte ⫼ 3.80 – **31 rm** ⊑ 36.00/46.00 **st.** – SB (weekends only) 50.00 **st.**

🏠 **Edwardian House,** 15 Shakespeare Rd, MK40 2DZ, ℰ 45281 – TV ⫼◻️wc ⫼wc ℗ ◪ AE
14 rm ⊑ 32.50/40.00 **st.**

at Houghton Conquest S : 6 ½ m. by A 6 – ✉ ✆ 0234 Bedford :

XX **Knife and Cleaver,** MK45 3LA, ℰ 740387 – ℗. ◪ VISA
closed Sunday and Bank Holiday lunch – M 10.50 **t.** (dinner)and a la carte 10.50/13.80 **t.**

at Turvey W : 7 m. on A 428 – ✉ Bedford – ✆ 023 064 Turvey :

XX **Laws** with rm, MK43 8DB, ℰ 213, ⟪ – TV ⫼◻️wc ℗. ◪ VISA
M (closed Sunday dinner to non residents) (bar lunch Monday and Saturday) a la carte 11.45/13.00 **t.** ⫼ 3.00 – **8 rm** ⊑ 35.00/65.00 **t.**

at Clapham NW : 2 m. on A 6 – ✉ ✆ 0234 Bedford :

🏯 **Woodlands Manor** ◈, Green Lane, MK41 6EP, ℰ 63281, Telex 825007, ⟪ – TV ☎ ℗. 🛄 ◪ AE VISA ◈
M (closed lunch Saturday and Bank Holidays) 9.25/13.50 **t.** and a la carte ⫼ 4.75 – ⊑ 5.50 – **21 rm** 37.50/63.00 **t.**, **1 suite** 83.50 **t.** – SB (weekends only) 57.00 **st.**

MICHELIN Distribution Centre, Hammond Rd, Elms Farm Industrial Estate, MK41 0LG, ℰ 213491

AUSTIN-ROVER-DAIMLER-JAGUAR 120 Goldington Rd ℰ 55221
BMW, ROLLS ROYCE-BENTLEY Shuttleworth Rd, Goldington ℰ 60412
FORD 8-10 The Broadway ℰ 58391
FORD Hudson Rd ℰ 40041
HONDA, VOLVO Windsor Rd ℰ 45454
MERCEDES-BENZ,VAUXHALL-OPEL Barker's Lane ℰ 50011
NISSAN 180 Goldington Rd ℰ 60121
RENAULT 87 High St., Clapham ℰ 54257
SAAB,SCIMITAR Station Rd, Oakley ℰ 023 02 (Oakley) 3118

BEESTON Cheshire 402 403 404 L 24 – pop. 221 – ✉ Tarporley – ✆ 0829 Bunbury.

♦London 186 – Chester 15 – ♦Liverpool 40 – Shrewsbury 32.

XXX **Wild Boar Inn** (Embassy) with rm, CW6 9NW, on A 49 ℰ 260309, Telex 61455, ⟪ – TV ⫼◻️wc ℗. ◪ 🛄 AE ⑩ VISA
M 9.75/14.50 **t.** and a la carte 14.10/25.35 **t.** ⫼ 3.00 – ⊑ 4.50 – **30 rm** 30.00/40.00 **t.** – SB 58.00 **st.**

XXX **Rembrandt,** Whitchurch Road, Spurstow, CW6 9PD, on A 49 ℰ 260281 – ℗. ◪ ⑩ VISA
closed Sunday dinner, Monday and Bank Holidays – M 10.20 **st.** and a la carte ⫼ 3.55.

BEESTON Notts. 402 403 404 Q 25 – see Nottingham.

BELBROUGHTON Heref. and Worc. 403 404 N 26 – see Stourbridge (West Midlands).

84

BELFORD Northumb. **401 402** O 17 — pop. 943 — ECD : Thursday — ☎ 066 83.
◆London 335 — ◆Edinburgh 71 — ◆Newcastle-upon-Tyne 49.

  🏠 **Blue Bell,** Market Sq., NE70 7NE, ℰ 543, ☞ — TV ⏢wc ℗ 🅿. 🔼 ℀ ① VISA. ℀
  M 8.00/12.00 **t.** and a la carte ⓘ 2.50 — **15 rm** ⩘ 22.00/28.00 **t.** — SB 56.00/62.00 **st.**

BELPER Derbs. **402 403 404** P 24 — pop. 17 328 — ✉ ☎ 077 382.
◆London 141 — Derby 8 — ◆Manchester 55 — ◆Nottingham 17.

  XX **Remy,** 84 Bridge St., DE5 1AZ, ℰ 2246 — ▤. 🔼 ① VISA
  closed lunch Monday and Saturday, Sunday, 1 week January and 2 weeks August — **M** 16.00 **t.**
  ⓘ 3.00.

BEMBRIDGE I.O.W. **403 404** Q 31 — see Wight (Isle of).

BENLLECH Gwynedd **402 403** H 24 — pop. 1 948 — ECD : Thursday — ☎ 0248 Tynygongl.
◆London 258 — Caernarfon 17 — Chester 70 — Holyhead 22.

  🏠 **Rhostrefor,** Amlwch Rd, LL74 8SR, on A 5025 ℰ 852347, 🔼, ☞ — TV ⏢wc ⽧wc ℗. 🔼
  M (bar lunch Monday to Saturday)/dinner 7.00 **st.** and a la carte ⓘ 2.85 — **15 rm**
  ⩘ 17.00/32.00 **st.** — SB (except summer and Bank Holidays) 43.00 **st.**

BEPTON West Sussex — see Midhurst.

BERKELEY Glos. **403 404** M 28 — pop. 1 498 — ECD : Wednesday — ☎ 0453 Dursley.
◆London 129 — ◆Bristol 20 — ◆Cardiff 50 — Gloucester 18.

  🏠 **Old School House,** Canonbury St., GL13 9BG, ℰ 811711 — TV ⏢wc ⽧wc ☎ ℗. 🔼 VISA.
  ℀
  closed 24 to 26 December — **M** *(closed Monday lunch)* a la carte lunch/dinner 13.00 **st.** ⓘ 3.25
  — **7 rm** ⩘ 25.00/39.00 **st.** — SB 54.00/56.00 **st.**

BERKHAMSTED Herts **404** S 28 — pop. 16 874 — ECD : Wednesday and Saturday — ☎ 044 27.
🛈 Library, Kings Rd ℰ 4545.
◆London 33 — Luton 16 — ◆Oxford 35.

  🏠 Hamberlin's ⧖ without rest., Tring Rd, Northchurch, HP4 3TL, NW : 1 ½ m. on A 41
  ℰ 75100, ☞ — TV ⽧wc ℗
  16 rm.

  🏠 **Swan,** 135-139 High St., HP4 3HH, ℰ 71451, Telex 82257 — ▤ rest TV ⏢wc ⽧wc ☎ ℗. 🔼
  VISA
  M 9.90 **t.** and a la carte ⓘ 4.00 — **16 rm** ⩘ 25.00/45.00 **st.** — SB (weekends only) 40.00/45.00 **st.**

AUSTIN-ROVER London Rd ℰ 71234   PEUGEOT-TALBOT Ringshall, Little Gaddesden ℰ
CITROEN Lower Kings Rd ℰ (04427) 2232   2273/2777/2384
FORD 33 High St. ℰ 71171

BERKSWELL West Midlands **403 404** P 26 — see Coventry.

BERWICK-UPON-TWEED Northumb. **401 402** O 16 — pop. 12 772 — ECD : Thursday — ☎ 0289.
See : City Walls★ 16C.
Envir. : Norham Castle★ (12C) SW : 7 m.
🛈₈ Goswick, Beal ℰ 87256, S : 5 m. — 🛈₈ Magdalene Fields ℰ 305109.
🛈 Castlegate Car Park ℰ 307187 (summer only).
◆London 349 — ◆Edinburgh 57 — ◆Newcastle-upon-Tyne 63.

  🏨 **King's Arms,** 43 Hide Hill, TD15 1EJ, ℰ 307454, Telex 8811232 — TV ⏢wc ⽧wc ☎. 🔼 🔼
  ① VISA
  M 5.50/10.50 **st.** and a la carte ⓘ 3.00 — **36 rm** ⩘ 32.00/48.00 **st.** — SB (weekends only) 52.00 **st.**

  🏠 **Turret House,** Etal Rd, Tweedmouth, TD15 2EG, S : ¾ m. by A 1167 on B 6354 ℰ 307344, ☞
  — TV ⏢wc ☎ ℗. 🔼 🔼 ① VISA
  M 5.50/10.85 **st.** ⓘ 3.50 — **10 rm** ⩘ 28.00/45.00 **st.** — SB 50.00/58.00 **st.**

AUSTIN-ROVER Tweedside Trading Estate ℰ 307561   VAUXHALL 12 Silver St. ℰ 307436
RENAULT Golden Sq. ℰ 307371   VOLVO Tweed St. ℰ 307537

When travelling for business or pleasure
in England, Wales, Scotland and Ireland :

— use the series of five maps
  (nos **401 402 403 404** and **405**) at a scale of 1:400 000
— they are the perfect complement to this Guide
  as towns underlined in red on the maps will be found in this Guide.

BETWS-Y-COED Gwynedd 402 403 I 24 – pop. 654 – ECD : Thursday – ✆ 069 02.

Envir. : Fairy Glen and Conway Falls★ *AC*, SE : 2 m. – Swallow Falls★ *AC*, NW : 2 m. – Nanty-gwryd valley★ W : by Capel Curig.

⌢ ✆ 556, ½ m. off A 5.

🛈 Royal Oak Stables ✆ 426465 (summer only).

◆London 226 – Holyhead 44 – Shrewsbury 62.

🏠 **Royal Oak,** Holyhead Rd, LL24 0AY, ✆ 219 – 📺 🛏wc ☎ 🅿 🔄 🆎 ⓞ 𝖵𝖨𝖲𝖠. 🍴
closed 25 and 26 December – **M** 7.00/11.00 **t.** and a la carte ⌕ 5.50 – **21 rm** 🖙 35.00/52.00 **t.** – SB (except Christmas) 64.00/68.00 **st.**

🏠 **Waterloo,** LL24 0AR, on A 5 ✆ 411 – 📺 🛏wc 🅰 🅿 🔄 🆎 ⓞ 𝖵𝖨𝖲𝖠. 🍴
closed 3 days at Christmas – **M** (bar lunch Monday to Saturday)/dinner 9.25 **t.** and a la carte ⌕ 2.95 – **28 rm** 🖙 18.50/44.00 **t.** – SB (except Bank Holidays) 49.00/59.00 **st.**

⌂ Park Hill, Llanrwst Rd, LL24 0HD, NE : 1 m. by A 5 on A 470 ✆ 540, ≼ Vale of Conwy, 🔲, 🍴
– 🛏wc 🛏wc 🅿
11 rm.

at Pont-y-Pant SW : 4 ½ m. on A 470 – ✉ ✆ 069 06 Dolwyddelan :

🏠 **Plas Hall,** LL25 0PJ, ✆ 206, 🏊, 🍴 – 📺 🛏wc ☎ ♿ 🅿 🔄 🆎 ⓞ 𝖵𝖨𝖲𝖠. 🍴
closed 25 and 26 December – **M** (lunch by arrangement) 6.50/9.75 **t.** and a la carte ⌕ 3.60 –
16 rm 🖙 21.50/56.00 **t.** – SB (except Easter and summer) 40.00/54.00 **st.**

BEVERLEY Humberside 402 S 22 – pop. 19 368 – ECD : Thursday – ✉ ✆ 0482 Kingston-upon-Hull.

See : Minster★★ 13C-15C – St. Mary's Church★ 14C-15C.

⌢ Walkington Rd ✆ 867190.

🛈 30 Market Pl. ✆ 867430.

◆London 188 – ◆Kingston-upon-Hull 8 – ◆Leeds 52 – York 29.

🏠 **Beverley Arms** (T.H.F.), North Bar Within, HU17 8DD, ✆ 869241, Telex 597568 – 🔧 📺
🛏wc 🅰 🅿 🔄 🆎 ⓞ 𝖵𝖨𝖲𝖠
M 6.95/9.75 **st.** and a la carte ⌕ 3.40 – 🖙 5.65 – **61 rm** 45.00/55.00 **st.**

🏠 **Lairgate,** 30 Lairgate, HU17 8EP, ✆ 882141 – 📺 🛏wc 🛏wc ☎ 🅿 🔄 𝖵𝖨𝖲𝖠
closed 25 and 26 December – **M** 6.00/10.00 **t.** ⌕ 2.50 – **24 rm** 🖙 22.00/39.00 **t.** – SB (weekends only)(October-March) 40.00/53.00 **st.**

⌂ King's Head, Market Pl., HU17 9AH, ✆ 869241, Telex 527568 – 🅿 – **9 rm**.

at Tickton NE : 3 ½ m. by A 1035 – ✉ Kingston-upon-Hull – ✆ 0401 Leven :

🏠 **Tickton Grange,** HU17 9SH, ✆ 43666, 🍴 – 📺 🛏wc 🛏wc 🅰 🅿 ♿ 🔄 🆎 ⓞ 𝖵𝖨𝖲𝖠
M a la carte lunch/dinner 10.00 **t.** ⌕ 4.25 – 🖙 4.75 – **15 rm** 42.00/52.50 **t.** – SB (weekends only) 67.00/72.00 **st.**

AUSTIN-ROVER Barmston Rd, Swinemoor Ind Est.   FORD Wednesday Market ✆ 868311
✆ 867922   VAUXHALL-OPEL Swinemoor Lane ✆ 882207

BEWDLEY Heref. and Worc. 403 404 N 26 – pop. 8 696 – ECD : Wednesday – ✆ 0299.

⌢ Little Lakes Golf and Country Club, Lye Head ✆ 266385, W : 2¼ m. off A 456.

🛈 The Library, Load St. ✆ 403303.

◆London 140 – ◆Birmingham 20 – Worcester 16.

🏠 **Black Boy,** Kidderminster Rd, DY12 1AG, ✆ 402119, 🍴 – 🛏wc 🛏 🅿 🔄 🆎 𝖵𝖨𝖲𝖠
closed Christmas Day – **M** (closed Sunday dinner to non-residents) a la carte lunch/dinner
7.95 **t.** ⌕ 3.00 – **25 rm** 🖙 15.90/39.00 **t.** – SB (weekends only) 31.00/43.00 **t.**

✕✕ **Bailiff's House,** 68 High St., DY12 2DJ, ✆ 402691, « 17C Bailiff's House » – 🔄 🆎 𝖵𝖨𝖲𝖠
closed Monday lunch and Sunday dinner – **M** (lunch by arrangement Tuesday to Satur-day)/dinner 15.50 **t.** ⌕ 2.80.

BEXHILL East Sussex 404 V 31 – pop. 34 625 – ECD : Wednesday – ✆ 0424.

⌢ Cooden Beach ✆ 042 43 (Cooden) 2040.

🛈 De La Warr Pavilion, Marina ✆ 212023.

◆London 66 – ◆ Brighton 32 – Folkestone 42.

🏠 **Cooden Resort,** Cooden Sea Rd, Cooden Beach, TN39 4TT, W : 2 m. on B 2182
✆ 04243 (Cooden) 2281, Telex 877247, 🏊 heated, 🍴 – 📺 🛏wc 🛏wc ☎ 🅿 ♿ 🔄 🆎 ⓞ
𝖵𝖨𝖲𝖠 🍴
M 11.00/12.00 **t.** and a la carte – **32 rm** 🖙 37.50/60.00 **t.** – SB (weekends only) 66.00/72.00 **st.**

⌂ Chantry Close, 13 Hastings Rd, TN40 2HJ, ✆ 222024 – 🛏 🅿 🍴
April-October – **7 rm** 🖙 12.00/14.00 **st.**

AUDI, VW King Offa Way ✆ 212255   RENAULT London Rd ✆ 210485
AUSTIN-ROVER-DAIMLER-JAGUAR 57-69 London   TOYOTA Holliers Hill ✆ 213577
Rd ✆ 212000   FIAT, MAZDA Holliers Hill ✆ 213577
FORD ✆ 212727   VAUXHALL-OPEL Dorset Rd ✆ 211212
HONDA Sackville Rd ✆ 221330

BIBURY Glos. **403 404** O 28 – pop. 603 – ECD : Wednesday – ⊠ Cirencester – ✆ 028 574.

See : Arlington Row★ 17C.

◆London 86 – Gloucester 26 – ◆Oxford 30.

🏨 **Swan,** GL7 5NW, ✆ 204, « Garden and trout stream », ⌐ – 🆃🆅 ⌂wc 🅿. 🅰 VISA
M 10.25/13.75 t. ₰ 3.50 – 🖵 30.50/52.50 t. – SB 57.50/75.00 st.

🏨 **Bibury Court** ⌂, GL7 5NT, ✆ 337, ≼, « Tudor mansion », ⌐, 🌲, park – ⌂wc 🅿. 🅰
AE ① VISA
closed 24 to 30 December – **M** (bar lunch)/dinner a la carte 9.30/14.25 t. ₰ 2.50 – 🖵 3.25 –
16 rm 24.00/48.00 t. **1 suite** 65.00 t. – SB (November-March) 58.00/62.00 st.

BICKLEIGH Devon **403** J 31 – pop. 205 – ECD : Tuesday – ⊠ Tiverton – ✆ 088 45.

◆London 195 – Exeter 9 – Taunton 31.

⌂ **Bickleigh Cottage,** EX16 8RJ, on A 396 ✆ 230, 🌲 – ⌂wc 🅿. ❀
April-October – **10 rm** 🖵 11.50/30.00 t.

BIDDENDEN Kent **404** V 30 – pop. 2 229 – ⊠ Ashford – ✆ 0580.

◆London 51 – Folkestone 29 – Hastings 23 – Maidstone 14.

XX **West House,** 28 High St., TN27 8AH, ✆ 291341, Italian rest. – 🅿. 🅰 VISA
closed Sunday, Monday, 2 weeks after Easter and 2 weeks August-September – **M** 6.50/8.50
st. and a la carte 9.00/13.60 st. ₰ 2.25.

X **Ye Maydes,** 13-15 High St., TN27 8AL, ✆ 291306 – 🅰 AE
closed Sunday, Monday, first week February, last week July, first week September and first
week November – **M** 6.85/15.00 t. and a la carte 8.60/14.10 t. ₰ 2.80.

BIDEFORD Devon **403** H 30 The West Country G. – pop. 13 826 – ECD : Wednesday – ✆ 023 72.

See : The Bridge★★ – Burton Art Gallery★AC.

Envir. : Clovelly★★, W : 11 m. – Great Torrington : Dartington Glass★AC, SE : 7 m. – at Hartland
(≼★★★) Church★ Quay★ (≼★★), W : 12 m. – at Thornbury, Devon Museum of Mechanical Music★AC,
S : 15 m.

⌐ to the Isle of Lundy (Lundy Co.) 2-3 Weekly (2 h 30 mn).

🅸 The Quay ✆ 77676 (summer only).

◆London 231 – Exeter 43 – ◆Plymouth 58 – Taunton 60.

🏨 **Durrant House,** Heywood Rd, Northam, EX39 3QB, N : 1 m. on A 386 ✆ 72361, ⌱ heated –
🍽 rest 🆃🆅 ⌂wc 🅿. 🅰 AE ① VISA
M 4.50/8.25 t. and a la carte – **52 rm** 🖵 31.00/45.70 t. **2 suites** 47.50/60.00 st. – SB (weekends
only)(September-June) 47.00/57.20 st.

🏨 **Yeoldon House** (Best Western) ⌂, Durrant Lane, Northam, EX39 2RL, N : 1 ½ m. by A 386
✆ 74400, ≼ Torridge estuary, « Country house atmosphere », 🌲 – 🆃🆅 ⌂wc ⌂wc ☎ 🅿. 🅰
AE ① VISA. ❀
M (bar lunch)/dinner 10.50 t. and a la carte ₰ 3.20 – **10 rm** 🖵 31.50/53.00 t. – SB 52.50/69.50 st.

🏨 **Riversford** ⌂, Limers Lane, Northam, EX39 2RG, N : 1 m. by A 386 ✆ 74239, ≼, 🌲 – 🆃🆅
⌂wc 🅿. 🅰 AE ① VISA
M 5.40/8.85 st. and a la carte – **17 rm** 🖵 16.45/24.90 st. – SB (weekends only) 54.50/58.30 st.

🏨 Beaconside House ⌂, Landcross, EX39 5JL, S : 3 m. by A 386 on A 388 ✆ 77205, ≼, ⌱, 🌲,
park, ❀ – 🆃🆅 ⌂wc 🅿 – 9 rm.

⌂ **Orchard Hill,** Orchard Hill, EX39 2QY, N : ¾ m. by A 386 ✆ 72872, 🌲 – 🆃🆅 ⌂wc 🅿. ❀
closed 2 weeks November – **9 rm** 🖵 16.00/28.00 st.

at Instow N : 3 m. on A 39 – ⊠ Bideford – ✆ 0271 Instow :

🏨🏨 **Commodore,** Marine Par., EX39 4JN, ✆ 860347, ≼ Taw and Torridge estuaries, 🌲 – 🆃🆅 ☎
🅿. ⚿. 🅰 AE VISA. ❀
M 6.70/10.50 t. and a la carte ₰ 3.50 – **20 rm** 🖵 33.00/49.00 t.

at Eastleigh NE : 2 ½ m. by A 39 (via Old Barnstaple road) – ⊠ Bideford – ✆ 0271 Instow :

⌂ **Pines,** EX39 4PA, ✆ 860561, ≼, 🌲 – 🅿. 🅰 VISA. ❀
April-October – **8 rm** 🖵 14.00/23.00 st.

AUSTIN-ROVER 6 Queen St. ✆ 73304
PEUGEOT-TALBOT Bridgeland St. ✆ 71975 71976
RENAULT Kingsley Rd ✆ 72546

SAAB, HYUNDAI Meddon St. ✆ 72467
VAUXHALL-OPEL, BEDFORD Handy Cross ✆ 72282

BIDFORD-ON-AVON Warw. **403 404** O 27 – pop. 2 748 – ECD : Thursday – ⊠ Alcester –
✆ 0789.

◆London 103 – ◆Birmingham 25 – ◆Coventry 27 – ◆Oxford 50 – Worcester 22.

🏨 **White Lion,** High St., B50 4BQ, ✆ 773309 – 🆃🆅 ⌂wc 🅿. 🅰 AE
M (bar lunch Monday to Saturday)/dinner 15.00 t. – **15 rm** 🖵 17.00/32.00 t. – SB (weekends
only) 39.50/49.50 t.

BIGBURY-ON-SEA Devon 403 I 33 – pop. 559 – ECD : Thursday – ✉ Kingsbridge – ☎ 0548.

Kingsbridge ✆ 207, S : 1 m. on B 3392.

London 196 – Exeter 42 – Plymouth 17.

- **Seagulls**, Folly Hill, TQ7 4AR, ✆ 810331, ≤ Bigbury Bay and Bolt Head, – wc wc P. VISA
  Easter-mid October – **M** (bar lunch)/dinner 8.75 **st.** 1.90 – **10 rm** 16.00/36.00 **st.**
- **Henley**, Folly Hill, TQ7 4AR, ✆ 810240, ≤ Bigbury Bay and Bolt Head, – wc P
  Easter-September – **M** (bar lunch)/dinner 8.00 **t.** 2.00 – **9 rm** 20.00/42.00 **st.**

BILBROOK Somerset 403 J 30 – ✉ Minehead – ☎ 0984 Washford.

London 181 – Minehead 5 – Taunton 19.

- **Dragon House,** TA24 6HQ, ✆ 40215, « Part 18C house with gardens » – TV wc wc P. AE VISA
  M (bar lunch Monday to Saturday)/dinner 9.75 **t.** and a la carte 2.70 – **10 rm** 21.50/46.00 **t.**, **1 suite** 65.00 **t.** – SB 57.50/67.50 **st.**
- **Bilbrook Lawns,** TA24 6HE, ✆ 40331, – TV wc wc P
  M *(closed Sunday dinner)* 4.85/5.50 **t.** and a la carte 2.75 – **13 rm** 13.50/30.00 **t.** – SB (except Christmas) 32.00/38.00 **st.**

BILLINGHAM Cleveland 402 Q 20 – pop. 36 855 – ✉ ☎ 0642 Stockton-on-Tees.

Sandy Lane ✆ 554494.

London 255 – Middlesbrough 3 – Sunderland 26.

- **Billingham Arms,** The Causeway, TS23 2HD, ✆ 553661, Telex 587746 – TV wc wc ☎ P. AE VISA
  M (bar lunch Saturday) 7.00/10.00 **st.** and a la carte 3.95 – **63 rm** 18.00/49.00 **t.** – SB (except Christmas)(weekends only) 88.00 **st.**

AUSTIN-ROVER Wolviston Rd ✆ 553959
FORD The Green ✆ 550415
RENAULT Central Garage ✆ 553071

BILLINGSHURST West Sussex 404 S 30 – pop. 4 877 – ECD : Wednesday – ☎ 040 381.

London 45 – Brighton 24 – Guildford 20 – Portsmouth 39.

- **Jennie Wren,** Groomsland House, Pulborough Rd, RH14 9EU, S : ½ m. on A 29 ✆ 2571, « 15C house » – P. AE VISA
  closed Saturday lunch, Sunday dinner, 2 weeks February and Bank Holidays – **M** 7.95 **t.** (lunch) and a la carte 9.80/14.50 **t.** 3.50.

FORD High St. ✆ 2537
MERCEDES-BENZ, PORSCHE, SCIMITAR High St. ✆ 3341

BINGLEY West Yorks. 402 O 22 – pop. 18 954 – ECD : Tuesday – ✉ ☎ 0274 Bradford.

London 204 – Bradford 6 – Skipton 13.

- **Bankfield** (Embassy), Bradford Rd, BD16 1TV, SE : 1 ½ m. on A 650 ✆ 567123, – TV wc ☎ P. AE VISA
  M (carving rest.) 9.50 **st.** and a la carte 3.00 – 5.00 – **69 rm** 39.00/48.00 **st.** – SB 59.00 **st.**

SCIMITAR Park Rd ✆ 563556

BIRKBY Cumbria – see Maryport.

BIRKENHEAD Merseyside 402 403 K 23 – pop. 99 075 – ECD : Thursday – ☎ 051 Liverpool.

Arrowe Park, Woodchurch ✆ 677 1527 – Prenton, Golf Links Rd ✆ 608 1053.

to Liverpool (Merseyside Transport) frequent services daily (7-8 mn).

Central Library, Borough Rd ✆ 652 6106.

London 222 – Liverpool 2.

Plan : see Liverpool p. 3

- **Bowler Hat,** 2 Talbot Rd, Oxton, L43 2HH, ✆ 652 4931, Telex 628761, – TV ☎ P. AE VISA AX
  M 9.50/11.70 **st.** and a la carte 3.25 – 4.50 – **29 rm** 47.85/60.50 **st.**, **1 suite** – SB (weekends only) 59.50/64.50 **st.**

FIAT Claughton Firs ✆ 653 8555
MAZDA Albion St., Wallasey ✆ 638 2234
MITSUBISHI, COLT New Chester Rd ✆ 645 1025
NISSAN Hoylake Rd ✆ 678 1060
RENAULT Borough Rd ✆ 608 9121
SEAT Park Rd North ✆ 647 9445
VAUXHALL-OPEL 6 Woodchurch Rd ✆ 652 2366

Dieser Führer ist kein vollständiges Hotel- und Restaurantverzeichnis.
Um den Ansprüchen aller Touristen gerecht zu werden, haben wir uns auf eine Auswahl in jeder Kategorie beschränkt.

BIRMINGHAM West Midlands **403 404** O 26 – pop. 1 013 995 – ECD : Wednesday – ✿ 021.

See : Museum and Art Gallery★★ JZ **M1** – Museum of Science and Industry★ JY **M2** – Cathedral (stained glass windows★ 19C) KYZ E.

📮 Cocks Moor Woods, Alcester Rd South, King's Heath ✆ 444 2062, S : 6 ½ m. by A 435 FX – 📮 Edgbaston, Church Rd ✆ 454 1736, S : 1 m. FX – 📮 Pype Hayes, Eachelhurst Rd, Walmley ✆ 361 1014, NE : 7 ½ m. DT – 📮 Warley, Lightwoods Hill, ✆ 429 2440, W : 5 m. BU.

✈ Birmingham Airport : ✆ 767 7153, E : 6 ½ m. by A 45 DU.

🛈 2 City Arcade ✆ 643 2514 – National Exhibition Centre ✆ 780 4141 – Birmingham Airport ✆ 767 5511.

◆London 122 – ◆Bristol 91 – ◆Liverpool 103 – ◆Manchester 86 – ◆Nottingham 50.

Town plans : Birmingham pp. 2-7
Except where otherwise stated see pp. 6 and 7

🏨🏨 **Albany** (T.H.F.), Smallbrook, Queensway, B5 4EW, ✆ 643 8171, Telex 337031, ≼, ☒, squash – 🛊 📺 🅆🅒 ☎ 🚃 🔌 🔼 🆎 ⓘ 💳 _JKZ_ **a**
M 9.45/8.65 **st.** and a la carte 🛆 3.40 – ⊒ 6.00 – **254 rm** 55.00/65.00 **st.**, **8 suites**.

🏨🏨 **Plough and Harrow** (Crest), 135 Hagley Rd, Edgbaston, B16 8LS, W : 1 ½ m. on A 456 ✆ 454 4111, Telex 338074, 🚣 – 🛊 📺 ☎ 🅿 🔌 🔼 🆎 ⓘ 💳 p. 4 EX **a**
M (see Plough and Harrow below) – ⊒ 7.25 – **44 rm** 68.00/83.50 **st.**, **3 suites** 110.00/145.00 **st.** – SB (weekends only) 98.00 **st.**

🏨🏨 **Midland** (Best Western), 128 New St., B2 4JT, ✆ 643 2601, Telex 338419 – 🛊 📺 🆆🅒 🔌 🔼 🆎 ⓘ 💳 🚍 _KZ_ **r**
M 9.50/11.50 **t.** and a la carte – **107 rm** ⊒ 45.00/67.00 **t.**, **2 suites** 85.00 **t.** – SB (weekends only)(except Christmas) 56.00/61.00 **st.**

🏨🏨 **Holiday Inn,** Central Sq., Holliday St., B1 1HH, ✆ 643 2766, Telex 337272, ≼, ☒ – 🛊 📺 ☎ 🔌 🅿 🔼 🆎 ⓘ 💳 _JZ_ **z**
M (buffet lunch) and a la carte 13.00/17.75 **t.** 🛆 3.20 – ⊒ 6.00 – **295 rm** 52.90/59.80 **st.**, **4 suites** 145.00/260.00 **st.** – SB (weekends only) 49.00/61.00 **st.**

🏨🏨 **Strathallan Thistle** (Thistle), 225 Hagley Rd, Edgbaston, B16 9RY, W : 2 m. on A 456 ✆ 455 9777, Telex 336680 – 🛊 📺 rest 📺 🆆🅒 🅿 🔌 🔼 🆎 ⓘ 💳 p. 4 EX **i**
M 8.00/11.00 **t.** and a la carte 🛆 2.50 – ⊒ 6.50 – **164 rm** 47.00/75.00 **st.**, **4 suites** 90.00 **st.**

🏨🏨 **Grand** (Q.M.H.), Colmore Row, B3 2DA, ✆ 236 7951, Telex 338174 – 🛊 📺 🆆🅒 🔌 🔼 🆎 ⓘ 💳 _JKY_ **c**
closed 25 to 30 December – **M** 8.50 **st.** and a la carte – **167 rm** ⊒ 58.00/68.00 **st.**, **2 suites** 90.00 **st.** – SB 55.00 **st.**

🏨🏨 **Royal Angus Thistle** (Thistle), St. Chad's, Queensway, B4 6HY, ✆ 236 4211, Telex 336889 – 🛊 📺 🆆🅒 🔌 ⓘ 💳 🚍 _KY_ **s**
M approx. 10.00 **t.** and a la carte 🛆 2.75 – ⊒ 5.25 – **137 rm** 47.00/75.00 **st.**, **2 suites** 85.00 **st.**

🏨 **Apollo,** 243-247 Hagley Rd, Edgbaston, B16 9RA, W : 2 ¼ m. on A 456 ✆ 455 0271, Telex 336759 – 🛊 rest 📺 🆆🅒 ☎ 🔌 🔼 🆎 ⓘ 💳 p. 4 EX **o**
M (closed Saturday lunch) 12.80/14.50 **st.** and a la carte 🛆 3.00 – ⊒ 5.50 – **130 rm** 44.75/58.50 **st.**, **2 suites** 59.75/64.75 **st.**

🏨 **Ladbroke International** (Ladbroke), New St., B2 4RX, ✆ 643 2747, Telex 338331 – 🛊 🚃 📺 🆆🅒 🔌 🔼 🆎 ⓘ 💳 _KZ_ **x**
⊒ 5.75 – **191 rm** 48.00/60.00 **st.**, **4 suites** – SB (weekends only) 63.00 **st.**

🏨 **Asquith House,** 19 Portland Rd, off Hagley Rd, Edgbaston, B16 9HN, W : 2 m. by A 456 ✆ 454 5282, « Attractive decor and furnishings », 🚣 – 📺 🆆🅒 🔌 🅿 🔼 🆎 p. 4 EX **c**
closed 1 week at Christmas – **M** (closed Sunday dinner) (residents only)(lunch by arrangement) 12.00/16.00 **st.** 🛆 2.40 – **10 rm** ⊒ 27.00/41.75 **st.** – SB (weekends only) 70.00/80.00 **st.**

🏨 **Berrow Court** ⬙, Berrow Drive off Westfield Rd, Edgbaston, B15 3UD, W : 3 m. by A 456 ✆ 454 1488, « Country house atmosphere », 🚣 – 🅿 💳 p. 4 EX **e**
closed 24 December-2 January – **M** (closed Saturday and Sunday) (dinner only)(residents only) 5.80 **st.** – **16 rm** ⊒ 20.50/32.50 **st.**

🏨 **Hagley Court,** 229 Hagley Rd, Edgbaston, B16 9RP, W : 2 m. on A 456 ✆ 454 6514 – 📺 🆆🅒 🆆🅒 🔌 🅿 🔼 💳 p. 4 EX **s**
closed 24 December-2 January – **M** (closed Friday to Sunday) (dinner only) 7.25 **st.** and a la carte 🛆 2.25 – **25 rm** ⊒ 16.00/37.00 **st.**

🏨 **Cobden,** 166-174 Hagley Rd, Edgbaston, B16 9NZ, W : 2 m. on A 456 ✆ 454 6621, Group Telex 339715, 🚣 – 🛊 📺 🆆🅒 🆆🅒 ☎ 🅿 🔌 🔼 🆎 ⓘ 💳 p. 4 EX **n**
closed Christmas and New Year – **M** 6.00/8.50 **st.** – **210 rm** ⊒ 23.50/45.00 **st.**

🏨 **Fountain Court,** 339-343 Hagley Rd, Edgbaston, B17 8NH, W : 2 ½ m. on A 456 ✆ 429 1754, 🚣 – 📺 🆆🅒 🆆🅒 🅿 🔌 EX **u**
M (residents only)(bar lunch)/dinner 6.95 🛆 2.95 – **28 rm** ⊒ 16.50/34.50 – SB (weekends only) 54.00 **st.**

XXX **Plough and Harrow** (Crest), (at Plough and Harrow H.) 135 Hagley Rd, Edgbaston, B16 8LS, W : 1 ½ m. on A 456 ✆ 454 4111, Telex 338074, 🚣 – 🅿 🔼 🆎 ⓘ 💳 EX **a**
M 16.50/22.50 **st.** and a la carte 24.75/34.75 **st.**

XXX **Jonathans',** 16-20 Wolverhampton Rd, B68 0LH, W : 4 m. by A 456 ✆ 429 3757, English rest., « Victoriana » – 🔼 🆎 ⓘ 💳 p. 2 BU **e**
closed Saturday lunch, 26 December and 1 January – **M** 7.90/16.90 **st.** and a la carte 10.30/16.30 **st.** 🛆 2.80.

P.T.O. →

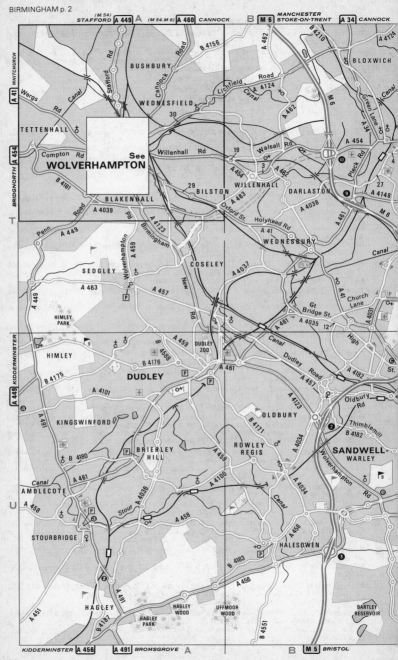

BIRMINGHAM AND WOLVERHAMPTON
ENLARGED AREA

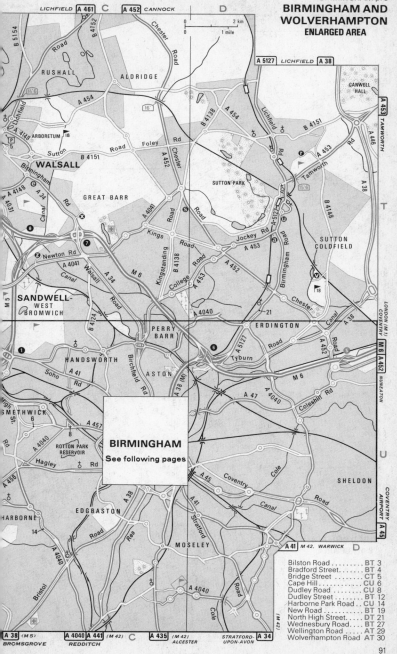

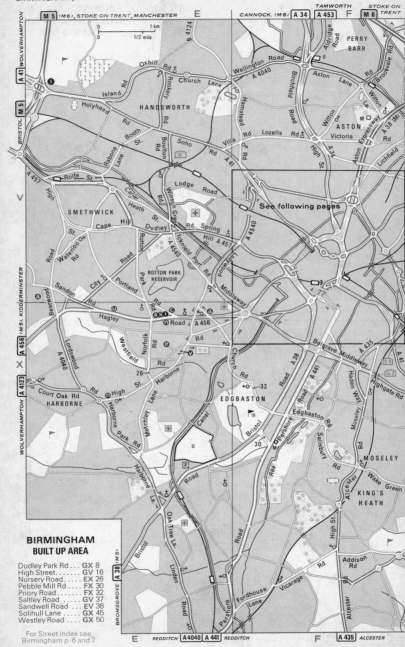

For Street Index see
Birmingham p. 6 and 7

92

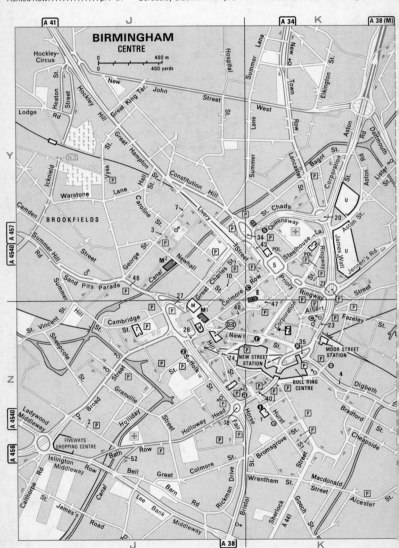

XX **Rajdoot,** 12-22 Albert St., B4 7UD, ℰ 643 8805, Indian rest. – ⛰ 壓 ⓞ 𝑉𝐼𝑆𝐴   KZ **c**
closed lunch Sunday and Bank Holidays and 25-26 December – **M** 5.00/11.50 **t.** and a la carte
11.60/15.90 **t.** 🍷 3.00.

XX **Sloans,** Chad Sq., off Harborne Rd, Edgbaston, B15 3TQ, W : 2 ¾ m. by A 456 ℰ 455 6697 –
⛰ 壓 𝑉𝐼𝑆𝐴   p. 4
closed Saturday lunch, Sunday, first week January and Bank Holidays – **M** 19.50 **t.** and a la
carte 16.60/19.50 **t.**

XX **Henry Wong,** 283 High St., Harborne, B17 9QH, W : 3 ¾ m. by A 456 ℰ 427 9799, Chinese-
Cantonese rest.. ⛰ 壓 ⓞ 𝑉𝐼𝑆𝐴   EX **n**
closed Sunday, 1 week August and 24 to 26 December – **M** 8.60 **st.** (dinner) and a la carte
12.60/18.00 **st.** 🍷 5.80.

XX **Dynasty,** 93-103 Hurst St., B5 4TE, ℰ 622 1410, Chinese rest. – ⛰ 壓 ⓞ 𝑉𝐼𝑆𝐴   KZ **e**
M 5.50/10.50 **t.** and a la carte 8.50/11.10 **t.** 🍷 2.80.

XX **Lorenzo,** 3 Park St., Digbeth, B5 5JD, ℰ 643 0541, Italian rest. – ⛰ 壓 ⓞ 𝑉𝐼𝑆𝐴   KZ **o**
closed Saturday lunch, Monday dinner, Sunday, 3 weeks July-August and Bank Holidays – **M**
a la carte 10.30/15.20 **t.** 🍷 3.10.

X **Maharaja,** 23-25 Hurst St., B5 4AS, ℰ 622 2641, Indian rest. – ▤. ⛰ 壓 ⓞ 𝑉𝐼𝑆𝐴   KZ **i**
closed Sunday and last 2 weeks July – **M** 7.50 **t.** (dinner) and a la carte 4.55/10.00 **t.** 🍷 3.05.

X **Pinocchio's,** 8 Chad Sq., off Harborne Rd, B15 3TQ, W : 2¾ m. by A 456 ℰ 454 8672, Italian
rest. – ⛰ 壓 ⓞ 𝑉𝐼𝑆𝐴   p. 4   EX **v**
closed Sunday – **M** 6.75 **t.** (lunch) and a la carte 10.35/15.00 **t.** 🍷 5.50.

MICHELIN Distribution Centre, Valepits Rd, Garretts Green, B33 0YD, ℰ 784 7900 p. 5 HX

AUSTIN-ROVER Essex St. ℰ 622 2851
AUSTIN-ROVER Aston Hall Rd, Aston ℰ 328 0833
AUSTIN-ROVER 71 Aston Rd North, Aston ℰ
359 2011
AUSTIN-ROVER Queslett Rd,Great Barr ℰ 360 5445
CITROEN Barnes Hill, Weoley Castle ℰ 427 5231
COLT 205 Lozells Rd ℰ 551 7717
FORD 156-182 Bristol St. ℰ 622 2777
FORD Long Acre, Aston ℰ 327 4791
FORD Granby Av., Garretts Green ℰ 784 8585
JAGUAR Bristol St. ℰ 622 1122
LADA Wood End Lane, Erdington ℰ 373 5805
MAZDA Rookery Rd, Handsworth ℰ 554 9333
MERCEDES-BENZ Charles Henry St. ℰ 622 3031
NISSAN Walkers Heath Rd, Kings Norton ℰ
451 1411
NISSAN Chester Rd, Erdington ℰ 382 8181

NISSAN 4 Birmingham Rd ℰ 358 7011
PEUGEOT, TALBOT Summer Lane, Newtown ℰ
359 4848
RENAULT 1300 Bristol Rd South ℰ 475 5241
ROLLS-ROYCE Stratford Rd, Shirley ℰ 745 5566
SKODA, DAIHATSU, HYUNDAI 1520 Stratford Rd,
Hall Green ℰ 744 1144
SKODA, MAZDA 37 Stoney Lane, Yardley ℰ 754 7877
SKODA Coleshill Rd, Sutton Coldfield ℰ 354 6283
TALBOT, PEUGEOT Charlotte St. ℰ 236 4382
TALBOT 30 High St, Deriford ℰ 772 4388
TOYOTA 138 Soho Hill, Handsworth ℰ 554 6311
VAUXHALL-OPEL 86 Orphanage Rd, Erdington ℰ
373 5241
VOLVO Bristol St. ℰ 622 4491
VW, AUDI Digbeth ℰ 643 7341

Except where otherwise stated see pp. 2 and 3

at Streetly N : 7 m. on A 452 – ✉ Sutton Coldfield – ☏ 021 Birmingham :

🏠 **Parson and Clerk** without rest., Chester Rd North, B73 6SP, S : 1 ½ m. on A 452 ℰ 353 7785
– 📺 🚿wc ☎ 🅿 ⛰ 壓 ⓞ 𝑉𝐼𝑆𝐴 🎿   CT **s**
30 rm ⊏⊐ 28.75/34.50 **st.**

at Walmley NE : 6 m. by B 4148 – ✉ Sutton Coldfield – ☏ 021 Birmingham :

🏨 **Penns Hall** (Embassy) 🦢, Penns Lane, B76 8LH, ℰ 351 3111, Telex 335789, 🗨, 🖼 – ▤ 📺
☎ 🅿 🛁 ⛰ 壓 ⓞ 𝑉𝐼𝑆𝐴 🎿   DT **v**
M a la carte 14.25/21.25 **st.** 🍷 3.35 – ⊏⊐ 5.00 – **115 rm** 48.00/57.00 **st.**, **5 suites** 80.00/95.00 **st.**
– SB (weekends only) 55.00/59.00 **st.**

AUSTIN-ROVER Chester Rd ℰ 353 3231
BMW Jockey Rd, Boldmere ℰ 354 8131
CITROEN Old Kingsbury Rd, Minworth ℰ 351 4367
DAIHATSU, FIAT, LANCIA 35 Sutton New Rd,
Erdington ℰ 350 1301
HONDA Bromford Lane ℰ 328 4211

MAZDA 504-508 College Rd, Erdington ℰ 373 2542
SAAB Eachelhurst Rd, Erdington ℰ 351 1027
TALBOT, PEUGEOT Newport Rd, Castle Bromwich
ℰ 747 4712
VAUXHALL 364 Chester Rd, Castle Bromwich ℰ
749 2222

at Castle Bromwich NE : 6 m. by A 47 – ✉ ☏ 021 Birmingham :

🏨 Bradford Arms Motel, Chester Rd, B36 0AG, ℰ 747 0227 – ▤ 📺 🚿wc ☎ 🅿   p. 5   HV **a**
30 rm.

at Sutton Coldfield NE : 8 m. by A 38 – ✉ Sutton Coldfield – ☏ 021 Birmingham :

🏨 **Belfry** (De Vere) 🦢, Lichfield Rd, Wishaw, B76 9PR, E : 3 m. on A 446 ℰ 0675 (Curd-
worth) 70301, Telex 338848, ≼, 🏊, 🖼, 🖼, park, 🎾, squash – ▤ ▤ rest 📺 ☎ 🅿 🛁 ⛰ 壓
ⓞ 𝑉𝐼𝑆𝐴 🎿   by A 38   DT
M 11.50 **st.** and a la carte 🍷 4.00 – **168 rm** ⊏⊐ 75.00/95.00 **st.** – SB (weekends only)
85.00/105.00 **st.**

🏨 **Moor Hall** (Best Western) 🦢, Moor Hall Drive, Four Oaks, B75 6LN, NE : 1 m. by A 453
ℰ 308 3751, Telex 335127, 🖼 – 📺 🚿wc 🖨 🅿 🛁 ⛰ 壓 ⓞ 𝑉𝐼𝑆𝐴 🎿   DT **r**
M 10.50/15.95 **t.** 🍷 3.95 – **50 rm** ⊏⊐ 40.00/52.00 **t.** – SB (weekends only) 52.00/56.00 **st.**

⌂ **Standbridge,** 138 Birmingham Rd, B72 1LY, ℰ 354 3007, 🖼 – 🍴 🅿   DT **a**
closed 25 May-1 June and Christmas-New Year – **9 rm** ⊏⊐ 15.50/29.15 **st.**

XX **Le Bon Viveur,** 65 Birmingham Rd, B72 1QF, ℰ 355 5836 – ⛰ 壓 ⓞ 𝑉𝐼𝑆𝐴   DT **u**
closed Sunday, Monday, 3 weeks August and Bank Holidays – **M** 6.25 **t.** (lunch) and a la carte
11.80/16.35 **t.** 🍷 3.10.

AUSTIN-ROVER Maney Corner ☎ 354 7601
AUSTIN-ROVER 10 Birmingham Rd ☎ 355 5537
DAIHATSU 35 Sutton New Rd ☎ 350 1301
RENAULT 62 Chester Rd ☎ 352 0022
VAUXHALL Lichfield Rd ☎ 308 8282
VOLVO 127 Chester Rd ☎ 353 3191
VW, AUDI 45-51 Kings Rd ☎ 355 1261

at National Exhibition Centre E : 9 ½ m. on A 45 – DU – ✉ ☎ 021 Birmingham :

Birmingham Metropole, Blackfirs Lane, Bickenhill, B40 1PP, ☎ 780 4242, Telex 336129, <, squash – 🛗 ▤ TV ☎ ♿ P. 🏊. ◼ AE ⊙ VISA
M 9.50/19.00 **st.** and a la carte 🍾 3.90 – ☕ 4.00 – **498 rm** 57.00/85.00 **st.**, **9 suites** 185.00/235.00 **st.** – SB (weekends only) 55.00 **st.**

Warwick, Blackfirs Lane, Bickenhill, B40 1PP, ☎ 780 4242, Telex 336129, squash – 🛗 TV 🛁wc ☎ P. ◼ AE ⊙ VISA
Exhibitions only – **M** (rest. see **Birmingham Metropole H.**) – ☕ 4.00 – **196 rm** 48.00/65.00 **st.**

Arden, Coventry Rd, Bickenhill, B92 0EH, S : ½ m. on A 45 ✉ Solihull ☎ 067 55 (Hampton-in-Arden) 3221, Telex 334913 – 🛗 TV 🛁wc ☎ P. 🏊. ◼ AE ⊙ VISA
closed 3 days at Christmas – **M** 7.50 **st.** and a la carte 🍾 3.50 – ☕ 3.50 – **46 rm** 25.00/39.50 **st.** – SB (weekends only) 48.00 **st.**

at Acocks Green SE : 4 ½ m. on A 41 – DU – ✉ ☎ 021 Birmingham :

Kerry House, 946 Warwick Rd, B27 6QG, ☎ 707 0316 – TV 🚿wc P
closed 1 week Christmas – **23 rm** ☕ 17.25/28.00 **st.**

ALFA-ROMEO 683 Stratford Rd, Sparkhill ☎ 778 1295
AUSTIN-ROVER 884 Warwick Rd ☎ 706 8271
AUSTIN-ROVER Warwick Rd, Tyseley ☎ 706 4331
CITROEN 2 Warwick Rd ☎ 707 3122
DAIHATSU, SKODA 1520 Stratford Rd, Hall Green ☎ 744 1144
FIAT, LANCIA, LOTUS, SAAB 979 Stratford Rd, Hall Green ☎ 778 2323
FSO 438 Stratford Rd, Spartihill ☎ 773 8646
LADA, RELIANT 723-725 Stratford Rd, Sparkhill ☎ 777 6164
RENAULT High St., Bordesley ☎ 773 8251
TOYOTA 32-38 Coventry Rd, Bordesley ☎ 772 5916
VAUXHALL 291 Shaftmoor Lane, Hall Green ☎ 777 1074
VAUXHALL-OPEL 870 Stratford Rd, Sparkhill ☎ 777 3361

at Sheldon SE : 6 m. on A 45 – HX – ✉ ☎ 021 Birmingham :

Wheatsheaf, 2225 Coventry Rd, B26 3EH, ☎ 742 6201 – TV 🚿wc ☎ P. 🏊. ◼ AE ⊙ VISA. 🐕 p. 5 HX **a**
M 6.00/6.50 **s.** and a la carte 🍾 3.75 – **84 rm** ☕ 35.00/45.00 **st.**

CITROEN The Radleys ☎ 742 1142
PEUGEOT-TALBOT 2119 Coventry Rd ☎ 742 5533

at Birmingham Airport SE : 7 m. on A 45 – DU – ✉ ☎ 021 Birmingham :

Excelsior (T.H.F.), Coventry Rd, Elmdon, B26 3QW, ☎ 743 8141, Telex 338005 – ▤ TV P. 🏊. ◼ AE ⊙ VISA
M 7.50/11.25 **st.** and a la carte 🍾 3.40 – ☕ 6.00 – **141 rm** 47.00/57.00 **st.**, **3 suites**.

FIAT Station Rd, Marston ☎ 779 5140

at Northfield SW : 6 m. by A 38 – CU – ✉ ☎ 021 Birmingham :

Norwood, 87 Bunbury Rd, B31 2ET, ☎ 475 3262, 🌳 – P
closed Christmas – **12 rm** ☕ 16.95/33.50 **st.**

CITROEN Hallan St., Balsall Heath, Kings Heath ☎ 440 4606
FORD 82 St. Mary's Row, Moseley, Kings Heath ☎ 449 3771
NISSAN 57 Walkers Heath Rd ☎ 451 1411
SKODA 307 Northfield Rd, Harborne, Kings Heath ☎ 427 4050
VAUXHALL 16 Ryland St., Edgbaston, Kings Heath ☎ 455 7171

at Smethwick W : 3 ½ m. by A 456 – ✉ ☎ 021 Birmingham :

Franzl's, 151 Milcote Rd, Bearwood, B67 5BN, ☎ 429 7920, Austrian rest. – ◼ VISA
closed Sunday, Monday, first 3 weeks August and first week January – **M** (dinner only) a la carte 8.85/12.25 **t.** 🍾 3.20. p. 4 EV **a**

at West Bromwich NW : 6 m. on A 41 – ✉ West Bromwich – ☎ 021 Birmingham :

West Bromwich Moat House (Q.M.H.) Birmingham Rd, B70 6RS, W : 1 m. by A 41 ☎ 553 6111, Telex 336232 – 🛗 ▤ rest TV 🛁wc ☎ P. 🏊. ◼ AE ⊙ VISA BU **c**
M 8.90/9.50 **st.** and a la carte 🍾 2.95 – **181 rm** ☕ 47.00/61.00 **st.** – SB (weekends only) 46.00 **st.**

AUSTIN-ROVER High St. ☎ 553 0778
FERRARI, FIAT Birmingham Rd ☎ 553 7509
FORD 377 High St. ☎ 553 1881
VAUXHALL-OPEL Spon Lane ☎ 553 3777
VOLVO 127 Hill Top ☎ 502 3802

at Great Barr NW : 6 m. on A 34 – ✉ Great Barr – ☎ 021 Birmingham :

Post House (T.H.F), Chapel Lane, B43 7BG, ☎ 357 7444, Telex 338497, 🏊 heated – TV 🛁wc ☎ P. 🏊. ◼ AE ⊙ VISA CT **x**
M 8.50/15.00 **st.** and a la carte 🍾 3.40 – ☕ 5.65 – **204 rm** 47.00/55.00 **st.**

Barr, Pear Tree Drive, Newton Rd, B43 6HS, W : 1 m. by A 4041 ☎ 357 1141, Telex 336406, 🌳 – TV 🛁wc ☎ P. 🏊. ◼ AE ⊙ VISA. 🐕 CT **z**
M 7.50/9.50 **st.** and a la carte 🍾 3.75 – **114 rm** ☕ 35.50/55.00 **st.** – SB (weekends only) 44.00/80.00 **st.**

BIRTLE Greater Manchester 402 ② 404 ⑩ – see Bury.

BISHOP AUCKLAND Durham 401 402 P 20 – pop. 23 560 – ECD : Wednesday – ☎ 0388.
ᵀ₈ High Plains ℰ 602198, NE : 1 m. on A 689.

♦London 253 – ♦Carlisle 73 – ♦Middlesbrough 24 – ♦Newcastle-upon-Tyne 28 – Sunderland 25.

   🏠 **Park Head,** New Coundon, DL14 8AL, NE : 1¾ m. by A 689 on A 688 ℰ 661727 – 📺 🖾wc
   ⁿ⁄ₘwc ⊗ 🅿 . 🔼 AE ⑩ VISA
   M (a la carte lunch)/dinner 10.50 t. ⅊ 2.50 – **12 rm** ⊑ 28.00/38.00 t.

DAIHATSU ℰ 832184   RENAULT ℰ 6027
FORD ℰ 605184

BISHOP'S CASTLE Salop 403 L 26 – pop. 1 810 – ☎ 0588.

♦London 182 – ♦Birmingham 71 – Shrewsbury 24.

   🏠 Castle, Market Sq., SD9 5DG, ℰ 638403 – 🅿
   7 rm.

BISHOP'S STORTFORD Herts. 404 U 28 – pop. 22 535 – ECD : Wednesday – ☎ 0279.
✈ Stansted Airport : ℰ 502380, Telex 81102, NE : 3 ½ m.

🅱 Council Offices, The Causeway ℰ 55261 ext 251.

♦London 34 – ♦Cambridge 27 – Chelmsford 19 – Colchester 33.

   🏠 Brook House, 29 Northgate End, CM23 2LD, ℰ 57892, ☛ – 📺 🖾wc ⁿ⁄ₘwc ☎ 🅿 . ⸘
   24 rm.

   ✕ **Michael Man,** 88 South St., ℰ 505799, Chinese (Peking, Canton, Szechuan) rest. – 🔼 AE
   ⑩ VISA
   M 12.50 t. and a la carte.

AUSTIN-ROVER-DAIMLER-JAGUAR 123-129 South   PEUGEOT-TALBOT 26 Northgate End ℰ 53494
St. ℰ 58441   RENAULT Northgate End ℰ 53127
CITROEN Dunmow Rd ℰ 54335   VAUXHALL-OPEL, VOLVO The Causeway ℰ 52304
DAIHATSU, LANCIA London Rd ℰ 54181   VW, AUDI Dane St. ℰ 54680
FORD London Rd ℰ 52214

BISHOP'S TAWTON Devon 403 H 30 – see Barnstaple.

BLACKBURN Lancs. 402 M 22 – pop. 109 564 – ECD : Thursday – ☎ 0254.
ᵀ₈ Beardwood Brow, ℰ 51122 – ᵀ₈ Pleasington ℰ 21028, W : 3 m.

🅱 Town Hall ℰ 55201 ext 214 and 53277 ext 248.

♦London 228 – ♦Leeds 47 – ♦Liverpool 39 – ♦Manchester 24 – Preston 11.

   🏨 **Blackburn Moat House** (Q.M.H.), Yew Tree Drive, Preston New Rd, BB2 7BE, NW : 2 m. at
   junction A 677 and A 6119 ℰ 64441, Telex 63271 – 🔌 📺 🖾wc ☎ 🅿 . 🔺 . 🔼 AE ⑩ VISA
   M 5.50/8.95 st. and a la carte ⅊ 3.85 – **98 rm** ⊑ 39.50/49.50 st., **2 suites** 48.00/59.50 st. – SB
   (weekends only) 55.00 st.

   🏠 Woodlands, 363 Preston New Rd, BB2 7AA, NW : 1 ¼ m. on A 677 ℰ 691122 – 📺 🖾wc 🅿
   M (Greek rest.) – **14 rm**.

   at Mellor NW : 4 m. by A 677 – ✉ Blackburn – ☎ 025481 Mellor :

   🏠 **Millstone,** Church Lane, BB2 7JR, ℰ 3333 – 📺 🖾wc ⁿ⁄ₘwc ☎ 🅿 . 🔺 . 🔼 AE ⑩ VISA
   M 7.50/10.50 t. and a la carte ⅊ 3.50 – **16 rm** ⊑ 34.00/46.00 st., **1 suite** 64.00 st.

AUSTIN-ROVER-DAIMLER-JAGUAR Park Rd ℰ   TALBOT Whalley New Rd ℰ 661616
662721   TOYOTA Accrington Rd ℰ 57333
FIAT 52-56 King St. ℰ 52981   VAUXHALL Quarry St., Eanam ℰ 51191
FORD Montague St. ℰ 57021   VAUXHALL-OPEL Montague St. ℰ 53885
RENAULT Gt. Harwood ℰ 886590   VW, AUDI 854 Whalley New Rd ℰ 40621

BLACKPOOL Lancs. 402 K 22 – pop. 146 297 – ECD : Wednesday – ☎ 0253.
See : Illuminations★★ (late September and early October) – Tower★ (⅜★) AC AY A.
ᵀ₈ Blackpool North Shore, Devonshire Rd ℰ 52054, N : 1 ½ m. from main station BY – ᵀ₈ Blackpool
Park, Stanley Park ℰ 33960, E : 1 ½ m. BY – ᵀ₈ Poulton-le-Fylde, Myrtle Farm, Breck Rd ℰ 0253
(Poulton) 893150, E : 3 m. by A 586 BY.

✈ Blackpool Airport : ℰ 43061, S : 3 m. by A 584.

🅱 1 Clifton St. ℰ 21623 and 25212 (weekdays only) – 87a Coronation St. ℰ 21891.

♦London 246 – ♦Leeds 88 – ♦Liverpool 56 – ♦Manchester 51 – ♦Middlesbrough 123.

Plan opposite

   🏨 **Imperial,** North Shore, North Promenade, FY1 2HB, ℰ 23971, Telex 677376, ≼, 🔲 – 🔌 📺
   ☎ 🅿 . 🔺 . 🔼 AE ⑩ VISA   AY c
   M (carving rest.) 7.00/9.50 t. and a la carte ⅊ 3.00 – **159 rm** ⊑ 50.00/70.00 t., **7 suites** 100.00 t.
   – SB 70.00/80.00 st.

   🏨 **Pembroke,** North Promenade, FY1 2JQ, ℰ 23434, Telex 677469, ≼, 🔲 – 🔌 📺 ☎ 🅿 . 🔺 . 🔼
   AE ⑩ VISA   AY x
   M (carving lunch) 9.00/10.00 st. and a la carte ⅊ 4.25 – **201 rm** ⊑ 40.00/70.00 t., **6 suites**
   155.00/250.00 t.

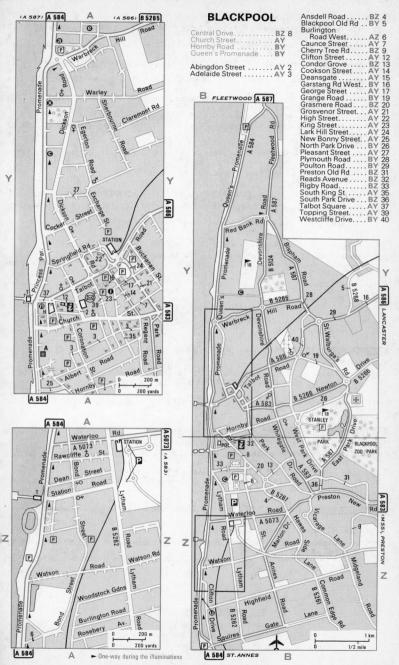

BLACKPOOL

Central Drive . . . . BZ 8
Church Street . . . . AY
Hornby Road . . . . BY
Queen's Promenade . . . . BY

Abingdon Street . . . . . . AY 2
Adelaide Street . . . . AY 3

Ansdell Road . . . . . . BZ 4
Blackpool Old Rd . . BY 5
Burlington
  Road West . . . . . AZ 6
Caunce Street . . . . AY 7
Cherry Tree Rd. . . . BZ 9
Clifton Street . . . . . AY 12
Condor Grove . . . . BZ 13
Cookson Street . . . AY 14
Deansgate . . . . AY 15
Garstang Rd West . . BY 16
George Street . . . . . AY 17
Grange Road . . . . . BY 19
Grasmere Road . . . BZ 20
Grosvenor Street . . AY 21
High Street . . . . AY 22
King Street . . . . AY 23
Lark Hill Street . . . . AY 24
New Bonny Street . . AY 25
North Park Drive . . BY 26
Pleasant Street . . . AY 27
Plymouth Road . . . BY 28
Poulton Road . . . . . BY 29
Preston Old Rd . . . BY 31
Reads Avenue . . . . BZ 32
Rigby Road . . . . . . BZ 33
South King St. . . . . AY 35
South Park Drive . . BZ 36
Talbot Square . . . . AY 37
Topping Street . . . . AY 39
Westcliffe Drive . . . BY 40

► One-way during the illuminations

99

🏨 **Savoy,** Queens Promenade, FY2 9SJ, ✆ 52561, Telex 67570 – |፮| 📺 ⇔wc 🅿 🅟 🚗 ◪ 🝙
🅞 *VISA*   AY **a**
M 5.00/9.00 **st.** and a la carte 🍷 2.50 – **127 rm** ⬳ 22.00/44.00 **st.** – SB (except September and October) 60.00/80.00 **st.**

🏨 **New Clifton,** Talbot Sq., FY1 1ND, ✆ 21481, Group Telex 67415 – |፮| 📺 ⇔wc ☎ 🚗 ◪
◪ 🅞 *VISA*   AY **n**
M 5.95/7.95 **t.** and a la carte 🍷 2.50 – **78 rm** ⬳ 36.00/55.00 **t.**, **1 suite** 55.00/80.00 **t.** – SB 48.00/62.00 **st.**

🏨 **Warwick** (Best Western), 603-609 New South Promenade, FY4 1NG, ✆ 42192, ◪ – 📺
⇔wc 🅟 🚗 ◪ ◪ 🅞 *VISA*   BZ **u**
M (bar lunch)/dinner 6.95 **st.** – **52 rm** ⬳ 21.50/42.00 **st.** – SB 49.50/67.50 **st.**

🏨 **Motel Mimosa** without rest., 24a Lonsdale Rd, FY1 6EE, ✆ 41906 – 📺 ⇔wc ⫚wc 🅟 ◪
VISA 🕭   BZ **c**
15 rm ⬳ 13.95/27.90 **st.**

🛏 **Sunray,** 42 Knowle Av., off Queens Promenade, FY2 9TQ, ✆ 51937 – 📺 ⫚wc 🅟   BY **c**
closed 15 December-5 January – **9 rm** ⬳ 16.00/32.00 **t.**

🛏 **Denely,** 15 King Edward Av., FY2 9TA, ✆ 52757 – ⫚ 🅟 🕭   AY **e**
9 rm ⬳ 9.00/28.00.

at Little Thornton NE : 5 m. by A 586 – BY – off A 588 – ✉ 🕙 0253 Blackpool :

XX **River House** 🦢 with rm, Skippool Creek, Wyre Rd, FY5 5LF, ✆ 883497, ≼, 🛋 – 📺 🅟 🅟
◪ ◪
M (booking essential) a la carte 14.50/18.00 **t.** 🍷 2.75 – **4 rm** ⬳ 25.00/30.00 **t.** – SB (weekends only) 55.00/60.00 **t.**

at Little Singleton NE : 6 m. by A 586 – BY – on A 585 – ✉ 🕙 0253 Blackpool :

🏨 **Mains Hall** 🦢, 86 Mains Lane, FY6 7LE, ✆ 885130, 🛋 – ⇔wc ⫚wc 🅟 ◪
closed 31 December-2 January – **M** *(closed Sunday)* (dinner only) 10.50 **st.** 🍷 3.50 – **7 rm** ⬳ 16.50/40.00 **st.**

AUSTIN-ROVER, DAIMLER-JAGUAR Vicarage Lane
✆ 67811
AUSTIN-ROVER Cherry Tree Rd ✆ 67811
AUSTIN-ROVER 159 Devonshire Rd ✆ 34301
BMW Bloomfield Rd ✆ 402541
FIAT 79/83 Breck Rd, Poulton-le-Fylde ✆ 882571
FORD Whitegate Drive ✆ 63333

HONDA Devonshire Rd ✆ 35816
LADA St. Annes Rd ✆ 405119
MERCEDES-BENZ Church St. ✆ 22257
MERCEDES-BENZ Church St. ✆ 28436
PEUGEOT-TALBOT Squires Gate Lane ✆ 45544
VW, AUDI Central Drive ✆ 401228

BLACKWOOD (COED-DUON) Gwent **403** K 29 – pop. 13 255 – ECD : Thursday – 🕙 0495.
♦London 158 – ♦Cardiff 15 – Newport 13.

🏨 **Maes Manor** 🦢, Maesrudded, NP2 0AG, N : 1 ¼ m. by A 4048 turning at Rock Inn ✆ 224551,
🛋, park – 📺 ⇔wc 🅟 🅟 🚗 ◪ ◪ 🅞 *VISA*
23 rm.

FIAT High Bank ✆ 0443 831703

RENAULT Newbridge Rd, Pontllanfraith ✆ 0495 225423

BLAKENEY Norfolk **404** X 25 – pop. 1 559 – ECD : Wednesday – ✉ Holt – 🕙 0263 Cley.
♦London 127 – King's Lynn 37 – ♦Norwich 28.

🏨 **Blakeney** (Best Western), The Quay, NR25 7NE, ✆ 740797, ≼, ◪, 🛋 – 📺 ⇔wc 🅟 🅟 🚗
52 rm.

🏨 **Manor,** The Quay, NR25 7ND, ✆ 740376, 🛋 – 📺 ⇔wc 🍴 🅟
closed December – **M** (buffet lunch)/dinner 10.00 **st.** 🍷 2.50 – **22 rm** ⬳ 22.00/60.00 **st.** – SB (except summer) 35.00/52.00 **st.**

BLANCHLAND Northumb. **401 402** N 19 – ECD : Monday and Tuesday – ✉ Consett (Durham)
– 🕙 043 475.
♦London 298 – ♦Carlisle 47 – ♦Newcastle-upon-Tyne 24.

🏨 **Lord Crewe Arms** 🦢, DH8 9SP, ✆ 251, « Part 13C abbey », 🛋 – 📺 ⇔wc ⫚wc ☎ 🅟
🚗 ◪ ◪ 🅞 *VISA*
M (bar lunch Monday to Saturday)/dinner 11.00 **t.** 🍷 4.00 – **15 rm** ⬳ 35.00/55.50 **t.** – SB 56.00/69.00 **st.**

Gebruik voor uw reizen in Engeland, Schotland, Wales en Ierland :

— de vijf kaarten nrs. **401**, **402**, **403**, **404** en **405** (schaal 1:400 000)
— zij vormen een uitstekende aanvulling op deze gids
  omdat de plaatsen die op de kaarten rood onderstreept zijn,
  in deze gids zijn opgenomen.

BLANDFORD FORUM Dorset **403 404** N 31 The West Country G. – pop. 7 249 – ECD : Wednesday – ✆ 0258 Blandford.

See : Site★.

Envir. : Royal Blandford Signals Museum★ *AC*, NE : 2 m. off B 3082.

🏇 Ashley Wood, The Wimborne Rd ✆ 52283, E : 2 m. on B 3082.

🗓 West St. ✆ 51989.

♦London 124 – Bournemouth 17 – Dorchester 17 – Salisbury 24.

🏨 **Crown** 1 West St., DT11 7AJ, ✆ 56626, 🍴 – 📺 🛏wc ☎ **P**. 🝙 **AE** **VISA**
M 9.75 t. – **28 rm** 🖙 34.00/50.00 t. – SB (weekends only) 49.00/55.00 **st.**

XX **La Belle Alliance** with rm, Portman Lodge, Whitecliff Mill St., DT11 3BP, ✆ 52842 – 📺 🛏wc **P**. 🝙 **AE** ⓪ **VISA**
closed Sunday dinner except Bank Holidays and first 2 weeks January – **M** (lunch by arrangement)/dinner 16.00 **st.** ⏶ 2.75 – **5 rm** 🖙 24.00/40.00 **st.** – SB 48.00/60.00 **st.**

at Tarrant Monkton NE : 5 ½ m. by A 354 – ✉ Blandford Forum – ✆ 025 889 Tarrant Hinton :

XX **Langtons** with rm, DT11 8RX, ✆ 225 – 📺 🛏wc ☎ **P**. 🝙 **AE** ⓪ **VISA**
M (dinner only and Sunday lunch) a la carte 8.75/10.75 t. ⏶ 2.60 – **6 rm** 🖙 19.50/30.00 t.

FERRARI, JAGUAR Pimperne ✆ 51211   RENAULT St. Leonards Av. ✆ 52311

BLAWITH Cumbria – pop. 101 – ✉ Ulverston – ✆ 022 985 Lowick Bridge.

♦London 290 – ♦Carlisle 66 – Kendal 28 – Lancaster 43.

🏨 **Highfield,** LA12 8EG, on A 5084 ✆ 238, ≤, 🍴 – 📺 🛏wc 🛏wc **P**. 🝙 **VISA**
closed 1 to 7 January – **M** (bar lunch Monday to Saturday)/dinner 10.50 **t.** and a la carte ⏶ 2.95 – **11 rm** 🖙 21.50/43.00 t. – SB 50.00/60.00 **st.**

BLOCKLEY Glos. **403 404** O 27 – pop. 1 729 – ECD : Thursday – ✉ Moreton-in-Marsh – ✆ 0386.

♦London 89 – ♦Birmingham 40 – Gloucester 29 – ♦Oxford 33.

🏨 **Lower Brook House** 🦢, Lower St., GL56 9DS, ✆ 700286, « Converted 17C cottages », 🍴
– 📺 🛏wc 🛏wc **P**. 🍴
closed January – **M** a la carte 5.00/13.50 t. ⏶ 2.75 – **8 rm** 🖙 (dinner included) 36.00/80.00 t. – SB (November-March)(weekends only) 65.00/67.50 **st.**

BLOFIELD Norfolk **404** Y 26 – see Norwich.

BLOXHAM Oxon. **403 404** P 28 – see Banbury.

BLUE ANCHOR Somerset – see Dunster.

BLUNDELLSANDS Merseyside **402 403** K 23 – see Liverpool.

BLUNSDON Wilts. **403 404** O 29 – see Swindon.

BLYTH Notts. **402 403 404** Q 23 – pop. 1 897 – ECD : Wednesday – ✉ Worksop – ✆ 090 976.

♦London 154 – ♦Leeds 41 – Lincoln 29 – ♦Nottingham 31 – ♦Sheffield 21.

🏩 Fourways, High St., S81 8EW, ✆ 235 – **P**. 🝙 **AE** **VISA** 🍴
9 rm 🖙 19.00/26.00 t.

BODINNICK-BY-FOWEY Cornwall – see Fowey.

BODMIN Cornwall **403** F 32 The West Country G. – pop. 11 992 – ECD : Wednesday – ✆ 0208.

See : St. Petroc Church★.

Envir. : Lanhydrock★★ *AC*, S : 3 m. – Bodmin Moor★★ – St. Endellion Church★★, NW : 12 m. – Pencarrow House★ *AC*, NW : 4 m. – Cardinham Church★, NE : 5 m. – Blisland★ (Church★), NE : 6 m. – St. Mabyn Church★, N : 6 m. – St. Tudy★, N : 8 m.

🗓 Shire House, Mount Folly Sq. ✆ 4159.

♦London 273 – Exeter 63 – Penzance 47 – ♦Plymouth 30.

🏨 **Westberry,** Rhind St., PL31 2EL, ✆ 2772 – 📺 🛏wc 🛏wc ☎ **P**. 🝙 ⓪ **VISA**
closed Christmas and New Year – **M** (closed lunch Saturday and Sunday) (bar lunch)/dinner 6.30 t. and a la carte ⏶ 2.30 – **23 rm** 🖙 15.00/30.00 t.

at Tredethy N : 5 m. by A 389 off B 3266 – ✉ Bodmin – ✆ 020 884 St. Mabyn :

🏨 **Tredethy Country** 🦢, PL30 4QS, ✆ 262, ≤, « Country house atmosphere », ⌇ heated, 🍴, park – 🛏wc 🛏wc **P**. 🍴
closed 24 December-31 January – **M** (bar lunch)/dinner 7.50 t. and a la carte ⏶ 2.50 – **11 rm** 🖙 24.00/52.00 t. – SB (winter only) 40.00 **st.**

AUSTIN-ROVER Liskeard Rd ✆ 3145

BOGNOR REGIS West Sussex 404 R 31 – pop. 50 323 – ECD : Wednesday – © 0243.

🛈 1-2 Place St-Maur des Fossés, Belmont St. ℰ 823140.

♦London 65 – ♦Brighton 29 – ♦Portsmouth 24 – ♦Southampton 37.

🏨 **Royal Norfolk**, The Esplanade, PO21 2LH, ℰ 826222, Telex 477575, ≤, ⟂ heated, 🎬, 🎯 –
🔄 📺 ⇆wc 🅿 👍 🗲 ⅀ ⓞ 𝗩𝗜𝗦𝗔
M 7.75/10.50 **st.** and a la carte – **52 rm** ⊇ 42.00/57.00 **st.**, **2 suites** 75.00 **st.** – SB 52.00/72.00 **st.**

AUSTIN-ROVER 65 Aldwick Rd ℰ 864041
FORD Lennox St. ℰ 864641
PEUGEOT-TALBOT 131 Elmer Rd, Middleton-on-Sea
ℰ 024 369 (Middleton-on-Sea) 2432

VW, AUDI 126 Felpham Way ℰ 024 369 (Middleton-on-Sea) 3185

BOLHAM Devon 403 J 31 – see Tiverton.

BOLTON Greater Manchester 402 404 M 23 – pop. 143 960 – ECD : Wednesday – © 0204.

Envir. : Hall I'Th'Wood★ (16C) *AC*, N : 1 ½ m.

🔃 Bolton Municipal, Links Rd, Lostock ℰ 42336 – 🔃 Dunscar, Longworth Lane, Bromley Cross ℰ 53321, N : 3 m. off A 666 – 🔃 Lostock Park, ℰ 43067, W : 3 ½ m.

🛈 Town Hall, ℰ 22311 ext 211/485 and 384174.

♦London 214 – Burnley 19 – ♦Liverpool 32 – ♦Manchester 11 – Preston 23.

🏨 **Crest** (Crest), Beaumont Rd, BL3 4TA, SW : 2 ½ m. on A 58 ℰ 651511, Telex 635527 – 📺
🔄wc ⊞ 🅿. 👍 🗲 ⅀ ⓞ 𝗩𝗜𝗦𝗔
M 7.55/11.95 **t.** and a la carte – ⊇ 5.85 – **100 rm** 46.50/56.50 **st.** – SB (weekends only) 51.00/54.00 **st.**

🏨 **Pack Horse** (De Vere), Nelson Sq., Bradshawgate, BL1 1DP, ℰ 27261, Telex 635168 – 🔄 📺
🔄wc 🕿. 👍 🗲 ⅀ ⓞ 𝗩𝗜𝗦𝗔
M (carving rest.) 7.75/9.75 **st.** and a la carte ⧓ 3.95 – **74 rm** ⊇ 48.00/56.00 **st.**

at Egerton N : 3 ½ m. by A 673 on A 666 – ✉ © 0204 Bolton :

🏨 **Egerton House** ⟋, Blackburn Rd, BL7 9PL, ℰ 57171, ≤, 🎬, park – 📺 🔄wc 🕿 🅿. 🗲 ⅀ ⓞ 𝗩𝗜𝗦𝗔
closed 29 and 30 December – **M** *(closed lunch Saturday)* 8.50 **st.** (lunch) and a la carte – **25 rm** ⊇ 30.00/60.00 **st.** – SB (weekends only) 60.00/75.00 **st.**

at Bromley Cross N : 4 m. by A 676 – ✉ © 0204 Bolton :

🏨 **Last Drop Village,** Hospital Rd, BL7 9PZ, ℰ 591131, Telex 635322, ▨, 🎬 – 📺 🔄wc 🕿 🅿. 👍 🗲 ⅀ ⓞ 𝗩𝗜𝗦𝗔
M 7.50/15.00 **t.** and a la carte ⧓ 3.95 – **80 rm** ⊇ 35.00/66.00 **t.**, **3 suites** 60.00/70.00 **t.** – SB (weekends only) 60.00/65.00 **st.**

AUSTIN-ROVER-DAIMLER-JAGUAR Manchester Rd ℰ 32241
COLT 154-160 Crook St. ℰ 24686
FORD 54-56 Higher Bridge St. ℰ 24474
HYUNDAI, SUBARU Thynne St. ℰ 32511
OPEL Halliwell Rd ℰ 26566

PEUGEOT-TALBOT, CITROEN, LANCIA 157 Bradshawgate ℰ 31323
TOYOTA Radcliffe Rd ℰ 382234
VW, AUDI Blackburn Rd ℰ 31464
VW, AUDI St. Helens Rd ℰ 62131

BOLTON ABBEY North Yorks. 402 O 22 – pop. 122 – ✉ Skipton – © 075 671.

See : Bolton Priory★ (ruins) and woods (the Strid★ and nature trails in upper Wharfedale).

♦London 216 – Harrogate 18 – ♦Leeds 23 – Skipton 6.

🏨 **Devonshire Arms** ⟋, BD23 6AJ, on A 59 at Bolton Bridge ℰ 441, Telex 51218, ≤, « Restored former coaching inn », ⟋ – 📺 🕿 ⅃ 👍 🗲 ⅀ ⓞ 𝗩𝗜𝗦𝗔
M (buffet lunch)/dinner 15.50 **t.** and a la carte 14.50/19.50 **t.** ⧓ 3.90 – **38 rm** ⊇ 52.00/65.00 **t.** – SB 80.00/84.00 **st.**

BONCATH Dyfed 403 G 27 – ✉ © 023 974.

♦London 247 – Carmarthen 27 – Fishguard 17.

↥ **Pantyderi Farm** ⟋, SA37 0JB, W : 2 ¾ m. by B 4332 ℰ 227, ≤, ⟂, 🎬, park – 🅿
7 rm

BONCHURCH I.O.W. 403 404 Q 32 – see Wight (Isle of) : Ventnor.

BONTDDU Gwynedd 402 403 I 25 – see Dolgellau.

BONT-FAEN = Cowbridge.

BOOTLE Merseyside 402 ③ 403 ② – see Liverpool.

BOREHAM STREET East Sussex 404 V 31 – see Herstmonceux.

BOROUGHBRIDGE North Yorks. 402 P 21 – pop. 1 835 – ECD : Thursday – ☎ 090 12.

🛈 Fishergate ℰ 3373 (summer only).

◆London 216 – ◆Leeds 26 – ◆Middlesbrough 35 – York 17.

🏨 **Crown**, Horsefair, YO5 9LB, ℰ 2328 – 🗐 📺 ☎ ὐ ℗ 🏌 ⚡ ΑΕ ① 𝑉𝐼𝑆𝐴
M 9.50/12.50 **t.** and a la carte – **43 rm** ⛛ 40.00/71.50 **t.**, **1 suite** 70.00/110.00 **t.** – SB 64.00/80.00 **st.**

🏨 **Three Arrows** (Embassy) ⊗, Horsefair, YO5 9LL, ℰ 2245, 🗪, park – 📺 ⇔wc ☎ ℗ ⚡ ΑΕ ① 𝑉𝐼𝑆𝐴
M 6.50/10.50 **st.** ⫶ 3.00 – ⛛ 5.00 – **17 rm** 32.00/41.50 **st.** – SB (except Christmas) 61.00 **st.**

↑ **Farndale**, Horsefair, YO5 9AH, ℰ 3463 – ⇔wc ⫟wc ℗
13 rm ⛛ 10.00/24.00 **st.**

XXX **Fountain House**, St. James Sq., YO5 9AR, ℰ 2241 – ℗ ⚡ ① 𝑉𝐼𝑆𝐴
closed Sunday, Monday and 3 weeks January-February – **M** (dinner only) 18.00 **t.** ⫶ 3.00.

BORROWDALE Cumbria 402 K 20 – see Keswick.

BOSCASTLE Cornwall 403 F 31 The West Country G. – ☎ 084 05.

See : Site★.

◆London 260 – Bude 14 – Exeter 59 – ◆Plymouth 43.

🏠 **Bottreaux House**, PL35 0BG, on B 3266 ℰ 231 – 📺 ⇔wc ⫟wc ℗ ⚡ 𝑉𝐼𝑆𝐴
M (no smoking)(bar lunch)/dinner a la carte 8.00/11.50 **t.** ⫶ 3.00 – **7 rm** ⛛ 17.00/31.50 **t.** – SB (September-June) 45.00 **st.**

↑ **St. Christopher's Country House**, High St., PL35 0BD, S : ½ m. by B 3266 ℰ 412 – ⫟wc ℗
March-November – **8 rm** ⛛ 11.00/17.00 **st.**

↑ **Valency House**, The Harbour, PL35 0HD, ℰ 288, 🗪 – ℗ ⚡ ΑΕ 𝑉𝐼𝑆𝐴 ⊛
March-November – **7 rm** ⛛ 11.00/22.00 **st.**

X **Riverside** with rm, The Harbour, PL35 0HE, ℰ 216 – ⇔wc ⫟wc ℗ ⚡ ⊛
closed December-mid February – **M** a la carte 8.55/10.95 **t.** ⫶ 3.00 – **10 rm** ⛛ 14.50/29.00 **t.** – SB 45.00 **st.**

BOSHAM West Sussex 404 R 31 – see Chichester.

BOSTON Lincs. 402 404 T 25 – pop. 33 908 – ECD : Thursday – ☎ 0205.

See : St. Botolph's Church★★ 14C.

🛈 28 South St. ℰ 56656 (summer only).

◆London 122 – Lincoln 35 – ◆Nottingham 55.

🏨 **New England**, 49 Wide Bargate, PE21 6SH, ℰ 65255 – 📺 ⇔wc ☎ ℗ 🏌 ⚡ ΑΕ ① 𝑉𝐼𝑆𝐴
M (carving rest.) approx. 9.25 **t.** ⫶ 3.35 – **25 rm** ⛛ 39.50/49.50 **t.** – SB (weekends only) 54.00/58.00 **st.**

AUSTIN-ROVER-DAIMLER Wide Bargate ℰ 66677
COLT, LADA, RELIANT Frith Bank ℰ 62230
FIAT London Rd ℰ 55500
FORD 57 High St. ℰ 60404
NISSAN Main Ridge East ℰ 53737

PEUGEOT, TALBOT Grantham Rd ℰ 69020
TOYOTA Tawney St. ℰ 68626
VAUXHALL Butterwick ℰ 760421
VOLVO West St. ℰ 69288
VW, AUDI-NSU ℰ 63867

BOTALLACK Cornwall – see St. Just.

BOTLEY Hants. 403 404 Q 31 – pop. 2 156 – ECD : Thursday – ✉ Hedge End, Southampton – ☎ 048 92.

◆London 83 – ◆Portsmouth 17 – ◆Southampton 6 – Winchester 11.

🏨 **Botleigh Grange** ⊗, Grange Rd, Hedge End, SO3 2GA, W : 1 m. on A 334 ℰ 5611, ≼, 🗪, 🗪, park – 📺 ⇔wc ⫟wc ☎ ℗ 🏌 ⚡ ΑΕ 𝑉𝐼𝑆𝐴
M 6.00/7.00 **st.** and a la carte – **45 rm** ⛛ 27.00/60.00 **st.** – SB 62.00/65.00 **st.**

XX **Cobbett's**, 13-15 The Square, SO3 2EA, ℰ 2068 – ℗ ⚡ 𝑉𝐼𝑆𝐴
closed Saturday and Monday lunch, Sunday, 2 weeks in summer, 2 weeks in winter and Bank Holidays – **M** 9.00 **t.** (lunch) and a la carte 13.00/18.50 **t.** ⫶ 3.60.

AUDI, VW Shamblehurst Lane ℰ 3434

AUSTIN-ROVER Southampton Rd ℰ 5111

BOTTESFORD Leics. 402 404 R 25 – pop. 2 085 – ECD : Wednesday – ☎ 0949.

◆ London 116 – Grantham 75 – Lincoln 26 – ◆ Leicester 32 – ◆ Nottingham 18.

XX **Thatch**, 26 High St., NG13 0AA, ℰ 42330, Italian rest. – ℗ ⚡ ΑΕ ① 𝑉𝐼𝑆𝐴
closed Sunday – **M** (lunch by arrangement)/dinner a la carte 9.65/15.95 **t.** ⫶ 3.05.

BOUGHTON MONCHELSEA Kent – see Maidstone.

BOURNE Lincs. **402 404** S 25 − pop. 7 672 − ECD : Wednesday − ✪ 0778.

Envir. : Spalding Parish Church ★ E : 10 m. − Ayscoughfee Hall ★ 15C E : 10 m.

◆London 101 − ◆Leicester 42 − Lincoln 35 − ◆Nottingham 42.

🏨 **Toft House,** Main Rd, Toft, PE10 0JT, SW : 3 m. on A 6121 ℰ 077 833 (Witham-on-the-Hill) 614, 🏮, squash − 📺 ⌷wc �📶wc 🅿. ⚫ VISA ⚙

　 M *(closed Sunday dinner)* 4.95/6.90 **t.** and a la carte ⌢ 2.25 − **22 rm** ⊑ 17.25/34.50 **t.**

AUSTIN-ROVER　Thurlby Rd ℰ 422892　　　　　FORD　Spalding Rd ℰ 424464
AUSTIN-ROVER　North St ℰ 422129　　　　　　NISSAN　Rippingale ℰ 07785 (Dowsby) 777

BOURNE END Herts. **404** S 28 − see Hemel Hempstead.

BOURNEMOUTH Dorset **403 404** O 31 The West Country G. − pop. 142 829 − ECD : Wednesday and Saturday − ✪ 0202.

See : Museums★ *AC* DX, DZ **M.**

🔵 Meyrick Park ℰ 20862 CY − 🔵 Queen's Park, Queen's Park South Drive ℰ 36198, NE : 2 m. CV.

✈ Hurn Airport : ℰ 578646, Telex 41345, N : 5 m. by Hurn Rd DV.

🏢 Westover Rd ℰ 291715 and 290883 − ◆London 114 − ◆Bristol 76 − ◆Southampton 34.

Plans on following pages

🏛 **Carlton,** Meyrick Rd, East Overcliff, BH1 3DN, ℰ 22011, Telex 41244, ≼, ⤓ heated, 🏮 − 🛗
　 📺 ✦ 🕭 ⇔ 🅿. 🔒 🔃 AE ⓘ VISA ⚙　　　　　　　　　　　　　　　　　　　EZ **a**
　 M 11.50/17.00 **t.** and a la carte ⌢ 3.70 (see also **La Causerie** below) − ⊑ 6.50 − **55 rm** 57.00/89.00 **t.**, **4 suites** 145.00/165.00 **t.** − SB (except Christmas, New Year and Easter) 116.00/160.00 **st.**

🏛 **Royal Bath** (De Vere), Bath Rd, BH1 2EW, ℰ 25555, Telex 41375, ≼, ⤓ heated, 🏮 − 🛗 📺
　 📺 ✦ ⇔ 🅿. 🔒 🔃 AE ⓘ VISA ⚙　　　　　　　　　　　　　　　　　　　　DZ **a**
　 M (see **Oscars** below) − **135 rm** ⊑ 55.00/145.00 **st.**, **8 suites** 145.00/160.00 **st.** − SB (weekends only) 98.00/106.00 **st.**

🏛 **Highcliff** (Best Western), 105 St. Michael's Rd, West Cliff, BH2 5DU, ℰ 27702, ≼, ⤓ heated,
　 🏮, ⚘ − 🛗 📺 ✦ 🅿. 🔒 🔃 AE ⓘ VISA　　　　　　　　　　　　　　　　　CZ **z**
　 M 7.50/11.50 **st.** and a la carte ⌢ 5.25 − **108 rm** ⊑ 38.00/92.00 **st.**, **3 suites** 50.00/92.00 **st.** − SB 66.00/76.00 **st.**

🏛 **Palace Court,** Westover Rd, BH1 3BZ, ℰ 27681, Telex 418451, ≼ − 🛗 📺 🕭 🅿. 🔒 🔃 AE
　 ⓘ VISA　　　　　　　　　　　　　　　　　　　　　　　　　　　　　　　　　DZ **c**
　 M 10.50 **t.** and a la carte ⌢ 4.00 (see also **La Taverna** below) − **107 rm** ⊑ 35.00/52.00 **t.**, **2 suites** 105.00 **t.**

🏛 **Marsham Court** (De Vere), Russell Cotes Rd, East Cliff, BH1 3AB, ℰ 22111, Group Telex
　 41420, ≼, ⤓ heated − 🛗 📺 🕭 🅿. 🔒 🔃 AE ⓘ VISA ⚙　　　　　　　　　DZ **e**
　 M 8.50/10.50 **st.** and a la carte ⌢ 3.50 − **80 rm** ⊑ 35.00/70.00 **st.**, **2 suites** 90.00/110.00 **st.** − SB (weekends only) 68.00 **st.**

🏨 **Cliff End,** Manor Rd, East Cliff, BH12 3EX, ℰ 309711, ⤓ heated, 🏮, ⚘ − 🛗 📺 ⌷wc �📶wc
　 🕭 🅿. 🔃 AE　　　　　　　　　　　　　　　　　　　　　　　　　　　　　　CX **v**
　 M 6.00/8.95 **st.** ⌢ 2.95 − **40 rm** ⊑ 26.00/52.00 **st.** − SB (September-May) 49.50 **st.**

🏨 **Crest** (Crest), Meyrick Rd, The Lansdowne, BH1 2PR, ℰ 23262, Telex 41232 − 🛗 📺 ⌷wc
　 🕭 🅿. 🔒 🔃 AE ⓘ VISA　　　　　　　　　　　　　　　　　　　　　　　　DY **a**
　 M 7.50/11.50 **st.** and a la carte − ⊑ 5.95 − **102 rm** 49.00/59.00 **st.** − SB (weekends only) 66.00/78.00 **st.**

🏨 **Burley Court,** 29 Bath Rd, BH1 2NP, ℰ 22824, ⤓ heated − 🛗 📺 ⌷wc ⊛ ✦ 🅿. 🔃 VISA
　 closed January − **M** (bar lunch)/dinner 8.50 **st.** and a la carte − **40 rm** ⊑ 16.50/52.50 **st.** − SB (weekends only)(except summer) 42.00/50.00 **st.**　　　　　　　　　　　　　　　　　　　　DY **i**

🏨 **Courtlands** (Best Western), 16 Boscombe Spa Rd, East Cliff, BH5 1BB, ℰ 302442, Telex
　 41344, ⤓ heated − 🛗 📺 ⌷wc �📶wc 🕭 🅿. 🔒 🔃 AE ⓘ VISA　　　　　　CX **o**
　 closed 28 December-5 January − **M** 6.75/10.25 **st.** ⌢ 2.95 − **45 rm** ⊑ 21.20/37.60 **st.** − SB (November-mid May) 48.75/58.90 **st.**

🏨 **Anglo-Swiss,** 16 Gervis Rd, East Cliff, BH1 3EQ, ℰ 24794, Group Telex 8954665, ⤓ heated,
　 🏮 − 🛗 📺 ⌷wc 🕭 🅿. 🔒 🔃 AE ⓘ VISA　　　　　　　　　　　　　　　　EY **e**
　 M (bar lunch in summer)/dinner 9.00 **st.** ⌢ 3.75 − **64 rm** ⊑ 33.00/60.00 **st.** − SB (weekends only) 52.50/66.00 **st.**

🏨 **Durley Hall,** 7 Durley Chine Rd, Westcliff, BH2 5JS, ℰ 766886, ⤓ heated, 🏮 − 🛗 📺
　 ⌷wc �📶wc 🕭 🅿. 🔃 VISA　　　　　　　　　　　　　　　　　　　　　　　CZ **s**
　 M (bar lunch)/dinner 8.00 **t.** and a la carte ⌢ 2.50 − **80 rm** ⊑ 25.00/76.00 **t.** − SB (except Easter and Christmas) 42.00/72.00 **st.**

🏨 **Winterbourne,** Priory Rd, BH2 5DJ, ℰ 296366, ≼, ⤓ heated − 🛗 📺 ⌷wc �📶wc 🅿. 🔃 VISA
　 closed January − **M** (bar lunch)/dinner 7.50 **t.** ⌢ 4.60 − **41 rm** ⊑ 21.00/47.00 **t.** − SB (October-April) 39.00/50.00 **st.**　　　　　　　　　　　　　　　　　　　　　　　　　　　　　　CZ **n**

🏨 **Chesterwood,** East Overcliff Drive, BH1 3AR, ℰ 28057, ≼, ⤓ heated − 🛗 📺 ⌷wc �📶wc
　 🕭 🅿. 🔃 ⓘ VISA　　　　　　　　　　　　　　　　　　　　　　　　　　　EZ **i**
　 closed January − **M** 5.00/9.00 **t.** ⌢ 2.90 − **52 rm** ⊑ 19.50/52.00 **st.** − SB (24 October-May) 42.00/49.00 **st.**

🏨 **East Cliff Court,** East Overcliff Drive, BH1 3AN, ℰ 24545, ≼, ⤓ heated − 🛗 📺 ⌷wc �📶wc
　 🕭 🅿. 🔃 VISA　　　　　　　　　　　　　　　　　　　　　　　　　　　　　EZ **e**
　 M 7.50/9.75 **t.** and a la carte ⌢ 3.60 − **69 rm** ⊑ 21.50/84.00 **t.** − SB 43.00/56.00 **st.**

🏨 **Heathlands,** 12 Grove Rd, East Cliff, BH1 3AY, ℰ 23336, ⬛ heated – ▮▮ TV ⌷wc ☎ ㋘ ㋪.
🅿 ㋐ AE ⓪ *VISA*
EZ **c**
M 6.50/8.50 **st.** and a la carte ↥ 3.75 – **116 rm** ⇌ 30.00/60.00 **st.** – SB (except Bank Holidays)(weekends only) 46.00/55.00 **st.**

🏨 **Cliffeside,** 32 East Overcliff Drive, BH1 3AQ, ℰ 25724, ≼, ⬛ heated – ▮▮ TV ⌷wc ▥wc ☎
🅿 ㋐ ㋠ *VISA*
EZ **v**
M 5.95/8.95 **t.** ↥ 2.00 – **64 rm** ⇌ 19.00/50.00 **t.** – SB (October-May) 46.00/54.00 **st.**

🏨 **Queens,** Meyrick Rd, Eastcliff, BH1 3DL, ℰ 24415, Group Telex 418297 – ▮▮ TV ⌷wc ☎ 🅿.
㋠ *VISA*
EYZ **r**
M 6.00/9.95 **t.** ↥ 2.80 – **110 rm** ⇌ 20.00/52.00 **t.** – SB (October-April) 54.00 **st.**

🏨 **Bournemouth Moat House** (Q.M.H.), Knyveton Rd, BH1 3QQ, ℰ 293311, ⬛ heated –
TV ⌷wc ☎ 🅿 ㋐ AE ⓪ *VISA*
CX **e**
M 7.50/9.50 **st.** and a la carte – **151 rm** ⇌ 33.00/48.00 **st.** – SB 52.50/58.00 **st.**

🏛 **Cliff House,** 113 Alumhurst Rd, Alum Chine, BH4 8HS, ℰ 763003, ≼ – ▮▮ TV ⌷wc ▥wc ㋘
⫿⫿
BX **s**
March-October – **M** (dinner only) 8.00 **st.** ↥ 1.75 – **10 rm** ⇌ 15.50/37.00 **st.** – SB (March-May and October) 45.00/49.00 **st.**

🏛 **Hinton Firs,** 9 Manor Rd, East Cliff, BH1 3HB, ℰ 25409, ⬛ heated – ▮▮ TV ⌷wc 🅿. ㋠ *VISA*.
⫿⫿
EY **n**
M (bar lunch)/dinner 6.75 **st.** ↥ 2.50 – **56 rm** ⇌ 15.50/46.00 **st.** – SB (October-mid May) 37.00/46.20 **st.**

🏛 **Miramar,** 19 Grove Rd, East Overcliff, BH1 3AL, ℰ 26581, ≼, 🌿 – ▮▮ TV ⌷wc ▥wc ☎ 🅿
㋠ AE *VISA*
DZ **u**
M 6.00/9.50 ↥ 4.50 – **42 rm** ⇌ 22.50/52.00 – SB (except summer)(weekends only) 48.30/55.20 **st.**

🏛 Cottonwood, 79 Grove Rd, East Cliff, BH1 3AP, ℰ 23183, ≼, 🌿 – ▮▮ TV ⌷wc ▥wc 🅿
EY **y**
30 rm

🏛 **Chinehead,** 31 Alumhurst Rd, BH4 8EN, ℰ 761693 – ⌷wc 🅿. *VISA*
BX **n**
M (dinner only) 5.00 **st.** ↥ 2.60 – **27 rm** ⇌ 11.00/40.00 **st.**

🛏 **Alumcliff,** 121 Alumhurst Rd, Alum Chine, BH4 8HS, ℰ 764777, ≼ – TV ⌷wc ▥wc 🅿. ㋠
㋠ *VISA*
BX **a**
16 rm ⇌ 18.50/58.00 **t.**

🛏 **Valberg,** 1a Wollstonecraft Rd, Boscombe, BH5 1JQ, ℰ 34644, 🌿 – ▥wc 🅿. ⫿⫿
CX **s**
closed last 2 weeks November – **10 rm** ⇌ 10.00/21.00 **s.**

🛏 **Stonecroft,** 6 Wollstonecraft Rd, Boscombe, BH5 1JQ, ℰ 309390, 🌿 – ▥wc 🅿
CX **u**
March-October – **8 rm** ⇌ 10.00/26.00 **st.**

🛏 **Naseby Nye,** 10 Byron Rd, Boscombe Overcliff, BH5 1JD, ℰ 34079, 🌿 – ⌷wc 🅿
DX **z**
13 rm ⇌ 13.00/30.00 **st.**

🛏 **Tudor Grange,** 31 Gervis Rd, BH1 3EE, ℰ 291472, 🌿 – ⌷wc 🅿
EY **o**
12 rm ⇌ 11.50/34.00 **st.**

🛏 **Wood Lodge,** 10 Manor Rd, East Cliff, BH1 3EY, ℰ 290891, 🌿 – ⌷wc ▥wc 🅿. ㋠ *VISA*. ⫿⫿
EY **z**
Easter-October – **15 rm** ⇌ 9.75/34.00 **st.**

🛏 **Mariners,** 22 Clifton Rd, Southbourne, BH6 3PA, ℰ 420851 – 🅿
EX **c**
March-October – **15 rm** ⇌ 8.00/18.00 **s.**

XXX **La Causerie** (at Carlton H.), Meyrick Rd, East Overcliff, BH1 3DN, ℰ 22011, Telex 41244 –
🅿 ㋠ AE ⓪ *VISA*
EZ **a**
closed Saturday lunch and Sunday – **M** 11.50/17.00 **t.** and a la carte 14.35/21.15 **t.** ↥ 3.70.

XXX **Oscars** (De Vere) (at Royal Bath H.), Bath Rd, BH1 2EW, ℰ 25555, Telex 41375 – 🅿
DZ **a**
M 11.00/17.00 **t.** and a la carte 15.70/23.60 **st.** ↥ 5.00.

XX ✿ **Provence,** 91 Belle Vue Rd., Southbourne, BH6 3DH, ℰ 424421, French rest. – ㋠ ⓪ *VISA*
EX **s**
closed Sunday – **M** (dinner only) a la carte 16.80/19.80 **st.**
Spec. Homard au beurre de basilic, Filet de barbue au pamplemousse rose, Magret de canard à la poire William.

XX **La Taverna** (at Palace Court H.), Westover Rd, BH1 3BZ, ℰ 27681, Telex 418451 – 🅿. ㋠ AE
⓪ *VISA*
DZ **c**
closed Sunday – **M** 10.50 **t.** and a la carte 15.45/20.30 **t.** ↥ 4.00.

X **Sophisticats,** 43 Charminster Rd, BH8 8UE, ℰ 291019
BV **a**
closed Sunday, Monday, 3 weeks January, last week June and last week October – **M** (dinner only) a la carte 11.35/13.85 **t.** ↥ 2.60.

X **Crust,** Bourne Av., The Square, BH2 5AE, ℰ 21430 – ㋠ ⓪ *VISA*
CY **o**
closed 25 and 26 December – **M** 5.95 **t.** (lunch) and a la carte 8.80/12.55 **t.** ↥ 3.00.

AUSTIN-ROVER 235 Castle Lane West, Redhill ℰ 510201
AUSTIN-ROVER 14 Carbery Row ℰ 423243
BENTLEY, ROLLS ROYCE Ringwood Rd ℰ 570575
BMW Exeter Rd ℰ 24433
CITROEN, PEUGEOT, TALBOT 43 Holdenhurst Rd ℰ 26566
DAIMLER-JAGUAR 38 Poole Hill ℰ 510252
FIAT 674 Wimborne Rd ℰ 512121
FORD Poole Rd ℰ 762442

LANCIA 318-320 Holdenhurst Rd ℰ 33304
MERCEDES BENZ Wallisdown Rd ℰ 525111
PORSCHE, JAGUAR 382/386 Charminster Rd ℰ 510252
SEAT 25-27 Palmerston Rd, Boscombe ℰ 37206
VAUXHALL Castle Lane West ℰ 526434
VAUXHALL-OPEL Poole Rd ℰ 763361

VOLVO 33 R. L. Stephenson Av. ℰ 763344

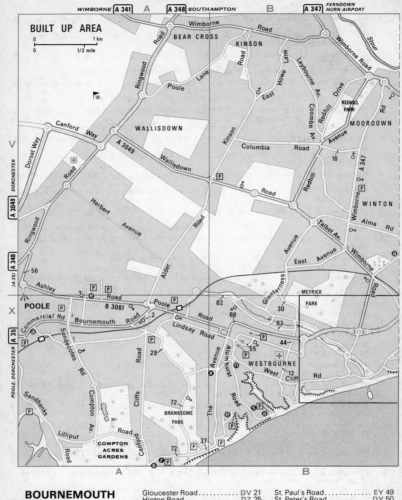

BOURNEMOUTH

Town plans : the names of main shopping streets are indicated in red
at the beginning of the list of streets.

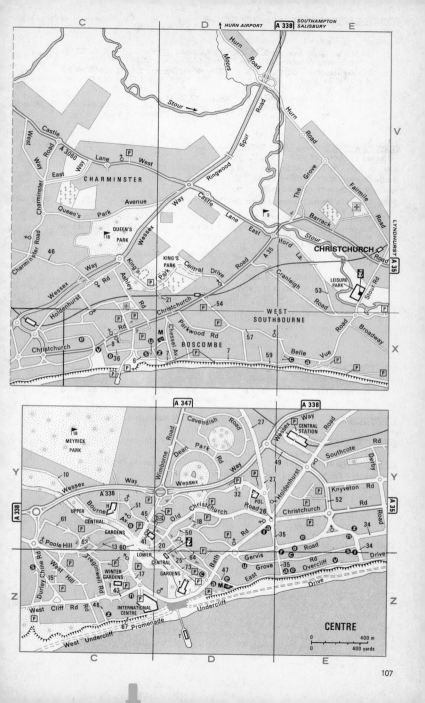

♦London 91 – ♦Birmingham 47 – Gloucester 24 – ♦Oxford 36.

🏦 **Old Manse,** Sherborne St., GL54 2BX, ☏ 20642, � – 📺 🛏wc ⇌wc ☎ 🅿. 🄾 𝑽𝑰𝑺𝑨. ❀
closed 2 weeks January – ⊊ 2.75 – **12 rm** 22.50/47.00 **t.** – SB 53.00/60.00 **st.**

🏠 **Brookside,** Riverside, GL54 2BS, ☏ 20371, � – 📺 🛏wc ⇌wc 🅿. 🄾 𝗔𝗘 ⓪ 𝑽𝑰𝑺𝑨
M 6.00/9.00 **t.** ⌕ 3.30 – **10 rm** ⊊ 17.50/42.00 **t.** – SB (except Christmas and second week of March) 47.00/51.00 **st.**

✗ **Rose Tree,** Riverside, GL54 2BX, ☏ 20635 – 🄾 𝗔𝗘 ⓪ 𝑽𝑰𝑺𝑨
closed Tuesday to Saturday lunch October-April, Sunday dinner, Monday and mid January-mid February – **M** (bar lunch Tuesday to Saturday)/dinner 9.25/15.95 **t.** ⌕ 3.25.

FORD Lansdowne Rd ☏ 20366

See : St. Peter, St. Paul and St. Thomas of Canterbury Church★.

🄯 Lower Car Park ☏ 832047 (summer only).

♦London 214 – Exeter 14 – ♦Plymouth 32.

🏦 **Coombe Cross,** Coombe Cross, TQ13 9EY, on B 3344 ☏ 832476, � – 📺 🛏wc ☎ 🅿. 🄾 𝗔𝗘 𝑽𝑰𝑺𝑨 ⊊ ❀
M (bar lunch)/dinner 10.95 **st.** ⌕ 2.75 – **25 rm** ⊊ 21.95/39.90 **st.** – SB 44.00/50.00 **st.**

🏦 **Edgemoor** ⌕, Haytor Rd, TQ13 9LE, ☏ 832466, � – ⇌wc 🅿. 🄾 𝗔𝗘 ⓪ 𝑽𝑰𝑺𝑨. ❀
M (bar lunch)/dinner 9.50 **st.** ⌕ 2.75 – **18 rm** ⊊ 18.25/39.50 **st.** – SB (except 24 December-2 January) 42.50/54.50 **st.**

🏠 **Front House,** East St., TQ13 9EL, ☏ 832202, � – 📺 🛏wc 🅿
6 rm ⊊ 11.00/21.00 **st.**

at Haytor NW : 1 ½ m. on B 3344 – ✉ Bovey Tracey – ✪ 036 46 Haytor :

🏰 **Bel Alp House** ⌕, TQ13 7XX, NW : 1 m. on Widecombe Rd ☏ 217, ≼ Countryside, « Country house atmosphere », �, ❀ – 🍴 📺 ⇌wc ⇌wc 🅿. 🄾 𝑽𝑰𝑺𝑨
M (booking essential) 12.00/17.00 **t.** ⌕ 3.00 – **9 rm** ⊊ 36.00/60.00 **t.** – SB (except summer) 84.00/90.00 **st.**

☞ *Michelin puts no plaque or sign on the hotels and restaurants mentioned in this Guide.*

♦London 265 – Durham 3 – ♦Middlesbrough 20.

🏦 **Bowburn Hall,** DH6 5NT, E : 1 m. ☏ 770311, � – 📺 ⇌wc ☎ 🅿. 🄾 𝗔𝗘 ⓪ 𝑽𝑰𝑺𝑨
M (bar lunch)/dinner 8.45 **st.** ⌕ 3.00 – **20 rm** ⊊ 32.00/38.00 **st.**

🏌 Downshire Easthampstead Park, Wokingham ☏ 422682 SW : 3 m.

🄯 Central Library, Town Sq., ☏ 423149.

♦London 35 – Reading 11.

🏰 **Ladbroke** (Ladbroke), Bagshot Rd, RG12 3QJ, S : 2 m. on A 322 ☏ 424801, Telex 848058 – 🍴 🍴 rest 📺 ⇌wc ☎ & 🅿. ⚠. 🄾 𝗔𝗘 ⓪ 𝑽𝑰𝑺𝑨. ❀
M *(closed Saturday lunch)*/dinner 10.95 ⌕ 3.70 – ⊊ 6.00 – **147 rm** 52.50/65.00 **st.** – SB (weekends only) 63.00 **st.**

AUSTIN-ROVER London Rd ☏ 50411   VAUXHALL Lovelace Rd ☏ 481925
NISSAN Downshire Way ☏ 426500

🏌 Phoenix Park, Thornbury ☏ 667573, E : on A 647 BX – 🏌 Bradford Moor, Scarr-Hall, Pollard Lane ☏ 638313 BX.

✈ Leeds and Bradford Airport : ☏ 0532 (Rawdon) 503431, Telex 557868 NE : 6 m. by A 658 BX.

🄯 Central Library, Princes Way ☏ 753678 – City Hall ☏ 753678.

♦ London 212 – ♦Leeds 9 – ♦Manchester 39 – ♦Middlesbrough 75 – ♦Sheffield 45.

Plan of Enlarged Area : see Leeds

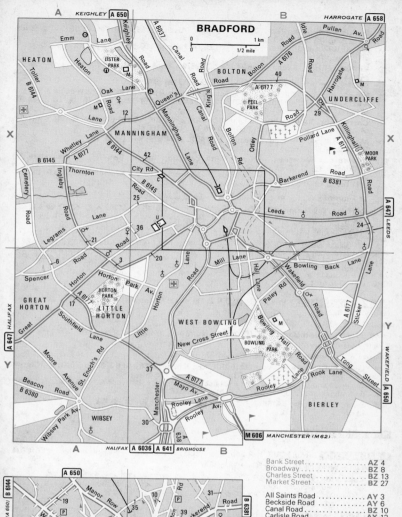

BRADFORD

1 km
1/2 mile

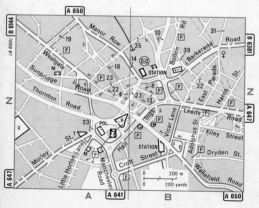

🏨 **Stakis Norfolk Gardens** (Stakis), Hall Ings, BD1 5SH, ℰ 734734, Telex 517573 – |⚑| 🍽 rest
📺 🅿 ⚙ 🅿 🖿 🔄 AE ⓪ VISA
M 7.00/10.00 **t.** and a la carte 🍷 3.75 – ⚏ 3.90 – **126 rm** 45.00/58.00 **t.**, **3 suites** 70.00/90.00 **t.** –
SB (weekends only) 46.00/54.00 **st.**

BZ **e**

🏨 **Victoria** (T.H.F.), Bridge St., BD1 1JX, ℰ 728706, Telex 517456 – |⚑| 📺 ⌷wc 🏮wc ☎ 🅿
⚙ 🔄 AE VISA
M (carving rest.) 8.00/8.65 **st.** 🍷 3.50 – ⚏ 5.65 – **59 rm** 39.00/48.50 **st.**

BZ **c**

🏨 **Novotel Bradford, Euroway Trading Estate, Merrydale Rd, BD4 6SA, S : 3 ½ m. by A 641 and
A 6117 off M 606 ℰ 683683, Telex 517312, ⚿ heated – |⚑| 📺 ⌷wc ☎ ⚙ 🅿 ⚙ 🔄 AE ⓪ VISA
M 8.00 **st.** and a la carte – **136 rm**

on plan of Leeds AX **a**

🏨 **Cartwright**, 308 Manningham Lane, BD8 7AX, ℰ 499908 – 📺 ⌷wc 🏮wc 🅿 VISA
M 4.50/6.50 **st.** and a la carte 🍷 2.50 – **12 rm** ⚏ 24.00/38.00 **st.**

BX **a**

🏠 **Maple Hill** ⟆, 3 Park Drive, Heaton, BD9 4DP, ℰ 44061, 🌿 – 📺 🅿 VISA
10 rm ⚏ 16.50/26.50 **st.**

AX **o**

✗✗✗ **Restaurant Nineteen** with rm, North Park Rd, Heaton, BD9 4NT, (at Belvedere H.)
ℰ 492559 – 📺 🏮 🔄 AE ⓪ VISA 🐾
closed Sunday, Monday, 1 week August and 1 week January – **M** (dinner only) 19.50 **t.** 🍷 4.60
– **12 rm** ⚏ 19.00/30.00 **st.**

AX **n**

at Thornton W : 5 ¼ m. on B 6145 – AX – ✉ ✆ 0274 Bradford :

✗✗✗ **Cottage,** 869 Thornton Rd, BD13 3NW, W : 1 m. on B 6145 ℰ 832752 – 🅿 🔄 AE ⓪ VISA
closed Saturday lunch and Sunday – **M** 11.50 **t.** (dinner) and a la carte 11.65/21.45 **t.** 🍷 4.10.

AUSTIN-ROVER-DAIMLER-JAGUAR Canal Rd ℰ
733488
BMW Oak Lane ℰ 495521
CITROEN Whetley Hill ℰ 495543
COLT St. Enoch's Rd ℰ 722234
FIAT Keighley Rd, Frizinghall ℰ 490031
FORD 44 Bowland St. ℰ 725131
FORD 146-148 Tong St. ℰ 681601

MERCEDES-BENZ Thornton Rd ℰ 494122
NISSAN 88 Thornton Rd ℰ 727302
POLONEZ, FSO 341 Leeds Rd ℰ 726812
PORSCHE, VAUXHALL-OPEL Parry Lane ℰ 392321
SAAB Apperley Lane, Yeadon ℰ 0532 (Leeds) 502231
VOLVO 221 Sunbridge Rd ℰ 721720
VW, AUDI-NSU Ingleby Rd ℰ 494100

BRADFORD-ON-AVON Wilts. 403 404 N 29 The West Country G. – pop. 8 921 – ECD : Wednesday – ✆ 022 16.

See : Site★★ – Saxon Church of St. Lawrence★★ – Bridge★.

Envir. : Great Chalfield Manor★ *AC* (Church★), NE : 2 m. – Westwood Manor★ *AC*, SW : 1 ½ m.

🛈 Waterlands, 34 Silver St. ℰ 2495/5797.

◆London 118 – ◆Bristol 24 – Salisbury 35 – Swindon 33.

🏨 **Leigh Park,** Leigh Rd West, BA15 2RA, NE : 1 m. by A 363 and B 3109 on B 3105 ℰ 3433, 🌿,
🐾 – 📺 ⌷wc 🏮wc 🅿 ⚙ 🔄 VISA 🐾
closed 25 and 26 December – **M** *(closed Sunday dinner to non residents and Saturday)* (lunch
by arrangement) 5.75/9.50 **t.** 🍷 2.50 – **20 rm** ⚏ 26.00/40.00 **t.**

🏠 **Swan,** 1 Church St., BA15 1LN, ℰ 2224 – 📺 ⌷wc 🏮wc 🅿 🔄 ⓪ VISA
13 rm ⚏ 27.50/35.00 **t.**

BRADFORD-ON-TONE Somerset 403 K 30 – see Taunton.

BRADWORTHY Devon 403 G 31 – pop. 821 – ECD : Wednesday – ✉ Holsworthy – ✆ 040 924.

◆London 251 – Barnstaple 27 – Exeter 50 – ◆Plymouth 47.

✗✗ **Lake Villa** ⟆ with rm, EX22 7SQ, E : ½ m. ℰ 342, 🌿, 🐾 – 📺 ⌷wc 🏮wc 🅿 🐾
M *(closed Monday to non residents)* (booking essential)(bar lunch)/dinner a la carte
7.50/12.00 **t.** – **7 rm** ⚏ 15.00/35.00 **st.** – SB (October-March) 45.00 **st.**

BRAINTREE Essex 404 V 28 – pop. 30 975 – ECD : Thursday – ✆ 0376.

🛈 King Lane, Stisted ℰ 24117, E : 2 m. off A 120.

◆London 45 – ◆Cambridge 38 – Chelmsford 12 – Colchester 15.

🏨 **White Hart (whitbread),** Bocking End, CM7 6AB, ℰ 21401 – 📺 ⌷wc ☎ 🅿 ⚙ 🔄 AE
⓪ VISA 🐾
closed Christmas Day – **M** 10.00 **t.** and a la carte – **35 rm** ⚏ 40.00/48.00 **t.** – SB (weekends
only)(except Bank Holidays) 54.00/58.00 **st.**

FORD Rayne Rd ℰ 21202
MAZDA Rayne Rd ℰ 42159

VAUXHALL-OPEL 277-281 Rayne Rd ℰ 21456
VOLVO Skitts Hill ℰ 47797

BRAITHWAITE Cumbria 401 402 K 20 – see Keswick.

BRAMHOPE West Yorks. 402 P 22 – see Leeds.

BRAMLEY Surrey 404 S 30 – see Guildford.

BRAMPTON Cumbria **401 402** L 19 – pop. 3 686 – ECD : Thursday – ☎ 069 77.

Envir. : Lanercost : Priory★ (14C ruins) *AC*, NE : 3 m. – Bewcastle (churchyard Runic Cross★ 8C) N : 12 m.

🛄 Talkin Tarn ♟ 2255, SE : 1 m. on B 6413.

🎫 Moot Hall, Market Place ♟ 3433 (summer only).

♦ London 317 – ♦Carlisle 9 – ♦Newcastle-upon-Tyne 49.

   🏛 **Farlam Hall** ♠, CA8 2NG, SE : 2 ¾ m. on A 689 ♟ 069 76 (Hallbankgate) 234, ≼, « Gardens » – 📺 ⇌wc ℗. 🌫 🅰🅴 *VISA*. ⋘
    closed Monday and Tuesday December-January, February and first 3 weeks November – **M** (dinner only) 15.50 **t.** – **13 rm** ⇌ (dinner included) 50.00/110.00 **t.** – SB (November-April) 80.00/90.00 **st.**

   🏵 **Howard Arms,** Front St., CA8 1NG, ♟ 2357 – 📺 ⇌wc ⸐wc. 🌫 🅰🅴 *VISA*
    M (bar lunch)/dinner 9.50 **t.** and a la carte ⓘ 3.00 – **11 rm** ⇌ 18.00/34.00 **t.** – SB 34.00/40.00 **st.**

   at Talkin S : 2 m. by B 6413 – ✉ ☎ 06977 Brampton :

   XX **Tarn End** ♠ with rm, Talkin Tarn, CA8 1LS, ♟ 2340, ≼Talkin Tarn, ☞ – 📺 ⇌wc ℗. 🌫 🅰🅴 ⓞ *VISA*. ⋘
    closed February – **M** *(Easter-November)(closed Monday lunch and Sunday dinner)* (lunch by arrangement)/dinner 16.00 **t.** and a la carte ⓘ 4.50 – **6 rm** ⇌ 17.00/45.00 **t.** – SB 62.00 **st.**

BRAMSHAW Hants. **403 404** P 31 – pop. 611 – ECD : Tuesday – ✉ Lyndhurst – ☎ 0703 Southampton.

♦London 93 – Salisbury 13 – ♦Southampton 11 – Winchester 21.

   🏠 **Bramble Hill** ♠, Bramble Hill, SO43 7JG, W : ½ m. ♟ 813165, ≼, « Former hunting lodge », ☞, park – ⇌wc ℗. 🌫 *VISA*
    M (bar lunch)/dinner 9.00 **t.** and a la carte ⓘ 2.50 – **16 rm** ⇌ 25.00/55.00 **t.**

BRANDON Warw. **403 404** P 26 – see Coventry.

BRANSCOMBE Devon **403** K 32 The West Country G. – pop. 506 – ECD : Thursday – ✉ Seaton – ☎ 029 780.

♦London 167 – Exeter 20 – Lyme Regis 11.

   🏛 **Ye Olde Masons Arms,** EX12 3DJ, ♟ 300, « 14C inn », ☞ – 📺 ⇌wc ☎ ℗. 🌫 *VISA*
    M (bar lunch Monday to Saturday)/dinner 14.00 **t.** ⓘ 3.10 – **21 rm** ⇌ 19.50/64.00 **t.** – SB (winter only) 50.00/75.00 **st.**

BRANSTON Lincs **402 404** S 24 - see Lincoln.

BRANSTON Staffs. – see Burton-upon-Trent.

BRATTON Wilts. **403 404** N 30 – see Westbury.

BRAUNSTONE Leics. **402 403 404** Q 26 – see Leicester.

BRAUNTON Devon **403** H 30 – pop. 9 004 – ECD : Wednesday – ☎ 0271.

♦London 226 – Exeter 47 – Taunton 58.

   ↑ **Brookdale,** 62 South St., EX33 2AN, ♟ 812075 – ℗. ⋘
    8 rm ⇌ 9.00/24.00 **st.**

   XX **Otter's,** 30 Caen St., EX33 1AA, ♟ 813633 – 🌫 *VISA*
    closed Sunday, 2 weeks February and 2 weeks October – **M** a la carte 10.25/12.50 **st.** ⓘ 2.75.

   at Wrafton SE : ½ m. on A 361 – ✉ ☎ 0271 Braunton :

   🏠 **Poyers,** EX33 2DN, ♟ 812149, ☞ – 📺 ⇌wc ⸐wc ℗. 🌫 🅰🅴 ⓞ *VISA*
    closed 24 December-third week in January – **M** (dinner only) 9.00 **t.** and a la carte ⓘ 2.40 – **10 rm** ⇌ 23.00/38.50 **t.** – SB 50.10 **st.**

Camping or Caravanning in France ?

Your holiday will be more enjoyable if you use the Michelin Guide

''Camping Caravaning France''

It includes :

    – A comprehensive selection of sites classified according to the nature and comfort of their amenities

    – Notes on charges, local rules and conditions, insurances etc...

    – Location maps

The Guide is revised annually - get this year's edition.

BRAY-ON-THAMES Berks. 🗺️ R 29 – pop. 9 427 – ✉️ ✪ Maidenhead.
♦London 34 – Reading 13.

🏠 **Chauntry House,** High St., SL6 2AB, ☏ 73991, ≼ – 📺 ⬛wc 🏠wc 🅿️ ⬛ AE VISA
M (dinner only)a la carte 10.35/13.75 **t.** ᗐ 3.00 – **9 rm** ⌖ 48.00/60.00 **t.**

XXXX ✿✿✿ **Waterside Inn,** Ferry Rd, SL6 2AT, ☏ 20691, Telex 8813079, ≼, French rest.,
« Thames-side setting », ☀️ – 🅿️ ⬛ AE ⓿ VISA
closed Tuesday lunch, Sunday dinner 19 October-Easter, Monday, 26 December-14 February
and Bank Holidays – **M** 20.00/36.00 **st.** and a la carte 25.30/38.30 **st.** ᗐ 5.10
Spec. Tronçonnettes de homard poêlées minute au porto blanc, Caneton Juliette (April-September), Soufflé
chaud aux mirabelles (October-March).

XX **Hind's Head,** High St., SL6 2AB, ☏ 26151, ☀️ – 🅿️ ⬛ AE ⓿ VISA
M (closed Sunday dinner) 14.50/21.50 **st.**

BRECHFA Dyfed 🗺️ H 28 – ✉️ Carmarthen – ✪ 026 789.
♦London 223 – Carmarthen 11 – ♦Swansea 30.

XX Ty Mawr ⑀ with rm, Abergorlech Rd, SA32 7RA, ☏ 332, ⚓, ☀️ – ⬛wc 🅿️
5 rm.

BRECON (ABERHONDDU) Powys 🗺️ J 28 – pop. 7 166 – ECD : Wednesday – ✪ 0874.
See : Cathedral★ 13C.
Envir. : Bwlch (≼★ of the Usk Valley), SE : 8 ½ m. – Road★ from Brecon to Hirwaun – Road★ from
Brecon to Merthyr Tydfil – Craig-y-Nos (Dan-yr-Ogof Caves★), SW : 18 m.
🏌️ Newton Park ☏ 2004, W : ¾ m. on A 40 – 🏌️ Panoyre Park, Cradoc ☏ 3658, NW : 2 m.
🅱️ Watton Mount ☏ 4437 (summer only) – Market Car Park ☏ 2485 and 5692 (summer only).
♦London 171 – ♦Cardiff 40 – Carmarthen 31 – Gloucester 65.

🏠 **Wellington,** The Bulwark, LD3 7AD, ☏ 5225 – 📺 ⬛wc ☎️ ᗐ⬛ ⬛ AE VISA ⚒️
M a la carte 4.15/9.10 **st.** – **21 rm** ⌖ 23.00/40.00 **st.** – SB 51.50 **st.**

BREDWARDINE Heref. and Worc. 🗺️ L 27 – pop. 177 – ✉️ Hereford – ✪ 098 17 Moccas.
♦London 150 – Hereford 12 – Newport 51.

🏠 **Red Lion,** HR3 6BU, ☏ 303, ⚓, ☀️ – ⬛wc 🅿️ ⬛ AE ⓿ VISA
M (bar lunch)/dinner 11.50 **t.** ᗐ 3.25 – **10 rm** ⌖ 12.00/48.00 **t.** – SB 19.00/28.00 **st.**

BRENDON Devon 🗺️ I 30 – see Lynton.

BRENT KNOLL Somerset 🗺️ L 30 – pop. 1 092 – ECD : Wednesday and Saturday – ✉️ High-
bridge – ✪ 0278 Bridgwater.
🅱️ Brent Knoll Picnic Area (M5 Southbound) ☏ Edingworth (093 472) 466 (summer only).
♦London 151 – ♦Bristol 33 – Taunton 21.

🏠 **Battleborough Grange,** Bristol Rd, TA9 4HJ, on A 38 ☏ 760208, ☀️ – 📺 ⬛wc 🏠wc ☎️
🅿️ ⬛ AE ⓿ VISA ⚒️
M (closed Sunday dinner in winter) (lunch by arrangement) a la carte 8.10/11.50 **st.** ᗐ 2.80 –
11 rm ⌖ 18.00/36.00 **st.** – SB (except summer)(weekends only) 45.00/55.00 **st.**

BRENTWOOD Essex 🗺️ V 29 – pop. 51 212 – ECD : Thursday – ✪ 0277.
🏌️ King George's playing fields, Ingrave Rd ☏ 218850.
♦London 22 – Chelmsford 11 – Southend-on-Sea 21.

🏢 **Brentwood Moat House** (Q.M.H.), London Rd, CM14 4NR, SW : 1 ¼ m. on A 1023
☏ 225252, Telex 995182, ☀️ – ᗐ⬛ 🅿️ ᗐ⬛ ⬛ AE ⓿ VISA ⚒️
M a la carte 17.00/21.00 **t.** ᗐ 3.00 – ⌖ 6.00 – **37 rm** 51.00/66.00 **st.** – SB (weekends only)
70.00/80.00 **st.**

🏠 **Post House** (T.H.F.), Brook St., CM14 5NF, SW : 1 ¾ m. on A 1023 ☏ 210888, Telex 995379,
⚒️ heated – ᗐ⬛ 📺 ⬛wc ☎️ ᗐ⬛ 🅿️ ᗐ⬛ ⬛ AE ⓿ VISA
M 8.50/12.50 **st.** and a la carte ᗐ 2.90 – ⌖ 5.65 – **120 rm** 52.00/60.00 **st.**

BRERETON Cheshire – see Holmes Chapel.

BRIDGE Kent 🗺️ X 30 – see Canterbury.

EUROPE on a single sheet
Michelin map no 🗺️🗺️🗺️.

BRIDGEND (PEN-Y-BONT) Mid Glam. **403** J 29 – pop. 31 008 – ECD : Wednesday – ✆ 0656.
♦London 177 – ♦Cardiff 20 – ♦Swansea 23.

🏨 **Heronston,** Ewenny, CF35 5AW, S : 2 m. on B 4265 ✆ 68811, Telex 498232, ▨ – 📺 🛏wc
☎ 🅿 🕭 🖸 AE ⑩ VISA
M 8.50 t. – **40 rm** ⬡ 36.00/48.00 st. – SB (weekends only) 55.00 st.

at Coychurch (Llangrallo) E : 2 ¼ m. by A 473 – ⊠ ✆ 0656 Bridgend :

XXX **Coed-y-Mwstwr** ⚘ with rm, CF35 6AF, N : 1 m. ✆ 860621, ≼, ⬍ heated, 🎯, park, ❧ –
📺 🛏wc ✆ 🅿 🕭 🖸 AE ⑩ VISA 🔥 ﬗ
M *(closed Saturday lunch and Sunday dinner)* 14.95 st. and a la carte 🍴 3.25 – ⬡ 7.50 – **15 rm**
30.00/55.00 st.

MICHELIN Distribution Centre, Brackla Industrial Estate, CF31 2BD, ✆ **62343**

AUSTIN-ROVER Brackla Ind. Est. ✆ 0656 3376
FIAT Tremains Rd ✆ 2984

VAUXHALL, OPEL Maesteg Rd ✆ 55007
VOLVO Ogmore Rd, Ewenny ✆ 59821

BRIDGNORTH Salop **403 404** M 26 – pop. 10 332 – ECD : Thursday – ✆ 074 62.
Envir. : Claverley (Parish church : wall paintings★ 13C-15C) E : 5 m. – Much Wenlock : Wenlock
priory★ (ruins 11C) *AC*, NW : 8 ½ m.

🛝 Stanley Lane ✆ 3315, N : 1 m.
🅩 Bridgnorth Library, Listley St. ✆ 3358.
♦London 146 – ♦Birmingham 26 – Shrewsbury 20 – Worcester 29.

⌂ **Croft,** St. Mary's St., WV16 4DW, ✆ 2416 – 🛏wc ﬙wc. 🖸 VISA
7 rm ⬡ 15.00/32.00 st.

X **Old Colonial,** 3 Bridge St., Low Town, WV15 6AF, ✆ 66510, Indian rest.

at Worfield NE : 4 m. by A 454 – ⊠ Bridgnorth – ✆ 074 64 Worfield :

🏨 **Old Vicarage** ⚘, WV15 5JZ, ✆ 497, 🎯 – 📺 🛏wc ﬙wc ☎ 🅿 🖸 AE ⑩ VISA
M 10.95/14.95 t. 🍴 3.45 – **10 rm** ⬡ 36.00/49.50 t. – SB 57.50 st.

at Hampton Loade SE : 6¼ m. by A 442 – ⊠ Bridgnorth – ✆ 0746 Quatt :

XX **Haywain,** ✆ 780404 – 🅿 🖸 🖸 VISA
M *(closed Sunday dinner and Monday)* 10.00/17.50 t.

AUSTIN-ROVER 52 West Castle St. ✆ 2207
RENAULT Northgate ✆ 3332

VW, AUDI Hollybush Rd ✆ 4343

When visiting Scotland,

use the Michelin Green Guide '' Scotland ''.

– Detailed descriptions of places of interest

– Touring programmes

– Maps and street plans

– The history of the country

– Photographs and drawings of monuments, beauty spots, houses...

BRIDGWATER Somerset **403** L 30 The West Country G. – pop. 30 782 – ECD : Thursday –
✆ 0278.
See : Site★ – Castle St.★ – St. Mary's★ – Admiral Blake Museum★*AC*.
Envir. : Stogursey Priory Church★★, NW : 14 m. by A 39 – Westonzoyland Church★★, SE : 3 m. –
North Petherton Church Tower★★, S : 3 m.
🅩 Town Hall, High St. ✆ 427652/424391 ext 419 (summer only).
♦London 160 – ♦Bristol 39 – Taunton 11.

🏨 **Watergate,** 10-11 West Quay, TA6 3DB, ✆ 423847 – 📺 ﬙wc. 🖸 AE ⑩ VISA ﬗ
M *(closed Sunday and Bank Holidays)* 8.00 t. and a la carte 🍴 2.50 – **8 rm** ⬡ 22.00/
36.00 t.

X **Old Vicarage** with rm, 45 St. Mary's St., TA6 3EQ, ✆ 458891, 🎯 – 📺 🛏wc ☎ 🅿 🖸 AE
VISA
closed 26 December-3 January – **M** *(closed Sunday lunch)* 5.00 t. (lunch) and a la carte
9.75/13.95 t. 🍴 2.25 – **10 rm** ⬡ 25.00/32.50 t.

at West Huntspill N : 6 m. on A 38 – ⊠ Highbridge – ✆ 0278 Burnham-on-Sea :

🏨 **Sundowner,** 74 Main Rd, TA9 3QU, on A 38 ✆ 784766 – 📺 🛏wc ﬙wc 🅿 🖸 AE ⑩ VISA
M *(closed Monday lunch and Sunday dinner)* 4.60 t. and a la carte 🍴 3.85 – **8 rm** ⬡ 22.00/
36.00 t.

XX **Huntspill Villa** with rm, 82 Main Rd, TA9 3QX, on A 38 ✆ 782291 – 📺 🛏wc 🅿 🖸 AE ⑩
M *(closed lunch Monday and Saturday and Sunday dinner)* a la carte 9.75/12.10 t. 🍴 3.30 –
6 rm ⬡ 22.50/40.00 t. – SB (weekends only) 55.00/65.00 st.

at Chilton Polden NE : 6 ¼ m. by A 39 – ⊠ ❀ 0278 Bridgwater :

✕ **Wilton Farmhouse,** 9 Goose Lane, TA7 9ED, ℰ 722134 – **P**. ⑩ **VISA**
closed Sunday, Monday and Tuesday to Thursday in winter – **M** (lunch by arrangement)/dinner 10.00 ⓛ 2.65.

at North Petherton S : 3 m. on A 38 – ⊠ ❀ 0278 Bridgwater :

🏠 **Walnut Tree Inn,** TA6 6QA, ℰ 662255 – **TV** ⇔wc ☎ **P**. ⚓. 🔼 **AE** ⑩ **VISA**. ⅙
M 7.50/9.00 **t**. and a la carte ⓛ 2.20 – **20 rm** ⊊ 29.00/50.00 **t**. – SB (weekends only) 54.00/64.00 **st**.

AUSTIN-ROVER Market St. ℰ 422125
BMW High St., Cannington ℰ 652228
CITROEN Main Rd, Cannington ℰ 0278 (Combwich) 652233

FORD 37 Frian St. ℰ 451332
RENAULT 52 Eastover ℰ 422218
VOLVO Bristol Rd ℰ 455333

BRIDLINGTON Humberside **402** T 21 – pop. 28 426 – ECD : Thursday – ❀ 0262.

See : Priory Church★ 12C-15C.

Envir. : Burton Agnes Hall★ (Elizabethan) *AC*, SW : 6 m.

🏌 Belvedere ℰ 72092, S : 1 ½ m. on A 165 – 🏌 Flamborough Head ℰ 850333, NE : 5 m.

🅱 Garrison St. ℰ 673474 and 679626.

◆ London 236 – ◆Kingston-upon-Hull 29 – York 41.

🏨 **Expanse,** North Marine Drive, YO15 2LS, ℰ 675347, ⩻ – 🛗 **TV** ⇔wc ☜ **P**. 🔼 **AE** ⑩ **VISA**. ⅙
M 5.25/8.00 **t**. ⓛ 2.95 – **48 rm** ⊊ 26.00/48.00 **t**. – SB 56.00/64.00 **st**.

🏠 **Monarch,** South Marine Drive, YO15 3JJ, ℰ 674447, ⩻ – 🛗 ⇔wc ☜ **P**. 🔼 **AE** ⑩
VISA. ⅙
17 April-19 October – **M** (bar lunch Monday to Saturday)/dinner 7.50 **t**. and a la carte ⓛ 3.00 –
44 rm.

FORD Hamilton Rd ℰ 675336
NISSAN Quay Rd ℰ 670331
TALBOT 74 Pessingby Rd ℰ 678141

VAUXHALL-OPEL 52-60 Quay Rd ℰ 672022
VOLVO Pinfold Lane ℰ 670351

BRIDPORT Dorset **403** L 31 **The West Country G.** – pop. 10 615 – ECD : Thursday – ❀ 0308.

Envir. : Parnham House★★*AC*, N : 6 m. on A 3066.

🏌 Bridport and West Dorset, West Bay ℰ 22597, S : 1 ½ m.

🅱 32 South St. ℰ 24901 (summer only).

◆London 150 – Exeter 38 – Taunton 33 – Weymouth 19.

↑ **Roundham House,** Roundham Gdns, West Bay Rd, DT6 4BD, ℰ 22753, ⩬ – **TV** ⇔wc
⛩wc **P**. 🔼. ⅙
8 rm ⊊ 15.50/34.00 **t**.

↑ **Britmead House,** 154 West Bay Rd, DT6 4EG, S : 1 m. by B 3157 ℰ 22941 – **TV** ⇔wc **P**.
🔼 **VISA**
closed 23 December-9 February – **6 rm** ⊊ 18.00/30.00 **st**.

at Nettlecombe NE : 4 m. off A 3066 – ⊠ Bridport – ❀ 030 885 Powerstock :

☖ Marquis of Lorne ⅍, DT6 3SY, ℰ 236, ⩬ – ⛩wc **P**. ⅙
closed Christmas night – **6 rm** ⊊ 13.50/30.00 **t**. – SB 39.00/44.00 **st**.

at Shipton Gorge SE : 3 m. off A 35 – ⊠ ❀ 0308 Bridport :

✕✕ **Innsacre Farmhouse** ⅍ with rm, Shipton Lane, DT6 4LJ, N : 1 m. ℰ 56137, ⩬ – **TV**
⇔wc **P**. 🔼 **AE** ⑩ **VISA**
M 8.25/16.00 **st**. ⓛ 3.00 – **7 rm** ⊊ 16.00/40.00 **st**. – SB (except winter) 42.50/66.50 **st**.

at West Bexington SE : 7 ½ m. by B 3157 – ⊠ Bridport – ❀ 0308 Burton Bradstock :

🏠 **Manor,** Beach Rd, DT2 9DF, ℰ 897616, ⩻, ⩬ – **TV** ⇔wc ⛩wc **P**. 🔼 **AE** **VISA**. ⅙
M 8.45/10.95 **t**. ⓛ 2.50 – **10 rm** ⊊ 19.90/36.00 **t**. – SB 50.00/55.50 **st**.

at West Bay S : 1 ½ m. on B 3157 – ⊠ ❀ 0308 Bridport :

🏠 **Haddon House,** DT6 4EN, ℰ 23626 – **TV** ⇔wc ⛩wc ☎ **P**. 🔼 **AE** ⑩ **VISA**
M 6.75/12.00 **st**. – **13 rm** ⊊ 27.50/40.00 **st**.

at Chideock W : 3 m. on A 35 – ⊠ Bridport – ❀ 029 789 Chideock :

↑ **Betchworth House,** Main St., DT6 6JW, ℰ 478, ⩬ – ⛩wc **P**. ⅙
6 rm ⊊ 12.00/30.00 **st**.

✕✕ **Chideock House** with rm, Main St., DT6 6JN, ℰ 242 – **TV** ⇔wc **P**. 🔼 **AE** **VISA**
M *(closed Monday lunch)* (lunch by arrangement)(grill rest. Sunday and Monday) 10.25
st. and a la carte 10.65/12.95 **st**. ⓛ 2.50 – **9 rm** ⊊ 16.00/32.00 **st**. – SB 46.00/50.00 **st**.

See : Royal Pavilion★ (interior★★) *AC* CZ − Aquarium★ *AC* CZ **A** − Booth Museum (bird collection)★ BV **M** − Preston Manor (Chinese collection★) BV **D** − The Lanes CZ.

Envir. : Stanmer Park (site★) N : 3 ½ m. by A 27 CV − Clayton (church of St. John the Baptist : frescoes★ 14C) N : 6 m. by A 23 BV.

↖ East Brighton, Roedean ℰ 604838 CV − ↖ Dyke, Dyke Rd ℰ 079 156 (Poynings) 296, N : by Dyke Rd BV − ↖ Dyke Rd ℰ 556482 BV.

✈ Shoreham Airport : ℰ 452304 W : 8 m. by A 27 A.

🛈 Marlborough House, 54 Old Steine ℰ 23755 − Sea Front, Kings Rd ℰ 23755 (summer only).

🛈 at Hove : Town Hall, Norton Rd ℰ 775400.

♦London 53 − ♦Portsmouth 48 − ♦Southampton 61.

Plans on following pages

🏰 **Grand** (De Vere), Kings Rd, BN1 2FW, ℰ 21188, Telex 877410, ≤, 🖼 − 🛗 📺 ☎. 🏊. 🔄 🆎 ⓪ 𝘝𝘐𝘚𝘈 BZ **v**
M 12.00 **st.** and a la carte 12.00/24.00 **st.** ⅄ 5.00 − **160 rm** ⊊ 55.00/130.00 **st.**, **8 suites** 190.00/250.00 **st.** − SB 100.00 **st.**

🏨 **Brighton Metropole**, Kings Rd, BN1 2FU, ℰ 775432, Telex 877245, ≤, 🖼 − 🛗 📺 ☎ Ⓟ. 🏊. 🔄 🆎 ⓪ 𝘝𝘐𝘚𝘈. ⚘ BZ **s**
M 10.65/11.50 **t.** and a la carte ⅄ 4.25 − ⊊ 5.10 − **328 rm** 52.00/89.00 **t.**, **16 suites** 165.00/280.00 **t.** − SB (weekends only) 65.00 **st.**

🏨 **Norfolk Resort**, 149 Kings Rd, BN1 2PP, ℰ 738201, Telex 877247, 🖼 − 🛗 ▤ rest 📺 ☎ Ⓟ. 🏊. 🔄 🆎 ⓪ 𝘝𝘐𝘚𝘈 BZ **r**
M 7.75/11.50 **st.** and a la carte ⅄ 4.00 − **117 rm** ⊊ 43.00/58.00 **st.** − SB (weekends only) 54.00/58.00 **st.**

🏨 **Granville**, 125 King's Rd, BN1 2FA, ℰ 26302, ≤ − 🛗 📺 ⇌wc ☎. 🏊. 🔄 🆎 ⓪ 𝘝𝘐𝘚𝘈 BZ **n**
M 7.50/13.95 **t.** and a la carte ⅄ 3.30 − ⊊ 5.30 − **25 rm** 47.50/110.00 **t.** − SB (weekends only) 73.50/115.00 **st.**

🏨 **Old Ship**, King's Rd, BN1 1NR, ℰ 29001, Telex 877101, ≤ − 🛗 📺 ⇌wc ☎ ⇦. 🏊. CZ **n**
M 12.00/13.50 **st.** and a la carte − **153 rm** ⊊ 49.00/60.00 **st.**, **1 suite** 100.00 **st.** − SB (weekends only)(except Christmas and Easter) 80.00 **st.**

🏨 **Sheridan**, 64 King's Rd, BN1 1NA, ℰ 23221, ≤ − 🛗 📺 ⇌wc ☎. 🔄 🆎 ⓪ 𝘝𝘐𝘚𝘈 BZ **e**
M Seafood rest. ⅄ 3.00 − **58 rm** ⊊ 40.00/65.00 **st.**, **2 suites** 90.00/110.00 **st.** − SB 70.00/90.00 **st.**

🏨 **Royal Crescent**, 100 Marine Par., BN2 1AX, ℰ 606311, Telex 87253, ≤ − 🛗 📺 ⇌wc ☎. 🏊. 🔄 🆎 ⓪ 𝘝𝘐𝘚𝘈 CV **a**
M 6.50/8.50 **t.** and a la carte ⅄ 3.00 − **50 rm** ⊊ 35.00/50.00 **st.**, **4 suites** 60.00/80.00 **st.** − SB 40.00/60.00 **st.**

🏨 **Topps**, 17 Regency Sq., BN1 2FG, ℰ 729334 − 🛗 📺 ⇌wc ☎. 🔄 🆎 ⓪ 𝘝𝘐𝘚𝘈. ⚘ BZ **i**
closed 1 to 21 January − **M** (closed Sunday and Wednesday) (dinner only) 9.95 **st.** ⅄ 2.35 − **12 rm** ⊊ 30.00/70.00 **st.** − SB (weekends only) 75.00/92.00 **st.**

🏨 **The Twenty One**, 21 Charlotte St., BN2 1AG, ℰ 686450 − 📺 🛗wc. 🔄 🆎 ⓪ 𝘝𝘐𝘚𝘈 CV **i**
closed 25 December-mid January − **M** (closed dinner Sunday and Wednesday) (bar lunch)/dinner 18.00 **t.** ⅄ 3.50 − **6 rm** ⊊ 28.00/45.00 **st.** − SB (weekends only) 66.00/78.00 **st.**

🏠 **Marina House**, 8 Charlotte St., BN2 1AG, ℰ 605349 − 📺 🛗wc CV **n**
10 rm ⊊ 11.50/29.50 **st.**

XX **La Marinade**, 77 St. Georges Rd, Kemp Town, BN2 1EF, ℰ 600992 − ▤. 🔄 🆎 ⓪ 𝘝𝘐𝘚𝘈 CV **c**
closed Sunday dinner, Monday, 16 August-2 September and 25-26 December − **M** 6.50 **t.** (lunch) and a la carte 10.20/13.55 **t.** ⅄ 2.50.

XX **Chardonnay**, 33 Chesham Rd, Kemp Town, ℰ 672733, French rest. − 🆎 ⓪ 𝘝𝘐𝘚𝘈 CV **e**
closed Tuesday lunch, Sunday, Monday, 2 weeks February and 1 week August − **M** 6.50 **t.** (lunch) and a la carte 11.80/13.75 **t.** ⅄ 3.75.

XX **French Cellar**, 37 New England Rd, BN1 4GG, ℰ 603643, French rest. − 🔄 🆎 ⓪ 𝘝𝘐𝘚𝘈 CX **a**
closed Sunday, August and Bank Holidays − **M** (dinner only) 16.75 **t.** and a la carte 9.40/18.40 **t.** ⅄ 3.10.

XX **Stubbs**, 14 Ship St., BN1 1AD, ℰ 204005 − 🔄 🆎 ⓪ 𝘝𝘐𝘚𝘈 CZ **v**
closed lunch Monday and Saturday and 2 weeks January − **M** 8.95 **t.** (lunch) and a la carte 11.60/18.05 **t.** ⅄ 4.95.

X **Le Grandgousier**, 15 Western St., BN1 2PG, ℰ 772005, French rest. − 🆎 BY **x**
closed Saturday lunch, Sunday and 24 December-1 January − **M** 10.00 **st.** ⅄ 2.60.

X **Orchard**, 33 Western St., BN1 2PG, ℰ 776618 − 🔄 🆎 ⓪ 𝘝𝘐𝘚𝘈 BZ **o**
closed Sunday, Monday and 23 to 27 December − **M** (dinner only) 10.95 **t.** ⅄ 3.00.

X **Foggs**, 5 Little Western St., BN1 2PU, ℰ 735907 − 🔄 🆎 𝘝𝘐𝘚𝘈 BY **a**
M (dinner only) a la carte 9.00/12.00 **t.** ⅄ 2.50.

P.T.O. →

BRIGHTON AND HOVE

BUILT UP AREA

1 km
1/2 mile

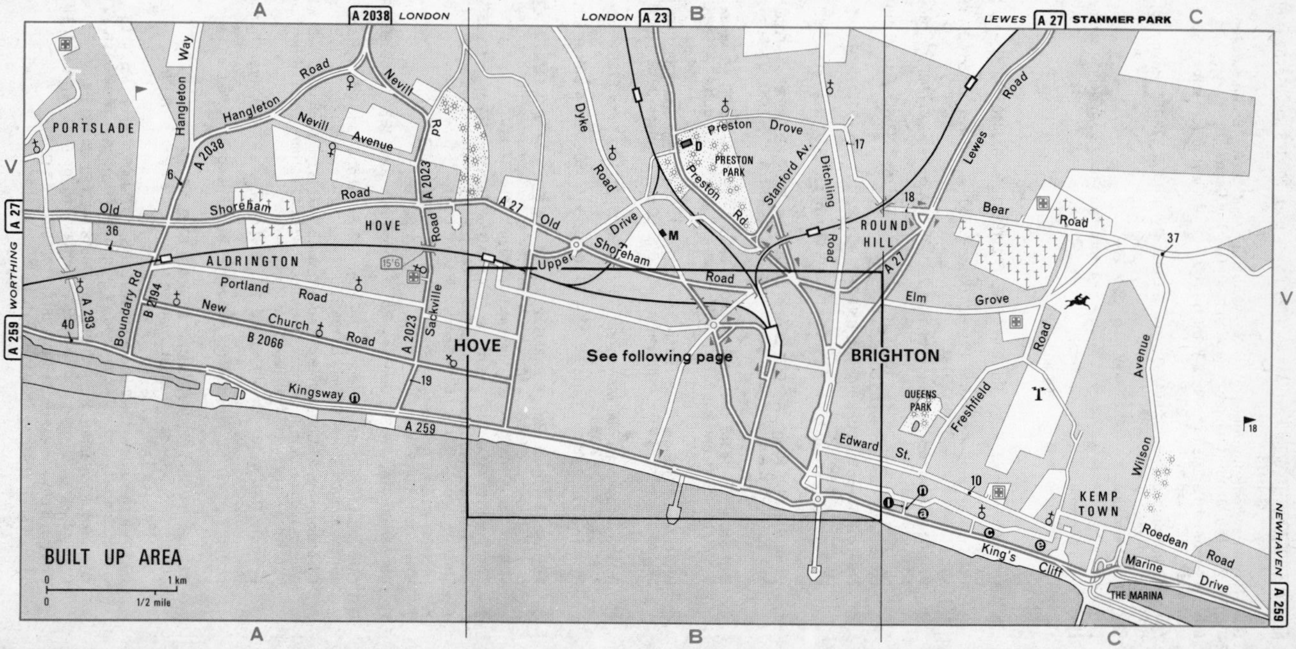

BRIGHTON
AND HOVE
CENTRE

For names of numbered streets,
see previous page.

117

at Hove – ⊠ Hove – ☺ 0273 Brighton :

🏨 **Dudley** (T.H.F.), Lansdowne Pl., BN3 1HQ, ℰ 736266, Telex 87537 – |注| ▤ rest 🖵 ☎ ⇦ 🅿.
🚲 ⚞ 🆔 *VISA*   AY o
M (buffet lunch)/dinner 12.75 **st.** and a la carte ⓝ 3.40 – ⌨ 5.65 – **80 rm** 49.00/62.00 **st., 2 suites**.

🏨 **Sackville** (Best Western), 189 Kingsway, BN3 4GU, ℰ 736292, Telex 877830, ≼ – |注| 🖵
⌨wc ☎ ⇦ 🚲 ⚞ 🆔 *VISA*   AV n
M 9.50 **t.** and a la carte – **45 rm** ⌨ 41.50/67.50 **st.** – SB (weekends only) 66.00/72.00 **st.**

🏨 **Courtlands**, 19-27 The Drive, BN3 3JE, ℰ 731055, Telex 87574, 🔲 – |注| 🖵 ⌨wc 洲wc ☎ 🅿.
⚞ 🆔 *VISA*   AY c
M 9.50/12.00 **t.** and a la carte ⓝ 3.50 – **57 rm** ⌨ 35.00/57.50 **st.** – SB (weekends only)
60.00/65.00 **st.**

🏨 **Whitehaven**, 34 Wilbury Rd, BN3 3JP, ℰ 778355, 🚗 – 🖵 ⌨wc 洲wc ☎. ⚞ 🆔 *VISA*. 😤
M *(closed Sunday lunch)* 7.50/8.50 **t.** and a la carte ⓝ 2.90 – **17 rm** ⌨ 40.00/55.00 **t.** – SB
(weekends only) 59.50/66.00 **st.**   AX c

XXX **Eaton**, 13 Eaton Gdns, BN3 3TN, ℰ 738921, English rest. – 🅿. ⚞ 🆔 *VISA*   AX a
closed Sunday dinner, Good Friday and Christmas Day – **M** 11.50/15.00 **t.** and a la carte ⓝ 3.50.

X **Fig Leaf**, 37 Waterloo St., BN3 1AY, ℰ 732383 – ▤. ⚞ *VISA*   BY i
closed Sunday, Monday, first 2 weeks September and first week January – **M** (dinner only)
12.50 **t.** ⓝ 2.50.

ALFA-ROMEO Old Shoreham Rd, Portslade ℰ 411020	MERCEDES-BENZ Victoria Rd ℰ 414911
AUSTIN-ROVER-DAIMLER-JAGUAR 200 Dyke Rd ℰ 553061	NISSAN 21/29 Preston Rd ℰ 685985
	RENAULT Stephenson Rd ℰ 692111
AUSTIN-ROVER 233 Preston Rd ℰ 553021	SKODA Longridge Av., Saltdean ℰ 31061
BMW 1a Lewes Rd ℰ 604131	VAUXHALL-OPEL Old Shoreham Rd, Portslade ℰ 422552
FIAT, LANCIA 100 Lewes Rd ℰ 508966	VOLVO, SUBARU, LANCIA 270-272 Old Shoreham Rd ℰ 737555
FORD 90-96 Preston Rd ℰ 550211	
MAZDA 373 Kingsway, Hove ℰ 413833	

BRIMSCOMBE Glos. 🔢🔢 N 28 – see Stroud.

When visiting the West Country,
*use the **Michelin Green Guide " England-The West Country ".***

– Detailed descriptions of places of interest
– Touring programmes by county
– Maps and street plans
– The history of the region
– Photographs and drawings of monuments, beauty spots, houses...

BRISTOL Avon 🔢🔢 M 29 **The West Country G.** – pop. 413 861 – ECD : Wednesday and
Saturday – ☺ 0272.

See : Site★★★ – Clifton Suspension Bridge★★★ AY – Cabot Tower Area★★ (The Georgian
House★★★ AC CZ – Red Lodge★ AC DZ D) – St. Nicholas Church Museum★★ AC DZ M1 – Theatre
Royal★★ DZ T – Quakers Friars★★ AC EZ K – St. Mary Redcliffe Church★★ DZ – Industrial
Museum★★ AY M2 – S.S Great Britain ★ AC AY A – Bristol Zoological Garden★★ AC AY –
Clifton Roman Catholic Cathedral off SS Peter and Paul★★ AY B – Cathedral★ DZ – Lord Mayors
Chapel★ AC DZ E – City Museum and Art Gallery★ AC CZ M – John Wesleys New Room★ AC DZ G.

Envir. : Blaise Castle House Museum★ AC AX M3 Blaise Hamlet★, NW : 5 m. by B4057 AX – at
Chew Magna★ Stanton Drew Stone Circles★ AC, S : 8 m. by A37 BY.

🆃8 Carsons Rd, Mangotsfield ℰ 565501, NE : 6 m. by B 4465 BX.

✈ Bristol Airport : ℰ 027 587 (Lulsgate) 4441/6, SW : 7 m. by A 38 AY.

🚂 ℰ 291001 ext 2479.

🅱 Colston House, Colston St. ℰ 293891/20767.

♦London 121 – ♦Birmingham 91.

Plans on following pages

🏩 **Holiday Inn,** Lower Castle St., Old Market, BS1 3AD, ℰ 294281, Telex 449720, 🔲 – |注| ▤
🖵 ☎ 👍 🅿. 🚲 ⚞ 🆔 *VISA*. 😤   EZ s
M (carving lunch) 11.95/12.50 **st.** and a la carte ⓝ 4.95 – ⌨ 6.50 – **284 rm** 48.50/60.50 **s.**

🏨 **Ladbroke Dragonara** (Ladbroke), Redcliffe Way, BS1 6NJ, ℰ 20044, Telex 449240 – |注|
▤ rest 🖵 ☎ 👍 🅿. 🚲 ⚞ 🆔 *VISA*. 😤   DEZ n
M *(closed Saturday)* a la carte approx. 10.95 ⓝ 3.70 – ⌨ 6.25 – **196 rm** 54.50/66.00 **st., 2 suites**
80.00 **st.** – SB (weekends only) 65.00 **st.**

🏨 **Grand** (Mt. Charlotte), Broad St., BS1 2EL, ℰ 291645, Telex 449889 – |注| 🖵 ☎ 🅿. 🚲 ⚞ 🆔
VISA   DZ a
M 8.95/9.50 **st.** ⓝ 3.00 – **178 rm** ⌨ 52.00/63.00 – SB (weekends only) 54.00 **st.**

🏬 **Unicorn** (Rank), Prince St., BS1 4QF, ☎ 294811, Telex 44315 – 📶 📺 ⇔wc ☎ ⇦. 🛗 🔼
AE 🛈 VISA — DZ **i**
M *(closed Saturday lunch)* 6.85/9.60 **st.** and a la carte ⅋ 3.00 – **192 rm** ⥿ 44.50/64.00 st.,
2 suites 72.50/80.00 **st.**

🏬 **St. Vincent Rocks,** Sion Hill, Clifton, BS8 4BB, ☎ 739251, Telex 444932, ≤ – 📺 ⇔wc
📶wc ☎ 🛗 AE 🛈 VISA — AY **c**
M *(closed Saturday lunch)* 8.95 **t.** and a la carte ⅋ 3.35 – **46 rm** ⥿ 44.00/54.00 **t.**

🏬 **Avon Gorge** (Mt. Charlotte), Sion Hill, Clifton, BS8 4LD, ☎ 738955, Telex 444237, ≤ – 📶 📺
⇔wc ☎ ☻. 🛗 🔼 AE 🛈 VISA — AY **x**
M 8.25 **st.** ⅋ 3.00 – **81 rm** ⥿ 41.50/55.25 **st.** – SB (weekends only) 54.00 **st.**

🏠 **Westbury Park,** 37 Westbury Rd, BS9 3AU, ☎ 620465 – 📺 ⇔wc 📶wc ☻ — AX **r**
M a la carte lunch/dinner 7.95 **t.** ⅋ 2.95 – **9 rm** ⥿ 18.50/32.00 **t.**

⬆ **Downlands,** 33 Henleaze Gdns, BS9 4HH, ☎ 621639 – 📺 — AX **s**
8 rm ⥿ 11.00/22.00 **s.**

⬆ **Oakfield,** 52-54 Oakfield Rd, Clifton, BS8 2BG, ☎ 735556 – ☻ — AY **n**
closed 23 December-1 January – **27 rm** ⥿ 14.50/22.00 **st.**

XXX **Harvey's,** 12 Denmark St., BS1 5DQ, ☎ 277665 – 🍽. 🔼 AE 🛈 VISA — DZ **c**
closed Saturday lunch, Sunday and Bank Holidays – **M** a la carte 16.00/21.55 **t.**

XX **Barbizon,** 43-45 Corn St., BS1 1HT, ☎ 22658, French rest. – 🔼 AE 🛈 VISA — DZ **x**
closed Saturday lunch, Sunday, August and Bank Holidays – **M** 7.75 **t.** (lunch) and a la carte
10.10/13.80 ⅋ 2.75.

XX **Du Gourmet,** 43 Whiteladies Rd, BS8 2LS, ☎ 736230 – 🔼 AE 🛈 VISA — AY **v**
closed Saturday lunch, Sunday, Monday and 24 December-1 January – **M** a la carte 9.35/14.55 **t.**
⅋ 2.70.

XX ✿ **Les Semailles,** 9 Druid Hill, Stoke Bishop, BS9 1EW, ☎ 686456, French rest. – 🔼
VISA — AX **a**
closed Sunday, Monday, last 2 weeks July, 25 December-1 January and Bank Holidays – **M**
(booking essential) 9.50 **st.** (lunch) and a la carte 16.40/23.40 **st.**
Spec. Hure de saumon d'Ecosse et fenouil en gaspacho de légumes frais (Summer), Rognons de veau en croûte
de sel aux échalotes et poireaux confits, Sabayon glacé aux pointes d'asperges confites (Summer).

XX **Rajdoot,** 83 Park St., BS1 5PJ, ☎ 28033, Indian rest. – 🔼 AE 🛈 VISA — CZ **u**
closed lunch Sunday and Bank Holidays – **M** 11.50 **t.** and a la carte 8.80/12.10 **t.** ⅋ 3.00.

XX **La Taverna Dell'Artista,** 33 King St., BS1 4DZ, ☎ 297712, Italian rest. – 🔼 AE VISA — DZ **s**
closed Sunday and Monday – **M** a la carte 5.65/11.95 **t.** ⅋ 2.75.

X **Bistro Twenty One,** 21 Cotham Road, Kingsdown, BS6 5TZ, ☎ 421744 — AY **z**
closed Sunday, Monday, 1 week Easter, 3 weeks August and 1 week Christmas – **M** (booking
essential)(dinner only) a la carte 10.15/13.25 **t.** ⅋ 2.85.

X **Ganges,** 368 Gloucester Rd, Horfield, BS7 8TP, ☎ 45234, Indian rest. – 🔼 AE 🛈 VISA — AX **e**
closed 25 and 26 December – **M** 6.50/9.50 **t.** and a la carte ⅋ 4.95.

X **Danton,** 2 Upper Byron Pl., The Triangle, BS8 1JY, ☎ 28314 – 🔼 AE 🛈 VISA — CZ **e**
closed Saturday lunch, Tuesday dinner, Sunday, 1 week Easter and 1 week August – **M** a la
carte 6.65/14.10 **t.** ⅋ 2.95.

X **Edwards,** 24 Alma Vale Rd, Clifton, BS8 2HY, ☎ 741533 – 🔼 VISA — AY **i**
*closed Saturday lunch, Sunday, 5 days Easter, last 2 weeks July, 5 days Christmas and Bank
Holidays* – **M** a la carte 5.70/12.10 **t.** ⅋ 2.25.

at Hambrook NE : 5 ½ m. by M 32 on A 4174 – ⊠ ✿ 0272 Bristol :

🏬 **Crest** (Crest), Filton Rd, BS16 1QX, ☎ 564242, Telex 449376, park – 📶 🍽 rest 📺 ☎ 🔖 ☻.
🛗 🔼 AE 🛈 VISA — BX **o**
M 12.25 **st.** and a la carte ⅋ 6.50 – ⥿ 6.30 – **151 rm** 57.00/68.50 **st.** – SB (weekends only)
78.00/82.00 **st.**

at Winterbourne N : 6 ¾ m. by M 32 on B 4058 – BX – ⊠ Bristol – ✿ 0454 Winterbourne :

XXX **Grange** ⬭ with rm, Northwoods, BS17 1RP, NW : 2 m. by B 4057 on B 4427 ☎ 777333, Telex
449205, ≤, 🍽, park – 📺 ⇔wc ☎ ☻. 🛗 🔼 AE 🛈 VISA
M 13.00/16.00 **t.** and a la carte 15.85/21.75 **t.** ⅋ 5.00 – **32 rm** 45.00/55.00 **t.**, **4 suites**
75.00/85.00 **t.** – SB (weekends only) 58.00/62.00 **st.**

MICHELIN Distribution Centre, Pennywell Rd, BS5 0UB, ☎ 559802 BY

AUSTIN-ROVER 74-80 Staple Hill Rd ☎ 654776
AUSTIN-ROVER-DAIMLER-JAGUAR, ROLLS
ROYCE 11-15 Merchants Rd. Clifton ☎ 730361
BMW 33 Zetland Rd ☎ 292402
CITROEN, FIAT 724 Fishponds Rd ☎ 657247
FIAT 168-176 Coronation Rd ☎ 631101
FORD 175-185 Muller Rd, Horfield ☎ 513333
FORD College Green ☎ 293881
FORD 135 High St. ☎ 670011
MAZDA, ALFA ROMEO 676 Fishponds Rd ☎ 655439

MERCEDES-BENZ 20 Whitehouse St. ☎ 669331
RENAULT Vale Lane ☎ 665070
RENAULT Station Rd, Kingswood ☎ 569911
RENAULT Marlborough St. ☎ 421816
TOYOTA Gloucester Rd, Patchway ☎ 693704
VAUXHALL-OPEL, BEDFORD Gloucester Rd ☎ 694331
VOLVO 84 Downend Rd ☎ 574474
VOLVO Berkeley Pl. ☎ 277355

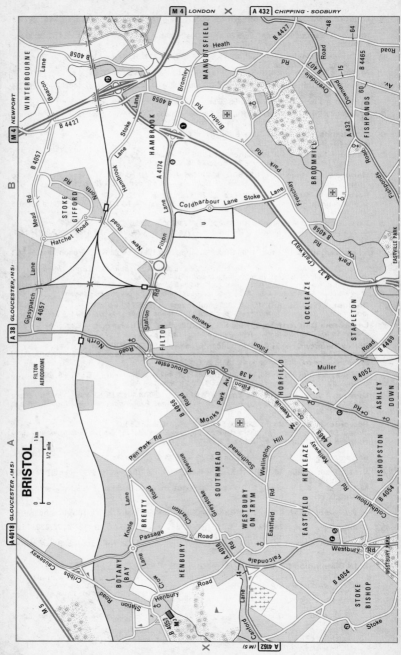

BRISTOL

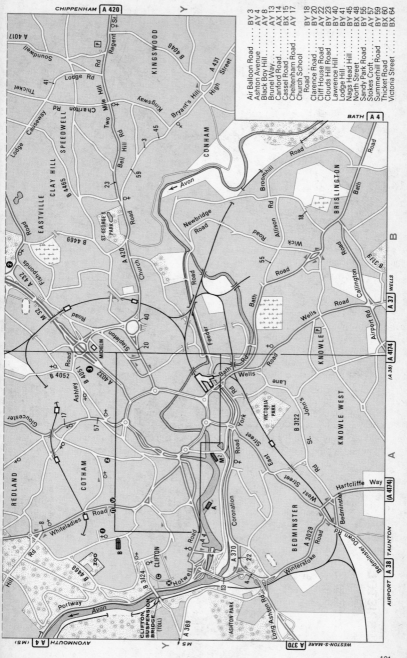

CHIPPENHAM A 420

Air Balloon Road . . . . . . BY 3
Ashton Avenue . . . . AV 4
Black Boy Hill . . . . AY 8
Brunel Way . . . . AX 13
Canford Road . . . . AX 14
Cassel Road . . . . BX 15
Cheltenham Road . . . . . . AY 17
Church School
Road . . . . BY 18
Clarence Road . . . . BY 20
Cliff House Road . . . . . . AY 22
Clouds Hill Road . . . . . . BY 23
Lawrence Hill . . . . BY 40
Lodge Hill . . . . BY 41
Nags Head Hill . . . . BY 45
North Street . . . . BX 48
Sandy Park Road . . . . . . BY 55
Stokes Croft . . . . AY 57
Summerhill Road . . . . . . BY 59
Thicket Road . . . . BX 60
Victoria Street . . . . BX 64

BATH A 4

121

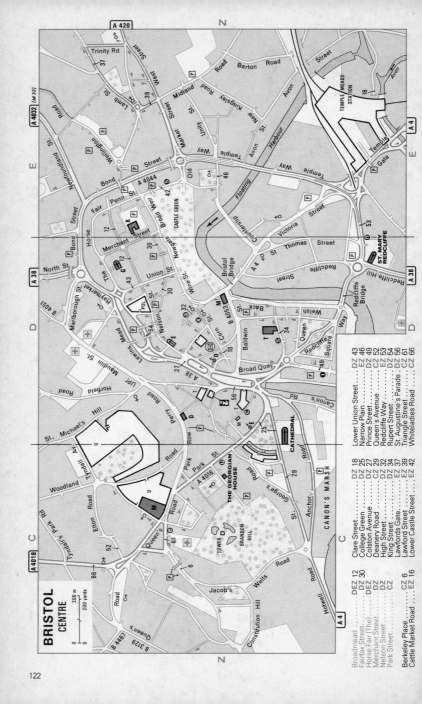

BRISTOL
CENTRE

0   200 m
0   200 yards

N

BRIXHAM Devon ⌧ J 32 The West Country G. – pop. 15 171 – ECD : Wednesday – ✆ 080 45.

Envir. : Berry Head★ (≼★★★), E : 2 m.

🛈 The Old Market House, The Quay ℰ 2861/8444.

♦London 230 – Exeter 30 – ♦Plymouth 32 – Torquay 8.

🏨 **Quayside,** 41-49 King St., TQ5 9TJ, ℰ 55751, ≼ harbour – 📺 ⇱wc ☎ 🅿. ⚞ 𝖠𝖤 ⓞ 𝘝𝘐𝘚𝘈. ✿

 M (bar lunch Monday to Saturday)/dinner 10.55 **t.** and a la carte ⌂ 3.50 – **32 rm** ⊠ 24.00/62.00 **t.** – SB 43.00/80.00 **st.**

🕿 Smuggler's Haunt, 1 Church Hill East, TQ5 8HH, ℰ 3050 – ⇱wc
 14 rm.

AUSTIN-ROVER Milton St. ℰ 2474 RENAULT New Rd ℰ 2266
FORD Churston Ferrers ℰ 0803 (Churston) 842245

BROAD CAMPDEN Glos. – see Chipping Campden.

BROADSTAIRS Kent ⌧ Y 29 – pop. 21 551 (inc. St. Peter's) – ECD : Wednesday – ✆ 0843 Thanet.

See : Bleak House (stayed in by Charles Dickens) *AC.*

🛈 Pierremont Hall, 67 High St. ℰ 68399.

♦London 78 – ♦Dover 21 – Maidstone 47.

🏨 **Castlemere,** 15 Western Esplanade, CT10 1TD, ℰ 61566, ≼, ☞ – 📺 ⇱wc ▥wc ☎ 🅿. ⚞ 𝘝𝘐𝘚𝘈

 M *(closed for lunch November-April)* (bar lunch)/dinner 9.50 **st.** ⌂ 2.85 – **36 rm** ⊠ 22.10/49.00 **st.** – SB 50.50/58.20 **st.**

🏠 **Royal Albion,** Albion St., CT10 1LU, ℰ 68071, Telex 965761, ≼, ☞ – 📺 ⇱wc ▥wc ☎ 🅿. ⚞. 𝖠𝖤 ⓞ 𝘝𝘐𝘚𝘈

 M 7.50/9.75 **t.** and a la carte ⌂ 2.50 – **19 rm** ⊠ 35.00/60.00 **st.** – SB (except July and August) 96.00/100.00 **st.**

⇞ **Bay Tree,** 12 Eastern Esplanade, CT10 1DR, ℰ 62502, ≼ – 🅿
 9 rm ⊠ 12.75/28.00 **st.**

⇞ **Keston Court,** 14 Ramsgate Rd, CT10 1PS, ℰ 62401 – 🅿. 𝖠𝖤. ✿
 9 rm ⊠ 10.50/22.00.

XX **Marchesi,** 18 Albion St., CT10 1LU, ℰ 62481, ≼ – 🅿. ⚞ 𝖠𝖤 ⓞ 𝘝𝘐𝘚𝘈
 closed 26 to 28 December – **M** 7.25/9.50 **t.** and a la carte 10.35/13.85 **t.** ⌂ 2.50.

AUDI, VW St. Peter's Rd ℰ 62333 HYUNDAI Ramsgate Rd ℰ 63531

BROADSTONE Dorset ⌧ ⌧ O 31 – see Wimborne Minster.

BROADWATER Herts. – see Stevenage.

For business or tourist interest :
MICHELIN Red Guide : Main Cities EUROPE.

BROADWAY Heref. and Worc. ⌧ ⌧ O 27 – pop. 1 931 – ECD : Thursday – ✆ 0386.

🛈 The Green ℰ 852937 (summer only).

♦London 93 – ♦Birmingham 36 – Cheltenham 15 – Worcester 22.

🏰 **Lygon Arms,** High St., WR12 7DU, ℰ 852255, Telex 338260, « Part 15C inn », ☞, ✿ – 📺 ☎ 🕹 ⇦☞ 🅿. ⚞ 𝖠𝖤 ⓞ 𝘝𝘐𝘚𝘈
 M 13.50/21.00 **t.** and a la carte – ⊠ 6.00 – **64 rm** 70.00/115.00 **t.**, **5 suites** 165.00/200.00 **t.**

🏨 **Broadway,** The Green, WR12 7AB, ℰ 852401, ☞ – 📺 ⇱wc ☎ 🅿. ⚞ 𝖠𝖤 ⓞ 𝘝𝘐𝘚𝘈. ✿
 M (bar lunch Monday to Saturday)/dinner 10.95 **t.** and a la carte ⌂ 2.70 – **24 rm** ⊠ 24.00/56.00 **st.** – SB (winter only)(weekends only) 44.00/76.00 **st.**

🏠 **Collin House** ⌂, Collin Lane, WR12 7PB, NW : 1 ¼ m. by A 44 ℰ 858354, ≼, « Country house atmosphere », ⬈ heated, ☞ – ⇱wc 🅿. ⚞ 𝘝𝘐𝘚𝘈. ✿
 closed 24 to 26 December – **M** (bar lunch Monday to Saturday)/dinner 13.00 **st.** ⌂ 2.60 – **7 rm** ⊠ 28.50/67.00 **st.** – SB (November-March) 67.00/72.00 **st.**

⇞ **Half Way House,** 89 High St., WR12 7AL, ℰ 852237 – 🅿
 6 rm ⊠ 17.00/30.00 **s.**

XX **Hunters Lodge,** High St., WR12 7DT, ℰ 853247, ☞ – 🅿. ⚞ 𝖠𝖤 ⓞ 𝘝𝘐𝘚𝘈
 closed Sunday dinner, Monday, first 2 weeks February and first 2 weeks August – **M** 7.50 **t.** (lunch) and a la carte 14.55/16.65 **t.** ⌂ 2.95.

 at Willersey (Glos.) N : 2 m. on A 46 – ⌧ ✆ 0386 Broadway :

🏠 **Old Rectory** ⌂ without rest., Church St., WR12 7PM, ℰ 853729, « Tasteful decor », ☞ – 📺 ⇱wc ▥wc 🅿. ⚞ 𝘝𝘐𝘚𝘈. ✿
 6 rm ⊠ 29.00/59.00 **t.**

at Willersey Hill (Glos.) E : 2 m. by A 44 – ⊠ ✿ 0386 Broadway :

🏛 **Dormy House,** WR12 7LF, ℰ 852711, Telex 338275, ☞ – 🖸 ☎ 🄿 🄿 ⅍ 🖭 🝌 ⓪ 𝘝𝘐𝘚𝘈 ⅍
   M (bar lunch Saturday) 14.50/19.00 **t.** and a la carte – **48 rm** ⊑ 45.00/90.00, **3 suites**
   99.00/140.00 – SB (weekends only) 98.00 **st.**

at Buckland (Glos.) SW : 2 ¼ m. by A 46 – ⊠ ✿ 0386 Broadway :

🏛 **Buckland Manor** ⑤, WR12 7LY, ℰ 852626, « Country house atmosphere », ⚓ heated, ☞,
   park, ⅍ – 🖸 ☎ 🄿 𝘝𝘐𝘚𝘈 ⅍
   closed 3 weeks January-February – **M** a la carte 14.60/23.15 **t.** – **11 rm** ⊑ 85.00/130.00 **t.**

AUSTIN-ROVER Willersey ℰ 852338

■ BROCKENHURST Hants. 408 404 P 31 – pop. 2 939 – ECD : Wednesday – ✿ 0590 Lymington.
🔝 Brockenhurst Manor, Sway Rd ℰ 233332, S : ¾ m. on B 3055.
♦London 99 – Bournemouth 17 – ♦Southampton 14 – Winchester 27.

🏛 **Rhinefield House** ⑤, Rhinefield Rd, W : 3 ½ m. on Rhinefield Way ℰ 22922,
   Telex 266628, ⚓ heated, 🖾, ☞, park – 🖸 ⇔wc ☎ 🄿 ⅍ 🖭 🝌 ⓪ 𝘝𝘐𝘚𝘈 ⅍
   M 8.50/23.50 **st.** and a la carte ⅃ 3.60 – **32 rm** ⊑ 47.50/62.50 **st.** – SB 64.50/80.50 **st.**

🏛 **Ladbroke Balmer Lawn** (Ladbroke), Lyndhurst Rd, SO42 7ZB, ℰ 23116, Telex 477649, ≼,
   ⚓ heated, ☞, ⅍, squash – 🕮 🖸 ⇔wc ☎ 🄿 ⅍ 🖭 𝘝𝘐𝘚𝘈 ⅍
   M (closed Saturday lunch) 9.00 ⅃ 3.70 – **58 rm** ⊑ 41.50/60.00 **st.** – SB (weekends only) 69.50 **st.**

🏛 **Carey's Manor,** Lyndhurst Rd, SO42 7RH, ℰ 23551, Telex 47442, Dancing Friday and Saturday, 🖾, ☞ – 🖸 ⇔wc ☎ & 🄿 ⅍ 🖭 🝌 ⓪ 𝘝𝘐𝘚𝘈 ⅍
   M 9.70/12.70 **t.** and a la carte ⅃ 3.90 – **57 rm** ⊑ 43.95/63.90 **t.** – SB 73.70/79.70 **st.**

🏛 **Forest Park,** Rhinefield Rd, SO42 7ZG, ℰ 22844, Group Telex 477802, ⚓ heated, ☞, ⅍ –
   🖸 ⇔wc ☎ 🄿 🖭 🝌 ⓪ 𝘝𝘐𝘚𝘈 ⅍
   M 7.45/15.85 **t.** and a la carte – **36 rm** ⊑ 34.00/46.00 **t.** – SB 63.00/66.00 **st.**

🏛 **Whitley Ridge** ⑤, Beaulieu Rd, SO42 7QL, E : 1 m. on B 3055 ℰ 22354, ≼, ☞, ⅍ – 🖸
   ⇔wc 🝌wc 🄿 🖭 🝌 ⓪ 𝘝𝘐𝘚𝘈 ⅍
   closed January – **M** (bar lunch residents only)/dinner 10.50 **st.** and a la carte ⅃ 3.25 – **15 rm**
   ⊑ 33.00/55.00 **st.** – SB (except Bank Holidays) 52.00/68.00 **st.**

🏛 **Watersplash,** The Rise, SO41 7ZP, ℰ 22344, ⚓ heated, ☞ – ⇔wc & 🄿 ⅍ 🖭
   25 rm ⊑ 21.00/45.00 **t.** – SB 48.00/56.00 **st.**

XX **Le Poussin** with rm, 57-59 Brookley Rd, SO42 7RB, ℰ 23063, French rest. – ⇔wc 🝌wc 🖭
   𝘝𝘐𝘚𝘈
   closed Monday lunch and Sunday – **M** 8.95/16.95 **t.** and a la carte ⅃ 3.25 – **4 rm** ⊑ 25.00/40.00
   – SB 75.00/100.00 **st.**

AUSTIN-ROVER Sway Rd ℰ 23344   PEUGEOT Waters Green ℰ 23113
MAZDA Brockley Rd ℰ 23122   SAAB, HONDA 24 Brookley Rd ℰ 23464

■ BROME Suffolk 404 X 26 – pop. 265 – ⊠ ✿ 0379 Eye.
♦London 86 – ♦Cambridge 50 – ♦Ipswich 20 – ♦Norwich 22.

🏛 **Oaksmere** ⑤, IP23 8AJ, ℰ 870326, « Part 16C country house », ☞, park – 🖸 🝌wc 🄿 🖭
   🝌 ⓪ 𝘝𝘐𝘚𝘈
   M a la carte 11.40/18.45 **t.** ⅃ 4.50 – **5 rm** ⊑ 29.50/49.50 **st.** – SB (weekends only) 55.00/65.00 **st.**

■ BROMLEY CROSS Greater Manchester 402 404 M 23 – see Bolton.

■ BROMPTON BY SAWDON North Yorks. 402 S 21 – pop. 1 827 – ⊠ ✿ 0723 Scarborough.
♦London 242 – ♦Kingston-upon-Hull 44 – Scarborough 8 – York 31.

XX **Brompton Forge,** YO13 9DP, ℰ 85409 – 🄿
   closed lunch Tuesday, Friday and Saturday, Sunday dinner, Monday and 2 weeks February –
   M 8.00/11.00 **st.** ⅃ 3.20.

■ BROMSGROVE Heref. and Worc. 403 404 N 26 – pop. 24 576 – ECD : Thursday – ✿ 0527.
🄰 47-49 Worcester Rd ℰ 31809 – ♦London 117 – ♦Birmingham 14 – ♦Bristol 71 – Worcester 13.

🏛 **Perry Hall** (Embassy), 13 Kidderminster Rd, B61 7JN, ℰ 31976, ☞ – 🖸 ⇔wc 🝌wc ☎ 🄿
   ⅍ 🖭 🝌 ⓪ 𝘝𝘐𝘚𝘈
   M 7.50/8.50 **st.** and a la carte ⅃ 2.55 – ⊑ 5.00 – **52 rm** 38.00/47.50 **st.** – SB (weekends only)
   50.00/55.00 **st.**

🏛 **Pine Lodge,** 85 Kidderminster Rd, B61 9AB, W : 1 m. on A 448 ℰ 33033, ⚓ heated, ☞ – 🖸
   ⇔wc ☎ 🄿 🖭
   M (grill rest. only) 8.50/9.50 **st.** and a la carte ⅃ 3.20 – **59 rm** ⊑ 34.00/44.00 **st.**

XXX **Grafton Manor** ⑤ with rm, Grafton Lane, B61 7HA, SW : 1 ¾ m. by Worcester Rd ℰ 31525,
   « 16C and 18C manor », ⸙, ☞, park – 🖸 ⇔wc ☎ 🄿 🖭 🝌 ⓪ 𝘝𝘐𝘚𝘈 ⅍
   M (dinner only and Sunday lunch)/dinner 19.25 **t.** ⅃ 3.75 – ⊑ 5.75 – **8 rm** 44.00/80.00 **t.**,
   1 suite 110.00 **t.**

AUSTIN-ROVER 52 Birmingham Rd ℰ 72212   RENAULT 17-21 Worcester Rd ℰ 79898
LADA Windsor St. ℰ 75210   VAUXHALL-OPEL 137 Birmingham Rd ℰ 71244
PEUGEOT-TALBOT 184 Worcester Rd ℰ 72552

BROOK Hants. 403 404 P 31 – ECD : Tuesday – ✉ Lyndhurst – ☎ 0703 Southampton.
18, Bramshaw ✆ 813433.
♦London 92 – Bournemouth 24 – ♦Southampton 14.

Bell, SO34 7HE, ✆ 812214, 18, – TV wc P. AE VISA
M 7.50/9.75 **t.** and a la carte 4.20 – **12 rm** 27.00/54.00 **t.**

BROOKMANS PARK Herts. 404 T 28 – pop. 4 020 – ☎ 0707 Potters Bar.
♦London 21 – Luton 21.

Villa Rosa, 3 Great North Rd, SE : 1 ¾ m. on A 1000 ✆ 51444, Italian rest. – P. AE VISA
closed Saturday lunch and Sunday – **M** a la carte 8.50/16.90 **t.** 3.00.

BROUGHTON Lancs. 402 L 22 – see Preston.

BROXTED Essex – see Thaxted.

BRUSHFORD Somerset 403 J 30 – pop. 486 – ✉ ☎ 0398 Dulverton.
♦London 195 – Exeter 24 – Minehead 18 – Taunton 24.

Carnarvon Arms, TA22 9AE, ✆ 23302, heated, , , park, – TV wc P. VISA
M 6.75/12.00 **t.** and a la carte 2.95 – **26 rm** 28.00/60.00 **t.**, **1 suite** 40.00/80.00 **t.** – SB (June-October)(except Bank Holidays) 55.00/62.00 **st.**

Three Acres Captain's Country , TA22 9AR, ✆ 23426, – wc P
25 March-December – **M** (bar lunch)/dinner 10.00 **s.** 2.20 – **7 rm** 16.00/34.00 **s.**

BRUTON Somerset 403 404 M 30 – pop. 1 759 – ☎ 0749.
♦London 118 – ♦Bristol 27 – Bournemouth 44 – Salisbury 35 – Taunton 36.

Grants with rm, High St., BA10 0EQ, ✆ 813395 – wc. VISA.
closed January – **M** *(closed Sunday and Monday)* (dinner only) 12.95 **t.** 2.80 – **3 rm** 14.00/24.00 **t.**

Clogs, 95 High St., BA10 0AR, ✆ 812255, Dutch Indonesian rest.
closed Monday lunch, Sunday, 1 week April and 1 week September – **M** (dinner only)(booking essential) a la carte 9.50/12.50 **t.** 2.90.

BRYHER Cornwall 403 ⑳ – see Scilly (Isles of).

BRYNBUGA = Usk.

BUCKDEN Cambs. 404 T 27 – ✉ ☎ 0480 Huntingdon.
♦London 65 – Bedford 15 – ♦Cambridge 20 – Northampton 31.

George, Great North Rd, PE18 9XA, ✆ 810307, – TV wc ☎ P
15 rm.

BUCKDEN North Yorks. 402 N 21 – pop. 223 – ✉ Skipton – ☎ 075 676 Kettlewell.
♦London 241 – Kendal 47 – ♦Leeds 44 – Preston 55 – York 63.

Low Greenfield , Langstrothdale Chase, BD23 5JN, NW : 6 ¾ m. by Hawes road ✆ 858, ≤, « Converted farmhouse », , , park – P
Easter-October except August – **3 rm** 15.00/30.00 **st.**

BUCKFASTLEIGH Devon 403 I 32 The West Country G. – pop. 2 355 – ECD : Wednesday – ☎ 0364.
See : Buckfast Abbey (the Sacrament Chapel★).
♦London 223 – Exeter 23 – ♦Plymouth 20.

Furzeleigh Mill, Dart Bridge, TQ11 0JP, NE : ¾ m. on old A 38 ✆ 43476, – wc wc P
16 rm.

BUCKHURST HILL Essex 404 ㊸ – pop. 11 147 – ECD : Wednesday – ☎ 01 London.
♦London 13 – Chelmsford 25.

Plan : see Greater London (North-East)

Roebuck (T.H.F.), North End, IG9 5QY, ✆ 505 4636 – TV wc ☎ P. . AE VISA
M 8.50/10.00 **st.** and a la carte 3.40 – 5.65 – **23 rm** 43.00/53.00 **st.** – SB (weekends only) 48.00/60.00 **st.**
GU **u**

Do not lose your way in Europe, use the Michelin
Main Road maps, scale : 1 inch : 16 miles.

BUCKINGHAM Bucks. 🔢🔢 Q 27 — pop. 6 439 — ECD : Thursday — ☏ 0280.

Envir. : Claydon House★ (Rococo interior★★ : Chinese Room★★ staircase★★★, Florence Nightingale Museum) *AC*, SE : 8 m. — Stowe School 18C (south front★, Marble Saloon★, park : monuments★ 18C, ⬉★ from the Lake Pavilions) *AC*.

♦London 64 — ♦Birmingham 61 — Northampton 20 — ♦Oxford 25.

🏨 **White Hart** (T.H.F.), Market Sq., MK18 1NL, ☏ 815151 — 📺 🛁wc ☎ 🅿. 🅰. 🔜 AE ⓞ VISA
M 5.25/8.95 **st.** and a la carte 🍷 2.95 — 🖵 5.65 — **19 rm** 42.50/52.00 **st.**

AUSTIN-ROVER Motorworks ☏ 812121   VAUXHALL-OPEL School Lane ☏ 814242

BUCKLAND Glos. 🔢🔢 O 27 — see Broadway (Heref. and Worc.).

BUCKLAND IN THE MOOR Devon The West Country G. — pop. 93 — ✉ ☏ 0364 Ashburton.

♦London 225 — Exeter 25 — ♦Plymouth 28.

🏠 **Buckland Hall** 📶, TQ13 7HL, ☏ 52679, ⬉ countryside and Holne Moor, 🐎, park — 📺 🛁wc 🅿. 🔜 AE VISA
M (bar lunch)/dinner 9.25 **t.** — **6 rm** 🖵 21.00/37.00 **t.** — SB 44.00/55.50 **st.**

BUCKLERS HARD Hants. 🔢🔢 P 31 — see Beaulieu.

BUCKLOW HILL Cheshire 🔢🔢🔢 M 24 — see Knutsford.

BUDE Cornwall 🔢 G 31 The West Country G. — pop. 2 679 — ECD : Thursday — ☏ 0288.

See : The breakwater★★ ⬉ ★ from Compass Point★.

Envir. : Poughill★ (Church★★), N : 2 ½ m. — at Poundstock★ (⬉★★, church★★, Gildhouse★), S : 4 ½ m. — Morwenstowe Church★ (cliffs★★), N : 11 m. — Stratton Church★, E : 1 ½ m. — Launcells Church★, E : 3 m. — Kilkhampton Church★, NE : 5 ½ m. — Jacobstowe Church★, S : 7 m.

🏌 Burn View ☏ 2006 — 🏌 Holsworthy ☏ 0409 (Holsworthy) 253177, E : 8 ½ m.

🅩 The Crescent car park ☏ 4240 (summer only) — A 39, Stamford Hill, Stratton ☏ 3781 (summer only).

♦London 252 — Exeter 51 — ♦Plymouth 44 — Truro 53.

🏨 **Strand** (T.H.F.), The Strand, EX23 3RA, ☏ 3222 — 🛗 📺 🛁wc ☎ 🅿. 🔜 AE ⓞ VISA
M (bar lunch)/dinner 8.75 **st.** and a la carte 🍷 3.40 — 🖵 5.65 — **40 rm** 34.00/48.00 **st.**

🏨 **Hartland,** Hartland Terr., EX23 8JY, ☏ 2509, ⬉, ⬛ heated — 🛗 📺 🛁wc 🅿
Easter-October and 4 days at Christmas — **M** 6.90/7.80 **t.** and a la carte 🍷 2.70 — **29 rm** 🖵 23.00/44.00 **t.**

🏠 **Camelot,** Downs View, EX23 8RS, ☏ 2361, 🐎 — 📺 🛁wc 🍴wc 🅿. 🔜 VISA. 🐾
March-October — **M** (bar lunch)/dinner 10.00 **t.** 🍷 3.00 — **14 rm** 🖵 22.00/44.00 **t.**

🏠 **Bude Haven,** Flexbury Av., EX23 8NS, ☏ 2305, 🐎 — 🛁wc 🍴wc 🅿. 🔜 VISA
closed mid December-mid January — **M** (bar lunch)/dinner 6.50 **st.** and a la carte 🍷 2.25 — **11 rm** 🖵 12.50/31.00 **st.**

🏠 **Reeds** 📶, Northcott Mouth road, Poughill, EX23 9EL, NE : 1 ¼ m. ☏ 2841, 🐎, park — 🛁wc 🅿. 🐾
closed Tuesday to Friday and Christmas Day — **M** (dinner only) 17.50 **st.** — **3 rm** 🖵 30.00/50.00 **st.**

🏡 **Teeside,** 2 Burn View, EX23 8BY, ☏ 2351 — 🐾
March-October — **6 rm** 🖵 8.00/18.00.

🏡 **Meva Gwin,** Upton, EX23 0LY, S : 1¼ m. on coast road ☏ 2347, ⬉ — 🛁wc 🅿. 🐾
18 April-26 September — **13 rm** 🖵 10.00/26.00 **st.**

AUSTIN-ROVER Bencoolen Rd ☏ 2146   FORD, POLSKI-FIAT Bencoolen Rd ☏ 4616

BUDLEIGH SALTERTON Devon 🔢 K 32 The West Country G. — pop. 4 346 — ECD : Thursday — ☏ 039 54.

🅩 Rolle Mews Car Park, Fore St. ☏ 5275 (summer only).

♦London 215 — Exeter 16 — ♦Plymouth 55.

🏡 **Long Range,** 5 Vales Rd, by Raleigh Rd, EX9 6HS, ☏ 3321, 🐎 — 📺 🅿. 🐾
closed winter — **9 rm** 🖵 10.00/29.00 **t.**

AUSTIN-ROVER 10-12 High St. ☏ 2277

BUILTH WELLS (LLANFAIR-YM-MUALLT) Powys 🔢 J 27 — pop. 2 225 — ☏ 0982.

🅩 Groe car park ☏ 553307 (summer only).

♦London 197 — Brecon 22 — ♦Cardiff 63 — ♦Swansea 63 — Shrewsbury 70.

🏠 **Caer Beris Manor** 📶, Garth Rd, LD2 3NP, W : ¾ m. by A 483 ☏ 552601, ⬉, « 19C mock-tudor house », ⬅, park — 🛁wc 🍴wc 🅿
15 rm.

🏡 **Llanfair,** 1, The Strand, LD2 3BG, ☏ 553253, 🐎 — 📺 🍴wc 🅿. VISA. 🐾
March-November — **9 rm** 🖵 8.00/19.00.

FIAT Garth ☏ 05912 287   PEUGEOT May Rd ☏ 0982 553647
FORD Station Rd ☏ 0982 552639

BUNWELL Norfolk 404 X 26 – pop. 797 – ECD : Monday and Wednesday – ☎ 095 389.
♦London 102 – ♦Cambridge 51 – ♦Norwich 16.

   🏠 **Bunwell Manor** ⚘, Bunwell St., NR16 1QU, NW : 1 m. ℰ 317, 🍽 – 📺 ⌷wc �📶wc 🅿. 🖼
      AE VISA
      M 6.00/10.00 st. and a la carte ⬧ 2.30 – **11 rm** ⊇ 26.00/38.00 t. – SB 90.00/94.00 st.

BURFORD Oxon. 403 404 P 28 – pop. 1 371 – ECD : Wednesday – ☎ 099 382.
See : St. John's Church★ 12C-14C – Envir. : Swinbrook (church : Fettiplace Monuments★)
E : 3 ½ m. – Cotswold Wildlife Park★ AC, S : 2 m. – Northleach : SS. Peter and Paul's Church :
South Porch and the brasses★ (Perpendicular) NW : 7 ½ m.
🛈 Swindon Rd ℰ 2583, S : ½ m. on A 361.
🎭 The Brewery, Sheep St. ℰ 3558.
♦London 76 – ♦Birmingham 55 – Gloucester 32 – ♦Oxford 20.

   🏠🏠 **Bay Tree**, Sheep St., OX8 4LW, ℰ 3137, 🍽 – 📺 ⌷wc ⚑wc 🅿. 🖼 AE VISA ⌘
      closed 25 and 26 December – **M** 6.50/15.50 t. ⬧ 2.95 – **22 rm** ⊇ 24.50/60.00 t.. **1 suite** 60.00 t.
      – SB (November-April) 60.00/75.00 st.

   🏠 **Golden Pheasant**, High St., OX8 4RJ, ℰ 3223 – 📺 ⌷wc ⚑wc 🍴 ⅙ 🖼 AE VISA ⌘
      M 9.25/11.75 st. and a la carte ⬧ 3.75 – **12 rm** ⊇ 25.00/42.50 st. – SB 42.50/62.50 st.

   🏠 **Lamb Inn**, Sheep St., OX8 4LR, ℰ 3155, 🍽 – ⌷wc ⚑wc
      M (closed Sunday dinner to non-residents) (bar lunch Monday to Saturday)/dinner 16.00 st.
      ⬧ 2.95 – **14 rm** ⊇ 20.00/65.00 st. – SB (weekends only) 48.00/66.00 st.

   🏠 **Inn For All Seasons**, The Barringtons, OX8 4TN, W : 3 ¼ m. on A 40 ℰ 045 14 (Win-
      drush) 324, 🍽 – 📺 ⌷wc 🅿. 🖼 AE VISA
      M (bar lunch Monday to Friday)/dinner 10.50 t.and a la carte ⬧ 2.65 – **9 rm** ⊇ 35.00/55.00 t. –
      SB (November-July) 59.00/64.00 st.

   🏠 **Corner House**, High St., OX8 4RJ, ℰ 3151 – 📺 ⌷wc ⚑wc
      March-October – **M** (closed Sunday lunch) a la carte 5.30/9.50 t. ⬧ 1.60 – **9 rm** ⊇ 19.00/34.00 t.

   🏠 **Highway**, High St., OX8 4RG, ℰ 2136 – 📺 ⌷wc ⚑wc. 🖼 AE ⑩ VISA
      M (bar lunch)/dinner 11.00 st. ⬧ 3.25 – **10 rm** ⊇ 20.00/37.00 st. – SB 50.00/55.00 st.

BURGHFIELD Berks. 403 404 Q 29 – see Reading.

BURLEY Hants. 403 404 O 31 – pop. 1 492 – ECD : Wednesday – ✉ Ringwood – ☎ 042 53.
🛈₉ ℰ 2431.
♦London 102 – Bournemouth 17 – ♦Southampton 17 – Winchester 30.

   🏠 **Moorhill House** ⚘, BH24 4AG, ℰ 3285, 🖾, 🍽 – 📺 ⌷wc ⚑wc ☎ 🅿. 🖼 AE ⑩ VISA
      M (lunch by arrangement)/dinner 11.00 st. ⬧ 3.40 – **24 rm** ⊇ 24.00/48.00 st. – SB 48.00/64.00 st.

   🏠 **Tree House**, The Cross, Ringwood Rd, BH24 4BA, ℰ 3448, 🍽 – 📺 ⚑wc 🅿. 🖼 AE ⑩ VISA
      M (closed Sunday dinner) (bar lunch)/dinner 6.00 t. ⬧ 2.75 – **11 rm** ⊇ 18.50/49.00 t. – SB
      (November-Easter) 46.00 st.

BURN BRIDGE North Yorks. – see Harrogate.

BURNHAM Bucks. 404 S 29 – ECD : Thursday – ☎ 062 86.
♦London 33 – ♦Oxford 37 – Reading 17.

   🏠🏠 **Grovefield** ⚘, Taplow Common Rd, SL1 8LP, ℰ 3131, 🍽 – 📱 📺 ⌷wc ☎ 🅿. 🎿. 🖼 AE
      ⑩ VISA
      M (closed Saturday lunch, Sunday dinner and Bank Holidays) 10.00 t. (lunch) and a la carte
      12.85/19.95 t. ⬧ 2.75 – **33 rm** ⊇ 55.00/65.00 t. – SB (weekends only) 61.00 st.

   🏠🏠 **Burnham Beeches**, Grove Rd, Burnham Beeches, SL1 8DP, NW : 1 m. by Britwell Rd ℰ
      3333, Telex 849041, 🍽, park, ⌘ – 📺 ⌷wc ☎ 🅿. 🎿. 🖼 AE ⑩ VISA
      M (closed Saturday lunch) 10.50/13.50 t. and a la carte ⬧ 3.25 – **46 rm** ⊇ 55.00/85.00 st. – SB
      (weekends only) 69.00/79.00 st.

CITROEN 46-48 High St. ℰ 5255   VAUXHALL-OPEL 71 Stomp Rd ℰ 4994

BURNHAM MARKET Norfolk 404 W 25 – pop. 943 – ☎ 0328 Fakenham.
♦London 128 – ♦Cambridge 71 – ♦Norwich 36.

   ✗ **Fishes**, Market Pl., PE31 8HE, ℰ 738588, Seafood – 🖼 AE ⑩ VISA
      closed Sunday dinner October-June, Monday, 24 to 28 December and 12 to 29 January – **M**
      7.45 t. (lunch) and a la carte 9.80/16.15 t.

BURNHAM-ON-CROUCH Essex 404 W 29 – pop. 6 268 – ECD : Wednesday – ☎ 0621 Maldon.
♦London 52 – Chelmsford 19 – Colchester 32 – Southend-on-Sea 25.

   ✗✗ **Contented Sole**, 80 High St., CM0 8AA, ℰ 782139
      closed Monday, last 2 weeks July and 20 December-18 January – **M** 6.75 st. (lunch)
      and a la carte 10.90/15.00 st. ⬧ 3.00.

AUSTIN-ROVER, FORD Station Rd ℰ 782130

BURNLEY Lancs. 🗺️ N 22 – pop. 76 365 – ✪ 0282.

Envir. : Towneley Hall★ (16C-18C) SE : 1 m.

🏌️ Towneley, Towneley Park, Todmorden Rd ✆ 38473, E : 1 ½ m. – 🏌️ Glen View ✆ 21045 – 🏌️ Marsden Park, Townhouse Rd, Walton Lane, Nelson ✆ 0282 (Nelson) 67525, N : 4 m. – 🏌️ Marsden Heights, Brierfield, Nelson ✆ 0282 (Nelson) 64583, N : 2 m.

🎫 William Thompson Recreation Centre, Red Lion St. ✆ 25011.

◆London 236 – Bradford 32 – ◆Leeds 37 – ◆Liverpool 55 – ◆Manchester 25 – ◆Middlesbrough 104 – Preston 22 – ◆Sheffield 68.

🏨 **Oaks** (Best Western), Colne Rd, Reedley, BB10 2LF, NE : 2½ m. on A 56 ✆ 414141, 🔲, 🛋️ –
📺 🅿️ 🛁. and a la carte 🍷 3.75 – **32 rm** 🍴 46.00/58.00 **st.** – SB (weekends only)
71.00/75.00 **st.**

🏨 **Rosehill House,** Rosehill Av., Manchester Rd, BB11 2PW, ✆ 53931, 🛋️ – 📺 🚪wc 🚿wc
🛁 🅿️. 🔲 ㏂ 🆚 – **20 rm** 🍴 30.00/40.00 **st.**
M 8.95 **st.** and a la carte 🍷 3.50 – **20 rm** 🍴 30.00/40.00 **st.**

AUSTIN-ROVER Todmorden Rd ✆ 36131
DATSUN Accrington Rd ✆ 27328

RENAULT Trafalgar St. ✆ 33311
VAUXHALL Accrington Rd ✆ 27321

BURNSALL North Yorks. 🗺️ O 21 – pop. 116 – ECD : Monday and Thursday – ✉️ Skipton –
✪ 075 672.

◆London 223 – Bradford 26 – ◆Leeds 29.

🏨 **Red Lion,** BD23 6BU, ✆ 204 – 🚪wc 🚿wc 🅿️. ❄️
M (bar lunch Monday to Saturday)/dinner 7.30 t. 🍷 3.00 – **12 rm** 🍴 17.00/34.00 **t.**

🏠 **Manor House,** BD23 6BW, ✆ 231, 🍽️, 🛋️ – 🅿️
closed 7 to 30 November – **7 rm** 🍴 10.00/20.00 **st.**

BURPHAM West Sussex 🗺️ S 30 – see Arundel.

BURRINGTON Devon 🗺️ I 31 – pop. 482 – ECD : Saturday – ✪ 0769 High Bickington.

◆London 260 – Barnstaple 14 – Exeter 28 – Taunton 50.

🏨 **Northcote Manor** (Best Western) 🦢, EX37 9LZ, NW : 1 m. ✆ 60501, ≤, 🛋️ – 📺 🚪wc 🚿
🅿️. 🔲 ㏂ 🆚. ❄️
16 March-October – **M** (bar lunch)/dinner 12.00 **st.** 🍷 3.00 – **11 rm** 🍴 27.00/54.00 **st.** – SB
62.00/69.00 **st.**

BURTON-UPON-TRENT Staffs. 🗺️ 🗺️ 🗺️ O 25 – pop. 59 040 – ECD : Wednesday – ✪ 0283.

🏌️ Branston, Burton Rd ✆ 43207, SW : 1½ m. on A 521.

🎫 Town Hall, King Edward Square ✆ 45454.

◆London 128 – ◆Birmingham 29 – ◆Leicester 27 – ◆Nottingham 27 – Stafford 27.

🏠 **Edgecote,** 179 Ashby Rd, DE15 0LB, SE : 1 m. on A 50 ✆ 68966, 🛋️ – 🅿️
11 rm 🍴 12.50/26.00 **st.**

at Rolleston-on-Dove N : 4 m. by A 38 – ✉️ ✪ 0283 Burton-upon-Trent :

XXX **Brookhouse Inn** 🦢 with rm, Brookside, DE13 9AA, ✆ 814188, « Tastefully furnished part
17C house », 🛋️ – 📺 🚪wc 🚿wc 🅿️. 🔲 ㏂ 🆚 🆚 –
closed 24 December-7 January and Bank Holidays – **M** (closed Saturday lunch and Sunday)
6.00 t. (lunch) and a la carte 12.05/16.85 t. 🍷 3.00 – **16 rm** 🍴 39.00/55.00 **st.** – SB (weekends
only) 70.00 **st.**

at Newton Solney NE : 3 m. by A 50 on B 5008 – ✉️ ✪ 0283 Burton-upon-Trent :

🏨 **Newton Park** (Embassy) 🦢, DE15 0SS, ✆ 703568, ≤, 🛋️ – 📺 🚪wc 🚿 🅿️. 🛁. 🔲 ㏂ 🆚
🆚
M (closed Saturday lunch and Sunday dinner to non-residents) 6.50/10.50 **st.** and a la carte
🍷 3.10 – 🍴 5.00 – **27 rm** 34.00/40.00 **st.** – SB 53.00 **st.**

at Branston SW : 1 ½ m. on A 5121 – ✉️ ✪ 0283 Burton-upon-Trent :

🏨 **Riverside Inn** 🦢, Riverside Drive, off Warren Lane, DE14 3EP, ✆ 63117, 🛋️ – 📺 🚪wc 🚿
🅿️. 🔲 ㏂ 🆚
M 8.50/9.85 t. and a la carte 🍷 3.25 – **22 rm** 🍴 29.50/45.00 t. – SB (weekends only)
44.00/50.00 **st.**

AUSTIN-ROVER-JAGUAR Moor St. ✆ 45353
CITROEN Tollgate ✆ 212454
FIAT Derby Rd ✆ 64891
FORD Horninglow St. ✆ 61081
LADA Woodside Rd ✆ 760363
NISSAN Scalpcliffe Rd ✆ 66677

RENAULT 118 Horninglow Rd ✆ 67811
SCIMITAR, LOTUS, CITROEN Station Rd ✆ 813593
SKODA Main St. ✆ 217513
VOLVO New St. ✆ 31331
VW, AUDI Tutbury Rd ✆ 31336

BURY Greater Manchester 402 N 23 403 ② 404 N 23 – ✪ 061 Manchester.

♦London 211 – ♦Leeds 45 – ♦Liverpool 35 – ♦Manchester 9.

at Birtle E : 3 m. off B 6222 – ⊠ Bury – ✪ 061 Manchester

🏠 **Normandie** ⟨⟩, Elbut Lane, BL9 6UT, ℰ 764 3869 – 🛒 📺 ⌷wc 🏠wc ☎ Ⓟ. 🔺 AE ⓪ VISA
⟨⟩
closed 1 to 14 Januaray – **M** *(closed lunch Saturday and Sunday)* 14.50 **t.** (dinner) and a la
carte 🍴 3.00 – ⌷ 4.85 – **4 rm** 37.00/42.00 **t.** – SB (weekends only) 62.15 **st.**

BURY ST. EDMUNDS Suffolk 404 W 27 – pop. 30 563 – ECD : Thursday – ✪ 0284.

See : St. Mary's Church★ 15C (the Angel roof★★).

Envir. : Ickworth House★ (18C) *AC*, SW : 3 m.

🏌 Lark Valley, Fornham St. Martin ℰ 63426, off A 134 on B 1106.

🛈 Abbey Gardens, Angel Hill ℰ 64667 (summer only).

♦London 79 – ♦Cambridge 27 – ♦Ipswich 26 – ♦Norwich 41.

🏰 **Angel**, 3 Angel Hill, IP33 1LT, ℰ 3926, Telex 81630 – 📺 🛒 Ⓟ. 🔺 AE ⓪ VISA ⟨⟩
M 11.00 **t.** and a la carte – ⌷ 5.00 – **36 rm** 40.00/55.00 **t.**, **1 suite** 65.00/75.00 **t.**

🏠 **Suffolk** (T.H.F.), 38 The Buttermarket, IP33 1DC, ℰ 3995 – 📺 ⌷wc ☎. 🔺 AE ⓪ VISA
M 5.25/8.75 **st.** and a la carte 🍴 3.40 – ⌷ 5.65 – **40 rm** 42.00/52.00 **st.**

✗ **Bradleys**, St. Andrews St. South, ℰ 703825 – VISA
closed Sunday, Monday and 2 weeks Christmas – **M** (lunch by arrangement)(booking essential)/dinner a la carte 13.05/21.95 **t.** 🍴 3.05.

at Bradfield Combust SE : 4 ½ m. on A 134 – ⊠ Bury St. Edmunds – ✪ 028 486 Sickles-
mere :

✗✗ **Bradfield House**, Sudbury Rd, IP30 0LR, ℰ 301, ☞ – Ⓟ. ⓪ VISA
closed Sunday dinner and Monday – **M** (dinner only and Sunday lunch) a la carte 11.25/16.00 **t.**
🍴 4.20.

at Whepstead S : 4 ½ m. by A 143 on B 1066 – ⊠ Bury St. Edmunds – ✪ 028 486 Sickles-
mere :

🏠 **Hammonds** ⟨⟩, Bull Lane, Pinford End, IP29 5NU, by Hawkstead rd and Pinford End rd
ℰ 8867, ≼, « 15C thatched Gothic hall cottage », ☞ – 📺 ⌷wc Ⓟ. ⟨⟩
M (dinner only)(booking essential) 8.50 🍴 3.50 – **5 rm** ⌷ 18.95/45.00.

AUSTIN-ROVER 76 Risbygate St. ℰ 31015
FIAT, LANCIA Mildenhall Rd ℰ 3280
FORD 5 Fornham Rd ℰ 2332
RENAULT Bury Rd, Horringer ℰ 028 488 (Horringer)
362

VAUXHALL-OPEL Cotton Lane ℰ 5621
VOLVO, NISSAN Out Risbygate ℰ 62444
VW, AUDI Northern Way ℰ 63441

BUTTERMERE Cumbria 402 K 20 – pop. 194 – ⊠ Cockermouth – ✪ 059 685.

See : Lake★.

♦London 306 – ♦Carlisle 35 – Kendal 43.

🏠 **Bridge**, CA13 9UZ, ℰ 252, ≼ – ⌷wc 🏠wc Ⓟ
closed 4 January-1 February – **M** (bar lunch)/dinner 10.25 **t.** 🍴 3.45 – **19 rm** ⌷ (dinner included) 27.00/62.00 **t.** – SB (November-March, except Christmas) 54.00 **st.**

BUXTON Derbs. 402 403 404 O 24 – pop. 19 502 – ECD : Wednesday – ✪ 0298.

Envir. : Tideswell (Parish Church★ 14C) NE : 9 m.

🏌 Buxton and High Peak, Townend ℰ 3453, NE : on A 6 – 🏌 Cavendish, Gadley Lane ℰ 3494, ¾ m.
Buxton Station.

🛈 The Cresent ℰ 5106.

♦London 172 – Derby 38 – ♦Manchester 25 – ♦Stoke-on-Trent 24.

🏠 **Lee Wood** (Best Western), 13 Manchester Rd, SK17 6TQ, on A 5002 ℰ 70421, Telex 669848,
☞ – 📺 ⌷wc 🏠wc Ⓟ. 🔺 AE ⓪ VISA
M (bar lunch)/dinner 10.00 **t.** and a la carte 🍴 2.50 – **41 rm** ⌷ 35.00/49.00 **t.** – SB 59.00/68.00 **st.**

⌂ **Hartington**, 18 Broad Walk, SK17 6JR, ℰ 2638 – ⌷wc 🏠wc ⴵ. 🔺 ⟨⟩
closed 24 December-3 January – **17 rm** ⌷ 12.00/33.00 **t.**

FORD 127 London Rd ℰ 3816
HONDA, SAAB Leek Rd ℰ 2494

RENAULT The Old Court House ℰ 3947
VAUXHALL-OPEL Leek Rd ℰ 3466

BWLCHTOCYN Gwynedd 402 403 G 25 – see Abersoch.

CADNAM Hants. 403 404 P 31 – pop. 1 882 – ECD : Wednesday – ✪ 0703 Southampton.

♦London 91 – Salisbury 16 – ♦Southampton 8 – Winchester 19.

🏠 **Bartley Lodge** ⟨⟩, Lyndhurst Rd, SO4 2NR, on A 337 ℰ 812248, ≼, ⟨⟩, ☞, park – 📺
⌷wc 🏠wc Ⓟ. VISA
M *(closed Sunday dinner)* (bar lunch)/dinner 11.95 **t.** and a la carte 🍴 2.50 – **18 rm**
⌷ 25.00/45.00 **st.**

CAERDYDD = Cardiff.

CAERFFILI = Caerphilly.

CAERFYRDDIN = Carmarthen.

CAERGYBI = Holyhead.

CAERNARFON Gwynedd 402 403 H 24 – pop. 9 271 – ECD : Thursday – ⓒ 0286 Llanwnda.
See : Castle★★★ 13C-14C (Royal Welsh Fusiliers Regimental museum★) *AC* – City walls★.
Envir. : SE : Snowdon (ascent and ❅★★★) 1 h 15 mn by Snowdon Mountain Railway (*AC*) from Llanberis (Pass★★) SE : 13 m. – Dinas Dindle★ SW : 5 m.
🛪 Llanfaglan *P* 3783, SW : 1 ¾ m. – 🛥 The Slate Quay *P* 2232 (summer only).
♦London 249 – Birkenhead 76 – Chester 68 – Holyhead 30 – Shrewsbury 85.

　🏠　**The Stables,** Llanwnda, LL54 5SD, SW : 3 ½ m. by A 487 on A 499 *P* 830711, 🔟, ⌺ – 📺
　　　🅿wc ⓦⓒ 🅿. 🔼 🆎 *VISA*
　　　M 6.50/10.00 t. and a la carte ▯ 3.25 – **12 rm** ⌷ 29.00/46.00 t. – SB (weekends only) 55.00/60.00 st.

CAERPHILLY (CAERFFILI) Mid Glam. 403 K 29 – pop. 28 681 – ECD : Wednesday – ⓒ 0222.
See : Castle★★ 13C – 🛪 Castell Heights, Blangwynlais, SW : 2 m.
🛈 Park Lane *P* 863378 (summer only).
♦London 157 – ♦Cardiff 8 – Newport 11.

　　　Hotels and restaurants see : **Cardiff.**S : 8 m., **Newport (Gwent)** E : 11 m.

CAERSWS Powys 403 J 26 – ECD : Thursday – ✉ Newtown – ⓒ 068 684.
♦London 202 – Aberystwyth 38 – Newtown 6.

　🏠　**Maesmawr Hall** ⌂, SY17 5SF, E : 1 m. on A 489 *P* 255, ≤, « 16C manor house in large garden », ⌑, park – 🅿wc ⓦwc 🅿. 🔼 🆎 ⓪ *VISA*
　　　M 6.25/11.50 and a la carte – **19 rm** ⌷ 25.00/45.00 t. – SB 47.00/52.00 st.

AUSTIN-ROVER Central Garage *P* 345　　　　　　　VOLVO Trefeglwys *P* 055 16 (Trefeglwys) 202

CALCOT Glos. – see Tetbury.

CALNE Wilts. 404 O 29 – ⓒ 0249.
♦London 91 – ♦Bristol 33 – Swindon 17.

　🏠　**Chilvester Hill House,** SN11 OLP, W : ¾ m. on A 4 *P* 813981, 🔟 heated, ⌺ – 📺 🅿wc
　　　🅿. 🆎 *VISA*. ✎
　　　M (dinner only) 12.50/15.50 – **3 rm** ⌷ 25.00/46.00 st.

CALSTOCK Cornwall 403 H 32 – pop. 4 079 – ✉ – ⓒ 0821 Tavistock.
♦London 246 – Exeter 48 – ♦Plymouth 22.

　🏠　**Danescombe Valley** ⌂, Lower Kelly, PL18 9RY, W : ½ m. *P* 832414, ≤ River Tamar, « Country house atmosphere » – 🅿wc. ✎
　　　April-October and Christmas – **M** (restricted lunch)/dinner 14.00 **st.** ▯ 2.50 – **7 rm** ⌷ 25.00/48.00 st.

CAMBERLEY Surrey 404 R 29 – pop. 45 108 – ECD : Wednesday – ⓒ 0276.
Envir. : Sandhurst (Royal Military Academy : Royal Memorial Chapel★) NW : 1 ½ m.
♦London 40 – Reading 13 – ♦Southampton 48.

　🏨　**Frimley Hall** (T.H.F.), off Portsmouth Rd via Lime Av., GU15 2BG, E : ¾ m. off A 325 *P* 28321, Telex 858446, ⌺ – 📺 🅿. 🟰. 🔼 🆎 ⓪ *VISA*
　　　M 9.75/12.95 **st.** and a la carte ▯ 3.40 – ⌷ 6.50 – **66 rm** 47.00/57.00 st.

　✕　**Villa Romana,** 20 Park St., GU15 3PL, *P* 24370, Italian rest. – 🔼 🆎 ⓪ *VISA*
　　　closed Sunday – **M** a la carte 8.25/11.50 **st.** ▯ 2.75.

AUSTIN-ROVER London Rd *P* 63443

CAMBRIDGE Cambs. 404 U 27 – pop. 87 111 – ECD : Thursday – ⓒ 0223.
See : Colleges Quarter★★★ : King's College★★ (King's Chapel★★★) Z – Queens' College★★ (Cloister Court) Z – St. John's College★★ (Gateway★) Y – Fitzwilliam Museum★★ *AC* Z M1 – Trinity College★★ (Wren Library★★, Chapel★, Great Court and Gate★) Y – Holy Sepulchre★ (12C round church) Y E – Senate House★ Z S – The Backs★ YZ – Jesus College (Chapel★) Y K – Christ's College (Gatehouse★) YZ A.
Envir. : Anglesey Abbey 12C (interior★★ and park★ *AC*) NE : 6 m. by A 1303 X and B 1102.
🛪 Cambridgeshire Hotel, Bar Hill *P* 0954 (Crafts Hill) 80555, NW : 5 ½ m. by A 1307 X.
🛫 Cambridge Airport : *P* 61133, E : 2 m. on A 1303 X.
🛈 Wheeler St. *P* 322640.
♦London 55 – ♦Coventry 88 – ♦Kingston-upon-Hull 137 – ♦Ipswich 54 – ♦Leicester 74 – ♦Norwich 61 – ♦Nottingham 88 – ♦Oxford 100.

130

CAMBRIDGE

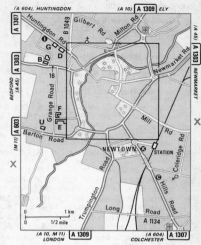

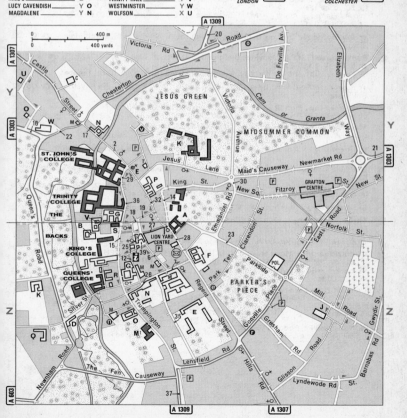

131

🏨🏨 **Garden House** (Best Western), Granta Pl., off Mill Lane, CB2 1RT, 𝒫 63421, Telex 81463, ≼, 🛱 – 🔟 ☎ 🅟 🏖 🔜 🖭 ⚪ Z n
M 10.50/19.95 **t.** and a la carte 🍷 2.75 – ⚏ 4.00 – **117 rm** 50.00/70.00 **t.**, **4 suites** 150.00 **t.** – SB (except Christmas)(weekends only) 81.95/86.35 **t.**

🏨🏨 **University Arms,** Regent St., CB2 1AD, 𝒫 351241, Telex 817311 – 📶 🔟 ☎ ♿ 🅟 🏖 – 🔜 🖭 Z e ⚪ 𝘝𝘐𝘚𝘈
M 5.50/9.20 **st.** and a la carte 🍷 2.50 – ⚏ 4.50 – **113 rm** 38.00/52.00 **st.**, **1 suite** 90.00 **st.** – SB (except summer)(weekends only) 53.00/57.00 **st.**

🏨 **Arundel House,** 53 Chesterton Rd, CB4 3AN, 𝒫 67701 – 🔟 ⊂wc ⊞wc ☎ 🅟 🏖 – 🔜 🖭 ⚪ 𝘝𝘐𝘚𝘈 Y u
closed 25 and 26 December – **M** 7.25/8.55 **t.** and a la carte 🍷 1.90 – ⚏ 1.85 – **73 rm** 19.50/46.00 **t.** – SB (weekends only)(April-October) 48.50/52.00 **st.**

🏨 **Gonville,** Gonville Pl., CB1 1LY, 𝒫 66611 – 📶 ⊟ rest 🔟 ⊂wc ⚆ 🅟 🏖 – 🔜 🖭 ⚪ 𝘝𝘐𝘚𝘈 Z r
closed Christmas – **M** 6.95/8.75 **st.** and a la carte 🍷 3.50 – **62 rm** ⚏ 38.00/52.00 **st.** – SB (weekends only) 53.00/57.00 **st.**

🏨 **Centennial,** 63-69 Hills Rd, CB2 1PG, 𝒫 314652 – 🔟 ⊂wc ⊞ ☎ 🅟 🔜 🖭 ⚪ 𝘝𝘐𝘚𝘈 ✂
closed 25 December-2 January – **M** (lunch by arrangement) 6.25/7.25 **t.** and a la carte 🍷 2.25 – **22 rm** ⚏ 24.00/36.00 **t.** – SB (weekends only)(except summer) 34.00/39.00 **st.** X x

🏨 **Helen,** 167-169 Hills Rd, CB2 2RJ, 𝒫 246465 – 🔟 ⊂wc ⊞wc ☎ 🅟 🔜 𝘝𝘐𝘚𝘈 ✂ X c
closed 10 December-6 January – **M** (dinner only) 9.00 **t.** – **23 rm** ⚏ 20.00/38.00 **st.**

🏠 **Ashley,** 74 Chesterton Rd, CB4 1ER, 𝒫 350059, 🛱 – 🔟 ⊞wc ☎ 🅟 🔜 𝘝𝘐𝘚𝘈 ✂ Y o
closed 25 and 26 December – **10 rm** ⚏ 17.50/29.00 **st.**

🏠 **May View,** 12 Park Par., CB5 8AL, 𝒫 66018 – ✂ Y v
closed 18 December-2 January – **6 rm** ⚏ 23.00/28.00 **st.**

🍴🍴 **Cambridge Lodge** with rm, 139 Huntingdon Rd, CB3 0DQ, 𝒫 352833 – 🔟 ⊂wc ⊞wc ☎ 🅟 🔜 🖭 ⚪ 𝘝𝘐𝘚𝘈 X i
(closed Saturday lunch) – **M** 11.25/14.75 **t.** and a la carte 14.10/20.50 **t.** 🍷 3.25 – **11 rm** ⚏ 35.00/60.00 **st.**

at Impington N : 2 m. on B 1049 at junction of A 45 – X – ✉ Cambridge – 🕿 022 023 Histon :

🏨🏨 **Post House** (T.H.F.), Lakeview, Bridge Rd, CB4 4PH, 𝒫 7000, Telex 817123, 🔜, 🛱 – ⊟ 🔟 ☎ 🅟 🏖 🔜 🖭 ⚪ 𝘝𝘐𝘚𝘈
M 10.70/12.95 **st.** and a la carte 🍷 3.40 – ⚏ 5.65 – **120 rm** 53.00/66.00 **st.**, **1 suite**.

at Fowlmere S : 8 ¾ m. by A 1309 – X – and A 10 on B 1368 – ✉ Royston – 🕿 076 382 Fowlmere :

🍴🍴 **Chequers Inn,** High St., SG8 7SR, 𝒫 369 – 🅟 🔜 🖭 ⚪ 𝘝𝘐𝘚𝘈
closed 25 and 26 December – **M** a la carte 14.20/24.05 **st.** 🍷 3.00.

🍴🍴 **Maguire's,** High St., SG8 7SR, 𝒫 444 – 🅟 🔜 🖭 ⚪ 𝘝𝘐𝘚𝘈
closed 25 and 26 December – **M** 10.50/15.00 **t.** 🍷 2.75.

at Duxford S : 9 ½ m. by A 1309 – X – A 1301 and A 505 on B 1379 – ✉ Duxford – 🕿 0223 Cambridge :

🏨 **Duxford Lodge,** Ickleton Rd, CB2 4RU, 𝒫 836444, Telex 817438, 🛱 – 🔟 ⊂wc ☎ 🅟 🏖 – 🔜 🖭 ⚪ 𝘝𝘐𝘚𝘈
M (closed Saturday lunch) 10.50/14.50 **st.** and a la carte – **16 rm** ⚏ 40.00/70.00 **st.** – SB (except Christmas and New Year)(weekends only) 70.00/90.00 **st.**

at Madingley W : 4 ½ m. by A 1303 – X – ✉ 🕿 0954 Madingley :

🍴🍴 **Three Horseshoes,** High St., CB3 8AB, 𝒫 210221, 🛱 – 🅟 🔜 🖭 ⚪ 𝘝𝘐𝘚𝘈
M a la carte 13.55/17.75 **t.** 🍷 2.95.

at Bar Hill NW : 5 ½ m. by A 1307 – X – on A 604 – ✉ Bar Hill – 🕿 0954 Crafts Hill :

🏨 **Cambridgeshire Moat House** (Q.M.H.), Huntingdon Rd, CB3 8EU, 𝒫 80555, Telex 817141, 🔜, 🏊, ✂, squash – 🔟 ⊂wc ☎ 🅟 🏖 🔜 🖭 ⚪ 𝘝𝘐𝘚𝘈
M (bar lunch Saturday) 11.50 **t.** and a la carte 🍷 3.35 – **100 rm** ⚏ 46.00/59.00 **t.** – SB (weekends only) 73.00 **st.**

ALFA-ROMEO,SUZUKI Babraham Rd 𝒫 247072
AUSTIN-ROVER-DAIMLER-JAGUAR 400 Newmarket Rd 𝒫 65111
BEDFORD, OPEL-VAUXHALL 137 Histon Rd 𝒫 66751
CITROEN Newmarket Rd, Duxford 𝒫 832136
HONDA Cheddars Lane 𝒫 359151

LANCIA,SUZUKI,FIAT 315 Mill Rd 𝒫 242222
MERCEDES-BENZ 121-129 Perne Rd 𝒫 247268
RENAULT 217 Newmarket Rd 𝒫 351616
TOYOTA 1 Union Lane 𝒫 356225
VAUXHALL-OPEL Elizabeth Way 𝒫 321321
VOLVO Harston 𝒫 870123
VW, AUDI 383 Milton Rd 𝒫 354472

CANNOCK Staffs. 402 403 404 N 25 – pop. 54 503 – ECD : Thursday – ☎ 054 35.
◆London 135 – ◆Birmingham 20 – Derby 36 – ◆Leicester 51 – Shrewsbury 32 – ◆Stoke-on-Trent 28.

🏛 **Roman Way,** Watling St., Hatherton, WS11 1SH, SW : 1 ¼ m. by A 460 on A 5 ℰ 72121 –
📺 🛏wc 🚿wc ☎ 🅿. 🅰 🆎 ⓞ 𝘝𝘐𝘚𝘈
M 6.25 **t.** and a la carte – **24 rm** 🛏 30.00/41.00 **t.** – SB (weekends only) 50.00 **st.**

AUSTIN-ROVER Wolverhampton Rd ℰ 6326
FIAT Highfield Rd., Chasetown ℰ 05436(Burnt-
wood)5544
FORD Watling St. ℰ 0922(Cheslyn Hay)417014
PEUGEOT-TALBOT 40 Longford Rd,Bridgetown ℰ
4111

RENAULT 173 Walsall Rd ℰ 72504
VAUXHALL-OPEL Watling St. ℰ 5361
VW AUDI Delta Way ℰ 6216

☛   *There is no paid publicity in this Guide.*

CANTERBURY Kent 404 X 30 – pop. 34 546 – ECD : Thursday – ☎ 0227.
See : Christ Church Cathedral★★★ (Norman crypt★★, Bell Harry Tower★★, Great Cloister★★, ⩽★
from Green Court) Y – King's School★ Y **B** – Mercery Lane★ Y – Weavers★ (old houses) Y **D.**
Envir. : Patrixbourne (St. Mary's Church : south door★) SE : 3 m. by A 2 Z.
🛈 13 Longmarket CTI 2JS ℰ 66567.
◆London 59 – ◆Brighton 76 – ◆Dover 15 – Maidstone 28 – Margate 17.

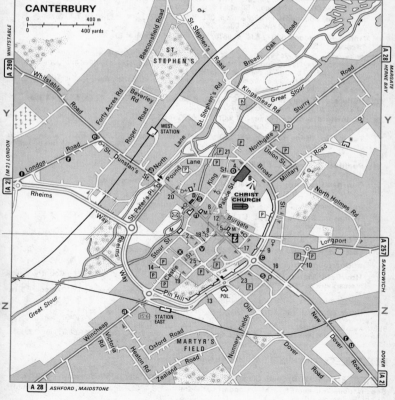

133

🏨 **County,** High St., CT1 2RX, ℰ 66266, Telex 965076 – 🛗 ▤ rest 📺 ☎ ⟺ 🅿 🏛 🔼 🇦🇪 ⓞ *VISA*   Y n
   M (see Sullys below) – ⌑ 5.50 – **74 rm** 42.00/60.00 t., **1 suite** 100.00 t.

🏨 **Chaucer** (T.H.F.), Ivy Lane, CT1 1TT, ℰ 464427, Telex 965096 – 📺 ⌑wc ☎ 🅿 🏛 🔼 🇦🇪 ⓞ *VISA*   Z c
   M a la carte 13.95/17.50 **st.** 🍷 3.40 – ⌑ 5.65 – **43 rm** 44.00/55.00 **st.**
   16 rm.

🏨 **Falstaff** (Whitbread), 8-12 St. Dunstan's St., CT2 8AF, ℰ 462138 – 📺 ⌑wc ☎ 🅿 🏛   Y a
   16 rm.

🏨 **Slatters,** St. Margarets St., CT1 2TR, ℰ 463271 – 🛗 📺 ⌑wc ☎ 🅿 🔼 🇦🇪 ⓞ *VISA*   Z v
   M 5.25/7.50 **st.** and a la carte 🍷 2.50 – **32 rm** ⌑ 39.00/53.00 **st.** – SB (except Christmas) 64.00 **st.**

🏨 **Canterbury,** 71 New Dover Rd, CT1 3DZ, ℰ 450551 – 🛗 📺 ⌑wc 🛗wc ☎ 🅿 🔼 🇦🇪 ⓞ *VISA*   Z u
   M 6.50/8.50 t. and a la carte – **27 rm** ⌑ 30.00/40.00 **st.** – SB (except summer) 40.00/44.00 **st.**

🏨 **Victoria (Berni),** 59 London Rd, CT2 8JY, ℰ 459333, ⇷ – 📺 ⌑wc ☎ 🅿 🔼 🇦🇪 ⓞ *VISA*   Y i
   ⌬
   M (grill rest. only) 12.00 t. 🍷 3.25 – **21 rm** ⌑ 26.00/45.00 t.

🏨 **Pointers,** 1 London Rd, CT2 8LR, ℰ 456846 – 📺 ⌑wc 🛗 ☎ 🅿 🔼 🇦🇪 ⓞ *VISA*   Y e
   closed 23 December-20 January – **M** (dinner only) 9.00 **st.** 🍷 3.00 – **14 rm** ⌑ 20.00/40.00 t. –
   SB 40.00/46.00 **st.**

🏨 **Ebury,** 65-67 New Dover Rd, CT1 3DX, ℰ 68433, ⇷ – 📺 ⌑wc 🛗wc ☎ 🅿 🔼 🇦🇪 ⓞ *VISA*   Z r
   closed 24 December-14 January – **M** *(closed Sunday)* (dinner only) 9.50 t. 🍷 2.80 – **15 rm**
   ⌑ 25.00/38.00 t. – SB (except Sunday) 40.00/47.50 **st.**

🏠 **Highfield,** Summer Hill, Harbledown, CT2 8NH, ℰ 462772, ⇷ – 🛗wc 🅿 🔼 *VISA* ⌬
   March-November – **10 rm** ⌑ 13.00/29.00.   by Rheims way   Y

🏠 **Ann's,** 63 London Rd, CT2 8JZ, ℰ 68767, ⇷ – 📺 ⌑wc 🛗wc 🅿 ⌬   Y r
   19 rm ⌑ 17.50/35.00 t.

XXX ❀ **Seventy-Four,** 74 Wincheap, CT1 3RS, ℰ 67411 – 🅿 🔼 🇦🇪 ⓞ *VISA*   X a
   closed Saturday lunch, Sunday, 1 week Easter, 2 weeks August-September and Bank Holidays
   – **M** 12.00/28.00 t. and a la carte 17.30/23.00 t. 🍷 4.00
   Spec. Parcel of fresh foie gras wrapped in salmon on a bed of crisp vegetables. Whole roast lobster in a rich red
   wine sauce. Tartlet of raspberries with a gooseberry and calvados ice-cream (spring).

XXX **Sully's,** (at County H.) High St., CT1 2RX, ℰ 66266, Telex 965076 – ▤ 🅿 🔼 🇦🇪 ⓞ *VISA*   Y n
   M 9.00/12.50 t. and a la carte 12.30/17.50 t.

XX **Waterfield's,** 5a Best Lane, CT1 2JB, ℰ 450276 – 🔼 *VISA*   Y s
   closed Monday lunch and Sunday – **M** a la carte 8.70/14.00 t. 🍷 2.50.

XX **Tuo e Mio,** 16 The Borough, CT1 2JD, ℰ 61471, Italian rest. – 🔼 🇦🇪 ⓞ *VISA*   Y o
   closed Tuesday lunch, Monday and 18 August-9 September – **M** 7.00 t. (lunch) and a la carte
   9.25/14.00 t. 🍷 2.50.

XX **Beehive,** 52 Dover St., CT1 3HD, ℰ 61126, Italian rest. – 🔼 🇦🇪 ⓞ *VISA*   Z s
   closed Sunday – **M** 5.95 t. (lunch) and a la carte 9.15/11.20 t. 🍷 2.50.

X **Georges Brasserie,** 71-72 Castle St., CT1 2QD, ℰ 65658 – 🔼 🇦🇪 *VISA*   Z x
   closed Sunday – **M** 10.50 t. and a la carte 7.40/13.70 t. 🍷 2.70.

   at Fordwich NE : 3 m. by A 28 – Y – ✉ ❀ 0227 Canterbury :

🏨 George and Dragon, King St., CT2 0BX, ℰ 710661, ⇷ – 📺 ⌑wc ☎ 🅿 🔼 🇦🇪 ⓞ *VISA*
   M (grill rest. only) – **13 rm** ⌑ 17.50/34.00.

   at Bridge SE : 3 m. by (A 2) Z – ✉ ❀ 0227 Canterbury :

🏠 East Bridge Country, Bridge Hill, CT4 5AS, ℰ 830808 – 🛗wc 🅿 – **4 rm.**

   at Chartham Hatch W : 3 ¼ m. by A 28 – Z – ✉ ❀ 0227 Canterbury :

🏨 **Howfield Manor** ⌂, Howfield Lane, CT4 7HQ, SE : 1 m. ℰ 738294, « Country house
   atmosphere », ⇷ – ⌑wc 🛗wc 🅿 🔼 *VISA*. ⌬
   closed mid December-mid January – **M** (dinner only) (booking essential) 13.00 **st.** – **5 rm**
   ⌑ 32.50/50.00 **st.** – SB (November-mid March) 57.00/60.00 **st.**

AUSTIN-ROVER-DAIMLER-JAGUAR 28-30 St.   RENAULT Northgate ℰ 65561
Peters St. ℰ 66161   SUBARU, SEAT Island Rd ℰ 710431
BMW Vauxhall Rd ℰ 454341   TOYOTA Union St. ℰ 455553
FIAT, CITROEN, VAUXHALL 41 St. Georges Pl. ℰ   VAUXHALL-OPEL Ashford Rd, Chartham ℰ 731331
66131   VOLVO Mill Rd, Sturry ℰ 710481

CARBIS BAY Cornwall 🄰🄾🄳 D 33 – see St. Ives.

CARDIFF (CAERDYDD) South Glam. 🄰🄾🄳 K 29 – pop. 262 313 – ECD : Wednesday – ❀ 0222.
See : National Museum★★ BY M – Llandaff Cathedral★ AY B – St. Fagan's Castle (Folk Museum)★
AC, by St. Fagans Rd. AY.
🏌 Llanishen Cwm Lisuane ℰ 755078, N : 7 m. on A 469 A.
✈ Cardiff-Wales Airport ℰ 0446 (Rhoose) 711911 (day) 711914 (night) SW : 8 m. by A 48 AZ –
Terminal : Central Bus Station.
🅱 3 Castle St. ℰ 27281.
♦London 155 – ♦Birmingham 110 – ♦Bristol 46 – ♦Coventry 124.

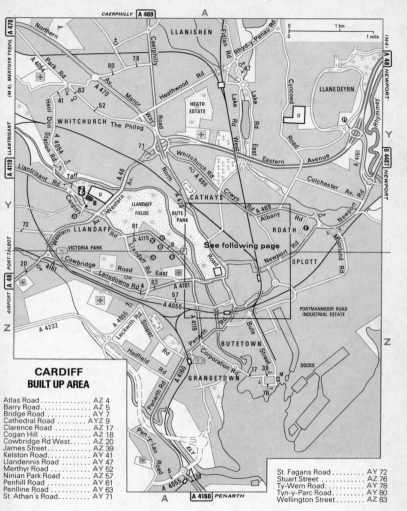

CARDIFF
BUILT UP AREA

Park (Mt. Charlotte), Park Pl., CF1 3UD, ℰ 383471, Telex 497195 – ﴾⊡⋕ TV ☎ ⏚. 🅰. 🔼 🆎 ⓞ VISA
BZ **c**
M 7.95/9.95 **t.** and a la carte ⏚ 3.45 – **108 rm** ⌁ 49.95/61.25 **t.**, **6 suites** 71.50/90.00 **t.** – SB (weekends only) 52.00/57.00 **st.**

Holiday Inn, Mill Lane, CF1 1EZ, ℰ 399944, Group Telex 497365, ≼, 🔼, squash – ⋕ ▤ TV
☎ & ⏚. 🅰. 🔼 🆎 ⓞ VISA
BZ **s**
M 11.75 **st.** and a la carte 17.00/22.00 **st.** ⏚ 4.00 – ⌁ 6.50 – **182 rm** 48.00/58.00 **s.**, **4 suites** 130.00 **s.** – SB (weekends only) 69.00/79.00 **st.**

Inn on the Avenue (Stakis), Circle Way East, Llanedeyrn, CF3 7XF, NE : 3 m. on A 48
ℰ 732520, Telex 497582, 🔼 – ⋕ ▤ rest TV ☎ ⏚. 🅰. 🔼 🆎 ⓞ VISA
AY **n**
closed Christmas Day – **M** 8.00/9.95 **t.** and a la carte ⏚ 3.25 – **145 rm** ⌁ 41.50/52.00 **st.** – SB 50.00/56.00 **st.**

Angel (Norfolk Cap), Castle St., CF1 2QZ, ℰ 32633, Telex 498132 – ⋕ TV ☎ ⏚. 🅰. 🔼 🆎 ⓞ
VISA ⌘
BZ **a**
M 9.00 **t.** and a la carte ⏚ 3.00 – **97 rm** ⌁ 49.00/65.00 **st.**, **1 suite** 80.00/95.00 **st.** – SB 56.00/70.00 **st.**

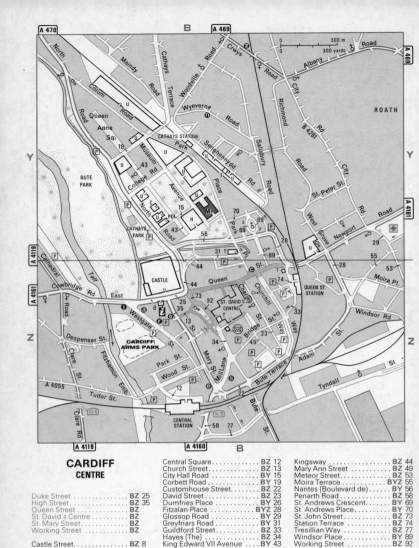

CARDIFF
CENTRE

Royal, St. Mary St., CF1 1LL, ℰ 383321 – 🛗 📺 ➡wc ☎. ⅍. 🔺 🅰🅴 ⓪ 𝘝𝘐𝘚𝘈. ❄ BZ **e**
M (carving rest.) 9.00 **st.** and a la carte ⅋ 3.50 – ☲ 5.50 – **63 rm** 27.50/55.00 **st.** – SB (weekends only) 55.00/59.00.

Post House (T.H.F.), Church Rd, CF2 7XA, NE : 4 m. by A 48 ℰ 731212, Telex 497633 – 🛗 📺
➡wc 🖭 � 🅿. ⅍. 🔺 🅰🅴 ⓪ 𝘝𝘐𝘚𝘈 on A 48 AY
M 6.95/8.95 **st.** and a la carte ⅋ 3.40 – ☲ 5.65 – **150 rm** 44.00/54.00 **st.**

Crest (Crest), Castle St., CF1 2XB, ℰ 388681, Telex 497258 – 🛗 📺 ➡wc ☎ 🅿. ⅍. 🔺 🅰🅴
⓪ 𝘝𝘐𝘚𝘈 BZ **i**
M 7.50/11.95 **st.** and a la carte – ☲ 5.85 – **159 rm** 45.00/63.00 **st.**, **1 suite** 83.00 **st.** – SB (weekends only) 58.00/66.00 **st.**

Ferrier's, 130-132 Cathedral Rd, CF1 9LQ, ℰ 383413 – 📺 ⅲ 🅿. 🔺 🅰🅴 ⓪ 𝘝𝘐𝘚𝘈 AY **e**
closed 2 weeks at Christmas – **M** (closed dinner Friday, Saturday and Sunday) (bar lunch)/
dinner a la carte 6.20/8.85 **t.** ⅋ 2.00 – **27 rm** ☲ 19.00/36.00 **t.**

136

♔ **Beverley,** 75-77 Cathedral Rd, CF1 9PG, ℰ 43443 – 📺 ⌷wc ⋔wc ☎ 🅿   AZ **o**
M a la carte 6.60/10.65 t. ⌷ 2.85 – **18 rm** ⌷ 31.00/39.00 **st.**

⋔ **Abbey,** 151 Cathedral Rd, CF1 9PJ, ℰ 390896 – 📺 ⋔wc. 🔌 _VISA_   AY **o**
26 rm ⌷ 16.00/36.00 **st.**

⋔ **Princes,** 10 Princes St., Roath, CF2 3PR, ℰ 491732 – ✀   AY **r**
6 rm ⌷ 12.00/20.00.

⋔ **Preste Gaarden,** 181 Cathedral Rd, CF1 9PN, ℰ 28607 – 📺. ✀   AY **x**
9 rm ⌷ 52.00/24.00 **st.**

XX **Spanghero's,** Westgate House, Westgate St., CF1 1DD, ℰ 382423 – 🔌 _AE_ _VISA_   BZ **r**
closed Saturday lunch, Monday dinner, Sunday and last 2 weeks August – **M** 9.95/19.75 **t.** and
a la carte 9.20/23.85 **t.**

XX **La Chaumière,** 44 Cardiff Rd, Llandaff (behind Maltsters Arms), CF5 2XX, ℰ 555319 –
🔌 _AE_ ⓞ   AY **a**
closed Saturday lunch, Sunday dinner and first 2 weeks January – **M** 9.95 **t.** (dinner) and a la
carte 10.35/12.65 **t.** ⌷ 3.00.

X **Gibson's,** 8 Romilly Crescent, Canton, CF1 9NR, ℰ 41264, Bistro – 🔌 _AE_ ⓞ _VISA_   AZ **a**
closed Sunday and Bank Holidays – **M** 7.95/15.50 **st.** and a la carte 11.70/15.35 **st.** ⌷ 3.00.

X **Blas-ar-Gymru,** 48 Crwys Rd, CF2 4NN, ℰ 382132 – 🔌 _AE_ ⓞ _VISA_   BY **z**
closed Saturday lunch, Sunday, 5 to 19 January and Bank Holidays – **M** 5.95 **t.** (lunch) and a la
carte 8.15/12.95 **t.** ⌷ 3.00.

X **Armless Dragon,** 97 Wyeverne Rd, Cathays, CF2 4BG, ℰ 382357 – 🔌 _AE_ ⓞ _VISA_   BY **n**
closed Saturday lunch, Sunday, Christmas-New Year and Bank Holidays – **M** a la carte
9.90/13.80 **t.**

X **Thai House,** 23 High St., CF1 2BZ, ℰ 387404, Thai rest. – _AE_ ⓞ _VISA_   BZ **o**
closed Sunday – **M** a la carte 10.40/16.90 **t.**

**at Castleton (Cas-Bach)** (Gwent) NE : 7 m. on A 48 – AY – ✉ Cardiff – ☎ 0633 Castleton :

🏠 Ladbroke Wentloog Castle (Ladbroke), CF3 8UO, ℰ 680591 – 📺 ⌷wc ⋔wc 🅿 🅰. 🔌
_AE_ ⓞ _VISA_. 🔌
54 rm ⌷ 37.00/44.00 **st.** – SB (weekends only) 59.50 **st.**

AUSTIN-ROVER 52 Penarth Rd ℰ 43571
AUSTIN-ROVER Rhiwbina ℰ 623232
AUSTIN-ROVER-DAIMLER-JAGUAR 501 Newport
Rd ℰ 495591
FORD 505 Newport Rd ℰ 490511
FORD 281 Penarth Rd ℰ 21071
PORSCHE, ROLLS ROYCE Cowbridge Road West ℰ
592363

RENAULT Llantrisant Rd ℰ 562345
RENAULT 325 Penarth Rd ℰ 383122
SAAB, SKODA Crwys Rd ℰ 485725
TOYOTA 516 Cowbridge Rd ℰ 561212
TOYOTA Dyfrig Rd ℰ 564028
VAUXHALL-OPEL, HONDA, CITROEN Sloper Rd ℰ
387221
VOLVO Newport Rd, St. Mellons ℰ 777183

CARDIGAN (ABERTEIFI) Dyfed 🔢 G 27 – pop. 3 815 – ECD : Wednesday – ☎ 0239.
Envir. : Mwnt (site★) N : 6 m. – Gwbert-on-Sea (cliffs ≼★) NW : 3 m. – Cilgerran (castle★ 13C) _AC_
SE : 4 m.

🏌 Gwbert-on-Sea ℰ 612035, NW : 3 m.

🛈 3 Heathfield Pendre ℰ 613230 (summer only).

♦London 250 – Carmarthen 30 – Fishguard 19.

X **Rhyd-Garn-Wen** 🈹 with rm, SA43 3NW, SW : 2 ¾ m. by A 487 on Cilgerran rd ℰ 612742,
🚗 – ⋔wc 🅿. ✀
Easter-September – **M** (dinner only) 13.50 **s.** ⌷ 2.50 – **3 rm** ⌷ 23.00/40.00 **st.**

**at Cilgerran** SE : 3 ½ m. by A 478 on Cilgerran road – ✉ ☎ 0239 Cardigan :

X **Castle Kitchen,** High St., SA43 2SG, ℰ 615055
M _(closed lunch in winter)_ (booking essential)(restricted lunch) a la carte 5.90/10.00 ⌷ 1.95.

**at Gwbert-on-Sea** NW : 3 m. on B 4548 – ✉ ☎ 0239 Cardigan :

🏨 **Cliff** 🈹, SA43 1PP, ℰ 613241, Telex 48440, ≼ bay and countryside, 🟦 heated, 🎣, ⚲, 🚗,
squash – 📺 ⌷wc ⋔wc 🅿 🅰. 🔌 _AE_ ⓞ _VISA_
closed January – **M** (bar lunch Monday to Saturday)/dinner 9.50 **st.** and a la carte ⌷ 2.90 –
70 rm ⌷ 25.00/60.00 **st.** – SB (October-May) 56.00/65.00 **st.**

AUSTIN-ROVER Aberystwyth Rd ℰ 612365   FIAT St. Dogmaels ℰ 612025

When travelling for business or pleasure
in England, Wales, Scotland and Ireland :

– use the series of five maps
  (nos 🔢 🔢 🔢 🔢 and 🔢) at a scale of 1:400 000
– they are the perfect complement to this Guide
  as towns underlined in red on the maps will be found in this Guide.

CARLISLE Cumbria **401 402** L 19 – pop. 72 206 – ECD : Thursday – 🕿 0228.

See : Castle★ (12C) *AC* AY – Cathedral★ 12C-14C AY E – ⓕ Aglionby 🖉 022 872 (Scotby) 303 E : 2 m. by A 69 BY – ⓕ Stoney Holme 🖉 34856 E : 1 m. by St. Aidan's Rd BY.

🛪 🖉 022 873 (Crosby-on-Eden) 629, Telex 64476 by A 7 BY and B 6264 – **Bus Station, Lowther Street** – 🚊 🖉 44711.

🖪 The Old Town Hall, Greenmarket 🖉 25517.

◆London 317 – ◆Blackpool 95 – ◆Edinburgh 101 – ◆Glasgow 100 – ◆Leeds 124 – ◆Liverpool 127 – ◆Manchester 122 – ◆Newcastle-upon-Tyne 59.

CARLISLE

Botchergate		BZ
Castle Street		BY 6
English Street		BY 13
Scotch Street		BY 19
Annetwell Street		AY 2

Bridge Street	AY 3
Brunswick Street	BZ 4
Caldcotes	AY 5
Charlotte Street	AZ 7
Chiswick Street	BY 8
Church Street	AY 10
Eden Bridge	BY 12
Lonsdale Street	BY 14
Lowther Street	BY 15

Port Road	AY 16
St. Aidan's Road	BY 17
St. Nicholas Street	BZ 18
Spencer Street	BY 20
Tait Street	BZ 21
Victoria Viaduct	ABZ 24
West Tower Street	BY 26
West Walls	ABY 27
Wigton Road	AZ 29

🏦 **Swallow Hilltop** (Swallow), London Rd, CA1 2PQ, SE : 1 m. on A 6 🖉 29255, Telex 64292, 🔲 – 🛉 📺 ⌷wc 🕿 🅿. 🔥 🔼 🖭 ⓪ 𝗩𝗜𝗦𝗔
by A 6 BZ
M 7.50/10.00 **st.** and a la carte ⌷ 3.95 – **110 rm** ⊠ 27.00/60.00 **st.** – SB 54.00/67.00 **st.**

🏦 **Ladbroke Crown and Mitre** (Ladbroke), English St., CA3 8HZ, 🖉 25491, Telex 64183, 🔲 – 🛉 📺 ⌷wc 🕾 🅿. 🔥 🔼 🖭 ⓪ 𝗩𝗜𝗦𝗔. 🛠
BY **a**
M 7.75/15.50 ⌷ 3.70 – ⊠ 6.00 – **94 rm** 33.00/46.00 **st.**

🏨 **Cumbria Park**, 32 Scotland Rd, CA3 9DG, N : 1 m. on A 7 🖉 22887 – 📺 ⌷wc 🛏wc 🅿. 🔼 𝗩𝗜𝗦𝗔. 🛠
by A 7 BY
closed 25 and 26 December – **M** 7.00/10.00 **t.** and a la carte ⌷ 3.00 – **42 rm** ⊠ 27.00/60.00 **t.**

at Kingstown N : 3 m. at junction 44 of A 7 – BY – and M 6 – ⊠ 🕿 0228 Carlisle :

🏦 **Crest** (Crest), Kingstown, CA4 0HR, 🖉 31201, Telex 64201 – 📺 ⌷wc 🕿 🅿. 🔥 🔼 🖭 ⓪ 𝗩𝗜𝗦𝗔
M (closed Saturday lunch) 8.50/11.50 **st.** and a la carte – ⊠ 5.85 – **98 rm** 46.00/56.00 **st.** – SB (weekends only) 64.00/70.00 **st.**

at Crosby-on-Eden NE : 4 ½ m. by A 7 – BY – on B 6264 – ⊠ Carlisle – 🕿 022 873 Crosby-on-Eden :

🛠🛠 **Crosby Lodge** 🦢 with rm, CA6 4QZ, 🖉 618, ≼, « 18C country mansion », 🌤 – 📺 ⌷wc 🛏wc 🅿. 🖭 ⓪ 𝗩𝗜𝗦𝗔. 🛠
closed 24 December-third week January – **M** (closed Sunday dinner) 10.75/15.50 **t.** and a la carte ⌷ 3.50 – **11 rm** ⊠ 38.00/55.00 **t.** – SB (weekends only)(October-March) 60.00 **st.**

at Faugh E : 8 ¼ m. by A 69 – BY – ⊠ Carlisle – ☎ 022 870 Hayton :

🏚 **String of Horses Inn,** Heads Nook, CA4 9EG, ✆ 297, « Elaborately furnished 17C inn », ⊠ heated – 🍽 rest 📺 ⌂wc 🚿wc 🅟 🔼 AE ⓪ VISA 🐾
M (bar lunch)/dinner 12.95 **t.** and a la carte ⒤ 2.75 – **13 rm** ⊊ 37.00/68.00 **t.** – SB (October-April) 62.00/80.00 **st.**

at Wetheral SE : 6 ¼ m. by A 6 – BZ – on B 6233 – ⊠ Carlisle – ☎ 0228 Wetheral :

🏨 **Crown** (Best Western), CA4 8ES, ✆ 61888, Telex 64175, ☞ – 📺 ⌂wc ☎ 🅟 🔼 🔼 AE ⓪
VISA
M (bar lunch Saturday) 8.00/14.00 **st.** and a la carte ⒤ 3.75 – **50 rm** ⊊ 47.00/69.00 **st.** – SB 69.00/74.00 **st.**

XX **Fantails,** The Green, CA4 8ET, ✆ 60239 – 🅟 🔼 AE ⓪ VISA
closed Sunday, Monday and February – **M** a la carte 5.95/16.65 **t.** ⒤ 3.50.

AUSTIN-ROVER-DAIMLER-JAGUAR Rosehill Estate ✆ 24387
CITROEN, SAAB Willowholme Estate ✆ 26617
FIAT Church St., Caldewgate ✆ 25092
FORD Hardwick Circus ✆ 24234
LADA Cecil St. ✆ 25051

MERCEDES-BENZ Victoria Viaduct ✆ 28234
NISSAN Lowther St. ✆ 25555
RENAULT Church St. ✆ 22423
VAUXHALL-OPEL Viaduct Estate ✆ 29401
VOLVO Victoria Viaduct ✆ 28234
VW, AUDI-NSU Lowther St. ✆ 26104

CARLYON BAY Cornwall 403 F 33 – see St. Austell.

CARMARTHEN (CAERFYRDDIN) Dyfed 403 G 28 – pop. 13 860 – ECD : Thursday – ☎ 0267.
🏌 Blaenycoed Rd ✆ 87214, NW : 4 m.
🛈 Lammas St. ✆ 231557 (summer only).
♦London 220 – Fishguard 45 – ♦Swansea 27.

🏨 **Ivy Bush Royal** (T.H.F.), 11-13 Spilman St., SA31 1LG, ✆ 235111, Telex 48520 – 🛗 📺 ⌂wc 🟦wc ☎ 🅟 🔼 🔼 AE ⓪ VISA
M 7.00/10.00 **st.** and a la carte ⒤ 3.40 – ⊊ 5.65 – **79 rm** 38.00/48.00 **st., 1 suite.**

X **Hoi San,** 15 Queen St., SA31 1JT, ✆ 231100, Chinese-Cantonese rest. – 🔼 AE ⓪ VISA
closed 3 days at Christmas – **M** 4.95/11.00 **t.** and a la carte 7.80/17.90 **t.**

AUSTIN-ROVER, LAND-ROVER, SHERPA Pensarn Rd ✆ 5252
FIAT Pensarn ✆ 6633

FORD The Bridge ✆ 6482
HONDA, TOYOTA Priory St. ✆ 4171
NISSAN Penguin Court ✆ 7356

CARNKIE Cornwall – see Redruth.

CARTMEL Cumbria 402 L 21 – see Grange-over-Sands.

CAS-BACH = Castleton.

CAS-BLAIDD = Wolf's Castle.

CASNEWYDD-AR-WYSG = Newport.

CASTELL NEWYDD EMLYN = Newcastle Emlyn.

CASTERTON Cumbria – see Kirkby Lonsdale.

CASTLE ACRE Norfolk 404 W 25 – pop. 777 – ☎ 076 05.
See : Priory** (ruins 11C - 14C) *AC.*
♦London 101 – King's Lynn 20 – ♦Norwich 31.

Hotels see : King's Lynn NW : 20 m., *Swaffham* S : 4 m.

CASTLE BROMWICH West Midlands 403 404 O 26 – see Birmingham.

CASTLE CARY Somerset 403 404 M 30 – pop. 2 599 – ECD : Thursday – ☎ 0963.
♦London 125 – ♦Bristol 28 – Taunton 31 – Yeovil 13.

🏨 **George,** Market Pl., BA7 7AH, ✆ 50761 – 📺 ⌂wc 🟦wc ☎ 🔼 🔼 AE ⓪ VISA
closed 24, 25 and 31 December – **M** (bar lunch) a la carte 9.00/14.00 **t.** ⒤ 2.90 – **17 rm** ⊊ 25.00/35.00 **t.** – SB (November-March) 60.00 **st.**

Pour les 🏨🏨, 🏨, 🏨, nous ne donnons pas le détail de l'installation, ces hôtels possédant, en général, tout le confort.

⌂wc 🟦wc

☎

CASTLE COMBE Wilts. 408 404 N 29 The West Country G. – pop. 347 – ⊠ Chippenham – ☎ 0249.

See : Site★★ – ◆London 110 – ◆Bristol 23 – Chippenham 6.

🏨 **Manor House** (Best Western) ⤷, SN14 7HR, ℰ 782206, Telex 449115, « Part 14C manor house in park », 🔄 heated, ⤷, 🎾, ✹ – 📺 ☎ 🅿 🔼 🆎 ⓪ 𝚅𝙸𝚂𝙰
M 9.50/18.00 t. and a la carte ⅄ 3.50 – **33 rm** ⊐ 40.00/89.00 st. – SB (November-March)(except Christmas week) 79.00/82.00 st.

at Ford S : 1 ¾ m. – ⊠ Chippenham – ☎ 0249 Castle Combe :

🏨 **White Hart Inn**, SN14 8RP, ℰ 782213, 🔄 heated – 📺 ⌷wc ⌁wc 🅿 🔼 ✹
M (closed 25 and 26 December) (bar lunch Monday to Saturday)/dinner 10.50 t. ⅄ 3.95 – **11 rm** ⊐ 30.00/44.00 t. – SB 53.00/58.00 st.

CASTLE DONINGTON Leics. 402 408 404 P 25 – pop. 5 854 – ⊠ ☎ 0332 Derby.

✈ East Midlands, ℰ 810621, Telex 37543.

◆London 123 – ◆Birmingham 38 – ◆Leicester 23 – ◆Nottingham 13.

🏨 **Donington Manor**, High St., DE7 2PP, ℰ 810253, Telex 377208 – 📺 ⌷wc ⌁wc ☎ 🅿 🔓 🔼 🆎 ⓪ 𝚅𝙸𝚂𝙰 ✹
closed 26 to 31 December – **M** 4.90/6.50 st. and a la carte ⅄ 3.20 – **38 rm** ⊐ 30.00/47.00 st.

VAUXHALL-OPEL Station Rd ℰ 810221

CASTLETON (CAS-BACH) Gwent 408 K 29 – see Cardiff (South Glam.).

CASTLETON North Yorks. 402 R 20 – ⊠ Whitby – ☎ 0287.

◆London 258 – ◆Middlesbrough 18 – York 61.

🏨 **Moorlands**, 55 High St., YO21 2DB, ℰ 60206, ≤, – ⌁wc 🅿
M (bar lunch Monday to Saturday)/dinner a la carte 10.75/14.50 t. ⅄ 2.50 – **10 rm** ⊐ 16.00/34.00.

CAVENDISH Suffolk 404 V 27 – pop. 973 – ⊠ Sudbury – ☎ 0787 Glemsford.

◆London 66 – ◆Cambridge 29 – ◆Ipswich 28.

XX **Alfonso's**, The Green, CO10 8BB, ℰ 280372, Italian rest. – 🔼 🆎 ⓪
closed Monday lunch and Sunday dinner – **M** 9.50 st. and a la carte 10.00/13.00 st. ⅄ 3.50.

CAWSAND Cornwall 408 H 33 – ⊠ ☎ 0752 Plymouth.

◆London 253 – ◆Plymouth 10 – Truro 53.

🏨 **Criterion** ⤷, Garrett St., PL10 1PD, ℰ 822244, ≤ Plymouth Sound, « Converted fishermen's cottages » – 📺 ⌁wc 🔼 𝚅𝙸𝚂𝙰
M (bar lunch)/dinner 10.00 t. ⅄ 2.65 – **8 rm** ⊐ 15.50/36.00 t.

CEINEWYDD = New Quay.

CERNE ABBAS Dorset 408 404 M 31 The West Country G. – pop. 573 – ☎ 030 03.

See : Site★ – ◆ London 137 – Dorchester 8 – Salisbury 49 – Yeovil 16.

XX **Old Market House**, 25 Long St., DT2 7JG, ℰ 680 – 🔼 🆎
closed Sunday dinner and Monday – **M** 12.50 t. (dinner) and a la carte 8.75/11.25 t.

CHADLINGTON Oxon. 408 404 P 28 – pop. 749 – ☎ 060 876.

◆London 74 – Cheltenham 32 – ◆Oxford 18 – Stratford-upon-Avon 25.

🏨 **Chadlington House**, OX7 3LZ, ℰ 437, 🌺, – 📺 ⌷wc ⌁wc 🅿 🔼 𝚅𝙸𝚂𝙰 ✹
March-November – **M** (bar lunch)/dinner 11.50 t. ⅄ 2.70 – **10 rm** ⊐ 22.50/50.00 t. – SB 46.00/59.00 st.

CHAGFORD Devon 408 I 31 The West Country G. – pop. 1 400 – ECD : Wednesday – ☎ 064 73.

Envir. : Castle Drogo★ AC, NE : 2 m. – ◆London 218 – Exeter 17 – ◆Plymouth 28.

🏨 ✿ **Gidleigh Park** ⤷, TQ13 8HH, NW : 2 m. by Gidleigh Rd ℰ 2367, ≤ Vale and woodland, « Country house atmosphere », 🌺, park, ✹ – 📺 ☎ 🅿 🔼 🆎 ⓪ 𝚅𝙸𝚂𝙰
M (booking essential) 17.00/27.00 s. and a la carte lunch ⅄ 3.50 – ⊐ 5.00 – **14 rm** 70.00/125.00 s.
Spec. Terrine of fresh duck foie gras, Sea bass with chanterelles, Calfs kidney and sweetbread with cassis sauce.

🏨 **Teignworthy Country House** ⤷, Frenchbeer, TQ13 8EX, SW : 2 ½ m. by Fernworthy Rd, off Thornworthy Rd ℰ 3355, ≤, « Country house atmosphere », 🌺, park, ✹ – 📺 ⌷wc ☎ 🅿 🔼 𝚅𝙸𝚂𝙰 ✹
M (restricted lunch)(booking essential) 22.00 t. (dinner) and a la carte 13.50/22.00 t. ⅄ 4.20 – **9 rm** ⊐ 48.50/77.00 t. – SB (winter only) 89.00/119.00 st.

🏨 **Thornworthy House** ⤷, Thornworthy, TQ13 8EY, SW : 3 m. by Fernworthy Rd on Thornworthy Rd ℰ 3297, ≤, « Country house atmosphere », 🌺, park, ✹ – ⌷wc 🅿 ✹
closed January and February – **M** (booking essential)(bar lunch)/dinner 12.00 st. ⅄ 3.00 – **6 rm** ⊐ 20.00/40.00 st. – SB (except Easter and summer) 55.00 st.

🏨 **Torr House** ⤷, Thornworthy, TQ13 8DX, SW : 1 ½ m. by Fernworthy Rd on Thornworthy Rd ℰ 2228, 🌺 – ⌁wc 🅿
4 rm ⊐ 18.00/28.00 t.

🏛 *at Sandypark* NE : 1 ½ m. on A 382 – ⊠ 🕸 064 73 Chagford :

🏛 **Mill End** 🏊, TQ13 8JN, on A 382 ℰ 2282, « Country house with water mill », 🐟, 🐎 – 📺
⊟wc ☎ 🚗 🅿. 🔌 AE ⓪ VISA
closed 10 days Christmas – **M** (lunch by arrangement) 11.00/13.00 t. ▮ 3.50 – **17 rm**
⊆ 26.00/58.00 t. – SB 60.00/80.00 st.

🏛 **Great Tree** (Best Western) 🏊, TQ13 8JS, on A 382 ℰ 2491, ≤, « Country house atmosphere », 🐎, park – 📺 ⊟wc 🅿. 🔌 AE ⓪ VISA
closed 27 December-1 February – **M** 7.00/15.00 s. ▮ 3.50 – **14 rm** ⊆ 29.00/65.00 t. – SB
70.00/80.00 st.

🏛 *at Easton Cross* NE : 1 ½ m. – ⊠ 🕸 064 73 Chagford :

🏛 **Easton Court,** TQ13 8JL, on A 382 ℰ 3469, « 15C thatched house », 🐎 – ⊟wc 🛁wc 🅿.
🔌 AE ⓪ VISA
M (dinner only) 15.00 s. ▮ 3.25 – **8 rm** ⊆ 18.00/50.00 t. – SB (except Christmas) 54.00/70.00 st.

RENAULT New St. ℰ 2226

CHALE I.O.W. – see Wight (Isle of).

CHALFORD Glos. 403 404 N 28 – pop. 4 125 – ⊠ Stroud – 🕸 0453 Brimscombe.
♦London 105 – ♦Bristol 40 – Gloucester 14 – Swindon 22.

🏛 **Springfield House,** London Rd, GL6 8NW, on A 419 ℰ 883555, 🐎 – 📺 ⊟wc 🐶 🅿. 🔌
AE ⓪ VISA
closed 1 to 14 January – **M** 8.50/13.50 t. ▮ 2.95 – **8 rm** ⊆ 26.00/46.00 – SB 66.00/80.00 st.

CHANCERY (RHYDGALED) Dyfed 403 H 26 – see Aberystwyth.

CHAPEL-EN-LE-FRITH Derbs. 402 403 404 O 24 – pop. 7 090 – ⊠ Stockport (Cheshire) –
🕸 0298.
🏊 Manchester Rd ℰ 812118 – ♦ London 176 – ♦ Manchester 22 – Derby 42 – ♦ Sheffield 24.

🏛 **King's Arms,** Market Place, SK12 6EN, ℰ 812105 – 📺 🅿. 🔌 AE ⓪ VISA
M *(closed Christmas Day)* (bar lunch)/dinner 8.00 st. and a la carte ▮ 2.00 – **11 rm**
⊆ 12.50/23.00 st. – SB (except Bank Holidays) 30.00 st.

CHAPEL STILE Cumbria 402 K 20 – see Ambleside.

CHAPELTOWN North Yorks. 402 403 404 P 23 – see Sheffield.

CHARD Somerset 403 L 31 The West Country G. – pop. 9 357 – ECD : Wednesday – 🕸 046 06.
Envir. : Ilminster★ St. Mary's Church★★, N ; 5 m. – Cricket St. Thomas Wildlife park★, E : 3 m. –
Forde Abbey★, SE : 4 m. – Barrington Court★AC, NE : 8 m. – Clapton Court Gardens★AC,
E : 11 m.
♦London 180 – Exeter 31 – ♦Southampton 85 – Taunton 16.

🏛 George, 15 Fore St., TA20 1PH, ℰ 3413 – 📺 ⊟wc 🛁wc 🅿 – **20 rm**.

CHARLBURY Oxon. 403 404 P 28 – pop. 2 637 – 🕸 0608.
♦London 72 – ♦Birmingham 50 – ♦Oxford 15.

🏛 **Bell at Charlbury** (Best Western), Church St., OX7 3AP, ℰ 810278 – 📺 ⊟wc 🐶 🅿. 🔌 AE
⓪ VISA
M 7.50/12.95 t. and a la carte ▮ 2.70 – **13 rm** ⊆ 32.00/50.00 t. – SB 61.00/70.00 st.

CHARLESTOWN Cornwall 403 F 33 – see St. Austell.

CHARLTON West Sussex 404 R 31 – see Chichester.

CHARMOUTH Dorset 403 L 31 – pop. 1 121 – ECD : Thursday – ⊠ Bridport – 🕸 0297.
♦London 157 – Dorchester 22 – Exeter 31 – Taunton 27.

🏛 **White House,** 2 Hillside, The Street, DT6 6PJ, ℰ 60411 – 📺 ⊟wc ☎ 🅿. 🔌 VISA
M 12.50 st. (dinner) and a la carte ▮ 2.95 – **7 rm** ⊆ 23.50/51.00 st. – SB 55.00/65.00 st.

🏛 **Fernhill,** Fernhill, DT6 6BX, W : ¾ m. by A 35 on A 3052 ℰ 60492, ⅃ heated, 🐎 – ⊟wc
🛁wc 🅿. 🔌 VISA
M (bar lunch)/dinner 10.95 t. and a la carte – **15 rm** ⊆ 19.00/42.00 t. – SB (except August)
46.00/58.00 st.

🏠 **Newlands House,** Stonebarrow Lane, DT6 6RA, ℰ 60212, 🐎 – 📺 ⊟wc 🛁wc 🅿
March-October – **12 rm** ⊆ 16.00/32.00 st.

🏠 **Hensleigh,** Lower Sea Lane, DT6 6LW, ℰ 60830 – 📺 ⊟wc 🛁wc 🅿
April-October – **10 rm** ⊆ 13.00/30.00 st.

🏠 **Sea Horse,** Higher Sea Lane, DT6 6BB, ℰ 60414, ≤, 🐎 – ⊟wc 🅿. 🔌 VISA
10 rm ⊆ 12.00/30.50 t.

CHARNOCK RICHARD Lancs. 402 404 M 23 – pop. 2 000 – ECD : Wednesday – ☎ 0257
Coppull – ⌊ᵣₐ Duxbury Park, Chorley ℰ 025 72 (Chorley) 65380, E : 2 m.
◆London 215 – ◆Liverpool 26 – ◆Manchester 24 – Preston 10.

   🏨 **TraveLodge** (T.H.F.) without rest., Mill Lane, PR7 5LQ, on M 6 ℰ 791746, Telex 67315 – 📺
       ⇌wc ☞ ᶜ ᴮ 🅿 ◻ AE ⓪ *VISA*
       102 rm ⊂⊐ 33.00/40.00 **st.**

CHARTHAM HATCH Kent 404 X 30 – see Canterbury.

CHEDINGTON Dorset 403 L 31 – pop. 96 – ⊠ Beaminster – ☎ 093 589 Corscombe.
◆ London 148 – Dorchester 17 – Taunton 25.

   🏛 **Chedington Court** ⌖, DT8 3HY, ℰ 265, ≼ countryside, « Country house in landscaped
       gardens », park – 📺 ⇌wc ☞ ᴮ 🅿 ◻ 🖧
       closed January and February – **M** (dinner only) 17.50 **st.** ᵭ 3.40 – **10 rm** ⊂⊐ 34.40/81.60 **st.** –
       SB 66.00/102.00 **st.**

CHELFORD Cheshire 402 403 404 N 24 – ⊠ Macclesfield – ☎ 0625.
◆London 189 – ◆Liverpool 39 – ◆Manchester 17 – ◆Stoke on Trent 23.

   🏠 **Dixon Arms**, Knutsford Rd, SK11 9AZ, ℰ 861313 – 📺 �𝄢wc ☎ 🅿 ◻ AE ⓪ *VISA*
       closed 24 December-2 January – **M** (bar lunch)/dinner 8.95 **t.** and a la carte ᵭ 2.85 – **10 rm**
       ⊂⊐ 36.00/42.00 **st.**

CHELMSFORD Essex 404 V 28 – pop. 91 109 – ECD : Wednesday – ☎ 0245.
◆London 33 – ◆Cambridge 46 – ◆Ipswich 40 – Southend-on-Sea 19.

   🏨 **South Lodge**, 196 New London Rd, CM2 0AR, ℰ 264564, Telex 99452 – 📺 ⇌wc ☎ 🅿 🖧
       ◻ AE ⓪ *VISA*
       M 9.50 **t.** and a la carte ᵭ 3.50 – ⊂⊐ 5.00 – **41 rm** 31.00/49.00 **st.**

   🏠 **County**, 29 Rainsford Rd, CM1 2QA, ℰ 266911 – 📺 ⇌wc ☞ ᴮ 🅿 🖧 ◻ AE ⓪ *VISA*
       closed 27 to 31 December – **M** 6.90/7.90 **t.** and a la carte ᵭ 3.50 – **52 rm** ⊂⊐ 21.00/52.50 **t.**

   ↰ **Oaklands**, 240 Springfield Rd, CM2 6BP, ℰ 352004, 🖾 – 📺 ᑖwc ᑲ 🅿 🖧
       closed 3 weeks at Christmas – **10 rm** ⊂⊐ 14.00/28.00.

   ↰ **Tanunda**, 217-219 New London Rd, CM2 0AJ, ℰ 354295, 🖾 – 📺 ⇌wc ᑖwc 🅿
       closed 1 week at Christmas – **20 rm** ⊂⊐ 16.75/33.50 **st.**

   ✗ **Rose of India**, Rainsford Rd, CM1 2QD, ℰ 352990, Indian rest. – ◻ *VISA*
       M 3.95/7.95 **t.** and a la carte ᵭ 2.75.

   at Great Baddow SE : 3 m. by A 130 – ⊠ ☎ 0245 Chelmsford :

   🏛🏛 **Pontlands Park** ⌖, West Hanningfield Rd, CM2 8HR, ℰ 76444, Telex 995411, ≼, 🔲, 🖾,
       park – 📺 🅥 ☎ 🅿 ◻ AE ⓪ *VISA*
       M (closed lunch Monday and Saturday and Sunday dinner) 12.00/15.00 **t.** – ⊂⊐ 7.00 – **19 rm**
       45.00/80.00 **st.** – SB (weekends only) 45.00/80.00 **st.**

   at High Easter NW : 10 m. by A 414 off A 1060 – ⊠ Chelmsford – ☎ 024 531 Good Easter :

   ✗✗ **Punch Bowl**, CM1 4QW, ℰ 222 – 🅿 ◻ AE ⓪ *VISA*
       closed Sunday dinner and Monday – **M** (lunch by arrangement Tuesday to Saturday) 8.50/15.50
       t. and a la carte 15.00/18.15 **t.** ᵭ 2.75.

AUSTIN-ROVER, RENAULT 74 Main Rd, Broomfield   RENAULT Southend Rd, Sandon ℰ 71113
ℰ 440571   VAUXHALL-OPEL Eastern Approach ℰ 466333
CITROEN, LANCIA Galley Wood ℰ 268366   VAUXHALL-OPEL Moulsham Lodge ℰ 351611
FORD 39 Robjohns Rd ℰ 264111   VOLVO Colchester Rd, Springfield ℰ 468151

CHELSWORTH Suffolk – pop. 133 – ⊠ – ☎ 0449 Bildeston.
◆London 68 – Colchester 21 – ◆Ipswich 16.

   ☎ **Peacock Inn**, The Street, IP7 7HU, ℰ 740758 – 📺 🅿 🖧
       M (buffet lunch)/dinner 11.00 **t.** and a la carte ᵭ 2.75 – **5 rm** ⊂⊐ 15.00/22.00 **t.**

CHELTENHAM Glos. 403 404 N 28 – pop. 87 188 – ECD : Wednesday and Saturday – ☎ 0242.
See : Pittville Park★ A – Municipal Art Gallery and Museum★ B M – Envir. : Elkstone (Parish
Church : doorway★ and arches★ 12C) SE : 7 m. by A 435 A – Sudeley Castle★ (12C - 15C) AC, NE :
6 m. by A 46. A.
⌊ᵣₐ Cleeve Hill ℰ 024 267 (Bishop's Cleeve) 2025, N : 3 m. by A 46. A.
🛈 Municipal Offices, The Promenade ℰ 522878.
◆London 99 – ◆Birmingham 48 – ◆Bristol 40 – Gloucester 9 – ◆Oxford 43.

Plan opposite

   🏛🏛 **Queen's** (T.H.F.), Promenade, GL50 1NN, ℰ 514724, Telex 43381, 🖾 – 🕻 📺 🅿 🖧 ◻ AE
       ⓪ *VISA*   B n
       M 8.95/12.95 **st.** and a la carte ᵭ 3.40 – ⊂⊐ 6.00 – **77 rm** 53.00/65.00 **st.**

   🏛🏛 **Golden Valley Thistle** (Thistle), Gloucester Rd, GL51 0TS, W : 2 m. on A 40 ℰ 32691, Telex
       43410, 🖾 – 🕻 📺 ☎ 🅿 ◻ AE ⓪ *VISA* 🖧   by A 40   A
       M 8.75/11.50 **t.** and a la carte – ⊂⊐ 5.95 – **99 rm** 48.00/75.00 **st.**

142

CHELTENHAM

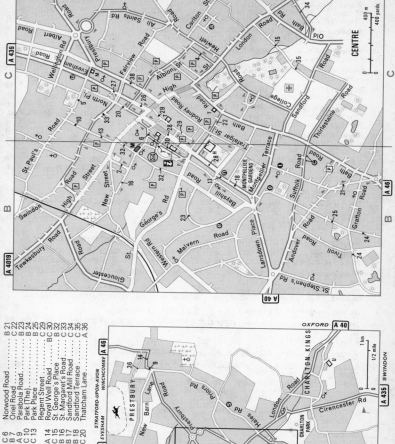

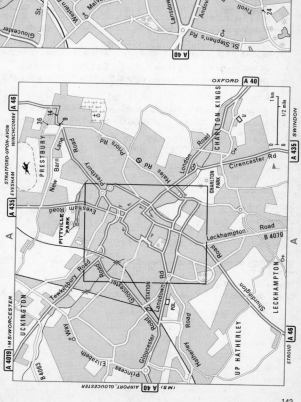

Wyastone, Parabola Rd, GL50 3BG, ℰ 45549 – 📺 ➖wc 🛁wc ☎ 🅿 🔝 🅰🅴 ⓞ 𝘝𝘐𝘚𝘈 ⛱
M *(closed Monday lunch and Sunday to non-residents)* a la carte 9.80/14.75 **st.** – ☲ 4.00 –
13 rm 36.00/50.00 **st.** – SB (weekends only) 70.00 **st.**   B e

Abbottslee, Priory Walk, GL52 6DU, ℰ 515255 – 🅿 ⛱   C a
closed 25 and 26 December – **6 rm** ☲ 11.00/20.00 **st.**

Hannaford's, 20 Evesham Rd, GL52 2AB, ℰ 515181 – 📺 🛁wc. 🔝 𝘝𝘐𝘚𝘈 ⛱   C u
11 rm ☲ 17.00/35.00 **st.**

Hollington House, 115 Hales Rd, GL52 6ST, ℰ 519718 – 📺 🛁wc 🅿   A s
closed Christmas – **7 rm** ☲ 16.00/32.00 **t.**

Willoughby, 1 Suffolk Sq., GL50 2DR, ℰ 522798, 🌳 – 📺 🛁 🅿   B o
closed 2 weeks Christmas and New Year – **9 rm** ☲ 13.00/30.00 **st.**

Redmond's, 12 Suffolk Rd, GL50 2AQ, ℰ 580323 – 🔝 🅰🅴 ⓞ 𝘝𝘐𝘚𝘈   B c
closed Monday lunch, Sunday and 2 weeks August-September – **M** (restricted lunch) 10.25 **st.**
(lunch) and a la carte 14.00/19.25 **st.** 🍷 2.90.

Twelve, 12 Suffolk Par., GL50 2AB, ℰ 584544 – 🔝 🅰🅴 ⓞ 𝘝𝘐𝘚𝘈   B i
closed Sunday dinner, Monday and Bank Holidays – **M** 7.25 **t.** (lunch) and a la carte
11.00/12.50 **t.** 🍷 2.50.

La Ciboulette, 24-26 Suffolk Rd, GL50 2AQ, ℰ 573449 – 🍽 🔝 🅰🅴 𝘝𝘐𝘚𝘈   B c
closed Sunday, Monday, Easter week, 2 weeks August and 1 week Christmas – **M** 9.30 **t.**
(lunch) and a la carte 13.40/19.60 **t.** 🍷 3.30.

at Southam NE : 3 m. on A 46 – A – ✉ ☎ 0242 Cheltenham :

De La Bere (Best Western), GL52 3NH, ℰ 37771, Telex 43232, « Tudor manor house »,
➖ heated, 🌳, park, 🎾, squash – 📺 ☎ 🅿 🛁 🔝 🅰🅴 ⓞ 𝘝𝘐𝘚𝘈
M 11.95/12.95 **t.** and a la carte 🍷 2.95 – ☲ 4.00 – **43 rm** 45.00/74.00 **st.** – SB (except March,
Christmas and New Year) 68.00/75.00 **st.**

at Cleeve Hill NE : 4 m. on A 46 – A – ✉ Cheltenham – ☎ 024 267 Bishop's Cleeve :

Rising Sun, GL52 3PX, ℰ 6281, ≤, 🌳 – 📺 ➖wc ☎ 🅿 🛁 🔝 🅰🅴 ⓞ 𝘝𝘐𝘚𝘈 ⛱
M 9.95 **st.** and a la carte 🍷 3.40 – **24 rm** ☲ 22.00/48.00 **st.** – SB (weekends only) 56.00 **st.**

Malvern View with rm, GL52 3PR, ℰ 2017, ≤ Malvern hills, 🌳 – 📺 ➖wc 🛁wc 🅿 🔝 𝘝𝘐𝘚𝘈
⛱
closed 3 weeks Christmas-New Year – **M** *(closed Sunday to non residents)* (dinner only)
14.25 **st.** 🍷 4.00 – **7 rm** ☲ 30.00/42.50 **t.** – SB (weekends only)(November-March) 62.50 **st.**

at Andoversford SE : 6 m. on A 40 – A – ✉ ☎ 0242 Cheltenham :

Old Cold Comfort, Kilkenny, GL54 4LR, SW : 1 ½ m. on A 436 ℰ 820349, ≤, 🌳 – 🅿 🔝
8 rm ☲ 15.00/35.50 **st.**

at Shurdington SW : 3 ¾ m. on A 46 – A – ✉ ☎ 0242 Cheltenham :

Greenway ⛱, GL51 5UG, ℰ 862352, Telex 437216, ≤, « Country house, gardens », park –
📺 ☎ 🅿 🔝 🅰🅴 ⓞ 𝘝𝘐𝘚𝘈 ⛱
closed 28 December-9 January – **M** *(closed lunch Saturday and Bank Holiday Mondays)*
(Sunday dinner residents only) 15.00/22.00 **st.** – **19 rm** ☲ 60.00/115.00 **st.** – SB (weekends
only)(winter only) 97.50/137.50 **st.**

AUSTIN-ROVER Princess Elizabeth Way ℰ 520441
CITROEN, PEUGEOT-TALBOT 16-28 Bath Rd ℰ 515391
COLT 60-66 Fairview Rd ℰ 513880
FORD 71-93 Winchcombe St. ℰ 527061
HONDA 172 Leckhampton Rd ℰ 524348
LADA, YUGO, ALFA-ROMEO Stoke Orchard ℰ 024 268 (Combe Hill) 428
LANCIA Swindon Rd ℰ 32167
MAZDA Bath Rd ℰ 523879
MERCEDES-BENZ Princess Elizabeth Way ℰ 380777

RENAULT Montpellier Spa Rd ℰ 521651
RENAULT Montpellier Spa Rd ℰ 521121
ROLLS ROYCE-BENTLEY Rutherford Way ℰ 515374
SAAB, SUZUKI High St., Prestbury ℰ 44247
SEAT Charlton Kings ℰ 521131
SUBARU Bouncers Lane, Prestbury ℰ 35705
TOYOTA 38 Suffolk Rd ℰ 527778
VAUXHALL-OPEL 379 High St. ℰ 522666
VAUXHALL-OPEL Albion St. ℰ 525252
VOLVO Bishops Cleeve ℰ 674851
VW, AUDI North St. ℰ 515301

CHENIES Bucks. **404** S 28 – pop. 2 240 – ECD : Thursday – ✉ Rickmansworth (Herts.) –
☎ 092 78 Chorleywood.

◆London 30 – Aylesbury 18 – Watford 7.

Bedford Arms Thistle (Thistle), WB3 6EQ, ℰ 3301, « 16C inn », 🌳 – 📺 ☎ 🅿 🔝 🅰🅴 ⓞ
𝘝𝘐𝘚𝘈
M a la carte 15.50/17.50 **t.** 🍷 5.00 – ☲ 6.95 – **10 rm** 50.00/75.00 **st.**

In this guide

a symbol or a character, printed in red or **black**, in **bold** or light
type, does not have the same meaning.
Pay particular attention to the explanatory pages (pp. 12 to 19).

CHEPSTOW Gwent 403 404 M 29 – pop. 9 039 – ECD : Wednesday – ✪ 029 12.

See : Castle★ (stronghold) *AC*.

🆔 The Gatehouse, High St. ℰ 3772 (summer only) – ♦London 131 – ♦Bristol 17 – ♦Cardiff 28 – Gloucester 34.

🏨 **George** (T.H.F.), Moor St., NP6 5DB, ℰ 5363 – 📺 ⌂wc 🅿 🔊 AE ⓪ *VISA*
M (buffet lunch)/dinner 9.50 **st.** and a la carte ⓘ 3.75 – ☲ 5.65 – **15 rm** 40.50/48.00 **st.**

🏨 **Castle View,** 16 Bridge St., NP6 5EZ, ℰ 70349, ☞ – 📺 ⌂wc ☎. 🔊 AE ⓪ *VISA*
M 10.50 **st.** and a la carte ⓘ 3.50 – **10 rm** ☲ 27.00/45.00 **st.** – SB 52.00/56.00 **st.**

🏨 **Beaufort,** Beaufort Sq., NP5 5EP, ℰ 2497 – 📺 ⌂wc 🏵wc 🅿. 🔊 AE ⓪ *VISA* 🔅
M (bar lunch)/dinner 7.50 **t.** and a la carte ⓘ 2.95 – **18 rm** ☲ 20.00/40.00 **t.**

AUSTIN-ROVER   Station Rd ℰ 3159
FORD   Newport Rd ℰ 8155

PEUGEOT, TALBOT   Tutshill ℰ 3131
VAUXHALL-OPEL   St. Lawrence Rd ℰ 3889

CHERITON BISHOP Devon 403 I 31 – pop. 587 – ECD : Wednesday – ✉ Exeter – ✪ 064 724.

♦London 211 – Exeter 10 – ♦Plymouth 51.

🛖 **Old Thatch Inn,** EX6 6HG, ℰ 204 – 📺 🏵 🅿. 🔊
M a la carte 3.35/6.75 **t.** ⓘ 2.65 – **4 rm** ☲ 12.50/24.75 **st.** – SB (except summer and Christmas) 21.00/22.00 **st.**

CHESTER Cheshire 402 403 L 24 – pop. 80 154 – ECD : Wednesday – ✪ 0244.

See : Cathedral★★ 14C-16C (choir stalls and misericords★★) – St. John's Church★ 12C D – The Rows★ – City Walls★ – Grosvenor Museum (Roman gallery★) M1.

Envir. : Upton (Chester Zoo★★) *AC*, N : 3 m. by A 5116 – 🚍 Upton-by-Chester, Upton Lane ℰ 381183, by A 5116 – 🚍 Vicars Cross, Littleton ℰ 335174, E : 2 m. by A 51.

🆔 Town Hall, Northgate St. ℰ 40144 ext 2111/2250 – Chester Visitor Centre, Vicars Lane ℰ 313126.

♦London 207 – Birkenhead 7 – ♦Birmingham 91 – ♦Liverpool 19 – ♦Manchester 40 – Preston 52 – ♦Sheffield 76 – ♦Stoke-on-Trent 38.

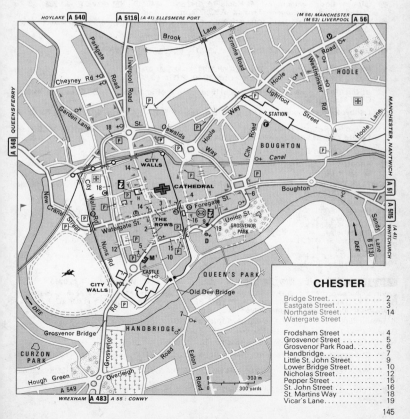

CHESTER

Chester Grosvenor, Eastgate St., CH1 1LT, ✆ 24024, Telex 61240 – 🛗 🍴 rest 📺 ☎ 🕭 🅿. 🔼 🔝 🚗
a
closed 25 and 26 December – **M** 16.00 **t.** and a la carte 🛢 5.50 – 🖵 7.50 – **104 rm** 56.00/105.00 **t.,**
5 suites 135.00/215.00 **t.** – SB (weekends only) 110.00/125.00 **st.**

Queen (T.H.F.), City Rd, CH1 3AH, ✆ 28341, Telex 617101, 🐎 – 🛗 📺 🅿. 🔼 🔝 AE ⓪ VISA r
M 6.85/9.25 **st.** and a la carte 🛢 3.40 – 🖵 5.65 – **91 rm** 44.00/54.00 **st.**

Mollington Banastre (Best Western), Parkgate Rd, CH1 6NN, NW : 2 m. on A 540
✆ 851471, Telex 61686, 🔼, 🐎, squash – 🛗 📺 🚾wc ☎ 🅿. 🔼 🔝 VISA
M 8.85/13.75 **s.** and a la carte 🛢 3.85 – **67 rm** 🖵 52.50/74.00 **st.** – SB (except Christmas)
65.00/75.00 **st.**

Post House (T.H.F.), Wrexham Rd, CH4 9DL, S : 2 m. on A 483 ✆ 674111, Telex 61450, 🐎 –
📺 🚾wc ☎ 🅿. 🔼 🔝 AE ⓪ VISA
M (buffet lunch Monday to Saturday)/dinner 11.95 **st.** and a la carte 🛢 3.40 – 🖵 5.65 – **62 rm**
45.00/55.00 **st.**, **1 suite**

Blossoms, St. John St., CH1 1HL, ✆ 23186, Telex 61113 – 🛗 📺 🚾wc 🅿. 🔼 🔝 AE ⓪
VISA
e
M 7.45/8.45 **st.** and a la carte 🛢 2.75 – **71 rm** 🖵 45.00/66.00 **st.**, **1 suite** 90.00 **st.** – SB (except
Christmas and New Year)(weekends only) 58.00/69.00 **st.**

Chester Court, 48 Hoole Rd, CH2 3NL, ✆ 20779 – 📺 🚾wc 🍴wc 🅿. 🔼 AE ⓪ VISA v
closed 24 December-2 January – **19 rm** 🖵 26.40/34.00 **t.**

City Walls, City Walls Rd, CH1 2LU, ✆ 313416 – 🛗 📺 🚾wc ☎. 🔼 🔝 VISA o
M (dinner only) 8.95 **t.** and a la carte 🛢 2.85 – 🖵 3.50 – **16 rm** 24.00/34.00 **t.** – SB (except Bank
Holidays) 46.00/49.00 **st.**

Cromwell Court without rest., 5-7 St. Martin's Way, CH1 2NR, ✆ 49202 – 📺 🍴wc ☎ 🅿.
🔼 🔝 VISA
c
🖵 3.50 – **11 rm** 24.00/32.00 **t.**

Gloster Lodge without rest., 44 Hoole Rd, CH2 3NL, ✆ 48410 – 📺 🚾wc 🅿. 🔼 VISA v
closed 24 to 31 December – **8 rm** 🖵 19.50/32.50 **st.**

Redland, 64 Hough Green, CH4 8JY, SW : 1 m. on A 549 ✆ 671024, « Victorian town house »
– 🍴wc 🅿. 🕭
closed January and February – **10 rm** 🖵 19.00/34.00 **st.**

Green Bough, 60 Hoole Rd, CH2 3NL, ✆ 26241 – 📺 🚾wc 🍴wc 🅿 i
11 rm.

✕ **Pippa's,** 58 Watergate St., CH1 2LA, ✆ 313721 – 🔼 AE VISA u
closed Sunday – **M** 14.75 **t.** and a la carte 12.50/18.05 **t.** 🛢 3.50.

at Backford Cross N : 4 ½ m. by A 5116 junction A 41 and A 5117 – ✉ Chester – ☎ 0244
Great Mollington

Ladbroke (Ladbroke), CH1 6PE, ✆ 851551, Telex 61552 – 📺 🚾wc ☎ 🕭 🅿. 🔼 🔝 AE ⓪
VISA 🕭
M *(closed Saturday lunch)* (buffet lunch)/dinner 9.95 🛢 3.70 – 🖵 5.50 – **121 rm** 45.00/55.00 **st.,**
1 suite 72.00 **st.** – SB (weekends only) 64.00 **st.**

at Christleton E : 2 m. on A 41 – ✉ ☎ 0244 Chester :

Abbots Well (Embassy), Whitchurch Rd, CH3 5QL, ✆ 332121, Telex 61561, 🐎 – 📺 🚾wc 🚗
🔼 🔝 – **127 rm**.

MICHELIN Distribution Centre, Sandycroft Industrial Estate, Glendale Av., Sandycroft, Deeside,
CH5 2QP, ✆ 537373 by A 548

AUSTIN-ROVER Victoria Rd ✆ 381246
BMW Chester Rd ✆ 311404
CITROEN Border House ✆ 672977
COLT Chester Rd ✆ 534347
DAIMLER-JAGUAR, ROLLS-ROYCE, RENAULT,
LOTUS 8 Russell St. ✆ 25262
FIAT, SUZUKI Sealand Rd ✆ 374440
FORD Bridge Gate ✆ 20444
FORD Station Rd ✆ 813414

FORD Station Rd, Queensferry ✆ 813414
MERCEDES-BENZ 36 Tarvin Rd ✆ 47441
NISSAN Hamilton Pl. ✆ 317661
SAAB Western Av. ✆ 375744
TOYOTA Welsh Rd ✆ 813633
VAUXHALL-OPEL Boughton ✆ 24611
VAUXHALL-OPEL 21-25 Garden Lane ✆ 46955
VAUXHALL-OPEL, BEDFORD Parkgate Rd ✆ 372666

CHESTERFIELD Derbs. 🄰🄾🄸 🄰🄾🄳 🄰🄾🄳 P 24 – pop. 73 352 – ECD : Wednesday – ☎ 0246.
Envir. : Chatsworth✶✶✶ : site✶✶, house✶✶✶ (Renaissance), garden✶✶✶ *AC*, W : 7 m. – Hardwick
Hall✶✶ 16C (Tapestries and embroideries✶✶) *AC*, SE : 8 m. – Bolsover Castle✶ (17C) *AC*, E : 6 m. –
Worksop (Priory Church : Norman nave✶) NE : 14 m.
🍺 Tapton Park, Murray House, Crow Lane, Tapton ✆ 73887.
🛈 The Peacock Tourist Information and Heritage Centre, Low Pavement ✆ 207777.
♦London 152 – Derby 24 – ♦Nottingham 25 – ♦Sheffield 12.

Chesterfield (Best Western), Malkin St., S41 7UA, ✆ 71141, Telex 547492 – 🛗 📺 ☎ 🚗
🔼 🔝 AE ⓪ VISA
M 6.50/8.75 **t.** and a la carte 🛢 2.95 – **61 rm** 🖵 38.50/54.00 **t.** – SB (except Christmas)(weekends
only) 55.00/57.00 **st.**

Portland, West Bars, S40 1AY, ✆ 34502 – 📺 🚾wc 🚗 🅿
24 rm.

AUSTIN-ROVER 221 Sheffield Rd ☎ 77241
BMW Pottery Lane ☎ 208681
CITROEN, AUDI Sheffield Rd ☎ 451611
DATSUN High St. Brimington ☎ 209171
FIAT 300 Northwingfield Rd ☎ 850686
FORD Chatsworth Rd ☎ 76341
PEUGEOT-TALBOT 361 Sheffield Rd ☎ 450383

PORSCHE, AUDI-VW Broombank Rd ☎ 451611
SAAB Sheffield Rd ☎ 451800
VAUXHALL 464 Chatsworth Rd ☎ 79201
VAUXHALL, RENAULT Chesterfield Rd, Staveley ☎ 473286
VOLVO Whittington Moor ☎ 453655

CHESTER-LE-STREET Durham **401 402** P 19 – pop. 34 776 – ECD : Wednesday – ☎ 0385.
Envir. : Lumley Castle★ (14C), E : 1 m. – Beamish (North of England open Air Museum★) *AC*, NW : 3 m.

☉ Lumley Park ☎ 883218, E : 1 m. off B 1284.

♦London 275 – Durham 7 – ♦Newcastle-upon-Tyne 8.

🏛 **Lumley Castle,** DH3 4NX, E : 1 m. on B 1284 ☎ 891111, Telex 537433, « 13C castle », 🚲, park – 📺 ➡wc 🚻wc ☎ 🅿. 🕿 🔼 AE ⓞ VISA
  closed 25 and 26 December – **M** 6.95/10.95 **st.** and a la carte ▮ 5.65 – **54 rm** ☲ 39.50/59.75 **st.,**
  1 suite 95.00/125.00 **st.** – SB (weekends only) 64.00/90.00 **st.**

MICHELIN Distribution Centre, Drum Rd Industrial Estate, Drum Rd, DH3 2AF, ☎ 091 (Tyneside) 410 7762

AUSTIN-ROVER Newcastle Rd ☎ 882267
COLT Picktree Lane ☎ 882761
NISSAN Pelton Rd ☎ 881813

FORD 187 Front St. ☎ 884221
VAUXHALL Hopgarth ☎ 886111

CHESTERTON Oxon. **403 404** Q 28 – pop. 1 120 – ⊠ ☎ 0869 Bicester.

♦London 65 – Northampton 33 – ♦Oxford 13.

XX **Woods,** Bignell View, OX6 8UE, on A 4095 ☎ 241444, 🚲 – 🅿. 🔼 AE ⓞ VISA
  closed Sunday dinner and Monday – **M** 17.75 **t.** ▮ 2.55.

☛ *Use this year's Guide.*

CHICHESTER West Sussex **404** R 31 – pop. 26 050 – ECD : Thursday – ☎ 0243.
See : Cathedral★ 11C-15C BZ **A** – Market Cross★ BZ **B**.
Envir. : Fishbourne Roman Palace (mosaics★) *AC* W : 2 m. AZ **R** – Goodwood House★ (18C) *AC*, NE : 4 m. by A 27 AY and A 285.

☉ Goodwood ☎ 527491, NE : 4½ m. off A 27.

🛈 The Council House, St. Peter's Market, West St. ☎ 775888.

♦London 69 – ♦Brighton 31 – ♦Portsmouth 18 – ♦Southampton 30.

CHICHESTER

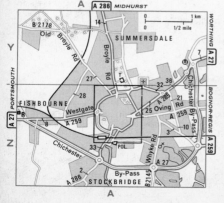

Dolphin and Anchor (T.H.F.), West St., PO19 1QE, ℰ 785121 – 📺 🛁 📼 AE ⓪ VISA
BZ **a**
M 8.95/10.55 **st.** and a la carte ⬧ 3.40 – ⌘ 5.65 – **54 rm** 45.00/56.00 **st.**

Chichester Lodge, Westhampnett Roundabout, PO19 4UL, on A 27 ℰ 786351, 🌲 – 📺
AY **u**
🗄wc ☎ 🅿 🛁 📼 AE VISA
closed Christmas – **M** 8.00/11.00 **t.** and a la carte ⬧ 3.20 – **43 rm** ⌘ 40.00/55.00 **t.** – SB
56.00/58.00 **st.**

Bedford, Southgate, PO19 1DP, ℰ 785766 – 📺 🎛 📼 AE ⓪ VISA
BZ **i**
M (closed Sunday) (bar lunch)/dinner a la carte 5.80/10.00 **st.** ⬧ 3.00 – **27 rm** ⌘ 19.50/40.00 **st.**
– SB (except summer) 44.00/50.00 **st.**

Ship, North St., PO19 1NH, ℰ 782028, Telex 86276 – 🎛 📺 🗄wc 🅿 📼 AE ⓪ VISA 🌿
M (buffet lunch Monday to Saturday)/dinner 8.75 **t.** and a la carte ⬧ 3.20 – **36 rm**
BY **r**
⌘ 34.00/48.00 **t.** – SB (except Bank Holidays) 62.00/72.00 **st.**

XX **Clinchs'** with rm, 4 Guildhall St., PO19 1NJ, ℰ 789915, « Tastefully furnished town house »
BY **s**
– 📺 🗄wc 🎛wc ☎ 🅿 📼 AE ⓪ VISA 🌿
closed Christmas – **M** (closed Sunday) (dinner only) 16.50 **t.** ⬧ 3.75 – **7 rm** ⌘ 40.00/55.00 **t.**

at Chilgrove N : 6 ½ m. by A 286 – AY – on B 2141 – ✉ Chichester – ✪ 024 359 East
Marden :

XX **White Horse Inn,** 1 High St., PO18 9HX, ℰ 219, English rest. – 🅿 📼 AE ⓪ VISA
closed Sunday dinner, Monday, 3 weeks February and 1 week October – **M** 12.95/15.95 **t.**
⬧ 3.45.

at Charlton N : 6 ¼ m. by A 286 – AY – ✉ Chichester – ✪ 024 363 Singleton :

⌂ **Woodstock House,** PO18 0HU, ℰ 666, 🌲 – 🗄wc 🎛wc 🅿 🌿
Mid February-mid November – **11 rm** ⌘ 17.00/40.00 **t.**

at Goodwood NE : 3 ½ m. by A 27 AY on East Dean Rd – ✉ ✪ 0243 Chichester :

Goodwood Park (Best Western), PO18 0QB, ℰ 775537, Telex 869173, 🌲 – 📺 🗄wc ☎ 🛁
🅿 🛁 📼 AE ⓪ VISA
M 9.50/14.50 **st.** and a la carte ⬧ 3.50 – **50 rm** ⌘ 42.00/60.00 **st.**, **5 suites** 90.00 **st.** – SB
60.00/88.00 **st.**

at Bosham W : 4 m. by A 27 – AZ – ✉ ✪ 0243 Chichester :

Millstream (Best Western), Bosham Lane, PO18 8HL, ℰ 573234, « Tasteful decor », 🌲 –
📺 🗄wc ☎ 🅿 📼 AE ⓪ VISA
M 9.50 **t.** (dinner) and a la carte 11.50/14.00 **t.** ⬧ 2.50 – **29 rm** ⌘ 32.00/68.00 **st.** – SB
59.00/75.00 **st.**

AUSTIN-ROVER Westhampnett Rd ℰ 781331
FIAT Northgate ℰ 784844
FORD The Hornet ℰ 788100
MERCEDES-BENZ Quarry Lane ℰ 776111
PEUGEOT-TALBOT-CITROEN 113 The Hornet ℰ
782293

RENAULT Delling Lane, Bosham ℰ 573271
TOYOTA Tangmere By-Pass (A 27) ℰ 773855
VAUXHALL-OPEL, BEDFORD, FIAT City Service
Centre, Terminus Rd ℰ 774321
VW, AUDI 51-54 Bognor Rd ℰ 787684

CHIDDINGFOLD Surrey 🔢 S 30 – pop. 2 209 – ✪ 042 879 Wormley.
◆London 45 – ◆Brighton 40 – Guildford 12.

XXX **Crown Inn** with rm, The Green, Petworth Rd, GU8 4TX, ℰ 2255, « 13C inn » – 📺 🗄wc ☎
🅿 📼 AE ⓪ VISA
closed Christmas night – **M** 12.00 **t.** and a la carte 18.95/22.95 **t.** ⬧ 4.00 – ⌘ 3.00 – **8 rm**
35.00/65.00 **t.**

CHIDEOCK Dorset 🔢 L 31 – see Bridport.

CHILGROVE West Sussex 🔢 R 31 – see Chichester.

CHILLINGTON Devon 🔢 I 33 – see Kingsbridge.

CHILTON POLDEN Somerset – see Bridgwater.

CHINNOR Oxon. 🔢 R 28 – pop. 5 432 – ✪ 0844 Kingston Blount.
◆London 45 – ◆Oxford 19.

at Sprigg's Alley E : 2 m. – ✉ Chinnor – ✪ 024 026 Radnage :

X **Sir Charles Napier Inn,** OX9 4BX, by Bledlow Ridge Rd ℰ 3011, 🌲 – 🅿 AE ⓪
closed 4 days late summer and 4 days after Christmas – **M** (closed Sunday dinner and
Monday) 7.50/9.50 **t.** and a la carte 10.75/16.75 **t.** ⬧ 2.75.

Für die 🏨 , 🏨 , 🏨 , geben wir keine Einzelheiten
über die Einrichtung an,
da diese Hotels im allgemeinen jeden Komfort besitzen.

🗄wc 🎛wc

☎

CHIPPENHAM Wilts. **403 404** N 29 The West Country G. – pop. 21 325 – ECD : Wednesday – ✆ 0249.

See : Yelde Hall★ *AC* – Envir. : Biddestone★, W : 4 ½ m. – Sheldon Manor★ *AC*, W : 1 ½ m. – Bowood House★ *AC* (Library ≼★ of the Park), SE : 5 m.

🖿 Malmesbury Rd ✆ 652040, N : 1 m.

🎫 The Neeld Hall, High St. ✆ 657733.

◆London 93 – ◆Bristol 27 – ◆Southampton 64 – Swindon 21.

🏠 **Angel** (Norfolk Cap.), 8 Market Pl., SN15 3HD, ✆ 652615, Group Telex 23241 – 📺 🛏wc ☎ 🅿 🏄 🏧 🆎 ⓪ *VISA*
M 7.00/8.50 **st.** and a la carte ⑂ 3.00 – **43 rm** ⊊ 23.00/45.00 **st.** – SB 40.00/45.00 **st.**

FIAT New Rd ✆ 652215
FORD Cocklebury Rd ✆ 653255
RENAULT London Rd ✆ 651131

VAUXHALL-OPEL 16-17 The Causeway ✆ 654321
VOLVO Malmesbury Rd ✆ 652016

CHIPPERFIELD Herts. **404** ㊼ – pop. 1 764 – ECD : Wednesday – ⊠ ✆ 092 77 Kings Langley.

◆ London 27 – Hemel Hempstead 5 – Watford 6.

🏠 **Two Brewers Inn** (T.H.F.), The Common, WD4 9BS, ✆ 65266 – 📺 🛏wc ☎ 🅿 🏄 🆎 ⓪ *VISA*
M 9.50/13.00 **st.** and a la carte ⑂ 3.00 – ⊊ 5.65 – **20 rm** 48.00/58.00 **st.**

CHIPPING Lancs. **402** M 22 – pop. 1 376 – ⊠ Preston – ✆ 099 56.

◆London 233 – Lancaster 30 – ◆Leeds 54 – ◆Manchester 40 – Preston 12.

🏠 **Gibbon Bridge Country House** ⑊, PR3 2TQ, E : 1 m. on Clitheroe Rd ✆ 456, ≼, ᾟ – 📺 🛏wc ☎ 🅿 🏄 *VISA* ⑊
M 5.95 **t.** (lunch)/dinner a la carte – **7 rm** ⊊ 20.00/30.00 **t.** – SB (except Christmas) 36.00 **st.**

CHIPPING CAMPDEN Glos. **403 404** O 27 – pop. 1 936 – ECD : Thursday – ✆ 0386 Evesham.

See : High Street★ – Envir. : Hidcote Manor Garden★ *AC*, NE : 2 ½ m.

🎫 Woolstaplers Hall Museum, High St. ✆ 840289 (summer only).

◆London 93 – Cheltenham 21 – ◆Oxford 37 – Stratford-upon-Avon 12.

🏠 **King's Arms**, The Square, GL55 6AW, ✆ 840256, ᾟ – 🛏wc. 🏧 *VISA*
M (bar lunch Monday to Saturday)/dinner 13.25 **st.** ⑂ 4.00 – **14 rm** ⊊ 25.00/60.00 **st.** – SB (weekends only)(November-March) 54.00/62.00 **st.**

🏠 **Noel Arms**, High St., GL55 6AT, ✆ 840317 – 🛏wc 🛏wc 🅿 🏧 *VISA* ⑊
M 7.50/11.50 **t.** and a la carte ⑂ 3.50 – **19 rm** ⊊ 33.00/43.50 **t.** – SB (November-April) 95.00/110.00 **st.**

✕ **Caminetto**, Old Kings Arms Pantry, High St., GL55 6AG, ✆ 840934, Italian rest. – 🏧 *VISA*
closed Monday lunch and Sunday – **M** a la carte 5.80/13.40 **t.** ⑂ 3.20.

at Mickleton N : 3 ¼ m. by B 4035 and B 4081 on A 46 – ⊠ Chipping Campden – ✆ 038 677 Mickleton :

🏠 **Three Ways**, Chapel Lane, GL55 6SB, ✆ 231 – 📺 🛏wc 🅿 ⑂ ⚹ 🅿 🏄 🏧 🆎 ⓪ *VISA*
closed 1 to 11 January – **M** (bar lunch Monday to Saturday)/dinner 10.00 **t.** ⑂ 2.95 – **37 rm** ⊊ 28.00/46.00 **t.** – SB (weekends only) 52.00/58.00 **st.**

at Broad Campden S : 1 ¼ m. by B 4081 – ⊠ Chipping Campden – ✆ 0386 Evesham :

🏠 **Malt House** ⑊, GL55 6UU, S : ¼ m. ✆ 840295, ᾟ – 📺 🛏wc. 🏧 *VISA* ⑊
closed 24 December-1 January – **M** (closed Sunday) (dinner only) 14.50 **t.** – **6 rm** ⊊ 20.00/56.00 **t.**

AUSTIN-ROVER High St. ✆ 840213
CITROEN Sheep St. ✆ 840221

FORD Mickleton ✆ 038 677 (Mickleton) 270

CHIPPING NORTON Oxon. **403 404** P 28 – pop. 5 003 – ECD : Thursday – ✆ 0608.

🎫 22 New St. ✆ 41320.

◆London 77 – ◆Birmingham 44 – Gloucester 36 – ◆Oxford 21.

🏠 **White Hart** (T.H.F.), High St., OX7 5AD, ✆ 2572 – 📺 🛏wc ☎ 🅿 🏧 🆎 ⓪ *VISA*
M (bar lunch Monday to Saturday)/dinner 8.50 **st.** and a la carte ⑂ 2.90 – ⊊ 5.65 – **21 rm** 34.00/44.00 **st.**

✕✕ **La Madonette**, 7 Horse Fair, OX7 5AL, ✆ 2320 – 🏧 *VISA*
closed Sunday, Monday and 25 December-2 January – **M** (dinner only) a la carte 13.25/20.35 **t.** ⑂ 2.55.

AUSTIN-ROVER London Rd ✆ 2014

VAUXHALL-OPEL Burford Rd ✆ 2461

CHIPSTEAD Surrey **404** T 30 – pop. 7 177 (inc. Hooley and Woodmansterne) – ✆ 073 75 Downland.

◆London 15 – Reigate 6.

✕✕✕ **Dene Farm**, Outwood Lane, CR3 3NP, on B 2032 ✆ 52661, ᾟ – 🅿 🏧 🆎 ⓪ *VISA*
closed Saturday lunch, Sunday dinner, Monday, 2 weeks August and 2 weeks January – **M** 15.75 **st.** and a la carte 19.75 **st.**

BMW Outwood Lane ✆ 56789

CHISLEHAMPTON Oxon. – ⊠ Oxford – ✆ 0865 Stadhampton.
♦London 55 – ♦Oxford 7.

  🏠 **Coach and Horses,** OX9 7UX, ✆ 890255 – 📺 🛁wc 🚿wc ☎ & 🅿
    M *(closed Saturday lunch and Sunday to non-residents)* 9.00 **t.** and a la carte – **9 rm**
    🛏 35.00/61.00 **st.** – SB (weekends only) 39.50/55.00 **st.**

CHITTLEHAMHOLT Devon **403** I 31 – pop. 259 – ⊠ Umberleigh – ✆ 076 94.
♦London 216 – Barnstaple 14 – Exeter 28 – Taunton 45.

  🏨 **Highbullen** ⑤, EX37 9HD, ✆ 561, ≤, ⤴ heated, 🗻, ⅂ₛ, ⟋, 🚗, park, ⚒, squash – 📺
    M (buffet lunch)/dinner 11.50 **st.** ↕ 2.95 – 🛏 1.00 – **35 rm** 26.50/53.00 **st.** – SB (weekdays
    only) 60.00/70.00 **st.**

CHOLLERFORD Northumb. **401 402** N 18 – ⊠ Hexham – ✆ 043 481 Humshaugh.
♦London 303 – ♦Carlisle 36 – ♦Newcastle-upon-Tyne 21.

  🏨 **George (Swallow),** NE46 4EW, ✆ 611, Group Telex 53168, ≤, « Riverside gardens », 🗻, ⟋
    – 📺 🛁wc 🅿 🅿 ⚙ ⚞ 🔼 AE ⓞ VISA
    M 7.40/10.50 **st.** and a la carte ↕ 3.75 – **54 rm** 🛏 38.00/55.00 **st.** – SB 62.00/70.00 **st.**

CHORLEY Lancs. **402 404** M 23 – pop. 33 465 – ECD : Wednesday – ✆ 025 72.
♦London 222 – ♦Blackpool 30 – ♦Liverpool 32 – ♦Manchester 26.

  at Whittle-le-Woods N : 2 m. on A 6 – ✆ 025 72 Chorley :

  🏨 **Shaw Hill H. Golf and Country Club** ⑤, Preston Road, PR6 7PP, ✆ 69221, ≤, ⅂ₛ – 📺
    🛁wc 🅿 🅿 ⚙ ⚞ 🔼 AE ⓞ VISA
    M (bar lunch Saturday) 10.95/10.00 **t.** and a la carte ↕ 2.80 – 🛏 5.00 – **22 rm** 40.00/60.00 **t.** –
    SB 75.00/90.00 **st.**

  at Adlington S : 3 m. on A 6 – ⊠ Chorley – ✆ 0257 Adlington :

  🏠 **Glad Mar** ⑤, Railway Rd, PR6 9NE, ✆ 480398, 🚗 – 📺 🛁wc 🚿 🅿 🔼 VISA ⚒
    M (bar lunch)/dinner 7.80 **t.** and a la carte ↕ 2.80 – **13 rm** 🛏 23.00/34.00 **t.**

CHRISTCHURCH Dorset **403 404** O 31 – pop. 32 854 – ECD : Wednesday – ✆ 0202.
See : Site★ – Priory★ – **Envir. :** Hengistbury Head★ (≤★★), SW : 4 m. by B 3059.
⅂ₛ Ilford Bridge, Barrack Rd ✆ 473912, W : on A 5.
🛈 30 Saxon Sq. ✆ 471780.
♦London 111 – Bournemouth 6 – Salisbury 26 – ♦Southampton 24 – Winchester 39.

  🏛 **King's Arms,** 18 Castle St., BH23 1DT, ✆ 484117 – 🔔 📺 🛁wc 🚿wc ☎ 🅿 ⚞ 🔼 AE ⓞ
    VISA
    M (carving rest.) 5.65 **t.** and a la carte ↕ 3.00 – **32 rm** 🛏 21.50/41.50 **t.** – SB (weekends only)
    53.00 **t.**

  ↑ **Park House,** 48 Barrack Rd, BH23 1PF, ✆ 482124, 🚗 – 🅿 🔼 VISA ⚒
    9 rm 🛏 12.50/37.50 **st.**

  ✕ **Splinters,** 12 Church St., BH23 1BW, ✆ 483454 – AE ⓞ VISA
    closed Sunday and 25-26 December – **M** (dinner only) a la carte 13.65/16.25 **t.** ↕ 2.75.

  at Mudeford SE : 2 m. – ⊠ ✆ 0202 Christchurch :

  🏨 **Avonmouth** (T.H.F.), BH23 3NT, ✆ 483434, ≤ Christchurch harbour, ⤴ heated, 🚗 – 📺
    🛁wc ⚙ 🅿 ⚞ 🔼 AE ⓞ VISA
    M (buffet lunch Monday to Saturday)/dinner 8.75 **st.** and a la carte ↕ 3.40 – 🛏 5.65 – **41 rm**
    40.00/62.00 **st.**

  ↑ **The Pines,** 39 Mudeford, BH23 3NQ, ✆ 482393 – 📺 🚿wc 🅿
    14 rm 🛏 13.50/32.00 **st.**

AUSTIN-ROVER Highcliffe ✆ 042 52 (Highcliffe)   FORD Lyndhurst Rd ✆ 042 52 (Highcliffe) 71371
77703   VW, AUDI 105 Summerford Rd ✆ 476871
CITROEN Barrack Rd ✆ 479351

CHRISTLETON Cheshire **402 403** L 24 – see Chester.

CHURCH STRETTON Salop **403** L 26 – pop. 2 932 – ECD : Wednesday – ✆ 0694.
⅂ₛ Links Rd ✆ 722281.
🛈 Church St. ✆ 722535 (summer only).
♦London 166 – ♦Birmingham 46 – Hereford 39 – Shrewsbury 14.

  🏨 **Stretton Hall** ⑤, Old Shrewsbury Rd, All Stretton, SY6 6HG, NE : 1 m. on B 4370 ✆ 723224,
    🚗 – 📺 🛁wc 🚿 & 🅿 🔼 🅿 🔼 AE ⓞ VISA
    M 6.50/9.50 **t.** and a la carte ↕ 3.50 – **13 rm** 🛏 32.00/43.00 **st.** – SB (weekends only)(weekdays
    in winter) 52.00 **st.**

  ↑ **Mynd House,** Ludlow Rd, Little Stretton, SY6 6RB, SW : 1 m. on B 4370 ✆ 722212, ≤, 🚗 –
    🛁wc 🔼 🔼 VISA
    closed 16 December-31 January – **13 rm** 🛏 15.00/31.00 **t.**

CHURT Surrey 404 R 30 — see Farnham.

CILGERRAN Dyfed 403 G 27 — see Cardigan.

CIRENCESTER Glos. 403 404 O 28 — pop. 13 491 — ECD : Thursday — ☎ 0285.
See : Parish Church★ (Perpendicular) — Corinium Museum★.
Envir. : Chedworth (Roman Villa ★) *AC*, N : 7 m.
🛞 Cheltenham Rd ✆ 2465, N : 1 ½ m.
🛈 Corn Hall, Market Pl. ✆ 4180.
◆London 97 — ◆Bristol 37 — Gloucester 19 — ◆Oxford 37.

🏛 **Fleece**, Market Pl., GL7 4NZ, ✆ 68507 — 📺 ⇔wc ☎ 🅿. 🔼 🆔 ⓞ *VISA*
closed 25 and 26 December — **M** 8.25/12.45 st. and a la carte ↕ 3.25 — ⌧ 4.95 — **25 rm** 39.50/49.50 st. — SB (weekends only) 56.00 st.

🏛 **King's Head** (Best Western), 24 Market Pl., GL7 2NR, ✆ 3322, Telex 43470 — 🔄 📺 ⇔wc ☎ 🅿. 🔒 🔼 🆔 ⓞ *VISA*
closed 27 to 30 December — **M** 7.85/10.25 st. and a la carte ↕ 4.50 — **70 rm** ⌧ 36.00/58.00 st. — SB 50.00/70.00 st.

🏠 **Corinium Court,** 12 Gloucester St., GL7 2DG, ✆ 69711 — 📺 ⇔wc ▥wc ☎ 🅿. 🔼 🆔 ⓞ *VISA*
M (closed Sunday dinner) (bar lunch)/dinner a la carte 12.05/15.40 t. ↕ 3.50 — **12 rm** ⌧ 38.00/48.00 t.

⚲ **La Ronde,** 52-54 Ashcroft Rd, GL7 1QX, ✆ 4611 — 📺 ▥wc. ⌘
10 rm ⌧ 18.50/34.50 t.

⚲ **Wimborne,** 91 Victoria Rd, GL7 1ES, ✆ 3890 — 📺 ⇔wc 🅿. ⌘
5 rm ⌧ 17.50/25.00 st.

at Ewen SW : 3 ¼ m. by A 429 — ✉ Cirencester — ☎ 028 577 Kemble :

🍴 **Wild Duck Inn,** GL7 6BY, ✆ 364, ⇞ — 📺 ⇔wc 🅿. 🔼 🆔 ⓞ *VISA*. ⌘
M 8.50/11.50 t. and a la carte ↕ 4.95 — ⌧ 3.50 — **8 rm** 32.00/42.00 t., **1 suite** 50.00/60.00 t. — SB (weekends only) 60.00 st.

at Stratton NW : 1 ¼ m. on A 417 — ✉ ☎ 0285 Cirencester :

🏛 **Stratton House,** Gloucester Rd, GL7 2LE, ✆ 61761, ⇞ — ⇔wc ▥wc ⊗ 🅿. 🔒 🔼 🆔 ⓞ *VISA*
M 7.50/10.50 st. and a la carte ↕ 3.30 — **26 rm** ⌧ 31.50/46.50 st. — SB 79.00/84.00 st.

AUSTIN-ROVER Tetbury Rd ✆ 2614
CITROEN Perrotts Brook ✆ 028 583 (North Cerney) 219
COLT Love Lane ✆ 5799
NISSAN Chesterton Lane ✆ 2196

PEUGEOT-TALBOT Victoria Rd ✆ 3460
RENAULT Gloucester Rd ✆ 68007
VAUXHALL-OPEL Lovelane Trading Estate ✆ 3314
VOLVO 10 Love Lane ✆ 69112

CLACTON-ON-SEA Essex 404 X 28 — pop. 39 618 — ECD : Wednesday — ☎ 0255.
See : Sea front (gardens)★.
🛈 Central Seafront, Marine Parade ✆ 423400 (summer only).
◆London 71 — Chelmsford 38 — Colchester 16.

🏠 **Kings Cliff,** 55 Kings Par., Esplanade, Holland-on-Sea, CO15 5JB, NE : 1 ½ m. ✆ 812343, ⪕ — 📺 ⇔wc ▥wc 🅿. 🔼 ⌘
M 5.50/7.25 st. and a la carte ↕ 1.75 — **16 rm** ⌧ 25.00/45.00 t. — SB (except summer)(weekends only) 55.00/75.00 st.

AUSTIN-ROVER 107 Old Rd ✆ 424128
BEDFORD, OPEL-VAUXHALL 65 High St. ✆ 420444

CITROEN 67 Frinton Rd ✆ 812205
FORD St John's Rd ✆ 425487

CLANFIELD Oxon. 403 404 P 28 — pop. 822 — ECD : Wednesday and Saturday — ☎ 036 781.
◆London 76 — ◆Oxford 20 — Swindon 17.

🍴 **Plough at Clanfield** with rm, Bourton Rd, OX8 2RB, on A 4095 ✆ 222, Group Telex 449848, « Small Elizabethan manor house », ⇞ — 📺 ⇔wc ▥wc ☎ 🅿. 🔼 🆔 ⓞ *VISA*. ⌘
M (booking essential) 9.95/18.95 t. — **7 rm** ⌧ 49.50/75.00 t. — SB (except 1 week March and Christmas) 64.90/77.90 st.

CLAPHAM Beds. 404 S 27 — see Bedford.

CLAPPERSGATE Cumbria — see Ambleside.

CLAUGHTON Lancs. 402 M 21 — pop. 121 — ✉ Lancaster — ☎ 0468 Hornby.
◆London 254 — Kendal 25 — Lancaster 6 — ◆Leeds 63.

🏛 **Old Rectory,** LA2 9LA, on A 683 ✆ 21455, ⇞ — 📺 ⇔wc 🅿. 🔼 *VISA*. ⌘
M (closed Sunday) (lunch by arrangement)/dinner 14.85 t. — **12 rm** ⌧ 34.50/49.50 t.

CLAVERDON Warw. 403 404 O 27 — see Henley-in-Arden.

CLAVERING Essex 404 U 28 – pop. 1 076 – ✪ 079 985.
◆London 44 – ◆Cambridge 25 – Colchester 44 – Luton 29.

   ✗ **Cricketers**, CB11 4QT, ✆ 442 – **P**. 🖭 VISA
    M (bar lunch Monday to Saturday)/dinner 12.50 t.

CLAWTON Devon 403 H 31 – pop. 300 – ✉ Holsworthy – ✪ 040 927 North Tamerton.
◆London 240 – Exeter 39 – ◆Plymouth 36.

   🏠 **Court Barn** ⑤, EX22 6PS, W : ½ m. ✆ 219, « Gardens » – ➖wc ⑪wc **P**. 🖭 AE ① VISA
    M 4.25/10.50 **st.** and a la carte ⑧ 2.95 – **8 rm** ⇆ 18.00/36.00 – SB 44.00/50.00 **st.**

CLAYGATE Surrey 404 ⑫ – see Esher.

CLAYTON-LE-MOORS Lancs 402 M 22 – pop. 5 484 – ECD : Wednesday – ✉ ✪ 0254 Accrington.
◆London 232 – Blackburn 3.5 – Lancaster 37 – ◆Leeds 44 – Preston 14.

   🏨 **Dunkenhalgh**, Blackburn Rd, BB5 5JP, W : 1 ½ m. on A 678 ✆ 398021, Telex 63282, ✿, park
   – 🖭 ➖wc 🚿 ⑪. 🖭 AE ① VISA
    M 7.00/12.00 **st.** and a la carte ⑧ 3.95 – **50 rm** ⇆ 41.00/55.00 **st.**, **1 suite** 48.00/63.00 **st.** – SB
    (weekends only) 47.00/52.00 **st.**

CLAYWORTH Notts. 402 404 R 23 – pop. 275 – ✉ ✪ 0777 Retford.
◆London 150 – ◆Leeds 49 – Lincoln 26 – ◆Nottingham 38 – ◆Sheffield 29.

   🏠 **Royston Manor** ⑤, St. Peters Lane, DN22 9AA, ✆ 817484, ≤, ✿ – 🖭 ➖wc ⑪wc ☎ **P**.
   🖭 AE ① VISA
    M (closed Saturday lunch) a la carte approx. 4.35 **st.** ⑧ 3.00 – **12 rm** ⇆ 23.00/38.00 **st.** – SB
    (weekends only) 44.00 **st.**

CLEARWELL Glos. – see Coleford.

CLEETHORPES Humberside 402 404 U 23 – pop. 33 238 – ECD : Thursday – ✪ 0472.
🛈 43 Alexandra Rd ✆ 697472.
◆London 171 – Boston 49 – Lincoln 38 – ◆Sheffield 77.

Plan : see Great Grimsby

   🏨 **Kingsway**, Kingsway, DN35 0AE, ✆ 601122, ≤ – 🛉 🖭 ➖wc ☜ ⇦ **P**. 🖭 AE ① VISA
   ❀
    BZ **a**
    closed 25 and 26 December – **M** 7.50/10.00 **st.** and a la carte ⑧ 3.25 – **55 rm** ⇆ 34.50/55.00 **st.**
    – SB (weekends only) 58.00 **st.**

   🏠 **Wellow**, Kings Rd, DN35 0AQ, ✆ 695589 – 🖭 ➖wc ☜ **P**
    Y
    10 rm.

CITROEN 76-80 Brereton Av. ✆ 56417   LANCIA 421 Grimsby Rd ✆ 698991

CLEEVE HILL Glos. 403 404 N 28 – see Cheltenham.

CLEOBURY MORTIMER Salop 403 404 M 26 – pop. 1 883 – ✪ 0299.
◆London 147 – ◆Birmingham 29 – Shrewsbury 35.

   🏠 **Redfern**, Lower St., DY14 8AA, ✆ 270395, Telex 335176 – 🖭 ➖wc 🚿 ☎ **P**. 🖭 AE ①
   VISA
    M 6.00/9.25 **st.** and a la carte ⑧ 3.00 – **11 rm** ⇆ 26.00/40.00 **st.** – SB (except Christmas)
    48.00/50.50 **st.**

CLEVEDON Avon 403 L 29 The West Country G. – pop. 17 875 – ECD : Wednesday – ✪ 0272.
See : Site* (≤ from park benches**) – Clevedon Court*AC.
◆London 138 – ◆Bristol 15 – Taunton 34.

   🏨 **Walton Park**, 1 Wellington Terr., BS21 7BL, ✆ 874253, ≤, ✿ – 🛉 🖭 ➖wc ⑪wc ☎ ⇦
   P. 🖭 AE ① VISA
    M a la carte 9.00/11.25 **t.** – **35 rm** ⇆ 27.00/47.00 **t.** – SB (except Christmas)(weekends only)
    49.00/53.95 **st.**

AUSTIN-ROVER Old Church Rd ✆ 872201

CLIFFORD CHAMBERS Warw. – see Stratford-upon-Avon.

CLIMPING West Sussex 404 S 31 – pop. 925 – ✉ Littlehampton – ✪ 0903 Arundel.
◆London 64 – Bognor Regis 5 – ◆ Brighton 23.

   🏨 **Bailiffscourt** ⑤, Climping St., BN17 5RW, ✆ 723511, Telex 877870, «Reconstructed
   medieval house », ⅃, ✿, park, ✗ – 🖭 ➖wc **P**. 🚿 🖭 AE ① VISA
    M 10.50/17.50 **st.** and a la carte – **20 rm** ⇆ 50.00/120.00 **st.**

CLIVEDEN Berks. 404 R 29 – see Maidenhead.

152

CLOWNE Derbs. 402 403 404 Q 24 — pop. 6 846 — ECD : Wednesday — ✆ 0246 Chesterfield.
♦London 156 — Derby 40 — Lincoln 35 — ♦Nottingham 30 — ♦Sheffield 12.

🏛 **Van Dyk,** Worksop Rd, S43 4TD, N : ¾ m. on A 619 🖉 810219 — TV ⌂wc 🏦wc ☎ 🅿 🛁.
🔃 AE VISA
M *(closed Sunday dinner)* 9.95 **t.** and a la carte — 🖵 5.50 — **16 rm** 29.00/48.00 **t.** — SB (except Christmas and New Year)(weekends only) 79.00/89.00 **st.**

CLUN Salop 403 KL 26 — pop. 817 — ✉ Craven Arms — ✆ 058 84.
♦London 178 — ♦Birmingham 60 — Shrewsbury 29.

🏤 **Sun Inn,** High St., SY7 8JB, 🖉 559 — 🏦wc 🅿 🔃 🌿
M a la carte 6.00/8.50 **t.** — **7 rm** 🖵 13.00/30.00 **t.** — SB (November-April)(weekdays only) 30.00/40.00 **st.**

✗ **Old Post Office** with rm, 9 The Square, SY7 8HA, 🖉 687, ⇐ — 🌿
closed February — **M** *(closed Sunday and Monday to non residents)* (restricted lunch in summer)/dinner 13.50 **t.** 🍷 3.00 — **3 rm** 🖵 13.50/30.00 **t.**

COATHAM MUNDEVILLE Durham 402 P 20 — see Darlington.

COBHAM Surrey 404 S 30 — pop. 13 920 — ECD : Wednesday — ✆ 0932.
Envir. : Wisley gardens★★ *AC*, SW : 4 m. by A 3 AZ.
♦London 24 — Guildford 10.

Plan : see Greater London (South-West)

🏛 **Ladbroke Seven Hills** (Ladbroke), Seven Hills Rd South, KT11 1EW, W : 1 ½ m. by A 245 🖉 64471, Telex 929196, 🏊 heated, 🌲, park, ✾, squash — 🛗 TV ⌂wc ☎ 🅿 🛁 🔃 AE ⓸ VISA 🌿
M a la carte 11.00/13.95 🍷 3.70 — 🖵 6.00 — **111 rm** 57.00/72.50 **st., 3 suites** 90.00 **st.**

✗✗ **San Domenico,** Portsmouth Rd, KT11 1EL, SW : 1 m. on A 3 🖉 63006, Italian rest., 🌲 — 🅿
🔃 AE ⓸ VISA
closed Sunday dinner and Bank Holidays — **M** a la carte 12.00/16.30 **t.** 🍷 2.75.

by A 3   AZ

AUDI-VW 42 Portsmouth Rd 🖉 4493   BMW 22 Portsmouth Rd 🖉 7141
AUSTIN-ROVER Stoke Rd 🖉 4244

COCKERMOUTH Cumbria 401 402 J 20 — pop. 7 074 — ECD : Thursday — ✆ 0900.
🚩 Riverside Car Park, Market St. 🖉 822634 (summer only).
♦London 306 — ♦Carlisle 25 — Keswick 13.

🏛 **Trout,** Crown St., CA13 0EJ, 🖉 823591, 🦢, 🌲 — TV ⌂wc 🏦wc ☎ 🅿 🔃 VISA
closed Christmas Day — **M** 6.50/11.00 **t.** and a la carte 🍷 3.00 — **16 rm** 🖵 25.00/39.00 **t.** — SB (weekends only) 46.00/50.00 **st.**

🏠 **Wordsworth,** Main St., CA13 9JS, 🖉 822757 — TV ⌂wc 🏦wc 🅿 🔃 VISA 🌿
closed Christmas Day — **M** (bar lunch)/dinner 8.00 **t.** and a la carte 🍷 3.00 — **18 rm** 🖵 17.00/35.00 **t.** — SB (weekends only)(except Bank Holidays) 48.00/58.00 **st.**

at Great Broughton W : 2 ¾ m. by A 66 — ✉ ✆ 0900 Cockermouth :

🏛 **Broughton Craggs** 🦢, CA13 0XW, 🖉 824400, 🌲 — TV ⌂wc 🏦wc ☎ 🅿 🔃 AE VISA 🌿
M 6.00/10.00 **t.** and a la carte 🍷 3.00 — **10 rm** 🖵 29.00/40.00 **t.** — SB (weekends only except Bank Holidays) 45.00 **st.**

BMW, VOLVO Derwent St. 🖉 823666   FORD Lorton St. 🖉 822033

COED-DUON = Blackwood.

COGGESHALL Essex 404 W 28 — pop. 3 505 — ECD : Wednesday — ✉ Colchester — ✆ 0376.
♦London 49 — Braintree 6 — Chelmsford 16 — Colchester 9.

🏛 **White Hart,** Market End, CO6 1NH, 🖉 61654, « Part 14C Guild Hall » — TV ⌂wc ☎ 🅿 🔃 AE ⓸ VISA 🌿
closed August and 2 weeks Christmas — **M** *(closed lunch Monday and Saturday, Sunday dinner and Friday)* a la carte 18.00/22.00 **st.** — **18 rm** 🖵 35.00/60.00 **st.**

COLCHESTER Essex 404 W 28 — pop. 87 476 — ECD : Thursday — ✆ 0206.
See : Roman Walls★.
Envir. : Layer Marney (Marney Tower★ 16C) SW : 7 m.
🏌 Birch Grove, Layer Rd 🖉 020 634 (Layer-de-la-Haye) 276, S : 2 m.
🚩 Town Hall, High St. 🖉 46379 and 712233.
♦London 52 — ♦Cambridge 48 — ♦Ipswich 18 — Luton 76 — Southend-on-Sea 41.

🏛 **George** (Q.M.H.), 116 High St., CO1 1TD, 🖉 578494 — TV ⌂wc ☎ 🅿 🛁 🔃 AE ⓸ VISA
M (carving rest.) 8.25 **st.** 🍷 2.50 — **47 rm** 🖵 39.00/49.00 **st.** — SB (weekends only) 56.00 **st.**

🏠 **Rose and Crown,** East St., CO1 2TZ, 🖉 866677, « Part 15C inn » — TV ⌂wc 🏦wc ☎ 🅿
28 rm, 2 suites.

✗ **Bistro 9,** 9 North Hill, CO1 1OZ, 🖉 576466 — 🔃 VISA
closed Sunday and Monday — **M** 10.00 **st.** and a la carte 7.25/9.95 **t.** 🍷 2.85.

153

COLCHESTER

MICHELIN Distribution Centre, 97 Gosbecks Rd, CO2 9JT, ✆ 578451/4

AUDI, VW Wyncol Rd ✆ 855000
AUSTIN-ROVER East Gates ✆ 867484
AUSTIN-ROVER-DAIMLER-JAGUAR Elmstead Rd ✆ 862811
BMW 10 Osborne St ✆ 577287
CITROEN Butt Rd ✆ 576803
FERRARI, PORSCHE Auto Way, Ipswich Rd ✆ 855500

FIAT, TOYOTA Gosbecks Rd ✆ 46455
FORD Magdalen St. ✆ 571171
HONDA, LADA, RELIANT, SEAT ✆ 867298
NISSAN Cowdray Av. ✆ 576291
RENAULT 78 Military Rd ✆ 577295
TALBOT, PEUGEOT Wimpole Rd ✆ 570197
VAUXHALL-OPEL Ipswich Rd ✆ 844422
VOLVO Autoway, Ipswich Rd ✆ 855055

COLEBROOK Devon – see Plymouth.

COLEFORD Glos. 408 404 M 28 – pop. 8 246 – ECD : Thursday – ✆ 0594 Dean.
[18] Coalway Rd ✆ 0594 (Dean) 32583, ½ m. on Parkend Rd.
♦London 143 – ♦ Bristol 28 – Gloucester 19 – Newport 29.

🏛 **Speech House** (T.H.F.), Forest of Dean, GL16 7EL, NE : 3 m. on B 4226 ✆ 22607, ☞ – TV ⇌wc ℗ ☒ AE ⓪ VISA
M 6.50/8.95 **st.** and a la carte ⓰ 3.40 – ⊆ 5.65 – **13 rm** 44.00/52.00 **st.**

🏛 **Lambsquay** ⬎, Perrygrove Rd, GL16 8QB, S : 1 m. on B 4228 ✆ 33127, ☞ – TV ⇌wc ℗ ☒ VISA
M (closed Sunday dinner) 10.00 ⓰ 3.25 – **9 rm** ⊆ 15.00/44.00 – SB 49.00/51.00 **st.**

at Clearwell S : 2 m. by B 4228 – ☒ Coleford – ✆ 0594 Dean :

🏛 **Clearwell Castle** ⬎, GL16 8LG, ✆ 32320, « Neo-Gothic mansion », ☞, park – TV ⇌wc ☎ ℗ ⚠ ☒ AE VISA ⅏
M 10.50/17.50 **t.** and a la carte ⓰ 3.00 – **8 rm** ⊆ 35.00/80.00 **t.**

⌂ **Tudor Farm,** ✆ 33046 – ℗ ⅏
closed January – **4 rm** ⊆ 16.50/25.00 **st.**

AUSTIN-ROVER, LAND ROVER-RANGE ROVER
Market Pl. ✆ 2468

FORD High St ✆ 32747
NISSAN ✆ 33517

COLESHILL Warw. 408 404 O 26 – pop. 6 038 – ECD : Monday and Thursday – ☒ Birmingham – ✆ 0675.
♦London 113 – ♦Birmingham 8 – ♦Coventry 11.

🏛 **Swan,** High St., B46 3BL, ✆ 62212 – TV ▥wc ☎ ℗ ⚠ ☒ AE ⓪ VISA ⅏
M 6.00/6.50 **s.** and a la carte ⓰ 3.75 – **34 rm** ⊆ 29.00/39.00 **st.**

🏛 **Coleshill** (Whitbread), 152 High St., B46 3BG, ✆ 65527 – TV ⇌wc ▥wc ℗ ☒ AE ⓪ VISA
M (closed Saturday lunch) 7.50/9.50 **st.** and a la carte ⓰ 3.10 – **15 rm** ⊆ 38.00/46.00 **st.** – SB (except Christmas)(weekends only) 52.00/56.00 **st.**

✗ **Blythe's,** 19 High St., B46 1AY, ✆ 62266 – ℗ ☒ ⓪ VISA
closed Saturday lunch, Sunday, Monday, last 2 weeks August and 2 to 9 January – **M** 8.00/14.50 **t.** and a la carte lunch 5.35/8.25 **t.** ⓰ 2.90.

COLLYWESTON Northants. 402 404 S 26 – see Stamford (Lincs.).

COLWALL Heref. and Worc. – see Great Malvern.

COLWYN BAY (BAE COLWYN) Clwyd 402 408 I 24 – pop. 27 002 – ECD : Wednesday – ✆ 0492.
See : Zoo★.
Envir. : Bodnant gardens★★ AC, SW : 6 m.
[18] Abergele and Pensarn, Tan-y-Goppa Rd, Abergele ✆ 0745 (Abergele) 824034, E : 6 m. – [5],[5] Old Colwyn, Woodland Av. ✆ 515581.
🛈 Prince of Wales Theatre ✆ 30478 – Colwyn Bay Hotels and Guest Houses Association ✆ 515719 (summer only) – 77 Conway Rd ✆ 31731.
♦London 237 – Birkenhead 50 – Chester 42 – Holyhead 41.

🏛 **Norfolk House,** 36 Princes Drive, LL29 8PF, ✆ 531757, ☞ – ▤ TV ⇌wc ▥wc ☜ ℗ ⚠ ☒ AE ⓪ VISA
M (bar lunch)/dinner 12.00 **t.** and a la carte – **27 rm** ⊆ 26.50/38.00 **t.** – SB (weekends only) 45.00 **st.**

🏛 **Hopeside,** 63-67 Prince's Drive, West End, LL29 8PW, ✆ 33244 – TV ⇌wc ▥wc ☜ ℗ ☒ AE ⓪ VISA
closed 2 weeks Christmas and New Year – **M** (bar lunch)/dinner 11.50 **st.** ⓰ 1.80 – **19 rm** ⊆ 18.00/32.00.

🏛 **Lyndale,** 410 Abergele Rd, Old Colwyn, LL29 9AB, E : 1¾ m. on A 547 ✆ 515429 – TV ⇌wc ▥wc ☎ ℗ ☒ AE
M (bar lunch Monday to Saturday)/dinner 8.50 **st.** and a la carte ⓰ 3.25 – **14 rm** ⊆ 23.00/39.00 **st.** – SB 46.00/56.00 **st.**

154

at Penmaenhead E : 2¼ m. on A 547 – ⊠ ✆ 0492 Colwyn Bay :

🏨 **Hotel 70°** (Best Western), Old Colwyn, LL29 9LD, ✆ 516555, Telex 61362, ⇐ – 🔟 ☎ 🅿 &.
🖾 AE ⓞ *VISA*
closed 22 December-4 January – **M** 9.85/12.85 **st.** and a la carte ▯ 3.95 – **41 rm**
⊆ 39.00/60.00 **st.**, **1 suite** 85.00/95.00 **st.** – SB 65.00/75.00 **st.**

at Rhos-on-Sea (Llandrillo-yn-Rhos) NW : 1 m. – ⊠ ✆ 0492 Colwyn Bay :

🏚 **Ashmount,** College Av., LL28 4NT, ✆ 45479 – 🔟 ⇔wc ▥wc ☎ & 🅿. 🖾 AE ⓞ *VISA*
M (bar lunch)/dinner 7.50 **st.** ▯ 2.75 – **18 rm** ⊆ 18.00/37.00 **st.**

↥ **Cabin Hill,** 12 College Av., LL28 4NT, ✆ 44568 – 🔟 ▥wc. ⚘
March-October – **10 rm** ⊆ 11.00/28.00 **st.**

AUSTIN-ROVER 394 Abergele Rd ✆ 515292
FORD Conwy Rd ✆ 2201
PEUGEOT 268 Conwy Rd ✆ 44278

PORSCHE, MERCEDES-BENZ Abergele Rd ✆ 30456
VAUXALL Conwy Rd ✆ 30271
VW, AUDI Penrhyn Av. ✆ 46722

COLYTON Devon 403 K 31 The West Country G. – pop. 2 435 – ✆ 0297.
See : Site★ – St. Andrew's Church★.
◆London 160 – Exeter 23 – Lyme Regis 7.

↥ **Grove,** South St., EX13 6ER, ✆ 52438, 🚗 – ▥wc 🅿
closed Christmas – **7 rm** ⊆ 9.25/21.00 **st.**

COMBE MARTIN Devon 403 H 30 The West Country G. – pop. 2 279 – ECD : Wednesday –
⊠ Ilfracombe – ✆ 027 188.
🛈 Sea Cottage, Cross St. ✆ 3319 (summer only).
◆London 218 – Exeter 56 – Taunton 58.

🏚 **Coulsworthy Country House** ⚘, EX34 0PD, SE : 2 ½ m. by A 399 on road to Hunters Inn
✆ 2463, ⇐, ⊒ heated, 🚗, ⚘ – ▥wc ▥wc 🅿
closed 16 December - 9 February – **M** *(closed Sunday dinner)* (bar lunch Monday to Saturday)/dinner 12.50 **st.** – **10 rm** ⊆ (dinner included) 22.00/84.00 **st.**

🏚 **Rone House,** King St., EX34 0AD, ✆ 3428 – 🔟 ⇔wc ▥wc 🅿. 🖾
closed November-24 December – **M** (bar lunch)/dinner 8.50 **t.** – **10 rm** ⊆ 10.50/30.00 **t.**

↥ **Britannia,** Moorey Meadow, Seaside, EX34 0DG, ✆ 2294 – 🅿
10 rm ⊆ 13.00/28.50 **st.**

XX **La Gallerie** with rm, Victoria St., EX34 0JT, ✆ 2566, « Antique collection » – 🔟 ▥wc 🅿. 🖾
AE ⓞ *VISA*. ⚘
closed Monday and Tuesday November-Easter – **M** *(closed Sunday dinner)* (dinner only and
Sunday lunch)/dinner 10.40 **t.** and a la carte 12.00/15.10 **t.** ▯ 3.50 – **3 rm** ⊆ 23.00 **st.**

AUSTIN-ROVER Borough Rd ✆ 2391

VAUXHALL-OPEL Borough Rd ✆ 3257

COMPTON Surrey 404 S 30 – see Guildford.

CONGLETON Cheshire 402 403 404 N 24 – pop. 23 482 – ECD : Wednesday – ✆ 0260.
🛝 Astbury, Peel La., Astbury ✆ 272772, S : 1 ½m.
🛈 Town Hall, High St. ✆ 271095.
◆London 183 – ◆Liverpool 50 – ◆Manchester 25 – ◆Sheffield 46 – ◆Stoke-on-Trent 13.

🏨 **Lion and Swan,** Swan Bank, CW12 1JR, ✆ 273115, « 16C inn » – 🔟 ⇔wc ▥wc ☎ 🅿. 🖾
AE ⓞ *VISA*
M 4.95/9.50 **t.** and a la carte ▯ 3.00 – **13 rm** ⊆ 25.00/35.00 **t.**

CONISTON Cumbria 402 K 20 – pop. 1 713 – ✆ 0966.
🛈 1 Yewdale Rd ✆ 41533 (summer only).
◆London 285 – ◆Carlisle 55 – Kendal 22 – Lancaster 42.

🏚 **Sun** ⚘, LA21 8HQ, ✆ 41248, ⇐, ⚘ – ▥wc 🅿. 🖾 *VISA*
closed January and February – **M** (bar lunch)/dinner 11.50 **t.** ▯ 3.00 – **10 rm** ⊆ 25.00/48.00 **st.**
– SB (November-April) 50.00/60.00 **st.**

AUSTIN-ROVER Broughton Rd ✆ 41253

CONSTANTINE BAY Cornwall 403 E 32 – see Padstow.

Pour vos déplacements en Grande-Bretagne :
— *cinq cartes détaillées nos* **401**, **402**, **403**, **404**, **405** *à 1/400 000*
— *utilisez-les conjointement avec ce guide,*
    un souligné rouge signale toutes les localités citées dans ce guide.

ONWY Gwynedd **402 403** I 24 – pop. 3 649 – ECD : Wednesday – ✪ 049 263.

e : Site✶✶ – Castle✶✶ (13C) *AC* – St. Mary's Church✶ 14C – **Envir. :** Sychnant Pass✶ W : 2 ½ m.

🚃 Penmaenmawr ✆ 0492 (Penmaenmawr) 623330 W : 4 m.

🅩 Snowdonia National Park, Visitor Centre, Castle St. ✆ 2248 (summer only).

◆London 241 – Caernarfon 22 – Chester 46 – Holyhead 37.

🏨 **Bryn Cregin Garden,** Ty Mawr Rd, Deganwy, LL31 9UR, NE : 2 m. by A 55 on A 546
✆ 0492 (Deganwy) 85266, ≼, 🛋 – 🆃🆅 ⌷wc ⋒wc ☎ 🅿 🄴 VISA 🛇
closed January – **M** *(closed Monday lunch)* 3.25/9.50 **t.** and a la carte ⏦ 3.85 – **16 rm**
🖴 20.00/44.00 **t.,** **1 suite** 42.00/50.00 **t.**

🏨 **Sychnant Pass,** Sychnant Pass Rd, LL32 8BJ, SW : 1 ¾ m. ✆ 6868, 🛋 – 🆃🆅 ⌷wc ⋒wc 🖭
🅿 🄰 🄴 VISA
closed January and November – **M** *(bar lunch)/dinner* 14.95 **st.** ⏦ 2.75 – **10 rm** 🖴 30.00/50.00 **st.**
– SB 49.00/62.00 **st.**

🏨 **Castle** (T.H.F.), High St., LL32 8DB, ✆ 2324 – 🆃🆅 ⌷wc 🖭 🅿. 🄰 🄴 ⓞ VISA
M *(buffet lunch)/dinner* 9.50 **st.** and a la carte ⏦ 3.90 – 🖴 5.65 – **25 rm** 38.50/51.00 **st.**

🏨 **Castle Bank,** Mount Pleasant, LL32 8NY, ✆ 3888, ≼ – 🆃🆅 ⋒wc 🅿. 🛇
closed January – **M** *(dinner only and Sunday lunch)* 6.00/9.50 **t.** ⏦ 3.00 – **9 rm** 🖴 16.50/35.00 **t.**
– SB (October-mid May) 43.00/56.00 **st.**

⌂ **Llys Gwilym,** 3 Mountain Rd (off Cadnant Park), LL32 8PU, ✆ 2351 – 🛇
6 rm 🖴 9.50/18.00.

at Roewen S : 3 m. by B 5106 – ✉ Conwy – ✪ 0492 Twyn-y-Groes :

⌂ **Tir-y-Coed** 🌫, LL32 8TP, ✆ 650219, ≼, 🛋 – 🆃🆅 ⌷wc 🅿
closed December and January – **7 rm** 🖴 15.10/32.60 **t.**

at Tal-y-Bont S : 5 ¾ m. on B 5106 – ✉ Conwy – ✪ 049 269 Dolgarrog :

🏨 **Lodge,** LL32 8YX, ✆ 766 – 🆃🆅 ⌷wc ☎ 🅿. 🄰 🄴 ⓞ VISA
M 7.50/12.50 **t.** and a la carte ⏦ 2.85 – **10 rm** 🖴 25.00/40.00 **st.** – SB 50.00/55.00 **st.**

COOKHAM Berks. **404** R 29 – pop. 5 865 – ECD : Wednesday and Thursday – ✉ Maidenhead
– ✪ 062 85 Bourne End.

Envir. : Cliveden House✶ 19C (Park✶✶) *AC* SE : 2 m.

◆London 32 – High Wycombe 7 – Reading 16.

✗ Cookham Tandoori, High St., SL6 9SL, ✆ 22584, Indian rest.

CITROEN High St. ✆ 22984

COPDOCK Suffolk **404** X 27 – see Ipswich.

COPTHORNE West Sussex **404** T 30 – see Crawley.

CORBRIDGE Northumb. **401 402** N 19 – pop. 2 757 – ECD : Thursday – ✪ 043 471.

Envir. : Corstopitum Roman Fort✶ *AC*, NW : 1 ½ m.

🅩 Vicar's Pele Tower, Market Pl. ✆ 2815 (summer only).

◆London 300 – Hexham 3 – ◆Newcastle-upon-Tyne 18.

☎ **Riverside,** Main St., NE45 5LE, ✆ 2942 – ⋒wc 🅿
closed January – **M** *(closed Sunday) (booking essential) (dinner only)* 9.50 **st.** ⏦ 3.15 – **11 rm**
🖴 17.00/31.00 **st.** – SB (October-May) (except Sunday) 34.00/46.00 **st.**

✗✗✗ **Ramblers Country House,** Tinklers Bank, Farnley, NE45 5RN, S : 1 m. on Riding Mill Rd
✆ 2424, German rest. – 🅿. 🄰 🄴 ⓞ VISA
closed Sunday, Monday, 1 week February and 2 weeks September – **M** *(dinner only)* 9.85 **t.**
and a la carte 11.90/13.65 **t.** ⏦ 2.60.

AUSTIN-ROVER Main St. ✆ 2068   SUBARU Stagshaw ✆ 043 472 (Great Whittington)
216

CORNHILL-ON-TWEED Northumb. **401 402** N 17 – pop. 312 – ECD : Thursday – ✪ 0890 Cold-
stream.

◆London 345 – ◆Edinburgh 49 – ◆Newcastle-upon-Tyne 59.

⌂ **Coach House,** Crookham, TD12 4TD, E : 4 m. on A 697 ✆ 089 082 (Crookham) 293, 🛋
⌷wc 🚼 🅿
March-October – **11 rm** 🖴 14.00/32.00 **t.**

CORPUSTY Norfolk **404** X 25 – pop. 1 234 – ✉ Heydon – ✪ 026 387 Saxthorpe.

◆London 134 – ◆Cambridge 77 – ◆Norwich 16.

🏠 Cropton Hall 🌫, NR11 6RX, S : 1 m. on Heydon Rd ✆ 869, 🏊, 🛋 – 🆃🆅 ⌷wc ⋒wc 🅿
8 rm.

CORRIS Gwynedd **402 403** I 26 – see Machynlleth (Powys).

CORSE LAWN Heref. and Worc. – see Tewkesbury (Glos.).

156

CORSHAM Wilts. 403 404 N 29 The West Country G. – pop. 11 259 – ECD : Wednesday – 🕿 0249 – See : Corsham Court★★★ AC.

🖪 Methuen Arms Hotel, High St. ℰ 714867 – ♦London 110 – ♦Bristol 22 – Swindon 25.

🏤 **Rudloe Park,** Leafy Lane, SN13 0PA, W : 2 m. by B 3353 on A 4 ℰ 0225 (Bath) 810555, ≼, 🐎
– 📺 ⇌wc ☎ 🅿. 🏄. 🔄 🖭 ⑳ 𝘝𝘐𝘚𝘈.
M 8.50/9.75 t. and a la carte ⓪ 3.25 – **8 rm** ⇌ 37.50/65.00 t. – SB (weekends only) 77.00/88.00 st.

✗ **Weavers Loft,** 1 High St., SN13 0ES, ℰ 713982 – 🔄 ⑳ 𝘝𝘐𝘚𝘈
closed Saturday lunch, Sunday and Monday – **M** 15.00 st. and a la carte 11.25/14.00 t. ⓪ 2.80.

CORTON Wilts. 403 404 N 30 – see Warminster.

COSHAM Hants. 403 404 Q 31 – see Portsmouth and Southsea.

COVENTRY West Midlands 403 404 P 26 – pop. 318 718 – ECD : Thursday – 🕿 0203.
See : St. Michael's Cathedral★★★ (1962) : tapestry★★★ AV – Old Cathedral★ (ruins) AV **A** – St. John's Church★ 14C-15C AV **B** – Old houses★ 16C-17C AV DEF.
🇳 Brandon Wood, Brandon Lane ℰ 0203 (Wolston) 543141,SE : 6 m. by A 428 BY – 🇳 Sphinx, Siddeley Av.ℰ 458890 BY – 🇳 The Grange, Copsewood ℰ 451465, E : 3 m. on A 428 BY.
✈ Coventry Airport : ℰ 301717, S : 3 ½ m. by Coventry Rd, Telex 31646 BZ.
🖪 Central Landing Library, Smithford Way ℰ 20084.
♦London 100 – ♦Birmingham 18 – ♦Bristol 96 – ♦Nottingham 52.

Plans on following pages

🏩 **De Vere** (De Vere), Cathedral Sq., CV1 5RP, ℰ 51851, Telex 31380 – 🛗 ▤ rest 📺 ☎ 🅿. 🏄.
🔄 🖭 ⑳ 𝘝𝘐𝘚𝘈.   AV **n**
M 7.50/10.00 st. and a la carte ⓪ 3.65 – **190 rm** ⇌ 55.00/67.50 st., **10 suites** 68.00/89.50 st. – SB (weekends only) 55.00 st.

🏩 **Leofric** (Embassy), Broadgate, CV1 1LZ, ℰ 21371, Telex 311193 – 🛗 📺 ☎. 🏄. 🔄 🖭 ⑳
𝘝𝘐𝘚𝘈. 🦐   AV **c**
M 9.50 st. and a la carte ⓪ 2.85 – ⇌ 5.00 – **91 rm** 44.00/53.00 st., **5 suites** 70.00/90.00 st. – SB 55.00/107.00 st.

🏨 **Hylands** (Best Western), 153 Warwick Rd, CV3 6AU, ℰ 501600, Telex 312388 – ▤ rest 📺
⇌wc ☎ 🅿. 🔄 🖭 ⑳ 𝘝𝘐𝘚𝘈   AYZ **z**
closed 25 and 26 December – **M** (closed Saturday lunch) (carving rest.) 6.75/7.45 t. and a la carte – **56 rm** ⇌ 36.15/47.15 st. – SB (weekends only)(except Christmas) 42.50 st.

🏛 **Merrick Lodge,** 80-82 St. Nicholas St., CV1 4BP, ℰ 553940 – 📺 🖫wc 🅿. 🔄 🖭 ⑳ 𝘝𝘐𝘚𝘈
M 6.50/8.50 st. and a la carte – **13 rm** ⇌ 25.00/45.00 st.   AV **a**

⌂ **Fairlight,** 14 Regent St., CV1 3EP, ℰ 24215   AV **i**
closed 24 December-2 January – **11 rm** ⇌ 10.00/19.00 s.

✗✗ Grandstand, Coventry City F.C., King Richard St., CV2 4FW, ℰ 27053 – ▤ 🅿   BY **a**

✗ **Herbs** with rm, 28 Lower Holyhead Rd, CV1 3AU, ℰ 555654, Vegetarian rest. – 🦐   AV **o**
M (closed Sunday) (dinner only) a la carte 6.45/7.20 t. – **7 rm** ⇌ 12.50/20.00 t.

at Longford N : 4 m. on A 444 – ✉ 🕿 0203 Coventry :

🏨 **Novotel,** Wilsons Lane, CV6 6HL, ℰ 365000, Telex 31545, 🏊 heated, squash – 🛗 ▤ 📺
⇌wc ☎ 🖪. 🏄. 🔄 🖭 ⑳ 𝘝𝘐𝘚𝘈   BV **v**
M 7.50/8.75 st. and a la carte ⓪ 3.65 – ⇌ 4.50 – **100 rm** 40.50/47.50 st. – SB (weekends only) 63.50/87.50 st.

at Walsgrave on Sowe NE : 3 m. on A 46 – ✉ 🕿 0203 Coventry :

🏩 **Crest** (Crest), Hinckley Rd, CV2 2HP, NE : ½ m. on A 46 ℰ 613261, Telex 311292 – 🛗 ▤ rest
📺 📹 🖪. 🏄. 🔄 🖭 ⑳ 𝘝𝘐𝘚𝘈   BX **e**
M (bar lunch Saturday) 9.25/11.50 st. and a la carte ⓪ 3.25 – ⇌ 6.15 – **152 rm** 49.50/59.50 st., **2 suites** 90.00 st. – SB (weekends only) 56.00/64.00 st.

at Brandon E : 6 m. on A 428 – BZ – ✉ 🕿 0203 Coventry :

🏨 **Brandon Hall** (T.H.F.) 🦐, Main St., CV8 3FW, ℰ 542571, Telex 31472, 🐎, park, squash –
📺 ⇌wc 📹 🅿. 🔄 🖭 ⑳ 𝘝𝘐𝘚𝘈
M 6.95/9.95 st. and a la carte ⓪ 3.40 – ⇌ 5.65 – **60 rm** 44.50/54.50 st.

at Willenhall SE : 3 m. on A 423 – ✉ 🕿 0203 Coventry :

🏨 **Chace Crest** (Crest), London Rd, CV3 4EQ, ℰ 303398, Telex 311993, 🐎 – 📺 ⇌wc 📹 🅿.
🏄. 🔄 🖭 ⑳ 𝘝𝘐𝘚𝘈   BZ **u**
M (closed Saturday lunch) 8.50/10.95 st. and a la carte – ⇌ 5.55 – **68 rm** 49.00/59.00 st. – SB (weekends only) 58.00 st.

at Berkswell W : 6 ½ m. on A 4023 – AY – ✉ 🕿 0203 Coventry :

✗✗✗ **Nailcote Hall** 🦐 with rm, Nailcote Lane, CV7 7DE, S : 1 ½ m. on A 4023 ℰ 466174, 🐎 – 📺
⇌wc 🅿. 🔄 🖭 ⑳. 🦐
closed 1 week Easter, 1 week August and 1 week Christmas – **M** (closed Sunday and Bank Holidays) a la carte 12.00/19.25 t. ⓪ 3.00 – ⇌ 7.50 – **4 rm** 50.00/80.00 t.

COVENTRY

Broadgate............. AV 6
Corporation Street..... AV
Shopping Precincts....

Bayley Lane........... AV 3
Bishop Street......... AV 5
Burges............... AV 7
Earl Street........... AV 10
Fairfax Street......... AV 12
Far Gosford Street..... AV 13

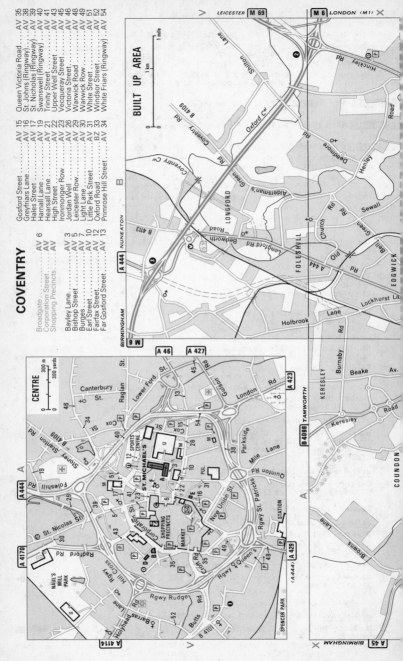

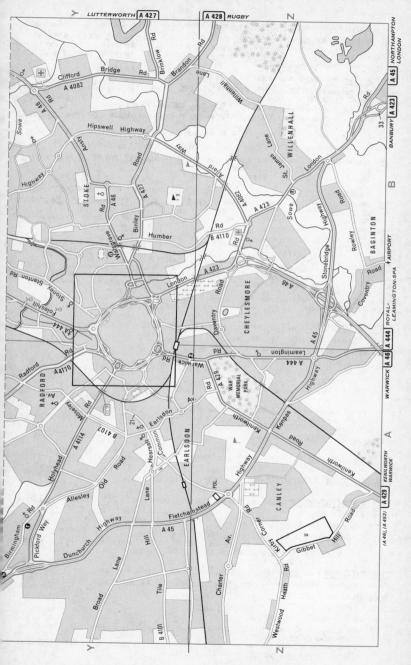

at Balsall Common W : 6 ¾ m. by A 4023 on B 4101 AY – ⊠ Coventry – 🕿 0676 Berkswell :

🏠 **Haigs,** 273 Kenilworth Rd, CV7 7EL, 🕿 33004, 🍴 – 📺 🖂wc ⏿wc 🅿 🚗 AE ⓪ VISA ⚬
closed 26 December-5 January and 1 week August – **M** (closed weekday lunch and Sunday dinner to non-residents) 6.70/8.25 **st.** and a la carte 🍷 2.50 – **14 rm** 🖃 16.50/37.75 **st.** – SB (weekends only) 48.00/56.00 **st.**

at Allesley NW : 3 m. on A 4114 – ⊠ 🕿 0203 Coventry :

🏨 **Post House** (T.H.F.), Rye Hill, CV5 9PH, 🕿 402151, Telex 31427 – ▐ ▬ rest 📺 🖂wc 🕿 🅿
🚗 🔼 AE ⓪ VISA
AXY s
M 7.50/10.50 **st.** and a la carte 🍷 3.40 – 🖃 5.65 – **190 rm** 44.00/52.00 **st.**

🏨 **Allesley,** Birmingham Rd, CV5 9GP, 🕿 403272, Group Telex 312549 – 📺 🖂wc ⏿wc 🕿 🅿
AY r
🚗 🔼 AE ⓪ VISA
M 8.50/9.75 **st.** and a la carte 🍷 2.55 – **88 rm** 🖃 37.50/50.00 **t.** – SB (weekends only) 55.00 **st.**

at Keresley NW : 3 m. on B 4098 – AX – ⊠ Coventry – 🕿 020 333 Keresley :

🏨 **Royal Court,** Tamworth Rd, CV7 8JG, 🕿 334171, Group Telex 312549, 🍴 – ▐ ▬ rest 📺
🖂wc ⏿wc 🕿 🕭 🅿 🚗 🔼 AE ⓪ VISA
M a la carte 9.20/13.40 **t.** – **99 rm** 🖃 32.75/44.00 **t.**

at Meriden NW : 6 m. by A 45 on B 4102 – AX – ⊠ Coventry – 🕿 0676 Meriden :

🏨 **Manor** (De Vere), Main Rd, CV7 7NH, 🕿 22735, Telex 311011, ⌇ heated, 🍴 – 📺 🖂wc 🕿
🚗 🔼 AE ⓪ VISA
M (bar lunch Saturday) 8.50/10.00 **st.** and a la carte 🍷 3.25 – **32 rm** 🖃 47.00/60.00 **st.** – SB (weekends only) 50.00 **st.**

AUSTIN-ROVER Lockhurst Lane 🕿 688851
AUSTIN-ROVER Warwick Rd 🕿 28661
AUSTIN-ROVER, LAND ROVER-RANGE ROVER Kenpas Highway 🕿 411515
BMW 138 Sutherland Av. 🕿 461441
DAIHATSU Goodyens Lane 🕿 362259
FIAT 324 Station Rd Balsall Common 🕿 0676 (Berkswell) 33145
HONDA 207 Wheelwright Lane, Exhall 🕿 364004
LADA Binley Rd 🕿 452777

MAZDA Browns Lane 🕿 404293
MERCEDES-BENZ Humber Rd 🕿 306234
NISSAN 149 Far Gosford St. 🕿 24552
NISSAN 105 Foleshill Rd 🕿 26417
PEUGEOT-TALBOT 136 Daventry Rd 🕿 503522
RELIANT, SKODA 90 Paynes Lane 🕿 20475
TOYOTA Bennetts Rd, Keresley 🕿 334204
VAUXHALL-OPEL Raglan St. 🕿 25361
VOLVO London Rd 🕿 303132
VW, AUDI Spon End 🕿 56325

COWBRIDGE (BONT-FAEN) South Glam. 🔢 J 29 – pop. 3 525 – ECD : Wednesday – 🕿 044 63.
Envir. : Old Beaupré Castle* 14C, SE : 3 m.
♦London 169 – ♦Cardiff 12 – ♦Swansea 27.

🏨 **Bear,** High St., CF7 7AF, 🕿 4814 – 📺 🖂wc 🕿 🅿 🚗 🔼 AE ⓪ VISA
M (bar lunch)/dinner 8.95 **t.** and a la carte 🍷 2.65 – **31 rm** 🖃 22.00/37.00 **t.** – SB (weekends only) 44.90 **st.**

XX **Off the Beeton Track,** 1 Town Hall Sq., 🕿 3599 – 🔼 AE VISA
closed Sunday dinner and Monday – **M** 11.50 **t.** and a la carte 10.90/13.00 **t.** 🍷 3.00.

X **Basil's Brasserie,** 2 Eastgate, CF7 7DG, 🕿 3738, Bistro – 🅿 🔼 VISA
closed Sunday, Monday, 2 weeks August-September, 1 week Christmas and Bank Holidays –
M a la carte 6.95/11.35 **t.**

AUSTIN-ROVER St. Mary Church 🕿 0446 2391   RENAULT High St. 🕿 0446 2599

COWES I.O.W. 🔢 🔢 PQ 31 – see Wight (Isle of).

COYCHURCH (LLANGRALLO) Mid Glam. 🔢 J 29 – see Bridgend.

CRACKINGTON HAVEN Cornwall 🔢 G 31 The West Country G. – ECD : Tuesday – ⊠ Bude –
🕿 084 03 St. Gennys.
♦London 262 – Bude 11 – Truro 42.

🏠 **Coombe Barton,** EX23 0JG, 🕿 345, ≤, – 🖂wc 🅿 🔼 VISA
Mid March-mid October – **M** (bar lunch)/dinner 8.75 **t.** and a la carte 🍷 2.75 – **10 rm**
🖃 14.50/33.00 **t.** – SB (except July and August) 35.00/41.00 **st.**

CRANBROOK Kent 🔢 V 30 – pop. 3 593 – ECD : Wednesday – 🕿 0580.
Envir. : Sissinghurst : castle* 16C (≤*, 78 steps), gardens** AC, NE : 1 ½ m.
🏌 Benenden Rd 🕿 712833.
🖪 Vestry Hall, Stone St. 🕿 712538 (summer only).
♦London 53 – Hastings 19 – Maidstone 15.

🏨 **Willesley,** Angley Rd, TN17 2LE, N : ¾ m. on B 2189 at junction with A 229 🕿 713555, 🍴 –
📺 🖂wc 🕿 🅿 🔼 AE ⓪ VISA
closed first week February – **M** 6.75/10.50 **st.** and a la carte 🍷 2.85 – **16 rm** 🖃 35.00/52.00 **st.** –
SB (except summer)(weekends only) 55.00/57.00 **st.**

🏠 **Kennel Holt** ⚘, Goudhurst Rd, Flishinghurst, TN17 2PT, NW : 2 ¼ m. by A 229 on A 262 ℰ 712032, ≤, « Country house atmosphere and gardens » – 📺 ⇌wc 🛁wc Ⓟ ⚘ *closed 23 December-26 January* – **M** (dinner only) 9.50 **t.** – **8 rm** ⇌ 28.00/72.00 **t.** – SB (November-March)(weekends only) 58.00/69.00 **st.**

AUSTIN-ROVER Cranbrook Rd, Staplehurst ℰ 892093

FORD Stone St. ℰ 712121
RENAULT Wilsley Pound ℰ 713262

CRANTOCK Cornwall **408** E 32 – see Newquay.

CRAWLEY West Sussex **404** T 30 – pop. 80 113 – ECD : Wednesday – ✆ 0293.

🏌 Cottesmore, Buchan Hill ℰ 28256, S : 4 m. on plan of Gatwick Z – 🏌 Gatwick Manor ℰ 24470, N : 5 m. on plan of Gatwick Y.

◆London 33 – ◆Brighton 21 – Lewes 23 – Royal Tunbridge Wells 23.

Plan of Enlarged Area : see Gatwick

CRAWLEY

🏨 **George** (T.H.F.), High St., RH10 1BS, ☎ 24215, Telex 87385 – 📺 🛏wc ☎ 🅿 🔄 🔌 🆎 ⓪ 𝗩𝗜𝗦𝗔   BY **o**
M 7.20/9.95 **st.** and a la carte ⓘ 3.40 – ⇌ 5.65 – **76 rm** 49.00/57.00 **st.**

🏨 **Crest** (Crest), Langley Drive, Tushmore Roundabout, RH11 7SX, ☎ 29991, Telex 877311 – 📧 📺 🛏wc ☎ 🅿 🔄 🔌 🆎 ⓪ 𝗩𝗜𝗦𝗔   BY **n**
M 8.25/12.25 **t.** and a la carte ⓘ 4.25 – ⇌ 5.85 – **230 rm** 51.00/61.00 **t.** – SB (weekends only) 62.00/70.00 **st.**

🏛 **Goffs Park**, 45-47 Goffs Park Rd, RH11 8AX, ☎ 35447, Group Telex 87415, ☛ – 📺 🛏wc ⋔wc ☎ 🅿 🔌 🆎 ⓪ 𝗩𝗜𝗦𝗔   AZ **s**
M 7.50/8.00 **st.** and a la carte ⓘ 3.75 – **59 rm** ⇌ 39.00/54.50 **st.**

🏛 **Grange**, 15 Brighton Rd, RH10 6AE, ☎ 35191 – 📺 ⋔wc ☎ 🅿   BZ **a**
39 rm.

at Copthorne NE : 4 ½ m. on A 264 – BY – 📧 Crawley – 🕐 0342 Copthorne :

🏛🏛 **Copthorne**, Copthorne Rd, RH10 3PG, ☎ 714971, Telex 95500, ☛, park, squash – 📺 ☎ 🔌 🔄 🔌 🆎 ⓪ 𝗩𝗜𝗦𝗔 ✍
M 12.95/9.50 **st.** and a la carte ⓘ 7.75 – ⇌ 5.95 – **223 rm** 55.00/65.00 **st.**, **2 suites** 85.00/95.00 **st.** – SB (weekends only) 75.00/79.00 **st.**

at Pound Hill E : 3 m. by A 264 – BY – on B 2036 – 📧 🕐 0293 Crawley :

🏛 **Barnwood**, Balcombe Rd, RH10 4RU, ☎ 882709, ☛ – 📺 ⋔wc ☎ 🅿 🔌 🔄 🆎 ⓪ 𝗩𝗜𝗦𝗔 ✍
M *(closed Bank Holiday lunch)* 6.50/9.50 **t.** ⓘ 3.00 – **40 rm** ⇌ 32.00/40.00 **t.**
            see plan of Gatwick   Z **a**

AUSTIN-ROVER Copthorne ☎ 713933
BEDFORD, OPEL-VAUXHALL Fleming Way ☎ 29771
CITROEN 163-165 Three Bridges Rd ☎ 25533
FORD Worth Park Av., Three Bridges ☎ 28381
PEUGEOT-TALBOT Barton ☎ 543232

RENAULT Orchard St. ☎ 23323
SAAB Turners Hill ☎ 715467
SKODA Balcombe Rd ☎ 882620
VW, AUDI Overdene Drive ☎ 515551

▇▇▇▇ **CREWE** Cheshire 𝟒𝟎𝟐 𝟒𝟎𝟑 𝟒𝟎𝟒 M 24 – pop. 59 097 – ECD : Wednesday – 🕐 0270.
Envir. : Sandbach (Two Crosses★ 7C, in Market Place) NE : 10 m.
🛈🔋 Fields Rd ☎ 584099, E : 2 ¼ m. off A 534.
🚗 ☎ 214343.
🅱 Delamere House, Delamere St., ☎ 583191.
♦London 174 – Chester 24 – ♦Liverpool 49 – ♦Manchester 36 – ♦Stoke-on-Trent 15.

🏨 **Crewe Arms** (Embassy), Nantwich Rd, CW1 1DW, ☎ 213204 – 📺 🛏wc ☎ 🅿 🔄 🔌 🔄 🆎 ⓪ 𝗩𝗜𝗦𝗔
M (carving rest.) 8.50 **st.** and a la carte ⓘ 2.75 – ⇌ 5.00 – **35 rm** 37.50/42.50 **st.** – SB (weekends only) 50.00/60.00 **st.**

ALFA-ROMEO Newcastle Rd ☎ 665138
CITROEN Woolstanwood ☎ 213495
FIAT, NISSAN Cross Green ☎ 583437
PEUGEOT, TALBOT 613 Crewe Rd, Wistaston ☎ 664111

SEAT West St. ☎ 214317
VOLVO Earle St. ☎ 587711
VW, AUDI Oak St. ☎ 213241

▇▇▇▇ **CREWKERNE** Somerset 𝟒𝟎𝟑 L 31 The West Country G. – pop. 6 018 – ECD : Thursday – 🕐 0460.
♦London 145 – Exeter 38 – ♦Southampton 81 – Taunton 20.

🏛 **Old Parsonage**, 55-59 Barn St., TA18 8BP, ☎ 73516 – 📺 🛏wc ⋔wc ☎ 🅿 🔄 🆎 ⓪ 𝗩𝗜𝗦𝗔
closed 25 December-4 January – **M** (closed Sunday to non-residents) 15.00 **t.** ⓘ 2.20 – **10 rm** ⇌ 27.50/49.50 **t.** – SB (weekends only) (except Bank Holidays) 44.80/57.60 **st.**

at Haselbury Plucknett NE : 2 ¾ m. by A 30 on A 3066 – 📧 🕐 0460 Crewkerne :

⌂ **Oak House**, North St., TA18 7RB, ☎ 73625, « 16C thatched cottage », ☛ – ⋔wc 🅿
Easter-October – **8 rm** ⇌ 15.00/35.00 **st.**

▇▇▇▇ **CRICCIETH** Gwynedd 𝟒𝟎𝟐 𝟒𝟎𝟑 H 25 – pop. 1 535 – ECD : Wednesday – 🕐 076 671.
See : Castle ≼★★ AC.
🛈🔋 Ednyfed Hill ☎ 2154.
🅱 The Square ☎ 2489.
♦London 249 – Caernarfon 17 – Shrewsbury 85.

🏨 **Bron Eifion Country House** ⑊, LL52 0SA, W : ½ m. on A 497 ☎ 2385, ≼, « 19C country house in large garden », park – 🛏wc ⋔wc ☎ 🅿 – **24 rm**.

🏛 **Plas Isa**, Porthmadog Rd, LL52 0HP, ☎ 2443 – 📺 🛏wc ☎ 🅿 🔌 🆎 ⓪ 𝗩𝗜𝗦𝗔 ✍
M 6.00/8.50 **st.** and a la carte ⓘ 4.50 – **12 rm** ⇌ 20.00/40.00 **st.**

⌂ **Glyn-y-Coed**, Portmadoc Rd, LL52 0HL, ☎ 2870 – 🅿
closed 2 weeks October, Christmas and New Year – **10 rm** ⇌ 11.00/22.00 **t.**

✗ **Moelwyn** with rm, 27-29 Mona Terr., LL52 0HG, ≼ – ⋔wc 🅿 🔌 𝗩𝗜𝗦𝗔 ✍
April-October – **M** (closed Sunday dinner April and October) 10.50 **t.** (dinner) and a la carte 7.45/11.75 **t.** ⓘ 3.00 – **6 rm** ⇌ 9.50/21.00 **t.** – SB (except summer) 37.00/40.00 **st.**

AUDI, MERCEDES-BENZ, VW Caernarfon Rd ☎ 2516   VOLVO Penamser Rd ☎ Portmadoc 3717
FIAT Ala Rd, Pwllheli ☎ 612827

162

CRICK Northants. 403 404 Q 26 – see Rugby.

CRICKHOWELL Powys 403 K 28 – pop. 1 979 – ECD : Wednesday – ☎ 0873.
Envir. : Tretower Court and Castle★, NW : 2 ½ m.
♦London 169 – Abergavenny 6 – Brecon 14 – Newport 25.

🏨 **Gliffaes Country House** ⑤, NP8 1RH, W : 3 ¾ m. by A 40 ℘ 0874 (Bwlch) 730371, ≤, « Country house and gardens on the banks of the River Usk », ⑤, park, ⚲ – ⌷wc ᥍wc
🅿 ⒶⒺ *VISA* ⌾
closed 31 December-13 March – **M** 6.50/12.75 **st.** ⓛ 2.50 – **19 rm** ⌷ 19.50/53.00 **st.**

🏨 **Bear,** High St., NP8 1BW, ℘ 810408, 🚗 – ⌷wc ᥍wc 🅿 ⒶⒺ *VISA*
M *(closed Sunday)* (bar lunch)/dinner a la carte 11.50/14.75 **t.** ⓛ 3.60 – **12 rm** ⌷ 20.00/
47.00 **t.**

CROMER Norfolk 404 X 25 – pop. 4 197 – ECD : Wednesday – ☎ 0263.
🛈 Town Hall, Prince of Wales Rd ℘ 512497.
♦London 132 – ♦Norwich 23 – Peterborough 76.

🏨 Craigside, St. Mary's Rd, NR27 9DJ, ℘ 511025, ⑤ heated, 🚗 – ᥍wc 🅿 ⒶⒺ *VISA*
22 rm ⌷ 12.50/31.00 **t.**

CROSBY-ON-EDEN Cumbria 401 402 L 29 – see Carlisle.

CROSSBUSH West Sussex – see Arundel.

CROWBOROUGH East Sussex 404 U 30 – pop. 17 008 – ECD : Wednesday – ☎ 089 26.
♦London 45 – ♦Brighton 25 – Maidstone 26.

🏨 Crest, Beacon Rd, TN6 1AD, on A 26 ℘ 2772 – 🛗 📺 ⌷wc ᥍wc 📞 🅿 🏌
30 rm.

AUSTIN-ROVER Beacon Rd ℘ 2777   TALBOT Church Rd ℘ 3424
FORD Crowborough Hill ℘ 2175

CROWTHORNE Berks. 404 R 29 – pop. 19 166 – ECD : Wednesday – ✉ ☎ 0344.
♦London 42 – Reading 15.

🏨 **Waterloo** (Anchor), Dukes Ride, RG11 7NW, on B 3348 ℘ 777711, Telex 848139 – 📺 ⌷wc
᥍wc ☎ 🅿 🏌 ⒶⒺ ⑩ *VISA* ⌾
M 9.75/9.50 **st.** and a la carte ⓛ 3.35 – **58 rm** ⌷ 49.50/59.50 **st.** – SB (weekends only)
57.00/65.00 **st.**

CROXDALE Durham – see Durham.

CROYDE Devon 403 H 30 The West Country G. – ☎ 0271.
♦London 232 – Barnstaple 10 – Exeter 50 – Taunton 61.

🏨 **Kittiwell House,** St. Mary's Road, EX33 1PG, ℘ 890247, « 16C thatched Devon longhouse »
– ⌷wc ᥍wc 🅿 ⒶⒺ *VISA*
closed February – **M** (bar lunch Monday to Saturday)/dinner 7.60 **t.** and a la carte – **14 rm**
⌷ 14.00/54.00 **t.** – SB (except summer) 36.00/42.00 **st.**

🏨 **Baggy Point** ⑤, Baggy Point, EX33 1PA, ℘ 890204, ≤ Appledore, Lundy Island and cliff,
🚗 – ⌷wc 🅿 ⒶⒺ *VISA*
March-October – **M** (bar lunch)/dinner 8.50 **st.** ⓛ 2.95 – **11 rm** ⌷ 15.00/46.00 **st.** – SB (except
summer) 39.60/55.00 **st.**

CRUDWELL Wilts. 403 404 N 29 – see Malmesbury.

CRUG-Y-BAR Dyfed 403 I 27 – ECD : Saturday – ✉ Llanwrda – ☎ 055 83 Talley.
♦London 213 – Carmarthen 26 – ♦Swansea 36.

🏨 **Glanrannell Park** ⑤, SA19 8SA, SW : ½ m. by B 4302 ℘ 230, ≤, ⑤, 🚗, park – ⌷wc
🅿
April-October – **M** *(closed Sunday lunch)* (bar lunch)/dinner 10.00 **t.** ⓛ 3.00 – **8 rm**
⌷ 19.00/35.00 **t.**

CUCKFIELD West Sussex 404 T 30 – pop. 2 650 – ECD : Wednesday – ☎ 0444 Haywards
Heath.
♦London 40 – ♦Brighton 15.

🏨 Ockenden Manor, Ockenden Lane, RH17 5LD, ℘ 416111, « Part 16C manor », 🚗 – 📺 ⌷wc
☎ 🅿
10 rm. 2 suites.

CUFFLEY Herts. 404 T 28 – pop. 4 875 – ECD : Thursday – ✪ 0707 Potter's Bar.

♦London 16 – ♦Cambridge 44 – Luton 26.

⚐⚐ **Ponsbourne** ☜, Ponsbourne Park, Newgate Street Village, SG13 8QZ, N : 3 m. by B 157 ℰ 875221, Telex 299912, ≼, ⌇, ☛, park, ❤ – ☎ Ⓟ ⚐ ⚐ AE ⓪ VISA
M *(closed Sunday dinner to non-residents)* 12.00/16.50 **st.** and a la carte – **32 rm** ⌸ 35.00/60.00 **st.**

CUMNOR Oxon. 403 404 P 28 – see Oxford.

CWMBRAN Gwent 403 K 29 – pop. 44 592 – ECD : Wednesday – ✪ 063 33.

☞ Greenmeadow, Treherbert Rd ℰ 69321.

♦London 149 – ♦Bristol 35 – ♦Cardiff 17 – Newport 5.

⚐⚐ **Parkway,** Cwmbran Drive, NP44 3UW, S : 1 m. by A 4051 ℰ 71199 – ☎ ☛ ⚐ Ⓟ ⚐ ⚐ AE ⓪ VISA
M (carving lunch) 8.95 **st.** and a la carte ⌁ 3.35 – **46 rm** ⌸ 28.95/52.95 **st., 1 suite** 58.95/88.35 **st.** – SB (weekends only) 55.00/72.65 **st.**

⚐ **Commodore,** Mill Lane, Llan-yr-Afon, NP44 8SH, S : 1 m. via Llanfrechfa Way ℰ 4091 – ▯
☎ ☐wc ☛ ⚐ ⚐ ⚐ AE VISA
M a la carte 10.20/17.25 ⌁ 2.25 – **60 rm** ⌸ 32.00/52.00 **st.** – SB (weekends only) 52.90 **st.**

FIAT 10-11 Court Rd Ind. Est. ℰ 06333 72711
FORD Avon Rd ℰ 06333 5255
TOYOTA Maendy Way ℰ 06333 2253

DALLINGTON East Sussex 404 V 31 – pop. 286 – ✉ Heathfield – ✪ 042 482 Brightling.

♦London 59 – ♦Brighton 26 – Hastings 14 – Maidstone 34.

✗ **Little Byres,** Christmas Farm, Battle Rd, Wood's Corner, TN21 9LE, on B 2096 ℰ 230 – Ⓟ ⚐ VISA
closed Sunday and January – **M** (dinner only) 14.00 **t.** ⌁ 3.00.

DARESBURY Cheshire 402 403 404 M 23 – pop. 353 – ✉ ✪ 0925 Warrington.

♦London 197 – Chester 16 – ♦Liverpool 22 – ♦Manchester 25.

⚐⚐ **Lord Daresbury** (De Vere), Chester Rd, WA4 4BB, on A 56 ℰ 67331, Telex 629330, ⚐, squash – ▯ ☎ ☛ ⚐ Ⓟ ⚐ ⚐ AE ⓪ VISA
M 10.50/11.50 **st.** and a la carte ⌁ 4.00 – **141 rm** ⌸ 37.50/79.00 **t., 3 suites** 75.00/95.00 **t.** – SB (weekends only) 69.00/79.00 **st.**

DARLINGTON Durham 402 P 20 – pop. 85 519 – ECD : Wednesday – ✪ 0325.

☞ Blackwell Grange, Briar Close ℰ 464464, S : 1 m. on A 66 – ☞ Stressholme, Snipe Lane, ℰ 461002, S : 2 m.

✈ Tees-side Airport : ℰ 332811, E : 6 m. by A 67.

☷ District Library, Crown St. ℰ 469858.

♦London 251 – ♦Leeds 61 – ♦Middlesbrough 14 – ♦Newcastle-upon-Tyne 35.

⚐⚐ **Blackwell Grange Moat House** (Q.M.H.) ☜, Blackwell Grange, DL3 8QH, SW : 2 m. on A 66 ℰ 460111, Telex 587272, ☛, ❤ – ▯ ☎ ☛ ⚐ Ⓟ ⚐ ⚐ AE ⓪ VISA
M 8.75/10.95 **st.** and a la carte ⌁ 3.25 – **98 rm** ⌸ 45.00/75.00 **st., 2 suites** 80.00/90.00 **st.** – SB (weekends only) 50.00/60.00 **st.**

⚐ **King's Head** (Swallow), Priestgate, DL1 1NW, ℰ 380222, Telex 587112 – ▯ ☎ ☐wc ☛ Ⓟ ⚐ ⚐ AE ⓪ VISA
M 7.50/9.50 **st.** and a la carte ⌁ 3.95 – **60 rm** ⌸ 41.00/54.00 **st.** – SB (weekends only and July-August) 52.00/56.00 **st.**

⚐ **Stakis White Horse** (Stakis), Harrowgate Hill, DL1 3AD, N : 2 ¼ m. on A 167 ℰ 487111 – ▯ ☎ ☐wc ☛ Ⓟ ⚐ ⚐ VISA
M (buffet lunch)/dinner 7.50 **t.** and a la carte ⌁ 3.25 – ⌸ 3.90 – **40 rm** 35.00/45.00 **t.** – SB 36.00/48.00 **st.**

✗✗ **Bishop's House,** 38 Coniscliffe Rd, DL3 7RG, ℰ 286666 – ⚐ AE VISA
closed Saturday lunch, Sunday, 24 December-3 January and Bank Holidays – **M** 9.00/13.00 **t.** ⌁ 3.60.

at Coatham Mundeville N : 4 m. by A 167 – ✉ Darlington – ✪ 0325 Aycliffe :

⚐ **Hall Garth Country House** ☜, DL1 3LU, ℰ 313333, « Country house atmosphere », ⌇ heated, ☛, ❤ – ☎ ☐wc ☐wc ☛ Ⓟ ⚐ ⚐ AE ⓪ VISA
closed 22 December-2 January – **M** *(closed Sunday dinner)* 10.75/13.95 **t.** ⌁ 2.90 – ⌸ 3.25 – **20 rm** 34.00/56.00 **t., 2 suites** 58.00 **t.** – SB (weekends only) 62.00 **st.**

at Tees-side Airport E : 5 ½ m. by A 67 – ✉ ✪ 0325 Darlington :

⚐ **St. George** (Mt. Charlotte), DL2 1RH, ℰ 332631, Telex 58664, squash – ☎ ☐wc ☛ Ⓟ ⚐ ⚐ AE ⓪ VISA
M (bar meals Saturday lunch and Sunday dinner) 8.50 **st.** (dinner)and a la carte ⌁ 3.25 – **58 rm** ⌸ 36.75/47.25 **st.** – SB (weekends only) 47.50 **st.**

at Neasham SE : 6 ½ m. by A 66 off A 167 – ⊠ ☏ 0325 Darlington :

Newbus Arms ⑤, Hurworth Rd, DL2 1PE, W : ½ m. ℘ 721071, ⛫, squash – TV ⇔wc ☎ Ⓟ. ⛓. AE ⓞ VISA. ✻
M 17.50 **t.** and a la carte ♁ 4.55 – **15 rm** ⊐ 45.00/55.00 **t.** – SB (weekends only)(except Christmas) 70.00 **st.**

at Stapleton S : 3 m. by A 66 – ⊠ ☏ 0325 Darlington :

✗ **Bridge Inn,** DL2 2QQ, ℘ 50106 – Ⓟ. AE ⓞ VISA
closed Saturday lunch, Sunday dinner and Monday – **M** (lunch by arrangement) 7.50/15.00 **t.** and a la carte ♁ 3.50.

at Headlam NW : 6 m. by A 67 – ⊠ Gainford – ☏ 0325 Darlington :

Headlam Hall ⑤, DL2 3HA, ℘ 730238, ←, « Part Jacobean mansion », ⛫, park, ✻ – TV ⇔wc ⩚wc ☎ Ⓟ. AE VISA
closed 24 December-2 January – **M** (restricted lunch) a la carte 9.75/14.75 **st.** ♁ 2.50 – **13 rm** ⊐ 30.00/45.00 **st.**, **3 suites** 40.00/65.00 **st.** – SB (October-July)(weekends only) 45.00/65.00 **st.**

CITROEN 163 Northgate ℘ 468753
FIAT Woodland Rd ℘ 483251
FORD St. Cuthberts Way ℘ 467581
LADA Albert Rd ℘ 485759
NISSAN Haughton Rd ℘ 463384
HONDA Chestnut St. ℘ 485141
TOYOTA Neasham Rd. ℘ 482141
VAUXHALL Chestnut St. ℘ 466155
VAUXHALL-OPEL Whessoe Rd ℘ 466044
VW, AUDI 28-56 West Auckland Rd, Faverdale ℘ 53737

DARTINGTON Devon 403 I 32 – see Totnes.

DARTMOUTH Devon 403 J 32 The West Country G. – pop. 5 282 – ECD : Wednesday and Saturday – ☏ 080 43.

See : Site★★ (←★) – Dartmouth Castle (←★★★) *AC*.
Envir. : Start Point (←★), S : 15 m. including 1 m. on foot.
Royal Avenue Gardens ℘ 4224 (summer only).
♦London 236 – Exeter 36 – ♦Plymouth 35.

Royal Castle, 11 The Quay, TQ6 9PS, ℘ 2397, ← – TV ⇔wc ⩚wc ☎. VISA
M (bar lunch)/dinner 13.00 **t.** ♁ 3.15 – **20 rm** ⊐ 24.95/58.00 **st.** – SB (except Christmas and Easter) 59.90/69.90 **st.**

Dart Marina (T.H.F.), Sandquay, TQ6 9PH, ℘ 2580, ← – TV ⇔wc ☎ Ⓟ. AE ⓞ VISA
M 7.20/14.00 **st.** and a la carte ♁ 3.40 – ⊐ 5.65 – **35 rm** 38.00/54.00 **st.**, **1 suite**.

Townstal Farm, Townstal Rd, TQ6 9HY, NW : 1 m. on A 379 ℘ 2300, ⛫ – Ⓟ. ✻
⊐ 1.00 – **7 rm** 16.00/22.00 **st.**

Three Feathers, 51 Victoria Rd, TQ6 9RT, ℘ 4694 – TV ⩚ Ⓟ. ✻
5 rm ⊐ –/18.00 **st.**

✗✗ ✿ **Carved Angel,** 2 South Embankment, TQ6 9BH, ℘ 2465, ←
closed Sunday dinner, Monday and January – **M** 15.00/25.00 **st.** and a la carte 16.00/21.50 **st.** ♁ 3.75
Spec. Porbeagle Shark cooked in butter with lemon and parsley (summer), Charcoal grilled brochette of beef, marinaded with ginger and orange, Rhubarb in a honey and saffron custard (spring and summer).

✗ **Bistro 33,** 33 Lower St., TQ6 9AN, ℘ 2882
closed Sunday, Monday and 2 to 16 February – **M** (restricted lunch July-September) a la carte 11.25/15.00 **st.** ♁ 2.25.

at Stoke Fleming SW : 3 m. on A 379 – ⊠ Dartmouth – ☏ 0803 Stoke Fleming :

Stoke Lodge, TQ6 0RA, ℘ 770608, ←, ⛱ heated, ⛫ – TV ⇔wc ⩚wc ☎ Ⓟ
24 rm.

Endsleigh, New Rd, TQ6 0NR, ℘ 770381 – ⩚wc Ⓟ
M (bar lunch Monday to Saturday)/dinner 6.00 **t.** and a la carte – **8 rm** ⊐ 11.50/30.00 **t.**

at Strete SW : 6 m. on A 379 – ⊠ Dartmouth – ☏ 0803 Stoke Fleming :

✗ **Laughing Monk,** TQ6 0RN, ℘ 770639 – Ⓟ. AE ⓞ VISA
closed Sunday and 2 weeks January – **M** (dinner only) (booking essential) a la carte 10.75/13.50 **t.** ♁ 2.70.

DAWLISH Devon 403 J 32 The West Country G. – pop. 8 030 – ECD : Thursday and Saturday – ☏ 0626.

18 Warren ℘ 862255, E : 1 ½ m.
The Lawn ℘ 863589.
♦London 215 – Exeter 13 – ♦Plymouth 40 – Torquay 11.

Langstone Cliff ⑤, Dawlish Warren, EX7 0NA, N : 2 m. by A 379 ℘ 865155, ⛱ heated, ⛱, ⛫, ✻ – ⧉ TV ⇔wc ☎ ♿ Ⓟ. ⛓. AE ⓞ VISA
M 6.50/8.50 **st.** ♁ 3.20 – **64 rm** ⊐ 22.00/50.00 **st.** – SB 54.00/60.00 **st.**

Lynbridge, 8 Barton Villas, The Bartons, EX7 9QJ, ℘ 862352, ⛫ – Ⓟ. ✻
Easter-October – **8 rm** ⊐ 9.50/21.00 **st.**

DEDDINGTON Oxon. 403 404 Q 28 – pop. 1 617 – ✪ 0869.

♦London 72 – ♦Birmingham 46 – ♦Coventry 33 – ♦Oxford 18.

🏠 **Holcombe,** High St., OX5 4SL, ℰ 38274 – 📺 ⌷wc ⩍wc 🅿 🕾 ➚ AE ⓞ VISA
  closed 24 to 28 December – **M** 11.50 t. – **13 rm** ⊆ 33.00/43.00 t. – SB 44.00/58.00 st.

DEDHAM Essex 404 W 28 – pop. 1 905 – ECD : Wednesday – ✉ ✪ 0206 Colchester.

🔒 Countryside Centre, Duchy Barn, The Drift ℰ 323447 (summer only).

♦London 63 – Chelmsford 30 – Colchester 8 – ♦Ipswich 12.

🏠 **Maison Talbooth** ⅀ without rest., Stratford Rd, CO7 6HN, W : ½ m. ℰ 322367, Group Telex 987083, ≼, – 📺 🕾 🅿 ➚ AE ⓞ VISA ⅍
  ⊆ 4.00 – **10 rm** 60.00/100.00 st., **1 suite** 110.00 st.

✕✕✕ **Le Talbooth,** Gun Hill, CO7 6HP, W : 1 m. ℰ 323150, Group Telex 987083, ≼, « Tudor house on riverside », 🚅 – 🅿 ➚ AE ⓞ VISA
  M 11.50/24.00 t. and a la carte 18.00/24.00 t. 🍷 3.60.

✕✕ **Dedham Vale** with rm, Stratford Rd, CO7 6HW, W : ¾ m. ℰ 322273, Group Telex 987083, ≼,
  🚅 – 📺 ⌷wc 🕾 🅿 ➚ AE ⓞ VISA ⅍
  M *(closed Saturday lunch and Sunday dinner)* (smörgasbord lunch)/dinner a la carte 12.50/20.00 t. 🍷 3.20 – ⊆ 4.00 – **6 rm** 50.00/80.00 st.

DENBIGH (DINBYCH) Clwyd 402 403 J 24 – pop. 7 710 – ECD : Thursday – ✪ 074 578 Llanynys.

♦London 217 – Chester 29 – Shrewsbury 55.

🏠 **Bryn Morfydd** ⅀, Llanrhaedr, LL16 4NP, SE : 3 ¼ m. by A 525 ℰ 280, ≼ Vale of Clwyd, ⅃ heated, 🏊, 🚅, park, ✂ – 📺 ⌷wc ⩍wc ⊛ 🅿 ⛳ ➚ AE ⓞ VISA
  M 3.50/12.50 st. and a la carte 🍷 2.70 – **29 rm** ⊆ 25.00/35.00 st. – SB 45.00 st.

DENHOLME West Yorks. 402 0 22 – pop. 2 369 – ✉ ✪ 0274 Bradford.

♦London 220 – Burnley 22 – ♦Leeds 17 – ♦Manchester 39.

🏠 **Five Flags,** Manywell Heights, BD13 5EA, N : 1 m. on A 629 ℰ 834188, 🚅 – 📺 ⌷wc ⊛
  🅿 ⛳ ➚ AE ⓞ VISA ⅍
  M 8.50/9.50 and a la carte 🍷 7.65 – **26 rm** ⊆ 39.50/51.00 t., **2 suites** 55.00/63.50 t.

DENTON Greater Manchester 402 403 404 N 23 – pop. 37 784 – ECD : Tuesday – ✉ ✪ 061 Manchester.

♦London 204 – ♦Manchester 6 – ♦Sheffield 34.

🏠 **Old Rectory** ⅀, Meadow Lane, Haughton Green, M34 1GD, S : 2 m. by A 6017 ℰ 336 7516, Telex 668615, 🚅 – 📺 ⌷wc 🕾 🅿 ➚ AE ⓞ VISA ⅍
  closed 1 week at Christmas and Bank Holidays – **M** *(closed Saturday lunch and Sunday)* a la carte 7.50/11.50 st. 🍷 2.50 – **26 rm** ⊆ 31.00/45.00 st. – SB (weekends only) 50.00 st.

DERBY Derbs. 402 403 404 P 25 – pop. 218 026 – ECD : Wednesday – ✪ 0332.

Envir. : Kedleston Hall★★ (18C) *AC*, NW : 5 m. by Kedleston Rd X – Melbourne (St. Michael's Church : Norman nave★) S : 8 m. by A 514 X.

🔒 Breadsall Priory, Moor Rd, Morley ℰ 832235, NE : 3 m. off A 38 X.

✈ East Midlands, Castle Donington ℰ 810621, Telex 37543, SE : 12 m. by A 6 X.

🔒 Reference Library, The Wardwick ℰ 31111 ext 2185/6 or 46124 (evenings and Saturday).

♦London 132 – ♦Birmingham 40 – ♦Coventry 49 – ♦Leicester 29 – ♦Manchester 62 – ♦Nottingham 16 – ♦Sheffield 47 – ♦Stoke-on-Trent 35.

Plan opposite

🏠 **Pennine** (De Vere), Macklin St., DE1 1LF, ℰ 41741, Telex 377545 – 🛗 📺 ⌷wc ⩍wc 🕾 ⛳
  ➚ AE ⓞ VISA
  M (carving lunch) 3.65/7.25 t. and a la carte 🍷 3.45 – **100 rm** ⊆ 43.00/51.00 st. – SB 50.00 st. Z e

🏠 **Gables,** 119 London Rd, DE1 2QR, ℰ 40633 – 📺 ⌷wc 🕾 🅿 ➚ AE VISA ⅍ Z o
  closed 1 week at Christmas – **M** 7.00/10.00 t. and a la carte – **62 rm** ⊆ 18.00/42.00 t.

🏠 **Midland,** Midland Rd, DE1 2SQ, ℰ 45894, 🚅 – 📺 ⌷wc 🕾 🅿 ➚ AE ⓞ VISA ⅍
  closed 25 and 26 December – **M** 12.00 t. (dinner) and a la carte 🍷 4.95 – **62 rm** ⊆ 25.00/49.00 t.,
  1 suite 49.00/70.00 t. Z i

✕✕ **La Gondola,** 220 Osmaston Rd, DE3 8JX, ℰ 32895, Italian rest. Dancing (Saturday) – 🅿 ➚
  AE ⓞ VISA X c
  closed Sunday dinner – **M** 5.00/7.50 st. and a la carte 9.50/16.20 st. 🍷 3.75.

at Shardlow S : 6 m. on A 6 – X – ✉ ✪ 0332 Derby :

✕ La Marina, Derby Rd, ℰ 792553, Italian rest. – 🅿

at Littleover SW : 2 ½ m. on A 5250 – ✉ ✪ 0332 Derby :

🏠 **Crest** (Crest), Pasture Hill, DE3 7BA, ℰ 514933, Telex 377081, 🚅 – 📺 ⌷wc 🕾 🅺 🅿 ⛳
  ➚ AE ⓞ VISA X a
  M *(closed Saturday lunch)* (carving lunch) 6.95/11.50 t. and a la carte – ⊆ 6.15 – **66 rm** 49.50/65.00 st., **2 suites** 90.00 st. – SB (weekends only) 66.00/70.00 st.

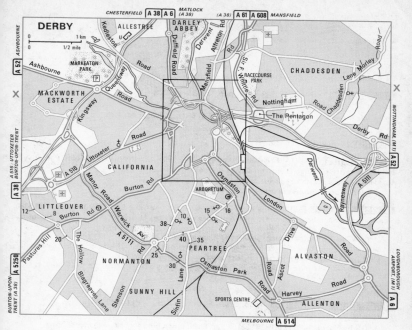

DERBY

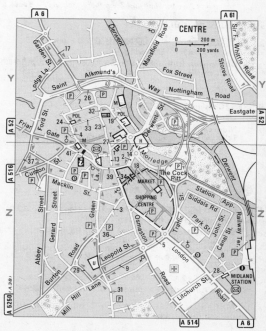

CENTRE

DERBY

AUDI, VW 23-33 Ashbourne Rd ℰ 31282
AUSTIN-ROVER Derwent St. ℰ 31166
AUSTIN-ROVER 152-160 Burton Rd ℰ 43224
BMW King St. ℰ 369511
CITROEN, DAIHATSU Alfreton Rd ℰ 381502
FORD Normanton Rd ℰ 40271
MAZDA Nottingham Rd ℰ 666101
MERCEDES-BENZ Pentagon Island ℰ 383131

NISSAN Burton Rd ℰ 369723
PEUGEOT-TALBOT Ascot Drive ℰ 361626
RENAULT 1263 London Rd, Alvaston ℰ 71847
SAAB 34-39 Duffield Rd ℰ 32706
TOYOTA St. Alkmunds Way ℰ 49536
VAUXHALL-OPEL Pentagon Island, Nottingham Rd ℰ 362661
VOLVO Kedleston Rd ℰ 32625

DERSINGHAM Norfolk 402 404 V 25 – pop. 3 263 – ✪ 0485.
♦London 110 – ♦Cambridge 53 – ♦Norwich 46.

↑ **Westdene House,** 60 Hunstanton Rd, PE31 6HQ, ℰ 40395, ↙ – ℗. ⌘
  March-October – **5 rm** ⊊ 12.50/27.00.

DEVERON Cornwall – see Truro.

DEVIL'S BRIDGE (PONTARFYNACH) Dyfed 403 I 26 – ✉ Aberystwyth – ✪ 097 085 Ponterwyd.
See : Nature Trail (Mynach Falls and Devil's Bridge)**.
♦London 230 – Aberystwyth 12 – Shrewsbury 66.
    Hotels see : Aberystwyth W : 12 m.

DEVIZES Wilts. 403 404 O 29 The West Country G. – pop. 12 430 – ECD : Wednesday – ✪ 0380.
See : Site* – St. John's Church** – Market Place* – Devizes Museum* AC – Envir. : Potterne :
Porch House**, S : 2 m. on A 360.
🛆 North Wilts., Bishop's Cannings ℰ 038 086 (Cannings) 627, N : 5 m.
🎏 Canal Centre, Couch Lane ℰ 71069 (summer only) – ♦London 98 – ♦Bristol 38 – Salisbury 25 – Swindon 19.

  🏛 **Bear,** Market Pl., SN10 1HS, ℰ 2444 – 📺 ⌿wc ☎ ℗. ◪ Æ VISA
    closed 26 December – **M** 7.75/9.25 **t.** and a la carte ₰ 3.50 – **27 rm** ⊊ 27.00/50.00 **t.** – SB
    (weekends only) 53.00/56.00 **st.**

FORD New Park St. ℰ 3456

DIDDLEBURY Salop 403 L 26 – pop. 526 – ✉ Craven Arms – ✪ 058 476 Munslow.
♦ London 169 – ♦ Birmingham 46.

  ↑ **Glebe Farm** ≫, SY7 9DH, ℰ 221, « Part Elizabethan house », ↙ – ℗. ⌘
    closed first 2 weeks June and 7 November-February – **6 rm** ⊊ 15.00/38.00 **st.**

DINBYCH-Y-PSYGOD = Tenby.

DINNINGTON South Yorks. 402 403 404 Q 23 – pop. 1 870 – ✉ Sheffield – ✪ 0909.
♦London 166 – Lincoln 37 – ♦Sheffield 12.

  🏛 **Dinnington Hall,** Falcon Way off B 6060, S31 7NY, ℰ 569661, ↙ – 📺 ⌿wc ⋔wc ☎ & ℗.
    ◪ Æ ⑩ VISA
    M (closed Sunday and Bank Holidays) (dinner only) 22.65 **st.** and a la carte ₰ 3.55 – ⊊ 5.25 –
    10 rm 38.00/60.00 **st.**

DISLEY Cheshire 402 403 404 N 23 – pop. 3 425 – ECD : Wednesday – ✉ Stockport – ✪ 066 32.
♦London 187 – Chesterfield 35 – ♦Manchester 12.

  🏛 **Moorside** (Best Western) ≫, Mudhurst Lane, Higher Disley, SK12 2AP, SE : 2 m. ℰ 4151,
    Telex 665170, ≼ – 📺 ⌿wc ⋔wc ☎ ℗. ♨. ◪ Æ ⑩ VISA
    M 7.75/13.50 **st.** and a la carte ₰ 3.00 – ⊊ 5.00 – **41 rm** 30.00/60.00 **st.**, **1 suite** 70.00/100.00 **st.**
    – SB (weekends only) 54.00/60.00 **st.**

  ✕ **The Ginnel,** 3 Buxton Old Rd, SK12 2BB, ℰ 4494 – ◪ Æ ⑩ VISA
    closed Sunday dinner, Monday and 1 to 8 January – **M** 5.75 **t.** (lunch) and a la carte 9.75/13.25 **t.**
    ₰ 2.75.

MAZDA Fountain Sq. ℰ 2327   RENAULT 159 Buxton Rd ℰ 2105

DISS Norfolk 404 X 26 – pop. 5 463 – ECD : Tuesday – ✉ ✪ 0379.
♦London 98 – ♦Ipswich 25 – ♦Norwich 21 – Thetford 17.

  ✕✕ **Salisbury House** with rm, 84 Victoria Rd, IP22 3JG, ℰ 4738, « Victorian house with period
    furniture, garden » – ⋔wc ℗
    closed 1 week spring, 1 week autumn, 2 weeks at Christmas and Bank Holidays – **M** (closed
    Sunday and Monday to non-residents) (dinner only and Sunday lunch)/dinner 15.00 **st.** – **3 rm**
    ⊊ 27.50/37.50 **st.**

    at Scole E : 2 m. by A 1066 on A 143 – ✉ ✪ 0379 Diss :

  🏛 **Scole Inn** (Best Western), Main St., IP21 4DR, ℰ 740481, « 17C inn » – 📺 ⌿wc ☎ ℗. ♨.
    ◪ Æ ⑩ VISA
    M 8.00/9.00 **t.** and a la carte ₰ 2.50 – **20 rm** ⊊ 30.00/50.00 **t.** – SB 50.00/54.00 **st.**

AUSTIN-ROVER Victoria Rd ℰ 3141   VAUXHALL-OPEL 142-144 Victoria Rd ℰ 2241
FORD Park Rd ℰ 2311

168

DITTON PRIORS Salop 403 404 M 26 — pop. 550 — ✉ Bridgnorth — ✆ 074 634.

♦London 154 — ♦Birmingham 34 — Ludlow 13 — Shrewsbury 21.

XX **Howard Arms** ⟍ with rm, WV16 6SQ, ℰ 200, 🍴 – 🅿. ✻
    closed Sunday dinner, Monday, 2 weeks August and 2 weeks September – **M** (dinner only and Sunday lunch)/dinner 17.50 **t.** ⌕ 3.50 – **2 rm** ⌷ 20.00/32.00 **t.**

DODDISCOMBSLEIGH Devon — see Exeter.

DOLGELLAU Gwynedd 402 403 I 25 — pop. 2 261 — ECD : Wednesday — ✆ 0341.

Envir. : N : Precipice walk★★, Torrent walk★, Rhaiadr Ddu (Black waterfalls★), Coed-y-Brenin Forest★ – E : Bwlch Oerddrws★ on road★ from Cross Foxes Hotel to Dinas Mawddwy – S : Cader Idris (road★★ to Cader Idris : Cregenneu lakes) – Tal-y-Llyn Lake★★.

🏌 Pencefn Rd ℰ 422603.

🅾 Snowdonia National Park Visitor Centre, The Bridge ℰ 422888 (summer only).

♦London 221 — Birkenhead 72 — Chester 64 — Shrewsbury 57.

🏨 **Golden Lion Royal,** Lion St., LL40 1DN, ℰ 422579, 🍴 – 📺 ⌂wc ☎ 🅿. 🔼 AE ① VISA
    M (bar lunch)/dinner 8.50 **t.** – **25 rm** ⌷ 27.00/45.00 **t.**, **2 suites** 66.00 **t.**

🏨 **Royal Ship,** Queen Sq., LL40 1AR, ℰ 422209 – 🔀 ⌂wc 🅿. 🔼 VISA
    M 5.00/8.75 **t.** and a la carte – ⌷ 4.00 – **23 rm** 13.00/39.00 **t.** – SB 33.50/50.00 **st.**

at Penmaenpool W : 2 m. on A 493 – ✉ ✆ 0341 Dolgellau :

X **George III** with rm, LL40 1YD, ℰ 422525, ⩻ Mawddach estuary and mountains – 📺 ⌂wc
    🅿. 🔼 AE ① VISA
    closed Christmas and New Year – **M** *(closed Sunday dinner to non-residents)* (bar lunch Monday to Saturday)/dinner a la carte 8.90/15.10 **t.** – **12 rm** ⌷ 30.00/50.00 **t.** – SB (November-April) 48.40/60.50 **st.**

at Bontddu W : 5 m. on A 496 – ✉ Dolgellau – ✆ 034 149 Bontddu :

🏛 **Bontddu Hall,** LL40 2SU, ℰ 661, ⩻ Mawddach estuary and mountains, « Victorian mansion in large gardens » – 📺 ⌂wc 🅿. 🔼 AE ① VISA
    closed January-mid March – **M** (buffet lunch)/dinner 13.00 **st.** and a la carte 10.50/15.95 **st.**
    ⌕ 3.00 – **22 rm** ⌷ 23.50/55.00 **st.**, **2 suites** 65.00 **st.** – SB (except summer) 65.00/75.00 **st.**

XX **Borthwnog Hall** with rm, LL40 2TT, E : 1 m. on A 496 ℰ 271, ⩻, « Part Regency house on banks of Mawddach estuary », 🍴, park – 🅿. 🔼 AE VISA. ✻
    M *(closed Sunday dinner October-June)* (booking essential) (lunch by arrangement to non-residents)/dinner 8.00 **t.** and a la carte ⌕ 2.55 – **3 rm** ⌷ 20.00/34.00 **t.** – SB (November-May)(except Bank Holidays) 37.50/45.00 **st.**

FORD Arran Rd ℰ 423441   NISSAN Bala Rd ℰ 422681

DOLWYDDELAN Gwynedd 402 403 I 24 — pop. 480 — ECD : Thursday — ✆ 069 06.

♦London 232 — Holyhead 51 — Dolgellau 24 — LLandudno 27.

🏨 **Elen's Castle,** LL25 0EJ, on A 470 ℰ 207, ⩻, ⟍, 🍴 – ⌂wc 🚿wc 🅿
    April-September – **M** (bar lunch)/dinner 6.00 **t.** ⌕ 1.30 – **10 rm** ⌷ 14.70/33.60 **t.** – SB 41.80/43.80 **st.**

DONCASTER South Yorks. 402 403 404 Q 23 — pop. 74 727 — ECD : Thursday — ✆ 0302.

🏌 Crookhill Park, Conisbrough ℰ 0709 (Rotherham) 862979, W : 3 m. on A 630.

🅾 Central Library, Waterdale ℰ 734309.

♦London 173 — ♦Kingston-upon-Hull 46 — ♦Leeds 30 — ♦Nottingham 46 — ♦Sheffield 19.

🏨 **Danum** (Swallow), High St., DN1 1DN, ℰ 62261, Telex 547533 – 🔀 📺 ⌂wc 🚿wc ☎ 🅿. 🛗
    🔼 AE ① VISA
    M 7.25/8.95 **st.** and a la carte ⌕ 3.95 – **66 rm** ⌷ 42.00/54.00 **st.**, **2 suites** 60.00 **st.** – SB (week-ends only) 53.00 **st.**

🏨 **Grand St. Leger** (Best Western), Bennetthorpe, DN2 6AX, S : 1 ½ m. on A 638 ℰ 64111 –
    📺 ⌂wc ☎ 🅿. 🛗. 🔼 VISA. 🛗
    M 5.95/7.95 **t.** and a la carte – **14 rm** ⌷ 43.00/52.00 **t.** – SB (weekends only) 65.00 **st.**

🏨 Earl of Doncaster, Bennetthorpe, DN2 6AD, SE : ½ m. on A 638 ℰ 61371, Telex 547923 – 🔀
    📺 ⌂wc ☎ 🅿. 🛗. 🔼 AE ① VISA
    53 rm ⌷ 39.50/49.50 **st.**

🏩 Punch's (Embassy), Bawtry Rd, Bessacarr, DN4 7BS, SE : 3 m. on A 638 ℰ 535235 – 📺 ⌂wc
    ☎ 🅿. 🛗
    25 rm

⌂ **Ashlea,** 81 Thorne Rd, DN1 2ES, ℰ 63374 – 📺 🚿wc 🅿. ✻
    8 rm ⌷ 11.50/32.00 **s.**

DONCASTER

at Rossington S : 6 m. on A 638 – ⊠ ✪ 0302 Doncaster :

🏠 **Mount Pleasant,** Great North Rd, DN11 0HP, on A 638 ✆ 868219, 🍴 – TV ➘wc 🛏wc ☎
📶 🚗 📺. 🔊
closed Christmas Day – **M** 7.00/9.00 **t.** and a la carte ⒜ 2.75 – **28 rm** ⌁ 14.50/47.00 **t.**

at Sprotbrough W : 3 ½ m. by A 630 – ⊠ ✪ 0302 Doncaster :

✗✗ **Edelweiss,** 4 Main St., DN5 7PJ, ✆ 853923 – 🔊 AE ⓞ VISA
closed Monday – **M** 6.75/10.75 **t.** and a la carte 8.60/16.00 **t.** ⒜ 3.00.

BMW Wheatley Hall Rd ✆ 69191
LANCIA Springwell Lane ✆ 854674
RENAULT Selby Rd, Thorne ✆ 0405 (Thorne) 8121100

TOYOTA Old Thorn Rd, Hatfield ✆ 840348
VW, AUDI York Rd Roundabout ✆ 64141

DONHEAD ST. ANDREW Wilts. – see Shaftesbury (Dorset).

DONYATT Somerset 403 L 37 – pop. 311 – ⊠ ✪ 046 05 Ilminster.
◆London 147 – Exeter 33 – Taunton 11 – Yeovil 17.

✗ **Thatchers Pond,** TA19 0RG, ✆ 3210, « 15C thatched cottage », 🍴 – 📶. 🔊 VISA
closed Sunday dinner, Monday and January-mid February – **M** (buffet only) 10.20/11.75 **t.**

DORCHESTER Dorset 403 404 M 31 The West Country G. – pop. 13 734 – ECD : Thursday –
✪ 0305.
See : Site★ – Dorset County Museum★*AC*.
Envir. : Bere Regis : St. John the Baptist Church★★★, NE : 11 m. by A 35 – Maiden Castle★★ (≤★)
AC, SW : 2 m. by A 354 – Puddletown Church★, NE : 5 m. by A 35 – Athelhampton★*AC*, NE : 6 m.
on A 35 – Moreton Church★, E : 10 m.
🏌 Came Down ✆ 030 581 (Upwey) 2531, S : 2 m.
🚩 7 Acland Rd ✆ 67992.
◆London 135 – Bournemouth 27 – Exeter 53 – ◆Southampton 53.

🏠 **King's Arms,** 30 High East St., DT1 1HF, ✆ 65353 – TV ➘wc 🛏wc ☎ 📶. 🚗 🔊 AE VISA
M 6.00/12.00 **st.** and a la carte ⒜ 3.25 – **26 rm** ⌁ 30.00/45.50 **t.** – SB (except summer)(weekends
only) 50.00 **st.**

🏠 **Casterbridge** without rest., 49 High East St., DT1 1HU, ✆ 64043 – TV ➘wc 🛏wc. 🔊 AE ⓞ
VISA. 🚗
closed 25 and 26 December – **15 rm** ⌁ 20.00/38.00 **t.**

🏠 **King's Arms,** 30 High East St., DT1 1HF, ✆ 65353 – TV ➘wc 🛏wc ☎ 📶. 🚗 🔊 AE VISA
M 6.00/12.00 **st.** and a la carte ⒜ 3.25 – **26 rm** ⌁ 30.00/45.50 **t.** – SB (except summer) (weekends
only) 50.00 **st.**

at Owermoigne SE : 7 m. by A 352 – ⊠ Dorchester – ✪ 0305 Warmwell :

🏠 **Owermoigne Moor** 🐾, 32 Moreton Rd, DT2 8DX, N : 1 ½ m. ✆ 852663, ≤, 🍴, park – 📶
M (lunch by arrangement) 6.00/10.00 ⒜ 2.50 – **6 rm** ⌁ 15.00/25.00.

AUSTIN-ROVER 21-26 Trinity St. ✆ 63031
BMW North Sq. ✆ 67411
CITROEN, LAND ROVER, PEUGEOT, TALBOT, RANGE
ROVER Puddletown ✆ 84456
FIAT, MERCEDES-BENZ Trinity St. ✆ 64494

FORD Prince of Wales Rd ✆ 62211
NISSAN London Rd ✆ 66066
VAUXHALL 6 High East St. ✆ 63913
VOLVO Bridport Rd ✆ 65555

DORCHESTER Oxon. 403 404 Q 29 – pop. 1 045 – ✪ 0865 Oxford.
See : Abbey Church★ 14C.
◆London 51 – Abingdon 6 – ◆Oxford 8 – Reading 17.

🏛 **White Hart,** 26 High St., OX9 8HN, ✆ 340074, « Tastefully converted 17C coaching inn »
TV ➘wc ☎ 📶. 🔊 AE ⓞ VISA. 🚗
M 8.50/17.50 **t.** and a la carte ⒜ 5.50 – **20 rm** ⌁ 48.00/68.00 **st.**, **4 suites** 75.00/95.00 **st.** – SB
(except May)(weekends only) 75.00/85.00 **st.**

🏠 **George,** High St., OX9 8HH, ✆ 340404 – TV ➘wc 🚗 📶. 🚗 🔊 AE ⓞ VISA. 🚗
closed Christmas – **M** 12.00 **t.** (dinner) and a la carte ⒜ 2.30 – **17 rm** ⌁ 33.00/65.00 **t.** – SB
(weekends only) 58.50/66.50 **st.**

DORKING Surrey 404 T 30 – pop. 14 602 – ECD : Wednesday – ✪ 0306.
Envir. : Box Hill ≤★★ NE : 2 ½ m. – Polesden Lacey★★ (19C) *AC*, NW : 4 ½ m.
◆London 26 – ◆Brighton 39 – Guildford 12 – Worthing 33.

🏛 **Burford Bridge** (T.H.F.), Box Hill, RH5 6BX, N : 1 ½ m. on A 24 ✆ 884561, Telex 859507,
🏊 heated, 🍴 – 📶 ☎ 📶. 🚗 🔊 AE ⓞ VISA
M 13.50/16.00 **st.** and a la carte ⒜ 5.00 – ⌁ 6.00 – **48 rm** 58.00/73.00 **st.**

🏛 **White Horse** (T.H.F.), High St., RH4 1BE, ✆ 881138, 🏊 heated – TV ➘wc ☎ 📶. 🚗 🔊 AE
VISA
M 8.50/10.50 **st.** and a la carte ⒜ 3.70 – ⌁ 5.65 – **68 rm** 44.00/55.00 **st.**

✗ **Le Bistro,** 84 South St., RH4 2EZ, ✆ 883239, French rest. – 🔊 AE ⓞ VISA
closed Saturday lunch, Sunday, 1-2 January and Bank Holidays – **M** a la carte 9.70/21.00 **st.**
⒜ 3.40.

AUSTIN-ROVER 105 South St. ✆ 882244

VAUXHALL-OPEL Reigate Rd ✆ 885022

DORMINGTON Heref. and Worc. – see Hereford.

DORRINGTON Salop 402 403 L 26 – see Shrewsbury.

DOVER Kent 404 Y 30 – pop. 33 461 – ECD : Wednesday – ☎ 0304.

See : Castle★★ 12C (≤★) *AC* Y.

Envir. : Barfreston (Norman Church★ 11C : carvings★★) NW : 6 ½ m. by A 2 Z – Bleriot Memorial E : 1 ½ m. Z **A**.

🚢 Shipping connections with the Continent : to France (Boulogne) (Sealink) (Townsend Thoresen) (Hoverspeed) – to France (Calais) (Sealink) (Hoverspeed) (Townsend Thoresen) – to Belgium (Oostende) (Townsend Thoresen) – to Belgium (Zeebrugge) (Townsend Thoresen).

🚢 to Belgium (Oostende) (Townsend Thoresen, Jetfoil).

🅘 Townwall St. 🕾 205108 – ◆London 76 – ◆Brighton 84.

DOVER

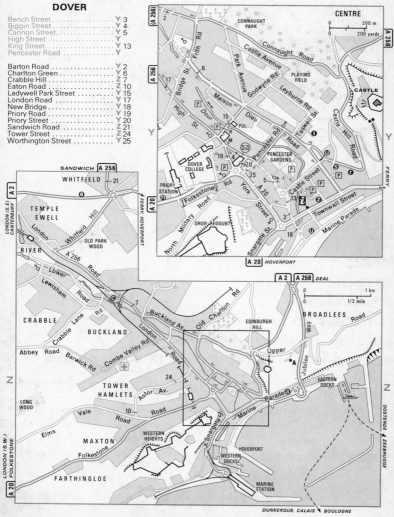

171

🏨 **Dover Moat House** (Q.M.H.), Townwall St., CT16 1SZ, 𝄞 203270, Telex 96458, ⬚ – ⧉ ▤
📺 🕿 👤 🅿 🏖 🔥 ⑩ 𝑽𝑰𝑺𝑨   **Y z**
M 9.50 **st.** and a la carte ⅄ 2.50 – ⟷ 4.75 – **79 rm** 42.50/52.00 **st.** – SB (weekends only)
61.00/64.00 **st.**

🏨 **White Cliffs,** Seafront, CT17 9BW, 𝄞 203633, Telex 965422, ≼ – ⧉ 📺 ⌷wc 🔥wc 🕿 ⇔
⬛ 🄰🄴 ⑩ 𝑽𝑰𝑺𝑨   **Y a**
closed 24 to 26 December – **M** 5.95/6.50 **t.** and a la carte ⅄ 3.75 – **62 rm** ⟷ 27.00/50.00 **t.** – SB
(weekends only)(October-May) 50.00 **st.**

🏠 **St. James,** 2 Harold St., CT16 1SF, 𝄞 204579 – 📺 ⌷wc 🔥wc ⇔. ⬛ 🄰🄴 ⑩ 𝑽𝑰𝑺𝑨   **Y i**
M (lunch by arrangement) 9.50 **st.** (dinner) and a la carte ⅄ 3.60 – **15 rm** ⟷ 13.00/32.00 **st.** –
SB (October-March) 36.00/38.00 **st.**

🏠 **Cliffe Court,** 25-26 Marine Par., CT16 1LU, 𝄞 211001, ≼ – 📺 ⌷wc 🔥wc 🅿. ⬛ 🄰🄴 ⑩ 𝑽𝑰𝑺𝑨
🎙   **Z a**
M 6.50/6.95 **t.** and a la carte ⅄ 2.50 – **25 rm** ⟷ 23.00/35.00 **st.**

🏠 **Mildmay,** 78 Folkestone Rd, CT17 9SF, 𝄞 204278 – 📺 ⌷wc 🅿. ⬛ 🄰🄴 ⑩ 𝑽𝑰𝑺𝑨. 🎙   **Y n**
closed February – **M** (dinner only) a la carte 7.20/10.50 **st.** – **21 rm** ⟷ 24.50/36.00 **st.** – SB
40.00/44.00 **st.**

🏠 **Hubert House,** 9 Castle Hill Rd, CT16 1QW, 𝄞 202253 – 📺 🔥wc 🅿. ⬛ ⑩ 𝑽𝑰𝑺𝑨   **Y s**
closed October – **M** (closed Sunday) (dinner only) 6.50 **t.** and a la carte ⅄ 2.25 – **8 rm**
⟷ 16.00/28.00 **t.**

🏠 **Beulah House,** 94 Crabble Hill, London Rd, CT17 0SA, 𝄞 824615, 🌳 – ⇔ 🅿. 🎙   **Z c**
8 rm ⟷ 14.00/24.00 **s.**

🏠 **Number One,** 1 Castle St., CT16 1QH, 𝄞 202007 – 📺 🔥wc ⇔   **Y u**
5 rm ⟷ 16.00/26.00 **st.**

🏠 **St. Martins,** 17 Castle Hill Rd, CT16 1QW, 𝄞 205938 – 📺 🔥. ⬛. 🎙·   **Y r**
closed Christmas – **8 rm** ⟷ 15.00/24.00 **st.**

at Whitfield N : 3 ½ m. on A 256 – ✉ ✪ 0304 Dover :

🏨 **Dover Motel,** Singledge Lane, CT16 3LF, 𝄞 821222, Telex 965866 – ▤ rest 📺 ⌷wc 🕿 🔥
🅿. ⬛ 🄰🄴 ⑩ 𝑽𝑰𝑺𝑨   **Z o**
M 8.95/11.95 **t.** and a la carte ⅄ 3.75 – ⟷ 4.15 – **67 rm** 39.00/49.00 **t.**, **1 suite** 45.00/55.00 **t.** –
SB (weekends only)(October-June) 64.00 **st.**

at St. Margaret's Bay NE : 4 m. by A 258 – Z – and B 2058 – ✉ ✪ 0304 Dover :

🏠 **Granville** 🎙, Hotel Rd, off Granville Rd, CT15 6DX, 𝄞 852212, ≼ sea and coastline, 🌳 –
⌷wc ⇔ 🅿. ⬛ 🄰🄴 ⑩ 𝑽𝑰𝑺𝑨
M 6.00/7.50 **t.** and a la carte ⅄ 2.50 – ⟷ 3.75 – **20 rm** 17.00/31.00 **t.**

🏠 **Cliffe Tavern,** High St., CT15 6AT, 𝄞 852749 – 📺 ⌷wc 🅿. ⬛ 🄰🄴 ⑩ 𝑽𝑰𝑺𝑨
M 9.85 **t.** and a la carte – ⟷ 4.00 – **12 rm** 18.00/48.00 **t.**

FORD Woolcomber St. 𝄞 206518   VAUXHALL Castle St. 𝄞 203001
RELIANT South Rd 𝄞 206160   VW, AUDI 1 Crabble Hill 𝄞 206710
TOYOTA Eric Rd, Buckland 𝄞 201235

DOWNTON Wilts. 🅰🅾🅼 🅰🅾🅴 O 31 – see Salisbury.

DRAYTON Norfolk 🅰🅾🅴 X 25 – see Norwich.

DRENEWYDD = Newtown.

DRENEWYDD YN NOTAIS (NOTTAGE) Mid Glam. – see Porthcawl.

DRIFFIELD Humberside 🅰🅾🄶 S 21 – see Great Driffield.

DROITWICH Heref. and Worc. 🅰🅾🅷 🅰🅾🅴 N 27 – pop. 18 025 – ECD : Thursday – ✪ 0905.
🅸 Heritage Way 𝄞 774312 – ◆London 129 – ◆Birmingham 20 – ◆Bristol 66 – Worcester 6.

🏨 **Château Impney,** WR9 0BN, NE : 1 m. on A 38 𝄞 774411, Group Telex 336673, « Reproduction 16C French château », 🌳, park, ✗ – ⧉ 📺 🅿. 🏖. ⬛ 🄰🄴 ⑩ 𝑽𝑰𝑺𝑨
closed Christmas – **M** 9.00/12.00 **st.** and a la carte ⅄ 3.95 – ⟷ 6.95 – **67 rm** 64.95/69.95 **st.**

🏨 **Raven,** St. Andrews St., WR9 8DU, 𝄞 772224, Group Telex 336673, 🌳 – ⧉ 📺 🅿. 🏖. ⬛ 🄰🄴
⑩ 𝑽𝑰𝑺𝑨
closed Christmas – **M** 9.00/12.00 **st.** and a la carte ⅄ 3.95 – ⟷ 6.95 – **55 rm** 29.95/68.85 **st.**

AUSTIN-ROVER St. Georges Sq. 𝄞 775123   FORD 141-149 Worcester Rd 𝄞 772132

DRONFIELD Derbs. 🅰🅾🅱 🅰🅾🅷 🅰🅾🅴 P 24 – pop. 22 641 – ECD : Wednesday – ✉ Sheffield (South
Yorks) – ✪ 0246.
◆ London 158 – Derby 30 – ◆ Nottingham 31 – ◆ Sheffield 6.

🏠 **Manor,** 10-15 High St., S18 6PY, 𝄞 413971 – 📺 🔥wc 🅿. ⬛ 𝑽𝑰𝑺𝑨
closed 26 December-31 January – **M** (closed Monday lunch, Sunday dinner and Bank Holidays
to non-residents) (bar lunch)/dinner a la carte 8.70/12.95 **st.** ⅄ 2.75 – **10 rm** ⟷ 27.50/35.00 **t.**

DULVERTON Somerset **403** J 30 The West Country G. – pop. 1 301 – ECD : Thursday – ☎ 0398.
See : Site★.

Envir. : Tarr Steps★★, NW : 6 m. by B 3223.

♦London 198 – Barnstaple 27 – Exeter 26 – Minehead 18 – Taunton 27.

  🏨 **Ashwick House** ⌖, TA22 9QD, NW : 4 ¼ m. by B 3223 ♒ 23868, ≼, « Country house atmosphere », 屛 – 📺 ⇔wc 🅿. ⚙
    M *(closed Sunday and Monday to non-residents)* (dinner only and Sunday lunch)/dinner 9.50 t. ⌗ 3.40 – **6 rm** ⊠ 36.00/60.00 t. – SB 49.50/60.50 st.

DUNCHURCH Warw. **403 404** Q 26 – pop. 2 409 – ⊠ ☎ 0788 Rugby.

♦London 90 – ♦Coventry 12 – ♦Leicester 24 – Northampton 26.

  🏨 **Dun Cow,** The Green, CV22 6NJ, ♒ 810233, Telex 312242, « 16C inn » – 📺 ⇔wc 🗊wc ☎
    🅿. ⚙ 🆎 ① **VISA**
    M 7.95/8.95 **st.** and a la carte ⌗ 3.50 – **23 rm** ⊠ 31.00/60.00 st. – SB (weekends only) 55.00/74.00. st.

VW, AUDI Coventry Rd ♒ 816868

DUNSTABLE Beds. **404** S 28 – pop. 48 436 – ECD : Thursday – ☎ 0582.
See : Priory Church of St. Peter (West front★).

Envir. : Whipsnade Park★ (zoo) ≼★★ *AC*, S : 3 m.

🆚 Tilsworth, Dunstable Rd ♒ 0525 (Leighton Buzzard) 210721, N : 2 m. on A 5.

🆉 The Library, Vernon Pl. ♒ 608441/2.

♦London 40 – Bedford 24 – Luton 4.5 – Northampton 35.

  🏨 **Old Palace Lodge,** Church St., LU5 4RT, ♒ 62201 – ⫴ ▦ rest 📺 ⇔wc ☎ 🅿. ⚙. 🆐 🆎
    ① **VISA**. ⚙
    M 18.00 **t.** (dinner) and a la carte ⌗ 3.00 – ⊊ 4.75 – **49 rm** 45.00/50.00 st. – SB (weekends only) 72.00/92.00 st.

  🏨 **Highwayman,** London Rd, LU6 3DX, SE : 1 m. on A 5 ♒ 61999 – 📺 ⇔wc 🗊wc ☎ 🅿. 🆐
    🆎 ① **VISA**
    M (buffet lunch Monday to Saturday and a la carte) 7.25/9.75 t. ⌗ 2.75 – **37 rm** ⊠ 30.00/40.00 st. – SB (weekends only) 60.00 st.

AUSTIN-ROVER London Rd ♒ 696111   VW, AUDI Common Rd, Kensworth ♒ 872182
FORD 55 London Rd ♒ 67811

DUNSTER Somerset **403** J 30 The West Country G. – pop. 793 – ECD : Wednesday – ⊠ Minehead – ☎ 0643.

See : Site★★ – Castle★★*AC* (upper rooms ≼★ from window) – Dunster Castle Water Mill★*AC* – Dovecote★ – St. Georges Church★.

Envir. : Cleeve Abbey★★*AC*, SE : 5 m. on A 39 – Wheddon Cross (Vantage Point★), SW : 6 m.

♦London 184 – ♦Bristol 61 – Exeter 40 – Taunton 22.

  🏨 **Luttrell Arms** (T.H.F.), 36 High St., TA24 6SG, ♒ 821555, 屛 – 📺 ⇔wc ⚙. 🆐 🆎 ① **VISA**
    M (buffet lunch Monday to Saturday)/dinner 9.75 **st.** and a la carte ⌗ 3.40 – ⊊ 5.65 – **21 rm** 45.00/55.00 st.

  🏨 **Exmoor House,** 12 West St., TA24 6SN, ♒ 821268, 屛 – 📺 🗊wc. 🆐 🆎 ① **VISA**
    closed December and January – **M** (dinner only) 10.25 t. ⌗ 2.40 – **6 rm** ⊠ 24.50/39.00 t. – SB 46.00/54.00 st.

    at Blue Anchor SE : 3 ½ m. by A 39 on B 3191 – ⊠ Minehead – ☎ 0643 Dunster :

  ↑ **Langbury,** TA24 6LB, ♒ 821375, ⛲, 屛 – 📺 🗊wc 🅿
    March-October – **9 rm** ⊠ 12.00/30.00 st.

DURHAM Durham **401 402** P 19 – pop. 38 105 – ECD : Wednesday – ☎ 0385.

See : Cathedral★★★ (Norman) (Chapel of the Nine Altars★★) B – University (Gulbenkian Museum of Art and Archaeology★★ *AC*) by Elvet Hill Rd A – Castle★ (Norman chapel★) *AC* B.

🆚 Low Job's Hill, Crook ♒ 0388 (Bishop Auckland) 762429, SW : 10 m. by A 690 A – 🆚 South Moor, The Middles, Craghead ♒ 0207 (Stanley) 32848, NW : 8 m. by Framwelgate Peth A and B 6532.

🆉 13 Claypath ♒ 43720/47641.

♦London 267 – ♦Leeds 77 – ♦Middlesbrough 23 – Sunderland 12.

Plan on next page

  🏨 **Royal County** (Swallow), Old Elvet, DH1 3JN, ♒ 66821, Group Telex 538238 – ⫴ 📺 ⌗ 🅿.
    ⚙. 🆐 🆎 ① **VISA**   B
    M 7.25/10.50 **st.** and a la carte ⌗ 3.95 – **120 rm** ⊠ 48.50/58.00 st. – SB (weekends only) 70.00 st.

  🏨 **Three Tuns** (Swallow), New Elvet, DH1 3AQ, ♒ 64326 – 📺 ⇔wc ⚙ 🅿. 🆐. 🆎 ① **VISA**
    M 8.00/10.00 **st.** – **54 rm** ⊠ 44.00/56.00 st. – SB (weekends only) 64.00 st.   B e

    at Croxdale S : 3 m. by A 1050 on A 167 – B – ⊠ ☎ 0385 Durham :

  🏨 **Bridge,** DH1 3SP, ♒ 780524, Telex 538156 – 📺 ⇔wc 🅿. ⚙. 🆐 🆎 ① **VISA**. ⚙
    M a la carte 7.70/9.95 **st.** ⌗ 3.30 – **46 rm** ⊠ 19.50/42.00 st. – SB (weekends only) 43.00 st.

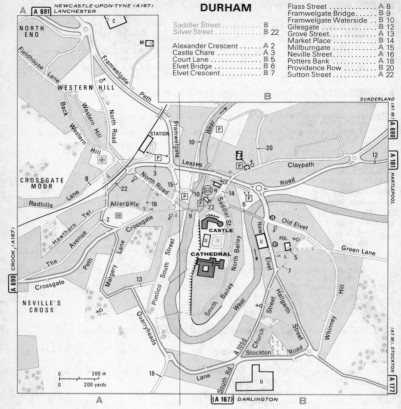

DURHAM

ALFA-ROMEO 81 New Elvet 📞 47777
AUSTIN-ROVER 74 New Elvet 📞 47278
AUSTIN-ROVER Gilesgate Moor 📞 67231
CITROEN Croxdale 📞 0388 (Spennymoor) 814671
FORD Nevilles Cross 📞 46655

RENAULT Langley Moor 📞 69666
VAUXHALL Claypath 📞 42511
VOLVO Sawmills Lane 📞 780866
VW, AUDI 20 Alma Rd, Gilesgate Moor 📞 67215
YUGO Pity Me 📞 44000

DUXFORD Cambs. 404 U 27 – see Cambridge.

DYMCHURCH Kent 404 W 30 – pop. 3 327 – ◎ 0303 Hythe.
♦London 72 – ♦Brighton 65 – ♦Dover 19.

↑ **Chantry,** Sycamore Gdns, TN29 0LA, 📞 873137, 雨, – 🚿wc ℗. ⁑
March-October – **8 rm** ⌁ 12.00/32.00 **st.**

EAGLESCLIFFE Cleveland 402 P 20 – see Stockton-on-Tees.

EARL SHILTON Leics. 403 404 Q 26 – pop. 16 484 – ECD : Wednesday – ✉ Leicester – ◎ 0455.
♦London 107 – ♦Birmingham 35 – ♦Coventry 16 – ♦Leicester 9 – ♦Nottingham 35.

🏠 **Fernleigh,** 32 Wood St., LE9 7ND, 📞 47011 – 📺 🛁wc ☎ ℗ 🅰 VISA
M 4.95/6.95 **st.** and a la carte ⅄ 4.95 – **13 rm** ⌁ 27.00/36.00 **t.** – SB (weekends only)
40.00/72.00 **st.**

FIAT Flood St. 📞 43046

EARL STONHAM Suffolk 404 X 27 – ✉ Stowmarket – ◎ 0449 Stonham.
♦London 81 – ♦Cambridge 47 – ♦Ipswich 10 – ♦Norwich 33.

✕✕ **Mr. Underhill's,** IP14 5DW, Junction of A 140 and A 1120 📞 711206 – ℗ 🅰 VISA
closed Saturday lunch, Sunday, Monday and Bank Holidays – **M** (lunch by arrangement)
(booking essential) 14.95/16.95 **t.** ⅄ 4.00.

174

EASINGWOLD North Yorks. **402** Q 21 — pop. 3 468 — ⊠ York — ☎ 0347.
♦London 217 — ♦Middlesbrough 37 — York 14.

🏛 George, Market Pl., ☎ 21698 — 📺 ⌷wc ℗
17 rm.

at Raskelf W : 2 ¾ m. — ⊠ York — ☎ 0347 Easingwold :

🏛 **Old Farmhouse,** YO6 3LF, ☎ 21971 — ⌷wc ⋔wc ℗
closed 21 December-16 January — **M** (dinner only)(residents only) 8.00 **t.** and a la carte ₤ 2.50
— **10 rm** ⊐ 17.50/30.00 **t.** — SB (November-March) 38.00/40.00 **st.**

EAST BERGHOLT Suffolk **404** X 28 — pop. 2 757 — ⊠ ☎ 0206 Colchester (Essex).
♦London 59 — Colchester 9 — ♦Ipswich 8.5.

XX Fountain House, The Street, CO7 6TB, ☎ 298232, « 15C cottage » — ℗.

EASTBOURNE East Sussex **404** U 31 — pop. 86 715 — ECD : Wednesday — ☎ 0323.
See : Grand Parade★ X.

Envir. : Beachy Head★ (cliff), ☀★ SW : 3 m. Z — Seven Sisters★ (cliffs) from Birling Gap, SW : 5 m.
Z — Charleston Manor★ *AC*, W : 8 m. by A 259 Z — W : scenic road★ from Eastdean by A 259 Z up to
Wilmington by Westdean — Wilmington : The Long Man★ : prehistoric giant figure, NW : 7 m. by
A 27 Y.

🏌, 🏌 Royal Eastbourne, Paradise Drive ☎ 30412 Z — 🏌 Eastbourne Downs, East Dean Rd ☎20827 Z.
🛈 3 Cornfield Terr. ☎ 27474/21333 ext 1184/7 — Seafront, Grand Parade ☎ 647724 (summer only) — Terminus
Rd, Precinct, ☎ 21333 ext 1184/7 — at Pevensey, Castle Car Park, High St. ☎ 0323 (Eastbourne) 761444.
♦London 68 — ♦Brighton 25 — ♦Dover 61 — Maidstone 49.

Plan on next page

🏨 **Grand** (De Vere), King Edward's Par., BN21 4EQ, ☎ 22611, Telex 87332, ≼, 🛆 heated, 🎿 —
📺 ☎ ♣ . 🛆 AE ① VISA
M a la carte lunch/dinner 16.00 **st.** ₤ 4.00 — **164 rm** ⊐ 60.00/135.00 **st.**, **15 suites** 110.00/210.00
st. — SB (weekends only and all June-August) 100.00/210.00 **st.**
Z x

🏨 **Cavendish** (De Vere), 37-40 Grand Par., BN21 4DH, ☎ 27401, Telex 87579, ≼ — 🕿 📺 ♣ ♿
℗ 🛆 AE ① VISA
M 8.00/13.50 **st.** and a la carte — **114 rm** ⊐ 46.00/98.00 **st.**, **4 suites** 80.00/120.00 **st.** — SB
87.00/99.00 **st.**
X r

🏨 **Queen's** (De Vere), Marine Par., BN21 3DY, ☎ 22822, Telex 877736, ≼ — 🕿 📺 ☎ ℗. 🛆.
AE ① VISA
M 9.00/11.00 **st.** and a la carte — **108 rm** ⊐ 42.00/86.00 **st.**, **2 suites** — SB (weekends only and
all June-September) 76.00/80.00 **st.**
V e

🏨 **Hydro,** Mount Rd, BN20 7HZ, ☎ 20643, ≼, 🛆 heated, 🎿 — 🕿 📺 ℗. 🛆 VISA. ✄
M 5.95/6.95 **st.** ₤ 2.25 — **100 rm** ⊐ 20.00/54.00 **t.** — SB (weekends only) 45.00/49.00 **st.**
Z e

🏛 **Lansdowne** (Best Western), King Edward's Par., BN21 4EE, ☎ 25174, ≼ — 🕿 📺 ⌷wc ⋔wc
℗ ⇔. 🛆 AE ① VISA
closed 1 to 11 January — **M** (bar lunch)/dinner 9.00 **st.** and a la carte ₤ 3.25 — **136 rm**
⊐ 23.00/60.00 **st.** — SB (except summer) 41.00/55.00 **st.**
Z z

🏛 **Wish Tower** (T.H.F.), King Edward's Par., BN21 4EB, ☎ 22676, ≼ — 🕿 📺 ⌷wc ⋔wc ♣ ♿. 🛆 AE
① VISA
M (buffet lunch)/dinner 9.50 **st.** and a la carte ₤ 3.40 — ⊐ 5.65 — **73 rm** 35.00/47.00 **st.**
Z r

🏛 **Chatsworth,** Grand Par., BN21 3YR, ☎ 30327, ≼ — 🕿 📺 ⌷wc ⋔wc ♿. 🛆 VISA
closed January-mid March — **M** (bar lunch Monday to Saturday)/dinner 8.25 **t.** ₤ 3.00 — **45 rm**
⊐ 24.60/59.80 **t.** — SB (except Easter, Christmas and New Year) 53.00/58.00 **st.**
X n

🏛 **Sandhurst,** Grand Par., BN21 4DJ, ☎ 27868, ≼ — 🕿 📺 ⌷wc ⋔wc ℗. 🛆 AE ① VISA
M 6.25/7.95 **st.** ₤ 2.95 — **64 rm** ⊐ 20.00/56.00 **t.** — SB (November-April) 52.00/70.00 **st.**
X o

🏛 **Princes,** 12-20 Lascelles Terr., BN21 4BL, ☎ 22056 — 🕿 📺 ⌷wc ☎. ⇔. 🛆 AE ① VISA
closed January — **M** 6.00/8.50 **st.** ₤ 3.50 — **50 rm** ⊐ 34.50/65.00 **st.** — SB (except summer)(weekdays only) 48.00/52.00 **st.**
X z

🏛 **Farrar's,** 3-5 Wilmington Gdns, BN21 4JN, ☎ 23737, 🎿 — 🕿 📺 ⌷wc ⋔wc ℗. 🛆 AE VISA
M 5.00/7.50 **t.** ₤ 2.25 — **42 rm** ⊐ 19.00/52.00 **t.** — SB (except summer) 42.00/46.00 **st.**
X s

🏛 **Mandalay,** 16 Trinity Trees, BN21 3LE, ☎ 29222 — 📺 ⌷wc ⋔wc ℗. 🛆 VISA. ✄
M (*closed Sunday*) (chinese rest.) (bar lunch)/dinner 4.50 **t.** and a la carte — **12 rm**
⊐ 16.50/39.00 **t.**, **1 suite** — SB (October-May) 32.00/35.00 **st.**

🏛 **Oban,** King Edward's Par., BN21 4DS, ☎ 31581 — 🕿 📺 ⌷wc ⋔wc
April-October — **M** 4.50/7.50 **t.** ₤ 3.00 — **31 rm** ⊐ 18.00/36.00 **t.** — SB 36.00/44.00.
X a

🏛 **Croft,** 18 Prideaux Rd, BN21 2NB, ☎ 642291, 🛆 heated, 🎿, ✗ — 📺 ⌷wc ℗. 🛆 AE ①
VISA. ✄
M (*closed Saturday lunch*) 6.95/7.50 and a la carte ₤ 3.50 — **9 rm** ⊐ 16.50/59.00 **t.**
Y c

↑ **Cherry Tree,** 15 Silverdale Rd, BN20 7AJ, ☎ 22406 — 📺 ⋔wc. ✄
10 rm ⊐ 13.50/33.00 **t.**
Z u

↑ **Traquair,** 25 Hyde Gdns, BN21 4PX, ☎ 25198 — 📺 ⋔wc. 🛆 AE ① VISA
11 rm ⊐ 13.50/26.00 **t.**
V x

↑ **Hanburies,** 4 Hardwick Rd, BN21 4NY, ☎ 30698 — 📺 ⌷wc. ✄
14 rm ⊐ 13.50/33.00 **t.**
X c

EASTBOURNE

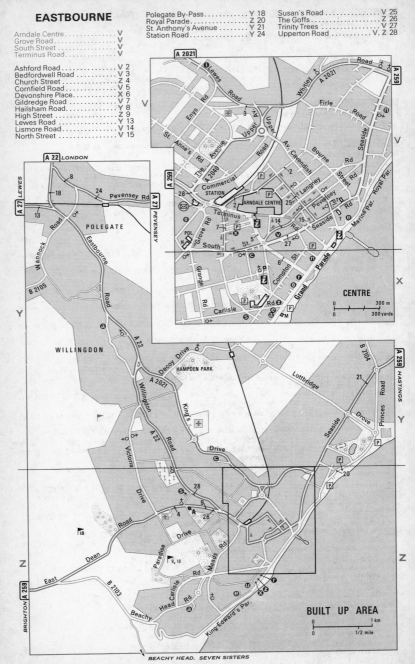

CENTRE

0   300 m
0   300 yards

BUILT UP AREA

0   1 km
0   1/2 mile

BEACHY HEAD. SEVEN SISTERS

176

⚗ **Orchard House,** 10 Old Orchard Rd, BN21 1DB, ✆ 23682 – 📺 ⊟wc ∭wc. ⚗   V **o**
7 rm ☞ 13.00/30.00 t.

⚗ **Nirvana,** 32 Redoubt Rd, BN22 7DL, ✆ 22603 – ⚗   V **n**
April-October and Christmas – **9 rm** ☞ 9.00/22.00 st.

⚗ **Delladale Lodge,** 35 Lewes Rd, BN21 2BU, ✆ 25207, ☕ heated – ∭wc ℗. ⚗   V **i**
April-October – **10 rm** ☞ 18.50/30.00 st.

XX **Crimples Flemish Room,** 42-44 Meads St., BN20 7RG, ✆ 26805 – 🔲 *VISA*   Z **a**
*closed Sunday dinner, Monday, 1 week March, 2 weeks October, 25-26 December and
1 January* – **M** 3.95/8.95 t. and a la carte ▯ 1.95.

X **Byron's,** 6 Crown St., Old Town, BN21 1NX, ✆ 20171 – AE ⓞ *VISA*   Z **s**
closed Saturday lunch, Sunday and 1 week at Christmas – **M** a la carte 10.25/12.85 t. ▯ 2.30.

X **Brown's,** 17 Carlisle Rd, BN21 4BT, ✆ 28837 – 🔲 AE ⓞ *VISA*   X **e**
*closed Sunday except lunch in Summer, Monday, 1 week February, 10 days August, 3 days
October and Bank Holidays* – **M** 8.20/17.80 t. and a la carte ▯ 3.40.

at Willingdon N : 2 ¾ m. on A 22 – ✉ ☎ 0323 Eastbourne

🏠 **Chalk Farm** ⚘, Coopers Hill, BN20 9JD, ✆ 503800, ≤, ☞ – ⊟wc ℗. 🔲 ⚗   Y **a**
M 6.50 st. (dinner) and a la carte ▯ 2.85 – **8 rm** ☞ 16.00/40.00 st.

at Pevensey NE : 5 m. by A 259 – Y – on A27 – ✉ ☎ 0323 Eastbourne :

🏠 **Priory Court,** Castle Rd., BN24 5LG, ✆ 763150, ☞ – 📺 ⊟wc ℗. 🔲 AE *VISA*
9 rm ☞ 19.00/45.00 t.

at Jevington NW : 6 m. by A 259 – Z – on B 2105 – ✉ ☎ 032 12 Polegate :

XX **Hungry Monk,** The Street, BN26 5QF, ✆ 2178, « Part Elizabethan Cottages » – ℗
closed 24 to 26 December – **M** (dinner only and Sunday lunch) (booking essential) 11.50
▯ 2.80.

at Wilmington NW : 6 ½ m. by A 22 on A 27 – Y – ✉ ☎ 032 12 Polegate :

⚗ **Crossways,** BN26 5SG, ✆ 2455, ☞ – 📺 ℗
8 rm ☞ 15.00/34.00 st.

AUSTIN-ROVER, ROLLS ROYCE Meads Rd ✆ 30201
CITROEN, SAAB 8-14 Seaside ✆ 640139
FIAT Ashford Rd ✆ 640101
FORD Lottbridge Drove ✆ 37171
LADA, SUBARU Susans Rd ✆ 639589
NISSAN 46 Pevensey Rd ✆ 37339

PEUGEOT-TALBOT East Dean ✆ 3053
RELIANT, SKODA Pevensey Bay Rd ✆ 761150
RENAULT 18 Lottbridge Drove ✆ 37233
VAUXHALL, RELIANT 336-8 Seaside ✆ 30663
VW, AUDI Burlington Rd ✆ 640114

EAST BUCKLAND Devon **403** I 30 – see South Molton.

EAST CHINNOCK Somerset – see Yeovil.

EAST DEREHAM Norfolk **404** W 25 – pop. 11 798 – ☎ 0362 Dereham.
◆London 109 – ◆Cambridge 57 – King's Lynn 27 – ◆Norwich 16.

🏨 **Phoenix** (T.H.F.), Church St., NR19 1DL, ✆ 2276 – 📺 ⊟wc 🅿 ℗. 🔲 AE ⓞ *VISA*
M 7.50/9.50 st. and a la carte ▯ 3.40 – ☞ 5.65 – **24 rm** 38.50/50.00 st.

🏠 **King's Head,** 42 Norwich St., NR19 1AD, ✆ 3842, ⚗ – 📺 ⊟wc ∭wc ℗. 🔲 AE ⓞ *VISA*
M 8.20/ a la carte ▯ 2.65 – **15 rm** ☞ 23.00/34.00 t.

AUSTIN-ROVER Two Oaks Garage Beetley ✆ 860219   FORD High St. ✆ 2281
AUSTIN-ROVER Norwich Rd ✆ 2293

EAST GRINSTEAD West Sussex **404** T 30 – pop. 23 867 – ECD : Wednesday – ☎ 0342.
Envir. : Hever Castle★ (13C-20C) and gardens★★ *AC*, NE : 10 m.
◆London 32 – ◆Brighton 29 – Eastbourne 33 – Lewes 21 – Maidstone 32.

🏨 **Felbridge,** London Rd, RH19 2BH, NW : 1 ½ m. on A 22 ✆ 26992, Telex 95156, ☕ heated, 🔲,
☞ – 📺 ⊟wc 🅿 ℗. ⚗. 🔲 AE ⓞ *VISA*
M *(closed Saturday lunch)* (carving lunch)/dinner 12.00 st. ▯ 4.00 – **50 rm** ☞ 43.00/58.00 st. –
SB (weekends only) 60.00 st.

XX **Woodbury House** with rm, Lewes Rd, RH19 3UD, SE : ½ m. on A 22 ✆ 313657, ☞ – 📺
∭wc ☎ ℗. 🔲 AE ⓞ *VISA*. ⚗
closed 25 and 26 December – **M** *(closed Sunday dinner)* 9.50 t. and a la carte 14.80 t. ▯ 2.70 –
7 rm ☞ 27.50/50.00 t.

at Gravetye SW : 4 ½ m. by B 2110 – ✉ East Grinstead – ☎ 0342 Sharpthorne :

🏛 **Gravetye Manor** ⚘, Vowels Lane, RH19 4LJ, ✆ 810567, Telex 957239, ≤, « 16C Manor
house with gardens and grounds by William Robinson », ⚒, park – 📺 ℗. ⚗
M *(closed to non-residents Christmas night)* (booking essential) 15.00 s. (lunch) and a la carte
19.50/27.40 s. ▯ 6.00 – ☞ 6.00 – **14 rm** 45.00/100.00 s.

AUSTIN-ROVER King St. ✆ 24666   FORD 220 London Rd ✆ 24344

EAST HORSLEY Surrey 404 S 30 – pop. 5 864 – ECD : Thursday – ✉ Leatherhead – ✆ 048 65.
♦London 29 – Guildford 7.

🏨 **Thatchers** (Best Western), Epsom Rd, KT24 6TB, on A 246 ✆ 4291, ⚊ heated, 🐾 – 📺 ☎
🅿 🛄 🔼 AE ⓪ VISA 🕸
M 11.25/12.25 **t.** and a la carte – ⊆ 4.75 – **29 rm** 48.00/60.00 **st.** – SB (weekends only)(except
Christmas) 65.00/70.00 **st.**

EAST LANGTON Leics. – see Market Harborough.

EASTLEIGH Devon 403 H 30 – see Bideford.

EASTLEIGH Hants. 403 P 31 – pop. 58 585 – ECD : Wednesday – ✆ 0703.
🏌 Fleming Park, Magpie La. ✆ 612797.
🎫 Town Hall Centre, Leigh Rd ✆ 614646 ext 3067.
♦London 74 – Winchester 8 – ♦Southampton 4.

🏨 **Crest** (Crest), Leigh Rd, SO5 5PG, ✆ 619700, Telex 47606 – 🛗 🍽 rest 📺 ☎ 🕭 🅿 🛄 🔼 AE
⓪ VISA
M 9.00/16.25 **st.** and a la carte 🍴 3.25 – ⊆ 6.45 – **120 rm** 54.00/76.00 **st.**, **3 suites** 85.00/95.00
st. – SB (weekends only) 62.00/70.00 **st.**

EAST MOLESEY Surrey 404 ⑫ – see Esher.

EASTON CROSS Devon 403 I 31 – see Chagford.

EASTON GREY Wilts. 403 404 N 29 – see Malmesbury.

EAST PORTLEMOUTH Devon 403 I 33 – see Kingsbridge.

EAST PRESTON West Sussex 404 S 31 – see Worthing.

EAST WITTERING West Sussex 404 R 31 – pop. 3 503 – ✆ 0243 Chichester.
♦London 74 – ♦Brighton 37 – ♦Portsmouth 25.

✗ **Clifford's Cottage,** Bracklesham Lane, Bracklesham Bay, PO20 8JA, E : ¼ m. by B 2179 on
B 2198 ✆ 670250 – 🅿 🔼 AE ⓪ VISA
closed Sunday dinner, Tuesday, first 2 weeks February and last 2 weeks October – **M** (lunch by
arrangement)/dinner 10.50 **st.** and a la carte 🍴 3.25.

EBBERSTON North Yorks. 402 S 21 – pop. 425 – ✉ ✆ 0723 Scarborough.
♦London 243 – Scarborough 9 – York 31.

⌂ **Foxholm,** Main St., YO13 9NJ, off A 170 ✆ 85550, 🐾 – 🚿wc 🅿
March-October and Christmas – **10 rm** ⊆ 13.00/30.00 **t.**

EDWALTON Notts. 402 403 404 Q 25 – see Nottingham.

EGERTON Greater Manchester 402 ② 403 ② 404 ⑨ – see Bolton.

EGHAM Surrey 404 S 29 – pop. 21 337 – ECD : Thursday – ✆ 0784.
♦London 29 – Reading 21.

🏨 **Runnymede,** Windsor Rd, TW20 0AG, on A 308 ✆ 36171, Telex 934900, ≤ – 🛗 🍽 rest 📺 ☎
🅿 🛄
(Dancing Friday and Saturday) **124 rm**.

🏨 **Great Fosters,** Stroude Rd, TW20 9UR, S : 1 ¼ m. by B 388 ✆ 33822, Telex 944441, ≤,
« Elizabethan mansion with extensive gardens », ⚊ heated, park, ✗ – 📺 ☎ 🅿 🛄 🔼 AE
⓪ VISA 🕸
M 11.50/16.50 **t.** and a la carte 🍴 3.00 – **44 rm** ⊆ 43.50/82.50 **t.**, **2 suites** 82.50/88.00 **t.** – SB
(November-April) (weekends only) 72.50/82.50 **st.**

✗✗ **La Bonne Franquette,** 5 High St., TW20 9EA, ✆ 39494, French rest., 🐾 – 🅿 🔼 AE ⓪ VISA
closed Saturday lunch – **M** 12.50 **st.** (lunch) and a la carte 16.55/23.85 **st.** 🍴 3.75.

✗✗ **Bailiwick,** Wick Rd, Englefield Green, TW20 0HN, SW : 2 ½ m. by A 30 ✆ 32223 – 🔼 AE ⓪
VISA
closed Sunday dinner – **M** 15.00 **t.** and a la carte 15.10/30.10 **t.** 🍴 3.25.

✗ **Trattoria il Borgo,** 15 The Precinct, ✆ 33544, Italian rest. – 🔼 AE VISA
closed Sunday – **M** a la carte 8.00/14.50 **t.** 🍴 3.00.

AUSTIN-ROVER The Causeway ✆ 36191   PEUGEOT-TALBOT 186 High St. ✆ 38787
FERRARI Egham-by-pass ✆ 36431

EGLWYSFACH Dyfed 403 I 26 – see Machynlleth (Powys).

ELLESMERE Salop 402 403 L 25 – pop. 2 474 – ECD : Thursday – ✪ 069 171.
♦London 181 – Chester 24 – Shrewsbury 17 – ♦Stoke-on-Trent 33.

🏠 **Grange** ⟍, Grange Rd, SY12 9DE, N : 1 m. on A 528 ℰ 3495, ℛ – 📺 ⌂wc ☎ ᵹ. 🅿. ⊠ ⑩ VISA
M (bar lunch)/dinner 11.00 **st.** ▯ 3.00 – **15 rm** ⊊ 27.00/47.00 **st.** – SB (October-May) 50.00/65.00 **st.**

ELSTEAD Surrey 404 R 30 – pop. 2 633 – ✪ 0252.
♦London 43 – Guildford 9 – ♦Portsmouth 41.

XXX **Bentleys,** Elstead Mill, GU8 6LE, on B 3001 ℰ 702310, « Converted watermill », ℛ – ▤ 🅿.
⊠ 🗚 VISA
closed Sunday dinner – **M** 8.50 **t.** (lunch) and a la carte 13.50/18.00 **t.** ▯ 3.00.

ELSTREE Herts 404 T 29 – pop. 5 296 – ✪ 01 London.
♦London 18 – Luton 20.

XXX **Battleaxes** (T.H.F.), Butterfly Lane, WD6 3AD, NW : 2 m. by A 411 and Aldenham Rd
ℰ 953 1049 – 🅿. ⊠ 🗚 ⑩ VISA
closed Sunday dinner and Monday – **M** 10.50 **t.** (lunch) and a la carte 13.65/21.35 **t.** ▯ 3.65.

ELTERWATER Cumbria – see Ambleside.

ELY Cambs. 404 U 26 – pop. 9 006 – ECD : Tuesday – ✪ 0353.
See : Cathedral** 11C-16C (Norman nave***, lantern***).
🖾 Ely City, Cambridge Rd ℰ 2751.
🛈 Public Library, Palace Green ℰ 2062.
♦London 74 – ♦Cambridge 16 – ♦Norwich 60.

🏠 **Lamb** (Q.M.H.), 2 Lynn Rd, CB7 4EJ, ℰ 3574 – 📺 ⌂wc ☎ 🅿. ⊠ 🗚 ⑩ VISA
closed 25 to 29 December – **M** 7.50 **st.** and a la carte ▯ 3.25 – **32 rm** ⊊ 36.00/46.00 **st.** – SB (weekends only) 54.00 **st.**

🏠 **Fenlands Lodge,** Soham Rd, Stuntney, CB7 5TR, SE : 3 m. on A 142 ℰ 67047, ℛ – 📺
⌂wc ☎ 🅿. ⊠ 🗚 ⑩ VISA
M 7.00/9.00 and a la carte ▯ 4.00 – **9 rm** ⊊ 35.00/45.00 – SB (October-April) 69.00 **st.**

X **Old Fire Engine House,** 25 St. Mary's St., CB7 4ER, ℰ 2582, English rest. – 🅿
closed Sunday dinner, 2 weeks at Christmas and Bank Holidays – **M** a la carte 7.85/11.00 **t.**
▯ 3.10.

X **Peking Duck,** 26 Fore Hill, CB7 4AF, ℰ 2948, Chinese rest. – 🗚
closed Tuesday lunch, Monday and 25-26 December – **M** 10.50 **t.** and a la carte 9.90/15.10 **t.**
▯ 3.80.

AUSTIN-ROVER Lynn Rd ℰ 2981
FORD Station Rd ℰ 61181
NISSAN 64 St. Mary's St. ℰ 2300

VOLVO The Slade, Witcham ℰ 778403
VW, AUDI 16-18 St. Mary's St. ℰ 61272

EMBOROUGH Somerset 403 404 M 30 – pop. 163 – ✉ Bath (Avon) – ✪ 0761 Stratton-on-the-Fosse.
♦London 127 – ♦Bristol 15 – Taunton 33.

🏠 **Court,** The Broadway, Lynch Hill, BA3 4SA, E : ¼ m. on B 3139 ℰ 232237, ℛ, ✻ – 📺
⌂wc 🎜wc 🅿. ⊠ VISA
M 9.75 **st.** and a la carte ▯ 2.95 – **9 rm** ⊊ 27.50/39.50 **st.** – SB (weekends only)(except Bank Holidays) 51.50/55.00 **st.**

EMSWORTH Hants. 404 R 31 – pop. 17 604 (inc. Southbourne) – ECD : Wednesday – ✪ 0243.
♦London 75 – ♦Brighton 37 – ♦Portsmouth 10.

🏢 **Brookfield,** 93-95 Havant Rd, PO10 7LF, ℰ 373363, ℛ – 📺 ⌂wc ☎ 🅿. ▵. ⊠ 🗚 ⑩ VISA.
✻
closed 24 December-1 January – **M** 7.55 **t.** and a la carte ▯ 2.65 – **31 rm** ⊊ 35.20/47.30 **st.** – SB (weekends only)(except summer) 50.00 **st.**

X **36 North Street,** 36 North St., PO10 7DG, ℰ 375592 – ⊠ 🗚 ⑩ VISA
closed Sunday and 23 December-13 January – **M** (lunch by arrangement)/dinner a la carte 15.30/19.55 **t.** ▯ 3.25.

EPPING Essex 404 U 28 – pop. 10 148 – ECD : Wednesday – ✪ 0378.
See : Forest*.
Envir. : Waltham Abbey (Abbey*) W : 6 m.
♦London 20 – ♦Cambridge 40 – Chelmsford 18.

🏢 **Post House** (T.H.F.), High Rd, Bell Common, CM16 4DG, S : ¾ m. on B 1393 ℰ 73137, Telex 81617, ℛ – 📺 ⌂wc ☎ 🅿. ▵. ⊠ 🗚 ⑩ VISA
M 7.95/10.75 **st.** and a la carte ▯ 3.90 – ⊊ 5.65 – **82 rm** 49.50/58.00 **st.**

RENAULT High Rd ℰ 72266

EPSOM Surrey 404 ㉚ – pop. 65 830 (inc. Ewell) – ECD : Wednesday – ✆ 037 27.
Envir. : Chessington Zoo★ *AC*, NW : 3 ½ m.
◻ Longdown Lane South, Epsom Downs ✆ 21666.
♦London 17 – Guildford 16.

↷ **White House,** Downs Hill Rd, off Ashley Rd, KT18 5HW, ✆ 22472, 舞 – ⌂wc 眞 🅿. ⌗
15 rm ⇌ 17.50/31.00.

✗ River Kwai, 4 East St., ✆ 41475, Thai rest.

AUSTIN-ROVER 4 Church St. ✆ 26611
CITROEN Walton-on-the-Hill ✆ 073 781 (Tadworth)
3811
FORD East St. ✆ 26246
FIAT 38 Upper High St. ✆ 25611

MAZDA 5 Ruxley Lane, Ewell ✆ 01 393 0202
RENAULT Nonsuch Ind Est ✆ 28391
VAUXHALL 48 Upper High St. ✆ 25920
VW, AUDI Reigate Rd ✆ 073 73 (Burgh Heath) 60111

ERMINGTON Devon 403 I 32 – ✉ Ivybridge – ✆ 0548 Modbury.
♦London 233 – Exeter 37 – ♦Plymouth 13 – Torquay 23.

🏛 **Ermewood House,** Totnes Rd, PL21 9NS, on B 3210 ✆ 830741, 舞 – 📺 ⌂wc 眞wc 🅿. ▨
▲ ① *VISA*
M (bar lunch)/dinner 15.00 **t.** and a la carte ♨ 3.80 – **10 rm** ⇌ 21.00/52.00 **t.** – SB (weekends only) 56.00 **st.**

ESHER Surrey 404 S 29 – pop. 46 688 (inc. Molesey) – ECD : Wednesday – ✆ 0372.
◻ Moore Place, Portsmouth Rd ✆ 63533 BZ.
♦London 20 – ♦Portsmouth 58.

Plan : see Greater London (South-West)

✗✗ **Good Earth,** 14-16 High St., KT10 9RT, ✆ 62489, Chinese rest. – ▤. ▲ ▣ ① *VISA*   BZ **e**
closed 24 to 27 December – **M** 15.95 **t.** and a la carte 9.20/16.85 **t.** ♨ 2.50.

✗✗ Le Pierrot, 63 High St., KT10 9RQ, ✆ 63191, French rest. – ▤.   BZ **o**

at East Molesey N : 2 m. by A 309 – ✉ East Molesey – ✆ 01 London :

✗✗ **Lantern,** 20 Bridge Rd, KT8 9AH, ✆ 979 1531, French rest. – ▲ ▣ ① *VISA*   BZ **i**
closed lunch Monday and Saturday, Sunday, August and Bank Holidays – **M** 11.95/15.95 **t.**
and a la carte 13.40/16.80 **t.** ♨ 3.15.

✗✗ **Le Chien Qui Fume,** 107 Walton Rd, KT8 0DR, ✆ 979 7150, French rest. – ▲ ▣ ① *VISA*
closed Sunday, 2 weeks August and Bank Holidays – **M** 6.50 **t.** (lunch) and a la carte
12.80/21.60 **t.** ♨ 2.90.   BZ **c**

✗ New Anarkali, 160 Walton Rd, ✆ 979 5072, Indian rest.   BZ **a**

at Claygate SE : 1 m. by A 244 – ✉ ✆ 0372 Esher

✗✗✗ **Les Alouettes,** High St., KT10 0JW, ✆ 64882, French rest. – ▲ ▣ ① *VISA*   BZ **n**
closed Saturday lunch, Sunday and Bank Holidays – **M** 14.50/17.50 **t.**

✗ **Reads,** 4 The Parade, KT10 0NU, ✆ 65105 – ▲ ▣ ① *VISA*   BZ **r**
closed Saturday lunch, Sunday, Monday and first 2 weeks June – **M** 6.50 **t.** (lunch)/dinner a la
carte 11.65/13.40 **t.** ♨ 2.95.

AUSTIN-ROVER 94 Hare Lane, Claygate ✆ 62996   VAUXHALL Kingston By-Pass, Hinchley Wood ✆ 01
                                                        (London) 398 0123

ESKDALE GREEN Cumbria 402 K 20 – pop. 457 – ECD : Wednesday and Saturday – ✉ Holmrook – ✆ 094 03.
♦London 312 – ♦Carlisle 59 – Kendal 60.

🏛 **Bower House Inn** ⌂, CA19 1TD, W : ¾ m. ✆ 244, 舞 – 📺 ⌂wc 🅿
closed Christmas night – **M** (bar lunch)/dinner 18.50 **t.** ♨ 3.50 – **15 rm** ⇌ 23.50/60.00 **t.**

ETON Berks. 404 S 29 – see Windsor.

ETON WICK Berks. – see Windsor.

ETTINGTON Warw. 403 404 P 27 – see Stratford-upon-Avon.

EVERSHOT Dorset 403 404 M 31 – pop. 224 – ✉ Dorchester – ✆ 093 583.
♦London 149 – Bournemouth 39 – Dorchester 12 – Salisbury 53 – Taunton 30 – Yeovil 10.

🏨 **Summer Lodge** ⌂, Summer Lane, DT2 0JR, ✆ 424, « Country house atmosphere »,
☒ heated, 舞 – ⌂wc ☎ & 🅿. ▨ *VISA*
closed December-January – **M** (dinner only) 15.00 **t.** ♨ 2.95 – **12 rm** ⇌ 40.00/70.00 **t.** – SB
70.00/90.00 **st.**

☖ **Acorn Inn,** DT2 0JW, ✆ 228 – 📺 🅿. *VISA*
M a la carte 5.50/13.50 **t.** ♨ 1.95 – **8 rm** ⇌ 15.00/32.00 **t.**

180

EVESHAM Heref. and Worc. 🔢🔢 O 27 – pop. 15 069 – ECD : Wednesday – 📞 0386.

🏛 The Almonry Museum, Abbey Gate ℰ 6944.

◆London 99 – ◆Birmingham 30 – Cheltenham 16 – ◆Coventry 32.

🏨 **Evesham,** Coopers Lane, off Waterside (A 44), WR11 6DA, ℰ 49111, Telex 339342, 🍴 – 📺
🕪wc 🝙wc 🅿 🔼 🖭 *VISA*
closed 25 and 26 December – **M** (buffet lunch)/dinner a la carte 8.55/13.55 **st.** 🍷 2.90 – **34 rm**
🛏 40.00/55.00 **st.** – SB (weekends only) 50.00/76.00 **st.**

🏨 **Northwick Arms** (Whitbread), Waterside, WR11 6BT, ℰ 40322 – 📺 🕪wc 🝙wc 📞 🅿 🔼
25 rm

🏨 **Waterside,** 56-59 Waterside (A 44), WR11 6JZ, ℰ 2420 – 📺 🕪wc 🝙wc 🅿 🔼 🖭 *VISA*
M 5.50/7.50 **t.** and a la carte 🍷 2.90 – **13 rm** 🛏 23.00/40.00 **t.** – SB 47.00/50.00 **st.**

AUSTIN-ROVER Abbey Rd ℰ 6173	FORD Market Pl. ℰ 2525
BEDFORD, VAUXHALL-OPEL 70 High St. ℰ 2614	MAZDA Broadway Rd ℰ 6261
BMW, VW, AUDI Harvington ℰ 870612	NISSAN Cheltenham Rd ℰ 47103
FIAT 3 Cheltenham Rd ℰ 2301	SKODA Sedgeberrow ℰ 881208

EWEN Glos. 🔢🔢 O 28 – see Cirencester.

EXETER Devon 🔢 J 31 The West Country G. – pop. 88 235 – 📞 0392.

See : Site** – Cathedral** AZ **A** – Maritime Museum** *AC* AZ – Royal Albert Memorial
Museum* *AC* AZ **M2**.

Envir. : Killerton House** *AC*, N : 7 m. by B 3181 BY – Crediton (Holy Cross Church*), NW : 8 m. by
A 377 AY – Cullompton*, St. Andrews Church*, NE : 14 m. by B 3181 BY.

🏌 Downes Crediton ℰ 036 32 (Crediton) 3991, NW : 7 ½ m. by A 377 AY.

✈ Exeter Airport : ℰ 67433, Telex 42648, E : 5 m. by A 30 BY – Terminal : St. David's and Central
Stations.

🏢 Civic Centre, Dix's Field ℰ 72434 – Exeter Services Area (M 5) Sandygate, ℰ 37581 (summer only).

◆London 201 – Bournemouth 83 – ◆Bristol 83 – ◆Plymouth 46 – ◆Southampton 110.

Plan on next page

🏨 **Buckerell Lodge** (Crest), Topsham Rd, EX2 4SQ, SE : 1 m. on B 3182 ℰ 52451, Telex 42410,
🍴 – 📺 🕪wc 🝙wc 🅿 🔼 🖭 *VISA* 🎿
M 10.50/12.25 **st.** 🍷 6.20 – **54 rm** 46.50/56.50 **st.** – SB (weekends only) 64.00 **st.**
BY **a**

🏨 **St. Olaves Court,** Mary Arches St., EX4 3AZ, ℰ 217736, 🍴 – 📺 🕪wc 🝙wc 📞 🅿 AZ **e**
12 rm

🏛 **Royal Clarence** (Norfolk Cap.), Cathedral Yard, EX1 1HD, ℰ 58464, Group Telex 23241 – 📶
📺 🕪wc 🝙wc 📞 🔼 – **62 rm, 1 suite**. AZ **z**

🏨 **White Hart,** 65-66 South St., EX1 1EE, ℰ 79971, « Part 14C inn » – 📶 📺 🕪wc 🝙wc 📞 🅿
🔼 🖭 🗽 *VISA*
AZ **n**
closed 24 to 26 December – **M** 6.75 **t.** (lunch) and a la carte 9.25/28.00 **t.** – **62 rm**
🛏 23.65/52.80 **t.**, **2 suites** 67.00 **t.**

🏨 **Rougemont** (Mt. Charlotte), Queen St., EX4 3SP, ℰ 54982, Telex 42455 – 📶 📺 🕪wc 📞 🅿
🔼 🔼 🖭 🗽 *VISA*
AZ **x**
M 5.00/8.25 **st.** 🍷 3.00 – **68 rm** 🛏 36.75/50.00 **st.** – SB (weekends only) 56.00 **st.**

🏨 **Imperial,** St. David's Hill, EX4 4JX, ℰ 211811, Telex 42551, 🍴 – 📺 🕪wc 📞 🚗 🅿 🔼
🔼 🖭 🗽 *VISA*
AZ **v**
M 8.50/15.00 **t.** and a la carte 🍷 2.60 – **26 rm** 🛏 25.00/48.00 **t.** – SB (weekends only)(except
summer) 50.00/65.00 **st.**

🏨 **Exeter Moat House** (Q.M.H.), 398 Topsham Rd, EX2 6HE, S : 2 ½ m. at junction of A 379
and B 3182 ℰ 039 287 (Topsham) 5441 – 📺 🕪wc 🝙wc 📞 🅿 🔼 🖭 🗽 *VISA*
BY **o**
M *(closed Saturday lunch)* (bar lunch)/dinner 8.50 **t.** and a la carte 🍷 3.25 – **44 rm**
🛏 30.00/48.00 **st.** – SB 46.00/55.00 **st.**

🏨 **St. Andrews,** 28 Alphington Rd, EX2 8HN, ℰ 76784 – 📺 🕪wc 🝙wc 📞 🅿 🔼 🖭 *VISA*
closed 1 week at Christmas – **M** (dinner only) a la carte 7.35/10.10 **st.** 🍷 3.25 – **16 rm**
🛏 23.00/40.00 **st.** – SB (weekends only)(November-March) 40.00/50.00 **st.**
AY **a**

🏨 **Great Western,** St. David's Station Approach, EX4 4NU, ℰ 74039 – 📺 🕪wc 🝙wc 📞 🅿 🔼
🖭 🔘 *VISA*
AZ **c**
M 4.25/7.50 **t.** 🍷 2.75 – **39 rm** 🛏 16.50/31.00 **t.** – SB (weekends only) 41.00/48.00 **st.**

🏨 **Red House,** 2 Whipton Village Rd, EX4 8AR, ℰ 56104 – 📺 🕪wc 🝙wc 📞 🅿 🔼 🖭 🔘 *VISA*
M 7.00/12.00 **st.** and a la carte 🍷 2.60 – **12 rm** 🛏 22.50/39.50 **st.** – SB (weekends only)
50.00/60.00 **st.**
BY **r**

🏠 **Sylvania House,** 64 Pennsylvania Rd, EX4 6DF, ℰ 75583 – 📺 🝙wc 🅿 *VISA* 🎿
8 rm 🛏 10.50/25.00 **st.**
AY **e**

🏠 **Glendale,** 8 St. Davids Hill, EX4 3RQ, ℰ 74350 – 📺 🝙wc 🅿 🔼 *VISA* 🎿
10 rm 🛏 12.00/26.00 **st.**
AZ **o**

🏠 **Park View,** 8 Howell Rd, EX4 4LG, ℰ 71772 – 📺 🕪wc 🝙wc 📞 🅿 🔼 🔘
15 rm 🛏 12.50/28.00 **t.**
AZ **i**

🏠 **Trenance House,** 1 Queens Cres., York Rd, EX4 6AY, ℰ 73277 – 📺 🝙 🅿 🔼 *VISA*
14 rm 🛏 12.00/22.00 **t.**
BZ **o**

🍴🍴 King Tandoori, 94-95 South St., EX1 1EN, ℰ 56992, Indian rest.
AZ **r**

EXETER

at Huxham N : 5 m. by A 377 — AY — off A 396 — ⊠ Exeter — ✪ 039 284 Stoke Canon :

XX **Barton Cross,** EX5 4EJ, ✆ 245, « Part 16C thatched cottage », 🖼 – 🅿 🖭 🆎 ⓪ 𝗩𝗜𝗦𝗔
closed Sunday dinner, Monday and January – **M** (restricted lunch)/dinner 13.00 **t.** and a la
carte 5.75/10.20 **t.** ⌀ 3.00.

at Pinhoe NE : 2 m. by A 30 — BY — ⊠ ✪ 0392 Exeter :

🏠 **Gipsy Hill** ⤢, Gipsy Hill Lane, via Pinn Lane, EX1 3RN, ✆ 65252, 🖼 – 📺 ➰wc ☎ 🅿 ⚒
🖪 🆎 ⓪ 𝗩𝗜𝗦𝗔
M 5.50/7.50 **st.** and a la carte ⌀ 2.75 – **19 rm** ⪥ 31.00/42.00 **st.** – SB (weekends only) 50.00 **st.**

at Whimple NE : 9 m. by A 30 — BY — ⊠ Exeter — ✪ 0404 Whimple :

🏠 **Woodhayes** ⤢, EX5 2TD, ✆ 822237, « Country house atmosphere », 🖼 – 📺 ➰wc 🅟
⪥ 🅿 🖪 🆎 ⓪ 𝗩𝗜𝗦𝗔 ⚒
closed 2 weeks mid January – **M** *(closed Sunday and Monday dinner to non residents)* (lunch
by arrangement) 16.00/19.50 **st.** ⌀ 2.95 – **7 rm** ⪥ 45.00/70.00 **st.** – SB (November-Easter, except
Christmas and New Year) 90.00 **st.**

at Kennford S : 5 m. on A 38 — AY — ⊠ ✪ 0392 Exeter :

🏠 **Exeter Court,** Kennford Services, EX6 7UX, ✆ 832121, Telex 42443 – 📺 ➰wc 🅟 🅿 ⚒
🖪 🆎 ⓪ 𝗩𝗜𝗦𝗔
M (grill rest. only) 7.50 **st.** and a la carte ⌀ 3.20 – **61 rm** ⪥ 36.00/48.00 **st.** – SB 50.00 **st.**

🏠 **Fairwinds,** EX6 7UD, ✆ 832911 – 📺 ➰wc 🅟wc 🅿 🖪 𝗩𝗜𝗦𝗔 ⚒
closed 18 to 30 December – **M** (lunch by arrangement)/dinner 8.35 **t.** ⌀ 2.15 – **8 rm**
⪥ 18.00/35.00 **t.** – SB 37.00/45.00 **st.**

at Doddiscombsleigh SW : 7 ½ m. by A 38 – AY – ⊠ Exeter – ✪ 0647 Christow :

🏛 **Nobody Inn** ⤢, EX6 7PS, ✆ 52394, « 16C inn », 🖼 – ➰wc 🅟wc 🅿 🖪 𝗩𝗜𝗦𝗔 ⚒
M *(closed dinner Sunday and Monday)* (bar lunch)/dinner a la carte 8.30/10.80 **t.** ⌀ 2.40 – **7 rm**
⪥ 10.00/30.00 **t.**

at Ide W : 3 m. by A 30 – AY – ⊠ ✪ 0392 Exeter :

XX **Old Mill,** 20 High St., ✆ 59480 – 🅿 🖪 🆎 𝗩𝗜𝗦𝗔
closed Sunday, 25-26 December and 1 January – **M** 6.50/10.95 **t.** and a la carte 13.05/17.75 **t.**
⌀ 2.75.

MICHELIN Distribution Centre, Kestrel Way, Sowton Industrial Estate, EX2 7LH, ✆ 77246 by
Honiton Road BY

AUSTIN-ROVER 55 Sidwell St. ✆ 78342
AUSTIN-ROVER 84-88 Sidwell St. ✆ 54923
AUSTIN-ROVER Honiton Rd ✆ 68187
DAIMLER-JAGUAR, LAND-ROVER-RANGE-ROVER
Marsh Barton Rd ✆ 37152
BMW Pinhill, Pinhoe ✆ 69595
CITROEN, FIAT, MERCEDES-BENZ Trusham Rd,
Marsh Barton ✆ 77311
FORD 9 Marsh Barton Rd ✆ 50141

MAZDA Alphinbrook Rd ✆ 57737
MITSUBISHI 66 Polsloe Rd ✆ 57990
RENAULT Summerland St. ✆ 77225
TOYOTA 37 Marsh Green Rd, Marsh Barton ✆ 34761
VAUXHALL-OPEL, BEDFORD 8 Marsh Barton Rd,
Marsh Barton Trading Estate ✆ 34851
VOLVO Longbrook Terr. ✆ 215691
VW, AUDI Haven Rd ✆ 30321

EXFORD Somerset 403 J 30 The West Country G. – pop. 409 – ECD : Thursday – ⊠ Minehead
– ✪ 064 383.

See : Exmoor National Park★★ – Church★.

Envir. : Dunkery Beacon★★★ (⩽★★★), N : 4 ½ m. – Winsford★, SE : 8 m. – at Oare, Doone Valley★,
NW : 8 m. plus 6 m. return on foot – Luccombe★ (Church★), NE : 9 m.

♦London 194 – Exeter 35 – Minehead 13 – Taunton 32.

🏠 **Crown,** TA24 7PP, ✆ 554 – 📺 ➰wc 🅟 🅿 🖪 🆎 𝗩𝗜𝗦𝗔
M (bar lunch Monday to Saturday)/dinner 13.75 **t.** ⌀ 3.25 – **18 rm** ⪥ (dinner included) 40.00/80.00 **t.** – SB (weekends only)(May-August and November-February) 66.00/75.00 **st.**

EXMOUTH Devon 403 J 32 The West Country G. – pop. 28 037 – ECD : Wednesday – ✪ 0395.

Envir. : A La Ronde★ *AC,* N : 2 m. – Bicton★, The Gardens★ *AC,* NE : 8 m.

🖪 Alexandra Terr. ✆ 263744 (summer only).

♦London 210 – Exeter 11.

🏠 **Devoncourt** ⤢, 16 Douglas Av., by Rolle Rd, EX8 2EX, ✆ 272277, ⩽, « Sub-tropical gardens », ⤢ heated, 🏊, 🖼, ✽ – ⦚ 📺 ➰wc 🅟 🅿 🖪 🆎 𝗩𝗜𝗦𝗔 ⚒
M 6.50/7.25 **t.** and a la carte ⌀ 3.00 – **68 rm** ⪥ 28.00/48.00 **t.** – SB (weekends only)(except
summer) 45.00/49.80 **st.**

🏠 **Imperial** (T.H.F.), The Esplanade, EX8 2SW, ✆ 274761, ⩽, 🏊 heated, 🖼, ✽ – ⦚ 📺 ➰wc
🅟 🆎 𝗩𝗜𝗦𝗔
M (buffet lunch Monday to Saturday)/dinner 9.50 **st.** and a la carte ⌀ 3.40 – ⪥ 5.65 – **58 rm**
40.00/55.00 **st.**

🏠 **Royal Beacon,** The Beacon, EX8 2AF, ✆ 264886, ⩽ – ⦚ 📺 ➰wc ☎ ⪥ 🅿 🖪 🆎 ⓪ 𝗩𝗜𝗦𝗔
M 6.25/9.50 **st.** and a la carte ⌀ 3.00 – **32 rm** ⪥ 25.45/55.30 **st.**

183

🏛 **Balcombe House** 🐾, 7 Stevenstone Rd, EX8 2EP, NE : 1 m. by A 376 ℰ 266349, 🖼 – 📺
🗄wc ⅍ & 🅟
April-October – **M** (bar lunch)/dinner 7.50 **t**. ⅋2.50 – **12 rm** ⌖ 15.50/38.50 **t**. – SB
45.00/48.00 **st**.

🏛 **Carlton Lodge**, Carlton Hill, EX8 2AJ, ℰ 263314 – 📺 ⬛wc 🗄wc 🅟
M (bar lunch)/dinner 7.30 **st**. ⅋3.05 – **6 rm** ⌖ 15.00/29.50 **st**. – SB (except June-September)(weekends only) 65.00/80.00 **st**.

⌂ **Palm Trees**, 72 Victoria Rd, EX8 1DP, ℰ 271055 – 🗄. ◪ 𝘝𝘐𝘚𝘈
16 rm ⌖ 7.50/20.00 **s**.

at Lympstone N : 3 m. by A 376 – ✉ ✿ 0395 Exmouth :

XXX **River House,** The Strand, EX8 5EY, ℰ 265147, ≼ Exe Estuary – ◪ 𝘈𝘌 𝘝𝘐𝘚𝘈
closed Sunday dinner, Monday, 25 to 27 December and 1-2 January – **M** 17.75 **t**. ⅋3.45.

AUSTIN-ROVER The Parade ℰ 72258 272758   RENAULT 4 Church Rd ℰ 263888
FORD Withycombe Village Rd ℰ 277633 272617   VAUXHALL-OPEL Salterton Rd ℰ 264366

EYAM Derbs. 🅰🅾🅱 🅰🅾🅴 O 24 – pop. 923 – ✉ Sheffield (South Yorks.) – ✿ 0433 Hope Valley.
See : Celtic Cross* 8C – ◆London 163 – Derby 29 – ◆Manchester 32 – ◆Sheffield 12.

🏛 **Miners Arms**, Water Lane, S30 1RG, ℰ 30853 – 🅟. 🛥
closed Christmas Day – **M** *(closed Sunday dinner and Monday to non residents)* 3.95/11.75 **t**.
⅋3.20 – ⌖3.00 – **4 rm** 11.00/29.00 **t**. – SB (weekends only) 43.50 **st**.

EYNSHAM Oxon. 🅰🅾🅱 🅰🅾🅴 P 28 – pop. 4 339 – ✿ 0865 Oxford.
◆London 65 – ◆Birmingham 65 – Gloucester 40 – Northampton 43.

XX **Edward's**, 4 Lombard St., OX8 1HT, ℰ 880777 – ◪ 𝘝𝘐𝘚𝘈
closed Saturday lunch, Sunday dinner, 24 to 27 December and 2 to 14 January – **M** a la carte
8.10/11.50 **t**. ⅋2.10.

FAIRFORD Glos. 🅰🅾🅱 🅰🅾🅴 O 28 – pop. 2 408 – ECD : Saturday – ✿ 0285 Cirencester.
See : St. Mary's Church (stained glass windows** 15C-16C).
◆London 99 – ◆Bristol 46 – Gloucester 28 – ◆Oxford 27.

🏛 **Hyperion House**, London St., GL7 4AH, ℰ 712349, 🖼 – 📺 ⬛wc & 🅟 ◪ 𝘈𝘌 ⑩ 𝘝𝘐𝘚𝘈
M (bar lunch)/dinner 15.00 **st**. and a la carte ⅋3.50 – **21 rm** ⌖ 30.00/45.00 **st**. – SB
55.00/65.00 **st**.

🏛 Bull, Market Pl., GL7 4AA, ℰ 712535, 🐾, 🖼 – 📺 ⬛wc – **17 rm**.

AUSTIN-ROVER The Bridge, Milton St. ℰ 712222   RENAULT London Rd ℰ 712219

FALFIELD Avon 🅰🅾🅱 🅰🅾🅴 M 29 – pop. 657 – ✿ 0454.
◆London 129 – ◆Bristol 16 – Gloucester 18 – Newport 30.

🏛 **Park**, GL12 8DR, S : 1 m. on A 38 ℰ 260550, 🖼 – 📺 ⬛wc 🗄wc 🐾 🅟 ◪ 𝘈𝘌 ⑩ 𝘝𝘐𝘚𝘈
M *(closed Sunday)* 12.50 **t**. and a la carte ⅋3.50 – ⌖ 4.75 – **10 rm** 25.00/45.00 **t**. – SB (except
spring and winter)(weekends only) 55.00 **st**.

FALLOWFIELD Greater Manchester 🅰🅾🅴 ③ 🅰🅾🅱 ③ 🅰🅾🅴 ⑩ – see Manchester.

FALMOUTH Cornwall 🅰🅾🅱 E 33 The West Country G. – pop. 17 810 – ECD : Wednesday – ✿ 0326.
See : Site** – Pendennis Castle* (≼**)AC B.
Envir. : Glendurgan Garden**AC, S : 3½ m. by Swanpool Rd A – Helston Flora Day Flurry Dance**,
SW : 11 m. by A 39 A – Mawnan Parish Church*, (≼**), SW : 4 m. by Trescobeas Rd A – at
Gweek, Seal Sanctuary*, setting*AC, SW : 8 m. by A 39 A – Carn Brea (≼*), NW : 9 m. by A 39 A
– at Wendron, Poldark Mine*, W : 9 m. by A 39 A – at Culdrose, Cornwall Aero Park*AC, SW :
10 m. by A 39 A – at Redruth, Tolgus Tin Streaming*AC, NW : 11 m. by A 39 A.

🛈 Swanpool Rd ℰ 311262 A – 🛈 Budock Vean Hotel ℰ 0326 (Mawnan Smith) 250288, SW : 7 m. by
Trescobeas Rd A.
🛈 Town Hall, The Moor ℰ 312300.
◆London 308 – Penzance 26 – ◆Plymouth 65 – Truro 11.

Plan opposite

🏨 **Falmouth**, TR11 4NZ, ℰ 312671, Telex 45262, ≼, ⬛ heated, 🖼 – ▐📺 🅟 ⚐. ◪ 𝘈𝘌 ⑩ 𝘝𝘐𝘚𝘈
closed 2 weeks at Christmas – **M** 6.50/11.50 **st**. and a la carte ⅋2.75 – **73 rm** ⌖ 27.30/84.00 **st**.
1 suite 85.60/99.50 **st**.   B x

🏨 **Greenbank**, Harbourside, TR11 2SR, ℰ 312440, Telex 45240, ≼ harbour – ▐📺 🐾 ⚐ 🅟.
◪ 𝘈𝘌 ⑩ 𝘝𝘐𝘚𝘈   A a
closed 24 December-12 January – **M** 7.50/12.00 **t**. and a la carte ⅋3.25 – **42 rm** ⌖ 32.00/80.00 **t**.
– SB (weekends only) 69.00/72.00 **st**.

🏨 **Royal Duchy**, Cliff Rd, TR11 4NX, ℰ 313042, ≼, ◪, 🖼 – ▐📺 🐾 🅟 ◪ 𝘈𝘌 ⑩ 𝘝𝘐𝘚𝘈 🛥
M 4.95/7.50 **t**. and a la carte – **42 rm** ⌖ 24.15/62.10 **t**. – SB (except May-September, Christmas
and New Year) 43.70/55.20 **st**.   B a

FALMOUTH

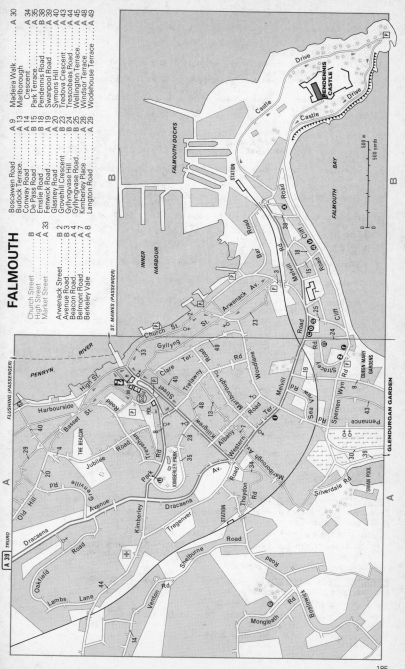

🏛 **Green Lawns,** Western Terr., TR11 4QJ, ℰ 312734, Telex 45169, 🔲 – 📺 ➚wc ☎ 🅿 ⚿ A i
🔜 AE ⓞ *VISA*
closed 24 to 30 December – **M** 7.50/10.00 t. and a la carte ⓘ 2.60 – **41 rm** ⊆ 18.40/54.05 t. –
SB (October-May) 56.80/74.05 **st.**

🏛 **St. Michaels,** Gyllyngvase Beach, Seafront, TR11 4NB, ℰ 312707, Telex 45540, ≼, 🔲, ⬎,
🔜 – 📺 ⌐wc ⌐wc ☎ 🅿 🔜 AE ⓞ *VISA* z
M (bar lunch)/dinner 12.00 t. and a la carte ⓘ 4.80 – **75 rm** ⊆ 29.50/80.00 t. – SB (November-
April) 72.00 **st.**

🏛 **Falmouth Beach,** Gyllyngvase Beach, Seafront, TR11 4NA, ℰ 318084, Telex 45540, ≼ – ⫿
📺 ➚wc ⌐wc ☎ 🅿 🔜 AE ⓞ *VISA* A r
M (bar lunch)/dinner 14.50 t. and a la carte ⓘ 4.80 – **67 rm** ⊆ 29.50/80.00 t. – SB (November-
April) 72.00 **st.**

🏠 **Penmere Manor** (Best Western) ⏉, Mongleath Rd, TR11 4PN, ℰ 314545, Telex 45266,
🔟 heated, 🔜 – 📺 ➚wc ⌐wc ☎ 🅿 🔜 AE ⓞ *VISA* A e
closed 21 to 27 December – **M** (bar lunch)/dinner 11.00 **st.** – **33 rm** ⊆ 27.50/54.00 **st.** – SB
50.00/69.00 **st.**

🏠 **Crill House** ⏉, Golden Bank, TR11 5BL, SW : 2 ½ m. by Swanpool Rd ℰ 312994, 🔟 heated,
🔜 – ➚wc 🅿 🔜 ⓞ *VISA* by Boslowick Rd A
April-mid October – **M** (bar lunch)/dinner 9.25 t. and a la carte ⓘ 3.55 – **11 rm** ⊆ 21.50/51.00 t.

🏠 **Carthion,** Cliff Rd, TR11 4AP, ℰ 313669, ≼, 🔜 – 📺 ➚wc ⌐wc 🅿 🔜 AE ⓞ *VISA* B v
March-October – **M** (bar lunch)/dinner 9.00 t. ⓘ 2.15 – **18 rm** ⊆ 18.00/45.00 t.

🏠 **Broadmead,** 68 Kimberley Park Rd, TR11 3DD, ℰ 315704 – 📺 ➚wc ☜ 🔜 *VISA* A u
closed Christmas and New Year – **M** (bar lunch) (booking essential)/dinner 10.00 ⓘ 2.75 –
12 rm ⊆ 15.00/46.00 **st.** – SB (except summer) 38.00/50.00 **st.**

🏠 **Rosemullion,** Gyllyngvase Hill, TR11 4DF, ℰ 314690 – ➚wc ⌐wc 🅿 🎇 B c
May-September – **13 rm** ⊆ 11.50/23.00 st.

🏠 **Gyllyngvase House,** Gyllyngvase Rd, TR11 4DJ, ℰ 312956, 🔜 – 📺 ➚wc ⌐wc 🅿 🎇
16 rm ⊆ 11.50/38.00 t. B s

🏠 **Cotswold House,** 49 Melvill Rd, TR11 4DF, ℰ 312077 – ➚wc 🔟 🅿 🎇 B o
11 rm ⊆ 9.50/22.00 st.

🏠 **Tresillian House,** 3 Stracey Rd, TR11 4DW, ℰ 312425 – 📺 ➚wc ⌐wc 🅿 🎇 A n
March-October – **12 rm** ⊆ 13.50/27.00 t.

at Mawnan Smith SW : 5 m. by Trescobeas Rd – A – off B 3291 – ✉ ✪ 0326 Falmouth :

🏛 **Meudon** ⏉, TR11 5HT, E : ½ m. ℰ 250541, Telex 45478, « ≼ Terraced gardens landscaped
by Capability Brown » – 📺 ☎ 🅿 🔜 AE ⓞ *VISA*
Mid February-mid November – **M** 15.00 t. (dinner) and a la carte 8.00/21.00 t. ⓘ 4.00 – **30 rm**
⊆ 30.00/68.00 t. – SB 70.00/90.00 **st.**

🏛 **Budock Vean** ⏉, TR11 5LG, ℰ 250288, ≼, 🔲, 🕤, 🔜, park, 🎿 – ⫿ ☎ 🅿 ⚿ 🔜 AE ⓞ
VISA 🎇
closed January and February – **M** (bar lunch Monday to Saturday)/dinner 12.00 t. and a la
carte 12.75/18.75 t. – **53 rm** ⊆ 21.00/57.00 t. – SB 59.00/97.00 **st.**

🏛 **Nansidwell Country House** ⏉, TR11 5HU, E : ¼ m. on Mawnan Church rd ℰ 250340, ≼,
« Gardens », park, 🎿 – ➚wc 🅿 🔜 AE ⓞ *VISA*
closed January and February – **M** (bar lunch)/dinner 12.50 t. – **18 rm** ⊆ 30.00/84.00 t.

🏠 **Trelawne** ⏉, Maenporth Rd, TR11 5HS, E : ¾ m. ℰ 250226, 🔲, 🔜 – 📺 ➚wc ⌐wc 🅿 🔜
AE ⓞ *VISA*
closed January and February – **M** (bar lunch)/dinner 10.90 **st.** ⓘ 2.50 – **16 rm** ⊆ 22.00/62.00 **st.**
– SB (November-March) 52.00 **st.**

BMW Falmouth Rd, Penryn ℰ 032 67 (Penryn) 2641   TOYOTA North Parade ℰ 313029
FORD Ponsharden ℰ 72011

FAREHAM Hants. 🔢🔢 Q 31 – pop. 55 563 (inc. Portchester) – ECD : Wednesday – ✪ 0329.
Envir. : Porchester castle★ (ruins 3C - 12C), Keep ≼★ *AC*, SE : 2 ½ m.
🅩 Ferneham Hall, Osborn Rd ℰ 221342.
♦London 77 – ♦Portsmouth 9 – ♦Southampton 13 – Winchester 19.

🏛 **Red Lion** (Whitbread), East St., PO16 0BP, ℰ 239611 – 📺 ➚wc ☎ 🅿 ⚿ 🔜 AE ⓞ *VISA* 🎇
M a la carte 7.75/13.55 **st.** ⓘ 3.20 – **33 rm** ⊆ 40.00/50.00 **st.** – SB (weekends only) 56.00 **st.**

AUSTIN-ROVER, LOTUS Newgate Lane ℰ 282811

FARINGDON Oxon. 🔢🔢 P 29 – pop. 4 646 – ECD : Thursday – ✪ 0367.
🅩 Car Park, Southampton St. ℰ 22191 (summer only).
♦London 79 – ♦Bristol 55 – ♦Oxford 17 – Reading 34.

🏠 **Bell,** Market Pl., SN7 7HP, ℰ 20534 – 📺 ➚wc 🔜 AE ⓞ *VISA*
M 15.95 **st.** and a la carte – ⊆ 3.25 – **11 rm** 19.75/31.75 t. – SB 47.00/50.60 **st.**

🏯 Faringdon, Market Pl., SN7 7HL, ℰ 20536 – 📺 ➚wc ⌐wc ☎
12 rm.

TOYOTA Church St. ℰ 22070   PEUGEOT, TALBOT Marlborough St. ℰ 21212

FARNBOROUGH Hants. 🅰🅾🅰 R 30 – pop. 48 063 – ECD : Wednesday – 🕾 0252.

See : St. Michael's Abbey church★ 19C (Imperial crypt *AC*).

🛅 Southwood, Ively Rd 🖉 548700, W : 1 m.

🖻 Country Library, Pinehurst Av. 🖉 513838 ext 24.

♦London 41 – Reading 17 – ♦Southampton 44 – Winchester 33.

🏨 **Queens** (T.H.F.), Lynchford Rd, GU14 6AZ, S : 1 ½ m. on Farnborough Rd (A 325) 🖉 545051, Group Telex 859637, 🔲 – 📺 🍽 wc 📞 🅿. 🛆. 🔼 AE 🛈 *VISA*
M 11.00/15.00 **st.** and a la carte ⅄ 4.25 – **110 rm** 🖵 49.00/59.00 **st.** – SB (weekends only) 62.00/66.00 **st.**

🏠 **Falcon**, 68 Farnborough Rd, GU14 6TH, S : ¾ m. on A 325 🖉 545378 – 📺 🍽 wc 🅿. 🛆. 🛠
M 7.50 **st.** ⅄ 2.80 – **30 rm** 🖵 35.00/45.00 **st.**

FORD   Elles Rd 🖉 544344

FARNE ISLANDS Northumb. 🅰🅾🅱 🅰🅾🅲 P 17.

See : Islands★★ (Sea Bird Sanctuary and grey seals, by boat from Seahouses *AC*).

   Hotels see : Bamburgh.

FARNHAM Surrey 🅰🅾🅰 R 30 – pop. 34 541 – ECD : Wednesday – 🕾 0252.

See : Castle keep 12C (square tower★) *AC*.

Envir. : Birdworld★ (zoological bird gardens) *AC*, SW : 3 ½ m.

🖻 Locality Office, South St. 🖉 048 68 (Godalming) 4104 ext 554.

♦London 45 – Reading 22 – ♦Southampton 39 – Winchester 28.

🏨 **Bush,** The Borough, GU9 7NN, 🖉 715237, Telex 858764, 🛠 – 📺 🍽 wc 📞 🅿. 🛆. 🔼 AE 🛈 *VISA*
M 8.75 **st.** (lunch)and a la carte 8.35/11.45 **t.** ⅄ 3.35 – **65 rm** 🖵 49.00/66.00 **t.** – SB (weekends only) 60.00/65.00 **st.**

🏠 Bishop's Table (Best Western), 27 West St., GU9 7DR, 🖉 710222, 🛠 – 📺 🍽 wc 📞
16 rm.

🏠 **Trevena House** 🛅, Alton Rd, GU10 5ER, SW : 1 ¾ m. on A 31 🖉 716908, ≼, ⵣ heated, 🛠, 🛠 – 📺 🍽 wc ⁂wc 📞 🅿. 🛆. 🔼 AE 🛈 *VISA* 🛠
closed 24 December-8 January – **M** *(closed Sunday and Bank Holidays)* (bar lunch, residents only)/a la carte 8.60/13.95 **t.** ⅄ 3.00 – **19 rm** 🖵 34.50/50.00 **st.**

XX **Tirolerhof**, 84 West St., 🖉 723277, Austrian rest. – 🔼 AE *VISA*
closed Sunday, Monday and 1 week January – **M** (dinner only) a la carte 10.50/13.90 **t.** ⅄ 2.60.

   at Seale E : 4 m. on A 31 – ✉ Farnham – 🕾 025 18 Runfold :

🏠 **Hog's Back** (Embassy), GU10 1EX, on A 31 🖉 2345, ≼ – 📺 🍽 wc 🕭 🅿. 🛆. 🔼 AE 🛈 *VISA*
M 9.75 **st.** and a la carte ⅄ 3.15 – 🖵 5.00 – **50 rm** 50.00/60.00 **st.** – SB 59.00/64.00 **st.**

   at Churt S : 5 ¾ m. on A 287 – ✉ Farnham – 🕾 025 125 Frensham :

🏨 **Frensham Pond** 🛅, GU10 2QB, N : 1 ½ m. by A 287 🖉 3175, Telex 858610, ≼, « Lake-side setting », 🔲, squash – 📺 🍽 wc 📞 🅿. 🛆. 🔼 AE 🛈 *VISA* 🛠
M 14.00/16.00 **t.** and a la carte ⅄ 3.50 – **19 rm** 🖵 50.00/64.00 **t.**, **1 suite** 88.00 **t.** – SB (weekends only except Christmas and Bank Holidays) 72.00 **st.**

🏨 **Pride of the Valley Inn** (Best Western) 🛅, Jumps Rd, GU10 2LE, E : 1 ½ m. via Hale House Lane 🖉 042 873 (Hindhead) 5799, 🛠 – 📺 🍽 wc 📞 🅿. 🔼 AE 🛈 *VISA*
M 7.80/8.50 **t.** and a la carte ⅄ 3.50 – **12 rm** 🖵 35.00/45.00 **st.**, **1 suite** 55.00 **st.** – SB 58.00/60.00 **st.**

AUSTIN-ROVER East St. 🖉 716201   VW, AUDI West St. and Crondall Lane 🖉 715616

FARRINGTON GURNEY Avon 🅰🅾🅱 🅰🅾🅰 M 30 – pop. 587 – ✉ Bristol – 🕾 0761 Temple Cloud.

♦London 132 – Bath 13 – ♦Bristol 12 – Wells 8.

🏠 **Country Ways** 🛅, Marsh Lane, BS18 5TT, 🖉 52449, 🛠 – 📺 🍽 wc 📞 🅿. 🔼 AE 🛈 *VISA*
closed 2 weeks February and 2 weeks Christmas – **M** *(closed Sunday dinner)* (bar lunch)(residents only)/dinner 13.00 **st.** ⅄ 2.50 – **6 rm** 🖵 28.30/44.80 **st.** – SB 59.00/62.00 **st.**

XX **Old Parsonage** with rm, Main St., BS18 5UB, 🖉 52211, 🛠 – 🍽 wc 🅿. 🛠
closed 17 April and 25 to 28 December – **M** *(closed Sunday dinner and Monday to non-residents)* (booking essential) a la carte 10.50/14.00 **t.** ⅄ 3.00 – **3 rm** 🖵 20.00/40.00 **t.**

   at Ston Easton S : 1 ¼ m. on A 37 – ✉ Bath – 🕾 076 121 Chewton Mendip :

🏰 **Ston Easton Park** 🛅, BA3 4DF, 🖉 631, ≼, « Palladian country house », 🛠, park – 📺 📞 🅿. 🔼 AE 🛈 *VISA* 🛠
M 14.50 **t.** (lunch) and a la carte 19.50/26.00 **t.** ⅄ 3.50 – 🖵 5.00 – **20 rm** 60.00/180.00 **st.** – SB (weekdays only) (November-March) 110.00/140.00 **st.**

FAR SAWREY Cumbria 🅰🅾🅲 L 20 – see Hawkshead.

FAUGH Cumbria – see Carlisle.

FAVERSHAM Kent 404 W 30 – pop. 15 914 – ECD : Thursday – ✆ 0795.

🏛 Fleur de Lis Heritage Centre, 13 Preston St. 𝒫 534542.

◆London 52 – ◆Dover 26 – Maidstone 21 – Margate 25.

  XX **Reads,** Painters Forstal, ME13 0EE, SW : 2 ¼ m. by A 2 𝒫 535344 – 🅿 ⒶⒺ ⓄⒹ 𝘝𝘐𝘚𝘈
      closed Sunday – **M** 9.00 **t.** (lunch) and a la carte 15.50/20.10 **t.** ⌗ 2.25.

FAWKHAM Kent – pop. 4 324 (inc. Hartley) – ✆ 0474 Ash Green.

◆London 22 – Maidstone 16.

  🏨 **Brands Hatch Place,** DA3 8NQ, 𝒫 872239, 🔲, 🐎, ⚒, squash – 📺 ⌁wc 🛏wc ☎ 🅿 🏌
    🔄 ⒶⒺ ⓄⒹ 𝘝𝘐𝘚𝘈 ✁
    M *(closed lunch Saturday and Sunday to non residents)* 10.50/12.50 **t.** and a la carte ⌗ 3.00 –
    ⌑ 4.75 – **29 rm** 43.00/60.00 **t.** – SB (weekends only) (except Christmas) 60.00 **st.**

FAWLEY Bucks. 404 R 29 – see Henley-on-Thames (Oxon.).

FELINDRE FARCHOG (VELINDRE) Dyfed 403 F 27 – see Newport (Dyfed).

FELINHELI = Port Dinorwic.

FELIXSTOWE Suffolk 404 Y 28 – pop. 24 207 – ECD : Wednesday – ✆ 0394.

⛴ Shipping connections with the Continent : to Belgium (Zeebrugge) (Townsend Thoresen).

⛴ to Harwich (Orwell & Harwich Navigation Co.) 5-8 daily (except weekends) (15 mn).

🏛 91 Undercliffe Rd West 𝒫 282126 and 276770.

◆London 84 – ◆Ipswich 11.

  🏨🏨 Orwell Moat House (Q.M.H.), Hamilton Rd, IP11 7DX, 𝒫 285511, 🐎 – 🛗 📺 ☎ 🅿 🏌
    60 rm, 1 suite.

  XX **Sherebangla,** 7 Hamilton Rd, IP11 7AX, 𝒫 274343, Indian rest. – 🔄 ⒶⒺ 𝘝𝘐𝘚𝘈
    M a la carte 6.75/10.40 **t.** ⌗ 3.10.

AUSTIN-ROVER Crescent Rd 𝒫 283221

FELSTED Essex 404 V 28 – pop. 2 509 – ✆ 0371 Great Dunmow.

◆London 44 – ◆Cambridge 30 – Colchester 18 – Chelmsford 11.

  XX **Boote House,** Chelmsford Rd, CM6 3DH, 𝒫 820279 – 🔄 ⒶⒺ ⓄⒹ 𝘝𝘐𝘚𝘈
    closed dinner Sunday, Monday, Tuesday, first 2 weeks February and first 2 weeks September –
    M (dinner only and Sunday lunch)/dinner a la carte 10.65/19.95 **t.** ⌗ 3.20.

FERNDOWN Dorset 403 404 O 31 – pop. 23 921 – ECD : Wednesday – ✆ 0202.

◆London 108 – Bournemouth 6 – Dorchester 27 – Salisbury 23.

  🏨🏨 **Dormy** (De Vere), New Rd, BH22 8ES, on A 347 𝒫 872121, Telex 418301, 🔲, 🐎, ⚒, squash
    – 🛗 🔄 rest 📺 ☎ & 🅿 🏌 🔄 ⒶⒺ ⓄⒹ 𝘝𝘐𝘚𝘈
    M 10.00/12.00 **t.** and a la carte – **133 rm** ⌑ 50.00/70.00 **t.**, **5 suites** 150.00/200.00 **t.** – SB (week-
    ends only) 90.00/95.00 **st.**

  🏠 **Coach House Motel,** Wimbourne Rd, Tricketts Cross, BH22 9NW, on A 31 𝒫 871222 – 📺
    ⌁wc 🛏wc ☎ 🅿 🔄 ⒶⒺ ⓄⒹ 𝘝𝘐𝘚𝘈
    M (bar lunch)/dinner 7.50 **t.** and a la carte ⌗ 2.95 – **44 rm** ⌑ 28.00/45.00 **t.** – SB (weekends
    only) 49.00/55.00 **st.**

    at Longham SW : 1 m. – ✉ Wimborne – ✆ 0202 Ferndown :

  🏨 **Bridge House,** 2 Ringwood Rd, BH22 9AN, 𝒫 578828, Telex 418484 – 📺 ⌁wc 🛏wc ☎ 🅿
    🔄 ⒶⒺ 𝘝𝘐𝘚𝘈 ✁
    closed 25 and 26 December – **M** a la carte 9.00/14.75 **t.** ⌗ 3.05 – ⌑ 3.50 – **25 rm** 28.00/80.00 **t.**

AUSTIN-ROVER 553 Ringwood Rd 𝒫 872212   TOYOTA Ringwood Rd 𝒫 872201
COLT Victoria Rd 𝒫 871131   VAUXHALL-OPEL Wimborne Rd East 𝒫 872055
RENAULT Ringwood Rd 𝒫 893589

FINDON West Sussex 404 S 31 – see Worthing.

FISHBOURNE I.O.W. 403 404 Q 31 Shipping Services : see Wight (Isle of).

Pleasant hotels and restaurants
are shown in the Guide by a red sign.

Please send us the names
of any where you have enjoyed your stay.

Your Michelin Guide will be even better.

🏨🏨🏨 ... 🏠

XXXXX ... X

FISHGUARD (ABERGWAUN) Dyfed **403** F 28 – pop. 2 903 – ECD : Wednesday – 🕿 0348.

Envir. : Porthgain (cliffs ✳✳✳) SW : 10 m. – Goodwick (≤✳✳) NW : 1 ½ m. – Strumble Head (≤✳✳ from the lighthouse) NW : 5 m. – Trevine (≤✳✳) SW : 8 m. – Bryn Henllan (site✳) NE : 5 m.

🚢 to Ireland (Rosslare) (Sealink) 1-3 daily (3 h 30 mn).

🛈 Town Hall 🖉 873484 (summer only)

◆London 265 – ◆Cardiff 114 – Gloucester 176 – Holyhead 169 – Shrewsbury 136 – ◆Swansea 76.

🏠 **Cartref,** High St., SA65 9AW, 🖉 872430 – ➩wc 🛁wc 🅿. 🔼 VISA. ⌀
M (bar lunch)/dinner 7.50 t. ▌ 2.65 – **13 rm** ⇌ 16.00/35.00 t.

🏠 **Blair Athol,** Windy Hall, SA65 9DP, 🖉 873147 – TV 🅿. ⌀
closed January and February – **M** (dinner only)(booking essential) 6.50 t. and a la carte ▌ 4.10 – **9 rm** ⇌ 14.50/30.00 st.

at Llanychaer SE : 2 ¼ m. on B 4313 – ✉ Fishguard – 🕿 034 882 Puncheston :

✗ **Penlan Oleu** ⌂ with rm, SA65 9TL, SE : 2 m. by B 4313 off Puncheston rd 🖉 314, ≤, « Converted farmhouse », ☞ – ➩wc 🛁wc 🅿. 🔼 VISA. ⌀
closed Sunday lunch and 25-26 December – **M** (booking essential) a la carte 9.25/10.75 **st.** ▌ 2.50 – **5 rm** ⇌ (dinner included) 28.00/56.00 st.

at Goodwick (Wdig) NW : 1 ½ m. – ✉ 🕿 0348 Fishguard :

🏨 **Fishguard Bay,** Quay Rd, SA64 0BT, 🖉 873571, 🔻 heated, park – 🛎 ➩wc 🕿 ⅙ 🅿. 🚗. 🔼 AE ⓪ VISA
M 7.50/9.50 t. and a la carte ▌ 2.50 – **62 rm** ⇌ 24.00/55.00 t.

AUSTIN-ROVER Clive Rd 🖉 872253

FITTLEWORTH West Sussex **404** S 31 – pop. 895 – ECD : Wednesday – ✉ Pulborough – 🕿 079 882.

◆London 52 – ◆Brighton 28 – Chichester 15 – Worthing 17.

🏠 **Swan,** Lower High St., RH20 1EN, 🖉 429, ☞ – 🛁 🅿. 🔼 AE ⓪ VISA
M 15.00 t. ▌ 3.50 – **7 rm** ⇌ 20.00/40.00 st. – SB 45.00/50.00 st.

FLAMBOROUGH Humberside **402** T 21 – pop. 1 588 – ECD : Wednesday – 🕿 0262 Bridlington.

◆London 240 – ◆Kingston-upon-Hull 34 – Scarborough 18 – York 45.

🏠 **Timoneer Country Manor** ⌂, South Landing, YO15 1AG, off Lighthouse Rd 🖉 850219, ☞ – TV ➩wc 🛁wc 🅿. 🔼 AE ⓪ VISA
M 6.25/10.50 t. and a la carte ▌ 3.75 – **10 rm** ⇌ 25.90/47.30 t. – SB (except Christmas and Bank Holidays) 51.50/56.65 st.

FLAMSTEAD Herts. **404** S 28 – pop. 1 407 – ✉ St. Albans – 🕿 0582 Luton.

◆London 32 – Luton 5.

🏨 **Hertfordshire Moat House** (Q.M.H.), London Rd, AL3 8HH, on A 5 🖉 840840 – TV ➩wc 🕿 🅿. 🚗. 🔼 AE ⓪ VISA
M (bar lunch Saturday) 11.50 **st.** and a la carte ▌ 3.75 – **97 rm** ⇌ 49.00/59.00 st. – SB 60.00 st.

FLEET Hants. **404** R 30 – pop. 27 406 – ECD : Wednesday – 🕿 0252 Farnborough.

◆London 46 – Guildford 14 – Reading 16 – ◆Southampton 42.

🏨 **Lismoyne** ⌂, Church Rd, GU13 8NA, 🖉 628555, ☞ – TV ➩wc 🕿 🅿. 🚗. 🔼 AE ⓪ VISA
M 7.90/8.90 st. and a la carte ▌ 3.55 – **39 rm** ⇌ 30.00/52.00 st.

AUSTIN-ROVER 66 Albert St. 🖉 613303

FLEETWOOD Lancs. **402** K 22 – pop. 27 899 – ECD : Wednesday – 🕿 039 17.

🏌 Fleetwood, Princes Way 🖉 3661, W : from Promenade.

🚢 to the Isle of Man : Douglas (Isle of Man Steam Packet Co.) July-August, 2 weekly (3 h 15 mn).

🛈 Marine Hall, The Esplanade 🖉 71141.

◆London 245 – ◆Blackpool 10 – Lancaster 28 – ◆Manchester 53.

🏨 **North Euston,** The Esplanade, FY7 6BN, 🖉 6525 – 🛎 TV ➩wc 🛁wc 🕿 🅿. 🚗. 🔼 AE ⓪ VISA
M 6.15/9.40 t. and a la carte ▌ 2.65 – **57 rm** ⇌ 24.00/41.00 t. – SB (weekends only) 47.00 st.

FORD West View 🖉 2292

FLITWICK Beds. **404** S 27 – pop. 8 421 – 🕿 0525.

◆London 45 – Bedford 13 – Luton 12 – Northampton 28.

✗✗✗ **Flitwick Manor** ⌂ with rm, Church Rd, off Dunstable Rd, MK45 1AE, 🖉 712242, Telex 825562, ≤, « 18C manor house », ☞, ✗ – TV ➩wc 🕿 🅿. 🔼 AE ⓪ VISA. ⌀
closed 25 and 26 December – **M** (closed Sunday dinner to non residents) (Seafood) 10.80/18.90 t. and a la carte 16.90/23.35 ▌ 3.45 – **8 rm** ⇌ 55.00/120.00 st.

FOLKESTONE Kent 404 X 30 – pop. 42 949 – ECD : Wednesday and Saturday – ☎ 0303.

See : Site★ – Envir. : The Warren★ (cliffs) E : 2 m. by A 20 X – Acrise Place★ *AC*, NW : 6 m. by A 260 X – 18 Sene Valley , Folkestone and Hythe,Sene, ✆ 68513, N : 2 m. from Hythe on B 2065, W : by A 259 X – Shipping Connections to France (Boulogne) (Sealink).

ℹ Harbour St. ✆ 58594 – Pedestrian Precinct, Sandgate Rd ✆ 53840 (summer only).

♦London 76 – ♦Brighton 76 – ♦Dover 8 – Maidstone 33.

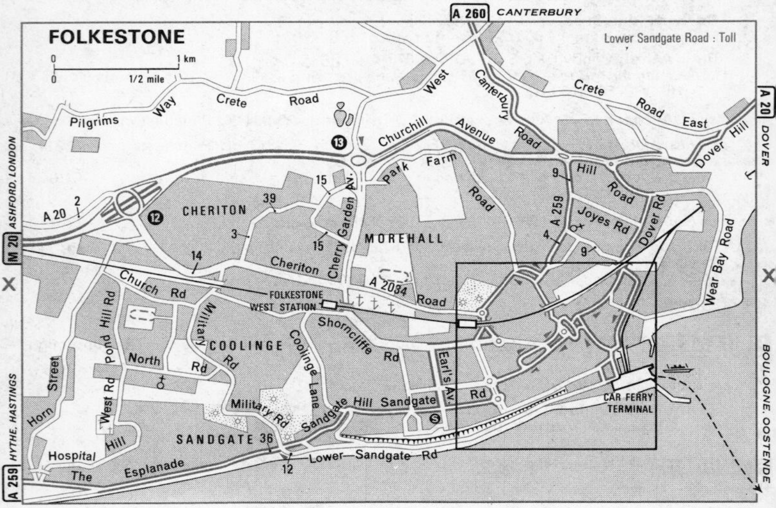

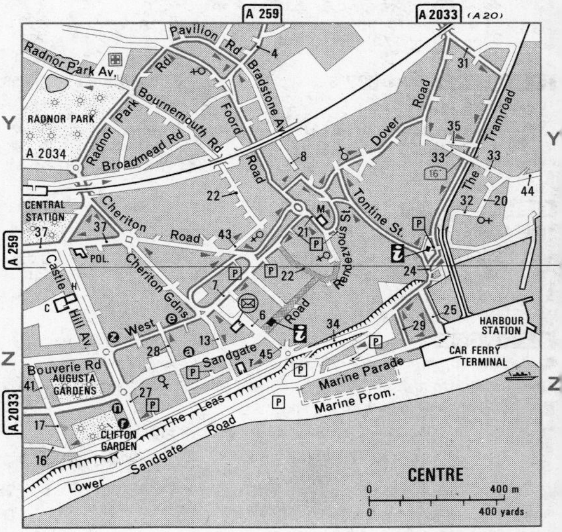

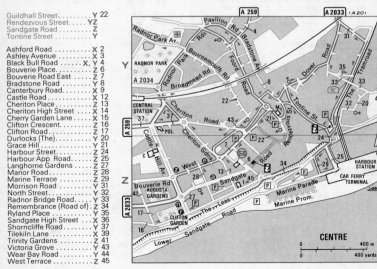

🏨 **Burlington,** Earl's Av., CT20 2HR, ✆ 55301, <, 🌳 – |\$| TV 🛁wc ☎ P. 🏌. AE ⓓ VISA **M** 6.75/10.25 **st.** and a la carte 🍷 2.60 – **57 rm** ☕ 28.00/52.00 **st.** – SB 52.00/58.00 **st.** X **s**

🏨 Clifton, The Leas, CT20 2EB, ✆ 41231, <, 🌳 – |\$| TV 🛁wc ☎. 🏌. **58 rm**. Z **r**

🏠 **Banque** without rest., 4 Castle Hill Av., CT20 2QT, ✆ 53797 – TV 🛁wc ☎. AE ⓓ VISA **12 rm** ☕ 17.00/34.00 **t.** Z **z**

XX **Emilio's Portofino,** 124a Sandgate Rd, CT20 2BT, ℰ 55762, Italian rest. – 🔼 AE ⓞ
VISA
Z **a**
closed Monday and Bank Holidays – **M** 6.50 **t.** (lunch) and a la carte 9.70/15.40 **t.** ₰ 2.70.

XX **La Tavernetta,** Leaside Court, Clifton Gdns, CT20 2EY, ℰ 54955, Italian rest. – 🔼 AE ⓞ
VISA
Z **n**
closed Sunday and Bank Holidays – **M** 6.50 **t.** (lunch) and a la carte 9.50/12.85 **t.** ₰ 3.35.

X **Paul's,** 2a Bouverie Rd West, CT20 2RX, ℰ 59697 – 🔼 AE *VISA*
Z **e**
closed Sunday, 2 weeks summer and 1 week winter – **M** a la carte 9.65 **t.** ₰ 2.75.

AUSTIN-ROVER 141-143 Sandgate Rd ℰ 55101
COLT 1-3 Park Rd ℰ 75114
FORD 104 Foord Rd ℰ 41234
NISSAN Shorncliffe Industrial Estate ℰ 39656

RENAULT Sandgate Rd ℰ 55331
VAUXHALL Sandgate Rd ℰ 53103
VAUXHALL Caesars Way, Cheriton ℰ 53103
VOLVO Park Farm Industrial Estate ℰ 42027

FONTMELL MAGNA Dorset 403 404 N 30 – see Shaftesbury.

FORD Wilts. – see Castle Combe.

FORDINGBRIDGE Hants. 403 404 O 31 – pop. 3 026 – ECD : Thursday – ✆ 0425.
See : St. Mary's Church★ 13C.
Envir. : Breamore House★ (Elizabethan) *AC*, N : 2 m.
◆London 101 – Bournemouth 17 – Salisbury 11 – Winchester 30.

XX **Hour Glass,** Salisbury Rd, Burgate, SP6 1LX, N : 1 m. on A 338 ℰ 52348, « 14C thatched
cottage » – **P.** 🔼 AE *VISA*. ⌚
closed Sunday and Monday – **M** (dinner only) 15.50 **st.** ₰ 3.85.

at Stuckton SE : 1 m. by B 3078 – ✉ ✆ 0425 Fordingbridge :

X **Three Lions Inn,** Stuckton Rd, SP6 2HF, ℰ 52489 – **P.** 🔼 *VISA*
closed Monday – **M** (booking essential)(restricted lunch)/dinner a la carte 11.95/19.00 **t.** ₰ 3.25.

FORDWICH Kent 404 X 30 – see Canterbury.

FOREST ROW East Sussex 404 U 30 – pop. 3 842 – ECD : Wednesday – ✆ 034 282.
🖈 Royal Ashdown Forest ℰ 2018.
◆London 35 – ◆Brighton 26 – Eastbourne 30 – Maidstone 32.

🏨 **Ashdown Forest,** Chapel Lane, RH18 5BB, E : 1 m. by B 2110 ℰ 4866, 🖈 – 📺 ⛉wc **P.**
🔼 *VISA*. ⌚
M 8.50 **st.** (lunch) and a la carte 13.75/17.50 **st.** ₰ 2.80 – **10 rm** ⇄ 29.50/40.50 **st.** – SB
74.00/83.00 **st.**

🏨 **Chequers Inn,** The Square, RH18 5ES, ℰ 4394 – 📺 ⛉wc ☎ ⇦⇨ **P.** 🔼 AE ⓞ *VISA*. ⌚
M 9.65/11.80 **st.** and a la carte ₰ 3.75 – ⇄ 4.00 – **16 rm** 21.50/31.50 **t.** – SB (weekends only)
42.00 **st.**

at Wych Cross S : 2 ½ m. on A 22 – ✉ ✆ 034 282 Forest Row :

🏨 **Roebuck** (Embassy), RH18 5JL, ℰ 3811, Telex 957088, 🖈 – 📺 ⛉wc ☎ **P.** ⛴ 🔼 AE ⓞ
VISA
M 8.95 **st.** and a la carte ₰ 3.00 – ⇄ 5.00 – **28 rm** 37.50/48.50 **st.** – SB (weekends only) 56.00 **st.**

FOSSEBRIDGE Glos. 403 404 O 28 – pop. 1 706 – ✉ ✆ 028 572.
◆London 88 – Gloucester 23 – ◆Oxford 31 – Swindon 21.

🏤 **Fossebridge Inn,** GL54 3JS, ℰ 310, 🖈 – ⛉wc **P.** 🔼 AE ⓞ *VISA*
M (bar lunch)/dinner 9.25/11.50 **t.** ₰ 3.00 – **10 rm** ⇄ 31.50/42.00 **t.** – SB (except summer)
53.00/65.00 **st.**

FOWEY Cornwall 403 G 32 The West Country G. – pop. 2 092 – ECD : Wednesday – ✆ 072 683.
See : Site★★.
🎫 Harliquinade, 30 Fore St. ℰ 3308.
◆London 277 – Newquay 24 – ◆Plymouth 34 – Truro 22.

🏨 **Fowey** ⌣, The Esplanade, PL23 1HX, ℰ 2551, ≤ Fowey estuary and Polruan, 🖈 – |🛗| 📺
⛉wc ⌗wc ☎ **P.** 🔼 AE ⓞ *VISA*
M *(Sunday dinner buffet only)* (bar lunch)/dinner 9.00 **st.** ₰ 2.50 – **29 rm** ⇄ 24.00/66.00 **st.** –
SB (except summer) 46.00 **st.**

🏨 **Marina,** The Esplanade, PL23 1HY, ℰ 3315, ≤ Fowey river and harbour – 📺 ⛉wc. 🔼 AE
ⓞ *VISA*
March-October – **M** (bar lunch)/dinner a la carte 10.00/13.00 **t.** ₰ 2.50 – **12 rm** ⇄ 18.00/54.00 **t.**
– SB (except summer) 48.00/58.00 **st.**

XX **Food for Thought**, 4 Town Quay, PL23 1AT, ℰ 2221, ⬱ – ⚊ _VISA_
closed Sunday, January and February – **M** (booking essential)(dinner only) 11.95 **t.** and a la carte 10.85/17.40 **t.** ▯ 3.50.

XX **Cordon Bleu**, 3 The Esplanade, PL23 1HY, ℰ 2359.

X **Al Fresco**, The Esplanade, PL23 1JA, ℰ 3249, ⬱, Seafood – **℗** ⚊ AE ⓞ _VISA_
closed Sunday October-June, Monday except Bank Holidays and 1 week at Christmas – **M** (booking essential) a la carte 7.80/12.95 **t.** ▯ 2.25.

at Golant N : 3 m. by B 3269 – ✉ ✿ 072 683 Fowey :

🏡 **Cormorant** ⬱, PL23 1LL, ℰ 3426, ⬳ River Fowey, ▨, ⬱, – TV ⊟wc ☎ ℗ _VISA_
M (bar lunch)/dinner a la carte 9.05/11.00 **t.** ▯ 3.85 – **11 rm** �⊇ 21.50/48.00 **t.**

at Bodinnick-by-Fowey E : ¼ m. via car ferry – ✉ Fowey – ✿ 072 687 Polruan :

🏡 **Old Ferry Inn**, PL23 1LY, ℰ 237, ⬳ Fowey estuary and town, « Part 16C inn » – TV ⊟wc ℗. _VISA_
closed December and January – **M** _(closed October-March)_ (bar lunch)/dinner 12.00 **t.** ▯ 3.40 – **12 rm** ⊇ 19.00/50.00 **t.**

FOWLMERE Cambs. 🚹🚹🚹 U 27 – see Cambridge.

FOWNHOPE Heref. and Worc. 🚹🚹🚹 🚹🚹🚹 M 27 – pop. 1 362 – ✉ Hereford – ✿ 043 277.
◆London 132 – ◆Cardiff 46 – Hereford 6 – Gloucester 27.

🏠 **Green Man Inn**, HR1 4PE, ℰ 243 – TV ⊟wc ▯wc ℗
M (bar lunch)/dinner 10.00 **st.** and a la carte ▯ 2.95 – **14 rm** ⊇ 17.50/29.00 **st.** – SB 40.00/47.00 **st.**

⌂ **Bowens Farmhouse**, HR1 4PS, on B 4224 ℰ 430, ⬱ – ⊟wc ▯wc ℗. ⬌
closed 15 December-1 February – **10 rm** ⊇ 12.75/27.50 **t.**

FRAMFIELD East Sussex 🚹🚹🚹 U 31 – see Uckfield.

FRAMLINGHAM Suffolk 🚹🚹🚹 X 27 – pop. 1 830 – ECD : Wednesday – ✉ Woodbridge – ✿ 0728.
See : Castle ramparts* (Norman ruins) _AC_.
◆London 92 – ◆Ipswich 19 – ◆Norwich 42.

🏡 **Crown** (T.H.F.), Market Hill, IP13 9AN, ℰ 723521, « 16C inn » – TV ⊟wc ☎ ℗ ⚊ AE ⓞ _VISA_
M (buffet lunch)/dinner 9.15 **st.** and a la carte ▯ 3.40 – ⊇ 5.65 – **15 rm** 42.00/54.00 **st.**

X **Market Place**, 18 Market Hill, IP13 9BB, ℰ 724275. ⚊ _VISA_
closed Sunday, Monday and 3 weeks in January – **M** (restricted lunch) a la carte 8.45/12.20 **st.** ▯ 2.40.

FORD Market Hill ℰ 723215

FRESHFORD Avon – see Bath.

FRESHWATER BAY I.O.W. 🚹🚹🚹 🚹🚹🚹 P 31 – see Wight (Isle of).

FRESSINGFIELD Suffolk 🚹🚹🚹 X 26 – pop. 831 – ✉ Eye – ✿ 037 986.
◆London 103 – ◆Ipswich 30 – ◆Norwich 23.

X **Fox and Goose**, IP21 5PB, ℰ 247 – ℗, ⚊ AE ⓞ _VISA_
closed Sunday dinner November-March, Tuesday, 27 January-10 February and 23 to 26 December – **M** (booking essential) 15.00 **t.** and a la carte 12.95/23.75 **t.**

FRIETH Bucks. – see Henley-on-Thames (Oxon.).

FRINTON-ON-SEA Essex 🚹🚹🚹 X 28 – pop. 12 507 (inc. Walton) – ECD : Wednesday – ✿ 025 56.
◆London 72 – Chelmsford 39 – Colchester 17.

🏡 **Maplin**, Esplanade, CO13 9EL, ℰ 3832, ⬱, ⊼ heated – TV ⊟wc ☎ ℗ ⚊ AE ⓞ _VISA_
closed January – **M** 10.00/12.00 **st.** and a la carte ▯ 3.50 – **11 rm** ⊇ 23.00/50.00 **st.**

⌂ **Uplands**, 41 Hadleigh Rd, CO13 9HQ, ℰ 4889, ⬱ – ℗. ⬌
closed 7 January-28 February – **8 rm** ⊇ 13.00/26.00 **s.**

AUSTIN-ROVER Connaught Av. ℰ 4311
FORD Connaught Av. ℰ 77137

PEUGEOT, TALBOT Thorpe Rd ℰ 4383
TOYOTA Frinton Rd, Kirby Cross ℰ 79191

FRODSHAM Cheshire 🚹🚹🚹 🚹🚹🚹 🚹🚹🚹 L 24 – pop. 9 143 – ✉ Warrington – ✿ 0928.
◆London 203 – Chester 11 – ◆Liverpool 21 – ◆Manchester 29 – ◆Stoke on Trent 42.

🏡 **Old Hall**, Main St., WA6 7AB, ℰ 32052 – TV ⊟wc ☎ ⚊ AE ⓞ _VISA_
M 6.50/9.50 **t.** and a la carte 6.80/12.65 **t.** ▯ 2.95 – **25 rm** ⊇ 37.50/50.00 **st.**, **1 suite** 50.00/65.00 **st.**

FROME Somerset **403 404** N 30 **The West Country** G. – pop. 19 678 – ECD : Thursday – ☎ 0373.
Envir. : Farleigh Hungerford Castle★ *AC*, (St. Leonards Chapel★), N : 11 m. by A 361 and A 36 –
Longleat House★★★ *AC*, SE : 7 m.
🅿 Cattle Market Car Park ☎ 67271 (summer only).
◆London 115 – ◆Bristol 28 – ◆◆Southampton 51 – Taunton 43.

🏨 **Mendip Lodge**, Bath Rd, BA11 2HP, N : ½ m. on A 361 ☎ 63223, Telex 44832, ≼, 🐎 – 📺
🚻wc 🅿. 🛁. 🔼 🅰🅴 ⓞ 🆅🅸🆂🅰
M 10.50 t. and a la carte – 🍽 4.00 – **40 rm** 34.00/48.50 t. – SB (except Bank Holidays)
57.00/69.00 st.

FULWOOD Lancs. **402** L M 22 – see Preston.

GAINSBOROUGH Lincs. **402 404** R 23 – pop. 20 326 – ECD : Wednesday – ☎ 0427.
See : Old Hall★★ (15C) *AC*.
🅿 Trinity Centre, Trinity St. ☎ 617242.
◆London 150 – Lincoln 19 – ◆Nottingham 42 – ◆Sheffield 34.

Hotels and Restaurant see : Bawtry NW : 12 m., *Scunthorpe* NE : 17 m.

AUSTIN-ROVER North St. ☎ 2251
FORD Trinity St. ☎ 3146

VAUXHALL-OPEL 35 Trinity St. ☎ 611570

GALMPTON Devon – ⊠ ☎ 0803 Brixham.
◆London 229 – ◆Plymouth 32 – Torquay 6.

🏛 **Lost and Found Inn** ⅀, Maypool, TQ5 0ET, by Greenway Rd ☎ 842442, ≼River Dart and
valley, – 📺 🚻wc 🗄wc 🅿. 🔼 🅰🅴 ⓞ 🆅🅸🆂🅰
M 10.00/12.50 t. and a la carte 🍴 2.40 – **16 rm** 🍽 42.75/67.00 t.

GANAREW Heref. and Worc. – see Monmouth (Gwent).

GARFORTH West Yorks. **402** P 22 – see Leeds.

GARGRAVE North Yorks. **402** N 22 – ⊠ ☎ 0756 Skipton.
◆London 221 – Burnley 21 – ◆Leeds 30.

⌂ **Kirk Syke**, BD23 3RA, ☎ 78356 – 🗄wc 🅿. ⅍
8 rm 🍽 14.00/24.00 st.

GATESHEAD Tyne and Wear **401 402** P 19 – pop. 91 429 – ECD : Wednesday – ☎ 091 Tyneside.
🅁 Ravensworth, Mossheaps, Wrekenton ☎ 487 6014 – 🅁 Whickham, Hollinside Park ☎ 488 7309,
SW : 5 m.
🅿 Central Library, Prince Consort Rd ☎ 477 34789.
◆London 282 – Durham 16 – ◆Middlesbrough 38 – ◆◆Newcastle-upon-Tyne 1 – Sunderland 11.

Plan : see Newcastle-upon-Tyne

🏨 **Springfield** (Embassy), Durham Rd, NE9 5BT, S : ½ m. on A 6127 ☎ 477 4121 – 📺 🚻wc ☎
🅿. 🛁. 🔼 🅰🅴 ⓞ 🆅🅸🆂🅰
M 7.50 st. and a la carte 🍴 3.00 – 🍽 5.00 – **40 rm** 34.50/44.50 st. – SB (weekends only)
52.00/69.50 st.

BX **s**

🏨 **Five Bridges** (Swallow), High Street West, NE8 1PE, ☎ 477 1105, Telex 53534 – 🛗 📺
🚻wc ☎ 🅿. 🛁. 🔼 🅰🅴 ⓞ 🆅🅸🆂🅰
M 7.50/9.75 st. and a la carte 🍴 3.95 – **106 rm** 🍽 25.00/55.00 st. – SB (weekends only and all
July and August) 50.00 st.

CZ **r**

🏠 **Eslington Villa**, 8 Station Rd, Low Fell, NE9 6DR, ☎ 487 6017 – 📺 🚻wc 🐎 🅿
M (dinner only) 8.50 t. and a la carte 🍴 3.00 – **8 rm** 🍽 24.50/31.50 t.   by A 6127 BX

AUDI, VW Bensham Rd ☎ 4784545
AUSTIN-ROVER Low Fell ☎ 4872118

FORD Eslington Park ☎ 4607464
TOYOTA St. James Sq. ☎ 4784333

GATWICK AIRPORT West Sussex **404** T 30 – ⊠ West Sussex – ☎ 0293 Gatwick.
✈ ☎ 0293 (Crawley) 28822 and ☎ 01 (London) 668 4211.
◆ London 29 – ◆Brighton 28.

Plan on next page

🏨 **Gatwick Hilton International**, Gatwick Airport, RH6 0LL, ☎ 518080, Telex 877021, 🔲 –
🛗 🗐 📺 🐎 🛁. 🅿. 🛁. 🔼 🅰🅴 ⓞ 🆅🅸🆂🅰
M 10.75/16.50 t. and a la carte 🍴 4.65 – 🍽 6.75 – **333 rm** 72.00/88.00 t., **2 suites** 150.00/
250.00 t.

Y **u**

🏨 **Gatwick Penta**, Povey Cross Rd ⊠Horley (Surrey), RH6 0BE, ☎ 785533, Telex 87440, 🐎 – 🛗
🛗 📺 ☎ 🐎 🅿.
260 rm, 1 suite.

Y **a**

🏨 **Post House** (T.H.F.), Povey Cross Rd ⊠Horley (Surrey), RH6 0BA, ☎ 771621, Telex 877351,
🔥 heated – 🗐 rest 📺 🐎 🛁. 🅿. 🛁. 🔼 🅰🅴 ⓞ 🆅🅸🆂🅰
M 12.95/14.95 st. and a la carte 🍴 3.40 – 🍽 5.65 – **148 rm** 53.00/66.00 st.

Y **c**

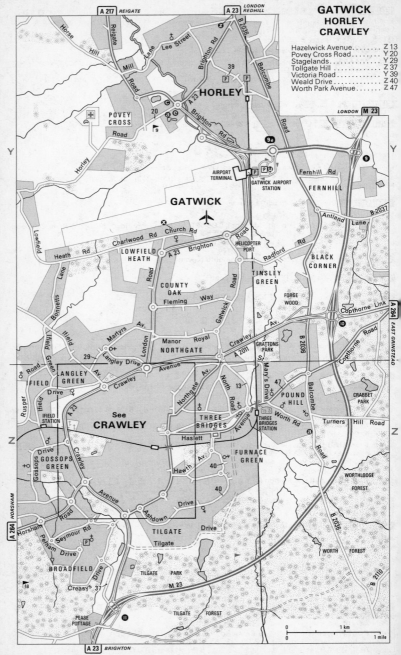

🏨 **Gatwick Moat House** (Q.M.H.), Longbridge Roundabout ⊠Horley (Surrey), RH6 0AB, ℰ
785599, Telex 877138 – 🛔 ▤ 🔟 ⌂wc 🏛 ℗. 🏄. 🔼 🔼 🔼 ⓪ 𝑉𝐼𝑆𝐴 Y e
M 7.50/9.50 t. and a la carte 🖺 2.65 – ⊆ 5.75 – **121 rm** 45.75/61.50 **st.** – SB (weekends only)
71.50 **st.**

🏨 **Gatwick Concorde** (Q.M.H.), Church Rd, Lowfield Heath, RH11 0PQ, ℰ 33441, Telex 87287
– 🛔 ▤ 🔟 ⌂wc ☎ ℗. 🏄. 🔼 🔼 🔼 ⓪ 𝑉𝐼𝑆𝐴 Y x
M (bar lunch)/dinner 9.50 t. and a la carte 🖺 2.65 – ⊆ 5.75 – **92 rm** 45.75/61.50 **st.**, **3 suites**
85.00/120.00 **st.** – SB (weekends only) 71.50 **st.**

GERRARDS CROSS Bucks. 🗺️ S 29 – pop. 19 447 (inc. Chalfont St.Peter) – ECD : Wednesday
– 🕾 0753 – ♦London 22 – Aylesbury 22 – ♦Oxford 36.

🏨 **Bull** (De Vere), Oxford Rd, SL9 7PA, on A 40 ℰ 885995, Telex 847747, 🐎 – 🔟 ⌂wc ☎ ℗.
🏄. 🔼 🔼 ⓪ 𝑉𝐼𝑆𝐴
M 13.25/14.50 **st.** and a la carte 🖺 3.50 – **98 rm** ⊆ 65.00/85.00 **st.** – SB (weekends only) 75.00 **st.**

🏠 Ethorpe, Packhorse Rd, FL9 8HX, ℰ 882039, 🐎 – 🔟 ⌂wc ☎ ℗
M (grill rest.) – **28 rm**.

BMW 31-33 Station Rd ℰ 888321   TALBOT Oxford Rd ℰ 882545

GIGGLESWICK North Yorks. – see Settle.

GILLAN Cornwall 🗺️ E 33 The West Country G. – see Helford.

GILLINGHAM Dorset 🗺️ 🗺️ N 30 – pop. 5 379 – 🕾 074 76.
♦London 116 – Bournemouth 34 – ♦Bristol 46 – ♦Southampton 52.

🍴🍴 **Stock Hill House** 🦢 with rm, Wyke, SP8 5NR, W : 1 ½ m. on B 3081 ℰ 3626, « Victorian
country house », 🔟, 🐎, park – 🔟 ⌂wc 🇫wc 🐎 ℗ – 🔼
closed late January-1 March – **M** (closed Monday to non residents) 10.00/16.00 **st.** 🖺 3.85 –
7 rm ⊆ 40.00/80.00 **st.** – SB (weekdays only) 65.00/90.00 **st.**

at Milton on Stour N : 1 ½ m. by B 3095 on B 3092 – ⊠ 🕾 074 76 Gillingham :

🏠 **Milton Lodge** 🦢, SP8 4PR, ℰ 2262, 🔼 heated, 🐎 – 🔟 ⌂wc 🐎 ℗ 🔼
M (bar lunch)/dinner 10.00 t. 🖺 4.00 – **10 rm** ⊆ 25.00/54.00 t. – SB 55.00/66.00 **st.**

GISBURN Lancs. 🗺️ N 22 – pop. 435 – ECD : Wednesday – ⊠ Clitheroe – 🕾 020 05.
🏌️ Ghyll, Ghyll Brow, Barnoldswick ℰ 0282 (Earby) 842466, SE : 5 ½ m.
♦London 243 – ♦Manchester 37 – Preston 25.

🏨 Stirk House, BB7 4LJ, SW : 1 m. on A 59 ℰ 581, Telex 635238, 🔼, 🐎, squash – 🔟 ⌂wc ☎
℗. 🏄 – **50 rm**.

GITTISHAM Devon 🗺️ K 31 – pop. 233 – ECD : Thursday – ⊠ 🕾 0404 Honiton.
♦London 164 – Exeter 14 – Sidmouth 9 – Taunton 21.

🏨 **Combe House** 🦢, EX14 0AD, ℰ 2756, ≼, « Country house atmosphere », 🐚, 🐎, park –
🔟 ☎ ℗. 🔼 🔼 ⓪ 𝑉𝐼𝑆𝐴
closed 12 January-27 February – **M** (bar lunch Monday to Saturday)/dinner a la carte
17.50/20.00 **st.** 🖺 3.10 – **12 rm** ⊆ 37.00/71.50 **st.**, **1 suite** 92.50 **st.**

GLASBURY Powys 🗺️ K 27 – pop. 289 – 🕾 049 74.
♦London 184 – ♦Birmingham 74 – Brecon 12 – Hereford 25.

🏠 **Llwynaubach Lodge**, HR3 5PT, on B 4350 ℰ 473, 🔼, 🐚, 🐎 – 🔟 ⌂wc ℗. 🔼 𝑉𝐼𝑆𝐴
M (closed Sunday dinner to non residents) 7.50/12.50 t. and a la carte 🖺 3.00 – **6 rm**
⊆ 24.80/43.00 t. – SB (except Summer and Bank Holidays)(weekends only) 57.00 **st.**

GLASTONBURY Somerset 🗺️ L 30 The West Country G. – pop. 6 751 – ECD : Wednesday –
🕾 0458 – See : Site★★★ – Abbey★★★AC – St. John the Baptist Church★★ – Somerset Rural Life
Museum★★AC – Glastonbury Tor★ (≼★★★).
🚩 1 Marchant's Buildings, Northload St. ℰ 32954 (summer only).
♦London 136 – ♦Bristol 26 – Taunton 22.

🏠 **George and Pilgrims,** 1 High St., BA6 9DP, ℰ 31146, « Part 15C inn » – 🔟 ⌂wc 🇫wc ☎.
🔼 🔼 ⓪ 𝑉𝐼𝑆𝐴
M 8.50/11.50 **s.** and a la carte 🖺 3.10 – **14 rm** ⊆ 33.00/58.00 t. – SB 60.00/72.00 **st.**

🍴🍴 **No 3** with rm, 3 Magdalene St., BA6 9EW, ℰ 32129, 🐎 – ℗. 🔼 ⓪ 𝑉𝐼𝑆𝐴
closed Monday, Tuesday and January – **M** (dinner only and Sunday lunch) (booking essential)
19.00 t. 🖺 3.00 – **2 rm** ⊆ 25.00/35.00 t.

RENAULT Beckery Rd ℰ 32741

GLOUCESTER

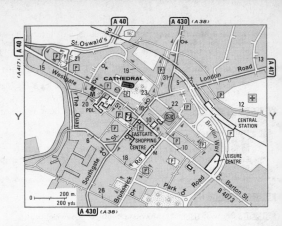

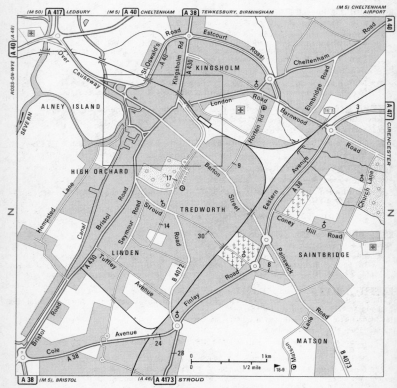

GLOUCESTER Glos. **403** **404** N 28 – pop. 106 526 – ECD : Thursday – ✆ 0452.

See : Cathedral★★ 12C-14C (Great Cloister★★★ 14C) Y – Bishop Hooper's Lodging (Folk Museum)★ 15C Y **M.**

🏌, 🏌 Gloucester Hotel and Country Club, Matson Lane ✆ 25653, S : 2 m. Z.

🏛 St Michael's Tower, The Cross ✆ 421188.

◆London 106 – ◆Birmingham 52 – ◆Bristol 38 – ◆Cardiff 66 – ◆Coventry 57 – Northampton 83 – ◆Oxford 48 – ◆Southampton 98 – ◆Swansea 92 – Swindon 35.

Plan opposite

🏨 **Crest** (Crest), Crest Way, Barnwood, GL4 7RX, E : 3 m. on A 417 ✆ 613311, Telex 437273 – 📺 📶wc ☎ 🅿 ⅙ 🏋 🔟 AE ⓞ VISA ⅙
                                by A 417   Z
M 8.25/11.50 **st.** and a la carte – ⊑ 5.85 – **100 rm** 49.50/59.50 **st.** – SB (weekends only) 64.00/74.00 **st.**

🏨 **Gloucester Hotel and Country Club** (Embassy), Robinswood Hill, Matson Lane, GL4 9EA, SE : 3 m. by B 4073 ✆ 25653, Telex 43571, 🏌, 🏌, squash – 📺 📶wc ☎ ⅙ 🅿 ⅙ 🔟 AE ⓞ VISA ⅙
                                                    Z c
M *(closed Saturday lunch)* (bar lunch)/dinner 15.00 **st.** and a la carte ⅙ 3.20 – ⊑ 6.00 – **73 rm** 48.40/62.00 **st.** – SB (except Christmas, Easter and Cheltenham Gold Cup week) 68.00/78.00 **st.**

↑ **Rotherfield House,** 5 Horton Rd, GL1 3PX, ✆ 410500 – 📺 📶wc 🅿 🔟 AE VISA   Z n
    closed 3 days at Christmas – **9 rm** ⊑ 13.80/29.90 t.

↑ **Lulworth,** 12 Midland Rd, GL1 4UF, ✆ 21881 – 📺 🅿   Z e
    8 rm ⊑ 10.00/15.00.

✗ **College Green,** 7-11 College St., GL1 2NE, ✆ 20739 – 🔟 AE VISA   Y a
    closed dinner Monday and Tuesday, Sunday and Bank Holidays – **M** 7.90 **st.** (lunch) and a la carte 9.95/15.05 **st.** ⅙ 2.50.

at Upton St. Leonards SE : 3 ½ m. on B 4073 – ⊠ ✆ 0452 Gloucester :

🏨 **Hatton Court** (Best Western), Upton Hill, GL4 8DE, ✆ 617412, Group Telex 449848, ≼ Severn Valley, ⅄ heated, ☞ – ▤ rest 📺 📶wc 📶wc ☎ 🅿 ⅙ 🔟 AE ⓞ VISA ⅙
M 9.50/16.50 **st.** – **24 rm** ⊑ 45.00/78.00 **st.** – SB (weekends only) 65.00/75.00 **st.**
                                           by B 4073   Z

at Minsterworth W : 5 m. by A 40 on A 48 – Z – ⊠ Gloucester – ✆ 045 275 Minsterworth :

↑ **Severn Bank,** Main Rd, GL2 8JH, ✆ 357, ≼, ☞ – 📺 🅿 ⅙
    closed 24 December – **6 rm** ⊑ 12.00/24.00 s.

AUDI, VW Eastern Av. ✆ 25177
AUSTIN-ROVER Mercia Rd ✆ 416565
BEDFORD, PANTHER LIMA, VAUXHALL Shepherd Rd, Cole Av. ✆ 26711
BMW Kingsholm Rd ✆ 23456
CITROEN 143 Westgate St. ✆ 23252
FORD Bristol Rd ✆ 5221731
LAND ROVER Wotton-Under-Edge ✆ 0453 (Dursley) 844131
MAZDA Old Bristol Rd ✆ 720332

NISSAN Eastern Av. ✆ 423691
PEUGEOT-TALBOT, DAIHATSU, FIAT Bristol Rd ✆ 29755
RENAULT St. Oswalds Rd ✆ 35051
SAAB Montpelier ✆ 22404
TOYOTA London Rd ✆ 21555
VAUXHALL-OPEL Cole Av. ✆ 26711
VAUXHALL-OPEL Priory Rd ✆ 24912
VOLVO 100 Eastgate St. ✆ 25291
VW, AUDI Eastern Av. ✆ 25177

In July and August, hotels are often overcrowded and staff overworked.
You will be more satisfied if you go in other months.

GOATHLAND North Yorks. **402** R 20 – pop. 442 – ECD : Wednesday and Saturday – ⊠ ✆ 0947 Whitby.

◆London 248 – ◆Middlesbrough 36 – York 38.

🏛 **Mallyan Spout** ⅙, YO22 5AN, ✆ 86206, ☞ – 📺 📶wc 🅿, AE ⓞ VISA
    M (bar lunch)/dinner 11.00 **t.** and a la carte ⅙ 2.65 – **22 rm** ⊑ 25.00/40.00 **t.** – SB 50.00/57.00 **t.**

↑ **Whitfield House** ⅙, Darnholm, YO22 5LA, NW : ¾ m. ✆ 86215, ☞ – 📶wc 📶wc
    closed mid December-mid January – **10 rm** ⊑ 12.25/29.00 **t.**

↑ **Heatherdene** ⅙, The Common, YO22 5AN, ✆ 86334, ≼, ☞ – 📶wc 🅿 ⅙
    6 rm ⊑ 14.00/29.00 s.

GODALMING Surrey **404** S 30 – pop. 18 758 – ECD : Wednesday – ✆ 048 68.

◆London 38 – Guildford 5 – ◆Southampton 51.

↑ **Meads,** 65 Meadrow, GU7 3HS, N : ½ m. on A 3100 ✆ 21800 – 📶wc 🅿 AE VISA
    15 rm ⊑ 16.00/33.00 **t.**

✗✗ **Inn on the Lake** with rm, GU7 1RH, on A 3100 ✆ 5575, ☞ – 📺 📶wc ☎ 🅿 ⅙ ⅙
    M 12.50 **t.** and a la carte ⅙ 2.75 – **16 rm** ⊑ 40.00/65.00 **t.** – SB (weekends only) 60.00/80.00 **st.**

at Hascombe SE : 3 ½ m. on B 2130 – ⊠ Godalming – ✆ 048 632 Hascombe :

✗ White Horse, GU8 4JA, ✆ 258, ☞ – 🅿

NISSAN The Wharf ✆ 5201
RENAULT Farncombe ✆ 7743 24 hr breakdown on 23169

VAUXHALL Portsmouth Rd ✆ 5666

GODSTONE Surrey 404 T 30 – pop. 2 567 – ✿ 0342 South Godstone.
◆London 22 – ◆Brighton 36 – Maidstone 28.

XXX **La Bonne Auberge,** Tilburstow Hill, South Godstone, RH9 8JY, S : 2 ¼ m. ℰ 892318, French rest., 🍴 – 🅿. 🔄 🅰🅴 ⓪ 𝓥𝓘𝓢𝓐
closed Sunday dinner and Monday – **M** 18.00/23.00 **st.** and a la carte 19.00/24.00 **st.** ⌕ 3.25.

VAUXHALL Eastbourne Rd ℰ 842000

GOLANT Cornwall 403 G 32 – see Fowey.

GOLCAR West Yorks. – see Huddersfield.

GOMSHALL Surrey 404 S 30 – see Guildford.

GOODRICH Heref. and Worc. 403 404 M 28 – see Ross-on-Wye.

GOODWICK (WDIG) Dyfed 403 F 27 – see Fishguard.

GOODWOOD West Sussex 404 R 31 – see Chichester.

GORDLETON Hants. – see Lymington.

GORLESTON-ON-SEA Norfolk 404 Z 26 – see Great Yarmouth.

GOSFORTH Cumbria 402 J 20 – pop. 1 701 – ⊠ Seascale – ✿ 094 05.
Envir. : E : Wast Water★, Wasdale Head (site★) – ◆London 314 – Kendal 62 – Workington 20.

🏠 **Gosforth Hall,** CA20 1AZ, ℰ 322, 🔄, 🍴 – 📺 ⌘wc 🅿. 🅰🅴. 🍸
M a la carte 5.05/9.95 **t.** ⌕ 2.00 – **12 rm** 🔄 20.00/30.00 **t.**. **1 suite** 50.00 **t.** – SB (weekends only)(except Christmas and New Year) 48.00 **st.**

at Wasdale Head NE : 9 m. – ⊠ Gosforth – ✿ 094 06 Wasdale :

🏠 **Wasdale Head Inn** 🍃, CA20 1EX, ℰ 229, ≤ Wasdale Head – ⌘wc 🔊wc ☎ 🅿. 🔄 𝓥𝓘𝓢𝓐
closed 15 November-28 December – **M** (bar lunch)/dinner 10.50 **t.** ⌕ 2.75 – **10 rm** 🔄 (dinner included) 32.50/66.00 **t.**

GOSFORTH Tyne and Wear 401 402 P 18 – see Newcastle-upon-Tyne.

GOUDHURST Kent 404 V 30 – pop. 2 673 – ECD : Wednesday – ⊠ Cranbrook – ✿ 0580.
◆London 45 – Hastings 22 – Maidstone 13.

🏠 **Star and Eagle,** High St., TN17 1AL, ℰ 211512, « 14C inn » – 📺 ⌘wc 🕿 🅿. 🔄 🅰🅴 ⓪ 𝓥𝓘𝓢𝓐
M (bar lunch)/dinner 10.00 **t.** and a la carte ⌕ 3.60 – **11 rm** 🔄 27.00/42.00 **t.** – SB (October-March) 45.00/50.00 **st.**

🏠 **Green Cross,** Station Rd, TN17 1HA, W : 1 m. on A 262 ℰ 211200, 🍴 – 🅿 – **6 rm**.

GOVETON Devon 403 I 33 – see Kingsbridge.

GRANGE-IN-BORROWDALE Cumbria 402 K 20 – see Keswick.

GRANGE-OVER-SANDS Cumbria 402 L 21 – pop. 3 864 – ECD : Thursday – ✿ 044 84.
Envir. : Cartmel (Priory Church★ 12C chancel★★) NW : 3 m.
🏌 Meathop Rd ℰ 3180, ½ m. Grange Station – 🏌 Grange Fell, Cartmell Rd ℰ 2536.
🅱 Victoria Hall, Main St. ℰ 4026 (summer only).
◆London 268 – Kendal 13 – Lancaster 24.

🏠 **Graythwaite Manor** 🍃, Fernhill Rd, LA11 7JE, ℰ 2001, ≤ gardens and sea, « Extensive flowered gardens », park, 🍴 – 📺 ⌘wc ☎ 🍸 🅿. 🔄 𝓥𝓘𝓢𝓐. 🍸
M *(closed 25 and 26 December to non-residents)* 6.50/12.00 **t.** ⌕ 2.50 – **24 rm** 🔄 (dinner included) 31.50/70.00 **st.** – SB (November-April) 45.00/55.00 **st.**

🏠 **Cumbria Grand,** Lindale Rd, LA11 6EN, ℰ 2331, ≤, 🍴, park, 🍴 – 📶 📺 ⌘wc 🐾 🅿. 🔄 🅰🅴 ⓪ 𝓥𝓘𝓢𝓐
M 5.95/9.00 **t.** and a la carte ⌕ 3.00 – **120 rm** 🔄 24.00/44.00 **t.** – SB 55.00/61.00 **st.**

🏠 **Netherwood** 🍃, Lindale Rd, LA11 6ET, ℰ 2552, ≤, 🍴 – ⌘wc 🍸 🅿. 🔄
M 4.95/7.65 **st.** ⌕ 2.35 – **23 rm** 🔄 17.00/39.00 **st.** – SB (November-March)(weekends only) 44.00/49.50 **st.**

🏠 **Somerset House,** Kents Bank Rd, LA11 7EY, ℰ 2631 – 🍸
April-October – **8 rm** 🔄 10.50/21.00.

at Witherslack NE : 5 m. by B 5277 off A 590 – ⊠ ✿ 044 852 Witherslack :

XX **Old Vicarage** 🍃 with rm, Church Rd, LA11 6RS, ℰ 381, 🍴 – 📺 ⌘wc 🔊wc ☎ 🅿. 🔄 🅰🅴 ⓪ 𝓥𝓘𝓢𝓐. 🍸
closed 1 week at Christmas – **M** (dinner only)(booking essential) 15.50 **t.** ⌕ 2.20 – **7 rm** 🔄 39.50/59.00 **t.** – SB (except summer) 69.00 **st.**

at Kents Bank SW : 1 ¾ m. by B 5277 – ⊠ ✆ 044 84 Grange-over-Sands :

⚤ **Kents Bank**, 96 Kentsford Rd, LA11 7BB, ✐ 2054, ≤ – ⊜wc 🅿 🔼 VISA
8 rm ⇌ 15.00/34.00 t.

at Cartmel NW : 3 m. – ⊠ Grange-over-Sands – ✆ 044 854 Cartmel :

🏛 **Aynsome Manor** ⌂, LA11 6HH, NE : ½ m. ✐ 276, « Country house atmosphere », 🚗 –
⊜wc 🅿 🔼 AE VISA
closed 2 to 23 January – **M** (closed Sunday dinner to non residents) (dinner only and Sunday
lunch)/dinner 13.00 t. 🍷 3.00 – **13 rm** ⇌ (dinner included) 31.50/66.00 t. – SB (mid October-mid
May) 46.00/54.00 st.

🏛 **Ivy House,** Aynsome Rd, LA11 6HF, ✐ 543, 🚗 – 📺 ⊜wc 🁃wc 🅿 ⌘
March-October – **M** (dinner only) 11.50 st. – **6 rm** ⇌ 27.75/40.50 st.

⚤ **Priory,** The Square, LA11 6QB, ✐ 267 – 🚗 🅿 ⌘
May-October, Christmas and New Year – **M** a la carte 7.95/11.30 t. 🍷 3.75 – **9 rm**
⇌ 18.00/42.00 t. – SB 52.00/70.00 st.

XX **Uplands** ⌂ with rm, Haggs Lane, LA11 6HD, E : 1 m. ✐ 248, ≤ Cartmel Sands, 🚗 – 📺
🁃wc 🅿 🔼 AE
closed 4 January-February – **M** (closed Monday lunch) (booking essential) 9.00/15.00 t. –
4 rm ⇌ 52.00/90.00 t.

BMW Lindale Hill ✐ 3751 VW, AUDI Lindale ✐ 4242
SUBARU, SEAT Lindale Corner ✐ 2282

GRANTHAM Lincs. 402 404 S 25 – pop. 30 700 – ECD : Wednesday – ✆ 0476.
See : St. Wulfram's Church★ 13C.
Envir. : Belton House★ (Renaissance) AC, NE : 2 m. – Belvoir Castle 19C (interior★) W : 8 m.
– 🔟 Stoke Rochford, Great North Rd ✐ 045 683 (Great Ponton) 275, S : 6 m. on A 1.
🅱 The Guildhall Yard, St. Peters Hill ✐ 66444.
♦London 113 – ♦Leicester 31 – Lincoln 29 – ♦Nottingham 24.

🏛 **George** (Best Western), High St., NG31 6NN, ✐ 63286, Telex 378121 – 📺 ⊜wc 🁃wc ☎ 🅿
🛁 🔼 AE ⓞ VISA
M (bar lunch)/dinner 10.50 st. and a la carte 🍷 3.40 – **46 rm** ⇌ 35.00/55.00 st. – SB (weekends
only) 59.00 st.

🏛 **Angel and Royal** (T.H.F.), 4 High St., NG31 6PN, ✐ 65816, « 13C stone walled restaurant
and bar » – 📺 ⊜wc 🅿 🛁 🔼 AE VISA
M 6.45/9.25 st. and a la carte 🍷 3.40 – ⇌ 5.65 – **24 rm** 43.00/53.00 st.. **1 suite**.

🏛 **King's,** 130 North Par., NG31 8AU, ✐ 65881 – 📺 ⊜wc 🁃wc ☎ 🅿 🔼 AE ⓞ VISA
M 6.50/7.65 st. and a la carte 🍷 3.00 – **17 rm** ⇌ 21.00/40.00 st. – SB (weekdays only)
42.00/52.00 st.

at Barkston N : 3 ¾ m. on A 607 – ⊠ Grantham – ✆ 0400 Loveden :

XX **Barkston House** with rm, NG32 2NH, ✐ 50555, ⌘, 🚗 – 📺 ⊜wc ☎ 🅿 🔼 AE ⓞ VISA ⌘
closed Christmas – **M** (closed Saturday lunch, dinner Sunday and Monday and Bank Holidays
except Good Friday) a la carte 7.05/12.10 t. 🍷 2.50 – **2 rm** ⇌ 28.00/38.00 t. – SB (weekends
only) 55.00 st.

FORD 30-40 London Rd ✐ 65195 TOYOTA Great Ponton ✐ 047 683 261
NISSAN Barrowby High Rd ✐ 64443 VOLVO Barrowby Rd ✐ 4114
PEUGEOT-TALBOT 66 London Rd ✐ 62595 VW, AUDI, SUBARU Spittlegate ✐ 66416
RENAULT London Rd ✐ 61338

GRAPPENHALL Cheshire – see Warrington.

GRASMERE Cumbria 402 K 20 – ECD : Thursday – ✆ 096 65.
🅱 Red Bank Rd ✐ 245 (summer only).
♦London 282 – ♦Carlisle 43 – Kendal 18.

Plans : see Ambleside

🏨 **Wordsworth,** LA22 9SW, ✐ 592, Telex 65329, 🔲, 🚗 – ▮ 🍽 rest 📺 ☎ ⚹ 🅿 🛁 🔼 AE ⓞ
VISA ⌘
M 8.75/16.50 t. and a la carte 🍷 3.50 – **35 rm** ⇌ 39.00/88.00 t. – SB (November-March) BZ **s**
72.00/85.00 st.

🏛 **Michaels Nook Country House** ⌂, LA22 9RP, NE : ½ m. off A 591 ✐ 496, Group Telex
65329, ≤ mountains and countryside, « Antiques and gardens » – 📺 ⊜wc ☎ 🅿 ⌘
M (booking essential) 19.00/26.00 t. 🍷 3.25 – **11 rm** ⇌ (dinner included) 70.00/170.00 st.,
2 suites 195.00/225.00 st. – SB (weekdays only)(November-March except Christmas and New
Year) 95.00 st. AY **n**

🏛 **Swan** (T.H.F.), LA22 9RF, on A 591 ✐ 551, ≤, 🚗 – 📺 ⊜wc 🅿 🔼 AE ⓞ VISA AY **r**
M 7.50/12.00 st. and a la carte 🍷 3.70 – ⇌ 6.50 – **40 rm** 46.00/60.00 st.

🏛 **Gold Rill Country House** ⌂, Langdale Rd, LA22 9PU, ✐ 486, ≤, 🏊 heated, 🚗 – 📺
🔼 AE ⓞ 🅿 VISA ⌘ BZ **c**
March-November and 10 days Christmas – **M** (bar lunch)/dinner 14.00 t. 🍷 2.75 – **16 rm**
⇌ 36.00/90.00 t.

🏛 **White Moss House,** Rydal Water, LA22 9SE, S : 1 ½ m. on A 591 𝒫 295, 🍴 – 📺 🚿wc
🅿. 🌫
BY **e**
Mid March-mid November – **M** *(closed Sunday)* (dinner only) (booking essential) 16.95 **t.**
🍷 3.00 – **6 rm** 🖙 (dinner included) 45.50/99.00 **t.** – SB (weekdays only)(March, April and
November) 87.00 **st.**

🏛 **Rothay Garden,** Broadgate, LA22 9RH, 𝒫 334, 🍴 – 📺 🚿wc 🚿wc 🅿. 🔼 ᴀᴇ 𝘝𝘐𝘚𝘈 AY **e**
Mid February-November and New Year – **M** (bar lunch)/dinner 12.50 **t.** 🍷 2.50 – **16 rm** 🖙 (dinner included) 35.00/72.00 **t.** – SB (except winter) 54.00/72.00 **st.**

🏛 **Oak Bank,** Broadgate, LA22 9TA, 𝒫 217, 🍴 – 📺 🚿wc 🚿wc 🅿. 🔼 𝘝𝘐𝘚𝘈 BZ **e**
closed Christmas and New Year – **M** (bar lunch)/dinner 10.00 **t.** 🍷 3.00 – **14 rm** 🖙 18.00/48.00 **t.**
– SB (weekdays only)(except summer and Bank Holidays) 40.00/60.00 **st.**

🏛 **Grasmere,** Broadgate, LA22 9TA, 𝒫 277, 🍴 – 🚿wc 🚿wc 🅿. 𝘝𝘐𝘚𝘈 BZ **r**
March-November – **M** (bar lunch)/dinner 11.00 **t.** 🍷 2.50 – **12 rm** 🖙 24.00/44.00 **t.** – SB
52.00/60.00 **st.**

🏛 **How Foot Lodge** without rest., Town End, LA22 9SQ, on A 591 𝒫 366, <, 🍴 – 🚿wc 🚿wc
🅿. 🌫
AY **v**
April-October – **6 rm** 🖙 30.00/38.00 **st.**

↑ **Bridge House** 🌫, Stock Lane, LA22 9SN, 𝒫 425, 🍴 – 🚿wc 🅿. 🔼 𝘝𝘐𝘚𝘈. 🌫 BZ **n**
8 March-mid November – **12 rm** 🖙 (dinner included) 22.00/53.00 **t.**

↑ **Titteringdales,** Pye Lane, LA22 9RQ, 𝒫 439, 🍴 – 🚿wc 🅿 AY **x**
April-October – **7 rm** 🖙 12.00/29.00 **st.**

↑ **Rothay Lodge** 🌫, White Bridge, LA22 9RH, 𝒫 341, 🍴 – 🅿. 🌫 AY **o**
closed Christmas – **6 rm** 🖙 11.00/27.00 **st.**

GRASSINGTON North Yorks. 402 O 21 – pop. 1 220 – ECD : Thursday – ✉ Skipton – ☎ 0756.
♦London 240 – Bradford 30 – Burnley 28 – ♦Leeds 37.

🏨 **Grassington House,** The Square, BD23 5AQ, 𝒫 752406 – 🚿wc 🅿
March-October – **M** *(closed lunch Monday and Friday)* (bar lunch)/dinner 8.05 **st.** 🍷 2.95 –
18 rm 🖙 17.25/33.80 **t.** – SB (summer only)(weekends only) 46.00 **st.**

↑ **Lodge,** 8 Wood Lane, 𝒫 752518 – 🅿
closed January and February – **7 rm** 🖙 14.00/26.00 **st.**

at Threshfield SW : ½ m. on B 6265 – ✉ Skipton – ☎ 0756 Grassington :

🏛 **Wilson Arms,** Station Rd, BD23 5EL, SW : ½ m. on B 6265 𝒫 752666, 🍴 – 🛗 📺 🚿wc ☎
⟺ 🅿. 🔼 ᴀᴇ ⓞ 𝘝𝘐𝘚𝘈
closed 3 to 16 January – **M** 6.50/10.95 **t.** 🍷 3.00 – **28 rm** 🖙 27.00/60.00 **t.** – SB 55.00/70.00 **st.**

↑ **Greenways** 🌫, Wharfeside Av., BD23 5BF, 𝒫 752598, <, 🍴 – 🅿
April-October – **5 rm** 🖙 13.50/27.00 **st.**

GRAVESEND Kent 404 V 29 – pop. 53 450 – ECD : Wednesday – ☎ 0474.
⟺ to Tilbury (Sealink) frequent services daily (5 mn).
🛈 10 Parrock St. 𝒫 337600.
♦London 25 – ♦Dover 54 – Maidstone 16 – Margate 53.

🏨 **Tollgate Moat House** (Q.M.H.), Watling St., DA13 9RA, S : 2 m. at junction A 2 and A 227
𝒫 357655, Telex 966227 – 📺 🚿wc ☎ ᵭ 🅿. 🅰. 🔼 ᴀᴇ ⓞ 𝘝𝘐𝘚𝘈. 🌫
M (bar lunch)/dinner 7.25 **st.** and a la carte 🍷 2.60 – **114 rm** 🖙 29.50/48.50 **st.**

🏨 **Overcliffe,** 16 The Overcliffe, DA11 0EF, 𝒫 322131 – 📺 🚿wc ☎ 🅿. 🔼 ᴀᴇ ⓞ 𝘝𝘐𝘚𝘈
M a la carte 8.45/12.15 **t.** 🍷 2.50 – **19 rm** 🖙 36.00/45.00 **t.** – SB (weekends only)(except
December) 50.00/60.00 **st.**

🏛 **Clarendon Royal,** Royal Pier Rd, DA12 2BF, 𝒫 63151 – 📺 🚿wc ☎ 🅿
M (grill rest.) – **23 rm**

↑ **Cromer,** 194 Parrock St., DA12 1EW, 𝒫 61935 – 📺 🅿. 𝘝𝘐𝘚𝘈. 🌫
closed 24 December-2 January – **11 rm** 🖙 9.50/19.00 **st.**

ALFA ROMEO, HYUNDAI 50 Singlewell Rd 𝒫 66148
AUSTIN-ROVER The Grove 𝒫 322111
CITROEN, RELIANT Rochester Rd 𝒫 65211
FORD 1-3 Pelham Rd 𝒫 64411
RENAULT West St. 𝒫 67801
SKODA Meopham 𝒫 813562
TOYOTA High St., Northfleet 𝒫 57481
VW-AUDI Old Rd West 𝒫 357925

GRAVETYE East Sussex – see East Grinstead.

GRAYSHOTT Hants. 404 R 30 – pop. 2 048 – ✉ Hindhead (Surrey) – ☎ 042 873 Hindhead.
♦London 47 – Chichester 23 – Farnham 9 – Guildford 14 – ♦Portsmouth and Southsea 31.

✗ **Woods,** Headley Rd, GU26 6LB, 𝒫 5555 – 🔼 ᴀᴇ ⓞ 𝘝𝘐𝘚𝘈
closed Sunday and Monday – **M** (dinner only) a la carte 13.55/16.65 **t.** 🍷 2.40.

LANCIA, MASSERATI, SUBARU Headley Rd 𝒫 5363

GREAT AYTON North Yorks. 四〇② Q 20 – pop. 4 690 – ⊠ ✿ 0642 Middlesbrough.
◆London 245 – ◆Leeds 63 – ◆Middlesbrough 7 – York 48.

XXX **Ayton Hall** 🦢 with rm, Low Green, TS9 6BW, 𝒫 723595, « Tasteful decor », 🐎, ❀ – 📺
⌷wc ⇌ 🅿. 🔼 VISA 🔼
M 8.95/13.95 t. ⓐ 3.95 – **5 rm** ⌷ 50.00/79.00 t. – SB (weekends only) 75.00/92.50 st.

GREAT BADDOW Essex 四〇四 V 28 – see Chelmsford.

GREAT BARDFIELD Essex 四〇四 V 28 – pop. 1 030 – ⊠ Braintree – ✿ 0371 Great Dunmow.
◆London 49 – ◆Cambridge 30 – Chelmsford 20 – Colchester 26.

XX **Corn Dolly,** High St., CM7 4SP, 𝒫 810554, English rest. – 🔼 AE ⓪ VISA
closed Monday and Tuesday – **M** *(closed dinner Sunday and Bank Holidays)* 10.00 t.
(lunch)/dinner a la carte 12.65/18.90 t.

GREAT BARR West Midlands 四〇③ 四〇四 O 26 – see Birmingham.

GREAT BROUGHTON Cumbria 四〇① 四〇② J 19 – see Cockermouth.

GREAT DRIFFIELD Humberside 四〇② S 21 – pop. 8 970 – ECD : Wednesday – ⊠ York – ✿ 0377.
🏌 Driffield, Sunderlandwick 𝒫 43116.
◆London 201 – ◆Kingston-upon-Hull 21 – Scarborough 22 – York 29.

🏨 **Bell** (Best Western), 46 Market Pl., YO25 7AP, 𝒫 46661, squash – 📺 ⌷wc ☎ ♿ 🅿. 🔼. 🔼
AE ⓪ VISA
M (buffet lunch)/dinner a la carte 9.30/12.90 st. ⓐ 2.95 – **14 rm** ⌷ 33.00/47.75 st. – SB (week-
ends only) 55.00 st.

at Nafferton NE : 2 ½ m. on A 166 – ⊠ ✿ 0377 Great Driffield :

🏨 **Wold House** 🦢, Wold Rd, YO25 0LD, 𝒫 44242, 🏊 heated, 🐎 – ⌷wc 🌢wc 🅿
M (bar lunch Monday to Saturday)/dinner 9.50 st. and a la carte ⓐ 3.00 – **13 rm**
⌷ 17.50/30.00 st. – SB (except summer) 35.00/45.00 st.

GREAT DUNMOW Essex 四〇四 V 28 – pop. 4 026 – ECD : Wednesday – ✿ 0371.
◆London 42 – ◆Cambridge 27 – Chelmsford 13 – Colchester 24.

🏨 **Saracen's Head** (T.H.F.), High St., CM6 1AG, 𝒫 3901 – 📺 ⌷wc ⇌ 🅿. 🔼. 🔼 AE ⓪ VISA
M 7.50/9.75 st. and a la carte ⓐ 3.40 – ⌷ 5.65 – **24 rm** 46.00/56.00 st.. **1 suite.**
XXX **Starr,** Market Pl., CM6 1AX, 𝒫 4321 – 🅿. 🔼 AE ⓪ VISA
closed Saturday lunch, Sunday dinner, 3 weeks August and 25 December-9 January – **M** 12.95
t. (lunch) and a la carte 14.00/19.55 t. ⓐ 3.25.

BMW 81 High St. 𝒫 2884

GREAT GRIMSBY Humberside 四〇② 四〇四 T 23 – pop. 91 532 – ECD : Thursday – ✿ 0472.
Envir. : Thornton Curtis (St. Lawrence's Church★ : Norman and Gothic) NW : 16 m. by A 18 Y and
B 1211 – Thornton Abbey (ruins 14C) : the Gatehouse★ *AC*, NW : 18 m. by A 18 Y and B 1211.
✈ Humberside Airport : 𝒫 0652 (Barnetby)688456, W : 13 m. by A 8 Y.
🛈 Central Library, Town Hall Square 𝒫 53123/4.
◆London 172 – Boston 50 – Lincoln 36 – ◆Sheffield 75.

Plan on next page

🏨 **Humber Royal** (Crest), Littlecoates Rd, DN34 4LX, 𝒫 50295, ≼ – 📳 📺 🅿. 🔼. 🔼 AE ⓪
VISA
Y c
M (bar lunch Saturday) 7.45/12.25 st. and a la carte – ⌷ 6.15 – **52 rm** 51.00/61.00 st. – SB
(weekends only) 62.00 st.

🏨 **Crest** (Crest), St. James Sq., DN31 1EP, 𝒫 59771, Telex 527741 – 📳 📺 ⌷wc ⇌ 🅿. 🔼.
AE ⓪ VISA
AZ n
closed 1 week at Christmas – **M** 7.00/13.00 st. and a la carte ⓐ 4.00 – ⌷ 6.50 – **131 rm**
46.00/56.00 st. – SB (weekends only) 62.00/70.00 st.

XX **Regines,** 2 Osborne St., 𝒫 56737 – 🔼 AE VISA
AZ a
closed Sunday, Monday, first 2 weeks February and first 2 weeks August – **M** 7.95/8.95 t. and a
la carte 8.95/14.20 t. ⓐ 2.50.

AUSTIN-ROVER 415 Victoria St. 𝒫 56161
AUSTIN-ROVER Railway St. 𝒫 52461
BMW Laceby Rd 𝒫 71835
FIAT, SUBARU Wellowgate 𝒫 55951
FORD Corporation Rd 𝒫 58941
FSO Hainton Av. 𝒫 45655
HONDA Alexandra Rd 𝒫 58625
MERCEDES-BENZ Bradley Cross Rd 𝒫 79274
MITSUBISHI Rendel St. 𝒫 362021

NISSAN 210-212 Victoria St. 𝒫 53572 and 41281
PEUGEOT, TALBOT Park St. 𝒫 46011
RENAULT Chelmsford Av. 𝒫 70111
SAAB Heneage Rd 𝒫 48527
SKODA, ALFA ROMEO Rendel St. 𝒫 57362
TOYOTA Cromwell Rd 𝒫 52191
VAUXHALL-OPEL 123 Cromwell Rd 𝒫 46066
VAUXHALL-OPEL Brighowgate 𝒫 58486
VW, AUDI Convamore Rd 𝒫 55451

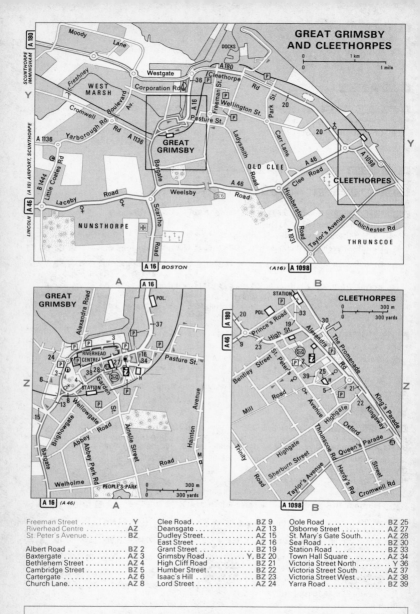

Für Ihre Reisen in Großbritannien

– 5 Karten (Nr. **401**, **402**, **403**, **404**, **405**) im Maßstab 1:400 000
– Die auf den Karten rot unterstrichenen Orte sind im Führer erwähnt,
  benutzen Sie deshalb Karten und Führer zusammen.

GREAT HARWOOD Lancs. 402 M 22 – pop. 10 968 – ✪ 0254.

◆London 236 – Blackburn 6 – Burnley 10 – ◆Manchester 26.

　　XX　**Tiffany,** 79 Church St., BB6 7QB, ✆ 889528 – △
　　　closed lunch Saturday and Sunday and Monday – **M** a la carte 16.15/20.45 **t.**

GREAT MALVERN Heref. and Worc. 403 404 N 27 – pop. 30 153 – ECD : Wednesday – ✪ 068 45.

See : Priory Church★ 11C B **B.**

🛈 Winter Gdns, Grange Rd ✆ 4700.

◆London 127 – ◆Birmingham 34 – ◆Cardiff 66 – Gloucester 24.

Plan on next page

🏤　**Foley Arms** (Best Western), Worcester Rd, WR14 4QS, ✆ 3397, Group Telex 437269, ≼, 🚗 –
　　📺 🚽wc 🛁wc ☎ 🅿 ⚓ B **a**
　　26 rm.

🏤　**Mount Pleasant,** Belle Vue Terr., WR14 4PZ, ✆ 61837, ≼, 🚗 – 📺 🚽wc 🛁wc ☎ 🅿 ⚓
　　🔔 AE ① VISA 🛳 B **e**
　　closed 25 and 26 December – **M** 5.95/6.95 **t.** and a la carte ◊ 3.25 – 🖵 4.00 – **14 rm** 26.00/35.00 **t.**
　　– SB 48.00/56.00 **st.**

🏠　**Cotford,** 51 Graham Rd, WR14 2JW, ✆ 2427, 🚗 – 📺 🚽wc 🅿 △ VISA
　　M (lunch by arrangement)/dinner 9.00 **st.** ◊ 2.50 – **14 rm** 🖵 16.00/37.00 **st.** B **o**

🏠　**Montrose,** 23 Graham Rd, WR14 2HU, ✆ 2335, 🚗 – 🛁wc 🅿 △ VISA B **i**
　　closed 20 December-6 January – **M** (dinner only) 8.00 **st.** ◊ 3.80 – **14 rm** 🖵 15.00/34.00 **st.** –
　　SB (except Easter and Bank Holidays) 38.00/45.00 **st.**

🏠　**Thornbury,** 16 Avenue Rd, WR14 3AR, ✆ 2278, 🚗 – 📺 🛁wc 🅿 △ VISA 🛳 B **c**
　　M *(closed Sunday dinner)* (bar lunch Monday to Saturday)/dinner 8.25 **t.** and a la carte ◊ 3.50
　　– **18 rm** 🖵 16.50/35.00 **t.** – SB 35.00/48.00 **st.**

🏠　**Sidney House,** 40 Worcester Rd, WR14 4AA, ✆ 4994, ≼ – 📺 🅿 △ AE ① VISA B **s**
　　7 rm 🖵 14.00/30.00 **st.**

🏠　**Bredon,** 34 Worcester Rd, WR14 4AA, ✆ 5323, ≼ – 📺 🚽wc 🛁wc ☎ 🅿 △ AE VISA B **u**
　　9 rm 🖵 18.00/40.00 **st.**

X　**Walmer Lodge** with rm, 49 Abbey Rd, WR14 3HH, ✆ 4139, 🚗 – 🚽wc 🛁wc 🅿 🛳 A **n**
　　closed Sunday, 2 weeks July-August, Christmas and New Year – **M** (dinner only)(booking
　　essential) 11.95 **t.** ◊ 2.80 – **8 rm** 🖵 16.10/29.90 **t.**

　　at Welland SE : 4 ½ m. by A 449 on A 4104 – ✉ Great Malvern – ✪ 0684 Hanley Swan :

🏠　**Holdfast Cottage** 🦢, Marlbank Rd, Welland, WR13 6NA, W : ¾ m. ✆ 310288, « 17C
　　country cottage », 🚗 – 🚽wc 🛁wc 🅿 A **x**
　　M (bar lunch, residents only)/dinner 11.25 **t.** ◊ 3.75 – **9 rm** 🖵 18.00/40.00 **t.** – SB (except
　　summer) 52.00/58.00 **st.**

　　at Malvern Wells S : 2 m. on A 449 – ✉ ✪ 068 45 Great Malvern :

🏤　**Cottage in the Wood** 🦢, Holywell Rd, WR14 4LG, ✆ 3487, ≼ Severn and Evesham Vales,
　　🚗 – 📺 🚽wc 🛁wc 🅿 △ VISA 🛳 A **z**
　　closed 24 to 30 December – **M** 8.50/15.00 **st.** and a la carte ◊ 3.75 – 🖵 4.00 – **20 rm**
　　40.00/85.00 **st.** – SB 65.00/95.00 **st.**

　　XX ✿ **Croque-en-Bouche,** 221 Wells Rd, WR14 4NF, ✆ 65612 – △ VISA A **u**
　　closed Sunday to Tuesday and Christmas – **M** (dinner only) (booking essential) 19.50 **st.** ◊ 3.00
　　Spec. Soupe au pistou (May-September), Crab mousse with a mango sauce, Leg of lamb with ginger, rosemary
　　and soy.

　　XX　**The Course,** 191-193 Wells Rd, WR14 4HE, ✆ 5065 – △ VISA A **o**
　　closed Sunday, 15 to 22 February, 25 December-3 January and Bank Holidays – **M** (dinner
　　only) 13.75 **t.** ◊ 2.95.

　　at Colwall S : 3 ¼ m. by A 449 on B 4218 – ✉ Great Malvern – ✪ 0684 Colwall :

🏠　**Colwall Park,** Walwyn Rd, WR13 6QG, ✆ 40206, Telex 335626 – 📺 🚽wc 🛁wc ☎ 🅿 ⚓
　　🔔 AE VISA A **r**
　　M 10.95 **t.** ◊ 2.75 – **20 rm** 🖵 28.50/47.50 **t.** – SB (except Bank Holidays) 59.00 **st.**

　　at Wynds Point S : 4 m. on A 449 – ✉ Great Malvern – ✪ 0684 Colwall :

🏠　**Malvern Hills,** British Camp, WR13 6DW, ✆ 40237, 🚗 – 📺 🚽wc 🅿 △ AE ① A **s**
　　M (bar lunch Monday to Saturday)/dinner 8.50 **st.** and a la carte ◊ 2.75 – **15 rm**
　　🖵 24.00/50.00 **st.** – SB (except Christmas and Bank Holidays) 55.00/60.00 **st.**

　　at West Malvern W : 2 m. on B 4232 – ✉ ✪ 068 45 Great Malvern :

🏠　**Broomhill,** West Malvern Rd, WR14 4AY, ✆ 64367, ≼ hills and countryside, 🚗 – 🚽wc
　　🛁wc 🅿 A **v**
　　March-October – **M** (bar lunch)/dinner 7.25 **t.** – **10 rm** 🖵 16.00/33.00 **t.** – SB (except summer)
　　32.00/40.00 **st.**

CITROEN　62 Court Rd ✆ 3391
FORD　203-207 Worcester Rd ✆ 69111
VAUXHALL-OPEL　Linktop ✆ 3336

VOLVO　Pickersleigh Rd ✆ 61498
VW, AUDI　Worcester Rd ✆ 3601

GREAT MALVERN

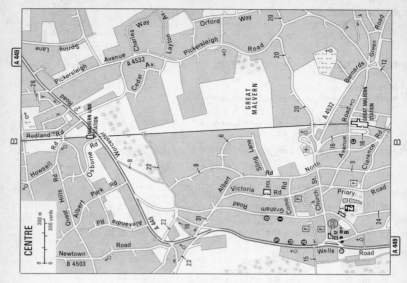

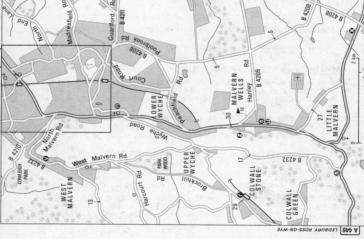

Town plans
roads most used
by traffic and those
on which guide listed
hotels and restaurants
stand are fully drawn ;
the beginning only
of lesser roads
is indicated.

GREAT MILTON Oxon. 408 404 Q 28 — see Oxford.

GREAT MISSENDEN Bucks. 404 R 28 — pop. 7 429 (inc. Prestwood) — ECD : Thursday — ☎ 024 06.
♦London 34 — Aylesbury 10 — Maidenhead 19 — ♦Oxford 35.

× **Atkins,** 107 High St., HP16 0BB, ✆ 5370 — ⊠ AE ⓪
closed Sunday, Monday, 2 weeks January and 2 weeks August — **M** (booking essential)(dinner only) a la carte 14.00/21.00 **t.**

GREAT SNORING Norfolk 404 W 25 — pop. 180 — ⊠ Fakenham — ☎ 032 872 Walsingham.
♦London 115 — ♦Cambridge 68 — ♦Norwich 28.

🏠 **Old Rectory** ⟨⟩, Barsham Rd, NR21 0HP, ✆ 597, « Country house atmosphere », ⇤ — 📺 ⌧wc 📶 🅿 ⚠ ⌘
closed 24 to 27 December — **M** (dinner only)(booking essential) 11.50 **t.** 🍷 2.95 — **6 rm** ⊏⊐ 35.00/58.00 **t.**

GREAT WITCHINGHAM Norfolk 404 X 25 — see Lenwade - Great Witchingham.

GREAT YARMOUTH Norfolk 404 Z 26 — pop. 54 777 — ECD : Thursday — ☎ 0493.
🚢 Shipping connections with the Continent : to The Netherlands (Scheveningen) (Norfolk Line).
🏢 1 South Quay ✆ 846345 — Marine Parade ✆ 842195 (summer only).
♦London 126 — ♦Cambridge 81 — ♦Ipswich 53 — ♦Norwich 20.

🏨 **Carlton,** 1-5 Kimberley Terr., Marine Par., NR30 3JE, ✆ 855234 — 🛗 📺 ☎ ⇌ 🅿 ⚠ ⊠ AE ⓪ VISA
M (bar lunch)/dinner 8.25 **st.** and a la carte 🍷 4.45 — **90 rm** ⊏⊐ 38.25/50.00 **st.**, **5 suites** 68.50/125.00 **st.** — SB (weekends only) 57.75/65.25 **st.**

🏨 **Star** (Q.M.H.), 24 Hall Quay, NR30 1HG, ✆ 842294 — 🛗 📺 ⌧wc ☎ 🅿 ⚠ ⊠ AE ⓪ VISA
M 7.45 **t.** and a la carte 🍷 3.75 — **42 rm** ⊏⊐ 35.00/50.00 **t.** — SB (weekends only) 44.00/46.00 **st.**

at Gorleston-on-Sea S : 3 m. on A 12 — ⊠ ☎ 0493 Great Yarmouth :

🏨 **Cliff** (Best Western), Cliff Hill, NR31 6DH, ✆ 662179, ⇤ — 📺 ⌧wc ⌧wc ☎ 🅿 ⚠ AE ⓪ VISA
M 6.00/8.00 **t.** and a la carte 🍷 3.40 — **30 rm** ⊏⊐ 32.50/53.00 **t.** — SB (weekends only) 46.00/52.50 **st.**

AUSTIN-ROVER North Quay ✆ 4266
CITROEN Main Rd, Repps ✆ 069 27 (Potter Heigham) 271/256
FORD South Gates Rd ✆ 844922

FORD 134 Lowestoft Rd, Gorleston-on-Sea ✆ 664151
RENAULT Drudge Rd ✆ 664158
VW, AUDI-NSU South Denes Rd ✆ 857711

GREAT YELDHAM Essex 404 V 27 — pop. 1 440 — ECD : Wednesday — ⊠ Halstead — ☎ 0787.
Envir. : Hedingham Castle (Norman Keep★) *AC*, SE : 2 ½ m.
♦London 56 — ♦Cambridge 27 — Chelmsford 23 — Colchester 21.

×× **White Hart,** Poole St., CO9 4HJ, ✆ 237250, « 15C timbered inn », ⇤ — 🅿 ⊠ AE ⓪ VISA
M 9.95 **t.** and a la carte 12.15/15.10 **t.** 🍷 3.25.

GRETA BRIDGE Durham 402 O 20 — ⊠ Barnard Castle — ☎ 0833 Teesdale.
♦London 253 — ♦Carlisle 63 — ♦Leeds 63 — ♦Middlesbrough 32.

🏨 **Morritt Arms,** DL12 9SE, ✆ 27232, ⟨⟩, ⇤ — 📺 ⌧wc ⇌ 🅿 ⊠ ⓪ VISA
M 8.00/12.00 **t.** 🍷 3.50 — **23 rm** ⊏⊐ 20.00/48.00 **t.** — SB (November-April) 47.00/49.00 **st.**

GRIMSBY Humberside 402 404 T 23 — see Great Grimsby.

GRIMSTHORPE Lincs. 402 404 S 25 — ⊠ Bourne — ☎ 077 832 Edenham.
♦London 105 — Lincoln 43 — ♦Nottingham 38.

× **Black Horse Inn** with rm, PE10 0LY, ✆ 247, English rest. — ⌧wc 🅿 ⊠ AE VISA
closed Sunday and 1 week Christmas — **M** (restricted lunch) 11.95 **t.** and a la carte — **4 rm** ⊏⊐ 25.00/50.00 **t.** — SB 50.00/55.00 **st.**

GRIMSTON Norfolk — see Kings Lynn.

GRINDLEFORD Derbs. 402 403 404 P 24 — ⊠ Sheffield (South Yorks.) — ☎ 0433 Hope Valley.
♦London 165 — Derby 31 — ♦Manchester 34 — ♦Sheffield 10.

🏨 **Maynard Arms,** Main Rd, S30 1HP, ✆ 30321, ≤, ⇤ — 📺 ⌧wc ☎ 🅿 ⚠ ⊠ AE ⓪ VISA
M 7.25/10.50 **t.** 🍷 2.50 — **13 rm** ⊏⊐ 32.00/42.00 **t.** — SB 52.00/59.00 **st.**

GRINDLETON Lancs. 402 M 22 — pop. 1 451 (inc. West Bradford) — ⊠ ☎ 020 07 Bolton-by-Bowland — ♦London 241 — ♦Blackpool 38 — Lancaster 25 — ♦Leeds 45 — ♦Manchester 33.

🏠 **Harrop Fold Country Farmhouse** ⟨⟩, Harrop Fold, BB7 4PJ, N : 2 ¾ m. by Slaidburn Rd ✆ 600, « 17C Longhouse », ⟨⟩ — 📺 ⌧wc 🅿 ⊠ VISA 🍷
M (dinner only) a la carte 6.50/12.30 **st.** 🍷 2.50 — **8 rm** ⊏⊐ 19.00/40.00 **st.** — SB 50.00/62.00 **st.**

205

GRIZEDALE Cumbria **402** K 20 – see Hawkshead.

GUILDFORD Surrey **404** S 30 – pop. 61 509 – ECD : Wednesday – ☎ 0483.
See : Cathedral★ (1961) Z **A**.
Envir. : Clandon Park★★ (Renaissance House) *AC*, E : 3 m. by A 246 Z.
🖸 Civic Hall, London Rd ☎ 575857 — ◆London 33 — ◆Brighton 43 — Reading 27 — ◆Southampton 49.

GUILDFORD

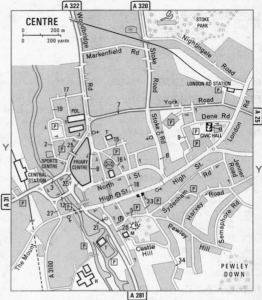

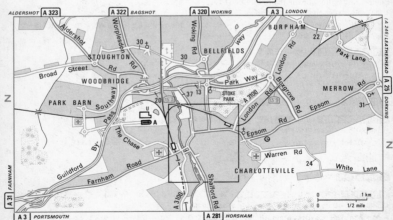

🏛 **Angel** (T.H.F.), High St., GU1 3DR, ☎ 64555, « 16C coaching inn » – 📺 🛏wc ☎. 🔔. 🔼 AE ① **VISA**
    M 7.50/12.50 **st.** and a la carte ⑃ 3.75 – ☲ 5.65 – **27 rm** 46.50/60.00 **st.** Y **a**

🏠 **Quinns** without rest., 78 Epsom Rd, GU1 2BX, on A 246 ☎ 60422, 🛋 – 📺 🛏wc 🕳wc 🅿. 🔼 AE ① **VISA**
    11 rm ☲ 24.00/42.00 **st.** Z **e**

✗ **Café de Paris,** 35 Castle St., GU1 3UQ, ℰ 34896, French rest. – ⚡ AE VISA   Y u
   closed Saturday lunch, Monday dinner and Sunday – **M** 7.95/8.95 **t.** and a la carte 5.90/15.00 **t.**
   🍴 3.10.

   at West Clandon NE : 5 m. by A 246 on A 247 – Z – ✉ 🏵 0483 Guildford :

✗✗ **Onslow Arms Inn,** The Street, GU4 7TE, ℰ 222447 – ℗ ⚡ AE ⑩ VISA
   closed Sunday dinner and Monday – **M** 8.50 **t.** (lunch) and a la carte 10.85/18.45 **t.** 🍴 3.75.

   at Shere E : 4 ¾ m. by A 25 – Z – ✉ Guildford – 🏵 048 641 Shere :

✗✗ **La Chaumiere,** Gomshall Lane, GU5 9HE, ℰ 2168 – ℗ ⚡ AE ⑩ VISA
   M 8.50 **t.** (lunch) and a la carte 11.50/19.05 **t.** 🍴 3.75.

   at Gomshall E : 5 ½ m. on A 25 – Z – ✉ Guildford – 🏵 048 641 Shere :

🏡 **Black Horse Inn,** Station Rd, GU5 9NP, on A 25 ℰ 2242, ⊸ – ℗ ⑩ VISA ⚞
   M *(closed Sunday dinner and Monday)* a la carte 4.65/11.70 **t.** 🍴 2.70 – **4 rm** ⇆ 16.10/32.20 **t.**

   at Peaslake SE : 8 ½ m. by A 25 – Z – ✉ Guildford – 🏵 0306 Dorking :

🏠 **Hurtwood Inn** (T.H.F.), Walking Bottom, GU5 9RR, ℰ 730851, ⊸ – 📺 🛏wc ☎ ℗ 🅰 ⚡
   AE ⑩ VISA
   M (bar lunch)/dinner 9.50 **st.** and a la carte 🍴 3.40 – ⇆ 5.65 – **18 rm** 39.00/53.00 **st.**

   at Bramley S : 3 m. on A 281 – Z – ✉ 🏵 0483 Guildford :

🏛 **Bramley Grange,** High St., GU5 0BL, ℰ 893434, Telex 859948, ⊸ – 📺 🛏wc ☎ ℗ 🅰 ⚡
   AE ⑩ VISA ⚞
   M 11.00 **st.** and a la carte 🍴 4.00 – **21 rm** ⇆ 49.00/65.00 **st.** – SB (weekends only) 75.00/95.00 **st.**

✗✗ **La Baita,** High St., GU5 0HB, ℰ 893392, Italian rest. – ℗ ⚡ AE ⑩ VISA
   closed Sunday – **M** a la carte 11.00/20.60 **t.**

   at Compton SW : 4 m. by A 3100 on B 3000 – Z – ✉ Guildford – 🏵 048 68 Godalming :

✗ **Withies Inn,** Withies Lane, GU3 1JA, ℰ 21158, ⊸ – ℗ ⚡ AE ⑩ VISA
   M *(closed Sunday dinner)* a la carte approx. 15.25 **t.** 🍴 3.00.

AUSTIN-ROVER, JAGUAR, ROLLS ROYCE Wood-
bridge Rd ℰ 69231
BEDFORD, VAUXHALL-OPEL Woking Rd ℰ 37731
BMW Moorfield Rd ℰ 502211

FORD Woodbridge Meadow ℰ 60601
MERCEDES-BENZ Aldershot Rd ℰ 60751
RENAULT Walnut Tree Close ℰ 577371
TOYOTA Pitch Pl. Worplesdon ℰ 234242

GUIST Norfolk 404 W 25 – pop. 209 – ✉ Fakenham – 🏵 036 284 Foulsham.
♦London 119 – ♦Cambridge 67 – King's Lynn 29 – ♦Norwich 20.

✗✗ **Tollbridge,** Dereham Rd, NR20 5NU, S : ½ m. on B 1110 ℰ 359, ≼, « Attractive setting on
   banks of River Wensum », ⊸ – ℗ VISA
   closed Sunday, Monday, 3 weeks January and first week October – **M** (booking essential)
   7.50 **t.** (lunch) and a la carte 10.25/11.75 **t.** 🍴 2.40.

AUSTIN-ROVER Norwich Rd ℰ 0328(Fakenham)2251
PEUGEOT-TALBOT Hempton Rd ℰ 0328(Fakenham)2226

VAUXHALL-OPEL Greenway Lane ℰ 0328 (Fakenham) 2200

GULWORTHY Devon 403 H 32 – see Tavistock.

GUNNISLAKE Cornwall 403 H 32 The West Country G. – pop. 2 154 – ECD : Wednesday –
🏵 0822 Tavistock.
Envir. : Cotehele House★★ *AC*, SW : 2 ½ m.
♦London 244 – Bude 37 – Exeter 43 – ♦Plymouth 20 – Tavistock 5.

🏡 **Cornish Inn,** The Square, PL18 9BW, ℰ 832475 – 🛏wc ℗ ⚡ AE ⑩ VISA
   M a la carte 7.00/9.30 **t.** – **10 rm** ⇆ 12.00/27.50 **t.**

GWBERT-ON-SEA Dyfed 403 F 27 – see Cardigan.

HACKNESS North Yorks. 402 S 21 – see Scarborough.

HADLEIGH Suffolk 404 W 27 – pop. 5 858 – 🏵 0473.
🏰 Toppiss Hall ℰ 822922.
♦London 72 – ♦Cambridge 49 – Colchester 17 – ♦Ipswich 10.

✗ **Weavers,** 25-27 High St., IP7 5AG, ℰ 827247 – ⚡ VISA
   closed Sunday, Monday and 1 week at Christmas – **M** (dinner only) a la carte 7.40/10.30 **t.**
   🍴 2.90.

✗ **Spinning Wheel,** 117-119 High St., IP7 5EJ, ℰ 822175 – ⚡ AE ⑩ VISA
   closed 26 December – **M** (booking essential Sunday dinner) a la carte 10.75/15.75 **t.** 🍴 3.00.

AUSTIN-ROVER 132 High St. ℰ 823525

HADLOW Kent 404 V 30 – pop. 2 655 – ⊠ Tonbridge – ✆ 0732.
♦London 34 – Maidstone 10 – Royal Tunbridge Wells 9.

  XX **La Cremaillère,** The Square, TN11 0DD, ✆ 851489, French rest. – 🖳 🖭 *VISA*
    closed Saturday lunch, Sunday, 1 week January, 1 week spring, 1 week summer and Bank
    Holidays – **M** (booking essential) 13.00 **t.** ⏳ 5.00.

HAILSHAM East Sussex 404 U 31 – pop. 12 774 – ECD : Thursday – ⊠ ✆ 0323.
🖪 Area Library, Western Rd ✆ 840604 – ♦London 57 – ♦Brighton 23 – Eastbourne 7 – Hastings 20.

  🏠 **Boship Farm,** Lower Dicker, BN27 4AT, NW : 3 m. by A 295 on A 22 ✆ 844826, ⌧ heated,
    ⌨, ⚹ – 🖭 ⇔wc ☎ 🅿. 🔼. 🖳 🖭 ⓞ *VISA*
    M 8.75/16.85 **t.** and a la carte – **47 rm** ⊑ 34.00/42.00 **t.** – SB (weekends only) 56.00 **st.**

HALE Greater Manchester 402 403 404 M 23 – see Altrincham.

HALEBARNS Greater Manchester – see Altrincham.

HALESWORTH Suffolk 404 Y 26 – ✆ 098 67.
♦London 111 – ♦Ipswich 32 – ♦Norwich 23.

  X **Bassetts,** 84 London Rd, IP19 8LS, on A 144 ✆ 3154 – 🖳 *VISA*
    closed Sunday, Monday and November – **M** a la carte 9.75/10.90 **st.** ⏳ 2.70.

HALIFAX West Yorks. 402 O 22 – pop. 76 675 – ECD : Thursday – ✆ 0422.
🖬 Halifax Bradley Hall, Holywell Green ✆ 0422 (Elland) 74108 – 🖬 West End, Highroad Well
✆ 53608, N : 3 m. – 🖬 Ryburn, Norland ✆ 831355, S : 3 m.
🖪 The Piece Hall ✆ 68725 – ♦London 205 – Bradford 8 – Burnley 21 – ♦Leeds 15 – ♦Manchester 28.

  🏠 **Holdsworth House,** Holmfield, HX2 9TG, N : 3 m. by A 629 ✆ 240024, Telex 51574, « Part
    17C house », – 🖭 ☎ ⅙ 🅿. 🔼. 🖳 🖭 ⓞ *VISA*
    closed 1 week at Christmas – **M** *(closed lunch Saturday and Sunday)* a la carte 13.75/17.00 **st.**
    ⏳ 3.50 – **40 rm** ⊑ 40.00/60.00 **st.**, **4 suites** 60.00/75.00 **st.** – SB (weekends only) 70.00/90.00 **st.**

AUSTIN-ROVER Huddersfield Rd ✆ 65944
FIAT, CITROEN Queens Rd ✆ 67711
FIAT, POLSKI Rochdale Rd ✆ 65036
FORD Skircoat Rd ✆ 65790
HONDA Boothtown ✆ 67516
PEUGEOT-TALBOT Skircoat Rd ✆ 53701

RENAULT Hope St. ✆ 59442
VAUXHALL Northgate ✆ 62851
VAUXHALL-OPEL 7 Horton St. ✆ 65846
VOLVO 354 Pellon Lane ✆ 61961
VW, AUDI Denholme Gate Rd, Hipperholme ✆ 205611

HALLAND East Sussex 404 U 31 – ECD : Wednesday – ⊠ Lewes – ✆ 082 584.
♦London 48 – ♦Brighton 16 – Eastbourne 16 – Royal Tunbridge Wells 19.

  🏠 **Halland Forge,** BN8 6PW, on A 22 ✆ 456, ⌨ – 🖭 ⇔wc 🍴wc ☎ 🅿. 🖳 🖭 ⓞ *VISA*. ⚹
    M 8.00/10.00 **t.** and a la carte ⏳ 2.90 – ⊑ 5.00 – **20 rm** 31.00/39.00 **t.** – SB 56.00/59.00 **st.**

HALSE TOWN Cornwall 403 D 33 – see St. Ives.

HALTWHISTLE Northumb. 401 402 M 19 – pop. 3 522 – ✆ 0498.
🖪 Sycamore St. ✆ 20351 (summer only) – ♦London 335 – ♦Carlisle 22 – ♦Newcastle 37.

  ⌂ **Ashcroft,** NE49 0DA, ✆ 20213, – 🅿. ⚹
    closed 21 December-6 January – **7 rm** ⊑ 9.00/18.00.

HAMBLE Hants. 403 404 Q 31 – pop. 2 936 – ✆ 0703 Southampton.
♦London 88 – ♦Portsmouth 20 – ♦Southampton 7 – Winchester 22.

  XX Beth's, The Quay, ✆ 454314, ≼.

PEUGEOT-TALBOT Hamble Lane ✆ 453757

HAMBLETON Leics. – see Oakham.

HAMBROOK Avon 403 404 M 29 – see Bristol.

HAMPTON LOADE Salop – see Bridgnorth.

HANDFORTH Cheshire 402 403 404 N 23 – see Wilmslow.

HANLEY Staffs. 402 403 404 N 24 – see Stoke-on-Trent.

HARBERTONFORD Devon 403 I 32 – pop. 970 – ⊠ Totnes – ✆ 080 423.
♦London 228 – Exeter 28 – ♦Plymouth 24 – Torquay 13.

  XX **Hungry Horse,** Old Rd, TQ9 7TA, ✆ 441 – 🅿. 🖳 🖭 ⓞ *VISA*
    closed Sunday, Monday, first 2 weeks June and first 2 weeks October – **M** (dinner only) a la
    carte 11.85/17.65 **t.**

HARLECH Gwynedd 402 403 H 25 – pop. 1 292 – ECD : Wednesday – ✆ 0766.

See : Castle★★ (13C) *AC*, site and ≼ from the castle★.

Envir. : Llanbedr (Cwm Bychan★) S : 3 ½ m. – Vale of Ffestiniog★ NE : 9 m.

☒ Royal St. David's ✆ 780203.

🛈 Snowdonia National Park Visitor Centre, High St. ✆ 780658 (summer only).

♦London 241 – Chester 72 – Dolgellau 21.

 🏨 **Maes-y-Neuadd** ⊗, Talsarnau, LL47 6YA, NE : 3 ½ m. by B 4573 ✆ 780200, ≼, « Part 14C country house », ⇘, ⚓, park – 📺 ⌂wc 🅿. 🐎 ☒ *VISA*
  closed 11 January-5 February – **M** (lunch Monday-Saturday by arrangement) 9.50/13.75 **st.**
  🍷 2.75 – **14 rm** ⊊ 25.00/60.00 **st.** – SB (mid October-mid April) 62.00/68.00 **st.**

 ✗ **The Cemlyn** with rm, High St., LL46 2YA, ✆ 780425, ≼ Harlech Castle, Cardigan Bay and Lleyn Peninsula – 📺 ☒ ⊙
  Mid March-October and Saturdays November-December – **M** (lunch by arrangement)/dinner 9.95 **t.** – **2 rm** ⊊ 8.50/21.00 **st.**

 at Talsarnau NE : 4 m. on A 496 – ✆ 0766 Harlech :

 ↰ **Gwrach Ynys**, LL47 6TS, SW : 1¼ m. on A 496 ✆ 780742, 🐎 – ⌂wc 🅿
  closed December and January – **7 rm** ⊊ 10.00/24.00 **st.**

HARLOW Essex 404 U 28 – pop. 79 150 – ECD : Wednesday – ✆ 0279.

♦London 22 – ♦Cambridge 37 – ♦Ipswich 20.

 🏨 **Green Man** (T.H.F.), Mulberry Green, Old Harlow, CM17 0ET, E : 2 ¼ m. by A 414 and B 183
  ✆ 442521, Group Telex 817972 – 📺 ⌂wc ☎ 🅿. 🐎 ☒ ☒ ⊙ *VISA*
  M *(closed Saturday lunch to non residents)* 8.75/9.75 **st.** and a la carte 🍷 3.35 – **55 rm**
  ⊊ 45.50/55.50 **st.**

HARNHAM Wilts. 403 404 O 30 – see Salisbury.

HAROME North Yorks. – see Helmsley.

HARPENDEN Herts. 404 S 28 – pop. 28 589 – ECD : Wednesday – ✆ 058 27.

♦London 32 – Luton 6.

 🏨 **Harpenden Moat House** (Q.M.H.), 18 Southdown Rd, AL5 1PE, ✆ 64111, 🐎 – 📺 ☎ 🅿.
  🐎. ☒ ☒ ⊙ *VISA*
  M 9.50/11.50 **st.** and a la carte 🍷 3.50 – ⊊ 4.50 – **56 rm** 41.00/52.00 **st.**, **3 suites** 65.00/75.00 **st.**
  – SB (weekends only) 65.00/70.00 **st.**

 🏨 **Glen Eagle**, 1 Luton Rd, AL5 2PX, ✆ 60271, Telex 925859, 🐎 – ⧆ 📺 ⌂wc ☎ 🅿. 🐎
  51 rm.

FORD,RELIANT,SCIMITAR Southdown Rd ✆ 5217   VAUXHALL-OPEL 17 Luton Rd ✆ 67776
RENAULT 74 High St. ✆ 4545   VOLVO Station Rd ✆ 64311

HARROGATE North Yorks. 402 P 22 – pop. 63 637 – ECD : Wednesday – ✆ 0423.

See : Harlow Car gardens★★ by B 6162 AZ – Envir. : Fountains Abbey★★★ (ruins 12C-13C, floodlit in summer), Studley Royal Gardens★★ – Fountains Hall★ (17C) *AC*, NW : 9 m. by A 61 AY.

☒ Oakdale, off Kent Rd ✆ 67126 AY – ☒ Crimple Valley, Hookstone Wood Rd ✆ 883485 by A 661 CZ.

🛈 Royal Baths Assembly Rooms, Crescent Rd ✆ 525666.

♦London 211 – Bradford 18 – ♦Leeds 15 – ♦Newcastle-upon-Tyne 76 – York 22.

Plan on next page

 🏨 **Majestic** (T.H.F.), Ripon Rd, HG1 2HU, ✆ 68972, Telex 57918, ⊠, 🐎, ✗, squash – ⧆ 📺 ☎
  🅿. 🐎. ☒ ☒ ⊙ *VISA*
  M 7.50/10.50 **st.** and a la carte 🍷 3.40 – ⊊ 6.00 – **156 rm** 49.00/59.00 **st.**, **10 suites**
                               AY **c**

 🏨 **Harrogate International** (Q.M.H.), Kings Rd, HG1 1XX, ✆ 500000, Telex 57575, ≼ – ⧆
  🗐 rest 📺 ☎ 🅿. 🐎. ☒ ☒ ⊙ *VISA*
  closed Christmas – **M** 8.00/8.75 **st.** 🍷 3.50 – **214 rm** ⊊ 50.00/65.00 **st.**, **9 suites** 80.00/90.00 **st.**
  – SB 60.00/68.00 **st.**   BY **x**

 🏨 **Old Swan** (Norfolk Cap.), Swan Rd, HG1 2SR, ✆ 500055, Telex 57922, 🐎, park, ✗ – ⧆ 📺
  ☎ ☎ 🅿. 🐎. ☒ ☒ ⊙ *VISA*
  M 9.00/11.00 **t.** and a la carte 🍷 4.95 – **137 rm** ⊊ 52.50/78.00 **st.**, **10 suites** 130.00/160.00 **st.** –
  SB 70.00 **st.**   AY **e**

 🏨 **Crown** (T.H.F.), Crown Pl., HG1 2RZ, ✆ 67755, Telex 57652 – ⧆ 📺 ☎ 🅿. 🐎. ☒ ☒ ⊙ *VISA*
  M 7.00/11.00 **st.** and a la carte 🍷 3.40 – ⊊ 6.00 – **122 rm** 47.00/57.00 **st.**, **6 suites**.
                               AZ **i**

 🏨 **St. George** (Swallow), 1 Ripon Rd, HG1 2SY, ✆ 61431, Telex 57995, ⊠ – ⧆ 📺 ⌂wc ☎ 🅿.
  🐎. ☒ ☒ ⊙ *VISA*
  M (buffet lunch)/dinner 9.75 **st.** and a la carte 🍷 3.00 – **84 rm** ⊊ 48.00/66.00 **st.** – SB
  65.00/69.00 **st.**   AY **o**

 🏨 **Studley**, 28 Swan Rd, HG1 2SE, ✆ 60425 – ⧆ 🗐 rest 📺 ⌂wc ☎ 🅿. ☒ ☒ ⊙ *VISA* ✗
  M *(closed Monday lunch)* a la carte 9.00/13.75 **t.** 🍷 2.65 – **39 rm** ⊊ 45.00/65.00 **st.**, **2 suites**
  75.00 **st.**   AZ **x**

209

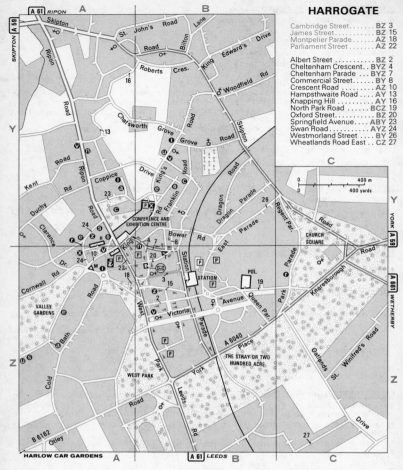

HARROGATE

🏨 **Russell,** 29-35 Valley Drive, HG2 0JN, ✆ 509866 – 💈 📺 ➪wc �𝅘wc ☎. ⟐. ⟐ 🄰🄴 ⓪ 𝘝𝘐𝘚𝘈
    closed 27 to 30 December – **M** (see **Hodgsons** below) – **34 rm** ⟐ 31.25/53.50 st.. **2 suites**
    63.50/69.50 **st.** – SB 61.00/66.00 **st.**   **AZ** **e**

🏨 **Balmoral,** 16-18 Franklin Mount, HG1 5EJ, ✆ 508208, « Antique furnishings » – 📺 ➪wc ☎
    14 rm. 1 suite.   **BY** **v**

🏨 Hospitality Inn (Mt. Charlotte), Prospect Pl., West Park, HE1 1LB, ✆ 64601, Telex 57530 – 💈
    📺 ➪wc 🅰 ⟐. ⟐ 🄰🄴 ⓪ 𝘝𝘐𝘚𝘈   **BZ** **v**
    M (bar lunch Monday to Saturday)/dinner 7.50 🍷 3.00 – **71 rm. 7 suites.**

🏨 **Grants,** 3-7 Swan Rd, HG1 2SS, ✆ 60666 – 💈 🍽 rest 📺 ➪wc ⟐wc ☎ 🕭 ⟐. ⟐ 🄰🄴 ⓪ 𝘝𝘐𝘚𝘈
    🌺   **AY** **s**
    M (bar lunch Saturday and Sunday) 8.95/9.95 **t.** and a la carte 🍷 2.85 – **17 rm** ⟐ 37.50/56.00 **t.**
    – SB 90.00 **st.**

🏠 **Alexandra Court** without rest., 8 Alexandra Rd, HG1 5JS, ✆ 502764 – 📺 ⟐wc ⟐   BY **o**
    12 rm ⟐ 23.00/38.00 **st.**

🏠 **Fern,** Swan Rd, HG1 2SS, ✆ 523866, Telex 57583 – 📺 ➪wc ☎. ⟐ 🄰🄴 ⓪ 𝘝𝘐𝘚𝘈. 🌺   AY **z**
    M (bar lunch)/dinner 14.95 **st.** and a la carte 🍷 2.75 – **28 rm** ⟐ 29.95/56.95 **st.** – SB (except
    summer) 49.95 **st.**

🏠 **Green Park,** Valley Drive, HG2 0JT, ✆ 504681 – 💈 📺 ➪wc ⟐wc 🅰 ⟐. 🏌 ⟐ 🄰🄴 ⓪ 𝘝𝘐𝘚𝘈
    M (bar lunch)/dinner 8.75 **t.** and a la carte – **44 rm** ⟐ 29.00/48.00 **t.** – SB (weekends only)
    47.50/52.50 **st.**   **AZ** **a**

🏠 **White House,** 10 Park Par., HG1 5AH, ℰ 501388 – 📺 ⌕wc ⌕wc ☎ 🅿 ◪ 🅰🄴 ◉ *VISA*
M (lunch by arrangement)/dinner 10.00 **t.** and a la carte ⌗ 3.00 – **15 rm** ⌷ 32.00/43.00 **t.** – SB 43.00 **st.**
CZ r

🏠 **Italia,** 53 King's Rd, HG1 5HJ, ℰ 67404 – 📺 ⌕wc ⌕ 🅿 ⌗ 🅰🄴 ◉ *VISA* ⌗
M *(closed Sunday dinner)* (bar lunch)/dinner 7.50 and a la carte ⌗ 3.50 – **25 rm** ⌷ 23.50/39.00 **s.** – SB (weekends only) 45.00 **st.**
BY u

🏠 **Britannia Lodge,** 16 Swan Rd, HG1 2SA, ℰ 508482 – 📺 ⌕wc ⌕wc 🅿 ◪ *VISA* ⌗ AYZ r
M (dinner only) 8.20 **t.** ⌗ 2.50 – **12 rm** ⌷ 23.00/40.00 **t.** – SB 49.00 **st.**

🏠 **Gables,** 2 West Grove Rd, HG1 2AD, ℰ 505625 – 📺 ⌕wc ⌕wc 🅿 ◪ 🅰🄴 *VISA* ⌗ BY i
M (bar lunch)/dinner 7.50 **t.** ⌗ 3.50 – **9 rm** ⌷ 21.50/43.00 **t.** – SB (weekends only) 50.00 **st.**

↑ **Woodhouse,** 7 Spring Grove, HG1 2HS, ℰ 60081 – 📺 ⌕wc ⌕wc. ⌗ AY a
closed 24 December-2 January – **9 rm** ⌷ 12.00/26.00 **st.**

↑ **Stoney Lea,** 13 Spring Grove, HG1 2HS, ℰ 501524 – 📺 ⌕wc ⌕wc 🅿. ⌗ AY i
closed 2 weeks at Christmas – **6 rm** ⌷ 16.00/28.00 **st.**

↑ **Garden House,** 14 Harlow Moor Drive, HG2 0JX, ℰ 503059 – 📺 ⌕wc ⌕ AZ u
8 rm ⌷ 13.00/28.00 **st.**

↑ **Alvera Court,** 76 Kings Rd, HG1 5JX, ℰ 505735 – 📺 ⌕wc ⌕wc BY e
11 rm.

↑ **Alexa House,** 26 Ripon Rd, HG2 2JJ, ℰ 501988 – 📺 ⌕wc ⌕wc ⌖ 🅿 ◪ *VISA* ⌗ AY n
closed 1 week at Christmas – **16 rm** ⌷ 13.00/32.00 **st.**

↑ **Arden House,** 69-71 Franklin Rd, HG1 5EH, ℰ 509224 – 📺 ⌕wc ☎ 🅿. ⌗ BY c
12 rm ⌷ 14.50/32.00 **t.**

↑ **Wessex,** 22-23 Harlow Moor Drive, HG2 0JY, ℰ 65890 – ⌕wc. ⌗ ◪ *VISA* AZ s
closed December – **13 rm** ⌷ 16.00/32.00 **t.**

↑ **Abbey Lodge,** 29-31 Ripon Rd, HG1 2JL, ℰ 69712 – 📺 ⌕wc ⌕wc 🅿. ⌗ AY v
11 rm ⌷ 13.00/30.00 **st.**

XXX **Hodgson's,** (at Russell H.) 29-35 Valley Drive, HG2 0JN, ℰ 509866 – ◪ 🅰🄴 ◉ *VISA* AY e
M (dinner only) 10.75 **st.** and a la carte 9.20/14.75 **st.** ⌗ 3.95.

XX **Shabab,** 1 John St., HG1 1JZ, ℰ 500250, Indian rest. – ◪ 🅰🄴 ◉ *VISA* BZ z
closed Sunday lunch and Christmas Day – **M** a la carte 5.70/9.20.

XX **Burdekins,** 21 Cheltenham Cres., HG1 1DH, ℰ 502610 – ◪ 🅰🄴 *VISA* BYZ n
closed Sunday and 25-26 December – **M** (dinner only) a la carte 9.70/13.65 **t.** ⌗ 2.45.

XX **Shrimps,** Swan Rd, HG1 2SE, ℰ 508111, Seafood – ▤ ◪ 🅰🄴 ◉ *VISA* AY x
closed Sunday – **M** (dinner only) 7.75 **t.** and a la carte 8.90/13.80 **t.** ⌗ 2.55.

X **Drum and Monkey,** 5 Montpellier Gdns, HG1 2TF, ℰ 502650, Seafood – ◪ *VISA* AZ v
closed Sunday and 24 December-2 January – **M** (booking essential) a la carte 7.35/16.55 **t.**

at Burn Bridge S : 4 m. by A 61 (turn right before junction with A 658) – BZ – ✉ ☎ 0423 Harrogate :

XX **Roman Court,** 55 Burn Bridge Rd, HG3 1PB, ℰ 879933, Italian rest. – 🅿 ◪ 🅰🄴 *VISA*
closed Sunday – **M** (dinner only) 8.50 **t.** and a la carte 9.25/16.60 **t.** ⌗ 3.00.

at Markington NW : 8 ¾ m. by A 61 – AY – ✉ ☎ 0423 Harrogate :

🏛 **Hob Green** ⌕, HG3 3PJ, SW : ½ m. ℰ 770031, Telex 57780, ≤, « Country house in extensive parkland », ⌗ – 📺 ⌕wc 🅿 ◪ 🅰🄴 ◉ *VISA*
M (buffet lunch Monday to Saturday)/dinner 15.00 **t.** ⌗ 3.50 – **11 rm** ⌷ 46.00/65.00 **t.** – SB 80.00 **st.**

AUSTIN-ROVER-DAIMLER-JAGUAR, ROLLS ROYCE 91 Leeds Rd ℰ 871263
FIAT Leeds Rd, Panna ℰ 879236
CITROEN, LANCIA Cheltenham Mount ℰ 68151
FORD Station Par. ℰ 88593

PEUGEOT-TALBOT, VAUXHALL-OPEL West Park ℰ 504601
RENAULT Pannal ℰ 879231
VOLVO East Parade ℰ 64567
VW, AUDI-NSU Ripon Rd ℰ 55141

HARTFORD Cheshire 𝟜𝟘𝟚 𝟜𝟘𝟛 𝟜𝟘𝟜 M 24 – pop. 4 000 – ☎ 0606 Northwich.

▨ Delamere Forest ℰ 0606 (Sandiway) 882807, SW : 2 m.

♦London 188 – Chester 15 – ♦Liverpool 31 – ♦Manchester 25.

🏛 Hartford Hall, School Lane, CW8 1PW, ℰ 75711, ⌗ – 📺 ⌕wc ☎ 🅿
21 rm. 1 suite.

AUDI, VW Station Rd, Northwich ℰ 0606 (Northwich) 6061
CITROEN Manchester Rd, Northwich ℰ 0606 (Northwich) 3816
FORD Chesterway, Northwich ℰ 0606 (Northwich) 6141

RENAULT Runcorn Rd, Barnton ℰ 0606 (Northwich) 77137
PEUGEOT-TALBOT 322 Chester Rd ℰ 0606 (Sandiway) 888188
VAUXHALL-OPEL-BEDFORD 9 London Rd, Northwich ℰ 0606 (Northwich) 3434

211

HARTLEPOOL Cleveland **402** Q 19 – pop. 91 749 – ECD : Wednesday – ✆ 0429.
⟦ﬔ⟧ Seaton Carew, Tees Rd ✆ 266249.
✈ Teesside Airport ✆ 0325 (Darlington) 332811, SW : 20 m.
🗗 H.M.S. Warrior, Coal Dock ✆ 266522 ext 375 – Civic Centre, Victoria Rd ✆ 266522 ext 375.
♦London 263 – Durham 19 – ♦Middlesbrough 9 – Sunderland 21.

 🏨 **Grand,** Swainson St., TS24 8AA, ✆ 266345 – ▮| 🔲 ⚏wc ☎. ⚙. ◪ Æ ⓞ 𝒱𝐼𝒮𝒜. ⚞
  closed 25-26 December and 1 January – **M** (bar lunch Monday to Saturday)/dinner 6.80
  st. and a la carte 🍷 3.05 – **44 rm** ⌷ 29.50/54.50 **st.** – SB (weekends only) 33,00/38.50 **st.**

AUSTIN-ROVER York Rd ✆ 274431   FORD Stockton Rd ✆ 264311
CITROEN Casebourne Rd ✆ 233031

HARTOFT END North Yorks. **402** R 21 – pop. 62 – ⊠ Pickering – ✆ 075 15 Lastingham.
♦London 243 – Scarborough 26 – York 32.

 🏠 **Blacksmith's Arms,** YO18 8EN, ✆ 331 – 🔲 ⚏wc ⓟ. ◪ 𝒱𝐼𝒮𝒜. ⚞
  M (bar lunch)/dinner 9.50 **t.** and a la carte 🍷 3.05 – **12 rm** ⌷ 15.50/40.00 **t.** – SB (October-March)
  40.00/53.00 **st.**

HARWICH and DOVERCOURT Essex **404** X 28 – pop. 17 245 – ECD : Wednesday – ✆ 025 55
(4 fig.) or 0255 (6 fig.).

 ⟦≈⟧ Shipping connections with the Continent : to Germany (Hamburg) (DFDS Seaways) – to
Denmark (Esbjerg) (DFDS Seaways) – from Parkeston Quay to The Netherlands (Hoek van Holland)
(Sealink) – to Sweden (Göteborg) (DFDS Seaways) – to Norway (Kristiansand) (Fred Olsen Lines
KDS) summer only.
 ⟦≈⟧ to Felixstowe (Orwell & Harwich Navigation Co.) 5-8 daily (except weekends)(15 mn).
🗗 Parkeston Quay ✆ 506139 (summer only).
♦London 78 – Chelmsford 41 – Colchester 20 – ♦Ipswich 23.

 🏨 **Tower,** Main Road, Dovercourt, CO12 3PJ, ✆ 504952 – 🔲 ⚏wc ⚏|wc ☎ ⓟ. ◪ Æ ⓞ 𝒱𝐼𝒮𝒜
  M 5.75 **t.** (lunch) and a la carte 9.00/16.25 **t.** – **15 rm** ⌷ 25.00/44.00 **t.**

 🏠 **Cliff,** Marine Par., Dovercourt, CO12 3RE, ✆ 503345, ≼ – 🔲 ⚏wc ⚏| ☎ ⓟ. ◪ Æ ⓞ 𝒱𝐼𝒮𝒜
  ⚞
  M *(closed 25-26 December)* 5.00/7.00 **t.** and a la carte 🍷 2.25 – **30 rm** ⌷ 23.00/40.00 **t.**, **1 suite**
  40.00/60.00 **t.**

 XX **Pier at Harwich,** The Quay, CO12 3HH, ✆ 503363, ≼, Seafood – ◪ Æ ⓞ 𝒱𝐼𝒮𝒜
  M 7.75 **t.** (lunch) and a la carte 10.25/14.00 **t.** 🍷 4.10.

FORD 113 High St., Dovercourt ✆ 0255 502537   SKODA 22 Station Rd ✆ 0255 506006

HASCOMBE Surrey – see Godalming.

HASELBURY PLUCKNETT Somerset **403** L 31 – see Crewkerne.

HASLEMERE Surrey **404** R 30 – pop. 10 544 – ECD : Wednesday – ✆ 0428.
Envir. : Petworth House★★★ 17C (paintings★★★ and carved room★★★) *AC*, SE : 11 m.
♦London 47 – ♦Brighton 46 – ♦Southampton 44.

 🏯 **Lythe Hill** ⟦🐾⟧, Petworth Rd, GU27 3BQ, E : 1 ½ m. on B 2131 ✆ 51251, Telex 858402, ≼, ⟦≈⟧,
  ⟦🌳⟧, park, ⚞ – 🔲 ☎ ⓟ. ⚙. ◪ Æ ⓞ 𝒱𝐼𝒮𝒜
  M a la carte 11.50/17.50 – ⌷ 4.50 – **38 rm** 50.00/75.00 **st.**, **11 suites** 75.00/130.00 **st.** – SB
  (except Bank Holidays) 72.00/77.00 **st.**

 XXX **Auberge de France** (at Lythe Hill H.), Petworth Rd, GU27 3BQ, E : 1 ½ m. on B 2131
  ✆ 51251, Telex 858402, ≼, French rest., ⟦🍴⟧ – ⓟ. ◪ Æ ⓞ 𝒱𝐼𝒮𝒜
  closed Tuesday lunch and Monday – **M** a la carte 12.75/19.00 **t.**

 XX **Morels,** 25-27 Lower St., GU27 2NY, ✆ 51462, French rest. – ◪ Æ ⓞ 𝒱𝐼𝒮𝒜
  *closed Saturday lunch, Sunday, Monday, February, 2 weeks September-October and Bank
  Holidays* – **M** 11.00/13.00 **t.** and a la carte 18.00/21.40 **t.** 🍷 3.00.

 X **Shrimptons,** 2 Grove Cottages, Midhurst Rd, Kingsley Green, GU27 3AL, SW : 1 ¼ m. on
  A 286 ✆ 3539 – ◪ Æ ⓞ 𝒱𝐼𝒮𝒜
  closed Sunday, Christmas Day and 1 January – **M** 14.50 **t.** (dinner) and a la carte 12.00/14.45 **t.**

AUSTIN-ROVER Grayswood Rd ✆ 2303   VAUXHALL-OPEL West St. ✆ 3333
FORD Havenford ✆ 3222   VW, AUDI Hindhead Rd ✆ 53811
PEUGEOT-TALBOT High St. ✆ 52552

HASSELL STREET Kent – see Wye.

HASSOP Derbs. – see Bakewell.

HASTINGS and ST. LEONARDS East Sussex 404 V 31 – pop. 74 979 – ✪ 0424.

See : Norman Castle (ruins) ✳★★ *AC* BZ – Alexandra Park★ AY – White Rocks gardens ≼★ ABZ – Public Museum and Art Gallery (Pottery★, Durbar Hall★) BZ **M**.

🚩 Beauport Park, St. Leonards, ℰ 52977, NW : 3 m. by B 2159 AY.

🖪 4 Robertson Terr. ℰ 424242 – The Fishmarket ℰ 425641 (summer only).

♦London 65 – ♦Brighton 37 – Folkestone 37 – Maidstone 34.

HASTINGS AND ST. LEONARDS

King's Road	**AZ** 22
London Road	**AZ**
Norman Road	**AZ**
Queen's Road	**BZ**
Robertson Street	**BZ** 27
Wellington Place	**BZ** 35

Bourne (The)	**BY** 4
Cambridge Gardens	**BZ** 5
Castle Street	**BZ** 7
Castle Hill Road	**BZ** 8
Cornwallis Gardens	**BZ** 9
Cornwallis Terrace	**BZ** 10
Denmark Place	**BZ** 13
Dorset Place	**BZ** 15
Gensing Road	**AZ** 16
George Street	**BY** 18

Grosvenor Crescent	**AY** 19
Harold Place	**BZ** 20
Marine Court	**AZ** 23
Rock-a-Nore Road	**BY** 30
St. Helen's Park Road	**BY** 31
Sedlescombe Road South	**AY** 32
Silchester Road	**AZ** 33
Warrior Square	**BZ** 34
Wellington Square	**BZ** 36
White Rock Road	**BZ** 38

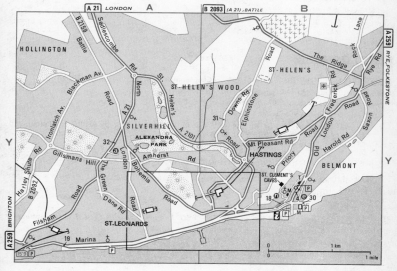

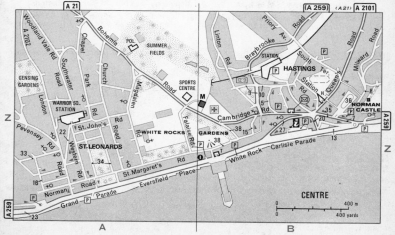

CENTRE

🏨 **Beauport Park** ॐ, Battle Rd, TN38 8EA, NW : 3 ½ m. at junction A 2100 and B 2159 ☎ 51222, Telex 957126, ⇐, « Formal garden », ⅃ heated, park, ⅍ – ▤ rest 📺 ⌂wc ☎ **P**. 🏍 🔝 **AE** ⊙ **VISA** on B 2159 AY
M 8.50/9.95 **st.** and a la carte ⅄ 3.00 – **23 rm** ⌸ 38.00/52.00. **st.** – SB (weekends only) 56.90/62.50 **st.**

↑ **Chimes**, 1 St. Matthews Gdns, Silverhill, TN38 0TS, ☎ 434041, ⅊ – 📺 ⌂wc AY **a**
9 rm.

↑ **Norton Villa,** Hill St., Old Town, TN34 3HU, ☎ 428168, ⇐ – **P**. ⅍ BY **n**
Easter-October – **4 rm** ⌸ 16.00/20.00. **st.**

XX **Röser's,** 64 Eversfield Pl., TN37 6DB, ☎ 712218 – 🔝 **AE** ⊙ **VISA** BZ **i**
closed Saturday lunch, Sunday, first 2 weeks January and Bank Holidays – **M** 9.95 **st.** (lunch) and a la carte 10.25/18.95 **t.** ⅄ 3.00.

X **Coach House,** 60a All Saints St., Old Town, TN34 3BN, ☎ 428080 – 🔝 **AE** ⊙ **VISA** BY **e**
closed lunch Monday to Saturday except December – **M** (dinner only and Sunday lunch)/dinner 12.60 **t.** and a la carte 8.20/12.60 **t.**

AUSTIN-ROVER Sedlescombe Rd North ☎ 754444
CITROEN London Rd ☎ 427746
DAF, VOLVO 100 Battle Rd ☎ 423451
FIAT, LANCIA, MAZDA West Marina ☎ 433533
FORD Bohemia Rd ☎ 422727

LANCIA Sedlescombe Rd North ☎ 440511
PEUGEOT-TALBOT Bexhill Rd ☎ 431276
RENAULT 109-111 Sedlescombe Rd North ☎ 432982
VAUXHALL 36-39 Western Rd, St. Leonards ☎ 424545

HATCH BEAUCHAMP Somerset 🗹🗹🗹 K 30 – see Taunton.

HATFIELD Herts. 🗹🗹🗹🗹 T 28 – pop. 33 174 – ECD : Monday and Thursday – ✪ 070 72.
See : Hatfield House✱✱✱ *AC* (gardens✱ and Old Palace✱).
⛳ Bedwell Park, Essendon ☎ 0707 (Potters Bar) 42624, E : 3 m.
♦London 27 – Bedford 38 – ♦Cambridge 39.

🏨 **Comet** (Embassy), 301 St. Albans Rd West, AL10 9RH, SW : 1 m. by A 1057 at junction with A 1 and A 414 ☎ 65411 – 📺 ⌂wc ☎ **P**. 🏍 🔝 **AE** ⊙ **VISA**
M (carving rest.) 8.00 **st.** ⅄ 2.55 – ⌸ 5.00 – **57 rm** 42.00/47.50 **st.** – SB (weekends only) 50.00 **st.**

XXX **Salisbury,** 15 The Broadway, Old Hatfield, AL9 5JB, ☎ 62220 – 🔝 **AE** ⊙ **VISA**
closed Saturday lunch, Sunday dinner, Monday, first 2 weeks January and Bank Holidays except Christmas Day – **M** 11.50/19.50 **st.** and a la carte 17.05/22.20 **st.** ⅄ 4.95.

ALFA-ROMEO, HONDA, TALBOT, PEUGEOT By-Pass ☎ 64521

AUSTIN-ROVER 1 Great North Rd ☎ 64366
LANCIA 42 Beaconsfield Rd ☎ 71226

HATHERLEIGH Devon 🗹🗹🗹 H 31 – pop. 1 355 – ECD : Wednesday – ✉ ✪ 0837 Okehampton.
⛳ at Okehampton, Tors Rd, ☎ 0837 (Okehampton) 2113, SE : 7 m.
♦London 230 – Exeter 29 – ♦Plymouth 38.

🏨 **George,** Market St., EX20 3JN, ☎ 810454, « 15C inn », ⅃ heated – ⌂wc 🎞wc **P**. 🔝 **VISA**
M (bar lunch)/dinner a la carte 8.55/14.75 **t.** ⅄ 3.65 – **11 rm** ⌸ 23.50/40.00 **t.**

at Sheepwash NW : 5 ½ m. by A 3072 – ✉ Beaworthy – ✪ 040 923 Black Torrington :

🏨 **Half Moon Inn,** The Square, EX21 5NE, ☎ 376, « 17C inn », ⅊ – 📺 ⌂wc **P**. 🔝 **VISA**
closed January and February – **M** (bar lunch)/dinner 9.50 **t.** ⅄ 2.65 – **14 rm** ⌸ 17.50/39.00 **t.** – SB 54.00/60.00 **st.**

HATHERSAGE Derbs. 🗹🗹🗹 🗹🗹🗹 🗹🗹🗹🗹 P 24 – pop. 1 966 – ECD : Wednesday – ✉ Sheffield (South Yorks.) – ✪ 0433 Hope Valley.
♦London 165 – ♦Manchester 33 – ♦Sheffield 10.

🏨 **George** (Whitbread), Main Rd, S30 1BB, ☎ 50436 – 📺 ⌂wc 🍴 **P**. 🔝 **AE** **VISA**
M 8.00 **t.** (lunch) and a la carte 10.80/13.20 **t.** – **18 rm** ⌸ 40.85/49.45 **t.** – SB (weekends only) 60.00 **st.**

↑ **Highlow Hall** ॐ, S30 1AX, S : 1 ½ m. by B 6001 on Abney Rd ☎ 50393, ⇐, ⅊ – **P**
May-October – **6 rm** ⌸ 12.50/18.50 **t.**

AUSTIN-ROVER Main Rd ☎ 50341

HAVANT Hants. 🗹🗹🗹🗹 R 31 – pop. 50 098 – ECD : Wednesday – ✪ 0705.
🄯 1 Park Rd South ☎ 480024 (summer only).
♦London 70 – ♦Brighton 39 – ♦Portsmouth 9 – ♦Southampton 22.

🏨 **Bear** (Whitbread), 15 East St., PO9 1AA, ☎ 486501 – 🔊 📺 ⌂wc 🎞wc ☎ **P**. 🏍 🔝 **AE** ⊙ **VISA**. ⅍
M 8.00/10.00 **t.** and a la carte ⅄ 3.50 – **35 rm** ⌸ 40.00/55.00. **t.** – SB (weekends only) 56.00/70.00 **st.**

FORD New Rd ☎ 482161

214

HAVERFORDWEST (HWLFFORDD) Dyfed **403** F 28 – pop. 13 572 – ECD : Thursday – ✆ 0437.

Envir. : SW : Martin's Haven ※★★ – St. Ann's Head★★ by Dale ≪★.

🖪 Pembrokeshire Coast National Park Centre, 40 High St. ✆ 3110 (summer only).

♦London 250 – Fishguard 15 – ♦Swansea 57.

🏛 **Mariners,** Mariners Sq., SA61 2DU, ✆ 3353 – 🖵 �␣wc 🏦wc ☎ 🅿. 🔼 🅰🅴 ⑩ *VISA*
M (bar lunch Monday to Saturday)/dinner 8.60 **t.** and a la carte 🍴 3.25 – **29 rm** ⬡ 27.00/40.00 **t.**
– SB (weekends only) 45.00/60.00 **st.**

🕿 **Elliotts Hill** 🍴, Crow Hill Rd, SA62 6HT, NW : 1 ½ m. on B 4330 ✆ 4720, 🌫, ※ – 🅿. *VISA*
M 4.50/7.00 **st.** and a la carte approx. 7.55 **st.** 🍴 2.00 – **18 rm** ⬡ 13.00/26.00 **s.** – SB (weekends only)(except June-August) 36.80/39.10 **st.**

AUSTIN-ROVER-DAIMLER-JAGUAR Salutation Sq.   RENAULT Fishguard Rd ✆ 2468
✆ 4511   VAUXHALL-OPEL Bridgend Sq. ✆ 2717
FORD Dew St. ✆ 3772

HAWES North Yorks. **402** N 21 – pop. 1 177 – ✆ 096 97.

🖪 National Park Centre, Station Yard ✆ 450 (summer only).

♦London 253 – Kendal 27 – ♦Leeds 72 – ♦York 65.

🏛 **Simonstone Hall** 🍴, Simonstone, DL8 3LY, N : 1 ½ m. on Muker rd ✆ 255, ≪, « Country house atmosphere », 🌫 – ➣wc 🅿. 🔼 ⑩
M (bar lunch)/dinner 11.75 **t.** and a la carte 🍴 3.20 – **10 rm** ⬡ 21.50/51.00 **t.** – SB (November-mid April, except Easter, Christmas and New Year) 55.50/62.00 **st.**

🏠 **Stone House** 🍴, Sedbusk, DL8 3PT, N : 1 m. by Muker rd on Askrigg rd ✆ 571, 🌫 – 🖵 ➣wc 🏦wc 🅿. *VISA*
Mid March-November, Christmas and New Year – **M** (dinner only) 9.50 **t.** 🍴 2.80 – **12 rm** ⬡ 20.00/40.00 **t.**

𝕏𝕏 **Cockett's** with rm, Market Place, DL8 3RD, ✆ 312 – 🖵 🏦wc. 🔼 *VISA*. ※
closed 10 November-20 December – **M** (dinner only) 15.00 **t.** 🍴 3.50 – **7 rm** ⬡ 25.00/36.50 **t.**

HAWKCHURCH Devon **403** L 31 – see Axminster.

HAWKHURST Kent **404** V 30 – pop. 3 192 – ECD : Wednesday – ✆ 058 05.

Envir. : Bedgebury Pinetum★ *AC*, NW : 2 m.

♦London 47 – Folkestone 34 – Hastings 14 – Maidstone 19.

🏛 **Tudor Arms** (Best Western), Rye Rd, TN18 5DA, E : 1 ½ m. on A 268 ✆ 2312, ≪, « Gardens » – 🖵 ➣wc 🏦wc 🅿. 🔼 🅰🅴 ⑩ *VISA*
M 8.50/9.00 **st.** and a la carte 🍴 3.50 – **13 rm** ⬡ 25.00/58.00 **st.** – SB (except Christmas and Easter) 64.00/69.00 **st.**

AUSTIN-ROVER Horns Rd ✆ 2020

HAWKRIDGE Somerset **403** J 30 – ✉ Dulverton – ✆ 064 385 Winsford.

♦London 203 – Exeter 32 – Minehead 17 – Taunton 32.

🏛 **Tarr Steps** 🍴, TA22 9PY, NE : 1 ½ m. ✆ 293, ≪, ⌇, 🌫, park – ➣wc 🅿. 🅰🅴 *VISA*
Mid March-mid November – **M** (bar lunch Monday to Saturday)/dinner 11.50 **t.** 🍴 2.25 – **15 rm** ⬡ 19.50/39.00 **t.**

HAWKSHEAD Cumbria **402** L 20 – pop. 660 – ECD : Thursday – ✉ Ambleside – ✆ 096 66.

🖪 Brown Cow Laithe ✆ 525 (summer only).

♦London 283 – ♦Carlisle 52 – Kendal 19.

🏛 **Tarn Hows** 🍴, LA22 0PR, NW : 1 ½ m. on Ambleside rd ✆ 330, ≪, ⌛ heated, 🌫, park, ※ – ➣wc ⊗ 🅿. 🔼 🅰🅴 ⑩ *VISA*
closed 12 January-14 February – **M** (bar lunch)/dinner 15.00 **st.** and a la carte 🍴 2.00 – **23 rm** ⬡ 22.00/66.00 **t.** – SB (except summer) 56.00/75.00 **st.**

🏠 **Highfield House** 🍴, Hawkshead Hill, LA22 0PN, W : ½ m. on B 5285 ✆ 344, ≪, 🌫 – 🖵 ➣wc 🅿
11 rm ⬡ 14.00/32.00 **st.**

🏠 **Rough Close** 🍴, LA22 0QF, S : 1½ m. on Newby Bridge road ✆ 370, 🌫 – 🅿. ※
April-October – **6 rm** ⬡ 14.50/25.00 **t.**

at Far Sawrey SE : 2 ½ m. on B 5285 – ✉ Ambleside – ✆ 096 62 Windermere :

🏠 **West Vale,** LA22 0LQ, ✆ 2817, ≪ – 🏦wc 🅿
8 rm ⬡ 11.00/26.50 **t.**

at Grizedale SW : 2 ¾ m. – ✉ Ambleside – ✆ 096 66 Hawkshead :

🏡 **Grizedale Lodge** 🍴, LA22 0QL, ✆ 532 – 🖵 ➣wc 🏦wc 🅿. 🔼 *VISA*. ※
closed January-mid February – **M** (bar lunch)/dinner 9.50 **t.** 🍴 2.50 – **6 rm** ⬡ 18.50/35.00 **t.** – SB (except summer) 39.00/45.00 **st.**

HAWORTH West Yorks. 🔢🔢🔢 O 22 – pop. 5 041 – ECD : Tuesday – ✉ Keighley – ☎ 0535.
See : Brontë Parsonage Museum★ *AC*.
🛈 2-4 West Lane ✆ 42329 – ◆London 213 – Burnley 22 – ◆Leeds 22 – ◆Manchester 34.

- ☆ **Old White Lion**, 6 West Lane, BD22 8DU, ✆ 42313 – 🖵wc ⓜwc 🅿. 🖾 🖾 ⓞ 𝘝𝘐𝘚𝘈
  M (bar lunch)/dinner 7.50 **t.** and a la carte 🈪 3.45 – **11 rm** 🖂 17.50/31.00 **t.** – SB (weekends only)(except Bank Holidays) 28.75/31.25 **st.**

- ✗ **Weaver's**, 15 West Lane, BD22 8DU, ✆ 43822 – 🖾 🖾 𝘝𝘐𝘚𝘈
  closed Sunday dinner, Monday, last week in June, first 2 weeks July and 24 to 31 December –
  M 6.95/7.95 **t.** and a la carte 7.60/14.25 **t.** 🈪 2.60.

HAYDOCK Merseyside 🔢🔢🔢 🔢🔢🔢 🔢🔢🔢 M 23 – pop. 17 372 – ✉ Newton-Le-Willows – ☎ 0942 Ashton-in-Makerfield.
◆London 198 – ◆Liverpool 17 – ◆Manchester 18.

- 🏨 **Post House** (T.H.F.), Lodge Lane, WA12 0JG, NE : 1 m. on A 49 ✆ 717878, Telex 677672 – 📳
  📺 ☎ 🈁 🅿. 🖾 🖾 ⓞ 𝘝𝘐𝘚𝘈
  M 7.40/9.25 **st.** and a la carte 🈪 3.40 – 🖂 5.65 – **98 rm** 49.00/59.00 **st.**

HAYLING ISLAND Hants. 🔢🔢🔢 R 31 – pop. 12 410 – ECD : Wednesday – ☎ 0705.
🛈 32 Seafront ✆ 467111 (summer only) – ◆London 77 – ◆Brighton 45 – ◆Southampton 28.

- 🏨 **Post House** (T.H.F.), Northney Rd, PO11 0NQ, ✆ 465011, Telex 86620, ≼, ⅀ heated – 📺
  🖵wc 🈁 🅿. 🖾 🖾 ⓞ 𝘝𝘐𝘚𝘈
  M 7.95/10.95 **st.** and a la carte 🈪 3.00 – 🖂 5.65 – **96 rm** 48.00/57.00 **st.**

- 🏠 **Newtown House**, Manor Rd, PO11 0QR, ✆ 466131, ⅀ heated, 🚣, ✗ – 📺 🖵wc ⓜwc ☎
  🅿. 🖾 🖾 ⓞ 𝘝𝘐𝘚𝘈. ✼
  closed 24 December-3 January – **M** (closed Monday lunch) 6.25/8.25 **t.** and a la carte 🈪 3.00 –
  26 rm 🖂 32.00/48.00 **t.** – SB (weekends only) 48.00/50.00 **st.**

HAY-ON-WYE Powys 🔢🔢🔢 K 27 – pop. 1 578 – ECD : Tuesday – ☎ 0497.
🛈 Car Park ✆ 820144 (summer only) – ◆London 154 – Brecon 16 – Hereford 21 – Newport 62.

- 🏠 **Old Black Lion**, 26 Lion St., HR3 5AD, ✆ 820841 – 📺 🖵wc ⓜwc 🅿. 🖾
  M a la carte 8.45/9.90 **st.** 🈪 2.75 – **10 rm** 🖂 13.00/35.50 **st.** – SB (except Bank Holidays) 40.00/51.00 **st.**

- ✗ **Lion's Corner House**, 39 Lion St., HR3 5AA, ✆ 820175.

AUSTIN-ROVER, LAND ROVER, RANGE ROVER   FORD Broad St. ✆ 820548
Church St. ✆ 820404

HAYTOR Devon – see Bovey Tracey.

HEACHAM Norfolk 🔢🔢🔢 🔢🔢🔢 V 25 – see Hunstanton.

HEADLAM Durham – see Darlington.

HEATHROW AIRPORT – see Hillingdon (Greater London).

HEDDONS MOUTH Devon 🔢🔢🔢 I 30 – see Lynton.

HELFORD Cornwall 🔢🔢🔢 E 33 – ✉ Helston – ☎ 032 623 Manaccan.
◆London 324 – Falmouth 15 – Penzance 22 – Truro 27.

- ✗✗ **Riverside** ⌂ with rm, TR12 6JU, ✆ 443, ≼, « Converted cottages in picturesque setting »,
  🚣 – 📺 🖵wc 🅿. ✼
  Mid March-October – **M** (closed lunch to non-residents) (booking essential)/dinner 25.00 **st.**
  🈪 4.00 – **7 rm** 45.00/67.00 **st.**

  at Gillan S : 3 m. – ✉ Helston – ☎ 032 623 Manaccan :

  - 🏠 **Tregildry** ⌂, TR12 6HG, ✆ 378, ≼, 🚣 – 🖵wc 🅿. 🖾 𝘝𝘐𝘚𝘈
    Easter-October – **M** (bar lunch)/dinner 9.50 **t.** and a la carte 🈪 2.75 – **11 rm** 🖂 20.00/50.00 **t.**

HELMSLEY North Yorks. 🔢🔢🔢 Q 21 – pop. 1 399 – ECD : Wednesday – ☎ 0439.
See : Castle★ (ruins 12C) *AC* – Envir. : Rievaulx Abbey★★ (ruins 12C-13C) *AC*, NW : 2 ½ m. –
Byland Abbey★ (ruins 12C) SW : 6 m. by Ampleforth.
🛈 9 Church St. ✆ 70401.
◆London 234 – ◆Middlesbrough 29 – York 24.

- 🏨 **Black Swan** (T.H.F.), Market Pl., YO6 5BJ, ✆ 70466, « 16C inn », 🚣 – 📺 🅿. 🈁 🖾 🖾 ⓞ
  𝘝𝘐𝘚𝘈
  M 9.00/13.50 **st.** and a la carte 🈪 3.80 – 🖂 5.65 – **38 rm** 46.00/60.00 **st.**

- 🏠 **Feversham Arms** (Best Western), 1 High St., YO6 5AG, ✆ 70766, 🚣, ✗ – 📺 🖵wc 🌐
  🅿. 🈁 🖾 🖾 ⓞ 𝘝𝘐𝘚𝘈
  M (bar lunch Tuesday to Saturday)/dinner 15.00 **t.** 🈪 4.50 – **20 rm** 🖂 37.00/48.00 **t.** – SB 50.00/64.00 **st.**

⚘ **Feathers,** Market Pl., YO6 5BH, ☎ 70275, ⇗ – 📺 ⛉wc ⛉wc 🅿. ⬛ 🆎 ⑩ 𝑉𝐼𝑆𝐴
closed 2 weeks Christmas and New Year – **M** 5.50/9.50 **t.** and a la carte ⑃ 3.00 – **18 rm**
⊊ 16.00/38.00 **st.** – SB (October-June) 42.00/47.00 **st.**

⚘ **Crown,** Market Pl., YO6 5BJ, ☎ 70297, ⇗ – 📺 ⛉wc ⇐⇒ 🅿. ⬛ 𝑉𝐼𝑆𝐴
M 4.90/8.60 **t.** ⑃ 2.90 – **15 rm** ⊊ 18.50/41.00 **t.** – SB (except summer) 43.50/48.50 **st.**

⌂ **Beaconsfield,** Bondgate, YO6 5BW, ☎ 71346 – 📺 🅿. ⅍
6 rm ⊊ 16.00/27.00 **st.**

at Harome E : 2 ½ m. by A 170 – ⊠ York – ✪ 0439 Helmsley :

🏛 **Pheasant,** YO6 5JG, ☎ 71241 – 📺 ⛉wc 🅿
closed January and February – **M** (bar lunch)/dinner 11.00 **t.** – **11 rm** ⊊ 25.00/40.00 **t.**

at Nawton E : 3 ¼ m. on A 170 – ⊠ York – ✪ 0439 Helmsley :

⌂ **Plumpton Court,** High St., YO6 5TT, ☎ 71223, ⇗ – ⛉wc 🅿. ⅍
March-October – **8 rm** ⊊ 16.00/25.00 **st.**

at Nunnington SE : 6 ¼ m. by A 170 off B 1257 – ⊠ York – ✪ 043 95 Nunnington :

XX **Ryedale Lodge** ⅏ with rm, YO6 5XB, W : 1 m. ☎ 246, ≼, « Converted railway station »,
⅌, ⇘, – 📺 ⛉wc 🅿. ⬛ 𝑉𝐼𝑆𝐴. ⅍
closed January – **M** (dinner only) 16.75 **t.** ⑃ 2.75 – **7 rm** ⊊ 35.50/54.00 **t.** – SB 70.00/78.00 **st.**

▮**HELSTON**▮ Cornwall **403** E 33 ✪ 0326.
♦London 311 – Falmouth 13 – Penzance 13 – ♦Plymouth 71.

🏮 **Nansloe Manor** ⅏, Meneage Rd, TR13 0SB, ☎ 574691, ⇗ – 📺 ⛉wc ⛉wc ☎ 🅿. ⬛
𝑉𝐼𝑆𝐴
closed 24 to 28 December – **M** (bar lunch Monday to Saturday)/dinner a la carte 9.10/14.00 **t.**
⑃ 2.45 – **7 rm** ⊊ 15.00/48.00 **t.** – SB (November-March) 45.00 **st.**

▮**HEMEL HEMPSTEAD**▮ Herts. **404** S 28 – pop. 80 110 – ECD : Wednesday – ✪ 0442.
▮18▮ Little Hay, Little Hay Farm, Bovington ☎ 833798 off A 41 at Box Lane.
🛈 Pavilion, Marlowes ☎ 64451.
♦London 30 – Aylesbury 16 – Luton 10 – Northampton 46.

🏛 **Post House** (T.H.F.), Breakspear Way, HP2 4UA, E : 2 ½ m. by A 414 on A 4147 ☎ 51122,
Telex 826902, ⇗ – ⅻ 📺 ⛉wc ☎ 🅿. ⬛. ⬛ 🆎 ⑩ 𝑉𝐼𝑆𝐴
M 7.50/9.50 **st.** and a la carte ⑃ 3.40 – ⊊ 5.65 – **107 rm** 48.50/58.50 **st.**

X **Casanova,** 75 Waterhouse St., HP1 1LE, ☎ 47482, Italian rest. – ⬛ 🆎 ⑩ 𝑉𝐼𝑆𝐴
closed Saturday lunch, Sunday and Bank Holidays – **M** a la carte 11.45/14.15 **t.** ⑃ 2.60.

at Bourne End W : 2 ¼ m. on A 41 – ⊠ Hemel Hempstead – ✪ 044 27 Berkhamsted :

🏛 **Hemel Hempstead Moat House** (Q.M.H.), London Rd, HP1 2RJ, ☎ 71241 – 📺 ⛉wc ⇐
🅿. ⬛. ⬛ 🆎 ⑩ 𝑉𝐼𝑆𝐴
M 7.75/8.25 **st.** and a la carte ⑃ 3.00 – **40 rm** ⊊ 38.50/46.50 **st.** – SB (weekends only)
52.00/56.00 **st.**

AUSTIN-ROVER London Rd ☎ 42841
BEDFORD, FIAT, VAUXHALL-OPEL Two Waters Rd
☎ 51212

FORD Redbourne Rd ☎ 63013
PEUGEOT-TALBOT High St. ☎ 54561/50401
TOYOTA Queensway ☎ 51466

▮**HENDY-GWYN**▮ = Whitland.

▮**HENLADE**▮ Somerset – see Taunton.

▮**HENLEY-IN-ARDEN**▮ Warw. **403** **404** O 27 – pop. 2 636 – ECD : Thursday – ✪ 056 42.
♦London 104 – ♦Birmingham 15 – Stratford-upon-Avon 8 – Warwick 8.5.

🏛 **Yew Trees,** 154 High St., B95 5BN, ⊠ Solihull ☎ 4636, Telex 334264, ⅏ heated, ⇗ – 📺
⛉wc ⛉wc ☎ 🅿. ⬛ 🆎 ⑩ 𝑉𝐼𝑆𝐴. ⅍
M 9.00/11.00 **t.** and a la carte ⑃ 3.95 – **8 rm** ⊊ 48.00/70.00 **t.** – SB (weekends only)
68.00/76.00 **st.**

⌂ **Ashleigh House,** Whitley Hill, B95 5DL, E : 1 ¾ m. on B 4095 ☎ 2315, ⇗ – 📺 ⛉wc 🅿. ⅍
10 rm ⊊ 20.00/35.00 **st.**

XX Beaudesert, Birmingham Rd, B95 5QR, ⊠ Solihull N : 1 m. on A 34 ☎ 2675 – 🅿.

XX **Le Filbert Cottage,** 64 High St., B95 5BX, ☎ 2700, French rest. – ⬛ 🆎 ⑩ 𝑉𝐼𝑆𝐴
closed Sunday and Bank Holidays, except Christmas Day lunch – **M** 8.50/20.00 **t.** and a la
carte 13.70/17.40 **t.**

at Claverdon E : 3 m. on B 4095 – ⊠ Henley-in-Arden – ✪ 092 684 Claverdon :

🏮 **Ardencote Country** ⅏, Shrewley Rd, CV35 8LT, N : ½ m. by Lyle Green ☎ 3111, ⬛, ⇗,
⅍ – 📺 ⛉wc ☎ 🅿. ⬛ ⑩ 𝑉𝐼𝑆𝐴
closed 24,25,31 December and 1 January – **M** (bar lunch Monday to Saturday)/dinner a la
carte 9.00/10.50 **st.** ⑃ 2.00 – ⊊ 4.05 – **11 rm** 30.00/35.00 **s.** – SB 54.50/59.50 **st.**

HENLEY-ON-THAMES Oxon. **404** R 29 – pop. 10 910 – ECD : Wednesday – ☎ 0491.

Envir. : Greys Court★ *AC*, NW : 2 ½ m.

🏌 Huntercombe, Nuffield ℰ 641207, W : 6 m. on A 423.

🛈 Town Hall, Market Place ℰ 578034.

◆London 40 – ◆Oxford 23 – Reading 9.

🏨 **Red Lion,** Hart St., RG9 2AR, ℰ 572161, ←, – 📺 ⌂wc ☎ 🅿. 🝇 🝓 VISA. ⁝
M 8.50/10.00 **st.** and a la carte – **27 rm** ⌷ 28.00/60.00 **st.** – SB (weekends only)(November-April) 50.00/55.00 **st.**

🏨 **Regency House** without rest., 4 River Terr., RG9 1BG, ℰ 571133, ←, – 📺 ⌂wc 🛋wc ☎. 🝓 VISA. ⁝
closed 25 and 26 December – **M** (booking essential) 17.50 **st.** ▮ 2.80 – **6 rm** ⌷ 35.00/58.00 **st.** – SB (weekends only) 60.00/90.00 **st.**

🏠 **Thamesmead House,** Remenham Lane, RG9 2LR, E : ½ m. by A 423 ℰ 574745 – 🛋wc 🅿.
🝓 VISA
8 rm ⌷ 17.50/37.50 **t.**

XX **Flohr's** with rm, 15 Northfield End, RG9 2JG, ℰ 573412 – 📺 🝇 🝓 ⓞ VISA
M (closed Sunday dinner) 8.50/14.50 **t.** and a la carte – **9 rm** ⌷ 21.50/59.00 **t.**

XX **Gaylord Tandoori,** 60 Bell St., RG9 2BN, ℰ 575157, Indian rest.

X **Chef Peking,** 10 Market Pl., RG9 2AH, ℰ 578681, Chinese-Peking rest. – 🍽.

at Fawley (Bucks.) N : 3 ½ m.by A 4155 – ✉ Henley-on-Thames – ☎ 049163 Turville Heath :

X **Walnut Tree,** Fawley Green, RG9 6JE, ℰ 360 – 🅿. 🝇 VISA
closed Christmas Day – **M** a la carte 7.30/11.95 **t.**

at Frieth (Bucks.) NE : 7 ½ m. by A 4155 – ✉ Henley-on-Thames – ☎ 0494 High Wycombe :

X **Yew Tree,** RG9 6RJ, ℰ 882330 – 🅿. 🝇 🝓 ⓞ VISA
M (booking essential) 9.50/10.50 **t.** and a la carte.

BMW 49 Station Rd ℰ 577933   FIAT 66 Bell St. ℰ 573077

🖙 To go a long way quickly, use **Michelin maps** at a scale of 1:1 000 000.

HEREFORD Heref. and Worc. **403** L 27 – pop. 48 277 – ECD : Thursday – ☎ 0432.

See : Cathedral★★ 12C-13C (the Mappa Mundi★ 13C) A **A** – The Old House★ 17C A **B**.

Envir. : Abbey Dore★ (12C-17C) SW : 12 m. by A 465 B.

🏌 Holmer Rd ℰ 271639. B.

🛈 Shirehall, 1a St. Owen St. ℰ 268430.

◆London 133 – ◆Birmingham 51 – ◆Cardiff 56.

HEREFORD

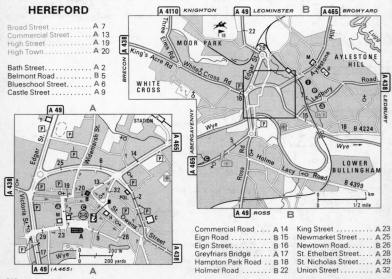

🏛 **Green Dragon** (T.H.F.), Broad St., HR4 9BG, ℰ 272506, Telex 35491 – 🛊 ⌷ 📺 ⇔ – 🔬 ⅏. 🔼 🖭
⊙ 💳 A a
M 5.75/11.50 **st.** and a la carte 🍴 3.40 – � 5.65 – **88 rm** 43.00/52.00 **st.**, **1 suite**.

🏛 **Hereford Moat House** (Q.M.H.), Belmont Rd, HR2 7BP, SW : 1 ½ m. on A 465 ℰ 54301 –
📺 ⌷wc 🔥 🔥 ⅏ ⅏. 🔬 🔼 ⅏ 💳 🖭 B c
M *(closed lunch Saturday and Bank Holidays)* 7.50/9.00 **st.** and a la carte 🍴 2.95 – **32 rm**
⊏⊐ 39.00/48.00 **st.** – SB (weekends only) 55.00 **st.**

🏚 **Litchfield Lodge**, 32 Bodenham Rd, HR1 2TS, ℰ 273258 – 📺 ⌷wc 🎋wc ⅏. 🛇 B e
14 rm.

🏠 **Ferncroft**, 144 Ledbury Rd, HR1 2TB, ℰ 265538, 🌺 – 📺 🎋wc ⅏. 🔼 💳. 🛇 B a
closed mid December-mid January – **11 rm** ⊏⊐ 14.00/35.00 **t.**

🏠 **Somerville**, 12 Bodenham Rd, HR1 2TS, ℰ 273991, 🌺 – 📺 🎋wc ⅏. 🛇 B i
10 rm ⊏⊐ 13.50/33.50 **st.**

✕ **Effy's**, 96 East St., HR1 2LW, ℰ 59754 – 🔼 🔼 ⊙ 💳 A c
closed Sunday and Bank Holidays – **M** (buffet lunch in summer)/dinner 16.00 **t.** and a la carte
11.50 **s.** 🍴 3.50.

at Dormington E : 5 ¼ m. on A 438 – B – ✉ ✪ 0432 Hereford :

🏚 **Dormington Court**, HR1 4DA, ℰ 850370, 🍃, 🌺 – 📺 ⅏. 🔬 🔼 🔼 ⊙ 💳
M (restricted lunch)/dinner a la carte approx. 9.10 **t.** 🍴 2.75 – **6 rm** ⊏⊐ 15.00/24.00 **t.** – SB
37.00/39.00 **st.**

at Much Birch S : 5 ½ m. on A 49 – B – ✉ Hereford – ✪ 0981 Golden Valley :

🏛 **Pilgrim**, HR2 8HJ, on A 49 ℰ 540742, ≼, 🌺 – 📺 ⌷wc 🎋wc 🕿 ⅏. 🔬 🔼 🔼 ⊙ 💳
closed 28 December-8 January – **M** 12.00 **t.** and a la carte 🍴 3.10 – **18 rm** ⊏⊐ 37.50/55.00 **t.** –
SB 64.00/70.00 **st.**

ALFA ROMEO, SUBARU Conningsby St. ℰ 53471
AUSTIN-ROVER Callow G 92 ℰ 273074
BEDFORD, OPEL-VAUXHALL Blackfriars St. ℰ
267441
BMW White Cross Rd ℰ 272589
CITROEN 38 St. Martin St. ℰ 272545
DAIHATSU ℰ 441
FIAT Bath St. ℰ 274134
FORD Commercial Rd ℰ 276494
HONDA Steels Corner ℰ 267151
LADA, SAAB Kings Acre Rd ℰ 266974

LANCIA Whitestone ℰ 850464
LAND ROVER, RANGE ROVER Muchgowarne ℰ
053186(Bosbury)605
PEUGEOT-TALBOT 101-105 St. Owen St. ℰ 276268
RELIANT Bridge St. ℰ 272341
SKODA, SCIMITAR ℰ 272341
TOYOTA Mill St. ℰ 276727
VOLVO 14-15 Commercial Rd ℰ 276275
VW, AUDI Harrow Rd ℰ 59234
YUGO ℰ 056884(Boddenham)337

HERNE BAY Kent 👰 X 29 – pop. 26 523 – ECD : Thursday – ✪ 0227.
Envir. : Reculver (church twin towers★ *AC*) E : 3 m.
🛈 William St. ℰ 361911.
◆London 63 – ◆Dover 24 – Maidstone 32 – Margate 13.

🏠 **Northdown**, 14 Cecil Park, CT6 6DL, ℰ 372051, 🌺 – 📺 ⅏. 🛇
5 rm ⊏⊐ 13.00/28.00 **st.**

✕ **L'Escargot**, 22 High St., CT6 5LH, ℰ 372876 – 🔼 💳
*closed lunch Saturday and Bank Holidays, Sunday except dinner in summer and 2 weeks
February* – **M** 6.80/7.80 **t.** and a la carte 🍴 2.80.

HERSTMONCEUX East Sussex 👰 U 31 – pop. 2 246 – ✪ 032 181 (4 fig.) or 0323 (6 fig.).
See : Castle 15C (home of the Royal Greenwich Observatory) site and grounds★★ *AC*.
Envir. : Michelham Priory (site★) *AC*, SW : 6 m.
◆London 63 – Eastbourne 12 – Hastings 14 – Lewes 16.

✕✕ **Sundial**, Gardner St., BN27 4LA, ℰ 832217, French rest., « Converted 16C cottage », 🌺 –
⅏. 🔼 ⊙ 💳
closed Sunday dinner, Monday, mid August-10 September and 25 December-20 January – **M**
12.50/16.50 **t.** and a la carte 16.45/20.70 **t.** 🍴 3.50.

at Boreham Street SE : 2 m. on A 271 – ✉ ✪ 0323 Herstmonceux :

🏛 **White Friars** (Best Western), Boreham St., BN27 4SE, ℰ 832355, 🌺 – 📺 ⌷wc 🕿 ⅏. 🔼
🔼 ⊙ 💳
closed 1 to 29 January – **M** (bar lunch Monday and Tuesday) 6.50/7.50 **st.** and a la carte 🍴 3.85
– **20 rm** ⊏⊐ 29.50/52.00 **st.** – SB 57.00/68.00 **st.**

AUSTIN-ROVER Boreham St. ℰ 832353   FIAT Cowbeech ℰ 833321

HERTFORD Herts. 👰 T 28 – pop. 21 350 – ECD : Thursday – ✪ 0992.
🛈 Vale House, 43 Cowbridge ℰ Bishop' Stortford (0279) 55261 ext 487.
◆London 24 – ◆Cambridge 35 – Luton 26.

✕✕ **Marquee**, 1 Bircherley Green, SG14 1BN, ℰ 558999 – 🔼 🔼 ⊙ 💳
M 7.50 **t.** (lunch) and a la carte 12.25/22.75 **t.**

AUSTIN-ROVER First Av. ℰ Harlow (0279) 27541   PEUGEOT-TALBOT North Rd ℰ 53044

HERTINGFORDBURY Herts. 404 T 28 – pop. 658 – ⊠ ❀ 0992 Hertford.

♦London 26 – Luton 18.

🏨 **White Horse** (T.H.F.), Hertingfordbury Rd, SG14 2LB, ✆ 56791, 🐎 – 📺 ⊟wc ☎ 🅿 🏌.
🔄 AE ⓪ VISA
M 9.60/10.95 **st.** and a la carte 🍴 3.40 – ⊊ 5.65 – **30 rm** 46.00/57.00 **st.**

HESWALL Merseyside 402 403 K 24 – pop. 31 037 – ECD : Wednesday – ⊠ Wirral – ❀ 051 Liverpool.

♦London 223 – Birkenhead 6.5 – Chester 12 – ♦Liverpool 9 – ♦Manchester 48.

XX Les Bougies, 106 Telegraph Rd, L60 0AQ, ✆ 342 6673 – 🅿.

HETHERSETT Norfolk 404 X 26 – see Norwich.

HEVERSHAM Cumbria 402 L 21 – pop. 741 – ECD : Thursday and Saturday – ⊠ ❀ 044 82 Milnthorpe.

♦London 259 – Kendal 6 – Lancaster 15.

🏨 **Blue Bell,** The Princes' Way, LA7 7EE, on A 6 ✆ 3159, 🐎 – 📺 ⊟wc 🎏wc 🅿 🔄 AE VISA
closed 25 and 26 December – **M** 5.50/11.00 **st.** and a la carte 🍴 2.75 – **26 rm** ⊊ 30.00/41.00 **st.**
– SB (weekends only)(October-June) 50.00/52.00 **st.**

HEXHAM Northumb. 401 402 N 19 – pop. 8 914 – ECD : Thursday – ❀ 0434.

See : Abbey Church★ 13C – Envir. : Hadrian's Wall★★ with its forts and milecastles (Chesters Fort★, museum *AC*) NW : 5 ½ m. – Housesteads Fort★★, museum *AC*, NW : 14 m. – Derwent Reservoir (site★) SE : 7 m. – Vindolanda★ (fort and town) *AC*, NW : 14 ½ m.

🏌 Spital Park ✆ 603072.

🅩 The Manor Office, Hallgate ✆ 605225.

♦London 304 – ♦Carlisle 37 – ♦Newcastle-upon-Tyne 21.

🏨 **Beaumont,** Beaumont St., NE46 3LT, ✆ 602331 – 📺 ⊟wc 🎏wc ☎ 🏌 🔄 AE ⓪ VISA 🛎
M 6.25/7.95 **st.** and a la carte 🍴 3.25 – **20 rm** ⊊ 25.00/37.00 **st.**

🏠 **County,** Priestpopple, NE46 1PS, ✆ 602030 – 📺 🎏wc. 🔄 AE VISA
M 6.50/14.00 **t.** and a la carte 🍴 2.90 – **10 rm** ⊊ 20.00/34.00 **t.** – SB (weekends only)(winter only) 40.00 **st.**

X **Pine Kitchen,** Battle Hill, NE46 1BB, ✆ 606688 – 🔄 AE ⓪ VISA
closed Tuesday dinner except July-September – **M** 6.50 **t.** (lunch) and a la carte 5.55/11.50 **t.**
🍴 2.30.

at Wall N : 4 m. on A 6079 – ⊠ Hexham – ❀ 043 481 Humshaugh :

🏩 **Hadrian,** NE46 4EE, ✆ 232, 🐎 – 📺 ⊟wc 🎏 🅿 🔄
M 6.75 **st.** (lunch) and a la carte 7.50/11.90 **st.** 🍴 2.85 – **9 rm** ⊊ 18.00/38.00 **st.** – SB 46.00/56.00 **st.**

at Langley W : 8 m. by B 6305 on A 686 – ⊠ Hexham – ❀ 043484 Haydon Bridge :

🏨 **Langley Castle** 🦢, NE47 5LU, ✆ 8888, ≤, « 14C castle », 🐎, park – 📺 ⊟wc ☎ 🅿 🔄 AE VISA
M 8.50/12.50 **t.** and a la carte 🍴 4.00 – **8 rm** 30.25/57.50 **t.**

AUSTIN-ROVER Alemouth Rd ✆ 605151
FIAT Tyne Mills ✆ 603013
FORD Priestpopple ✆ 603516
MAZDA Tynemills ✆ 605544
NISSAN Haugh Lane ✆ 604527

RENAULT West Rd ✆ 603861
SUZUKI Priestpopple ✆ 603615
VAUXHALL Parkwell ✆ 602411
VOLVO Gilesgate ✆ 605825

HEYSHAM Lancs. 402 L 21 – ECD : Wednesday – ❀ 0524.

🛥 to the Isle of Man : Douglas (Isle of Man Steam Packet Co.) 2-3 daily (3 h 45 mn).

♦London 251 – ♦Blackpool 33 – ♦Carlisle 74 – Lancaster 8.

↖ **Carr Garth,** 18 Bailey Lane, LA3 2PS, ✆ 51175, 🐎 – 🅿
Easter-mid October – **10 rm** ⊊ 9.25/16.50.

HIGHAM Derbs. 402 403 404 P 24 – pop. 4 803 (inc. Shirland) – ⊠ ❀ 0773 Alfreton.

♦London 147 – Derby 16 – ♦Nottingham 20 – ♦Sheffield 20.

🏠 **Higham Farm,** Main Rd, DE5 6EH, on B 6013 ✆ 833812, 🦃 – 📺 ⊟wc 🎏wc 🐎 🅿 🔄 AE ⓪ VISA
M 5.50/8.95 **t.** 🍴 3.40 – **12 rm** ⊊ 35.50/49.50 – SB (weekends only) 48.40/65.40 **st.**

HIGHCLERE Hants. 403 404 P 29 – pop. 1 939 – ⊠ Newbury (Berks.) – ❀ 0635.

♦London 65 – ♦Oxford 31 – ♦Southampton 32 – Swindon 32.

XX **Yew Tree Inn** with rm, Andover Rd, RG15 9SE, on A 343 ✆ 253360 – 📺 ⊟wc 🎏wc 🅿 🔄 VISA 🛎
M (lunch by arrangement) 14.95 **t.** – **4 rm** ⊊ 28.00/34.00 **t.**

HIGH EASTER Essex **404** V 28 – see Chelmsford.

HIGH OFFLEY Salop **402 403 404** N 25 – see Newport.

HIGHWORTH Wilts. **403 404** O 29 – pop. 8 020 – ✆ 0367 Faringdon.
♦London 88 – Gloucester 33 – ♦Oxford 25 – Swindon 5.

 ✗✗ **Inglesham Forge,** SN6 7QY, N : 2 ½ m. by A 361 ☞ 52298 – ℗. 🖾 AE ⓪ VISA
  *closed lunch Monday and Saturday, Sunday, last 2 weeks August, 25 to 31 December and
  Bank Holidays* – **M** 10.50 **st.** (lunch) and a la carte 13.50/19.00 **st.**

HIGH WYCOMBE Bucks. **404** R 29 – pop. 69 575 – ECD : Wednesday – ✆ 0494.
Envir. : Hughenden Manor★ (site★, Disraeli Museum) *AC*, N : 1 m. – West Wycombe (Manor
House★ 18C, *AC*, St. Lawrence's Church : from the tower 74 steps, *AC*, ☀★) NW : 2 ½ m.
🛈 Council Offices, Queen Victoria Rd ☞ 26100.
♦London 34 – Aylesbury 17 – ♦Oxford 26 – Reading 18.

 🏨 **Crest** (Crest), Crest Rd, HP11 1TL, SW : 1 ½ m. by A 404 ☞ 442100, Telex 83626 – 📺 ⇌wc
  ☎ & ℗. 🖾 AE ⓪ VISA. 🛠
  M 8.95/11.95 **st.** and a la carte 🍷 6.25 – ⇌ 6.30 – **108 rm** 54.50/65.00 **st.** – SB (weekends only)
  60.00/68.00 **st.**

 ✗✗ Peking Chef, 21a High St., ☞ 21644, Chinese-Peking rest.

MICHELIN Distribution Centre, Thomas Rd, Wooburn Green, HP10 0PE, ☞ 06285 (Bourne End)
27472

TOYOTA Littleworth Rd, Downley ☞ 35811   VAUXHALL-OPEL West Wycombe Rd ☞ 32545
VAUXHALL-OPEL London Rd ☞ 30021

HILLSFORD BRIDGE Devon – see Lynton.

HINCKLEY Leics. **402 403 404** P 26 – pop. 35 510 – ECD : Thursday – ✆ 0455.
♦London 103 – ♦Birmingham 31 – ♦Coventry 12 – ♦Leicester 14.

 🏨 **Sketchley Grange** 🦢, Sketchley Lane, Burbage, LE10 3HU, SE : 2 m. by A 447 ☞ 634251,
  🛠 – 📺 ⇌wc 🛏wc ☎ ℗. 🖾 AE ⓪ VISA
  M *(closed Sunday)* (dinner only) 9.00 **t.** and a la carte 🍷 3.40 – **10 rm** ⇌ 31.00/40.00 **t.** – SB
  (weekends only) 50.00/60.00 **st.**

HINDHEAD Surrey **404** R 30 – pop. 6 174 – ECD : Wednesday – ✆ 042 873.
See : Devil's Punch Bowl (≼★).
♦London 46 – Guildford 12 – ♦Portsmouth 28.

 🏨 Hindhead Motor without rest., GU26 6TF, on A 3 Portsmouth Rd ☞ 6666 – 📺 ⇌wc ☎ ℗.
  🛏 – **16 rm**.

HINDON Wilts. **403 404** N 30 – pop. 489 – ECD : Saturday – ✉ Salisbury – ✆ 074 789.
♦London 107 – Bath 28 – Bournemouth 40 – Salisbury 15.

 🏨 **Lamb at Hindon,** SP3 6DP, ☞ 225, 🛠 – ⇌wc ℗. 🖾. 🛠
  closed 25 and 26 December – **M** 8.50/11.50 **t.** and a la carte 🍷 3.20 – **16 rm** ⇌ 18.00/40.00 **st.**
  – SB (October-March) 44.00/50.00 **st.**

HINTLESHAM Suffolk **404** X 27 – pop. 554 – ✆ 047 387.
♦London 76 – Colchester 18 – ♦Ipswich 5.

 ✗✗✗ **Hintlesham Hall** 🦢 with rm, IP8 3NS, ☞ 268, ≼, « Georgian country house with 16C
  origins », 🛠, park, ✗ – 📺 ⇌wc ☎ ℗. 🛈. 🖾 AE ⓪ VISA. 🛠
  closed Saturday lunch and 26 January-9 February – **M** 13.95/23.00 **st.** and a la carte
  16.95/22.20 **st.** 🍷 3.95 – **11 rm** ⇌ 45.00/105.00 **st.** – SB (except summer) 87.50/115.00 **st.**

HITCHIN Herts. **404** T 28 – pop. 33 480 – ECD : Wednesday – ✆ 0462.
🛈 Library, Paynes Park ☞ 34738 and 50133 – ♦London 40 – Bedford 14 – ♦Cambridge 26 – Luton 9.

 🏨 **Sun,** Sun St., SG5 1AF, ☞ 32092 – 📺 ⇌wc 🛏wc ☎ ℗. 🛈. 🖾 AE ⓪ VISA. 🛠
  M (carving rest.) 5.65 **t.** – **32 rm** ⇌ 35.50/45.50 **t.**

 🏨 **Lord Lister,** Park St., SG4 9AH, ☞ 32712 – 📺 ⇌wc 🛏 ℗. 🖾 AE ⓪ VISA. 🛠
  M (dinner only) a la carte approx. 7.05 **t.** 🍷 2.60 – **21 rm** ⇌ 22.00/45.00 **t.** – SB (weekends only)
  45.00 **st.**

 ✗ Raj Douth, 19a Hermitage Rd, 37674, Indian rest.

 at Little Wymondley SE : 2 ½ m. on A 602 – ✉ Hitchin – ✆ 0438 Stevenage :

 ✗✗ **Redcoats Farmhouse** 🦢 with rm, Redcoats Green, SG4 7JR, S : ½ m. by A 602 ☞ 729500,
  « Part 15C farmhouse », 🛠 – ⇌wc ℗. 🖾 AE ⓪ VISA. 🛠
  closed Christmas and New Year – **M** *(closed Sunday and Bank Holidays)* a la carte 13.50/18.75 **t.**
  🍷 2.75 – **15 rm** ⇌ 21.00/48.00 **st.** – SB (weekends only) 60.00/67.00 **st.**

AUSTIN-ROVER Queen St. ☞ 50311   CITROEN High St., Graveley ☞ 0438 (Stevenage)
                                         316177

HOLFORD Somerset 408 K 30 – pop. 266 – ✉ Bridgwater – ☎ 027 874.

Envir. : Stogursey Priory Church★★, W : 4 ½ m.

◆London 171 – ◆Bristol 48 – Minehead 15 – Taunton 22.

🏛 **Combe House** ⟨⟩, TA5 1RZ, SW : 1 m. ℰ 382, « Country house atmosphere », ◰, ☞, ℅ – ▥ ➡wc ℗ ◿ 🄰 ▨ **VISA** ℅
Mid February-mid November – **M** (bar lunch)/dinner 8.00 t. ⫘ 3.25 – **22 rm** ⊆ 16.50/35.00 t. – SB (except summer) 40.00/43.75 **st.**

🏛 Alfoxton Park ⟨⟩, TA5 1SG, W : 1 ½ m. ℰ 211, ⟨, ◿ heated, ☞, park, ℅ – ▥ ➡wc ℗. ℅
18 rm.

HOLMES CHAPEL Cheshire 402 403 404 M 24 – pop. 4 672 – ✉ Crewe – ☎ 0477.

◆London 181 – Chester 25 – ◆Liverpool 41 – ◆Manchester 24 – ◆Stoke-on-Trent 20.

🏛 **Holly Lodge,** 70 London Rd, CW4 7AS, on A 50 ℰ 37033 – ▥ ➡wc ℗ ◿ ⅙ ℗ 🄰 ▨ ▨ ⓪ **VISA**
M *(closed Saturday lunch and Bank Holidays)* 4.95/8.50 **t.** and a la carte ⫘ 3.25 – **32 rm** ⊆ 32.50/48.00 **st.** – SB (weekends only) 49.00 **st.**

🏛 **Old Vicarage,** Knutsford Rd, Cranage, CW4 7DE, NW : ½ m. on A 50 ℰ 32041 – ▥ ➡wc ☎ ℗ ▨ ▨ **VISA** ℅
M *(closed Saturday lunch)* 8.50/12.00 **st.** and a la carte ⫘ 3.50 – **8 rm** ⊆ 35.00/49.00 **st.** – SB (weekends only) 50.00 **st.**

at Twemlow Green NE : 1 ¾ m. on A 535 – ✉·☎ 0477 Holmes Chapel :

✕✕✕ **Yellow Broom,** Macclesfield Rd, CW4 8BL, ℰ 33289 – ℗ ▨ ▨ **VISA**
closed Sunday dinner and Monday – **M** (dinner only and Sunday lunch) (booking essential)/dinner 15.00 **t.** ⫘ 4.25.

at Brereton SE : 2 m. on A 50 – ✉ Sandbach – ☎ 0477 Holmes Chapel :

🏛 Bear's Head, Newcastle Rd, CW11 9RS, ℰ 35251, ☞, ℅ – ▥ ➡wc ⁞wc ☎ ℗
21 rm.

HOLMROOK Cumbria 402 J 20 – ✉ ☎ 094 04.

◆London 314 – Kendal 52 – Workington 24.

⌂ **Carleton Green** ⟨⟩, Saltcoats Rd, CA19 1YX, S : 1 m. by A 595 ℰ 608, ☞ – ➡wc ℗
March-October – **6 rm** ⊆ 10.00/21.00 **s.**

HOLT Norfolk 404 X 25 – pop. 2 502 – ECD : Thursday – ☎ 0263.

◆London 124 – King's Lynn 34 – ◆Norwich 22.

⌂ **Lawns,** 26 Station Rd, NR25 6BS, ℰ 713390, ☞ – ➡wc ℗
10 rm ⊆ 14.00/34.00.

HOLYHEAD (CAERGYBI) Gwynedd 402 403 G 24 – pop. 12 569 – ECD : Tuesday – ☎ 0407.

Envir. : South Stack (cliffs★) W : 3 ½ m. – Rhosneigr (site★) SE : 13 m.

⛴ to Ireland (Dun Laoghaire) (Sealink) 2 daily; (3 h 30 mn) – to Ireland (Dublin) (B & I Line) 1-2 daily (3 h 30 mn).

🛈 Marine Sq., Salt Island Approach ℰ 2622 (summer only).

◆London 269 – Birkenhead 94 – ◆Cardiff 215 – Chester 88 – Shrewsbury 105 – ◆Swansea 190.

HOLY ISLAND Northumb. 401 402 O 16 – pop. 190 – ☎ 0289 Berwick-upon-Tweed.

See : Castle (16C) ⟨★★ *AC* – Priory★ (ruins 12C) *AC*.

◆London 342 – Berwick-upon-Tweed 13 – ◆Newcastle-upon-Tyne 59.

Hotels see : Berwick-upon-Tweed NW : 13 m.

HOLYWELL (TREFFYNNON) Clwyd 402 403 K 24 – pop. 11 101 – ECD : Wednesday – ☎ 0352.

🛈 Little Chef Services, A 55 ℰ 780144 (summer only).

◆London 217 – Chester 19 – ◆Liverpool 34.

🏛 **Stamford Gate,** Halkyn Rd, CH8 7SJ, ℰ 712942 – ▥ ➡wc ℗ ▨ ▨ ⓪ **VISA** ℅
M 5.50/7.15 **st.** and a la carte ⫘ 2.80 – **12 rm** ⊆ 22.00/34.00 **st.**

HONITON Devon 403 K 31 The West Country G. – pop. 6 490 – ECD : Thursday – ☎ 0404.

See : All Hallows Museum★ *AC*.

Envir. : Farway Countryside Park (⟨★) *AC*, S : 3 m.

🛈 Angel Hotel car park, High St. ℰ 3716 (summer only).

◆London 186 – Exeter 17 – ◆Southampton 93 – Taunton 18.

at Stockland NE : 8 ½ m. by A 30 – ✉ Honiton – ☎ 040 486 Upottery :

🏛 Snodwell Farm ⟨⟩, Stockland Hill, Cotleigh, EX14 9HZ, W : 3 m. ℰ 263, ◿, ☞ – ➡wc ⁞wc ℗
10 rm.

at Wilmington E : 3 ½ m. on A 35 – ⊠ Honiton – ✿ 040 483 Wilmington :

🏠 **Home Farm,** EX14 9JR, on A 35 ℘ 278, « Converted 16C thatched farm house », 🚗 – 📺
🛏wc 🅿 ▲ AE ⑩ *VISA*
M 9.00/12.00 **t.** ⓘ 2.75 – **13 rm** ⌒ 23.50/59.00 **st.** – SB 55.00/65.00 **st.**

at Weston W : 2 m. by A 30 – ⊠ ✉ 0404 Honiton :

🏨 **Deer Park** ⌖, EX14 0PG, ℘ 2064, ≤, ⊥ heated, ⌇, 🚗, park, ✕, squash – 📺 🛏wc 🅿
🅿 ▲ AE ⑩ *VISA* ✕
M 7.00/13.50 **st.** and a la carte ⓘ 3.00 – ⌒ 6.00 – **31 rm** 27.50/70.00 **st.** – SB (except
August)(weekends only) 65.00/80.00 **st.**

HOOK Hants. 🗺️ R 30 – pop. 2 562 – ECD : Thursday – ✿ 025 672.
♦London 47 – Reading 13 – ♦Southampton 35.

🏠 **Oaklea,** London Rd, RG27 9LA, ℘ 2673, 🚗 – 🛏wc 🅿
10 rm ⌒ 17.00/35.00 **st.**

HOPE COVE Devon 🗺️ I 33 – see Salcombe.

HOPTON WAFERS Salop 🗺️ 🗺️ M 26 – pop. 948 – ⊠ Kidderminster – ✿ 0299 Cleobury
Mortimer.
♦London 150 – ♦Birmingham 32 – Shrewsbury 38.

✕ **Crown Inn,** DY14 0NB, on A 4117 ℘ 270372 – 🅿 ▲ *VISA*
closed Sunday dinner and Monday except Bank Holidays – **M** 10.50 **t.** and a la carte
approx. 12.95 **t.** ⓘ 3.00.

HORLEY Surrey 🗺️ T 30 – pop. 17 700 – ECD : Wednesday – ✿ 029 34 (4 and 5 fig.) or 0293
(6 fig.).
♦London 27 – ♦Brighton 26 – Royal Tunbridge Wells 22.

Plan : see Gatwick

🏨 **Chequers Thistle** (Thistle), Brighton Rd, RH6 8PH, ℘ 786992, Telex 877550, ⊥ – 📺 ☎ ৬
🅿 ▲ AE ⑩ *VISA* ✕
M 7.25/10.50 **t.** and a la carte ⓘ 3.00 – ⌒ 5.50 – **78 rm** 52.00/70.00 **st.** Y z

AUSTIN-ROVER Massetts Rd ℘ 785176   RENAULT 61 Brighton Rd ℘ 72566
FORD Hookwood Rd ℘ 782257
PEUGEOT Keppers Corner, Burstow ℘ 0342 (Cop-
thorne) 712017

HORNBY Lancs. 🗺️ M 21 – pop. 1 808 – ✿ 0468.
♦London 257 – Kendal 20 – Lancaster 9.

🏠 **Castle,** Main St., LA2 8JT, ℘ 21204 – 📺 🛏wc 🛏wc 🅿 ▲ AE *VISA*
M (bar lunch Monday to Saturday)/dinner 9.00 **t.** and a la carte ⓘ 2.50 – **12 rm** ⌒ 19.00/37.00 **t.**
– SB 43.00/48.00 **st.**

HORNCASTLE Lincs. 🗺️ 🗺️ T 24 – pop. 4 194 – ECD : Wednesday – ✿ 065 82.
♦London 140 – Lincoln 21.

✕✕ **Magpies,** 73-75 East St., LN9 6AA, on A 158 ℘ 7004 – ▲
closed Sunday dinner, Monday and 3 weeks September – **M** (lunch by arrangement Tuesday
to Saturday) 6.50/12.00 **t.** ⓘ 3.20.

AUSTIN-ROVER Spilsby Rd ℘ 2391   LANCIA Lincoln Rd ℘ 7667

HORNING Norfolk 🗺️ Y 25 – pop. 1 033 – ECD : Wednesday – ⊠ Norwich – ✿ 0692.
♦London 122 – Great Yarmouth 17 – ♦Norwich 11.

🏨 **Petersfield House** ⌖, Lower St., NR12 8PF, ℘ 630741, 🚗 – 📺 🛏wc 🛏wc ☎ 🅿 ▲ AE
⑩ *VISA*
M 7.50/9.50 **t.** and a la carte ⓘ 3.00 – **18 rm** ⌒ 33.00/45.00 **t.** – SB 60.00/66.00 **st.**

HORNS CROSS Devon 🗺️ H 31 – ECD : Wednesday – ⊠ Bideford – ✿ 023 75.
♦London 237 – Barnstaple 15 – Exeter 48.

🏨 **Foxdown Manor** ⌖, Foxdown, EX39 5PJ, S : 1 m. ℘ 325, ≤, « Country house atmosphere »,
⊥ heated, 🚗, park, ✕ – 📺 🛏wc 🅿 ▲ AE *VISA*
closed January-March – **M** (bar lunch)/dinner 9.75 **t.** and a la carte ⓘ 2.75 – **8 rm**
⌒ 25.00/70.00 **t.**, **1 suite** 100.00 **t.** – SB 50.00/64.00 **st.**

🏠 **Hoops Inn,** EX39 5DJ, W : ¾ m. on A 39 ℘ 222, 🚗 – 📺 🛏wc 🚿 🅿
M (bar lunch)/dinner 9.25 **t.** and a la carte ⓘ 2.80 – **14 rm** ⌒ 13.50/35.00 **t.** – SB (November-
March) 45.00 **st.**

HORSFORTH West Yorks. 🗺️ P 22 – see Leeds.

223

HORSHAM West Sussex 404 T 30 – pop. 38 356 – ECD : Monday and Thursday – ✆ 0403.

◆London 39 – ◆Brighton 23 – Guildford 20 – Lewes 25 – Worthing 20.

🏠 **Ye Olde King's Head,** 35 Carfax, RH12 1EG, 𝒫 53126 – 📺 ⊟wc 🛏wc ☞ 🄿 🔼 🄰🄴 🄾 𝗩𝗜𝗦𝗔
closed 25 and 26 December – **M** 6.55/9.85 **t.** and a la carte ₫ 3.60 – **43 rm** ⊷ 32.50/50.50 **t.** – SB (weekends only) 50.00 **st.**

at Lower Beeding SE : 3 ½ m. on A 281 – ⊠ Horsham – ✆ 040 376 Lower Beeding :

🏨 **South Lodge** ⊗, Brighton Rd, RH13 6PS, on A 281 𝒫 711, Telex 877765, ≼, ⊶, 🐎, park, ⚗ – 📺 ☎ 🄿. 🔼 🄰🄴 🄾 𝗩𝗜𝗦𝗔
M 11.50/22.50 **t.** and a la carte ₫ 4.00 – ⊷ 5.00 – **24 rm** 49.00/90.00 **t., 2 suites** 125.00 **t.** – SB (weekends only) 125.00 **st.**

🍴🍴🍴 **Cisswood House** with rm, Sandygate Lane, RH13 6NF, 𝒫 216, 🐎 – 📺 ⊟wc ☎ 🄿. 🔼 🄴 🄾 𝗩𝗜𝗦𝗔. ⚗
closed last 2 weeks August and 19 December-mid January – **M** 14.75 **t.** and a la carte 10.15/15.70 **t.** ₫ 3.50 – ⊷ 4.50 – **17 rm** 36.50/60.00 **st.**

AUSTIN-ROVER Springfield Rd 𝒫 54311	TOYOTA Slinfold 𝒫 790766
CITROEN Guildford Rd 𝒫 61393	VAUXHALL-OPEL Broadbridge Heath 𝒫 56464
FIAT Brighton Rd 𝒫 65637	VW, AUDI Plummers Plain 𝒫 76466
FORD The Bishopric 𝒫 54331	VOLVO Guildford Rd 𝒫 56381
RENAULT 108 Crawley Rd 𝒫 61146	

HORSHAM ST. FAITH Norfolk 404 X 25 – see Norwich.

HORTON Dorset 403 404 O 31 – see Wimborne Minster.

HORTON Northants. 404 R 27 – ⊠ ✆ 0604 Northampton.

◆London 66 – Bedford 18 – Northampton 6.

🍴🍴 **French Partridge,** Newport Pagnell Rd, NN7 2AP, 𝒫 870033 – 🄿
closed Sunday, Monday, 2 weeks Easter, mid July-first week August and 2 weeks at Christmas – **M** (dinner only) (booking essential) 15.00 **st.** ₫ 3.60.

HORTON-CUM-STUDLEY Oxon. 403 404 Q 28 – ECD : Wednesday – ⊠ Oxford – ✆ 086 735 Stanton St. John.

◆London 57 – Aylesbury 23 – ◆Oxford 7.

🏨 **Studley Priory** ⊗, OX9 1AZ, 𝒫 203, « Converted priory in park », 🐎, 🍴 – 📺 ⊟wc 🛏wc ☎ 🄿. 🔼 🄰🄴 🄾 𝗩𝗜𝗦𝗔. ⚗
closed first week January – **M** 14.50 **st.** and a la carte ₫ 3.00 – **19 rm** ⊷ 45.00/95.00 **st., 1 suite** 110.00 **st.** – SB (October-April) 75.00/95.00 **st.**

HOUGHTON CONQUEST Beds. 404 S 27 – see Bedford.

HOVE East Sussex 404 T 31 – see Brighton and Hove.

HOVINGHAM North Yorks. 402 R 21 – pop. 310 – ECD : Thursday – ⊠ York – ✆ 065 382.

◆London 235 – ◆Middlesbrough 36 – York 25.

🏨 **Worsley Arms,** YO6 4LA, 𝒫 234, 🐎 – ⊟wc ⇦ 🄿. 🔼 𝗩𝗜𝗦𝗔
closed 25 and 26 December – **M** 11.50/12.50 **t.** ₫ 2.75 – **12 rm** ⊷ 25.00/42.00 **t.** – SB 52.00/67.00 **st.**

HOWDEN Humberside 402 R 22 – pop. 3 227 – ECD : Thursday – ✆ 0430.

See : St. Peter's Church★ 12C-14C.

◆London 196 – ◆Kingston-upon-Hull 23 – ◆Leeds 37 – York 22.

🏠 **Bowmans,** Bridgegate, DN14 7JG, 𝒫 30805 – 📺 ⊟wc ☞ 🄿. 🔼 🄰🄴 🄾 𝗩𝗜𝗦𝗔. ⚗
M (closed Saturday lunch and Sunday dinner) 8.60 **t.** and a la carte – **13 rm** ⊷ 24.95/41.95 **t.**

HOWEY Powys – see Llandrindod Wells.

HOWTOWN Cumbria – see Ullswater.

HUDDERSFIELD West Yorks. 402 404 O 23 – pop. 147 825 – ECD : Wednesday – ✆ 0484.

🏌 Thick Hollins Hall, Meltham 𝒫 850227, SW : 5 m. – 🏌 Bradley Park, off Bradley Rd 𝒫 539988 N : 3 m. – 🏌 Longley Park, Maple St., off Somerset Rd 𝒫 22304.

🄳 3-5 Albion St. 𝒫 22133 and 23877 (Saturday only).

◆London 191 – Bradford 11 – ◆Leeds 15 – ◆Manchester 25 – ◆Sheffield 26.

🏨 **Ladbroke** (Ladbroke), Ainley Top, HD3 3RH, NW : 2 ½ m. at junction A 629 and A 640 𝒫 0422 (Elland) 75431, Telex 517346 – ⧉ ⊟ rest 📺 ☎ 🄿. 🔼 🄰🄴 🄾 𝗩𝗜𝗦𝗔 ⚗
M (closed Saturday lunch) (carving rest.) 9.95 ₫ 3.70 – ⊷ 5.50 – **119 rm** 45.00/54.00 **st.** – SB (weekends only) 63.00 **st.**

🏨 **George** (T.H.F.), St. George's Sq., HD1 1JA, 𝒫 25444 – ⧉ 📺 ⊟wc ☞ 🄿. 🔼 🄰🄴 🄾 𝗩𝗜𝗦𝗔
M 7.00/10.00 **st.** and a la carte ₫ 3.40 – ⊷ 5.65 – **62 rm** 37.00/42.00 **st.**

224

🏠 **Cote Royd,** 7 Halifax Rd, HD3 3AN, ℰ 547588, 🔲, 🛋 – 📺 ➰wc 🗯wc ☎ 🄿 ☒ AE ⓸
VISA, ✀
closed 24 December-1 January – **M** (dinner only) 8.50 **st.** and a la carte ◊ 2.50 – **21 rm**
☲ 31.00/40.00 **st.**

🏠 **Huddersfield,** 41 Kirkgate, HD1 1QT, ℰ 512111 – 📳 📺 ➰wc 🗯wc ☎ ☒ AE ⓸ **VISA**
M (restricted lunch Saturday and Sunday) 4.50/8.50 **st.** and a la carte ◊ 3.25 – **21 rm**
☲ 25.75/35.75 **st.**, **1 suite** 35.75/70.00 **st.**

XX **Shabab,** 37-39 New St., HD1 2BG, ℰ 549514, Indian rest. – ☒ AE ⓸ **VISA**
closed Sunday lunch and Christmas Day – **M** a la carte 5.70/9.20.

at Golcar W : 3 ½ m. by A 62 on B 6111 – ⊠ ✿ 0484 Huddersfield :

X **Weaver's Shed,** Knowl Rd, HD7 4AN, via Scar Lane ℰ 654284, « Converted 18C woollen
mill » – 🄿
closed Saturday lunch, Sunday dinner, Monday, first 2 weeks January and last 2 weeks July –
M a la carte 10.25/13.70 **t.** ◊ 3.25.

at Outlane NW : 4 m. on A 640 – ⊠ Huddersfield – ✿ 0422 Elland :

🏠 **Old Golf House,** New Hey Rd, HD3 3YP, ℰ 79311 – 📺 ➰wc ☏ 🄿 🔐 – **29 rm.**

ALFA-ROMEO, PEUGEOT, TALBOT Northgate ℰ
20822
AUSTIN-ROVER, JAGUAR, LAND ROVER, RANGE-
ROVER Southgate ℰ 535341
BMW Somerset Rd ℰ 515515
FORD Southgate ℰ 29675
JAGUAR, LAND ROVER, RANGE-ROVER Northgate
ℰ 535251

LANCIA Kirkheaton ℰ 29754
TOYOTA Fartown ℰ 514514
VAUXHALL-OPEL 386 Leeds Rd ℰ 518700
VOLVO Northgate ℰ 531362
VW, AUDI Bradford Rd ℰ 542001

HULL Humberside **402** S 22 – see Kingston-upon-Hull.

HUNGERFORD Berks. **403 404** P 29 – pop. 4 488 – ECD : Thursday – ✿ 0488.
Envir. : Littlecote House★ *AC*, NW : 3 ½ m.
🖥 West Berkshire, Chaddleworth ℰ 048 82 (Chaddleworth) 574, N : 2 ½ m.
♦London 74 – ♦Bristol 57 – ♦Oxford 28 – Reading 26 – ♦Southampton 46.

🏠 **Bear,** 17 Charnham St., RG17 0EL, on A 4 ℰ 82512, 🛋 – 📺 ➰wc 🗯wc ☎ 🄿 ☒ AE ⓸ **VISA**
✀
M *(closed 24 to 26 December)* 12.45/13.45 **t.** and a la carte – ☲ 4.25 – **28 rm** 42.50/47.50 **st.**,
6 suites 55.00/65.00 **st.** – SB (weekends only) 59.50 **st.**

BMW, SUZUKI Bath Rd ℰ 82772

HUNMANBY North Yorks. **402** T 21 – pop. 2 623 – ⊠ Filey – ✿ 0723 Scarborough.
♦London 198 – ♦Kingston-upon-Hull 40 – Scarborough 9 – York 41.

🏠 **Wrangham House,** 10 Stonegate, YO14 0NS, ℰ 891333, 🛋 – 📺 ➰wc 🗯wc 🄿 ☒ **VISA**
✀
March-mid November – **M** (dinner only) 10.50 **st.** – **9 rm** ☲ (dinner included) 28.00/58.00 **st.**
– SB (October-May) 50.00/52.00 **st.**

HUNSTANTON Norfolk **402 404** V 25 – pop. 3 990 – ECD : Thursday – ✿ 048 53.
🛈 The Green ℰ 2610.
♦London 120 – ♦Cambridge 60 – ♦Norwich 45.

🏠 **Le Strange Arms,** Golf Links Lane, PE36 6JJ, N : 1 m. by A 149 ℰ 34411, ≤, 🛋 – 📺 ➰wc
🗯wc ☎ 🄿 🔐 ☒ AE ⓸ **VISA**
M 10.00 **t.** and a la carte – **30 rm** ☲ 32.50/51.00 **t.** – SB (except Christmas and Bank Holidays)
55.00/64.00 **st.**

↥ **Claremont,** 35 Greevegate, PE36 6AF, ℰ 33171 – ✀
February-October – **7 rm** ☲ 9.00/18.00 **st.**

at Heacham S : 3 m. by A 149 – ⊠ Kings Lynn – ✿ 0485 Heacham :

🏠 **Holly Lodge,** Lynn Rd, PE31 7HY, ℰ 70790, « Country house atmosphere », 🛋 – ➰wc 🄿
☒ AE **VISA**, ✀
closed January – **M** *(closed Sunday dinner)* (dinner only and Sunday lunch) a la carte
9.50/13.25 **t.** ◊ 3.00 – **6 rm** ☲ 35.00/55.00 **t.** – SB 65.00/75.00 **st.**

AUSTIN-ROVER 12 Lynn Rd ℰ 33435

CITROEN, VAUXHALL Westgate ℰ 2508

HUNSTRETE Avon **403 404** M 29 – see Bath.

Pour parcourir l'Europe,
utilisez les cartes Michelin **Grandes Routes** à 1/1 000 000.

HUNTINGDON Cambs. 404 T 26 – pop. 14 395 – ECD : Wednesday – 🕿 0480.

See : Cromwell Museum – All Saint's Church (interior★) – Envir. : Hinchingbrooke House★ (Tudor mansion-school) W : 1 m. – Ramsey (Abbey Gatehouse★ 15C) NE : 11 ½ m.

🚇 St. Ives 🕿 64459, E : 5 m.

🖪 Huntingdon Library, Princes St. 🕿 52181 – ◆London 69 – Bedford 21 – ◆Cambridge 16.

🏨 **Old Bridge,** 1 High St., PE18 6TQ, 🕿 52681, Telex 32706 – 📺 ➯wc 🕿 🅿. ☒ AE ⓪ VISA
   M 15.25 st. and a la carte – **22 rm** ☲ 45.00/68.00 st.

🏨 **George** (T.H.F.), George St., PE18 6AB, 🕿 53096 – 📺 ➯wc 🕸 🅿. 🛋. ☒ AE ⓪ VISA
   M 5.25/9.25 st. and a la carte 🖔 3.40 – ☲ 5.65 – **24 rm** 42.00/51.00 st.

   at Wyton NE : 2 ¾ m. by A 141 and A 1123 – ⊠ – 🕿 0480 Huntingdon :

XX **Mario's Lodge,** Hartford Marina, PE17 2AA, W : ¾ m. on A 1123 🕿 50964, ≤, Italian rest. –
   🅿. ☒ AE ⓪ VISA
   closed Sunday dinner – **M** 6.95 t. and a la carte 11.55/13.80 t. 🖔 3.85.

AUSTIN-ROVER-LAND ROVER 1-3 Hartford Rd 🕿   BMW, VAUXHALL-OPEL Brookside 🕿 52694
56441

HURLEY-ON-THAMES Berks. 404 R 29 – ECD : Wednesday – ⊠ Maidenhead – 🕿 062 882
Littlewick Green.

◆London 38 – ◆Oxford 26 – Reading 12.

🏨 **Ye Olde Bell,** High St., SL6 5LX, 🕿 5881, Telex 847035, « Part 12C inn », 🐎 – 📺 🕿 🅿. 🛋.
   ☒ AE ⓪ VISA
   M 12.75/13.75 t. and a la carte 🖔 3.50 – ☲ 3.40 – **24 rm** 37.50/75.00 t., **2 suites** 70.00/85.00 t. –
   SB (except Easter and Christmas) 60.00 st.

HURSTBOURNE TARRANT Hants. 403 404 P 30 – pop. 709 – ⊠ Andover – 🕿 026 476.

◆London 77 – ◆Bristol 77 – ◆Oxford 38 – ◆Southampton 33.

XX **Esseborne Manor** ⚘ with rm, SP11 0ER, NE : 1 ½ m. on A 343 🕿 444, 🐎, ⚒ – 📺 ➯wc
   🕿 🅿. ☒ AE ⓪ VISA. ⚘
   closed 2 weeks at Christmas – **M** *(closed Saturday lunch and Sunday to non residents)* (lunch
   by arrangement) a la carte 13.40/17.25 st. 🖔 3.50 – **12 rm** ☲ 42.00/65.00 st. – SB (except
   winter) 75.00 st.

HURST GREEN Lancs. 402 M 22 – ⊠ Whalley – 🕿 025 486 Stonyhurst.

◆London 236 – Blackburn 12 – Burnley 13 – Preston 12.

🏨 **Shireburn Arms** ⚘, Whalley Rd, BB6 9QJ, 🕿 518, 🐎 – 📺 ➯wc 🅿. ☒ VISA
   M a la carte 9.70/15.75 st. 🖔 2.50 – **11 rm** ☲ 19.50/39.50 st. – SB (weekends only) 60.00/75.00 st.

HUSBANDS BOSWORTH Leics. 403 404 Q 26 – pop. 889 – ⊠ Lutterworth – 🕿 0858 Market
Harborough.

◆London 88 – ◆Birmingham 40 – ◆Leicester 14 – Northampton 17.

XX **Fernie Lodge,** Berridges Lane, LE17 6LE, 🕿 880551 – ▤ 🅿. ☒ VISA
   closed lunch Monday and Saturday and Sunday dinner – **M** (booking essential) 7.75/12.75 t.

HUTTON-LE-HOLE North Yorks. 402 R 21 – see Lastingham.

HUXHAM Devon – see Exeter.

HWLFFORDD = Haverfordwest.

HYDE Cheshire 402 403 404 N 23 – pop. 30 461 – 🕿 061 Manchester.

◆London 201 – ◆Manchester 10 – ◆Sheffield 34.

🏨 **Village,** Captain Clark Rd, off Dukinfield Rd, SK14 4QG, 🕿 368 1456, squash – ▤ 📺 ▥wc 🕿
   🕭 🅿. 🛋. ☒ 🅿. ☒ VISA
   M (grill rest. only) (bar lunch Saturday) a la carte 6.10/10.75 st. 🖔 2.80 – **37 rm** ☲ 30.00/36.00 st.

HYTHE Kent 404 X 30 – pop. 13 118 – ECD : Wednesday – 🕿 0303.

See : St. Leonard's Church (≤★ from the churchyard) – Canal.

🚇 Hythe Imperial, Princes Parade 🕿 67441 – ◆London 68 – Folkestone 6 – Hastings 33 – Maidstone 31.

🏨 **Hythe Imperial** (Best Western) ⚘, Princes Par., CT21 6AE, 🕿 67441, Telex 965082, ≤, ☒,
   🖪, ⚒, squash – ▤ 📺 🕿 🅿. 🛋. ☒ AE ⓪ VISA. ⚒
   M 10.00/13.50 t. and a la carte 🖔 3.50 – **83 rm** ☲ 38.00/100.00 st., **5 suites** 90.00/130.00 t. – SB
   (weekends only)(except Bank Holidays) 70.00/110.00 st.

🏨 **Stade Court** (Best Western), West Par., CT21 6DT, 🕿 68263, Telex 965082, ≤ – ▤ 📺 ➯wc
   ▥wc 🕸 🅿. ☒ AE ⓪ VISA
   M 7.25/11.50 st. and a la carte 🖔 3.00 – **32 rm** ☲ 26.50/52.00 st. – SB 56.00/76.00 st.

AUSTIN-ROVER 6-12 East St. 🕿 69335   PEUGEOT-TALBOT The Green 🕿 60511
FORD Stade St. 🕿 67726   SAAB 215 Seabrook Rd 🕿 38467

IBSLEY Hants. 🔢🔢 O 31 – see Ringwood.

ICKLESHAM East Sussex – pop. 2 235 – ✉ Winchelsea – ☎ 0424 Hastings.
♦London 69 – Folkestone 35 – Hastings 7.

⌂ **Snailham House** 🔲, Broad St., TN36 4AT, N : ½ m. 𝒫 814556, ≤, 🌳 – 🅿. 🎿
Easter-October – **7 rm** 🛏 10.00/22.00 **st.**

IDE Devon 🔢 J 31 – see Exeter.

IDE HILL Kent – see Sevenoaks.

IGHTHAM Kent – see Wrotham Heath.

ILFRACOMBE Devon 🔢 H 30 **The West Country G.** – pop. 9 966 – ECD : Thursday – ☎ 0271.
See : Capstone Hill★ (≤★) – Hillsborough (≤★★) – St. Nicholas' Chapel AC (≤★).
🏌 Hele Bay 𝒫 62176, E : 1 m.
Access to Lundy Island from Hartland Point by helicopter 𝒫 062 882 (Littlewick Green) 3431.
🅩 The Promenade 𝒫 63001 – ♦London 223 – Exeter 54 – Taunton 61.

🏡 **Langleigh** 🔲, Langleigh Rd, EX34 8EA, 𝒫 62629, « Country house atmosphere », 🌳 – 📺
🛏wc 🚿wc 🅿
closed December and January – **M** (bar lunch)/dinner 9.00 **st.** 🍷 2.60 – **8 rm** 🛏 15.00/40.00 **st.,**
2 suites 32.00/40.00 **st.**

🏡 **St. Helier,** Hillsborough Rd, EX34 9QQ, 𝒫 64906, 🌳 – 📺 🛏wc 🅿. 🔃 𝑽𝑰𝑺𝑨
May-September – **M** (bar lunch)/dinner 7.00 **st.** 🍷 2.50 – **24 rm** 🛏 14.00/31.00 **st.**

at Lee W : 3 ¼ m. by B 3231 – ✉ ☎ 0271 Ilfracombe :

🏨 **Lee Bay** (Best Western) 🔲, EX34 8LP, 𝒫 63503, ≤, 🌊 heated, 🌳, park – 📺 ☎ 🅿. 🔃 🅰🅴
① 𝑽𝑰𝑺𝑨
M 6.50/10.50 **t.** 🍷 3.50 – **50 rm** 🛏 34.00/40.00 – SB 77.00/89.70 **st.**

⌂ **Lee Manor** 🔲, EX34 8LR, 𝒫 63920, 🌳, park – 📺 🛏wc 🚿wc 🅿. 🎿
April-October and Christmas – **M** (bar lunch Monday to Saturday)/dinner 9.00 **t.** and a la carte
🍷 3.50 – **12 rm** 🛏 19.00/70.00 **t.**

PEUGEOT, TALBOT   West Down 𝒫 63104   RENAULT   Northfield Rd 𝒫 62075

ILKLEY West Yorks. 🔢🔢 O 22 – pop. 13 060 – ECD : Wednesday – ☎ 0943.
🏌 Middleton 𝒫 600214.
🅩 Station Rd 𝒫 602319 – ♦London 210 – Bradford 13 – Harrogate 17 – ♦Leeds 16 – Preston 46.

🏨 **Rombalds,** 11 West View, Wells Rd, LS29 9JG, 𝒫 603201, Telex 51593 – 📺 🛏wc 🚿wc ☎
🅿. 🔃 🅰🅴 ① 𝑽𝑰𝑺𝑨
M 16.50 **t.** (dinner) and a la carte 11.50/18.00 **t.** 🍷 3.75 – **18 rm** 🛏 38.00/60.00 **t.,** **2 suites**
82.00/92.00 **t.** – SB (except Christmas) 66.00/72.80 **st.**

🏡 **Grove,** 66 The Grove, LS29 9PA, 𝒫 600298 – 📺 🛏wc 🚿wc 🅿. 🔃 𝑽𝑰𝑺𝑨
M 6.50/8.50 **st.** 🍷 3.00 – **6 rm** 🛏 18.00/36.00 **st.** – SB 42.00/50.00 **st.**

⌂ **Moorview,** 104 Skipton Rd, LS29 9HE, W : ¼ m. on A 65 𝒫 600156, ≤, 🌳 – 📺 🚿wc 🅿. 🎿
closed mid December-mid January – **12 rm** 🛏 18.00/32.00.

XXX ⊛ **Box Tree,** 35-37 Church St., LS29 9DR, 𝒫 608484, « Ornate decor » – 🔃 🅰🅴 ① 𝑽𝑰𝑺𝑨
closed Sunday, Monday, 25-26 December and 1 January – **M** (dinner only)(booking essential)
17.50 **t.** and a la carte 17.00/23.00 **t.**
Spec. Terrine de fruits de mer en chemise verte au safran, Rondels d'agneau et sa garniture de legumes, Timbale
de fraises "Box Tree".

AUSTIN-ROVER   Ben Rhydding 𝒫 603261   VAUXHALL-OPEL   Bradford Rd, Menston 𝒫 0943
PEUGEOT-TALBOT   Skipton Rd 𝒫 608966   (Menston) 76122
VAUXHALL, GENERAL MOTORS   Skipton Rd 𝒫
607606

IMPINGTON Cambs. – see Cambridge.

INGATESTONE Essex 🔢🔢 V 28 – pop. 6 150 – ECD : Wednesday – ☎ 0277.
♦London 27 – Chelmsford 6.

🏨 **Ivy Hill,** Ivy Barn Lane, Margaretting, CM4 0EW, NE : 2 ¼ m. by A 12 𝒫 353040, 🌊 heated,
🌳, 🎿 – 📺 ☎ 🅿. 🔃 🅰🅴 ① 𝑽𝑰𝑺𝑨
M 10.50 **t.** and a la carte 11.70/20.10 **t.** 🍷 3.60 – 🛏 5.75 – **18 rm** 39.00/53.00 **t.**

INGLETON North Yorks. 🔢🔢 M 21 – pop. 1 769 – ✉ Carnforth – ☎ 0468.
🅩 Community Centre car park 𝒫 41049/41280 (summer only).
♦London 266 – Kendal 21 – Lancaster 18 – ♦Leeds 53.

⌂ **Oakroyd,** Main St., LA6 3HJ, 𝒫 41258, 🌳 – 🅿
7 rm 🛏 9.00/18.00 **t.**

INSTOW Devon 🔢 H 30 – see Bideford.

IPSWICH

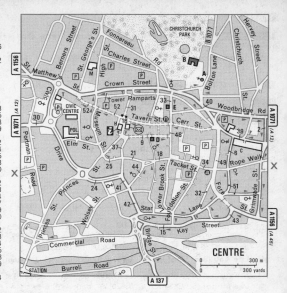

CENTRE

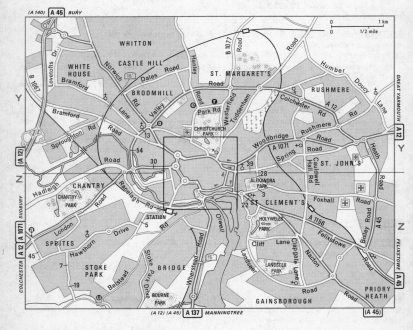

Red Lion   If the name of the hotel
is not in bold type,
on arrival ask the hotelier his prices.

228

IPSWICH Suffolk **404** X 27 – pop. 129 661 – ECD : Monday and Wednesday – ✆ 0473.

See : St. Margaret's Church (the roof★) X **A** – Christchurch Mansion (museum★) X **B** – Ancient House★ 16C X **D** – Pykenham House★ 16C X **E**.

🅑 Town Hall, Princes St. ✆ 58070.

♦London 76 – ♦Norwich 43.

Plan opposite

🏨 **Belstead Brook** ⛳, Belstead Rd, IP2 9HB, SW : 2 ½ m. ✆ 684241, Telex 987674, ☞, park –
📺 ☎ 🅿 ⚕ 🔥 AE ⓞ VISA   Z u
M 7.95/10.95 **st.** and a la carte ⓘ 3.20 – 🖃 5.50 – **33 rm** 46.00/60.00 **st.**, **6 suites** 75.00 **st.** – SB (weekends only) 93.00 **st.**

🏨 **Marlborough**, Henley Rd, IP1 3SP, ✆ 57677, ☞ – 📺 ☎ 🅿 ⚕ 🔥 AE ⓞ VISA   Y e
M (see **Marlborough rest.** below) – 🖃 5.25 – **22 rm** 40.00/55.00 **t.** – SB (weekends only)(except Christmas and New Year) 64.00/70.00 **st.**

🏨 **Post House** (T.H.F.), London Rd, IP2 0UA, SW : 2 ¼ m. on A 12 ✆ 690313, Telex 987150,
🦢 heated – 📺 📼 wc ⚕ 🅿 🔥 VISA   Z a
M 7.50/9.95 **st.** and a la carte ⓘ 3.40 – 🖃 5.65 – **118 rm** 44.00/53.00 **st.**

🏠 **Great White Horse**, Tavern St., IP1 3AH, ✆ 56558 – 📺 📼 wc ☎. ⚕. 🔥   X n
M (bar lunch)/dinner 8.50 **st.** and a la carte ⓘ 2.60 – 🖃 4.50 – **46 rm** 25.00/40.00 **st.** – SB 52.00 **st.**

🏚 **Bentley Tower**, 172 Norwich Rd, IP1 2PY, ✆ 212142 – 📺 📼 wc 🅿. 🔥 AE ⓞ VISA ☞   Y o
M (restricted lunch for residents only)/dinner 9.50 **st. 10 rm** 🖃 25.00/38.00 **t.**

↖ **Gables**, 17 Park Rd, IP1 3SX, ✆ 54252, ☞ – 🅿   Y r
12 rm 🖃 13.00/23.00 **st.**

XXX **Marlborough**, at Marlborough H, Henley Rd, IP1 3SP, ✆ 57677 – 🅿. 🔥 AE ⓞ VISA   Y e
M (residents only 25 December) 10.00/12.00 **t.** and a la carte 16.75/20.40 **t.** ⓘ 3.70.

XX **Rajasthan**, 6 Orwell Pl., IP4 1BB, ✆ 51397, Indian rest. – 🔥 AE ⓞ VISA   X a
closed 25 and 26 December – **M** 9.50 **t.** and a la carte ⓘ 2.90.

at Copdock SW : 4 m. on A 12 – Z – ✉ Ipswich – ✆ 047 386 Copdock :

🏨 **Ipswich Moat House** (Q.M.H.), London Rd, IP8 3JD, ✆ 444, Telex 987207, ☞ – 📺 📼 wc
☎ 🅿. ⚕. 🔥 AE ⓞ VISA
M (carving lunch) 7.95/8.95 **st.** and a la carte ⓘ 3.25 – 🖃 5.95 – **45 rm** 39.50/49.50 **st.** – SB (weekends only) 52.00/56.00 **st.**

AUDI, VW   88 Princes St. ✆ 214231
AUSTIN-ROVER   Barrack Lane ✆ 54202
AUSTIN-ROVER   Felixstowe Rd ✆ 75431
BMW   West End Rd ✆ 212456
FIAT, LANCIA   Burrel Rd ✆ 690321
FORD   Princes St. ✆ 55401
MAZDA, POLSKI   Fuchsia Lane ✆ 74535
MERCEDES-BENZ   Raneleigh Rd ✆ 221388

PEUGEOT-TALBOT, ALFA-ROMEO   Derby Rd ✆ 70101
RENAULT   301-305 Norwich Rd ✆ 43021
SAAB   Dales Rd ✆ 42547
SKODA   West End Rd ✆ 55461
TOYOTA   301-305 Woodbridge Rd ✆ 719221
VAUXHALL-OPEL   Knightsdale Rd ✆ 43044
VOLVO   Rushmore Rd ✆ 626767

IRONBRIDGE Salop **402 403 404** M 26 – pop. 2 477 – ✉ Telford – ✆ 095 245.

♦London 154 – ♦Birmingham 39 – Shrewsbury 17.

🏚 **Tontine**, The Square, TF8 7AQ, ✆ 2127 – 🔥 VISA
M 7.00 **t.** and a la carte ⓘ 2.50 – **11 rm** 🖃 14.00/28.00 **t.** – SB 31.00 **st.**

IVINGHOE Bucks. **404** S 28 – pop. 2 517 (inc. Pitstone) – ✉ Leighton Buzzard – ✆ 0296 Cheddington.

🛦 ✆ 668696 – ♦London 42 – Aylesbury 9 – Luton 11.

XXX **King's Head** (T.H.F.), Station Rd, LU7 9EB, ✆ 668388 – ▤ 🅿. 🔥 AE ⓞ VISA
M 12.25 **t.** (lunch) and a la carte 15.80/20.75 **t.** ⓘ 3.75.

IXWORTH Suffolk **404** W 27 – pop. 2 121 – ✉ Bury St. Edmunds – ✆ 0359 Pakenham.

♦London 85 – ♦Cambridge 35 – ♦Ipswich 25 – ♦Norwich 36.

X **Theobalds**, 68 High St., IP31 2HJ, ✆ 31707 – 🔥 VISA
closed Saturday lunch, Sunday dinner and Monday – **M** a la carte 11.50/15.75 **t.** ⓘ 2.70.

JAMESTON Dyfed **403** F 29 – see Manorbier.

JEVINGTON East Sussex **404** U 31 – see Eastbourne.

KENDAL Cumbria **402** L 21 – pop. 23 710 – ECD : Thursday – ✆ 0539.

See : Abbot Hall Art Gallery (Museum of Lakeland Life and Industry★) AC.

Envir. : Levens Hall★ (Elizabethan) AC and Topiary Garden★ AC, SW : 5 ½ m.

🛦 The Heights ✆ 24079 – 🛦 The Riggs ✆ 0587 (Sedbergh) 20993, E : 9 m.

🅑 Town Hall, Highgate ✆ 25758.

♦London 270 – Bradford 64 – Burnley 63 – ♦Carlisle 49 – Lancaster 22 – ♦Leeds 72 – ♦Middlesbrough 77 – ♦Newcastle-upon-Tyne 104 – Preston 44 – Sunderland 88.

KENDAL

🏨 **Woolpack** (Swallow), Stricklandgate, LA9 4ND, ℰ 23852, Group Telex 53168 – 📺 🛏wc
🛏wc 📵 🅿 🛄 ﹠ ⏣ ⓘ ▨
M 6.50/10.00 **st.** and a la carte ▯ 3.95 – **57 rm** 42.00/54.00 **st.** – SB (weekends only)
62.00/68.00 **st.**

🏨 **Garden House** ﹠, Fowling Lane, LA9 6PH, by A 685 ℰ 31131, 🌫 – 📺 🛏wc 🛏wc ☎ 🅿
🔺 ﹠ ⓘ ▨
closed 2 weeks at Christmas – **M** (closed lunch Saturday to Monday and Sunday dinner to
non residents) 13.50 **st.** ▯ 2.95 – **10 rm** 🛏 29.50/39.50 **st.** – SB 51.00/59.00 **st.**

🍴 **Castle Dairy,** 26 Wildman St., LA9 6EN, ℰ 21170, English rest., « Part 13C and 16C »
closed Sunday to Tuesday and August – **M** (booking essential) (dinner only) 12.00 ▯ 2.50.

at Underbarrow W : 3 ½ m. on Crosthwaite rd – ✉ Kendal – ✪ 044 88 Crosthwaite :

🏨 **Greenriggs Country House** ﹠, LA8 8HF, E : ½ m. ℰ 387, ﹤, « Country house atmosphere », 🌫 – 🛏wc 🅿
closed weekdays November-December and March, January and February – **M** (dinner only)
12.50 **t.** ▯ 2.00 – **13 rm** 🛏 21.00/38.00 **t.** – SB (weekends only)(November-May except Bank
Holidays) 53.00/63.00 **st.**

ALFA-ROMEO, FORD, MERCEDES BENZ Ings ℰ
0539 (Staveley) 821442
AUSTIN-ROVER Sandes Av. ℰ 28800
FIAT 113 Stricklandgate ℰ 20967
FORD Mintsfeet Ind. Est. ℰ 23534

PEUGEOT Kirkland ℰ 28822
RENAULT Kirkland ℰ 22211
VAUXHALL Sandes Av. ℰ 24420
VOLVO Station Rd ℰ 31313
VW, AUDI-NSU, PORSCHE Longpool ℰ 24331

KENILWORTH Warw. 🔢🔢🔢 🔢🔢🔢 P 26 – pop. 18 782 – ECD : Monday and Thursday – ✪ 0926.
See : Castle★ (12C) *AC.*
🆔 Crew Lane ℰ 54296.
🔖 Library, 11 Smalley Pl. ℰ 52595.
♦London 102 – ♦Birmingham 19 – ♦Coventry 5 – Warwick 5.

🏨 **De Montfort** (De Vere), The Square, CV8 1ED, ℰ 55944, Telex 311012 – 🎚 📺 ☎ 🅿 🛄 🔺
﹠ ⓘ ▨
M 8.50/9.75 **st.** and a la carte ▯ 3.90 – **95 rm** 🛏 49.50/67.50 **st.**, **1 suite** 112.50 **st.** – SB (weekends only) 58.00 **st.**

🏨 **Clarendon House,** 6-8 High St., Old Town, CV8 1LZ, ℰ 57668, Telex 311240 – 📺 🛏wc
🛏wc ☎ 🅿 🔺 ▨
M 8.50/10.50 **st.** and a la carte ▯ 4.50 – **32 rm** 🛏 27.50/50.00 **st.**

🏠 **Enderley,** 20 Queens Rd, CV8 1JQ, ℰ 55388. 🌫
5 rm 🛏 10.50/19.00 **st.**

🍴 **Diment,** 121-123 Warwick Rd, CV8 1HP, ℰ 53763 – 🅿 🔺 ﹠ ⓘ ▨
closed Saturday lunch, Sunday, Monday, 1 week Easter, first 3 weeks August and Bank Holidays
– **M** 5.95/11.75 **t.** and a la carte 11.65/14.85 **t.** ▯ 2.95.

🍴 **Bosquet,** 97a Warwick Rd, CV8 1HP, ℰ 52463 – ﹠ ▨
closed Saturday lunch, Sunday, last 2 weeks July, 24 December-2 January and Bank Holidays
– **M** (lunch by arrangement) 10.50 **st.** and a la carte 14.90/17.60 **st.** ▯ 3.00.

🍴 **Portofino,** 14 Talisman Sq., ℰ 57186, Italian rest. – 🔺 ﹠ ⓘ ▨
M 7.00/18.00 **t.** and a la carte ▯ 3.45.

🍴 **Ana's Bistro,** 121-123 Warwick Rd, CV8 1HP, ℰ 53763 – 🅿 🔺 ﹠ ⓘ ▨
closed Sunday, Monday, 1 week Easter, first 3 weeks August and Bank Holidays – **M** (dinner
only) a la carte 5.70/8.65 **t.** ▯ 2.40.

ALFA-ROMEO, LANCIA Station Rd ℰ 53073

TOYOTA Warwick Rd ℰ 54722

KENNFORD Devon 🔢🔢🔢 J 32 – see Exeter.

KENNINGTON Kent 🔢🔢🔢 W 30 – see Ashford.

KENTS BANK Cumbria 🔢🔢🔢 L 21 – see Grange-over-Sands.

KERESLEY West Midlands 🔢🔢🔢 🔢🔢🔢 P 26 – see Coventry.

KESWICK Cumbria 🔢🔢🔢 K 20 – pop. 4 777 – ECD : Wednesday – ✪ 0596.
See : Derwent Water★★ Y – **Envir. :** Castlerigg (stone circle) 🌟★ E : 2 m. Y **A.**
🆔 Threlkeld Hall ℰ 059 683 (Threlkeld) 324, E : 4 m. by A 66 Y.
🔖 Moot Hall, Market Sq. ℰ 72645.
♦London 294 – ♦Carlisle 31 – Kendal 30.

Plan opposite

🏨 **Underscar** ﹠, Applethwaite, CA12 4PH, N : 1 ½ m. by A 591 ℰ 72469, Telex 64354, ﹤
Derwent Water and mountains, 🌫, park – 📺 🛏wc 🛏wc ☎ 🅿 🔺 ﹠ ⓘ 🌫
closed mid December-mid February – **M** 7.50/15.50 **t.** ▯ 3.50 – **18 rm** 🛏 25.00/70.00 **t.** – SB
(winter only) 55.00/100.00 **st.**   by A 591   Y

🏨 **Royal Oak,** Station St., CA12 5HH, ℰ 72965 – 🎚 📺 🛏wc ☎ 🅿 – **43 rm.**   Z ⓘ

230

KESWICK

*North is at the top
on all town plans.*

*Les plans de villes
sont disposés
le Nord en haut.*

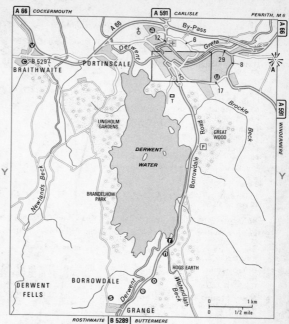

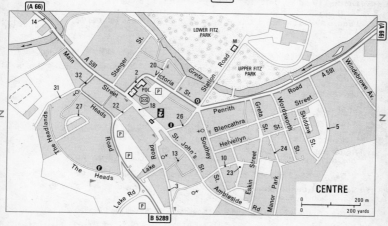

CENTRE

*When travelling for business or pleasure
in England, Wales, Scotland and Ireland :*

*– use the series of five maps
   (nos **401**, **402**, **403**, **404** and **405**) at a scale of 1:400 000*

*– they are the perfect complement to this Guide
   as towns underlined in red on the maps will be found in this Guide.*

Grange Country House ⛰, Manor Brow, Ambleside Rd, CA12 4BA, ✆ 72500, ≤, ⚘ – TV ⛀wc ⛆wc Ⓟ. ⊠ Y **u**
closed 24 and 25 December – **M** (bar lunch)/dinner 9.50 **t.** ♣ 2.90 – **12 rm** ⊐ 17.50/39.00 **t.** – SB (except summer and Bank Holidays) 48.00/56.00 **st.**

Gale ⛰, Underskiddaw, CA12 4PL, NW : 1 ¾ m. by A 591 ✆ 72413, ≤, ⚘ – ⛀wc ⛆wc Ⓟ. ⊠ VISA. ⚡ by A 591 Y
April-November – **M** (dinner only) 7.00 **st.** ♣ 1.60 – **13 rm** ⊐ 13.50/32.00 **st.**

Lyzzick Hall ⛰, , CA12 4PY, NW : 2 ½ m. on A 591 ✆ 72277, ≤, ⛱ heated, ⚘ – TV ⛀wc ⛆ Ⓟ. ⊠ AE ⦿ VISA. ⚡ By A 591 Y
M (bar lunch Monday to Saturday)/dinner 12.00 **t.** ♣ 2.20 – **20 rm** ⊐ 16.50/42.00 **t.** – SB (winter only) 38.00/46.00 **st.**

Highfield, The Heads, CA12 5ER, ✆ 72508, ≤ – ⛆wc Ⓟ Z **r**
Easter-October – **M** (bar lunch)/dinner 7.50 **t.** ♣ 2.50 – **19 rm** ⊐ 11.00/28.00 **t.**

Walpole, Station Rd, CA12 4NA, ✆ 72072 – TV ⛀wc ⛆wc Ⓟ Z **o**
M (bar lunch)/dinner 9.00 **t.** ♣ 3.00 – **17 rm** ⊐ 14.75/34.00 **t.** – SB 42.00/48.00 **st.**

Brackenrigg Country House, Thirlmere, CA12 4TF, SE : 3 m. on A 591 – Y – ✆ 72258, ⚘, ✂ – ⛆wc Ⓟ
6 rm.

Lairbeck ⛰, Vicarage Hill, CA12 5QB, ✆ 73373, ⚘ – ⛀wc Ⓟ. ⚡ Y **a**
12 rm ⊐ 13.50/38.00 **t.**

at Borrowdale S : 3 ¼ m. on B 5289 – ✉ Keswick – ☎ 059 684 Borrowdale :

Lodore Swiss ⛰, CA12 5UX, ✆ 285, Group Telex 64305, ≤ Derwent Water and mountains, ⛱ heated, ⛱, ⚘, park, ✂, squash – ⇕ TV ☎ ⇔ Ⓟ. AE. ⚡ Y **n**
Mid March - early November – (rest. see **Lodore Swiss** below) – **72 rm** ⊐ 34.00/68.00 **t.**, **1 suite** 115.00 **t.**

Borrowdale, CA12 5UY, ✆ 224, ≤, ⚘ – TV ⛀wc ⛆wc ☎ Ⓟ. ⊠ VISA Y **o**
M 7.25/12.00 **t.** and a la carte ♣ 3.30 – **35 rm** ⊐ 16.00/48.00 **t.** – SB (except summer) 100.00/112.00 **st.**

Mary Mount Country House ⛰ without rest., CA12 5UU, ✆ 223, Group Telex 64305, ≤ Derwent Water and mountains, ⚘, park – TV ⛀wc Ⓟ. AE. ⚡ Y **r**
closed 17 November-27 December – **12 rm** ⊐ 27.00/44.00 **t.**

Leathes Head ⛰, CA12 5UY, ✆ 247, ≤, ⚘ – ⛀wc ⛆wc Ⓟ. ⚡ Y **e**
12 rm ⊐ 16.50/35.00 **t.**

XXX **Lodore Swiss** (at Lodore Swiss H.), CA12 5UX, ✆ 285, Group Telex 64305 – Ⓟ. AE Y **n**
Mid March-early November – **M** (booking essential) 14.00 **t.** (dinner) and a la carte 7.40/17.00 **t.** ♣ 3.00.

at Grange-in-Borrowdale S : 4 ¾ m. by B 5289 – ✉ Keswick – ☎ 059 684 Borrowdale :

Borrowdale Gates Country House ⛰, CA12 5UQ, ✆ 204, ≤, ⚘ – TV ⛀wc ⛆wc Ⓟ. ⊠ AE ⦿ Y **s**
M (bar lunch)/dinner 11.95 **st.** ♣ 3.90 – **20 rm** ⊐ (dinner included) 34.00/64.00 **st.** – SB (winter only) 51.20 **st.**

at Rosthwaite S : 6 m. on B 5289 – Y – ✉ Keswick – ☎ 059 684 Borrowdale :

Scafell ⛰, CA12 5XB, ✆ 208, ⚘ – ⛀wc Ⓟ
closed 4 January-12 February – **M** (bar lunch Monday to Saturday)/dinner 11.00 **t.** and a la carte – **20 rm** ⊐ 18.85/42.00 **t.** – SB (November-April) 36.00/60.00 **st.**

Royal Oak ⛰, CA12 5XB, ✆ 214 – ⛀wc ⛆wc Ⓟ. ⊠
closed 29 November-28 December – **12 rm** ⊐ (dinner included) 21.00/42.00 **t.**

at Seatoller S : 8 m. on B 5289 – Y – ✉ Keswick – ☎ 059 684 Borrowdale :

Seatoller House, Borrowdale, CA12 5XN, ✆ 218, ≤ Borrowdale, ⚘ – ⛆wc Ⓟ
April-October – **9 rm** ⊐ 19.50/36.00 **t.**

at Braithwaite W : 2 m. on A 66 – ✉ Keswick – ☎ 059 682 Braithwaite :

Ivy House, CA12 5SY, on A 66 ✆ 338 – TV ⛀wc ⛆wc Ⓟ. ⊠ ⦿ VISA. ⚡ Y **c**
March-22 November – **M** (dinner only) 10.50 **t.** ♣ 2.60 – **8 rm** ⊐ 27.00/41.00 **t.**

Middle Ruddings, CA12 5RY, on A 66 ✆ 436, ⚘ – TV ⛀wc Ⓟ. ⊠ AE ⦿ VISA. ⚡ Y **v**
closed 4 January - mid February – **M** (bar lunch)/dinner 10.50 **st.** and a la carte ♣ 2.75 – **15 rm** ⊐ 22.50/54.00 **st.** – SB 60.00/74.00 **st.**

at Thornthwaite W : 3 ½ m. by A 66 – ✉ Keswick – ☎ 059 682 Braithwaite :

Thwaite Howe ⛰, CA12 5SA, ✆ 281, ≤ Skiddaw and Derwent Valley, ⚘ – TV ⛀wc Ⓟ. ⚡ Y **i**
March-October – **M** (lunch by arrangement) 5.00/8.50 **t.** ♣ 2.50 – **8 rm** ⊐ 27.00/44.00 **t.** – SB 50.00 **st.**

AUSTIN-ROVER High Hill ✆ 72768 FIAT Lake Rd ✆ 72064

KETTLEWELL North Yorks. 402 N 21 – pop. 361 (inc. Starbotton) – ECD : Tuesday and Thursday – ✉ Skipton – ☎ 075 676 – ♦London 237 – Bradford 33 – ♦Leeds 40.

- **Racehorses,** Town Foot, BD23 5QZ, ℘ 233 – wc wc **P**.
  M (bar lunch)/dinner 12.50 **t.** and a la carte 3.10 – **14 rm** 18.00/40.00 **t.** – SB (October-March) 48.00/53.00 **st.**
- **Bluebell,** Town Foot, BD23 5QX, ℘ 230 – TV wc
  M (bar lunch)/dinner 7.50 **st.** and a la carte 2.75 – **7 rm** 15.00/29.00 **st.** – SB (October-March)(weekends only) 44.00/48.00 **st.**

KEYNSHAM Avon 403 404 M 29 – pop. 16 452 – ECD : Wednesday – ✉ Bristol – ☎ 027 56.
♦London 127 – Bath 8 – ♦Bristol 4.

- **Grange,** 42 Bath Rd, BS18 1SN, ℘ 69181 – TV wc ☎ **P**. VISA.
  M a la carte 4.25/8.15 **t.** 2.15 – **31 rm** 25.00/44.00 **t.** – SB (weekends only) 53.60/62.60 **st.**

KEYSTON Cambs. 404 S 26 – pop. 252 (inc. Bythorn) – ✉ Huntingdon – ☎ 080 14 Bythorn.
♦London 75 – ♦Cambridge 29 – Northampton 24.

- XX **Pheasant Inn,** Village Loop Rd, PE18 0RE, ℘ 241 – **P**. AE VISA
  closed 3 days at Christmas – **M** 14.40 **st.**

KIDDERMINSTER Heref. and Worc. 403 404 N 26 – pop. 50 385 – ECD : Wednesday – ☎ 0562.
Library, Market St. ℘ 752832 – ♦London 139 – ♦Birmingham 17 – Shrewsbury 34 – Worcester 15.

- **Gainsborough House** (Best Western), Bewdley Hill, DY11 6BS, SW : 1 m. on A 456 ℘ 754041, Telex 333058, – TV wc ☎ **P**. AE VISA
  M 6.25/8.50 **t.** 3.95 – **42 rm** 35.75/51.50 **st.** – SB (weekends only) 45.50/50.00 **st.**

at Stone SE : 2 ½ m. on A 448 – ✉ Kidderminster – ☎ 056 283 Chaddesley Corbett :

- **Stone Manor**, DY10 4PJ, ℘ 555, Telex 335661, <, heated, , park, – TV ☎ **P**. AE VISA
  M 8.50 **t.** (lunch) and a la carte – 5.50 – **23 rm** 42.50/52.00 **st.**, **1 suite** 65.00/75.00 **st.** – SB (weekends only) 60.00/70.00 **st.**

ALFA-ROMEO Mill St. ℘ 3708
AUSTIN-ROVER Churchfields ℘ 752566
BMW Mustow Green ℘ 056 283 (Chaddesley Corbett)433
CITROEN, FIAT Worcester Rd ℘ 2202
FORD Worcester Rd ℘ 752661
LADA Plimsoll St. ℘ 2145
RENAULT, VW High St. ℘ 0299 (Cleobury Mortimer) 270352
VOLVO Stourport Rd ℘ 515832
VAUXHALL-OPEL Churchfields ℘ 748501
VW, AUDI Worcester Rd ℘ 745056

KIDLINGTON Oxon. 403 404 Q 28 – see Oxford.

KILDWICK North Yorks. 402 O 22 – ✉ Keighley – ☎ 0535 Cross Hills.
♦London 226 – Burnley 15 – ♦Leeds 23.

- **Kildwick Hall**, BD20 9AE, ℘ 32244, <, « Jacobean manor house », – TV **P**. AE VISA
  M (grill rest. lunch Monday to Saturday)/dinner 13.95 **st.** and a la carte 3.50 – **12 rm** 35.00/85.00 **st.** – SB 67.90/97.00 **st.**

KILSBY Northants. 403 404 Q 26 – see Rugby (Warw.).

KILVE Somerset – pop. 324 – ☎ 027 874 Holford.
♦London 172 – ♦Bristol 49 – Minehead 13 – Taunton 23.

- **Meadow House**, Sea Lane, TA5 1EG, ℘ 546, « Country house atmosphere », – TV wc **P**. VISA.
  M (dinner only) 14.00 **st.** 3.20 – **5 rm** 35.00/50.00 **st.**

KINGHAM Oxon. 403 404 P 28 – pop. 576 – ECD : Wednesday – ☎ 060 871.
♦London 81 – Gloucester 32 – ♦Oxford 25.

- **Mill**, OX7 6UH, ℘ 8188, Group Telex 849041, – TV wc ☎ **P**. AE VISA.
  M 8.95/13.50 **t.** and a la carte 4.30 – **20 rm** 28.00/46.00 **st.** – SB 64.00/70.00 **st.**
- **Conygree Gate,** Church St., OX7 6YA, ℘ 389, – **P**.
  March-October – **6 rm** 15.00/30.00 **st.**

KINGSBRIDGE Devon 403 I 33 The West Country G. – pop. 4 164 – ECD : Thursday – ☎ 0548.
See : Site★ – Boat Trip to Salcombe★★ *AC*.
The Quay ℘ 3195 – ♦London 236 – Exeter 36 – ♦Plymouth 20 – Torquay 21.

- **Crabshell Motor Lodge** without rest., Embankment Rd, TQ7 1JZ, ℘ 3301, < – TV wc **P**. AE VISA
  3.75 – **24 rm** 20.00/31.00 **t.**
- Vineyard, Embankment Rd, TQ7 1JN, ℘ 2520, – wc wc **P** – **11 rm**.
- **Harbour Lights,** 11-13 Ebrington St., TQ7 1DE, ℘ 2418,
  Easter-October – **5 rm** 12.50/25.00 **s.**

at Loddiswell N : 3 ½ m. by B 3196 – ✉ ☎ 0548 Kingsbridge :

XX **Lavinia's,** TQ7 4ED, N : 1 m. ✆ 550306, – Ⓟ. VISA
Easter-October – **M** *(closed Sunday and Monday)* (booking essential)(dinner only) 20.00 ₰ 3.40.

at Goveton NE : 2 ½ m. by A 381 – ✉ ☎ 0548 Kingsbridge :

Buckland-Tout-Saints (Best Western) , TQ7 2DS, ✆ 3055, ≤, « Queen Anne mansion », , park – TV wc wc ☎ Ⓟ. AE VISA
closed January-4 March – **M** 17.50 **t.** ₰ 3.50 – ☕ 3.50 – **13 rm** 49.50/80.00 **t.** – SB 66.00/100.00 **st.**

at East Portlemouth E : 6 ½ m. by A 379 – ✉ ☎ 054 884 Salcombe :

Gara Rock , TQ8 8PH, SE : ½ m. ✆ 2342, ≤, heated, , park, – wc wc Ⓟ. VISA
Easter-October – **M** (bar lunch)/dinner 9.00 **st.** and a la carte – **20 rm** ☕ 20.00/52.00 **t.** – SB (except summer) 46.00 **st.**

at Chillington SE : 5 m. on A 379 – ✉ Kingsbridge – ☎ 054 853 Frogmore :

White House, TQ7 2JX, ✆ 0548 (Kingsbridge) 580580, – wc wc Ⓟ.
April-October – **M** (bar lunch)/dinner 7.00 **st.** ₰ 2.50 – **8 rm** ☕ 14.00/46.00 **t.**

Oddicombe House, TQ7 2JD, ✆ 234, , – wc Ⓟ
Easter-October – **M** (bar lunch residents only, Monday to Saturday)/dinner 9.50 **t.** and a la carte ₰ 3.50 – **10 rm** ☕ 16.50/44.00 **t.**

at Torcross SE : 7 m. on A 379 – ✉ ☎ 0548 Kingsbridge :

The Venture, TQ7 2TQ, ✆ 580314, ≤ – TV
March-October – **5 rm** ☕ 13.00/26.00 **st.**

at Thurlestone W : 4 m. by A 381 – ✉ ☎ 0548 Kingsbridge :

Thurlestone (Best Western) , TQ7 3NN, ✆ 560382, ≤, heated, , 9, , park, , squash – rest TV ☎ Ⓟ. AE VISA
closed 4 to 10 January – **M** 13.50/22.00 **st.** and a la carte – **68 rm** ☕ 39.00/127.00 **st.** – SB (October-May) 82.00/100.00 **st.**

Furzey Close , TQ7 3NP, ✆ 560333, ≤, – TV wc wc Ⓟ
April-September – **M** (bar lunch)/dinner a la carte 11.00/14.70 **st.** ₰ 3.95 – **10 rm** ☕ 14.00/23.50 **st.**

AUSTIN-ROVER The Quay ✆ 2323

KINGSKERSWELL Devon 403 J 32 – pop. 3 471 – ✉ Torquay – ☎ 080 47.

♦London 219 – Exeter 21 – ♦Plymouth 33 – Torquay 4.

XX **Pitt House,** 2 Church End Rd, TQ12 5DS, ✆ 3374, « 15C Dower house », – Ⓟ. AE VISA
closed Saturday lunch, Sunday and 25 January-22 February – **M** (restricted lunch) a la carte 9.80/15.80 **t.** ₰ 3.90.

KING'S LYNN Norfolk 402 404 V 25 – pop. 37 323 – ECD : Wednesday – ☎ 0553.

See : St. Margaret's Church★ (17C, chancel 13C) – St. Nicholas' Chapel★ (Gothic) – **Envir. :** Houghton Hall★★ (18C) *AC*, NE : 15 m. – Sandringham House★ and park★★ *AC*, NE : 6 m.

18 Castle Rising ✆ 654, NE : 4 m. off A 164.

Saturday Market Place ✆ 763044 – ♦London 103 – ♦Cambridge 45 – ♦Leicester 75 – ♦Norwich 44.

Duke's Head (T.H.F.), Tuesday Market Pl., PE30 1JS, ✆ 774996, Telex 817349 – TV wc ☎ Ⓟ. AE VISA
M 11.00 **st.** (dinner) and a la carte ₰ 3.40 – ☕ 5.65 – **72 rm** 43.00/54.00 **st.**

Stuart House, 35 Goodwins Rd, PE30 5QX, ✆ 772169, – TV wc ☎ Ⓟ. VISA.
closed 24 December-5 January – **M** (bar lunch)/dinner 9.00 **t.** and a la carte – **21 rm** ☕ 20.00/39.50 **st.** – SB (weekends only) 40.00/48.00 **st.**

Russet House, 53 Goodwins Rd, PE30 5PE, ✆ 773098, – TV wc Ⓟ. VISA.
closed 24 December-2 January – **11 rm** ☕ 18.00/35.00 **t.**

at Grimston NE : 6 ¼ m. by A 148 – ✉ Kings Lynn – ☎ 0485 Hillington :

Congham Hall , Lynn Rd, PE32 1AH, ✆ 600250, ≤, « Country house atmosphere », heated, , park, – TV wc ☎ Ⓟ. AE VISA.
closed 24 December-10 January – **M** *(closed Saturday lunch and Sunday dinner to non-residents)* 10.50/26.50 **t.** ₰ 4.50 – **11 rm** ☕ 50.00/77.00 **t.**, **1 suite** 99.00 **t.** – SB (weekends only) 100.00/125.00 **st.**

AUSTIN-ROVER-DAIMLER-JAGUAR,LAND ROVER Church St. ✆ 763133
FORD Lynn Rd, Heacham ✆ 0485 (Heacham) 70243
RELIANT, MAZDA Valingers Rd ✆ 772255
RENAULT Hardwick Rd ✆ 772644
TOYOTA Tottenhill ✆ 810 306
VAUXHALL-OPEL North St. ✆ 773861

KINGSTON Devon 403 I 33 – pop. 317 – ✉ ☎ 0548 Kingsbridge.

♦London 237 – Exeter 41 – ♦Plymouth 11.

Trebles Cottage , TQ7 4PT, ✆ 810268, – wc Ⓟ.
March-October – **6 rm** ☕ 11.50/31.00 **st.**

KINGSTON-UPON-HULL

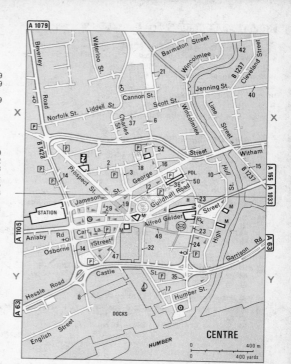

CENTRE

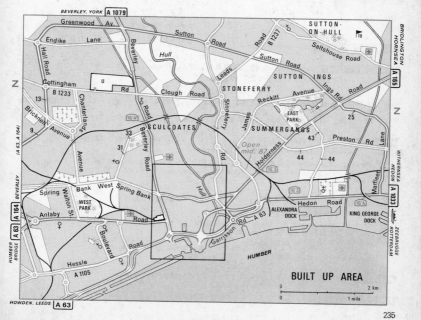

BUILT UP AREA

KINGSTON-UPON-HULL Humberside 402 S 22 – pop. 322 144 – ECD : Monday and Thursday – ☺ 0482 Hull.

Envir. : Burton Constable Hall★ (16C) *AC*, NE : 8 m. by A 165 Z – 🄽 Springhead Park, Willerby Rd ℰ 656309, W : by Spring Bank West Z – 🄽 Sutton Park, Salthouse Rd ℰ 74242, E : 3 m. Z.

🛫 Humberside Airport : ℰ 0652 (Barnetby) 688456, S : 19 m. by A 63 Z and A 15 via Humber Bridge – Terminal : Coach Service.

🚢 Shipping connections with the Continent : to The Netherlands (Rotterdam) and Belgium (Zeebrugge) (North Sea Ferries).

🛈 Central Library, Albion St. ℰ 223344 – Corporation Rd, King George Dock, Hedon Rd ℰ 702118.

♦London 183 – ♦Leeds 61 – ♦Nottingham 94 – ♦Sheffield 68.

Plan on preceding page

🏨 **Stakis Paragon** (Stakis), Paragon St., HU1 3PJ, ℰ 26462, Telex 592431 – 🛗 📺 ⌿wc ☎. 🄰 🔼 🄰🄴 ⓪ *VISA*   Y e
M (buffet lunch)/dinner 11.25 **st.** ▮ 3.60 – **125 rm** ⌷ 43.00/51.00 **st.** – SB (except Bank Holidays) 56.00.00.

XX **Cerutti's,** 10 Nelson St., HU1 1XE, ℰ 28501, Seafood – 🄿. 🔼   Y o
closed Saturday lunch, Sunday, 10 days Christmas and Bank Holidays – **M** a la carte 9.65/15.40 **t.** ▮ 3.45.

at North Ferriby W : 7 m. on A 63 – Z – ✉ Kingston-upon-Hull – ☺ 0482 Hull :

🏨 **Crest** (Crest), Ferriby High Rd, HU14 3LG, ℰ 645212, Telex 592558 – 📺 ⌿wc ☎ 🄿. 🄰. 🔼 🄰🄴 ⓪ *VISA* ⌾
M 8.50/18.95 **st.** and a la carte ▮ 4.00 – ⌷ 6.30 – **102 rm** 49.50/59.50 **st.** – SB (weekends only) 58.00/62.00 **st.**

at Willerby NW : 5 m. by A 63 – Z – off A 164 – ✉ Kingston-upon-Hull – ☺ 0482 Hull :

🏨 **Willerby Manor,** Well Lane, HU10 6ER, ℰ 652616, 🌫 – 📺 ⌿wc 🏧wc ▥ 🄿. 🄰. 🔼 *VISA*
M (closed Saturday lunch and Sunday dinner) 7.00/8.50 **t.** and a la carte ▮ 3.50 – ⌷ 3.75 – **41 rm** 32.50/45.00 **st.**

at Little Weighton NW : 11 m. by A 164 – Z – ✉ Cottingham – ☺ 0482 Hull :

🏨 **Rowley Manor** ⌾, HU20 3XR, SW : ½ m. by Rowley Rd ℰ 848248, ≼, 🌫 – 📺 ⌿wc 🏧wc ▥ 🄿. 🔼 🄰🄴 ⓪ *VISA*
M a la carte 7.75/13.00 **t.** ▮ 2.75 – **16 rm** ⌷ 35.00/60.00 **t.**

ALFA-ROMEO, LANCIA   Calvert Lane ℰ 572444
AUSTIN-ROVER   Boothferry Rd ℰ 506911
AUSTIN-ROVER   Springbank ℰ 227469
BMW   54 Anlaby Rd ℰ 25071
COLT   32 Princes Av. ℰ 42739
DAIHATSU, SAAB   Anlaby Rd ℰ 23773
FIAT   Holderness High Rd ℰ 701785
FIAT   96 Boothferry Rd ℰ 506976

FORD   172 Anlaby Rd ℰ 25732
HONDA   576 Springbank West ℰ 51250
MAZDA   300-302 Boothferry Rd, Hessle ℰ 645 283
NISSAN   Witham ℰ 24131
PEUGEOT-TALBOT   Anlaby ℰ 659362
TOYOTA   Clarence St. ℰ 20039
VAUXHALL-OPEL   230-236 Anlaby Rd ℰ 23681
VW,AUDI   Anlaby Rd ℰ 23631

KINGSTOWN Cumbria – see Carlisle.

KINGSWINFORD West Midlands 403 404 N 26 – ECD : Thursday – ☺ 0384.
♦London 135 – ♦Birmingham 14 – Stafford 22 – Worcester 32.

Plan : see Birmingham p. 2

🏠 **Summerhill House,** Swindon Rd, DY6 9XA, ℰ 295254, 🌫 – ⌿wc ▥ 🄿. 🔼 🄰🄴 ⓪ *VISA* ⌾   AU a
M (closed Saturday lunch) 6.00/6.50 **s.** and a la carte ▮ 3.75 – **10 rm** ⌷ 21.00/35.00 **st.**

KINGTON Heref. and Worc. 403 K 27 – pop. 2 040 – ECD : Wednesday – ☺ 0544.
♦London 152 – ♦Birmingham 61 – Hereford 19 – Shrewsbury 54.

X **Penrhos Court,** HR5 3LR, E : 1 ½ m. on A 44 ℰ 230720, « Converted 18C barn » – 🄿
closed Sunday dinner, Monday, Tuesday, January and February – **M** a la carte 9.50/17.00 **t.** ▮ 2.50.

KINTBURY Berks. 403 404 P 29 – pop. 2 034 – ✉ Newbury – ☺ 0488.
♦London 73 – Newbury 6 – Reading 23.

XX **Dundas Arms** with rm, Station Rd, RG15 0UT, ℰ 58263, ≼, « Canal and riverside setting », 🌫 – 📺 ⌿wc ☎ 🄿. 🔼 🄰🄴 ⓪ *VISA* ⌾
closed Christmas and New Year – **M** (closed Sunday, Monday and Bank Holidays) (booking essential) 10.50/14.50 **t.** and a la carte 16.70/19.00 **t.** ▮ 4.00 – **5 rm** ⌷ 38.00/45.00 **t.** – SB (except summer) 77.00/85.00 **st.**

KINVER Staffs. 403 404 N 26 – see Stourbridge (West Midlands).

KIRBY BELLARS Leics. 402 R 25 – see Melton Mowbray.

236

KIRKBY Merseyside 402 403 L 23 – pop. 52 825 – ECD : Wednesday – ✆ 051 Liverpool.

🏌 Liverpool Municipal, Ingoe Lane ✆ 546 5435.

🎫 Municipal Buildings, Cherryfield Drive ✆ 443 4024 and 489 6000.

♦London 214 – ♦ Blackpool 54 – ♦Liverpool 7 – ♦Manchester 31.

  🏨 **Crest** (Crest), East Lancs Rd, Knowsley, Prescot, L34 9HA, S : 1 ½ m. at junction A 580 and A 5207 ✆ 546 7531, Telex 629769 – 📺 ⇔wc 🅿 🏊 📶 🖭 ⓞ VISA
  M *(closed lunch Saturday, Sunday and Bank Holidays)* (grill rest. lunch) 8.50 **st.** (dinner) and a la carte – 🖵 5.25 – **50 rm** 35.00/40.00 **st.** – SB (weekends only) 55.00 **st.**

KIRKBY FLEETHAM North Yorks. 402 P 20 – pop. 406 (inc. Fencote) – ⊠ ✆ 0609 Northallerton.

♦London 236 – ♦Leeds 46 – ♦Middlesbrough 31 – ♦Newcastle-upon-Tyne 51 – York 37.

  🏨 **Kirkby Fleetham Hall** 🦢, DL7 0SU, N : 1 m. ✆ 748226, ≼, « Georgian country house », 🌲, park – 📺 ⇔wc 🅿 🖭 VISA. 🛇
  M (dinner only and Sunday lunch) 15.50 **st.** ⌽ 5.95 – **15 rm** 🖵 49.00/82.00 **st.**

KIRKBY LONSDALE Cumbria 402 M 21 – pop. 1 557 – ECD : Wednesday – ⊠ Carnforth – ✆ 0468.

🏌 Casterton Rd ✆ 71429, 1 m. on Sedbergh Rd.

🎫 18 Main St. ✆ 71603.

♦London 259 – ♦Carlisle 62 – Kendal 13 – Lancaster 17 – ♦Leeds 58.

  🏨 **Royal**, Main St., Market Sq., LA6 2AE, ✆ 71217 – 📺 ⇔wc 🅿
  M (bar lunch)/dinner 12.50 **st.** and a la carte ⌽ 2.75 – **22 rm** 🖵 22.50/37.50 **st.** – SB (October-March) 50.00 **st.**

  at Casterton NE : 1 ¼ m. on A 683 – ⊠ ✆ 0468 Kirkby Lonsdale :

  🏛 **Pheasant Inn**, LA6 2RX, ✆ 71230 – 📺 ⇔wc 🅿
  M 5.75/10.50 **t.** and a la carte ⌽ 3.75 – **14 rm** 🖵 19.50/32.00 **t.** – SB (except Christmas and New Year) 95.00/100.00 **st.**

KIRKBYMOORSIDE North Yorks. 402 R 21 – pop. 2 227 – ECD : Thursday – ✆ 0751.

🏌 Manor Vale ✆ 31525.

♦London 244 – Scarborough 26 – York 33.

  🏛 **George and Dragon,** 17 Market Pl., YO6 6AA, ✆ 31637, 🌲 – 📺 ⇔wc 🍴wc 🅿 📶 VISA
  closed 25 and 26 December – **M** 5.25 (lunch) and a la carte 6.55/11.15 ⌽ 3.10 – **20 rm** 🖵 20.00/36.00 – SB (December-Easter) 43.15/53.25.

NISSAN Pickering Rd ✆ 31551   VAUXHALL-OPEL Piercy End ✆ 31434
RENAULT New Rd ✆ 31401

KIRKBY STEPHEN Cumbria 402 M 20 – pop. 1 518 – ECD : Thursday – ✆ 07683.

Envir. : Brough (Castle ruins 12C-14C : keep ✳* *AC*) N : 4 m.

🎫 Bank House, 22 Market St. ✆ 71804.

♦London 285 – ♦Carlisle 48 – Kendal 24.

  🏛 **King's Arms,** Market Sq., CA17 4QN, ✆ 71378, 🌲 – 🅿 📶 VISA
  closed Christmas Day – **M** (bar lunch Monday to Saturday)/dinner 11.50 **t.** ⌽ 3.00 – **8 rm** 🖵 18.50/38.50 **t.** – SB (November-mid May except Bank Holidays) 40.00 **st.**

KIRKHAM Lancs. 402 L 22 – pop. 8 393 – ⊠ Preston – ✆ 0772.

♦London 240 – ♦Blackpool 9 – Preston 7.

  XX **Cromwellian,** 16 Poulton St., PR4 2AB, ✆ 685680
  closed Sunday dinner, Wednesday and last 2 weeks July – **M** (dinner only and Sunday lunch)/dinner 10.90 **t.** ⌽ 2.95.

KIRKOSWALD Cumbria 401 402 L 19 – pop. 730 – ⊠ Penrith – ✆ 076 883 Lazonby.

♦London 300 – ♦Carlisle 23 – Kendal 41 – Lancaster 58.

  🏛 **Prospect Hill** 🦢, CA10 1ER, N : ¾ m. ✆ 500, ≼, « Converted 18C farm buildings », 🌲 – ⇔wc 🅿 📶 🖭 ⓞ VISA. 🛇
  closed February – **M** (lunch by arrangement)/dinner a la carte 7.70/12.45 **t.** ⌽ 3.80 – **10 rm** 🖵 15.00/42.00 **t.**

KIRTON Notts. – see Ollerton.

KNAPTON Norfolk – see North Walsham.

Une voiture bien équipée, possède à son bord
des **cartes Michelin** à jour.

KNARESBOROUGH North Yorks. 402 P 21 – pop. 12 910 – ECD : Thursday – ✪ 0423 Harrogate.
🛏 Boroughbridge Rd ✆ 863219, N : 1 ½ m.
🅱 Market Place ✆ 866886 (summer only) — ♦London 217 – Bradford 21 – Harrogate 3 – ♦Leeds 18 – York 18.

  🏨 **Dower House** (Best Western), Bond End, HG5 9AL, ✆ 863302, ⚘ – 📺 ➡wc ᴔwc ☎ 🅿.
    🔲 AE ⓪ VISA ⛝
    closed 26 and 27 December – **M** *(closed Saturday lunch)* 13.60/16.75 **t.** and a la carte ⓵ 3.10 –
    20 rm ⇌ 30.00/50.00 **t.**, **1 suite** 59.50/65.00 **t.** – SB (weekends only) 58.00 **st.**

  XX **Schwallers**, 6-8 Bond End, HG5 9AQ, ✆ 863899 – 🔲 VISA
    closed Tuesday, 26 December and 1 January – **M** (dinner only and Sunday lunch)/dinner
    18.00 **t.** and a la carte ⓵ 3.00.

FORD York Place ✆ 862291

KNIGHTWICK Heref. and Worc. 403 404 M 27 – pop. 82 – ECD : Wednesday – ✉ Worcester
– ✪ 0886.
♦London 132 – Hereford 20 – Leominster 18 – Worcester 8.

  🏠 **Talbot**, WR6 5PH, on B 4197 ✆ 21235, ⚲, squash – ➡wc ᴔwc 🅿. 🔲 VISA
    M (bar lunch)/dinner a la carte 7.55/13.25 **st.** ⓵ 2.25 – **10 rm** ⇌ 13.50/34.50 **st.**

KNOWLE West Midlands 403 404 O 26 – pop. 16 850 – ECD : Thursday – ✉ Solihull – ✪ 056 45.
♦London 108 – ♦Birmingham 9 – ♦Coventry 10 – Warwick 11.

  🏨 **Greswolde Arms**, High St., B93 0LL, ✆ 2711 – 📺 ᴔwc ☎ 🅿. 🚗. 🔲 AE ⓪ VISA ⛝
    M 6.00/6.50 **s.** and a la carte ⓵ 3.75 – **18 rm** ⇌ 24.00/39.00 **st.**

  XX **Florentine**, 15 Kenilworth Rd, B93 0JB, ✆ 6449, Italian rest. – 🔲 AE ⓪ VISA
    closed Monday lunch, Sunday, August and Bank Holidays – **M** 6.00 **t.** (lunch) and a la carte
    8.10/11.60 **t.**

AUSTIN-ROVER 25 Station Rd ✆ 4221   VAUXHALL Grange Rd, Dorridge ✆ 6131

KNOWL HILL Berks. 404 R 29 – ✉ Twyford – ✪ 062 882 Littlewick Green.
♦London 38 – Maidenhead 5 – Reading 8.

  XX **Bird in Hand**, Bath Rd, RG10 9UP, ✆ 2781, ⚘ – 🅿. 🔲 AE ⓪ VISA
    M 8.75/10.50 **t.** and a la carte 13.00/18.00 **t.** ⓵ 3.00.

    at Warren Row NW : 1 m. – ✉ Knowl Hill – ✪ 062 882 Littlewick Green :

  XX **Warrener**, Wargrave, RG10 8QS, ✆ 2803, ⚘ – 🅿. 🔲 AE ⓪ VISA
    closed Saturday lunch, Sunday, Monday, last 2 weeks August and second week in January –
    M 12.50/21.50 **t.** ⓵ 3.00.

  X **Old House at Home**, Wargrave, RG10, ✆ 2995, English rest. – 🅿.

KNUTSFORD Cheshire 402 403 404 M 24 – pop. 13 628 – ECD : Wednesday – ✪ 0565.
Envir. : Tatton Hall★ (Georgian) and gardens★★ *AC*, N : 2 m. – Jodrell Bank (Concourse building-
radiotelescope *AC*) SE : 8 ½ m.
🅱 Council Offices, Toft Rd ✆ 2611.
♦London 187 – Chester 25 – ♦Liverpool 33 – ♦Manchester 18 – ♦Stoke-on-Trent 30.

  🏨 **Cottons**, Manchester Rd, WA16 0SU, NE : 1 ½ m. on A 50 ✆ 50333, Telex 669931, 🔲 – 🛗
    📺 ➡wc ⓺ & 🅿. 🚗. 🔲 AE ⓪ VISA
    M (bar lunch Saturday)/dinner 7.95 **t.** and a la carte ⓵ 3.75 – **60 rm** ⇌ 55.00/64.00 **st.**, **9 suites**
    65.00/90.00 **st.** – SB (weekends only) 69.00 **st.**

  🏨 **Royal George**, King St., WA16 6EE, ✆ 4151 – 🛗 📺 ➡wc ☎ 🅿. 🔲 AE ⓪ VISA ⛝
    M (grill rest. only) 7.00 **t.** and a la carte – **31 rm** ⇌ 30.00/45.50 **t.** – SB (weekends only)
    36.10/52.70 **st.**

  ↑ **Longview**, 55 Manchester Rd, WA16 0LX, ✆ 2119 – 📺 ᴔwc 🅿.
    closed Christmas and New Year – **14 rm** ⇌ 18.00/34.00 **st.**

  XXX **La Belle Epoque** with rm, 60 King St., WA16 6DT, ✆ 3060, « Art nouveau » – 📺 ➡wc 🅿.
    🔲 AE ⓪ VISA ⛝
    closed Sunday, first week January and Bank Holidays – **M** (dinner only)(booking essential)
    28.00 **st.** and a la carte 12.50/18.00 **t.** ⓵ 3.00 – ⇌ 4.50 – **5 rm** 28.00/38.00 **st.**

  X **David's Place**, 10 Princess St., WA16 6DD, ✆ 3356 – 🔲 AE VISA
    closed Sunday and Bank Holidays – **M** 10.50 **t.** (dinner) and a la carte 14.90/21.45 **t.** ⓵ 3.00.

    at Lower Peover S : 3 ½ m. by A 50 on B 5081 – ✉ Knutsford – ✪ 056 581 Lower Peover :

  X **Bells of Peover**, The Cobbles, ✆ 2269, ⚘ – 🅿.

    at Bucklow Hill NW : 3 ½ m. at junction A 556 and A 5034 – ✉ Knutsford – ✪ 0565
    Bucklow Hill :

  🏨 **Swan Inn** (De Vere), Chester Rd, WA16 6RD, ✆ 830295, Telex 666911 – 📺 ➡wc ᴔwc ☎
    🅿. 🚗. 🔲 AE ⓪ VISA
    M 7.50/9.50 **st.** and a la carte ⓵ 3.75 – **70 rm** ⇌ 49.50/60.00 **st.** – SB (weekends only)
    56.00/60.00 **st.**

ALFA-ROMEO, SEAT London Rd, Allostock ✆   RENAULT 21a Brook St. ✆ 4294
056 581 (Lower Peover) 2899   VOLVO Park Lane, Pickmere ✆ 056 589 (Pickmere)
FORD Garden Rd ✆ 4141   3254

LACOCK Wilts. 403 404 N 29 The West Country G. – pop. 1 289 – ✉ Chippenham – ☎ 024 973.
See : Site★ – Lacock Village : High St.★, St. Cyriac Church★, Fox Talbot Museum of Photography★ *AC* – Lacock Abbey★ *AC*.

♦London 109 – Bath 16 – ♦Bristol 30 – Chippenham 3.

✗ **Sign of the Angel** with rm, 6 Church St., SN15 2LA, ♫ 230, English rest., « 14C inn in National Trust village », ▦ – ⌂wc
closed 22 December-1 January – **M** (closed lunch Saturday and Bank Holidays and Sunday dinner) 15.00/17.50 t. ▯ 3.40 – **6 rm** ☐ 35.00/60.00 t. – SB (weekdays only)(except summer) 80.00 st.

LAKE VYRNWY Powys 402 403 J 25 – ☎ 069 173 Llanwddyn.

♦London 204 – Chester 52 – Llanfyllin 10 – Shrewsbury 40.

🏨 **Lake Vyrnwy** ◐, SY10 0LY, ✉ Llanwddyn via Oswestry, Salop ♫ 244, ≼ Lake Vyrnwy, « Country house atmosphere », ◥, ▦, park, ✗ – ▨ ⌂wc ⇔ ℗ ✦
closed February – **M** (buffet lunch Monday to Saturday)/dinner 8.90 st. ▯ 2.80 – **28 rm** ☐ 15.00/60.00 st. – SB (October-April except Easter and Christmas) 59.00/65.00 st.

LAMORNA COVE Cornwall 403 D 33 – ECD : Thursday – ✉ ☎ 0736 Penzance.
Envir. : Land's End★★ W : 7 ½ m.

♦London 323 – Penzance 5 – Truro 31.

🏨 **Lamorna Cove** ◐, TR19 6XH, ♫ 731411, ≼, ⬙ heated, ▦ – ▨ TV ⌂wc ▯wc ☎ ℗ ⬛ AE
⓪ VISA
closed December and January – **M** 7.50/11.50 st. and a la carte ▯ 3.50 – **18 rm** ☐ 23.50/36.00 st. – SB (except spring and summer) 51.90/69.90 st.

LAMPETER (LLANBEDR PONT STEFFAN) Dyfed 403 H 27 – pop. 1 908 – ECD : Wednesday – ☎ 0570.

🏌 Cilgwyn, Llangybi ♫ 057 045 (Llangybi) 286, NE : 4 m. off A 485.

♦London 223 – Brecon 41 – Carmarthen 22 – ♦Swansea 50.

🏨 **Black Lion Royal,** High St., SA48 7BG, ♫ 422172, ▦ – TV ⌂wc ℗ ▵ ⬛ VISA ✦
M (closed Sunday dinner to non residents) 7.00 t. and a la carte – **14 rm** ☐ 16.50/30.00 t.

LAMPHEY Dyfed – see Pembroke.

LANCASTER Lancs. 402 L 21 – pop. 43 902 – ECD : Wednesday – ☎ 0524.
🏢 7 Dalton Sq. ♫ 32878.

♦London 252 – ♦Blackpool 26 – Bradford 62 – Burnley 44 – ♦Leeds 71 – ♦Middlesbrough 97 – Preston 26.

🏨 **Post House** (T.H.F.), Waterside Park, Caton Rd, LA1 3RA, NE : 1 ¼ m. on A 683 ♫ 65999, Telex 65363, ◩, – ▨ TV ☎ ⬙ ℗ ▵ ⬛ AE ⓪ VISA
M 6.95/11.95 st. and a la carte ▯ 3.40 – ☐ 5.65 – **117 rm** 49.00/59.00 st.

AUSTIN-ROVER King St. ♫ 32233
FORD Parliament St. ♫ 63553

HYUNDAI, PONY Brookhouse ♫ 0524 (Caton) 770501
NISSAN Scotsforth Rd ♫ 36162

LANGLEY Northumb. – see Hexham

LANGSTONE Gwent 403 L 29 – see Newport.

LANREATH Cornwall 403 G 32 – pop. 449 – ✉ Looe – ☎ 0503.

♦London 269 – ♦Plymouth 26 – Truro 34.

🏨 **Punch Bowl Inn**, PL13 2NX, ♫ 20218, ▦ – TV ⌂wc ▦ ℗ ⬛ VISA
April-October – **M** 7.55 t. (dinner) and a la carte ▯ 2.50 – **18 rm** ☐ 12.00/36.80 t.

LAPFORD Devon 403 I 31 – pop. 875 – ECD : Wednesday – ✉ Crediton – ☎ 036 35.

♦London 218 – Exeter 17 – ♦Plymouth 63 – Taunton 54.

🏠 **Nymet Bridge House** ◐, EX17 6QX, NW : 1 ½ m. by A 377 ♫ 334, ▦ – ▯wc ℗ VISA ✦
April-October – **5 rm** ☐ 12.00/26.00.

LARKFIELD Kent 404 V 30 – see Maidstone.

LASTINGHAM North Yorks. 402 R 21 – pop. 108 – ECD : Wednesday – ✉ York – ☎ 075 15.

♦London 244 – Scarborough 26 – York 32.

🏨 **Lastingham Grange** ◐, YO6 6TH, ♫ 345, ≼, « Country house atmosphere », ▦ – TV ⌂wc ℗ ⬛ AE ⓪
closed mid December-February – **M** (bar lunch Monday to Saturday)/dinner 12.00 t. ▯ 2.25 – **12 rm** ☐ 33.75/67.00 t. – SB 84.50/94.50 st.

at Hutton-Le-Hole W : 2 m. – ✉ York – ☎ 075 15 Lastingham :

🏠 **Barn**, YO6 6UA, ♫ 311 – ▯wc ℗ ✦
Easter-October – **9 rm** ☐ 13.00/32.00 t.

239

LAVENHAM Suffolk 404 W 27 – pop. 1 658 – ECD : Wednesday – ✉ Sudbury – ☎ 0787.

See : SS. Peter and Paul's Church : the Spring Parclose★ (Flemish).

♦London 66 – ♦Cambridge 39 – Colchester 22 – ♦Ipswich 19.

🏨 **Swan** (T.H.F.), High St., CO10 9QA, ℰ 247477, « Part 14C timbered inn », ⊶ – 📺 🅿. 🏤. 🔄
AE ① VISA
M 7.75/12.50 **st.** and a la carte ⅄ 3.75 – ☲ 6.00 – **48 rm** 46.50/50.00 **st., 2 suites**.

XX **Great House** with rm, Market Pl., CO10 9QZ, ℰ 247431 – 📺 ⇌wc ☎. 🔄 AE VISA
closed 5 to 31 January – **M** (restricted lunch)/dinner 9.75 **t.** and a la carte 11.00/14.30 **t.** ⅄ 4.70
– **3 rm** ☲ 25.00/48.00 **t.** – SB (weekdays only) 100.65/120.45 **st.**

PEUGEOT, TALBOT Sudbury Rd ℰ 247228

LEAMINGTON SPA Warw. 403 404 P 27 – see Royal Leamington Spa.

LEDBURY Heref. and Worc. 403 404 M 27 – pop. 4 985 – ECD : Wednesday – ☎ 0531.

See : Church Lane★.

Envir. : Birtsmorton Court★ (15C) AC, SE : 7 m.

🛈 St. Katherine's, High St. ℰ 2461.

♦London 119 – Hereford 14 – Newport 46 – Worcester 16.

🏨 **Feathers,** High St., HR8 1DS, ℰ 5266, « Heavily timbered 16C inn », squash – 📺 ⇌wc ☎
🅿. 🔄 AE ①
M (buffet lunch)/dinner 8.20 **st.** and a la carte ⅄ 2.00 – **11 rm** ☲ 33.00/47.50 **st.** – SB (weekends only) 61.00 **st.**

🏠 **Royal Oak,** 5 The Southend, HR8 2EY, ℰ 2110 – 📺 ⇌wc 🅿. 🔄 VISA. ⅋
M (buffet lunch)/dinner a la carte 5.85/8.50 **st.** – **8 rm** ☲ 15.00/36.00 **t.**

at Wellington Heath N : 2 m. by B 4214 – ✉ ☎ 0531 Ledbury :

🏨 **Hope End Country House** ⌂, Hope End, HR8 1JQ, N : ¾ m. ℰ 3613, « Country house atmosphere », ⊶, park – ⇌wc 🅿. 🔄 VISA. ⅋
March-November – **M** (closed Monday and Tuesday) (dinner only) (booking essential) 18.00 **st.**
⅄ 4.00 – **7 rm** ☲ 53.00/68.00 **st.** – SB 90.00/100.00 **st.**

FORD New St. ℰ 2261

LEE Devon 403 H 30 – see Ilfracombe.

LES GUIDES VERTS MICHELIN

Paysages, monuments
Routes touristiques
Géographie, Économie
Histoire, Art
Itinéraires de visite
Plans de villes et de monuments.

LEEDS West Yorks. 402 P 22 – pop. 445 242 – ECD : Wednesday – ☎ 0532.

See : St. John's Church★ 17C DZ A.

Envir. : Temple Newsam House★ 17C (interior★★) AC, E : 4 m. CX D – Kirkstall Abbey★ (ruins 12C) AC, NW : 3 m. BV.

🛇 ⬜₈, ⬜₁₈ The Lady Dorothy Wood, The Lord Irwin, Temple Newsam Rd, Halton ℰ 645624, E : 3 m. CX – ⬜₁₈ Gotts Park, Armley Ridge Rd, ℰ 638232, W : 2 m. BV – ⬜₁₈ Middleton Park Municipal, Town St., Middleton ℰ 700449, S : 3 m. CX.

✈ Leeds and Bradford Airport : ℰ 0532 (Rawdon) 503431, Telex 557868 NW : 8 m. by A 65 and A 658 BV.

🛈 Central Library, Calverley St. ℰ 462453/4.

♦London 204 – ♦Liverpool 75 – ♦Manchester 43 – ♦Newcastle-upon-Tyne 95 – ♦Nottingham 74.

Plans on following pages

🏨 **Ladbroke Dragonara** (Ladbroke), Neville St., LS1 4BX, ℰ 442000, Telex 557143 – ⬦ ▤ rest
📺 ☎ & 🅿. 🏤. 🔄 AE VISA
DZ **r**
M a la carte approx. 11.25 ⅄ 3.70 – ☲ 5.75 – **234 rm** 54.50/65.00 **st.**

🏨 **Queen's** (T.H.F.), City Sq., LS1 1PL, ℰ 431323, Telex 55161 – ⬦ 📺 ⇌wc ⊚. 🏤. 🔄 AE ①
VISA
DZ **a**
M 8.50/9.00 **st.** and a la carte ⅄ 3.50 – ☲ 6.00 – **198 rm** 47.00/62.00 **st.**

🏨 **Metropole** (T.H.F.), King St., LS1 2HQ, ℰ 450841, Telex 557755 – ⬦ 📺 ⇌wc ⊚ 🅿. 🏤. 🔄
AE ① VISA
CZ **o**
M (carving rest.) 5.75/8.65 **st.** and a la carte ⅄ 3.40 – ☲ 5.65 – **110 rm** 40.00/50.00 **st.**

🏛 **Merrion,** Merrion Centre, 17 Wade Lane, LS2 8NH, ℰ 439191, Telex 55459 – ⃟ TV ⌁wc ☎
P. ⟷ ⟐ ⟐ **VISA**
DZ **x**
M 6.50/8.95 **st.** and a la carte ⟐ 3.50 – ⟷ 5.50 – **120 rm** 30.00/55.00 **st.** – SB (weekends only)
57.00/62.00 **st.**

🏠 **Aragon** ⟶, 250 Stainbeck Lane, LS7 2PS, ℰ 759306, ⟷ – TV ⌁wc ⟐wc **P.** ⟐ ⓞ
VISA
CV **c**
closed Christmas – **11 rm** ⟷ 14.50/28.00 **s.**

🏠 **Pinewood,** 78 Potternewton Lane, LS7 3LW, ℰ 622561, ⟷ – ⟐ **P.** ⟐ ⟷
AY **s**
closed 1 week Christmas – **11 rm** ⟷ 15.95/29.95 **t.**

🏠 **Ash Mount,** 22 Wetherby Rd, Oakwood, LS8 2QD, ℰ 654263 – **P.** ⟷
CV **u**
closed 1 week Christmas – **14 rm** ⟷ 13.35/29.50 **st.**

🏠 **Highfield,** 79 Cardigan Rd, LS6 1EB, ℰ 752193 – **P.**
AY **x**
10 rm ⟷ 11.65/23.00 **t.**

XXX Gardini's Terrazza, Minerva House, 16 Greek St., LS1 5RU, ℰ 432880, Italian rest. – ▦
CDZ **n**

XXX **Mandalay,** 8 Harrison St., LS1 6PA, ℰ 446453, Indian rest. – ▦. ⟐ ⟐ ⓞ **VISA**
DZ **e**
closed Saturday lunch and Sunday – **M** 4.75 **t.** and a la carte 8.40/11.90 **t.**

XX **Embassy,** 333 Roundhay Rd, LS8 4HT, NE : 2 ½ m. by A 58 ℰ 490562 – **P.** ⟐ ⟐ ⓞ
VISA
BY **v**
closed Sunday and Bank Holidays – **M** (dinner only) 11.80 **t.** and a la carte ⟐ 2.95.

XX **Shabab,** 2 Eastgate, LS2 7JL, ℰ 468988, Indian rest. – ▦. ⟐ ⟐ ⓞ **VISA**
DZ **v**
closed Sunday lunch and Christmas Day – **M** a la carte 5.30/9.50.

at Seacroft NE : 5 ½ m. at junction of A 64 and A 6120 – ✉ ✿ 0532 Leeds :

🏛 **Stakis Windmill** (Stakis), Ring Rd, LS14 5QP, ℰ 732323 – ⃟ ▤ rest TV ⌁wc ☎ ⅙ **P.** ⟐.
⟐ ⟐ ⓞ **VISA**
CV **a**
M (grill only) 5.95/10.75 **st.** ⟐ 3.40 – ⟷ 3.90 – **101 rm** 42.00/54.00 **st.**

at Garforth E : 6 m. at junction of A 63 and A 642 – CV – ✉ ✿ 0532 Leeds :

🏛 **Ladbroke** (Ladbroke), Wakefield Rd, LS25 1LH, ℰ 866556, Telex 556324 – TV ⌁wc ☎ ⅙
P. ⟐. ⟐ ⟐ ⓞ **VISA**
M (closed Saturday lunch) (carving rest.) 9.95 ⟐ 3.70 – ⟷ 5.50 – **142 rm** 44.00/53.00 **st.** – SB
(weekends only) 63.00 **st.**

at Oulton SE : 6 ¼ m. at junction of A 639 and A 642 – ✉ ✿ 0532 Leeds :

🏛 **Crest** (Crest), The Grove, LS26 8EW, ℰ 826201, Telex 557646 – TV ⌁wc ⟐ ⅙ **P.** ⟐ ⟐
VISA
CX **z**
M (closed lunch Saturday and Bank Holidays) 6.95/11.50 **st.** and a la carte – ⟷ 5.85 – **40 rm**
48.50/59.50 **st.** – SB (weekends only) 50.00/58.00 **st.**

at Horsforth NW : 5 m. by A 65 off A 6120 – ✉ ✿ 0532 Leeds :

XXX **Low Hall,** Calverley Lane, LS18 4EF, ℰ 588221, « Elizabethan manor », ⟷ – **P.** ⟐
VISA
BV **a**
closed Saturday lunch, Sunday, Monday, 25 to 30 December and Bank Holidays – **M** 8.50/16.00
st. and a la carte 16.50/24.25 **st.**

XX **Roman Garden,** Hall Lane, Hall Park, LS18 5JY, ℰ 587962, ⟨, Italian rest. – **P.** ⟐ ⟐
VISA
BV **i**
closed Saturday lunch, Sunday and Monday – **M** 6.25/8.75 **t.** and a la carte 9.80/16.50 **t.** ⟐ 2.75.

at Bramhope NW : 8 m. on A 660 – BV – ✉ ✿ 0532 Leeds :

🏛 **Post House** (T.H.F.), Otley Rd, LS16 9JJ, ℰ 842911, Telex 556367, ⟨ – ⃟ ▤ rest TV ⌁wc
⟐ ⅙ **P.** ⟐. ⟐ ⟐ ⓞ **VISA**
M (closed Saturday lunch) 7.25/14.50 **st.** and a la carte ⟐ 3.40 – ⟷ 5.65 – **120 rm** 50.00/
62.00 **st.**

🏛 **Parkway** (Embassy), Otley Rd, LS16 8AG, S : 2 m. on A 660 ℰ 672551, ⟷ – TV ⌁wc ⟐
P. ⟐. ⟐ ⟐ ⓞ **VISA**. ⟷
M 9.50 **st.** ⟐ 3.00 – ⟷ 5.00 – **39 rm** 44.00/53.00 **st.** – SB (weekends only) 59.00 **st.**

MICHELIN Distribution Centre, Gelderd Rd, LS12 6EU, ℰ **793911** BX

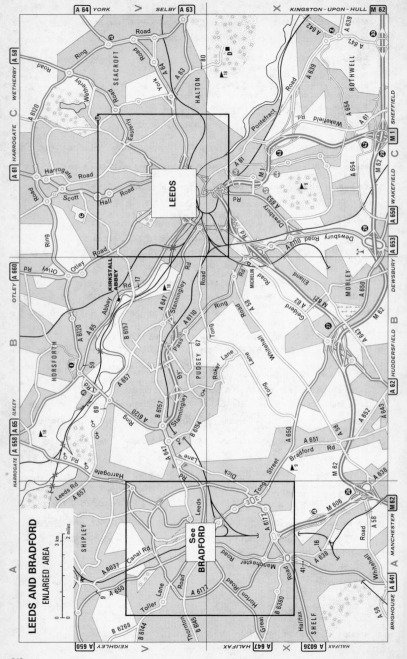

LEEDS AND BRADFORD
ENLARGED AREA

0 1 2 3 km
0   1   2 miles

LEEDS

See BRADFORD

KIRKSTALL ABBEY

A 58 WETHERBY
A 61 HARROGATE
A 660 OTLEY
A 65 ILKLEY
A 658 HARROGATE
A 650 KEIGHLEY
A 647 HALIFAX
A 6036 HALIFAX
A 641 BRIGHOUSE
M 62 MANCHESTER
A 653 DEWSBURY
A 650 WAKEFIELD
M 1 SHEFFIELD
A 62 HUDDERSFIELD

SHIPLEY
HORSFORTH
SEACROFT
HALTON
ROTHWELL
PUDSEY
MORLEY

242

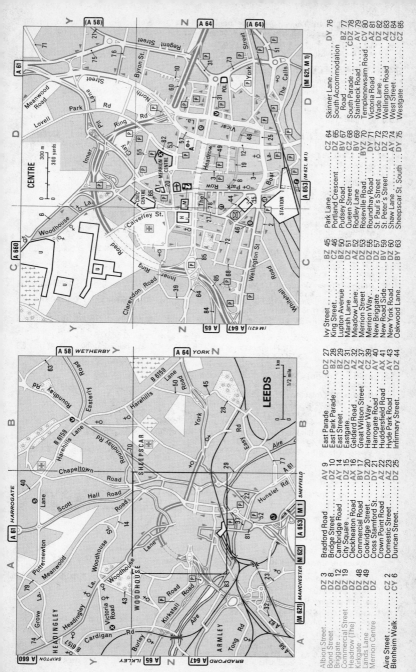

LEEMING BAR North Yorks. 402 P 21 – pop. 1 468 – ECD : Wednesday – ⊠ Northallerton – ✪ 0677 Bedale – ◆London 235 – ◆Leeds 44 – ◆Middlesbrough 30 – ◆Newcastle-upon-Tyne 52 – York 37.

🏠 **White Rose,** DL7 9AY, 𝒫 22707 – 📺 ⇌wc ⋔wc ☎ ✪ 🔼 AE ⑩ *VISA*
   M (bar lunch Monday to Saturday)/dinner 7.95 **t.** and a la carte ⅄ 3.25 – **12 rm** ⌑ 16.00/28.00 **t.**

LEE-ON-THE-SOLENT Hants. 403 404 Q 31 – pop. 7 068 – ECD : Thursday – ✪ 0705.
◆London 81 – ◆Portsmouth 13 – ◆Southampton 15 – Winchester 23.

🏠 **Belle Vue,** 39 Marine Par. East, PO13 2BW, 𝒫 550258 – 📺 ⇌wc ⋔wc ✪ 🔼 *VISA*
   closed 25 and 26 December – **M** (carving rest.) a la carte 5.20/13.20 **t.** – **32 rm** ⌑ 18.00/40.00 **t.**
   – SB 43.50/45.00 **st.**

NISSAN High St. 𝒫 551785

LEICESTER Leics. 402 403 404 Q 26 – pop. 324 394 – ECD : Monday and Thursday – ✪ 0533.
See : Museum of local archaeology, Jewry Wall and baths★ *AC* BY M1 – Museum and Art Gallery★
CY M2 – St. Mary de Castro's Church★ 12C BY A.

🏌 Leicestershire, Evington Lane 𝒫 738825 E : 2 m. AY – 🏌 Western Park, Scudamore Rd 𝒫 876158,
W : 4 m. AY – 🏌 Cambridge Rd, Whetstone 𝒫 861424 by A 426 AZ – ✈ East Midlands Airport :
Castle Donington 𝒫 0332 (Derby) 810621, Telex 37543, NW : 22 m. by A 50 AX and M1.
🛈 12 Bishop St. 𝒫 556699 – ◆London 107 – ◆Birmingham 43 – ◆Coventry 24 – ◆Nottingham 26.

Plans on following pages

🏨 **Holiday Inn,** 129 St. Nicholas Circle, LE1 5LX, 𝒫 531161, Telex 341281, 🔲 – 🛗 🍴 rest 📺 ☎
   🕭 🛗 🔼 AE ⑩ *VISA*   BY c
   M (buffet lunch)/dinner a la carte 14.00/25.00 **t.** – ⌑ 5.00 – **188 rm** 45.00/48.00 **st.**, **1 suite**
   115.00/130.00 **st.** – SB (weekends only) 72.00/80.00 **st.**

🏨 **Grand** (Embassy), 73 Granby St., LE1 6ES, 𝒫 555599, Group Telex 342244 – 🛗 🍴 rest 📺 ☎
   ✪ 🛗 🔼 AE ⑩ *VISA*   CY o
   closed 25 to 27 December – **M** (carving rest.) 8.50 **st.** and a la carte ⅄ 3.00 – ⌑ 5.00 – **93 rm**
   44.00/50.00 **st.**, **1 suite** 60.00 **st.** – SB (weekends only) 56.00 **st.**

🏨 **Belmont** (Best Western), De Montfort St., LE1 7GR, 𝒫 544773, Telex 34619 – 🛗 📺 ⇌wc ☎
   ✪ 🛗 🔼 AE ⑩ *VISA*   CY c
   M (closed Saturday lunch) 8.50/12.00 **st.** and a la carte ⅄ 3.95 – **60 rm** ⌑ 35.00/58.00 **st.** – SB
   (weekends only) 40.00/65.00 **st.**

🏨 **Queens,** Abbey St., LE1 3TE, 𝒫 50666, Telex 342434 – 🛗 📺 ⇌wc ⋔wc ☜ ✪ 🛗 🔼 AE
   ⑩ *VISA*   CX a
   M (carving rest.) 5.95/7.95 **t.** and a la carte ⅄ 2.50 – **73 rm** ⌑ 42.00/50.00 **t.**

🏨 **Ladbroke** (Ladbroke), Humberstone Rd, LE5 3AJ, 𝒫 20471, Telex 341460 – 🛗 🍴 rest 📺
   ⇌wc ☎ ✪ 🛗 🔼 AE ⑩ *VISA*   CX n
   M 9.25 ⅄ 3.70 – ⌑ 5.25 – **220 rm** 35.00/46.00 **st.**, **1 suite** – SB (weekends only) 63.00 **st.**

↑ **Spindle Lodge,** 2 West Walk, LE1 7NA, 𝒫 551380 – ✪   CY r
   closed Christmas – **12 rm** ⌑ 14.00/32.00 **st.**

↑ **Scotia,** 10 Westcotes Drive, LE3 0QR, 𝒫 549200 – 📺   AY e
   closed Christmas – **15 rm** ⌑ 15.00/30.00 **st.**

↑ **Rowans,** 290 London Rd, LE2 2AG, 𝒫 705364, 🚗 – 📺 ⋔ ✪ 🔼   AY i
   closed 23 December-4 January – **15 rm** ⌑ 15.50/25.00 **st.**

↑ **Burlington,** 3 Elmfield Av., Stoneygate, LE2 1RB, 𝒫 705112 – 📺 ⇌wc ⋔wc ✪ 🔼 *VISA*. 🍽
   closed Christmas and New Year – **17 rm** ⌑ 15.00/27.00 **st.**   AY a

✗✗ **Water Margin,** 76-78 High St., LE1 5YP, 𝒫 56422, Chinese-Cantonese rest. – 🍴 🔼 AE ⑩
   VISA   BY x
   M 2.20/8.00 **t.** and a la carte 5.40/22.50 **t.**

   at Rothley N : 5 m. by A 6 – AX – on B 5328 – ⊠ ✪ 0533 Leicester :

🏨 **Rothley Court** (Best Western) 🐾, Westfield Lane, LE7 7LG, W : ½ m. on B 5328 𝒫 374171,
   Telex 341995, ≼, « Part 12C house and chapel », 🚗 – 📺 ☎ ✪ 🛗 🔼 AE ⑩ *VISA*
   M (closed Saturday lunch) 10.50/16.50 **t.** and a la carte ⅄ 3.00 – **34 rm** ⌑ 42.00/68.50 **st.** – SB
   (weekends only)(except Christmas) 69.50/85.00 **st.**

↑ **Limes,** 35 Mount Sorrel Lane, LE7 7PS, 𝒫 302531 – ⋔wc ✪. 🍽
   10 rm ⌑ 17.50/25.00 **s.**

   at Oadby SE : 3 ¼ m. by A 6 – AY – on A 5096 – ⊠ ✪ 0533 Leicester :

🏠 **Leicestershire Moat House** (Q.M.H.), Wigston Rd, LE2 5QE, 𝒫 719441 – 🛗 📺 ⇌wc ☜
   ✪ 🛗 🔼 AE ⑩ *VISA*
   M (closed Saturday lunch) 8.00/9.00 **st.** and a la carte ⅄ 2.95 – **29 rm** ⌑ 38.00/50.00 **t.** – SB
   (weekends only) 48.00/58.00 **st.**

   at Whetstone S : 5 ½ m. by A 426 – AZ – ⊠ – ✪ 0533 Leicester :

✗✗✗ **Old Vicarage,** 123 Enderby Rd, LE8 3JY, 𝒫 771195 – ✪
   closed Saturday lunch, Sunday and Bank Holidays – **M** a la carte 8.05/11.55 ⅄ 3.00.

   at Braunstone SW : 2 m. on A 46 – BY – ⊠ ✪ 0533 Leicester :

🏨 **Post House** (T.H.F.), Braunstone Lane East, LE3 2FW, 𝒫 896688, Telex 341009 – 🛗 🍴 rest
   📺 ⇌wc ☜ 🕭 🛗 🔼 AE ⑩ *VISA*   AY u
   M (closed Saturday lunch) 6.95/9.75 **st.** and a la carte ⅄ 3.40 – ⌑ 5.65 – **172 rm** 45.00/52.00 **st.**

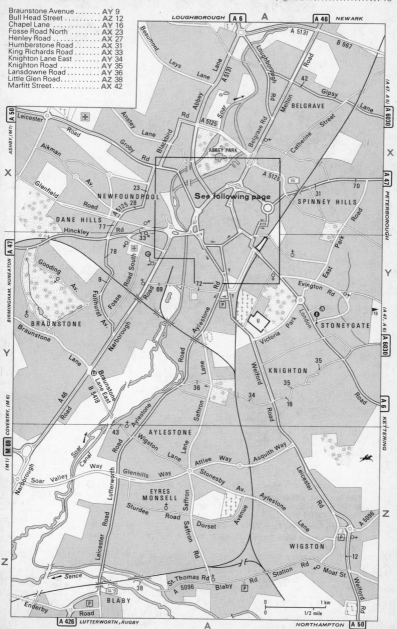

LEICESTER
BUILT UP AREA

See following page

245

LEICESTER
CENTRE

at Narborough SW : 6 m. by A 46 – AZ – and A 5096 on B 4114 – ⊠ ✪ 0533 Leicester :

Charnwood, 48 Leicester Rd, LE9 5DF, ℰ 862218, ☞ – TV ⌂wc ⌂wc ℗. ⬛ A℟ VISA
M (closed Sunday dinner to non residents) 5.25/7.50 t. and a la carte ⑃ 2.95 – **19 rm**
⊡ 28.50/38.00 t.

at Leicester Forest East W : 3 m. on A 47 – AY – ⊠ ✪ 0533 Leicester :

Leicester Forest Moat House (Q.M.H.), Hinckley Rd, LE3 3GH, ℰ 394661 – TV ⌂wc ☎ ℗.
⑃ – **29 rm**.

ALFA-ROMEO 2 Saxby St. ℰ 543300
AUDI, VW Dover St. ℰ 556262
AUSTIN-ROVER Leicester Rd ℰ 881601
AUSTIN-ROVER Parker Drive ℰ 352587
AUSTIN-ROVER 60-62 North Gate St. ℰ 28612
AUSTIN-ROVER Abbey Lane ℰ 669393
CITROEN 135-137 Queens Rd ℰ 709523
CITROEN, SUZUKI Lee Circle ℰ 25285
FORD Belgrave Gate ℰ 50111
FORD Conduit St. ℰ 544301

HONDA 7 Pike St. ℰ 56281
NISSAN Abbey Lane ℰ 666861
PEUGEOT, TALBOT Stoneygate Rd ℰ 700521
PORSCHE Coventry Rd at Narborough ℰ 848270
RENAULT, ROLLS ROYCE Welford Rd ℰ 548757
SKODA 252 Loughborough Rd, Mount Sorrel ℰ 661135
TALBOT 91 Abbey Lane ℰ 661501
VAUXHALL-OPEL Main St., Evington ℰ 730421
VOLVO 459 Aylestone Rd ℰ 831052

246

LEIGH Greater Manchester 402 403 404 M 23 – pop. 42 627 – ECD : Wednesday – ☎ 0942.
🏠 Kenyon Hall, Culcheth ✆ 092 576 (Culcheth) 3130, S : by A 574.
♦London 205 – ♦Liverpool 25 – ♦Manchester 12 – Preston 25.

🏨 **Greyhound** (Embassy), Warrington Rd, WN7 3XQ, S : 1 m. at junction A 580 and A 574
✆ 671256 – 🅿 📺 ⌧wc ☜ ⅋ 🅿 🔥 🅰 AE ⑩ VISA
M 7.35 st. and a la carte ⌟ 2.55 – ⌧ 5.00 – **54 rm** 40.00/48.00 st. – SB (weekends only)
42.00/48.00 **st.**

AUSTIN-ROVER Wigan Rd ✆ 671131
FIAT Small Brook Lane, Atherton ✆ 882201
FORD Brown St. Nth ✆ 673401

NISSAN 39 Plank Lane ✆ 602211
VAUXHALL-OPEL Wigan Rd ✆ 602931
VAUXHALL-OPEL 196 Chapel St. ✆ 671326

LELANT Cornwall – see St. Ives.

LENWADE-GREAT WITCHINGHAM Norfolk 404 X 25 – ECD : Wednesday – ✉ ☎ 0603 Norwich.
♦London 121 – Fakenham 14 – ♦Norwich 10.

🏠 **Lenwade House** 🦢, Fakenham Rd, NR9 5QP, ✆ 872288, ≼, « Country house atmosphere »,
🔺 heated, ≼, 🐎, park, 🎾, squash – 📺 ⌧wc ⒞wc ☎ 🅿 🔥 🅰 AE ⑩ VISA
M (closed Sunday) 5.95/9.95 **t.** and a la carte ⌟ 2.50 – ⌧ 3.75 – **13 rm** 26.50/36.50 **t.** – SB
(October-May) 53.00 **st.**

LEOMINSTER Heref. and Worc. 403 L 27 – pop. 8 637 – ECD : Thursday – ☎ 0568.
See : Priory Church★ 14C (the north aisle★ 12C).
Envir. : Berrington Hall★ (Georgian) AC, N : 3 m. – Croft Castle★ (15C) AC, NW : 6 m.
🛈 School Lane ✆ 2291 and 6460 – ♦London 141 – ♦Birmingham 47 – Hereford 13 – Worcester 26.

🏨 **Talbot** (Best Western), West St., HR6 8EP, ✆ 2121 – 📺 ⌧wc ⒞wc 🅿 🔥 🅰 AE ⑩ VISA
M 5.50/9.50 **st.** and a la carte ⌟ 3.00 – **28 rm** ⌧ 29.00/52.00 **st.** – SB 54.00/59.00 **st.**
🏠 **Royal Oak,** South St., HR6 8JA, ✆ 2610 – 📺 ⌧wc 🅿 🔥 🅰 AE ⑩ VISA
M 6.90/10.00 **st.** and a la carte ⌟ 3.00 – **16 rm** ⌧ 22.50/35.00 **st.**

at Stoke Prior SE : 2 m. by A 44 – ✉ ☎ 0568 Leominster :
✗ **Wheelbarrow Castle** with rm, HR6 0NB, ✆ 2219 – 🅿 🔥 🅰 VISA
closed Christmas Day – **M** a la carte 8.85/13.75 **t.** ⌟ 2.00 – **3 rm** ⌧ 10.50/18.00 **st.**

AUSTIN-ROVER South St. ✆ 2545
FORD 3-4 Etnam St. ✆ 2060

PEUGEOT-TALBOT The Bargates ✆ 2337
RENAULT West St. ✆ 2562

LETCHWORTH Herts. 404 T 28 – pop. 31 146 – ECD : Wednesday – ☎ 046 26 (4 and 5 fig.) or
0462 (6 fig.).
♦London 40 – Bedford 22 – ♦Cambridge 22 – Luton 14.

🏨 **Broadway,** The Broadway, SG6 3NZ, ✆ 685651 – 🅿 📺 ⌧wc ☎ 🅿 🔥 🅰 AE ⑩ VISA 🦢
closed Christmas and New Year – **M** (carving rest.) 7.50 **t.** ⌟ 2.85 – **37 rm** ⌧ 31.50/41.50 **t.**
🏨 **Letchworth Hall** 🦢, Letchworth Lane, SG6 3NP, S : 1 m. by A 505 ✆ 683747, Telex 825740,
≼, Dancing (Saturday), 🐎 – 📺 ⌧wc 🅿 🔥 🅰 AE ⑩ VISA ⅙ 🦢
closed 26 December – **M** 8.50 **t.** and a la carte ⌟ 3.00 – **42 rm** ⌧ 42.00/55.00 **t.**, **1 suite**
80.00/100.00 **t.** – SB (weekends only) 61.00/127.00 **st.**

AUSTIN-ROVER Works Rd ✆ 73161
FORD 18-22 Station Rd ✆ 83722

HONDA Norton Way North ✆ 78191
VW, AUDI Norton Way North ✆ 6341

LEWDOWN Devon 403 H 32 – ✉ ☎ 056 683.
♦London 238 – Exeter 37 – ♦Plymouth 22.

🏠 **Fox's Earth** 🦢, EX20 4PN, S : ¾ m. by Lewtrenchard Rd ✆ 256, « Country house atmosphere », 🔺, 🐎, park – 📺 ⌧wc 🅿 🅰 AE VISA ⅙
M (lunch by arrangement Monday to Saturday) 13.50/18.50 **t.** ⌟ 3.25 – ⌧ 4.50 – **8 rm**
30.00/66.00 **t.** – SB 80.00 **st.**

LEWES East Sussex 404 U 31 – pop. 14 499 – ECD : Wednesday – ☎ 0273.
See : Norman Castle (ruins) site and ≼★, 45 steps, AC – Anne of Cleves' House (1559) AC –
Envir. : Glynde Place (pictures★) AC, E : 3 ½ m. – Firle Place★ (mansion 15C-16C) AC, SE : 4 ½ m.
– Ditchling Beacon ≼★ W : 7 ½ m. – Glyndebourne Opera Festival (May-August) AC, E : 3 m.
🏠 Chapel Hill ✆ 473245, Opp. Junction Cliffe High/South St.
🛈 Lewes House, 32 High St. ✆ 471600 – ♦London 53 – Brighton 8 – Hastings 29 – Maidstone 43.

🏨 **Shelleys** (Mt. Charlotte), High St., BN7 1XS, ✆ 472361, 🐎 – 📺 ⌧wc ⒞wc 🅿 🔥 🅰 AE
⑩ VISA – **M** 9.00/10.00 **st.** ⌟ 3.00 – **21 rm.**
✗✗ **Trumps,** 19-20 Station St., BN7 2DB, ✆ 473906 – 🅰 AE ⑩ VISA
closed Monday and 27 to 30 December – **M** 11.95 **t.** ⌟ 3.50.
✗✗ **Kenwards,** Pipe Passage, 151a High St., BN7 1XU, ✆ 472343 – 🅰
closed Sunday, Monday, 1 week spring and 1 week autumn – **M** (dinner only) (booking
essential) a la carte 12.00/16.00 **st.** ⌟ 3.80.

AUSTIN-ROVER Brooks Rd ✆ 3186
FORD Station St. ✆ 4461

VW Western Rd ✆ 3221

LEYLAND Lancs. 402 L 22 – pop. 36 694 – ECD : Wednesday – ✪ 077 44.

♦London 220 – ♦Liverpool 31 – ♦Manchester 32 – Preston 6.

🏨 Ladbroke (Ladbroke), Leyland Way, PR5 3JX, E : ¾ m. on B 5256 ℘ 422922, Telex 677651 –
📺 ⌕wc ☎ & 🅿. 🔥. 🔼 AE ⓞ VISA
M (carving rest.) – **93 rm** 41.50/53.00 st. – SB (weekends only) 63.00 st.

AUSTIN-ROVER Preston Rd ℘ 52311
FORD Towngate ℘ 21766
PEUGEOT, TALBOT Golden Hill Lane ℘ 23416
SKODA Wigan Rd ℘ 423797

LICHFIELD Staffs. 402 403 404 O 25 – pop. 25 408 – ECD : Wednesday – ✪ 0543.

See : Cathedral★★ 12C-14C.

🛈 Donegal House, Bore St. ℘ 252109.

♦London 128 – ♦Birmingham 16 – Derby 23 – ♦Stoke-on-Trent 30.

🏨 George (Embassy), Bird St., WS13 6PR, ℘ 414822 – 📺 ⌕wc ⌕wc ☎ 🅿. 🔥 🔼 AE ⓞ VISA
M 8.00/9.50 st. and a la carte ⌗ 2.85 – ⌕ 5.25 – **39 rm** 42.00/50.00 st. – SB (weekends only)(except Christmas) 50.00/55.00 st.

🏨 Swan (Embassy) without rest., Bird St., WS13 6PW, ℘ 414851 – 📺 ⌕wc ⊕ 🅿. 🔥
31 rm

🏨 Little Barrow, Beacon St., WS13 7AR, ℘ 414500 – 📺 ⌕wc ☎ 🅿. 🔼 AE ⓞ VISA. ⬚
M 6.50/9.50 t. and a la carte ⌗ 3.50 – **24 rm** ⌕ 35.00/45.00 t. – SB (weekends only) 60.00 st.

🏠 Oakleigh House, 25 St. Chad's Rd, WS13 7LZ, ℘ 262688, ⌖ – 📺 ⌕wc ⌗wc 🅿. 🔼 VISA. ⬚
10 rm ⌕ 22.00/40.00 t.

🏠 Angel Croft, 3 Beacon St., WS13 7AA, ℘ 258737, ⌖ – 📺 ⌕wc ⌗wc ☎ 🅿. 🔼 ⓞ VISA. ⬚
closed 25 and 26 December – **M** (closed Sunday dinner) 12.00/12.50 t. ⌗ 3.20 – **21 rm**
⌕ 28.00/50.00 t.

⌂ Gaialands ⬚, 9 Gaiafields Rd, off Bulldog Lane, WS13 7LT, ℘ 263764, ⌖ – 🅿. ⬚
5 rm ⌕ 12.50/26.00 st.

✗ Thrales, 40-44 Tamworth St. (corner of Backcester Lane), ℘ 255091.

AUSTIN-ROVER St. John St. ℘ 414451
FORD Birmingham Rd ℘ 414566
MAZDA Birmingham Rd ℘ 414404

LIFTON Devon 403 H 32 – pop. 966 – ECD : Tuesday – ✪ 0566.

🛈 Launceston, St. Stephen ℘ 0566 (Launceston) 3442, W : 5 m.

♦London 238 – Bude 24 – Exeter 37 – Launceston 4 – ♦Plymouth 32.

🏨 Arundell Arms (Best Western), Fore St., PL16 0AA, on A 30 ℘ 84666, ⬚, ⌖ – 📺 ⌕wc
⌗wc ☎ 🅿. 🔼 🔼 AE ⓞ VISA
closed 22 to 27 December – **M** 8.50/13.50 t. and a la carte ⌗ 3.50 – **29 rm** ⌕ 23.50/56.00 t. –
SB 60.00/78.00 st.

LIMPSFIELD Surrey 404 U 30 – pop. 3 325 – ⊠ ✪ 088 33 Oxted.

♦London 24 – ♦Brighton 40 – Maidstone 25.

✗✗ Old Lodge, High St., RH8 0DR, ℘ 2996 – 🅿. 🔼 AE ⓞ VISA
closed Saturday lunch, Sunday dinner, Monday, 17 April and first 2 weeks January – **M**
18.50/25.00 st. ⌗ 3.75.

LINCOLN Lincs. 402 404 S 24 – pop. 79 980 – ECD : Wednesday – ✪ 0522.

See : Cathedral★★★ 11C-15C (Angel Choir★★, Library : Magna Carta AC) Y – Jew's House★★ 12C Y
– Castle★ (11C) AC Y – Newport Arch★ (Roman) Y E – Stonebow and Guildhall★ 15C-16C Z S.

Envir. : Doddington Hall★ (Elizabethan) AC, SW : 7 m. by A 15 Z and A 46.

🛈 Carholme ℘ 23725, 1 m. from town centre.

✈ Humberside Airport : ℘ 0652 (Barnetby) 688456, N : 32 m. by A 15 Y.

🛈 9 Castle Hill ℘ 29828 – 21 The Cornhill ℘ 32151 ext 504/5.

♦London 140 – Bradford 81 – ♦Cambridge 94 – ♦Kingston-upon-Hull 44 – ♦Leeds 73 – ♦Leicester 53 – ♦Norwich
104 – ♦Nottingham 38 – ♦Sheffield 46 – York 82.

Plan opposite

🏨 White Hart (T.H.F.), Bailgate, LN1 3AR, ℘ 26222, Telex 56304, « Antique furniture » – ⧗ 📺
⌔ 🅿. 🔥. 🔼 AE ⓞ VISA   Y c
M 9.50/16.00 st. and a la carte – ⌕ 5.65 – **49 rm** 50.00/61.00 st.. **8 suites**

🏨 Eastgate Post House (T.H.F.), Eastgate, LN2 1PN, ℘ 20341, Telex 56316, ⌖ – ⧗ 📺 ☎ &
🅿. 🔼 🔼 AE ⓞ VISA   Y a
M 7.95/9.50 st. and a la carte ⌗ 3.40 – ⌕ 5.65 – **71 rm** 47.00/59.00 st.

🏠 D'Isney Place without rest., Eastgate, LN2 4AA, ℘ 38881, ⌖ – 📺 ⌕wc ⌗wc ☎. 🔼 AE
ⓞ VISA   Y e
17 rm ⌕ 33.00/46.00 t.

🏠 Hillcrest, 15 Lindum Terr., LN2 5RT, ℘ 26341, ⬘, ⌖ – 📺 ⌗wc 🅿. 🔼 VISA   Y o
M (closed Sunday dinner) (bar lunch)/dinner a la carte 6.85/9.40 t. ⌗ 3.05 – **15 rm**
⌕ 21.00/36.00 t. – SB (weekends only)(October-April) 35.00/42.00 st.

248

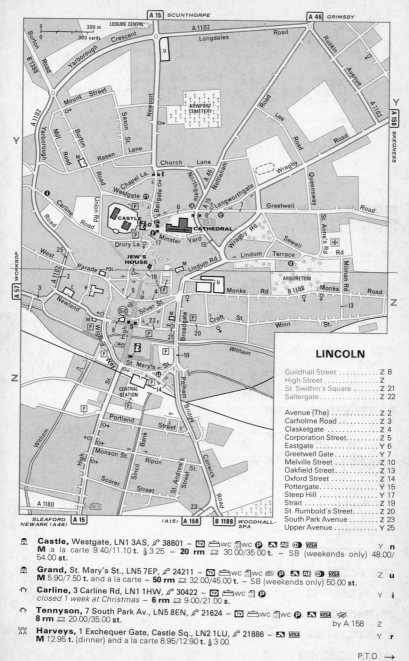

LINCOLN

🏛 **Castle,** Westgate, LN1 3AS, ℰ 38801 – 📺 ⇌wc 🛁wc 🅿 🅰 AE ⑩ VISA   Y **n**
M a la carte 9.40/11.10 **t.** ⅄ 3.25 – **20 rm** � 30.00/35.00 **t.** – SB (weekends only) 48.00/
54.00 **st.**

🏛 **Grand,** St. Mary's St., LN5 7EP, ℰ 24211 – 📺 ⇌wc 🛁wc ☜ 🅿 🅰 AE ⑩ VISA   Z **u**
M 5.90/7.50 **t.** and a la carte – **50 rm** � 32.00/45.00 **t.** – SB (weekends only) 50.00 **st.**

⌂ **Carline,** 3 Carline Rd, LN1 1HW, ℰ 30422 – 📺 ⇌wc 🛁 🅿   Y **i**
closed 1 week at Christmas – **6 rm** � 9.00/21.00 **s.**

⌂ **Tennyson,** 7 South Park Av., LN5 8EN, ℰ 21624 – 📺 ⇌wc 🛁wc 🅿 🅰 VISA ⌖
8 rm � 20.00/35.00 **st.**   by A 158   Z

XX **Harveys,** 1 Exchequer Gate, Castle Sq., LN2 1LU, ℰ 21886 – 🅰 VISA   Y **r**
M 12.95 **t.** (dinner) and a la carte 8.95/12.90 **t.** ⅄ 3.00.

P.T.O. →

at Washingborough E : 3 m. by B 1188 – Z – on B 1190 – ⊠ ✿ 0522 Lincoln :

🏠 **Washingborough Hall** ⬧, Church Hill, LN4 1BE, ✆ 790340, ⏏, ⌦ – ⊤⊽ ⊢wc ⋔wc ☎
℗ ⬛ ⒜⒠ ⓞ 𝘝𝘐𝘚𝘈
M (bar lunch Monday to Saturday)/dinner 8.50 **st.** ⒤ 3.00 – **12 rm** ⊇ 27.00/44.00 **t.** – SB
46.00 **st.**

at Branston SE : 3 m. on B 1188 – Z – ✿ 0522 Lincoln :

🏠🏠 **Moor Lodge,** Sleaford Rd, LN4 1HU, ✆ 791366 – ⊤⊽ ⊢wc ⋔wc ☎ ⅋ ℗ ⬛ ⒜⒠ ⓞ 𝘝𝘐𝘚𝘈
M (closed Saturday lunch) 7.50/9.50 **t.** and a la carte ⒤ 2.75 – **25 rm** ⊇ 35.00/48.00 **t.** – SB
52.00 **st.**

MICHELIN Distribution Centre, Tritton Rd, LN6 7RX, ✆ 684023 by A 1180 Z

AUSTIN-ROVER Outer Circle Rd ✆ 35771
BMW South Park Av. ✆ 21345
CITROEN 300 Wragby Rd ✆ 31195
DAIMLER-JAGUAR High St. ✆ 43637
FIAT 316-322 Wragby Rd ✆ 34805
FORD Wragby Rd ✆ 30101
HONDA, LANCIA Wragby Rd ✆ 31735
LADA, MAZDA Newark Rd, North Hykeham ✆ 681242

NISSAN 148 Newark Rd ✆ 42281
RENAULT 25 Wragby Rd ✆ 21252
SAAB 247 Lincoln Rd ✆ 681463
TALBOT, PEUGEOT 477 High St. ✆ 29131
VAUXHALL Outer Circle Rd ✆ 31785
VOLVO 314 Wragby Rd ✆ 29462/3
VW, AUDI 223 Newark Rd ✆ 31881

LISKEARD Cornwall **403** G 32 The West Country G. – pop. 6 213 – ECD : Wednesday – ✿ 0579.
See : Church★.
Envir. : St. Neot★ (Church★★), NW : 5 m.
◆London 261 – Exeter 59 – ◆Plymouth 18 – Truro 37.

🏠 **Country Castle** ⬧, Station Rd, PL14 4EB, SW : ¾ m. by B 3254 ✆ 42694, ⏏, ⌦ – ⊤⊽
⊢wc ⋔wc ☎ ℗ ⬛ 𝘝𝘐𝘚𝘈
closed November – **M** 7.50/9.00 **st.** ⒤ 2.90 – **10 rm** ⊇ 16.00/50.00 **st.** – SB 41.00/56.00 **st.**

🏠 **Lord Eliot,** Castle St., PL14 3AU, ✆ 42717 – ⊤⊽ ⊢wc ⋔wc ℗ ⬛ 𝘝𝘐𝘚𝘈
M 7.50 **st.** and a la carte 4.50/11.00 **st.** ⒤ 2.95 – **16 rm** ⊇ 26.50/39.00 **st.** – SB 36.00/60.00 **st.**

at St. Keyne S : 3 ½ m. on B 3254 – ⊠ ✿ 0579 Liskeard :

🏠 **Old Rectory** ⬧, PL14 4RL, ✆ 42617, ⌦ – ⊤⊽ ⊢wc ⋔wc ℗ ⬛ 𝘝𝘐𝘚𝘈
closed February – **M** (bar lunch)/dinner 15.00 **t.** ⒤ 2.50 – **9 rm** ⊇ 16.00/36.00 **t.** – SB (except
summer) 44.00/48.00 **st.**

LISS Hants. **404** R 30 – pop. 5 489 – ✿ 0730.
◆London 57 – ◆Portsmouth 22 – Reading 34.

✗✗ **Le Papillon,** 94 Station Rd., GU33 7AQ, ✆ 893363, ⌦ – ℗ ⬛ ⒜⒠ ⓞ 𝘝𝘐𝘚𝘈
closed Saturday lunch, Sunday and Monday – **M** (lunch by arrangement)/dinner 15.00 **t.**
⒤ 3.50.

LITTLE CHALFONT Bucks. **404** S 29 – pop. 4 093 – ✿ 024 04.
◆London 31 – Luton 20 – ◆Oxford 37.

✗✗ **Dynasty 1,** 9 Nightingales Corner, HP7 9PZ, ✆ 4038, Chinese-Peking rest. – ⬛ ⒜⒠ 𝘝𝘐𝘚𝘈
closed 20 April and 25-26 December – **M** 15.00/20.00 **t.** and a la carte 10.00/19.30 **t.**

LITTLE HAVEN Dyfed **403** E 28 – ECD : Thursday – ⊠ Haverfordwest – ✿ 043 783 Broad Haven.
◆London 258 – Haverfordwest 8.

🏠 **Haven Fort,** Settlands Hill, SA62 3LA, ✆ 401, ⬱ St. Brides Bay, ⌦ – ⊢wc ⋔wc ℗ ⬧
Mid March-mid October – **M** (bar lunch)/dinner 9.95 **t.** ⒤ 4.80 – **15 rm** ⊇ 18.50/37.00 **t.**

⋔ **Pendyffryn,** SA62 3LA, ✆ 337, ⬱ – ⊤⊽ ℗ ⬧
Mid May-September – **7 rm** ⊇ 11.00/18.00.

LITTLE KELYNACK Cornwall – see St. Just.

LITTLE LANGDALE Cumbria **402** K 20 – see Ambleside.

LITTLEOVER Derbs. **402 403 404** P 25 – see Derby.

LITTLE SINGLETON Lancs. – see Blackpool.

LITTLE THORNTON Lancs. **402** L 22 – see Blackpool.

LITTLE WEIGHTON Humberside **402** S 22 – see Kingston-upon-Hull.

LITTLE WYMONDLEY Herts. **404** T 28 – see Hitchin.

LIVERPOOL Merseyside **402 403** L 23 – pop. 538 809 – ECD : Wednesday – ✪ 051.

See : Walker Art Gallery★★ CY **M1** – City of Liverpool Museums★ CY **M2** – Anglican Cathedral★ (1904) CZ **A** – Roman Catholic Cathedral★ (1967) DZ **B**.

Envir. : Knowsley Safari Park★★ *AC*, NE : 8 m. by A 57 BX – Speke Hall★ (16C) *AC*, SE : 7 m. by A 561 BX.

🖸 Dunnings Bridge Rd, Bootle ✆ 928 1371, N : 5 m. by A 5036 AV – 🖸 Allerton Park ✆ 428 1046, S : 5 m. by B 5180 BX – 🖸 Childwall, Naylor's Rd, Gateacre ✆ 487 9982, E : 7 m. by B 5178 BX.

✈ Liverpool Airport : ✆ 494 0066, Telex 629323, SE : 6 m. by A 561 BX – **Terminal : Pier Head.**

⛴ to Ireland (Dublin) (B & I Line) 1 nightly (8 h 45 mn) – to Belfast (Belfast Car Ferries) 1 daily (9 h) – to Douglas (Isle of Man Steam Packet Co.) 1-2 weekly (summer only) (3 h).

⛴ to Birkenhead (Merseyside Transport) frequent services daily (7-8 mn) – to Wallasey (Merseyside Transport) frequent services daily (7-8 mn).

🛈 29 Lime St. ✆ 709 3631.

◆London 219 – ◆Birmingham 103 – ◆Leeds 75 – ◆Manchester 35.

Town plans : Liverpool pp. 2-5

🏨 **Liverpool Moat House** (Q.M.H.), Paradise St., L1 8JD, ✆ 709 0181, Telex 627270, ☒ – 📶
📧 📺 ☎ ᵹ ₫ 🏧 🔼 🅰🅴 ① 💳
closed 25 to 28 December – **M** 6.00/8.50 t. and a la carte – **253 rm** ⣥ 48.00/59.75, **7 suites** 74.00/160.00 – SB (weekends only) 56.50/67.00 **st.**
CZ **n**

🏨 **Atlantic Tower Thistle** (Thistle), 30 Chapel St., L3 9RE, ✆ 227 4444, Telex 627070, ⇐ – 📶
📧 📺 ☎ ℗ ₫ 🔼 🅰🅴 ① 💳
M 9.50 t. and a la carte ᶙ 3.20 – ⣥ 6.25 – **226 rm** 47.00/70.00 **st.**, **10 suites** 70.00 – SB (weekends only) 58.00 st.
CY **r**

🏨 **St. George's** (T.H.F.), St. John's Precinct, Lime St., L1 1NQ, ✆ 709 7090, Telex 627630 – 📶
📺 ☎ ᵹ ₫ 🔼 🅰🅴 ① 💳
M (carving rest.) 5.50/8.65 **st.** and a la carte ᶙ 3.40 – ⣥ 6.00 – **155 rm** 46.00/55.00 **st.**, **2 suites**.
CY **v**

🏨 **Crest** (Crest), Lord Nelson St., L3 5QB, ✆ 709 7050, Telex 627954 – 📶 📺 ⌷wc 🏧 ₫
M (bar lunch)/dinner 13.00 **st.** and a la carte ᶙ 3.00 – ⣥ 5.85 – **160 rm** 45.00/55.00 **st.**, **1 suite** 60.00/85.00 st. – SB (weekends only) 56.00 **st.**
CY **i**

🏩 **Green Park,** 4-6 Green Bank Drive, Sefton Park, L17 1AN, SE : 2 ½ m. by A 562 ✆ 733 3382,
😊 – 📺 ⌷wc �848wc ℗ 🔼 🅰🅴 ① 💳
M 6.00 t. and a la carte ᶙ 3.00 – **23 rm** ⣥ 13.00/32.00 **st.** – SB (weekends only) 34.50 st.
BX **u**

XXX Ristorante del Secolo, First Floor, 36-40 Stanley St., L2 6AL, ✆ 236 4004, Italian rest.
CY **x**

XXX Churchill's, Churchill House, Tithebarn St., L2 2PB, ✆ 227 3877 – 🔼 🅰🅴 ① 💳
closed Saturday lunch, Sunday and Bank Holidays – **M** 9.75/12.95 t. and a la carte 12.00/20.00 t. ᶙ 3.25.
CY **a**

XX **Jenny's Seafood,** Old Ropery, Fenwick St., L2 7NT, ✆ 236 0332, Seafood – 📧 🔼 🅰🅴 ①
💳
closed Saturday lunch, Monday dinner, Sunday, 25 December-2 January and Bank Holidays –
M 9.55 t. and a la carte 9.65/16.60 t. ᶙ 2.25.
CZ **e**

at Bootle N : 5 m. by A 565 – AV – ✉ ✪ 051 Liverpool :

🏨 **Park,** Park Lane West, L30 3SU, on A 5036 ✆ 525 7555, Telex 629772 – 📶 📺 ⌷wc �848wc
℗ ₫ 🔼 🅰🅴 ① 💳
M 5.00 **st.** and a la carte ᶙ 3.80 – **60 rm** 38.00/48.00 **st.**

at Blundellsands N : 6 ½ m. by A 565 – AV – ✉ ✪ 051 Liverpool :

🏨 **Blundellsands** (Whitbread), The Serpentine South, L23 6TN, ✆ 924 6515 – 📶 📺 ⌷wc ⎙
℗ ₫ 🔼 🅰🅴 ① 💳
M 7.50/10.00 **t.** and a la carte – **39 rm** ⣥ 40.00/45.00 **t.**

at Aigburth SE : 4 m. on A 561 – BX – ✉ ✪ 051 Liverpool :

🏨 **Grange,** 14 Holmefield Rd, L19 3PG, ✆ 427 2950, 🌊 – 📺 ⌷wc ☎ ℗ 🔼 🅰🅴 ① 💳 ❀
M (dinner only and Sunday lunch)/dinner 9.75 t. and a la carte ᶙ 2.90 – **25 rm** ⣥ 30.00/48.00 **st.**
– SB (weekends only) 51.50/67.50 **st.**

X **L'Alouette,** 2 Lark Lane, L17 8US, ✆ 727 2142, French rest. – 🔼 💳
closed Saturday lunch and Monday – **M** 5.50/15.00 **st.** and a la carte ᶙ 3.75.
BX **n**

AUSTIN-ROVER 72-74 Coronation Rd ✆ 924 6411
AUSTIN-ROVER Long Lane ✆ 523 3737
BMW Scotland Rd ✆ 207 7213
BMW Aigburth Rd ✆ 427 8086
CITROEN, MITSUBISHI Ullet Rd ✆ 727 1414
FIAT Coronation Rd ✆ 924 9101
FIAT East Prescot Rd ✆ 228 9151
FORD Linacre Lane ✆ 922 0070
FORD Prescot St. ✆ 260 9898
FORD Speke Hall Rd ✆ 486 2233
NISSAN Mersey Rd ✆ 924 6575
NISSAN Queen's Drive ✆ 523 9779
PEUGEOT-TALBOT Edge Lane ✆ 924 4210

RENAULT, SEAT Edge Lane ✆ 220 2611
SAAB 574 Aigburth Rd ✆ 427 3500
SKODA Durning Rd ✆ 263 7374
SKODA Bridge Rd ✆ 928 2515
TOYOTA Gale Rd ✆ 546 8228
TOYOTA 1 Aigburth Rd ✆ 727 2204
VAUXHALL-OPEL 215 Knowsley Rd ✆ 922 7585
VAUXHALL-OPEL Speke Hall Rd ✆ 486 8846
VAUXHALL-OPEL Derby Rd ✆ 933 7575
VOLVO Fox St. ✆ 207 4364
VW, AUDI Moor Lane, Thornton ✆ 931 2861
VW, AUDI Edge Lane ✆ 228 0919

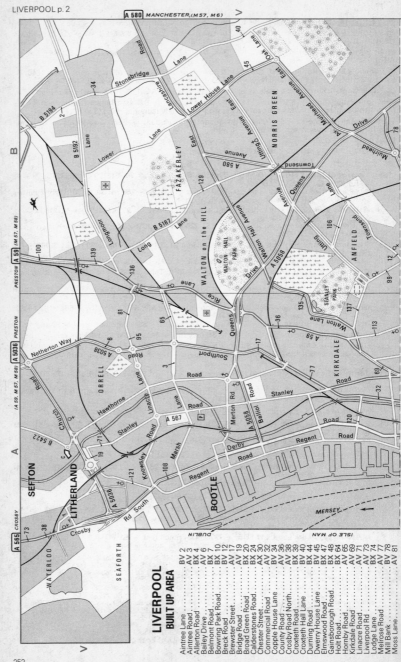

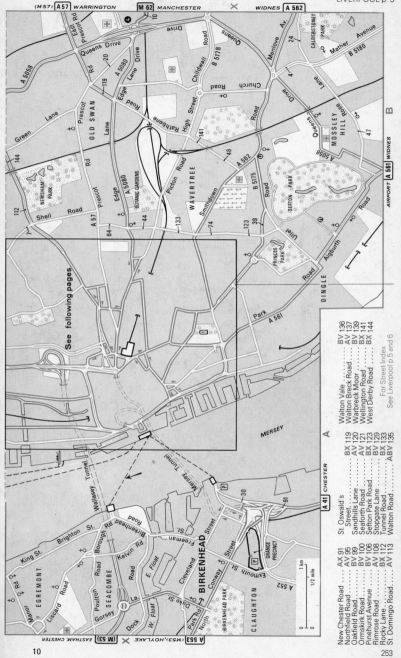

LIVERPOOL
CENTRE

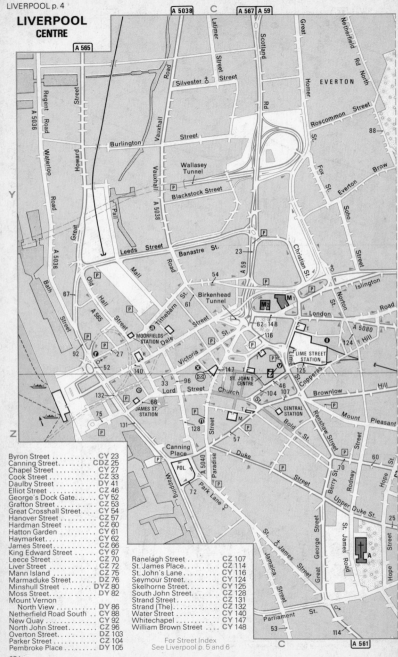

For Street Index
See Liverpool p. 5 and 6

254

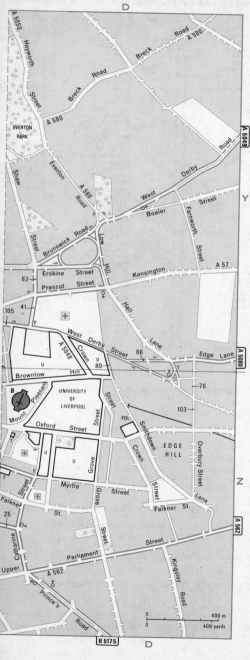

STREET INDEX

Concluded on next page

255

STREET INDEX TO LIVERPOOL TOWN PLANS (concluded)

☞ *Michelin n'accroche pas de panonceau aux hôtels et restaurants qu'il signale.*

LIVERSEDGE West Yorks. **402** O 22 — ✪ 0924 Heckmondwike.

◆London 197 — Bradford 7 — ◆Leeds 9 — ◆Manchester 37.

XX **Lillibet's** with rm, Ashfield House, 64 Leeds Rd, WF15 6HX, ℰ 404911, 🛪 – 📺 ⇨wc 🏲wc
🕸 🅿 📠 🖭 ① 𝗩𝗜𝗦𝗔 ⚘
closed Sunday, last 2 weeks July and 25 December-1 January – **M** (dinner only) 12.25 t. ᾇ 3.25
– **7 rm** 🖙 27.50/50.00 st.

LIZARD Cornwall **403** E 34 The West Country G. — ✪ 0326 The Lizard.

See : Lizard Peninsula★★ – **Envir. :** Kynance Cove★★★, NW : 1 ½ m. – Landewednack★, Church★,
E : ½ m. – Cury★, Church★, N : 6 ½ m. – Cadgwith★, NE : 4 m. – Ruan Minor (Church★), NE : 4 m.
– Gunwalloe Fishing Cove★, NW : 9 m. – Mawgan In Meneage Church★, N : 10 m.

◆London 326 — Penzance 24 — Truro 29.

🏠 **Housel Bay** ⑤, Housel Cove, TR12 7PG, ℰ 290417, ≼ Housel Cove, 🛪 – ⇨wc 🏲wc 🅿
📠 🖭 𝗩𝗜𝗦𝗔
M (bar lunch)/dinner 9.00 st. and a la carte ᾇ 3.00 – **27 rm** 🖙 24.00/50.00 st.

⌂ **Parc Brawse House** ⑤, Penmenner Rd, TR12 7NR, ℰ 290466, ≼, 🛪 – 🅿
Easter-October – **6 rm** 🖙 13.00/24.00.

⌂ **Penmenner House** ⑤, Penmenner Rd, TR12 7NR, ℰ 290370, ≼ – 🏲wc 🅿
April-October – **8 rm** 🖙 11.50/27.00 t.

LLANARMON DYFFRYN CEIRIOG Clwyd **402** **403** K 25 — pop. 137 — ⊠ Llangollen — ✪ 069 176.

◆London 196 — Chester 33 — Shrewsbury 32.

🏠 **Hand**, LL20 7LD, ℰ 666, ⌲, 🛪, ⚘ – ⇨wc 🅿 📠 🖭 ① 𝗩𝗜𝗦𝗔 ⚘
M (bar lunch Monday to Saturday)/dinner 11.95 t. – **13 rm** 🖙 32.00/50.00 t. – SB 70.00/78.00 st.

🏠 **West Arms**, LL20 7LD, ℰ 665, ⌲, 🛪 – ⇨wc 🏲 🅿 📠 🖭 ① 𝗩𝗜𝗦𝗔 ⚘
M (bar lunch)/dinner 10.50 st. ᾇ 2.95 – **12 rm** 🖙 22.00/38.00 t. – SB (September-May)
51.00/55.00 st.

LLANBEDR Gwynedd 402 403 H 25 – pop. 486 – ECD : Wednesday – ✆ 034 123.
♦London 262 – Holyhead 54 – Shrewsbury 100.

🏨 **Pensarn Hall** ⟡, LL45 2HS, N : ¾ m. on A 496 ℰ 236, ≤, ↝ – ▥ ➪wc ₱. ⚓
M 5.00/7.50 **st.** and a la carte ⓘ 2.25 – **7 rm** ⌂ 14.50/28.00 **st.**

🏠 **Ty Mawr** ⟡, LL45 2NH, ℰ 440, ↝ – ▥ ➪wc ⧖wc ₱
M (bar lunch)/dinner a la carte 8.00/10.00 **t.** ⓘ 2.70 – **10 rm** ⌂ 18.00/36.00 **t.** – SB 46.50 **st.**

LLANBEDR PONT STEFFAN = Lampeter.

LLANBERIS Gwynedd 403 H 24 – pop. 1 809 – ECD : Wednesday – ✆ 0286.
🛈 Oriel Eryri ℰ 870765 – ♦London 243 – Caernarfon 7 – Chester 65 – Shrewsbury 78.

🏠 **Pen y Gwryd** ⟡, Nant Gwynant, LL55 4NT, SE : 6 m. via Pass of Llanberis ℰ 870211, ≤ –
closed mid November-1 January and weekdays January-February – M (buffet lunch)/dinner
9.50 **st.** – **21 rm** ⌂ 12.60/27.20 **st.**

XX **Y Bistro**, 43-45 High St., LL55 4EU, ℰ 871278 – ▦ AE ⓞ VISA
closed Sunday, 3 weeks January and 1 week October – M (lunch by arrangement)(booking
essential)/dinner 18.50 **t.**

LLANDEILO Dyfed 403 I 28 – pop. 1 598 – ECD : Thursday – ✆ 0558.
Envir. : Talley (abbey and lakes★) N : 7 m.
🔟₈ Glynhir, Llandybie nr. Ammanford ℰ 0269 (Llandybie) 850472.
♦London 218 – Brecon 34 – Carmarthen 15 – ♦Swansea 25.

🏛 **Cawdor Arms**, Rhosmaen St., SA19 6EN, ℰ 823500, « Tasteful decor » – ▥ ➪wc ⧖wc
⚲ ₱. ▦ AE ⓞ VISA
M 13.00/15.00 **t.** and a la carte ⓘ 3.30 – **17 rm** ⌂ 36.00/57.50 **t.** – SB (weekends only)(except
Christmas) 65.00/75.00 **st.**

at Rhosmaen N : 1 m. on A 40 – ✉ ✆ 0558 Llandeilo :

X **Plough Inn**, SA19 6NP, ℰ 823431, Italian rest. – ₱ ▦ VISA
closed Sunday, first week November and Christmas Day – M a la carte 7.20/15.75 **t.**

AUSTIN-ROVER 28 Rhosmaen St. ℰ 823221

LLANDEWI SKIRRID Gwent – see Abergavenny.

LLANDRILLO-YN-RHOS (RHOS-ON-SEA) Clwyd – see Colwyn Bay.

LLANDRINDOD WELLS Powys 403 J 27 – pop. 4 232 – ECD : Wednesday – ✆ 0597.
🔟₈ ℰ 2010, E : 1 m.
🛈 Rock Park Spa ℰ 2600 – ♦London 204 – Brecon 29 – Carmarthen 60 – Shrewsbury 58.

🏛 **Metropole** (Best Western), Temple St., LD1 5DY, ℰ 2881, Telex 35237, ↝ – ▤ ▥ ➪wc ☎
₱. ▦ AE ⓞ VISA
M 9.00/11.00 **t.** ⓘ 3.60 – **121 rm** ⌂ 31.50/52.00 **t.**, **2 suites** 65.00/68.00 **t.** – SB 56.00/67.00 **st.**

🏠 **Griffin Lodge**, Temple St., LD1 5HF, ℰ 2432 – ⧖wc ₱ ▦ AE VISA
closed January – M 5.50 **t.** and a la carte ⓘ 3.00 – **8 rm** ⌂ 14.50/28.00 **t.** – SB (except July and
August) 30.00/34.00 **st.**

at Howey S : 1 ½ m. on A 483 – ✉ ✆ 0597 Llandrindod Wells :

🏠 **Corven Hall** ⟡, LD1 5RE, S : ½ m. by A 483 on Hundred House rd ℰ 3368, ↝ – ⧖wc ₱
closed 1 week at Christmas – **7 rm** ⌂ 12.00/19.00 **st.**

AUDI, VW Doldowlod ℰ 0597 810376   FORD Ridgebourne Service Station ℰ 0597 2249

LLANDUDNO Gwynedd 402 403 I 24 – pop. 13 202 – ECD : Wednesday except summer –
✆ 0492.
See : Great Orme's Head (≤★★ from the summit) by Ty-Gwyn Rd A – Tour of the Great Orme's
Head★★ – 🔟₈ Rhos-on-Sea Residential, Penryn Bay ℰ 49641 by A 546 B.
🛈 Chapel St. ℰ 76413 – Arcadia Theatre ℰ 76413 ext 264 (summer only) – Kiosk, North Promenade ℰ 76572
(summer only).
♦London 243 – Birkenhead 55 – Chester 47 – Holyhead 43.

Plan on next page

🏰 **Bodysgallen Hall** ⟡, LL30 1RS, SE : 2 ½ m. on A 470 ℰ 0492 (Deganwy) 84466, Telex
617163, ≤ gardens and mountains, « Part 17 C and 18 C hall with terraced gardens », park,
⚲ – ▥ ₱. ▦ AE ⓞ VISA ⚓   on A 470   B
M 8.50/16.50 **t.** and a la carte ⓘ 3.30 – ⌂ 5.00 – **28 rm** 50.00/95.00 **st.**, **9 suites** 75.00/95.00 **st.**
– SB (except summer) 90.00 **st.**

🏰 **Empire**, 73 Church Walks, LL30 2HE, ℰ 79955, Telex 617161, ▨ – ▤ ▥ ₱ ▦ AE ⓞ VISA
closed 2 weeks at Christmas and New Year – M 8.00/11.25 **st.** and a la carte ⓘ 3.25 – **56 rm**
⌂ 27.50/65.00 **st.** – SB 46.00/85.00 **st.**
                                                                                          A e

257

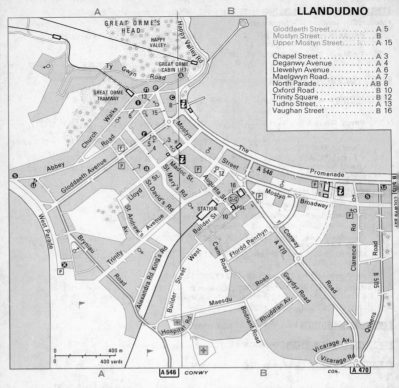

St. Tudno, Promenade, LL30 2LP, ☎ 74411, « Tasteful decor », ▨ – ⌷ TV ⌷wc ⌷wc ☎.
▨ VISA ⌷
closed 20 December-22 January – **M** (bar lunch Monday to Saturday)/dinner 14.50 **t.**
⌷ 3.25 – **21 rm** ⌷ 25.00/70.00 **t.** – SB (except Bank Holidays)(November-March) 52.00/
88.00 **st.**
A **c**

Gogarth Abbey, West Shore, LL30 2QY, ☎ 76211, ≤, ▨, ⌷ – TV ⌷wc ⌷wc **P.** ▨ AE
VISA ⌷
closed 24 December-23 January – **M** (bar lunch)/dinner 11.00 **t.** and a la carte ⌷ 3.50 – **41 rm**
⌷ 23.00/50.00 **t.**, **1 suite** 60.00/70.00 **t.** – SB 50.00/70.00 **st.**
A **s**

Dunoon, Gloddaeth St., LL30 2DW, ☎ 77078 – ⌷ TV ⌷wc **P**
Mid March-October – **M** 6.00/7.50 **st.** and a la carte ⌷ 2.25 – **57 rm** ⌷ 14.00/28.00 **st.** – SB
38.00/52.00 **st.**
A **r**

Bryn-y-Bia Lodge, Bryn-y-Bia Rd, Craigside, LL30 3AS, E : 1 ½ m. on A 546 ☎ 49644, ⌷ –
TV ⌷wc ⌷wc **P**
closed December and January – **M** (booking essential for lunch) 8.00/12.00 **t.** ⌷ 3.50 – **18 rm**
⌷ 18.00/40.00 **t.** – SB (October-May) 46.00/55.00 **st.**
by A 546 B

Bromwell Court, Promenade, 6 Craig-y-Don Par., LL30 1BG, ☎ 78416 – TV ⌷wc ⌷wc. ▨
VISA
closed 24 December-February – **M** (bar lunch)/dinner 9.50 **t.** ⌷ 3.50 – **11 rm** ⌷ 17.50/33.00 **t.**
– SB (October-May) 43.00/46.00 **st.**
B **u**

Headlands, Hill Terr., LL30 2LS, ☎ 77485, ≤ Llandudno and Ormes Bay – TV ⌷wc ⌷wc
P. ▨ ⓪ VISA
closed January and February – **M** (bar lunch)/dinner 10.00 **t.** and a la carte ⌷ 2.50 – **17 rm**
⌷ 18.00/36.00 **t.** – SB 50.00/55.00 **st.**
AB **a**

Clontarf, 1 Great Orme's Rd, West Shore, LL30 2AS, ☎ 77621 – ⌷wc **P.** ⌷
March-October – **10 rm** ⌷ 11.00/19.50 **t.**
A **u**

Sunnymede, West Par., West Shore, LL30 2BD, ☎ 77130 – TV ⌷wc ⌷wc **P.** ▨
VISA
6 March-7 November – **18 rm** ⌷ 13.00/34.00 **t.**
A **x**

⌂ **Cranleigh,** Great Orme's Rd, West Shore, LL30 2AR, ℘ 77688 – 🚻wc **P**
Easter-October – **13 rm** ⟷ 10.50/28.00. **st.**   A u

⌂ **Leamore,** 40 Lloyd St., LL30 2YG, ℘ 75552 – 📺 🚻wc. ✖
closed Christmas – **12 rm** ⟷ 12.00/28.00 **st.**   A o

✗✗ **Floral,** Victoria St., Craig y Don, LL30 1LJ, ℘ 75735 – ◪ ⓞ 𝑽𝑰𝑺𝑨
closed Saturday lunch and Monday – **M** a la carte 11.00/13.90 **t.** ⌕ 2.90.   B s

✗ **No. 1,** 1 Old Rd, LL30 2HA, ℘ 75424, Bistro.
closed Sunday – **M** 6.30/7.85 **t.** and a la carte 5.60/7.40 **t.** ⌕ 3.20.   A i

CITROEN Herkomer Rd ℘ 77607   PEUGEOT-TALBOT Conwy Rd ℘ 77461

LLANELLI Dyfed **👍👍👍** H 29 – pop. 45 336 – ECD : Tuesday – ☎ 0554.
Envir. : Kidwelly (Castle★★) *AC*, NW : 9 m.
♦London 206 – Carmarthen 20 – ♦Swansea 11.

🏨 **Stradey Park** (T.H.F.), Furnace, SA15 4HA, N : ¾ m. on B 4309 ℘ 758171, Telex 48521 – 📶
📺 🚻wc 🅿 😃 ◪ 🆔 ⓞ 𝑽𝑰𝑺𝑨
M 5.50/8.50 **st.** and a la carte ⌕ 3.40 – ⟷ 5.65 – **80 rm** 38.00/46.00 **st.**

🏨 **Diplomat,** Felinfoel Rd, SA15 3PJ, NE : 1 m. on A 476 ℘ 756156 – 📶 📺 ⌷wc 🚻 ☎ 🅿 😃.
◪ 🆔 ⓞ 𝑽𝑰𝑺𝑨
M *(closed Sunday dinner)* 5.95/10.00 **t.** and a la carte ⌕ 2.80 – **24 rm** ⟷ 29.00/41.00 **t.** – SB
(weekends only) 44.00 **st.**

AUSTIN-ROVER Vauxhall Rd ℘ 773371

LLANELWY = St. Asaph.

LLANFAIR-YM-MUALLT = Builth Wells.

LLANFYLLIN Powys **👍👍👍** K 25 – pop. 1 210 – ECD : Friday – ☎ 069 184.
♦London 188 – Chester 42 – Shrewsbury 24 – Welshpool 11.

🏚 **Bodfach Hall** 🦢, SY22 5HS, NW : 1 m. on B 4391 ℘ 272, ≼, « Country house in extensive
gardens », park – 📺 ⌷wc 🚻wc 🅿. ◪ 🆔 ⓞ
March-mid November – **M** (bar lunch Monday to Saturday)/dinner 9.50 **t.** – **9 rm**
⟷ 20.00/40.00 **t.** – SB (March-mid May) 49.00 **st.**

LLANGAMMARCH WELLS Powys **👍👍** J 27 – ECD : Wednesday – ☎ 059 12.
♦London 200 – Brecon 17 – Builth Wells 8.

🏨 **Lake** 🦢, LD4 4BS, E : ¾ m. ℘ 202, ≼, ⛳, ⌕, ☞, park, ✖ – 📺 ⌷wc ☎ 🅿. ◪ 🆔 𝑽𝑰𝑺𝑨
M (bar lunch)/dinner 15.00 **st.** – **20 rm** ⟷ 32.50/52.50 **st.**, **2 suites** 55.00/70.00 **st.** – SB
65.00/85.00 **st.**

LLANGOLLEN Clwyd **👍👍👍** K 25 – pop. 2 546 – ECD : Thursday – ☎ 0978.
See : Plas Newydd★★ (the house of the Ladies of Llangollen) *AC*.
Envir. : Horseshoe Pass★, NW : 4 ½ m. – Chirk Castle★ (gates★)*AC*, SE : 7 ½ m.
🔟 Vale of Llangollen, Holyhead Rd ℘ 860040, E : 1 ½ m.
🚹 Town Hall, ℘ 860828 (summer only).
♦London 194 – Chester 23 – Holyhead 76 – Shrewsbury 30.

🏨 **Bryn Howel,** LL20 7UW, E : 2 ¾ m. on A 539 ℘ 860331, ≼, ⌇, ☞ – 📺 ⌷wc ☎ 🅿. 😃. ◪
🆔 𝑽𝑰𝑺𝑨
closed Christmas Day – **M** 6.50/11.00 **st.** and a la carte – **35 rm** ⟷ 32.00/50.00 **st.**

🏨 **Royal** (T.H.F.), Bridge St., LL20 8PG, ℘ 860202, ≼, ⌇ – 📺 ⌷wc 🖨 🅿. 😃. ◪ 🆔 ⓞ 𝑽𝑰𝑺𝑨
M (bar lunch Monday to Saturday)/dinner 9.00 **st.** and a la carte ⌕ 3.40 – ⟷ 5.65 – **33 rm**
38.00/51.00 **st.**

☁ **Ty'n-y-Wern,** LL20 7PH, E : 1 m. on A.5 ℘ 860252, ≼, ☞ – 📺 ⌷wc 🅿. ◪ 𝑽𝑰𝑺𝑨
closed Christmas Day – **M** 8.50 **st.** (dinner) and a la carte ⌕ 2.80 – **10 rm** ⟷ 18.00/37.00 **st.**

✗ **Caesar's,** Deeside Lane, LL20 8NT, ℘ 860133, ≼ – ◪ 𝑽𝑰𝑺𝑨
closed Sunday in winter – **M** (dinner only) 12.95 **t.** ⌕ 2.40.

FORD Berwyn St. ℘ 860270

LLANGURIG Powys **👍👍** J 26 – pop. 620 – ECD : Thursday – ✉ Llanidloes – ☎ 055 15.
♦London 188 – Aberystwyth 25 – Carmarthen 75 – Shrewsbury 53.

⌂ **Old Vicarage,** SY18 6RN, ℘ 280, ☞ – 🅿. 𝑽𝑰𝑺𝑨
4 rm ⟷ 9.50/21.00 **st.**

LLANGYBI Gwent – see Usk.

LLANILLTUD FAWR = Llantwit Major.

LLANNEFYDD Clwyd 402 403 J 24 – ⊠ Denbigh – ✆ 074 579.

♦London 225 – Chester 37 – Shrewsbury 63.

   🏠 **Hawk and Buckle Inn**, LL16 5ED, ℰ 249, ≤ – 📺 ⇌wc ☎ ⊙ 🅿 🔼 AE ⊙ VISA ⋘
     M *(closed lunch Monday to Friday November-May)* (bar lunch)/dinner 9.50 **t.** ♦ 2.85 – **10 rm**
     ⊐ 23.00/34.00 **t.** – SB 46.00/56.00 **st.**

AUSTIN-ROVER Denbigh Rd ℰ 227

LLANRHIDIAN West Glam. – see Swansea.

LLANRWST Gwynedd 402 403 I 24 – pop. 2 908 – ECD : Thursday – ✆ 0492.

See : Gwydir Castle★.

Envir. : Capel Garmon (Burial Chamber★) SE : 6 m.

♦London 230 – Holyhead 50 – Shrewsbury 66.

   🏛 **Maenan Abbey**, N : 2 ½ m. on A 470, LL26 0UL, ℰ 049 269 (Dolgarrog) 247, ⋟, 🚗 – 📺
     ⇌wc 🛏wc 🚗 🅿 🔼 AE ⊙ VISA
     M 5.95/9.50 **t.** and a la carte ♦ 3.25 – **12 rm** ⊐ 20.00/40.00 **t.** – SB (except summer)
     40.00/42.00 **st.**

   XX **Meadowsweet** with rm, Station Rd, LL26 0DS, ℰ 640732, ≤ – 📺 🛏wc ☎ ⊙ 🔼 AE VISA
     M (closed lunch Monday to Saturday in winter) 10.50/14.95 **t.** ♦ 2.75 – **10 rm** ⊐ 21.00/39.00 **t.**
     – SB (except Bank Holidays) 54.00/70.00 **st.**

AUSTIN-ROVER Kerry Garage ℰ 640381   FORD Betws Rd ℰ 640684

LLANTWIT MAJOR (LLANILLTUD FAWR) South Glam. 403 J 29 – pop. 13 375 (inc. St. Athan) –
✆ 044 65.

♦London 175 – ♦Cardiff 18 – ♦Swansea 33.

   🏠 **West House**, West St., CF6 9SP, ℰ 2406, 🚗 – 📺 ⇌wc 🅿 🔼 VISA
     M a la carte 8.50/12.50 **t.** ♦ 4.90 – **19 rm** ⊐ 17.00/35.00 **t.** – SB (weekends only) 40.00/45.00 **st.**

TOYOTA 2 Colhugh St. ℰ 3466

LLANWENARTH Gwent – see Abergavenny.

LLANWRTYD WELLS Powys 403 J 27 – pop. 528 – ECD : Wednesday – ✆ 059 13.

See : Cambrian Mountains : road★★ from Llanwrtyd to Tregaron.

Envir. : Rhandir-mwyn (≤★ of Afon Tywi Valley) SW : 12 m.

🗒 The Bookshop ℰ 391.

♦London 214 – Brecon 32 – Carmarthen 39.

   🏠 **Lasswade House**, Station Rd, LD5 4RW, ℰ 515, ≤, ⬛, 🚗 – 📺 ⇌wc 🛏wc 🅿 🔼 VISA
     M (bar lunch Monday to Saturday)/dinner 12.50 **st.** ♦ 3.00 – **8 rm.**

   at Abergwesyn NW : 5 m. – ⊠ Builth Wells – ✆ 059 13 Llanwrtyd Wells :

   🏠 **Llwynderw** ⋟, LD5 4TW, ℰ 238, ≤ countryside and hills, « Georgian house with antique
     furnishings », 🚗 – ⇌wc 🅿 🔼 AE ⋘
     April-October – **M** (lunch by arrangement) 15.00/20.00 **t.** – **10 rm** ⊐ 55.00/75.00 **t.**

LLANYCHAER Dyfed 403 F 28 – see Fishguard.

LLWYNMAWR Clwyd 402 403 K 25 – ⊠ Llangollen – ✆ 069 172 Glyn Ceiriog.

♦London 192 – Shrewsbury 28 – Wrexham 15.

   🏠 **Golden Pheasant** ⋟, LL20 7BB, ℰ 281, Telex 35664, ≤, 🚗 – 📺 ⇌wc 🛏wc 🅿 🔼 AE VISA
     M 9.50/11.95 **st.** ♦ 4.00 – **18 rm** ⊐ 19.00/62.00 **st.** – SB (except Christmas) 60.00/79.00 **st.**

LODDISWELL Devon – see Kingsbridge.

LODDON Norfolk 404 Y 26 – pop. 2 508 – ECD : Wednesday – ✆ 0508.

♦London 121 – Great Yarmouth 16 – ♦Ipswich 48 – ♦Norwich 11.

   ↑ **Rackhams' Stubbs House**, Stubbs Green, NR14 6EA, SW : ¾ m. ℰ 20231, 🚗 – 🛏wc 🅿
     ⋘
     closed December and January – **9 rm** ⊐ 14.00/33.00 **t.**

LOFTUS Cleveland 402 R 20 – pop. 5 626 – ECD : Wednesday – ⊠ Saltburn by the Sea –
✆ 0287 Guisborough.

♦London 264 – ♦Leeds 73 – ♦Middlesbrough 17 – Scarborough 36.

   🏨 **Grinkle Park** ⋟, Easington, TS13 4UB, SE : 3 ½ m. by A 174 ℰ 40515, ≤, 🚗, park – 📺 ☎
     🅿 🔼 AE ⊙ VISA
     M 8.50/12.50 **st.** and a la carte ♦ 3.95 – **20 rm** ⊐ 40.00/55.00 **st.** – SB (weekends only)
     70.00/90.00 **st.**

LONDON

LONDON (Greater) **404** folds ㊷ to ㊹ — **London G.** — pop. 7 566 620 — ✪ 01.

✈ Heathrow, ✆ 759 4321, Telex 934892, p. 8 AY — **Terminal** : Airbus (A1) from Victoria, Airbus (A2) from Paddington — Underground (Piccadilly line) frequent service daily — Helicopter service to Gatwick Airport.

✈ Gatwick, ✆ 0293 (Crawley) 28822 and ✆ 01 (London) 668 4211, Telex 877725, p. 9 : by A 23 EZ and M 23 — **Terminal** : Coach service from Victoria Coach Station (Flightline 777) — Railink (Gatwick Express) from Victoria (24 h service) — Helicopter service to Heathrow Airport.

✈ Stansted, at Bishop's Stortford, ✆ 0279 (Bishop's Stortford) 502380, Telex 81102, NE : 34 m. off M 11 and A 120.

BA Air Terminal : Victoria Station, ✆ 834 2323, p. 30 BX.

British Caledonian Airways, Victoria Air Terminal : Victoria Station, SW1, ✆ 834 9411, p. 30 BX

🚉 Euston ✆ 387 8541 — King's Cross ✆ 833 2805 — Paddington ✆ 723 7000 ext 3148.

🛈 National Tourist Information Centre, Victoria Station Forecourt, SW1, ✆ 730 3488.
British Travel Centre, 12 Regent St., Picadilly Circus, SW1 ✆ 730 3400.
London Visitor and Convention Bureau Telephone Information Service ✆ 730 3485.
Teletourist ✆ 246 8041 (English), 246 8043 (French), 246 8045 (German).

The maps in this section of the Guide are based upon the Ordnance Survey of Great Britain with the permission of the Controller of Her Majesty's Stationery Office. Crown Copyright reserved.

SIGHTS

CURIOSITÉS

LE CURIOSITÀ

SEHENSWÜRDIGKEITEN

■ HISTORIC BUILDINGS AND MONUMENTS

Palace of Westminster★★★ : House of Lords★★, Westminster Hall★★ (hammerbeam roof★★★), Robing Room★, Central Lobby★, House of Commons★, Big Ben★, Victoria Tower★ p. 19 NX — Tower of London★★★ (Crown Jewels★★★, White Tower or Keep★★★, St. John's Chapel★★, Beauchamp Tower★) p. 20 QU.

Banqueting House★★ p. 19 NV — Buckingham Palace★★ (Changing of the Guard★★, Royal Mews★★) p. 30 BV — Kensington Palace★★ p. 18 JV — Lincoln's Inn★★ p. 31 FV — London Bridge★★ p. 20 QV — Royal Hospital Chelsea★★ p. 29 FU — St. James's Palace★★ p. 27 EP — South Bank Arts Centre★★ (Royal Festival Hall★, National Theatre★, County Hall★) p. 19 NV — The Temple★★ (Middle Temple Hall★) p. 15 NU — Tower Bridge★★ p. 20 QV.

Albert Memorial★ p. 28 CQ — Apsley House★ p. 26 BP — Bloomsbury★ p. 15 NT — Burlington House★ p. 27 EM — Charterhouse★ p. 16 PT — Commonwealth Institute★ p. 17 HX — Design Centre★ p. 27 FM — George Inn★, Southwark p. 20 QV — Gray's Inn★ p. 15 NT — Guildhall★ (Lord Mayor's Show★★) p. 16 PT — Imperial College of Science and Technology★ p. 28 CR — Dr Johnson's House★ p. 16 PTU A — Lancaster House★ p. 27 EP — Leighton House★ p. 17 GX — Linley Sambourne House★ p. 17 HX — Mansion House★ (plate and insignia★★) p. 16 QU P — The Monument★ (⚶★) p. 16 QU G — Royal Opera Arcade★ (New Zealand House) p. 27 FGN — Old Admiralty★ p. 19 MV — Royal Exchange★ p. 16 QU V — Royal Opera House★ (Covent Garden) p. 31 EV — Somerset House★ p. 31 EV — Staple Inn★ p. 15 NT Y — Stock Exchange★ p. 16 QTU — Westminster Bridge★ p. 19 NX.

■ CHURCHES

The City Churches

St. Paul's Cathedral★★★ (Dome ≼★★★) p. 16 PU.

St. Bartholomew the Great★★ (vessel★) p. 16 PT K — St. Dunstan-in-the-East★★ p. 16 QU F — St. Mary-at-Hill★★ (plan★, woodwork★★) p. 16 QU B — Temple Church★★ p. 15 NU.

All Hallows-by-the-Tower (font cover★★, brasses★) p. 16 QU Y — Christ Church★ p. 16 PT E — St. Andrew Undershaft (monuments★) p. 16 QU A — St. Bride★ (steeple★★) p. 16 PU J — St. Clement Eastcheap (panelled interior★★) p. 16 QU E — St. Edmund the King and Martyr (tower and spire★) p. 16 QU D — St. Giles Cripplegate★ p. 16 PT N — St. Helen Bishopsgate★ (monuments★★) p. 16 QTU R — St. James Garlickhythe (tower and spire★, sword rests★) p. 16 PU R — St. Katherine Cree (sword rest★) p. 16 QU J — St. Magnus the Martyr (tower★, sword rest★) p. 16 QU K — St. Margaret Lothbury★ (tower and spire★, woodwork★, screen★, font★) p. 16 QT S — St. Margaret Pattens (woodwork★) p. 16 QU N — St. Martin Ludgate (tower and spire★, door cases★) p. 16 PU B — St. Mary Abchurch★ (tower and spire★, dome★, reredos★) p. 16 QU X — St. Mary-le-Bow (tower and steeple★★) p. 16 PU G — St. Michael Paternoster Royal (tower and spire★) p. 16 PU D — St. Nicholas Cole Abbey (tower and spire★) p. 16 PU F — St. Olave★ p. 16 QU S — St. Peter upon Cornhill (screen★) p. 16 QU L — St. Stephen Walbrook★ (tower and steeple★, dome★) p. 16 QU Z — St. Vedast (tower and spire★, ceiling★) p. 16 PTU E.

Other Churches

Westminster Abbey★★★ (Chapel of Edward the Confessor★★, Henry VII Chapel★★★, Chapter House★★) p. 19 MX.

Southwark Cathedral★★ p. 20 QV.

Queen's Chapel★ p. 27 EP — St. Clement Danes★ p. 31 FV — St. James's★ p. 27 EM — St. Margaret's★ p. 19 NX A — St. Martin-in-the-Fields★ p. 31 DX — St. Paul's★ (Covent Garden) p. 31 DV — Westminster Roman Catholic Cathedral★ p. 19 MX B.

■ PARKS

Regent's Park★★★ p. 14 KS (terraces★★), Zoo★★★.

Hyde Park★★ p. 18 JU — St. James's Park★★ p. 19 MV.

Kensington Gardens★ p. 18 JV (Orangery★ A).

■ STREETS AND SQUARES

The City★★★ p. 16 PU.

Bedford Square★★ p. 15 MT — Belgrave Square★★ p. 30 AV — Burlington Arcade★★ p. 27 DM — The Mall★★ p. 27 FP — Piccadilly★★ p. 27 EM — The Thames★★ pp. 18-20 — Trafalgar Square★★ p. 31 DX — Whitehall★★ (Horse Guards★) p. 19 MV.

Barbican★ p. 16 PT — Bond Street★ pp. 26-27 CK-DM — Canonbury Square★ p. 16 PR — Carlton House Terrace★ p. 27 GN — Charing Cross★ p. 31 DX — Cheyne Walk★ p. 18 JZ — Fitzroy Square★ p. 15 LT — Jermyn Street★ p. 27 EN — Merrick Square★ p. 20 PX — Montpelier Square★ p. 29 EQ — Piccadilly Arcade★ p. 27 DEN — Portman Square★ p. 26 AJ — Queen Anne's Gate★ p. 19 MX — Regent Street★ p. 27 EM — St. James's Square★ p. 27 FN — St. James's Street★ p. 27 EN — Shepherd Market★ p. 26 CN — Strand★ p. 31 DX — Trinity Church Square★ p. 20 PX — Victoria Embankment★ p. 31 EX — Waterloo Place★ p. 27 FN.

■ MUSEUMS

British Museum★★★ p. 15 MT — National Gallery★★★ p. 27 GM — Science Museum★★★ p. 28 CR — Tate Gallery★★★ p. 19 MY — Victoria and Albert Museum★★★ p. 29 DR.

Courtauld Institute Galleries★★ p. 15 MT M — Museum of London★★ p. 16 PT M — National Portrait Gallery★★ p. 27 GM — Natural History Museum★★ p. 28 CS — Queen's Gallery★★ p. 30 BV — Wallace Collection★★ p. 26 AH.

Clock Museum★ (Guildhall) p. 16 PT — Geological Museum★ p. 28 CR — Imperial War Museum★ p. 20 PX — London Transport Museum★ p. 31 EV — Madame Tussaud's★ p. 14 KT M — Museum of Mankind★ p. 27 DM — National Army Museum★ p. 29 FU — Percival David Foundation of Chinese Art★ p. 15 MS M — Sir John Soane's Museum★ p. 15 NT M — Wellington Museum★ p. 26 BP.

■ OUTER LONDON

Hampton Court p. 8 BZ (The Palace★★★, gardens★★★) — Kew p. 9 CY Royal Botanic Gardens★★★ : Palm House★★, Temperate House★, Kew Palace or Dutch House★★, Orangery★, Pagoda★, Japanese Gateway★ — Windsor (Castle★★★) by A 4, M 4 AX.

Blackheath p. 11 GY terraces and houses★, Eltham Palace★ A — Brentford p. 8 BY Syon Park★★, gardens★ — Chiswick p. 9 CX Chiswick Mall★★, Chiswick House★ D, Hogarth's House★ E — Greenwich pp. 10 and 11 : Cutty Sark★★ FX F, National Maritime Museum★★ (Queen's House★★) FX M, Royal Naval College★★ (Painted Hall★, the Chapel★) FX G, Old Royal Observatory★ (Meridian Building : collection★★) GX K, Ranger's House★ FY N — Hampstead Kenwood House★★ (Adam Library★★, paintings★★) p. 5 EV P, Fenton House★ p. 13 GR — Hendon p. 5 CU Royal Air Force Museum★★ M — Hounslow p. 8 BX Osterley Park★★ — Lewisham p. 10 FY Horniman Museum★ M — Richmond pp. 8 and 9 : Richmond Park★★, ❋★★★ CY, Richmond Bridge★★ BY R, Richmond Green★★ BY S (Maids of Honour Row★★, Trumpeter's House★), Asgill House★ BY B, Ham House★★ BY V.

Dulwich p. 10 FY Dulwich College Picture Gallery★ X — Shoreditch p. 6 FV Geffrye Museum★ M — Tower Hamlets p. 6 FX St. Katharine Dock★ (HMS Discovery★) Y — Twickenham p. 8 BY Marble Hill House★ Z, Strawberry Hill★ A.

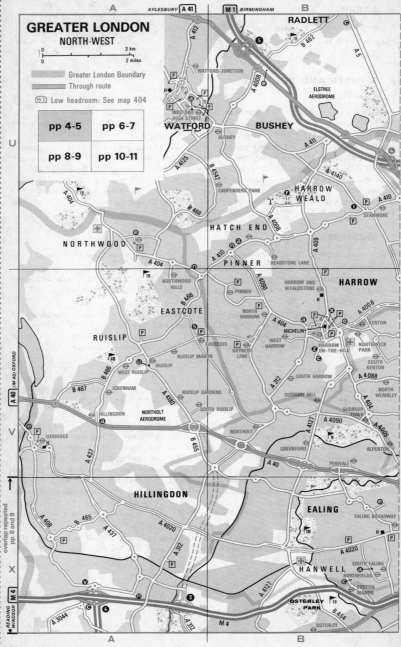

GREATER LONDON
NORTH-WEST

Greater London Boundary
Through route

16.2 Low headroom: See map 404

pp 4-5	pp 6-7
pp 8-9	pp 10-11

264

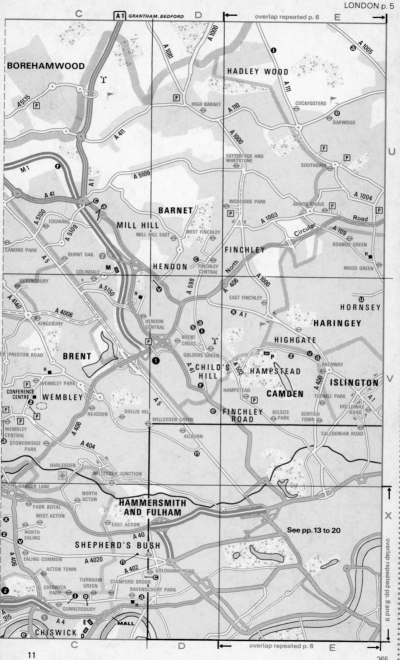

A1 GRANTHAM, BEDFORD

BOREHAMWOOD

HADLEY WOOD

COCKFOSTERS

OAKWOOD

HIGH BARNET

TOTTERIDGE AND
WHETSTONE

SOUTHGATE

BARNET

WOODSIDE PARK

ARNOS GROVE

Road

MILL HILL

WEST FINCHLEY

FINCHLEY

Circular

BOUNDS GREEN

EDGWARE

Mill Hill East

North

WOOD GREEN

CANONS PARK

BURNT OAK

HENDON

Finchley
Central

EAST FINCHLEY

QUEENSBURY

COLINDALE

HORNSEY

KINGSBURY

Hendon
Central

HARINGEY

PRESTON ROAD

Brent
Cross

HIGHGATE

BRENT

GOLDERS GREEN

HAMPSTEAD

ISLINGTON

CHILD'S
HILL

CAMDEN

ARCHWAY

WEMBLEY PARK

CONFERENCE
CENTRE

WEMBLEY

HAMPSTEAD

TUFNELL PARK

NEASDEN

DOLLIS HILL

FINCHLEY
ROAD

BELSIZE
PARK

HOLLOWAY
ROAD

WEMBLEY
CENTRAL

WILLESDEN GREEN

KENTISH
TOWN

STONEBRIDGE
PARK

KILBURN

CALEDONIAN ROAD

HARLESDEN

WILLESDEN JUNCTION

HANGER LANE

NORTH
ACTON

HAMMERSMITH
AND FULHAM

PARK ROYAL

WEST ACTON

EAST ACTON

See pp. 13 to 20

NORTH
EALING

EALING COMMON

SHEPHERD'S BUSH

ACTON TOWN

GOLDHAWK ROAD

CHISWICK
PARK

TURNHAM GREEN

STAMFORD BROOK

RAVENSCOURT PARK

GUNNERSBURY

CHISWICK

MALL

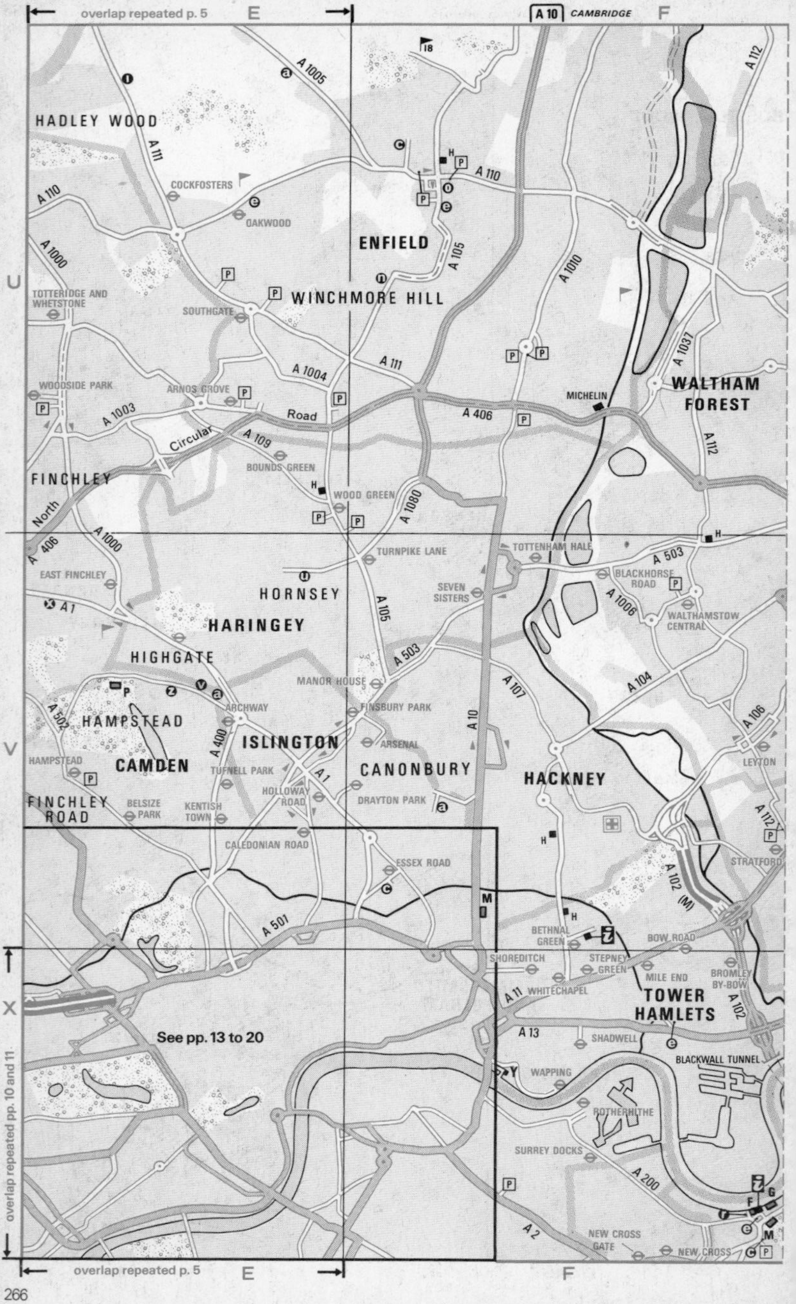
overlap repeated p. 5
E
A 10 CAMBRIDGE
F
HADLEY WOOD
A 1005
A 111
A 110
COCKFOSTERS
OAKWOOD
ENFIELD
A 105
A 1000
U
TOTTERIDGE AND WHETSTONE
SOUTHGATE
WINCHMORE HILL
A 1010
A 1037
A 112
A 1004
A 111
WOODSIDE PARK
ARNOS GROVE
A 1003
Road
A 406
MICHELIN
WALTHAM FOREST
Circular
A 109
BOUNDS GREEN
FINCHLEY
WOOD GREEN
A 1080
North
A 406
A 1000
TURNPIKE LANE
TOTTENHAM HALE
A 503
EAST FINCHLEY
BLACKHORSE ROAD
A 1006
HORNSEY
SEVEN SISTERS
A1
A 105
WALTHAMSTOW CENTRAL
HARINGEY
HIGHGATE
A 503
MANOR HOUSE
A 107
A 104
A 502
HAMPSTEAD
ARCHWAY
FINSBURY PARK
A 106
A 10
ISLINGTON
A 400
ARSENAL
V
HAMPSTEAD
CAMDEN
TUFNELL PARK
A1
CANONBURY
HACKNEY
LEYTON
HOLLOWAY ROAD
DRAYTON PARK
FINCHLEY ROAD
BELSIZE PARK
KENTISH TOWN
A 112
CALEDONIAN ROAD
STRATFORD
ESSEX ROAD
A 102 (M)
A 501
BETHNAL GREEN
BOW ROAD
SHOREDITCH
STEPNEY GREEN
MILE END
BROMLEY BY-BOW
X
A 11
WHITECHAPEL
TOWER HAMLETS
A 102
A 13
See pp. 13 to 20
SHADWELL
BLACKWALL TUNNEL
WAPPING
ROTHERHITHE
SURREY DOCKS
A 200
A 2
NEW CROSS GATE
NEW CROSS
overlap repeated pp. 10 and 11
overlap repeated p. 5
E
F

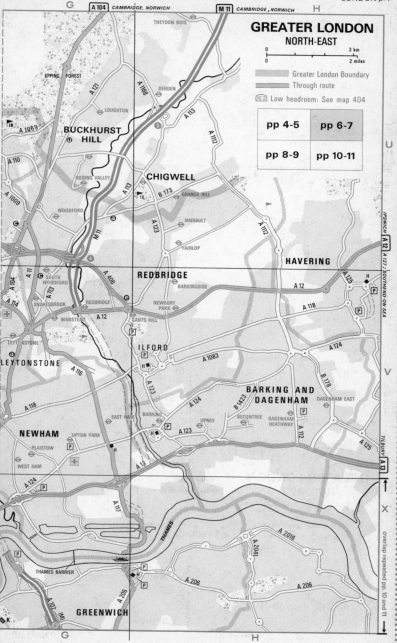

GREATER LONDON
NORTH-EAST

0   3 km
0   2 miles

Greater London Boundary
Through route

16.2 Low headroom: See map 404

| pp 4-5 | pp 6-7 |
| pp 8-9 | pp 10-11 |

267

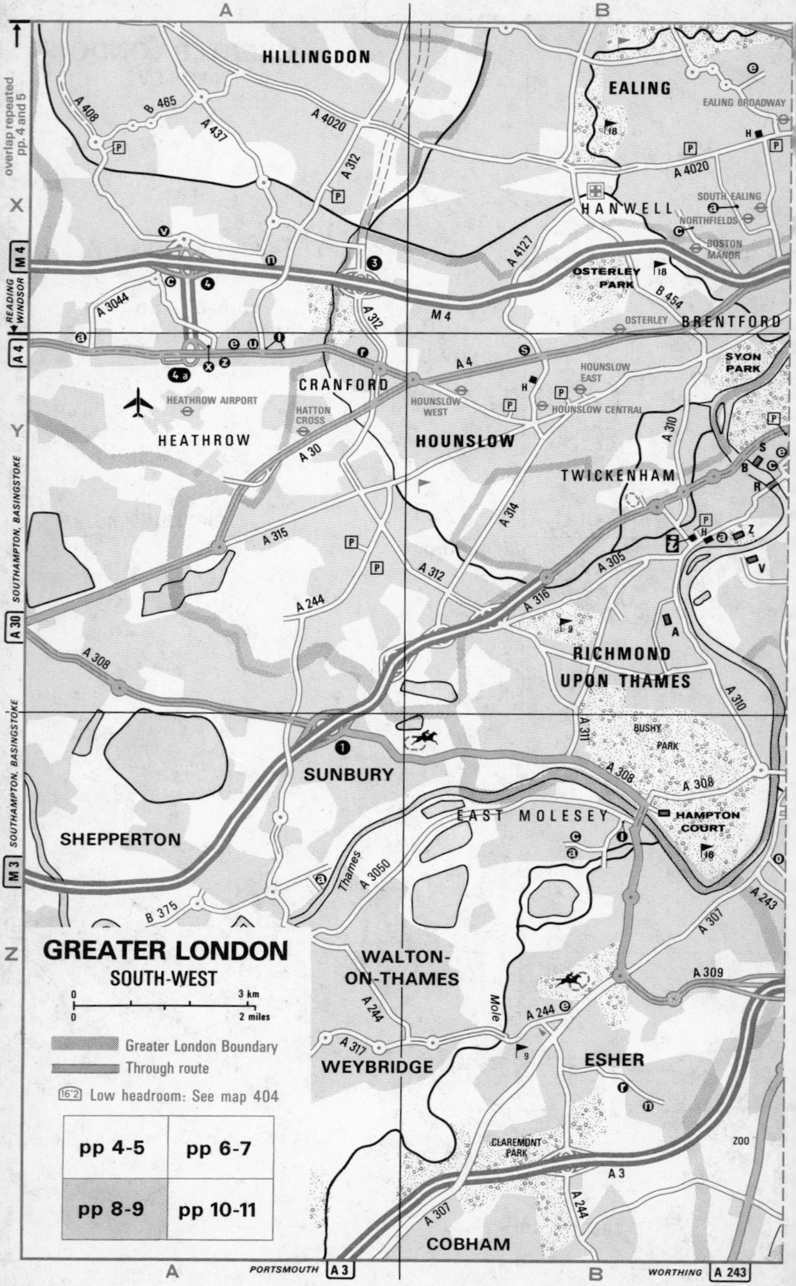

A   B

overlap repeated pp. 4 and 5

X

M4 READING WINDSOR

A4

Y

A30 SOUTHAMPTON, BASINGSTOKE

M3 SOUTHAMPTON, BASINGSTOKE

Z

HILLINGDON

EALING

EALING BROADWAY

HANWELL

SOUTH EALING
NORTHFIELDS
BOSTON MANOR

OSTERLEY PARK

OSTERLEY

BRENTFORD

SYON PARK

A 408
B 465
A 437
A 4020
A 312
A 4020
A 4127
A 4
M 4
A 3044
A 30
A 315
A 244
A 312
A 308
A 4
A 304
A 305
A 316
A 310
A 311
A 308
A 308
A 307
A 243
A 309
A 307
A 244
A 3
A 244
A 317
A 307

CRANFORD

HEATHROW AIRPORT

HATTON CROSS

HEATHROW

HOUNSLOW WEST

HOUNSLOW EAST

HOUNSLOW CENTRAL

HOUNSLOW

TWICKENHAM

RICHMOND UPON THAMES

BUSHY PARK

SUNBURY

SHEPPERTON

EAST MOLESEY

HAMPTON COURT

WALTON-ON-THAMES

WEYBRIDGE

ESHER

CLAREMONT PARK

COBHAM

Thames

Mole

B 375
A 3050
B 454

GREATER LONDON
SOUTH-WEST

0   3 km
0   2 miles

▬▬ Greater London Boundary
▬▬ Through route
16·2 Low headroom: See map 404

pp 4-5	pp 6-7
pp 8-9	pp 10-11

PORTSMOUTH A 3

WORTHING A 243

ZOO

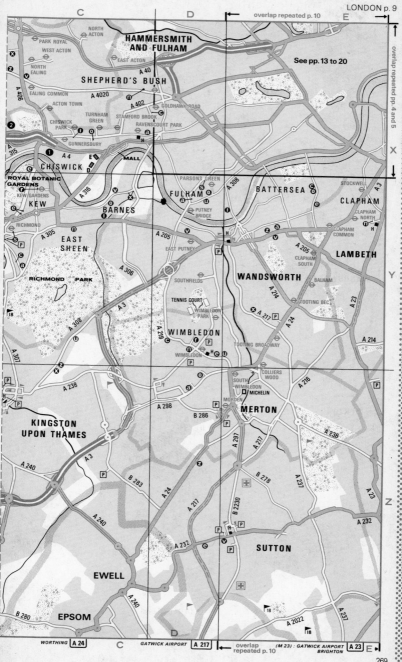

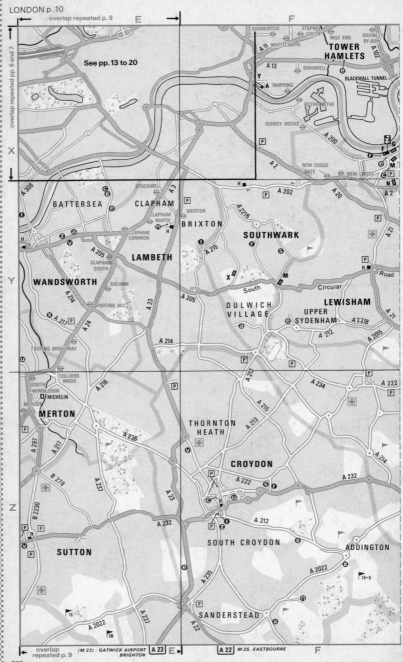

overlap repeated p. 9

See pp. 13 to 20

overlap repeated pp. 6 and 7

SHOREDITCH
STEPNEY
GREEN
MILE END
BROMLEY
BY-BOW

WHITECHAPEL
A 11
A 102

**TOWER
HAMLETS**

A 13
SHADWELL

BLACKWALL TUNNEL

WAPPING

ROTHERHITHE

SURREY DOCKS

A 200

NEW CROSS
GATE
NEW CROSS

A 2

STOCKWELL
A 3
A 202
A 20
A 21

BATTERSEA
CLAPHAM
BRIXTON

CLAPHAM
NORTH
BRIXTON

A 2216

SOUTHWARK

CLAPHAM
COMMON

A 215

LAMBETH

CLAPHAM
SOUTH

WANDSWORTH
A 205
BALHAM

South
Circular
Road

A 214
TOOTING BEC
A 205

A 217
A 24

DULWICH
VILLAGE

UPPER
SYDENHAM
LEWISHAM

A 2218

TOOTING BROADWAY

A 214
A 212
A 2015

A 212

SOUTH
WIMBLEDON
COLLIERS
WOOD
A 216

A 222

A 234

MORDEN
MICHELIN

MERTON

A 217

THORNTON
HEATH

A 213

A 214

A 297

B 278
A 237

CROYDON

A 232

A 23

A 222

SUTTON

A 232

A 212

SOUTH CROYDON

ADDINGTON

A 2022

18-9

A 235

A 18

SANDERSTEAD

A 2022
A 237
A 22

overlap
repeated p. 9

(M 23) : GATWICK AIRPORT
BRIGHTON
A 23 E

A 22 M 25, EASTBOURNE

F

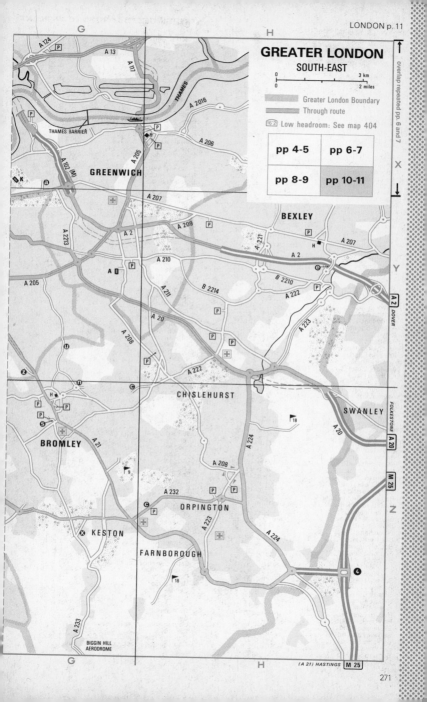

GREATER LONDON
SOUTH-EAST

0   3 km
0   2 miles

▨ Greater London Boundary
▨ Through route
16.2 Low headroom: See map 404

| pp 4-5 | pp 6-7 |
| pp 8-9 | pp 10-11 |

overlap repeated pp. 6 and 7

A 124
A 13
A 111
THAMES
A 2016
A 206
THAMES BARRIER
H
A 205
A 102 (M)
GREENWICH
K
A 207

BEXLEY
A 213
A 2
A 209
A 221
H
A 207
A 2
A 210
B 2210
A 1
A 211
B 2214
A 222
A 205
A 20
A 223
A 208
A 222

CHISLEHURST
H
SWANLEY
A 224
A 20
BROMLEY
A 21
18
A 208
9
A 232
ORPINGTON
A 223
KESTON
A 224
FARNBOROUGH
18
A 233
BIGGIN HILL
AERODROME

A 2 DOVER
FOLKESTONE A 20
M 25
4

Continued on next page

281

Continued on next page

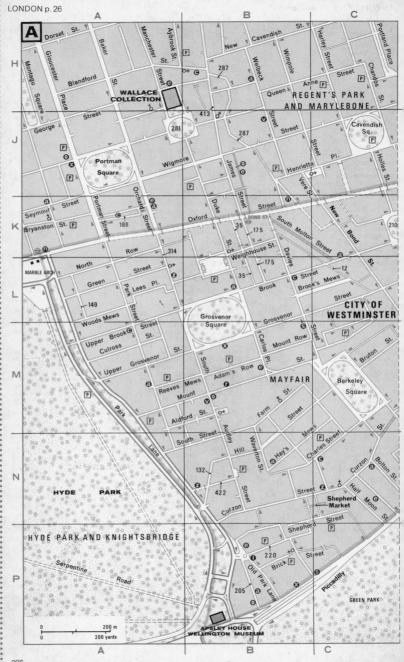

Oxford Street is closed to private traffic, Mondays to Saturdays :
from 7 am to 7 pm between Portman Street and St. Giles Circus

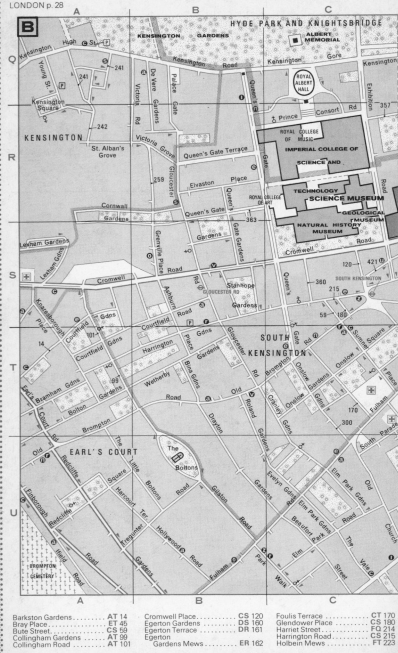

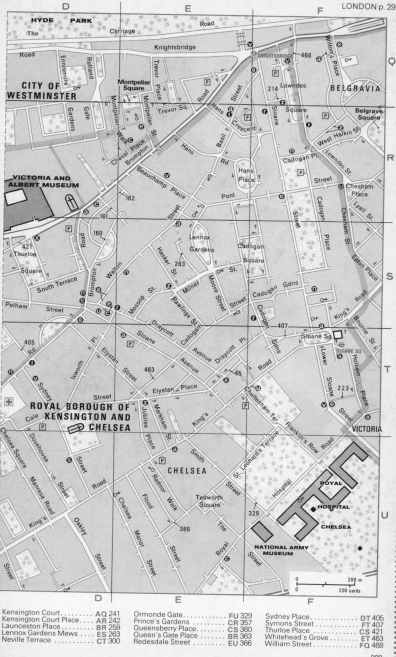

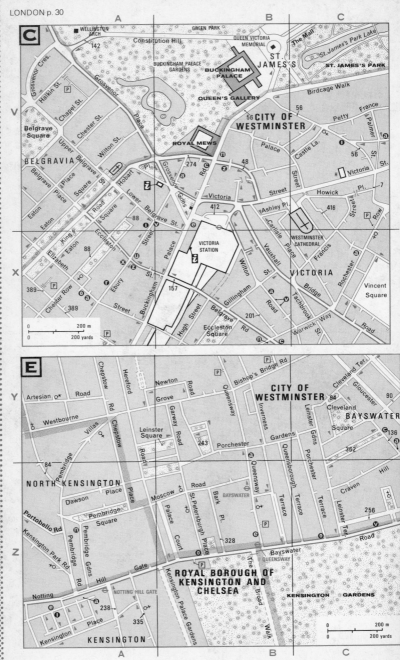

ALPHABETICAL LIST OF HOTELS AND RESTAURANTS
LISTE ALPHABÉTIQUE DES HOTELS ET RESTAURANTS
ELENCO ALFABETICO DEGLI ALBERGHI E RISTORANTI
ALPHABETISCHES HOTEL- UND RESTAURANTVERZEICHNIS

ALPHABETICAL LIST OF AREAS INCLUDED
LISTE ALPHABÉTIQUE DES QUARTIERS CITÉS
ELENCO ALFABETICO DEI QUARTIERI CITATI
LISTE DER ERWÄHNTEN BEZIRKE

STARRED ESTABLISHMENTS IN LONDON
LES ÉTABLISSEMENTS A ÉTOILES DE LONDRES
GLI ESERCIZI CON STELLE A LONDRA
DIE STERN-RESTAURANTS LONDONS

✿✿✿

	Area	Page
Le Gavroche	Mayfair	70

✿✿

	Area	Page
The Terrace	Mayfair	70
La Tante Claire	Chelsea	59
Simply Nico	Victoria	75

✿

	Area	Page			Area	Page
Connaught	Mayfair	69	Rue St. Jacques	Regent's Park and Marylebone	72
Capital	Chelsea	59				
90 Park Lane	Mayfair	70	Suntory	St. James's	73
Chelsea Room	Chelsea	59	L'Arlequin	Battersea	67
Le Soufflé	Mayfair	70	Lichfield's	Richmond	65
Waltons	Chelsea	59	Ma Cuisine	Chelsea	60
Chez Nico	Battersea	67	Le Mazarin	Victoria	76

FURTHER ESTABLISHMENTS WHICH MERIT YOUR ATTENTION
AUTRES TABLES QUI MÉRITENT VOTRE ATTENTION
ALTRE TAVOLE PARTICOLARMENTE INTERESSANTI
WEITERE EMPFEHLENSWERTE HÄUSER

M

Odins	Regent's Park and Marylebone	72	Ken Lo's Memories of China	Victoria	76
Bagatelle	Chelsea	60	Moghul Brasserie	Wembley	50
Hilaire	South Kensington	63	Partners 23	Sutton	66

RESTAURANTS CLASSIFIED ACCORDING TO TYPE

RESTAURANTS CLASSÉS SUIVANT LEUR GENRE

RISTORANTI CLASSIFICATI SECONDO IL LORO GENERE

RESTAURANTS NACH ART UND EINRICHTUNG GEORDNET

Borough	Area	Restaurant	Page
		BISTRO	
Islington	Islington	✗ **M'sieur Frog**	58
Westminster (City of)	Regent's Park & Marylebone	✗ **Langan's Bistro**	72
—	Victoria	✗ **Bumbles**	76
		DANCING	
Hammersmith	Fulham	✗✗ **Barbarella**	55
Westminster (City of)	Bayswater & Maida Vale	✗✗ **Concordia Notte**	68
—	Mayfair	✗✗✗ **Tiberio**	70
—	St. James's	✗✗✗✗✗ **Maxim's de Paris**	73
		SEAFOOD	
Barnet	Finchley	✗✗ **Fogareiro**	49
City of London	City of London	✗✗✗ **Wheeler's**	52
—	—	✗✗ **Bill Bentley's**	53
Croydon	Croydon	✗ **34 Surrey Street**	53
Harrow	Harrow-on-the-Hill	✗✗✗ **Wheeler's**	56
Kensington & Chelsea (Royal Borough of)	Chelsea	✗✗ **Poissonnerie de l'Avenue**	60
—	—	✗✗ **Suquet (Le)**	60
—	—	✗ **Wheelers**	60
—	Earl's Court	✗✗ **Croisette (La)**	61
—	—	✗✗ **Tiger Lee**	61
—	Kensington	✗ **Quai St. Pierre (Le)**	62
Westminster (City of)	Mayfair	✗✗✗✗✗ **Scott's**	70
—	Strand & Covent Garden	✗✗ **Frère Jacques**	74
—	—	✗✗ **Sheekey's**	74
—	—	✗ **Flounders**	75
—	—	✗ **Grimes**	75
—	Victoria	✗✗ **Hoizin**	76

Borough	Area		Restaurant	Page

CHINESE

Borough	Area		Restaurant	Page
Barnet	Finchley	✕	Peking Duck	49
—	Mill Hill	✕✕	Good Earth	49
	—	✕✕	Taicoon	49
Bromley	Bromley	✕	Peking Diner	50
Camden	Bloomsbury	✕✕	Mr Kai	51
—	Finchley Road	✕✕	Green Cottage II	51
—	Hampstead	✕✕✕	Zen W3	52
—	Swiss Cottage	✕✕	Lee Ho Fook	52
Croydon	Addington	✕✕	Willow	53
Ealing	Ealing	✕✕	Maxim	54
—	Hanwell	✕	Happiness Garden	54
Enfield	Winchmore Hill	✕✕	Dragon Garden	54
Greenwich	Greenwich	✕✕	Treasure of China	55
Hammersmith	Fulham	✕✕	Mao Tai	52
—	—	✕	Evergreen	55
Harrow	Hatch End	✕	Swan	56
—	Stanmore	✕✕	Buddha House	56
Kensington & Chelsea (Royal Borough of)	Chelsea	✕✕✕	Zen	59
—	—	✕✕	Good Earth	60
—	—	✕✕	Good Earth	60
—	—	✕✕	Hans	60
—	—	✕✕	Sampan	60
—	Earl's Court	✕✕	Tiger Lee	61
—	—	✕	Crystal Palace	61
—	Kensington	✕✕	I Ching	62
—	—	✕✕	Mama San	61
—	—	✕✕	Mandarin	62
—	—	✕	Sailing Junk	62
—	South Kensington	✕✕	Golden Chopsticks	63
—	—	✕✕	Pun	63
Merton	Wimbledon	✕✕	Confucius	64
—	—	✕✕	Winbledon Palace	64
Redbridge	Ilford	✕✕	Mandarin Palace	64
—	South Woodford	✕✕	Ho-Ho	64
Richmond-upon-Thames	Richmond	✕✕	Evergreen	65
—	—	✕✕	Kew Rendezvous	65
—	—	✕	Red Lion	65
Southwark	East Dulwich	✕	Mr Lui	66
Tower Hamlets	Linehouse	✕	Good Friends	66
Wandsworth	Clapham	✕	Jasmin	67
—	Putney	✕✕	Bayee House	67
Westminster (City of)	Bayswater & Maida Vale	✕✕✕	Bombay Palace	68
—	—	✕	Fortune Cookie	68
—	Mayfair	✕✕✕	Princess Garden	70
—	—	✕✕	Ho-Ho	70
—	—	✕✕	Mr Kai	70
—	Regent's Park & Marylebone	✕✕	Lords Rendezvous	72
—	Soho	✕✕	Mayflower	73
—	—	✕✕	Poons	73
—	—	✕	Fung Shing	73

Borough	Area	Restaurant	Page

CHINESE (continued)

—	—	✕ Gallery Rendezvous	73
—	—	✕ Joy King Lau	74
—	Strand & Covent Garden	✕ Happy Wok	75
—	—	✕ Poons of Covent Garden	75
—	Victoria	✕✕✕ Inn of Happiness	75
—	—	✕✕ Hunan	76
—	—	✕✕ Ken Lo's Memories of China	76
—	—	✕✕ Kym's	76

ENGLISH

Kensington & Chelsea (Royal Borough of)	Chelsea	✕✕ English Garden	59
—	—	✕✕ English House	60
Westminster (City of)	St. James's	✕✕ Greens	73
—	Strand & Covent Garden	✕✕✕ Simpson's-in-the-Strand	74
—	Victoria	✕✕✕ Lockets	75
—	—	✕ Tate Gallery Rest.	76

FRENCH

Barnet	Finchley	✕ La Madrague	49
Camden	Bloomsbury	✕✕✕ Etoile (L')	51
—	—	✕✕ Porte de la Cité	51
—	—	✕ Mon Plaisir	51
—	Hampstead	✕✕✕ Keats	52
City of London	City of London	✕✕ Poulbot (Le) (basement)	52
—	—	✕ Bastille (La)	53
—	—	✕ Bourse Plate (La)	53
—	—	✕ Bubb's	53
—	—	✕ Gamin (Le)	53
Hammersmith	Fulham	✕✕ Gastronome One	55
Hounslow	Chiswick	✕ Biba's	58
—	—	✕ Dordogne (La)	58
Kensington & Chelsea (Royal Borough of)	Chelsea	✕✕✕✕ ✿✿ Tante Claire (La)	59
—	—	✕✕✕ Français (Le)	59
—	—	✕✕ Bagatelle	60
—	—	✕✕ Gavvers	60
—	—	✕✕ ✿ Ma Cuisine	60
—	—	✕✕ Poissonnerie de l'Avenue	60
—	—	✕✕ St. Quentin	60
—	—	✕✕ Suquet (Le)	60
—	—	✕ Brasserie (La)	60
—	—	✕ Thierry's	60
—	Earl's Court	✕✕ Croisette (La)	61

Borough	Area	Restaurant		Page

FRENCH (continued)

Borough	Area	Restaurant		Page
Kensington & Chelsea (Royal Borough of)	Kensington	XXX	Belvedere	61
–	–	XXX	Ruelle (La)	61
–	–	XX	Crocodile (Le)	61
–	–	XX	Pomme d'Amour (La)	61
–	–	XX	Résidence (La)	61
–	–	X	Ark (The)	62
–	–	X	Quai St. Pierre (Le)	62
–	North Kensington	XX	Chez Moi	62
–	–	XX	Monsieur Thompsons	62
Richmond-upon-Thames	Barnes	X	Barnaby's	65
–	Richmond	XX	Chez Bubb	65
Southwark	Peckham Rye	XX	Auberge (L')	66
Wandsworth	Battersea	XXX	✿ Chez Nico	67
–	–	XX	✿ Arlequin (L')	67
Westminster (City of)	Belgravia	XX	Trou Normand (Le)	68
–	Mayfair	XXXXX	✿✿ Terrace (The)	70
–	–	XXXX	✿✿✿ Gavroche (Le)	70
–	Regents Park & Marylebone	XXX	✿ Rue St. Jacques	72
–	–	X	Aventure (L')	72
–	–	X	Bois St. Jean (Au)	72
–	–	X	Muscadet (Le)	72
–	St. James's	XXXXX	Maxims de Paris	73
–	–	XXXX	Ecu de France (A l')	73
–	Soho	XX	Jardin des Gourmets (Au)	73
–	–	X	Cafe Loire	74
–	Strand & Covent Garden	XXXX	Boulestin	74
–	–	XX	Chez Solange	74
–	–	XX	Interlude	74
–	–	XX	Tourment d'Amour	74
–	–	X	Café Pelican	75
–	–	X	Magnos Brasserie	75
–	Victoria	XXX	Auberge de Provence	75
–	–	XXX	✿✿ Simply Nico	75
–	–	XX	Ciboure	76
–	–	XX	Dolphin Brasserie	76
–	–	XX	✿ Mazarin (Le)	76
–	–	X	Poule au Pot (La)	76

GREEK

Borough	Area	Restaurant		Page
Camden	Bloomsbury	XXX	White Tower	51
Westminster (City of)	Bayswater & Maida Vale	X	Kalamaras Taverna	68

HUNGARIAN

Borough	Area	Restaurant		Page
Westminster (City of)	Soho	XX	Old Budapest	73
–	–	XX	Gay Hussar	73

Borough	Area		Restaurant	Page

INDIAN & PAKISTANI

Borough	Area		Restaurant	Page
Brent	Kilburn	✕	**Vijay**	50
—	Wembley	✕✕	**Moghul Brasserie**	50
Camden	Bloomsbury	✕✕	**Lal Qila**	51
—	Holborn	✕✕	**Bhatti**	52
—	Kentish Town	✕	**Bengal Lancer**	52
Croydon	Croydon	✕	**Khyber**	53
Hammersmith	Hammersmith	✕	**Aziz**	55
—	Shepherd's Bush	✕✕	**Shireen**	55
—	West Kensington	✕✕	**Koh-I-Noor**	55
Islington	Upper Holloway	✕	**Raj Vogue**	58
Kensington & Chelsea (Royal Borough of)	Chelsea	✕	**Nayab**	60
	Kensington	✕	**Malabar**	62
—	South Kensington	✕✕✕	**Bombay Brasserie**	63
—	—	✕✕	**Memories of India**	63
Kingston	Kingston	✕	**Modern India**	63
Merton	Wimbledon	✕✕	**Golden Tandoori**	64
Richmond-upon-Thames	Barnes	✕	**Gate of India**	65
Westminster (City of)	Bayswater & Maida Vale	✕✕✕	**Bombay Palace**	68
—	Belgravia	✕✕	**Salloos**	68
—	Hyde Park & Knightsbridge	✕✕✕	**Shezan**	68
—	Regent's Park & Marylebone	✕✕	**Gaylord**	72
—	—	✕✕	**Viceroy of India**	72
—	Soho	✕✕✕	**Red Fort**	73
—	—	✕✕	**Last Days of the Raj**	73
—	Victoria	✕✕✕	**Kundan**	75

ITALIAN

Borough	Area		Restaurant	Page
Barnet	Finchley	✕✕	**Luigi's " Belmont "**	49
Bromley	Bromley	✕✕	**Capisano**	50
—	Chislehurst	✕✕	**Mario**	50
—	Farnborough	✕✕	**Ombrello (L')**	50
—	Keston	✕✕	**Giannino's**	50
Camden	Hampstead	✕	**Villa Bianca**	52
Croydon	Sanderstead	✕	**Elio**	53
Ealing	Ealing	✕	**Gino's**	54
Hammersmith	Fulham	✕✕	**Barbarella**	55
Haringey	Highgate	✕✕	**San Carlo**	56
Harrow	Hatch End	✕✕	**Canaletto 2**	56
Hillingdon	Eastcote	✕	**Sambuca**	57
—	Northwood	✕✕	**Martini**	57
—	Uxbridge	✕✕✕	**Giovanni's**	58
Islington	Islington	✕✕	**Portofino**	58
Kensington & Chelsea (Royal Borough of)	Chelsea	✕✕✕	**Mario**	59
—	—	✕✕	**Beccofino**	60
—	—	✕✕	**Don Luigi**	60
—	—	✕✕	**Eleven Park Walk**	59
—	—	✕✕	**Finezza (La)**	59
—	—	✕✕	**Meridiana**	60
—	—	✕✕	**Ponte Nuovo**	60

Borough	Area		Restaurant	Page

ITALIAN (continued)

Borough	Area		Restaurant	Page
—	—	XX	San Frediano	60
—	—	XX	San Ruffillo	60
—	—	XX	Toto	60
—	Kensington	XX	Franco Ovest	62
—	—	XX	Paesana (La)	61
—	—	XX	Topo d'Oro	62
—	—	XX	Trattoo	62
—	—	X	Barbino (II)	62
Merton	Wimbledon	XX	San Lorenzo Fuoriporta	64
Richmond-upon-Thames	Barnes	X	Bellamore (II)	65
—	East Sheen	X	Tagliatelle (Le)	65
—	Richmond	XX	Bellini	65
Southwark	Dulwich Village	XX	Luigi's	66
Waltham Forest	Leytonstone	X	Trattoria Parmigiana	66
Westminster (City of)	Bayswater & Maida Vale	XX	Canaletto	68
—	—	XX	Concordia Notte	68
—	—	XX	San Marino	68
—	—	X	Concordia	68
—	Hyde Park & Knightsbridge	XX	Montpeliano	68
—	Mayfair	XXX	Tiberio	70
—	—	X	Trattoria Fiori	70
—	Regent's Park & Marylebone	XX	Loggia (La)	72
—	—	XX	Pavona (La)	72
—	—	XX	Tonino	72
—	—	X	Barbino (II)	72
—	—	X	Biagi's	72
—	Soho	XXX	Leonis Quo Vadis	73
—	—	XX	Rugantino	73
—	—	XX	Venezia	73
—	Strand & Covent Garden	X	Laguna	75
—	Victoria	XXX	Santini	75
—	—	XX	Gran Paradiso	76
—	—	XX	Villa Claudius	76
—	—	X	Fontana (La)	76
—	—	X	Mimmo d'Ischia	76
—	—	X	Villa Medici	76

JAPANESE

Borough	Area		Restaurant	Page
City of London	City of London	XX	Aykoku Kaku	52
—	—	X	Hana Guruma Bako	53
Kensington & Chelsea (Royal Borough of)	Kensington	XX	Hiroko	62
Westminster (City of)	Mayfair	XX	Miyama	70
—	—	XX	One Two Three	70
—	—	XX	Shogun	70
—	—	X	Ikeda	70
—	Regent's Park & Marylebone	XX	Asuka	72
—	—	XX	Masako	72
—	St. James's	XXX	❀ Suntory	73
—	Soho	XX	Fuji	73
—	Strand & Covent Garden	XX	Azami	74

Borough	Area	Restaurant	Page

KOREAN

Westminster (City of)	Soho	✗✗ **Kaya**	73

ORIENTAL

Barnet	Mill Hill	✗✗ **Hees**	49
Enfield	Enfield	✗ **Mr Choi**	54
Kensington & Chelsea (Royal Borough of)	Chelsea	✗✗ **T'ang**	60
Richmond-upon-Thames	Richmond	✗ **Kim's**	65

THAI

Kensington & Chelsea (Royal Borough of)	South Kensington	✗✗ **Tui**	63
Kingston	Kingston	✗ **Ayudhya**	63
Wandsworth	Tooting	✗ **Oh Boy**	67
Westminster (City of)	Regent's Park & Marylebone	✗ **Chaopraya**	72
—	Soho	✗ **Chiang Mai**	73

VEGETARIAN

Southwark	Southwark	✗ **Dining Room**	66

VIETNAMESE

Westminster (City of)	Soho	✗ **Nam Long**	74
—	—	✗ **Saigon**	74

RESTAURANTS OPEN ON SUNDAY (L : lunch - D : dinner) AND RESTAURANTS TAKING LAST ORDERS AFTER 11.30 p.m.

RESTAURANTS OUVERTS LE DIMANCHE (L : déjeuner - D : dîner) ET RESTAURANTS PRENANT LES DERNIÈRES COMMANDES APRÈS 23 h 30

RISTORANTI APERTI LA DOMENICA (L : colazione - D : pranzo) E RISTORANTI CHE ACCETTANO ORDINAZIONI DOPO LE 23. 30

RESTAURANTS, DIE SONNTAGS GEÖFFNET SIND (L : Mittagessen - D : Abendessen), BZW. BESTELLUNGEN AUCH NACH 23. 30 UHR ANNEHMEN

Borough	Area	Restaurant	Sunday	11.30 p. m.	Page
Barnet	Child's Hill	✕ Quincy's 84	L		49
—	Finchley	✕✕ Luigi's « Belmont »	L D		49
—	—	✕ Pelcing Duck	L D		49
—	Mill Hill	✕✕ Good Earth	L D		49
Brent	Kilburn	✕ Vijay	L D		50
—	Wembley	✕✕ Moghul Brasserie	L D		50
Camden	Bloomsbury	✕ Seven Dials		x	51
—	Finchley Road	✕ Sheridans	L D		51
—	Hampstead	✕✕✕ Zen W3	L D	x	52
—	—	✕ Chateaubriand (12.00)		x	52
—	Holborn	✕✕✕ Opera (L') (12.00)		x	52
—	—	✕✕ Bhatti	L D	x	52
—	Kentish Town	✕ Bengal Lancer (12.30)	L D	x	52
—	Swiss Cottage	✕✕ Lee Ho Fok	L D	x	52
—	—	✕✕ Peters	L	x	52
Croydon	Addington	✕✕ Willow	L D	x	53
—	Croydon	✕✕✕ Chateau Napoleon	L		53
—	—	✕ Khyber	L D		53
Ealing	Ealing	✕✕ Maxim (12.00)	D	x	54
—	—	✕ Gino's		x	54
Enfield	Southgate	✕✕ L'Oiseau Noir	L		54
Greenwich	Greenwich	✕✕ Papillon (Le)	L		55
Hammersmith	Fulham	✕✕ Barbarella (1.00)		x	55
—	—	✕✕ Gastronome One		x	55
—	—	✕✕ Hiders		x	55
—	—	✕✕ Mao Tai (11.45)	L D	x	55
—	—	✕ Evergreen	L D	x	55
—	—	✕ Perfumed Conservatory		x	55
—	Hammersmith	✕ Aziz (11.45)		x	55
—	Shepherd's Bush	✕✕ Shireen	L D	x	55

Borough	Area	Restaurant	Sunday	11.30 p. m.	Page
Haringey	Highgate	𝄂𝄂 **One Hampstead Lane**	L		56
—	—	𝄂𝄂 **San Carlo**	L D	x	56
Harrow	Hatch End	𝄂 **Swan**	L D	x	56
—	Stanmore	𝄂𝄂 **Buddha House**	L D	x	56
Hillingdon	Eastcote	𝄂 **Sambuca**	L	x	57
Islington	Islington	𝄂𝄂 **Frederick's**		x	58
—	—	𝄂𝄂 **Portofino**		x	58
—	—	𝄂𝄂 **Varnom's**	L		58
—	—	𝄂 **M'sieur Frog**		x	58
Kensington & Chelsea (Royal Borough of)	Chelsea	🏨 ✿ **Capital**	L D		59
—	—	𝄂𝄂𝄂𝄂 ✿ **Chelsea Room**	L D		59
—	—	𝄂𝄂𝄂𝄂 ✿ **Waltons**	L D	x	59
—	—	𝄂𝄂𝄂 **Mario**	L D	x	59
—	—	𝄂𝄂𝄂 **Turner's**	L D		59
—	—	𝄂𝄂𝄂 **Zen**	L D	x	59
—	—	𝄂𝄂 **Daphne's (12.00)**		x	59
—	—	𝄂𝄂 **Eleven Park Walk (2.00)**	L D	x	59
—	—	𝄂𝄂 **English Garden**	L D	x	59
—	—	𝄂𝄂 **English House**	L D	x	60
—	—	𝄂𝄂 **Good Earth**	L D		60
—	—	𝄂𝄂 **Good Earth**	L D	x	60
—	—	𝄂𝄂 **Han's**	L D		60
—	—	𝄂𝄂 **Ménage à Trois (12.15)**		x	60
—	—	𝄂𝄂 **Meridiana (12.00)**	L D	x	60
—	—	𝄂𝄂 **Pier 31**	L D	x	60
—	—	𝄂𝄂 **Poissonnerie de l'Avenue**		x	60
—	—	𝄂𝄂 **Ponte Nuovo (11.45)**	L D	x	60
—	—	𝄂𝄂 **Sampan**	L D	x	60
—	—	𝄂𝄂 **St. Quentin (12.00)**	L D	x	60
—	—	𝄂𝄂 **Suquet (Le)**	L D	x	60
—	—	𝄂𝄂 **Toto**	L D		60
—	—	𝄂 **Brasserie (La) (12.00)**	L D	x	60
—	—	𝄂 **Monkeys**	L D	x	60
—	—	𝄂 **Nayab (12.00)**	L D	x	60
—	—	𝄂 **Thierry's**		x	60
—	—	𝄂 **Wheelers**	L D		60
—	Earl's Court	𝄂𝄂 **Brinkley's**		x	61
—	—	𝄂𝄂 **Tiger Lee**	D		61
—	—	𝄂 **Crystal Palace**	L D	x	61
—	Kensington	🏨 **Royal Garden (Royal Roof)**		x	61
—	—	𝄂𝄂𝄂 **Ruelle (La)**		x	61
—	—	𝄂𝄂 **Franco Ovest**		x	62
—	—	𝄂𝄂 **Hiroko**	L D		62
—	—	𝄂𝄂 **Mandarin**	L D		62
—	—	𝄂𝄂 **Paesana (La) (11.45)**		x	61
—	—	𝄂𝄂 **Topo d'Oro**	L D	x	62
—	—	𝄂𝄂 **Trattoo**	L D	x	62
—	—	𝄂 **Ark (The)**	D	x	62
—	—	𝄂 **Barbino (Il) (12.00)**		x	62
—	—	𝄂 **Malabar**	L D		62
—	—	𝄂 **Quai St. Pierre (La)**		x	62

Borough	Area	Restaurant	Sunday	11.30 p. m.	Page
—	North Kensington	XXX Leith's (12.00)	D	x	62
—	—	XX Chez Moi		x	62
—	South Kensington	XXX Bombay Brasserie (12.00)	L D	x	63
—	—	XX Memories of India	L D		63
—	—	XX Pun	L D	x	63
—	—	XX Reads	L		63
—	—	XX Tui	L D		63
Lambeth	Herne Hill	X Au Provençal	D		64
Lewisham	Upper Sydenham	XX Hornimans	L		64
Merton	Wimbledon	XX San Lorenzo Fuoriporta	L D		64
—	—	XX Village	L		64
—	—	XX Wimbledon Palace	L D		64
Redbridge	Ilford	XX Mandarin Palace (12.00)	L D	x	64
—	South Woodford	XX Ho Ho	L D	x	64
Richmond-upon-Thames	Barnes	X Il Bellamore	L D	x	65
—	—	XX Sonnys	D		65
—	East Sheen	X Tagliatelle (Le)	L D		65
—	Kew	X Mange Tout (Le)	L		65
—	Richmond	XX Evergreen	L D	x	65
—	—	XX Kew Rendezvous	L D	x	65
—	—	X Kims	L D		65
—	—	X Red Lion	L D	x	65
Southwark	Dulwich	XX Luigis		x	66
—	Peckham Rye	XX L'Auberge	L		66
Tower Hamlets	Limehouse	X Good Friends	L D	x	66
Waltham Forest	Leytonstone	X Trattoria Parmigiana (12.00)		x	66
Wandsworth	Battersea	XX Alonso's		x	67
—	—	X Ransome's		x	67
—	Clapham	X Jasmin		x	67
—	—	X Pollyanna's (12.00)	L	x	67
—	Putney	XX Bayee House	L D		67
Westminster (City of)	Bayswater & Maida Vale	XXX Bombay Palace	L D	x	68
—	—	XX Concordia Notte (1.00)		x	68
—	—	XX San Marino		x	68
—	—	X Concordia (11.45)		x	68
—	—	X Fortune Cookie	L D		68
—	—	X Kalamaras Taverna		x	68
—	Belgravia	⚏⚏⚏ Berkeley (Restaurant)	L D		68
—	—	XX Trou Normande (Le)		x	68
—	Hyde Park & Knightsbridge	XXX Shezan		x	68
—	Mayfair	⚏⚏⚏ Claridges (Causerie)	L D		69
—	—	⚏⚏⚏ Inn on the Park (Four Seasons)	L D		69
		(Lanes 12.00)	L D	x	69
—	—	XXXXX ❀❀ The Terrace		x	70
—	—	XXXX ❀ Soufflé (Le)	L D	x	70
—	—	XXXX Scott's	D		70

Borough	Area	Restaurant		Sunday	11.30 p. m.	Page
—	—	XXX	Princess Garden	L D	x	70
—	—	XXX	Tiberio (1.00)		x	70
—	—	XX	Langen's Brasserie (11.45)		x	70
—	—	XX	Mr. Kai	L D		70
—	Regent's Park & Marylebone	XXX	Odins		x	72
—	—	XX	Gaylord	L D		72
—	—	XX	Loggia (La)		x	72
—	—	XX	Lords Rendezvous	L D		72
—	—	XX	Viceroy of India	L D	x	72
—	—	X	Aventure (L')	L D		72
—	—	X	Bois St. Jean (Au)	L D	x	72
—	—	X	Barbino (Il) (12.00)		x	72
—	—	X	Biagi's	L D		72
—	—	X	Langans Bistro		x	72
Westminster (City of)	St. James's	XXXX	Ecu de France (A l')	D	x	73
—	—	XX	Caprice (Le) (12.00)	L D	x	73
—	Soho	XXX	Bastide (La)		x	73
—	—	XXX	Leonis Quo Vadis	D		73
—	—	XXX	Red Fort	L D		73
—	—	XX	Chesa (Swiss Centre)	L D		73
—	—	XX	Jardin de Gourmets (Au)		x	73
—	—	XX	Kaya	D		73
—	—	XX	Last Days of the Raj	L D	x	73
—	—	XX	Old Budapest		x	73
—	—	XX	Poons		x	73
—	—	X	Cafe Loire		x	74
—	—	X	Chiang Mai	L D	x	73
—	—	X	Frith's		x	73
—	—	X	Fung Shing	L D	x	73
—	—	X	Gallery Rendezvous (11.45)	L D		73
—	—	X	Joy King Lau	L D		74
—	—	X	Saigon		x	74
—	Strand & Covent Garden	▲▲▲▲	Savoy (River)	L D		74
—	—	XXX	Inigo Jones		x	74
—	—	XX	Azami	L D		74
—	—	XX	Bates		x	74
—	—	XX	Chez Solange (12.15)	D	x	74
—	—	XX	Frere Jacques	L D	x	74
—	—	XX	Tourment d'Amour		x	74
—	—	X	Grimes		x	75
—	—	X	Happy Wok		x	75
—	—	X	Magnos Brasserie		x	75
—	—	X	Poons of Covent Garden		x	75
—	Victoria	XXX	Auberge de Provence	L D		75
—	—	XXX	Santini	D	x	75
—	—	XX	Ciboure		x	76
—	—	XX	Dolphin Brasserie (11.45)	L D		76
—	—	XX	Gran Paradiso		x	76
—	—	XX	Hoizin		x	76
—	—	XX	Kym's	L D	x	76
—	—	XX	✿ Mazarin (Le)		x	76
—	—	X	Fontana (La)	L D		76
—	—	X	Villa Medici		x	76

BOROUGHS and AREAS

Greater London is divided, for administrative purposes, into 32 boroughs plus the City ; these sub-divide naturally into minor areas, usually grouped around former villages or quarters, which often maintain a distinctive character.

✪ of Greater London : 01 except special cases.

BARNET pp. 4 and 5.

Child's Hill – ✉ NW2.

✗ **Quincy's 84,** 675 Finchley Rd, NW2 2JP, ℰ 794 8499 – 🍽. 🖭 *VISA*   DV **r**
closed Monday, first week September and 24 December-8 January – **M** (dinner only and Sunday lunch) 11.50/14.75 **t.** ⫶ 3.50.

Finchley – ✉ N3/N12/NW11.
🛇 Nether Court, Frith Lane ℰ 346 2436.

✗✗ **Luigi's Belmont,** 2-4 Belmont Par., Finchley Rd, NW11 6XP, at Temple Fortune ℰ 455 0210, Italian rest. – 🖭 AE ⓪ *VISA*   DV **a**
closed Monday – **M** 5.00 **t.** (lunch) and a la carte 8.90/14.70 **t.** ⫶ 2.50.

✗✗ **Fogareiro,** 16-18 Hendon Lane, N3, ℰ 346 0315, Seafood – 🖭 AE ⓪ *VISA*   DU **c**
closed Sunday – **M** 7.75 **t.** (lunch) and a la carte ⫶ 2.75.

✗ La Madrague, 816 Finchley Rd, NW11 6XL, at Temple Fortune ℰ 455 8853, French rest.
                                          DV **i**

✗ **Peking Duck,** 30 Temple Fortune Par., Finchley Rd, NW11, ℰ 455 9444, Chinese rest. – 🖭
AE ⓪ *VISA*   DV **s**
closed Tuesday – **M** 8.00 **t.** and a la carte 8.90/12.70 **t.** ⫶ 3.00.

Hendon – ✉ NW4/NW7.
🛇 off Sanders Lane ℰ 346 6023.

🏨 **Hendon Hall,** Ashley Lane, NW4 1HF, ℰ 203 3341, Telex 8956088, 🚗 – ⧈ 📺 ☎ 🅿. 🖄. 🖭
AE ⓪ *VISA*. ⁂   DV **v**
M 10.50 **st.** and a la carte ⫶ 4.00 – ⌑ 5.50 – **52 rm** 48.00/58.00 **st.**, **1 suite** 80.00 **t.** – SB (weekends only) 68.00/86.00 **st.**

🏨 TraveLodge (T.H.F.), NW7 3HB, at Scratchwood Service Area on M 1 ℰ 906 0611, Telex 8814796 – 🍽 rest 📺 ⌑wc 🕾 ⚹ 🅿. 🖄. 🖭 AE ⓪ *VISA*   CU **r**
97 rm ⌑ 39.50/50.50 **st.**

Mill Hill – ✉ NW7.
🛇 100 Barnet Way ℰ 959 2282.

✗✗ Taicoon, 655 Watford Way, NW7 3JR, at Apex Corner ℰ 959 5037, Chinese rest.   CU **c**
✗✗ **Good Earth,** 143-145 The Broadway, NW7 4RN, ℰ 959 7011, Chinese rest. – 🖭 AE ⓪ *VISA*
M 10.50/16.50 **t.** and a la carte 13.45/20.00 **t.**   CU **a**
✗✗ Hees, 27 The Broadway, NW7, ℰ 959 7109, Chinese (Peking, Szechuan) rest.   CU **a**

BEXLEY pp. 10 and 11.

Bexley – ✉ Kent – ✪ 0322 Crayford.

🏨 **Crest** (Crest), Black Prince Interchange, Southwold Rd, DA5 1ND, on A 2 ℰ 526900, Telex 8956539 – ⧈ 📺 ⌑wc 🕾 ⚹ 🅿. 🖄. 🖭 AE ⓪ *VISA*. ⁂   HY **e**
M 10.25/11.95 **st.** and a la carte ⫶ 3.90 – ⌑ 5.85 – **78 rm** 50.00/60.00 **st.** – SB (weekends only) 56.00/58.00 **st.**

BRENT pp. 4 and 5.

Kilburn.

✗ **Vijay,** 49 Willesden Lane, NW6 7RF, 🖉 328 1087, South Indian rest. – ▤. ⚒ AE ⓞ VISA
closed 25 and 26 December – **M** 6.00 and a la carte.   DV **n**

Wembley – ✉ Middx.

🇫 Horsenden Hill, Whitton Av. 🖉 902 4555.

🏨 **Ladbroke International** (Ladbroke), Empire Way, HA9 8DS, 🖉 902 8839, Telex 24837 – 🛗
▤ rest 📺 ☎ ᴕ ℗. ᴕ ⚒ AE ⓞ VISA   CV **z**
M 9.50/11.50 **t.** and a la carte ᦙ 3.25 – ⌷ 6.75 – **322 rm** 55.00/70.00 **t.** – SB (weekends only)
50.00/65.00 **st.**

✗✗ **Moghul Brasserie,** 525 High Rd, HA0 4AG, 🖉 903 6967, Indian rest. – ▤. ⚒ AE ⓞ VISA
closed Christmas Day – **M** a la carte 7.45/8.80 **t.**   CV **a**

BROMLEY pp. 10 and 11.

Bromley – ✉ Kent.

🇫 Magpie Hall Lane 🖉 462 7014.

🏨 **Bromley Court** ⬙, Bromley Hill, BR1 4JD, 🖉 464 5011, Telex 896310, ☞ – 🛗 📺 ➟wc
🕳wc ☎ ℗. ᴕ ⚒ AE ⓞ VISA   GY **z**
M 8.00/9.00 **t.** and a la carte ᦙ 3.00 – **130 rm** ⌷ 44.00/58.00 **t.**

⌂ **Grianan,** 23 Orchard Rd, BR1 2PR, 🖉 460 1795 – 📺 🕳wc ℗. ⬙
12 rm ⌷ 15.00/25.00 **st.**   GYZ **n**

✗ **Capisano,** 9 Simpsons Rd, BR2 9AP, 🖉 464 8036, Italian rest. – ⚒ AE VISA   GZ **s**
closed Sunday, Monday and 15 August-8 September – **M** 7.50 **t.** (lunch) and a la carte
9.60/13.50 **t.** ᦙ 2.80.

✗ **Peking Diner,** 71 Burnt Ash Lane, BRI 5AA, 🖉 464 7911, Chinese rest. – ⚒ AE ⓞ VISA
closed Sunday and Bank Holidays – **M** 10.00/15.00 **t.** ᦙ 2.00.   GY **u**

Chislehurst – ✉ Kent.

✗✗ **Mario,** 53 Chislehurst Rd, BR7 5NP, 🖉 467 1341, Italian rest. – ⚒ AE ⓞ VISA   GZ **c**
closed Monday lunch, Sunday and Bank Holidays – **M** 4.95/7.50 **t.** and a la carte 11.80 **t.**
ᦙ 2.75.

Farnborough – ✉ Kent – ☎ 0689 Farnborough.

🇫 High Elms, High Elms Rd 🖉 58175, off A 21 via Shire Lane.

✗✗ **L'Ombrello,** 360 Crofton Rd, Locks Bottom, BR6 7XX, 🖉 52286, Italian rest. – ⚒ AE ⓞ
VISA   HZ **c**
closed Sunday – **M** 7.25 **t.** (lunch) and a la carte 8.15/13.35 **t.** ᦙ 2.75.

Keston – ✉ Kent – ☎ 0689 Farnborough.

✗✗ Giannino's, 6 Commonside, BR4 2TS, 🖉 56410, Italian rest.   GZ **x**

*Groß-London (GREATER LONDON) besteht aus der City und 32 Verwaltungsbezirken
(Borough). Diese sind wiederum in kleinere Bezirke (Area) unterteilt, deren Mittelpunkt
ehemalige Dörfer oder Stadtviertel sind, die oft ihren eigenen Charakter bewahrt
haben.*

CAMDEN Except where otherwise stated see pp. 13-16.

Bloomsbury – ✉ NW1/W1/WC1.

🏨 **Russell** (T.H.F.), Russell Sq., WC1B 5BE, 🖉 837 6470, Telex 24615 – 🛗 📺 ☎. ᴕ ⚒ AE ⓞ
VISA   NT **o**
M (carving rest.) 10.50 **st.** and a la carte ᦙ 3.40 – ⌷ 6.50 – **316 rm** 57.00/72.00 **st.**

🏨 **Grafton,** 130 Tottenham Court Rd, W1P 9HP, 🖉 388 4131, Telex 297234 – 🛗 ▤ rest 📺 ☎.
ᴕ ⚒ AE ⓞ VISA. ⬙   LT **n**
M 10.00 **st.** and a la carte ᦙ 6.00 – ⌷ 6.00 – **159 rm** 59.90/79.90 **st.**

🏨 **Kenilworth,** 97 Great Russell St., WC1B 3LB, 🖉 637 3477, Telex 25842 – 🛗 📺 ☎. ᴕ ⚒ AE
ⓞ VISA ⬙   MT **a**
M 10.00 **st.** and a la carte 13.00/17.75 **st.** ᦙ 3.55 – ⌷ 6.00 – **180 rm** 59.90/79.90, **1 suite**

🏨 **Mountbatten,** Seven Dials, WC2H 9HD, 🖉 836 4300, Telex 298087 – 🛗 ▤ rest 📺 ☎. ᴕ.
⚒ AE ⓞ VISA. ⬙   p.31 DV **o**
M 10.50 **t.** and a la carte 14.50/21.50 **t.** – ⌷ 8.00 – **127 rm** 89.90/123.90 **st.**, **7 suites**
180.00/250.00 **st.** – SB (except summer) (weekends only)107.00 **st.**

Bonnington, 92 Southampton Row, WC1B 4BH, ☎ 242 2828, Telex 261591 – 🛗 📺 ☐wc ❀
⅚. 👗. ❄ 🅰🅴 ① 𝘝𝘐𝘚𝘈   NT **s**
M (buffet lunch)/dinner 8.50 **st.** and a la carte ⓘ 3.20 – **242 rm** ⊃ 31.35/66.00 **st.**

Bloomsbury Crest (Crest), Coram St., WC1N 1HT, ☎ 837 1200, Telex 22113 – 🛗 ▤ rest 📺
☐wc ☎ ⇦ ❷. ❄ 🅰🅴 ① 𝘝𝘐𝘚𝘈. ❄
MNS **c**
M 10.95 **st.** and a la carte – ⊃ 6.65 – **239 rm** 58.00/68.00, **2 suites** 120.00/140.00 – SB
(weekends only) 75.90/83.90 **st.**

Kingsley (Mt. Charlotte), Bloomsbury Way, WC1A 2SD, ☎ 242 5881, Telex 21157 – 🛗 📺
☐wc ☎. 👗. ❄ 🅰🅴 ① 𝘝𝘐𝘚𝘈. ❄   NT **r**
M (closed lunch Saturday and Sunday) a la carte approx. 12.50 **t.** ⓘ 3.10 – ⊃ 3.50 – **145 rm**
65.00/80.00 **st.**, **1 suite** 160.00 **st.**

Harlingford, 61-63 Cartwright Gdns, WC1H 9EL, ☎ 387 1551 – 📺. ❄ 𝘝𝘐𝘚𝘈. ❄   MS **n**
40 rm ⊃ 21.00/39.00 **st.**

Russell House, 11 Bernard St., WC1, ☎ 837 7686 – 📺 🗐wc   NT **e**
11 rm.

White Tower, 1 Percy St., W1P 0ET, ☎ 636 8141, Greek rest. – ▤. ❄ 🅰🅴 ① 𝘝𝘐𝘚𝘈   MT **u**
closed Saturday, Sunday, 3 weeks August, 1 week Christmas and Bank Holidays – **M** a la carte
12.10/21.50 **t.** ⓘ 3.25.

L'Etoile, 30 Charlotte St., W1P 1HJ, ☎ 636 7189, French rest.   LT **e**

Neal Street, 26 Neal Street, WC2 9PH, ☎ 836 8368 – ▤. ❄ 🅰🅴 ① 𝘝𝘐𝘚𝘈   p. 31 DV **s**
closed Saturday, Sunday and Christmas-New Year – **M** a la carte 14.60/26.10 **t.** ⓘ 4.35.

Seven Dials, 5 Neals Yard, off Monmouth St., WC2 9DP, ☎ 379 4955 – ❄ 🅰🅴 ① 𝘝𝘐𝘚𝘈
closed Saturday lunch, Sunday and Bank Holidays – **M** a la carte 12.55/16.70 **t.**   p.31 DV **a**

Porte de la Cité, 65 Theobalds Rd, WC1 8TA, ☎ 242 1154, French rest. – ▤. ❄ 🅰🅴 ① 𝘝𝘐𝘚𝘈
closed Saturday, Sunday, Easter, Christmas and Bank Holidays – **M** (lunch only) 16.50 **st.**
ⓘ 3.00.   NT **c**

Lal Qila, 117 Tottenham Court Rd, W1P 9HL, ☎ 387 4570, Indian rest.   LT **u**

Mon Plaisir, 21 Monmouth St., WC2H 9DD, ☎ 836 7243, French rest.   p. 31 DV **a**
closed Saturday lunch, Sunday, Christmas-New Year and Bank Holidays – **M** 8.95/18.00 **t.** and
a la carte 10.80/14.50 **t.** ⓘ 3.20.

Euston – ✉ NW1.

Kennedy (Mt. Charlotte), 43 Cardington St., NW1 2LP, ☎ 387 4400, Telex 28250 – 🛗 ▤ 📺
☐wc ☎. 👗. ❄ 🅰🅴 ① 𝘝𝘐𝘚𝘈. ❄   LS **r**
M 8.50 **st.** and a la carte ⓘ 3.35 – ⊃ 3.50 – **320 rm** 48.50/61.00 **st.**

Finchley Road – ✉ NW1/NW3.

Charles Bernard, 5 Frognal, NW3 6AL, ☎ 794 0101, Telex 23560 – 🛗 📺 ☐wc ☎ ❷. ❄ 🅰🅴
① 𝘝𝘐𝘚𝘈   GR **s**
M 9.80 **st.** and a la carte 7.25/10.75 **st.** ⓘ 2.60 – **57 rm** ⊃ 46.00/62.10 **st.** – SB (weekends only)
58.70 **st.**

Dawson House, 72 Canfield Gdns, NW6 3ED, ☎ 624 0079, ☞ – ❄   HR **a**
15 rm ⊃ 12.00/23.00 **st.**

Green Cottage II, 122a Finchley Rd, NW3 5HT, ☎ 794 3833, Chinese Vegetarian rest. – ▤
JR **u**

Sheridan's, 351 West End Lane, NW6 1LT, ☎ 794 3234 – ❄ 🅰🅴 ① 𝘝𝘐𝘚𝘈   pp. 4 and 5 DV **v**
closed Monday, 18 August-2 September and 1 to 15 January – **M** (dinner only and Sunday
lunch)/dinner a la carte 10.05/14.35 **t.** ⓘ 3.40.

Hampstead – ✉ NW3.

Ladbroke Clive (Ladbroke), Primrose Hill Rd, NW3 3NA, ☎ 586 2233 – 🛗 📺 ☎ ❷. 👗. ❄
🅰🅴 ① 𝘝𝘐𝘚𝘈   KR **q**
M (closed Saturday lunch) 9.50 **st.** and a la carte ⓘ 3.80 – ⊃ 6.50 – **84 rm** 60.00/86.00 **st.** – SB
(weekends only) 70.00/90.00 **st.**

Swiss Cottage, 4 Adamson Rd, NW3 3HP, ☎ 722 2281, Telex 297232, « Antique furniture
collection » – 🛗 📺 ☐wc 🗐wc ☎. ❄ 🅰🅴 ① 𝘝𝘐𝘚𝘈. ❄   JR **n**
M 7.50/10.50 **t.** and a la carte ⓘ 2.50 – **65 rm** 36.50/73.00 **t.**, **4 suites** 73.00 **t.**

Post House (T.H.F.), 215 Haverstock Hill, NW3 4RB, ☎ 794 8121, Telex 262494 – 🛗 📺
☐wc ❀ ❷. ❄ 🅰🅴 ① 𝘝𝘐𝘚𝘈   GR **r**
M 8.95 **st.** and a la carte ⓘ 3.40 – ⊃ 5.65 – **140 rm** 52.00/63.00 **st.**

Sandringham ⑤, 3 Holford Rd, NW3 1AD, ☎ 435 1569, ≤, ☞ – ❷. ❄   GR **u**
13 rm ⊃ 18.00/35.00 **st.**

Frognal Lodge, 14 Frognal Gdns (off Church Row), NW3 6UX, ☎ 435 8238, Telex 8812714 – 🛗
☐wc ❀   GR **v**
17 rm.

XXX **Keats,** 3-4 Downshire Hill, NW3 1NR, ℰ 435 3544, French rest. – ⊠ AE ⓞ VISA   GR i
closed Sunday and last 2 weeks August – **M** (dinner only) 19.00 **st.** and a la carte 18.30/23.00 **st.**
§ 9.00.

XXX **Zen W3,** 83 Hampstead High St., NW3 1RE, ℰ 794 7863, Chinese rest. – ⊠ AE ⓞ VISA
M a la carte 13.00/19.00 **t.**   GR a

X   **Villa Bianca,** 1 Perrin's Court, NW3 1QR, ℰ 435 3131, Italian rest.   GR c

X   **Chateaubriand,** 48 Belsize Lane, NW3 5AR, ℰ 435 4882 – ⊠ AE ⓞ VISA   GR n
closed Sunday – **M** (dinner only) 18.00 **t.** and a la carte 9.10/15.85 **t.** § 2.95.

| Holborn | – ⊠ WC2.

🏨 **Drury Lane Moat House** (Q.M.H.), 10 Drury Lane, High Holborn, WC2B 5RE, ℰ 836 6666,
Telex 8811395 – ⧉ ▤ TV ☎ ⤴. ⊠ AE ⓞ VISA ⥁   p. 31 DV c
M 11.30 **t.** and a la carte 15.35/16.60 **t.** § 3.50 – ☲ 6.75 – **129 rm** 68.00/98.00 **t.**, **1 suite** 156.00
t. – SB (weekends only) 76.00/80.00 **st.**

XXX **L'Opera,** 32 Great Queen St., WC2B 5AA, ℰ 405 9020 – ⊠ AE ⓞ VISA   p. 31 EV n
closed Saturday lunch, Sunday and Bank Holidays – **M** 18.00/25.00 **st.** and a la carte
15.45/21.40 **t.** § 3.00.

XX **Hodgsons,** 115 Chancery Lane, WC2, ℰ 242 2836 – ⊠ AE ⓞ VISA   NT a
closed Saturday, Sunday and Bank Holidays – **M** 10.95 **t.** and a la carte § 2.75.

XX **Bhatti,** 37 Great Queen St., WC2, ℰ 831 0817, Indian rest. – ⊠ AE ⓞ VISA   EV z
M 8.50/9.50 **t.** and a la carte 7.15/9.05 **t.** § 3.15.

| Kentish Town | – ⊠ NW5.

X   **Bengal Lancer,** 253 Kentish Town Rd, NW5 2JY, ℰ 485 6688, Indian rest. – ▤. ⊠ AE ⓞ
VISA   LR c
M 18.00 **t.** and a la carte 10.50/17.25 **t.** § 3.00.

| King's Cross | – ⊠ N1.

🏨 **Great Northern,** N1 9AN, ℰ 837 5454, Telex 299041 – ⧉ TV ⤳wc ☎. ⤴. ⊠ AE ⓞ VISA ⥁
closed Christmas – **M** 10.00/13.00 **st.** § 3.30 – **87 rm** ☲ 52.50/67.50 **st.**   MNS s

| Regent's Park | – ⊠ NW1.

🏨 **White House** (Rank), Albany St., NW1 3UP, ℰ 387 1200, Telex 24111 – ⧉ ▤ rest TV ☎ ⅓.
⤴. ⊠ AE ⓞ VISA. ⥁   LS o
M 9.00 **t.** and a la carte 10.00/20.50 **t.** – ☲ 7.00 – **580 rm** 62.00/90.00 **t.**, **9 suites** 160.00/
310.00 **t.**

| Swiss Cottage | – ⊠ NW3.

🏨 **Holiday Inn,** 128 King Henry's Rd, NW3 3ST, ℰ 722 7711, Telex 267396, ⬛ – ⧉ ▤ TV ☎ ⅓.
Ⓟ ⤴. ⊠ AE ⓞ VISA   JR a
M 13.50 **t.** (lunch) and a la carte 11.60/20.20 **t.** § 4.30 – ☲ 7.10 – **291 rm** 83.40/95.45 **st.**,
4 suites.

XX **Peter's,** 65 Fairfax Rd, NW6 4EE, ℰ 624 5804 – ⊠ AE ⓞ VISA   JR i
closed Saturday lunch, Sunday dinner and 26 December – **M** 12.00 (lunch) and a la carte
12.00/15.75 **t.** § 3.25.

XX **Lee Ho Fook,** 5-6 New College Par., Finchley Rd, NW3, ℰ 722 9552, Chinese rest. ⊠ AE ⓞ
VISA   JR c
M 15.00/20.00 **t.** and a la carte.

| CITY OF LONDON | Except where otherwise stated see p. 16.

🛈 St. Paul's Churchyard, EC4, ℰ 606 3030 ext 2456.

XXX **Corney and Barrow,** 109 Old Broad St., EC2N 1AP, ℰ 920 9560 – ▤. ⊠ AE ⓞ VISA   QT c
closed Saturday, Sunday and Bank Holidays – **M** (lunch only) a la carte 23.25/24.55 **st.** § 6.00.

XXX **Wheeler's,** 33 Foster Lane, EC2V 6HD, ℰ 606 8254, Seafood   PT o

XX **Le Poulbot** (basement), 45 Cheapside, EC2V 6AR, ℰ 236 4379, French rest. – ▤. ⊠ AE ⓞ
VISA   PU i
closed Saturday, Sunday, Christmas-New Year and Bank Holidays – **M** (lunch only) 24.50 **st.**
§ 5.80.

XX **Candlewick Room,** 45 Old Broad St., EC2N 1HT, ℰ 628 7929 – ⊠ AE ⓞ VISA   QT n
closed Saturday, Sunday and Bank Holidays – **M** (lunch only) 25.00 **st.** and a la carte
20.40/23.45 **t.**

XX **Corney and Barrow,** 118 Moorgate, EC2M 6UR, ℰ 628 2898 – ▤. ⊠ AE ⓞ VISA   QT a
closed Saturday, Sunday and Bank Holidays – **M** a la carte 16.75/22.95 **t.** § 4.00.

XX **Corney and Barrow,** 44 Cannon St., EC4N 6JJ, ℰ 248 1700 – ⊠ AE ⓞ VISA   PU r
closed Saturday, Sunday and Bank Holidays – **M** a la carte 16.65/20.45 **t.** § 4.00.

XX **Aykoku Kaku,** 9 Walbrook, EC4, ℰ 236 9020, Japanese rest.   PQU u

XX **Bill Bentley's,** Swedeland Court, 202-204 Bishopsgate, EC2M 4NR, ℰ 283 1763, Seafood –
🔄 AE ⓞ VISA
closed Saturday, Sunday and Bank Holidays – **M** (lunch only) a la carte 14.85/18.15 **t.** ⌀ 2.95. QT e

XX **Shares,** 12-13 Lime St., EC3M 7AA, ℰ 623 1843 – 🔄 AE ⓞ VISA
closed Saturday, Sunday and Bank Holidays – **M** (lunch only) 19.50 **t.** QU s

XX **Bill Bentley's,** 18 Old Broad St., EC2N 1DP, ℰ 588 2655, Seafood – 🔄 VISA
closed Saturday, Sunday and Bank Holidays – **M** (lunch only) a la carte 13.45/16.25 **t.** ⌀ 3.00. QT i

X **Bubb's,** 329 Central Market, Farringdon St., EC1A 9NB, ℰ 236 2435, French rest. –
closed Saturday, Sunday, 2 weeks August, 1 week Christmas-New Year and Bank Holidays –
M (booking essential) a la carte 16.45/20.50 **st.** ⌀ 3.80. PT a

X **La Bourse Plate,** 78 Leadenhall St., EC3A 3DN, ℰ 623 5159, French rest. – 🔄 AE ⓞ VISA
closed Saturday, Sunday – **M** (lunch only) 16.00 **st.** ⌀ 3.40. QU v

X **Le Gamin,** 32 Old Bailey, EC4M 7HS, ℰ 236 7931, French rest. – 🔄 AE ⓞ VISA
closed Saturday, Sunday – **M** (lunch only) 17.75 **st.** ⌀ 2.80. PU a

X **La Bastille,** 116 Newgate St., EC1A 7AE, ℰ 600 1134, French rest. – 🔄 AE ⓞ VISA
closed Saturday, Sunday, last week August, 1 week Christmas and Bank Holidays – **M** (lunch
only) 15.95 **st.** PT z

X **Hana Guruma Bako,** 49 Bow Lane, EC4M 9DL, ℰ 236 6451, Japanese rest. – 🔲 PU n

X **Whittington's,** 21 College Hill, EC4, ℰ 248 5855 – 🔲 🔄 AE ⓞ VISA
closed Saturday, Sunday and Bank Holidays – **M** (lunch only) a la carte 12.75/16.25 **t.** ⌀ 2.45. PU c

CROYDON pp. 10 and 11.

Addington – ✉ Surrey.

XX **Willow,** 88 Selsdon Park Rd, CR2 8JT, ℰ 657 4656, Chinese (Peking, Szechuan) rest. – 🅿.
🔄 AE ⓞ VISA
closed 25 to 28 December – **M** a la carte 10.15/19.20 **t.** ⌀ 3.80. FZ x

Croydon – ✉ Surrey.

🔄, 🔄, 🔄 Addington Court, Featherbed Lane ℰ 657 0281, E : 3 m. – 🔄 Coulsdon Court
Municipal ℰ 660 0468.

🔄 Central Library, Katherine St. ℰ 688 3627 ext 45/6.

🏨 **Holiday Inn,** 7 Altyre Rd, CR9 5AA, ℰ 680 9200, Telex 8956268, 🔲, squash – 🔲 🔲 📺 ☎ &.
🅿.
214 rm, 2 suites. FZ u

🏨 **Croydon Court,** Purley Way, CR9 4LT, ℰ 688 5185, Telex 893814, 🔄 – 📺 🔄wc ☎ 🅿. 🔄
🔄 AE ⓞ VISA
M *(closed Saturday lunch)* 10.95 **t.** and a la carte ⌀ 3.00 – **86 rm** 🔄 49.50/60.00 **t.** – SB
(weekends only) 56.00 **st.** FZ e

🔄 **Oakwood,** 69-71 Outram Rd, CR0 6XJ, ℰ 654 1000, 🔄 – 📺 🔄wc 🔄wc 🅿. 🔄 AE ⓞ VISA
M 7.50/9.00 **t.** – **14 rm** 🔄 35.00/46.00 **t.** – SB (weekends only) 50.00/74.00 **st.** FZ s

🔄 **Briarley,** 8-10 Outram Rd, CR0 6XE, ℰ 654 1000, 🔄 – 📺 🔄wc 🔄wc ☎ 🅿. 🔄 AE ⓞ VISA
M *(closed Sunday dinner)* (bar lunch Monday to Saturday)/dinner 8.50 **t.** and a la carte ⌀ 3.00
– **25 rm** 🔄 39.50/49.00 **t.** – SB (weekends only) 48.00/58.00 **st.** FZ r

XXX **Chateau Napoleon,** Coombe Lane, CR0 5RE, ℰ 680 6027 – 🅿. 🔄 AE ⓞ VISA
closed Sunday dinner – **M** 9.50/10.95 **st.** and a la carte 13.95/18.90 **st.** ⌀ 4.00. FZ o

X **Thirty Four Surrey Street,** 34 Surrey St., CR0 1RJ, ℰ 686 0586, Seafood. Live jazz FZ c

X **Dijonnais,** 299 High St., CR0 1QL, ℰ 686 5624 – 🔄 AE ⓞ VISA
closed Saturday lunch, Sunday, 10 days February, 2 weeks August and Bank Holidays –
M 5.50/12.50 **t.** and a la carte 10.50/13.25 **t.** ⌀ 3.00. FZ z

X **Khyber,** 284 High St., CR0 1NG, ℰ 686 1729, Indian rest. – 🔲. 🔄 AE ⓞ VISA
M 7.00/9.00 **t.** and a la carte 5.90/8.70 **t.** ⌀ 2.75. FZ i

Sanderstead – ✉ Surrey.

🔄 Selsdon Park Hotel, Addington Rd ℰ 657 4129.

🏨 **Selsdon Park** (Best Western), Addington Rd, CR2 8YA, ℰ 657 8811, Telex 945003, ≤,
🔲 heated, 🔲, 🔄, 🔄, park, 🔄, squash – 🔲 📺 & 🅿. 🔄. 🔄 AE ⓞ VISA FZ n
M 13.50/14.25 **st.** and a la carte ⌀ 5.75 – **150 rm** 🔄 62.00/106.00 **st.**, **4 suites** 190.00 **st.** – SB
(weekends only) 108.00/128.00 **st.**

X **Elio,** 17 Limpsfield Rd, CR2 9LA, ℰ 657 2953, Italian rest. – 🔄 AE ⓞ VISA
closed Sunday and Bank Holidays – **M** 8.75 **st.** and a la carte 11.75/14.65 **st.** ⌀ 3.50. FZ a

Thornton Heath – ✉ Surrey.

↑ **Dunheved,** 639-641 London Rd, CR4 6AZ, ℰ 684 2009, 🔄 – 🔄wc 🅿. 🔄 VISA. 🔄 FZ v
closed 25 and 26 December – **19 rm** 🔄 20.00/38.00 **st.**

EALING pp. 4 and 5.

Ealing – ⊠ W5.

🏨 **Carnarvon**, Ealing Common, W5 3HN, ℰ 992 5399, Telex 935114 – 🛗 📺 ➟wc ☎ 🅿️
🔬 . ⚘
145 rm
CX **v**

🏨 **Montpelier** ⬧, 9 Montpelier Av., W5 2XP, ℰ 991 1508, ✿ – 📺 ➟wc ⋔wc ☜ 🅿️. 🗚 🺥
⚘
M (bar lunch)/dinner 10.00 **st.** and a la carte – **9 rm** ⊊ 33.00/50.00 **st.**
BX **e**

🏨 **Kenton House**, 5 Hillcrest Rd, Hanger Hill, W5 2JL, ℰ 997 8436, Telex 8812544 – 📺 ➟wc
⋔wc ☎ 🅿️. 🖾 🗚 ⓞ 🺥 . ⚘
M (bar lunch)/dinner a la carte 8.55/12.35 **st.** ◊ 1.90 – **51 rm** ⊊ 31.75/47.75 **st.** – SB (weekends
only) 46.00 **st.**
CX **x**

XX **Maxim,** 153-155 Northfield Av., W13 9QT, ℰ 567 1719, Chinese (Peking) rest. – 🖾 🗚 ⓞ
🺥
closed Sunday lunch and 25-26 December – **M** 12.00/20.00 **t.** and a la carte 15.00/21.00 **t.**
◊ 2.50.
BX **a**

X **Gino's,** 4 The Mall, W5 2PJ, ℰ 567 3681, Italian rest. – 🖾 🗚 ⓞ 🺥
closed Saturday lunch, Sunday, Christmas and Bank Holidays – **M** 20.00 **t.** and a la carte
11.65/19.35 **t.**
CX **z**

Hanwell – ⊠ W7.

🏘 Brent Valley, Church Rd, Hanwell ℰ 567 1287.

X Happiness Garden, 22 Boston Par., Boston Rd, W7 2DG, ℰ 567 9314, Chinese rest.
BX **c**

During the season, particularly in resorts, it is wise to book in advance.
However, if you find you cannot take up a hotel booking you have made,
please let the hotel know immediately.
If you are writing to a hotel abroad enclose an International Reply Coupon
(available from Post Offices.)

ENFIELD pp. 6 and 7.

Enfield – ⊠ Middx.

🏘 Enfield Municipal, Beggars Hollow ℰ 363 4454, N : 1 m.

🏩 **Royal Chace**, 162 The Ridgeway, EN2 8AR, ℰ 366 6500, Telex 266628, ≤, ⌇, ✿ – 📺 ᵴ 🅿️.
🔬. 🖾 🗚 ⓞ 🺥 . ⚘
M 8.00/9.00 **st.** and a la carte ◊ 4.65 – ⊊ 4.00 – **92 rm** 41.00/52.00 **st.**
EU **a**

🏨 **Holtwhites**, 92 Chase Side, EN2 0QN, ℰ 363 0124, Telex 299670 – 📺 ➟wc ⋔wc ☎ 🅿️.
🗚 ⓞ 🺥
M (closed dinner Friday, Saturday and Sunday) (bar lunch)/dinner a la carte 8.55/17.05 **t.** ◊ 3.25
– **31 rm** ⊊ 36.00/62.00 **t.**
FU **c**

XXX Norfolk, 80 London Rd, EN2 6HU, ℰ 363 0979
FU **e**

X Mr. Choi, 14 London Rd, EN2 6EB, ℰ 363 0424, Chinese (Peking, Canton) rest.
FU **o**

Hadley Wood – ⊠ Herts.

🏩 **West Lodge Park** ⬧, off Cockfosters Rd, ⊠ Barnet, EN4 0PY, ℰ 440 8311, Telex 24734, ≤,
✿, park – 🛗 📺 ☎ 🅿️. 🔬. 🖾 🗚 ⓞ 🺥 . ⚘
M a la carte 9.90/17.75 **t.** ◊ 3.40 – **52 rm** ⊊ 50.00/63.00 **st.**
EU **i**

Southgate – ⊠ N 14.

XX **L'Oiseau Noir**, 163 Bramley Rd, N14, ℰ 367 1100 – 🅿️. 🖾 🗚 ⓞ 🺥
closed Sunday dinner and Monday – **M** 7.95/9.00 **t.** and a la carte 9.25/14.00 **t.** ◊ 2.75.
EU **e**

Winchmore Hill – ⊠ N21.

XX Dragon Garden, 869 Green Lanes, N21 2QS, ℰ 360 9125, Chinese rest.
FU **n**

MICHELIN Distribution Centre, Eley's Estate, Angel Rd, N18 3DQ, ℰ 803 7341

GREENWICH pp. 10 and 11.

Blackheath – ⊠ SE3.

🏨 **Bardon Lodge** without rest., 15-17 Stratheden Rd, SE3 7TH, ℰ 853 4051 – 📺 ⋔wc ☎ 🅿️. 🖾
🺥 . ⚘
28 rm ⊊ 26.00/45.00 **st.**
GX **a**

Greenwich – ✉ SE10.

🛈 Cutty Sark Gardens, near Greenwich Pier, SE10, ✆ 858 6376.

XX **Le Papillon,** 57 Greenwich Church St., SE10 9BL, ✆ 858 2668 – ⊠ 🖭 ⓞ 𝘝𝘐𝘚𝘈   FX **r**
closed Saturday lunch, Sunday dinner, 25 to 31 December and Bank Holidays – **M** (dinner only and Sunday lunch in summer) a la carte 11.00/15.25 **t.**

XX **Treasure of China,** 10 Nelson Rd, SE10, ✆ 858 9884, Chinese rest. – ▤. ⊠ 🖭 ⓞ 𝘝𝘐𝘚𝘈
closed 25 and 26 December – **M** 14.00/20.00 **t.** and a la carte ≬ 2.75.   FX **e**

X **Spread Eagle,** 2 Stockwell St., SE10 9JN, ✆ 853 2333 – ⊠ 🖭 ⓞ 𝘝𝘐𝘚𝘈   FX **c**
closed Saturday lunch, Sunday dinner and Bank Holidays – **M** 9.75 **st.** (lunch) and a la carte 12.50/16.45 **st.** ≬ 3.25.

HACKNEY – P.16.

Liverpool Street – ✉ EC2.

XX Equities, 1 Finsbury Av., EC2M 2PA, ✆ 247 1051 – ▤   QT **a**

HAMMERSMITH and FULHAM Except where otherwise stated see pp. 17-20.

Fulham – ✉ SW6.

XX **Hiders,** 755 Fulham Rd, SW6, ✆ 736 2331 – ⊠ 🖭 𝘝𝘐𝘚𝘈   pp. 8 and 9   DY **s**
closed Saturday lunch, Sunday, 3 weeks August, 25 December-1 January and Bank Holidays – **M** 13.50 **t.** ≬ 2.75.

XX **Mao Tai,** 58 New Kings Rd., Parsons Green, SW6, ✆ 731 2520, Chinese(Szechuan) rest. –
▤. ⊠ 🖭 𝘝𝘐𝘚𝘈   pp. 8 and 9   DY **o**
M 12.50 **t.** and a la carte 10.10/13.70 **t.**

XX **Le Gastronome,** 309 New Kings Rd SW6 4RS, ✆ 731 6993, French rest. – ⊠ 🖭 ⓞ 𝘝𝘐𝘚𝘈
closed Saturday lunch, Sunday and 25 December-1 January – **M** 16.50/18.50 (wine included) **st.**
pp. 8 and 9   DY **u**

XX **Barbarella,** 428 Fulham Rd, SW6 1DU, ✆ 385 9434, Italian rest., Dancing – ⊠ 🖭 ⓞ 𝘝𝘐𝘚𝘈
closed Sunday and Bank Holidays – **M** (dinner only) 14.00 **t.** and a la carte 11.20/16.50 **t.** ≬ 3.00.
HZ **x**

X **Perfumed Conservatory,** 182 Wandsworth Bridge Rd, SW6 1EX, ✆ 731 0732 – ⊠ 🖭
𝘝𝘐𝘚𝘈   pp. 8 and 9   EY **i**
closed Sunday, Monday, 1 week Christmas and Bank Holidays – **M** (dinner only) 19.00 **t.**

X **Evergreen,** 45 Fulham High St., SW6, ✆ 736 4372, Chinese(Peking) rest. – ⊠ 🖭 ⓞ 𝘝𝘐𝘚𝘈
M 12.00 **t.** and a la carte 9.50/12.00 **t.**   p.9   DY **a**

Hammersmith – ✉ W6/W12/W14.

🏛 **Novotel London,** 1 Shortlands, W6 8DR, ✆ 741 1555, Telex 934539 – ⊠ ▤ 📺 ☎ ⓖ ℗. 📶
⊠ 🖭 ⓞ 𝘝𝘐𝘚𝘈. ⌖
M 11.50 **st.** and a la carte – ⊆ 5.00 – **640 rm** 55.00/63.00 **st., 4 suites** 125.00 **st.**   GY **a**

⮝ **Hammersmith,** 186 Hammersmith Grove, W6 7HG, ✆ 743 0820 – 📺 ⇛wc 🎢wc. ⊠ 🖭
𝘝𝘐𝘚𝘈. ⌖
⊆ 2.00 – **16 rm** 25.00/38.00.   p.9   CDX **c**

X **Aziz,** 116 King St., W6, ✆ 748 1826, Indian rest. – ⊠ 🖭 ⓞ 𝘝𝘐𝘚𝘈   pp. 8 and 9   CX **a**
closed Sunday – **M** a la carte 8.40/11.60 **t.** ≬ 3.70.

Shepherd's Bush – ✉ W 12.

XX **Shireen,** 270 Uxbridge Rd, W12 8NR, ✆ 749 5927, Indian rest. – ▤. ⊠ 🖭 ⓞ 𝘝𝘐𝘚𝘈
closed 25 and 26 December – **M** a la carte 6.95/9.00 **t.**   pp. 8 and 9   CX **n**

West Kensington – ✉ SW6/W14.

🏛 **London West,** Lillie Rd, SW6 1UQ, ✆ 385 1255, Telex 917728 – ⊠ ▤ 📺 ⇛wc ☎ ℗. 📶
⊠ 🖭 ⓞ 𝘝𝘐𝘚𝘈   HZ **e**
M 10.00/12.00 **st.** and a la carte ≬ 3.50 – ⊆ 5.95 – **499 rm** 50.00/60.00 **st., 4 suites** 120.00 **st.**

XX **Koh-I-Noor,** 197-199 North End Rd, W14, ✆ 381 1364, Indian rest.   GZ **a**

14

HARINGEY pp. 6 and 7.

Highgate – ⊠ N6.

XX **San Carlo,** 2 High St., N6 5JL, ℰ 340 5823, Italian rest. – ◪ ◪ ◉ *VISA*   EV **v**
closed Monday and Bank Holidays – **M** 10.95 **st.** and a la carte 12.15/20.45 **st.** ⓐ 3.25.

XX **One Hampstead Lane,** 1 Hampstead Lane, N6, ℰ 340 4444 – ◪ ◪ ◉ *VISA*   EV **z**
closed Sunday dinner and Monday – **M** (dinner only and Sunday lunch)/dinner
14.95 **t.** and a la carte ⓐ 3.50.

Hornsey – ⊠ N8.

X **M'sieur Frog,** 36 The High St., N8 7NX, ℰ 340 2116 – ◪ *VISA*   EV **u**
closed Sunday, Monday, 3 weeks July-August and 1 week Christmas – **M** (dinner only) a la
carte 10.90/12.20 **t.** ⓐ 2.50.

HARROW pp. 4 and 5.

Central Harrow – ⊠ Middx.

🏛 **Monksdene,** 2-12 Northwick Park Rd, HA1 2NT, ℰ 427 2899, Telex 919171 – ◪ ⌷wc ☎
ⓟ. ◪ ◪ ◉ *VISA*. ⌘   BV **e**
M (closed Saturday) (carving lunch)/dinner a la carte approx. 12.45 **t.** ⓐ 2.50 – **70 rm**
⌷ 31.00/60.00 **st.** – SB (weekends only) 52.50/128.00 **st.**

🏛 **Harrow,** 12-22 Pinner Rd, HA1 4HZ, ℰ 427 3435, Telex 917898 – ◪ ⌷wc ⌷wc ☎ ⓟ. ◭
◪ ◪ ◉ *VISA*. ⌘   BV **a**
M 10.95 **t.** and a la carte – **95 rm** ⌷ 46.00/58.00 **st.** – SB (weekends only) 91.00/119.00 **st.**

🏛 **Cumberland,** 1 St. John's Rd, HA1 2EF, ℰ 863 4111 – ◪ ⌷wc ⌷wc ☎ ⓟ. ◪ ◪ ◉ *VISA*.
⌘   BV **x**
M 7.50/9.75 **st.** and a la carte ⓐ 2.95 – **79 rm** ⌷ 33.00/56.00 **st.** – SB (except Christmas)
(weekends only) 52.50/59.50 **st.**

Harrow-on-the-Hill – ⊠ Middx.

XXX **Wheeler's,** 51 High St., HA1 3LR, ℰ 864 6576, Seafood – ▤   BV **c**

X **Old Etonian,** 38 High St., HA1 3LL, ℰ 422 8482 – ◪ ◪ ◉ *VISA*   BV **z**
closed Saturday lunch, Sunday and Bank Holidays – **M** a la carte 11.65/16.55 **t.** ⓐ 2.95.

Harrow Weald – ⊠ Middx.

🏰 **Grims Dyke** (Best Western) ⌂, Old Redding, HA3 6SH, ℰ 954 4227, Group Telex 946240,
⌘, park – ◪ ⌷wc ⌷wc ☜ ⓟ. ◭ ◪ ◪ ◉ *VISA*   BU **r**
closed 26 to 30 December – **M** 13.50 **st.** and a la carte ⓐ 3.50 – ⌷ 5.75 – **48 rm** 50.00/63.00 **st.**
– SB (weekends only) 80.00/85.00 **st.**

Hatch End – ⊠ Middx.

XX **Canaletto 2,** 302 Uxbridge Rd, HA5 4HR, ℰ 428 4232, Italian rest. – ▤. ◪ ◉ *VISA*   BU **a**
closed Saturday lunch, Sunday and Bank Holidays – **M** a la carte 12.10/15.75 **t.** ⓐ 4.35.

X **Swan,** 322 Uxbridge Rd, ℰ 428 8821, Chinese (Peking) rest. – ▤. ◪ ◪ ◉ *VISA*   BU **n**
M 15.00 **t.**

Pinner – ⊠ Middx.

X **La Giralda,** 66-68 Pinner Green, HA5 2AB, ℰ 868 3429 – ◪ ◪ ◉ *VISA*   AUV **n**
closed Sunday, Monday and 3 weeks August – **M** 6.50/9.75 **t.** ⓐ 2.55.

Stanmore – ⊠ Middx.

XX **Buddha House,** 7-9 Stanmore Hill, ℰ 954 5326, Chinese rest. – ◪ ◪ ◉ *VISA*   BU **i**
M 12.00/15.00 **t.** and a la carte 10.30/13.50 **t.**

HAVERING pp. 6 and 7.

Hornchurch by A 12 – HU – on A 127 – ⊠ Essex – ☎ 040 23 Ingrebourne.

🏰 **Ladbroke** (Ladbroke), Southend Arterial Rd (A 127), RM11 3UJ, ℰ 46789, Telex 897315 – ◪
⌷wc ☎ ⓑ ⓟ. ◭ ◪ ◪ ◉ *VISA*
M (closed Saturday lunch) 9.95 ⓐ 3.70 – ⌷ 5.75 – **137 rm** 46.00/56.00 **st.** – SB (weekends
only) 63.00 **st.**

Romford by A 118 – HV – ⊠ Essex – ☎ 0708.

⌂ **Coach House,** 48 Main Rd, RM1 3DB, on A 118 ℰ 751901 – ◪ ⓟ. ⌘
16 rm ⌷ 18.50/38.50 **st.**

HILLINGDON pp. 4 and 8.

Eastcote – ✉ Middx.

✗ **Sambuca,** 113 Field End Rd, HA5 1QG, ✆ 866 7500, Italian rest. –  🄰🄴 ⑩ 𝘝𝘐𝘚𝘈
AV **s**
closed Sunday dinner, Monday, Christmas Day and Bank Holidays – **M** 6.50/
13.50 **t.** and a la carte ⑂ 2.50.

Heathrow Airport – ✉ Middx.

🚉 Heathrow Central Station, London Airport ✆ 730 3488.

🏨 **Sheraton Skyline,** Bath Rd, Harlington, Hayes, UB3 5BP, ✆ 759 2535, Telex 934254, « Exotic
indoor garden with ☒ » – 🛗 ▤ 📺 ☎ & 🄿 🛁 🄽 🄰🄴 ⑩ 𝘝𝘐𝘚𝘈
AY **u**
(rest. see **Colony Room** below) – ⌷ 6.90 – **355 rm** 72.80/82.90 **s., 5 suites** 165.00/470.00 **s.**

🏨 Heathrow Penta, Bath Rd, Hounslow, TW6 2AQ, ✆ 897 6363, Telex 934660, ≼, ☒ – 🛗 ▤ 📺
☎ & 🄿 🛁
AY **z**
670 rm, 9 suites.

🏨 **Excelsior** (T.H.F.), Bath Rd, West Drayton, UB7 0DU, ✆ 759 6611, Telex 24525, ☒ heated –
🛗 ▤ 📺 🛁 🄿 🄽 🄰🄴 ⑩ 𝘝𝘐𝘚𝘈
AY **x**
M 9.95 **st.** and a la carte ⑂ 3.40 – ⌷ 6.75 – **573 rm** 60.00/68.00 **st., 7 suites**.

🏨 **Holiday Inn,** Stockley Rd, West Drayton, UB7 9NA, ✆ 0895 (West Drayton) 445555, Telex
934518, ☒, ⋇ – 🛗 ▤ 📺 ☎ & 🄿 🛁 🄽 🄰🄴 ⑩ 𝘝𝘐𝘚𝘈
AX **v**
M 10.45 **st.** and a la carte – ⌷ 5.95 – **400 rm** 60.50/71.00 **st., 2 suites** 156.00/231.00 **st.**

🏨 **Sheraton Heathrow,** Colnbrook by-pass, West Drayton, UB7 0HJ, ✆ 759 2424, Telex
934331, ☒ – 🛗 ▤ 📺 ☎ & 🄿 🛁 🄽 🄰🄴 ⑩ 𝘝𝘐𝘚𝘈
AXY **a**
M a la carte 9.00/19.00 **t.** – ⌷ 7.00 – **405 rm** 59.00/70.00 **t., 5 suites** 120.00/147.00.

🏨 **Skyway** (T.H.F.), 140 Bath Rd, Hayes, UB3 5AW, ✆ 759 6311, Telex 23935, ☒ heated – 🛗
▤ rest 📺 ☎ & 🄿 🛁 🄽 🄰🄴 ⑩ 𝘝𝘐𝘚𝘈
AY **e**
M 12.50 **st.** and a la carte ⑂ 3.00 – ⌷ 6.50 – **412 rm** 50.00/60.00 **st.**

🏨 **Post House** (T.H.F.), Sipson Rd, West Drayton, UB7 0JU, ✆ 759 2323, Telex 934280 – 🛗 ▤
📺 ☎ & 🄿 🛁 🄽 🄰🄴 ⑩ 𝘝𝘐𝘚𝘈
AX **c**
M 10.50 **st.** and a la carte ⑂ 3.40 – ⌷ 6.50 – **597 rm** 54.00/64.50 **st.**

🏨 **Ibis,** 112-114 Bath Rd, Hayes, UB3 5AL, ✆ 759 4888 – ▤ 📺 ⇔wc ☎ & 🄿 🄽 🄰🄴 ⑩
𝘝𝘐𝘚𝘈
AY **i**
M 7.50 **st.** and a la carte ⑂ 3.50 – ⌷ 5.50 – **244 rm** 39.00/44.00 **st.**

🏨 **Ariel** (T.H.F.), Bath Rd, Hayes, UB3 5AJ, ✆ 759 2552, Telex 21777 – 🛗 ▤ 📺 ⇔wc ☎ & 🄿
🛁 🄽 🄰🄴 ⑩ 𝘝𝘐𝘚𝘈
AY **i**
M 9.95 **st.** and a la carte ⑂ 3.40 – ⌷ 6.50 – **177 rm** 51.00/62.00 **st.**

🏨 **Arlington,** Shepiston Lane, Hayes, UB3 1LP, ✆ 573 6162, Group Telex 935120 – ▤ rest 📺
⇔wc ⋒wc ☜ 🄿 🛁 🄽 🄰🄴 ⑩ 𝘝𝘐𝘚𝘈, ⋇
AX **n**
M *(closed lunch Saturday and Sunday)* 8.00 **t.** and a la carte – ⌷ 4.00 – **80 rm** 34.00/45.00 **t.**
– **SB** *(weekends only)* 56.00/76.00 **st.**

✗✗✗ **Colony Room** (at Sheraton Skyline H.), Bath Rd, Harlington, Hayes, UB3 5BP, ✆ 759 2535 –
AY **u**
M 16.50 **st.** (lunch) and a la carte 16.00/21.50 **st.** ⑂ 4.50.

Hillingdon – ✉ Middx. – ✆ 0895 Uxbridge.

🚉 22 High St., Uxbridge ✆ 50706.

🏨 **Master Brewer Motel,** Western Av., Hillingdon Circus, UB10 9BR, ✆ 51199 – 📺 ⇔wc ☎
🄿 🛁 🄽 🄰🄴 ⑩ 𝘝𝘐𝘚𝘈
AV **a**
M 6.00 **t.** and a la carte ⑂ 4.00 – ⌷ 3.95 – **106 rm** 42.00/50.00 **st.** – **SB** *(weekends only)* 55.00 **st.**

Northwood – ✉ Middx. – ✆ 092 74 Northwood.

🏌 Haste Hill, The Drive ✆ 22877.

✗✗ **Martini,** 27 Green Lane, ✆ 27052, Italian rest. – 🄽 🄰🄴 ⑩ 𝘝𝘐𝘚𝘈
AU **e**
closed Sunday and Bank Holidays – **M** a la carte 10.40/19.55 **t.**

Ruislip – ✉ Middx. – ☻ 089 56 Ruislip – ▥ Ickenham Rd ✎ 32004.

🏛 **Barn,** West End Rd, HA6 6JB, ✎ 36057, Telex 892514, 🛲 – 📺 ⇔wc ⊜ 🅿 ⊾ 🎫 ⓋⒾⓈⒶ
closed 24 December-2 January – **M** 6.95/8.50 **st.** and a la carte ⌂ 4.30 – ⊡ 4.00 – **52 rm**
32.00/45.00 **st.**
AV **u**

Uxbridge – ✉ Middx.

✕✕✕ **Giovanni's,** at Denham Lodge, Oxford Rd ✉ New Denham, Bucks., UB9 4AA, on A 4020
✎ 31568, Italian rest. – 🅿 ⊾ 🎫 ⓞ ⓋⒾⓈⒶ
closed Saturday lunch, Sunday and Bank Holidays – **M** a la carte 11.90/17.30 **st.** ⌂ 3.00.
AV **e**

HOUNSLOW pp. 8 and 9.

▥ Wyke Green, Syon Lane, Isleworth ✎ 560 8777, ½ m. from Gillettes Corner (A 4).

Chiswick – ✉ W4.

✕ **Biba's,** 313 Chiswick High Rd, W4 4HH, ✎ 995 3354, French rest. – ⊾ 🎫 ⓞ ⓋⒾⓈⒶ
closed Saturday lunch, Sunday, 3 weeks August and Bank Holidays – **M** 9.50 **st.** and a la carte
10.20/17.50 **t.** ⌂ 4.50.
CX **i**

✕ **La Dordogne,** 5 Devonshire Rd, W4 2EU, ✎ 747 1836, French rest. – ⊾ 🎫 ⓞ ⓋⒾⓈⒶ
closed Saturday lunch, Sunday, 2 weeks August, 1 week Christmas and Bank Holidays –
M a la carte 13.30/20.60 **t.** ⌂ 3.50.
CX **o**

Cranford – ✉ Middx.

🏛 **Berkeley Arms** (Embassy), Bath Rd, TW5 9QE, ✎ 897 2121, Telex 935728, 🛲 – 🔄 📺
⇔wc ☎ 🅿 ⌖ ⊾ 🎫 ⓞ ⓋⒾⓈⒶ ⚘
M (carving rest.) 9.25 **st.** and a la carte ⌂ 2.65 – ⊡ 5.00 – **41 rm** 43.00/52.00 **st.** – SB (weekends
only) 43.00 **st.**
AY **r**

Hounslow – ✉ Middx.

🏛 **Master Robert Motel,** 366 Great West Rd, TW5 0BD, ✎ 570 6261 – 📺 ⇔wc ⋔wc ☎ 🅿
⌖ ⊾ 🎫 ⓞ ⓋⒾⓈⒶ
M (grill rest. only) 6.00 **t.** and a la carte ⌂ 4.00 – ⊡ 3.95 – **63 rm** 42.00/50.00 **st.** – SB (weekends
only) 55.00 **st.**
BY **s**

ISLINGTON pp. 13-16.

Canonbury – ✉ N1.

✕ **Anna's Place,** 90 Mildmay Park, N1 4PR, ✎ 249 9379
closed Sunday, Monday, 2 weeks at Easter, August and 2 weeks at Christmas – **M** (booking
essential) a la carte 9.85/12.95 **t.**
pp. 6 and 7 FV **a**

Finsbury – ✉ WC1/EC1/EC2.

🏛 **London Ryan** (Mt. Charlotte), Gwynne Pl., King Cross Rd, WC1X 9QB, ✎ 278 2480, Telex
27728 – 🔄 ▤ rest 📺 ⇔wc ☎ 🅿 ⊾ 🎫 ⓞ ⓋⒾⓈⒶ ⚘
M (bar lunch)/dinner 8.50 **st.** and a la carte ⌂ 3.25 – ⊡ 3.50 – **211 rm** 47.25/57.75 **st.**
NS **a**

✕✕ **Rouxl Britannia,** Triton Court, 14 Finsbury Sq., EC2A 1RR, ✎ 256 6997 – ▤
M Le Restaurant (closed Saturday, Sunday and Bank Holidays) (lunch only) 14.00 **st.** – **Le Café**
(closed Saturday, Sunday and Bank Holidays) a la carte 6.00/16.50 **st.** ⌂ 3.50.
QT **x**

✕✕ **Café St. Pierre,** 29 Clerkenwell Green (1st floor), EC1, ✎ 251 6606 – ⊾ 🎫 ⓞ ⓋⒾⓈⒶ
closed Saturday, Sunday, 24 December-2 January and Bank Holidays – **M** 15.00 **st.** (dinner)
and a la carte 13.00/15.70 **t.** ⌂ 2.50.
PT **c**

Islington – ✉ N1.

✕✕ **Frederick's,** Camden Passage, N1 8EG, ✎ 359 2888, « Conservatory and walled garden » –
▤ ⊾ 🎫 ⓞ ⓋⒾⓈⒶ
closed Sunday, 17 and 20 April, 26 December, 1 January and Bank Holidays – **M** a la carte
12.60/16.60 **t.** ⌂ 3.25.
PR **a**

✕✕ **Varnom's,** 2 Greenman St., N1 8SB, ✎ 359 6707 – ▤ ⊾ 🎫 ⓞ ⓋⒾⓈⒶ
closed Saturday lunch, Sunday dinner and Monday – **M** 13.50 **t.** and a la carte 13.95/16.50 **t.**
⌂ 3.00.
p. 6 FV **c**

✕✕ **Portofino,** 39 Camden Passage, N1 8EA, ✎ 226 0884, Italian rest. – ▤ ⊾ 🎫 ⓞ ⓋⒾⓈⒶ
closed Sunday, 25-26 December, 1 January and Bank Holidays – **M** 12.00 **st.** and a la carte
9.70/16.90 ⌂ 3.00.
PR **o**

✕✕ **Julius's,** 39 Upper St., N1 0PN, ✎ 226 4380 – ▤
closed Saturday lunch and Sunday – **M** 6.95/7.95 **t.** and a la carte 12.70/15.20 **t.** ⌂ 2.45.
PR **i**

✕ **M'sieur Frog,** 31a Essex Rd, N1 2SE, ✎ 226 3495, Bistro – ⊾ ⓋⒾⓈⒶ
closed Sunday, 1 week July-August and 1 week at Christmas – **M** (dinner only) a la carte
14.45/16.90 **t.** ⌂ 2.50.
PR **n**

Upper Holloway – ✉ N19.

✕ Raj Vogue, 34 Highgate Hill, N19 5NL, ✎ 272 9091, Indian rest.
p.6 EV **a**

KENSINGTON and CHELSEA (Royal Borough of).

Chelsea – ✉ SW1/SW3/SW10 – Except where otherwise stated see pp. 28 and 29.

🏨🏨🏨 **Hyatt Carlton Tower,** 2 Cadogan Pl., SW1X 9PY, ℰ 235 5411, Telex 21944, ≤, 🐎, ✗ – 🛗
🍴 📺 🕭 🕭 🅿 🚗. 🔃 🖭 🗚 🕕 VISA ⚘
FR **n**
M (see Chelsea Room below) – **Rib Room** 17.50 **t.** (lunch) and a la carte 21.80/35.50 **t.** ↓ 7.50 –
⌁ 7.90 – **217 rm** 126.00/166.00 **t.**, **30 suites** 220.00/1000.00 **s.**

🏨🏨 **Sheraton Park Tower,** 101 Knightsbridge, SW1X 7RN, ℰ 235 8050, Telex 917222 – 🛗 🍴
📺 🕭 🕭 🅿 🚗. 🔃 🖭 🗚 🕕 VISA ⚘
FQ **v**
M 10.75/16.75 **t.** and a la carte 14.60/25.25 **t.** – ⌁ 8.00 – **295 rm** 127.85/161.00 **st.**, **16 suites**
316.25/345.00 **st.**

🏨🏨 ❀ **Capital,** 22-24 Basil St., SW3 1AT, ℰ 589 5171, Telex 919042 – 🛗 🍴 🖭 📺. 🔃 🗚 🕕 VISA
⚘
ER **a**
M 16.50/18.50 **st.** and a la carte 27.50/32.50 **st.** ↓ 6.00 – ⌁ 7.50 – **60 rm** 100.00/120.00 **st.**
Spec. Salade de pêcheurs tiède au Xérès, Carré d'agneau persillé aux herbes de Provence, Quenelles de poisson
fumé.

🏨🏨 **Basil Street,** 8 Basil St., SW3 1AH, ℰ 581 3311, Telex 28379 – 🛗 🖭 🕭. 🚗. 🔃 🗚 🕕 VISA
M 9.75 **t.** (lunch) and a la carte 14.45/18.75 **t.** ↓ 5.25 – ⌁ 5.80 – **95 rm** 36.30/86.50 **t.**, **1 suite**
144.00 **t.**
FQ **o**

🏨🏨 **Holiday Inn,** 17-25 Sloane St., SW1X 9NU, ℰ 235 4377, Telex 919111, 🔳 – 🛗 🍴 🖭 🕭. 🚗.
🔃 🗚 🕕 VISA ↓
FR **r**
M a la carte 10.75/18.55 **st.** ↓ 4.50 – ⌁ 5.95 – **198 rm** 93.00/118.00 **st.**, **4 suites** 245.00 **st.** – SB
(weekends only) 99.00 **st.**

🏨🏨 **Cadogan Thistle** (Thistle), 75 Sloane St., SW1X 9SG, ℰ 235 7141, Telex 267893 – 🛗 🖭 🕭.
↓. 🔃 🗚 🕕 VISA ⚘
FR **e**
M a la carte 11.00/15.50 **t.** ↓ 3.65 – ⌁ 6.75 – **68 rm** 85.00/125.00 **st.**, **5 suites** 135.00 **st.**

🏨🏨 **Royal Court** (Norfolk Cap.), Sloane Sq., SW1W 8EG, ℰ 730 9191, Telex 296818 – 🛗 🍴 rest
📺 🕭. 🔃 🗚 🕕 VISA ⚘
FST **a**
M 9.95/16.00 **st.** and a la carte 15.30/19.80 **t.** ↓ 3.50 – ⌁ 7.25 – **98 rm** 65.00/90.00 **st.**, **5 suites**
105.00/140.00 **st.** – SB (weekends only) 87.00 **st.**

🏨🏨 **L'Hotel** without rest., 28 Basil St., SW3 1AT, ℰ 589 6286, Telex 919042 – 🛗 📺 ⌁wc 🕭. 🗚.
12 rm 80.00/100.00 **st.**
ER **i**

🏨🏨 **Wilbraham** without rest., 1-5 Wilbraham Pl., Sloane St., SW1X 9AE, ℰ 730 8296 – 🛗 ⌁wc
🕭. ⚘
⌁ 4.00 – **56 rm** 26.00/57.00.
FS **n**

🏨 **Fenja** without rest., 69 Cadogan Gdns, SW3 2RB, ℰ 589 1183 – 🛗 ⌁wc 🕭. ⚘
FS **r**
16 rm.

🏨 **Willett** without rest., 32 Sloane Gdns, Sloane Sq., SW1W 8DJ, ℰ 824 8415 – 📺 ⌁wc
17 rm ⌁ 23.00/34.00 **s.**
FT **s**

🍴🍴🍴🍴 ❀ **Chelsea Room** (at Hyatt Carlton Tower H.), 2 Cadogan Pl., SW1X 9PY, ℰ 235 5411, Telex
21944 – 🅿. 🔃 🗚 🕕 VISA
FR **n**
M 19.50 **t.** (lunch) and a la carte 21.00/28.00 **t.** ↓ 4.75
Spec. Foie gras aux cassis, Fricassée de turbot et homard, Mignons de bœuf Arlequin.

🍴🍴🍴🍴 ❀ **Waltons,** 121 Walton St., SW3 2HP, ℰ 584 0204 – 🍴. 🔃 🗚 🕕 VISA
DS **a**
closed 4 days at Easter, 3 days at Christmas and Bank Holidays – **M** 12.65/20.15 **st.** and a la
carte 20.00/30.50 **t.** ↓ 3.50
Spec. Salmon-stuffed breast of chicken with basil cream sauce, Marbled terrine of turbot with a green herb
sauce, Pan fried medaillon of Scotch beef with stilton mousse.

🍴🍴🍴🍴 ❀❀ **La Tante Claire,** 68-69 Royal Hospital Rd, SW3 4HP, ℰ 352 6045, French rest. – 🍴. 🗚
🕕
EU **c**
closed Saturday, Sunday, 10 days at Easter, 3 weeks August-September, 10 days at Christmas-
New Year and Bank Holidays – **M** 19.00 **st.** (lunch) and a la carte 27.80/38.50 **st.**
Spec. Frivolités de la mer, Pied de cochon farci aux morilles, mousseline de broccoli, Croustade aux pommes
caramélisées.

🍴🍴🍴 ❀ **Zen,** Chelsea Cloisters, Sloane Av., SW3 3DW, ℰ 589 1781, Chinese rest. – 🍴. 🔃 🗚 🕕 VISA
ET **a**
closed 25 to 27 December – **M** a la carte 7.50/15.00 **t.**

🍴🍴🍴 **Le Français,** 257-259 Fulham Rd, SW3 6HY, ℰ 352 4748, French rest. – 🗚 VISA
CU **a**
closed Sunday and 4 days at Christmas – **M** 17.00 **st.** ↓ 7.00.

🍴🍴🍴 **Mario,** 260-262a Brompton Rd, SW3 2AS, ℰ 584 1724, Italian rest.
DS **n**

🍴🍴🍴 **Turner's,** 87-89 Walton St., SW3 3HP, ℰ 584 6711 – 🍴. 🔃 🗚 🕕 VISA
ES **n**
closed Monday and Bank Holidays – **M** 16.50/23.50 **st.** and a la carte ↓ 8.50.

🍴🍴 **Daphne's,** 110-112 Draycott Av., SW3 3AE, ℰ 589 4257 – 🔃 🗚 🕕 VISA
DS **e**
closed Saturday lunch, Sunday and Bank Holidays – **M** a la carte 10.80/18.00 **t.** ↓ 3.50.

🍴🍴 **La Finezza,** 62-64 Lower Sloane St., SW1, ℰ 730 8630, Italian rest.
FT **v**

🍴🍴 **Eleven Park Walk,** 11 Park Walk, SW10, ℰ 352 3449, Italian rest. – 🔃 🗚 🕕
CU **r**
M 15.20/20.20 **st.** and a la carte 14.30/18.50 **t.** ↓ 2.90.

🍴🍴 **English Garden,** 10 Lincoln St., SW3 2TS, ℰ 584 7272, English rest. – 🍴. 🔃 🗚 🕕 VISA
ET **x**
closed 17 April and 25-26 December – **M** a la carte 14.00/26.00 **st.** ↓ 3.75.

XX **English House,** 3 Milner St., SW3 2QA, ☎ 584 3002, English rest. – ⚡ AE ⓞ VISA ES z
closed 17 April and 25-26 December – **M** 12.50/18.50 **st.** and a la carte 14.00/26.50 **st.** ▯ 3.75.

XX **Toto,** Walton House, Walton St., SW3 2JH, ☎ 589 0075, Italian rest. – ⚡ AE VISA ES a
closed Easter and 4 days at Christmas – **M** a la carte 17.00/22.50 **t.** ▯ 3.00.

XX **Ponte Nuovo,** 126 Fulham Rd, SW3, ☎ 370 6656, Italian rest. – ⚡ AE ⓞ VISA CU e
closed Bank Holidays – **M** a la carte 10.00/18.00 **t.** ▯ 3.50.

XX **Gavvers,** 61-63 Lower Sloane St., SW1W 8DH, ☎ 730 5983, French rest. – ⚡ AE ⓞ
VISA FT e
closed Sunday, 25 December-4 January and Bank Holidays – **M** (dinner only) 18.75 **st.** ▯ 2.80.

XX **Poissonnerie de l'Avenue,** 82 Sloane Av., SW3 3DZ, ☎ 589 2457, French rest., Seafood –
⚡ AE ⓞ VISA DS u
closed Sunday, 24 December-5 January and Bank Holidays – **M** a la carte 14.25/19.75 **t.** ▯ 3.50.

XX **Ménage à Trois,** 15 Beauchamp Pl., SW3 1NQ, ☎ 589 4252 – ⚡ AE ⓞ VISA ER v
closed Sunday and 25-26 December – **M** (booking essential) 10.95/30.00 **t.** and a la carte
14.40/25.00 **t.** ▯ 3.15.

XX **St. Quentin,** 243 Brompton Rd, SW3 2EP, ☎ 589 8005, French rest. – ⚡ AE ⓞ VISA DR a
closed 1 week at Christmas – **M** 9.50/12.90 **t.** and a la carte 15.30/22.40 **t.**

XX **Bagatelle,** 5 Langton St., SW10 0JL, ☎ 351 4185, French rest. – ⚡ AE ⓞ VISA
closed Sunday, 1 week Christmas and Bank Holidays – **M** 14.00 **t.** (lunch) and a la carte
19.00/21.20 **t.** ▯ 3.10. pp. 17-20 JZ u

XX **Pier 31,** 31 Cheyne Walk, SW3 5HG, ☎ 352 5006 – ▤ ⚡ AE ⓞ VISA pp. 17-20 KZ c
closed 25 and 26 December – **M** 13.00 **t.** (lunch) and a la carte 15.25/18.95 **t.** ▯ 3.25.

XX **Meridiana,** 169 Fulham Rd, SW3 6SP, ☎ 589 8815, Italian rest. – ⚡ AE ⓞ VISA DT i
M 14.50 **t.** (lunch) and a la carte 13.50/25.25 **t.** ▯ 4.50.

XX **Good Earth,** 233 Brompton Rd, SW3 2EP, ☎ 584 3658, Chinese rest. – ⚡ AE ⓞ VISA DR c
closed 24 to 27 December – **M** 15.95 **t.** and a la carte 7.25/14.15 **t.** ▯ 2.50.

XX **Good Earth,** 91 King's Rd, SW3, ☎ 352 9231, Chinese rest. – ⚡ AE ⓞ VISA EU c
closed 24 to 27 December – **M** 15.95 **t.** and a la carte 9.20/16.85 **t.** ▯ 2.50.

XX **Han's,** 99-103 Fulham Rd, SW3, ☎ 581 8100, Chinese rest. – ▤ ⚡ AE ⓞ VISA DS o
M 8.50/15.00 **t.** and a la carte ▯ 3.00.

XX ✿ **Ma Cuisine,** 113 Walton St., SW3 2JY, ☎ 584 7585, French rest. – AE ⓞ DS a
closed Saturday, Sunday, 1 week Easter, 15 July-15 August and 1 week at Christmas – **M**
(booking essential) a la carte 13.00/17.30 **t.** ▯ 5.55
Spec. Quiche de poireaux et saumon, Aiguillettes de bœuf paloise, Mousse brûlée.

XX **Sails,** 4 Sydney St., SW3, ☎ 352 3433 – ▤ ⚡ AE ⓞ VISA DT v
closed Saturday lunch, Sunday, last 2 weeks August and Bank Holidays – **M** 8.75/15.50 **t.** and
a la carte 12.75/15.75 **t.** ▯ 2.75.

XX **Sampan,** 212 Fulham Rd, SW10, ☎ 351 5303, Chinese rest. – ⚡ AE ⓞ VISA BU o
M 6.50 **st.** (lunch)and a la carte 12.90/20.70 **st.**

XX **Don Luigi,** 316 King's Rd, SW3, ☎ 352 0025, Italian rest. CU i

XX **T'ang,** 294 Fulham Rd, SW10 9EW, ☎ 351 2599, Oriental cuisine. pp. 17-20 JZ a

XX **Le Suquet,** 104 Draycott Av., SW3 3AE, ☎ 581 1785, French rest., Seafood – AE ⓞ DS c
closed Christmas – **M** a la carte 13.00/34.00 **t.** ▯ 2.80.

XX **Beccofino,** 100 Draycott Av., SW3, ☎ 584 3600, Italian rest. – ⚡ AE VISA ES r
closed Sunday and Bank Holidays – **M** a la carte 12.20/24.50 **t.** ▯ 2.80.

XX **San Frediano,** 62-64 Fulham Rd, SW3 6HH, ☎ 584 8375, Italian rest. – ⚡ ⓞ VISA DT n
closed Sunday – **M** a la carte 10.55/12.65 **st.** ▯ 2.50.

XX **San Ruffillo,** 8 Harriet St., SW1 9JW, ☎ 235 3969, Italian rest. – ⚡ AE ⓞ VISA FQ z
closed Sunday and Bank Holidays – **M** 15.00 **t.** and a la carte approx. 12.25 **t.** ▯ 2.50.

X **Dan's,** 119 Sydney St., SW3 6NR, ☎ 352 2718 – AE ⓞ VISA DU s
closed Saturday lunch, Sunday and 1 week at Christmas – **M** 13.50 **t.** (dinner) and a la carte
approx. 11.20 **t.** ▯ 3.75.

X **Wheelers,** 33c King's Rd, SW3 4LX, ☎ 730 3023, Seafood – ⚡ AE ⓞ VISA FT u
M 9.50 **t.** (lunch) and a la carte 13.25/23.00 **t.** ▯ 3.00.

X **Monkey's,** 1 Cale St., Chelsea Green, ☎ 352 4711 ET z
closed first week February, last 3 weeks August and 25-26 December – **M** 8.00/15.00 **t.**

X **Nayab,** 9 Park Walk, SW10 OAJ, ☎ 352 2137, Indian rest. – ⚡ AE ⓞ VISA BU z
closed 25-26 December, 1 January and Bank Holidays – **M** a la carte 11.75/15.65 **t.** ▯ 3.75.

X **Thierry's,** 342 King's Rd, SW3, ☎ 352 3365, French rest. – AE ⓞ VISA CU c
closed Sunday, Easter, 15 August-1 September, Christmas and Bank Holidays – **M** 7.00 **t.**
(restricted lunch) and ▯ 2.95.

X **La Brasserie,** 272 Brompton Rd, SW3 2AW, ☎ 584 1668, French rest. – ⚡ AE ⓞ VISA DS s
closed 24 to 26 December – **M** a la carte 10.20/13.10 **t.** ▯ 5.90.

*Le Grand Londres (GREATER LONDON) est composé de la City et de 32 arrondisse-
ments administratifs (Borough) eux-mêmes divisés en quartiers ou villages ayant
conservé leur caractère propre (Area).*

Earl's Court – ⊠ SW5/SW10 – Except where otherwise stated see pp. 28 and 29.

🏥 **Barkston,** 34-44 Barkston Gdns, SW5 0EW, ℘ 373 7851, Telex 8953154 – 🛗 📺 ⇌wc ☎.
📷 🔼 🅰🅴 ⓪ 𝗩𝗜𝗦𝗔   AT **c**
M (buffet lunch)/dinner 12.00 **st.** and a la carte ⓘ 3.95 – ⌧ 5.00 – **80 rm** 40.00/50.00 **st.**

🏥 **Hogarth,** 27-35 Hogarth Rd, SW5 0QQ, ℘ 370 6831, Telex 8951994 – 🛗 🍽 rest 📺 ⇌wc
🍴wc ☎. 🔼 🅰🅴 ⓪ 𝗩𝗜𝗦𝗔   AS **a**
M (bar lunch)/dinner a la carte 8.50/11.00 **st.** ⓘ 3.00 – ⌧ 3.50 – **85 rm** 39.50/49.50 **st.** – SB
(weekends only) (November-April) 46.00/56.00 **st.**

🏠 Town House, 44-48 West Cromwell Rd, SW5 9QL, ℘ 373 4546 – 📺 🍴wc ☎. 🔼 🅰🅴 ⓪ 𝗩𝗜𝗦𝗔.
                                                  pp. 17-20 HY **o**
40 rm ⌧ 25.00/50.00 **st.**

XX **Tiger Lee,** 251 Old Brompton Rd, SW5 9HP, ℘ 370 2323, Chinese rest., Seafood – 🍽. 🔼 🅰🅴
⓪ 𝗩𝗜𝗦𝗔   AU **n**
closed Christmas Day – **M** (dinner only) a la carte 15.50/24.00 **t.**

XX L'Olivier, 116 Finborough Rd, SW10, ℘ 370 4183   AU **c**

XX **Brinkley's,** 47 Hollywood Rd, SW10 9HY, ℘ 351 1683 – 🍽. 🔼 🅰🅴 ⓪ 𝗩𝗜𝗦𝗔   BU **a**
closed Sunday, Easter and Christmas – **M** (dinner only) 14.00 **t.**

XX La Croisette, 168 Ifield Rd, SW10 9AF, ℘ 373 3694, French rest., Seafood   AU **a**

XX **L'Artiste Affamé,** 243 Old Brompton Rd, SW5 9HP, ℘ 373 1659 – 🔼 🅰🅴 ⓪ 𝗩𝗜𝗦𝗔   AU **r**
closed Sunday, 24 to 26 December and Bank Holidays – **M** 12.50 **t.** and a la carte 10.85/17.80 **t.**
ⓘ 3.75.

X **Crystal Palace,** 10 Hogarth Pl., SW5 0QT, ℘ 373 0754, Chinese (Peking, Szechuan) rest. –
🔼 🅰🅴 ⓪ 𝗩𝗜𝗦𝗔   pp. 17-20 HY **a**
M 11.50 **t.** and a la carte ⓘ 2.80.

En saison, surtout dans les stations fréquentées, il est prudent de retenir à l'avance.
Cependant, si vous ne pouvez pas occuper la chambre que vous avez retenue,
prévenez immédiatement l'hôtelier.
Si vous écrivez à un hôtel à l'étranger, joignez à votre lettre
un coupon-réponse international (disponible dans les bureaux de poste).

Kensington – ⊠ SW7/W8/W11/W14 – Except where otherwise stated see pp. 17-20.

🏨 **Royal Garden** (Rank), Kensington High St., W8 4PT, ℘ 937 8000, Telex 263151, ≤ – 🛗 🍽 📺
☎ 🅿 📷 🔼 🅰🅴 ⓪ 𝗩𝗜𝗦𝗔 ✂   pp. 28 and 29 AQ **c**
M Royal Roof (closed Sunday) (Dancing) 19.00/22.00 **st.** and a la carte ⓘ 4.00 – ⌧ 8.00 –
395 rm 89.00/125.00 **st.**, **38 suites** 125.00/300.00 **st.**

🏨 **Kensington Palace Thistle** (Thistle), De Vere Gdns, W8 5RA, ℘ 937 8121, Telex 262422 –
🛗 🍽 rest 📺 ☎. 📷 🔼 🅰🅴 ⓪ 𝗩𝗜𝗦𝗔. ✂   pp. 28 and 29 BQ **a**
M a la carte 15.00/20.00 **t.** ⓘ 3.45 – ⌧ 6.25 – **298 rm** 54.00/95.00 **st.**

🏨 **Hilton International,** 179-199 Holland Park Av., W11 4UL, ℘ 603 3355, Telex 919763 – 🛗 🍽
📺 ☎ 🔥 🅿. 📷 🔼 🅰🅴 ⓪ 𝗩𝗜𝗦𝗔. ✂   GV **s**
M 13.50 **t.** and a la carte 17.00/20.00 **t.** ⓘ 3.20 – ⌧ 7.50 – **606 rm** 62.00/81.00 **t.**

🏨 **London Tara** (Best Western), Scarsdale Pl., W8 5SR, ℘ 937 7211, Telex 918834 – 🛗 🍽 📺
☎ 🔥 🅿. 📷 🔼 🅰🅴 ⓪ 𝗩𝗜𝗦𝗔. ✂   HX **u**
M 9.50 **t.** and a la carte ⓘ 3.80 – ⌧ 6.00 – **831 rm** 54.00/66.00 **st.**

🏨 **Kensington Close** (T.H.F.), Wrights Lane, W8 5SP, ℘ 937 8170, Telex 23914, 🔲, 🏊, squash
– 🛗 📺 ☎ 🅿. 📷 🔼 🅰🅴 ⓪ 𝗩𝗜𝗦𝗔. ✂   HX **c**
M (buffet lunch)/dinner a la carte 10.50/19.70 **st.** ⓘ 3.60 – ⌧ 6.25 – **529 rm** 48.00/59.00 **st.**

XXX **La Ruelle,** 14 Wright's Lane, W8 6TF, ℘ 937 8525, French rest. – 🔼 🅰🅴 ⓪ 𝗩𝗜𝗦𝗔   HX **i**
closed Saturday, Sunday, Christmas, New Year and Bank Holidays – **M** 11.00 **st.** (lunch) and a la
carte 18.40/25.20 **st.**

XXX Belvedere, Holland House, Holland Park, ℘ 602 1238, ≤, French rest., « 19C Orangery in
park », 🌳 – 🅿   GX **x**

XX **Le Crocodile,** 38c Kensington Church St., W8, ℘ 938 2501, French rest. – 🍽. 🔼 🅰🅴 ⓪ 𝗩𝗜𝗦𝗔
closed Saturday lunch and Sunday – **M** 14.00/17.95 **t.** and a la carte ⓘ 4.50.   HV **a**

XX **Clarke's,** 124 Kensington Church St., W8, ℘ 221 9225 – 🍽. 🔼 𝗩𝗜𝗦𝗔   HV **o**
closed Saturday, Sunday, 10 days Easter, 3 weeks August and 10 days Christmas – **M**
13.00/19.00 **st.** ⓘ 3.50.

XX **La Pomme d'Amour,** 128 Holland Park Av., W11 4UE, ℘ 229 8532, French rest. – 🍽. 🔼 🅰🅴
⓪ 𝗩𝗜𝗦𝗔   GV **e**
closed Saturday lunch, Sunday and Bank Holidays – **M** 9.75 **t.** (lunch) and a la carte
12.35/16.50 **t.** ⓘ 4.25.

XX La Résidence, 148 Holland Park Av., W11 4UE, ℘ 221 6090, French rest. – 🍽   GV **z**

XX **La Paesana,** 30 Uxbridge St., W8 7TA, ℘ 229 4332, Italian rest. – 🍽. 🅰🅴 ⓪ 𝗩𝗜𝗦𝗔
closed Sunday, 17 to 20 April, 25-26 December and Bank Holidays – **M** a la carte 10.90/13.65 **t.**
ⓘ 2.40.   pp. 30 and 31 AZ **i**

XX Mama San, 11 Russell Gdns, W14, ℘ 602 0312, Chinese rest. – 🍽   GX **e**

XX **Hiroko** (at Hilton International H.), 179-199 Holland Park Av., W11 4UL, *𝄢* 603 5003, Japanese rest. – **Ⓟ** 🅺 AE ① VISA GV **s**
closed Monday lunch, 25 and 26 December, 1 to 4 January and Bank Holidays – **M** 10.00/21.00 **t.** and a la carte 11.85/17.10 **st.** ⅄ 4.80.

XX **I Ching**, 40 Earls Court Rd, W8 6EJ, *𝄢* 937 7047, Chinese rest. – ▤ HX **a**

XX **Trattoo**, 2 Abingdon Rd, W8 6AF, *𝄢* 937 4448, Italian rest. – ▤. 🅺 AE ① VISA HX **e**
closed Easter and Christmas – **M** a la carte 8.95/15.85 **t.** ⅄ 3.00.

XX **Franco Ovest**, 3 Russell Gdns, W14 8EZ, *𝄢* 602 1242, Italian rest. – 🅺 AE ① VISA GX **u**
closed Saturday lunch and Sunday – **M** 16.50 **st.** and a la carte 12.65/17.90 **t.** ⅄ 3.00.

XX **Topo d'oro**, 39 Uxbridge St., W8, *𝄢* 727 5813, Italian rest. – ▤. 🅺 AE ① VISA
closed 25 and 26 December – **M** 14.00 **t.** and a la carte 12.20/14.60 **t.** ⅄ 2.80.
pp. 30 and 31 AZ **a**

XX **Mandarin**, 197c Kensington High St., W8, *𝄢* 937 1551, Chinese rest. – ▤. 🅺 AE ① VISA
M 8.30/15.80 **t.** and a la carte 16.60/23.90 **t.** HX **s**

X **The Ark**, Kensington Court, 35 Kensington High St., W8 5BA, *𝄢* 937 4294, French rest. – ▤.
🅺 ① VISA pp. 28 and 29 AQ **s**
closed Sunday lunch, 4 days at Easter and 4 days at Christmas – **M** a la carte 9.35/12.80 **t.**
⅄ 2.20.

X **Sailing Junk**, 59 Marloes Rd, W8 6LE, *𝄢* 937 5833, Chinese rest. HX **x**

X **Le Quai St. Pierre**, 7 Stratford Rd, W8, *𝄢* 937 6388, French rest., Seafood – AE ① HX **r**
closed Monday lunch and Sunday – **M** a la carte 20.00/27.50 **t.**

X **Il Barbino**, 32 Kensington Church St., W8, *𝄢* 937 8752, Italian rest. – 🅺 AE ① VISA HV **o**
closed Saturday lunch, Sunday and Bank Holidays – **M** a la carte 9.30/15.10 **t.** ⅄ 2.70.

X **Malabar**, 27 Uxbridge St., W8, *𝄢* 727 8800, Indian rest. – 🅺 VISA p.30 AZ **e**
closed last week August and 25 to 27 December – **M** a la carte 9.15/15.90 **t.** ⅄ 2.85.

North Kensington – ✉ W2/W10/W11 – Except where otherwise stated see pp. 13-16.

🏠 **Portobello**, 22 Stanley Gdns, W11 2NG, *𝄢* 727 2777, Telex 21879, « Attractive town house in Victorian terrace » – ⓘ TV ➞wc ⓜwc ☎. 🅺 AE ① VISA GU **n**
closed 24 December-2 January – **M** (residents only) a la carte 11.50/13.05 **s.** ⅄ 3.05 – ☲ 6.00 –
25 rm 40.25/103.50 **st.**

🏠 **Pembridge Court**, 34 Pembridge Gdns, W2 4DX, *𝄢* 229 9977, Telex 298363 – ▤ rest TV
➞wc ⓜwc ☎. 🅺 AE ① VISA pp. 30 and 31 AZ **n**
M *(closed Sunday and Bank Holidays)* (dinner only) a la carte 8.70/13.25 **t.** ⅄ 3.25 – **29 rm**
☲ 37.00/80.00.

XXX **Leith's**, 92 Kensington Park Rd, W11 2PN, *𝄢* 229 4481 – ▤. 🅺 AE ① VISA GU **e**
closed 4 days at Christmas – **M** (dinner only) 29.50 **st.**

XX **Chez Moi**, 1 Addison Av., Holland Park, W11 4QS, *𝄢* 603 8267, French rest. – 🅺 AE ① VISA
closed Sunday, 2 weeks August, 2 weeks at Christmas and Bank Holidays – **M** (dinner only)
16.50 **t.** and a la carte 12.50/21.00 **t.** ⅄ 5.50. pp. 17-20 GV **n**

XX **Monsieur Thompsons**, 29 Kensington Park Rd, W11 2EU, *𝄢* 727 9957, French rest. GU **a**

PARIS-BORDEAUX 1895 — 1ᵉʳᵉ VOITURE sur PNEUS MICHELIN

South Kensington – ✉ SW5/SW7/W8 – pp. 28 and 29.

🏨 **Gloucester** (Rank), 4-18 Harrington Gdns, SW7 4LH, *𝄢* 373 6030, Telex 917505 – ⓘ ▤ TV ☎
& **Ⓟ** 🏋 🅺 AE ① VISA ✂ BS **r**
M 14.50/17.00 **t.** and a la carte ⅄ 5.50 – ☲ 7.75 – **531 rm** 90.00/120.00 **t.**, **12 suites** 200.00/600.00 **t.**

🏨 **Norfolk** (Norfolk Cap.), 2-10 Harrington Rd, SW7 3ER, *𝄢* 589 8191, Telex 268852 – ⓘ ▤ rest
TV ☎ & 🅺 AE ① VISA ✂ CS **e**
M 11.75/15.00 **st.** and a la carte – ☲ 7.25 – **97 rm** 65.00/90.00 **st.**, **4 suites** 115.00/170.00 **st.**

🏨 **London International** (Swallow), 147c Cromwell Rd, SW5 0TH, *𝄢* 370 4200, Telex 27260 –
ⓘ TV ☎ **Ⓟ** 🏋 🅺 AE ① VISA AS **c**
M 15.00/30.00 **st.** and a la carte ⅄ 6.00 – ☲ 3.50 – **416 rm** 52.00/68.00 **st.** – SB 73.00 **st.**

🏨 **Rembrandt,** 11 Thurloe Pl., SW7 2RS, 🕾 589 8100, Telex 295828, ⬜ – 🛗 🖭 🖭 🕾 🏊 🔌
AE ⓿ VISA. ⚘
DS x
M 11.50 st. ⬧ 3.50 – ⬚ 6.75 – **200 rm** 57.00/80.00 st., **1 suite** 57.00/105.00 st.

🏨 **Gore** (Best Western), 189 Queen's Gate, SW7 5EX, 🕾 584 6601, Telex 296244, « Attractive
decor » – 🛗 🖭 🖭 ⇔wc 🖭wc 🕾. 🔌 AE ⓿ VISA
BR n
M (closed Saturday) (coffee shop) a la carte 9.00/15.00 t. ⬧ 3.00 – ⬚ 6.00 – **54 rm**
54.00/110.00 st.

🏨 Vanderbilt, 68-86 Cromwell Rd, SW7 5BT, 🕾 589 2424, Telex 919867 – 🛗 🖭 ⇔wc 🖭wc 🕾.
BS v
230 rm.

🏨 **John Howard,** 4 Queen's Gate, SW7 5EH, 🕾 581 3011, Telex 8813397 – 🛗 🖭 ⇔wc
🖭wc 🕾. 🔌 AE ⓿ VISA. ⚘
BQ i
M 20.00/25.00 st. and a la carte ⬧ 6.50 – ⬚ 6.50 – **44 rm** 45.00/82.50 st., **1 suite** 95.00/170.00
st.

🏨 **Embassy House** (Embassy), 31-33 Queen's Gate, SW7 5JA, 🕾 584 7222, Telex 8813387 – 🛗
🖭 ⇔wc 🖭wc 🕾. 🔌 AE ⓿ VISA
BR e
M (closed lunch Saturday and Sunday) (restricted lunch) 5.75/10.25 st. – **69 rm**
⬚ 50.00/62.00 st., **1 suite** 167.00 st.

🏨 **Regency,** 100-105 Queen's Gate, SW7 5AG, 🕾 370 4595, Telex 267594 – 🛗 🖭 ⇔wc 🕾. 🔌
🔌 AE ⓿ VISA. ⚘
CT e
M 10.50 st. and a la carte ⬧ 3.30 – ⬚ 6.00 – **188 rm** 55.00/77.00 st.

🏠 **Number Sixteen** without rest., 15-17 Sumner Pl., SW7 3EG, 🕾 589 5232, Telex 266638,
« Attractively furnished Victorian town houses », 🌿 – 🛗 ⇔wc 🖭wc 🕾. 🔌 AE ⓿ VISA. ⚘
CT c
32 rm 33.00/85.00 st.

🏠 **Alexander** without rest., 9 Sumner Pl., SW7 3EE, 🕾 581 1591, Telex 917133, 🌿 – 🖭 ⇔wc
🖭wc 🕾. 🔌 AE ⓿ VISA. ⚘
CT a
40 rm ⬚ 50.00/80.00 st.

🏠 **Number Eight** without rest., Emperor's Gate, SW7 4HH, 🕾 370 7516 – 🖭 ⇔wc 🖭wc 🕾. 🔌
AE ⓿ VISA
BS o
14 rm ⬚ 33.00/40.00 s.

XXX **Bombay Brasserie,** Courtfield Close, 140 Gloucester Rd, SW7 4QH, 🕾 370 4040, Indian
rest., « Raj-style decor, conservatory garden » – 🔌 AE ⓿ VISA
BS a
closed 26 to 28 December – **M** (buffet lunch) 8.95/17.50 t. and a la carte.

XX **Reads,** 152 Old Brompton Rd, SW5 0BE, 🕾 373 2445 – ⬛ 🔌 AE ⓿ VISA
BT n
closed Sunday dinner and Bank Holidays – **M** 10.50 t. (lunch) and a la carte 18.85/25.55 t.

XX **Hilaire,** 68 Old Brompton Rd, SW7 3LQ, 🕾 584 8993 – 🔌 AE ⓿ VISA
CT n
closed Saturday lunch, Sunday and Bank Holidays – **M** (booking essential) 14.00/21.00 t.
⬧ 4.00.

XX Golden Chopsticks, 1 Harrington Rd, SW7, 🕾 584 0855, Chinese rest. – ⬛
CS z

XX **Tui,** 19 Exhibition Rd, SW7 2HE, 🕾 584 8359, Thai rest. – 🔌 AE ⓿ VISA
CZ u
M a la carte 10.10/15.30 t. ⬧ 6.75.

XX **Memories of India,** 18 Gloucester Rd, SW7 4RB, 🕾 589 6450, Indian rest. – 🔌 AE ⓿ VISA
BR s
M 10.50 t. and a la carte 4.05/8.75 t.

XX **Pun,** 53 Old Brompton Rd, SW7 3JX, 🕾 225 1609, Chinese rest. – ⬛ 🔌 AE ⓿ VISA
CST r
M 5.50/12.80 t. and a la carte ⬧ 3.20.

X Chanterelle, 119 Old Brompton Rd, SW3 3RN, 🕾 373 5522
BT v

KINGSTON UPON THAMES p. 9.

🛈 Heritage Centre, Fairfield West 🕾 546 5386.

Kingston – ✉ Surrey.

🏨 **Kingston Lodge,** 88 Kingston Hill, KT2 7NP, 🕾 541 4481, 🌿 – 🖭 ⇔wc 🕾 🔌 ♿ Ⓟ 🏊 🔌
AE ⓿ VISA
CY u
M (closed Saturday lunch) 11.95 t. and a la carte ⬧ 3.35 – **64 rm** ⬚ 54.00/64.00 st., **1 suite**
95.00/160.00 st. – SB (weekends only) 66.00/69.00 st.

X Ayudhya, 14 Kingston Hill, KT2 7NH, 🕾 549 5984, Thai rest.
CYZ z

X Modern India, 10 Kingston Hill, KT2 7NH, 🕾 546 4632, Indian rest.
CZ x

Surbiton – ✉ Surrey.

XX **Chez Max,** 85 Maple Rd, KT6 4AW, 🕾 399 2365 – 🔌 AE ⓿ VISA
BZ o
closed Saturday lunch, Sunday, Monday, 2 weeks August and 2 weeks after Christmas – **M**
(booking essential) 16.50/22.50 t. and a la carte ⬧ 3.75.

Pour les 🏨🏨🏨, 🏨🏨, 🏨, nous ne donnons pas
le détail de l'installation,
ces hôtels possédant, en général, tout le confort.

⇔wc 🖭wc

☎

LAMBETH pp.10 and 11.

Brixton – ⊠ SW9.

✗ **Twenty Trinity Gardens,** 20 Trinity Gdns., SW9 8DP, ☎ 733 8838 – 𝘝𝘐𝘚𝘈   EY **n**
closed Saturday lunch, Sunday and 25 to 30 December – **M** 12.50 **t.**

Herne Hill – ⊠ SE24.

✗ **Au Provençal,** 295 Railton Rd, SE24 0JP, ☎ 274 9163 – 𝘝𝘐𝘚𝘈   FY **i**
closed 25-26 December and 1 January – **M** (dinner only) 10.95 **t.** and a la carte ⚬ 2.00.

Waterloo – ⊠ SE1.

✗ RSJ, 13a Coin St., SE1, ☎ 928 4554   pp. 17-20   PV **e**

LEWISHAM – pp. 10 and 11.

Upper Sydenham – ⊠ SE26.

✗✗ **Hornimans,** 124 Kirkdale, SE26 4BB, ☎ 291 2901 – 🔼 𝘝𝘐𝘚𝘈   FY **e**
closed Saturday lunch, Sunday dinner, Monday and 25 December - 13 January – **M** 10.50 **st.**
(dinner) and a la carte 8.50/12.50 **st.** ⚬ 2.30.

LONDON HEATHROW AIRPORT – see Hillingdon, London p. 51.

MERTON pp. 8 and 9.

Merton – ⊠ SW19.

✗ **Les Amoureux,** 156 Merton Hall Rd, SW19 3PZ, ☎ 543 0567 – 🔼 AE   DZ **a**
closed Sunday – **M** (dinner only) a la carte 11.25/14.25 **t.** ⚬ 3.00.

Wimbledon – ⊠ SW19.

⌂ **Worcester House,** 38 Alwyne Rd, SW19 7AE, ☎ 946 1300 – 📺 🚿wc. 🔼 AE ⓞ 𝘝𝘐𝘚𝘈 �
9 rm ⊑ 28.75/47.15 **t.**   DY **r**

✗✗ **Village Restaurant,** 8 High St., SW19 5DX, ☎ 947 6477 – 🔼 AE 𝘝𝘐𝘚𝘈   DY **c**
closed lunch Monday and Saturday, Sunday dinner, 4 weeks August and Bank Holidays – **M**
12.50/18.50 **st.**

✗✗ **San Lorenzo Fuoriporta,** 38 Worple Rd Mews, SW19 4DB, ☎ 946 8463, Italian rest. – 🔼
AE ⓞ 𝘝𝘐𝘚𝘈   DY **n**
closed Bank Holidays – **M** a la carte 12.50/17.50 **t.**

✗✗ **Wimbledon Palace,** 88 The Broadway, SW19 1RH, ☎ 540 4505, Chinese (Peking, Szechuan)
rest. – 🍽 🔼 AE ⓞ 𝘝𝘐𝘚𝘈   DY **e**
closed Saturday lunch and 25-26 December – **M** 9.00/16.00 **t.** and a la carte 10.00/15.00 **t.**
⚬ 3.20.

✗✗ Confucius, 162 The Broadway, SW19 1RX, ☎ 542 5272, Chinese (Peking, Canton) rest.   DEY **u**

✗✗ Golden Tandoori, 57 Hartfield Rd, SW19, ☎ 542 0240, Indian rest.   DZ **o**

MICHELIN Distribution Centre, Deer Park Rd, Merton, SW19 3UD, ☎ 540 9034/7 South London
Branch (Merton) p. 9

REDBRIDGE pp. 6 and 7.

Ilford – ⊠ Essex.

✗✗ **Mandarin Palace,** 559 Cranbrook Rd, Gants Hill, ☎ 550 7661, Chinese (Peking, Canton)
rest. – 🍽 🔼 AE 𝘝𝘐𝘚𝘈   GV **e**
M 4.00/15.00 **t.** and a la carte 13.80/21.80 **t.**

South Woodford – ⊠ Essex.

✗✗ **Ho-Ho,** 20 High Rd, E18 2QL, ☎ 989 1041, Chinese rest. – 🔼 AE ⓞ 𝘝𝘐𝘚𝘈   GV **c**
M 7.00/17.00 **t.** and a la carte 9.30/12.75 **t.** ⚬ 5.50.

Woodford – ⊠ Essex.

🏦 **Woodford Moat House** (Q.M.H.), 30 Oak Hill, Woodford Green, IG8 9NY, ☎ 505 4511, 🚗
– 🛗 📺 🚿wc 🚿wc 🚬 🅿 🔼 AE ⓞ 𝘝𝘐𝘚𝘈   GU **c**
M (bar lunch Saturday)/dinner 9.10 **t.** and a la carte ⚬ 3.00 – **99 rm** ⊑ 42.50/52.00 **st.** – SB
(weekends only) 50.00 **st.**

🏦 Prince Regent, Manor Rd, Woodford Bridge, IG8 8AE, E : ¾ m. ☎ 504 7635, 🚗 – 🍽 rest 📺
🚿wc 🚿wc 🚬 🅿 🔼 �   GU **a**
10 rm.

RICHMOND-UPON-THAMES pp. 8 and 9.

Barnes – ✉ SW13.

XX **Sonny's**, 94 Church Rd, SW13 0DQ, ✆ 748 0393. 🆘 VISA
CY **x**
closed Sunday dinner – **M** 7.95 t. **(lunch)** and a la carte 9.25/12.75 t. ⌀ 2.50.

X **Barnaby's**, 39b High St., SW13 9LN, ✆ 878 4750, French rest.
CY **v**
closed lunch Saturday and Monday, Sunday, Easter, September, Christmas and Bank Holidays
– **M** (booking essential) a la carte 12.00/13.70 st. ⌀ 3.10.

X Gate of India, 60 Church Rd, SW13 0DQ, ✆ 748 6793, Indian rest.
CY **x**

X **Il Bellamore**, 5 White Hart Lane, SW13 0PX, ✆ 876 3335, Italian rest. – 🆘 AE ① VISA
closed 25 and 26 December – **M** 6.95 t. and a la carte ⌀ 2.10.
CY **o**

East Sheen – ✉ Surrey.

XX **Crowther's**, 481 Upper Richmond Rd West, SW14 7PU, ✆ 876 6372 – ▤. 🆘 AE
CY **n**
*closed Saturday lunch, Sunday, Monday, 1 week February, 2 weeks August-September and
25-26 December* – **M** (booking essential) 12.50/18.00 t. ⌀ 4.55.

X **Le Tagliatelle**, 180 Upper Richmond Road West, SW14 8AW, ✆ 878 8143, Italian rest. – 🆘
VISA
M 5.95 st. (lunch) and a la carte 8.10/11.40 t. ⌀ 2.80.
CY **i**

Kew – ✉ Surrey.

X **Le Mange Tout**, 3 Royal Par. (Station Approach), TW9 3QB, ✆ 940 9304 – ▤. 🆘 AE ① VISA
closed Saturday lunch, Sunday dinner, 25-26 December, 1-2 January and Bank Holidays –
M 10.85 t. and a la carte ⌀ 2.95.

X **Jasper's Bun in the Oven**, 11 Kew Green, TW7 3AA, ✆ 940 3987 – 🆘 AE ① VISA CX **e**
closed Sunday, Easter, Christmas and Bank Holidays – **M** 9.95 t. and a la carte 9.10/15.95 t.
⌀ 3.50.

Richmond – ✉ Surrey.

🛝, 🛝 Richmond Park ✆ 876 3205.

🛈 Central Library, Little Green ✆ 940 9125.

🏨 **Petersham**, Nightingale Lane, Richmond Hill, TW10 6RP, ✆ 940 7471, Telex 928556, ← – 🛗
📺 ⇆wc 🅿 🏖 🆘 AE ① VISA 🛞
CY **c**
M 12.50/14.50 t. and a la carte ⌀ 3.50 – **54 rm** ⇌ 55.00/65.00 st. – SB 75.00/90.00 st.

🏨 **Richmond Gate** without rest., Richmond Hill, TW10 6RP, ✆ 940 0061, Telex 928556, 🚗 –
📺 ⇆wc 🅿 🏖 🆘 ① VISA 🛞
CY **a**
50 rm ⇌ 55.00/65.00 st.

XX Chez Bubb, Riverside House, Water Lane, ✆ 948 7733, ←, French rest.
BY **c**

XX ✿ **Lichfield's**, 13 Lichfield Terr., Sheen Rd, TW9 1DP, ✆ 940 5236 – ▤. 🆘 AE
CY **s**
closed Saturday lunch, Sunday, Monday, first 2 weeks September and 1 week Christmas –
M (booking essential) 17.50/26.00 st. ⌀ 3.50
Spec. Lamb with chick pea souffle, Roast duck, Iced butterscotch meringue cake.

XX **Kew Rendezvous**, 110 Kew Rd, TW9 2PQ, ✆ 948 4343, Chinese (Peking) rest. – ▤. 🆘 AE
① VISA
CY **e**
closed 25 and 26 December – **M** 10.50/15.00 t. and a la carte.

XX **Evergreen**, 102-104 Kew Rd, TW9 2PQ, ✆ 940 9044, Chinese rest. – ▤. 🆘 AE ① VISA
M 10.10 t. and a la carte 5.00/12.90 t.
CY **e**

XX **Bellini**, 12 The Quadrant, TW9, ✆ 940 0086, Italian rest. – ① VISA
BY **e**
closed Saturday lunch and Sunday – **M** a la carte 13.40/16.15 ⌀ 3.60.

X Kim's, 12 Red Lion St., TW9 1RW, ✆ 948 5777, Malaysian, Singaporean rest. – ▤
CY **s**

X **Red Lion**, 18 Red Lion St., TW9 1RW, ✆ 940 2371, Chinese (Peking) rest. – 🆘 AE ① VISA
closed 25 and 26 December – **M** 10.00 t. and a la carte 7.30/8.50 t. ⌀ 3.30.
CY **s**

Twickenham – ✉ Middx.

🛈 District Library, Garfield Rd ✆ 892 0032.

XX **Cézanne**, 68 Richmond Rd, TW1 3BE, ✆ 892 3526 – 🆘 AE VISA
BY **a**
closed Saturday lunch, Sunday and Bank Holidays – **M** a la carte 10.30/13.90 t. ⌀ 2.25.

Do not mix up :

Comfort of hotels : 🏨🏨🏨🏨 ... 🏠, 🏡, 🏠
Comfort of restaurants : XXXXX X
Quality of the cuisine : ✿✿✿, ✿✿, ✿, M

SOUTHWARK pp. 10 and 11.

Dulwich – ⊠ SE21.

✕✕ **Luigi's,** 129 Gipsy Hill, SE19 1QS, ℰ 670 1843, Italian rest. – ⚊ AE ⓪ *VISA*   FY **a**
closed Saturday lunch, Sunday, August and Bank Holidays – **M** a la carte 11.60/14.70 **t.** ⓐ 3.50.

East Dulwich – ⊠ SE22.

✕ Mr Lui, 148 Lordship Lane, SE22, ℰ 693 8266, Chinese (Peking) rest. – ▤   FY **r**

Peckham Rye – ⊠ SE22.

✕✕ **L'Auberge,** 44 Forest Hill Rd, SE22, ℰ 299 2211, French rest. – ⚊ *VISA*   FY **s**
closed Sunday dinner, Monday and 3 weeks August – **M** (dinner only and Sunday lunch)/dinner
13.50 **t.** ⓐ 2.25.

Southwark – ⊠ SE1.

✕ **Dining Room,** Winchester Walk, London Bridge, SE1, off Cathedral St. ℰ 407 0337, Vegetarian rest.   pp. 17-20. PQV **a**
closed Saturday, Sunday and Monday – **M** 9.50 **st.** and a la carte approx. 8.00 **t.**

SUTTON pp. 8 and 9.

🛈 Oak Sports Centre, Woodmansterne Rd, Carshalton ℰ 643 8363.

Sutton – ⊠ Surrey.

☎ **Thatched House,** 135 Cheam Rd, SM1 2BN, ℰ 642 3131, ☞ – ⊺⊽ 🛁wc ⓟ ⚊ *VISA*   DZ **e**
M (dinner only) 9.65 **t.** ⓐ 3.10 – **18 rm** ⊊ 23.00/39.50 **st.**

↑ **Dene,** 39 Cheam Rd, SM1 2AT, ℰ 642 3170, ☞ – ⊺⊽ ⊏⊐wc 🛁wc ⓟ ⅋
19 rm ⊊ 14.95/41.40 **t.**   EZ **v**

✕✕ **Partners 23,** 23 Stonecot Hill, SM3 9HB, ℰ 644 7743 – ⚊ AE ⓪ *VISA*   DZ **z**
closed Saturday lunch, Sunday, Monday, 2 weeks August and last week December –
M (booking essential) 13.25/18.00 **t.** ⓐ 3.50.

TOWER HAMLETS – pp. 6 and 7.

Limehouse – ⊠ E14.

✕ **Good Friends,** 139-141 Salmon Lane, E14 7PG, ℰ 987 5541, Chinese rest. – ⚊ AE ⓪
VISA   FX **e**
closed 25 and 26 December – **M** 12.00 **t.** and a la carte approx. 11.00 **t.** ⓐ 3.00.

WALTHAM FOREST pp. 6 and 7.

🛈 at Chingford, 158 Station Rd ℰ 529 5708.

Leytonstone – ⊠ E11.

✕ **Trattoria Parmigiana,** 715 High Rd, E11 4RD, ℰ 539 1700, Italian rest. – ⚊ AE ⓪
VISA   GV **a**
closed Sunday – **M** a la carte 11.30/14.60 **t.** ⓐ 2.90.

When travelling for business or pleasure
in England, Wales, Scotland and Ireland :

— use the series of five maps
(nos **401**, **402**, **403**, **404** and **405**) at a scale of 1:400 000

— they are the perfect complement to this Guide
as towns underlined in red on the maps will be found in this Guide.

WANDSWORTH pp. 8 and 9.

Battersea – ✉ SW8/SW11.

XXX ⊛ **Chez Nico**, 129 Queenstown Rd, SW8 3RH, ☎ 720 6960, French rest. – ⚒ ⓞ *VISA*   EY **c**
closed lunch Saturday and Monday, Sunday, 4 days at Easter, 3 weeks July-August, 1 week at Christmas and Bank Holidays – **M** (booking essential) 14.50 **st.** (lunch) and a la carte 26.65/31.95 **st.** ₪ 6.00
Spec. Terrine de riz de veau et de morilles garnie d'une petite salade de mâche, Filets de rouget persillés au parfum de céleris, Savarin aux fruits et glace vanille, sirop de citron.

XX ⊛ **L'Arlequin**, 123 Queenstown Rd, SW8 3RH, ☎ 622 0555, French rest. – ▤ ⚒ AE ⓞ *VISA*
closed Saturday, Sunday, 3 weeks August, 1 week at Christmas and Bank Holidays – **M** (booking essential) 12.50 **st.** (lunch) and a la carte 22.20/30.50 **st.** ₪ 5.00   EY **o**
Spec. Mi-cuit de saumon au vinaigre de framboise (February-August), Galette de pigeonneau fermier, Assiette gourmande.

XX **Alonso's**, 32 Queenstown Rd, SW8 3RX, ☎ 720 5986 – ▤ ⚒ AE ⓞ *VISA*   EY **e**
closed Saturday lunch and Sunday – **M** 9.75/12.75 **t.** and a la carte.

X **Ransome's**, 35-37 Parkgate Rd, SW11, ☎ 223 1611 – ℗ ⚒ AE ⓞ *VISA*   pp. 17-20   KZ **e**
closed Saturday lunch, Sunday and Bank Holidays – **M** 9.75/15.00 **t.** ₪ 3.00.

Clapham – ✉ SW11.

X **Pollyanna's**, 2 Battersea Rise, SW11 1ED, ☎ 228 0316 – ⚒ AE *VISA*   EY **a**
closed Sunday dinner, 24 to 27 December and 1 January – **M** (dinner only and Sunday lunch)/dinner 10.95 **t.** and a la carte 11.90/19.50 **t.** ₪ 3.00.

X **Jasmin**, 50 Battersea Rise, SW11 1EG, ☎ 228 0336, Chinese rest. – ⚒ AE ⓞ *VISA*   EY **z**
closed Sunday – **M** a la carte 9.20/10.50 **t.** ₪ 2.50.

X **La Bouffe**, 13 Battersea Rise, SW11 1HG, ☎ 228 3384 – ▤ ⚒ *VISA*   EY **v**
closed Saturday lunch, Sunday and 24 to 30 December – **M** 5.00/12.95 **t.** and a la carte ₪ 2.50.

Putney – ✉ SW15.

XX **Bayee House**, 100 Upper Richmond Rd, SW15 1EL, ☎ 789 3161, Chinese (Peking) rest. –
▤ ⚒ AE ⓞ *VISA*   DY **v**
closed 23 to 25 December – **M** 20.00/35.00 **t.** and a la carte 11.50/18.80 **t.** ₪ 3.00.

XX Wild Thyme, 96 Felsham Rd, SW15, ☎ 789 3323   DY **x**

Tooting – ✉ SW17.

X **Oh Boy**, 843 Garratt Lane, SW17 0PG, ☎ 947 9760, Thai, French rest. – ⚒ AE ⓞ *VISA*   EY **x**
closed Sunday and last 2 weeks August – **M** (booking essential)(dinner only) a la carte 9.65/12.65 **t.** ₪ 3.30.

WESTMINSTER (City of)

Bayswater and Maida Vale – ✉ W2/W9 – Except where otherwise stated see pp. 30 and 31.

🏨 **Royal Lancaster** (Rank), Lancaster Terr., W2 2TY, ☎ 262 6737, Telex 24822, ≤ – ᛰ ▤ rest
📺 ☎ ₰ ℗ ⚷ ⚒ AE ⓞ *VISA* ₰   DZ **e**
M 12.50/16.95 **t.** and a la carte – ⊇ 8.50 – **418 rm** 95.00/112.00 **t.**, **20 suites** 200.00/650.00 **st.**

🏨 **White's** (Mt. Charlotte), Bayswater Rd, 90-92 Lancaster Gate, W2 3NR, ☎ 262 2711, Telex
24771 – ᛰ ▤ 📺 ☎ ℗ ⚷ ⚒ AE ⓞ *VISA*   CZ **v**
M 25.00 **t.** and a la carte ₪ 5.00 – ⊇ 7.00 – **55 rm** 95.00/115.00 **t.**, **3 suites** 250.00 **t.** – SB (weekends only) 112.00/135.00 **st.**

🏨 **London Metropole**, Edgware Rd, W2 1JU, ☎ 402 4141, Telex 23711, ≤ – ᛰ ▤ 📺 ☎ ℗
⚷ ⚒ AE ⓞ *VISA* ₰   pp. 13-16   JT **c**
M (carving lunch)/dinner a la carte approx. 18.00 **s.** – ⊇ 7.25 – **586 rm** 64.00/84.00 **st.**, **9 suites** 159.00 **st.**

🏨 **Hospitality Inn** (Mt. Charlotte), 104 Bayswater Rd, W2 3HL, ☎ 262 4461, Telex 22667, ≤ –
ᛰ 📺 ☎ ℗ ⚷ ⚒ AE ⓞ *VISA* ₰   CZ **o**
M 6.75/9.00 **st.** and a la carte ₪ 3.50 – ⊇ 6.50 – **175 rm** 55.00/85.00 **st.**, **1 suite**.

🏨 **London Embassy** (Embassy), 150 Bayswater Rd, W2 4RT, ☎ 229 1212, Telex 27727 – ᛰ ▤
📺 ⌴wc ₰ ⚷ ⚒ AE ⓞ *VISA*   BZ **o**
M (carving rest.) 9.75 **st.** and a la carte ₪ 3.30 – ⊇ 5.00 – **192 rm** 59.00/82.00 **st.**, **1 suite** 110.00 **st.**

🏨 **Colonnade**, 2 Warrington Cres., W9 1ER, ☎ 286 1052, Telex 298930 – ᛰ 📺 ⌴wc ⋔wc ☎.
⚒ AE ⓞ *VISA*   pp. 13-16   JT **e**
M *(closed Friday and Saturday)* (dinner only) 12.50 **t.** ₪ 2.80 – **53 rm** ⊇ 35.50/55.00 **t.**

🏨 **Mornington Lancaster** (Best Western) without rest., 12 Lancaster Gate, W2 3LG, ☎
262 7361, Telex 24281 – ᛰ 📺 ⌴wc ☎. ⚒ AE ⓞ *VISA*   DZ **s**
closed 22 December - 2 January – ⊇ 3.00 – **63 rm** 30.00/73.00 **st.**

⌂ **Dylan,** 14 Devonshire Terr., Lancaster Gate, W2 3DW, ℰ 723 3280 – ⇔wc ▥wc. 🅰🅴 ⓞ 𝗩𝗜𝗦𝗔.
⚘
18 rm ⊊ 22.00/40.00 **t.**   CY **c**

⌂ **Parkwood,** 4 Stanhope Pl., W2 2HB, ℰ 402 2241, Group Telex 8812714 – 📺 ⇔wc ☎. ⚘
18 rm.   FY **e**

⌂ **Allandale,** 3 Devonshire Terr., Lancaster Gate, W2 3DN, ℰ 723 8311 – 📺 ⇔wc ▥wc. 🖪
ⓞ 𝗩𝗜𝗦𝗔. ⚘   CY **a**
20 rm ⊊ 20.00/35.00.

XXX **Bombay Palace,** 50 Connaught St., Hyde Park Sq., W2, ℰ 723 8855, North Indian rest. – 🖪
🅰🅴 ⓞ 𝗩𝗜𝗦𝗔   EY **a**
M 9.95/10.50 **t.** and a la carte 10.50/13.50 **t.** ⱷ 5.50.

XX **San Marino,** 26 Sussex Pl., W2 2TH, ℰ 723 8395, Italian rest. – 🖪 🅰🅴 ⓞ 𝗩𝗜𝗦𝗔   EY **u**
closed Sunday and Bank Holidays – **M** a la carte 11.75/18.35 **t.** ⱷ 3.50.

XX **Concordia Notte,** 29-31 Craven Rd, W2 3BX, ℰ 402 4985, Italian rest., Dancing – 🖪 🅰🅴 ⓞ
𝗩𝗜𝗦𝗔   DY **r**
closed Sunday and Bank Holidays – **M** a la carte 18.50/25.00 **t.** ⱷ 4.00.

XX **Canaletto,** 451 Edgware Rd, W2 1TH, ℰ 262 7027, Italian rest. – 🖪 🅰🅴 ⓞ 𝗩𝗜𝗦𝗔
closed Saturday lunch and Sunday – **M** a la carte 11.60/16.70 **t.** ⱷ 5.50.   pp. 13-16   JT **v**

X **Concordia,** 29-31 Craven Rd, W2 3BX, ℰ 723 3725, Italian rest. – 🖪 🅰🅴 ⓞ 𝗩𝗜𝗦𝗔   DY **r**
closed Sunday and Bank Holidays – **M** 20.00 **t.** and a la carte 10.50/14.00 **t.** ⱷ 2.55.

X Fortune Cookie, 1 Queensway, W2 4QJ, ℰ 727 7260, Chinese (Peking) rest.   BZ **e**

X Kalamaras Taverna, 76-78 Inverness Mews, W2 3JQ, ℰ 727 9122, Greek rest.   BY **a**

Belgravia – ⊠ SW1 – Except where otherwise stated see pp. 28 and 29.

🏨 **Berkeley,** Wilton Pl., SW1X 7RL, ℰ 235 6000, Telex 919252, 🏊 – 🛗 🖃 📺 ☎ ⓧ ⇦ – 🖪. 🖪
🅰🅴 ⓞ 𝗩𝗜𝗦𝗔   FQ **e**
M Restaurant (closed Saturday) a la carte 21.50/27.00 **st.** ⱷ 3.40 – **Buttery** (closed Sunday,
August and Bank Holidays (buffet lunch)/dinner a la carte 15.25/20.00 **st.** ⱷ 3.40 – ⊊ 4.50 –
160 rm 120.00/195.00 **st.**, **26 suites**.

🏨 **Lowndes Thistle** (Thistle), 21 Lowndes St., SW1X 9ES, ℰ 235 6020, Telex 919065 – 🛗 📺
☎. 🖪 🅰🅴 ⓞ 𝗩𝗜𝗦𝗔   FR **i**
M a la carte 16.00/20.00 **t.** – ⊊ 7.00 – **79 rm** 85.00/135.00 **st.**

🏨 **Sheraton-Belgravia,** 20 Chesham Pl., SW1X 8HQ, ℰ 235 6040, Telex 919020 – 🛗 🖃 📺 ☎.
🖪 🅰🅴 ⓞ 𝗩𝗜𝗦𝗔. ⚘   FR **u**
M (closed lunch Saturday and Bank Holidays) 16.00/20.00 **t.** ⱷ 3.50 – ⊊ 7.50 – **89 rm**
90.00/120.00 **t.**, **7 suites** 185.00/220.00 **t.**

XX **Motcombs,** 26 Motcomb St., SW1X 8JU, ℰ 235 6382 – 🖪 🅰🅴 ⓞ 𝗩𝗜𝗦𝗔   FR **z**
closed Sunday – **M** a la carte 13.85/17.60 **t.** ⱷ 3.50.

XX Salloos, 62-64 Kinnerton St., SW1 8ER, ℰ 235 4444, Indian and Pakistani rest. – 🖃   FQ **a**

XX **Le Trou Normand,** 27 Motcomb St., SW1, ℰ 235 1668, French rest. – 🖪 🅰🅴 ⓞ 𝗩𝗜𝗦𝗔   FR **z**
closed Sunday and 2 weeks at Christmas – **M** 14.50/23.50 **t.**

Hyde Park and Knightsbridge – ⊠ SW1/SW7 – pp. 28 and 29.
🛈 Harrods, Knightsbridge, SW1 ℰ 730 3488.

🏨 **Hyde Park** (T.H.F.), 66 Knightsbridge, SW1Y 7LA, ℰ 235 2000, Telex 262057, ≼ – 🛗 🖃 📺
☎. 🖪 🅰🅴 ⓞ 𝗩𝗜𝗦𝗔   EQ **v**
M 14.50/20.00 **st.** and a la carte ⱷ 5.45 – ⊊ 9.00 – **180 rm** 135.00/150.00 **st.**, **20 suites**.

XXX **Shezan,** 16-22 Cheval Pl., Montpelier St., SW7 1ES, ℰ 589 7918, Indian and Pakistani rest. –
🖃. 🖪 🅰🅴 ⓞ 𝗩𝗜𝗦𝗔   ER **c**
closed Sunday and Bank Holidays – **M** 9.75 **st.** and a la carte 8.75/15.00 **st.** ⱷ 5.50.

XX Montpeliano, 13 Montpelier St., SW7 1HQ, ℰ 589 0032, Italian rest.   ER **e**

Mayfair – ✉ W1 – pp. 26 and 27.

🏨🏨🏨 **Claridge's**, Brook St., W1A 2JQ, 𝒫 629 8860, Telex 21872 – 🛗 🗐 📺 🕿 🕭, 🔼 🅰🅴 ⓘ 🆅🅸🆂🅰, 🛠
M a la carte 28.50/36.20 st. 🛉 3.40 – **Causerie** 13.50 st. (lunch) and a la carte 22.30/34.80 st. 🛉 3.40 – 🖙 11.50 – **205 rm** 110.00/195.00 st., **55 suites** 310.00/600.00 st.
BL c

🏨🏨🏨 **Dorchester**, Park Lane, W1A 2HJ, 𝒫 629 8888, Telex 887704 – 🛗 🗐 📺 🕿 🕭 🚙, 🔼 🅰🅴 ⓘ 🆅🅸🆂🅰, 🛠
BN z
M (see **The Terrace** below) – **Grill** 17.00 st. and a la carte 🛉 3.60 – 🖙 9.00 – **275 rm** 145.00/175.00 st., **66 suites** 250.00/800.00 st.

🏨🏨🏨 **Grosvenor House** (T.H.F.), Park Lane, W1A 3AA, 𝒫 499 6363, Telex 24871, 🔽 – 🛗 📺 📺 🕿 🕭, 🅿 🕭, 🔼 🅰🅴 ⓘ 🆅🅸🆂🅰, 🛠
AM
M (see **90 Park Lane** below) – 🖙 9.50 – **468 rm** 115.00/140.00 st., **50 suites**.

🏨🏨🏨 **Inn on the Park**, Hamilton Pl., Park Lane, W1A 1AZ, 𝒫 499 0888, Telex 22771 – 🛗 🗐 📺 🕿 🕭, 🚙, 🔼 🅰🅴 ⓘ 🆅🅸🆂🅰
BP a
M **Four Seasons** 20.50/22.50 st. and a la carte 29.50/34.50 st. 🛉 6.50 – **Lanes** 21.00 st. (lunch) and a la carte 20.50/22.50 st. 🛉 6.50 – 🖙 8.25 – **228 rm** 135.00/165.00 s., **19 suites** 260.00/615.00 s.

🏨🏨🏨 **Le Meridien**, Piccadilly, W1V 0BH, 𝒫 734 8000, Telex 25795, 🔽, squash – 🛗 🗐 📺 🕿 🕭, 🔼 🅰🅴 ⓘ 🆅🅸🆂🅰, 🛠
EM a
M 18.15/27.50 st. and a la carte 🛉 6.00 – 🖙 8.60 – **284 rm** 125.00/150.00 st., **19 suites** 210.00/450.00 st.

🏨🏨 🕸 **Connaught**, 16 Carlos Pl., W1Y 6AL, 𝒫 499 7070 – 🛗 🗐 rest 📺 🕿 🔼, 🛠
BM e
M (booking essential) a la carte 23.25/40.30 t. 🛉 3.70 – **90 rm**, **24 suites**
Spec. Pâté de turbot froid au homard, sauce pudeur, Rendez-vous du pêcheur, sauce légère au parfum d'Armorique, Salmis de canard strasbourgeoise en surprise.

🏨🏨 **Athenaeum** (Rank), 116 Piccadilly, W1V 0BJ, 𝒫 499 3464, Telex 261589 – 🛗 🗐 rest 📺 🕿, 🔼 🅰🅴 ⓘ 🆅🅸🆂🅰, 🛠
CP s
M 17.50 st. (lunch) and a la carte 16.35/26.90 st. 🛉 4.50 – 🖙 8.00 – **112 rm** 117.00/140.00 st., **6 suites** 200.00/240.00 st.

🏨🏨 **Brown's** (T.H.F.), 29-34 Albemarle St., W1A 4SW, 𝒫 493 6020, Telex 28686 – 🛗 📺 🕿, 🔼 🅰🅴 ⓘ 🆅🅸🆂🅰
DM e
M 22.00/23.00 st. and a la carte 🛉 4.25 – 🖙 9.25 – **125 rm** 99.00/130.00 st., **5 suites**.

🏨🏨 **May Fair** (Inter-Con.), Stratton St., W1A 2AN, 𝒫 629 7777, Telex 262526 – 🛗 🗐 📺 🕿 🔼 🅰🅴 ⓘ 🆅🅸🆂🅰
DN z
M 16.00/23.50 t. and a la carte 🛉 5.70 – 🖙 8.80 – **322 rm** 123.00/144.00, **24 suites** 273.00/700.00.

🏨🏨 **Marriott**, Duke St., Grosvenor Sq., W1A 4AW, 𝒫 493 1232, Telex 268101 – 🛗 🗐 📺 🕿 🕭, 🅿 🕭, 🔼 🅰🅴 ⓘ 🆅🅸🆂🅰
BL a
M a la carte 17.30/26.00 t. – 🖙 8.00 – **228 rm** 125.00/160.00 t., **9 suites** 230.00/800.00 t.

🏨🏨 **Inter-Continental** (Inter-Con.), 1 Hamilton Pl., Hyde Park Corner, W1V 0QY, 𝒫 409 3131, Telex 25853 – 🛗 🗐 📺 🕿 🕭, 🚙, 🕭, 🛠
BP o
491 rm, **15 suites**.

🏨🏨 **Britannia** (Inter-Con.), Grosvenor Sq., W1A 3AN, 𝒫 629 9400, Telex 23941 – 🛗 🗐 📺 🕿, 🔼 🅰🅴 ⓘ 🆅🅸🆂🅰, 🛠
BM x
M 15.50 t. and a la carte 🛉 4.50 – 🖙 9.20 – **354 rm** 105.00/130.00 s., **12 suites** 400.00 s.

🏨🏨 **Westbury** (T.H.F.), New Bond St. (entrance on Conduit St.), W1A 4UH, 𝒫 629 7755, Telex 24378 – 🛗 🗐 📺 🕿 🕭, 🅿 🕭, 🔼 🅰🅴 ⓘ 🆅🅸🆂🅰
DM a
M 25.00 st. and a la carte 20.65/27.50 st. 🛉 5.45 – 🖙 8.75 – **240 rm** 95.00/110.00 st., **15 suites**.

🏨🏨 **Londonderry**, Park Lane, W1Y 8AP, 𝒫 493 7292, Telex 263292 – 🛗 🗐 📺 🕿 🚙, 🔼 🅰🅴 ⓘ 🆅🅸🆂🅰, 🛠
BP i
M 19.00 st. and a la carte 21.55/29.95 st. 🛉 4.10 – 🖙 8.50 – **150 rm** 132.25/161.00 st., **12 suites** 207.00/400.00 st.

🏨🏨 **London Hilton on Park Lane**, 22 Park Lane, W1A 2HH, 𝒫 493 8000, Telex 24873, ≼ London – 🛗 🗐 📺 🕿 🕭, 🅿 🕭, 🔼 🅰🅴 ⓘ 🆅🅸🆂🅰
BP e
M 19.75/26.70 t. and a la carte 🛉 6.50 – 🖙 9.00 – **501 rm** 110.00/157.00, **54 suites** 240.00/760.00.

🏨🏨 **Holiday Inn**, 3 Berkeley St., W1X 6NE, 𝒫 493 8282, Telex 24561 – 🛗 🗐 📺 🕿 🚙, 🕭, 🔼 🅰🅴 ⓘ 🆅🅸🆂🅰, 🛠
DN r
M 12.50/32.00 st. and a la carte 🛉 4.00 – 🖙 8.00 – **185 rm** 97.00/110.00 st., **7 suites** 220.00/360.00 st. – SB (weekends only) 126.00/150.00 st.

🏨🏨 **Park Lane**, Piccadilly, W1Y 8BX, 𝒫 499 6321, Telex 21533 – 🛗 🗐 📺 🕿 🅿, 🕭, 🔼 🅰🅴 ⓘ 🆅🅸🆂🅰
BP x
M 13.50/19.50 st. and a la carte 17.95/22.45 st. 🛉 4.00 – 🖙 7.50 – **323 rm** 99.95/119.95 st., **54 suites** 150.00/400.00 st.

🏨🏨 **Chesterfield**, 35 Charles St., W1X 8LX, 𝒫 491 2622, Telex 269394 – 🛗 🗐 🕿, 🔼 🅰🅴 ⓘ 🆅🅸🆂🅰, 🛠
CN c
M (buffet lunch Saturday and Sunday)/a la carte 15.00/23.00 t. 🛉 5.00 – 🖙 7.50 – **112 rm** 95.00/115.00 t., **1 suite** 200.00/350.00 t.

XXXXX ✿✿ **The Terrace,** (at Dorchester H.), Park Lane, W1A 2HJ, ℰ 629 8888, Telex 887704, French
rest. – ≣. ⚠ AE ⓪ VISA   BN z
   closed Sunday – **M** (dinner only) 35.00 **st.** and a la carte 17.70/28.70 **st.** ⅋ 3.60
   Spec. Parfait de foies de volailles aux truffes, Symphonie de fruits de mer, Sole farcie à la brunoise de légumes
   gratinée.

XXXXX Mirabelle, 56 Curzon St., W1Y 8DL, ℰ 499 4636, ≉ – ≣   CN a

XXXXX ✿ **90 Park Lane** (T.H.F.), (at Grosvenor House H.), Park Lane, W1A 3AA, ℰ 409 1290, Telex
24871 – ≣. ⚠ AE ⓪ VISA   AM a
   closed Saturday lunch, Sunday and Bank Holidays – **M** 22.50/42.50 **st.** and a la carte
   28.45/46.20 **st.** ⅋ 7.50
   Spec. Loup de mer en croûte, Marbre de foie gras au poivre vert, Suprême de volaille à la Thai.

XXXX ✿✿✿ **Le Gavroche,** 43 Upper Brook St., W1P 1PS, ℰ 408 0881, French rest. – ≣. ⚠ AE ⓪
VISA   CN c
   closed Saturday, Sunday, 23 December-2 January and Bank Holidays – **M** (booking essential)
   19.50/40.00 **st.** and a la carte 28.00/44.00 **st.** ⅋ 5.60
   Spec. Soufflé suissesse, Assiette du boucher, Sablé aux fraises.

XXXX ✿ **Le Soufflé** (at Inter-Continental H.), 1 Hamilton Pl., Hyde Park Corner, W1V 0QY, ℰ
409 3131, Telex 25853 – ≣ ⇔. ⚠ AE ⓪ VISA   BP o
   M *(closed Saturday lunch)* 19.00/29.50 st. and a la carte
   Spec. Le medley du gourmand, Le jumelé d'agneau en croûte de poivre aux deux sauces, Le soufflé aux fruits de
   la passion.

XXXX Scott's, 20 Mount St., W1Y 6HE, ℰ 629 5248, Seafood – ≣. ⚠ AE ⓪ VISA   BM r
   closed Sunday lunch, Christmas and Bank Holidays – **M** a la carte 20.75/36.45 **t.**

XXX Princess Garden, 8-10 North Audley St., W1Y 1WF, ℰ 493 3223, Chinese (Peking) rest. –
≣. ⚠ AE ⓪ VISA   AL z
   M 20.00/35.00 and a la carte ⅋ 4.00.

XXX Tiberio, 22 Queen St., W1X 7PJ, ℰ 629 3561, Italian rest., Dancing – ⚠ AE ⓪ VISA   CN z
   closed Saturday lunch and Sunday – **M** a la carte 13.50/27.75 **t.** ⅋ 4.00.

XX Greenhouse, 27a Hay's Mews, W1X 7RJ, ℰ 499 3331 – ⚠ AE ⓪ VISA   BN a
   closed Saturday lunch, Sunday, 24 December-5 January and Bank Holidays – **M** a la carte
   13.60/18.70 **t.** ⅋ 3.05.

XX Langan's Brasserie, Stratton St., W1X 5FD, ℰ 491 8822 – ⚠ AE ⓪ VISA   DN e
   closed Saturday lunch, Sunday and Bank Holidays – **M** (booking essential) a la carte
   10.80/17.40 **t.** ⅋ 4.15.

XX Miyama, 38 Clarges St., W1Y 7PJ, ℰ 499 2443, Japanese rest. – ≣. ⚠ AE ⓪ VISA   CN e
   closed Saturday lunch, Sunday and Bank Holidays – **M** 7.00/24.00 **t.** and a la carte.

XX Mr. Kai, 65 South Audley St., W1Y 5FD, ℰ 493 8988, Chinese (Peking) rest. – ≣. ⚠ AE ⓪
VISA   BM v
   M a la carte 20.00/30.00 **t.**

XX Shogun (at Britannia H.), Adams Row, W1, ℰ 493 1255, Telex 8813271, Japanese rest.   BM x

XX Ho-Ho, 29 Maddox St., W1, ℰ 493 1228, Chinese rest. – ≣. ⚠ AE ⓪ VISA   DL x
   closed Sunday and Bank Holidays – **M** 8.50/18.60 **t.** and a la carte.

XX One Two Three, 27 Davies St., W1 1LN, ℰ 409 0750, Japanese rest. – ≣. ⚠ AE ⓪ VISA
   closed Saturday, Sunday and Bank Holidays – **M** 9.90/25.00 **t.** and a la carte ⅋ 2.80.   BM s

X Ikeda, 30 Brook St., W1Y 1AG, ℰ 629 2730, Japanese rest. – ≣. ⚠ AE ⓪ VISA   CKL a
   closed Saturday and Sunday – **M** 8.90/25.00 **t.** and a la carte.

X Trattoria Fiori, 87-88 Mount St., W1Y 5HG, ℰ 499 1447, Italian rest. – ⚠ AE ⓪ VISA   BM o
   closed Sunday and Bank Holidays – **M** 25.30 **t.** and a la carte 16.35/24.25 **t.** ⅋ 2.80.

Regent's Park and Marylebone – ⊠ NW1/NW6/NW8/W1 – Except where otherwise
stated see pp. 26 and 27.
🛈 Selfridges, Oxford St., W1 ℰ 730 3488.

🏨 **Churchill,** 30 Portman Sq., W1A 4ZX, ℰ 486 5800, Telex 264831 – ▮ ≣ 📺 ☎ 🕭 Ⓟ ◭. ⚠
AE ⓪ VISA. ✻   AJ x
   M a la carte 15.20/26.80 **st.** ⅋ 2.85 – ⊊ 7.50 – **487 rm** 120.00/135.00 **s.,** **39 suites** 220.00/
   525.00 **s.**

🏨🏨 **Montcalm,** Great Cumberland Pl., W1A 2LF, 🖉 402 4288, Telex 28710 – 🛗 📺 🏧 🕭.
AE ⑩ VISA
pp. 30 and 31   FY   x
M 15.00/35.00 **st.** and a la carte ⬧ 3.65 – ⥲ 5.50 – **116 rm** 115.00/137.00 **st.**

🏨🏨 Portman Inter-Continental (Inter-Con.), 22 Portman Sq., W1H 9FL, 🖉 486 5844, Telex 261526
– 🛗 ▤ 📺 🕭 & ℗. 🏧
AJ   o
278 rm. 8 suites.

🏨🏨 **Holiday Inn,** 134 George St., W1H 6DN, 🖉 723 1277, Telex 27983, 🔲 – 🛗 ▤ 🏧 🕭.
🏧. 🔼 AE ⑩ VISA
pp. 30 and 31   FY   i
M approx. 13.50 **st.** and a la carte – ⥲ 7.10 – **241 rm** 105.00/127.00 **st.**, **2 suites** 300.00/
500.00 **st.**

🏨🏨 **Selfridge Thistle** (Thistle), 400 Orchard St., W1H 0JS, 🖉 408 2080, Telex 22361 – 🛗 ▤ 📺
🕭 & ⑩. 🔼 AE ⑩ VISA
AK   e
M a la carte 22.00/28.00 **t.** ⬧ 3.95 – ⥲ 6.75 – **298 rm** 90.00/125.00 **st.**

🏨🏨 **Ladbroke Westmoreland** (Ladbroke), 18 Lodge Rd, NW8 7JT, 🖉 722 7722, Telex 23101 –
🛗 ▤ 📺 ⑩ 🕭. 🔼 AE ⑩ VISA
pp. 13-16   JS   v
M (carving rest.) 13.00 **t.** and a la carte ⬧ 3.50 – ⥲ 7.50 – **347 rm** 73.00/100.00 **t.** – SB (weekends
only) 75.00/95.00 **st.**

🏨🏨 **Clifton Ford,** 47 Welbeck St., W1M 8DN, 🖉 486 6600, Telex 22569 – 🛗 📺 🕭. 🏧. 🔼 AE ⑩
VISA
BH   a
M 10.50/10.75 **st.** and a la carte ⬧ 4.00 – ⥲ 7.50 – **220 rm** 68.00/88.00 **st.**, **2 suites** 150.00/300.00
st.

🏨🏨 **St. George's** (T.H.F.), Langham Pl., W1N 8QS, 🖉 580 0111, Telex 27274, ≼ – 🛗 📺 🕭. 🔼 AE
⑩ VISA
pp. 13-16   LT   a
M 13.50/14.50 **st.** and a la carte ⬧ 3.40 – ⥲ 7.25 – **85 rm** 78.00/100.00 **st.**, **3 suites.**

🏨🏨 **Cumberland** (T.H.F.), Marble Arch, W1A 4RF, 🖉 262 1234, Telex 22215 – 🛗 📺 🕭 &. 🏧. 🔼
AE ⑩ VISA. ⛛
pp. 13-16   LT   n
M (carving rest.) 16.00/18.00 **st.** and a la carte ⬧ 3.40 – ⥲ 6.50 – **894 rm** 72.00/92.00 **st.**, **9 suites.**

🏨 **Durrants,** 26-32 George St., W1H 6BJ, 🖉 935 8131, Telex 894919 – 🛗 📺 ⥽wc 🕭. 🏧. 🔼
AE ⑩ VISA
AH   e
M a la carte 13.20/17.30 **t.** ⬧ 3.25 – ⥲ 6.00 – **96 rm** 40.00/78.00 **st.**, **3 suites** 90.00/150.00 **st.**

🏨 **Sherlock Holmes** (Ladbroke), 108 Baker St., W1M 1LB, 🖉 486 6161, Telex 8954837 – 🛗 📺
⥽wc 🕭. 🏧. 🔼 AE ⑩ VISA
pp. 13-15   KT   a
M 11.25 **t.** and a la carte ⬧ 3.80 – ⥲ 6.75 – **125 rm** 75.00/100.00 **t.**

🏨 **Savoy Court,** Granville Pl., W1H 0EH, 🖉 408 0130, Telex 8955515 – 🛗 📺 ⥽wc 🛁wc 🕭 &.
🔼 AE ⑩ VISA
AK   c
M (buffet lunch)/dinner 9.50 **t.** and a la carte 11.00/18.05 **st.** ⬧ 3.00 – ⥲ 6.00 – **97 rm**
52.90/74.90 **st.**

🏨 **Dorset Square,** 39-40 Dorset Sq., NW1 6QN, 🖉 723 7874, Telex 263964, « Attractively furnished Regency town house » – 🛗 📺 ⥽wc 🛁wc 🕭. 🔼 AE ⑩ VISA
pp. 13-16   KT   s
M a la carte 14.50/19.50 **t.** – ⥲ 8.00 – **30 rm** 55.00/90.00 **t.**

🏨 **Regent Crest** (Crest), Carburton St., W1P 8EE, 🖉 388 2300, Telex 22453 – 🛗 ▤ rest 📺
⥽wc ⑩. 🏧. 🔼 AE ⑩ VISA. ⛛
pp. 13-16   LT   i
M 14.75 **st.** and a la carte ⬧ 3.75 – ⥲ 7.95 – **317 rm** 63.00/86.00 **st.**, **6 suites** 140.00/180.00 **st.**
– SB (weekends only) 58.00/66.00 **st.**

🏨 **Berners,** 10 Berners St., W1A 3BE, 🖉 636 1629, Telex 25759 – 🛗 ▤ rest 📺 ⥽wc 🕭 &. 🏧.
🔼 AE ⑩ VISA. ⛛
FJ   r
M (carving rest.) 10.75 **st.** and a la carte ⬧ 3.50 – ⥲ 6.95 – **233 rm** 72.00/99.00 **st.**

🏨 **Stratford Court,** 350 Oxford St., W1N 0BY, 🖉 629 7474, Telex 22270 – 🛗 📺 ⥽wc 🕭. 🔼
AE ⑩ VISA. ⛛
BK   n
M (carving rest.) 9.00 **st.** ⬧ 2.75 – ⥲ 6.00 – **131 rm** 59.90/79.90 **st.**

🏨 **Londoner,** 57-59 Welbeck St., W1M 8HS, 🖉 935 4442, Telex 894630 – 🛗 📺 ⥽wc 🕭. 🔼 AE
⑩ VISA. ⛛
BJ   v
M 9.50 **st.** and a la carte ⬧ 3.00 – ⥲ 7.00 – **142 rm** 65.00/85.00 **st.**

🏨 **Harewood,** Harewood Row, NW1 6SE, 🖉 262 2707, Telex 297225 – 🛗 📺 ⥽wc 🕭. 🔼 AE
⑩ VISA. ⛛
pp. 13-16   KT   x
M (grill rest. only) 8.00/8.50 **st.** and a la carte ⬧ 4.00 – ⥲ 4.00 – **93 rm** 48.50/65.00 **st.**

🏨 **Bryanston Court,** 56-60 Great Cumberland Pl., W1H 7FD, 🖉 262 3141, Group Telex 262076
– 🛗 📺 ⥽wc 🛁wc 🕭. 🔼 AE ⑩ VISA. ⛛
pp. 30 and 31   FY   z
M (closed Saturday, Sunday and Bank Holidays) a la carte 9.50/13.75 **t.** ⬧ 3.00 – ⥲ 5.00 –
53 rm 45.00/60.00 **st.**

🏨 **Hallam** without rest., 12 Hallam St., W1N 5LJ, 🖉 580 1166 – 🛗 📺 ⥽wc 🛁wc 🕭. 🔼 AE ⑩
VISA. ⛛
pp. 13-16   LT ⋅r
23 rm ⥲ 35.00/50.00 **st.**

🏨 **Concorde** without rest., 50 Great Cumberland Pl., W1H 7FD, 🖉 402 6169, Group Telex
262076 – 🛗 📺 ⥽wc 🛁wc 🕭. 🔼 AE ⑩ VISA. ⛛
pp. 30 and 31   FY   n
⥲ 5.00 – **28 rm** 36.00/46.00 **st.**

🏨 Blandford without rest., 80 Chiltern St., W1M 1PS, 🖉 486 3103 – 🛗 ⥽wc 🛁wc 🕭
KT   i
33 rm.

🛏 **Portman Court,** 28-30 Seymour St., W1H 5WD, 🖉 402 5401 – 📺 ⥽wc 🛁 🈂. 🔼 VISA. ⛛
30 rm ⥲ 26.00/45.00 **st.**
AK   a

331

XXX **Odins,** 27 Devonshire St., W1N 1RS, ℰ 935 7296 – AE   pp. 13-16 KT **n**
closed Saturday lunch, Sunday and Bank Holidays – **M** 12.50 **t.** (lunch) and a la carte 17.10/25.80 **t.**

XXX ❀ **Rue St. Jacques,** 5 Charlotte St., W1P 1HD, ℰ 637 0222, French rest. – 🍽, 🖪 AE ⓪ VISA
closed Saturday lunch, Sunday, 1 week at Christmas and Bank Holidays – **M** 15.00 **t.** (lunch) and a la carte 23.75/36.25 **t.**   pp. 13-16 MT **c**
Spec. Charlotte de coquilles St. Jacques, sauce légère, Le perdreau rôti aux deux sauces, Biscuit aux deux parfums.

XX **Gaylord,** 79-81 Mortimer St., W1N 7TB, ℰ 580 3615, Indian and Pakistani rest. – 🍽, 🖪 AE ⓪ VISA   pp. 13-16 LT **c**
M 7.75/8.50 **t.** and a la carte 🍷 3.20.

XX La Pavona, 5-7 Blandford St., W1H 3AF, ℰ 486 9696, Italian rest. – 🍽   BH **c**

XX **Lords Rendezvous,** 24 Finchley Rd, NW8 6ES, ℰ 586 4280, Chinese (Peking) rest. – 🖪 AE ⓪ VISA   pp. 13-16 JR **r**
closed 25 and 26 December – **M** 20.00 **t.** and a la carte 10.80/15.50 **t.**

XX Masako, 6-8 St. Christopher's Pl., W1M 5HB, ℰ 935 1579, Japanese rest. – 🍽   BJ **e**

XX **Asuka,** Berkeley Arcade, 209a Baker St., NW1 6AB, ℰ 486 5026, Japanese rest. – 🖪 AE ⓪ VISA   pp. 13-16 KT **u**
closed Saturday lunch, Sunday, last week December and Bank Holidays – **M** a la carte 14.40/23.00 **st.**

XX Tonino, Berkeley Court, 12 Glentworth St., NW1 5PG, ℰ 935 4220, Italian rest.   pp. 13-16 KT **c**

XX **Viceroy of India,** 3-5 Glentworth St., NW1 5PG, ℰ 486 3401, Indian rest. – 🖪 AE ⓪ VISA
closed 25 December – **M** 8.50/9.95 **t.** and a la carte 🍷 3.50.   pp. 13-16 KT **o**

XX **La Loggia,** 68 Edgware Rd, W2 2EG, ℰ 723 0554, Italian rest. – 🍽, 🖪 AE ⓪ VISA
closed Sunday and Bank Holidays – **M** a la carte 11.50/18.00 **t.** 🍷 2.95. pp. 30 and 31 FY **a**

X Le Muscadet, 25 Paddington St., W1M 3RF, ℰ 935 2883, French rest. – 🍽 pp. 13-16 KT **e**

X **L'Aventure,** 3 Blenheim Terr., NW8 4JS, ℰ 624 6232, French rest. – AE VISA
closed 25 to 30 December – **M** a la carte 12.50/15.80 **t.** 🍷 3.25.   pp. 13-16 JR **s**

X **Au Bois St. Jean,** 122 St. John's Wood High St., NW8 7SG, ℰ 722 0400, French rest. – 🖪 VISA   pp. 13-16 JS **e**
closed Saturday lunch, Easter and Christmas – **M** 12.00/14.75 **st.** 🍷 3.00.

X **Langan's Bistro,** 26 Devonshire St., W1N 1RS, ℰ 935 4531 – AE   pp. 13-16 KT **r**
closed Saturday lunch, Sunday and Bank Holidays – **M** 20.00 **t.** and a la carte 11.05/13.20 **t.**

X **Biagi's,** 39 Upper Berkeley St., W1H 7PG, ℰ 723 0394, Italian rest. – 🖪 AE ⓪ VISA
closed Bank Holidays – **M** a la carte 8.05/12.55 **t.** 🍷 2.65.   pp. 30 and 31 FY **c**

X **Il Barbino,** 64 Seymour St., W1H 5AF, ℰ 402 6866, Italian rest. – 🖪 AE ⓪ VISA
closed Saturday lunch, Sunday and Bank Holidays – **M** a la carte 9.30/15.10 **t.** 🍷 2.70.
pp. 30 and 31 FY **r**

X **Chaopraya,** 22 St. Christopher's Place, W1M 5DH, ℰ 486 0777, Thai rest. – 🖪 AE ⓪ VISA   BJ **o**
closed Saturday lunch, Sunday and Bank Holidays – **M** 10.00 **t.** and a la carte 🍷 3.20.

St. James's – ✉ W1/SW1/WC2 – pp. 26 and 27.

🏨 **Ritz,** Piccadilly, W1V 9DG, ℰ 493 8181, Telex 267200, « Elegant restaurant in Louix XV style » – 🛗 🔺 🔟 ☎ 🖪 AE ⓪ VISA ✂
M 19.50/29.50 **st.** and a la carte 🍷 6.75 – ☲ 9.25 – **128 rm** 130.00/190.00 **st.**, **14 suites** 320.00/590.00 **st.**   DN **a**

🏨 **Stafford** ⌂, 16-18 St. James's Pl., SW1A 1NJ, ℰ 493 0111, Telex 28602 – 🛗 🔟 ☎ 🔺 AE ⓪ VISA 🔺
M 17.00/20.00 **st.** and a la carte 🍷 4.30 – ☲ 7.50 – **62 rm** 115.00/155.00 **st.**, **5 suites** 175.00/350.00 **st.**   DN **u**

🏨 **Dukes** ⌂, 35 St. James's Pl., SW1A 1NY, ℰ 491 4840, Telex 28283 – 🛗 🔟 ☎ 🖪 AE ⓪ VISA 🔺
M 17.50 **t.** (lunch) and a la carte 23.00/28.00 **t.** – ☲ 8.00 – **52 rm** 110.00/145.00 **t.**, **16 suites** 200.00/450.00 **t.**   EP **x**

🏨 **Cavendish** (T.H.F.), Jermyn St., SW1Y 6JF, ℰ 930 2111, Telex 263187 – 🛗 🍽 rest 🔟 ☎ 🔺 🅿 🔺 🖪 AE ⓪ VISA
M (bar lunch Saturday) 14.00 **st.** (lunch) and a la carte 18.00/26.25 **st.** 🍷 4.50 – ☲ 8.00 – **253 rm** 81.00/101.00 **st.**   EN **i**

🏨 **Royal Trafalgar Thistle** (Thistle), Whitcomb St., WC2H 7HG, ℰ 930 4477, Telex 298564 – 🛗 🍽 rest 🔟 ⌿wc ☎ 🖪 AE ⓪ VISA   GM **r**
M a la carte 10.50/15.50 **t.** 🍷 3.85 – ☲ 6.25 – **108 rm** 60.00/95.00 **st.**

🏨 **Pastoria** without rest., 3-6 St. Martin's St., WC2H 7HL, ℰ 930 8641, Telex 25538 – 🛗 🔟 ⌿wc ☎ 🖪 AE ⓪ VISA 🔺   GM **v**
☲ 6.00 – **54 rm** 60.00/80.00 **st.**

XXXXX Maxim's de Paris, 32-34 Panton St., SW1, ℰ 839 4809, French rest., Dancing – ▤   GM a

XXXX **A L'Ecu de France,** 111 Jermyn St., SW1Y 6HB, ℰ 930 2837, French rest. – ▤. ◪ ᴬᴱ ◉
VISA
closed lunch Saturday and Sunday – **M** 14.75/21.75 **st.** and a la carte ⌁ 5.50.   FM z

XXX ✿ **Suntory,** 72-73 St. James's St., SW1A 1PH, ℰ 409 0201, Japanese rest. – ▤. ◪ ᴬᴱ ◉
VISA
closed Sunday and Bank Holidays – **M** 25.00 **t.** and a la carte 12.20/26.20 **t.**   EP z
Spec. Teppan-Yaki, Shabu-Shabu, Tempura.

XX **Le Caprice,** Arlington House, Arlington St., SW1A 1RT, ℰ 629 2239 – ▤. ◪ ᴬᴱ ◉ *VISA*
closed Saturday lunch and 24 December-2 January – **M** a la carte 11.00/15.25 **t.**   DN c

XX Green's, 36 Duke St., SW1Y 6BR, ℰ 930 4566, English rest. – ▤   EN n

▣ **Soho** – ✉ W1/WC2 – pp. 26 and 27.

XXX **La Bastide,** 50 Greek St., W1V 5LQ, ℰ 734 3300 – ◪ ᴬᴱ ◉ *VISA*   GK e
closed Saturday lunch, Sunday and Bank Holidays – **M** 12.50 **t.** and a la carte 14.60/16.40 **t.**

XXX **Red Fort,** 77 Dean St., W1V 5HA, ℰ 437 2525, Indian rest. – ◪ ᴬᴱ ◉ *VISA*   FJK r
closed 25 and 26 December – **M** a la carte 7.40/14.85 **t.**

XXX **Leonis Quo Vadis,** 26-29 Dean St., W1V 6LL, ℰ 437 9585, Italian rest. – ◪ ᴬᴱ ◉ *VISA* FK u
closed lunch Saturday and Sunday. 25 December, 1 January – **M** a la carte 12.20/19.65 **t.**

XX **Au Jardin des Gourmets,** 5 Greek St., Soho Sq., W1V 5LA, ℰ 437 1816, French rest. – ◪
ᴬᴱ ◉ *VISA*   GJ a
closed lunch Saturday and Bank Holidays, Sunday, Easter and Christmas – **M** 12.50/23.50 **t.**
and a la carte 14.15/23.45 **t.** ⌁ 2.75.

XX **L'Escargot,** 48 Greek St., W1V 5LQ, ℰ 437 2679 – ◪ ᴬᴱ ◉ *VISA*   GK e
closed Saturday lunch, Sunday, Easter, Christmas and Bank Holidays – **M** a la carte
approx. 18.00 **t.**

XX **Gay Hussar,** 2 Greek St., W1V 6NB, ℰ 437 0973, Hungarian rest. – ▤   GJ c
closed Sunday – **M** 10.50 **t.** (lunch) and a la carte 14.00/19.50 **t.** ⌁ 3.50.

XX **Chesa (Swiss Centre),** 2 New Coventry St., W1V 3HG, ℰ 734 1291 – ▤. ◪ ᴬᴱ ◉ *VISA*
M 15.00/18.50 **st.** ⌁ 1.30.   GM n

XX **Venezia,** 21 Great Chapel St., W1V 3AQ, ℰ 437 6506, Italian rest. – ◪ ᴬᴱ ◉ *VISA*   FJ a
closed Saturday lunch, Sunday and Bank Holidays – **M** a la carte 10.80/13.50 **t.** ⌁ 2.50.

XX **Kaya,** 22-25 Dean St., W1V 5AL, ℰ 437 6630, Korean rest. – ▤. ◪ ᴬᴱ ◉ *VISA*   FJ i
closed lunch Saturday and Sunday – **M** 17.00 **t.** and a la carte ⌁ 3.30.

XX **Last Days of the Raj,** 42-43 Dean St., W1V 5AR, ℰ 439 0972, Indian rest. – ▤. ◪ ᴬᴱ ◉
VISA   FK n
M 15.00/18.00 **st.** and a la carte 9.15/12.50 **st.**

XX **Poons,** 4 Leicester St., WC2, ℰ 437 1528, Chinese rest. – ▤   GM i
closed Sunday and Christmas – **M** 6.00 **t.** and a la carte 4.20/11.00 **t.**

XX **Old Budapest,** 6 Greek St., W1, ℰ 437 2006, Hungarian rest. – ◪ ᴬᴱ *VISA*   GJ c
closed Sunday and Bank Holidays – **M** 9.00/15.60 **t.** and a la carte 10.60/15.60 **t.** ⌁ 4.50.

XX Rugantino, 26 Romilly St., W1V 5TQ, ℰ 437 5302, Italian rest.   GK u

XX Mayflower, 68-70 Shaftesbury Av., W1, ℰ 734 9207, Chinese (Canton) rest. – ▤   FL o

XX Fuji, 36-40 Brewer St., W1R 3HP, ℰ 734 0957, Japanese rest.   FL c

X Alastair Little, 49 Frith St., W1, ℰ 734 5183   FK o

X **Frith's,** 14 Frith St., W1V 5TS, ℰ 439 3370 – ◪ ᴬᴱ ◉ *VISA*   FGK s
closed Saturday lunch and Sunday – **M** 18.00 **t.**

X **Chiang Mai,** 48 Frith St., W1, ℰ 437 7444, Thai rest. – ◪ ᴬᴱ *VISA*   FGK o
M a la carte 6.75/9.75 **st.** ⌁ 2.75.

X **Fung Shing,** 15 Lisle St., WC2H 7BE, ℰ 437 1539, Chinese (Canton) rest. – ◪ ᴬᴱ ◉
VISA   GL a
M 8.00/15.00 **t.** and a la carte 9.70/14.00 **t.**

X **Gallery Rendezvous,** 53-55 Beak St., W1R 3LF, ℰ 734 0445, Chinese (Peking) rest. – ▤.
◪ ᴬᴱ ◉ *VISA*   EL a
M a la carte approx. 9.00 ⌁ 3.20.

✗ **Joy King Lau,** 3 Leicester St., WC2H 7BL, ☎ 437 1132, Chinese rest. – 🅰🅴 ⓞ   GM **e**
   M a la carte 12.50/20.80 **t.** ⌊ 2.25.

✗ **Saigon,** 45 Frith St., W1V 5TE, ☎ 437 7109, Vietnamese rest. – 🔄 🅰🅴 ⓞ 𝑉𝐼𝑆𝐴   FGK **x**
   closed Sunday and Bank Holidays – **M** 11.00 **t.** and a la carte approx. 12.00 **t.**

✗ **Cafe Loire,** 12 Great Marlborough St., W1, ☎ 434 2666, French rest. – 🔄 🅰🅴 ⓞ 𝑉𝐼𝑆𝐴   EK **e**
   closed Saturday lunch, Sunday and Bank Holidays – **M** 11.65/15.60 **t.** ⌊ 3.20.

✗ **Nam Long,** 40 Frith St., W1, ☎ 439 1835, Vietnamese rest. – 🔄 𝑉𝐼𝑆𝐴   GK **v**
   closed Sunday and Bank Holidays – **M** 14.00 **t.** and a la carte 10.00/13.90 **t.** ⌊ 2.50.

✗ Diamond, 23 Lisle St., WC2, ☎ 437 2517, Chinese (Canton) rest. – ▤   GL **a**

Strand and Covent Garden – ✉ WC2 – p. 31.

🏨 **Savoy,** Strand, WC2R 0EU, ☎ 836 4343, Telex 24234 – 🛗 📺 ☎ ⇔ 🅰 🔄 🅰🅴 ⓞ 𝑉𝐼𝑆𝐴
   ⌘   EX **a**
   M Grill *(closed Saturday lunch and Sunday)* a la carte 18.40/29.70 **st.** ⌊ 3.40 – **River** 18.15/
   31.35 **st.** and a la carte ⌊ 3.40 – ⌷ 8.25 – **200 rm** 120.00/195.00 **st.**, **48 suites** 230.00/450.00 **st.**

🏨 **Howard,** 12 Temple Pl., WC2R 2PR, ☎ 836 3555, Telex 268047 – 🛗 ▤ 📺 ☎ ⇔ 🅰 🔄 🅰🅴
   ⓞ 𝑉𝐼𝑆𝐴 ⌘   FV **e**
   M a la carte 20.10/33.00 **st.** – ⌷ 9.00 – **141 rm** 145.00/161.00 **st.**, **2 suites** 170.00/299.00 **st.**

🏨 **Waldorf** (T.H.F.), Aldwych, WC2B 4DD, ☎ 836 2400, Telex 24574 – 🛗 ▤ rest 📺 ☎ 🅰 🔄
   🅰🅴 ⓞ 𝑉𝐼𝑆𝐴   EV **x**
   closed Christmas and New Year – **M** *(closed Saturday lunch, Sunday and Bank Holidays)*
   16.50/19.50 **st.** and a la carte ⌊ 5.60 – ⌷ 7.25 – **310 rm** 73.00/90.00 **st.**

✗✗✗✗ **Boulestin,** 1a Henrietta St., WC2E 8PS, ☎ 836 7061, French rest. – ▤. 🔄 🅰🅴 ⓞ 𝑉𝐼𝑆𝐴   EV **r**
   closed Saturday lunch, Sunday, last 3 weeks August, 1 week Christmas and Bank Holidays –
   M 14.50 **t.** (lunch) and a la carte 19.20/25.00 **t.** ⌊ 5.00.

✗✗✗ **Inigo Jones,** 14 Garrick St., WC2E 9BJ, ☎ 836 6456 – ▤. 🔄 🅰🅴 ⓞ 𝑉𝐼𝑆𝐴   DV **e**
   closed Saturday lunch, Sunday, 24 December-5 January and Bank Holidays – **M** 16.25 **t.**
   (lunch) and a la carte ⌊ 5.85.

✗✗✗ **Simpson's-in-the-Strand,** 100 Strand, WC2R 0EW, ☎ 836 9112, English rest. – ▤. 🔄 🅰🅴
   ⓞ 𝑉𝐼𝑆𝐴   EV **o**
   closed Sunday, Easter, 25 December and Bank Holidays – **M** a la carte 14.00/19.50 **st.** ⌊ 3.00.

✗✗✗ **Thomas de Quincey's,** 36 Tavistock St., WC2E 7PB, ☎ 240 3972 – 🔄 🅰🅴 ⓞ 𝑉𝐼𝑆𝐴   EV **c**
   closed Saturday lunch, Sunday and Bank Holidays – **M** a la carte 18.55/24.95 **t.** ⌊ 3.60.

✗✗ **Interlude,** 7-8 Bow St., WC2E 7AH, ☎ 379 6473, French rest. – ▤. 🔄 🅰🅴 ⓞ 𝑉𝐼𝑆𝐴   DEV **x**
   closed Saturday lunch and Sunday – **M** 17.50/30.00 **st.** ⌊ 3.00.

✗✗ **Tourment d'Amour,** 19 New Row, WC2N 4LA, ☎ 240 5348, French rest. – 🔄 🅰🅴 ⓞ
   𝑉𝐼𝑆𝐴   DV **z**
   closed Saturday lunch, Sunday and Christmas – **M** 18.00 **t.**

✗✗ Sheekey's, 28-32 St. Martin's Court, WC2N 4AL, ☎ 240 2565, Seafood – ▤   DV **v**

✗✗ **Chez Solange,** 35 Cranbourn St., WC2H 7AD, ☎ 836 5886, French rest. – ▤. 🔄 🅰🅴 ⓞ
   𝑉𝐼𝑆𝐴   DV **i**
   closed Sunday lunch – **M** 13.00 **t.** and a la carte 14.75/20.00 **t.**

✗✗ **Bates,** 11 Henrietta St., WC2, ☎ 240 7600 – 🔄 🅰🅴 ⓞ 𝑉𝐼𝑆𝐴   DV **u**
   closed Saturday lunch, Sunday and Bank Holidays – **M** 15.00 **st.** and a la carte 12.90/20.20 **t.**

✗✗ Azami, 13-15 West St., WC2H 9BL, ☎ 240 0634, Japanese rest.   pp. 26 and 27   GK **z**

✗✗ **Frère Jacques,** 38 Longacre, WC2, ☎ 836 7823, Seafood – ▤. 🔄 🅰🅴 ⓞ 𝑉𝐼𝑆𝐴   DV **n**
   M a la carte 11.45/20.50 **t.** ⌊ 3.25.

✗ **Poons of Covent Garden,** 41 King St., WC2E 8JS, ℰ 240 1743, Chinese (Canton) rest. –
AE ⓞ VISA   DV r
closed Sunday and 24 to 27 December – **M** a la carte 6.50/15.75 **t.** ⓘ 4.50.

✗ **Café Pelican,** 45 St. Martins Lane, WC2N 4EJ, ℰ 379 0309, French rest., « Art deco »
            DX e

✗ **Magnos Brasserie,** 65A Long Acre, WC2E 9JH, ℰ 836 6077, French rest. – 🔁 AE VISA
closed Saturday lunch, Sunday and 24 December-2 January – **M** 8.45 **st.** (dinner) and a la
carte 13.70/20.90 **t.** ⓘ 4.45.   EV e

✗ **Laguna,** 50 St. Martin's Lane, WC2N 4EA, ℰ 836 0960, Italian rest. – 🔁 AE ⓞ VISA   DV z
closed Sunday and Bank Holidays – **M** 7.50/8.50 and a la carte ⓘ 2.35.

✗ **Flounders,** 19 Tavistock St., WC2, ℰ 836 3925, Seafood – 🔲   EV a

✗ **Happy Wok,** 52 Floral St., WC2, ℰ 836 3696, Chinese rest. – 🔁 AE ⓞ VISA   DV x
closed Sunday – **M** 19.00 **t.** and a la carte 6.50/10.80 **t.**

✗ **Grimes,** 6 Garrick St., WC2R 9BH, ℰ 836 7008, Seafood – 🔁 AE ⓞ VISA   DV e
closed Saturday lunch, Sunday, 24 to 27 December and Bank Holidays – **M** a la carte
13.35/14.85 **t.** ⓘ 2.60.

Le Grand Londres (GREATER LONDON) *est composé de la City et de 32 arrondisse-*
ments administratifs (Borough) eux-mêmes divisés en quartiers ou villages ayant
conservé leur caractère propre (Area).

Victoria – ⊠ SW1 – Except where otherwise stated see p. 30.

🏨 **St. James Court,** Buckingham Gate, SW1 6AF, ℰ 834 6655, Telex 938075 – 🕼 🔳 rest ☎.
🏋 🔁 AE ⓞ VISA. ✂   CV v
M (see **Auberge de Provence** and **Inn of Happiness** below) – �byₐ 8.00 – **391 rm** 95.00/135.00 **s.**,
10 suites 140.00/165.00 **s.**

🏨 **Goring,** 15 Beeston Pl., Grosvenor Gdns, SW1W 0JW, ℰ 834 8211, Telex 919166 – 🕼 🔳 📺
☎. 🏋 🔁 AE ⓞ VISA. ✂   BV a
M 14.00/16.00 **s.** and a la carte ⓘ 5.00 – �byₐ 7.00 – **90 rm** 75.00/115.00 **st.**, **4 suites** 150.00 **st.**

🏨 **Royal Horseguards Thistle** (Thistle), 2 Whitehall Court, SW1A 2EX, ℰ 839 3400, Telex
917096 – 🕼 🔳 rest 📺 ☎. 🏋 🔁 AE ⓞ VISA. ✂   pp. 17-20 NV a
M a la carte 18.00/25.00 **t.** ⓘ 3.50 – �byₐ 6.75 – **284 rm** 70.00/100.00 **t.**, **6 suites.**

🏨 **Stakis St. Ermin's** (Stakis), Caxton St., SW1H 0QW, ℰ 222 7888, Telex 917731 – 🕼 🔳 rest
📺 ☎. 🏋 🔁 AE ⓞ VISA. ✂   CV a
M (carving rest.) 11.50 **t.** and a la carte – �byₐ 6.75 – **250 rm** 71.50/93.50 **t.**, **6 suites** 150.00 **t.**

🏨 **Royal Westminster Thistle** (Thistle), 49 Buckingham Palace Rd, SW1W 0QT, ℰ 834 1821,
Telex 916821 – 🕼 🔳 🏋 🔁 AE ⓞ VISA. ✂   BV z
M 14.95/21.95 **t.** and a la carte ⓘ 4.00 – �byₐ 7.00 – **118 rm** 85.00/135.00 **st.**, **18 suites.**

🏨 **Grosvenor,** 101 Buckingham Palace Rd, SW1W 0SJ, ℰ 834 9494, Telex 916006 – 🕼 🔳 rest 📺
⊏ᵂᶜ ☎. 🏋 – **365 rm.**   BV e

🏨 **Rubens,** Buckingham Palace Rd, SW1W 0PS, ℰ 834 6600 – 🕼 🔳 rest 📺 ⊏ᵂᶜ ☎. 🏋
M (carving rest.) – **191 rm.**   BV n

🏨 **Ebury Court,** 26 Ebury St., SW1W 0LU, ℰ 730 8147 – 🕼 ⊏ᵂᶜ ☎. 🔁 VISA   AV i
M a la carte 8.50/14.10 **t.** ⓘ 2.10 – **39 rm** ⊏ 36.00/67.00 **t.**

🏨 **Hamilton House,** 60-64 Warwick Way, SW1V 1SA, ℰ 821 7113 – 📺 ⊏ᵂᶜ ☎. 🔁 VISA   BX n
M *(closed Saturday)* (grill rest. only) (dinner only) a la carte approx. 5.80 **t.** ⓘ 1.50 – **40 rm**
⊏ 28.00/50.00 **st.** – SB (November-March) 44.00/52.00 **st.**

🏠 **Chesham House,** 64-66 Ebury St., SW1W 9QD, ℰ 730 8513 – 📺. AE ⓞ VISA. ✂   AX x
23 rm ⊏ 20.00/36.00 **st.**

🏠 **Elizabeth,** 37 Eccleston Sq., SW1V 1PB, ℰ 828 6812 – 🔟. ✂   pp. 17-20 LY c
24 rm ⊏ 22.00/50.00 **st.**

🏠 **Collin House,** 104 Ebury Rd, SW1W 9QD, ℰ 730 8031 – 📺 🔟ᵂᶜ. ✂   AX r
11 rm ⊏ 27.00/38.00 **t.**

✗✗✗ 🕸🕸 **Simply Nico,** 48a Rochester Row, SW1, ℰ 630 8061, French rest. – 🔁 AE ⓞ VISA
closed Saturday, Sunday, 3 weeks August and 1 week Christmas – **M** (booking essential)
28.00/33.00 **t.** ⓘ 6.50   CX a
Spec. Terrine de foie gras et sa gelée au Sauternes, Suprême de canard au fumet de cèpes, Tulipe à la vanille.

✗✗✗ **Auberge de Provence,** (at St. James Court H.) Buckingham Gate, SW1 6AF, ℰ 834 6655,
Telex 938075, French rest. – 🔳. 🔁 AE ⓞ VISA   CV i
M 15.00 **t.** and a la carte ⓘ 4.00.

✗✗✗ **Inn of Happiness,** (at St James Court H.) Buckingham Gate, SW1 6AF, ℰ 834 6655, Telex
938075, Chinese rest.   CV i

✗✗✗ **Lockets,** Marsham Court, Marsham St., SW1P 4JY, ℰ 834 9552, English rest. – 🔁 AE ⓞ
VISA   pp. 17-20 MY z
closed Saturday lunch Sunday and Bank Holidays – **M** a la carte 11.65/16.65 **t.** ⓘ 3.00.

✗✗✗ **Kundan,** 3 Horseferry Rd, SW1P 2AN, ℰ 834 3434, Indian and Pakistani rest. – 🔁 AE ⓞ
VISA   pp. 17-20 NXY a
closed Sunday and Bank Holidays – **M** 12.00/15.00 **t.** ⓘ 7.50.

✗✗✗ **Santini,** 29 Ebury St., SW1W 0NZ, ℰ 730 4094, Italian rest. – 🔳. 🔁 AE ⓞ VISA   ABV v
closed lunch Saturday and Sunday – **M** 11.00 **t.** (lunch) and a la carte 15.90/21.50 **t.** ⓘ 4.00.

XX **Ken Lo's Memories of China,** 67-69 Ebury St., SW1W 0NZ, ℰ 730 7734, Chinese rest. –
🍽. 🔼 AE ⓪ VISA   AX u
closed Sunday and Bank Holidays – **M** 16.50/21.50 **t.** and a la carte 12.45/17.90 **t.**

XX ❀ **Le Mazarin,** 30 Winchester St., SW1V 4UZ, ℰ 828 3366, French rest. – 🍽. 🔼 AE ⓪
closed Sunday, 1 week at Christmas and Bank Holidays – **M** (dinner only) 22.50 **st.** ♦ 4.00
Spec. Fricassée de poulet fermier au basilic, Tranchettes d'onglet poêlé aux échalotes, Mousse au café et ses
noisettes croustillantes.   pp. 17-20 LZ i

XX **Kym's,** 70-71 Wilton Rd, SW1V 1DE, ℰ 828 8931, Chinese (Szechuan, Hunan) rest. – 🍽. 🔼
AE VISA   BX v
closed 25 and 26 December – **M** 7.50/10.50 **t.** and a la carte 8.20/12.40 **t.** ♦ 2.75.

XX **Villa Claudius,** 10a The Broadway, SW1, ℰ 222 3338, Italian rest. – 🔼 AE ⓪ VISA
closed Saturday, Sunday, Easter, Christmas and Bank Holidays – **M** 10.00 **t.** and a la carte
12.75/15.20 **t.** ♦ 2.75.   pp. 17-20 MX a

XX **Dolphin Brasserie,** Dolphin Square, Chichester St., SW1V 3LX, ℰ 828 3207, French rest.,
« Maritime Theme » – 🔼 AE ⓪ VISA   pp. 17-20 LZ e
M 12.80/18.50 **t.** ♦ 3.80.

XX **Pomegranates,** 94 Grosvenor Rd, SW1V 3LG, ℰ 828 6560 – 🔼 AE VISA   pp. 17-20 LMZ a
closed Saturday lunch and Sunday – **M** 17.50/19.50 **t.** ♦ 3.90.

XX **Eatons,** 49 Elizabeth St., SW1W 9PP, ℰ 730 0074 – 🔼 AE ⓪ VISA   AX a
closed Saturday, Sunday and Bank Holidays – **M** a la carte 11.20/13.30 **s.** ♦ 3.20.

XX **Ciboure,** 21 Eccleston St., SW1W 9LX, ℰ 730 2505, French rest. – 🔼 AE ⓪ VISA AX z
closed Saturday lunch and Sunday – **M** 12.50/18.50 **t.** and a la carte 14.90/17.75 **t.**

XX **Hoizin,** 72-73 Wilton Rd, SW1V 1DE, ℰ 630 5107, Seafood – 🍽. 🔼 AE VISA   BX v
closed Sunday – **M** a la carte 8.10/17.20 **t.**

XX Hunan, 51 Pimlico Rd, SW1W 8WE, ℰ 730 5712, Chinese rest.   pp. 17-20 KZ a

XX **Gran Paradiso,** 52 Wilton Rd, SW1V 1DE, ℰ 828 5818, Italian rest. – 🔼 AE ⓪ VISA BX a
closed Saturday lunch, Sunday and Bank Holidays – **M** a la carte 11.00/13.50 **t.** ♦ 2.30.

X **La Fontana,** 101 Pimlico Rd, SW1W 8PH, ℰ 730 6630, Italian rest. – AE ⓪ VISA
closed Bank Holidays – **M** a la carte 12.80/16.40 ♦ 3.30.   pp. 28 and 29 FT o

X La Poule au Pot, 231 Ebury St., SW1W 8UT, ℰ 730 7763, French rest.   pp. 17-20 KY n

X **Mimmo d'Ischia,** 61 Elizabeth St., SW1W 9PP, ℰ 730 5406, Italian rest.   AX o
M a la carte approx. 13.50 **t.** ♦ 3.60.

X **Tate Gallery Rest.,** Tate Gallery, Millbank, SW1P 4RG, ℰ 834 6754, English rest., « Rex
Whistler murals » – 🍽   pp. 17-20 NY c
closed Sunday, 17 April, 24 to 27 December, 1 January and Bank Holidays – **M** (lunch only) a
la carte 8.10/16.80 **t.** ♦ 3.90.

X **Bumbles,** 16 Buckingham Palace Rd, SW1W 0QP, ℰ 828 2903, Bistro – 🔼 AE ⓪ VISA
closed Saturday lunch, Sunday and Bank Holidays – **M** 10.25 **t.** and a la carte 10.65/13.45 **t.**
♦ 2.50.   BV c

X **Villa Medici,** 35 Belgrave Rd, SW1, ℰ 828 3613, Italian rest. – 🔼 AE ⓪ VISA   BX c
closed Saturday lunch, Sunday and Bank Holidays – **M** a la carte 10.20/15.10 **t.** ♦ 2.70.

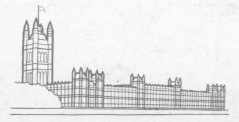

CAR REPAIRS IN LONDON

RÉPARATION DE VOITURES A LONDRES

RIPARAZIONE DI VETTURA A LONDRA

KFZ-REPARATUR IN LONDON

In the event of a breakdown in London, the location of the nearest dealer for your make of car can be obtained by calling the following numbers between 9am and 5pm.

En cas de panne à Londres, vous pouvez obtenir l'adresse du plus proche concessionnaire de votre marque d'automobile en appelant les numéros suivants entre 9 heures et 17 heures.

In caso di guasto a Londra, Vi sara' possibile ottenere l'indirizzo del concessionario della vostra marca di automobile, chiamando i seguenti numeri dalle ore 9.00 alle ore 17.00.

Im Pannenfall können Sie die Adresse der nächstgelegenen Reparaturwerkstatt ihrer Automarke zwischen 9 Uhr und 17 Uhr unter folgenden Telefon-Nr. erfahren.

ALFA ROMEO	Alfa Romeo (GB) Ltd P.O. Box 5 Poulton Close Dover, Kent (0304) 212 500	**AUSTIN ROVER**	(includes Morris, Triumph, MG, Vanden Plas) Kennings Northern The Hyde Colindale NW9 (01) 205 5402
BMW	BMW (GB) Ltd Ellesfield Av. Bracknell Berks. RG12 4TA (0344) 426 565	**CITROEN**	Citroen Cars Ltd Mill St. Slough Berks. SL2 5DE (0753) 23808
COLT- MITSUBISHI	Colt Car Co. Ltd Watermore Cirencester Glos. GL7 1LS (0285) 5777 ext 204/5	**DATSUN- NISSAN**	Datsun (UK) Ltd New Rd Durrington Worthing West Sussex (0903) 68561
FIAT	Fiat Information Service PO Box 39 Windsor Berkshire SL4 3SP 0753 856 307	**FORD**	Ford Motor Co. Ltd Becket House Chapel High Brentwood Essex CM14 4BY (0277) 251100
HONDA	Honda (UK) Ltd Power Rd Chiswick London W4 5YT (01) 747 1400	**JAGUAR**	H.R. Owen Ltd Lyttleton Rd Barnet London (01) 458 7111
LAND ROVER- RANGE ROVER	Land Rover Ltd Lode Lane Solihull West Midlands (021) 743 4242 ex. 3389/4746	**MAZDA**	Mazda Cars (UK) Ltd Mount Ephraim Tunbridge Wells Kent TN5 8BS (0892) 40123

MERCEDES BENZ
Mercedes Benz (UK) Ltd
403 Edgware Rd
Colindale
London NW9
(01) 205 1212

PORSCHE
Porsche Cars (GB) Ltd
23-30 Richfield Av.
Reading
Berks. RG1 8PH
(0734) 303 666

RELIANT
Reliant Motor PLC
Watling St.
Twogate
Tamworth
Staffs.
(0827) 250 000

RENAULT
Renault Ltd
Western Av.
Acton
London W3 ORZ
(01) 992 3481

SAAB
Saab (GB) Ltd
Saab House
Fieldhouse Lane
Marlow
Bucks.
(06284) 6977

SKODA
Skoda (GB) Ltd
150 Goswell Rd
London EC1
(01) 253 7441

TALBOT-PEUGEOT
Warwick Wright Motors
Ltd
Chiswick Roundabout
North Circular Rd
Chiswick
London W4
(01) 995 1466

TOYOTA
Toyota (GB) Ltd
The Quadrangle
Redhill
Surrey RH1 1PS
(0737) 68585

VAUXHALL-OPEL
Hamilton Motors Ltd
466-490 Edgware Rd
London W2 1EL
(01) 723 0022
(01) 961 1177
(24 hr recovery)

VOLKSWAGEN-AUDI
V.A.G. (UK) Ltd
Yeomans Drive
Blakelands
Milton Keynes
Bucks. MK14 5AN
(0908) 679121

VOLVO
Volvo Concessionnaires
Ltd
Raeburn Rd South
Ipswich
Suffolk IP3 OES
(0473) 715131 ext 3459

LONGBRIDGE Warw. – see Warwick.

LONG EATON Derbs. 402 403 404 Q 25 – see Nottingham (Notts.).

LONGFORD West Midlands 403 404 P 26 – see Coventry.

LONGHAM Dorset – see Ferndown.

LONGHORSLEY Northumb. 401 402 O 18 – see Morpeth.

LONG MELFORD Suffolk 404 W 27 – pop. 2 739 – ECD : Thursday – ✆ 0787 Sudbury.
See : Holy Trinity Church★ 15C.
♦ London 62 – ♦Cambridge 34 – Colchester 18 – ♦Ipswich 24.

　🏠　**Bull** (T.H.F.), Hall St., CO10 9JG, ℰ 78494, « Part 15C coaching inn » – 📺 �wc 🐾 🅿. 🖭
　　　🅰🅴 🕥 *VISA*
　　　M (buffet lunch)/dinner a la carte 10.95/23.90 **st.** ≀ 3.40 – ⟷ 5.65 – **27 rm** 44.00/56.00 **st.**

　🏠　**Black Lion,** The Green, CO10 9DN, ℰ 312356, ☞ – 📺 �wc ☎ 🅿. 🖭 🅰🅴 🕥 *VISA*. ⅝
　　　M *(closed Sunday dinner and Monday)* 12.00/15.00 **t.** ≀ 2.00 – **8 rm** ⟷ 29.00/45.00 **t.** –
　　　SB (weekends only) 46.00/57.00 **st.**

　♨　**Crown Inn,** Hall St., CO10 9JL, ℰ 77666 – 📺 �wc. 🖭 🅰🅴 🕥 *VISA*
　　　M 6.50/15.00 **t.** and a la carte ≀ 3.00 – **13 rm** ⟷ 20.00/42.00 **t.** – SB (October-May) 47.00/89.00 **st.**

　✗✗✗　**Chimneys,** Hall St., CO10 9JR, ℰ 79806, « Part 16C cottage », ☞ – 🖭 *VISA*
　　　closed Sunday dinner and Monday – **M** 9.50 **t.** (lunch) and a la carte 17.00/20.35 **t.** ≀ 3.25.

LONGNOR Staffs. 402 403 404 O 24 – pop. 381 – ✉ Buxton – ✆ 029 883.
♦ London 161 – Derby 29 – ♦Manchester 31 – ♦Stoke-on-Trent 22.

　♨　**Ye Olde Cheshire Cheese,** High St., SK17 0NS, ℰ 218 – 🅿. 🖭 🅰🅴 🕥 *VISA*. ⅝
　　　M *(closed Sunday dinner and Monday)* 6.00/11.50 **t.** and a la carte ≀ 3.50 – **5 rm**
　　　⟷ 15.00/25.00 **st.**

LOOE Cornwall 403 G 32 The West Country G. – pop. 4 279 – ECD : Thursday – ✆ 050 36.
See : Site★ – Monkey Sanctuary★ AC.
🏌18 Looe Bin Down ℰ 050 34 (Widegates) 247, E : 3 m.
🛈 The Guildhall, Fore St. ℰ 2072 (summer only).
♦ London 264 – ♦Plymouth 21 – Truro 39.

　🏠　**Rock Towers,** Marine Drive, Hannafore Rd, West Looe, PL13 2DQ, ℰ 2140, ≤ Looe Bay and
　　　harbour – �wc 🅿
　　　27 rm.

　🏠　**Klymiarven** ⌕, Barbican Hill, East Looe, PL13 1BH, ℰ 2333, ≤ Looe and harbour, 🏊 heated,
　　　☞ – 📺 �wc 🎞wc 🅿
　　　closed December-February – **M** (bar lunch)/dinner 8.00 **t.** ≀ 2.90 – **13 rm** ⟷ 14.00/39.50 **t.** –
　　　SB (except November) 40.50/52.50 **st.**

　🏠　**Fieldhead,** Portruan Rd, Hannafore, PL13 2DR, ℰ 2689, ≤ Looe Bay, 🏊 heated, ☞ – �wc
　　　🎞 🅿. 🖭 🅰🅴 🕥 *VISA*. ⅝
　　　closed December and January – **M** 4.50/7.50 **t.** and a la carte ≀ 2.95 – **14 rm** ⟷ 17.00/42.00 **t.**
　　　– SB (except summer) 40.00/50.00 **st.**

　✗✗　**Trelaske Country** ⌕ with rm, Polperro Rd, Trelaske, PL13 2JS, W : 2 ¼ m. by A 387
　　　ℰ 2159, ≤, ☞ – 🎞wc 🅿. 🖭 🅰🅴 🕥 *VISA*
　　　closed 5 January-5 February – **M** *(closed Sunday dinner and Monday)* (bar lunch)/dinner
　　　10.25 **t.** and a la carte 10.10/12.85 **t.** ≀ 3.25 – **4 rm** ⟷ 22.35/32.70 **t.** – SB (September-April)
　　　42.00/44.00 **st.**

　at Sandplace N : 2 ¼ m. on A 387 – ✉ ✆ 050 36 Looe :

　🏠　**Polraen Country House,** PL13 1PJ, ℰ 3956, ☞ – 🎞wc 🅿. 🖭 *VISA*
　　　M (bar lunch)/dinner 13.00 **st.** ≀ 2.95 – **5 rm** ⟷ 25.00/35.00 **st.** – SB (October-April)(except
　　　Easter and Christmas) 45.00 **st.**

　at Widegates NE : 3 ½ m. on B 3253 – ✉ Looe – ✆ 050 34 Widegates :

　⌂　**Coombe Farm** ⌕, PL13 1QN, ℰ 223, ≤ countryside, 🏊 heated, ☞, park – 🅿. ⅝
　　　March-October – **8 rm** ⟷ 15.00/29.00 **st.**

　at Talland Bay SW : 4 m. by A 387 – ✉ Looe – ✆ 0503 Polperro :

　🏠　**Talland Bay** ⌕, PL13 2JB, ℰ 72667, ≤, « Country house atmosphere », 🏊 heated, ☞ – 📺
　　　�wc ☎ 🅖. 🅿 ⅝
　　　closed mid December-mid February – **M** (bar lunch in winter)(buffet lunch in summer)/
　　　dinner 11.00 **t.** and a la carte ≀ 2.50 – **23 rm** ⟷ (dinner included) 28.50/106.00 **t.**, **1 suite** – SB
　　　(14 February-12 April and 21 October-12 December) 59.00/62.00 **st.**

　🏠　**Allhays Country House** ⌕, PL13 2JB, ℰ 72434, ≤, ☞ – 📺 �wc 🎞 🅿. 🖭. ⅝
　　　M (bar lunch Monday to Saturday)/dinner 8.70 **st.** and a la carte ≀ 2.75 – **6 rm** ⟷ 13.50/39.00 **st.**

LORTON Cumbria – ✪ 090 085.
♦London 307 – ♦Carlisle 29 – Keswick 14.

🏠 **Hollin House** ⬦, Church Lane, CA13 9UN, ℰ 656, ≤, « Converted rectory », 🍴 – Ⓟ. ☒
VISA ⬦
March-October – **M** (dinner only) 9.00 **st.** ▮ 2.10 – **6 rm** ⌷ 17.00/34.00 **st.**

LOSTWITHIEL Cornwall **403** G 32 **The West Country G.** – pop. 1 972 – ECD : Wednesday –
✪ 0208 Bodmin.
Envir. : Restormel Castle*★ AC* (✳★), N : 1 ½ m.
🅱 Community Centre, Liddicoat Rd ℰ 872207.
♦ London 273 – ♦Plymouth 30 – Truro 23.

🏠 **Carotel Motel,** 17 Castle Hill, PL22 0DD, on A 390 ℰ 872223, ⎏ heated – 📺 ⇌wc ⋔wc ☎
Ⓟ. ☒ 🅰🄴 ⑩ *VISA*
M (bar lunch)/dinner 10.50 **st.** and a la carte ▮ 3.00 – ⌷ 3.00 – **32 rm** 20.00/30.00 **st.** – SB
40.00/45.00 **st.**

✕ **Trewithen,** 3 Fore St., PL22 0AD, ℰ 872373 – ☒ ⑩ *VISA*
closed Monday in winter, Sunday, May and 1 week after Christmas – **M** (dinner only) a la carte
9.40/12.80 **t.** ▮ 4.25.

LOUGHBOROUGH Leics. **402 403 404** Q 25 – pop. 44 895 – ECD : Wednesday – ✪ 0509.
🏌 Longcliffe, Snells Nook Lane Nanpantan ℰ 23129, SW : 3 m. off B 5350.
🅱 John Storer House, Wards End ℰ 230131.
♦ London 117 – ♦Birmingham 41 – ♦Leicester 11 – ♦Nottingham 15.

🏨 **King's Head** (Embassy), High St., LE11 2QL, ℰ 233222 – ▤ 📺 ⇌wc ⋔wc ☎ Ⓟ. 🅰 ☒ 🅰🄴
⑩ *VISA*. ✄
M (carving rest.) 7.95 **st.** ▮ 3.00 – ⌷ 5.00 – **86 rm** 38.00/47.00 **st.** – SB (weekends only)
48.00/53.00 **st.**

🏨 **Cedars,** Cedar Rd, LE11 2AB, S : 1 m. off Leicester Rd ℰ 214459, ⎏ heated, 🍴 – 📺 ⇌wc
⋔wc ☎ Ⓟ. ☒ 🅰🄴 ⑩ *VISA*
closed 25 to 28 December – **M** *(closed Sunday dinner to non-residents)* 5.50 **t.** (lunch) and a la
carte 8.05/11.50 **t.** ▮ 3.00 – **37 rm** ⌷ 17.00/40.00 **t.** – SB (weekends only) 42.00/50.00 **st.**

✕✕✕ **Roger Burdell,** The Manor House, 11-12 Sparrow Hill, LE11 1BT, ℰ 231813 – ☒ 🅰🄴 ⑩
VISA
closed Monday lunch, Sunday and Bank Holidays – **M** 10.50/19.50 **st.** ▮ 4.50.

at Quorn SE : 3 m. on A 6 – ✉ ✪ 0509 Loughborough :

🏨 **Quorn Country,** Charnwood House, 66 Leicester Rd, LE12 8BB, ℰ 415050, 🍴 – ▤ 📺 ☎
🕭 Ⓟ. 🅰. ☒ 🅰🄴 ⑩ *VISA*
M 8.95/11.95 **st.** and a la carte ▮ 3.50 – **19 rm** ⌷ 53.00/69.00 **st.**, **3 suites** 105.00 **st.** –
SB (weekends only) 55.00/65.00 **st.**

🏠 **Quorn Grange,** 88 Wood Lane, LE12 8DB, ℰ 412167, 🍴 – 📺 ⇌wc Ⓟ. ☒ 🅰🄴 ⑩
VISA
M *(closed Monday lunch and Sunday dinner)* 12.50 **t.** and a la carte ▮ 3.10 – **7 rm**
⌷ 34.00/50.00 **t.** – SB (weekends only) 60.00/70.00 **st.**

AUSTIN-ROVER-JAGUAR Woodgate ℰ 262710
COLT Southfield Rd ℰ 212330
FIAT Station Rd ℰ 05097 (Kegworth) 2523
MAZDA Balley Rd ℰ 266901
PEUGEOT Nottingham Rd ℰ 212949

RENAULT Nottingham Rd ℰ 267657
TOYOTA Pinfold Gate ℰ 215731
VAUXHALL-OPEL Woodgate ℰ 213030
VOLVO Derby Rd ℰ 217777
VW, AUDI 28 Market St. ℰ 217080

LOUTH Lincs. **402 404** U 23 – pop. 13 019 – ECD : Thursday – ✪ 0507.
See : St. James' Church★ 15C.
🏌 Crowtree Lane ℰ 603681.
♦ London 155 – Boston 33 – Great Grimsby 17 – Lincoln 26.

🏠 **Priory,** Eastgate, LN11 9AJ, ℰ 602930, 🍴 – 📺 ⇌wc ⋔wc Ⓟ. ☒ *VISA*. ✄
closed 23 December-2 January – **M** *(closed Sunday to non-residents)* (dinner only) 7.95 **st.**
and a la carte ▮ 3.50 – **12 rm** ⌷ 20.00/45.00 **t.**

AUSTIN-ROVER Newmarket ℰ 605661
FORD Fairfield Rd, Industrial Estate ℰ 606737

VOLVO Grimsby Rd ℰ 603451
VW, AUDI Orme Lane ℰ 605284

LOWER BEEDING West Sussex **404** T 30 – see Horsham.

LOWER PEOVER Cheshire **402 403 404** M 24 – see Knutsford.

LOWER SLAUGHTER Glos. **403 404** O 28 – see Stow-on-the-Wold.

LOWER SWELL Glos. **403 404** O 28 – see Stow-on-the-Wold.

340

LOWESTOFT Suffolk 404 Z 26 – pop. 59 430 – ECD : Thursday – ☼ 0502.

🛈 The Esplanade ℰ 65989.

◆ London 116 – ◆Ipswich 43 – ◆Norwich 30.

⌂ **Rockville**, 6 Pakefield Rd, NR33 0HS, ℰ 81011 – 📺 🚻wc. 🔼 *VISA*. ॐ
8 rm ⇌ 12.50/26.00 st.

at Oulton NW : 2 m. by B 1074 – ⊠ ☼ 0502 Lowestoft :

🏛 **Parkhill** ॐ, Parkhill, NR32 5DQ, N : ½ m. on A 1117 ℰ 730322, 🐎 – 📺 🚻wc ☎ 🅿 🏄 🔼
AE *VISA*
M *(closed Sunday lunch)* 15.00/16.00 **st.** and a la carte ▯ 3.50 – **12 rm** ⇌ 30.00/40.00 **st.** –
SB (weekends only) 60.00/80.00 **st.**

AUSTIN-ROVER 97-99 London Rd South ℰ 61711
FORD Whapload Rd ℰ 653553
TALBOT, PEUGEOT Beccles Rd, Oulton Broad ℰ
63622

VAUXHALL-OPEL, BEDFORD London Rd South
ℰ 3512
VW, AUDI Cooke Rd, South Lowestoft Industrial
Estate ℰ 2583

LOWESWATER Cumbria 402 K 20 – pop. 231 – ECD : Thursday – ⊠ Cockermouth – ☼ 090 085
Lorton.

◆ London 305 – ◆Carlisle 33 – Keswick 12.

🏛 **Scale Hill** ॐ, CA13 9UX, ℰ 232, ≼, 🐎 – 🚻wc ♿ 🅿
closed 5 January -7 March – **M** (bar lunch)/dinner 11.00 **st.** ▯ 2.55 – **14 rm** ⇌ 18.00/50.00 **st.**

LOWICK GREEN Cumbria 402 K 21 – see Ulverston.

LOW LAITHE North Yorks. – see Pateley Bridge.

LOW ROW North Yorks. – ⊠ ☼ 0748 Richmond.

◆ London 256 – ◆Carlisle 64 – ◆Leeds 66 – ◆Middlesbrough 39.

⚓ **Punch Bowl Inn,** DL11 6PF, ℰ 86317, ≼ – 🚻wc 🏧wc 🅿 🔼 AE ⓞ *VISA*
M (bar lunch)/dinner 10.00 **st.** ▯ 2.65 – **15 rm** ⇌ 23.00/41.00 **st.** – SB (except summer)
(weekdays only) 55.00 **st.**

LUDLOW Salop 403 L 26 – pop. 7 496 – ECD : Thursday – ☼ 0584.

See : Castle★ (ruins 11C-16C) *AC* – Parish Church★ 13C – Feathers Hotel★ early 17C – Broad
Street★ 17C.

Envir. : Stokesay Castle★ (13C) *AC*, NW : 6 ½ m.

🛇 Bromfield ℰ 058 477 (Bromfield) 285, N : 2 m. on A 49.

🛈 Castle St. ℰ 3857 (summer only).

◆ London 162 – ◆Birmingham 39 – Hereford 24 – Shrewsbury 29.

🏛 **Feathers,** Bull Ring, SY8 1AA, ℰ 5261, Telex 35637, « Part Elizabethan house » – 🕌 📺 ☎
🅿 🏄 🔼 AE ⓞ *VISA*. ॐ
M 8.50/13.50 **t.** and a la carte ▯ 3.25 – **37 rm** ⇌ 45.00/75.00 **st.** – SB (November-March)
77.00/90.00 **st.**

🏛 **Overton Grange** ॐ, Hereford Rd, SY8 4AD, S : 1 ¾ m. on old A 49 ℰ 3500, 🐎 – 📺 🚻wc
🏧wc ☎ 🅿 🏄 🔼 AE ⓞ *VISA*
M 9.00 **t.** and a la carte ▯ 3.25 – **17 rm** ⇌ 15.50/40.00 **st.** – SB (except Christmas) 42.00/
49.00 **st.**

🏛 **Angel,** 8 Broad St., SY8 1NG, ℰ 2581 – 📺 🚻wc ☎ 🅿 🔼 AE ⓞ *VISA*
M 6.50/9.50 **t.** and a la carte ▯ 2.80 – **17 rm** ⇌ 35.00/60.00 **st.** – SB 55.00/70.00 **st.**

⌂ **Cecil,** Sheet Rd, SY8 1LR, ℰ 2442, 🐎 – 🅿
11 rm ⇌ 11.00/22.00 **st.**

AUSTIN-ROVER Corve St. ℰ 2301
FORD Temeside Ind Est. ℰ 5553

NISSAN Sheet Rd ℰ 2774
VOLVO, SUBARU, HYUNDAI Bromfield Rd ℰ 4666

LUDWELL Wilts. – see Shaftesbury (Dorset).

LUNDY (Isle of) Devon 403 FG 30 The West Country G. – pop. 52 – ☼ 062 882 Littlewick
Green.

See : Site ★★.

Helicopter service to Ilfracombe (Hartland Point) ℰ 3431.

⇌ to Bideford (Lundy Co.) 2-3 weekly (2 h 30 mn).

⚓ **Millcombe House** ॐ, EX39 2LY, ℰ 5925, ≼ Island, Channel
M (dinner only) 8.50 **st.** ▯ 2.00 – **7 rm** ⇌ (dinner included) 20.00/50.00 **st.**

LUTON Beds. 404 S 28 – pop. 163 209 – ECD : Wednesday – 🕿 0582.

See : Luton Hoo★ (Wernher Collection★★) and park★ *AC*.

🏌 Stockwood Park, London Rd ℰ 413704, S : 1 m. on A 6.

✈ Luton International Airport : ℰ 36061, Telex 826409, E : 1 ½ m. – **Terminal : Luton Bus Station.**

🛈 Central Library, St. George's Sq. ℰ 32629.

♦London 35 – ♦Cambridge 36 – ♦Ipswich 32 – ♦Oxford 45 – Southend-on-Sea 63.

🏨 **Strathmore Thistle** (Thistle), Arndale Centre, LU1 2TR, ℰ 34199, Telex 825763 – 🛗 📺 ☎ 🄿 🔬 ☒ 🄰🄴 *VISA* 🛳
    M 11.00/12.50 **t.** and a la carte ♨ 3.25 – ☲ 5.95 – **151 rm** 48.00/78.00 **st.**, **3 suites** 85.00 **st.** –
    SB (weekends only) 62.00 **st.**

🏨 **Chiltern** (Crest), Waller Av., Dunstable Rd, LU4 9RU, NW : 2 m. on A 505 ℰ 575911, Telex
    825048 – 🛗 🟰 rest 📺 ☎ ♿ 🄿 🔬 ☒ 🄰🄴 ⑩ *VISA*
    M *(closed lunch Saturday and Bank Holidays)* 9.00/12.25 **st.** – ☲ 6.15 – **93 rm** 50.50/59.50 **st.**
    – SB (weekends only) 62.00 **st.**

🏨 **Crest** (Crest), 641 Dunstable Rd, LU4 8RQ, NW : 2 ¾ m. on A 505 ℰ 575955, Telex 826283 –
    🛗 📺 ⇔wc ☎ 🄿 🔬 ☒ 🄰🄴 *VISA* 🛳
    closed 25 December-2 January – **M** 9.55/10.95 **st.** and a la carte ♨ 2.90 – ☲ 5.85 – **133 rm**
    47.50/56.50 **st.** – SB (weekends only) 60.00 **st.**

🏨 **Leaside**, 72 New Bedford Rd, LU3 1BT, ℰ 417643 – 📺 ⇔wc ☎ 🄿 🔬 ☒ 🄰🄴 ⑩ *VISA* 🛳
    closed 25 and 26 December – **M** *(closed Sunday dinner)* 11.50 **t.** and a la carte ♨ 2.75 – **13 rm**
    ☲ 33.00/39.00 **st.** – SB 80.50/90.50 **st.**

🏨 Red Lion, Castle St., LU1 3AA, ℰ 27337 – 📺 ⇔wc ☏ 🄿 – **48 rm**

⌂ **Humberstone**, 616-618 Dunstable Rd, LU4 8RT, NW : 2 ½ m. on A 505 ℰ 574399 – 📺 ⇔wc
    🄿 🛳
    closed 25 and 26 December – **13 rm** ☲ 14.95/33.90 **s.**

BMW 80-88 Marsh Rd ℰ 576622	VAUXHALL-OPEL 15 Hitchin Rd ℰ 454666	
FORD 326-340 Dunstable Rd ℰ 31133	VAUXHALL-OPEL 540-550 Dunstable Rd ℰ 575944	
LAND-ROVER,JAGUAR Latimer Rd ℰ 411311	VAUXHALL Memorial Rd ℰ 572577	
NISSAN Leagrave Rd ℰ 571221	VW-AUDI Castle St. ℰ 417505	
RENAULT 619 Hitchin Rd ℰ 35332		

LUTTERWORTH Leics. 403 404 Q 26 – 🕿 045 55.

♦London 93 – ♦Birmingham 34 – ♦Coventry 14 – ♦Leicester 16.

🏨 **Denbigh Arms,** High St., LE17 4AD, ℰ 3537 – 📺 ⇔wc ☎ 🄿 🔬 ☒ 🄰🄴 ⑩ *VISA* 🛳
    M *(closed 26 December and 1 January)* 8.50/11.50 **st.** ♨ 3.00 – **34 rm** ☲ 45.00/58.00 **st.** –
    SB (weekends only) 60.00 **st.**

LYDDINGTON Leics. – see Uppingham.

LYME REGIS Dorset 403 L 31 The West Country G. – pop. 4 510 – ECD : Thursday – 🕿 029 74.

See : Site ★ – The Cobb ★.

🏌 Timber Hill ℰ 2043.

🛈 The Guildhall, Bridge St. ℰ 2138.

♦London 160 – Dorchester 25 – Exeter 31 – Taunton 27.

🏨 **Mariners,** Silver St., DT7 3HS, ℰ 2753, Telex 46491, 🚗 – 📺 ⇔wc ⋔wc 🄿 🔬 ☒ 🄰🄴 ⑩ *VISA*
    🛳
    March-October – **M** (bar lunch)/dinner 11.50 **t.** ♨ 3.00 – **16 rm** ☲ 23.00/50.00 **t.** – SB (March-
    May and October) 51.50/56.00 **t.**

🏨 **Alexandra,** Pound St., DT7 3HZ, ℰ 2010, ≼, 🚗 – 📺 ⇔wc ⋔wc 🄿 🔬 ☒ 🄰🄴 ⑩ *VISA*
    closed January and first week February – **M** 6.50/10.25 **st.** and a la carte – **26 rm**
    ☲ 22.00/65.00 **t.** – SB (except summer) 44.00/58.00 **st.**

🏨 **Kersbrook,** Pound Rd, DT7 3HX, ℰ 2596, 🚗 – ⇔wc ⋔wc 🄿 🔬 🄰🄴 *VISA*
    closed January and December – **M** (bar lunch)/dinner 9.50 **t.** and a la carte ♨ 2.60 – **13 rm**
    ☲ 18.50/33.00 **t.** – SB (except summer and Bank Holidays) 42.00/50.00 **st.**

    at Rousdon (Devon) W : 3 m. on A 3052 – ⊠ 🕿 029 74 Lyme Regis :

🏨 **Orchard Country,** DT7 3XW, ℰ 2972, 🚗 – ⇔wc ⋔wc 🄿 🔬 *VISA*
    Mid April-October and Christmas – **M** (bar lunch)/dinner 8.50 **st.** ♨ 2.75 – **14 rm**
    ☲ 20.00/42.00 **t.** – SB 44.00/47.00 **st.**

    at Uplyme (Devon) NW : 1 ¼ m. on A 3070 – ⊠ 🕿 029 74 Lyme Regis :

🏨 **Devon** (Best Western), Lyme Rd, DT7 3TQ, ℰ 3231, ≼, ⍐ heated, 🚗, park – 📺 ⇔wc 🄿
    🔬 🄰🄴 ⑩ *VISA*
    April-October and Christmas – **M** (bar lunch)/dinner 10.50 **t.** ♨ 3.20 – **21 rm** ☲ 26.50/61.00 **t.**
    – SB 58.00/62.00 **t.**

Do not lose your way in Europe, use the Michelin
Main Road maps, scale : 1 inch : 16 miles.

LYMINGTON Hants. 408 404 P 31 – pop. 11 614 – ECD : Wednesday – ✆ 0590.

🚢 to the Isle of Wight : Yarmouth (Sealink) frequent services daily (30 mn).

♦London 104 – Bournemouth 18 – ♦Southampton 19 – Winchester 32.

🏨 **Stanwell House,** 15 High St., SO4 9AA, ℰ 77123, Telex 477463, 🥘 – 📺 🛏wc ☎. 🖘 🖾
   🕮 VISA 🖾
   closed 24 to 26 December – **M** (rest. see **Railings** below) – **33 rm** 🖙 31.00/58.00 **t.** –
   SB (except summer) 68.00 **st.**

XX **Railings,** (at Stanwell House H.) 15 High St., SO4 9AA, ℰ 77123 – 🖘 🖾 ⓪ VISA
   closed 24 to 26 December – **M** 10.00/15.00 **t.** and a la carte 11.50/15.00 **t.** 🍷 3.75.

X **Limpets,** 9 Gosport St., SO4 9BG, ℰ 75595 – 🖘 🖾
   closed Sunday and Monday October-April and December – **M** (dinner only) a la carte
   11.40/18.50 **t.**

   at Mount Pleasant NW : 2 m. by A 337 – ✉ ✆ 0590 Lymington :

🏨 **Passford House** 🌲, Mount Pleasant Lane, SO41 8LS, ℰ 682398, ≼, 🏊 heated, 🖾, 🥘,
   park, 🏌 – 📺 ☎ ❷. 🖧. 🖘 🖾 VISA
   M 12.25/17.55 **t.** and a la carte 🍷 3.00 – **54 rm** 🖙 39.00/72.00 **t.**, **1 suite** 126.00 **t.** – SB (except
   summer) 66.00/78.00 **st.**

   at Gordleton NW : 3 ½ m. by A 337 – ✉ Sway – ✆ 0590 Lymington :

XX **Gordleton Mill** with rm, Silver St., SO4 1DJ, W : ½ m. ℰ 682219, « Riverside setting », 🥘
   – 📺 🛏wc 📶wc ❷
   closed January – **M** *(closed Sunday and Monday)* a la carte 15.00/19.55 **t.** – **8 rm**
   🖙 20.00/48.00 **t.**

   at Sway NW : 4 m. by A 337 on B 3055 – ✉ ✆ 0590 Lymington :

🏠 **White Rose,** Station Rd, SO41 6BA, ℰ 682754, 🏊, 🥘, park – ⌸ 📺 🛏wc ❷. 🖘 VISA
   M 10.50 **st.** and a la carte 🍷 3.10 – **13 rm** 🖙 22.50/50.00 **st.** – SB (except August and September)
   44.00/59.00 **st.**

SEAT Sway ℰ 059 068 (Sway) 2212

LYMM Cheshire 402 403 404 M 23 – pop. 10 036 – ECD : Wednesday – ✆ 092 575.

🏌 Whitbarrow Rd ℰ 2177.

♦ London 193 – Chester 24 – ♦Liverpool 23 – ♦Manchester 15.

🏨 **Lymm** (De Vere), Whitbarrow Rd, WA13 9AQ, ℰ 2233, Telex 629455, 🥘 – 📺 🛏wc 📶wc
   ☎ ❷. 🖧. 🖘 🖾 ⓪ VISA
   M *(closed Saturday lunch)* 10.50 **st.** and a la carte 🍷 3.40 – **69 rm** 🖙 49.50/57.00 **st.** –
   SB (weekends only) 55.00 **st.**

LYMPSTONE Devon 408 J 32 – see Exmouth.

LYNDHURST Hants. 408 404 P 31 – pop. 2 828 – ECD : Wednesday – ✆ 042 128.

See : New Forest★.

🏌 New Forest ℰ 2450.

🛈 Main Car Park ℰ 2269 (summer only).

♦London 95 – Bournemouth 20 – ♦Southampton 10 – Winchester 23.

🏨 **Parkhill** 🌲, Beaulieu Rd, SO4 7FZ, SE : 1 ¼ m. by B 3056 ℰ 2944, ≼, « Tastefully furnished
   country house », 🏊 heated, 🥘, park – 📺 🛏wc ☎ ❷. 🖧. 🖘 🖾 ⓪ VISA
   closed 28 December-12 January – **M** 8.25/13.25 **t.** and a la carte 🍷 3.25 – **22 rm** 🖙 28.00/57.00 **t.**
   – SB 63.00/83.00 **st.**

🏨 **Crown** (Best Western), 9 High St., SO43 7NF, ℰ 2922 – ⌸ 📺 🛏wc ☎ ❷. 🖘 🖾 ⓪ VISA
   M (buffet lunch Saturday) 9.25 **st.** and a la carte 🍷 2.25 – **43 rm** 🖙 37.00/61.00 **st.**, **1 suite**
   76.00/79.00 **st.** – SB (weekends only) 62.00/70.00 **st.**

🏠 Pikes Hill Forest Lodge, Pikes Hill, Romsey Rd, SO4 7AS, ℰ 3677, 🏊 heated, 🥘 – 📺 🛏wc
   📶wc ❷ ⬥ ❷. 🖘 🖾 ⓪ VISA
   M (bar lunch)/dinner 9.50 **t.** and a la carte 🍷 4.75 – **20 rm**.

🏠 **Forest Point,** Romsey Rd, SO43 7AR, ℰ 2420 – 📺 🛏wc 📶wc ☎ ❷. 🖘 🖾 ⓪ VISA
   M (dinner only and bar lunch Easter-September) 8.50 **t.** (dinner) and a la carte 🍷 3.40 – **9 rm**
   🖙 23.00/44.00 **t.** – SB (except Bank Holidays) 49.00/56.00 **st.**

↑ **Ormonde House,** Southampton Rd, SO4 7BT, ℰ 2806, 🥘 – 📺 🛏wc ❷. 🖘 🖾 VISA. 🍽
   closed December-mid January – **15 rm** 🖙 13.80/33.00 **st.**

↑ **Whitemoor House,** Southampton Rd, SO4 7BU, ℰ 2186 – ❷
   5 rm 🖙 14.00/24.00 **s.**

   at Woodlands NE : 3 ½ m. by A 35 – ✉ ✆ 042 129 Ashurst :

🏠 **Woodlands Lodge** 🌲, Bartley Rd, SO4 2GN, ℰ 2257, 🥘 – 📺 🛏wc ❷. 🖧. 🖘 VISA. 🍽
   closed Christmas – **M** (bar lunch)/dinner 11.00 **st.** 🍷 3.00 – **11 rm** 🖙 20.00/60.00 **st.** –
   SB (except summer) 48.00/60.00 **st.**

AUSTIN-ROVER 77 High St. ℰ 2861   VAUXHALL-OPEL Romsey Rd ℰ 2609

LYNMOUTH Devon 408 I 30 – see Lynton.

LYNTON Devon 400 I 30 The West Country G. – pop. 2 075 (inc. Lynmouth) – ECD : Thursday – ✪ 0598.

See : Site ★ (≤★★) – Envir. : Valley of the Rocks ★, W : 1 m. – Watersmeet ★, E : 1 ½ m.

🖪 Town Hall, Lee Rd ✆ 2225.

◆London 206 – Exeter 59 – Taunton 44.

🏨 **Lynton Cottage** 🦢, North Walk, EX35 6ED, ✆ 52342, ≤ bay and Countisbury hill, 🛱 – 📺
🗀wc 🗋wc ☎ 🅿. 🛪 ᴁ ⓞ 𝘝𝘐𝘚𝘈
closed January and February – **M** (bar lunch)/dinner 9.75 **t.** and a la carte 🔧 3.95 – **21 rm**
🖙 17.50/64.00 **t.** – SB (except summer) 40.00/55.00 **st.**

🏨 **Hewitt's** 🦢, North Walk, EX35 6HJ, ✆ 52293, ≤ bay and Countisbury hill, « Country house
atmosphere », 🛱, park – 📺 🗀wc 🅿. 🛪 ᴁ ⓞ 𝘝𝘐𝘚𝘈. ⌘
M (bar lunch Monday to Saturday)/dinner 13.50 **st.** and a la carte 🔧 3.00 – **12 rm**
🖙 16.00/50.00 **st.** – SB (except summer and Bank Holidays) 55.00/75.00 **st.**

🏠 **Crown,** Sinai Hill, EX35 6AG, ✆ 52253 – 📺 🗀wc 🅿. 🛪 ᴁ ⓞ 𝘝𝘐𝘚𝘈
closed January – **M** (bar lunch)/dinner 9.95 **st.** and a la carte 🔧 3.20 – **16 rm** 🖙 20.50/47.00 **t.**
– SB 51.00/58.00 **st.**

🏠 **Chough's Nest** 🦢, North Walk, EX35 6HJ, ✆ 53315, ≤ bay and Countisbury hill – 🗀wc
🗋wc. ⌘
Easter-October – **M** (dinner only) 7.00 **t.** 🔧 2.00 – **12 rm** 🖙 14.00/28.00 **t.** – SB 40.00 **st.**

🏠 **Neubia House,** Lydiate Lane, EX35 6AH, ✆ 52309 – 📺 🗀wc 🗋wc 🅿
closed December and January – **M** (dinner only) 8.00 **t.** 🔧 2.80 – **12 rm** 🖙 15.75/33.70 **t.**

☖ **Seawood** 🦢, North Walk, EX35 6HJ, ✆ 52272, ≤ – 📺 🗀wc 🗋wc 🅿
March-October – **M** (dinner only) 9.00 **t.** 🔧 2.20 – **12 rm** 🖙 12.00/29.00 **st.**

☖ **Castle Hill House,** Castle Hill, EX35 6JA, ✆ 52291 – 📺 🗀wc 🗋. 🛪 𝘝𝘐𝘚𝘈
April-October – **M** 8.00/12.50 **t.** and a la carte 🔧 2.35 – **9 rm** 🖙 14.00/36.00 **st.** – SB (except
summer) 40.00/45.00 **st.**

☖ **Rockvale,** EX35 6HW, off Lee Rd ✆ 52279 – 📺 🗀wc 🅿. 𝘝𝘐𝘚𝘈
M (bar lunch)/dinner 8.00 **st.** 🔧 3.50 – **8 rm** 🖙 17.00/34.00 **st.** – SB 43.00/49.00 **st.**

⌂ **Pine Lodge** 🦢, Lynway, EX35 6AX, ✆ 53230, ≤, 🛱 – 🗋wc 🅿
Easter-October – **8 rm** 🖙 11.00/25.00 **st.**

at Lynmouth – ✉ Lynmouth – ✪ 0598 Lynton :

🏨 Tors 🦢, EX35 6NA, ✆ 53236, ≤ Lynmouth and bay, 🔲 heated, 🛱 – 🛗 📺 🗀wc ☎ 🅿. ⌘
39 rm

🏠 **Rising Sun,** The Harbour, EX35 6EQ, ✆ 53223, « 14C thatched inn », 🛱 – 📺 🗀wc 🗋wc.
🛪 ᴁ 𝘝𝘐𝘚𝘈
closed 6 December-14 February – **M** (bar lunch Monday to Saturday)/dinner 9.50 **st.**
and a la carte 🔧 3.65 – **17 rm** 🖙 25.50/51.00 **st.**, **1 suite** 60.00 **st.** – SB (except summer)
48.00/60.00 **st.**

🏠 **Bath,** EX35 6EL, ✆ 52238 – 🗀wc 🅿. 🛪 ᴁ ⓞ 𝘝𝘐𝘚𝘈
closed December-February – **M** (bar lunch)/dinner 9.00 **st.** and a la carte 🔧 3.40 – **24 rm**
🖙 11.50/40.00 **st.** – SB 35.00/52.00 **st.**

☖ **Beacon** 🦢, Countisbury Hill, EX35 6ND, E : ½ m. on A 39 ✆ 53268, ≤, 🛱 – 📺 🗀wc 🗋wc
🅿. ⌘
Mid March-October – **M** 4.75/9.00 **st.** and a la carte 🔧 2.30 – **7 rm** 🖙 16.00/31.00 **st.** – SB
36.00/41.00 **st.**

⌂ **Heatherville** 🦢, Tors Park, EX35 6NB, by Tors Rd ✆ 52327 – 🗋wc 🅿. ⌘
April-October – **8 rm** 🖙 12.00/27.00 **t.**

⌂ Countisbury Lodge 🦢, Countisbury hill, EX35 6NB, ✆ 52388, ≤ – 🗀wc 🗋wc 🅿
8 rm.

at Brendon E : 4 m. by A 39 – ✉ Lynton – ✪ 059 87 Brendon :

☖ **Stag Hunters** 🦢, High St., EX35 1PS, ✆ 222, 🛱 – 📺 🗀wc 🅿 🛪 ᴁ ⓞ 𝘝𝘐𝘚𝘈
closed January-mid March – **M** 10.50 **t.** 🔧 2.95 – **22 rm** 🖙 25.00/40.00 **t.**

at Hillsford Bridge S : 4 ½ m. by A 39 – ✉ ✪ 0598 Lynton :

☖ **Combe Park** 🦢, EX35 6LE, ✆ 52356, 🛱 – 🗀wc 🗋wc 🅿
closed January-mid February – **M** (dinner only) 11.00 **t.** 🔧 2.10 – **9 rm** 🖙 21.00/36.00 **t.**

at Woody Bay W : 3 ¼ m. via Coast road – ✉ ✪ 059 83 Parracombe :

🏠 **Woody Bay** 🦢, EX31 4QX, ✆ 264, ≤ woody bay – 🗀wc 🅿. 🛪 𝘝𝘐𝘚𝘈
closed January-mid February – **M** (bar lunch)/dinner 9.25 **t.** and a la carte 🔧 2.75 – **14 rm**
🖙 17.00/46.00 **t.** – SB 44.00/60.00 **st.**

at Martinhoe W : 4 ¼ m. via Coast road – ✉ ✪ 059 83 Parracombe :

🏠 **Old Rectory** 🦢, EX31 4QT, ✆ 368, ≤ – 🗀wc 🗋wc 🅿
Easter-mid October – **M** (dinner only) 10.50 **t.** 🔧 3.30 – **10 rm** 🖙 18.00/36.00 **t.**

at Heddon's Mouth W : 5 ¾ m. by B 3234 off A 39 – ✉ ✪ 059 83 Parracombe :

🏨 **Heddon's Gate** 🦢, EX31 4PZ, via coast road and Martinhoe ✆ 313, ≤, 🛱, park – 📺
🗀wc 🗋wc 🅿. 🛪 ᴁ
April-October – **M** (bar lunch)/dinner 15.00 **t.** 🔧 2.90 – **16 rm** 🖙 23.80/50.50 **t.**, **3 suites**
52.50 **t.**

LYTHAM ST ANNE'S Lancs. 402 L 22 – pop. 39 599 – ECD : Wednesday – ✆ 0253 St. Anne's –
☕ St. Anne's Old Links, Highbury Rd ✆ 723597.
🗓 St. Anne's Sq. ✆ 725610 and 721222.
◆London 237 – ◆Blackpool 7 – ◆Liverpool 44 – Preston 13.

🏨 **Grand,** 77 South Promenade, FY8 1NB, ✆ 721288, Telex 67481 – 📶 📺 ⇔wc ☎ 🅿 🚗 🔼
AE ① VISA
M 5.75/9.25 **t.** and a la carte 🛇 3.15 – **40 rm** ⊑ 43.00/56.00 **t.** – SB (except Christmas and New Year) 60.00/70.00 **st.**

🏨 **Dalmeny,** 19-33 South Promenade, FY8 1LX, ✆ 712236, 🔲, squash – 📶 📺 ⇔wc ☎ 🅿 🚗
🔼 VISA ✎
closed 24 to 26 December – **M** 8.00/10.50 **t.** and a la carte 🛇 2.75 – ⊑ 3.75 – **84 rm** 30.00/50.00 **t.**
– SB 50.00/70.00 **st.**

at Lytham SE : 3 m. – ⊠ ✆ 0253 Lytham :

🏨 **Clifton Arms** (Whitbread), West Beach, FY8 5QJ, ✆ 739898, Telex 677463 – 📶 📗 rest 📺
☎ 🅿 🚗 AE ① VISA
M 6.95/9.50 **t.** and a la carte – **45 rm** ⊑ 45.00/70.00 **t.** – SB (weekends only) 55.00/65.00 **st.**

AUSTIN-ROVER-DAIMLER Kings Rd ✆ 728051
FORD Preston Rd ✆ 733261
RENAULT Heyhouse Lane ✆ 726799
RENAULT Sefton Rd ✆ 726821
VAUXHALL Heeley Rd ✆ 726714

MACCLESFIELD Cheshire 402 403 404 N 24 – pop. 47 525 – ECD : Wednesday – ✆ 0625.
☕ The Hollins ✆ 23227, SE : off A 523.
🗓 Town Hall, Market Pl. ✆ 21955 ext 114/5.
◆London 186 – Chester 38 – ◆Manchester 18 – ◆Stoke-on-Trent 21.

🏠 Sutton Hall ◔, Bullocks Lane, Sutton, SK11 0HE, SE : 2 m. by A 523 ✆ 3211, 🐎 – 📺 ⇔wc
☎ 🅿
9 rm

⌂ **Fourways Diner Motel,** Cleulow Cross, Wincle, SK11 0QL, SE : 4 ½ m. on A 54
✆ 026 07 (Wincle) 228, ⇔, 🐎 – 📺 ⇔wc 🚿wc 🅿 🔼 VISA
7 rm ⊑ 20.00/30.00 **t.**

✗ **Olivers Bistro,** 101-103 Chestergate, SK11 6DU, ✆ 32003 – 🔼 VISA
closed Sunday – **M** (dinner only) 8.50 **t.** and a la carte 9.40/11.95 **st.** 🛇 2.85.

AUSTIN-ROVER Hobson St. ✆ 615555
FIAT London Rd ✆ 28866
FORD Hibel Rd ✆ 27766
HONDA Beech Lane ✆ 23592
PEUGEOT, TALBOT Waters Green ✆ 22226
RENAULT Davenport St. ✆ 23677
VAUXHALL, OPEL 98 Chestergate ✆ 22909
VW-AUDI Crossall St. ✆ 23036

MACHYNLLETH Powys 402 403 I 26 – pop. 1 952 – ECD : Thursday – ✆ 0654.
Envir. : NW : Cader Idris (road★★ to Cader Idris : Cregenneu lakes) – Aberangell Clipiau (site★)
NE : 10 m. – SE : Llyfnant Valley ★ via Glaspwll.
🗓 Canolfan Owain Glyndwr ✆ 2401.
◆London 220 – Shrewsbury 56 – Welshpool 37.

🏨 **Wynnstay** (T.H.F.), Maengwyn St., SY80 8AE, ✆ 2941 – 📺 ⇔wc 🖘 🅿 🔼 AE ① VISA
M (bar lunch Monday to Saturday)/dinner 18.45 **st.** 🛇 3.40 – ⊑ 5.65 – **26 rm** 39.00/46.00 **st.**

🏠 **Plas Dolguog** ◔, SY20 8UJ, E : 1 ½ m. by A 489 ✆ 2244, ⇔, « 17C country house », ◔, 🐎
– ⇔wc 🅿 🔼 VISA ✎
M (closed lunch to non-residents) a la carte 7.80/12.15 **t.** 🛇 2.95 – **7 rm** ⊑ 27.00/49.00 **t.** –
SB 51.00/62.00 **st.**

✗ **Janie's,** 57 Maengwyn St., SY20 8EE, ✆ 2126
Easter-mid October – **M** (closed Sunday except Bank Holidays) (dinner only) a la carte
8.20/12.95 **t.** 🛇 2.95.

at Corris (Gwynedd) N : 5 ¼ m. on A 487 – ⊠ Machynlleth (Powys) – ✆ 065 473 Corris :

🏠 **Braich Goch,** SY20 9RD, on A 487 ✆ 229, ⇔, 🐎 – 🚿wc 🅿 🔼
M 5.50/6.00 **st.** and a la carte 🛇 3.20 – **6 rm** ⊑ 13.00/30.00 **st.** – SB (October-April except
Easter and Christmas) 30.00/38.00 **st.**

at Eglwysfach (Dyfed) SW : 6 m. on A 487 – ⊠ Machynlleth (Powys) – ✆ 065 474 Glan-
dyfi :

🏨 **Ynyshir Hall** ◔, SY20 8TA, ✆ 209, ⇔, « Country house in large gardens », park – 📺
⇔wc 🅿 🔼 VISA
closed last week April and first week November – **M** 9.50/11.50 **st.** and a la carte 🛇 2.75 – **9 rm**
⊑ 26.50/56.00 **st.** – SB (November-April) 58.00 **st.**

AUSTIN-ROVER Station Garage ✆ 2108
FORD ✆ 065 04 (Dinas Mawddwy) 326

MADINGLEY Cambs. 404 U 27 – see Cambridge.

MAENORBYR = Manorbier.

MAIDENCOMBE Devon 403 J 32 – see Torquay.

MAIDENHEAD Berks. **404** R 29 – pop. 59 809 – ECD : Thursday – ✆ 0628.

🏛 Central Library, St. Ives Rd ℘ 781110.

♦London 33 – ♦Oxford 32 – Reading 13.

🏨🏨 **Crest** (Crest), Manor Lane, SL6 2RA, ℘ 23444, Telex 847502, 🔲, 🍴, squash – 📶 📺 🆚 ಈ. 🅿 ⛽ 🔟 🅰🅴 ① 𝗩𝗜𝗦𝗔 🦽
M (rest. see **Shoppenhangers Manor** below) – ⌿ 6.15 – **189 rm** 61.00/74.00 st., **2 suites** 90.00 st. – SB (weekends only) 90.00 st.

🏨🏨 **Fredrick's,** Shoppenhangers Rd, SL6 2PZ, ℘ 35934, 🍴 – 📺 🅿 🅿 ⛽. 🔟 🅰🅴 ① 𝗩𝗜𝗦𝗔 🦽
M (rest. see **Fredrick's** below) – **38 rm** ⌿ 59.50/78.00 st., **1 suite** 145.00 st.

🏨 **Thames Riviera,** at the bridge, Bridge Rd, SL6 8DW, ℘ 74057, Telex 846687 – 📺 ⛛wc ☎ 🅿 ⛽. 🔟 🅰🅴 ① 𝗩𝗜𝗦𝗔 🦽
M 8.50/10.75 **t.** and a la carte ⑀ 3.00 – **52 rm** ⌿ 52.50/75.00 **t.** – SB (weekends only) 59.00/68.00 **st.**

🏠 **Bear,** 8-10 High St., SL6 1QJ, ℘ 25183 – 📺 🍴 🕳. 🔟 𝗩𝗜𝗦𝗔 🦽
M (buffet rest.) a la carte 4.90/5.90 **st.** ⑀ 2.05 – **12 rm** ⌿ 27.00/38.00 **st.**

XXX **Fredrick's** (at Fredrick's H.), Shoppenhangers Rd, SL6 2PZ, ℘ 24737, 🍴 – ▤ 🅿. 🔟 🅰🅴 ① 𝗩𝗜𝗦𝗔
closed Saturday lunch – **M** 25.50/35.00 **st.** ⑀ 4.25.

XXX **Shoppenhangers Manor** (Crest) (at Crest H.), Manor Lane, SL6 2RA, ℘ 23444, Telex 847502, 🍴 – 🅿. 🔟 🅰🅴 ① 𝗩𝗜𝗦𝗔
M 10.95/11.95 **st.** and a la carte 15.75/21.25 **st.**

XX Jasmine Peking, 29 High St., SL6 1JG, ℘ 20334, Chinese rest.

X La Peking, 1a Glynwood House, Bridge Av., SL6 1RR, ℘ 73655, Chinese rest.

X **Maidenhead Chinese,** 45-47 Queen St., SL6 1LT, ℘ 24545, Chinese-Peking rest. – 🔟 🅰🅴 ① 𝗩𝗜𝗦𝗔
closed Sunday – **M** 11.00/15.00 **t.** and a la carte 9.20/16.80 **t.**

at Cliveden NE : 4 ½ m. by A 4 via Berry Hill – ✉ Taplow – ✆ 06286 Burnham :

🏰 **Cliveden** ⛳, SL6 0JF, ℘ 68561, Telex 846562, « Mid-Victorian stately home – ≼ National Trust Gardens and parterre », 🔲 heated, 🎾, squash – 📶 🔟 🅰🅴 ① 𝗩𝗜𝗦𝗔 🦽
M 26.60/35.60 **st.** ⑀ 7.00 – **25 rm** ⌿ 120.00/200.00 **st.**, **7 suites** 250.00/350.00 **st.**

BMW 84 Altwood Rd ℘ 37611		MAZDA 7 Bath Rd ℘ 32339	
FORD Bath Rd, Taplow ℘ 29711		ROLLS ROYCE 128 Bridge Rd ℘ 33188	
HONDA 14-20 Bath Rd ℘ 21331		VAUXHALL Braywick Rd ℘ 75461	

MAIDSTONE Kent **404** V 30 – pop. 86 067 – ECD : Wednesday – ✆ 0622.

See : All Saints' Church★ – Carriage Museum★ *AC* – Chillington Manor (Museum and Art Gallery★).

Envir. : Leeds Castle★ *AC*, SE : 4 ½ m. – Aylesford (The Friars carmelite priory : great courtyard★) NW : 3 ½ m. – Coldrum Long Barrow (prehistoric stones) site★ : NE : 1 m. from Trottiscliffe plus 5 mn walk, NW : 12 m.

🏕 Cobtree Manor Park, Chatham Park, Sandling ℘ 53276, N : ¼ m.

🏛 The Gatehouse, Old Palace Gardens, Mill St. ℘ 671361 ext 169 and 673581.

♦London 36 – ♦Brighton 64 – ♦Cambridge 84 – Colchester 72 – Croydon 36 – ♦Dover 45 – Southend-on-Sea 49.

🏠 **Grange Moor,** 4-8 St. Michael's Rd (off Tonbridge Rd), ME16 8BS, ℘ 677623 – 📺 🍴wc ☎ 🅿 𝗩𝗜𝗦𝗔
M 6.50 **t.** and a la carte ⑀ 3.40 – **34 rm** ⌿ 23.00/40.00 **t.** – SB (weekends only) 45.00/52.50 **st.**

🏠 **Rock House,** 102 Tonbridge Rd, ME16 8SL, ℘ 51616 – 🅿. 🔟 𝗩𝗜𝗦𝗔 🦽
closed 24 December-1 January – **10 rm** ⌿ 14.25/24.50 **st.**

🏠 **Carval,** 56-58 London Rd, ME16 8QL, ℘ 62100 – 📺 🅿. 🔟 🅰🅴 ① 𝗩𝗜𝗦𝗔 🦽
8 rm ⌿ 12.50/28.00 **st.**

at Bearsted E : 3 m. by A 249 – ✉ ✆ 0622 Maidstone :

XX **Sueffle,** The Green, ME14 4DN, ℘ 37065 – 🅿. 🔟 🅰🅴 ① 𝗩𝗜𝗦𝗔
closed lunch Saturday and Good Friday, Monday dinner, Sunday and Bank Holidays – **M** 9.95 **st.** (lunch) and a la carte 13.20/25.70 **st.** ⑀ 3.00.

at Boughton Monchelsea S : 4 ½ m. by A 229 on B 2163 – ✉ ✆ 0622 Maidstone :

🏠 **Tanyard** ⛳, Wierton Hill, ME17 4JT, S : 1 ½ m. by Park Lane ℘ 44705, ≼, « 14C Tannery standing in orchards », 🍴 – 📺 🍴wc 🅿. 🔟 🅰🅴 ① 𝗩𝗜𝗦𝗔 🦽
Mid March-October – **M** (dinner only) 13.80 **st.** ⑀ 3.25 – **5 rm** ⌿ 34.50/46.00 **st.**

at Wateringbury SW : 4 ½ m. on A 26 – ✉ ✆ 0622 Maidstone :

🏨 Wateringbury, Tonbridge Rd, ME18 5NS, ℘ 812632 – 📺 🍴wc ☎ 🅿
28 rm.

at Larkfield W : 3 ¼ m. on A 20 – ✉ Larkfield – ✆ 0732 West Malling :

🏨 Larkfield, 812 London Rd, ME20 6HJ, ℘ 846858, Telex 957420 – ▤ rest 📺 ⛛wc ☎ ಈ 🅿. ⛽. 🔟 🅰🅴 ① 𝗩𝗜𝗦𝗔
M (closed Saturday lunch) 9.95/11.00 **t.** and a la carte ⑀ 3.00 – **52 rm**.

XXX **Wealden Hall,** 773 London Rd, ME20 6DE, ℘ 840259 – 🅿. 🔟 🅰🅴 ① 𝗩𝗜𝗦𝗔
closed Sunday dinner – **M** 7.95/9.95 **st.** and a la carte 13.30/18.00 **st.** ⑀ 3.75.

AUSTIN-ROVER-DAIMLER-JAGUAR Bircholt Rd *&*
65461
BMW Broadway *&* 686666
ALFA-ROMEO Bow Rd, Wateringbury *&* 812358
COLT Forstal Rd, Aylesford *&* 76421
FIAT, LANCIA 29 Union St. *&* 52439
FORD Ashford Rd *&* 56781
HONDA Upper Stone St. *&* 53096
LADA Loose Rd *&* 52584

NISSAN Ashford Rd, Harrietsham *&* 859363
PEUGEOT, TALBOT Mill St. *&* 53333
RENAULT Ashford Rd *&* 54744
SAAB Linton Rd, Loose *&* 46629
VAUXHALL-OPEL, MERCEDES-BENZ Park Wood,
Sutton Rd *&* 55531
VAUXHALL London Rd, Ditton *&* 0732 (West Mal-
ling) 844922
VW, AUDI Upper Stone St. *&* 50821

MALDON Essex **404** V 28 – pop. 14 638 – ECD : Wednesday – ✆ 0621.
🅱 2 High St. *&* 56503.
♦London 42 – Chelmsford 9 – Colchester 17.

🏨 **Blue Boar** (T.H.F.), Silver St., CM9 7QE, *&* 52681 – 📺 🛏wc 📶 🅿. 🔥. 🔼 AE ⓞ 𝘝𝘐𝘚𝘈
M 9.60/8.95 **st.** and a la carte 🍷 3.40 – 🖙 5.65 – **23 rm** 39.00/48.00 st.

🍴 **Benbridge,** The Square, Heybridge, CM9 7LT, *&* 57666 – 📺 🛏wc 🕋wc 📶 🅿. 🔼 AE ⓞ
𝘝𝘐𝘚𝘈
M 4.20 **t.** (lunch) and a la carte 7.75/14.10 **t.** 🍷 2.25 – **14 rm** 🖙 21.50/31.00 st. – SB (weekends
only) 46.00/60.00 st.

✗ **Francine's,** 1a High St., CM9 7PB, *&* 56605 – 🔼 𝘝𝘐𝘚𝘈
closed Sunday, Monday, 2 weeks August and 1 week at Christmas – **M** (dinner only) (booking
essential) a la carte 12.35/15.05 **t.** 🍷 3.25.

AUSTIN-ROVER Heybridge *&* 52468
BMW Spital Rd *&* 52131

FORD 1 Spital Rd *&* 52345
VAUXHALL-OPEL 127-131 High St. *&* 52424

MALHAM North Yorks. **402** N 21 – pop. 130 – ✉ Skipton – ✆ 072 93 Airton.
♦London 231 – Burnley 32 – ♦Leeds 42 – York 58.

🍴 **Buck Inn,** BD23 4DA, *&* 317 – 🅿
M (bar lunch)/dinner 7.00 **st.** and a la carte 🍷 2.70 – **10 rm** 🖙 13.00/42.00 **t.** – SB (except
summer and Bank Holidays) 34.00 st.

MALMESBURY Wilts. **403 404** N 29 – pop. 4 220 – ECD : Thursday – ✆ 066 62.
See : Site ★ – Market Cross ★★ – Abbey ★.
🅱 Town Hall, Cross Hayes *&* 2143/3748.
♦London 108 – ♦Bristol 28 – Gloucester 24 – Swindon 19.

🏨 Old Bell, Abbey Row, SN16 0BW, *&* 2344, 🚗 – 📺 🛏wc 🕋wc ☎ 🅿. 🔥. 🔼 AE ⓞ 𝘝𝘐𝘚𝘈
M 8.70/14.50 **st.** and a la carte 🍷 3.50 – **19 rm, 1 suite**.

at Crudwell N : 4 m. on A 429 – ✉ ✆ 066 67 Crudwell :

🏨 **Mayfield House,** SN16 9EW, *&* 409, 🚗 – 📺 🛏wc 🕋wc 🅿. 🔼 𝘝𝘐𝘚𝘈
M (bar lunch Monday to Saturday)/dinner 8.50 **t.** and a la carte 🍷 2.50 – **21 rm** 🖙 19.00/39.00 t.
– SB 40.00/52.00 st.

at Easton Grey W : 2 m. on B 4040 – ✉ ✆ 066 62 Malmesbury :

🏰 Whatley Manor ⌲, SN16 0RB, E : ½ m. on B 4040 *&* 2888, Telex 449380, ≼, « 18C Manor
house », ⌁ heated, 🎾, 🚗, park, ✗ – 📺 ☎ 🅿. 🔥
25 rm.

PEUGEOT-TALBOT Gloucester Rd *&* 3434

MALPAS Cheshire **402 403** L 24 – pop. 1 522 – ✆ 0948.
♦London 77 – ♦Birmingham 60 – Chester 15 – Shrewsbury 26 – ♦Stoke-on-Trent 30.

✗✗ **Market House,** Church St., SY14 8NU, *&* 860400, 🚗 – 🔼 𝘝𝘐𝘚𝘈
closed Sunday dinner, Monday, 1 week March and 2 weeks August – **M** (lunch by arrangement)/dinner a la carte 7.85/13.45 **t.** 🍷 3.75.

MALTON North Yorks. **402** R 21 – pop. 4 033 – ECD : Thursday – ✆ 0653.
Envir. : Castle Howard★★ (18C) AC, SW : 6 m. – Flamingo Park Zoo★ AC, N : 4 ½ m.
🅸 Malton and Norton, Welham Park *&* 2959.
🅱 28-30 Castlegate *&* 7638.
♦London 229 – ♦Kingston-upon-Hull 36 – Scarborough 24 – York 17.

🏨 **Talbot** (T.H.F.), Yorkersgate, YO17 0AA, *&* 4031 – 📺 🛏wc 📶 🚗 🅿. 🔼 AE ⓞ 𝘝𝘐𝘚𝘈
M 6.50/9.50 **st.** and a la carte 🍷 3.40 – 🖙 5.65 – **23 rm** 42.00/50.00 st.

at Amotherby W : 2 ½ m. on B 1257 – ✉ ✆ 0653 Malton :

⌂ **Quarry,** YO17 0TG, *&* 3623, ≼, 🚗 – 🅿.
March-November – **6 rm** 🖙 9.00/18.00 st.

AUSTIN-ROVER Wintringham *&* 09442 (Rillington)
242

BMW Church St., Norton *&* 5151
VOLVO Horse Market Rd *&* 3019

MALVERN Heref. and Worc. **403 404** N 27 – see Great Malvern.

MALVERN WELLS Heref. and Worc. **403 404** N 27 – see Great Malvern.

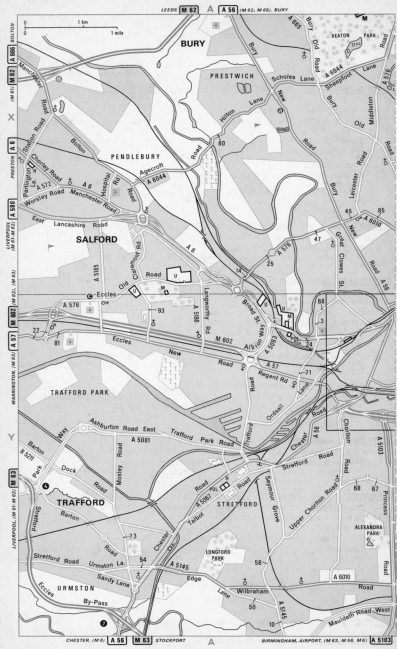

A 666 BOLTON
M 62
(M 61)
PRESTON A 6
A 580
LIVERPOOL (M 61-M 62)
M 602
A 57
WARRINGTON, (M 63)
M 63
LIVERPOOL (M 61-M 62)

X

Y

0 1 km
1 mile

BURY

HEATON PARK

PRESTWICH

Scholes Lane

A 6044

Sheepfoot Lane

A 576

Middleton

Hilton Lane

New

Bury

Old

Leicester Road

Road

Bury

New

Road A 56

80

Manchester Road

PENDLEBURY

Bolton Road

Agecroft
A 6044

Chorley Road

Partington La.
Worsley Road
A 572
Manchester Road
Hospital Rd

East Lancashire Road

SALFORD

A 5185

Old Clarendon Rd

Road

A 6

14

25

A 576

47

45 85
A 6010

Great Clowes St.

Langworthy Rd

A 5188

88

Road A 56

Eccles

A 576

93

M 602

Eccles

81

22

New Road

Broad St

A 5063

U
M
POL

3

24

A/b¹on Way

A 57

71

Regent Rd

Ordsall Lane

TRAFFORD PARK

Way

Barton

B 5211

Dock Road

Mosley Road

Ashburton Road East
A 5081

Trafford Park Road

Trafford Road

Chester Road

A 56

Stretford Road

Chorlton Road

A 5103

68 67

Princess Road

TRAFFORD

Barton

Stretford

Road

Road
A 5067

STRETFORD

Talbot Road

73

Chester

Seymour Grove

Upper Chorlton Road

ALEXANDRA PARK

54

Stretford Road
Urmston La.
A 5145

Sandy Lane

Edge Lane

LONGFORD PARK

56

A 6010 Road

URMSTON

Eccles By-Pass

Wilbraham

50

A 5145

10

Mauldeth Road West

4

7

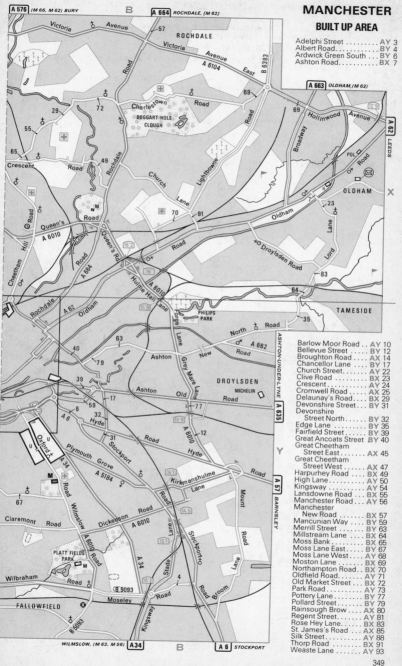

MANCHESTER
BUILT UP AREA

See : Town Hall★ 19C DZ **H** – City Art Gallery★ DZ **M** – Whitworth Art Gallery★ BY **M** – Cathedral 15C (chancel★) DZ **B** – John Ryland's Library (manuscripts★) CZ **A**.

Envir. : Heaton Hall★ (18C) *AC*, N : 5 m. AX **M**.

☖ Heaton Park, ✆ 798 0295, N : by A 576 ABX – ☖ Fairfield Golf and Sailing, Booth Rd, Audenshaw, ✆ 370 1641, E : by A 635 BY.

✈ Manchester International Airport ✆ (061) 489 3000 or 489 2404 (British Airways), S : 10 m. by A 5103 AY and M 56 – **Terminal :** Coach service from Victoria Station.

🛈 Town Hall Extension, Lloyd St. ✆ 234 3157/8 – Manchester International Airport, International Arrivals Hall ✆ 437 5233.

◆London 202 – ◆Birmingham 86 – ◆Glasgow 221 – ◆Leeds 43 – ◆Liverpool 35 – ◆Nottingham 72.

Plans on preceding pages

🏨 **Piccadilly** (Embassy), Piccadilly Plaza, M60 1QR, 🖉 236 8414, Telex 668765, ← – 🛗 📺 ☎ 🅿
🕍 📇 ☑ ⑩ 𝗩𝗜𝗦𝗔 ⚭
M 11.50 **t.** and a la carte 14.95/24.40 **t.** 🍷 3.75 – 🖙 6.25 – **250 rm** 65.00/75.00 **st.**, **9 suites**
150.00/180.00 **st.** – SB (weekends only) 70.00 **st.**
DZ **s**

🏨 **Portland Thistle** (Thistle), Portland St., Piccadilly Gdns., M1 6DP, 🖉 228 3400, Telex 669157
– 🛗 📺 ☎ 🕍 📇 ☑ ⑩ 𝗩𝗜𝗦𝗔
M 8.50/12.00 **t.** 🍷 5.50 – 🖙 7.95 – **219 rm** 60.00/95.00 **st.**, **1 suite** 115.00 **st.**
DZ **v**

🏨 **Grand** (T.H.F.), Aytoun St., M1 3DR, 🖉 236 9559, Telex 667580 – 🛗 📺. 🕍 📇 ☑ ⑩ 𝗩𝗜𝗦𝗔
M (carving rest.) 8.65 **st.** and a la carte 🍷 3.40 – **140 rm** 🖙 57.00/67.50 **st.**, **2 suites**.
DZ **u**

🏠 **Hazeldean**, 467 Bury New Rd, M7 ONX, 🖉 792 6667 – 📺 ⥾wc 🅗wc 🅿 📇 ☑ ⑩ 𝗩𝗜𝗦𝗔. ⚭
closed 25 and 26 December – **M** (bar lunch Monday to Saturday)/dinner 12.00 **t.** and a la carte
🍷 3.20 – **21 rm** 🖙 27.85/45.55 **st.** – SB (weekends only) 56.10/65.85 **st.**
AX **a**

↑ **New Central**, 144-146 Heywood St., M8 7PD, 🖉 205 2169 – 🅗 🅿. ⚭
closed 23 December-1 January – **10 rm** 🖙 16.25/29.50 **st.**
BX **e**

↑ **Sabre d'Or**, 392 Wilbraham Rd, Chorlton-cum-Hardy, M21 1UH, S : 5 m. by A 5103 on
A 6010 🖉 881 5055 – 🅿 📇 🅝 𝗩𝗜𝗦𝗔 – **9 rm** 🖙 16.00/22.00 **st.**
AY **c**

XXX **Terrazza**, 14 Nicholas St., M1 4FE, 🖉 236 4033, Italian rest. – 📇 ☑ ⑩ 𝗩𝗜𝗦𝗔
closed Sunday and Bank Holidays – **M** 5.95/12.50 **t.** and a la carte 7.60/13.00 **t.** 🍷 2.95.
DZ **r**

XX **Isola Bella**, 6a Booth St., M2 4AW, 🖉 236 6417, Italian rest. – 📇 ☑ ⑩ 𝗩𝗜𝗦𝗔
closed Sunday and Bank Holidays – **M** 18.00 **t.** and a la carte 10.40/12.80 **t.** 🍷 3.60.
DZ **e**

XX **Gaylord**, Amethyst House, Marriott's Court, Spring Gardens, M2 1EA, 🖉 832 6037, Indian
rest. – 📇 ☑ 𝗩𝗜𝗦𝗔
closed 25 December and 1 January – **M** 3.95/7.95 **t.** and a la carte 5.35/6.65 **t.** 🍷 3.75.
DZ **c**

XX **Leen Hong**, 35 George St., M1 4HQ, 🖉 228 0926, Chinese rest. – 📇 ⑩
M a la carte 5.25/9.70 **t.**
DZ **z**

XX **Rajdoot**, St. James' House, South King St., M2 6DW, 🖉 834 2176, Indian rest. – 📇 ☑
𝗩𝗜𝗦𝗔 – closed Sunday lunch and 25-26 December – **M** 4.00/9.50 **t.** and a la carte 🍷 2.95
CZ **c**

XX Assam Gourmet, 17a Bloom St., Indian rest.
DZ **n**

X **Truffles**, 63 Bridge St., M3 3BQ, 🖉 832 9393 – 📇 ☑ ⑩ 𝗩𝗜𝗦𝗔
CZ **n**
closed Saturday lunch, Sunday, Monday, first 2 weeks August and Bank Holidays – **M** 9.95 **t.**
(lunch) and a la carte 13.00/19.40 **t.** 🍷 2.85.

X **Market**, 30 Edge St., M4 1HN, 🖉 834 3743, Bistro – 📇 ☑
DZ **o**
closed Sunday, Monday, 1 week spring, August and 1 week after Christmas – **M** (dinner only)
a la carte 7.60/11.90 **t.** 🍷 2.50.

X **Mina**, 63 George St., 🖉 228 2598, Japanese rest. – 📇 ☑ ⑩ 𝗩𝗜𝗦𝗔
DZ **i**
M 13.00/18.00 **t.** and a la carte 11.00/18.00 **t.** 🍷 3.00.

X Yang Sing, 34 Princess St., 🖉 236 2200, Chinese rest.
DZ **a**

at Fallowfield S : 3 m. on B 5093 – ✉ ⊙ 061 Manchester :

🏨 **Willow Bank,** 340 Wilmslow Rd, M14 6AF, 🖉 224 0461, Telex 668222 – 📺 ⥾wc 🅿. 📇
☑ ⑩ 𝗩𝗜𝗦𝗔 – **M** 4.50/7.50 **st.** and a la carte 🍷 3.00 – 🖙 4.50 – **123 rm** 28.00/40.00 **st.** –
SB (weekends only) 53.00/56.00 **st.**
BY **x**

at Northenden S : 6 ½ m. by A 5103 – AY – off M 56 – ✉ ⊙ 061 Manchester :

🏨 **Post House** (T.H.F.), Palatine Rd, M22 4FH, 🖉 998 7090, Telex 669248 – 🛗 📺 ⥾wc 🅗 ᴴ
🅿. 📇 ☑ ⑩ 𝗩𝗜𝗦𝗔
M 7.50/10.25 **st.** and a la carte 🍷 3.50 – 🖙 5.65 – **200 rm** 50.00/58.00 **st.**

at Manchester Airport S : 9 m. by A 5103 – AY – off M 56 – ✉ ⊙ 061 Manchester :

🏨 **Excelsior** (T.H.F.), Ringway Rd, Wythenshawe, M22 5NS, 🖉 437 5811, Telex 668721, ⽔ heated – 🛗 ☰ 📇 ☎ 🅗 🅿. 🕍 📇 ☑ ⑩ 𝗩𝗜𝗦𝗔
M 8.50/10.50 **st.** and a la carte 🍷 3.70 – 🖙 6.00 – **304 rm** 56.00/66.00 **st.**, **4 suites**.

XXX **Moss Nook,** Ringway Rd, Moss Nook, M22 5NA, 🖉 437 4778 – 🅿. 📇 ☑ ⑩ 𝗩𝗜𝗦𝗔
closed lunch Saturday and Monday, Sunday, 2 weeks Christmas and Bank Holidays – **M**
16.50 **t.** and a la carte 17.90/24.45 **t.**

MICHELIN Distribution Centre, Ferris St., off Louisa St., Openshaw, M11 1BS, 🖉 223 2010 and
3274 BY

ALFA-ROMEO 123 a/b Jersey St. 🖉 205 2213
AUSTIN-ROVER Gill St. 🖉 205 2792
AUSTIN-ROVER 208 Bury New Rd 🖉 792 4343
BMW 325-327 Deansgate 🖉 832 8781
BMW 45 Upper Brook St. 🖉 273 1571
CITROEN, FIAT, LANCIA Ashton Old Rd 🖉 273 4411
FORD 292 Bury New Rd 🖉 792 6161
FORD 391 Palatine Rd 🖉 998 3427
FORD Oxford Rd 🖉 224 7301
FORD 660 Chester Rd 🖉 872 2201
FORD 3-5 New Wakefield St. 🖉 236 4168
HONDA Liverpool St. 🖉 737 3540
MAZDA Oldham Rd, Ashton 🖉 330 8135
MAZDA 54, Sackville St. 🖉 228 6727
MERCEDES-BENZ Upper Brook St. 🖉 273 8123
MORGAN, RELIANT, RENAULT Ashley Rd, Hale 🖉
941 1916

NISSAN Victoria Rd 🖉 330 3840
NISSAN Regent Rd, Salford 🖉 832 6041
PEUGEOT, TALBOT Chester Rd 🖉 834 6677
PORSCHE Bury New Rd at Whitefield 🖉 796 7414
RENAULT Blackfriars Rd 🖉 832 6121 770 Chester
Rd 🖉 865 1151
SAAB Water St. 🖉 832 6566
TOYOTA Greenside Lane 🖉 370 2145
TOYOTA Moseley Rd 🖉 224 6265
VAUXHALL-OPEL 292 Bury New Rd 🖉 792 4321
VAUXHALL-OPEL Blackfriars Rd 🖉 834 8200
VAUXHALL-OPEL 80-90 Port St., Gt Ancoats St. 🖉
236 4311
VAUXHALL-OPEL 799 Chester Rd 🖉 872 2141
VOLVO Rowsley St. 🖉 223 7272
VW, AUDI Ashton Old Rd 🖉 273 4361
VW, AUDI Stamford Rd 🖉 320 5454

MANNINGTREE Essex **404** X 28 – pop. 3 909 – ✆ 0206 Colchester.

•London 67 – Colchester 9 – •Ipswich 12.

XX Bucks, Cattawade, CO11 1RG, N : 1 ½ m. by B 1352 off A 137 ✆ 392571 – 🅿.

X **Clodd's,** 3-5 South St., CO11 1BA, ✆ 394102 – 🔼 *VISA*
closed Sunday, Monday and 5 to 18 October – **M** 7.50 **t.** and a la carte 7.50/10.85 **t.** ⌂ 2.90.

MANORBIER (MAENORBYR) Dyfed **403** F 29 – pop. 1 154 – ECD : Saturday – ✆ 083 482.
See : Castle* (13C) *AC.*

•London 253 – Carmarthen 33 – Haverfordwest 18.

🏠 **Castle Mead** ⚘, SA70 7TA, ✆ 358, ≼ Manorbier Bay, 🚳 – ⌂wc 🅿. 🅰🅴
Easter-October – **M** (bar lunch)/dinner 7.50 **st.** ⌂ 2.60 – **11 rm** ⌂ 15.50/35.00 **st.**

at Jameston W : 2 m. on A 4139 – ✉ ✆ 083 482 Manorbier :

🏠 **Tudor Lodge** ⚘, SA70 7SS, ✆ 320, 🚳 – 📺 ⌂wc 🍴wc 🅿. 🔼 *VISA*
closed January and February – **M** (bar lunch) 9.00 **t.** and a la carte ⌂ 3.95 – **10 rm**
⌂ 13.00/33.00 **t.** – SB (weekends only)(winter only) 39.00/46.00 **st.**

MARAZION Cornwall **403** D 33 The West Country G. – pop. 1 366 – ECD : Wednesday – ✉
✆ 0736 Penzance.

•London 318 – Penzance 3 – Truro 26.

🏠 **Mount Haven,** Turnpike Rd, TR17 0DQ, on A 394 ✆ 710249, ≼ St. Michael's Mount and
Mount's Bay – 📺 ⌂wc ☎ 🅿. 🔼 *VISA* ⚘
closed Christmas – **M** (bar lunch Monday to Saturday)/dinner 10.00 **t.** ⌂ 3.50 – **17 rm**
⌂ 17.50/37.00 **t.** – SB (except July and August) 45.00/49.00 **st.**

at Perranuthnoe SE : 1 ¾ m. by A 394 – ✉ ✆ 0736 Penzance :

⌂ **Ednovean House** ⚘, TR20 9LZ, ✆ 711071, ≼ St. Michael's Mount and Mount's Bay, 🚳 –
🍴wc 🅿
6 rm ⌂ 13.50/34.50 **t.**

MARKET DEEPING Lincs. **402** **404** T 25 – pop. 9 621 – ✆ 0778.

•London 94 – •Cambridge 44 – •Leicester 41 – Lincoln 42.

☎ **Deeping Stage,** 16 Market Pl., PE6 8EA, ✆ 343234, 🚳 – 🅿. 🅰🅴 ⓞ *VISA*. ⚘
M (Dancing Saturday) 6.00 **t.** and a la carte – **8 rm** ⌂ 16.00/30.00 **st.**

MARKET DRAYTON Salop **402** **403** **404** M 25 – pop. 9 003 – ECD : Thursday – ✆ 0630.

•London 161 – •Birmingham 44 – Chester 33 – Shrewsbury 19 – •Stoke-on-Trent 16.

☎ **Corbet Arms,** 8 High St., TF9 1PY, ✆ 2037 – 📺 ⌂wc 🍴wc ☎ 🅿. 🔼 🅰🅴 ⓞ *VISA*
M (carving lunch)/dinner 8.50 **t.** and a la carte ⌂ 2.25 – **12 rm** ⌂ 20.00/36.00 **t.** –
SB 36.50/48.00 **st.**

FORD Shrewsbury Rd ✆ 2027   VAUXHALL, VOLVO Cheshire St. ✆ 2444
RENAULT Shrewsbury Rd ✆ 4257

MARKET HARBOROUGH Leics. **404** R 26 – pop. 15 852 – ECD : Wednesday – ✆ 0858.
📕 Pen Lloyd Library, Adam and Eve St. ✆ 62649/62699.

•London 88 – •Birmingham 47 – •Leicester 15 – Northampton 17.

🏠 **Three Swans,** 21 High St., LE16 7NJ, ✆ 66644 – 📺 ⌂wc 🍴wc ☎ 🅿. 🔼 🅰🅴 ⓞ *VISA*
M (closed Sunday dinner) 6.50 **t.** (lunch) and a la carte 11.20/14.00 **t.** – **18 rm** ⌂ 36.50/48.00 **t.**

at East Langton N : 4 m. by A 6 off B 6047 – ✉ ✆ 0858 84 East Langton :

X **Bell Inn,** Main St., LE16 7TW, ✆ 567 – 🅿. 🔼 *VISA*
closed Sunday dinner – **M** 7.50/12.50 **t.** and a la carte 10.85/12.95 **t.** ⌂ 3.25.

at Marston Trussell (Northants.) W : 3 ½ m. by A 427 – ✉ ✆ 0858 Market Harborough :

🏠 **Sun Inn** ⚘, Main St., LE16 9TY, ✆ 65531 – 📺 ⌂wc 🍴wc ☎ 🅿. 🔼 🅰🅴 ⓞ *VISA*
M 7.00/15.00 **t.** ⌂ 3.50 – **10 rm** ⌂ 30.00/40.00 **t.** – SB 55.00/65.00 **st.**

ALFA-ROMEO Main St. ✆ 66984   VAUXHALL-OPEL Springfield St. ✆ 67177
FORD Leicester Rd ✆ 66688   VW-AUDI Northampton Rd ✆ 65511
RENAULT Abbey St. ✆ 32530

MARKET RASEN Lincs. **402** **404** T 23 – pop. 3 050 – ECD : Thursday – ✆ 0673.

•London 159 – Great Grimsby 20 – Lincoln 16.

🏠 **Limes,** Gainsborough Rd, LN8 3JN, ✆ 842357, 🚳, squash – 📺 ⌂wc 🍴wc ☎ 🅿. 🔼 ⓞ
VISA
M (closed Saturday lunch) a la carte 7.35/13.50 **t.** ⌂ 2.75 – **15 rm** ⌂ 32.00/40.00 **t.** –
SB (weekends only) 60.00/80.00 **st.**

XX **Carafe,** 5 King St., LN8 3BB, ✆ 843427 – 🔼 🅰🅴 ⓞ
closed Sunday, Monday, 2 weeks August and 2 weeks after Christmas – **M** 5.00/15.00 **t.** and a
la carte 10.10/13.80 **t.** ⌂ 2.80.

AUSTIN-ROVER Market Pl. ✆ 842355   RENAULT Willingham Rd ✆ 842951

352

MARKET WEIGHTON Humberside **402** S 22 – pop. 3 775 – ECD : Thursday – ✉ York – ☎ 0696.
◆London 208 – ◆Kingston-upon-Hull 18 – ◆Leeds 40 – York 19.

　🏠　Londesborough Arms, High St., YO4 3AH, ✗ 72219 – 📺 🛏wc ⋔wc ☎ 🅿
　　14 rm.

MARKINGTON North Yorks. **402** P 21 – see Harrogate.

MARLBOROUGH Wilts. **403 404** O 29 The West Country G. – pop. 5 330 – ECD : Wednesday –
☎ 0672.

See : Site ★.

Envir. : Savernake Forest★★ (Grand Avenue★★★), SE : 2 m. off A 346 – The Ridgeway Path★★,
85 miles starting from Overton Hill near Avebury including White Horse ⩤★ – West Kennett Long
Barrow★, W : 4 ½ m. – Silbury Hill★, W : 6 m. – Pewsey : Vale of Pewsey★, S : 7 m. on A 3455 – at
Avebury★, The Stones★, Church★, W : 7 m. – Wilton Windmill★AC, S : 9 m. by A 346 on A 338 – at
Great Bedwyn, Crofton Beam Engines★AC, on Kennet and Avon Canal, SE : 10 m.

🄹₈ The Common ✗ 52147, N : 1 m.

🅱 St. Peter's Church, High St. ✗ 53989 (summer only).

◆London 84 – ◆Bristol 47 – ◆Southampton 40 – Swindon 12.

　🏠　Ivy House, High St., SN8 1HJ, ✗ 53188 – 📺 🛏wc ☎ 🅿 🔼 *VISA* . 🍽
　　M (restricted dinner Sunday) 11.50/12.50 t. and a la carte ⅃ 4.50 – 12 rm ⌣ 33.50/58.00 t. –
　　SB 50.00/70.00 st.

　🏠　Castle and Ball (T.H.F.), High St., SN8 1LZ, ✗ 55201 – 📺 🛏wc ☎ 🅿 ᴁ. 🔼 🆎 ⓞ *VISA*
　　M 10.20/19.65 st. and a la carte ⅃ 3.40 – ⌣ 5.65 – 36 rm 43.00/51.00 st.

AUSTIN-ROVER　80-83 High St. ✗ 52076　　　　　　　　　　PORSCHE　London Rd ✗ 52001

MARLOW Bucks. **404** R 29 – pop. 18 584 – ECD : Wednesday – ☎ 062 84.

🅱 Caravan, Higginson Park, Pound Lane ✗ 3597.

◆London 35 – Aylesbury 22 – ◆Oxford 29 – Reading 14.

　🏛　Compleat Angler (T.H.F.), Marlow Bridge, Bisham Rd, SL7 1RG, ✗ 4444, Telex 848644, ⩤
　　River Thames, « Riverside setting and gardens », 🌂, 🍽 – 📺 ☎ 🅿 🔼 🆎 *VISA* –
　　M 20.00 st. (lunch) and a la carte 19.00/32.00 st. ⅃ 6.00 – ⌣ 8.00 – 46 rm 75.00/90.00 t.,
　　4 suites.

　✗　Hare and Hounds, Henley Rd, SL7 2DF, SW : ¾ m. on A 4155 ✗ 3343 – 🅿 🔼 🆎
　　closed Sunday – M a la carte 13.00/16.75 t. ⅃ 2.80.

AUSTIN-ROVER　Oxford Rd ✗ 6333

MARSTON TRUSSELL Northants. – see Market Harborough (Leics.).

MARTINHOE Devon – see Lynton.

MARTON Cleveland – see Middlesbrough.

MARYPORT Cumbria **401 402** J 19 – pop. 9 890 – ECD : Wednesday – ✉ ☎ 0900.
◆London 334 – ◆Carlisle 28 – Workington 6.

　　at Birkby NE : 1 ½ m. on A 596 – ✉ ☎ 0900 Maryport :

　✗✗　Retreat, CA15 6RG, ✗ 814056, 🍽 – 🅿 🔼 *VISA*
　　closed Monday and Christmas Day – M 7.00/11.00 t. and a la carte 5.85/12.65 t. ⅃ 3.00.

MARY TAVY Devon **403** H 32 – see Tavistock.

MASHAM North Yorks. **402** P 21 – pop. 976 – ECD : Thursday – ✉ Ripon – ☎ 0677 Bedale.
◆London 231 – ◆Leeds 38 – ◆Middlesbrough 37 – York 32.

　🏛　Jervaulx Hall ⬏, HG4 4PH, NW : 5 ½ m. on A 6108 ✗ 60235, ⩤, « Converted manor house,
　　country house atmosphere », 🌂, park – 🛏wc ৬ 🅿
　　March-November – M (dinner only) 13.00 st. ⅃ 3.25 – 8 rm ⌣ 39.00/74.00 t. – SB (October-
　　May) 60.00/70.00 st.

　⋔　Bank Villa, HG4 4DB, on A 6108 ✗ 0765 (Ripon) 89605, 🌂 – ⋔
　　March-October – 7 rm ⌣ 13.50/22.00 st.

In addition to establishments indicated by
XXXXX ... X ,
many hotels possess
good class restaurants.

MATLOCK Derbs. 402 403 404 P 24 – pop. 13 706 – ECD : Thursday – ✆ 0629.
See : Site★.
Envir. : Riber Castle (ruins) ≼★ (Fauna Reserve and Wildlife Park *AC*) SE : 2 ½ m.
🛈 The Pavilion ℘ 55082.
♦London 153 – Derby 17 – ♦Manchester 46 – ♦Nottingham 24 – ♦Sheffield 24.

  🏥 **Riber Hall** ⬩, Riber, DE4 5JU, SE : 3 m. by A 615 ℘ 2795, ≼, « Elizabethan manor house »,
    🚗 – 📺 ⌷wc ☎ 🅿. 🔼 🆎 ⓞ 𝚅𝙸𝚂𝙰. ✼
    M 12.00 t. (lunch) and a la carte 21.50/26.50 t. ⌕ 3.40 – ⌷ 4.00 – **11 rm** 47.00/62.00 t. –
    SB (mid October-mid April) 87.00/111.00 **st**.

  at Matlock Bath S : 1 ½ m. on A 6 – ✉ ✆ 0629 Matlock :

  🏥 **New Bath** (T.H.F.), New Bath Rd, DE4 3PX, ℘ 3275, ⌇ heated, 🔲, 🚗, ✼ – 📺 ⌷wc ☎
    🅿. ⌕ 🔼 🆎 ⓞ 𝚅𝙸𝚂𝙰. ✼
    M 7.95/11.20 **st**. and a la carte ⌕ 3.40 – ⌷ 5.65 – **56 rm** 42.00/54.00 **st**.

AUSTIN-ROVER Bakewell Rd ℘ 3291   FORD 41 Causeway Lane ℘ 2231

MATLOCK BATH Derbs. 402 403 404 P 24 – see Matlock.

MAWGAN Cornwall 403 E 33 – ✉ Helston – ✆ 032 622.
♦London 317 – Falmouth 18 – Penzance 19 – Truro 22.

  ✖ **Yard Bistro**, Trelowarren, TR12 6AF, SE : 1 ½ m. by B 3293 ℘ 595, « Converted coach
    house » – 🅿
    closed Sunday dinner, Monday except Bank Holidays and 20 December-15 March – **M** a la
    carte 8.00/11.40 t.

MAWGAN PORTH Cornwall 403 E 32 – ECD : Wednesday – ✉ Newquay – ✆ 0637 St. Mawgan.
♦London 293 – Newquay 7 – Truro 20.

  🏠 **Tredragon**, TR8 4DQ, ℘ 860213, ≼ Mawgan Porth, 🔲, 🚗 – ⌷wc ⌷wc 🅿. 🔼 𝚅𝙸𝚂𝙰
    Easter-October – **M** *(closed Sunday dinner)* (bar lunch Monday to Saturday)/dinner 7.00 **st**.
    ⌕ 2.80 – **30 rm** ⌷ 13.00/42.00 **st**.

MAWNAN SMITH Cornwall 403 E 33 – see Falmouth.

MAYFIELD East Sussex 404 U 30 – pop. 1 784 – ECD : Wednesday – ✆ 0435.
♦London 46 – ♦Brighton 25 – Eastbourne 22 – Lewes 17 – Royal Tunbridge Wells 9.

  ✖ **Old Brew House**, High St., TN20 6AG, ℘ 872342 – 🆎 ⓞ 𝚅𝙸𝚂𝙰
    *closed Tuesday after Bank Holidays, Sunday, Monday, 2 weeks August-September and
    24 December-2 January* – **M** (dinner only and Saturday lunch) 6.50/13.50 t. ⌕ 4.60.

MEASHAM Leics. 402 403 404 P 25 – pop. 4 184 – ECD : Wednesday – ✆ 0530.
♦London 122 – ♦Birmingham 25 – ♦Leicester 21 – ♦Nottingham 26.

  🏠 Measham Inn, Tamworth Rd, DE12 7DY, ℘ 70095 – 📺 ⌷wc ☎ 🅿
    31 rm.

MELBOURN Cambs. 404 U 27 – pop. 3 846 – ✉ ✆ 0763 Royston (Herts.).
♦London 44 – ♦Cambridge 10.

  ✖✖ **Pink Geranium**, 25 Station Rd, SG8 6DX, ℘ 60215, « Attractively converted cottage », 🚗
    – 🅿. 🔼 🆎 𝚅𝙸𝚂𝙰
    closed Saturday lunch, Sunday, Monday, last 2 weeks August and Bank Holidays – **M** 7.25 t.
    (lunch) and a la carte 14.00/16.50 t. ⌕ 2.50.

  ✖✖ **Sheen Mill** with rm, Station Rd, SG8 6DH, ℘ 61393, ≼, 🚗 – 📺 ⌷wc 🅿. 🔼 🆎 ⓞ 𝚅𝙸𝚂𝙰. ✼
    closed Bank Holidays – **M** *(closed Sunday dinner)* (Dancing Saturday) 7.50 t. (lunch) and a la
    carte 11.65/17.45 t. ⌕ 2.50 – **7 rm** ⌷ 32.50/55.00 **st**.

MELKSHAM Wilts. 403 404 N 29 – pop. 13 248 – ECD : Wednesday – ✆ 0225.
🛈 Round House, 25 Church St. ℘ 707424.
♦London 113 – ♦Bristol 25 – Salisbury 35 – Swindon 28.

  ✖✖✖ **Beechfield House** with rm, Beanacre, SN12 7PU, N : 1 m. on A 350 ℘ 703700, Telex 444969,
    ≼, « Country house and gardens », ⌇ heated, ⬩ park, ✼ – 📺 ⌷wc ☎ 🅿. 🔼 🆎 ⓞ 𝚅𝙸𝚂𝙰
    ✼
    M 12.95 **st**. (lunch) and a la carte 18.45/24.00 **st**. ⌕ 4.50 – **16 rm** ⌷ 45.00/90.00 **st**. –
    SB (November-March) 87.50 **st**.

  at Shaw NW : 1 ¼ m. on A 365 – ✉ Melksham – ✆ 0225 Shaw :

  ↥ **Shaw Farm**, Bath Rd, SN12 8EF, on A 365 ℘ 702836, ⌇ heated, 🚗 – ⌷wc 🅿. 🔼 🆎 𝚅𝙸𝚂𝙰
    ✼
    closed 25 and 26 December – **12 rm** ⌷ 15.50/31.00 **st**.

AUSTIN-ROVER Lancaster Rd ℘ 702256

MELLOR Lancs. − see Blackburn.

MELTHAM West Yorks. 402 404 O 23 − pop. 7 098 − ✉ ✿ 0484 Huddersfield.
🔞 Thick Hollins Hall ✆ 850227, E : 1 m.
♦London 192 − ♦Leeds 21 − ♦Manchester 23 − ♦Sheffield 26.

   🏦 **Durker Roods,** Bishops Way, HD7 3AG, ✆ 851413, ☞ − 🆅 ⊟wc �🚻wc ☎ 🅿. 🏄. 🔼 AE
     ① VISA
     closed Christmas night − **M** *(closed Saturday lunch and Sunday dinner)* 6.00/8.00 **t.**
     and a la carte ▯ 3.00 − **32 rm** �码 25.00/40.00 **t.** − SB (weekends only) 45.00 **st.**

MELTON MOWBRAY Leics. 402 404 R 25 − pop. 23 379 − ECD : Thursday − ✿ 0664.
🔞 Thorpe Arnold ✆ 62118, NE : 2 m.
🅱 Carnegie Museum, Thorpe End. ✆ 69946.
♦London 113 − ♦Leicester 15 − Northampton 45 − ♦Nottingham 18.

   🏦 **George,** High St., LE13 0TR, ✆ 62112 − 🆅 ⊟wc �🚻wc ☎ 🅿. 🏄.
     20 rm.

   🏦 **Harboro,** Burton St., LE13 1AF, ✆ 60121, Group Telex 858875 − 🆅 ⊟wc �🚻wc ☎ 🅿. 🏄. 🔼
     AE ① VISA
     M 9.50 **t.** and a la carte ▯ 3.35 − **28 rm** �码 39.00/51.50 **t.** − SB (weekends only) 55.00 **st.**

   🏛 **Quorn Lodge,** 46 Asfordby Rd, LE13 0HR, ✆ 66660 − 🆅 ⊟wc �🚻wc ☎ 🅿. 🔼 AE ① VISA
     🐾
     M 8.00/17.50 **st.** and a la carte − **10 rm** �码 30.00/65.00 **st.** − SB (weekends only) 105.00/130.00 **st.**

   🏠 **Westbourne House,** Nottingham Rd, LE13 0NP, ✆ 69456, ☞ − 🅿. 🐾
     closed 24 December-2 January − **16 rm** ⊑ 14.00/27.00 **t.**

   at Kirby Bellars W : 2 ¾ m. on A 607 − ✉ ✿ 0664 Melton Mowbray :

   ✕✕ **Kirby Gatehouse,** LE14 2DU, ✆ 813028, ☞ − 🅿.

AUSTIN-ROVER ✆ 60266   TALBOT 26 Victoria St. ✆ 62235
FIAT Mill St. ✆ 60141   VOLVO 56 Scalford Rd ✆ 63241

MENTMORE Bucks. 404 R 28 − pop. 196 − ✉ Leighton Buzzard − ✿ 0296 Cheddington.
♦London 46 − Aylesbury 10 − Luton 15.

   🏛 **The Stable Yard** without rest., LU7 0QG, ✆ 661488, « Attractive 19C stable and coach yard »
     − 🆅 🅿
     5 rm.

   ✕✕ **Stag Inn,** The Green, LU7 0QF, ✆ 668423, ☞ − 🅿. 🔼 AE ① VISA
     closed Monday − **M** 7.50 **t.** (lunch) and a la carte 14.90/21.30 **t.** ▯ 3.50.

MERE Wilts. 403 404 N 30 **The West Country G.** − pop. 2 201 − ECD : Wednesday − ✿ 0747.
Envir. : Stourhead House★★★ *AC*, NW : 3 m.
🅱 The Square, Church St. ✆ 860341.
♦London 113 − Exeter 65 − Salisbury 26 − Taunton 40.

   🏛 **Old Ship,** Castle St., BA12 6JE, ✆ 860258 − 🆅 ⊟wc �🚻wc ☎ 🅿. 🔼 VISA
     M a la carte 8.20/13.80 **t.** ▯ 3.00 − **24 rm** ⊑ 23.50/40.00 **st.** − SB 52.00/56.00 **st.**

AUSTIN-ROVER Salisbury St. ✆ 860244   CITROEN Castle St. ✆ 860404

MERE BROW Lancs. 402 L 23 − ✉ Preston − ✿ 077 473 Hesketh Bank.
♦London 221 − ♦Liverpool 22 − Preston 11 − Southport 6.

   ✕ **Crab and Lobster,** behind the Leigh Arms, Tarleton, PR4 6LA, ✆ 2734, Seafood − 🅿
     closed Sunday, Monday and Christmas-late January − **M** (dinner only) a la carte 9.75/15.00 **t.**

MERIDEN West Midlands 403 404 P 26 − see Coventry.

MERSHAM Kent − see Ashford.

MEVAGISSEY Cornwall 403 F 33 **The West Country G.** − pop. 1 896 − ECD : Thursday − ✿ 0726.
See : Site ★★.
♦London 287 − Newquay 21 − ♦Plymouth 44 − Truro 20.

   🏛 **Trevalsa Court** 🐾, School Hill, Polstreath, PL26 6TH, ✆ 842468, ≼, ☞ − 🆅 ⊟wc �🚻wc
     🅿. 🔼 AE ① VISA
     closed mid December-mid January − **M** (bar lunch)/dinner 7.00 **t.** and a la carte ▯ 3.00 − **10 rm**
     ⊑ 15.00/38.50 **t.**

   🏠 **Mevagissey House,** Vicarage Hill, PL26 6SZ, ✆ 842427, ☞ − 🆅 �🚻wc 🅿. 🐾
     March-October − **6 rm** ⊑ 14.00/33.00.

MICKLETON Glos. 403 404 O 27 − see Chipping Campden.

MIDDLEHAM North Yorks. 402 O 21 – pop. 737 – ECD : Thursday – ☎ 0969 Wensleydale.
♦London 233 – Kendal 45 – ♦Leeds 47 – York 45.

🏛 **Miller's House,** Market Pl., DL8 4NR, ℰ 22630, 🚗 – 📺 ⌂wc 🅿 🔼 ✗
 closed December and January – **M** (dinner only) 10.00 **st.** 🍷 2.50 – **6 rm** ⫴ 20.00/38.00 **st.** –
 SB (except summer) 50.00 **st.**

MIDDLESBROUGH Cleveland 402 Q 20 – pop. 158 516 – ECD : Wednesday – ☎ 0642.
🏌 Middlesbrough Municipal, Ladgate Lane ℰ 315533, S : by Acklam Rd AZ.
✈ Teesside Airport : ℰ 0325 (Darlington) 332811, SW : 13 m. by A 66 AZ and A 19 on A 67.
🅱 125 Albert Rd ℰ 245750/245432 ext 3580.
♦London 246 – ♦Kingston-upon-Hull 89 – ♦Leeds 66 – ♦Newcastle-upon-Tyne 41.

MIDDLESBROUGH

🏨 **Ladbroke Dragonara** (Ladbroke), Fry St., TS1 1JH, ℰ 248133, Telex 58266 – 🕃 📺 ⌨wc
☎ 🅿 ⅏ 🔄 ⁄Ⅎ ⓪ 𝘝𝘐𝘚𝘈 ⅏   BY **c**
M *(closed lunch Saturday and Sunday)* (carving rest.) 9.75 🅙 3.70 – ⌲ 6.00 – **140 rm**
40.00/51.00 **st.**, **3 suites** – SB (weekends only) 63.00 **st.**

🏨 **Baltimore,** 250 Marton Rd, TS4 2EZ, ℰ 224111, Telex 58517 – 📺 ⌨wc ☎ 🅿 🔄 ⁄Ⅎ ⓪ 𝘝𝘐𝘚𝘈
M *(closed Saturday lunch)* 6.50/6.95 **st.** and a la carte – ⌲ 3.75 – **31 rm** 27.50/40.50 **st.**,
1 suite 60.00/80.00 **st.** – SB (weekends only) 39.00/69.00 **st.**   BZ **e**

🏨 **Marton Way Motel,** Marton Rd, TS4 3BS, S : 2 m. on A 172 ℰ 817651, Telex 587783 – 📺
⌨wc ⊕ 🅿 ⅏ 🔄 ⁄Ⅎ ⓪ 𝘝𝘐𝘚𝘈   BZ **a**
closed Christmas night – **M** (carving rest.) 4.95 **st.** and a la carte – **53 rm** ⌲ 32.00/44.00 **st** –
SB (weekends only) 43.00/50.00 **st.**

⌂ **Grey House,** 79 Cambridge Rd, TS5 5NL, ℰ 817485, ⋉ – 📺 🔥wc 🅿   AZ **n**
closed Christmas and New Year – **10 rm** ⌲ 14.00/28.00 **s.**

at Marton SE : 4 m. on A 172 – BZ – ✉ ☎ 0642 Middlesbrough :

🏨 **Blue Bell** (Swallow), Acklam Rd, TS5 7HL, W : 1 ¾ m. on B 1380 ℰ 593939, Group Telex
53168 – 🕃 📺 ⌨wc ⊕ 🅿 🔄 ⁄Ⅎ ⓪ 𝘝𝘐𝘚𝘈
M 4.75/9.00 **st.** and a la carte 🅙 3.95 – **60 rm** ⌲ 39.00/46.00 **st.** – SB (weekends only) 50.00 **st.**

AUSTIN-ROVER 336 Stokesley Rd, Marton ℰ 317171	TALBOT Marton Rd ℰ 242873
CITROEN Linthorpe Rd ℰ 822884	TOYOTA Eastbourne Rd ℰ 816658
FIAT Longlands Rd ℰ 244651	VAUXHALL-OPEL Marton Rd ℰ 243415
RENAULT Newport Rd ℰ 249346	VW, AUDI Park End ℰ 317971
SKODA Eston Grange ℰ 452436	

MIDDLETON IN TEESDALE Durham 𝟜𝟘𝟙 𝟜𝟘𝟚 N 20 – pop. 1 132 – ECD : Wednesday – ☎ 0833
Teesdale – Envir. : High Force★★ (waterfalls) *AC*, NW : 5 m.
🛈 1 Market Pl. ℰ 40806.

◆London 268 – ◆ Carlisle 40 – ◆Leeds 68 – ◆Middlesbrough 41 – ◆Newcastle-upon-Tyne 49.

🏡 **Teesdale,** Market Pl., DL12 0QG, ℰ 40264 – 📺 ⌨wc 🅿 𝘝𝘐𝘚𝘈
M (bar lunch Monday to Saturday)/dinner 9.20 **t.** and a la carte 🅙 3.15 – **14 rm** ⌲ 18.95/37.90 **t.**
– SB (except summer and Bank Holidays) 47.50/49.50 **st.**

at Romaldkirk SE : 4 m. on B 6277 – ✉ Barnard Castle – ☎ 0833 Teesdale :

🏨 Rose and Crown, DL12 9EB, ℰ 50213 – 📺 ⌨wc 🔥wc ⊕ 🅿
15 rm

FORD ℰ 40213

MIDDLETON STONEY Oxon. 𝟜𝟘𝟛 𝟜𝟘𝟜 Q 28 – pop. 238 – ECD : Saturday – ✉ Bicester –
☎ 086 989.
◆London 66 – Northampton 30 – ◆Oxford 12.

🏡 **Jersey Arms Inn,** Ardley Rd, OX6 8SE, ℰ 234 – 📺 ⌨wc ☎ 🅿 🔄 ⁄Ⅎ ⓪ 𝘝𝘐𝘚𝘈 ⅏
M *(closed Sunday dinner to non-residents)* 11.50 **t.** and a la carte 🅙 3.75 – **14 rm**
⌲ 32.00/43.00 **t.**, **4 suites** 39.00/55.00 **t.** – SB 60.00/65.00 **st.**

MIDDLE WALLOP Hants. 𝟜𝟘𝟛 𝟜𝟘𝟜 P 30 – ✉ Stockbridge – ☎ 0264 Andover.
◆London 80 – Salisbury 11 – ◆Southampton 21.

🏨 **Fifehead Manor,** SO20 8EG, on A 343 ℰ 781565, « 16C converted manor house », ⋉ – 📺
⌨wc 🔥wc ⅙ 🅿 🔄 ⁄Ⅎ ⓪ 𝘝𝘐𝘚𝘈
closed 2 weeks at Christmas – **M** 18.00 **st.** and a la carte 🅙 3.50 – **16 rm** ⌲ 36.00/65.00 **st.** –
SB (November-Easter) 65.00/70.00 **st.**

✕✕ **Old Drapery Stores** with rm, Station Rd, SO20 8HN, ℰ 781301, ⋉ – 📺 🔥 🅿 🔄 ⁄Ⅎ ⓪ 𝘝𝘐𝘚𝘈
⅏
closed 26 December and 1 January – **M** *(closed Saturday lunch and Sunday)* a la carte
11.80/13.55 **t.** – **4 rm** ⌲ 18.00/40.00 **st.**

MIDHURST West Sussex 𝟜𝟘𝟜 R 31 – pop. 5 991 – ECD : Wednesday – ☎ 073 081.
See : Cowdray House (Tudor ruins)★ *AC* – Envir. : Uppark★ (17C-18C) *AC*, SW : 12 m.
🖽 Cowdray Park ℰ 2088, NE : 1 m. on A 272 – 🖽 at Petersfield ℰ 0730 (Petersfield) 67732, W : 10 m.
◆London 57 – ◆Brighton 38 – Chichester 12 – ◆Southampton 41.

🏨🏨 **Spread Eagle** (Best Western), South St., GU29 9NH, ℰ 6911, Telex 86853, « 15C hostelry »
– 📺 ☎ 🅿 🔄 ⁄Ⅎ ⓪ 𝘝𝘐𝘚𝘈
M 10.50/14.50 **st.** and a la carte 🅙 4.25 – **29 rm** ⌲ 45.00/92.50 **st.** – SB 70.00/80.00 **st.**

✕ **Maxine's,** Red Lion St., GU29 9PB, ℰ 6271 – 🔄 ⁄Ⅎ ⓪ 𝘝𝘐𝘚𝘈
closed Monday lunch, Tuesday and 15 February-4 March – **M** 7.95 **st.** and a la carte
11.00/15.00 **st.** 🅙 3.65.

✕ **Mida,** Wool Lane, GU29 9BY, ℰ 3284
closed Sunday, Monday, 1 week spring and 1 week winter – **M** (booking essential) a la carte
approx. 20.00.

at Bepton SW : 2 ¼ m. by A 286 – ✉ ☎ 073 081 Midhurst :

Park House ⛰, GU29 0JB, ☎ 2880, heated, ⛰, ✂ – TV wc wc P
M (dinner only) 12.50 – **11 rm** 28.75/69.00 **t.**

at Trotton W : 3 ¼ m. on A 272 – ✉ Petersfield (Hants.) – ☎ 073 080 Rogate :

Southdowns ⛰, GU31 5JN, S : 1 m. ☎ 521, – TV wc ☎ P. AE VISA
M 7.50 **t.** and a la carte 2.75 – **8 rm** 25.00/45.00 **t.** – SB (except Christmas) 39.00/49.00 **st.**

AUSTIN-ROVER Petersfield Rd ☎ 2443 RENAULT Rumbolds Hill ☎ 2162

MILDENHALL Suffolk 404 V 26 – pop. 9 794 – ECD : Thursday – ☎ 0638.
♦London 73 – ♦Cambridge 22 – ♦Ipswich 38 – ♦Norwich 41.

Bell (Best Western), High St., IP28 7EA, ☎ 717272 – TV wc ☎ P. AE VISA
M a la carte 7.30/13.00 **t.** – **18 rm** 24.00/39.00 **t.** – SB (weekends only) 52.00 **st.**

MILFORD HAVEN (ABERDAUGLEDDAU) Dyfed 403 E 28 – pop. 13 927 ☎ 064 62.
♦London 258 – Carmarthen 39 – Fishguard 23.

Lord Nelson, Hamilton Terr., SA73 2AL, ☎ 5341, – TV wc wc ☎ P. AE VISA
M (bar lunch)/dinner 7.95 **t.** – **29 rm** 26.00/37.00 **t.**

Wanderer Bistro, 27 Hamilton Terr., SA73 3JJ, ☎ 7594
closed Sunday dinner and Monday – **M** (restricted lunch) 5.00/10.00 **st.** and a la carte 6.95/10.15 **st.** 2.80.

MILFORD-ON-SEA Hants. 403 404 P 31 – pop. 3 953 – ECD : Wednesday – ✉ Lymington – ☎ 0590.
♦London 109 – Bournemouth 15 – ♦Southampton 24 – Winchester 37.

South Lawn, Lymington Rd, SO41 0RF, ☎ 43911, – TV wc ☎ P. VISA.
closed mid December-mid January – **M** (dinner only and Sunday lunch) 9.50 **t.** 3.50 – **24 rm** 27.50/48.00 **t.** – SB (except summer) 55.00 **st.**

Westover Hall, Park Lane, SO4 0PT, ☎ 43044, ≤ Solent and the Needles, « Restored Victorian mansion » – TV wc wc ☎ P. AE VISA
M 7.00/10.00 **t.** 2.75 – **11 rm** 19.00/60.00 **t.** – SB (except summer)(weekends only) 41.00/49.00 **t.**

MILNROW Greater Manchester 402 404 N 23 – pop. 11 647 – ✉ Rochdale (Lancs.) – ☎ 045 77 Saddleworth.
♦London 222 – ♦Manchester 14 – Rochdale 2.

Moorcock, Huddersfield Rd, OL16 3TJ, SE : 3 m. on A 640 ☎ 2659, ≤ – P. AE VISA
closed Sunday dinner and Monday – **M** 8.75 **t.** and a la carte 10.85/23.40 **t.** 4.50.

MILTON ABBAS Dorset 403 404 N 31 The West Country G. – pop. 433 – ✉ Blandford – ☎ 0258.
See : Village★.
♦London 127 – Bournemouth 23 – Weymouth 19.

Milton Manor ⛰, DT11 0AZ, ☎ 880254, ≤, « Country house atmosphere », , park – wc wc P. VISA.
April-October – **M** (bar lunch)/dinner 9.00 **t.** 2.75 – **12 rm** 23.00/50.00 **t.**

MILTON DAMEREL Devon 403 H 31 – pop. 454 – ✉ Holsworthy – ☎ 040 926.
♦London 249 – Barnstaple 21 – ♦Plymouth 48.

Woodford Bridge, EX22 7LL, N : 1 m. on A 388 ☎ 481, « Part 15C inn », , , , ✂, squash – ☎ P.
M (bar lunch)/dinner 14.00 **st.** and a la carte 3.25 – **23 rm** 17.00/63.00 **st.** – SB (October-May) 54.00/73.00 **st.**

MILTON KEYNES Bucks. 404 R 27 – pop. 93 305 – ☎ 0908.
Abbey Hill, Two Mile Ash ☎ 563845, W : 2 m. off A 5.
Saxon Court, 502 Avebury Boulevard ☎ 678361 and 664666.
♦London 56 – ♦Birmingham 72 – Bedford 16 – Northampton 18 – ♦Oxford 37.

Post House (T.H.F.), 500 Saxon Gate, Milton Keynes Central, MK9 2HQ, ☎ 667722, Telex 826842, – TV ☎ P. AE VISA
M 9.50/12.50 **st.** and a la carte 3.40 – 5.95 – **163 rm** 47.50/120.00 **st.**

at Woughton on the Green SE : 2 m. by A 509 off A 4146 – ✉ ☎ 0908 Milton Keynes :

Woughton House, MK6 3LR, ☎ 661919, – TV wc wc ☎ P – **20 rm**.

at Stony Stratford NW : 5 m. – ✉ ❀ 0908 Milton Keynes :

※※ **Stratfords,** 7 St. Paul's Court, 118 High St.,, MK11 1LJ, ℰ 566577, « Converted Victorian church » – **Ⓟ** 🖪 🄰🄴 ⓞ 𝘝𝘐𝘚𝘈
closed Saturday lunch, Sunday dinner, Monday and 3 to 13 January – **M** 10.50/15.75 **t.** and a la carte.

※ Akber Tandoori, 10-12 Wolverton Rd, ℰ 562487, Indian rest. – 🍽.

AUDI 3 Denbigh Rd ℰ 641535
AUSTIN-ROVER 32 Aylesbury St. ℰ 643636
FIAT Unit 15, Erica Rd ℰ 320355
FORD Bilton Rd ℰ 74011
FORD Stratford Rd ℰ 313117

LADA 9 London Rd ℰ 562361
NISSAN Tavistock St. ℰ 75388
PEUGEOT-TALBOT 125 Buckingham Rd ℰ 643322
SAAB Old Stratford Rd ℰ 562194
TOYOTA 84 Newport Rd ℰ 313383

MILTON ON STOUR Dorset 🄽🄾🄳 🄽🄾🄴 N 30 – see Gillingham.

MINEHEAD Somerset 🄽🄾🄳 J 30 **The West Country G.** – pop. 8 449 – ECD : Wednesday – ❀ 0643.
See : Site ★ – Higher Town : Church Steps ★ – St. Michael's Church ★ – West Somerset Railway★ – Envir. : Selworthy★ : Church★★ (⪕★★★ from Church of Dunkery Beacon), W : 4½ m. – Timberscombe Church★, S : 5 m.

🛈 Warren Rd ℰ 2057 – 🄱 Market House, The Parade ℰ 2624.
◆London 187 – ◆Bristol 64 – Exeter 43 – Taunton 25.

🏠 **Northfield** (Best Western) ⌇, Northfield Rd, TA24 5PU, ℰ 5155, « ⪕ gardens », 🖪 – 🌭 📺 ⌂wc ☎ & **Ⓟ** 🖪 🄰🄴 ⓞ 𝘝𝘐𝘚𝘈
M 7.50/12.95 **t.** and a la carte ⸙ 3.00 – **27 rm** ⚌ 30.25/75.50 **t.**

🏠 **Benares** ⌇, Northfield Rd, TA24 5PT, ℰ 2340, ☞ – 📺 ⌂wc **Ⓟ** 🖪 🄰🄴 ⓞ 𝘝𝘐𝘚𝘈
March-October and Christmas – **M** (bar lunch)/dinner 9.75 **t.** ⸙ 2.75 – **21 rm** ⚌ 17.00/40.00 **t.** – SB 47.00/58.00 **st.**

🏠 **Beach** (T.H.F.), The Avenue, TA24 5AP, ℰ 2193, ⅃ heated – 📺 ⌂wc ☎ **Ⓟ** 🖪 🄰🄴 ⓞ 𝘝𝘐𝘚𝘈
M (buffet lunch)/dinner 10.00 **st.** and a la carte ⸙ 3.40 – ⚌ 5.65 – **34 rm** 36.00/45.00 **st.**

🏠 **Merton,** Western Lane, The Parks, TA24 8BZ, ℰ 2375, ☞ – 📺 ⌂wc ⧏wc & **Ⓟ** 🖪 🄰🄴 ⓞ 𝘝𝘐𝘚𝘈
April-October – **M** (bar lunch)/dinner 8.00 **st.** ⸙ 2.45 – **12 rm** ⚌ 11.00/37.40 **st.**

🏠 **Beaconwood** ⌇, Church Rd, North Hill, TA24 5SB, ℰ 2032, ⪕ sea and Minehead, ⅃ heated, ☞ – 📺 ⌂wc ⧏wc **Ⓟ** 🖪 𝘝𝘐𝘚𝘈
closed January and February – **M** (bar lunch)/dinner 8.25 **st.** ⸙ 2.40 – **16 rm** ⚌ 14.80/37.60 **st.** – SB (except July-September) 40.00/47.00 **st.**

🏠 **Remuera,** Northfield Rd, TA24 5QH, ℰ 2611, ☞ – 📺 ⌂wc **Ⓟ** 🖪
April-October – **M** (bar lunch)/dinner 7.00 ⸙ 3.50 – **8 rm** ⚌ 17.00/24.00.

🏠 **York,** 48 The Avenue, TA24 5AN, ℰ 5151 – ⌂wc ⧏wc ☎ **Ⓟ** 🖪 🄰🄴 ⓞ 𝘝𝘐𝘚𝘈 ⌇
M (grill rest. only) a la carte 6.05/10.50 **st.** ⸙ 2.60 – **22 rm** ⚌ 12.00/30.00 **st.** – SB 34.00/44.00 **st.**

🏠 **Mentone,** The Parks, TA24 8BS, ℰ 5229, ☞ – 📺 ⌂wc ⧏wc. ⌇
April-October – **9 rm** ⚌ 15.00/30.00 **t.**

🏠 **Woodbridge,** 12-14 The Parks, TA24 8BS, ℰ 4860 – ⧏wc **Ⓟ** 🖪 🄰🄴 ⓞ 𝘝𝘐𝘚𝘈
9 rm ⚌ 13.75/22.10 **t.**

at Middlecombe W : 1 ½ m. on A 39 – see Minehead.

🏠 **Periton Park** ⌇, TA24 8SW, ℰ 5970, ⪕, « Country house atmosphere », ☞, park – 📺 ⌂wc & **Ⓟ** 🖪 🄰🄴 ⓞ 𝘝𝘐𝘚𝘈
closed first 2 weeks November – **M** (lunch by arrangement)/dinner 13.50 **st.** – **7 rm** ⚌ 25.50/61.00 **st., 1 suite** 61.00/75.00 **st.** – SB 70.00/88.00 **st.**

FIAT, VAUXHALL Townsend Rd ℰ 3379
RENAULT Blue Anchor ℰ 821571

VW, AUDI-NSU Mart Rd Industrial Estate ℰ 6868

MINSTER-IN-THANET Kent 🄽🄾🄴 Y 29 – see Ramsgate.

MINSTER LOVELL Oxon. 🄽🄾🄳 🄽🄾🄴 P 28 – pop. 1 364 – ✉ ❀ 0993 Witney.
◆London 72 – Gloucester 36 – ◆Oxford 16.

🏠 **Old Swan** ⌇, Main St., Old Minster, OX8 5RN, ℰ 75614, « 14C inn », ☞ – 📺 ⌂wc ☎ **Ⓟ** 🖪 🄰🄴 𝘝𝘐𝘚𝘈 ⌇
M (a la carte lunch)/dinner 14.00 **t.** ⸙ 2.95 – **10 rm** ⚌ 38.00/55.00 **t.** – SB (October-March) 60.00/75.00 **st.**

MINSTERWORTH Glos. 🄽🄾🄳 🄽🄾🄴 N 28 – see Gloucester.

MISKIN Mid Glamorgan – ✉ Cardiff – ❀ 0443 Pontypridd.
◆London 169 – ◆Cardiff 22 – ◆Swansea 31.

🏠 **Miskin Manor,** CF7 8ND, E : 1 ¾ m. by A 4119 (Groes Faen road) ℰ 224204, « Local stone building in attractive formal grounds », ☞, park – 📺 ⌂wc ☎ **Ⓟ** 🖪 🄰🄴 ⓞ 𝘝𝘐𝘚𝘈 ⌇
M *(closed Saturday lunch and Sunday dinner to non residents)* 10.50/12.50 **t.** and a la carte ⸙ 3.50 – ⚌ 5.00 – **10 rm** 43.00/60.00 **t.**

MITHIAN Cornwall **408** E 33 − see St. Agnes.

MOLD (YR WYDDGRUG) Clwyd **402 408** K 24 − pop. 8 487 − ECD : Thursday − ✆ 0352.
🛅 Pant-y-Mwyn ✆ 740318, W : 4 m. − 🛅 Old Padeswood, Station Rd ✆ 0244 (Buckley) 547401,
E : 2 m. on A 5118.
🛈 Town Hall, Earl St. ✆ 59331 (summer only).
◆ London 211 − Chester 12 − ◆ Liverpool 29 − Shrewsbury 45.

 🏨 **Bryn Awel,** Denbigh Rd, CH7 1BL, on A 541 ✆ 58622 − 📺 ⌂wc ☎ 🅿. ⟠ 𝑉𝐼𝑆𝐴
 M 6.00 **t.** and a la carte ⌖ 2.75 − **18 rm** ⊑ 24.00/42.00 **t.** − SB (weekends only) 38.00/44.00 **st.**

MONK FRYSTON North Yorks. **402** Q 22 − pop. 737 − ✉ Lumby − ✆ 0977 South Milford.
Envir. : Selby Abbey Church★★ 12C-16C, E : 8½ m. − Carlton Towers★ (19C) *AC*, SE : 14½ m.
◆London 190 − ◆Kingston-upon-Hull 42 − ◆Leeds 13 − York 20.

 🏨 **Monk Fryston Hall,** LS25 5DU, ✆ 682369, « Italian garden », park − 📺 ⌂wc ☎ 🅿. ⚐
 24 rm.

 🏨 **Selby Fork,** LS25 5LF, W : 2 ¼ m. by A 63 on A 1 ✆ 682711, Group Telex 557074, ⬛, ⚒ −
 📺 ⌂wc ⫟wc ☎ & 🅿. ⟠ 𝐴𝐸 ⓪ 𝑉𝐼𝑆𝐴
 M (carving rest.) 9.90 **st.** and a la carte ⌖ 2.95 − **109 rm** ⊑ 41.50/51.50 **st.** − SB (weekends
 only) 59.50/64.00 **st.**

MONKTON COMBE Avon − see Bath.

MONMOUTH (TREFYNWY) Gwent **408** L 28 − pop. 7 379 − ECD : Thursday − ✆ 0600.
Envir. : SE : Wye Valley★ − Raglan (castle★ 15C) SW : 7 m. − Skenfrith (castle and church★)
NW : 6 m.
🛈 National Trust Visitor Centre, Church St. ✆ 3899.
◆London 147 − Gloucester 26 − Newport 24 − ◆Swansea 64.

 🏨 **King's Head,** Agincourt Sq., NP5 3DY, ✆ 2177, Telex 497294 − 📺 ⌂wc ⫟wc ☎ 🅿. ⚐. ⟠
 𝐴𝐸 ⓪ 𝑉𝐼𝑆𝐴
 M 9.00/13.50 **t.** and a la carte ⌖ 3.50 − ⊑ 6.00 − **25 rm** 40.00/52.00 **t.** − SB 55.00/65.00 **st.**

 🍴 **Leasbrook** ⌂, Dixton, NP5 3SN, NE : ¾ m. on A 40 ✆ 2831, ⟿ − ⫟ 🅿. ⚒
 closed late December-late January − **M** (buffet lunch)/dinner 8.50 **st.** and a la carte ⌖ 2.40 −
 7 rm ⊑ 20.50/34.00 **st.** − SB (except Bank Holidays) 48.00 **st.**

 at Ganarew (Heref and Worc) NE : 3 m. by A 40 − ✉ ✆ 0600 Monmouth (Gwent) :

 🏨 **Ganarew House** ⌂, NP5 3SS, ✆ 890442, ≤, ⟿ − 📺 ⌂wc ⫟wc 🅿
 M (booking essential) (bar lunch)/dinner 10.00 **t.** and a la carte ⌖ 2.80 − **9 rm** ⊑ 16.50/32.00 **t.**
 − SB (except summer) 48.00 **st.**

 at Whitebrook S : 8 ½ m. by A 466 − ✉ ✆ 0600 Monmouth :

 🍴🍴 **Crown at Whitebrook** ⌂ with rm, NP5 4TX, ✆ 860254, ⟿ − ⌂wc ⫟wc ☎ 🅿. ⟠ 𝐴𝐸 ⓪
 𝑉𝐼𝑆𝐴
 M 17.50 **st.** ⌖ 5.40 − **12 rm** ⊑ 27.00/43.00 **st.** − SB 62.00/73.00 **st.**

AUSTIN-ROVER St. James Sq. ✆ 2773   MERCEDES-BENZ 8 Wonastow Rd ✆ 3118
FORD Redbrook Rd ✆ 2366   SUZUKI, CITROEN Wonastow Rd ✆ 2896

MONTACUTE Somerset **408** L 31 − see Yeovil.

MONTGOMERY (TREFALDWYN) Powys **408** K 26 − pop. 1 035 − ✆ 068 681.
◆ London 194 − ◆ Birmingham 71 − Chester 53 − Shrewsbury 30.

 🍴 Dragon, SY15 6PA, ✆ 476, ⬛ − 📺 ⌂wc ⫟wc 🅿
 15 rm.

MORECAMBE Lancs. **402** L 21 − pop. 41 432 − ECD : Wednesday − ✆ 0524.
See : Marineland★ *AC*.
🛅 Clubhouse ✆ 412841, on sea front.
🛈 Marine Rd Central ✆ 414110.
◆London 248 − ◆Blackpool 29 − ◆Carlisle 66 − Lancaster 4.

 🏨 **Midland,** Marine Rd, LA4 4BZ, ✆ 417180, ≤ − ⫼ 📺 ⌂wc ⫟wc ☎ 🅿. ⚐. ⟠ 𝐴𝐸 ⓪ 𝑉𝐼𝑆𝐴
 M 6.25/9.00 **t.** and a la carte ⌖ 3.50 − **46 rm** ⊑ 27.50/42.00 **t.** − SB (weekends only) 48.00 **st.**

 🏨 **Strathmore,** Marine Rd East, East Promenade, LA4 5AP, ✆ 421234, Group Telex 57515, ≤ −
 ⫼ 📺 ⌂wc ⫟wc ☎ & 🅿. ⟠ 𝐴𝐸 ⓪ 𝑉𝐼𝑆𝐴. ⚒
 closed 2 weeks at Christmas − **M** 6.00/6.50 **s.** and a la carte ⌖ 3.50 − **55 rm** ⊑ 17.50/46.00 **t.** −
 SB (except summer)(weekends only) 42.50/46.00 **st.**

 🏨 **Elms,** Princes Crescent, Bare, LA4 6DD, ✆ 411501, ⟿ − ⫼ 📺 ⌂wc ☎ 🅿. ⟠ 𝐴𝐸 ⓪ 𝑉𝐼𝑆𝐴.
 ⚒
 M 4.75/8.00 **st.** and a la carte ⌖ 2.50 − **39 rm** ⊑ 22.50/45.00 **st** − SB (weekends only)
 51.00/64.00 **st.**

⌂ **Channings,** 455 Marine Rd, Promenade, Bare, ℰ 417925 – ▭ ⌂wc ⃚wc. ◪ ⓞ 𝘝𝘐𝘚𝘈
M (dinner only) 7.00 **st.** ≬ 2.50 – **20 rm** ⊇ 17.50/28.00 **st.**

⌂ **Warwick,** 394 Marine Rd East, ℰ 418151 – ▭ ⃚wc. ◪ ⒜⒠ ⓞ 𝘝𝘐𝘚𝘈
23 rm ⊇ 10.10/24.00 **st.**

⌂ **Prospect,** 363 Marine Rd, East Promenade, LA4 5AQ, ℰ 417819 – ▭ ⌂wc. 𝘝𝘐𝘚𝘈
April-October – **14 rm** ⊇ 9.00/14.00 **s.**

AUSTIN-ROVER Marine Drive Central ℰ 414078
TOYOTA West Gate ℰ 413891
VAUXHALL Bare Lane ℰ 410205

VOLVO Marlborough Rd ℰ 417437
VW, AUDI Heysham Rd ℰ 415833

MORETONHAMPSTEAD Devon ⁴⁰³ I 32 The West Country G. – pop. 1 420 – ECD : Thursday –
✉ Newton Abbot – ☎ 0647.

☖ Manor House Hotel ℰ 40355.

♦London 213 – Exeter 12 – ♦Plymouth 38.

🏨 **Manor House** ⌖, TQ13 8RE, SW : 2 m. on B 3212 ℰ 40355, Telex 42794, ≼, ☖, ⌇, ⚒,
park, ⚒, squash – ⫞ ▭ ⌖ & ⓟ. ⚐ ◪ ⒜⒠ ⓞ 𝘝𝘐𝘚𝘈
M (buffet lunch)/dinner 14.50 **st.** and a la carte ≬ 3.50 – **69 rm** ⊇ 46.00/92.00 **st., 1 suite** –
SB (weekends only) 97.00 **st.**

⌂ **Wray Barton Manor** ⌖, TQ13 8SE, SE : 1½ m. on A 382 ℰ 40246, ≼, ⚒ – ▭ ⌂wc ⓟ.
⚒
5 rm ⊇ 11.00/25.00 **st.**

MORETON-IN-MARSH Glos. ⁴⁰³ ⁴⁰⁴ O 28 – pop. 2 545 – ECD : Wednesday – ☎ 0608.
Envir. : Chastleton House★★ (Elizabethan) *AC*, SE : 3½ m.

🅳 Council Offices, High St. ℰ 50881.

♦London 86 – ♦Birmingham 40 – Gloucester 31 – ♦Oxford 29.

🏨 **Manor House,** High St., GL56 0LJ, ℰ 50501, Telex 837151, « 16C manor house, gardens »,
◪, ⌇ – ▭ ▭ ⌂wc ⃚wc ☎ ⓟ. ⚐ ◪ ⒜⒠ ⓞ 𝘝𝘐𝘚𝘈. ⚒
M 9.00/14.00 **t.** ≬ 2.95 – **40 rm** ⊇ 23.00/57.50 **t.** – SB (November-April) 62.50/75.50 **st.**

🏛 **Redesdale Arms,** High St., GL56 0AN, ℰ 50308 – ▭ ⌂wc ⃚wc ☎ ⓟ. ◪ ⒜⒠
M 6.95/8.95 **t.** and a la carte ≬ 3.05 – **18 rm** ⊇ 25.75/45.00 **t.** – SB (except Christmas)
58.00/67.50 **st.**

🏛 **White Hart Royal** (T.H.F.), High St., GL56 0BA, ℰ 50731 – ▭ ⌂wc ⊛ ⓟ. ⚐ ◪ ⒜⒠ ⓞ
𝘝𝘐𝘚𝘈
M (bar lunch Monday to Saturday)/dinner 8.95 **st.** and a la carte ≬ 3.40 – ⊇ 5.65 – **24 rm**
40.00/50.00 **st.**

⌂ **Moreton House,** High St., GL56 0LQ, ℰ 50747 – ▭ ⃚wc ⓟ. ◪
8 rm ⊇ 12.50/25.00 **t.**

PEUGEOT-TALBOT London Rd ℰ 50585

RENAULT Little Compton ℰ 74202

MORPETH Northumb. ⁴⁰¹ ⁴⁰² O 18 – pop. 14 301 – ECD : Thursday – ☎ 0670.
Envir. : Brinkburn Priory (site★, church★ : Gothic) *AC*, NW : 10 m.
☖ Newbiggin-by-the-Sea ℰ 817344, E : 9 m. – ☖ The Common ℰ 2065.
🅳 The Chantry, Bridge St. ℰ 511323.

♦London 301 – ♦Edinburgh 93 – ♦Newcastle-upon-Tyne 15.

🏛 **Queen's Head,** Bridge St., NE61 1NB, ℰ 512083 – ▭ ⌂wc ⃚ ⊛ ⓟ
23 rm.

at Longhorsley NW : 7½ m. by A 192 on A 697 – ✉ ☎ 0670 Morpeth :

🏨 **Linden Hall** ⌖, NE65 8XF, N : 1 m. on A 697 ℰ 56611, Telex 538224, ≼, « Country house in
extensive grounds », ⚒, park, ⚒ – ⫞ ▭ ⌖ & ⓟ. ⚐ ◪ ⒜⒠ ⓞ 𝘝𝘐𝘚𝘈
M 9.50 **st.** (lunch) and a la carte 11.40/18.00 **st.** – **45 rm** ⊇ 52.50/62.50 **st.** – SB (weekends
only) 76.50 **st.**

AUSTIN-ROVER Hillgate ℰ 57441
FORD 53-55 Bridge St. ℰ 519611
PEUGEOT, TALBOT Ellington ℰ 860327

RENAULT Clifton ℰ 512538
VAUXHALL Bridge End ℰ 512115
VW, AUDI Castle Sq. ℰ 519011

MORTEHOE Devon ⁴⁰³ H 30 – see Woolacombe.

Do not mix up :

Comfort of hotels	:	🏨🏨🏨🏨 ... 🏛, 🏚, ⌂
Comfort of restaurants	:	XXXXX X
Quality of the cuisine	:	❀❀❀, ❀❀, ❀, **M**

MOULSFORD Oxon. 403 404 Q 29 – pop. 494 – ✪ 0491 Cholsey.

◆London 58 – ◆Oxford 17 – Reading 13 – Swindon 37.

🏦 **Beetle and Wedge** ⌖, Ferry Lane, OX10 9JF ℰ 651381, ≼, ☞ – 📺 ⌷wc ☎ 🅿. 🔼 🆀 ⑩ 🆅🆂🅰
closed 25 and 26 December – **M** 8.50/10.95 **t.** and a la carte ⫴ 3.25 – **15 rm** ⟷ 38.00/54.00 **t.** –
SB (weekends only) 60.00/65.00 **st.**

MOULTON Northants. 404 R 27 – see Northampton.

MOULTON North Yorks. 402 P 20 – ✉ Richmond – ✪ 032 577 Barton.

◆London 243 – ◆Leeds 53 – ◆Middlesbrough 25 – ◆Newcastle-upon-Tyne 43.

XX **Black Bull Inn,** DL10 6QJ, ℰ 289, « Brighton Belle Pullman coach » – 🅿. 🔼 🆀 🆅🆂🅰
closed Sunday and 24 to 31 December – **M** 7.00 **t.** (lunch) and a la carte 9.75/20.75 **t.** ⫴ 3.00.

MOUNT PLEASANT Hants. 403 404 P 31 – see Lymington.

MOUSEHOLE Cornwall 403 D 33 The West Country G. – ECD : Wednesday except summer – ✉
✪ 0736 Penzance.

See : Site★.

◆London 321 – Penzance 3 – Truro 29.

🏨 **Lobster Pot,** South Cliff, TR19 6QX, ℰ 731251, ≼, – 📺 ⌷wc ⌷wc 🅿. 🔼 🆀 🆅🆂🅰
closed mid January-mid March – **M** 7.00/11.55 **st.** and a la carte ⫴ 3.50 – **26 rm**
⟷ 15.00/43.00 **st.**

🏦 **Carn Du** ⌖, Raginnis Hill, TR19 6SS, ℰ 731233, ≼ Mounts Bay, ☞ – ⌷wc 🅿. 🔼 🆀 🆅🆂🅰
closed 5 January-16 March – **M** (bar lunch)/dinner 9.20 **t.** ⫴ 2.75 – **7 rm** ⟷ 19.00/41.00 **t.**

🛏 **Tavis Vor,** The Parade, TR19 6PR, ℰ 731306, ≼ Mounts Bay, ☞ – ⌷wc. ⌖
Mid March-mid October – **7 rm** ⟷ 11.50/29.00 **st.**

MUDEFORD Dorset 403 404 O 31 – see Christchurch.

MUCH BIRCH Heref. and Worc. – see Hereford.

MULLION Cornwall 403 E 33 The West Country G. – pop. 1 958 – ECD : Wednesday – ✉ Helston
– ✪ 0326.

See : Mullion Cove★★★ (Church★).

◆London 323 – Falmouth 21 – Penzance 21 – Truro 26.

🏨 **Polurrian** ⌖, TR12 7EN, SW : ½ m. ℰ 240421, ≼ Mounts Bay, ⛱ heated, 🔲, ☞, ⚒,
squash – 📺 ⌷wc ☎ 🅿. 🔼 🆀 ⑩ 🆅🆂🅰
April-October – **M** 8.00/11.50 **st.** and a la carte ⫴ 2.35 – **42 rm** ⟷ 20.00/72.00 **st.** –
SB 59.00/89.00 **st.**

MUMBLES West Glam. 403 I 29 – ECD : Wednesday – ✉ ✪ 0792 Swansea.

See : Mumbles Head★.

Envir. : Cefn Bryn (⁎★★★ from the reservoir) W : 12 m. – Rhosili (site and ≼ ★★★) W : 18 m. –
W : Oxwich Bay★.

◆London 202 – ◆Swansea 6.

🏨 **Osborne** (Embassy), Rotherslade Rd, Langland Bay, SA3 4QL, W : ¾ m. ℰ 366274, ≼ – 🛗
📺 ⌷wc ☎ 🅿. 🔼 🆀 ⑩ 🆅🆂🅰
M *(closed Sunday dinner to non residents)* 5.50/8.50 **st.** and a la carte ⫴ 4.45 – **36 rm**
⟷ 28.25/60.00 **st.** – SB (weekends only) 42.00/57.00 **st.**

🏨 **Langland Court** ⌖, 31 Langland Court Rd, Langland Bay, SA3 4TD, W : 1 m. ℰ 61545, ☞ –
📺 ⌷wc ⌷wc ☎ ⇐ 🅿. 🏛
21 rm.

🏨 **Norton House,** 17 Norton Rd, SA3 5TQ, ℰ 404891 – 📺 ⌷wc ⌷wc ☞ 🅿. 🏛 🔼 🆅🆂🅰
⌖
closed 28 December-4 January – **M** (dinner only) 10.50 **st.** and a la carte 10.40/15.25 **t.** – ⟷
4.50 – **16 rm** 29.00/49.00 **st.**

🏦 **Old School House,** 37 Nottage Rd, Newton, SA3 4SU, W : 1 m. ℰ 61541 – 📺 ⌷wc ⌷wc 🅿.
🔼 🆀 ⑩ 🆅🆂🅰
closed 24 to 26 December – **M** *(closed Sunday dinner)* (dinner only and Sunday lunch)/dinner
9.95 **st.** and a la carte ⫴ 4.95 – **8 rm** ⟷ 25.00/40.00 **t.** – SB (weekends only) 45.00 **st.**

🛏 **Wittemberg,** 2 Rotherslade Rd, Langland, SA3 4QN, W : ¾ m. ℰ 69696 – 📺 ⌷wc 🅿.
closed 1 week at Christmas – **11 rm** ⟷ 17.50/30.00 **st.**

MUNGRISDALE Cumbria 401 402 L 19 20 – pop. 336 – ⊠ Penrith – ✆ 059 683 Threlkeld.
♦London 301 – ♦Carlisle 33 – Keswick 8.5 – Penrith 13.

🏩 **Mill** ⌂, CA11 0XR, 𝒫 659, 🚗 – 📺 ⌷wc **℗**
March-October – **M** 6.00/10.00 **t.** ⌷ 2.95 – **8 rm** ⌷ 14.00/38.50 **t.** – SB (March-May) 38.50/48.50 **st.**

NAFFERTON Humberside 402 S 21 – see Great Driffield.

NANTWICH Cheshire 402 403 404 M 24 – pop. 11 867 – ECD : Wednesday – ✆ 0270.
🛈 Council Offices, Beam St. 𝒫 623914.
♦London 176 – Chester 20 – ♦Liverpool 45 – ♦Stoke-on-Trent 17.

🏨 **Rookery Hall** ⌂, Worleston, CW5 6DQ, N : 2 ½ m. by A 51 on B 5074 𝒫 626866, Telex 367169, ≼, « 19C country house », ⇘, park, ⚒ – 📺 ☎ **℗**. 🔙 🅰 ⅭⅬ ⓪ *VISA* ⌷
closed 19 January-12 February – **M** (booking essential) 12.95/25.00 **t.** and a la carte ⌷ 6.50 –
11 rm ⌷ 57.50/120.00 **t.**, **1 suite** 140.00/155.00 **t.** – SB (October-March) 122.50/170.00 **st.**

❌❌ **Churche's Mansion**, 150 Hospital St., CW5 5RY, 𝒫 625933, « 16C half-timbered house »,
🚗 – **℗**. 🔙 🅰 ⓪ *VISA*
closed Christmas – **M** 6.50/14.50 **t.** ⌷ 3.35.

AUSTIN-ROVER London Rd 𝒫 623151
FORD Crewe Rd 𝒫 623739
HONDA Whitchurch Rd 𝒫 780300

SAAB Welsh Row 𝒫 627678
VAUXHALL-OPEL Station Rd 𝒫 624027

NARBERTH (ARBERTH) Dyfed 403 F 28 – ⊠ ✆ 0834.
♦London 241 – Carmarthen 21 – Fishguard 26.

🏠 **Plas Hyfryd**, Moorfield Rd, SA67 7AB, 𝒫 860653, 🔥 heated, 🚗 – 📺 ⌷wc �filwc ☎ **℗**. 🔙 *VISA*
M *(closed Sunday lunch)* (lunch by arrangement) 10.95 **st.** ⌷ 2.60 – **12 rm** ⌷ 24.75/34.50 **st.** –
SB (except Easter, summer and Christmas) 43.00 **st.**

NARBOROUGH Leics. 403 404 Q 26 – see Leicester.

NASSINGTON Northants. 404 S 26 – see Peterborough (Cambs.).

NATIONAL EXHIBITION CENTRE West Midlands 403 404 O 26 – see Birmingham.

NAWTON North Yorks. – see Helmsley.

NEASHAM Durham 402 P 20 – see Darlington.

NEATISHEAD Norfolk 404 Y 25 – pop. 524 – ✆ 0692 Horning.
♦London 122 – North Walsham 8.5 – ♦Norwich 11.

❌❌ **Barton Angler Lodge** with rm, Irstead Rd, NR12 8XP, E : ¾ m. 𝒫 630740, 🚗 – 📺 fillwc **℗**.
🔙 🅰 *VISA*
M *(closed Sunday)* (bar lunch)/dinner a la carte approx. 14.00 **t.** ⌷ 2.75 – **7 rm** ⌷ 22.00/48.00 **t.**

NEEDHAM MARKET Suffolk 404 X 27 – pop. 3 420 – ECD : Tuesday – ⊠ ✆ 0449.
♦ London 77 – ♦ Cambridge 47 – ♦ Ipswich 8.5 – ♦ Norwich 38.

🏠 **Limes**, 99 High St., IP6 8DQ, 𝒫 720305 – 📺 ⌷wc ☜ **℗**. 🔙 🅰 ⓪ *VISA*
closed 25 and 26 December – **M** 8.50/9.00 **st.** and a la carte ⌷ 2.65 – **11 rm** ⌷ 33.00/52.00 **st.**
– SB (weekends only) 52.00/54.50 **st.**

NEFYN Gwynedd 402 403 G 25 – pop. 2 236 – ECD : Wednesday – ✆ 0758.
See : Site ★.
🛈₆ 𝒫 720218, W : 1 ½ m.
♦London 265 – Caernarfon 20.

🏩 **Caeau Capel** ⌂, Rhodfa'r Mor, LL53 6EB, 𝒫 720240, 🚗 – ⌷wc **℗**. 🔙 *VISA*
Easter-October – **M** (bar lunch)/dinner 7.95 **t.** ⌷ 1.85 – **23 rm** ⌷ 12.65/36.80 **t.**
AUSTIN-ROVER Church St. 𝒫 720206

NETTLECOMBE Dorset – see Bridport.

Red Lion

Si le nom d'un hôtel figure en petits caractères,
demandez à l'arrivée
les conditions à l'hôtelier.

NEWARK-ON-TRENT Notts. 402 404 R 24 – pop. 33 143 – ECD : Thursday – ✪ 0636.

🖪 The Ossington, Beast Market Hill, Castlegate ✆ 78962.

◆London 127 – Lincoln 16 – ◆ Nottingham 20 – ◆ Sheffield 42.

🏨 **Robin Hood,** Lombard St., NG24 1XB, ✆ 703858 – 📺 🛏wc ⊛ Ⓟ 🏄 🔼 AE ⓪ VISA
   closed 25 and 26 December – **M** a la carte 9.45/11.45 t. ₰ 3.35 – **20 rm** � 37.00/50.00 t. –
   SB (weekends only) 51.00/57.00 **st.**

🏨 **Grange,** 73 London Rd, at corner of Charles St., NG24 1RZ, ✆ 703399, ☞ – 📺 🛏wc Ⓟ 🔼
   VISA 🌤
   closed 23 December-3 January – **M** (dinner only) a la carte 6.30/8.30 **st.** ₰ 2.50 – **8 rm**
   ⊏ 17.50/33.50 **st.** – SB (weekends only) 40.00 **st.**

🏨 **Clinton Arms,** 44 Market Pl., NG24 1EG, ✆ 72299 – 📺 🛏wc 🗒wc
   18 rm.

AUSTIN-ROVER 69 Northgate ✆ 703413
FIAT Sleaford Rd ✆ 703405
FORD Farndon Rd ✆ 704131
LADA London Rd ✆ 704937
NISSAN Lombard St. ✆ 77533

RENAULT Clinton St. ✆ 704619
SKODA London Rd ✆ 705845
VAUXHALL-OPEL 116 Farndon Rd ✆ 705431
VW, AUDI Northern Rd ✆ 704484

NEWBRIDGE Cornwall – see Penzance.

NEWBURY Berks. 403 404 Q 29 – pop. 31 488 – ECD : Wednesday – ✪ 0635.

🖪 District Museum, The Wharf ✆ 30267.

◆London 67 – ◆ Bristol 66 – ◆ Oxford 28 – Reading 17 – ◆ Southampton 38.

🏛 **Elcot Park Country House** (Best Western) 🌤, RG16 8NJ, W : 5 m. by A 4 ✆ 0488 (Kintbury) 58100, Telex 846448, ≤, ☞, park, 🎾 – 📺 🛏 Ⓟ 🏄 🔼 AE ⓪ VISA
   M 8.50/14.50 t. and a la carte ₰ 3.75 – **30 rm** ⊏ 50.00/85.00 t. – SB 79.50/89.50 **st.**

🏨 **Chequers** (T.H.F.), 7-8 Oxford St., RG13 1JB, ✆ 38000, Telex 849205, ☞ – 📺 🛏wc ☎ Ⓟ
   🏄 🔼 AE ⓪ VISA
   M 9.45 **st.** and a la carte ₰ 3.70 – ⊏ 5.65 – **60 rm** 45.00/57.00 **st.**

✗ **Sapient Pig,** 29 Oxford St., RG13 1JG, ✆ 47425 – 🔼 VISA
   closed Saturday lunch, Sunday and Bank Holidays. – **M** a la carte 11.80/16.25 t.

AUSTIN-ROVER London Rd ✆ 41100
RENAULT London Rd ✆ 41020

VW-AUDI 22 Newtown Rd ✆ 41911

NEWBY BRIDGE Cumbria 402 L 21 – ECD : Saturday – ✉ Ulverston – ✪ 0448.

◆London 270 – Kendal 16 – Lancaster 27.

🏨 **Swan,** LA12 8NB, ✆ 31681, Telex 65108, ≤, ☜, ☞ – 📺 🛏wc ☎ Ⓟ 🏄 🔼 AE ⓪ VISA
   🌤
   closed 3 to 13 January – **M** 7.00/12.50 t. and a la carte ₰ 3.75 – **36 rm** ⊏ 32.50/54.00 t., **1 suite**
   40.50/65.00 t. – SB (October-March)(weekends only) 56.00/76.00 **st.**

🏨 **Whitewater,** The Lakeland Village, LA12 8PX, SW : 1 ½ m. by A 590 ✆ 31133, Telex 54173 –
   📳 📺 🛏wc ☎ & Ⓟ 🏄 🔼 AE ⓪ VISA 🌤
   M 6.50/9.95 t. and a la carte – **34 rm** ⊏ 46.00/57.00 t. – SB 69.00/85.00 **st.**

NEWBY WISKE North Yorks. – see Northallerton.

NEWCASTLE EMLYN (CASTELL NEWYDD EMLYN) Dyfed 403 G 27 – pop. 1 230 – ECD : Wednesday – ✪ 0239.

Envir. : Cenarth Falls★ W : 3 m.

Exc. : E : Teifi Valley★.

◆London 240 – Carmarthen 20 – Fishguard 29.

🏨 **Emlyn Arms,** Bridge St., SA38 9DU, ✆ 710317 – 📺 🛏wc ☎ Ⓟ 🔼 AE ⓪ VISA
   M 6.70 t. and a la carte ₰ 2.75 – **38 rm.**

FORD New Rd ✆ 710245

🏌 Newcastle Municipal, Keele Rd ℰ 627596, NW : 2 m. on A 525 V.

🛈 Area Reference Library, Ironmarket ℰ 618125.

◆London 161 – ◆Birmingham 46 – ◆Liverpool 56 – ◆Manchester 43.

Plan of Built up Area : see Stoke-on-Trent

🏨 **Clayton Lodge** (Embassy), Clayton Rd, Clayton, ST5 4AF, S : 1 ¼ m. on A 519 ℰ 613093 – 📺 🗕 🗕wc ☎ 📶. 🅿 🗛 🗛 ⓓ VISA   V e
M 8.25/9.50 **st.** and a la carte 🛢 3.00 – 🗌 5.00 – **50 rm** 39.00/45.00 **st.** – SB (weekends only) 55.00/60.00 **st.**

🏨 **Thomas Forshaw**, Liverpool Rd, Cross Heath, ST5 9DX, N : 2 m. on A 34 ℰ 612431, Telex 36681 – 🗔 rest 📺 🗕wc 📶 🕭
🅿 🗛 🗛   U a
74 rm.

🏨 **Post House** (T.H.F.), Clayton Rd, Clayton, ST5 4DL, S : 2 m. on A 519 ℰ 625151, Telex 36531 – 📺 🗕 🗕wc 📶 🅿 🗛 🗛 🗛 ⓓ VISA   V n
M (buffet lunch Saturday) 7.45/9.75 **st.** and a la carte 🛢 3.40 – 🗌 5.65 – **125 rm** 47.00/57.00 **st.**

🏠 **Grove Court,** 100 Lancaster Rd, ST5 1DS, ℰ 614406, 🚗 – 📺 🗕wc 📶 🗛 VISA   o
11 rm 🗌 15.50/28.00 t.

AUSTIN-ROVER Brook Lane ℰ 618461
BMW Pool Dam ℰ 620811
CITROEN, PEUGEOT-TALBOT Hassell St. ℰ 614621
CITROEN Brunswick St. ℰ 614791
FIAT Higherland ℰ 622141
FORD London Rd ℰ 621199
RENAULT High St., Wolstanton ℰ 626284
VAUXHALL-OPEL Higherland ℰ 610941

VOLVO Knutton Rd, Wolstanton ℰ 625333
VW, AUDI Brunswick St. ℰ 617321

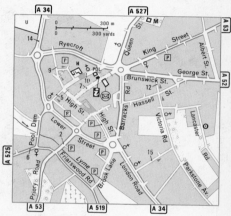

NEWCASTLE-UNDER-LYME CENTRE

High Street
Blackfriars Road 2

Church Street 5
Higherland 6
Iron Market 7
Liverpool Road 9
Merrial Street 10
North Street 12
Upper Green 14
Vessey Terrace 15

🏌 Gosforth Park, High Gosforth Park ℰ 364867, AV – 🏌 Broadway East, Gosforth, ℰ 856710, N : 3 m. by Kenton Rd AV – 🏌 Whorlton Grange, Westerhope, ℰ 869125, W : 5 m. by B 6324 AV.

✈ Newcastle Airport : ℰ 2860966, Telex 537831 NW : 5 m. by A 696 AV – Terminal : Bus Assembly : Central Station Forecourt – 🚗 ℰ 611234 ext 2621.

🚢 Shipping connections with the Continent : to Norway (Bergen, Stavanger) (Norway Line) summer only – to Denmark (Esbjerg) (DFDS Seaways) summer only – to Sweden (Götenborg) (DFDS Seaways) summer only.

🛈 Central Library, Princess Sq. ℰ 610691 – Blackfriars, Monk St. ℰ 615367.

◆London 276 – ◆Edinburgh 105 – ◆Leeds 95.

Plans on following pages

🏨 **Swallow** (Swallow), 1 Newgate Arcade, Newgate St., NE1 5SX, ℰ 232 5025, Telex 538230 – 🗐 📺 🗕wc 📶 🅿 🗛 🗛 🗛 VISA   CZ o
M 7.00/9.25 **st.** and a la carte 🛢 3.85 – **93 rm** 🗌 46.50/60.00 **st.** – SB (weekends only) 55.00/60.00 **st.**

🏨 **Crest** (Crest), New Bridge St., NE1 8BS, ℰ 232 6191, Telex 53467 – 🗐 🗔 rest 📺 🗕wc ☎ 🕭 🅿 🗛 🗛 🗛 ⓓ VISA   CY n
M 7.35/11.50 **st.** and a la carte – 🗌 5.85 – **178 rm** 49.00/56.50, **1 suite** – SB (weekends only) 58.00 **st.**

🏨 **Imperial** (Swallow), Jesmond Rd, NE2 1PR, ℰ 281 5511, Telex 537972, 🗔 – 🗐 📺 🗕wc ☎ 🅿 🗛 🗛 🗛 ⓓ VISA   CY c
M 6.00/9.75 **st.** and a la carte 🛢 3.60 – **127 rm** 🗌 46.50/56.50 **st.** – SB (weekends only and weekdays in July and August) 110.00 **st.**

🏨 **County Thistle** (Thistle), Neville St., NE99 1AH, ℰ 232 2471, Telex 537873 – 🗐 📺 🗕wc ☎. 🗛 🗛 🗛 ⓓ VISA   CZ a
M 8.75/11.50 **t.** and a la carte – 🗌 6.25 – **115 rm** 39.00/57.00 **st.**

P.T.O. →

NEWCASTLE-UPON-TYNE

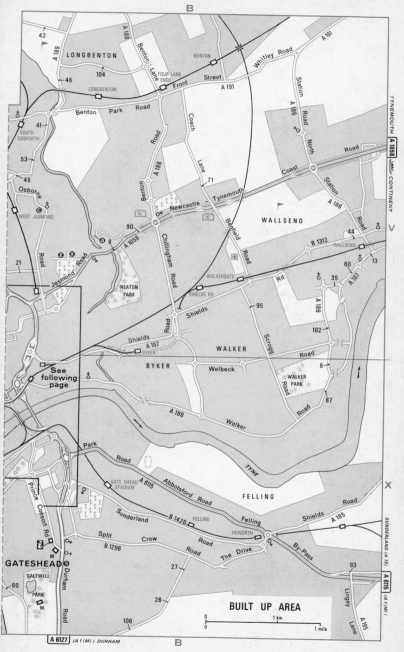

BUILT UP AREA

0   1 km
0   1 mile

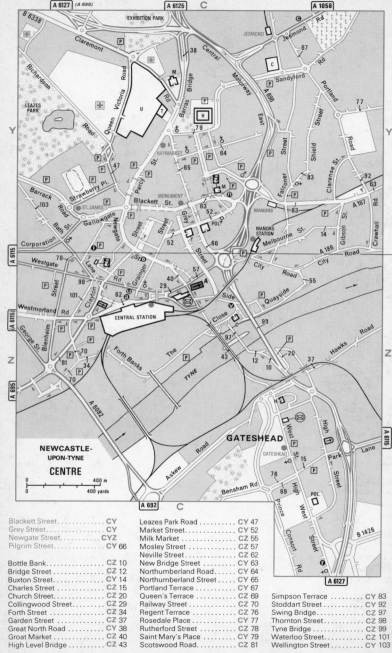

NEWCASTLE-
UPON-TYNE
CENTRE

0   400 m
0   400 yards

🏠 **New Kent,** 127 Osborne Rd, Jesmond, NE2 2TB, ℰ 281 1083 – 📺 ➡wc 🐾 🅿. 🔼 🅰🔢 ⓞ
VISA. 🦌
                                    BV **c**
 M *(closed Sunday dinner)* (dinner only and Sunday lunch)/dinner 10.90 **st.** and a la carte ▯ 3.50
 – **32 rm** ☲ 18.90/24.90 **t.** – SB (weekends only) 59.60 **st.**

🏠 **Avenue,** 2 Manor House Rd, Jesmond, NE2 2LU, ℰ 091 (Tyneside) 281 1396 – 🔼 🅰🔢 ⓞ
🦌
                                    BV **x**
 closed Christmas Day – **9 rm** ☲ 15.50/25.00 **s.**

🏠 **Westland,** 27 Osborne Av., Jesmond, NE2 1JR, ℰ 091 (Tyneside) 281 0412 – ➡wc BV **z**
 16 rm ☲ 16.25/29.90 **t.**

🏠 **Clifton Cottage,** Dunholme Rd, NE4 6XE, ℰ 091 (Tyneside) 273 7347 – 📺 🅿   AX **e**
 6 rm ☲ 11.00/20.00 **st.**

✕✕ **Fisherman's Wharf,** 15 The Side, NE1 3JE, ℰ 232 1057, Seafood – 🔼 🅰🔢 ⓞ **VISA** CZ **v**
 closed Saturday lunch, Sunday, and Bank Holidays – **M** 8.90 **t.** (lunch) and a la carte
 14.70/19.10 **t.** ▯ 3.50.

✕✕ **Fisherman's Lodge,** Jesmond Dene, Jesmond, NE7 7BQ, ℰ 091 (Tyneside) 281 3281,
 Seafood – 🅿. 🔼 🅰🔢 ⓞ **VISA**   BV **a**
 closed Saturday lunch, Sunday, 25 December-2 January and Bank Holidays – **M** 10.00 **t.**
 (lunch) and a la carte 13.40/27.50 **t.** ▯ 3.50.

✕✕ **Ming Dynasty,** 41 Stowell St., NE1 4XQ, ℰ 261 5787, Chinese - Peking rest. – 🔼 🅰🔢 ⓞ
VISA   CY **i**
 M 4.50/11.00 **t.** and a la carte ▯ 3.50.

✕ Mario, 59 Westgate Rd, NE1 1SG, ℰ 232 0708, Italian rest.   CZ **u**

 at Gosforth N : 4 ¾ m. on A 6125 – AV – ✉ ⊙ 0632 Newcastle-upon-Tyne :

🏨 **Gosforth Park Thistle** (Thistle), High Gosforth Park, NE3 5HN, on B 1318 ℰ 236 4111,
 Telex 53655, ≼, 🔲, 🌿, park, squash – 🛗 📺 ☎ & 🅿. 🅰. 🔼 🅰🔢 ⓞ **VISA**
 M 9.50/13.50 **t.** and a la carte ▯ 2.00 – ☲ 6.50 – **178 rm** 58.00/90.00 **st.**, **5 suites** 105.00 **st.**

 at Seaton Burn N : 8 m. on A 6125 – AV – ✉ Newcastle-upon-Tyne – ⊙ 0632 Wideopen :

🏨 **Holiday Inn,** Great North Rd, NE13 6BP, N : ¾ m. on junction with A 1 ℰ 236 5432, Telex
 53271, 🔲 – 🛗 📺 ☎ & 🅿. 🅰. 🔼 🅰🔢 ⓞ **VISA**
 M 11.75/11.95 **t.** and a la carte ▯ 4.30 – ☲ 6.50 – **150 rm** 49.50/59.50 **s.**, **1 suite** 122.50 **s.**

 at Wallsend NE : 6 m. on A 1058 – BV – ✉ Newcastle-upon-Tyne – ⊙ 091 Tyneside :

🏨 Newcastle Moat House (Q.M.H.), Coast Rd, NE28 9HP, at junction with A 1 ℰ 262 8989, Telex
 53583 – 🛗 📺 ➡wc 🐾 🅿. 🅰.
 closed 24 to 26 December – **158 rm**.

 at Newcastle Airport NW : 6 m. on A 696 – AV – ✉ Woolsington – ⊙ 0661 Ponteland :

🏨 **Stakis Airport** (Stakis), Woolsington, NE13 8DJ, ℰ 24911, Telex 537121 – 🛗 📺 ➡wc 🐾
 & 🅿. 🅰. 🔼 🅰🔢 ⓞ **VISA**
 M 5.95/8.95 **st.** and a la carte ▯ 3.40 – ☲ 3.90 – **98 rm** 41.00/48.00 **st.** – SB 46.00/54.00 **st.**

ALFA-ROMEO, YUGO Diana St. ℰ 322314	NISSAN Benfield Rd ℰ 2659171
AUSTIN-ROVER Etherstone Av. ℰ 2663311	PORSCHE Melbourne St. ℰ 612591
AUSTIN-ROVER Newburn Rd ℰ 2674449	RENAULT Shiremoor ℰ 2532318
AUSTIN-ROVER Westgate Rd ℰ 2737901	RENAULT Scotswood Rd ℰ 2730101
CITROEN Westgate Rd ℰ 2737821	SUBARU 87 Osborne Rd ℰ 811677
FIAT Railway St. ℰ 2732131	TALBOT Benton Rd ℰ 2666361
FORD Market St. ℰ 611471	VAUXHALL Two Ball Lonnen ℰ 2741000
FORD Scotswood Rd ℰ 2735121	VAUXHALL Great North Rd ℰ 363176
ISUZU Jesmond ℰ 370658	VAUXHALL Dunn St. ℰ 273 5201
LAND ROVER Comington ℰ 2676271	VOLVO Brunton Lane ℰ 2867111
MITSUBISHI, SEAT Longbenton ℰ 2668223	VOLVO Jesmond Rd ℰ 2815151

NEWDIGATE Surrey 🔟🔟🔟 T 30 – pop. 1 444 – ⊙ 030 677.
♦London 32 – ♦Brighton 32 – Guildford 18.

✕✕ **Forge,** Parkgate Rd, RH5 5DZ, N : 1 m. ℰ 582 – 🅿. 🅰🔢 ⓞ
 closed Sunday and Monday – **M** 6.90 **t.** and a la carte 11.35/15.40 **t.** ▯ 3.20.

NEWHAVEN East Sussex 🔟🔟🔟 U 31 – pop. 10 697 – ECD : Wednesday – ⊙ 0273.
🚲 Peacehaven, Brighton Rd ℰ 514049.
🚢 Shipping connections with the Continent : to France (Dieppe) (Sealink).
♦London 63 – ♦Brighton 9 – Eastbourne 14 – Lewes 7.

FORD Drove Rd ℰ 515303   VAUXHALL-OPEL Avis Way ℰ 5941

NEWLYN Cornwall 🔟🔟🔟 D 33 – see Penzance.

I prezzi	Per ogni chiarimento sui prezzi qui riportati, consultate le spiegazioni alla p. 32.

NEWMARKET Suffolk **404** V 27 – pop. 15 861 – ECD : Wednesday – ✆ 0638.

☗ Links, Cambridge Rd ✆ 662708, SW : 1 m.

◆London 64 – ◆Cambridge 13 – ◆Ipswich 40 – ◆Norwich 48.

🏨 **Newmarket Moat House** (Q.M.H.), Moulton Rd, CB8 8DY, ✆ 667171 – 🛗 📺 🅿. 🎿. 🔽 AE ① VISA
M *(closed lunch Saturday and Bank Holidays)* 9.50 **st.** and a la carte 🍷 2.85 – **44 rm** ⊑ 40.00/52.00 **st.** – SB (weekends only) 58.00 **st.**

🏨 **White Hart**, High St., CB8 8JP, ✆ 663051 – 📺 ☐wc ☎ 🅿. 🎿. 🔽 VISA
M 6.05/7.50 **t.** and a la carte – **21 rm** ⊑ 20.00/48.00 **st.** – SB (weekends only)(except Christmas) 52.00 **st.**

at Six Mile Bottom (Cambs.) SW : 6 m. on A 1304 – ✉ Newmarket – ✆ 063 870 Six Mile Bottom :

🏨 **Swynford Paddocks**, CB8 0UE, ✆ 234, Telex 817438, ≼, « Country house », 🐎, park, 🎾
– 📺 ☎ 🅿. 🔽 AE ① VISA
M 9.75 **t.** (lunch) and a la carte 14.20/20.20 **t.** 🍷 3.50 – **15 rm** ⊑ 48.00/75.00 **st.** – SB (weekends only) 83.00/89.50 **st.**

TOYOTA Bury Rd ✆ 662130
VAUXHALL-OPEL All Saints Rd ✆ 663121

VOLVO Dullingham ✆ 063 876 (Stetchworth) 244

NEW MILTON Hants. **403 404** P 31 – ECD : Wednesday – ✆ 0425.

◆London 106 – Bournemouth 12 – ◆Southampton 21 – Winchester 34.

🏰 ✆ **Chewton Glen** ⌂, Christchurch Rd, BH25 6QS, W : 2 m. by A 337 and Ringwood Rd on Chewton Farm Rd ✆ 042 52 (Highcliffe) 5341, Telex 41456, ≼, « Gardens », 🏊 heated, park, 🎾 – 📺 🅿. 🎿. 🔽 AE ① VISA. 🍸
M 15.00/30.00 **st.** and a la carte 🍷 4.00 – ⊑ 5.50 – **44 rm** 90.00/145.00 **st.**. **11 suites** 155.00/260.00 **st.** – SB (2 November-15 April) 135.00/190.00 **st.**
Spec. Loup de mer mouginoise (April-September), Homard de pays Robert Morley, Poêlée de langoustines et ris de veau.

AUSTIN-ROVER Old Milton Rd ✆ 614665
COLT Christchurch Rd ✆ 611198

NISSAN 25 Station Rd ✆ 620660
RENAULT 53 Lymington Rd ✆ 612296

NEWPORT I.O.W. **403 404** Q 31 – see Wight (Isle of).

NEWPORT (CASNEWYDD-AR-WYSG) Gwent **403** L 29 – pop. 115 896 – ECD : Thursday – ✆ 0633.

Envir. : Caerleon : Roman Amphitheatre★ *AC*, NE : 3 m.

🛈 Museum and Art Gallery, John Frost Sq ✆ 842962.

◆London 145 – ◆Bristol 31 – ◆Cardiff 12 – Gloucester 48.

🏨 **Celtic Manor**, Coldra Woods, NP6 2YA, E : 3 m. on A 48 ✆ 413000, Telex 498037, ≼ – 📺 ☎
🅿. 🎿. 🔽 AE ① VISA. 🍸
M (restricted lunch) 7.95/15.00 **t.** and a la carte 🍷 2.75 – **17 rm** ⊑ 58.00/75.00 **t.** – SB (weekends only)(except Bank Holidays) 68.00 **st.**

🏨 **Ladbroke** (Ladbroke), The Coldra, Chepstow Rd, NP6 2YG, E : 3 m. on A 48 ✆ 412777, Telex 497205 – 📺 ☐wc ☎ 🅿. 🎿
M (buffet rest.) 10.25 🍷 3.70 – ⊑ 5.50 – **119 rm** 42.00/52.50 **st.** – SB (weekends only) 63.00 **st.**

🏨 **Kings**, High St., NP9 1QU, ✆ 842020, Telex 497330 – 🛗 📺 ☐wc ☎ 🅿. 🎿. 🔽 AE ① VISA.
🍸
M (carving lunch) 6.95/9.45 **t.** and a la carte 🍷 3.00 – **47 rm** ⊑ 39.00/49.00 **t.** – SB (week ends only) 49.00/56.00 **st.**

✗ **Fratelli**, 173b Caerleon Rd, NP9 7FX, E : 1 m. ✆ 64602, Italian rest. – 🔽 AE VISA
closed Saturday lunch, Sunday, 3 weeks August, 1 week at Christmas and Bank Holidays –
M a la carte 7.85/14.00 **t.** 🍷 3.50.

at Langstone E : 4 ½ m. on A 48 – ✉ Newport – ✆ 0633 Llanwern :

🏨 **New Inn**, Chepstow Rd, NP6 2JN, ✆ 412426 – 📺 ☐wc ☎ 🅿. 🎿. 🔽 AE ① VISA. 🍸
M *(closed Saturday lunch)* 5.50/5.95 **s.** and a la carte 🍷 3.75 – **34 rm** ⊑ 25.00/39.75 **st.**

AUSTIN-ROVER Shaftesbury St. ✆ 858451
AUSTIN-ROVER Bassaleg Rd ✆ 63717
AUSTIN-ROVER Bassaleg Rd ✆ 53771

FORD Lee Way Industrial Estate ✆ 278020
NISSAN Spytty Rd ✆ 273414

Besonders angenehme Hotels oder Restaurants
sind im Führer   gekennzeichnet.

Sie können uns helfen, wenn Sie uns die Häuser angeben,
in denen Sie sich besonders wohl gefühlt haben.

Jährlich erscheint eine komplett überarbeitete Ausgabe
aller Roten Michelin-Führer.

🏰🏨 ... 🏠

XXXXX ... X

NEWPORT (TREFDRAETH) Dyfed **403** F 27 – pop. 1 224 – ECD : Wednesday – ☎ 0239.

See : Site★.

Envir. : Pentre Ifan (burial chamber★) SE : 4 ½ m.

🖪 Newport ✍ 820244.

🛂 Pembrokeshire Coast National Park Centre, East St. ✍ 820912 (summer only).

♦London 258 – Fishguard 7.

  ✗ **Cnapan** with rm, East St., on A 487, SA42 0WF, ✍ 820575, 🚗 – ᵀⱽ 📶wc Ⓟ. ⚞ VISA. �│
    closed Tuesday Easter-October and February – **M** *(closed to non residents November-Easter)*
    (Easter-October wholefood lunch only)(booking essential) a la carte 9.45/11.10 st. 🍷 3.00 –
    5 rm ⌿ 13.50/27.00 **st.**

    at Velindre (Felindre Farchog) E : 2 ¾ m. on A 487 – ✉ Cardigan – ☎ 0239 Newport :

  🏠 **Salutation Inn**, SA41 3UY, ✍ 820564, 🚗 – ᵀⱽ 📶wc Ⓟ. ⚞ VISA
    M (bar lunch Monday to Saturday)/dinner 8.50 **st.** and a la carte 🍷 2.50 – **8 rm** ⌿ 18.00/32.00 **t.**
    – SB 44.00 **st.**

NEWPORT Salop **402 403 404** M 25 – pop. 10 339 – ECD : Thursday – ☎ 0952.

🛂 9 St. Mary's St. ✍ 814109.

♦London 150 – ♦Birmingham 33 – Shrewsbury 18 – ♦Stoke-on-Trent 21.

  🏠 **Royal Victoria**, St. Mary's St., TF10 7BJ, ✍ 810831 – ᵀⱽ ⌿wc Ⓟ
    22 rm.

    at High Offley NE : 7 ¼ m. by A 519 – ✉ ☎ 0785 74 Woodseaves :

  ✗ **Royal Oak**, Grubb St., ST20 0NE, ✍ 579 – Ⓟ. ⚞ ᴀᴇ ⓞ VISA
    closed Sunday dinner, Monday, 3 weeks August-September and Bank Holidays – **M** (dinner
    only and Sunday lunch)/dinner 15.00 **t.** 🍷 3.50.

FORD Browns Garage ✍ 811076

NEWPORT PAGNELL Bucks. **404** R 27 – pop. 10 733 – ECD : Thursday – ☎ 0908.

♦London 57 – Bedford 13 – Luton 21 – Northampton 15.

  🏠 **TraveLodge** (T.H.F.) without rest., M 1 Service Area 3, MK16 8DS, W : 1 ½ m. by A 422 on
    M 1 ✍ 610878, Telex 826186 – ᵀⱽ ⌿wc ☎ Ⓟ. 🏊 ⚞ ᴀᴇ ⓞ VISA
    97 rm ⌿ 33.00/44.00 **st.**

  🏠 **Swan Revived**, High St., MK16 8AR, ✍ 610565, Telex 826801 – 🛗 ᵀⱽ ⌿wc 📶wc ☎ Ⓟ. 🏊
    ⚞ ᴀᴇ ⓞ VISA
    M a la carte 5.90/10.30 **t.** 🍷 3.00 – **31 rm** ⌿ 22.50/36.00 **st.**

PEUGEOT High St. ✍ 611715

NEWQUAY Cornwall **403** E 32 The West Country G. – pop. 13 905 – ECD : Wednesday – ☎ 063 73
(4 and 5 fig.) or 0637 (6 fig.).

Envir. : Pentire Points and Kelsey Head★ (≼★★) SW : 5 m. by A 3075 Y – Trerice Manor★ *AC*
S : 3 ½ m. by A 392 Y.

🖪 Perranporth ✍ 087 257 (Perranporth) 2454, SW : 6 m. by A 3075 Y – 🖪 Tower Rd ✍ 4354 Z.

✈ Newquay Civil Airport : ✍ 063 74 (St. Mawgan) 551, NE : 6 m. by A 3059 Y.

🛂 Cliffe Rd ✍ 871345/6.

♦London 291 – Exeter 83 – Penzance 34 – ♦Plymouth 48 – Truro 14.

    Plan on next page

  🏨🏨 **Bristol**, Narrowcliff, TR7 2PQ, ✍ 875181, ≼, ⚞ – 🛗 ᵀⱽ Ⓟ. ⚞ ᴀᴇ ⓞ VISA   Z r
    M 7.00/10.50 **st.** and a la carte 🍷 2.50 – **95 rm** ⌿ 23.50/54.50 **st.** – SB (except summer)
    (weekends only) 55.00 **st.**

  🏨🏨 **Riviera** (Best Western), Lusty Glaze Rd, TR7 3AA, ✍ 874251, ≼, ⚒ heated, 🚗, squash – 🛗
    ᵀⱽ Ⓟ. ⚞ ᴀᴇ VISA. �│   Z o
    M 7.00/9.50 **t.** and a la carte 🍷 3.00 – **50 rm** ⌿ 27.50/58.50 **t.** – SB (weekends only)(except
    Bank Holidays) 50.00/70.00 **st.**

  🏠🏠 **Trebarwith**, Island Cres., TR7 1BZ, ✍ 872288, ≼ bay and coast, ⚞, 🚗 – ᵀⱽ ⌿wc 📶wc Ⓟ.
    ⚞ VISA. �│   Z a
    April-October – **M** (bar lunch)/dinner 9.50 **st.** 🍷 5.50 – **43 rm** ⌿ 18.00/56.00 **st.**

  🏠🏠 **Windsor**, Mount Wise, TR7 2AY, ✍ 875188, ⚒ heated, ⚞, 🚗, squash – ᵀⱽ ⌿wc Ⓟ. ⚞
    VISA. �│   Z n
    Easter-October – **M** (bar lunch)/dinner 10.50 **st.** and a la carte 🍷 3.00 – **45 rm** ⌿ 20.00/65.00 **st.**

  🏠🏠 **Kilbirnie**, Narrowcliff, TR7 2RS, ✍ 875155, ⚞ – ᵀⱽ ⌿wc ☎ Ⓟ. ⚞ VISA   Z e
    closed 21 to 29 December – **M** (bar lunch)/dinner 9.00 **st.** and a la carte 🍷 2.50 – **69 rm**
    ⌿ 17.00/51.50 **st.** – SB (except summer) 42.00/45.50 **st.**

  🏠🏠 **Mordros**, 4 Pentire Av., TR7 1PA, ✍ 876700, ⚒ heated – ᵀⱽ ⌿wc Ⓟ. �│   Y x
    M a la carte 6.50/10.00 **st.** 🍷 3.00 – **30 rm** ⌿ 17.50/54.00 **st.** – SB 30.00/48.00 **st.**

P.T.O. →

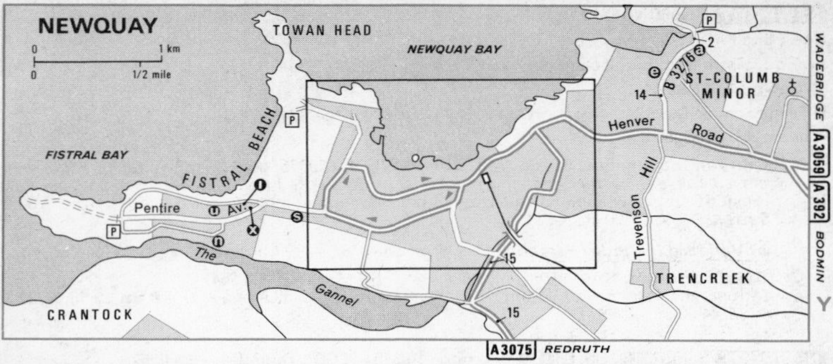

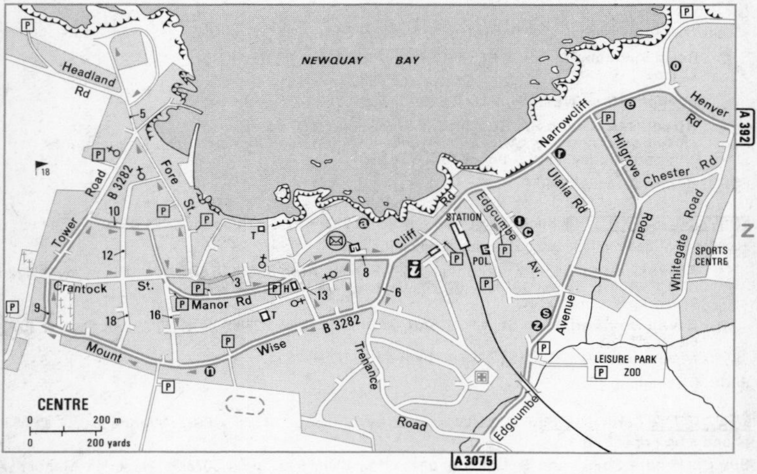

Bank Street . . . . Z 3
East Street . . . . Z 8
Fore Street . . . . Z

Alexander Road . . . . Y 2
Beacon Road . . . . Z 5
Berry Road . . . . Z 6
Higher Tower Road . . . . Z 9
Hope Terrace . . . . Z 10
Jubilee Street . . . . Z 12
Marcus Hill . . . . Z 13
Porth Way . . . . Y 14
Trevemper Road . . . . Y 15
St. Georges Road . . . . Z 16
St. John's Road . . . . Z 18

Corisande Manor, Riverside Av., Pentire, TR7 1PL, 872042, Gannel Estuary, – wc wc — Y **n**
3 May-10 October – **M** (bar lunch)/dinner 6.00 **t.** 2.25 – **19 rm** 15.00/44.00 **t.** – SB 36.00/48.00 **st.**

Porth Veor Manor, 56 Porth Way, TR7 3LW, 873274, , – wc wc . VISA — Y **e**
closed mid November-mid December and January – **M** 6.00/10.75 **t.** and a la carte 2.75 – **16 rm** 20.50/39.00 **t.** – SB (except June-September) 42.00/50.00 **st.**

Water's Edge, Esplanade Rd, Pentire, TR7 1QA, 872048, Fistral Bay, – wc wc . — Y **u**
Easter and 7 May-4 October – **M** (bar lunch)/dinner 9.50 **t.** 2.25 – **20 rm** (dinner included) 13.80/48.30 **t.**

Bewdley, 10 Pentire Rd, TR7 1NX, 872883, , heated – wc wc . VISA — Y **s**
March-mid November – **M** (bar lunch)/dinner 8.50 **st.** 3.00 – **31 rm** 14.50/27.00 **st.** – SB (weekends only) 33.00/48.00 **st.**

Porth Enodoc, 4 Esplanade Rd, Pentire, TR7 1PY, 872372, Fistral Bay – wc . — Y **i**
Easter-October – **12 rm** 12.00/28.00 **t.**

Pasadera, 15 Edgcumbe Av., TR7 2NJ, 873235 – . — Z **i**
Easter-mid October – **16 rm** 9.20/10.35 **st.**

Wheal Treasure, 72 Edgcumbe Av., TR7 2NN, 874136 – wc . — Z **z**
May-September – **9 rm** (dinner included) 13.00/33.00 **st.**

↑ **Copper Beech,** 70 Edgcumbe Av., TR7 2NN, ✆ 873376 – ⊟wc ⋔wc **P.** 🅰 🆎 ⓪   Z s
    Easter-October – **15 rm** ⌼ 10.35/27.60.

↑ **Pendeen,** 7 Alexandra Rd, Porth, TR7 3ND, ✆ 873521, 🚗 – 🆃🆅 ⊟wc ⋔wc **P.** ⌘   Y a
    April-September – **15 rm** ⌼ 11.50/33.00 **s.**

↑ **Hepworth,** 27 Edgcumbe Av., TR7 2NJ, ✆ 873686, 🚗 – ⋔wc **P.** ⌘   Z c
    Easter-September – **13 rm** ⌼ 9.20/27.00 **t.**

    at St. Columb Minor NE : 3 m. by A 3059 – Y – ✉ ☎ 0637 Newquay :

🏨 **Cross Mount,** 60 Church St., TR7 3EX, ✆ 872669 – ⊟wc ⋔wc **P.** 🅰 🆅🆂🅰 ⌘
    closed November and Christmas – **M** *(closed Monday dinner)* 6.00/7.00 **t.** and a la carte ⌖ 2.30
    – **12 rm** ⌼ 13.00/29.00 **t.**

    at Crantock SW : 4 m. by A 3075 – Y – ✉ Newquay – ☎ 0637 Crantock :

🏛 **Fairbank,** West Pentire Rd, TR8 5SA, ✆ 830424, ≼, 🚗 – ⊟wc ⋔wc **P.** 🅰 ⓪ 🆅🆂🅰
    ⌘
    April-October – **M** (bar lunch)/dinner 7.45 **t.** – **29 rm** ⌼ 17.00/20.00 **t.** – SB 31.00/38.00 **st.**

🏛 **Crantock Bay** ⌂, West Pentire, TR8 5SE, W : ¾ m. ✆ 830229, ≼ Crantock Bay, 🚗 – 🆃🆅
    ⊟wc **P.** 🆅🆂🅰
    April-October – **M** (buffet lunch)/dinner 7.95 **t.** ⌖ 2.40 – **29 rm** ⌼ 15.00/52.00 **t.**

AUSTIN-ROVER Quintrell Downs ✆ 2410   VOLVO Newlyn East ✆ 087 251 (Mitchell) 347
FIAT Tower Rd ✆ 2378

NEW QUAY (CEINEWYDD) Dyfed �403 G 27 – ✉ ☎ 0545.
♦London 234 – Aberystwyth 24 – Carmarthen 31 – Fishguard 39.

🏨 **Black Lion,** Glanmor Terr., SA45 9PT, ✆ 560209, ≼, 🚗 – 🆃🆅 ⊟wc ⋔wc **P.** 🅰 🆎 ⓪
    🆅🆂🅰
    M *(closed Sunday October-May)* (bar lunch)/dinner a la carte 7.25/13.70 **t.** ⌖ 2.85 – **7 rm**
    ⌼ 28.00/40.00 **st.** – SB 38.00/50.00 **st.**

NEW ROMNEY Kent �404 W 31 – pop. 4 547 – ECD : Wednesday – ☎ 0679.
Envir. : Lydd (All Saints' Church tower : groined vaulting★) SW : 3 ½ m. – Brookland (St. Augustine's
Church : belfry★ 15C, Norman font★) W : 6 m.
🄰 2 Littlestone Rd ✆ 64044.
♦London 71 – Folkestone 14 – Hastings 23 – Maidstone 33.

🏨 **Blue Dolphins,** Dymchurch Rd, TN28 8BE, ✆ 63224 – ⋔ **P.** 🅰 🆅🆂🅰 ⌘
    M *(closed Sunday)* (dinner only) 12.95 **t.** ⌖ 2.70 – **8 rm** ⌼ 13.25/25.00 **st.**

FORD The Avenue, Littlestone ✆ 62184   RENAULT Sussex Rd ✆ 2404

NEWTON FERRERS Devon �403 H 33 The West Country G. – pop. 1 609 – ☎ 0752 Plymouth.
♦London 242 – Exeter 42 – ♦Plymouth 11.

🏛 **Court House** ⌂, Court Rd, PL8 1AQ, ✆ 872324, ⊐ heated, 🚗 – ⊟wc **P.**
    11 rm.

    at Battisborough Cross E : 3 m. – ✉ ☎ 075 530 Holbeton :

🏛 **Alston Hall** ⌂, PL8 1HN, ✆ 259, ≼, ⊐, 🚗, ⌘ – 🆃🆅 ⊟wc ☎ **P.** 🅰 🆎 ⓪ 🆅🆂🅰 ⌘
    M 13.50/14.50 **t.** – **9 rm** ⌼ 39.50/67.50 **st.** – SB (except summer and Bank Holidays)
    65.00/80.00 **st.**

NEWTON SOLNEY Derbs. �402 �403 �404 P 25 – see Burton-upon-Trent (Staffs.).

NEWTOWN (DRENEWYDD) Powys �403 K 26 – pop. 8 906 – ECD : Thursday – ☎ 0686.
🄰 St. Davids House ✆ 25580.
♦London 196 – Aberystwyth 44 – Chester 56 – Shrewsbury 32.

🏛 **The Bear,** Broad St., SY16 2LU, ✆ 26964, Telex 35250 – 🆃🆅 ⊟wc ⋔wc ☎ **P.** 🅰 🆎 ⓪
    🆅🆂🅰
    M 6.95/8.70 **t.** and a la carte – **36 rm** ⌼ 23.50/46.00 **t.** – SB (weekends only)(except Christmas
    and New Year) 55.00/61.00 **st.**

🏛 **Elephant and Castle,** Broad St., SY16 2BQ, ✆ 26271 – 🆃🆅 ⊟wc ☎ **P.** 🅰 🆎 ⓪ 🆅🆂🅰
    closed 24 and 25 December – **M** 7.00/11.00 **st.** and a la carte – **21 rm** ⌼ 20.00/40.00 **st.**

    at Abermule (Aber-Miwl) NE : 4 ½ m. on A 483 – ✉ ☎ 068 686 Abermule :

🏛 **Dolforwyn Hall** ⌂, Dolforwyn, SY15 6JG, N : ½ m. on A 483 ✆ 221 – 🆃🆅 ⊟wc ⋔wc
    7 rm.

AUDI, VW Abermule ✆ 068 686 (Abermule) 615   FORD Pool Rd ✆ 25514

NORMAN CROSS Cambs. ⁴⁰⁴ T 26 – see Peterborough.

NORTHALLERTON North Yorks. ⁴⁰² P 20 – pop. 13 566 – ECD : Thursday – ☎ 0609.
Envir. : Bedale, Leyburn Rd (Parish church★ 13C-14C) SW : 7 ½ m.
🛏 at Bedale ✆ 0677 (Bedale) 22451, SW : 7 ½ m.
🛈 207 High St. ✆ 774324.

◆London 238 – ◆Leeds 48 – ◆Middlesbrough 24 – York 33.

🏨 **Golden Lion** (T.H.F.), High St., DL7 8PP, ✆ 2404 – 📺 ➹wc ☎ 🅿 🔥 🔼 Æ ⑩ 𝘝𝘐𝘚𝘈
M 6.00/9.00 st. and a la carte ⓘ 3.20 – 💷 5.65 – **29 rm** 43.50/50.00 st.

XX **McCoys at the Tontine** with rm, Staddlebridge, DL6 3JB, NE : 8 ½ m. by A 684 on A 19 ✆ 060 982 (East Harlsey) 671, « 1930's decor » – 🖃 📺 ➹wc ☎ 🅿 🔼 Æ ⑩ 𝘝𝘐𝘚𝘈
closed 24 to 26 December and 1 January – M (closed Sunday) (dinner only) 24.00 t. and a la carte 9.65/32.50 ⓘ 7.95 – **6 rm** 💷 50.00/70.00 t.

XX **Romanby Court,** 5 Romanby Court, High St., DL7 8PG, ✆ 774918 – 🔼 𝘝𝘐𝘚𝘈
closed Sunday and Monday – M a la carte 8.25/16.25 t. ⓘ 3.25.

at Newby Wiske S : 2 ½ m. by A 167 – 🖂 ☎ 0609 Northallerton :

🏨 **Solberge Hall** (Best Western) ⑤, DL7 9ER, ✆ 779191, 🌫, park – 📺 ➹wc ☎ 🅿 🔼 Æ ⑩ 𝘝𝘐𝘚𝘈
M 7.50/12.50 and a la carte ⓘ 3.00 – **15 rm** 💷 40.00/66.00 st. – SB (except Christmas and New Year) 50.00/76.00 st.

AUSTIN-ROVER Brompton Rd ✆ 3891   HONDA, SAAB East Rd ✆ 3921

NORTHAMPTON Northants. ⁴⁰⁴ R 27 – pop. 154 172 – ☎ 0604.
See : Church of the Holy Sepulchre★ 12C × A – Central Museum and Art Gallery (collection of footwear★) × M.
Envir. : Brixworth (All Saints Church★ 7C Saxon) N : 7 m. by A 508 Y – Earls Barton (All Saints Church : 10C Saxon tower★) NE : 5 m. by A 45 Y – Castle Ashby★ (16C-17C) AC, NE : 8 m. by A 428 Z.
🛏 Delapre, Eagle Drive ✆ 64036 Z.
🛈 21 St. Giles St. ✆ 22677.

◆London 69 – ◆Cambridge 53 – ◆Coventry 34 – ◆Leicester 42 – Luton 35 – ◆Oxford 41.

Plan opposite

🏨 **Swallow** (Swallow), Eagle Drive, NN4 0HW, SE : 2 m. by A 428 on A 45 ✆ 68700, Telex 31562, 🔲 – 🗏 rest 📺 ☎ & 🅿 🔥 🔼 Æ ⑩ 𝘝𝘐𝘚𝘈   Z **a**
M 9.50 st. and a la carte ⓘ 3.80 – **122 rm** 💷 65.00 – SB (weekends only) 62.00/70.00 st.

🏨 Northampton Moat House (Q.M.H.), Silver St., NN1 2TA, ✆ 22441, Telex 311142 – 🛗 📺 🅿.   X **n**
134 rm. 4 suites

XX Royal Bengal, 39-41 Bridge St., ✆ 38617, Indian rest.   X **s**

XX **Dunkley's,** Castle Ashby Station, Cogenhoe, NN7 1ND, E : 8 ¼ m. by A 428 and A 45 on Castle Ashby road ✆ 810546, « Converted station warehouse » – 🅿 🔼 Æ ⑩ 𝘝𝘐𝘚𝘈
closed Saturday lunch, Sunday dinner and 25-26 December – M 7.50/13.50 t. and a la carte 12.95/19.30 t. ⓘ 2.70.

X **Napoleon's Bistro,** 9-11 Welford Rd, Kingsthorpe, NN2 8AE, N : 1 ¾ m. by A 508 on A 50 ✆ 713899 – 🔼 Æ ⑩ 𝘝𝘐𝘚𝘈   Y **c**
closed Sunday and 14 to 28 July – M 5.70 t. (lunch) and a la carte 9.95/14.30 t. ⓘ 3.00.

X **Ca d'Oro,** 334 Wellingborough Rd, NN1 4ES, ✆ 32660, Italian rest. – 🔼 Æ ⑩ 𝘝𝘐𝘚𝘈   Z **e**
closed Saturday lunch and Sunday – M a la carte 8.10/19.20 t. ⓘ 2.75.

at Spratton N : 7 m. by A 508 off A 50 Y – 🖂 ☎ 0604 Northampton :

🏨 **Broomhill** ⑤, Holdenby Rd, NN6 8LD, SW : 1 m. by A 50 ✆ 845959, ≤, 🔄 heated, 🌫, park, ❧ – 📺 ➹wc ☎ 🅿 🔼 Æ ⑩ 𝘝𝘐𝘚𝘈
closed Christmas – M (closed Sunday dinner to non residents) 7.50/13.00 t. and a la carte ⓘ 2.75 – **6 rm** 💷 40.00/50.00 t.

at Weston Favell NE : 3 ½ m. by A 4500 – 🖂 ☎ 0604 Northampton :

🏨 **Westone Moat House** (Q.M.H.), Ashley Way, NN3 3EA, ✆ 406262, Telex 312587, 🌫 – 🛗 🗏 rest 📺 ☎ 🅿 🔥 🔼 Æ ⑩ 𝘝𝘐𝘚𝘈   Y **a**
closed 26 December-1 January – M (closed Saturday lunch) 7.50/8.50 st. and a la carte ⓘ 3.00 – **65 rm** 💷 40.00/50.00 st., **1 suite** 60.00 st. – SB (except Christmas and New Year)(weekends only) 54.00 st.

at Moulton NE : 4 ½ m. by A 43 – Y – 🖂 ☎ 0604 Northampton :

🏠 **Poplars,** 33 Cross St., NN3 1RZ, ✆ 43983, 🌫 – 📺 🎬wc 🅿 🔼 🈁
closed 1 week at Christmas – **21 rm** 💷 18.00/34.00 st.

AUSTIN-ROVER Weedon Rd ✆ 54041
AUSTIN-ROVER 46-50 Sheep St. ✆ 35471
CITROEN 194-200 Kingsthorpe Grove ✆ 713202
DAIMLER, JAGUAR, NISSAN 592 Wellingborough Rd ✆ 401141

MERCEDEZ-BENZ 42-50 Harborough Rd ✆ 250151
RENAULT Bedford Rd ✆ 39645
TOYOTA 348 Wellingborough Rd ✆ 31086
VOLVO Bedford Rd ✆ 21363

NORTHAMPTON

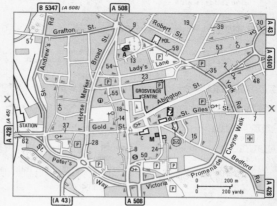

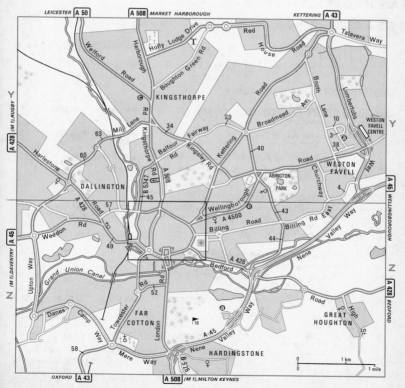

375

NORTH BOVEY Devon **403** I 32 – pop. 368 – ⊠ Newton Abbot – ✆ 0647 Moretonhampstead.
♦London 214 – Exeter 13 – ♦Plymouth 31 – Torquay 21.

🏠 **Glebe House** ⍟, TQ13 8RA, ✆ 40544, ≼, 🐾, park – ➭wc 🚿wc **P**. 🔼 _VISA_
   closed January and February – **M** (bar lunch residents only)/dinner 12.50 **t.** and a la carte
   ⓘ 2.75 – ⌘ 4.50 – **9 rm** 10.00/20.00 **t.**

🏠 **Blackaller House** ⍟, TQ13 8QY, ✆ 40322, ≼, 🐾 – ➭wc **P**. 🔼 _AE_ _VISA_
   March-November – **M** (dinner only) 12.25 **st.** ⓘ 2.85 – **5 rm** ⌘ 17.95/41.15 **st.**

NORTH CAVE Humberside **402** S 22 – pop. 1 728 – ✆ 043 02.
♦London 206 – ♦Kingston upon Hull 17 – ♦Leeds 46 – York 28.

XX **Sundial,** 18 Westgate, HU15 2NJ, ✆ 2537, English rest. – 🔼 _AE_ _VISA_
   closed Sunday, Monday, 2 weeks February and last week July – **M** (dinner only) a la carte
   9.45/12.75 **t.** ⓘ 3.00.

NORTHENDEN Greater Manchester **402** ㉝ **403** ③ **404** ⑩ – see Manchester.

NORTH FERRIBY Humberside **402** S 22 – see Kingston-upon-Hull.

NORTHFIELD West Midlands **403** ㉒ **404** ㉘ – see Birmingham.

NORTHIAM East Sussex **404** V 31 – pop. 1 657 – ECD : Wednesday – ⊠ Rye – ✆ 079 74.
♦London 55 – Folkestone 36 – Hastings 12 – Maidstone 27.

🏛 **Hayes Arms,** Village Green, TN31 6NN, ✆ 3142, « Part Tudor and Georgian country house »
   🐾 – 📺 ➭wc 🚿wc **P**. 🔼 _AE_ _VISA_
   closed 18 January-8 February – **M** (bar lunch)/dinner 10.50 **st.** ⓘ 2.75 – **7 rm** ⌘ 27.00/50.00 **st.**
   – SB 59.00/63.00 **st.**

NORTH PETHERTON Somerset **403** K 30 – see Bridgwater.

NORTH STIFFORD Essex **404** ㊹ – ⊠ Grays – ✆ 0375 Grays Thurrock.
♦London 22 – Chelmsford 24 – Southend-on-Sea 20.

🏛 **Stifford Moat House** (Q.M.H.), High Rd, RM16 1UE, ✆ 371451, 🐾, ✖ – 📺 ➭wc ☎ **P**.
   🏊 🔼 _AE_ _VISA_
   M _(closed Saturday lunch)_ 12.50 **st.** and a la carte ⓘ 3.25 – ⌘ 4.95 – **64 rm** 40.00/52.00 **st.** –
   SB (weekends only) 55.00 **st.**

NORTH STOKE Oxon. – see Wallingford.

NORTH WALSHAM Norfolk **403** **404** Y 25 – pop. 7 929 – ECD : Wednesday – ✆ 0692.
♦London 125 – ♦Norwich 16.

⌂ **Beechwood House,** 20 Cromer Rd, NR28 0HD, ✆ 403231, 🐾 – ➭wc 🚿wc **P**
   closed 24 December-6 January – **11 rm** ⌘ 13.50/32.00 **t.**

   at Knapton NE : 3 ½ m. on B 1145 – ⊠ North Walsham – ✆ 0263 Mundesley :

🏠 Knapton Hall, NR28 0SB, ✆ 720405, ⌇ heated, 🐾 – 📺 ➭wc ☎ **P**
   8 rm.

NORWICH Norfolk **404** Y 26 – pop. 169 814 – ✆ 0603.
See : Cathedral** 11C-12C (bosses** of nave vaulting) Y – Castle (museum**) _AC_ Z **M** –
St. Peter Mancroft's Church* (Perpendicular) Z B – Sainsbury Centre for Visual Arts* (University
of East Anglia) _AC_, by B 1108 X.
Envir. : Norfolk Wildlife Park* _AC_, NW : 12 m. by A 1067 V – Blickling Hall* (Jacobean) N : 12 m.
by A 140 V.
🛫 ✆ 411923, Telex 97209, N : 3 ½ m. by A 140 V.
🛈 Augustine Steward House, 14 Tombland ✆ 666071.
♦London 109 – ♦Kingston-upon-Hull 148 – ♦Leicester 117 – ♦Nottingham 120.

Plan opposite

🏰 **Maid's Head** (Q.M.H.), Tombland, NR3 1LB, ✆ 628821, Telex 975080 – 🛗 📺 **P**. 🏊 🔼 _AE_
   _①_ _VISA_   Y c
   M 7.00/9.50 **t.** and a la carte ⓘ 3.45 – **79 rm** ⌘ 40.50/63.00 **t.** – SB (weekends only)
   57.00/61.00 **st.**

🏛 **Nelson,** Prince of Wales Rd, NR1 1DX, ✆ 628612, Telex 975203, ≼ – 🛗 ▤ rest 📺 ➭wc 🚿
   🔥 🔼 🔼 _AE_ _①_ _VISA_ ✖   Z a
   M 8.95 **st.** and a la carte ⓘ 3.15 – **122 rm** ⌘ 45.50/55.50 **st.**, **3 suites** 61.50 **st.** – SB 61.00 **st.**

🏛 **Post House** (T.H.F.), Ipswich Rd, NR4 6EP, S : 2 ¼ m. on A 140 ✆ 56431, Telex 975106,
   ⌇ heated – 📺 ➭wc 🔥 🏊 🔼 _AE_ _①_ _VISA_   on A 140   X
   M 8.95/12.00 **st.** and a la carte ⓘ 3.40 – ⌘ 5.65 – **120 rm** 44.00/53.00 **st.**

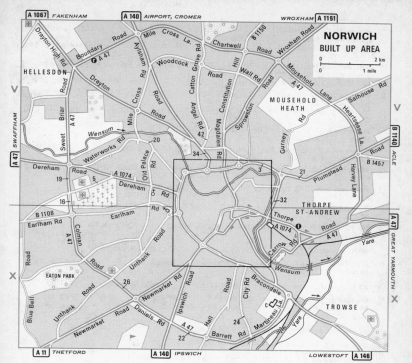

NORWICH BUILT UP AREA

0   2 km
0   1 mile

A 1067 FAKENHAM   A 140 AIRPORT, CROMER   WROXHAM A 1151

HELLESDON

MOUSEHOLD HEATH

THORPE ST-ANDREW

TROWSE

EATON PARK

A 11 THETFORD   A 140 IPSWICH   LOWESTOFT A 146

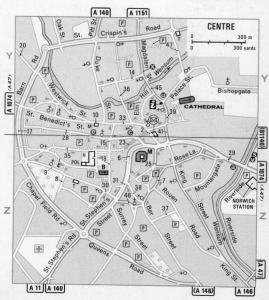

CENTRE

0   300 m
0   300 yards

A 140   A 1151

CATHEDRAL

Bishopgate

NORWICH STATION

A 11   A 140   A 146   A 146

🏨 **Norwich** (Best Western), 121-131 Boundary Rd, NR3 2BA, on A 47 ✆ 410431, Telex 975337 –
📺 🍴wc 🚗 & 🅿 🚪 🏛 🅰🅴 🕦 𝗩𝗜𝗦𝗔 🍽
M (carving lunch) 8.95 **st.** and a la carte 🍷 3.15 – **102 rm** ⇌ 39.00/49.00 **st.**, **3 suites** 53.00 **st.** –
SB 52.50 **st.**

    V r

🏨 **Sprowston Hall,** Wroxham Rd, NR7 8RP, NE : 3 ¼ m. on A 1151 ✆ 410871, 🦌, park – 📺
📺 🍴wc 🅿, 🚪 🏛 🅰🅴 🕦 𝗩𝗜𝗦𝗔
M 7.50/9.25 **t.** and a la carte – **40 rm** ⇌ 37.50/55.00 **t.** – SB (weekends only) 57.00/62.00 **st.**

    Z a

🏨 **Lansdowne** (Embassy), 116 Thorpe Rd, NR1 1RU, ✆ 620302 – 📶 📺 🍴wc 🍴wc ☎ 🅿, 🚪
🏛 🅰🅴 🕦 𝗩𝗜𝗦𝗔
M (closed Saturday lunch) 8.00 **st.** and a la carte 🍷 2.55 – ⇌ 5.00 – **38 rm** 36.00/45.00 –
SB 54.00 **st.**

    X i

🏠 **Riverside,** 11-12 Riverside Rd, NR1 1SQ, ✆ 623978 – 📺
10 rm ⇌ 12.00/24.00 **st.**

    Z s

🏠 **Conway,** 2 Aspland Rd, NR1 1SH, ✆ 624761 – 📺 🏛 🅰🅴 🕦 𝗩𝗜𝗦𝗔 🍽
9 rm ⇌ 11.00/26.00 **st.**

    Z v

XX **Marco's,** 17 Pottergate, NR2 1DS, ✆ 624044, Italian rest. – 🏛 🅰🅴 🕦 𝗩𝗜𝗦𝗔
closed Sunday, Monday and August – **M** a la carte 9.90/18.50 **t.**

    YZ e

XX **Brasted's,** 8-10 St. Andrew's Hill, NR2 1AD, ✆ 625949 – 🏛 🅰🅴 🕦 𝗩𝗜𝗦𝗔
closed Saturday lunch and Sunday dinner – **M** a la carte 12.10/14.55 **t.** 🍷 3.30.

    Y c

X **Bombay,** 9-11 Magdalen St., NR3 1LE, ✆ 666618, Indian rest. – 🏛 🅰🅴 🕦 𝗩𝗜𝗦𝗔
M a la carte 4.50/7.35 **t.**

    Y x

X **Bombay,** 43 Timber Hill, NR1 3LA, ✆ 620305, Indian rest. – 🏛 🅰🅴 🕦 𝗩𝗜𝗦𝗔
M a la carte 4.50/7.35 **t.**

 at Horsham St. Faith N : 4 ½ m. by A 140 – V – ✉ ✿ 0603 Norwich :

🏠 **Elm Farm Chalet,** 55 Norwich Rd, NR10 3HH, ✆ 898366, 🦌 – 📺 🍴wc 🅿. 🏛 𝗩𝗜𝗦𝗔 🍽
15 rm ⇌ 17.00/30.00 **st.**

 at Thorpe St. Andrew E : 2 ½ m. on A 47 – X – ✉ ✿ 0603 Norwich :

🏨 **Oaklands,** 89 Yarmouth Rd, NR7 0HH, ✆ 34471, 🦌 – 📺 🍴wc ☎ 🅿 🏛 🅰🅴 🕦 𝗩𝗜𝗦𝗔
M (lunch a la carte)/dinner 10.95 **t.** 🍷 2.00 – **42 rm** ⇌ 25.00/45.00 **st.** – SB (weekends only)
45.00/48.50 **st.**

 at Blofield E : 7 ½ m. by A 47 – X – ✉ ✿ 0603 Norwich :

XX La Locanda, Fox Lane, NR13 4LW, ✆ 713787, Italian rest. – 🅿.

 at Hethersett SW : 6 m. on A 11 – X – ✉ ✿ 0603 Norwich :

🏨 **Park Farm** 🌳, NR9 3DL, ✆ 810264, 🔲, 🦌, 🎾 – 📺 🍴wc 🍴wc ☎ 🅿. 🏛 𝗩𝗜𝗦𝗔 🍽
M (closed Sunday dinner to non-residents) 6.00/8.25 **t.** and a la carte 🍷 2.60 – **21 rm**
⇌ 33.00/50.00 **st.** – SB (weekends only)(except Bank Holidays) 60.00/90.00 **st.**

 at Drayton NW : 5 m. on A 1067 – V – ✉ ✿ 0603 Norwich :

XXX **Drayton Wood** 🌳 with rm, Drayton High Rd, NR8 6BL, SW : 1 ½ m. on A 1067 ✆ 409451,
🦌, park – 📺 🍴wc 🅿. 🏛 🅰🅴 🕦 🍽
closed 24 to 30 December – **M** (closed Sunday dinner) 8.00 **t.** (lunch) and a la carte 13.00/16.50 **t.**
🍷 3.00 – **4 rm** ⇌ 35.00/40.00 **t.**

AUDI-VW 79 Mile Cross Lane ✆ 410661/613631
ALFA-ROMEO, ISUZU, MERCEDES-BENZ, VW, AU-
DI Heigham Causeway, Heigham St. ✆ 612111
ASTON-MARTIN, AUSTIN-ROVER Ipswich Rd, Long
Stratton ✆ 0508 (Long Stratton) 30491
AUSTIN-ROVER 162 Cromer Rd ✆ 46946
AUSTIN-ROVER Norwich Rd, Stoke Holy Cross ✆
05086 (Framingham Earl) 2218
AUSTIN-ROVER Mile Cross Lane ✆ 483001
AUSTIN-ROVER,   DAIMLER-JAGUAR,   ROLLS
ROYCE 5 Prince of Wales Rd ✆ 628383
BMW 26-29 Cattlemarket St. ✆ 621471
CITROEN Earlham Rd ✆ 621393

FIAT, LANCIA, RELIANT Aylsham Rd ✆ 45345
FORD 39 Palace St. ✆ 624144
HONDA 36 Duke St. ✆ 629825
NISSAN Constitution Hill ✆ 43944
NISSAN 116-120 Prince of Wales Rd ✆ 613631
PORSCHE Vulcan Rd South ✆ 401814
RENAULT 22 Heigham St. ✆ 628911
TALBOT, VW, AUDI, PEUGEOT 116 Prince of Wales
Rd ✆ 628811
TOYOTA Rouen Rd ✆ 629655
VAUXHALL-OPEL Aylsham Rd, Mile Cross ✆ 414321
VAUXHALL-OPEL Mountergate ✆ 623111
VOLVO Westwick St. ✆ 626192

NOTTAGE (DRENEWYDD YN NOTAIS) Mid Glam. 🟥🟥🟥 I 29 – see Porthcawl.

When visiting the West Country,
use the **Michelin Green Guide " England-The West Country ".**

  – *Detailed descriptions of places of interest*

  – *Touring programmes by county*

  – *Maps and street plans*

  – *The history of the region*

  – *Photographs and drawings of monuments, beauty spots, houses...*

NOTTINGHAM Notts. **402 403 404** Q 25 – pop. 273 300 – ECD : Thursday – ✆ 0602.

See : Castle★ (Renaissance) and museum★ *AC* cz M.

Envir. : Newstead Abbey★★ 16C and gardens★★*AC*, N : 9 m. by B 683 AY – Wollaton Hall★ (16C) *AC*, W : 3 ½ m. AZ M.

☖ Wollaton Park ✆ 787574, W : 2 m. AZ – ☖ Bulwell Hall Park Links ✆ 278021, N : 5 m. AY.

✈ East Midlands Airport : Castle Donington ✆ 0332 (Derby) 810621, Telex 37543 SW : 15 m. by A 453 AZ.

🛈 18 Milton St. ✆ 470661 – Castle Gatehouse, Castle Rd ✆ 470661 (summer only).

🛈 at Long Eaton : Central Library, Tamworth Rd ✆ 0602 735426 – at West Bridgford : County Hall ✆ 823823.

◆London 135 – ◆Birmingham 50 – ◆Leeds 74 – ◆Manchester 72.

Plans on following pages

🏰 **Albany** (T.H.F.), St. James's St., NG1 6BN, ✆ 470131, Telex 37211 – 🛗 ▦ 📺 ☎. 🛎. 🔼 🗚
⓪ *VISA*
M 8.95/12.50 st. and a la carte ⅋ 3.40 – ⇄ 6.00 – **152 rm** 47.00/60.00 st., **1 suite**. CYZ a

🏨 **Royal Moat House International** (Q.M.H.), Wollaton St., NG1 5RH, ✆ 414444, Telex 37101, squash – 🛗 ▦ 📺 ☎ & 🛎. 🔼 🗚 ⓪ *VISA*
M 7.00/9.00 st. and a la carte ⅋ 3.60 – ⇄ 4.95 – **201 rm** 39.95/52.50 st., **1 suite**. CY e

🏨 **Strathdon Thistle** (Thistle), 44 Derby Rd, NG1 5FT, ✆ 418501, Telex 377185 – 🛗 ▦ rest 📺
🚻wc 🚻wc ☎. 🛎. 🔼 🗚 ⓪ *VISA*
M 7.50/10.20 t. and a la carte ⅋ 2.75 – ⇄ 5.75 – **69 rm** 42.00/90.00 st. CY c

🏨 Stakis Victoria (Stakis), Milton St., NG1 3PZ, ✆ 419561, Telex 37401 – 🛗 ▦ rest 📺 🚻wc 🚗.
🛎.
M (buffet lunch)/dinner 12.50 – **167 rm**. DY a

🏨 Savoy, 296 Mansfield Rd, NG5 2BT, ✆ 602621, Telex 377429 – 🛗 📺 🚻wc ☎ 🅿. 🛎. 🛄
125 rm. BY u

🏩 **Lucieville**, 349 Derby Rd, NG7 2DZ, ✆ 787389, 🍴 – 🚻wc 🅿. 🔼 *VISA* 🛄
closed 2 weeks at Christmas – **M** 9.00 t. and a la carte ⅋ 3.50 – **9 rm** ⇄ 27.50/40.00 t. AZ c

↥ **Royston**, 326 Mansfield Rd, NG5 2EF, ✆ 622947 – 📺 🚻wc 🅿. 🔼 🗚 ⓪. 🛄
14 rm ⇄ 16.75/35.00 st. BY e

↥ **Cotswold**, 332 Mansfield Rd, NG5 2EF, ✆ 623547 – 📺 🚻wc 🚻wc 🅿. 🔼 🗚 ⓪ *VISA*
17 rm ⇄ 15.00/32.00 st. BY c

✕✕ **Trattoria Conti**, 14-16 Wheeler Gate, NG1 2NB, ✆ 474056, Italian rest. – 🔼 🗚 ⓪
VISA
closed Sunday, 28 July-27 August and Bank Holidays – **M** 4.35/15.00 t. and a la carte ⅋ 2.50. CY n

✕ **Chand**, 26 Mansfield Rd, NG1 3GX, ✆ 474103, Indian rest. – 🔼 🗚 ⓪ *VISA*
M 3.00/5.50 t. and a la carte 5.95 t. DY i

at West Bridgford SE : 2 m. on A 52 – ✉ ✆ 0602 Nottingham :

🏨 **Windsor Lodge**, 116 Radcliffe Rd, NG2 5HG, ✆ 813773 – 📺 🚻wc 🚻wc ☎ 🅿. 🔼 🗚 *VISA*
🛄
closed 25 and 26 Decemer – **M** (closed Friday to Sunday) (bar lunch)/dinner 6.00 s. ⅋ 2.50 –
43 rm ⇄ 16.00/32.00 s. BZ x

at Edwalton S : 3 m. on A 606 – ✉ ✆ 0602 Nottingham :

🏨 **Edwalton Hall,** Village St., NG12 4AE, ✆ 231116, 🍴 – 📺 🚻wc ☎ 🅿. 🔼 🗚 ⓪
VISA
M a la carte 5.90/13.45 t. ⅋ 3.00 – **10 rm** ⇄ 16.50/40.00 s. BZ r

at Beeston SW : 4 ½ m. by A 52 on B 6006 – ✉ ✆ 0602 Nottingham :

✕ **Les Artistes Gourmands**, 61 Wollaton Rd, NG9 2NG, ✆ 228288, French rest. – 🔼 🗚 ⓪
VISA
closed lunch Saturday and August, Sunday dinner and 25 December-8 January –
M 9.50/15.80 st. ⅋ 4.60. AZ a

at Toton SW : 6 ½ m. on A 6005 – AZ – ✉ Nottingham – ✆ 0602 Long Eaton :

↥ **Manor**, Nottingham Rd, NG9 6EF, junction with B 6003 ✆ 733487 – 📺 🚻wc 🅿. 🔼 *VISA*
closed Christmas – **17 rm** ⇄ 16.50/32.00.

at Long Eaton (Derbs.) SW : 8 m. by A 52 on B 6002 – AZ – ✉ Nottingham – ✆ 0602 Long Eaton :

🏨 **Novotel Nottingham,** Bostocks Lane, NG10 4EP, ✆ 720106, Telex 377585, 🌊 heated, 🍴 –
🛗 ▦ 📺 🚻wc ☎ & 🅿. 🛎. 🔼 🗚 ⓪ *VISA*
M 6.50/13.00 st. and a la carte ⅋ 3.05 – ⇄ 4.50 – **109 rm** 39.50/45.00 st.

at Sandiacre (Derbs.) SW : 8 m. on A 52 – AZ – ✉ ✆ 0602 Nottingham :

🏨 **Post House** (T.H.F.), Bostocks Lane, NG10 5NJ, ✆ 397800, Telex 377378 – 📺 🚻wc ☎ 🅿.
🛎. 🔼 🗚 ⓪ *VISA*
M 5.50/9.75 st. and a la carte ⅋ 3.25 – ⇄ 5.65 – **107 rm** 48.00/56.00 st.

16

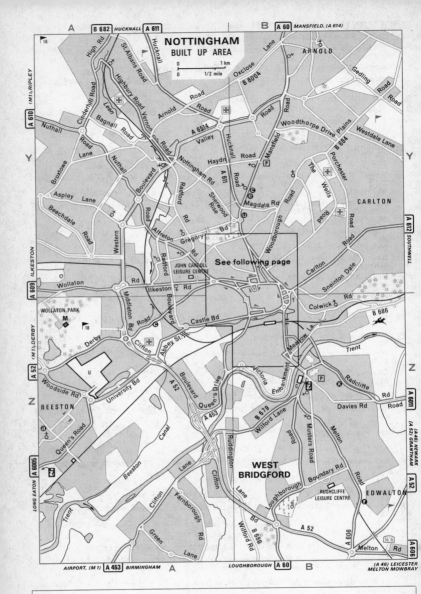

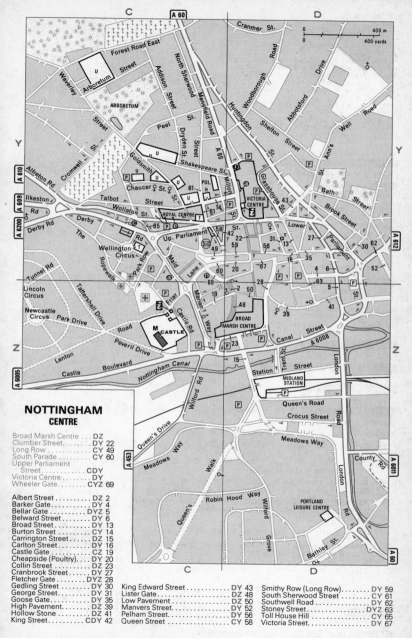

NOTTINGHAM
CENTRE

If you find you cannot take up a hotel booking you have made,
please let the hotel know immediately.

NOTTINGHAM

ALFA-ROMEO 499-509 Woodborough Rd ☏ 606674
AUSTIN-ROVER 136 Burton Rd, Carlton ☏ 617111
AUSTIN-ROVER, DAIMLER, ROLLS ROYCE-BENT-LEY Derby Rd ☏ 787701
AUSTIN-ROVER 199 Mansfield Rd, Arnold ☏ 204141
BMW 165 Huntingdon St. ☏ 582831
CITROEN,FIAT 333 Mansfield Rd ☏ 621000
COLT 61a Mansfield Rd ☏ 475635
DATSUN Woodborough Rd ☏ 623324
DATSUN Greasley St., Bulwell ☏ 272228
FIAT Wilford Rd, Ruddington ☏ 844114
FORD Derby Rd ☏ 476111
FORD Nottingham Rd, Stapleford ☏ 395000
FORD London Rd ☏ 506282
MAZDA Station Rd, Plumtree ☏ Plumtree (060 77) 5111 Loughborough Rd ☏ 822333

PEUGEOT-TALBOT Pasture Rd, Stapleford ☏ 394444
PEUGEOT-TALBOT Clifton Lane, Clifton ☏ 211228
RENAULT Ilkestone Rd ☏ 781938
RENAULT Sawley, Long Eaton ☏ 0602 (Long Eaton) 733124
SAAB Beechdale Rd ☏ 293023
SKODA 134-138 Loughborough Rd ☏ 814320
TOYOTA North Sherwood St. ☏ 474568
VAUXHALL-OPEL 5 Haywood Rd, Mapperley ☏ 603231
VAUXHALL-OPEL Main St., Bulwell ☏ 277031
VOLVO 50 Plains Rd ☏ 266336
VOLVO 131 Alfreton Rd ☏ 708181
VW, AUDI 180 Loughborough Rd ☏ 813813

NUNEATON Warw. ⁴⁰³⁴⁰⁴ P 26 – pop. 60 377 – ECD : Thursday – ☎ 0203.

Envir. : Arbury Hall★ (Gothic house 18C) *AC*, SW : 4 m.

🛈 Public Library, Church St. ☏ 384027.

♦London 107 – ♦Birmingham 25 – ♦Coventry 10 – ♦Leicester 18.

🏨 **Longshoot Motel,** Watling St., CV11 6JH, NE : 2 ½ m. on A 47 at junction with A 5 ☏ 329711, Telex 311100 – 📺 ➡wc ☎ ♿ ♿ 🅿 🔄 AE ⓞ *VISA* ⛵
    closed 2 weeks at Christmas – **M** (carving rest.) 5.45 – **47 rm** ⊑ 29.50/40.50 **t.**

🏠 **Chase,** Higham Lane, CV11 6AG, NE : 1 m. by A 47 ☏ 341013, 🌳 – 📺 ➡wc ⊛ 🅿 🔄 🔄 AE ⓞ *VISA* ⛵
    M 6.00/6.50 **s.** and a la carte ⌗ 3.75 – **28 rm** ⊑ 28.00/33.50.

at Sibson (Leics.) N : 7 m. on A 444 – ✉ ☎ 0827 Tamworth :

🏠 **Millers',** Main Rd, CV13 6LB, ☏ 880223 – 📺 ➡wc ⽔wc 🅿 🔄 🔄 AE ⓞ *VISA* ⛵
    closed 25 to 27 December – **M** *(closed lunch Saturday and Monday and Sunday dinner)* 7.75/12.95 **t.** – **12 rm** ⊑ 31.50/40.00 **t.** – SB (weekends only) 59.00 **st.**

AUSTIN-ROVER Weddington Rd ☏ 383471
FIAT Haunchwood Rd ☏ 382807
RENAULT Nuneaton Rd, Bulkington ☏ 383344

PEUGEOT-TALBOT 208-214 Edward St. ☏ 383339
TOYOTA 45 Attleborough Rd ☏ 382241

NUNNINGTON North Yorks. ⁴⁰² R 21 – see Helmsley.

OADBY Leics. ⁴⁰²⁴⁰³⁴⁰⁴ Q 26 – see Leicester.

OAKFORDBRIDE Devon – see Tiverton.

OAKHAM Leics. ⁴⁰²⁴⁰⁴ R 25 – pop. 7 914 – ECD : Thursday – ☎ 0572.

🛈 Public Library, Catmos St. ☏ 2918.

♦London 103 – ♦Leicester 26 – Northampton 35 – ♦Nottingham 28.

🏨 **Crown** (Best Western), 16 High St., LE15 6AP, ☏ 3631 – 📺 ➡wc ⊛ 🅿 🔄 🔄 AE ⓞ *VISA*
    closed 24 to 26 December – **M** 12.50 **t.** ⌗ 3.30 – **25 rm** ⊑ 34.00/42.00 **t.**, **1 suite** 45.00 **st.** – SB (weekends only) 46.00 **st.**

🏠 **Boultons,** 4 Catmose St., LE15 6HW, ☏ 2844, 🌳 – 📺 ➡wc ⽔wc 🅿 🔄 AE ⓞ *VISA*
    M 6.00/7.00 **st.** and a la carte ⌗ 3.50 – **14 rm** ⊑ 30.00/40.00 **st.** – SB 41.50/44.00 **st.**

✗ **Alphorn,** 30 Cold Overton Rd, LE15 6NT, ☏ 57469, Swiss rest. – 🔄 *VISA*
    closed Sunday, Monday, first 2 weeks February and first 2 weeks November – **M** a la carte 6.20/11.60 **st.** ⌗ 2.50.

at Hambleton E : 3 m. by A 606 – ✉ ☎ 0572 Oakham :

🏨🏨 ❀ **Hambleton Hall** ⌂, LE15 8TH, ☏ 56991, Telex 342888, ≤ Rutland water, 🔄, 🌳, park, ✗ – ▮🄿 📺 ☎ 🅿 🔄 🔄 AE ⓞ *VISA* ⛵
    M 25.00/32.00 **st.** and a la carte 19.50/26.00 **st.** ⌗ 5.50 – ⊑ 3.00 – **15 rm** 70.00/125.00 **st.**
    Spec. Fillet of smoked eel in a chardonnay jelly, Pot roasted squab with port and foie gras, Hambletons toasted rice pudding with a mango coulis.

AUSTIN-ROVER, LAND ROVER-RANGE ROVER Burley Rd ☏ 2657

OAKHILL Somerset ⁴⁰³⁴⁰⁴ M 30 – see Shepton Mallet.

OAKLEY Hants. ⁴⁰³⁴⁰⁴ Q 30 – see Basingstoke.

OBORNE Dorset ⁴⁰³⁴⁰⁴ M 31 – see Sherborne.

ODIHAM Hants. ❹❶❹ R 30 — pop. 3 002 — ECD : Wednesday — ✆ 025 671.

♦London 51 — Reading 16 — Winchester 25.

XX **King's**, 65 High St., RG25 1LF, ✆ 2559, Chinese rest. — 🔳 AE ⓞ VISA
 closed Sunday lunch — **M** 6.20/11.50 **t.** and a la carte 14.00/16.70 **t.**

MERCEDES-BENZ The Square ✆ 2294

ODSTOCK Wilts. ❹❶❸ ❹❶❹ O 30 — see Salisbury.

OKEHAMPTON Devon ❹❶❸ H 31 — ✆ 0837.

♦London 226 — Exeter 25 — ♦Plymouth 31.

at Sourton SW : 3 m. by A 30 on A 386 — ⊠ Okehampton — ✆ 083 786 Bridestowe :

🏛 **Collaven Manor** 🐾, EX20 4HH, S : ¾ m. on A 386 ✆ 217, ☞ — 📺 ⌂wc ℗ 🔳 VISA
 M 6.50/12.50 **t.** ⌂ 3.00 — **8 rm** ⌂ 15.50/35.00 **t.**

OLDHAM Greater Manchester ❹❶❷ ❹❶❹ N 23 — pop. 107 095 — ECD : Tuesday — ✆ 061 Manchester.

🔟 Crompton and Royton, High Barn ✆ 624 2154 — 🔟 Saddleworth, Uppermill ✆ 045 77 (Saddleworth)
2059, E : 5 m.

🅱 Local Studies Library, 84 Union St. ✆ 678 4654.

♦London 212 — ♦ Leeds 36 — ♦Manchester 7 — ♦Sheffield 38.

🏨 **Bower** (De Vere), Hollingwood Av., Chadderton, OL9 8DE, SW : 3 ¼ m. by A 62 on A 6104
 ✆ 682 7254, Telex 666883, ☞ — 📺 ⌂wc ⌂wc ☎ & ℗ 🔬 🔳 AE ⓞ VISA
 M *(closed Saturday lunch)* 15.00 **st.** — **66 rm** ⌂ 22.00/65.00 **st.**

MAZDA Oldham Rd, Springhead ✆ 624 3620   NISSAN Huddersfield Rd ✆ 624 6042

OLD SODBURY Avon — ECD : Thursday — ⊠ Bristol — ✆ 0454 Chipping Sodbury.

♦London 111 — ♦Bristol 16 — Gloucester 35.

↑ **Dornden,** Church Lane, BS17 6NB, ✆ 313325, ≼, ☞ — ⌂wc ℗
 closed 2 weeks October, Christmas and New Year — **9 rm** ⌂ 14.00/35.00 **t.**

OLLERTON Notts. ❹❶❷ ❹❶❸ ❹❶❹ Q 24 — pop. 11 303 (inc. Boughton) — ECD : Thursday —
⊠ Newark — ✆ 0623 Mansfield.

🔟 Woodhouse ✆ 0623 (Mansfield) 23521 SW : 7 m.

♦London 151 — ♦Leeds 53 — Lincoln 25 — ♦Nottingham 19 — ♦Sheffield 27.

🏮 **Hop Pole,** Main St., NG22 9AD, ✆ 822573 — 🗐 ℗ 🔳 AE VISA
 M (carving rest.) 7.50/8.50 **t.** ⌂ 2.85 — **12 rm** ⌂ 18.50/36.50 **t.**

at Kirton NE : 3 m. on A 6075 — ⊠ Newark — ✆ 0623 Mansfield :

↑ **Old Rectory,** Main St., NG22 9LP, ✆ 861540, ☞ — ℗ ⌖
 closed December — **10 rm** ⌂ 13.50/29.50 **s.**

ORFORD Suffolk ❹❶❹ Y 27 — pop. 665 — ECD : Wednesday — ⊠ Woodbridge — ✆ 0394.

♦London 93 — ♦Ipswich 20 — ♦Norwich 48.

🏛 **Crown and Castle** (T.H.F.), Market Hill, IP12 2LJ, ✆ 450205, ☞ — 📺 ⌂wc ⊜ ℗ 🔳 AE
 ⓞ VISA
 M (bar lunch Monday to Saturday)/dinner 8.95 **st.** ⌂ 3.40 — ⌂ 5.65 — **19 rm** 36.00/46.50 **st.**

ORMSKIRK Lancs. ❹❶❷ L 23 — ✆ 0704 Burscough.

♦London 219 — ♦Liverpool 12 — ♦Manchester 33 — Preston 18.

🏛 **Briars Hall,** Lathom, L40 5TH, NE : 4 m. by A 59 on A 5209 ✆ 892368, ☞ — 📺 ⌂wc ⌂wc
 ☎ ℗ 🔳 AE ⓞ VISA
 M 6.75/8.25 **t.** and a la carte ⌂ 3.25 — **9 rm** ⌂ 25.00/39.50 **t.** — SB (weekends only) 48.50 **st.**

OSWESTRY Salop ❹❶❷ ❹❶❸ K 25 — pop. 13 200 — ECD : Thursday — ✆ 0691.

🔟 at Llanymynech ✆ 0691 (Llanymynech) 830542, S : 5 m.

🅱 Little Chef rest., A 5, Babbinswood Whittington ✆ 662488 (summer only) — Library, Arthur St. ✆ 662753.

♦London 182 — Chester 28 — Shrewsbury 18.

🏨 **Wynnstay** (T.H.F.), Church St., SY11 2SZ, ✆ 655261, ☞ — 📺 ⌂wc ⊜ ℗ 🔬 🔳 AE ⓞ
 VISA
 M (bar lunch Saturday) 5.50/9.00 **st.** and a la carte ⌂ 3.40 — ⌂ 5.65 — **26 rm** 39.50/48.50 **st.**

🏛 **Sweeney Hall** 🐾, Morda, SY10 9EU, S : 1 ½ m. on A 483 ✆ 652450, ≼, ☞, park — ⌂wc ℗
 7 rm

🏛 **Ashfield**, Llwyn-y-Maen, Trefonen Rd, SY10 9DD, SW : 1 ½ m. ✆ 655200, ≼, ☞ — 📺
 ⌂wc ℗. ⌖
 M (bar lunch)/dinner 7.00 **t.** and a la carte ⌂ 3.50 — **12 rm** ⌂ 30.00/40.00 **t.** — SB (except
 Christmas and Bank Holidays) 80.00 **st.**

OSWESTRY

at Rhydycroesau W : 3 ½ m. on B 4580 – ⊠ 🏢 0691 Oswestry :

🏛 **Pen-y-Dyffryn Hall** �®, SY10 7DT, ℘ 653700, ≼, ⋺ – 🖵 ⌂wc ⋔wc **P**
M 5.00/10.00 t. and a la carte ▯ 3.00 – **6 rm** ⇋ 15.00/27.00 t. – SB (except Bank Holidays)
45.00/50.00 **st.**

AUSTIN-ROVER Lower Brook St. ℘ 652285
BMW Victoria Rd ℘ 652413
FORD Salop Rd ℘ 654141
HONDA ℘ 653491

PEUGEOT-TALBOT Willow St. ℘ 652301
VAUXHALL-OPEL Smithfield St. ℘ 652235
VOLVO West Felton ℘ 069 188 (Queens Head) 451

OTLEY Suffolk **404** X 27 – pop. 627 – ⊠ Ipswich – 🏢 047 339 Helmingham.
♦London 83 – ♦Ipswich 7.5 – ♦Norwich 43.

🏛 **Otley House** ®, IP6 9NR, ℘ 253, ≼, « Part 17C Suffolk longhouse », ⋺ – ⌂wc **P**. ⋘
closed 15 December-15 February – **M** (dinner only) 10.00 **st.** ▯ 2.70 – **4 rm** ⇋ 15.00/36.00 **st.**

OTLEY West Yorks. **402** O 22 – pop. 14 136 – 🏢 0943.
🛈 8 Boroughgate ℘ 465151.
♦London 216 – Harrogate 14 – ♦Leeds 12 – York 28.

🏛 **Chevin Lodge** ®, Yorkgate, LS21 3NU, S : 2 m. by East Chevin Rd ℘ 467818, Telex 51538,
« Pine log cabin », ⋺, park – ▤ rest 🖵 ⌂wc 🕿 & **P**. ▯▯ . 🖾 🅰🅴 𝘝𝘐𝘚𝘈
M 7.95/12.95 t. and a la carte ▯ 3.75 – **37 rm** ⇋ 52.95/69.95 t. – SB (weekends only)
69.50/75.50 **st.**

OTTERBURN Northumb. **401 402** N 18 – pop. 1 506 – ECD : Thursday – 🏢 0830.
♦London 314 – ♦Carlisle 54 – ♦Edinburgh 74 – ♦Newcastle-upon-Tyne 31.

🏛 **Percy Arms**, Main St., NE19 1NR, ℘ 20261, ⬎, ⋺ – 🖵 ⌂wc ⋔wc 🕿 **P**. ▯▯ . 🖾 🅰🅴 ⓞ
𝘝𝘐𝘚𝘈. ⋘
M (bar lunch)/dinner 12.00 t. and a la carte ▯ 2.50 – **30 rm** ⇋ 27.00/54.00 t. – SB (except Bank
Holidays) 58.00/64.00 **st.**

🏛 **Otterburn Tower**, NE19 1NB, ℘ 20620, « Crenellated Victorian house », park – ⌂wc **P**
🖾 🅰🅴 ⓞ 𝘝𝘐𝘚𝘈
M 7.50/9.00 t. and a la carte ▯ 2.75 – **12 rm** ⇋ 22.50/42.50 **s.** – SB 58.00/68.00 **st.**

OTTERY ST MARY Devon **403** K 31 The West Country G. – pop. 3 957 – ECD : Wednesday –
🏢 04) 481.
See : Site ★ – St. Mary's Church ★★.
🛈 Silver St. ℘ 3964.
♦London 167 – Exeter 12 – Bournemouth 71 – ♦Plymouth 53 – Taunton 23.

XX **The Lodge**, 17 Silver St., EX11 1DB, ℘ 2356 – 🅰🅴 ⓞ 𝘝𝘐𝘚𝘈
closed Sunday dinner, Monday and Bank Holidays – **M** (booking essential) 18.50 t. ▯ 3.00.

OULTON West Yorks. **402** ⑩ – see Leeds.

OULTON Suffolk – see Lowestoft.

OUNDLE Northants. **404** S 26 – pop. 3 225 – ECD : Wednesday – ⊠ Peterborough – 🏢 0832.
🛈 Market Pl. ℘ 74333.
♦London 89 – ♦Leicester 37 – Northampton 30.

🏛 **Talbot**, New St., PE8 4EA, ℘ 73621, Telex 32364, ⋺ – 🖵 ⌂wc 🕿 **P**. ▯▯ . 🖾 🅰🅴 ⓞ 𝘝𝘐𝘚𝘈
M 7.75/13.50 t. and a la carte ▯ 3.50 – **39 rm** ⇋ 43.00/53.00 t. . **1 suite** – SB (weekends only)
58.00/68.00 **st.**

X **Tyrrells**, 6-8 New St., PE8 4EA, ℘ 72347 – 🖾 𝘝𝘐𝘚𝘈
closed Sunday dinner and Monday – **M** a la carte 9.95/12.95 **st.** ▯ 3.50.

AUSTIN-ROVER 1 Station Rd ℘ 73542

AUSTIN-ROVER 1 Benefield Rd ℘ 73519

OUTLANE West Yorks. – see Huddersfield.

OWERMOIGNE Dorset **403 404** N 32 – see Dorchester.

OWLSWICK Bucks. **404** R 28 – ⊠ Aylesbury – 🏢 084 44 Princes Risborough.
♦London 47 – ♦Oxford 20.

🏛 **Shoulder of Mutton** ®, HP17 9RH, ℘ 4304, ⋺ – 🖵 ⌂wc ⊛ **P**. 🖾 🅰🅴 ⓞ 𝘝𝘐𝘚𝘈. ⋘
M (closed Sunday dinner to non-residents) (bar lunch)/dinner 9.50 t. and a la carte – **17 rm**
⇋ 30.00/40.00 t. – SB (weekends only) 50.00/56.00 **st.**

OXFORD Oxon. **408 404** Q 28 – pop. 113 847 – ECD : Thursday – ✆ 0865.

See : Colleges Quarter✦✦✦ : Merton College✦, (Old Library✦✦✦, hall✦, quadrangle✦, chapel windows and glass✦)BZ – Christchurch College✦ (hall✦✦, cathedral✦, quadrangle✦, tower✦) BZ – Bodleian Old Library✦✦ (painted ceiling✦✦) BZ **M2** – Divinity School (carved vaulting✦✦) BZ – Magdalen College✦✦ (cloister✦✦, chapel✦) BZ – New College (cloister✦, chapel✦) BZ Y – All Souls College (chapel✦) BZ A – University College (gateway✦) BZ V – Corpus Christi College (quadrangle and sundial✦) BZ E – Radcliffe Camera✦ BZ O – Sheldonian Theatre✦ BZ **M3** – High Street✦ BY **M1**. Ashmolean Museum✦✦ BY **M1**.

🖪 Banbury Rd ✆ 54415, N : by A 423 AY – 🖪 Southfield, Hill Top Rd ✆ 242158 AZ.

🛈 St. Aldates Chambers, St. Aldates ✆ 726871.

✦London 59 – ✦Birmingham 63 – ✦Brighton 105 – ✦Bristol 73 – ✦Cardiff 107 – ✦Coventry 54 – ✦Southampton 64.

Plans on following pages

Randolph (T.H.F.), Beaumont St., OX1 2LN, ✆ 247481, Telex 83446 – 🛗 📺 ☎ ⇔ 🄰. 🔼
BZ **n**
M 7.95/12.40 **st.** and a la carte ≬ 3.40 – 🖵 6.00 – **109 rm** 53.00/63.50 **st., 2 suites**.

Eastgate, Merton St., off High St., OX1 4BE, ✆ 248244, Telex 83302 – 🛗 📺 ⇔wc ☎ ℗. 🔼
AE ⓞ VISA. ✑
BZ **z**
M 9.25/13.75 **t.** and a la carte ≬ 3.35 – **42 rm** 🖵 52.00/65.00 **t.** – SB (weekends only) 69.60/76.00 **st.**

Oxford Moat House (Q.M.H.), Wolvercote Roundabout, OX2 8AL, N : 2 ½ m. at junction A 40 and A 4144 ✆ 59933, 🔲, squash – 📺 ⇔wc ☎ ℗. 🄰. 🔼 AE ⓞ VISA
AY **s**
M 5.95/8.25 **st.** – **155 rm** 🖵 52.00/62.00 **st.** – SB (weekends only) 66.00 **st.**

Ladbroke Linton Lodge (Ladbroke), 9-13 Linton Rd, off Banbury Rd, OX2 6UJ, ✆ 53461, Telex 837093, ✿ – 🛗 📺 ⇔wc ☎ ℗. 🄰. 🔼 AE ⓞ VISA. 🔼 ✿
AY **e**
M a la carte 9.75/14.50 ≬ 3.70 – 🖵 6.00 – **71 rm** 47.00/60.00 **st.** – SB (weekends only) 66.50 **st.**

TraveLodge (T.H.F.) without rest., Pear Tree Roundabout, Woodstock Rd, OX2 8JZ, N : 3 m. at junction of A 34 and A 43 ✆ 54301, Telex 83202, 🔲 heated – 📺 ⇔wc ☎ & ℗. 🄰. AE ⓞ VISA
AY **n**
100 rm 🖵 41.00/52.00 **st.**

Westwood Country ⚲, Hinksey Hill Top, OX1 5BG, SW : 2 ½ m. by A 4144 and A 423 ✆ 735408, ✿ – 📺 ⇔wc ≞wc & ℗. 🔼 AE ⓞ VISA. ✑
AZ **s**
closed Christmas and New Year – **M** (booking essential)(bar lunch)/dinner 10.50 **t.** ≬ 3.00 – **25 rm** 🖵 28.00/45.00 **t.** – SB 52.00/56.00 **st.**

Foxcombe Lodge, Fox Lane, Boars Hill, OX1 5DP, SW : 3 ¼ m. by A 4144 and A 423 ✆ 730746, ✿ – 📺 ⇔wc 🛗 ℗. 🔼 AE ⓞ VISA
AZ **v**
closed 25 to 27 December – **M** 12.50 **t.** and a la carte ≬ 2.50 – **19 rm** 🖵 30.00/80.00 **s.** – SB 40.00/60.00 **st.**

Old Black Horse, 102 St. Clements, OX4 1AR, ✆ 244691 – 📺 ⇔wc ℗. 🔼 VISA
AZ **c**
closed Christmas and New Year – **M** (closed Sunday) (dinner only) approx. 11.00 **t.** ≬ 2.85 – **8 rm** 🖵 30.00/48.00 **t.**

Earlmont, 322-324 Cowley Rd, OX4 2AF, ✆ 240236 – 📺 🛗 ℗. ✑
AZ **u**
11 rm 🖵 11.00/24.00 **st.**

Greengables, 326 Abingdon Rd, OX1 4TE, ✆ 725870, ✿ – 📺 ⇔wc & ℗. ✑
AZ **a**
8 rm 🖵 13.00/28.00 **t.**

Red Mullions, 23 London Rd, Headington, OX3 7RE, ✆ 64727 – 📺 ⇔wc 🛗wc ℗
✑
AY **o**
9 rm 13.00/30.00 **st.**

Burren, 374 Banbury Rd, Summertown, OX2 7PP, ✆ 513513 – 📺 🛗wc ℗. ✑
AY **c**
closed 24 December-2 January – **7 rm** 🖵 13.00/27.00 **t.**

Willow Reaches, 1 Wytham St., via Norrey's Av., OX1 4SU, ✆ 721545 – 📺 ⇔wc. AE ⓞ
VISA. ✑
AZ **e**
8 rm 🖵 15.00/31.00 **st.**

Elizabeth, 84 St. Aldates, OX1 1RA, ✆ 242230 – 🔼 AE ⓞ VISA
BZ **s**
closed Monday, 17 April and 24 to 31 December – **M** 11.00 **st.** (lunch) and a la carte 17.20/22.00 **st.** ≬ 4.75.

Le Petit Blanc, 61a Banbury Rd, OX2 6DE, ✆ 53540, French rest., « Victorian conservatory »
– ▤. 🔼 VISA
BY **i**
closed Wednesday lunch, Tuesday, 17 to 31 August and 24 December-6 January – **M** (booking essential) 17.50 **t.** (lunch) and a la carte 15.00/21.50 **t.** ≬ 2.60.

La Sorbonne, 1st floor, 130a High St., OX1 4DH, ✆ 241320, French rest. – 🔼 AE ⓞ
VISA
BZ **c**
closed Bank Holidays – **M** 18.00/25.00 **st.** and a la carte 15.50/20.90 **st.** ≬ 3.95.

Saraceno, 15 Magdalen St., OX1 3AE, ✆ 249171, Italian rest. – AE ⓞ VISA
BZ **u**
closed Sunday and Bank Holidays – **M** 15.00/20.00 **t.** and a la carte 10.40/14.20 **t.** ≬ 2.95.

at Kidlington N : 4 ½ m. on A 4237 – AY – ✉ Oxford – ✆ 086 75 Kidlington :

Bowood House, 238 Oxford Rd, OX5 1EB, ✆ 2839, 🔲 heated, ✿ – 📺 ⇔wc 🛗wc ℗. 🔼
VISA. ✑
closed 25 and 26 December – **9 rm** 🖵 14.00/31.50 **st.**

385

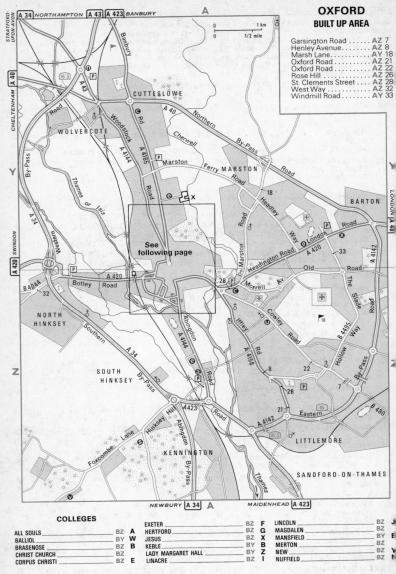

OXFORD
BUILT UP AREA

COLLEGES

at Great Milton SE : 12 m. by A 40 and A 329 Y – ⊠ Oxford – ☎ 084 46 Great Milton :

இது இது **Le Manoir aux Quat' Saisons** ⤶ with rm, Church Rd, OX9 7PD, ☎ 8881, ≤, « 15
and 16C manor house », ⤶ heated, 🌺, park, ✵ – 📺 ⤶wc ☎ 🅿 🔌 🅰🅴 ⓞ 🆅🆂🅰
✵

closed 24 December-22 January – **M** *(closed Tuesday lunch, Sunday dinner and Monda*
22.50/38.00 **st.** and a la carte 31.50/42.50 **st.** ⌁ 7.50 – **10 rm** ⥲ 95.00/230.00 **st.**, **1 suit**
230.00/250.00 **st.** – SB (weekdays only) 320.00 **st.**
Spec. Charlotte d'aubergines et poivrons doux aux filets mignons d'agneau, Pigeonneau de Norfolk en croûte
sel, Pomme soufflée au sabayon de cidre.

386

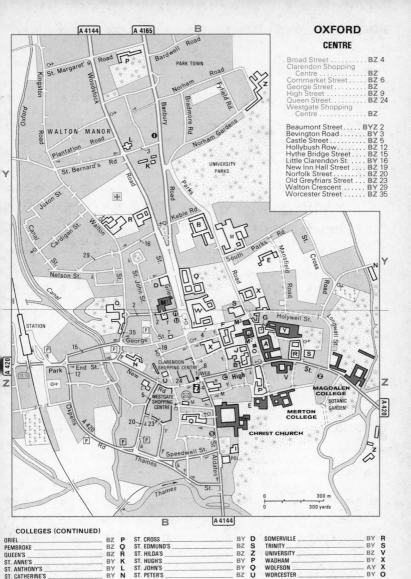

OXFORD

CENTRE

at Cumnor SW : 4 ½ m. by A 420 − AY − off B 4017 − ⊠ Oxford − ☎ 0865 Cumnor :

✗✗ **Bear and Ragged Staff,** Appleton Rd, OX2 9QH, ☎ 862329 − 🅿 🆘 🆎 ⓞ 𝑉𝐼𝑆𝐴
   M 12.95 t. and a la carte 12.20/17.70 t. ⌕ 2.50.

AUDI, VW Abingdon Rd ☎ 242241
AUSTIN-ROVER Oxford Rd, Kidlington ☎ 086 75
(Kidlington) 4363
CITROEN 281 Banbury Rd ☎ 512277
MERCEDES-BENZ Banbury Rd, Shipton-on-Cher-
well ☎ 086 75 (Kidlington) 71011

NISSAN 72 Rose Hill ☎ 774696
SAAB 75 Woodstock Rd ☎ 57028
VAUXHALL-OPEL Woodstock Rd ☎ 59955

PADSTOW Cornwall **403** F 32 The West Country G. – pop. 2 256 – ECD : Wednesday – 🔆 0841.

See : Site ★.

Envir. : Bedruthan Steps★★ *AC*, SW : 8 m. – Trevone (Cornwall Coast Path★★), W : 3 m. – Trevose Head★ (◄★★), W : 6 m.

♦London 288 – Exeter 78 – ♦Plymouth 45 – Truro 23.

🏠 **Metropole** (T.H.F.), Station Rd, PL28 8DB, ☏ 532486, ◄ Camel Estuary, ⌿ heated, ☞ – 🍽 📺 🛏wc 🅿 🅿. 🔳 🅰🅴 ⓪ 🆅🆂🅰
   M (buffet lunch)/dinner 8.95 **st.** and a la carte 🍴 3.40 – 🖙 5.65 – **43 rm** 38.00/55.00 **st.**, **1 suite**.

🏠 **Old Custom House Inn**, South Quay, PL28 8ED, ☏ 532359, ◄ Harbour and Camel Estuary – 📺 🛏wc ☎. 🔳 🅰🅴 ⓪ 🆅🆂🅰
   M (bar lunch)/dinner 11.25 **t.** and a la carte 🍴 2.20 – **25 rm** 🖙 30.00/44.00 **t.** – SB (except summer) 48.00 **st.**

🏠 Woodlands, Treator, PL28 8RV, W : 1 ¼ m. by A 389 on B 3276 ☏ 532426, ☞ – 🎐wc 🅿
   9 rm.

XX **Seafood** with rm, Riverside, PL28 8BY, ☏ 532485, ◄, Seafood – 📺 🛏wc. 🔳 🅰🅴 ⓪ 🆅🆂🅰
   19 March-19 December – **M** *(closed Sunday)* (dinner only) 12.95 **t.** and a la carte 🍴 3.20 – **8 rm** 30.00/60.00 **t.**, **1 suite**.

at Constantine Bay SW : 4 m. by B 3276 – ✉ 🔆 0841 Padstow :

🏠 **Treglos** ⌖, PL28 8JH, ☏ 520727, ◄, 🔳, ☞ – 🍽 ▤ rest 📺 ☎ ⇦ 🅿. 🔳 🆅🆂🅰
   11 March-6 November – **M** 6.95/10.95 **t.** and a la carte 🍴 2.95 – **44 rm** 🖙 22.50/75.00 **t.**, **3 suites** 56.00/96.00 **t.** – SB (except mid May-mid October) 66.00 **st.**

at Treyarnon Bay SW : 4 ¾ m. by B 3276 – ✉ 🔆 0841 Padstow :

🏠 **Waterbeach** ⌖, PL28 8JW, ☏ 520292, ◄, ☞, ✘ – 🛏wc 🎐wc 🅿. 🔳 🅰🅴 🆅🆂🅰 ✘
   March-November – **M** (bar lunch)/dinner 9.00 **t.** 🍴 1.50 – **16 rm** 🖙 16.00/60.00 **t.**

When visiting Scotland,
use the **Michelin Green Guide '' Scotland ''.**

– Detailed descriptions of places of interest
– Touring programmes
– Maps and street plans
– The history of the country
  – Photographs and drawings of monuments, beauty spots, houses...

PAIGNTON Devon **403** J 32 The West Country G. – pop. 39 565 – ECD : Wednesday – 🔆 0803.

See : Paignton Zoo★★ *AC*, by A 385 Z – Kirkham House★ *AC* Y B.

🎫 Festival Hall, Esplanade Rd ☏ 558383.

♦London 226 – Exeter 26 – ♦Plymouth 29.

Plan of Built up Area : see Torbay

🏠 **Redcliffe,** 4 Marine Drive, TQ3 2NL, ☏ 526397, ◄ Torbay, ⌿ heated, ☞ – 🍽 📺 🅿. 🏠. 🔳 🅰🅴 🆅🆂🅰   Y **n**
   M (bar lunch Monday to Saturday)/dinner 8.95 **t.** and a la carte 🍴 3.00 – **63 rm** 🖙 23.00/64.00 **t.** – SB 52.00/68.00 **st.**

🏠 **Palace** (T.H.F.), Esplanade Rd, TQ4 6BJ, ☏ 555121, ⌿ heated, ☞, ✘, squash – 🍽 📺 🅿. 🏠. 🔳 🅰🅴 ⓪ 🆅🆂🅰   Y **e**
   M (buffet lunch)/dinner 9.50 **st.** and a la carte 🍴 3.70 – 🖙 5.65 – **54 rm** 40.00/56.00 **st.**

🏠 **St. Ann's,** 6 Alta Vista Rd, Goodrington Sands, TQ4 6BZ, ☏ 557360, ◄, ⌿ heated, ☞ – 📺 🛏wc 🎐wc ☎ 🅿 🅿. 🔳 🆅🆂🅰   Z **o**
   April-October and December – **M** (bar lunch Monday to Saturday)/dinner 8.50 **t.** and a la carte 🍴 2.50 – **30 rm** 🖙 15.00/44.00 **t.** – SB 40.00/54.00 **st.**

🏠 **Sea Crest** ⌖, Roundham Cres., TQ4 6DF, ☏ 559849 – 🅿   Z **c**
   May-September – **8 rm** 🖙 7.50/16.00 **st.**

XX **Luigi,** 59 Torquay Rd, TQ3 3DT, ☏ 556185, Italian rest. – 🆅🆂🅰   Y **i**
   closed Monday lunch and 25-26 December – **M** 10.50 **t.** (dinner) and a la carte 6.85/15.75 **t.** 🍴 3.25.

BMW   349 Totnes Rd, Collaton St. Mary ☏ 558567
HONDA   Totnes Rd ☏ 554484
MERCEDES-BENZ, COLT   Bishop's Pl. ☏ 556234

TOYOTA   288 Torquay Rd ☏ 553415
VOLVO   59 Totnes Rd ☏ 559362

388

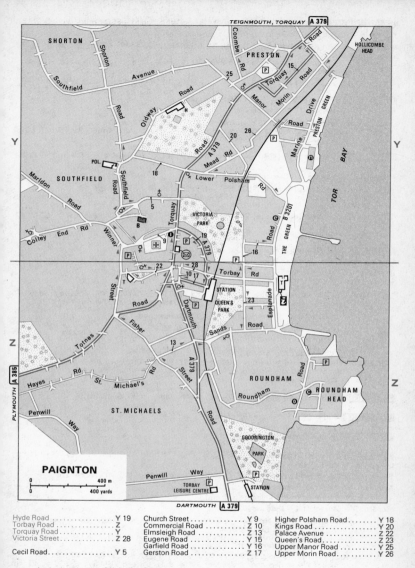

PAIGNTON

0 ——————— 400 m
0 ——————— 400 yards

☞ *Inclusion in the **Michelin Guide** cannot be achieved by pulling strings or by offering favours.*

PAINSWICK Glos. 🄓🄞🄓 🄓🄞🄓 N 28 – pop. 1 757 – ECD : Saturday – ⊠ Stroud – ☎ 0452.

🄩 The Library, Stroud Rd ℘ 812569.

◆London 107 – ◆Bristol 35 – Cheltenham 10 – Gloucester 7.

🏦 **Painswick** ⤸, Kemps Lane, Tibiwell, GL6 6YB, ℘ 812160, ≤, 🐎 – 📺 ⌁wc ☎ 🄿. 🔼 🄰🄴
① **VISA** ⛌
M *(closed Sunday dinner to non residents)* (buffet lunch)/dinner 14.50 t. ⌁ 4.00 – **15 rm**
⊠ 42.00/69.00 t. – SB (except Bank Holidays)(weekends only) 71.00/108.50 **st.**

389

PANGBOURNE Berks. 408 404 Q 29 – pop. 3 445 (inc. Whitchurch) – ECD : Thursday – ☎ 073 57.

♦London 56 – ♦Oxford 22 – Reading 6.

🏨 **Copper Inn** (Best Western), 2 Church Rd, RG8 7AR, ℰ 2244, ⇌ – 🖵 🚻wc ☎ 🅿 🏊 🛝
AE ① VISA ⚛
M 11.00 **t.** (lunch) and a la carte 15.45/21.00 **t.** ▯ 3.50 – ⇌ 4.50 – **21 rm** 44.00/54.00 **st.** –
SB (weekends only) 59.50/65.50 **st.**

AUSTIN-ROVER Reading Rd ℰ 2376   MERCEDES-BENZ Station Rd ℰ 3322

PANT MAWR Powys 408 I 26 – ⊠ ☎ 055 15 Llangurig.

♦London 219 – Aberystwyth 21 – Shrewsbury 55.

🏨 **Glansevern Arms,** SY18 6SY, on A 44 ℰ 240, ≤, ⛲ – 🖵 🚻wc 🅿
closed 20 to 30 December – **M** (closed Sunday dinner) (booking essential) 9.00/11.50 **t.** ▯ 2.50
– **7 rm** ⇌ 21.00/35.00 **t.** – SB (weekends only) 52.00 **st.**

PARKGATE Cheshire 402 408 K 24 – pop. 3 480 – ECD : Wednesday – ⊠ Wirral – ☎ 051
Liverpool.

♦London 206 – Birkenhead 10 – Chester 11 – ♦Liverpool 12.

🏨 **Ship,** The Parade, L64 6SA, ℰ 336 3931 – 🖵 🚻wc ⚏ 🅿 🏊 AE ① VISA ⚛
M 5.95/10.25 **t.** and a la carte ▯ 3.35 – **26 rm** ⇌ 38.00/48.00 **t.** – SB (weekends only)
55.00/59.00 **st.**

XX **Mr Chow's Eating House,** The Parade, L64 6SL, ℰ 336 2385, Chinese rest. – 🏊 AE ①
VISA
M (booking essential)(dinner only) 16.00 **t.** and a la carte.

PATELEY BRIDGE North Yorks. 402 O 21 – ⊠ ☎ 0423 Harrogate.

Envir. : Brimham Rocks★ E : 4 ½ m.

🛈 Southlands Car Park, off High St. ℰ 71147 (summer only).

♦London 225 – ♦Leeds 28 – ♦Middlesbrough 46 – York 32.

🏨 **Grassfield Country House** ⚘, Ramsgill Rd, HG3 5HL, ℰ 711412, ⇌ – 🚻wc 🏠wc 🅿
March-October – **M** (dinner only) 7.50 **st.** ▯ 2.80 – **9 rm** ⇌ 17.00/25.50 **st.**

at Low Laithe SE : 2 ¾ m. on B 6165 – ⊠ ☎ 0423 Harrogate :

XX **Dusty Miller,** Main Rd, HG3 4BU, ℰ 780837 – 🅿 🏊 VISA
closed Sunday and Monday – **M** (dinner only) a la carte 11.20/18.40 **t.** ▯ 3.50.

at Wath-in-Nidderdale NW : 2 ¼ m. – ⊠ ☎ 0423 Harrogate :

XX **Sportsman's Arms** ⚘ with rm, HG3 5PP, ℰ 711306, ⇌ – 🏠wc 🅿 🏊 AE ① VISA
M (closed Sunday dinner) (bar lunch Monday to Saturday)/dinner 12.50 **t.** and a la carte ▯ 3.60
– **6 rm** ⇌ 20.00/38.00 **t.**

PATTINGHAM Staffs. 402 408 404 N 26 – see Wolverhampton (W. Midlands).

PEASLAKE Surrey 404 S 30 – see Guildford.

PEASMARSH East Sussex 404 W 31 – see Rye.

PEMBROKE (PENFRO) Dyfed 408 F 28 – pop. 15 284 – ECD : Wednesday – ☎ 064 63 (4 fig.)
0646 (6 fig.) – **See :** Site★ – Castle★★.

Envir. : Lamphey (Bishop's palace★) AC, E : 2 m. – Carew (castle★ 13C) AC, NE : 4 ½ m.

🛡 Defensible Barracks, Pembroke Dock ℰ 3817.

⛴ to Ireland (Rosslare) (B & I Line) (4 h 15 mn).

♦London 252 – Carmarthen 32 – Fishguard 26.

🏨 **Underdown Country House** ⚘, Grove Hill, SA71 5PR, ℰ 683350, « Antiques and gardens » – 🖵 🚻wc 🏠wc 🅿 🏊 VISA ⚛
M (closed Sunday to non-residents) (booking essential) a la carte approx. 9.95 ▯ 2.50 – **6 rm**
⇌ 32.50/42.50 – SB 65.00/85.00 **st.**

🏨 **Old Kings Arms,** 13 Main St., SA71 4JS, ℰ 683611 – 🖵 🚻wc ⚏ 🅿 🏊 AE VISA
closed 25-26 December and 1 January – **M** a la carte 8.80/11.85 **t.** ▯ 2.30 – **21 rm**
⇌ 19.50/34.00 **t.**

🏠 **Coach House,** 116 Main St., SA71 4HN, ℰ 684602, ⇌ – 🖵 🚻wc ⚏ 🅿 🏊 AE ① VISA ⚛
M 5.90 **t.** and a la carte ▯ 2.80 – **14 rm** ⇌ 25.50/36.00 **t.**

↑ **High Noon,** Lower Lamphey Rd, SA71 4AB, ℰ 683736 – 🅿 ⚛
8 rm ⇌ 8.50/17.00 **st.**

at Lamphey E : 1 ¾ m. on A 4139 – ⊠ Pembroke – ☎ 0646 Lamphey :

🏨 **Court** (Best Western) ⚘, SA71 5NT, ℰ 672273, Telex 48587, 🔲, ⇌ – 🖵 🚻wc ☎ 🅿 🏊
🏊 AE ① VISA ⚛
M (bar lunch)/dinner 10.50 **st.** and a la carte ▯ 3.25 – **22 rm** ⇌ 32.50/52.50 **st.** –
SB 47.00/67.00 **st.**

at Pembroke Dock NW : 2 m. on A 4139 – ⊠ ✪ 0646 Pembroke :

🏨 **Cleddau Bridge,** Essex Rd, SA72 6UT, NE : 1 m. by A 4139 on A 477 (at Toll Bridge) ✆ 685961, ⚓ heated – 📺 ⇔wc ☎ 🅿 ⚒
24 rm. 3 suites.

AUSTIN-ROVER London Rd ✆ 0646 683143　　　　VAUXHALL-OPEL Greenford Garage ✆ 0646 7225

PEMBROKESHIRE (Coast) ** Dyfed **403** E 27 28.
See : From Cemaes Head to Strumble Head** : Newport (site★) – Bryn Henllan (site★) – Goodwick ≤★★ – Strumble Head (≤★★ from the lighthouse). From Strumble Head to Solva** : Trevine ≤★★ – Porthgain (cliffs ※★★★) – Abereiddy (site★) – St. David's Head** – Whitesand Bay★★ – Solva (site★). From Solva to Dale** : Newgale ≤★★ – Martin's Haven ※★★ – St. Ann's Head ≤★★ – Dale ≤★. From Dale to Freshwater West★ : Freshwater West (site★). From Freshwater West to Pendine Sands** (Stack Rocks★★) – St. Govan's Chapel (site★) – Freshwater East (site★) – Manorbier (castle★) – Tenby (site★★) – Amroth (site★) – Pendine Sands★.

PENANT Dyfed – see Aberaeron.

PENARTH South Glam. **403** K 29 – pop. 22 467 – ECD : Wednesday – ✪ 0222.
🛈 West House ✆ 707201 – Piermaster's Office, The Pier ✆ 706555 (summer only).
♦London 161 – ♦Cardiff 4.

🏨 **Walton House,** 37 Victoria Rd, CF6 2HY, ✆ 707782 – 📺 ⇔wc 🅿. 🔼 🅰🅴 ⓪ 𝘝𝘐𝘚𝘈
closed 25 and 26 December – **M** (bar lunch)/dinner 8.00 t. ⏶ 2.95 – **12 rm** ⇌ 16.50/34.00 t.

at Swanbridge S : 2 ½ m. by B 4267 – ⊠ Penarth – ✪ 0222 Sully :

XXX **Sully House** ⚓ with rm, Lavernock Beach Rd, St. Mary's Well Bay, CF6 2XR, ✆ 530448, ≤ – 📺 ⇔wc 🅿. 🔼 𝘝𝘐𝘚𝘈 ※
closed Saturday lunch, Sunday, 25-26 December and Bank Holidays – **M** 15.00 st. ⏶ 3.50 – **4 rm** ⇌ 30.00/40.00 st.

AUSTIN-ROVER Windsor Rd ✆ 703024

PENCRAIG Heref. and Worc – see Ross-on-Wye.

PENDOGGETT Cornwall **403** F 32 – ⊠ – ✪ 0208 Bodmin.
♦London 264 – Newquay 22 – Truro 30.

🏠 **Cornish Arms,** PL30 3HH, on B 3314 ✆ 880263, « Retaining 16C features », ⇌ – ⇔wc 🅿
7 rm.

PENFRO = Pembroke.

PENGETHLEY Heref. and Worc. **403** **404** M 28 – see Ross-on-Wye.

PENMAENHEAD Clwyd – see Colwyn Bay.

PENMAENPOOL Gwynedd **402** **403** I 25 – see Dolgellau.

PENMORFA Gwynedd – see Porthmadog.

PENRITH Cumbria **401** **402** L 19 – pop. 12 086 – ECD : Wednesday – ✪ 0768.
🛈 Robinson's School, Middlegate ✆ 67466 (summer only).
♦London 290 – ♦Carlisle 24 – Kendal 31 – Lancaster 48.

🏨 **North Lakes Gateway,** Ullswater Rd, CA11 8QT, S : 1 m. at M 6 junction 40 ✆ 68111, Telex 54257, 🔼, squash – 🛗 📺 ⇔wc ☎ 🅿. ⚒. 🔼 🅰🅴 ⓪ 𝘝𝘐𝘚𝘈
M 9.00/14.00 st. and a la carte ⏶ 3.00 – **57 rm** ⇌ 49.50/69.00 st. – SB 75.00/87.00 st.

🏨 **George,** Devonshire St., CA11 7SU, ✆ 62696 – 📺 ⇔wc �fiwc 🅿. ⚒. 🔼
closed 25-26 December and 1 January – **M** 8.00/10.00 t. ⏶ 2.50 – **31 rm** ⇌ 24.50/55.00 t. – SB (November-May except Bank Holidays) 75.00/85.00 st.

🏠 **Abbotsford,** Wordsworth St., CA11 7QY, ✆ 63940, ⇌ – 📺 ⇔wc ⓕwc 🅿. 🔼 🅰🅴 ⓪ 𝘝𝘐𝘚𝘈
M 5.00/8.00 st. and a la carte ⏶ 3.00 – **11 rm** ⇌ 18.50/33.00 st.

✗ **Passepartout,** 51 Castlegate, CA11 7HY, ✆ 65852 – 🔼 𝘝𝘐𝘚𝘈
closed Sunday except July-August and Bank Holidays, 25-26 December and late January-mid February – **M** (dinner only) 14.50 t. and a la carte 15.00/16.75 t. ⏶ 3.20.

AUDI, CITROEN, TALBOT Ullswater Rd ✆ 64545
AUSTIN-ROVER Victoria Rd ✆ 63666
FIAT King St. ✆ 64691

FORD Old London Rd ✆ 64571
RENAULT 11 King St. ✆ 62371
TOYOTA 15 Victoria Rd ✆ 64555

PENSHURST Kent **404** U 30 – pop. 1 749 – ✆ 0892.

See : Penshurst Place★ (and Tudor gardens★★ 14C) *AC*.

Envir. : Chiddingstone (castle : Egyptian and Japanese collections★ *AC*) NW : 5 m. – Hever Castle★ (13C) *AC*, W : 6 m.

♦London 38 – Maidstone 19 – Royal Tunbridge Wells 6.

  🏛 **Leicester Arms,** High St., TN11 8BT, ℰ 870551 – 📺 ⇌wc 🅿. ◪ 🆎 ⓪ *VISA*
      M *(closed Sunday dinner and Monday)* 7.50/9.50 **t.** and a la carte ⓐ 2.50 – **7 rm** �ABB 26.00/45.00 **t.**

PEN-Y-BONT = Bridgend.

PENZANCE Cornwall **403** D 33 The West Country G. – pop. 18 501 – ECD : Wednesday – ✆ 0736.

See : Site★ – Outlook★★★ – Western Promenade (≼★★★) YZ – Chapel St. ★ Y – Museum of Nautical Art★*AC* Y **M1.**

Envir. : St. Michael's Mount★★★, (≼★★) E : 5 m. by A 30 Y – Sancreed Church★★, Celtic Crosses★★, W : 4 m. by A 30 Z – St. Buryan★★ (Church Tower★★), SW : 4 ½ m. by A 30 Z – Chysauster★★*AC*, N : 4 ½ m. by B 3311 Y – Morvah, North Cornwall Coast Path (≼★★), NW : 6 ½ m. by B 3312 Y – Trengwainton Garden★★*AC*, NW : 2 m. by B 3312 Y – Prussia Cove★, SE : 9 m. by A 30 and A 394 Y – Land's End★ (cliff scenery★★★), SW : 10 m. by A 30 Z.

Access to the Isles of Scilly by helicopter ℰ 3871.

🚁 ℰ 65831.

⛴ to the Isles of Scilly : Hugh Town, St.Mary's (Isles of Scilly Steamship Co.) summer Monday to Saturday 1-2 daily ; winter 4 weekly (2 h 30 mn).

🛈 Alverton St. ℰ 62341 ext 292.

♦London 319 – Exeter 113 – ♦Plymouth 77 – Taunton 155.

Plan opposite

  🏛 **Queens,** Promenade, TR18 4HG, ℰ 62371, ≼ – 🅳 🅸 📺 ⇌wc 🛗wc 🅿   Z u
      71 rm.

  🏛 **Mount Prospect,** Britons Hill, TR18 3AE, ℰ 63117, ≼, ⌂ heated, 🐎 – 📺 ⇌wc 🛗wc ☎
      🅿. ◪ 🆎 ⓪ *VISA*   Y e
      M (bar lunch)/dinner 9.20 **st.** and a la carte ⓐ 3.00 – **26 rm** �ABB 26.00/42.00 **s.** – SB (October-March) 53.00/65.50 **st.**

  🏛 **Abbey,** Abbey St., TR18 4AR, ℰ 66906, « Attractively furnished 17C house », 🐎 – 📺
      ⇌wc 🛗wc 🅿   Y u
      M (dinner only) 12.00 **st.** – **6 rm** �ABB 35.00/65.00 **st.** – SB (weekends only)(November-February) 60.00/80.00 **st.**

  🏛 **Sea and Horses,** 6 Alexandra Terr., TR18 4NX, ℰ 61961 – 🛗wc 🅿. ◪ *VISA*. ⅍   Z s
      M (bar lunch)/dinner 7.25 **st.** ⓐ 2.50 – **11 rm** �ABB 13.50/30.00 **st.**

  🏛 **Alexandra,** Alexandra Terr., TR18 4NX, ℰ 62644, ≼ – 📺 ⇌wc 🛗wc ☎ 🅿. ◪ 🆎 *VISA*
      M (bar lunch)/dinner 7.00 **t.** and a la carte ⓐ 3.50 – **21 rm** �ABB 12.00/29.00 **t.** – SB 34.00/36.00 **st.**   Z a

  🛖 **Tarbert,** 11 Clarence St., TR18 2NU, ℰ 63758, 🐎 – 📺 🛗wc. ◪ 🆎 ⓪ *VISA*   Y i
      closed Christmas – **12 rm** �ABB 15.50/34.00 **st.**

  🛖 **Holbein House,** Alexandra Rd, TR18 4LZ, ℰ 65008, 🐎 – 📺 ⇌wc 🛗wc. *VISA*   Y n
      10 rm �ABB 12.00/30.00 **st.**

  🛖 **Dunedin,** Alexandra Rd, TR18 4LZ, ℰ 62652 – 📺   Y r
      closed December and January – **9 rm** �ABB 8.50/20.00 **t.**

  🛖 **Kimberley House,** 10 Morrab Rd, TR18 4EZ, ℰ 62727 – ◪ *VISA*. ⅍   Y s
      closed November and Christmas – **9 rm** �ABB 9.50/20.00 **st.**

  🛖 **Carnson House,** 2 East Terr., Market Jew St., TR18 2TD, ℰ 65589 – ◪ 🆎 ⓪ *VISA*. ⅍
      closed first 3 weeks February, 8 to 29 November and Christmas – **6 rm** �ABB 9.50/22.00 **st.**
                                                                 Y c

  🛖 **Estoril,** 46 Morrab Rd, TR18 4EX, ℰ 62468 – 📺 ⇌wc 🛗wc ☎. ◪ *VISA*. ⅍   Y o
      closed December and January – **10 rm** �ABB 15.50/32.00 **st.**

  XX **Harris's,** 46 New St., TR18 2LZ, ℰ 64408 – ◪ 🆎 ⓪ *VISA*   Y a
      closed Monday lunch, Sunday, 2 weeks February-March, 2 weeks November, 25-26 December and 1 January – **M** (restricted lunch) 5.00 **t.** and a la carte 9.45/15.25 **t.** ⓐ 2.95.

      at Newbridge NW : 3 m. on A 3071 – Y – ✉ ✆ 0736 Penzance :

  XX **Enzo,** TR20 8QH, ℰ 63777 – 🅿. ◪ 🆎 ⓪
      closed Sunday and 25-26 December – **M** (dinner only) (booking essential) a la carte 6.85/13.00 **t.**

      at Newlyn SW : 1 ½ m. on B 3315 – Z – ✉ ✆ 0736 Penzance :

  🏛 **Higher Faugan** ⌂, TR18 5NS, SW : ¾ m. on B 3315 ℰ 62076, « Country house atmos-
      phere », ⌂ heated, 🐎, park, ⅍ – 📺 ⇌wc ☎ 🅿. ◪ 🆎 ⓪. ⅍
      March-October – **M** (bar lunch)/dinner 10.35 **t.** ⓐ 3.00 – **11 rm** �ABB 23.00/56.00 **t.** – SB (March and April) 48.00 **st.**

AUSTIN-ROVER Newlyn ℰ 62038   PEUGEOT, TALBOT Hayle Terr. ℰ 753143

392

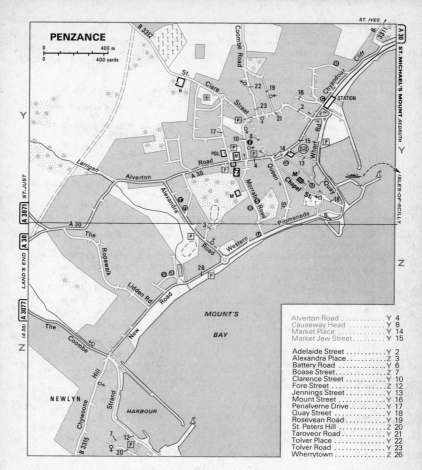

PENZANCE

Scale: 400 m / 400 yards

En saison, surtout dans les stations fréquentées, il est prudent de retenir à l'avance.
Cependant, si vous ne pouvez pas occuper la chambre que vous avez retenue,
prévenez immédiatement l'hôtelier.

Si vous écrivez à un hôtel à l'étranger, joignez à votre lettre
un coupon-réponse international (disponible dans les bureaux de poste).

PERRANUTHNOE Cornwall **403** D 33 – see Marazion.

PERSHORE Heref. and Worc. **403** **404** N 27 – pop. 6 850 – ECD : Thursday – © 0386.

🛈 Council Offices, 37 High St. ℘ 554711.

♦London 106 – ♦Birmingham 32 – Cheltenham 22 – Stratford-on-Avon 21 – Worcester 9.

🏨 **Angel,** 9 High St., WR10 1AF, ℘ 552046, 🍴 – 📺 🛁wc 🐾 🅿 🔼 AE ⓪ 💳 VISA
M 9.00 t. and a la carte 🛈 2.80 – **16 rm** 🖙 34.00/50.00 t., **1 suite** 50.00 t. – SB (weekends only)
57.00/67.00 **st.**

at Wyre Piddle NE : 2 m. by B 4082 and B 4083 on B 4084 – ⊠ Pershore – © 0386 Pershore :

🏨 **Avonside,** Main Rd, WR10 2JB, ℘ 552654, ≤, 🔼 heated, 🐟, 🍴 – 📺 🛁wc 🅿 🔼 💳 VISA
closed January – **M** (bar lunch)/dinner 9.90 **st.** 🛈 3.50 – **7 rm** 🖙 30.00/40.00 **st.** –
SB 50.00/60.00 **st.**

393

PETERBOROUGH Cambs. 402 404 T 26 – pop. 113 404 – ECD : Monday and Thursday – 🕓 0733.

See : Cathedral★★ 12C-13C (nave : painted roof★★★).

Envir. : Crowland : Abbey Church★ (8C ruins), Triangular Bridge★ 13C, NE : 8 m.

🏂 Thorpe Wood, Nene Parkway 🕿 267701, W : 3 m. on A 47 – 🏂 Ramsey 🕿 0487 (Ramsey) 813573, SE : 12 m. – 🖪 Central Library, Broadway 🕿 48343 and 43146 – Town Hall, Bridge St. 🕿 63141 or 63396 (Saturday only in summer).

♦London 85 – ♦Cambridge 35 – ♦Leicester 41 – Lincoln 51.

🏨 **Peterborough Moat House** (Q.M.H.), Thorpe Wood, PE3 6SG, SW : 2 ¼ m. at Roundabout 33 🕿 260000, Telex 32708 – 🛗 🔟 🚾wc 🚾 **🅿**. 🔈 🔄 🄰🄴 ⑩ 𝘝𝘐𝘚𝘈
M 8.25/9.50 **st.** and a la carte ᗰ 3.35 – 🖃 4.95 – **98 rm** 43.50/54.00 **st., 4 suites** 60.00/75.00 **st.** – SB (weekends only) 52.00 **st.**

🏨 **Bull** (Mt. Charlotte), Westgate, PE1 1RP, 🕿 61364 – 🔟 🚾wc 🚾 **🅿**. 🔄 🄰🄴 ⑩ 𝘝𝘐𝘚𝘈
M 7.95 **st.** and a la carte ᗰ 3.65 – **112 rm** 🖃 39.00/49.00 **st., 1 suite** 85.00 **st.** – SB (weekends only) 88.00 **st.**

🏨 **Newark**, 239 Eastfield Rd, PE1 4BH, 🕿 69811 – 🔟 🚾wc 🎶wc **🅿**
38 rm.

at Whittlesey SE : 7 m. on A 605 – ⌧ 🕓 0733 Peterborough :

🏠 **Falcon,** Paradise Lane, PE7 1BH, by St. Mary's St. 🕿 203247 – 🔟 🚾wc **🅿**. 🔄 🄰🄴 ⑩ 𝘝𝘐𝘚𝘈
M a la carte 9.10/12.20 **t.** ᗰ 2.90 – **8 rm** 🖃 22.00/39.50 **t., 1 suite** 35.00/47.00 **t.**

at Norman Cross S : 5 ¾ m. on A 15 at junction with A 1 – ⌧ 🕓 0733 Peterborough :

🏨 **Crest** (Crest), Great North Rd, PE7 3TB, 🕿 240209, Telex 32576 – 🔟 🚾wc 🎶wc 🚾 ᗩ 🔈 **🅿**. 🔈 🔄 🄰🄴 ⑩ 𝘝𝘐𝘚𝘈
M (carving lunch) 8.35 **st.** / dinner 11.50 **st.** and a la carte ᗰ 3.60 – 🖃 5.85 – **99 rm** 44.50/54.50 **st.** – SB (weekends only) 50.00/54.00 **st.**

at Nassington (Northants.) SW : 10 ¾ m. by A 47 – ⌧ Peterborough – 🕓 0780 Stamford :

✕✕ **Black Horse Inn,** 2 Fotheringhay Rd, PE8 6QU, 🕿 782324, 🍴 – **🅿**. 🔄 🄰🄴 ⑩ 𝘝𝘐𝘚𝘈
M a la carte 6.55/11.10 **st.** ᗰ 3.75.

at Wansford W : 8 ½ m. by A 47 – ⌧ Peterborough – 🕓 0780 Stamford :

🏨 **Haycock,** Great North Rd, PE8 6JA, 🕿 782223, Telex 32710, 🍴 – 🔟 🚾wc 🚾 **🅿**. 🔈 🔄 🄰🄴
🅿
M a la carte 16.65/19.15 **st.** – **26 rm** 🖃 48.00/73.00 **st.**

🏠 **Sibson House**, Great North Rd, PE8 6ND, SE : 1 ¾ m. on A 1 🕿 782227, ⊿, 🍴 – 🔟 🚾wc 🚾
12 rm.

ALFA-ROMEO, SUZUKI 659 Lincoln Rd 🕿 52141
AUSTIN-ROVER,LAND-ROVER,FREIGHT
ROVER,JAGUAR 7 Oundle Rd 🕿 66011
BMW Helpston Rd, Glinton 🕿 253333
FIAT, LANCIA Midland Rd 🕿 314431
FORD 27-53 New Rd 🕿 40104
MAZDA 50-64 Burghley Rd 🕿 65787

MERCEDES-BENZ High St., Eye 🕿 222363
NISSAN Oxney Rd 🕿 49336
PEUGEOT, TALBOT 343 Eastfield Rd 🕿 310900
RENAULT, VAUXHALL Bretton Way 🕿 264981
VAUXHALL-OPEL, BEDFORD, RENAULT Sturrock
Way 🕿 264981
VW, AUDI Oxney Rd 🕿 312213

PETERSFIELD Hants. 404 R 30 – pop. 10 078 – ECD : Thursday – 🕓 0730.

🏂 The Heath 🕿 67732, E : ½ m. – 🖪 Library, 27 The Square 🕿 63451.

♦ London 59 – ♦ Brighton 45 – Guildford 25 – ♦ Portsmouth 19 – ♦ Southampton 32 – Winchester 19.

🏨 **Langrish House** 🦢, Langrish, GU32 1RN, W : 3 ½ m. on A 272 🕿 66941, ≤, 🍴, park – 🔟 🚾wc 🚾 **🅿**. 🔄 🄰🄴 ⑩ 🏨
M *(closed Sunday and Bank Holidays)* (dinner only) a la carte 11.40/13.70 **t.** ᗰ 2.50 – 🖃 2.50 – **14 rm** 30.00/45.00 **t.** – SB (weekends only)(except summer) 48.00 **t.**

AUDI, VW Station Rd 🕿 62992
AUSTIN-ROVER 38 Collace St. 🕿 62206
HONDA Alton Rd, Steep 🕿 66341

SKODA Alton Rd, Froxfield 🕿 073 084 (Hawkley) 200
VOLVO 23 London Rd 🕿 64541

PETWORTH West Sussex 404 S 31 – pop. 2 003 – ECD : Wednesday – 🕓 0798.

See : Petworth House★★★ 17C (paintings★★★ and carved room★★★) *AC*.

♦London 54 – ♦Brighton 31 – ♦Portsmouth 33.

PEVENSEY East Sussex 404 V 31 – see Eastbourne.

PICKERING North Yorks. 402 R 21 – pop. 5 316 – ECD : Wednesday – 🕓 0751.

See : SS. Peter and Paul's Church (wall paintings★ 15C) – Norman castle★ (ruins) : ≤★ *AC*.

🖪 The Station, Park St. 🕿 73791 (summer only).

♦London 237 – ♦Middlesbrough 43 – Scarborough 19 – York 25.

🏠 **White Swan**, Market Place, YO18 7AA, 🕿 72288 – 🔟 🚾wc **🅿**. 🔄 𝘝𝘐𝘚𝘈
M 6.50/10.00 **st.** ᗰ 3.50 – **13 rm** 🖃 26.50/42.00 **t., 1 suite** 57.00 **t.** – SB (October-June)(except Bank Holidays) 58.00 **st.**

🏠 **Forest and Vale**, Malton Rd, YO18 7DL, 🕿 72722, 🍴 – 🔟 🚾wc 🎶wc **🅿**. 🔄 🄰🄴 ⑩ 𝘝𝘐𝘚𝘈
M 5.75/9.25 **t.** and a la carte ᗰ 2.80 – **23 rm** 🖃 26.00/40.00 **t.** – SB 52.00/66.00 **t.**

at Wrelton NW : 2 ½ m. on A 170 – ⊠ ✪ 0751 Pickering :

✗ **Huntsman** with rm, Main St., YO18 8PG, ✆ 72530 – ⇔wc **P**. ⅏
   closed 1 week February, 1 week November and 25 December – **M** *(closed Sunday dinner and Monday October-Easter)* (bar lunch)/dinner 12.75 **t**. and a la carte 9.50/12.75 **t**. – **3 rm** ⇌ 15.00/28.00 **t**. – SB (except July and August) 43.00 **st**.

FORD, MERCEDES-BENZ Eastgate ✆ 72251   FORD Middleton ✆ 72331

PICKHILL North Yorks. 402 P 21 – pop. 300 (inc. Roxby) – ⊠ ✪ 0845 Thirsk.
♦London 229 – ♦Leeds 41 – ♦Middlesbrough 30 – York 34.

   🏠 **Nags Head,** YO7 4JG, ✆ 567391 – 📺 ⇔wc ⋔wc **P**. 🔼 *VISA*
   M 6.50/12.50 **st**. – **8 rm** ⇌ 19.50/30.00 **st**.

PIDDLETRENTHIDE Dorset 403 404 M 31 – pop. 610 – ⊠ Dorchester – ✪ 030 04.
♦London 141 – ♦Bristol 54 – Exeter 62 – ♦Southampton 53.

   🏠 **Old Bakehouse,** DT2 7QR, S : 1 m. on B 3143 ✆ 305, ⊠ heated, 🐀 – 📺 ⇔wc **P**. 🔼
   VISA
   closed January – **M** (dinner only) 8.75 **t**. and a la carte – **10 rm** ⇌ 19.50/39.50 **t**.

PILLATON Cornwall 403 H 32 – pop. 464 – ⊠ Saltash – ✪ 0579 St. Dominick.
♦London 254 – ♦Plymouth 11.

   🏠 Weary Friar, PL12 6QS, ✆ 50238, « Part 12C inn » – 📺 ⇔wc **P**
   13 rm.

PINHOE Devon 403 J 31 – see Exeter.

PLAYDEN East Sussex – see Rye.

PLUCKLEY Kent 404 W 30 – pop. 1 109 – ✪ 023 384.
♦London 53 – Folkestone 25 – Maidstone 18.

   ↰ **Elvey Farm,** TN27 0SU, W : 3 m. by B 2077 off Mundy Boys Road ✆ 442 – 📺 ⇔wc ⋔wc
   P. ⊚. ⅏
   10 rm ⇌ 20.50/31.00 **t**.

PLYMOUTH Devon 403 H 32 The West Country G. – pop. 238 583 – ECD : Wednesday – ✪ 0752.

See : Site ✯✯ – Smeaton's Tower (≤✯✯) *AC* BZ – Royal Citadel✯ *AC* (The Ramparts ≤✯✯) BZ – City Museum and Art Gallery✯ *AC* BZ **M**.
Envir. : Buckland Abbey✯✯ *AC*, N : 7 m. by A 386 ABY – Antony House✯✯ *AC*, W : 5 m. by A 374 AY – Saltram House ✯✯ *AC* E : 3 ½ m. BY **A** – Yelverton Paperweight Centre✯ *AC*, N : 9 m. on A 386 ABY – Mount Edgcumbe (≤✯) *AC*, W : 9 m. by car ferry from Cremyll or passenger ferry from Stonehouse.

🛏 Whitsand Bay Hotel, Portwrinkle, Torpoint ✆ 0503 (St. Germans) 30276 W : 6 m. by A 374 AY – ⌐ₛ Elfordleigh, Plympton, ✆ 336428, E : 6 m. by A 374 BY.

✈ Roborough Airport : ✆ 772752, N : 3 ½ m. by A 386 ABY.

⛴ Shipping connections with the Continent : to France (Roscoff) (Brittany Ferries) – to Spain (Santander) (Brittany Ferries).

🛈 Civic Centre, Royal Parade ✆ 264851 and 264849 – 12 The Barbican ✆ 23806 (summer only).
♦London 242 – ♦Bristol 124 – ♦Southampton 161.

Plans on following pages

   🏨 **Holiday Inn,** Armada Way, PL1 2HJ, ✆ 662866, Telex 45637, ≤ city and Sound, 🔲 – ▐▌ 📺
   ☎ & **P**. 🔼 🔼 🔼 ⓪ *VISA*   BZ **s**
   M 10.45/8.95 **st**. and a la carte 🍷 5.00 – ⇌ 6.50 – **217 rm** 48.00/58.00, **3 suites** 114.00 –
   SB (weekends only) 75.00/93.00 **st**.

   🏨 **Mayflower Post House** (T.H.F.), Cliff Rd, The Hoe, PL1 3DL, ✆ 662828, Telex 45442, ≤
   Plymouth Sound, ⊠ heated – ▐▌ 📺 ⇔wc ☎ & **P**. 🔼 🔼 🔼 ⓪ *VISA*   AZ **v**
   M 8.25/11.75 **st**. and a la carte 🍷 3.75 – 5.65 – **106 rm** 48.50/58.50 **st**., **4 suites**.

   🏨 **Novotel Plymouth,** Marsh Mills Roundabout, PL6 8NH, ✆ 221422, Telex 45711, ⊠ heated
   – ▐▌ 🛏 rest 📺 ⇔wc ☎ & **P**. 🔼 🔼 🔼 ⓪ *VISA*   BY **i**
   M 7.50 (lunch) and a la carte 🍷 2.95 – ⇌ 4.50 – **100 rm** 40.50/47.00 **st**. – SB (weekends
   only) 52.00/56.00 **st**.

   🏨 **Astor,** 14-22 Elliott St., The Hoe, PL1 2PS, ✆ 225511 – ▐▌ 📺 ⇔wc ☎ & 🔼 🔼 🔼 ⓪ *VISA*
   ⅏   BZ **c**
   M *(closed Saturday lunch)* 5.65/8.10 **t**. and a la carte 🍷 2.95 – ⇌ 3.50 – **56 rm** 36.00/49.50 **t**. –
   SB (weekends only)(except Christmas) 52.00/56.00 **st**.

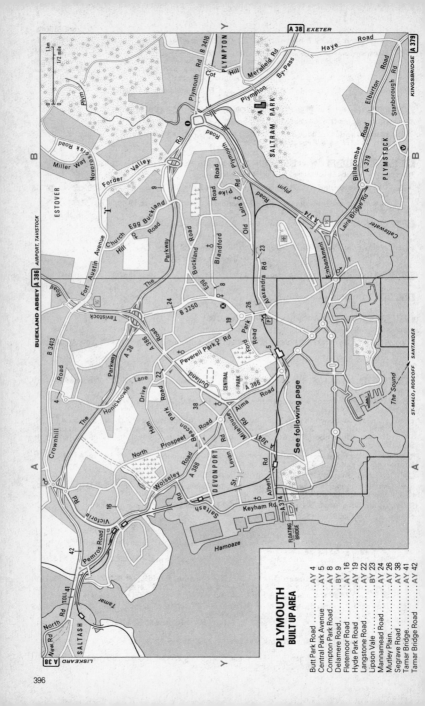

PLYMOUTH
BUILT UP AREA

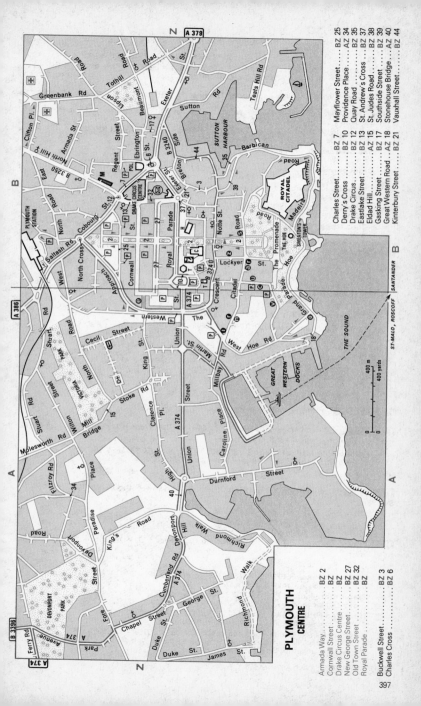

PLYMOUTH
CENTRE

397

🏠 **Georgian House,** 51 Citadel Rd, The Hoe, PL1 3AU, ✆ 663237 – 📺 ⮰wc ⣿wc. 🔌 AE ⓞ **VISA**　　　　　　AZ　**r**
M (bar lunch)/dinner 8.00 **t.** and a la carte 🍴 2.95 – **10 rm** ⌖ 19.95/29.50 **t.**

🏠 **Grosvenor,** 9 Elliott St., The Hoe, PL1 2PP, ✆ 260411 – 📺 ⮰wc ⣿wc ☎ 🔌 ⓞ **VISA** 🦌
M 7.50/9.50 **t.** and a la carte 🍴 2.75 – **14 rm** ⌖ 23.00/35.00 **t.** – SB (weekends only)
44.50/52.00 **st.**　　　　　　　　　　　　　　　　　　　　　　　　　　　　　　　BZ　**u**

🏠 **Merlin,** 2 Windsor Villas, Lockyer St., The Hoe, PL1 2QD, ✆ 228133 – 📺 ⣿wc 🅿. 🔌 AE ⓞ
VISA　　　　　　　　　　　　　　　　　　　　　　　　　　　　　　　　　　BZ　**z**
closed Christmas and New Year – **M** (closed Sunday and Bank Holidays) 6.50 **st.** (dinner) and
a la carte 🍴 2.85 – **24 rm** ⌖ 16.00/33.00 **st.**

↟ **Mooreton,** 71 Mannamead Rd, PL4 5ST, ✆ 266566 – 📺 ⣿wc 🅿. 🔌 **VISA** 🦌　　　AY　**x**
closed 23 December-2 January – **8 rm** ⌖ 21.85/34.50 **st.**

↟ **Sea Breezes,** 28 Grand Par., West Hoe, PL1 3DJ, ✆ 667205　　　　　　　　AZ　**o**
7 rm ⌖ 8.50/18.00 **st.**

↟ **Cranbourne,** 282 Citadel Rd, The Hoe, PL1 2PZ, ✆ 263858 – 📺 ⣿　　　　　BZ　**r**
closed 2 weeks at Christmas – **10 rm** ⌖ 9.00/16.00 **st.**

↟ **Carnegie,** 172 Citadel Rd, The Hoe, PL1 3BD, ✆ 225158 – ⣿. 🔌 AE ⓞ **VISA** 🦌　AZ　**n**
closed 1 week at Christmas – **9 rm** ⌖ 15.00/24.00 **st.**

↟ **Chichester,** 280 Citadel Rd, The Hoe, PL1 2PZ, ✆ 662746 – 📺 ⣿. **VISA**　　BZ　**a**
10 rm ⌖ 8.00/20.00 **st.**

✗ ❀ **Chez Nous,** 13 Frankfort Gate, PL1 1QA, ✆ 266793, French rest. – 🔌 AE ⓞ **VISA**　AZ　**e**
closed Sunday, Monday, 1 to 10 February, 1 to 10 September and Bank Holidays – **M** 16.20 **t.**
and a la carte 16.50/21.50 **t.** 🍴 4.00
Spec. Coquilles Saint Jacques au gingembre et petits légumes, Émincé de rognon et ris de veau aux morilles,
Poire et sa tuile au coulis au miel.

at Colebrook E : 6 ½ m. by A 374 – BY – ⌧ ❀ 0752 Plymouth :

🏠 Elfordleigh, Shaugh Prior Rd, PL7 5EB, N : 1 ½ m. by Boringdon Hill ✆ 336428, ≼, ⊿ heated,
🔲, 🟥, 🎯, park, ⛏ squash – 📺 ⮰wc ⣿wc ☎ 🅿. 🔌 AE ⓞ **VISA**
17 rm ⌖ 28.00/38.00 **st.**

at Plymstock SE : 3 m. on A 379 – ⌧ ❀ 0752 Plymouth :

🏠 **Highlands,** Dean Cross Rd, PL9 7AZ, ✆ 43643, ⊿ – 📺 ⮰wc ⣿wc 🅿. 🔌 **VISA**　　BY　**v**
M (restricted dinner Sunday) 4.50/6.90 **st.** and a la carte 🍴 2.60 – **13 rm** ⌖ 15.00/30.00 **st.**

ALFA-ROMEO　Weston Park Rd ✆ 266099
AUSTIN-ROVER, JAGUAR, LAND-ROVER　Union St.
✆ 263355
BMW　Union St. ✆ 669202
CITROEN　Colebrook Rd ✆ 336606
CITROEN　87 Crownhill Rd ✆ 772345
FORD　Millbay ✆ 668040

HONDA, SAAB　Albert Rd ✆ 51810
LANCIA　Colebrook, Plympton ✆ 336462
MERCEDES-BENZ　Crown Hill ✆ 785611
VAUXHALL-OPEL　Normandy Way ✆ 361251
VAUXHALL-OPEL　Bretonside ✆ 667111
VAUXHALL-OPEL　Cobourg St. ✆ 668886
VOLVO　Valley Rd, Plympton ✆ 338306

PLYMSTOCK Devon 🧾🧾🧾 H 32 – see Plymouth.

POCKLINGTON Humberside 🧾🧾🧾 R 22 – pop. 5 051 – ECD : Wednesday – ⌧ York – ❀ 075 92.
◆London 213 – ◆Kingston-upon-Hull 25 – York 13.

🏠 **Feathers,** 56 Market Pl., YO4 2UN, ✆ 3155 – 📺 ⮰wc 🅿. 🔌 AE ⓞ **VISA** 🦌
M 4.95/5.95 **t.** and a la carte 🍴 2.45 – **12 rm** ⌖ 23.00/38.00 **t.**

FORD　Hallgate ✆ 2768　　　　　　　　　　　　RENAULT　Kilnwick Rd ✆ 3221

POLKERRIS Cornwall 🧾🧾🧾 F 32 The West Country G. – ⌧ Fowey – ❀ 072 681 Par.
See : Site★.
◆London 277 – Newquay 22 – ◆Plymouth 34 – Truro 20.

✗ Rashleigh Inn, PL24 2TL, ✆ 3991, ≼ – 🅿.

POLPERRO Cornwall 🧾🧾🧾 G 33 The West Country G. – pop. 1 192 – ⌧ Looe – ❀ 0503.
See : Site ★.
◆London 271 – ◆Plymouth 28.

↟ **Lanhael House,** PL13 2PW, ✆ 72428, ≼, ⊿, 🎯 – 🅿. 🦌
March-October – **6 rm** ⌖ 16.00/26.00 **st.**

↟ **Claremont,** Fore St., PL13 2RG, ✆ 72241 – ⣿wc 🅿. **VISA**
Easter-October and 15 December-5 January – **9 rm** ⌖ 10.00/32.00 **st.**

✗✗ **House on Props,** Talland St., PL13 2RE, ✆ 72310 – 🔌 **VISA**
March-October – **M** (dinner only) a la carte 8.20/12.90 **t.**

✗ **Kitchen,** Fish Na Bridge, The Coombes, PL13 2RQ, ✆ 72780 – 🔌 AE ⓞ **VISA**
closed Monday, Sunday except summer and Tuesday to Thursday in winter – **M** (dinner only)
(booking essential) 10.95 **t.** 🍴 4.25.

PONTARFYNACH = Devil's Bridge.

PONT-AR-GOTHI Dyfed 403 H 28 – ✉ Carmarthen – ☏ 026 788 Nantgaredig.
♦London 218 – Carmarthen 6 – ♦Swansea 25.

⌂ Cothi Bridge, SA32 7NG, ☎ 251, ⩽, ⌒ – 📺 ⛀wc ⎍wc ☎ 🅟
11 rm.

PONTSHAEN Dyfed – ✉ Llandyssul – ☏ 054 555.
♦London 239 – Carmarthen 19 – Fishguard 37.

✕ **Farmhouse,** Castell Howell, SA44 4UA, N : 1 ½ m. off B 4459 ☎ 209, park – 🅟. ◪
closed Monday dinner in summer, Thursday dinner in winter and Sunday – **M** (bar lunch)/dinner a la carte 7.95/12.85 **st.** ♁ 2.50.

PONT-Y-PANT Gwynedd – see Betws-y-Coed.

POOLE Dorset 403 404 O 31 The West Country G. – pop. 122 815 – ECD : Wednesday – ☏ 0202.
See : Site★ – The Three Museums★ *AC* by A 35 AX.
Envir. : Compton Acres Gardens★★, (⩽★★★) *AC*, SE : 3 m. AX – Brownsea Island★, Baden Powell Stone (⩽★★) *AC*, by boat from Poole Quay or Sandbanks *AC*.
⛴ Shipping connections with the continent : to France (Cherbourg) (Brittany ferries) summer only.
ℹ Poole Quay ☎ 673322 – Arndale Centre.
♦London 116 – Bournemouth 4 – Dorchester 23 – Weymouth 28.

Plan : see Bournemouth

⌂ **Mansion House,** 11 Thames St., BH15 1JN, ☎ 685666, Telex 41495, « 18C town house, staircase » – ▤ rest 📺 ⛀wc ☎ 🅟. ♨. ◪ AE ◉ VISA by A 35 AX
closed 24 to 30 December – **M** *(closed Saturday lunch)* 10.35/14.75 **st.** and a la carte ♁ 3.40 – **19 rm** ⊒ 49.00/71.00 **st.** – SB (weekends only) 90.00 **st.**

⌂ **Hospitality Inn** (Mt. Charlotte), The Quay, BH15 1HD, ☎ 671200, ⩽ – ⇕ 📺 ⛀wc ☎ ♿ 🅟. ♨. ◪ AE ◉ VISA by A 35 AX
M (buffet lunch)/dinner 12.00 **st.** ♁ 3.00 – **68 rm** ⊒ 47.25/57.75 **st.** – SB (weekends only) 62.00 **st.**

⌂ **Dolphin,** 180 High St., BH15 1DU, ☎ 673612, Telex 417205 – ⇕ 📺 ⛀wc ⎍wc ☎ 🅟. ♨. ◪ AE ◉ VISA by A 35 AX
M (buffet lunch)/dinner 9.25 **st.** ♁ 2.95 – **68 rm** ⊒ 21.00/48.00 **t.** – SB (weekends only) 54.00/68.50 **st.**

⌂ Arndale Court, 62-64 Wimborne Rd, BH15 2BY, ☎ 683746 – 📺 ⎍wc 🅟 by A 3049 AV
18 rm.

⌂ **Sea Witch,** 47 Haven Rd, Canford Cliffs, BH13 7LH, ☎ 707697 – 📺 ⛀wc ⎍wc ☎ 🅟. ◪ AE VISA. ⚮ AX **o**
M *(closed Monday lunch, Christmas dinner and 1 January)* (closed Sunday dinner to non residents) 7.95/10.95 **st.** and a la carte ♁ 3.15 – **9 rm** ⊒ 24.00/39.00 **t.** – SB (except summer and Bank Holidays)(weekends only) 38.00/50.00 **st.**

⌂ **Redcroft** ⚘, 20 Pinewood Rd, Branksome Park, BH13 6JS, ☎ 763959 – ⛀wc 🅟. ⚮ BX **e**
10 rm ⊒ 15.40/33.80 **t.**

⌂ **Gables,** 19 Forest Rd, Branksome Park, BH13 6DQ, ☎ 760949, ⛱ – ⛀wc 🅟. ⚮ ABX **x**
April-September – **10 rm** ⊒ 15.00/40.00 **st.**

✕ **Le Chateau,** 13 Haven Rd, Canford Cliffs, BH13 7LE, ☎ 707400 – ◪ AE ◉ VISA AX **r**
closed Sunday and Monday – **M** 16.00 **st.** ♁ 3.75.

✕ **John B's,** 20 High St., BH15 1BP, ☎ 672440 – ◪ AE ◉ VISA by A 35 AX
closed Sunday – **M** (dinner only) 10.95 **t.** ♁ 2.60.

✕ **Isabel's,** 32 Station Rd, Lower Parkstone, BH14 8UD, ☎ 747885 – ◪ AE ◉ VISA AX **a**
closed Sunday, 25-26 December and first week January – **M** (dinner only) a la carte 9.90/14.40 **t.**

✕ **Edelweiss,** 232 Ashley Rd, Upper Parkstone, BH14 9BZ, ☎ 747703, Austrian rest. – ◪ AE ◉ VISA AX **e**
closed Monday – **M** (lunch by arrangement)/dinner 8.95 **t.** and a la carte 8.90/12.35 **t.** ♁ 2.95.

AUDI, VW Cabot Lane ☎ 745000
AUSTIN-ROVER The Quay ☎ 674187
CITROEN Broadstone ☎ 693501
CITROEN, PEUGEOT, TALBOT Blandford Rd ☎ 623636
VAUXHALL-OPEL Poole Rd, Branksome ☎ 763361

POOLEY BRIDGE Cumbria 401 402 L 20 – see Ullswater.

POOL IN WHARFEDALE West Yorks. 402 P 22 – pop. 1 706 – ✉ Otley – ☏ 0532 Arthington.
♦London 204 – Bradford 10 – Harrogate 8 – ♦Leeds 10.

✕✕✕ **Pool Court** with rm, Pool Bank, LS21 1EH, ☎ 842288, ⛱ – ▤ rest 📺 ⛀wc ☎ 🅟. ◪ AE ◉ VISA. ⚮
closed Sunday, Monday and 2 weeks Christmas – **M** (dinner only)(booking essential) 10.00 **t.** and a la carte 17.95/22.75 **t.** ♁ 5.95 – ⊒ 4.95 – **4 rm** 47.00/72.00 **t.**

PORLOCK Somerset **403** J 30 The West Country G. − pop. 1 453 (inc. Oare) − ECD : Wednesday − ☀ 0643.

See : Site★ − St. Dubricius Church★.

Envir. : St. Culbone★, NW : 5 m. including 3 m. return on foot.

♦London 190 − ♦Bristol 67 − Exeter 46 − Taunton 28.

 🏠 **Oaks**, TA24 8ES, ℰ 862265, ☞ − ☑ ⇐wc ⋔wc 🅿. 🆎 ⓪
  M (lunch by arrangement)/dinner 9.50 **st.** ᵻ 3.25 − **11 rm** ☑ 25.00/40.00 **st.** − SB 45.00/ 55.00 **st.**

  at Porlock Weir NW : 1 ½ m. − ✉ Minehead − ☀ 0643 Porlock :

 🏨 **Anchor and Ship**, TA24 8PB, ℰ 862636, ⇐ − ☑ ⇐wc ☎ 🅿. 🔼 🆎 *VISA*
  closed January − **M** 10.00 **t.** (dinner) and a la carte ᵻ 3.45 − **25 rm** ☑ 30.00/59.00 **st.** − SB 62.00/74.00 **st.**

PORT DINORWIC (FELINHELI) Gwynedd **402** **403** H 24 − ☀ 0248.

♦London 249 − Caernarfon 4 − Holyhead 23.

 ✕ **Seahorse**, 20 Snowdon St., LL56 4HQ, ℰ 670546 − 🔼 *VISA*
  closed Sunday, 1 week May, 2 weeks October, 24 to 26 December and 1 January − **M** (dinner only) a la carte 9.55/12.85 **t.** ᵻ 2.70.

  at Seion E : 2 ½ m. by A 487 and off B 4547 − ✉ Caernarfon − ☀ 0248 Port Dinorwic :

 ↑ **Ty'n Rhos Farm** ☜, Llanddeiniolen, LL55 3AE, ℰ 670489, ⇐, ☞ − ⇐wc 🅿. ✾
  closed Christmas and New Year − **9 rm** ☑ 14.00/32.00 **st.**

PORTHCAWL Mid Glam. **403** I 29 − pop. 15 162 − ECD : Wednesday − ☀ 065 671.

🅱 The Old Police Station, John St. ℰ 6639 (summer only).

♦London 183 − ♦Cardiff 28 − ♦Swansea 18.

 🏩 **Seabank** (Whitbread), The Promenade, CF36 3LU, ℰ 2261, ⇐ − 📶 ☑ ☎ 🅿. 🅰. 🔼 🆎 ⓪ *VISA* ✾
  M 6.25/8.75 **t.** and a la carte − **64 rm** ☑ 32.00/50.00 **t.** − SB (weekends only) 56.00/61.00 **st.**

 🏨 **Atlantic**, West Drive, CF36 3LT, ℰ 5011, ⇐ − 📶 ☑ ⇐wc ☎ 🅿. 🔼 🆎 ⓪ *VISA*
  M *(closed Sunday dinner)* 6.25/8.25 **t.** and a la carte ᵻ 3.20 − **18 rm** ☑ 33.00/44.00 **t.**

 🏠 **Seaways**, 26-30 Mary St., CF36 3YA, ℰ 3510 − ☑ ⇐wc ⋔wc 🅿. 🔼 🆎 ⓪ *VISA*
  M 3.25/5.25 **t.** and a la carte ᵻ 2.20 − **16 rm** ☑ 15.00/46.00 **t.** − SB 32.00/38.00 **st.**

 ↑ **Minerva**, 52 Esplanade Av., CF36 3YU, ℰ 2428 − ⇐wc
  8 rm ☑ 8.50/20.00 **st.**

  at Nottage (Drenewydd yn Notais) N : ¾ m. by A 4229 − ✉ ☀ 065 671 Porthcawl :

 🕯 **Rose and Crown**, Heol-y-Capel, CF36 3ST, ℰ 4850 − ☑ ⇐wc 🅿. 🔼 🆎 ⓪ *VISA* ✾
  M *(closed Sunday dinner)* (bar lunch)/dinner a la carte 6.50/8.50 **st.** ᵻ 3.80 − **7 rm** ☑ 23.00/35.00 **st.** − SB (weekends only) 43.00 **st.**

PORTHMADOG Gwynedd **402** **403** H 25 − pop. 2 865 − ECD : Wednesday − ☀ 0766.

🅂 Morfa Bychan ℰ 2037, W : 2 m..

🅱 High St. ℰ 2981 (summer only).

♦ London 245 − Caernarfon 20 − Chester 70 − Shrewsbury 81.

 🏨 Bodawen Country House ☜, N : ½ m. on A 487 ℰ 3422, ☞ − ☑ ⇐wc ⋔wc ☎ 🅿
  10 rm.

 🏠 **Royal Sportsman** (T.H.F.), High St., LL49 9HA, ℰ 2015 − ☑ ⇐wc ☜ 🅿. 🔼 🆎 ⓪ *VISA*
  M (bar lunch Monday to Saturday)/dinner 9.00 **st.** ᵻ 3.40 − ☑ 5.65 − **16 rm** 37.00/44.50 **st.**

  at Penmorfa NW : 2 m. on A 487 − ✉ ☀ 0766 Porthmadog :

 🏠 **Bwlch-y-Fedwen Country House**, LL49 9RY, ℰ 2975, « Tastefully renovated 17C inn » − ⇐wc 🅿. ✾
  April-October − **M** (residents only) (bar lunch) − **5 rm** ☑ (dinner included) 30.00/51.00 **t.**

PORT ISAAC Cornwall **403** F 32 The West Country G. − ECD : Wednesday − ☀ 0208 Bodmin.

♦London 266 − Newquay 24 − Tintagel 14 − Truro 32.

 🏨 **Port Gaverne**, Port Gaverne, PL29 3SQ, S : ½ m. ℰ 880244, « Retaining 17C features » − ⇐wc 🅿. 🔼 🆎 ⓪ *VISA*
  closed 11 January-28 February − **M** (buffet lunch)/dinner 9.75 **st.** and a la carte ᵻ 2.50 − **18 rm** ☑ 21.50/55.00 **st.** − SB (except Christmas, New Year and Bank Holidays) 52.00/60.00 **st.**

 ↑ **Archer Farm** ☜, Trewetha, PL29 3RU, SE : ½ m. by B 3276 ℰ 880522, ⇐, ☞ − ⋔wc 🅿
  April-December − **8 rm** ☑ 12.50/28.00.

400

PORTLAND Dorset **403 404** M 32 The West Country G. – pop. 12 405 – ECD : Wednesday – ✛ 0305 – See : Site ★ (vantage point ★★).

🛈 St. George's Centre, Reforne ✆ 823406.

♦London 149 – Dorchester 14 – Weymouth 6.

🏨 **Portland Heights** (Best Western), Yeates Corner, Wakeham, DT5 2EN, ✆ 821361, Telex 418493, ≼, ⨽ heated, squash – 🛗 📺 ⇌wc ☎ 🅿️ 🔥 ⚠ 🆔 𝗩𝗜𝗦𝗔
67 rm ⚏ 40.00/68.00 t. – SB (weekends only) 54.00/66.00 st.

🏨 **Pennsylvania Castle**, Pennsylvania Rd, Wakeham, DT5 1HZ, ✆ 820561, ≼, 🚗, – 📺 ⇌wc
🔥wc ☎ 🅿️ ⚠ 🆔 𝗩𝗜𝗦𝗔
M 8.50 t. and a la carte ⌆ 2.80 – **12 rm** ⚏ 29.50/42.00 t. – SB (weekends only)(September-June) 45.00/53.00 st.

FORD Easton Lane ✆ 820483

PORTLOE Cornwall **403** F 33 – ✉ ✛ 0872 Truro.

♦London 296 – St. Austell 15 – Truro 15.

🏠 **Lugger**, TR2 5RD, ✆ 501322, ≼ – 📺 ⇌wc 🔥wc 🅿️ ⚠ 🆔 𝗩𝗜𝗦𝗔, 🚫
March-November – **M** (bar lunch Monday to Saturday)/dinner 10.95 t. and a la carte ⌆ 2.85 –
20 rm ⚏ (dinner included) 31.00/75.00 t.

PORTSCATHO Cornwall **403** F 33 – ECD : Wednesday and Saturday – ✉ Truro – ✛ 087 258.

♦London 298 – Plymouth 75 – Truro 16.

🏨 **Rosevine** 🏖, Porthcurnick Beach, TR2 5EW, N : 2 m. by A 3078 ✆ 206, ≼, 🚗, – ⇌wc 🔥 ☎
🅿️ ⚠ 🆔 𝗩𝗜𝗦𝗔
Easter-October and Christmas – **M** (bar lunch)/dinner 12.00 st. ⌆ 2.30 – **16 rm** ⚏ 30.05/79.40 st.
– SB (except July and August) 55.00 st.

🏠 **Gerrans Bay**, Tregassick Rd, TR2 5ED, ✆ 338, 🚗, – ⇌wc 🅿️ ⚠ 🆔 𝗩𝗜𝗦𝗔
April-October and Christmas – **M** (bar lunch)/dinner 10.50 t. ⌆ 2.50 – **15 rm** ⚏ (dinner included) 21.00/57.00 st.

🏠 Roseland House 🏖, Rosevine, TR2 5EW, N : 2 m. by A 3078 ✆ 644, ≼ Gerrans Bay, 🚗 –
⇌wc 🅿️ – **18 rm**.

PORTSMOUTH and SOUTHSEA Hants. **403 404** Q 31 – pop. 174 218 – ECD : Monday, Wednesday and Thursday – ✛ 0705 – See : H.M.S. Victory★★★ BY and Victory Museum★ M1 AC – Royal Marines' Museum★, at Eastney AZ M2.

🏌 Great Salterns ✆ 664549. AY.

🚢 Shipping connections with the Continent : to France (Cherbourg) (Townsend Thoresen) (Sealink) – to France (Le Havre) (Townsend Thoresen) – to France (Saint-Malo and Caen) (Brittany Ferries) – to the Isle of Wight : Fishbourne (Sealink) 15-18 daily (45 mn) – to St. Helier, Jersey (Sealink) summer : 1 daily, winter : 6 weekly (8 h 45 mn) – to St. Helier, Jersey (Channel Island Ferries) 6-7 weekly (7 h 45 mn) – to St. Peter Port, Guernsey (Sealink) summer : 1 daily, winter 6 weekly (11 h 30 mn).

🚤 to the Isle of Wight : Ryde (Sealink from Portsmouth Harbour) frequent services daily (25 to 30 mn) – from Southsea to the Isle of Wight : Ryde (Hovertravel from Southsea Clarence Pier) summer frequent services daily; winter 8-12 daily (restricted Sundays) (9 mn).

🛈 The Hard ✆ 826722/3 – Clarence Esplanade, Southsea ✆ 754358 – Continental Ferry Terminal, Mile End ✆ 698111 (summer only).

♦London 78 – ♦Southampton 21.

Plans on following pages

🏨 **Crest** (Crest), Pembroke Rd, PO1 2TA, ✆ 827651, Telex 86397 – 🛗 📺 ⇌wc ☎ 🅿️ 🔥   BZ **o**
165 rm.

🏨 **Hospitality Inn** (Mt. Charlotte), South Parade, Southsea, PO4 0RN, ✆ 731281, Telex 86719, ≼ – 🛗 📺 ⇌wc ☎ 🅿️ 🔥 ⚠ 🆔 𝗩𝗜𝗦𝗔   BZ **r**
M 6.50/7.75 st. – **108 rm** ⚏ 44.50/57.75 st. – SB (weekends only) 54.00 st.

🏨 **Pendragon** (T.H.F.), Clarence Par., Southsea, PO5 2HY, ✆ 823201, Telex 86376 – 🛗 📺
⇌wc 📠 🅿️ ⚠ 🆔 𝗩𝗜𝗦𝗔   BZ **x**
M 8.50 st. (dinner) and a la carte ⌆ 3.40 – ⚏ 5.65 – **58 rm** 42.00/53.50 st.

🏠 Keppel's Head, 24-26 The Hard, PO1 3DT, ✆ 833231, Group Telex 858875 – 🛗 📺 ⇌wc 🔥wc
📠 🅿️ 🔥 – **25 rm**.   BY **a**

⌂ **White House**, 26 South Parade, PO5 2JF, ✆ 823709 – 📺 🔥wc. ⚠ 🆔 𝗩𝗜𝗦𝗔   BZ **i**
15 rm ⚏ 13.50/30.00 t.

⌂ **Goodwood House**, 1 Taswell Rd, Southsea, PO5 2RG, ✆ 824734 – 📺 🔥. 🚫   BZ **e**
closed 24 December-3 January – **8 rm** ⚏ 11.00/27.00.

✗ Le **Talisman**, 123 High St., Old Portsmouth, PO1 2HW, ✆ 811303 – 🔥 🆔 𝗩𝗜𝗦𝗔   BZ **v**
closed Sunday, Monday and 25 December-1 January – **M** a la carte 11.25/14.65 t. ⌆ 2.30.

✗ **Bistro Montparnasse**, 103 Palmerston Rd, Southsea, PO5 3PS, ✆ 816754 – 🔥 ⚠ 🆔 𝗩𝗜𝗦𝗔
closed Sunday – **M** (dinner only) a la carte 10.95/14.35 t. ⌆ 3.50.   BZ **a**

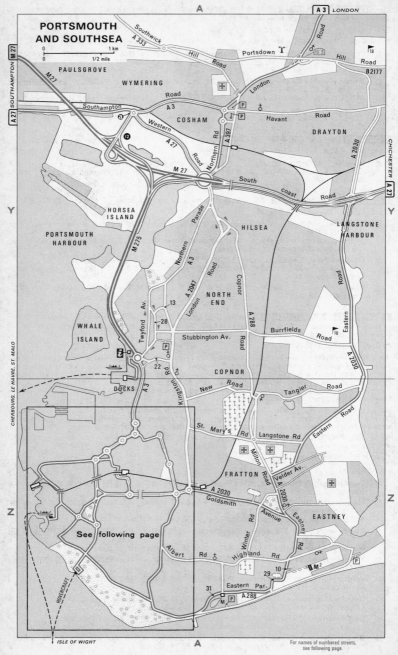

PORTSMOUTH AND SOUTHSEA

0 — 1 km
0 — 1/2 mile

PAULSGROVE

WYMERING

Southwick A 333

Hill Road

Portsdown

London Hill Road

B 2177

A 3 LONDON

M 27 SOUTHAMPTON A 27

M 27

Southampton A 3 Road

Western Road

A 27

COSHAM

Northern Rd

A 397

Havant Road

DRAYTON

A 2030

M 27

South coast Road

A 27 CHICHESTER

HORSEA ISLAND

PORTSMOUTH HARBOUR

Parade

Northern A 3 Road

London Road

Copnor Road

HILSEA

LANGSTONE HARBOUR

M 275

A 2047

NORTH END

Copnor Road

A 288

Burrfields Road

Eastern Road

A 2030

WHALE ISLAND

Twyford Av.

13

28

Stubbington Av.

COPNOR

New Road

Tangier Road

Eastern Road

Kingston Rd

22

DOCKS

A 3

St. Mary's Rd

Langstone Rd

Milton Road

FRATTON

Velder Av.

CHERBOURG, LE HAVRE, ST. MALO

See following page

A 2030

Goldsmith Avenue

A 2030

Eastney Rd

EASTNEY

Albert Rd

Winter Rd

Highland Rd

Eastern Par.

10

29

M 2

31

A 288

HOVERCRAFT

ISLE OF WIGHT

For names of numbered streets, see following page.

402

PORTSMOUTH AND SOUTHSEA

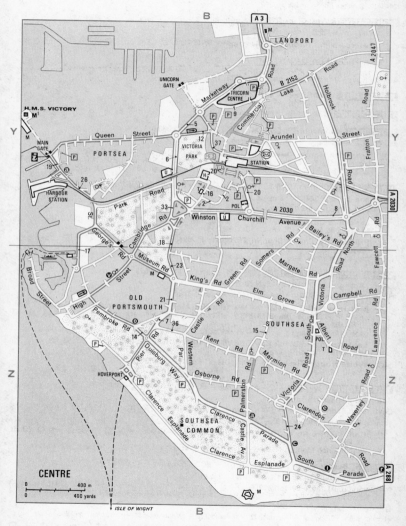

CENTRE

0 ————— 400 m
0 ————— 400 yards

ISLE OF WIGHT

Town plans: roads most used by traffic and those on which guide listed hotels and restaurants stand are fully drawn ; the beginning only of lesser roads is indicated.

PORTSMOUTH and SOUTHSEA

at Cosham N : 3 ¾ m. by A 3, M 275, M27 and A 27 – ✉ Portsmouth – 🕿 0705 Cosham :

🏨 **Holiday Inn,** North Harbour, PO6 4SH, 𝒫 383151, Telex 86611, ≼, 🔲, squash – 🏂 📺 🕿 🔥
📵 🗗 🛄 🖭 ⓪ 𝐕𝐈𝐒𝐀   AY **a**
M (buffet lunch)/dinner 12.50 **st.** and a la carte 🍴 4.75 – 🖙 6.50 – **170 rm** 49.95/60.95 **s.**

AUSTIN-ROVER Hambledon Rd 𝒫 070 14 (Water-   RENAULT 128 Milton Rd 𝒫 815151
looville) 2641   TALBOT Grove Rd South, Southsea 𝒫 823261
BMW 135-153 Fratton Rd 𝒫 827551   TOYOTA Gamble Rd 𝒫 660734
FIAT 117 Copnor Rd 𝒫 691621   VAUXHALL-OPEL London Rd, Hilsea 𝒫 661321
FORD Southampton Rd 𝒫 370944   VW, AUDI 41-53 Highland Rd 𝒫 815111
NISSAN Granada Rd, Southsea 𝒫 735311

PORT TALBOT West Glam. 🔢 I 29 – pop. 40 078 – ECD : Thursday – 🕿 0639.

♦London 187 – ♦Cardiff 32 – ♦Swansea 9.

🏠 **Twelve Knights** (Ladbroke), Margam Rd, SA13 1DB, SE : 2 m. on A 48 𝒫 882381 – 📺 🛏wc
🕿 📵 🗗 🛄 🖭 ⓪ 𝐕𝐈𝐒𝐀 🍴
🖙 4.60 – **11 rm** 33.00/42.00 **st.**

AUDI-VW Dan-y-Bryn Rd 𝒫 883733   VAUXHALL-OPEL Talbot Rd 𝒫 881962
AUSTIN-ROVER Fletchers of Cwmafon 𝒫 896378

POUND HILL West Sussex – see Crawley.

POUNDISFORD Somerset – see Taunton.

POWBURN Northumb. 🔢🔢 O 17 – ✉ Alnwick – 🕿 066 578.

♦London 312 – ♦Edinburgh 73 – ♦Newcastle-upon-Tyne 36.

🏨 **Breamish House** 🌙, NE66 4LL, 𝒫 266, ≼, ☞ – 📺 🛏wc 🍴wc 🖭 📵. 🍴
closed January – **M** (lunch by arrangement Monday to Saturday) 9.00/14.00 **t.** 🍴 2.75 – **10 rm**
🖙 25.00/50.00 **t.** – SB (October-April)(except Christmas and Bank Holidays) 59.00/66.00 **st.**

PRAA SANDS Cornwall 🔢 D 33 The West Country G. – ✉ 🕿 0736 Penzance.

🏐 Germoe Cross 𝒫 3445, N : 1 m. on A 394.

♦London 321 – Penzance 8 – Truro 24.

🏨 **Lesceave Cliff** 🌙, TR20 9TX, 𝒫 762325, ≼ Mount's Bay, ☞ – 📺 🛏wc 📵. 🔊 𝐕𝐈𝐒𝐀
M 5.00/7.50 🍴 4.25 – **26 rm** 🖙 18.00/56.00 **s.**

🏠 **Prah Sands,** Chy-an-Dour Rd, TR20 9SY, 𝒫 762438, ≼, 🔄 heated, ☞, 🍴 – 📺 🛏wc 🔥 📵.
🔊 𝐕𝐈𝐒𝐀
closed December and January – **M** 5.50/9.75 **t.** 🍴 3.00 – **20 rm** 🖙 15.00/45.00 **t.**

PRESTBURY Cheshire 🔢🔢🔢 N 24 – pop. 2 970 – 🕿 0625.

Envir. : Adlington Hall★ (15C) AC, N : 3 ½ m.

♦London 184 – ♦Liverpool 43 – ♦Manchester 17 – ♦Stoke-on-Trent 25.

🏨 **Mottram Hall** (De Vere) 🌙, Wilmslow Rd, Mottram St. Andrew, SK10 4QT, NW : 2 ¼ m.
on A 538 𝒫 828135, Telex 668181, ≼, « Part 18C mansion in park », ☞, 🍴 – 📺 📵 🕿 📵. 🗗 🔊
🛄 🖭 🍴
M 9.00/15.00 **st.** and a la carte – **71 rm** 🖙 55.00/70.00 **st.** – SB (weekends only) 72.00 **st.**

🕸🕸🕸 **Legh Arms and Black Boy,** The Village, SK10 4DG, 𝒫 829130 – 📵. 🔊 🛄 ⓪ 𝐕𝐈𝐒𝐀
M 8.00/10.50 **t.** and a la carte 🍴 3.75.

🕸🕸 **White House,** The Village, SK10 4DG, 𝒫 829376 – 🔊 🛄 ⓪
closed Monday and 4 to 20 January – **M** 6.95/10.95 **t.** and a la carte 9.60/25.70 **t.** 🍴 3.25.

PRESTEIGNE Powys 🔢 K 27 – pop. 1 490 – ECD : Thursday – 🕿 0544.

See : Church (Flemish Tapestry★).

Envir. : Old Radnor (church★) SW : 7 ½ m – 🏐 at Kington 𝒫 0544 (Kington) 230340, S : 7 m.

♦London 159 – Llandrindod Wells 20 – Shrewsbury 39.

🏨 **Radnorshire Arms** (T.H.F.), High St., LD8 2BE, 𝒫 267406, ☞ – 📺 🛏wc 🖭 🖙 🔊 🛄
⓪ 𝐕𝐈𝐒𝐀
M (bar lunch Monday to Saturday)/dinner 8.95 **st.** 🍴 3.40 – 🖙 5.65 – **16 rm** 40.00/49.00 **st.**

PRESTON Lancs. 🔢 L 22 – pop. 166 675 – ECD : Thursday – 🕿 0772.

Envir. : Samlesbury Old Hall★ (14C) AC, E : 2 ½ m.

🏐 Fulwood Hall Lane, Fulwood 𝒫 700011 – 🏐 Longridge, Fell Barn, Jeffrey Hill 𝒫 077 478 (Longridge)
3291, NE : 8 m. off B 6243 – 🏐 Fishwick Hall, Glenluce Drive, Farringdon Park, 𝒫 798300.

🎫 Town Hall, Lancaster Rd 𝒫 53731/54881 ext 6103.

♦London 226 – ♦Blackpool 18 – ♦Burnley 22 – ♦Liverpool 30 – ♦Manchester 34 – ♦Stoke-on-Trent 65.

🏨 **Crest** (Crest), The Ring Way, PR1 3AU, 𝒫 59411, Telex 677147 – 🏂 📺 🛏wc 🖭 📵. 🗗 🔊
🛄 ⓪ 𝐕𝐈𝐒𝐀
M 6.90/11.90 **st.** and a la carte 🍴 3.50 – 🖙 5.85 – **126 rm** 47.00/65.00 **st.** – SB (weekends only)
54.00/62.00 **st.**

at Fulwood N : 1½ m. on A 6 – ⊠ ✪ 0772 Preston :

⋔ **Briarfield,** 147 Watling Street Rd., off Garstang Rd, PR2 4AE, ℰ 700917 – 𝖳𝖵 ⋔wc ℗. ✸
closed 24 December-5 January – **9 rm** ⊐ 12.50/30.00 **st.**

at Broughton N : 3 m. on A 6 – ⊠ ✪ 0772 Preston :

🏛 **Broughton Park,** 418 Garstang Rd, PR3 5JB, ℰ 864087, Group Telex 67180, 🔲, 🐎 – 𝖳𝖵
⋔wc ⋔wc ☎ 🖕 ℗. 🅰. 🔼 𝖠𝖤 ⊚ 𝘝𝘐𝘚𝘈. ✸
M *(closed Saturday lunch)* 6.50/11.50 **t.** and a la carte 🍷 3.00 – **63 rm** ⊐ 45.00/52.00 **t.** –
SB (weekends only) 55.00 **st.**

at Barton N : 6 m. on A 6 – ⊠ Preston – ✪ 0772 Broughton :

🏛 **Barton Grange** (Best Western), Garstang Rd, PR3 5AA, ℰ 862551, Telex 67392, 🔲, 🐎, ✸
– 🖕 𝖳𝖵 ⋔wc ⋔wc ☎ ℗. 🅰. 🔼 𝖠𝖤 ⊚ 𝘝𝘐𝘚𝘈. ✸
M *(closed Saturday lunch, Sunday dinner and Bank Holidays)* 6.95/9.95 **st.** and a la carte 🍷 3.50
– **65 rm** ⊐ 30.00/55.00 **st.** – SB 54.00/60.00 **st.**

at Samlesbury E : 2½ m. at junction M 6 and A 59 – ⊠ Preston – ✪ 077 477 Samlesbury :

🏛 **Trafalgar,** Preston New Rd, PR5 0UL, E : 1 m. at junction A 59 and A 677 ℰ 351, Telex
677312, 🔲, squash – 🖕 𝖳𝖵 ⋔wc ⋔wc ☎ ℗. 🅰. 🔼 𝖠𝖤 ⊚ 𝘝𝘐𝘚𝘈. ✸
M 6.00/10.00 **st.** and a la carte 🍷 3.50 – **80 rm** ⊐ 43.85/57.50 **st.** – SB (weekends only)
59.00/65.00 **st.**

🏛 **Tickled Trout,** Preston New Rd, PR5 0UJ, ℰ 671, Telex 677625, ⪜, ⤳ – 𝖳𝖵 ⋔wc ☎ ℗.
🅰. 🔼 𝖠𝖤 𝘝𝘐𝘚𝘈
M 8.00/12.00 **t.** and a la carte 🍷 3.85 – **66 rm** ⊐ 45.00/60.00 **t.** – SB (weekends only)(except
December) 50.00/60.00 **st.**

at Bamber Bridge S : 5 m. on A 6 – ⊠ ✪ 0772 Preston :

🏛 **Novotel,** Reedfield Place, Walton Summit, PR5 6AB, SE : ¾ m. by A6 at junction with M6
ℰ 313331, Telex 677164, 🔟 heated, 🐎 – 🖕 𝖳𝖵 ⋔wc ☎ 🖕 ℗. 🅰. 🔼 𝖠𝖤 ⊚ 𝘝𝘐𝘚𝘈
M 6.50/9.50 **st.** and a la carte 🍷 3.40 – ⊐ 4.50 – **100 rm** 40.50/94.00 **st.** – SB (weekends only)
61.00 **st.**

MICHELIN Distribution Centre, Unit 20, Roman Way, Longridge Rd, Ribbleton, PR2 5BB, ℰ
651411

BMW Blackpool Rd, Ashton ℰ 724391	NISSAN Ribbleton Lane ℰ 704704
CITROEN Garstang Rd ℰ 718852	PEUGEOT-TALBOT. Blackpool Rd ℰ 735811
COLT Preston Rd ℰ 652323	RELIANT Blackpool Rd ℰ 726066
FIAT 306-310 Ribbleton Lane ℰ 792823	SKODA New Hall Lane ℰ 794491
FORD Penwortham ℰ 744471	TOYOTA 350 Blackpool Rd ℰ 719841
FORD Marsh Lane ℰ 54083	VAUXHALL Blackpool Rd ℰ 793054
HONDA Corporation St. ℰ 58862	VOLVO Strand Rd ℰ 50501
LADA Watling Street Rd ℰ 717262	VW, AUDI ℰ 702288

PRIORS HARDWICK Warw. 🟦🟦🟦 🟦🟦🟦 Q 27 – pop. 167 – ⊠ Rugby – ✪ 0327 Byfield.
◆London 94 – ◆Coventry 17 – Northampton 26 – Warwick 15.

✕✕✕ **Butchers Arms,** CV23 8SN, ℰ 60504, English rest., 🐎 – ℗
closed Saturday lunch and Sunday dinner – **M** 7.50 **s.** (lunch) and a la carte 9.50/18.25 **s.**
🍷 2.30.

PUDDINGTON Cheshire 🟦🟦🟦 🟦🟦🟦 K 24 – pop. 318 – ⊠ South Wirral – ✪ 051 Liverpool.
◆London 204 – Birkenhead 12 – Chester 8.

✕✕✕ **Craxton Wood** 🌿 with rm, Parkgate Rd, L66 9PB, on A 540 ℰ 339 4717, « ⪜ picturesque
grounds and gardens », park – 𝖳𝖵 ⋔wc ℗ 🖕 ℗. 🔼 𝖠𝖤 ⊚ 𝘝𝘐𝘚𝘈. ✸
closed Sunday, last 2 weeks August and Bank Holidays – **M** 9.50 **s.** (lunch) and a la carte
13.40 **s.** 🍷 3.95 – **14 rm** ⊐ 31.75/52.50 **s.**, **1 suite** 50.00/65.00 **s.**

PULBOROUGH West Sussex 🟦🟦🟦 S 31 – pop. 3 197 – ECD : Wednesday – ✪ 079 82.
Envir. : Hardham (church : wall paintings★ 12C) S : 1 m.
◆London 49 – ◆Brighton 25 – Guildford 25 – ◆Portsmouth 35.

🏠 **Chequers,** Church Pl., RH20 1AD, NE : ¼ m. on A 29 ℰ 2486, 🐎 – 𝖳𝖵 ⋔wc ⋔wc ℗. 🔼 𝖠𝖤
⊚ 𝘝𝘐𝘚𝘈
M (bar lunch)/dinner 8.50 **st.** 🍷 2.50 – **9 rm** ⊐ 25.00/40.00 **t.** – SB (except Christmas)
49.00/53.90 **st.**

✕✕ **Stane Street Hollow,** Codmore Hill, RH20 1BG, NE : 1 m. on A 29 ℰ 2819 – ℗
*closed Tuesday and Saturday lunch, Sunday, Monday, 2 weeks May, 3 weeks October and 24
December-5 January* – **M** (booking essential) 4.75 **t.** (lunch) and a la carte 10.95/13.75 **t.** 🍷 3.50.

AUSTIN-ROVER London Rd ℰ 2407   HONDA London Rd ℰ 079 881 (Bury) 691

PUTSBOROUGH Devon 🟦🟦🟦 H 30 – ⊠ Braunton – ✪ 0271 Croyde.
◆London 233 – Barnstaple 11 – Exeter 51 – Ilfracombe 9.

🏠 **Putsborough Sands,** EX33 1LB, ℰ 890555, ⪜, 🔲, squash – ⋔wc ℗. 🔼 𝖠𝖤 𝘝𝘐𝘚𝘈
April-September – **M** (bar lunch)/dinner 9.00 **t.** 🍷 2.80 – **54 rm** ⊐ 18.00/56.00 **t.** – SB (April-mid
July) 44.00/62.00 **st.**

QUORN Leics. – see Loughborough.

RADLETT Herts. 404 T 28 – pop. 7 749 – ECD : Wednesday – ✪ 092 76.

☋ at Aldenham, Radlett Rd ✆ 7775, SW : 3 m. BU.

◆London 21 – Luton 15.

Plan : see Greater London (North-West)

🏠 **Red Lion,** Watling St., WD7 7NP, ✆ 5341 – 📺 🛁wc 🚾 🅿. 🖭 🆎 ⓞ 𝘝𝘐𝘚𝘈 ⚘ BU **c**
   M a la carte 4.95/9.70 **t.** ᐦ 3.25 – **17 rm** 🖙 25.00/44.00 **t.** – SB (weekends only) 48.00/52.00 **st.**

AUSTIN-ROVER 411 Watling St. ✆ 5681   FORD 203-205 Watling St. ✆ 4851
BMW 74-76 Watling St. ✆ 4802

RAMPSIDE Cumbria 402 K 21 – see Barrow-in-Furness.

RAMSBOTTOM Greater Manchester 402 N 23 – pop. 16 334 – ✪ 070 682.

◆London 223 – ◆Blackpool 39 – Burnley 12 – ◆Leeds 46 – ◆Manchester 13 – ◆Liverpool 39.

🏨 **Old Mill,** Springwood St., off Carr St., BL0 9DS, ✆ 2991 – 📺 🛁wc ☎ 🅿. 🛆 🖭 🆎 ⓞ
   𝘝𝘐𝘚𝘈 ⚘
   M 5.50 **t.** (lunch) and a la carte 9.25/26.65 **t.** ᐦ 3.30 – **17 rm** 🖙 35.00/46.00 **st.** – SB (weekends only) 30.00/45.00 **st.**

✗ **Village,** 18 Market Pl., BL0 9HT, ✆ 5070, (No smoking) – 🖭 𝘝𝘐𝘚𝘈
   closed Sunday to Tuesday – **M** (booking essential) (dinner only) 16.50 **t.** ᐦ 3.00.

RAMSBURY Wilts. 403 404 P 29 – pop. 1 557 – ECD : Wednesday and Saturday – ✉ ✪ 0672 Marlborough.

◆London 79 – ◆Southampton 51 – Swindon 13.

✗✗ **Bell,** The Square, SN8 2PE, ✆ 20230, �たん – 🅿. 🖭 🆎 ⓞ 𝘝𝘐𝘚𝘈
   M 12.50 **t.** ᐦ 2.25.

RAMSGATE Kent 404 Y 30 – pop. 36 678 – ECD : Thursday – ✪ 0843 Thanet.

See : St. Augustine's Abbey Church (interior★).

Envir. : Minster-in-Thanet (abbey : remains★ 7C-12C) W : 4 ½ m. – Birchington-on-Sea : in Quex Park (Powell-Cotton Museum★ of African and Asian natural history and ethnology, AC), NW : 9 m.

🚢 Shipping connections with the Continent : to France (Dunkerque) (Sally Line).

🅱 Argyle Centre, Queen St. ✆ 591086.

◆London 77 – ◆Dover 19 – Maidstone 45 – Margate 4.5.

🏨 **Savoy,** 43 Grange Rd, CT11 9NA, ✆ 592637 – 📺 🛁wc 🚾 🅿. 🖭 🆎 ⓞ 𝘝𝘐𝘚𝘈 ⚘
   M 5.50 **st.** (lunch) and a la carte 7.00/12.00 **st.** ᐦ 2.60 – **23 rm** 🖙 15.00/31.00 **st.**

⌂ **Abbeygail,** 17 Penshurst Rd, East Cliff, CT11 8EG, ✆ 594154 – 🌊
   closed Christmas – **11 rm** 🖙 8.50/17.00 **s.**

   at Minster-in-Thanet W : 5 ½ m. by A 253 on B 2048 – ✉ ✪ 0843 Thanet :

✗✗ **Old Oak Cottage,** 53 High St., CT12 4BT, ✆ 821229 – 🅿. 🖭 🆎 ⓞ 𝘝𝘐𝘚𝘈
   closed Monday lunch and Sunday dinner – **M** 9.00 **t.** and a la carte 9.30/13.10 **t.** ᐦ 2.50.

AUSTIN-ROVER Grange Rd ✆ 583541   VAUXHALL West Cliff Rd ✆ 53877
FORD Boundary Rd ✆ 53784   VW, AUDI St. Lawrence ✆ 52333
RENAULT Margate Rd ✆ 52629

RANGEWORTHY Avon 403 404 M 29 – pop. 325 – ✉ Bristol – ✪ 045 422 Rangeworthy.

◆London 122 – ◆Bristol 13 – Gloucester 30 – Swindon 39.

🏠 **Rangeworthy Court** 🦢, Wooton Rd, BS17 5ND, ✆ 347, « Part 15C manor house », 🗵, 🌊
   – 🛁wc 🅿. 🖭 ⓞ
   closed 23 December-2 January – **M** (closed Sunday) (lunch by arrangement residents only)
   9.25 **t.** (dinner) ᐦ 2.85 – **14 rm** 🖙 18.50/35.00 **st.** – SB (weekends only) 38.50/48.50 **st.**

AUSTIN-ROVER Hatters Lane, Chipping Sodbury   BEDFORD, VOLVO West End Garage, Chipping
✆ 313181   Sodbury ✆ 318311

RASKELF North Yorks. – – see Easingwold.

RAVENSTONEDALE Cumbria 402 M 20 – pop. 501 – ECD : Thursday – ✉ Kirkby Stephen –
✪ 058 73 Newbiggin-on-Lune.

◆London 280 – ◆Carlisle 43 – Kendal 19 – Kirkby Stephen 5.

🏠 **Black Swan** 🦢, CA17 4NG, ✆ 204, 🌊 – 🛁wc 🅿. 🖭 🆎 𝘝𝘐𝘚𝘈
   closed January and February – **M** (closed Sunday dinner) (bar lunch Monday to Saturday)/dinner 12.00 **st.** and a la carte ᐦ 3.15 – **6 rm** 🖙 22.00/39.00 **st.** – SB (except summer)(weekends only) 46.00/51.00 **st.**

♨ **Fat Lamb,** Fell End, Crossbank, CA17 4LL, SE : 1 ¾ m. on A 683 ✆ 242 – 🛁wc ᕑ 🅿
   M 9.00 **t.** and a la carte ᐦ 2.25 – **9 rm** 🖙 17.00/34.00 **t.** – SB 46.00/52.00 **st.**

RAWTENSTALL Lancs. 402 404 N 22 – ECD : Tuesday – ✉ Rossendale – ✪ 0706 Rossendale.

◆London 230 – Blackburn 12 – ◆Leeds 40 – ◆Liverpool 49 – ◆Manchester 17.

🏠 High Croft, Haslingden Old Rd, BB4 8RR, ✆ 215808, 🗵 heated, 🌊 – 📺 🛁wc 🗐wc ☎ 🅿
   7 rm.

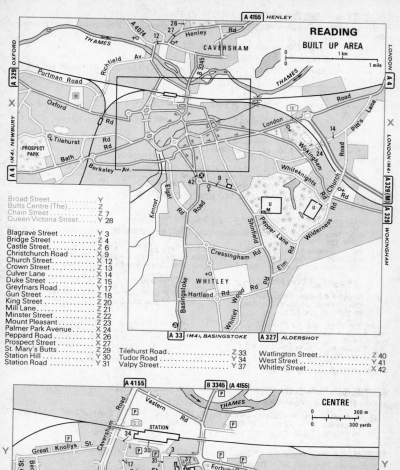

407

READING Berks. 403 404 Q 29 – pop. 194 727 – ✪ 0734.

Envir. : Stratfield Saye Park★ *AC*, S : 7 m. by A 33 ✕ – Mapledurham House★ *AC*, NW : 3 ½ m. by A 329 ✕.

🇫 Bearwood, Mole Rd, Sindlesham ✎ 760060 by A 329 ✕.

🅱 Civic Offices, Civic Centre ✎ 55911 and 592388.

◆London 43 – ◆Brighton 79 – ◆Bristol 78 – Croydon 47 – Luton 62 – ◆Oxford 28 – ◆Portsmouth 67 – ◆Southampton 46.

Plan on preceding page

🏨 **Ramada,** Oxford Rd, RG1 7RH, ✎ 586222, Telex 847785, 🖾 – 🛎 📺 ☎ ﴾ 🅿. 🕍 🔼 ⅍
① 𝑉𝐼𝑆𝐴 Z i
M 14.50/25.00 **t.** and a la carte 🍷 3.25 – ⌧ 5.85 – **200 rm** 64.00/72.00 **t.**, **1 suite** 140.00 **t.** –
SB (weekends only) 66.00 **st.**

🏨 **Post House** (T.H.F), Basingstoke Rd, RG2 0SL, S : 2 ½ m. on A 33 ✎ 875485, Telex 849160,
🖾 – 📺 🚽wc ☎ ﴾ 🅿. 🕍 🔼 ⅍ ① 𝑉𝐼𝑆𝐴 X a
M 10.50 **st.** and a la carte 🍷 3.80 – ⌧ 5.65 – **143 rm** 55.00/63.50 **st.**

🏠 **Upcross,** 68 Berkeley Av., RG1 6HY, ✎ 590796, 🌳 – 📺 🚽wc ⓜwc 🅿. 🔼 ⅍ 𝑉𝐼𝑆𝐴 Z c
closed 2 weeks at Christmas and New Year – **M** *(closed Friday, Saturday and Sunday dinner)*
(bar lunch)/dinner a la carte 8.00/9.75 **st.** 🍷 2.75 – **30 rm** ⌧ 24.00/42.00 **st.**

⚲ **Private House,** 98 Kendrick Rd, RG1 5DW, ✎ 874142 – 🅿. ⌖ X x
7 rm ⌧ 15.00/23.00 **st.**

at Shinfield S : 4 ¼ m. on A 327 – ✕ – ✉ ✪ 0734 Reading :

XXX ❀ **L'Ortolan** The Old Vicarage, Church Lane, RG2 9BY, ✎ 883783, French rest., 🌳 – 🅿. 🔼
⅍ ① 𝑉𝐼𝑆𝐴
closed Sunday dinner and Monday – **M** 16.50/23.50 **t.** 🍷 5.95
Spec. Saucisson de volaille au homard et son consommé, petite salade d'asperges, Panaché de veau aux trois
parfums, Délice de nougat glacé aux framboises et son coulis (June to August).

at Burghfield SW : 5 m. by A 4 – ✕ – ✉ ✪ 0734 Reading :

XX **Knight's Farm,** Berrys Lane, RG3 3XE, NE : 2 m. ✎ 52366, 🌳 – 🅿. 🔼 ⅍ ① 𝑉𝐼𝑆𝐴
closed Saturday lunch, Sunday, Monday, 2 weeks August and 2 weeks Christmas-New Year –
M 15.00/20.50 **t.** 🍷 3.50.

BMW   209-211 Shinfield Rd ✎ 871620
FIAT   Eaton Pl., Chatham St. ✎ 582521
FORD   160 Basingstoke Rd ✎ 875333
PEUGEOT-TALBOT   Christchurch Rd ✎ 875242
RANGE-ROVER, SAAB, JAGUAR   38 Portman Rd ✎
585011
RENAULT   Chatham St. ✎ 583322

RENAULT   Wokingham Rd ✎ 669456
TOYOTA   569-575 Basingstoke Rd ✎ 871278
VAUXHALL-OPEL   Vastern Rd ✎ 55501
VOLVO   406-412 London Rd ✎ 67321
VW, AUDI   Erleigh Rd ✎ 666111
VW, AUDI   Oxford Rd ✎ 418181

REDBOURN Herts. 404 S 28 – pop. 5 114 – ECD : Wednesday – ✉ St. Albans – ✪ 058 285.

◆London 31 – Luton 6 – Northampton 42.

🏨 **Aubrey Park,** Hemel Hempstead Rd, AL3 7AF, SW : 1 m. on B 487 ✎ 2105, Telex 825562,
🔼 heated, 🌳 – 📺 🚽wc ☎ 🅿. 🕍 🔼 ⅍ ① 𝑉𝐼𝑆𝐴
M 7.50/10.50 **st.** and a la carte 🍷 3.25 – ⌧ 6.00 – **80 rm** 43.00/65.00 **st.**

REDDITCH Heref. and Worc. 403 404 O 27 – pop. 61 639 – ECD : Wednesday – ✪ 0527.

🇫 Pitcheroak, Plymouth Rd ✎ 41054.

🅱 Civic Square, Alcester St. ✎ 60806.

◆London 111 – ◆Birmingham 15 – Cheltenham 33 – Stratford-upon-Avon 15.

🏨 **Southcrest** (Best Western) ⟆, Pool Bank, Southcrest District, B97 4JG, ✎ 41511, Telex
338455, 🌳 – 📺 🚽wc ⓜwc ☎ 🅿. 🕍 🔼 ⅍ ① 𝑉𝐼𝑆𝐴
closed 25 December-2 January – **M** *(closed Sunday dinner and Bank Holidays)* 8.50/9.50 **t.**
and a la carte 🍷 3.50 – **60 rm** ⌧ 38.00/46.00 **t.** – SB (weekends only) 48.00/52.00 **st.**

AUSTIN-ROVER   109 Alcester Rd, Studley ✎ 052 785
(Studley) 2297
AUSTIN-ROVER   Washford Drive ✎ 25055
CITROEN   Birmingham Rd ✎ 63636
FORD   Battens Drive ✎ 21212

SKODA   1124 Evesham Rd ✎ 052 789 (Astwood Bank)
2433
VOLVO   Clive Rd ✎ 69111
VW, AUDI   530 Evesham Rd, Crabe Cross ✎ 44554

REDHILL Surrey 404 T 30 – pop. 48 241 (inc. Reigate) – ECD : Wednesday – ✪ 0737.

◆London 22 – ◆Brighton 31 – Guildford 20 – Maidstone 34.

⚲ **Ashleigh House,** 39 Redstone Hill, RH1 4BG, on A 25 ✎ 64763, 🔼 heated, 🌳 – 🛏 🅿.
⌖
closed Christmas – **9 rm** ⌧ 16.50/30.00 **t.**

REDLYNCH Wilts. 403 404 O 31 – see Salisbury.

408

REDRUTH Cornwall 403 E 33 The West Country G. – pop. 29 560 (inc. Camborne) – ECD : Thursday – ✉ ☎ 0209.

◆London 301 – Penzance 18 – ◆Plymouth 61 – Truro 11.

at Carnkie SW : 1 ¼ m. by B 3297 – ✉ ☎ 0209 Redruth :

XX **Basset Count House,** TR16 6RZ, ℰ 215181 – **P**. AE VISA
closed Sunday dinner and Monday – **M** (lunch by arrangement Monday to Saturday)/dinner a la carte 10.70/13.50 **st.** ☖ 3.15.

REIGATE Surrey 404 T 30 – pop. 48 241 (inc. Redhill) – ECD : Wednesday – ☎ 073 72.

◆London 26 – ◆Brighton 33 – Guildford 20 – Maidstone 38.

🏨 **Bridge House,** Reigate Hill, RH2 9RP, ℰ 46801, ≼ – TV ⇌wc ☎ **P**. ⚠. ⋈ AE ⓪ VISA
🌦
M (closed Bank Holidays to non residents) 8.50/14.25 **t.** and a la carte ☖ 3.75 – ⬭ 3.75 – **30 rm** 31.50/52.00 **st.** – SB (weekends only) 72.00 **st.**

X **La Barbe,** 71 Bell St., RH2 7AN, ℰ 41966, French Bistro – ⋈ AE ⓪ VISA
closed lunch Monday and Saturday and Sunday – **M** 12.00/19.00 **st.** and a la carte ☖ 3.50.

RENISHAW Derbs. 402 403 404 P 24 – pop. 1 809 – ✉ Sheffield (South Yorks.) – ☎ 0246 Eckington.

◆London 157 – Derby 33 – ◆Nottingham 31 – ◆Sheffield 8.

🏨 **Sitwell,** Station Rd, S31 9WE, ℰ 435226, Telex 547303 – TV ☎ **P**. ⚠. ⋈ AE ⓪ VISA
M (closed Saturday lunch) 7.15/10.95 **t.** and a la carte ☖ 3.30 – ⬭ 3.95 – **31 rm** 25.50/45.00 **st.**, **1 suite** 45.00/55.00 **st.**

RHAEADR = Rhayader.

RHAYADER (RHAEADR) Powys 403 J 27 – pop. 1 672 – ECD : Thursday – ☎ 0597.

🛈 The Old Swan, West St. ℰ 810591 (summer only).

◆London 179 – Aberystwyth 34 – Carmarthen 75 – Shrewsbury 62.

🏨 **Elan Valley** ⮾, LD6 5HN, SW : 2 ½ m. on B 4518 ℰ 810448, ≼, ⮾ – ⇌wc **P**. AE
closed Christmas – **M** 7.00/8.00 **t.** ☖ 2.50 – **11 rm** ⬭ 19.50/35.00 **t.** – SB (winter only) 39.00/45.00 **st.**

RHOSMAEN Dyfed 403 I 28 – see Llandeilo.

RHOS-ON-SEA (LLANDRILLO-YN-RHOS) Clwyd 402 403 I 24 – see Colwyn Bay.

RHUTHUN = Ruthin.

RHYDAMAN = Ammanford.

RHYDGALED (CHANCERY) Clwyd 403 H 26 – see Aberystwyth (Dyfed).

RHYDYCROESAU Salop – see Oswestry.

RICHMOND North Yorks. 402 O 20 – pop. 7 596 – ECD : Wednesday – ☎ 0748.

See : Castle★ (Norman ruins) AC.

Envir. : Bolton Castle★ (15C) AC, ≼★, SW : 13 m.

🛈ₛ Bend Hagg ℰ 2457 – 🛈ₛ Catterick Garrison, Leyburn Rd ℰ 0748 (Richmond) 833268, S : 3 m.

🛈 Friary Gardens, Queens Rd ℰ 3525 (summer only).

◆London 243 – ◆Leeds 53 – ◆Middlesbrough 26 – ◆Newcastle-upon-Tyne 44.

🏨 **Howe Villa** ⮾, Whitcliffe Mill, DL10 4TJ, S : ½ m. by A 6108 ℰ 2559, ☀ – TV ⇌wc 🛁wc **P**. ⮾
Mid March-October – **4 rm** ⬭ (dinner included) 28.00/47.00.

🏨 **Frenchgate,** 59-61 Frenchgate, DL10 7AE, ℰ 2087, ☀ – TV ⇌wc 🛁wc **P**. ⋈ AE ⓪ VISA
closed mid December-mid February – **M** (closed Sunday lunch) (bar lunch)/dinner 8.00 **t.** and a la carte ☖ 2.40 – **13 rm** ⬭ 19.50/36.50 **t.** – SB (October-May) 42.00/44.00 **st.**

↑ **Whashton Springs Farm** ⮾, DL11 7JS, NW : 3 ½ m. by Ravensworth road ℰ 2884, « Working farm », ☀ – TV ⇌wc 🛁wc **P**. 🌦
closed December and January – **8 rm** ⬭ 12.00/24.00 **s.**

↑ Pottergate, 4 Pottergate, ℰ 3826 – TV
6 rm.

AUSTIN-ROVER Victoria Rd ℰ 2539   CITROEN Darlington Rd ℰ 3014

RINGWOOD Hants. 🄴🄾🄴 🄾🄾🄴 O 31 – pop. 10 941 – ECD : Monday and Thursday – 🕿 042 54.

🚲 Ringwood 🖉 042 53 (Burley) 2431, NE : 4 m.

♦London 102 – Bournemouth 11 – Salisbury 17 – ♦Southampton 20.

🏚 **Little Moortown House,** 244 Christchurch Rd, BH24 3AS, 🖉 3325 – 📺 🛁wc 🅿. 🔄 *VISA*
    M (dinner only) 7.50 t. 🛇 2.75 – **6 rm** ⌑ 17.00/34.00 t.

    at Ibsley N : 2 ½ m. on A 338 – ⊠ 🕿 042 54 Ringwood :

✕ **Old Beams,** Salisbury Rd, BH24 1AS, 🖉 3387, « 14C thatched cottage » – 🅿. 🔄 🄰🄴 *VISA*
    M 6.95 st. (lunch)and a la carte 8.50/13.50 st. 🛇 3.00.

    at Avon S : 4 m. on B 3347 – ⊠ Christchurch – 🕿 0425 Bransgore :

🏚 **Tyrrells Ford** 🏡, BH24 7BH, 🖉 72646, 🌿, park – 📺 🛁wc 🛁wc 🕿 🅿. 🔄 *VISA*. 🦌
    M (bar lunch Monday to Saturday)/dinner 11.95 t. and a la carte – **13 rm** ⌑ 27.50/50.00 t. –
    SB (except Bank Holidays) 60.00/70.00 **st.**

FIAT Salisbury Rd 🖉 6111   FORD Christchurch Rd 🖉 5432

RIPLEY Surrey 🄾🄾🄴 S 30 – pop. 1 903 – ECD : Wednesday – 🕿 0483 Guildford.

♦London 28 – Guildford 6.

✕✕✕ **Clock House,** 13 Portsmouth Rd, GU23 6AQ, 🖉 224777, 🌿 – 🔄 🄰🄴 🄾 *VISA*
    closed Saturday lunch, Sunday dinner and Monday – **M** 12.00/19.00 t. and a la carte 🛇 3.00.

RIPON North Yorks. 🄾🄾🄴 P 21 – pop. 13 036 – ECD : Wednesday – 🕿 0765.

See : Cathedral★ 12C-15C.

Envir. : Fountains Abbey★★★ (ruins 12C-13C, floodlit in summer) – Studley Royal Gardens★★ and
Fountains Hall★ (17C) *AC*, SW : 3 m. – Newby Hall★ (18C) *AC* (the tapestry room★★ and gardens★
AC) SE : 3 ½ m.

🚲 Palace Rd 🖉 3640, N : 1 m. on A 6108.

🄱 Wakemans House, Market Pl. 🖉 4625 (summer only).

♦London 222 – ♦Leeds 26 – ♦Middlesbrough 35 – York 23.

🏨 **Ripon Spa** (Best Western), Park St., HG4 2BU, 🖉 2172, Telex 57780, ≼, 🌿 – 🖃 📺 🛁wc
    🛁wc 🕿 🕭 🅿. 🔄 🄰🄴 🄾 *VISA*
    M 10.00/13.95 t. 🛇 3.40 – **41 rm** ⌑ 35.00/60.00 t.

🏚 **Crescent Lodge,** 42 North St., HG4 1EN, 🖉 2331 – 📺. 🦌
    closed 1 week at New Year – **6 rm** ⌑ 10.00/20.00 t.

✕ **New Hornblower,** Duck Hill, HG4 1BL, 🖉 4841 – 🔄 *VISA*
    closed Monday and February – **M** (dinner only) a la carte 8.25/10.70 t. 🛇 3.50.

FIAT, VAUXHALL Kirkby Rd 🖉 4491   TALBOT Blossom Gate 🖉 4268
FORD North St. 🖉 2324   VOLVO Palace Rd 🖉 2461
RENAULT Water Skellgate 🖉 2083

RIPPONDEN West Yorks. 🄾🄾🄴 O 22 – pop. 3 464 – ⊠ 🕿 0422 Halifax.

♦London 210 – Halifax 5 – Huddersfield 9 – ♦Leeds 21.

✕✕ **Over the Bridge,** Millfold, HX6 4LD, at junction of A 58 and B 6113 🖉 823722 – 🅿. 🄰🄴
    closed Bank Holidays – **M** (dinner only)(booking essential) 14.50 st. 🛇 3.50.

ROADE Northants. – pop. 2 703 – 🕿 0604.

♦London 66 – ♦Coventry 36 – Northampton 5.5.

✕ **Roadhouse,** 16 High St., NN7 2NW, 🖉 863372 – 🅿. 🔄 🄰🄴 *VISA*
    closed Saturday lunch, Sunday and Monday – **M** 8.50 t. (lunch) and a la carte 10.15/13.30 t.
    🛇 3.00.

ROBERTSBRIDGE East Sussex 🄾🄾🄴 V 31 – ⊠ 🕿 0580.

♦London 52 – Hastings 10.

✕✕ **Trompe L'œil,** 13 High St., TN32 5AE, 🖉 880362 – 🅿. 🔄 🄰🄴 🄾 *VISA*
    closed Saturday lunch, Sunday, Monday, first 2 weeks February, last 2 weeks October and
    25-26 December – **M** 8.95 t. and a la carte 12.20/15.70 t. 🛇 4.00.

ROCHDALE Greater Manchester 🄾🄾🄴 🄾🄾🄴 N 23 – pop. 97 292 – ECD : Tuesday – 🕿 0706.

♦London 212 – ♦Blackpool 53 – ♦Leeds 37 – ♦Liverpool 46 – ♦Manchester 13.

🏚 **Broadfield** 🏡, Sparrow Hill, OL16 1AF, 🖉 44085 – 📺 🛁wc 🛁wc 🕭 🅿. 🔄 🄰🄴 *VISA*
    M 5.00/6.75 t. and a la carte 🛇 3.20 – **18 rm** ⌑ 30.00/40.00 t. – SB (weekends only) 43.50 **st.**

CITROEN Yorkshire St. 🖉 54422   VAUXHALL-OPEL John St. 🖉 38491
FORD Oldham St. 🖉 32046

410

MICHELIN

More than a leap ahead

When the horseless carriage made its debut and 4mph was still considered such an awesome speed that vehicle owners had to employ flag walkers to march ahead of them, few people could have foreseen how important tyres would become in changing the face – and the pace – of 20th century travel.

By the 1900s, when the rattle and clatter of suspensionless and solid-tyred cars announced the future, the technical revolution that helped make comfortable personal mobility at 70mph run-of-the-mill had already taken place.

That was the invention in 1892 of the detachable pneumatic tyre, designed originally for bicycles. The company that made this invention famous is still a household name today.

Later, in 1948, the same company put into motion a second technical revolution that proved crucial in increasing vehicle speeds, performance and roadholding. That was the radial tyre.

Today the company supplies more car, truck and bus tyres in Britain and the rest of Western Europe than any other manufacturer. Michelin was there then as it is now, leading the way in modern tyre development.

1

Acclaimed reputation

Indeed, it is no idle boast to say that Michelin is miles ahead of its business rivals and takes pride in its reputation for tyres of quality, reliability, high performance and long life. There is a Michelin tyre for every task, from the child's pedal cycle to jet aircraft landing gear.

With 11,500 people, Michelin accounts for more than half the total employment in the British tyre manufacturing industry. The company's main manufacturing plant is in Stoke-on-Trent (est. 1927), producing semi-finished goods, steel cord and car tyres; its other British manufacturing operations are in Burnley (1960) and Ballymena (1969), producing truck tyres, and in Dundee (1972), producing car tyres.

The Michelin Commercial Headquarters is based in Harrow, not far from central London, and a network of 22 Commercial Distribution Centres throughout Britain and Ireland provides a high level of local service. Also in London is the Michelin Training and Information Centre, established in 1980 as a service to customers. The Centre is regarded as the best of its kind in British industry.

Commitment to quality

On a group scale, Michelin spends 5 per cent of total annual turnover on Research & Development, far more than any other European manufacturer. This commitment to R&D maintains Michelin's position as the frontrunner in radial tyre technology and enhances the quality of Michelin tyres.

There are 4,000 Michelin employees concentrating purely on tyre development, using some of the latest computer-aided design technology. Every year, on test, Michelin clock up a staggering 142,000,000 miles, 49,000,000 more than the distance between the earth and the sun.

A wide readership

An important aspect of Michelin, sometimes not connected directly with the company as a tyre manufacturer, is its publishing operation. In fact, the Red Guide you are reading is published by Michelin the tyre manufacturer. The Michelin group produces 65,000 maps and guides every working day and is Europe's largest publisher in this field.

Michelin radials for superb performance and roadholding

New generation Michelin radials are for drivers who enjoy their motoring and who look for the best possible performance from their cars. Whether in the fast lane or just cruising, you can be sure that Michelin radials will complement your car's performance with exceptional control and steering response and optimal roadholding. You might also appreciate the extra value of good mileage and fuel economy as well as the subtle sporting looks of our low profile range.

MX
are car tyres with safe sure handling, comfort and reliability.

MXL
radials, with their stylish wide section, give extra grip and stability along with improved fuel economy.

MXV
high speed, high performance radials provide outstanding braking power, precision handling and excellent grip with rapid water dispersal to prevent aquaplaning at speed.

XWX
radials are ideal for the powerful saloon car with their high acceleration capability and outstanding braking power, extra comfort, quiet running, high speed stability, and fuel economy.

MXX
radials for the ultra high performance sports cars give an extremely high level of grip, braking power, high torque transmission\and reliability.

TDX-E
are high efficiency radials designed for fuel\economy and extra ride comfort with a\built-in security factor – limited "run-on" capability after a deflation.

TRX
offer a unique radial tyre and rim combination with sustained high speed performance, exceptional steering response and remarkable comfort.

Michelin radials are not only a pleasure to drive and to behold, their quality ensures maximum reliability for confident motoring at speed.

When was the last time you checked your car's tyre pressures?

Last week? Very soon, any forget-fulness on the driver's part will be a thing of the past, for MTM will be doing the job!

MTM, which stands for Michelin Tyre Monitoring, is an ingenious microprocessor-based system that keeps an electronic check on car tyre pressures and gives a warning if anything is amiss.

The data are easily read in the normal driving position from a digital display on the dashboard, behind which is a central decoder that translates signals transmitted from pressure/temperature sensing devices in the wheels.

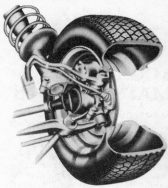

MTM, which is likely to become an original equipment option, runs off the car battery, continues to monitor when the car is parked and even gives a reminder if the spare wheel is in use. More important, MTM enhances safety.

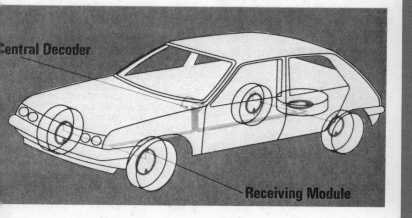

Central Decoder

Receiving Module

MICHELIN MAPS & GUIDES

At the end of the last century, motor cars were still a rarity, horse power still meant a flying mane, steel-bound wheels and a hard ride. But if motor cars were rare, route maps were almost unheard of and hotel and restaurant guide books simply did not exist.

The development of the pneumatic tyre was the one factor without which the motor car would have remained a noisy, slow and cumbersome toy with little future. The pneumatic tyre gave life to the motor car which at last made possible fast long-distance travel for the masses. André Michelin, one of the founders of Michelin, sensed the need for accurate information and in 1900, published the first Hotel and Restaurant Guide for France. The whole range of Michelin maps and guides available today stems from this first publication.

HOTEL AND RESTAURANT GUIDES

This Hotel and Restaurant Guide to Great Britain and Ireland is one of a world famous range of similar publications. The complete list is: Benelux, France, Germany, Great Britain and Ireland, Italy, Main Cities Europe, Spain and Portugal, Paris and London.

These guides are all prepared to the same standards and published annually. Easily understood symbols give details of the size and grade of the hotel or restaurant and the varying facilities available (see the reference pages at the front of this guide).

There is also a guide for the visitor to France who prefers the open air life – this is Camping and Caravaning in France, also revised annually.

GREEN TOURIST GUIDES

The first Michelin touring guides appeared before the First World War. In those days, they did not have a standard format; the shape and binding varied from guide to guide. Some of the earliest guides were of places to which even today a visit is an adventure. The guide of the 'Sunny Countries' featured parts of North Africa and Southern Europe.

Within a year of Armistice Day, a special series of tourist books was published which today are collectors' items. These are the Guides to the Battlefields. Through words and pictures depicting the horror and destruction at Amiens and Arras, Lille, the Marne Campaigns and Rheims, Soissons, the Somme, Verdun, Ypres and Yser, a multitude of visitors were helped to appreciate fully what had happened.

Today there are guides to many important cities: Paris, London, Rome, New York. To countries: Canada, Portugal, Spain, Austria, Germany, Greece, Italy, Belgium-Luxembourg, Switzerland and Holland. France is covered by six regional guides in English and twenty in the French language. For Great Britain there are The West Country and Scotland. In the USA, New England. All the guides, with the familiar green covers, are to a uniform standard.

All Green Tourist Guides are revised regularly (but not necessarily annually).

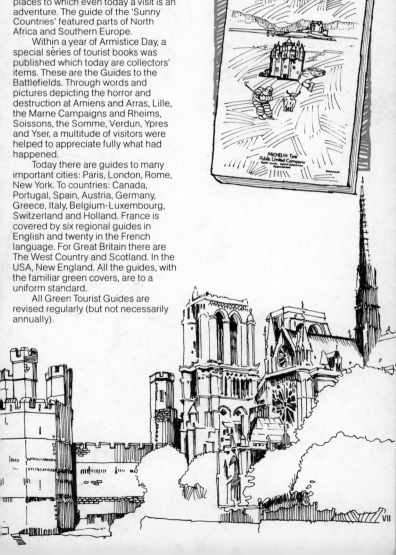

VII

MAPS

The Michelin archives contain many maps produced by the Company shortly after the first Michelin Red Guide, in other words, some 80 years ago. Like the Guide, the early maps were of France. However, as the coverage of the guides spread to cover the Mediterranean area and the British Isles, so did the maps. Indeed, in those areas that have never been blessed with motorways, an old Michelin map is still quite usable, (if you ignore the size of the towns and villages), because they were produced with such accuracy.

The range and scope of Michelin maps increase constantly and today cover the whole of Western Europe and Africa. Indeed, the Michelin Africa maps are the only true motoring maps of that vast continent.

Setting aside the rather special maps of specific areas, geological regions of France, city environs, historic events etc., the map range divides into three categories: main roads, regional maps and detailed maps. A single sheet map covers Europe from east to west and as far north as Bergen. There are main road maps of the whole of Western Europe. The biggest expansion in new Michelin maps, at this time, is of the regional maps. The British Isles are covered by five maps. There are 17 regional maps covering the whole of France. Spain and Portugal, the Benelux countries,

Switzerland and Austria are already in the series and the next countries to be included are Italy and West Germany. The detailed maps are primarily of France, the country being covered in 37 sheets.

We have said that the Michelin maps are for motorists; we believe that they are the only maps designed and

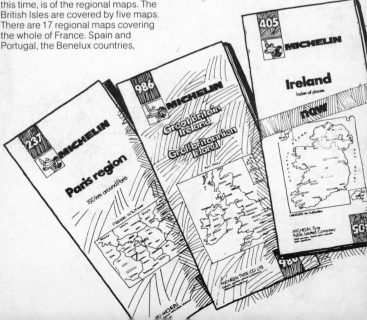

produced specifically with the driver in mind. They are famous not only for what they include but also for what is omitted. There is none of the clutter, so often associated with some other maps, which can make reference so difficult. On regional maps there is a generous overlap from sheet to sheet so that no town or place is on the fold.

'Motorist' does of course mean every type of driver from tourist to businessman. Truck drivers need good maps too. Michelin maps cater for all drivers. Recommended hotels and restaurants are cross-referenced in the appropriate Red Guide. Places of natural beauty and other tourist attractions are also indicated.

We could go on, but suffice it to say that we believe that our maps and guides, like our tyres, are the best. Changes are never made for cosmetic reasons only, but rather as a consequence of our regular reviews, constant research and the help we receive from our customers.

EUROPE
GREAT BRITAIN

AUSTRIA
BENELUX
FRANCE
GERMANY
GREECE
IRELAND
ITALY
PORTUGAL
SPAIN
SWITZERLAND
YUGOSLAVIA

AFRICA

IX

MICHELIN CELEBRATES THE CENTENARY OF THE AUTOMOBILE WITH AN HISTORIC GIFT TO THE NATIONAL MOTOR MUSEUM, BEAULIEU

To commemorate one hundred years of the car, Michelin has donated a set of ceramic panels, exact copies of the famous originals that decorate Michelin House in Chelsea, to the National Motor Museum at Beaulieu, Hampshire. The presentation to Lord Montagu of Beaulieu on behalf of the Museum Trust took place on Friday 18th July, 1986.

Michelin House, formerly the celebrated London headquarters of the tyre company, is decorated with ceramic panels encapsulating dramatic episodes from the early history of the automobile, particularly racing. The Khachadourian Gallery, Europe's leading automobile art dealer, in Pall Mall, London, commissioned a limited edition of 100 copies of each of the 34 panels and very appropriately, it is number 100 that Michelin has presented to the Museum.

These hand-painted ceramic tiles have been manufactured in Stoke-on-Trent, coincidentally Michelin's manufacturing headquarters in Great Britain. In order to faithfully reproduce the fine detail found on the original tiles, it was necessary to reintroduce certain glazing and tube lining techniques which are no longer used in production today.

Michelin's involvement with racing dates from 1891 when the Michelin brothers, André and Edouard, realised that splendid publicity could be gained by equipping racing cycles with their pneumatic tyres.

The company launched its newly developed pneumatic cycle tyre at the Paris-Brest Cycle Race in 1891 which was won by Charles Terront, as one of these panels depicts. 1895 marked another breakthrough in the history of the car when the Michelin brothers

1891 Paris – Brest. Ch. Terront

entered the Paris-Bordeaux-Paris race to champion the reliability of their pneumatic tyres for the horseless carriage. The car, named Lightning or l'Eclair because of its zig-zag progress down the road, completed the course, albeit in last position.

Michelin successfully challenged the German tyre manufacturer Continental in the 1901 Paris-Berlin race and, despite many obstacles, the race was won by Fournier on a Mors equipped with Michelin tyres. The following year, in the Paris-Vienna race, 61 of the 218 starters had Michelin tyres, which proved themselves in appalling conditions winning almost every class. The race was won by Marcel Renault.

Also illustrated in these ceramic panels is the notorious 'Race of Death' – the 1903 Paris-Madrid – which was to be the last great city-to-city race. They ended prematurely at Bordeaux after an alarming number of fatalities en route, including Marcel Renault. His brother Louis, depicted here, was awarded the race. Another panel records the remarkable feat of Fernand Gabriel on a heavy 12-litre Mors, who started the same race in 82nd position and doggedly drove through the carnage arriving in third place.

1895 Paris – Bordeaux. 1ere Voiture sur Pneus Michelin

1901 Paris – Berlin. Fournier sur Mors

1902 Paris – Vienna. Marcel Renault

The 1906 French Grand Prix was a triumph for Michelin, Renault and the detachable rim. The invention allowed mechanics to change the tyres in less than three minutes, a procedure that normally took 20 minutes. Szisz, the winner, was able to maintain an average speed of more than 62 mph over the 750 miler two-day race. In less than twenty years, Michelin had completely altered the course of racing history and by 1908 was regularly sweeping the boards at all the prestigious races in Europe.

1903 Paris – Madrid. Gabriel sur Mors

1903 Paris – Madrid. Louis Renault

1906 Grand-Prix A.C.F. Sarthe. Szisz sur Renault

The exhibit is housed in the main museum building and the National Motor Museum is open every day of the year, except Christmas Day. Beaulieu is located west of Southampton in the picturesque county of Hampshire.

ROCHESTER Kent 404 V 29 – pop. 23 840 – ECD : Wednesday – ✉ Chatham – ☎ 0634 Medway.
See : Castle★, ※★★ (142 steps) *AC* – Cathedral★ (interior★★) – Eastgate House★ 1590 – Fort Pitt Hill ≤★.
Envir. : Cobham Hall (Gilt Hall★) *AC*, W : 4 m.
ℹ Eastgate Cottage, Eastgate High St. ☎ 43666.
♦London 30 – ♦Dover 45 – Maidstone 8 – Margate 46.

Crest (Crest), Maidstone Rd, ME5 9SF, SE : 2 ½ m. by A 2 on A 229 ☎ 687111, Telex 965933 – rest TV wc ☎ & P. AE VISA
M 9.00/11.95 **st.** and a la carte 4.40 – 5.85 – **105 rm** 49.50/59.50 **st.** – SB (weekends only) 64.00/68.00 **st.**

AUSTIN-ROVER - JAGUAR 16 Medway St., Chatham ☎ 41122
AUSTIN-ROVER Commercial Rd, Strood ☎ 408451
FIAT, LANCIA Pier Rd, Gillingham ☎ 52333
NISSAN 100 Watling St. ☎ 576741
PEUGEOT, TALBOT High St. ☎ 42231
RELIANT Gundulph Rd, Chatham ☎ 41857
RENAULT Hoath Lane, Wigmore ☎ 31688
TOYOTA High St. ☎ 407788
VAUXHALL Station Rd, Strood ☎ 721021
VOLVO Wood St., Gillingham ☎ 402777
VW, AUDI 1 Ferndale Rd, Gillingham ☎ 572327

ROCHFORD Essex 404 W 29 – pop. 13 426 – ECD : Wednesday – ✉ ☎ 0702 Southend-on-Sea.
♦London 43 – Southend-on-Sea 4.

Hotel Renouf, Bradley Way, ☎ 541334 – TV wc ☎ P. AE VISA
M *(closed Saturday lunch)* 10.50/12.50 **t.** and a la carte 3.50 – **24 rm** 48.00/65.00 **t.**

XX **Renouf's,** 1 South St., SS4 1BL, ☎ 544393 – AE VISA
closed first 3 weeks January and 8 to 22 June – **M** (dinner only) 9.00 **t.** and a la carte 12.00/15.00 **t.** 3.50.

ROCK Cornwall 403 F 32 – ECD : Wednesday – ✉ Wadebridge – ☎ 020 886 Trebetherick.
♦London 288 – Newquay 22 – ♦Plymouth 45 – Truro 30.

St. Enodoc, PL27 6LA, ☎ 3394, ≤, squash – TV wc wc ☎ P. AE VISA
M (bar lunch Monday to Saturday)/dinner 8.25 **st.** and a la carte 2.95 – **13 rm** 19.00/43.00 **st.** – SB (October-April) 47.00/50.00 **st.**

Gleneglos, Trewint Lane, PL27 6LU, ☎ 2369, – TV wc P. VISA.
closed Christmas-early February – **M** *(closed Sunday dinner)* (dinner only and Sunday lunch) 9.50 **t.** and a la carte 2.60 – **6 rm** 26.00/36.00 **t.** – SB 46.00/50.00 **st.**

RODBOROUGH Glos. – see Stroud.

ROEWEN Gwynedd – see Conwy.

ROLLESTON-ON-DOVE Staffs. 402 403 404 P 25 – see Burton-upon-Trent.

ROMALDKIRK Durham 402 N 20 – see Middleton-in-Teesdale.

ROMSEY Hants. 403 404 P 31 – pop. 14 818 – ECD : Wednesday – ☎ 0794.
See : Abbey Church★ 12C-13C (interior★★).
18 Dunwood Manor, Shootash Hill ☎ 0794 (Lockerley) 40549, SE : 4 m. on A 27 – 18 Ampfield Par Three ☎ 68480, NE : on A 31 – 18 Romsey Rd ☎ 0703 (Southampton) 6673, S : on A 3057.
ℹ Bus Station car park, Broadwater Rd ☎ 512987 (summer only).
♦London 82 – Bournemouth 28 – Salisbury 16 – ♦Southampton 8 – Winchester 10.

White Horse (T.H.F.), Market Pl., SO5 8NA, ☎ 512431 – TV wc ☎ & P. AE VISA
M 7.75/10.50 **st.** and a la carte 3.40 – 5.65 – **33 rm** 43.00/55.00 **st.**

XX **Old Manor House,** 21 Palmerston St., SO51 8GF, ☎ 517353 – P. AE VISA
closed Sunday dinner, Monday, 3 weeks August-September and 24 December-30 January – **M** 6.95/18.00 **st.** 2.75.

AUSTIN-ROVER Winchester Rd ☎ 512850
PEUGEOT 45-55 Winchester Hill ☎ 513185
VAUXHALL-OPEL 24 Middlebridge St. ☎ 513806

ROSEDALE ABBEY North Yorks. 402 R 20 – ✉ Pickering – ☎ 075 15 Lastingham.
♦London 247 – ♦Middlesbrough 27 – Scarborough 25 – York 36.

Milburn Arms, YO18 8RA, ☎ 312, – TV wc wc P. VISA
M (bar lunch)/dinner 10.90 **t.** and a la carte 2.50 – **7 rm** 19.00/39.00 **t.** – SB (October-April except Easter) 42.00/48.00 **st.**

White Horse Farm, YO18 8SE, ☎ 239, ≤ – TV wc wc P. AE
closed Christmas Day – **M** (bar lunch Monday to Saturday)/dinner 12.50 **st.** 3.75 – **15 rm** 21.00/42.00 **t.** – SB 48.00/56.00 **st.**

ROSSINGTON South Yorks. 402 403 404 Q 23 – see Doncaster.

17

ROSS-ON-WYE Heref. and Worc. 408 404 M 28 – pop. 8 281 – ECD : Wednesday – ✆ 0989.
Envir. : Goodrich (Castle★ : ruins 12C-14C) *AC*, SW : 3 ½ m.
🖼 20 Broad St. ✆ 62768.
♦London 118 – Gloucester 15 – Hereford 15 – Newport 35.

🏛 **Chase** (Q.M.H.), Gloucester Rd, HR9 5LH, on A 40 ✆ 63161, � – ㏫ 🛁wc 🚿wc ☎ 🅿 🏄
40 rm.

🏛 **Royal** (T.H.F.), Palace Pound, Royal Par., HR9 5HZ, ✆ 65105, ≼, � – ㏫ 🛁wc ☎ 🅿 🏄
🔄 🆎 ① *VISA*
M 8.70/9.50 **st.** and a la carte 🍴 3.40 – ☲ 5.65 – **30 rm** 45.00/57.00 **st.**

🏛 **Chasedale**, Walford Rd, HR9 5PQ, ✆ 62423, � – 🛁wc 🅿 🔄 *VISA*
M 5.50/8.00 **st.** and a la carte 🍴 2.50 – **12 rm** ☲ 18.00/38.00 **st.** – SB 44.00/62.00 **st.**

↑ **Sunnymount** ⌂, Ryefield Rd, off Gloucester Rd (A 40), HR9 5LU, ✆ 63880, � – 🅿 *VISA*
🔄
closed 25 and 26 December – **6 rm** ☲ 13.00/23.00 **st.**

at Weston-Under-Penyard E : 2 m. on A 40 – ⊠ ✆ 0989 Ross-on-Wye :

🏛 Hunsdon Manor, HR9 7PE, ✆ 62748, � – ㏫ 🛁wc 🚿wc 🅿
12 rm.

at Pencraig SW : 3 ¾ m. on A40 – ⊠ Ross-on-Wye – ✆ 098 984 Llangarron :

🏛 **Pencraig Court**, HR9 6HR, ✆ 306, � – 🛁wc 🅿 🔄 🆎 *VISA* 🔄
closed Christmas and New Year – **M** (dinner only) 11.50 **st.** 🍴 2.60 – **11 rm** ☲ 20.00/40.00 **st.** –
SB (winter only) 50.00/72.00 **st.**

at Goodrich SW : 5 m. by A 40 on B 4229 – ⊠ Ross-on-Wye – ✆ 0600 Symonds Yat :

🏛 **Ye Hostelrie**, HR9 6HX, ✆ 890241, � – 🚿wc 🅿
M (bar lunch)/dinner 8.50 **st.** – **7 rm** ☲ 20.00/34.00 **st.**

at Pengethley NW : 4 m. on A 49 – ⊠ Ross-on-Wye – ✆ 098 987 Harewood End :

🏛 **Pengethley** (Best Western) ⌂, HR9 6LL, ✆ 211, ≼, ⏄ heated, �, park – ㏫ 🛁wc ☎ 㐃
🅿 🔄 🆎 ① *VISA*
M 12.50/19.50 **st.** 🍴 3.50 – **20 rm** ☲ 55.00/90.00 **st.** – SB 110.00/180.00 **st.**

AUSTIN-ROVER Cantilupe Rd ✆ 62400
FORD ✆ 62637
PEUGEOT-TALBOT High St. ✆ 62447

RENAULT Overross St. ✆ 63666
VW, AUDI Whitchurch ✆ 0600 (Monmouth) 890235

ROSTHWAITE Cumbria 402 K 20 – see Keswick.

ROSUDGEON Cornwall 408 D 33 – ⊠ ✆ 0736 Penzance.
♦London 321 – Penzance 6 – Truro 24.

✕ **Trevarrack Cottage**, Helston Rd, TR20 9PA, ✆ 762257 – 🅿 🔄 🆎 ① *VISA*
M 5.65/10.35 **t.** and a la carte 🍴 3.15.

ROTHAY BRIDGE Cumbria – see Ambleside.

ROTHBURY Northumb. 401 402 O 18 – pop. 1 694 – ECD : Wednesday – ⊠ Morpeth – ✆ 0669.
♦London 311 – ♦Edinburgh 84 – ♦Newcastle-upon-Tyne 29.

↑ **Orchard**, High St., NE65 7TL, ✆ 20684, � – 🔄
closed Christmas – **6 rm** ☲ 13.00/23.00 **st.**

ROTHERHAM South Yorks. 402 408 404 P 23 – pop. 122 374 – ECD : Thursday – ✆ 0709.
🏌 Thrybergh Park ✆ 850480, E : 3 m. – 🏌 Sitwell Park, Shrogs Wood Rd ✆ 0709 (Wickersley)
541046, E : 2 ½ m. – 🏌 Grange Park, Upper Wortley Rd ✆ 559497, NW : 3 m. by A 629 – 🏌 Pheonix,
Pavilion Lane, Brinsworth ✆ 363864.
🖼 Central Library and Arts Centre, Walker Pl. ✆ 382121 ext 3119/3199.
♦London 166 – ♦Kingston-upon-Hull 61 – ♦Leeds 36 – ♦Sheffield 6.

🏨 **Rotherham Moat House** (Q.M.H.), 102-104 Moorgate Rd, S60 2BG, ✆ 364902, Telex 547810
– 🔲 ㏫ 🅿 🏄 🔄 🆎 ① *VISA*
M *(closed Saturday lunch)* 6.00/10.75 **st.** and a la carte 🍴 3.50 – ☲ 4.75 – **62 rm** 20.00/44.00 **st.**
– SB (weekends only) 50.00 **st.**

AUSTIN-ROVER Doncaster Rd ✆ 373991
AUSTIN-ROVER, CITROEN 106 Barnsley Rd, Gold-
thorpe ✆ 893864
DATSUN West Bawtry Rd, Brinsworth ✆ 364204
FIAT 126 Fitzwilliam Rd ✆ 361666
FORD Sheffield Rd ✆ 60151
MAZDA High St., Rawmarsh ✆ 52278
PEUGEOT-TALBOT 132-138 Fitzwilliam Rd ✆ 382213

RENAULT Bawtry Rd, Wickersley ✆ 0709 (Wickers-
ley) 547641
TOYOTA 7-9 Canklow Rd ✆ 60681
VAUXHALL-OPEL 128 Wellgate ✆ 375571
VOLVO Bawtry Rd, Wickersley ✆ 0709 (Wickersley)
543462
VW-AUDI Brampton Rd, Wath ✆ 873366

ROTHERWICK Hants – see Basingstoke.

ROTHLEY Leics. 402 403 404 Q 25 – see Leicester.

ROTTINGDEAN East Sussex 404 T 31 – pop. 10 888 (inc. Saltdean) – ECD : Wednesday – ✉ ☎ 0273 Brighton.

◆London 58 – ◆Brighton 4 – Lewes 9 – Newhaven 5.

  🏠 **Olde Place,** High St., BN2 7HE, ✆ 31051 – 📺 ➡wc 📵 🅿. 🔼 AE VISA
    M *(closed Sunday dinner)* 9.50/11.50 **t.** and a la carte ▯ 3.00 – **20 rm** ⊃ 25.00/45.00 **st.** –
    SB 52.00/57.50 **st.**

  ✕ **My Cuisine,** 1 Meadow Par., BN2 7FA, N : ½ m. by Falmer Rd ✆ 33416 – 🔼 AE ⓞ VISA
    closed Sunday and Bank Holidays – **M** (dinner only) 14.00 **t.** ▯ 2.60.

ROUSDON Devon 403 L 31 – see Lyme Regis.

ROWSLEY Derbs. 402 403 404 P 24 – pop. 200 – ECD : Thursday – ✉ Matlock – ☎ 0629 Matlock.

◆London 157 – Derby 23 – ◆Manchester 40 – ◆Nottingham 30.

  🏠🏠 **Peacock** (Embassy), Bakewell Rd, DE4 2EB, ✆ 733518, « 17C stone house with antiques »,
    🔧, 🐎 – 📺 ➡wc ☎ 🅿. 🔼 AE ⓞ VISA 🦌
    M 8.25/16.75 **st.** ▯ 4.00 – ⊃ 5.50 – **20 rm** 38.00/51.00 **st.** – SB (October-May)(weekends only)
    59.00/64.00 **st.**

ROYAL LEAMINGTON SPA Warw. 403 404 P 27 – pop. 56 552 – ECD : Monday and Thursday – ☎ 0926.

🏌 Newbold-Comyn, Newbold Terrace East ✆ 21157, off Willes Rd.
🛈 Jephson Lodge, The Parade ✆ 311470 and 27072 ext 216.

◆London 99 – ◆Birmingham 23 – ◆Coventry 9 – Warwick 3.

  🏠🏠 **Manor House,** Avenue Rd, CV31 3NJ, ✆ 23251, Telex 311653 – 🛗 📺 ➡wc 🅿 🅿. 🔥 🔼 AE ⓞ VISA   i
    M (carving rest.) 9.50/10.75 **st.** and a la carte ▯ 3.35 – **53 rm** ⊃ 43.00/53.00 **st.** – SB (weekends only) 65.00/68.50 **st.**

  🏠🏠 **Regent** (Best Western), 77 The Parade, CV32 4AX, ✆ 27231, Telex 311715 – 🛗 📺 ➡wc ☎ 🅿. 🔥 🔼 AE ⓞ VISA   r
    M 7.35/10.00 **t.** and a la carte ▯ 3.25 – **80 rm** ⊃ 37.25/61.00 **t.**, **2 suites** – SB (weekends only) 49.00/53.00 **st.**

  🏠🏠 **Blackdown** 🦢, Sandy Lane off Stoneleigh Rd, CV32 6RD, N : 2 ¼ m. by A 452 ✆ 24761, 🐎 – 📺 ➡wc 🅿 🅿. 🔥 🔼 AE VISA   by A 452
    M 9.95/12.95 **t.** and a la carte ▯ 3.00 – **11 rm** ⊃ 40.00/55.00 **t.**

  🏠🏠 **Falstaff,** 16-20 Warwick New Rd, CV32 5JG, ✆ 312044 – 🛗 📺 ➡wc ▥wc 📵 🔥 🔼 AE ⓞ VISA
    M (bar lunch)/dinner 7.50 **st.** and a la carte ▯ 2.70 – **54 rm** ⊃ 27.00/44.00 **st.** – SB (weekends only) 44.00 **st.**

    plan of Warwick   Z u
    P.T.O. →

ROYAL LEAMINGTON SPA

COVENTRY A 452 | A 445 RUGBY | (A 445)

CENTRE
0   300 m
0   300 yards

413

🏨 **Lansdowne,** 87 Clarendon St., CV32 4PF, 🕿 21313, Telex 337556 – 🛗wc 🅿 ⚞ 🎏   **a**
M (dinner only) 9.65 **st.** ◗ 2.95 – **10 rm** ⚏ 19.95/35.90 **st.** – SB (except Christmas and New Year) 47.90/51.90 **st.**

🏨 **Beech Lodge,** 28 Warwick New Rd, CV32 5JJ, 🕿 22227 – 📺 🛗wc 🅿 ⚞ VISA
M *(closed Sunday dinner)* (dinner only, residents only) 9.00 **t.** ◗ 2.75 – **13 rm** ⚏ 23.25/42.00 **t.**
– SB (except Bank Holidays) 51.30/55.80 **t.**   plan of Warwick Z **s**

🏨 **Abbacourt,** 40 Kenilworth Rd, CV32 6JF, 🕿 311188, 🛋 – 📺 ⟱wc 🛗wc 🅿 ⚞ AE ⓞ
VISA   plan of Warwick Z **r**
M 5.00/12.00 **s.** and a la carte – **27 rm** ⚏ 19.00/45.00 **s.** – SB (weekends only) 54.00/70.00 **s.**

🏨 **Angel,** 143 Regent St., CV32 4NZ, 🕿 881296 – 📺 ⟱wc 🛗wc 🕿 🅿   **c**
16 rm.

⌂ **Buckland Lodge,** 35 Avenue Rd, CV31 3PG, 🕿 23843 – ⟱wc 🅿   **z**
closed Christmas and New Year – **11 rm** ⚏ 12.00/30.00 **st.**

XXX ⚙ **Mallory Court** ⟿ with rm, Harbury Lane, Bishop's Tachbrook, CV33 9QB, S : 2 m. by A 452 🕿 30214, Telex 317294, ≤, ⚒, 🛋, park, ✘, squash – 📺 ⟱wc 🕿 ⟲ ⚞ AE VISA
🎏   plan of Warwick Z **a**
closed 26 December-1 January – **M** (booking essential) 16.50/30.00 **st.** – ⚏ 6.95 – **9 rm** (dinner included) –/170.00 **st., 1 suite** (dinner included) 195.00 **st.** – SB (November-mid April except 31 January-4 February) 110.00/154.50 **st.**
Spec. Terrine de foie gras with sauternes jelly, Fillet of lamb with basil mousseline and charlotte of aubergine, Hot raspberry soufflé.

AUDI, VW Dormer Pl. 🕿 36511
AUSTIN-ROVER Station Approach 🕿 27156
CITROEN Warwick St. 🕿 35659
COLT Wood St. 🕿 24681
FORD Sydenham Drive 🕿 29411

PEUGEOT-TALBOT Spencer St. 🕿 30115
RENAULT Russell St. 🕿 21171
SAAB Lime Av. 🕿 23221
SKODA 4 Court St. 🕿 26011
VAUXHALL-OPEL Old Warwick Rd 🕿 20861

ROYAL TUNBRIDGE WELLS Kent **404** U 30 – pop. 57 699 – ECD : Wednesday – ☎ 0892.

See : The Pantiles★ (promenade 18C) B – Town Hall Museum (wood-mosaic articles★) B **M.**

Envir. : Scotney Castle Gardens (trees ★, Bastion view ★) *AC*, SE : 8 m. by B 2169 A.

🛈 Town Hall 🕿 26121.

♦London 36 – ♦Brighton 33 – Folkestone 46 – Hastings 27 – Maidstone 18.

ROYAL TUNBRIDGE WELLS

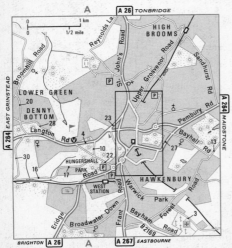

🏨 **Spa,** Mount Ephraim, TN4 8XJ, ℰ 20331, Telex 957188, ≼, ♨ heated, 🐾, park, ⚒ – ▮ 📺
☎ **🅿** ⚓ 🔼 AE ⓪ VISA
M 10.00 **t.** (lunch) and a la carte 🛦 3.15 – �< 5.50 – **75 rm** 42.50/65.00 **st., 4 suites** 65.00/
75.00 **st.** – SB (weekends only) 79.00/85.00 **st.**

🏨 **Russell,** 80 London Rd, TN1 1DZ, ℰ 44833, Telex 95177 – 📺 ➿wc 🛁wc ☎ **🅿** 🔼 AE ⓪
VISA. 🛥
A v
M (bar lunch)/dinner 10.50 **t.** and a la carte 🛦 3.00 – **20 rm** ➿ 38.00/50.00 **t.** – SB 63.90 **st.**
B a

XXX **Thackeray's House,** 85 London Rd, TN1 1EA, ℰ 37558, « Tastefully converted Regency
town house », 🐾 – 🔼 VISA
B s
closed Sunday, Monday and 18 to 29 August – **M** 9.85/19.85 **t.** and a la carte 16.85/23.00 **t.**
🛦 3.25.

X **Cheevers,** 56 High St., TN1 1XF, ℰ 45524 – 🔼 VISA
B c
closed Sunday, Monday, 1 week Easter and 2 weeks August – **M** (a la carte lunch)/dinner
13.95 **t.** 🛦 2.70.

at Southborough N : 2 m. on A 26 – A – ✉ 😀 0892 Royal Tunbridge Wells :

XX **Weavers,** London Rd, TN4 0PU, ℰ 29896 – **🅿** 🔼 AE ⓪ VISA
closed Sunday dinner, Monday and Bank Holidays – **M** 7.75/9.50 **t.** and a la carte 12.00/16.55 **t.**
🛦 3.50.

at Speldhurst NW : 3 ½ m. by A 26 – A – ✉ Royal Tunbridge Wells – 😀 089 286 Langton :

XX **George and Dragon Inn,** Barden Rd, TN3 0NN, ℰ 3125, « 13C inn » – **🅿**. 🔼 AE ⓪
VISA
closed Saturday lunch and Sunday dinner – **M** 10.00/16.75 **t.** and a la carte 13.00/19.00 **t.**
🛦 3.75.

AUSTIN-ROVER Crescent Rd ℰ 25266
AUSTIN-ROVER - DAIMLER - JAGUAR Mount Sion
ℰ 26463
BMW St. John's Rd ℰ 39355
CITROEN, FIAT, LANCIA 321 St. Johns Rd ℰ 35111
COLT, RELIANT Grosvenor Rd ℰ 27174
FORD Mount Ephraim ℰ 20323

FORD Commercial Rd, Paddock Wood ℰ (089 283)
Paddock Wood 6388
NISSAN 13-17 London Rd ℰ 29292
RENAULT Langton Rd ℰ 39466
PEUGEOT-TALBOT, ALFA-ROMEO 49 Mount Plea-
sant ℰ 27202
VW, AUDI Currie Rd ℰ 44733

RUAN-HIGH-LANES Cornwall **403** F 33 – see Veryan.

RUGBY Warw. **403 404** Q 26 – pop. 59 039 – ECD : Wednesday – 😀 0788.

Envir. : Stanford-on-Avon (castle 17C : park★ AC) NE : 5 m.

🛈 Public Library, St. Matthew's St. ℰ 2687.

♦London 88 – ♦Birmingham 33 – ♦Leicester 21 – Northampton 20 – Warwick 17.

🏨 **Three Horse Shoes,** Sheep St., CV21 3BX, ℰ 4585 – 📺 ➿wc 🛁wc 🕿. ⚓. 🔼 AE ⓪
VISA
M 8.95/12.50 **st.** and a la carte 🛦 3.75 – **31 rm** ➿ 45.00/55.00 **st., 1 suite** 55.00/65.00 **st.** –
SB (weekends only) 47.00/55.00 **st.**

🏩 **Carlton,** 130 Railway Terr., CV21 3HE, ℰ 3076 – 📺 ➿wc 🛁wc 🕿 **🅿** 🔼 VISA
closed Saturday lunch, Sunday dinner and Bank Holidays – **M** 5.65/6.65 **t.** and a la carte 🛦 2.95
– **12 rm** ➿ 17.00/34.00 **t.**

at Kilsby SE : 6 ¼ m. by A 428 on A 5 – ✉ Rugby – 😀 0788 Crick :

XX **Hunt House,** Main Rd, CV23 8XR, ℰ 823282, 🐾 – **🅿** 🔼 AE ⓪ VISA
closed Sunday and Monday – **M** (dinner only) 12.50 **t.** and a la carte 🛦 3.10.

at Crick SE : 6 m. on A 428 – ✉ 😀 0788 Rugby :

🏨 **Post House** (T.H.F.), NN6 7XR, W : ½ m. on A 428 ℰ 822101, Telex 311107 – 📺 **🅿** ⚓. 🔼
AE ⓪ VISA
M 8.25/10.25 **st.** and a la carte 🛦 3.40 – ➿ 5.65 – **96 rm** 46.00/55.00 **st.**

at West Haddon (Northants.) SE : 10 m. on A 428 – ✉ 😀 0788 87 West Haddon :

🏠 Pytchley, 23 High St., NN6 7AD, ℰ 209, 🐾 – 📺 ➿wc **🅿**
14 rm.

at Stretton Under Fosse NW : 7 ½ m. by A 426 and B 4112 on A 427 – ✉ 😀 0788 Rugby :

🏠 **Ashton Lodge** 🛥, CV23 0PJ, N : 1 m. by A 427 on B 4112 ℰ 832278, 🐾 – 📺 ➿wc 🛁wc
🅿 🔼 AE ⓪
M (closed Monday lunch and Sunday) (bar lunch)/dinner 8.75 and a la carte 🛦 2.25 – **11 rm**
➿ 22.50/38.00.

ALFA-ROMEO Cymbeline Way ℰ 810719
AUSTIN-ROVER Railway Terr. ℰ 3477
CITROEN 50 Albert St. ℰ 73671

HONDA Leicester Rd ℰ 60333
PEUGEOT-TALBOT Leicester Rd ℰ 62731
RENAULT 100 Railway Terr. ℰ 2660

RUGELEY Staffs. 402 403 404 O 25 – pop. 23 751 – ECD : Wednesday – ☎ 088 94.
Envir. : Blithfield Hall★ (Elizabethan) *AC*, N : 5 m.

◆London 135 – ◆Birmingham 23 – Stafford 9 – ◆Stoke-on-Trent 23.

at Armitage SE : 3 m. on A 513 – ⊠ Rugeley – ☎ 0543 Armitage :

XX **Old Farmhouse,** Armitage Rd, WS15 4AT, ℰ 490353 – 🗐 🅿. 🖾 🖭 ⓪ 𝘝𝘐𝘚𝘈
closed Sunday dinner and Monday – **M** 9.45/14.95 t. 🛢 2.50.

FORD Bradbury ℰ 76425

RUMWELL Somerset – see Taunton.

RUNCORN Cheshire 402 403 L 23 – pop. 63 995 – ECD : Wednesday – ☎ 092 85 (5 fig.) or 0928 (6 fig.).

🏌 Highfield Rd, Widnes ℰ 051 (Liverpool) 424 2995, N : 4 m.

🗓 57-61 Church St. ℰ 76776 and 69656.

◆London 202 – ◆Liverpool 14 – ◆Manchester 29.

🏨 **Crest** (Crest), Wood Lane, Beechwood, WA7 3HA, SE : ½ m. off junction 12 of M 56
ℰ 714000, Telex 627426 – 🗐 📺 🛏wc ☎ 🅿 🎿. 🖾 🖭 ⓪ 𝘝𝘐𝘚𝘈
M (carving lunch) 9.15/11.75 **st.** and a la carte 🛢 2.90 – ☲ 5.85 – **128 rm** 49.00/59.00 **st.** –
SB (weekends only) 56.00/64.00 **st.**

AUSTIN-ROVER Balfour St. ℰ 72271   MAZDA Picow Farm Rd ℰ 63099
FORD Victoria Rd ℰ 74333

RUSHDEN Northants. 404 S 27 – pop. 22 394 – ECD : Thursday – ☎ 0933.
See : Higham Ferrers (St. Mary's Church★ 13C-14C).

◆ London 72 – Bedford 13 – ◆ Cambridge 36 – ◆ Leicester 38 – Northampton 15.

🏠 **Westward,** Shirley Rd, NN10 9BY, ℰ 312376, ⟍ heated – 📺 🏠 🅿. 🌿
closed 23 December-3 January – **26 rm** ☲ 16.50/30.00 t.

AUSTIN-ROVER High St. South ℰ 59111

RUSHLAKE GREEN East Sussex 404 U 31 – ⊠ Heathfield – ☎ 0435.

◆London 57 – Eastbourne 14 – Hastings 15 – Royal Tunbridge Wells 21.

🏨 **Priory Country House** ⟍, TN21 9RG, N : 1 m. by Dallington Rd. ℰ 830553, Telex 957210,
≼, « 15C priory with country house atmosphere », ⟍, 🦌, park – 📺 🛏wc ☎ 🅿
closed 23 December-9 January – **M** (lunch by arrangement) 12.75/19.50 t. 🛢 4.00 – **15 rm**
☲ 39.00/100.00 t.

RUSPER West Sussex 404 T 30 – pop. 2 678 – ☎ 029 384.

◆London 30 – ◆Brighton 35 – Horsham 6.

XXX Ghyll Manor with rm, High St., RH12 4PX, ℰ 571, ≼, « Part Elizabethan manor », ⟍ heated,
🦌, park, ⅍ – 📺 🛏wc ☎ 🅿. 🎿
11 rm.

RUTHIN (RHUTHUN) Clwyd 402 403 K 24 – pop. 4 417 – ECD : Thursday – ☎ 082 42.
See : Church★.

🏌 at Pantymwyn ℰ 0352 (Mold) 740318, NE : 8 m. – 🏌 Pwllglas ℰ 2296, S : 2 ½ m.

🗓 Ruthin Craft Centre ℰ 3992.

◆London 210 – Birkenhead 31 – Chester 23 – Shrewsbury 46.

🏨 **Ruthin Castle** (Best Western) ⟍, Corwen Rd, LL15 2NU, ℰ 2664, Telex 61169, ≼,
« Reconstructed medieval castle », ⟍, 🦌, park – 🗐 🛏wc ☎ 🅿
M (bar lunch Monday to Saturday)/dinner 9.50 **t.** and a la carte – **58 rm** ☲ 31.00/59.00 **t.** –
SB 51.00/63.50 **st.**

🏨 **Castle (and Myddleton Arms),** St. Peter's Sq., LL15 1AA, ℰ 2479, Telex 617074 – 📺
🛏wc ☎ 🅿. 🎿 🖾 🖭 ⓪ 𝘝𝘐𝘚𝘈
M (bar lunch)/dinner 7.95 **t.** and a la carte 🛢 3.75 – **25 rm** ☲ 25.00/40.00 **t.** – SB (weekends
only) 42.00 **st.**

AUSTIN-ROVER Llanrhaeadr ℰ 074 578 (Llanynys)   NISSAN Well St. ℰ 2645
543

RYDAL Cumbria 402 L 20 – see Ambleside.

RYDE I.O.W. 403 404 Q 31 – see Wight (Isle of).

Le **carte stradali** Michelin
aggiornate viaggiano con l'accorto turista.

RYE East Sussex **404** W 31 – pop. 4 127 – ECD : Tuesday – ☎ 0797.

See : Old Town★ (chiefly : Mermaid Street) – Ypres Tower ≤★.

Envir. : Winchelsea (Church of St. Thomas the Martyr★ 1283 : Tombs★★ 12C) SW : 3 m. – Small Hythe (Ellen Terry's House★ *AC*) N : 7 ½ m.

🅱 48 Cinque Ports St., Ferry Rd ✆ 222293.

♦London 61 – ♦Brighton 49 – Folkestone 27 – Maidstone 33.

 🏛 **George** (T.H.F.), High St., TN31 7JP, ✆ 222114 – 📺 ⏤wc ☜ 🅿 🎿 🔼 🆎 ⓞ 𝚅𝙸𝚂𝙰 ⚘
  M 8.00/9.00 **st.** and a la carte ⓛ 3.40 – ⏤ 5.65 – **16 rm** 43.00/55.00 **st.**

 🏛 **Mermaid**, Mermaid St., TN31 7EY, ✆ 223065, Group Telex 957141, « 15C inn » – ⏤wc 🛁wc
  🅿 🆎 ⓞ 𝚅𝙸𝚂𝙰 ⚘
  closed midweek January-February – **M** 8.00/10.00 **t.** and a la carte ⓛ 3.30 – **28 rm**
  ⏤ 34.00/54.00 **t.** – SB (except Bank Holidays) 78.00/88.00 **st.**

 🏠 **Hope Anchor**, Watchbell St., TN31 7HA, ✆ 222216, ≤ – ⏤wc 🅿 🔼 🆎 ⓞ 𝚅𝙸𝚂𝙰
  M *(closed dinner in February)* (bar lunch)/dinner 8.10 **t.** and a la carte – **15 rm** ⏤ 21.00/39.00 **t.**

 ↑ **Old Vicarage**, 66 Church Sq., TN31 7HF, ✆ 222119, ⚘ – 📺 🔒 ⚘
  5 rm ⏤ 19.00/38.00 **st.**

 XX **Flushing Inn**, Market St., TN31 7LA, ✆ 223292, Seafood, « 15C inn with 16C mural » – 🔼
  🆎 ⓞ 𝚅𝙸𝚂𝙰
  closed Monday dinner, Tuesday and first 3 weeks January – **M** 9.00/15.00 **t.** and a la carte
  ⓛ 3.60.

 XX **Simmons**, 68 The Mint, TN31 7EW, ✆ 222026 – 🔼 🆎 ⓞ 𝚅𝙸𝚂𝙰
  closed Saturday lunch, Sunday dinner, Monday, 3 weeks February and 6 to 8 October –
  M 7.95/9.95 **t.** and a la carte 13.30/15.45 **t.** ⓛ 3.00.

 X **Landgate Bistro**, 5-6 Landgate, TN31 7LH, ✆ 222829 – 🔼 🆎 ⓞ 𝚅𝙸𝚂𝙰
  closed Sunday and Monday – **M** (dinner only) a la carte 8.00/11.80 **t.** ⓛ 1.95.

 at Playden N : 1 m. on A 268 – ✉ ☎ 0797 Rye :

 🏠 Playden Oasts, TN31 7UL, on A 268 ✆ 223502, 🐎 – 📺 ⏤wc 🛁wc ☎ 🅿 🔼 🆎 𝚅𝙸𝚂𝙰
  April-December – **M** a la carte 9.10/14.50 **t.** ⓛ 2.50 – **8 rm**.

 at Peasmarsh NW : 4 m. on A 268 – ✉ Rye – ☎ 079 721 Peasmarsh :

 🏠 **Flackley Ash** (Best Western), London Rd, TN31 6YH, ✆ 651, 🐎 – 📺 ⏤wc 🛁wc 🅿 🔼 🆎
  ⓞ 𝚅𝙸𝚂𝙰
  M (bar lunch)/dinner 9.50 **t.** and a la carte ⓛ 3.25 – **20 rm** ⏤ 37.00/56.00 **st.** – SB 50.00/70.00 **st.**

ALFA-ROMEO, CITROEN Cinque Ports St. ✆ 3196   RENAULT Rye Harbour Rd ✆ 4888
AUSTIN-ROVER-JAGUAR, LAND ROVER-RANGE
ROVER Fishmarket Rd ✆ 223334

SAFFRON WALDEN Essex **404** U 27 – pop. 11 879 – ECD : Thursday – ☎ 0799.

See : Parish Church★ (Perpendicular) – Audley End House★ (Jacobean : interior★★) *AC*.

🅱 Corn Exchange, Market Sq. ✆ 24282.

♦London 46 – ♦Cambridge 15 – Chelmsford 25.

 🏠 **Saffron**, 10-18 High St., CB10 1AY, ✆ 22676, Telex 81653 – 📺 ⏤wc 🛁wc ☜ 🅿 🔼 𝚅𝙸𝚂𝙰
  closed 24 to 30 December – **M** *(closed Sunday to non-residents)* 11.95 **st.** and a la carte ⓛ 2.55
  – ⏤ 2.50 – **18 rm** 17.50/42.00 **st.**

 X **Staircase**, 21 High St., CB10 1AT, ✆ 22226 – 🔼 𝚅𝙸𝚂𝙰
  M (dinner only) a la carte 10.50/24.05 **st.**

AUSTIN-ROVER High St. ✆ 27909   VAUXHALL-OPEL 13-15 Station St. ✆ 23238
AUSTIN-ROVER 66 High St. ✆ 23597

ST. AGNES Cornwall **403** E 33 The West Country G. – pop. 2 421 – ECD : Wednesday – ☎ 087 255.

See : St. Agnes Beacon★★ (☀★★).

♦London 302 – Newquay 12 – Penzance 26 – Truro 9.

 ♨ **Trevaunance Point** ⚓, Quay Rd, Trevaunance Cove, TR5 0RZ, ✆ 3235, ≤ bay and cliffs,
  – 📺 ⏤wc 🅿 🔼 🆎 ⓞ 𝚅𝙸𝚂𝙰 ⚘
  M 6.95/11.00 **t.** and a la carte ⓛ 3.50 – **10 rm** ⏤ 22.00/50.00 **t.** – SB (except summer)(weekends
  only) 59.50/63.50 **st.**

 ↑ **Sunholme** ⚓, Goonvrea Rd, Goonvrea, TR5 0NW, SW : 1 m. by B 3277 ✆ 2318, 🐎 – 🛁wc
  🅿 🔼 𝚅𝙸𝚂𝙰
  April-October – **10 rm** ⏤ 11.00/27.00 **t.**

 ↑ **Rosevean**, Rosemundy Rd, TR5 0UD, ✆ 2277, 🐎 – 🛁wc 🅿
  closed October – **9 rm** ⏤ 9.50/22.00 **s.**

 at Mithian E : 2 m. by B 3285 – ✉ ☎ 087 255 St. Agnes :

 🏠 **Rose-in-Vale** ⚓, TR5 0QD, ✆ 2202, ≤, ⚓ heated, 🐎 – ⏤wc 🛁wc 🅿 🔼 𝚅𝙸𝚂𝙰
  M (bar lunch)/dinner 7.95 **t.** and a la carte ⓛ 2.55 – **15 rm** ⏤ 13.50/30.00 **t.** – SB (October-May)
  36.50 **st.**

FORD Trevellas Garage, Trevellas ✆ 2372

ST. ALBANS Herts. 404 T 28 – pop. 76 709 – ECD : Thursday – ✪ 0727.

See : Site★★ – Cathedral and Abbey Church★ (Norman Tower★).

Envir. : Hatfield House★★★ *AC* (gardens★ and Old Palace★) E : 6 m. – Verulamium (Roman remains★ and museum) *AC*, W : 2 m.

ᕋ Batchwood Hall ℰ 52101.

🛈 37 Chequer St. ℰ 64511.

◆London 27 – ◆Cambridge 41 – Luton 10.

ᐰᐰ **Noke Thistle** (Thistle) Watford Rd., AL2 3DS, SW : 2 ½ m. at junction A 405 and B 4630
ℰ 54252, Telex 893834 – 📺 ☎ 🅟 🏦 🖭 AE ① VISA 🕸
M 10.25/14.25 **t.** and a la carte ⑂ 3.25 – 🖙 6.25 – **57 rm** 56.00/72.00 **st.**

🏛 **St. Michael's Manor** 🦢, Fishpool St., AL3 4RY, ℰ 64444, « Manor house, lake, ⪦ garden »,
park – 📺 ⇌wc 🏪wc ☎ 🅟 🏦 🖭 AE VISA 🕸
M (buffet dinner Sunday) 9.00/12.50 **t.** and a la carte ⑂ 3.25 – **26 rm** 🖙 45.50/58.00 **st.**

🏛 **Sopwell House** 🦢, Cottonmill Lane, AL1 2HQ, SE : 1 ½ m. by A 1081 and Mile House Lane
ℰ 64477, ⪼, park – 📺 ⇌wc ☎ 🅟 🏦 🖭 AE ① VISA 🕸
closed 27 to 30 December – **M** (closed Sunday dinner) 9.90/12.90 **t.** and a la carte – **29 rm**
🖙 33.00/64.90 **st.**, **1 suite** 79.00 **st.** – SB (weekends only) 58.00/70.00 **st.**

⋔ **Ardmore House**, 54 Lemsford Rd, AL1 3PR, ℰ 59313 – 📺 🏪wc 🅟 🕸
15 rm 🖙 20.70/36.80 **st.**

⋔ **Melford House**, 24 Woodstock Rd North, AL1 4QQ, ℰ 53642 – 🏪wc 🅟
12 rm 🖙 19.55/36.80 **st.**

✗ **La Province**, 13 George St., AL3 4ER, ℰ 52142, French rest. – 🖭 AE ① VISA
closed Saturday, Monday, 1 week after Easter, last 2 weeks August and 1 week at Christmas –
M 8.00 **t.** (lunch) and a la carte 12.25/13.80 **t.** ⑂ 3.00.

✗ **Langtry's**, London Rd, AL1 1SP, ℰ 61848, Seafood – 🖭 AE ① VISA
closed Sunday lunch, Sunday and 26 to 30 December – **M** a la carte 13.30/20.00 **t.** ⑂ 2.75.

✗ **Koh-I-Noor**, 8 George St., AL3, ℰ 53602, Indian rest.

AUSTIN-ROVER-DAIMLER-JAGUAR, ROLLS ROYCE-BENTLEY Acrewood Way, Hatfield Rd ℰ 66522
AUSTIN-ROVER Park St., Frogmore ℰ 72626
CITROEN, VAUXHALL-OPEL 66-70 High St., Potters Bar ℰ 0707 (Potters Bar) 42391
CITROEN 101 Holywell Hill ℰ 65756
FIAT Beech Rd ℰ 50871

FORD London Rd ℰ 59155
HONDA Catherine St. ℰ 54342
PEUGEOT-TALBOT 220 London Rd ℰ 63377
RENAULT 99-111 London Rd ℰ 52345
VAUXHALL-OPEL 100 London Rd ℰ 50601
VW, AUDI Valley Rd ℰ 36236
VW, AUDI 229-233 Hatfield Rd ℰ 36366

ST. ASAPH (LLANELWY) Clwyd 402 403 J 24 – pop. 3 156 – ECD : Thursday – ✪ 0745.

Envir. : Rhuddlan (castle★ 13C) *AC*, NW : 3 m.

◆London 225 – Chester 29 – Shrewsbury 59.

🏛 **Oriel House**, Upper Denbigh Rd, LL17 0LW, S : ¾ m. on A 525 ℰ 582716, ⪼ – 📺 ⇌wc
🏪wc 🆑 🅟 🏦 🖭 AE VISA 🕸
M 6.00/12.95 **st.** and a la carte ⑂ 3.00 – **18 rm** 🖙 28.50/44.00 **st.** – SB 58.00 **st.**

ALFA-ROMEO High St. ℰ 583475
PEUGEOT-TALBOT Bod Ewr Corner ℰ 582345

RENAULT The Roe ℰ 582233

ST. AUSTELL Cornwall 403 F 32 The West Country G. – pop. 20 267 – ECD : Thursday – ✪ 0726.

See : Holy Trinity★★.

Envir. : St. Austell Bay★★ (Gribbin Head ★★), E : 3 m. by A 3601 – Wheal Martyn Museum★★*AC*,
N : 2 m. on A 391 – Polkerris★, E : 9 m. by A 3082.

ᕋ Carlyon Bay ℰ 072 681 (Par) 4250, E : 2 m.

🚗 ℰ 01 (London) 723 7000 ext. 3148.

◆London 281 – Newquay 16 – ◆Plymouth 38 – Truro 14.

🏯 **White Hart**, Church St., PL25 4AT, ℰ 72100 – 📺 ⇌wc 🆑 🖭 AE ① VISA 🕸
closed 25-26 December – **M** 5.85/8.50 **st.** ⑂ 2.75 – **20 rm** 🖙 18.50/32.00 **st.** – SB (weekends
only)(except summer) 35.00 **st.**

at Tregrehan E : 2 ½ m. by A 390 – ⊠ St. Austell – ✪ 072 681 Par :

✗✗ **Boscundle Manor** 🦢 with rm, PL25 3RL, ℰ 3557, « Tastefully converted 18C manor »,
🟥 heated, ⪼, park – 📺 ⇌wc 🅟 🖭 AE VISA 🕸
closed mid December-mid February – **M** (closed Sunday dinner to non residents) (restricted
lunch residents only)/dinner 16.00 **st.** ⑂ 3.00 – **11 rm** 🖙 33.00/100.00 **st.**

at Carlyon Bay E : 2 ½ m. by A 3601 – ⊠ St. Austell – ✪ 072 681 Par :

ᐰᐰ **Carlyon Bay** 🦢, PL25 3RD, ℰ 2304, ⪦ Carlyon Bay, « Extensive gardens », 🟥 heated, 🟦,
ᕋ, park, 🕸 – ⇌ 📺 🅟 🖭 AE ① VISA
M 6.90/9.80 **t.** and a la carte – **69 rm** 🖙 33.55/84.70 – SB (except Easter, summer, Christmas
and New Year) 68.30/86.00 **st.**

🏛 **Porth Avallen** 🦢, Sea Rd, PL25 3SG, ℰ 2183, ⪦ Carlyon Bay, ⪼ – 📺 ⇌wc ☎ 🅟 🏦 🖭
AE ① VISA 🕸
closed 23 December-6 January – **M** 8.00/8.25 **st.** ⑂ 3.00 – **24 rm** 🖙 23.00/49.50 **st.**

418

at Charlestown SE : 2 m. by A 390 on A 391 – ⊠ ✆ 0726 St. Austell :

☆ **Pier House**, Harbour Front, PL25 3NJ, ✆ 75272, ← – ⌂wc **P**
M (bar lunch residents only)/dinner 6.50 **t.** and a la carte ⅃ 2.70 – **12 rm** ⌷ 12.50/31.00 **t.**

AUSTIN-ROVER Carlyon Bay ✆ 072 681 (Par) 2451   PEUGEOT-TALBOT Gwendra, St. Stephen ✆ 822566
CITROEN 77 Fore St. ✆ 850 241

ST. CLEARS (SANCLER) Dyfed **403** G 28 – ⊠ ✆ 0994.
♦London 229 – Carmarthen 9 – Fishguard 37.

☆ **Forge Motel**, E : ½ m. on A 40, SA33 4NA, ✆ 230300 – ⒯ ⌂wc ☎ **P**. ⌷ A̲E̲ VISA
closed 24 to 28 December – **M** (grill rest. only) a la carte 7.40/17.20 **t.** ⅃ 2.50 – **10 rm**
⌷ 22.50/34.00 **t.**

ST. COLUMB MAJOR Cornwall **403** F 32 – pop. 1 816 – ECD : Wednesday – ⊠ Newquay –
✆ 0637 St. Columb.
♦London 287 – Newquay 6 – ♦Plymouth 46 – Truro 16.

at Tregoose S : 2 ¾ m. by Newquay road and Tregaswith road – ⊠ Newquay – ✆ 0637
St. Columb :

✗ **Tregoose Old Mill** ⌂ with rm, ✆ 880559, ☞ – ⌷ ① VISA ⌾
M 18.00/25.00 – **4 rm** ⌷ 25.00/28.00.

ST. COLUMB MINOR Cornwall – see Newquay.

ST. DAVIDS (TYDDEWI) Dyfed **403** E 28 – pop. 1 428 – ECD : Wednesday – ✆ 0437.
See : Cathedral★ 12C (site★) – Bishops Palace★ AC.
Envir. : Porthgain (cliffs ✳★★★) NE : 7 m. – Whitesand Bay★★ and St. David's Head★★ NW : 2 m.
– Newgale (←★★) by Solva (site★) E : 7 m. – Abereiddy (site★) NE : 5 m.
🛈 Pembrokeshire Coast National Park Centre, City Hall ✆ 720747 (summer only).
♦London 266 – Carmarthen 46 – Fishguard 16.

🏛 **Warpool Court** ⌂, SA62 6BN, ✆ 720300, ← sea and countryside, ⌷, ⌘, ☞, ✗ – ⒯
⌂wc ⌁wc ☎ **P**. ⌷ A̲E̲ ① VISA
closed 4 January-12 February – **M** 11.00/20.00 **t.** and a la carte ⅃ 2.85 – **25 rm** ⌷ 27.00/67.00 **t.**
– SB 53.00/86.00 **st.**

🏛 **St. Non's**, Catherine St., SA62 6RJ, ✆ 720239, ☞ – ⒯ ⌂wc ☎ **P**. ⌷ A̲E̲ ① VISA
closed January – **M** (bar lunch)/dinner 10.50 **t.** and a la carte ⅃ 2.75 – **20 rm** ⌷ 17.00/45.00 **t.**
– SB (except summer) 39.00/60.00 **st.**

🏠 **Old Cross**, Cross Sq., SA62 6SP, ✆ 720387, ☞ – ⌂wc **P**
March-October – **M** (bar lunch)/dinner 9.00 **t.** and a la carte ⅃ 2.50 – **17 rm** ⌷ 15.00/45.00 **t.** –
SB (except summer) 40.00 **st.**

⌂ **Pen-Y-Daith**, 12 Millard Park, SA62 6QH, ✆ 720720 – **P**. ⌾
closed January and February – **8 rm** ⌷ 10.00/20.00 **s.**

ST. HELENS Merseyside **402 403** L 23 – pop. 114 397 – ECD : Thursday – ✆ 0744.
⌜₉ Sherdley Park ✆ 813149, E : 2 m. on A 570.
♦London 204 – ♦Liverpool 14 – ♦Manchester 21 – Preston 25.

🏛 Fleece (Greenall Whitley), 15 Church St., WA10 1BA, ✆ 26546, Telex 629811 – ⌷ ⒯ ⌂wc ☎
P. ⌸ – **73 rm**.

AUSTIN ROVER Prescot Rd ✆ 34441   NISSAN, VOLVO Mill Lane, Newton-le-Willows
AUSTIN ROVER Elephant Lane ✆ 811565   ✆ 092 52 (Newton-le-Willows) 4411
FIAT Gaskell St. ✆ 21961   PEUGEOT-TALBOT, CITROEN Knowsley Rd ✆ 32411
FORD City Rd ✆ 26381   RENAULT East Lancashire Rd ✆ 27373
LADA Dentons Green Lane ✆ 24748   SAAB Aspinal Pl. ✆ 55333
NISSAN Jackson St. ✆ 26681   VAUXHALL-OPEL Knowsley Rd ✆ 35221

ST. IVES Cornwall **403** D 33 The West Country G. – pop. 9 439 – ECD : Thursday – ✆ 0736
Penzance – See : Site ★★ – Barbara Hepworth Museum★★*AC* Y M1 – St. Ia Church★ Y A – Barnes
Museum of Cinematography★*AC* Y M2.
🛈 The Guildhall, Street-an-Pol ✆ 797600.
♦London 319 – Penzance 10 – Truro 25.

Plan on next page

🏛 **Garrack** ⌂, Burthallan Lane, Higher Ayr, TR26 3AA, ✆ 796199, ←, ⌷, ☞ – ⌂wc ⌁wc **P**.
⌷ A̲E̲ ① VISA   Y a
M 9.50 **t.** dinner and a la carte ⅃ 3.20 – **18 rm** ⌷ 17.25/50.60 **t.** – SB (except summer) 52.00 **st.**

🏛 **Porthminster** (Best Western), The Terrace, TR26 2BN, ✆ 795221, ←, ⌷ heated, ☞ – ⌷ ⒯
⌂wc ⌁wc **P**. ⌷ A̲E̲ ① VISA   Y s
M 9.60 **t.** (dinner) and a la carte ⅃ 3.00 – **50 rm** ⌷ 26.50/75.00 – SB (winter only except Bank
Holidays) 48.00 **st.**

P.T.O. →

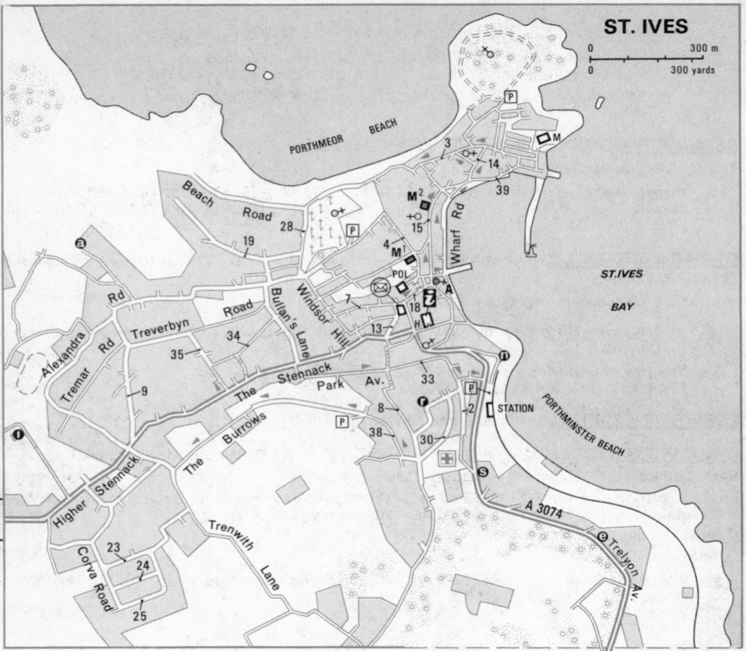

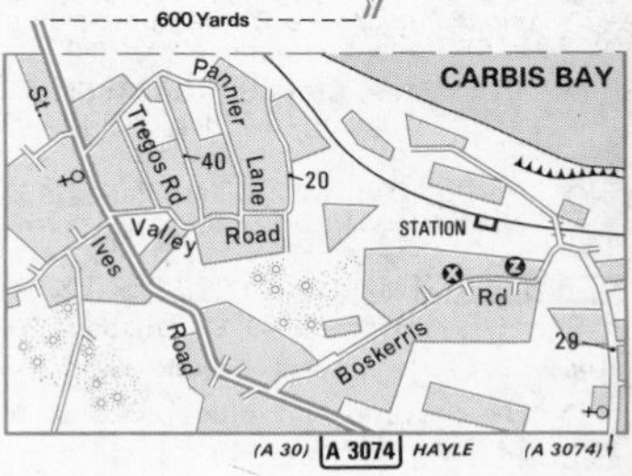

Fore Street . . . . Y 15
High Street . . . . Y 18

Albert Road . . . . Y 2
Back Road West . . . . Y 3
Barnoon Hill . . . . Y 4
Bedford Road . . . . Y 7
Bishop's Road . . . . Y 8
Carnellis Road . . . . Y 9
Chapel Street . . . . Y 13
Fish Street . . . . Y 14
Orange Lane . . . . Y 19
Parc Owles . . . . Z 20
Penwith Road . . . . Y 23
Porthia Crescent . . . . Y 24
Porthia Road . . . . Y 25
Porthmeor Hill . . . . . . Y 28
Porthrepta Road . . . . . Z 29
Talland Road . . . . Y 30
Tregenna Terrace . . . . Y 33
Trelawney Road . . . . . Y 34
Trerice Road . . . . Y 35
Trewidden Road . . . . . Y 38
Wharf (The) . . . . Y 39
Wheal Whidden . . . . . Z 40

Pedn-Olva, Porthminster Beach, TR26 2EA, ℘ 796222, ≤ coastline – wc wc Ⓟ. VISA. Y **n**
closed late January and early February – **M** (bar lunch)/dinner 7.00 **t.** 2.80 – **24 rm** (dinner included) 20.00/58.00 **t.** – SB (except summer) 44.00 **st.**

Dean Court, Trelyon Av., TR26 2AD, ℘ 796023, ≤ St. Ives and bay – TV wc wc Ⓟ. Y **e**
Mid April-mid October – **M** (dinner only) 6.00 **st.** 2.50 – **12 rm** 20.00/46.00 **st.** – SB (except summer) 42.00/48.00 **st.**

Old Vicarage, Parc-an-Creet, TR26 2ET, ℘ 796124, – wc Ⓟ. VISA Y **i**
closed 1 week at Christmas – **8 rm** 13.00/25.00 **t.**

Pedn Olva Rock, Porthminster Beach, TR26 2EA, ℘ 797710, ≤ – TV wc wc. Y **n**
closed mid December-mid February – **10 rm** 15.00/28.00 **t.**

Pondarosa, 10 Porthminster Terr., TR26 2DQ, ℘ 795875 – Ⓟ. Y **r**
March-October – **9 rm** 8.00/28.00 **st.**

at Carbis Bay S : 1 ¾ m. on A 3074 – ✉ St. Ives – 0736 Penzance :

Boskerris, Boskerris Rd, TR26 2NQ, ℘ 795295, ≤, heated, – wc Ⓟ. Z **x**
Easter-October – **M** (bar lunch)/dinner 10.00 **st.** 2.50 – **20 rm** 18.00/40.00 **t.** – SB (except summer) 47.00 **st.**

St. Uny, Boskerris Rd, TR26 2NQ, ℘ 795011, ≤, – wc Ⓟ. VISA. Z **z**
Easter-mid October – **M** (bar lunch)/dinner 9.50 **t.** 2.75 – **31 rm** 16.00/50.00 **t.**

at Lelant SE : 3 ¼ m. on A 3074 – Y – ⊠ Hayle – ✿ 0736 Penzance :

XX **Watermill,** Mill Down, Hayle, TR27 6LL, S : ½ m. by A 3074 ℰ 755019, 🚗 – 🅿 ⓐ AE ⓪ *VISA*

closed Tuesday – **M** (dinner only and Sunday lunch)/dinner 11.00 t. and a la carte 9.50/14.40 t. ⓵ 3.50.

AUSTIN-ROVER Long Stone Hill, Carbis Bay ℰ 0736 (Penzance) 795188

ST. IVES Cambs. 🄰🄾🄾 T 27 – pop. 13 431 – ECD : Thursday – ✿ 0480.
See : Bridge★ 15C.
◆London 75 – ◆Cambridge 14 – Huntingdon 6.

🏨 **Slepe Hall,** Ramsey Rd, PE17 4RB, ℰ 63122 – 📺 ⌷wc 🚿 🅿 ⓐ AE ⓪ *VISA*
closed 25 and 26 December – **M** 9.95 t. and a la carte ⓵ 2.95 – **14 rm** ⊊ 27.50/49.50 t. –
SB (weekends only) 59.00/82.50 **st.**

🏠 **St. Ives Motel,** London Rd, PE17 4EX, S : ¾ m. on A 1096 – ℰ 63857 – 📺 ⌷wc 🚿 🅿 ⓐ
AE ⓪ *VISA*
closed Christmas Day – **M** a la carte 7.55/14.05 t. ⓵ 3.20 – ⊊ 4.35 – **16 rm** 24.50/32.50 t.

AUSTIN-ROVER The Quadrant ℰ 62871   FORD Ramsey Rd ℰ 63184
FIAT, LANCIA Station Rd ℰ 62641

ST. JUST Cornwall 🄰🄾🄾 C 33 The West Country G. – pop. 1 903 – ECD : Thursday – ✿ 0736
Penzance.
See : Site★ – Church★ – Envir. : Cape Cornwall★ (≤★★), W : 1 ½ m. – Carn Euny★*AC*, SE : 3 m. –
Geevor Tin Mine★*AC*, N : 3 m.
◆London 325 – Penzance 7.5 – Truro 35.

🏠 **Boscean** 🦢, TR19 7QP, ℰ 788748, ≤, 🚗 – ⌷wc ⊞wc 🅿
closed January and February – **11 rm** ⊊ 14.00/38.00 t.

at Little Kelynack S : 1 ½ m. by A 3071 on B 3306 – ⊠ St. Just – ✿ 0736 Penzance :

XX **Old School,** TR19 7RH, ℰ 788911, 🚗 – 🅿 ⓐ AE ⓪
M (dinner only) a la carte 9.45/12.40 t. ⓵ 3.75.

at Botallack NW : 2 ¼ m. by B 3306 – ⊠ St. Just – ✿ 0736 Penzance :

XX **Count House,** TR19 7QQ, ℰ 788588, ≤ coastline – ⓐ AE ⓪ *VISA*
closed Sunday dinner and Tuesday in winter, Monday and 3 weeks February-March –
M (booking essential) (dinner only and Sunday lunch)/dinner a la carte 13.00/20.00 t. ⓵ 2.75.

ST JUST IN ROSELAND Cornwall – see St. Mawes.

ST. KEYNE Cornwall – see Liskeard.

ST LAWRENCE I.O.W. – see Wight (Isle of) : Ventnor.

ST. LEONARDS East Sussex 🄰🄾🄾 V 31 – see Hastings and St. Leonards.

ST. MARGARET'S BAY Kent 🄰🄾🄾 Y 30 – see Dover.

ST. MARY'S Cornwall 🄰🄾🄾 ㉚ – see Scilly (Isles of).

ST. MAWES Cornwall 🄰🄾🄾 E 33 The West Country G. – ⊠ Truro – ✿ 0326.
See : Site ★★ – Castle★*AC* (≤★) – Envir. : St. Just-in-Roseland Church★★★, N : 2 ½ m. by A 3078
– St. Anthony-in-Roseland (≤★★), 8 m. round peninsula.
◆London 299 – ◆Plymouth 56 – Truro 18.

🏨 **Tresanton** 🦢, 27 Lower Castle Rd, TR2 5DR, ℰ 270544, ≤ estuary, « Converted cottages »,
🚗 – ⌷wc 🅿 ⓐ AE ⓪ *VISA*
closed January and February – **M** (buffet lunch)/dinner 17.00 t. – **21 rm** ⊊ 35.50/76.00 t.,
1 suite 134.00 t. – SB (except summer) 80.00/100.00 **st.**

🏨 **Rising Sun,** The Square, TR2 5DJ, ℰ 270233 – ⌷wc 🅿 ⓐ ⓪ *VISA*
M (bar lunch)/dinner 11.50 t. ⓵ 2.25 – **16 rm** ⊊ 23.00/69.00 t.

🏨 **Idle Rocks,** Tredenham Rd, TR2 5AN, ℰ 270771, ≤ harbour and estuary – 📺 ⌷wc ⊞wc.
ⓐ AE ⓪ *VISA*
April-October – **M** (bar lunch)/dinner 10.95 t. and a la carte ⓵ 2.85 – **24 rm** ⊊ (dinner inclu-
ded) 29.50/76.00 t.

🏠 **St. Mawes,** The Seafront, TR2 5DW, ℰ 270266, ≤ – 📺 ⌷wc ⊞wc. ⓐ *VISA*
closed December and January – **M** 8.00/11.50 **st.** ⓵ 2.80 – **8 rm** ⊊ 18.00/44.00 **st.**

at St. Just in Roseland N : 2 ½ m. on A 3078 – ⊠ Truro – ✿ 0326 St. Mawes :

🏠 **Rose da Mar** 🦢, TR2 5JB, N : ¼ m. on B 3289 ℰ 270450, ≤, 🚗 – ⌷wc 🅿 🍽
April-October – **M** (dinner only) 9.50 t. ⓵ 2.35 – **8 rm** ⊊ 15.40/34.80 t.

ST. NEOTS Cambs. **404** T 27 – pop. 12 468 – ✆ 0480 Huntingdon.

See : St. Mary's Church★ 15C – ⚐18 Eynesbury Hardwicke, St. Neots Leisure Centre ✆ 215153, SE : 2 m.

◆London 60 – Bedford 11 – ◆Cambridge 17 – Huntingdon 9.

🏠 **Stephenson's Rocket Motel,** Crosshall Rd, NW : 1 m. on A 45 ✆ 72773 – 📺 🛏wc ☎
🅿 **🔊** **AE** **①** **VISA** **※**
closed 25 and 26 December – **M** (bar lunch Sunday) 7.50/12.50 **t.** and a la carte ⌾ 2.50
– ☲ 3.50 – **9 rm** 30.00/37.50 **t.**

XX **Chequers Inn,** St. Mary's St., Eynesbury, PE19 2TA, S : ½ m. on B 1043 ✆ 72116 – **🅿** **🔊** **AE**
① **VISA**
closed Christmas Night – **M** a la carte 13.00/20.40 **t.** ⌾ 3.75.

XX Raj Douth, 12 High St., ✆ 219626, Indian rest.

at Wyboston SW : 2 ½ m. by A 45 on A 1 – ⊠ St. Neots – ✆ 0480 Huntingdon :

🏠 **Wyboston Lakes Motel** without rest., Great North Rd, MK44 3AL, N : ½ m. at junction of
A 45 and A 1 ✆ 219949 – 📺 🛏wc **🅿** **🔊** **VISA** **※**
M 10.00/15.00 **t.** and a la carte ⌾ 3.00 – ☲ 3.00 – **38 rm** 29.90/32.40 **t.**

AUSTIN-ROVER 42 Huntingdon St. ✆ 73237   FORD Cambridge St. ✆ 73321

*Es ist empfehlenswert, **in der Hauptsaison** und vor allem*
in Urlaubsorten, Hotelzimmer im voraus zu bestellen.
Benachrichtigen Sie sofort das Hotel, wenn Sie ein bestelltes
Zimmer nicht belegen können.
Wenn Sie an ein Hotel im Ausland schreiben, fügen Sie Ihrem Brief
einen internationalen Antwortschein bei (im Postamt erhältlich).

SALCOMBE Devon **403** I 33 The West Country G. – pop. 1 968 – ECD : Thursday – ✆ 054 884.

Envir. : Kingsbridge ★, N : 5 m. by A 381 Y – Prawle Point (≤★★★), E : 16 m. around coast by A 381 Y – Sharpitor Overbecks Museum and Garden (≤★★) *AC*, SW : 2 m. by South Sands Z.

🛈 Main Rd ✆ 2736 (summer only).

◆London 243 – Exeter 43 – ◆Plymouth 27 – Torquay 28.

SALCOMBE

Town plans
roads most used
by traffic and those
on which guide listed
hotels and restaurants
stand are fully drawn ;
the beginning only
of lesser roads
is indicated.

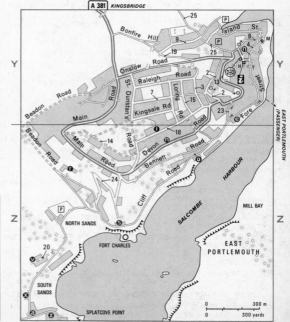

Marine, Cliff Rd, TQ8 8JH, ✆ **2251, Telex 45185,** ≤ **estuary,** heated, – TV ☎ P. AE VISA.
Y **e**
closed January-8 March – **M** (buffet lunch Monday to Saturday)/dinner 18.50 **t.** and a la carte 3.50 – **51 rm** 32.00/84.00 **t., 1 suite** 84.00/106.00 **t.** – SB (except summer) 64.00/72.00 **st.**

Tides Reach, South Sands, TQ8 8LJ, ✆ **3466,** ≤ **estuary,** , squash – TV ☎ P. AE VISA
Z **x**
March-mid November – **M** (buffet lunch)/dinner 13.25 **st.** and a la carte 3.50 – **42 rm** (dinner included) 42.50/106.00 **t.** – SB (except summer) 72.50/82.50 **st.**

South Sands, South Sands, TQ8 8LL, ✆ **3741,** ≤, – TV wc ☎ P. AE VISA
M 7.50/15.50 **t.** 2.40 – **29 rm** 35.00/65.00 **t.** – SB (September-May) 70.00 **st.** Z **a**

Bolt Head (Best Western), South Sands, TQ8 8LL, ✆ **3751,** ≤ **estuary,** heated – TV wc ☎ P. AE VISA
Z **z**
2 April-mid November – **M** (buffet lunch)/dinner 15.95 **st.** 3.50 – **29 rm** 29.00/92.00 **st.** – SB (spring and autumn only) 58.00/66.00 **st.**

St. Elmo, Sandhills Rd, TQ8 8JR, ✆ **2233,** ≤, heated, – TV wc wc P. VISA.
Z **r**
April-October – **M** (bar lunch)/dinner 12.50 **t.** – **23 rm** 25.00/60.00 **t.** – SB (except summer) 58.00/62.00 **st.**

Castle Point, Sandhills Rd, TQ8 8JP, ✆ **2167,** ≤ **estuary,** – TV wc wc P. VISA.
Z **s**
Easter-mid October – **M** (bar lunch)/dinner 9.95 **t.** 2.55 – **20 rm** 15.00/54.00 **t.**

Grafton Towers, Moult Rd, TQ8 8LG, ✆ **2882,** ≤ **estuary,** – TV wc wc P. VISA
Z **v**
April-September – **M** (bar lunch)/dinner 9.50 **t.** 3.00 – **15 rm** 15.00/49.00 **t.** – SB (spring only) 40.00/46.00 **st.**

Bay View, Bennett Rd, TQ8 8JJ, ✆ **2238,** ≤ **estuary** – P. VISA. Z **o**
March-October – **10 rm** 20.00/40.00 **t.**

Woodgrange, Devon Rd, TQ8 8HJ, ✆ **2439,** – TV wc wc P. AE VISA Z **n**
Mid March-mid October – **10 rm** 12.00/30.00 **st.**

Penn Torr, Herbert Rd, TQ8 8HN, ✆ **2234** – wc wc P. Z **i**
Easter-September – **10 rm** 11.00/26.00.

Wellingtons, 84-86 Fore St., TQ8 8BY, ✆ **3385** – AE VISA Y **n**
April-October – **M** *(closed Sunday in April, May and October)* (dinner only) 7.95 **t.** and a la carte 9.85/16.85 3.50.

at Soar Mill Cove SW : 3 m. via Cliff Rd – Y – ✉ Malborough – ☎ 0548 Kingsbridge :

Soar Mill Cove, TQ7 3DS, ✆ **561566,** ≤, heated, – TV wc P. VISA.
Mid March-mid October – **M** (bar lunch)/dinner 16.00 **t.** 4.00 – **14 rm** 30.00/96.00 **t.**

at Hope Cove W : 4 m. by A 381 – Y – ✉ ☎ 0548 Kingsbridge :

Cottage, TQ7 3HJ, ✆ **561555,** ≤ **Bolt Tail and Bigbury Bay,** – wc wc ☎ P
closed 2 to 30 January – **M** (bar lunch Monday to Saturday)/dinner 10.95 **st.** and a la carte 3.90 – **35 rm** 22.00/40.50 **st.** – SB (November-Easter) 39.30/60.90 **st.**

Lantern Lodge, TQ7 3HE, ✆ **561280,** ≤, , – wc wc P. AE VISA.
March-November – **M** (bar lunch)/dinner 13.00 **st.** 3.00 – **14 rm** 21.50/60.50 **st.**

Port Light, Bolberry Down, TQ7 3DY, SE : 1 ¾ m. ✆ **561384,** ≤, – wc P. VISA
Easter-October – **M** (bar lunch)/dinner 11.50 **t.** 3.50 – **6 rm** 16.15/45.70 **t.** – SB (except summer) 43.00/49.00 **st.**

" Short Breaks " (SB)

De nombreux hôtels proposent des conditions avantageuses
pour un séjour de deux nuits
comprenant la chambre, le dîner et le petit déjeuner.

SALISBURY Wilts. 403 404 O 30 **The West Country G.** – pop. 36 890 – ECD : Wednesday – ☎ 0722.

See : Site ★★★ – Cathedral★★★*AC* Z – The Close★ Z : Mompesson House★★*AC* Z **A,** Military Museum★★*AC* Z **M1** – Salisbury and South Wiltshire Museum★★*AC* Z **M2** – Sarum St. Thomas Church★ Y **B.**

Envir. : Stonehenge★★★*AC*, NW : 10 m. by A 345 Y – Wilton House★★★*AC*, W : 2 ½ m. by A 30 Y – Old Sarum★*AC* N : 2 m. by A 345 Y – at Wilton Village, Royal Wilton Carpet Factory★*AC*, W 2 ½ m. by A 30 Y – Heale House★*AC* N : 7 m. by Stratford Rd Y – Wardour Castle★*AC*, W : 10 m. by A 30. Y.

18, 9 Salisbury and South Wilts., Netherhampton ✆ 742645, by A 3094 Z – 18 High Post, Great Durnford ✆ 072 273 (Middle Woodford) 231, N : 4 m. by A 345. Y.

10 Endless St. ✆ 334956.

♦London 91 – Bournemouth 28 – ♦Bristol 53 – ♦Southampton 23.

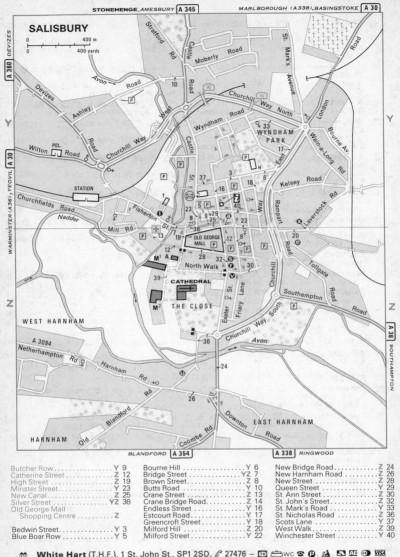

Butcher Row	Y 9
Catherine Street	Z 12
High Street	Z 19
Minster Street	Y 23
New Canal	Z 25
Silver Street	YZ 38
Old George Mall	
Shopping Centre	Z
Bedwin Street	Y 3
Blue Boar Row	Y 5

Bourne Hill	Y 6
Bridge Street	YZ 7
Brown Street	Z 8
Butts Road	Y 10
Crane Street	Z 13
Crane Bridge Road	Z 14
Endless Street	Y 16
Estcourt Road	Y 17
Greencroft Street	Y 18
Milford Hill	Z 20
Milford Street	Y 22

New Bridge Road	Z 24
New Harnham Road	Z 26
New Street	Z 28
Queen Street	Y 29
St. Ann Street	Z 30
St. John's Street	Z 32
St. Mark's Road	Y 33
St. Nicholas Road	Z 36
Scots Lane	Y 37
West Walk	Z 39
Winchester Street	Y 40

White Hart (T.H.F.), 1 St. John St., SP1 2SD, ℰ 27476 – 📺 📛wc ☎ 🅿 🔥 🔼 🅰🅴 ① 𝘝𝘐𝘚𝘈
M 6.95/10.50 **st.** and a la carte ⅃ 3.60 – ⊇ 5.65 – **68 rm** 45.00/57.50 **st.**   Z **s**

Old Bell Inn, 2 St. Ann St., SP1 2DN, ℰ 27958, « Converted 14C inn » – 🏠wc 🔼 🅰🅴 ① 𝘝𝘐𝘚𝘈
🛇   Z **v**
⊇ 3.50 – **7 rm** 38.00/44.00 **t.**

Cathedral, 7 Milford St., SP1 2AJ, ℰ 20144 – 🛗 ▦ rest 📺 📛wc 🏠 🔼 𝘝𝘐𝘚𝘈 🛇   Y **a**
M (buffet lunch)/dinner 6.75 **t.** and a la carte ⅃ 2.95 – **30 rm** ⊇ 23.50/48.50 **t.** – SB (except summer and Bank Holidays) 43.50/67.50 **st.**

Kings Arms, 9 St. John's St., SP1 2SB, ℰ 27629, « Part 13C and part 15C inn » – 📺 📛wc.
🔼 🅰🅴 ① 𝘝𝘐𝘚𝘈   Z **r**
M 5.95/8.00 **st.** and a la carte ⅃ 2.00 – **15 rm** ⊇ 22.50/44.00 **st.** – SB (except summer) 46.00/73.00 **st.**

424

↑ **Stratford Lodge,** 4 Park Lane, Castle Rd Y, SP1 3NP, ✎ 25177, 🚗 – 🆃🆅 ⇨wc 🗓wc 🅿. ⇔
closed December and January – **5 rm** ⇨ 18.00/30.00 **s.**

↑ **Byways House,** 31 Fowlers Rd, off Milford Hill, SP1 2QP, ✎ 28364, 🚗 – 🆃🆅 🗓wc 🅿. ⇔
17 rm ⇨ 11.00/26.00 **st.**
Z e

↑ **Glen Lyn,** 6 Bellamy Lane, Milford Hill, SP1 2SP, ✎ 27880 – 🆃🆅 🅿. ⇔
5 rm ⇨ 11.00/27.00 **s.**
YZ x

XX **Dutch Mill,** 58a Fisherton St., SP2 7RB, ✎ 23447 – 🆊 🆎 *VISA*
M 5.00 **t.** (lunch) and a la carte 10.20/11.80 **t.** 🍷 2.60.
Y i

at Redlynch SE : 8 ½ m. by A 338 – Z – off B 3080 – ✉ Salisbury – 🅰 0794 Romsey :

XX **Langley Wood** ⌛ with rm, Hamptworth Rd, SP5 2PB, SE : 1 ½ m. ✎ 390348, 🚗 – 🅿. 🆊
🆎 *VISA*
M *(closed Sunday dinner to non-residents)* (lunch by arrangement) a la carte 10.25/13.85 **t.**
🍷 2.30 – **3 rm** ⇨ 11.00/22.00 **t.**

at Odstock S : 2 ½ m. by A 338 – Z – ✉ 🅰 0722 Salisbury :

X **Yew Tree Inn,** SP5 4JE, ✎ 29786, 🚗 – 🅿. 🆊 🆎 ⓞ *VISA*
closed dinner Sunday and Monday – **M** (bar lunch Sunday and Monday) a la carte 6.50/15.75 **t.**
🍷 3.40.

at Downton S : 6 m. by A 338 – Z – ✉ 🅰 0725 Downton :

↑ **Warren,** 15 High St., SP5 3PG, ✎ 20263, 🚗 – 🅿
closed mid December-mid January – **6 rm** ⇨ 12.00/26.00 **t.**

at Harnham SW : 1 ½ m. by A 3094 – ✉ 🅰 0722 Salisbury :

🏩 **Rose and Crown** (Q.M.H.), Harnham Rd, SP2 8JQ, ✎ 27908, Telex 47224, ≤, « Riverside
location », 🚗 – 🆃🆅 ⇨wc 🗓 🔥 🅿. 🎿 🆊 🆎 ⓞ *VISA* ⇔
M 8.95/10.50 **st.** and a la carte 🍷 – **28 rm** ⇨ 50.95/76.95 **st.** – SB (weekends only) 73.00 **st.**
Z u

AUSTIN-ROVER 41-45 Winchester St. ✎ 336681
AUSTIN-ROVER, ROLLS ROYCE Southampton Rd
✎ 335251
BMW Harnham ✎ 24933
CITROEN Stephenson Rd ✎ 24136
FORD Castle St. ✎ 28443

NISSAN 114-120 Wilton Rd ✎ 28328
PEUGEOT, TALBOT Southampton Rd ✎ 335268
VAUXHALL-OPEL Brunell Rd ✎ 23522
VOLVO Telford Rd, Churchfields ✎ 333650
VW, AUDI 16 Lower Rd, Churchfields ✎ 27162

SAMLESBURY Lancs. 402 M 22 – see Preston.

SANCLER = St. Clears.

SANDIACRE Derbs. 402 403 404 Q 25 – see Nottingham (Notts.).

SANDPLACE Cornwall – see Looe.

SANDWICH Kent 404 Y 30 – pop. 4 184 – ECD : Wednesday – 🅰 030 46 (4 fig.) and 0304 (6 fig.).
🏌 18, 18, 19 Prince's, Sandwich Bay ✎ 612000 – 🅰 St. Peter's Church, Market St. ✎ 361161 ext 263/218.
♦London 72 – Canterbury 13 – ♦Dover 12 – Maidstone 41 – Margate 9.

🏩 **Bell,** The Quay, CT13 9EF, ✎ 613388 – 🆃🆅 ⇨wc 🅰 🅿 🔥 🆊 🆎 ⓞ *VISA*
M 6.50/11.50 **t.** and a la carte 🍷 4.25 – **28 rm** ⇨ 27.50/55.00 **st.** – SB (except Bank Holidays)
52.00/82.00 **st.**

ALFA-ROMEO ✎ 611654
FORD New St. ✎ 612308

LANCIA Harnet St. ✎ 613685
RENAULT Woodnesborough ✎ 812349

SANDYPARK Devon 403 I 31 – see Chagford.

SARISBURY Hants. 403 404 Q 31 – pop. 5 682 – ✉ Southampton – 🅰 048 95 Locks Heath.
♦London 90 – ♦Portsmouth 16 – ♦Southampton 6.

↑ **Dormy House,** 21 Barnes Lane, Sarisbury Green, SO3 6DA, S : 1 m. ✎ 2626, 🚗 – 🆃🆅 🗓wc
🅿. ⇔
7 rm ⇨ 9.00/22.00 **s.**

SAUNDERSFOOT Dyfed 403 F 28 – pop. 2 196 – ECD : Wednesday – 🅰 0834.
♦London 245 – Carmarthen 25 – Fishguard 34 – Tenby 3.

🏩 **St. Brides,** St. Brides Hill, SA69 9NH, ✎ 812304, Telex 48350, ≤ Saundersfoot Bay, 🏊 heated,
🚗 – 🆃🆅 ⇨wc 🗓wc 🅰 🅿 🔥 🆊 🆎 ⓞ *VISA*
M (restricted lunch) 6.45/12.95 **t.** and a la carte 🍷 3.75 – **48 rm** ⇨ 34.00/58.00 **t.** – SB (weekends
only) 45.00/65.00 **st.**

🏛 **Glen Beach** ⌛, Swallow Tree Woods, SA69 9DE, S : ½ m. by B 4316 ✎ 813430, ≤, 🚗 – 🆃🆅
⇨wc 🗓wc 🅿. 🆊 🆎 *VISA*
M (bar lunch)/dinner a la carte 8.00/14.50 **t.** 🍷 2.80 – **13 rm** ⇨ 21.00/50.00 **t.** – SB 45.00/60.00 **st.**

🏯 **Malin House,** St. Brides Hill, SA69 9NP, ✎ 812344, 🏊 heated, 🚗 – 🆃🆅 ⇨wc 🗓wc 🅿. *VISA*
⇔ – *April-October* – **M** (bar lunch)/dinner 7.00 **st.** 🍷 1.70 – **11 rm** ⇨ 13.00/26.00 **st.**

425

SAUNDERTON Bucks. 404 R 28 – ⊠ Aylesbury – ✪ 084 44 Princes Risborough.

♦London 42 – Aylesbury 9 – ♦Oxford 20.

  🏠 **Rose and Crown,** Wycombe Rd, HP17 9NP, N : on A 4010 ℰ 5299 – 📺 ⇔wc 🛁wc 🅿. 🔊
    AE 🆅🆂🅰
    closed 24 to 31 December – **M** *(closed lunch Monday and Saturday and Sunday dinner)*
    12.95 **t.** and a la carte 🍴 3.10 – **15 rm** ⇆ 25.00/55.00 **st.** – SB (except Christmas week) 45.50 **st.**

SAUNTON Devon 403 H 30 – ⊠ Braunton – ✪ 0271 Croyde.

♦London 230 – Barnstaple 8 – Exeter 48.

  🏨 **Saunton Sands,** EX33 1LQ, ℰ 890212, ≤ Saunton Sands, 🔲, 🌿, ✎, squash – 🖇 📺 🅿.
    M 6.90/12.65 **t.** and a la carte – **90 rm** ⇆ 32.50/81.65 **t.**, **3 suites** 50.60/103.50 **t.** – SB (except
    summer and Bank Holidays) 70.15/79.35 **st.**

  🏠 **Preston House,** EX33 1LG, ℰ 890472, ≤ Saunton Sands, 🌿 – ⇔wc 🛁wc 🅿. 🔊 🆅🆂🅰. ✎
    closed January and February – **M** (bar lunch)/dinner 8.50 **t.** and a la carte 🍴 3.10 – **12 rm**
    ⇆ 20.00/50.00 **t.**

SAWBRIDGEWORTH Herts. – ✪ 0279 Bishop's Stortford.

♦London 26 – ♦Cambridge 32 – Chelmsford 17.

  🏠 **Market House,** 42 Knight St., CM21 9AX, ℰ 722807 – 📺 🛁wc ☎ 🅿. 🔊 AE ① 🆅🆂🅰
    M 12.50/13.50 **t.** and a la carte 🍴 3.95 – **9 rm** ⇆ 39.50/49.50 **t.**

SAWLEY Lancs. 402 M 22 – pop. 179 – ⊠ ✪ 0200 Clitheroe.

♦ London 242 – ♦ Blackpool 39 – ♦ Leeds 44 – ♦ Liverpool 54.

  🏠 **Spread Eagle** ⌂, BB7 4NH, ℰ 41202, ↝ – 📺 ⇔wc 🛁wc ☎ 🅱 🅿. 🔊 AE ① 🆅🆂🅰. ✎
    M 7.50/11.50 **st.** and a la carte 🍴 3.00 – **9 rm** ⇆ 34.00/50.00 **st.** – SB (weekends only)
    60.00/70.00 **st.**

SCALBY North Yorks. 402 S 21 – see Scarborough.

SCARBOROUGH North Yorks. 402 S 21 – pop. 36 665 – ECD : Monday and Wednesday –
✪ 0723.

See : Castle 12C (≤★) *AC* Y.

🏌 North Cliff, North Cliff Av. ℰ 360786, NW : 2 m. by A 165 Y.

🄑 St. Nicholas Cliff ℰ 373333.

♦London 253 – ♦Kingston-upon-Hull 47 – ♦Leeds 67 – ♦Middlesbrough 52.

Plan opposite

  🏨 **Holbeck Hall** ⌂, Seacliff Rd, YO11 2XX, ℰ 374374, ≤, 🌿 – 📺 ☎ 🅿. 🔊 AE ① 🆅🆂🅰. ✎
    closed January-March – **M** 7.50/13.75 **t.** and a la carte 🍴 4.95 – **30 rm** ⇆ 28.75/69.00 **t.**, **2 suites**
    115.00/138.00 **t.** – SB 64.00/87.40 **st.**   by A 165   Z

  🏨 **Crown,** Esplanade, YO11 2AG, ℰ 373491, Telex 52277, ≤ – 🖇 📺 ☎ ⇐. 🄳. 🔊 AE ① 🆅🆂🅰
    M 6.50/10.95 **t.** and a la carte 🍴 3.00 – **80 rm** ⇆ 30.00/66.00 **t.**, **1 suite** 95.00/105.00 **t.** –
    SB 56.00/70.00 **st.**   Z i

  🏨 **Royal,** St. Nicholas St., YO11 2HE, ℰ 364333, 🔲 – 🖇 📺 ☎. 🄳. 🔊 AE ① 🆅🆂🅰. ✎
    M 7.00/12.00 **st.** and a la carte 🍴 2.50 – **137 rm** ⇆ 35.00/65.00 **st.**, **5 suites** 80.00/100.00 **st.** –
    SB (except Bank Holidays) 66.00 **st.**   Z c

  🏠 **St. Nicholas,** St. Nicholas Cliff, YO11 2EU, ℰ 364101, Telex 52351, ≤, 🔲 – 🖇 📺 ⇔wc ☎ 🅿.
    🄳. 🔊 AE ① 🆅🆂🅰   Z n
    M (bar lunch Monday to Saturday)/dinner 10.00 **t.** and a la carte 🍴 3.60 – **150 rm**, **5 suites.**

  🏠 **Palm Court,** St. Nicholas Cliff, YO11 2ES, ℰ 368161, Telex 527579, 🔲 – 🖇 📺 ⇔wc 🛁wc
    ⇐. 🄳. 🔊 AE ① 🆅🆂🅰. ✎   Z e
    M (bar lunch Monday to Saturday)/dinner 6.50 **t.** and a la carte 🍴 3.00 – **50 rm** ⇆ 24.00/42.00 **t.**
    – SB 56.00/59.00 **t.**

  ✗✗ **Grapevine,** 23 Valley Rd, YO11 2LY, ℰ 377088 – AE ① 🆅🆂🅰   Z a
    closed Sunday, 26 to 27 December and 1 to 2 January – **M** (dinner only) a la carte 9.85/14.95 **t.**
    🍴 3.50.

  ✗✗ **Lanterna,** 33 Queen St., YO11 1HQ, ℰ 363616, Italian rest. – 🔊 🆅🆂🅰   Y a
    closed Sunday, Monday and Bank Holidays – **M** (dinner only) a la carte 7.80/10.50 **t.** 🍴 2.75.

  at Scalby NW : 3 m. by A 171 – Z – ⊠ ✪ 0723 Scarborough :

  🏠 **Wrea Head** ⌂, YO13 0PB, by Barmoor Lane ℰ 378211, ≤, 🌿, park – 📺 ⇔wc 🛁wc ☎ 🅿.
    🔊 AE ① 🆅🆂🅰
    M 7.25/10.75 **st.** and a la carte 🍴 4.95 – **20 rm** ⇆ 20.00/50.00 **st.** – SB 60.00/70.00 **st.**

  at Hackness NW : 7 m. by A 171 – Z – ⊠ ✪ 0723 Scarborough :

  🏠 **Hackness Grange** (Best Western) ⌂, YO13 0JW, ℰ 82345, ≤, « 18C house », 🔲, ↝, 🌿,
    park, ✎ – 📺 ⇔wc ☎ 🅿. 🔊 AE ① 🆅🆂🅰. ✎
    M 8.00/13.50 **t.** and a la carte 🍴 3.30 – **27 rm** ⇆ 31.00/76.00 **t.** – SB 63.00/82.00 **st.**

AUSTIN-ROVER Seamer Rd ℰ 360221
CITROEN, DATSUN, PEUGEOT, TALBOT Northway ℰ 363533
FIAT Manor Rd ℰ 364111
FORD Vine St. ℰ 375581

LADA, DAIHATSU Pickering Rd. Westayton ℰ 862880
MAZDA Falconers Rd ℰ 360322
RENAULT Columbus Ravine ℰ 360791
VAUXHALL-OPEL Seamer Rd ℰ 360335

SCILLY (ISLES OF) Cornwall **403** ㉚ The West Country G. – pop. 2 653.

See : Site ★★.

Envir. : St. Martin's : Viewpoint ★★ – St. Agnes : Horsepoint ★.

Helicopter service from St. Mary's and Tresco to Penzance : ℰ 0736 (Penzance) 3871.

✈ St. Mary's Airport : ℰ 0720 (Scillonia)22677, E : 1 ½ m. from Hugh.

⇔ from Hugh Town, St. Mary's to Penzance (Isles of Scilly Steamship Co.) summer Monday/Saturday 1-2 daily; winter 4 weekly (2 h 30 mn).

🛈 Town Hall, St. Mary's ℰ 0720 (Scillonia) 22536.

Bryher – pop. 66 – ⊠ ✆ 0720 Scillonia.

See : Village on Watch Hill (≤★) – Hell Bay★.

🏠 **Hell Bay** ⟩, TR23 0PR, ℰ 22947, ⇜ – 📺 ▯wc. 🔌 **VISA** 🕱
April-October – **M** (bar lunch)/dinner a la carte 5.00/10.50 t. ▯ 2.50 – **11 rm** ⟳ (dinner included) 30.00/60.00 t.

427

St. Mary's – pop. 2 106 – ECD : Wednesday – ⊠ St. Mary's – ✪ 0720 Scillonia.
See : Garrison Walk★ (≤★★) – Peninnis Head ★.
🛬 ℰ 22692, N : 1 m. from Hugh Town.
🛈 Town Hall, ℰ 22536.

🏨 **Tregarthen's** (Best Western), TR21 0PP, ℰ 22540, ≤ Harbour and islands – 📺 📞wc ☎.
🔄 AE ① VISA ⅏
20 March-25 October – **M** (bar lunch)/dinner 11.00 **st.** 🍷 2.75 – **33 rm** ⅏ 22.50/61.00 **st.** –
SB 60.00/69.00 **st.**

🏨 **Godolphin,** Church St., TR21 0JR, ℰ 22316 – 📺 📞wc. 🔄 VISA ⅏
Mid March-11 October – **M** (bar lunch)/dinner 10.00 **t.** 🍷 2.80 – **31 rm** ⅏ 13.00/42.00 **t.**

🏨 **Star Castle** ⌂, TR21 0JA, ℰ 22317, « Elizabethan fortress », 🔄, 🌿, ⚒ – 📺 📞wc
March-October – **M** (bar lunch)/dinner 10.00 **t.** – **24 rm** ⅏ 28.00/62.00 **t.**

🏠 **Atlantic,** Hugh St., TR21 0PL, ℰ 22417, ≤ St. Mary's Harbour – 📞wc
April-September – **M** (bar lunch)/dinner 11.50 **t.** – **25 rm** ⅏ 25.00/53.00 **t.**

Tresco – pop. 285 – ⊠ Tresco – ✪ 0720 Scillonia.
See : Site★ – Abbey Gardens★*AC* – Lighthouse Way (≤★★).

🏨 **Island** ⌂, TR24 0PU, ℰ 22883, ≤ Islands, « Sub-tropical gardens », ⅃ heated, park – 📺
☎. ⅏
Mid March-mid October – **M** 16.50 **st.** (dinner) and a la carte 🍷 4.00 – **32 rm** ⅏ (dinner included) 37.00/130.00 **st.**, **1 suite** (dinner included) 134.00/152.00 **st.**

🏯 **New Inn** ⌂, TR24 0QQ, ℰ 22844, ≤, 🌿, 🌿 – 📞wc. ⅏
March-October – **M** (bar lunch)/dinner 15.00 **t.** 🍷 2.50 – **12 rm** ⅏ (dinner included) 25.00/69.00 **t.**

SCOLE Norfolk 🔢 X 26 – see Diss.

SCUNTHORPE Humberside 🔢 S 23 – pop. 79 043 – ECD : Wednesday – ✪ 0724.
Envir. : Normanby Hall★ (Regency) : Wildlife park★ *AC*, N : 4 m. – Barton-upon-Humber
(St. Mary's Church★ 12C, Old St. Peter's Church★ 10C-11C) NE : 13 ½ m. – 🛬 Kingsway ℰ 840945.
🛬 Humberside Airport : ℰ 0652 (Barnetby) 688456, E : 15 m. by A 18.
🛈 Central Library, Carlton St. ℰ 860161.
♦London 167 – ♦Leeds 54 – Lincoln 30 – ♦Sheffield 45.

🏨 **Wortley House,** Rowland Rd, DN16 1SU, ℰ 842223 – 📺 📞wc ☎ 🅿. 🚗. 🔄 AE ① VISA
M 7.50/10.50 **st.** and a la carte 🍷 3.00 – **28 rm** ⅏ 25.00/46.50 **st.** – SB (weekends only)
70.00/95.00 **st.**

🏠 **Royal,** Doncaster Rd, DN15 7DE, ℰ 868181, Telex 527479 – 📺 📞wc ☎ 🅿. 🚗. 🔄 AE ①
VISA
M *(closed Saturday lunch)* (carving rest.) a la carte 9.25/14.60 **st.** 🍷 3.35 – **33 rm**
⅏ 41.50/49.50 **st.** – SB (weekends only) 49.00 **st.**

AUSTIN-ROVER Glebe Rd ℰ 864181
BMW Old Crosby ℰ 864251
COLT Doncaster Rd ℰ 860212
FIAT Normanby Rd ℰ 861191
LADA Grange Lane North ℰ 851548
RENAULT 136-144 Ashby High St. ℰ 867474

TALBOT Smith St. ℰ 869323
TOYOTA Brigg Rd ℰ 842011
VAUXHALL-OPEL Moorwell Rd Industrial Estate
ℰ 843284
VAUXHALL-OPEL Winterton Rd ℰ 861083

SEACROFT West Yorks. 🔢 ⑩ – see Leeds.

SEAFORD East Sussex 🔢 U 31 – pop. 16 367 – ECD : Wednesday – ✪ 0323.
🛈 Station Approach ℰ 897426.
♦London 65 – ♦Brighton 14 – Folkestone 64.

XX **Bentley's,** 30a High St., BN25 1PL, ℰ 892220
closed Sunday dinner, Monday, Tuesday and February – **M** (dinner only and Sunday lunch)
6.00/10.50 **t.**

SEAHOUSES Northumb. 🔢 🔢 P 17 – pop. 1 709 (inc. North Sunderland) – ECD : Wednesday
– ✪ 0665 – 🛬 Beadnell Rd ℰ 720794.
🛈 16 Main St. ℰ 720424 (summer only).
♦London 328 – ♦Edinburgh 80 – ♦Newcastle-upon-Tyne 46.

🏠 **Beach House,** 12a St. Aidans, Seafront, NE68 7SR, ℰ 720337, ≤, 🌿 – 📺 📞wc 📶wc 🚿
🅿. 🔄 VISA
April-October – **M** (bar lunch residents only)/dinner 9.50 **t.** 🍷 3.25 – **14 rm** ⅏ 18.50/42.80 **t.** –
SB (April, May and October only) 47.00 **st.**

🏠 **St. Aidans,** Seafront, ℰ 720355, ≤ – 📺 📞wc 📶wc 🅿. 🔄 VISA
Mid February-mid November – **M** (bar lunch)/dinner 8.50 **st.** and a la carte 🍷 3.75 – **10 rm**
⅏ 12.00/39.00 **st.** – SB (except summer) 46.00/48.00 **st.**

🏯 **Olde Ship,** 9 Main St., NE68 7RD, ℰ 720200, 🌿 – 📺 📞wc 📶wc 🅿. ⅏
Easter-October – **M** (bar lunch)/dinner 7.00 **t.** 🍷 2.75 – **10 rm** ⅏ 14.50/32.00 **t.**

SEALE Surrey 404 R 30 − see Farnham.

SEATOLLER Cumbria − see Keswick.

SEATON Devon 403 K 31 − pop. 6 157 − ECD : Thursday − ✆ 0297.
🛈 The Esplanade ✆ 21660.
♦London 167 − Bournemouth 61 − Exeter 26 − Taunton 29.

⌂ **Thornfield,** 87 Scalwell Lane, EX12 2ST, ✆ 20039, ⚓ heated, ⚔ − 📺 🏠wc 🅿
9 rm ⊇ 12.00/27.00 st.

SEATON BURN Tyne and Wear 402 P 18 − see Newcastle-upon-Tyne.

SEAVIEW I.O.W. 403 404 Q 31 − see Wight (Isle of).

SEAVINGTON ST. MARY Somerset 403 L 31 − pop. 321 − ✉ Ilminster − ✆ 0460 South Petherton.
♦London 142 − Taunton 14 − Yeovil 11.

XX **Pheasant** ⟫ with rm, Water St., TA19 0QH, ✆ 40502, ⚔ − 📺 🏠wc ☎ 🅿. ⚓ ⚔
closed 26 December-3 January − **M** (dinner only) 9.50 **t.** and a la carte 12.85/16.85 **t.** ⓓ 3.50 −
10 rm ⊇ 40.00/55.00 **t.** − SB 68.75/74.25 st.

SEDBERGH Cumbria 402 M 21 − pop. 1 644 − ECD : Thursday − ✆ 0587.
🏌 The Riggs, ✆ 20993 S : 1 m.
🛈 National Park Centre, 72 Main St. ✆ 20125 (summer only).
♦London 284 − ♦Carlisle 49 − Kendal 10 − Lancaster 27 − Penrith 30.

🏠 **Oakdene Country,** Garsdale Rd, LA10 5JN, NE : 1 ½ m. on A 684 ✆ 20280, ≼, ⚔ − 🅿. ⚓
⚓ ⓪ 𝘝𝘐𝘚𝘈
closed 5 January-6 March − **M** (bar lunch)/dinner 9.85 **t.** and a la carte ⓓ 2.90 − **6 rm**
⊇ 13.50/33.00 **t.**

SEDGEFIELD Durham 401 402 P 20 − pop. 4 749 − ✉ Stockton-on-Tees (Cleveland) − ✆ 0740.
♦London 261 − Hartlepool 14 − ♦Middlesbrough 13 − ♦Newcastle-upon-Tyne 28.

🏨 **Hardwick Hall** ⟫, TS21 9EH, W : 1 ½ m. on A 177 ✆ 20253, ≼, ⚔, park − 📺 🏠wc ☎ 🅿. ⚔
17 rm
🍴 **Dun Cow Inn,** 43 Front St., TS21 3AT, ✆ 20894 − 📺 ⚙ 🅿. ⚓ ⚐ ⓪ 𝘝𝘐𝘚𝘈
M 6.90/10.50 **t.** and a la carte ⓓ 3.25 − **6 rm** ⊇ 27.00/32.00 **t.**

SEDLESCOMBE East Sussex 404 V 31 − pop. 1 315 − ✉ Battle − ✆ 042 487.
♦London 56 − Hastings 7 − Lewes 26 − Maidstone 27.

🏨 **Brickwall,** The Green, TN33 0QA, ✆ 253, ⚓ heated, ⚔ − 📺 🏠wc 🅿. ⚓ ⚐ ⓪ 𝘝𝘐𝘚𝘈
M 8.00/10.00 **st.** ⓓ 2.95 − **19 rm** ⊇ 30.00/43.00 **st.** − SB 53.00/57.50 **st.**
XX **Holmes House,** The Green, TN33 0QA, ✆ 450, ⚓ heated − ⚓ ⚐ ⓪ 𝘝𝘐𝘚𝘈
closed Saturday lunch, Sunday dinner and Monday − **M** 8.50/9.50 **st.** and a la carte
11.15/15.25 **st.** ⓓ 2.80.

SEION Gwynedd − see Port Dinorwic.

SELMESTON East Sussex 404 U 31 − pop. 187 − ✉ Polegate − ✆ 032 183 Ripe.
♦London 62 − ♦Brighton 14 − Hastings 23 − Lewes 7.5 − Maidstone 57.

XX **Sillett's Cottage,** Church Farm, BN26 6TZ, ✆ 343, « 17C farmhouse », ⚔ − 🅿. ⚓ ⚐ ⓪
𝘝𝘐𝘚𝘈
M 12.50 **t.** (dinner)/lunch a la carte 5.75/10.70 **t.**

SELSEY West Sussex 404 R 31 − pop. 7 540 − ECD : Wednesday − ✆ 0243.
♦London 78 − ♦Brighton 40 − Chichester 9.

🍴 **Thatched House,** 23 Warner Rd, off Clayton Rd, PO20 9DD, ✆ 602207, ≼, ⚔ − 🏠wc 🅿.
⚓ ⚐ ⓪ 𝘝𝘐𝘚𝘈 ⚔
M a la carte 8.00/17.55 **t.** − **7 rm** ⊇ 17.00/36.00 **st.**

SENNEN Cornwall 403 C 33 The West Country G. − pop. 772 − ✉ Penzance − ✆ 073 687.
See : Wayside Cross★ − Sennen Cove★ (≼★).
Envir. : Porthcurno★, SE : 4 m.
♦London 328 − Penzance 10 − Truro 36.

🏠 **Tregiffian** ⟫, TR19 7BE, NE : 2 ¼ m. by A 30 ✆ 408, ≼, ⚔ − 🏠wc 🏠wc 🅿. ⚓ ⓪ 𝘝𝘐𝘚𝘈 ⚔
March-October − **M** (bar lunch)/dinner 8.30 **t.** and a la carte ⓓ 3.30 − **8 rm** ⊇ 15.00/39.00 **t.** −
SB (except summer) 44.00 **st.**

SETTLE North Yorks. **402** N 21 – pop. 3 153 – ECD : Wednesday – © 072 92.

🛈 Town Hall, Cheapside ℘ 3617 (summer only).

♦London 238 – Bradford 34 – Kendal 30 – ♦Leeds 41.

- 🏨 **Falcon Manor,** Skipton Rd, BD24 9BD, ℘ 3814, ≤, ⇄ – TV ⊟wc ⊕ 🅿 ☒ ⓞ VISA
  M 6.50/10.50 **st.** and a la carte ⓘ 3.20 – **21 rm** ☲ 31.00/70.00 **st.** – SB 52.00/75.00 **st.**

- 🏨 **Royal Oak,** Market Pl., BD24 9ED, ℘ 2561 – TV ⊟wc ☎ 🅿
  M (bar lunch Monday to Saturday)/dinner a la carte 6.10/10.45 **st.** ⓘ 2.95 – ☲ 4.50 – **6 rm** 20.00/35.00 **st.**

  at Giggleswick NW : ¾ m. on A 65 – ✉ © 072 92 Settle :

- 🏠 **Woodlands** 🏖, The Mains, BD24 0AX, ℘ 2576, ≤, ⇄ – 🅿. ⅏
  closed Christmas and New Year – **8 rm** ☲ 17.00/38.00 **t.**

AUSTIN-ROVER Station Rd ℘ 2323

SEVENOAKS Kent **404** U 30 – pop. 24 493 – ECD : Wednesday – © 0732.

See : Knole★★ (15C-17C) *AC.*

Envir. : Lullingstone (Roman Villa : mosaic panels★) *AC*, N : 6 m.

🏌 Shoreham, Darenth Valley ℘ 095 92 (Otford) 2922, N : 3 m.

🛈 Buckhurst Lane ℘ 450305.

♦London 26 – Guildford 40 – Maidstone 17.

- 🏠 **Moorings,** 97 Hitchen Hatch Lane, TN13 3BE, ℘ 452589, ⇄ – TV 🕮wc 🅿. ☒ VISA. ⅏
  11 rm ☲ 19.55/29.90 **st.**

- XX **Le Chantecler,** 43 High St., TN13 1JF, ℘ 454662 – ☒ 🅰🅴 ⓞ VISA
  closed Saturday lunch, Sunday and Monday – **M** 8.50/11.50 **t.** and a la carte ⓘ 5.00.

- XX **Royal Oak** with rm, Upper High St., TN14 5PG, ℘ 451109 – TV ⊟wc 🕮wc ☎ 🅿 ☒ ⓞ VISA
  M (closed Saturday lunch and Sunday dinner) 8.50/15.00 **t.** ⓘ 3.30 – **21 rm** ☲ 35.00/40.00 **st.**

  at Ide Hill SW : 4 ¾ m. by A 2028 and A 25 on B 2042 – ✉ Sevenoaks – © 073 275 Ide Hill :

- XX **Churchill,** ℘ 500, ⇄ – 🅿 ☒ VISA
  closed Sunday dinner – **M** 18.00 **t.** ⓘ 3.50.

AUSTIN-ROVER, ROLLS ROYCE-BENTLEY London Rd ℘ 458177
BMW London Rd ℘ 450035
CITROEN Tonbridge Rd ℘ 453328
FORD The Vines ℘ 459911
NISSAN London Rd, Dunton Green ℘ 073 273 (Dunton Green) 292

RENAULT 71 St. Johns Hill ℘ 455174
SAAB Borough Green ℘ 883044
SKODA Seal Rd ℘ 454283
TOYOTA Badgers Mount ℘ 095 97 (Badgers Mount) 218
VAUXHALL-OPEL 128 Seal Rd ℘ 451337

SHAFTESBURY Dorset **403** **404** N 30 The West Country G. – pop. 4 831 – ECD : Wednesday and Saturday – © 0747.

See : ≤★ – Gold Hill★ – Local History Museum★*AC.*

Envir. : Wardour Castle★*AC*, NE : 5 m.

🛈 County Library, Bell St. ℘ 2256.

♦London 115 – Bournemouth 31 – ♦Bristol 47 – Dorchester 29 – Salisbury 20.

- 🏨 **Grosvenor** (T.H.F.), The Commons, SP7 8JA, ℘ 2282 – TV ⊟wc ☜. 🏖. ☒ 🅰🅴 ⓞ VISA
  M 8.50 **st.** and a la carte ⓘ 3.40 – ☲ 5.65 – **47 rm** 37.50/49.50 **st.**

- 🏨 **Royal Chase** (Best Western), Royal Chase Roundabout, SP7 8DB, junction of A 30 and A 350 ℘ 3355, ☒, ⇄ – TV ⊟wc ☎ 🅿 ☒ VISA
  M a la carte 6.20/12.65 **st.** ⓘ 3.25 – **32 rm** ☲ 31.50/62.00 **st.** – SB (except Christmas and New Year) 58.00/80.00 **st.**

  at Donhead St. Andrew (Wilts.) E : 3 ½ m. on A 30 – ✉ Shaftesbury – © 074 788 Donhead :

- X **Le Radier,** SP7 9LG, ℘ 324, French rest. – 🅿
  closed Sunday dinner and Monday – **M** (dinner only and Sunday lunch)(booking essential) 12.50 **st.**

  at Ludwell (Wilts.) E : 5 m. on A 30 – ✉ Shaftesbury (Dorset) – © 074 788 Donhead :

- 🏠 **Grove House,** SP7 9ND, on A 30 ℘ 365, ≤, ⇄ – ⊟wc 🕮wc 🅿. ☒ VISA
  closed 10 to 31 January – **M** (closed lunch Saturday and Sunday) 4.00/9.50 **t.** ⓘ 3.00 – **11 rm** ☲ 17.00/34.00 **t.** – SB 45.00/48.00 **st.**

  at Fontmell Magna S : 5 ¼ m. on A 350 – ✉ Shaftesbury – © 0747 Fontmell Magna :

- 🏠 **Estyard House,** SP7 0PB, ℘ 811460, ⇄ – 🅿
  closed November and Christmas – **6 rm** ☲ 10.75/21.50 **st.**

AUSTIN-ROVER Salisbury Rd ℘ 2295

SHALDON Devon **403** J 32 – see Teignmouth.

SHANKLIN I.O.W. 408 404 Q 32 – see Wight (Isle of).

SHARDLOW Derbs. 402 408 404 P 25 – see Derby.

SHAW Wilts. 408 404 N 29 – see Melksham.

SHEDFIELD Hants. 408 404 Q 31 – pop. 3 291 – ✉ Southampton – ☺ 0329 Wickham.
♦London 75 – ♦Portsmouth 13 – ♦Southampton 10.

🏨 Meon Valley Golf and Country Club (Best Western), Sandy Lane, SO3 2HQ, off A 334
    ⌖ 833455, Telex 86272, ≼, ⧄, ⯃, ☞, park, ﹪, squash – 📺 ⇔wc ☎ 🅿. 🏂
    54 rm

SHEEPWASH Devon 408 H 31 – see Hatherleigh.

SHEERNESS Kent 404 W 29 – pop. 11 087 – ECD : Wednesday – ☺ 0795.
See : ≼* from the pier.
Envir. : Minster (abbey : brasses*, effigied tombs*) SE : 2 ½ m.
⚓ Shipping connections with the Continent : to the Netherlands (Vlissingen) (Olau).
🛈 Bridge Rd Car Park ⌖ 665324.
♦London 52 – Canterbury 24 – Maidstone 20.

☎ **Royal,** The Broadway, ME12 1AB, ⌖ 662626 – 📺 ⇔wc. 🅽 𝘝𝘐𝘚𝘈
    closed 24 to 26 December – **M** 8.00 **t.** and a la carte 6.50/16.50 **t.** ⌗ 3.00 – **12 rm** ⊑ 20.00/35.00 **t.**

SKODA High St. ⌖ 662730

Sie suchen ein angenehmes, ruhiges Hotel ?
Blättern Sie nicht wahllos im Führer, sondern benutzen Sie die Karten,
die den verschiedenen Regionen vorangestellt sind.

SHEFFIELD South Yorks. 402 408 404 P 23 – pop. 470 685 – ECD : Thursday – ☺ 0742.
See : Abbeydale Industrial Hamlet* (steel and scythe works) *AC*, SW : by A 621 AZ.
⯃ Tinsley Park ⌖ 442237, E : by A 57 BZ – ⯃ Beauchief, Abbey Lane ⌖ 360648, SW : by B 6068 AZ.
🛈 Town Hall Extension, Union St. ⌖ 734671/2.
♦London 174 – ♦Leeds 36 – ♦Liverpool 80 – ♦Manchester 41 – ♦Nottingham 44.

Plans on following pages

🏨 **Hallam Tower Post House** (T.H.F.), Manchester Rd (A 57), S10 5DX, ⌖ 670067, Telex
    547293, ≼ – 🛗 📺 ☎ 🅿. 🏂 🅽 ᴀᴇ ⓞ 𝘝𝘐𝘚𝘈   AZ o
    M 7.50/10.00 **st.** and a la carte ⌗ 5.65 – **135 rm** 48.00/56.00 **st., 2 suites.**

🏨 **Grosvenor House** (T.H.F.), Charter Sq., S1 3EH, ⌖ 20041, Telex 54312 – 🛗 ▤ rest 📺 ☎ 🅿.
    🏂 🅽 ᴀᴇ ⓞ 𝘝𝘐𝘚𝘈   CZ a
    M 8.00/9.00 **st.** and a la carte ⌗ 3.40 – ⊑ 6.00 – **103 rm** 48.00/56.00 **st.**

🏨 **St. George** (Swallow), Kenwood Rd, S7 1NQ, ⌖ 583811, Telex 547030, ☞, park – 🛗 📺
    ⇔wc ⬢ & 🐕. 🏂 🅽 ᴀᴇ ⓞ 𝘝𝘐𝘚𝘈   AZ r
    M 7.50/9.50 **st.** and a la carte ⌗ 4.00 – **118 rm** ⊑ 36.00/60.00 **st.** – SB (weekends only)(except
    summer) 65.00/69.00 **st.**

🏨 **Rutland,** 452 Glossop Rd, S10 2PY, ⌖ 664411, Telex 547500 – 🛗 📺 ⇔wc ☎ 🅿. 🏂 🅽 ᴀᴇ
    ⓞ 𝘝𝘐𝘚𝘈   AZ e
    M 4.25/7.25 **st.** and a la carte ⌗ 2.65 – **90 rm** ⊑ 20.00/35.00 **st.** – SB (weekends only)
    43.00/44.00 **st.**

✗ **Nirmal's,** 193 Glossop Rd, S10 2GW, ⌖ 24054, North Indian rest. – 🅽 ᴀᴇ 𝘝𝘐𝘚𝘈   CZ n
    closed Sunday lunch – **M** a la carte 5.10/8.70 **t.** ⌗ 3.00.

✗ **Zing Vaa,** 55 The Moor, S1 4PF, ⌖ 22432, Chinese rest. – ▤. 🅽 ᴀᴇ ⓞ 𝘝𝘐𝘚𝘈   CZ r
    M 4.20/17.00 **t.** and a la carte.

at Chapeltown N : 6 m. on A 6135 – AY – ✉ ☺ 0742 Sheffield :

🏨 **Staindrop Lodge,** Lane End, S30 4UH, NW : ½ m. on High Green road ⌖ 846727 – 📺
    ⇔wc ☎ 🅿. 🏂 🅽 ᴀᴇ 𝘝𝘐𝘚𝘈. ⅏
    closed 25 and 26 December – **M** (closed Sunday dinner and Bank Holidays) 6.50/12.50 **t.** ⌗ 2.95
    – **12 rm** ⊑ 35.00/42.00 **t.** – SB (weekends only) 55.00 **st.**

✗✗ **Greenhead House,** 84 Buncross Rd, S30 4SF, ⌖ 469004 – 🅿. ᴀᴇ 𝘝𝘐𝘚𝘈
    closed Sunday, Monday, last 2 weeks February, first 2 weeks September and Christmas-New
    Year – **M** (dinner only) 15.00 **st.** ⌗ 3.75.

at Worrall NW : 4 ½ m. by A 61 off A 616 – AY – ✉ Sheffield – ☺ 074 286 Oughtibridge :

🏨 Middlewood Hall ⅏, Mowson Lane, S30 3AJ, ⌖ 3919, ≼, ☞, park – 📺 ⇔wc ⬚wc ☎ 🅿.
    🏂
    17 rm, 1 suite.

MICHELIN Distribution Centre, 12 Tinsley Park Close, S9 5LX, ⌖ 433264 BY

Barrow Road .... **BY** 4
Bawtry Road .... **BY** 5
Bradfield Road .... **AY** 7

Brocco Bank .... **AZ** 8
Broughton Lane .... **BY** 10
Burngreave Road .... **AY** 12
Handsworth Road .... **BZ** 24
Hemsworth Road .... **AZ** 27
Hollinsend Road .... **BZ** 28
Holywell Road .... **BY** 29
Main Road .... **BZ** 32

Meadow Hall Road.......... **BY** 33
Middlewood Road .... **AY** 34
Newhall Road .... **BY** 36
Rustlings Road .... **AZ** 39
Westbourne Road........... **AZ** 47
Western Bank .... **AZ** 48
Whitham Road .... **AZ** 49
Woodhouse Road........... **BZ** 50

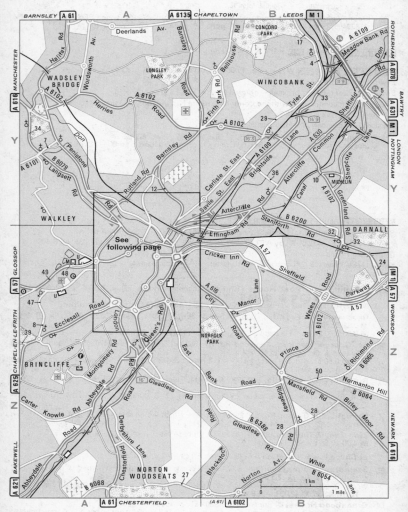

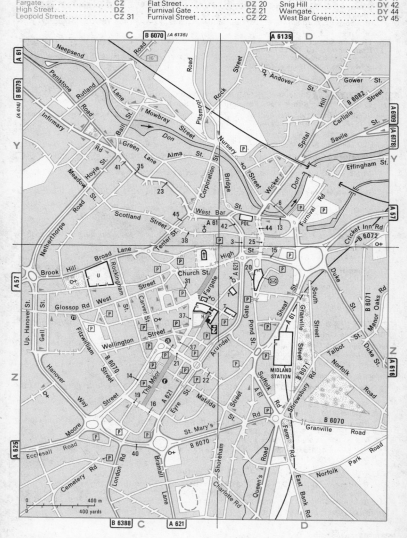

SHELDON West Midlands 403 @ 404 @ – see Birmingham.

SHEPPERTON Surrey 404 S 29 – pop. 9 643 – ✆ 0932 Walton-on-Thames.
♦London 25.

Plan : see Greater London (South-West)

🏨 **Shepperton Moat House** (Q.M.H.), Felix Lane, TW17 8NP, E : 1 ¼ m. on B 375 𝒫 241404,
Telex 928170, 🌳 – 🗲🛗 rest 📺 🚾wc ☎ 🅿 🛴 🔼 AE ⓞ VISA ⁓
    AZ **a**
M *(closed Saturday lunch)* 10.00 **st.** and a la carte 🍷 2.85 – **156 rm** ⇌ 45.00/57.00 **st.** –
SB (weekends only) 51.00 **st.**

XX **Thames Court,** Tow Path, Ferry Lane, TW17 9LJ, W : 1 ¼ m. by B 375 𝒫 221957, ≼ River
Thames, 🌳 – 🅿 🔼 AE ⓞ VISA
    by B 375 AZ
closed Saturday lunch, Sunday dinner, Monday, 1 week after Christmas and last week January
– **M** 8.50 **t.** and a la carte 9.50/13.70 **t.**

FORD Station Approach 𝒫 24811

SHEPTON MALLET Somerset 403 404 M 30 The West Country G. – pop. 6 197 – ECD : Wednes-
day – ✆ 0749 – **See** : Site ★ – SS. Peter and Paul's Church ★.
Envir. : Oakhill Manor★*AC*, N : 4 m. off A 37 – Evercreech Church Tower★, SE : 4 m. – Downside
Abbey★*AC*, N : 5 m. off A 37 and A 367 – Nunney★, W : 9 m. on A 361.
🛈 The Centre 𝒫 5258 (summer only).
♦London 127 – ♦Bristol 20 – ♦Southampton 63 – Taunton 31.

🏨 **Charlton House,** Charlton Rd, BA4 4PR, E : 1 m. on A 361 𝒫 2008, ≼, 🔼, 🌳, park, ⁓ – 📺
🛏🚾wc ☎ 🅿 🔼 AE ⓞ VISA ⁓
M 8.50/13.50 **st.** and a la carte 🍷 3.50 – **14 rm** ⇌ 35.50/45.00 **st.** – SB (except Christmas)
65.00/81.00 **st.**

XX **Bowlish House** with rm, Wells Rd, BA4 5JD, W : ½ m. on A 371 𝒫 2022, 🌳 – 📺 🛏🚾wc 🅿.
⁓
closed 24 to 27 December – **M** (dinner only) (booking essential) 14.00 **st.** 🍷 2.00 – ⇌ 2.50 –
5 rm 28.00/32.00 **st.**

X **Blostin's,** 29 Waterloo Rd, BA4 5HH, 𝒫 3648 – 🔼 ⓞ VISA
closed Sunday, first 2 weeks January, first week June and Bank Holidays – **M** (lunch by
arrangement)/dinner 9.95 **st.** and a la carte 12.40/14.40 **st.**

at Oakhill NE : 3 m. by A 37 on A 367 – ✉ ✆ 0749 Shepton Mallet :

XX **Oakhill House** ⁓ with rm, Bath Rd, BA3 5AQ, 𝒫 840180, 🌳 – 📺 🛏🚾wc 🅿. 🔼 AE ⓞ VISA
closed Saturday lunch, Sunday dinner and Monday – **M** 7.75 **t.** (lunch) and a la carte
11.65/17.10 **t.** 🍷 3.00 – **3 rm** ⇌ 25.00/40.00 **t.**

HONDA Townsend Rd 𝒫 4422   VW, AUDI High St. 𝒫 4091

SHERBORNE Dorset 403 404 M 31 The West Country G. – pop. 7 405 – ECD : Wednesday –
✆ 0935 – **See** : Site ★★★ – Abbey ★★★ – Sherborne Castle ★★*AC*.
Envir. : Sandford Orcas Manor House★*AC*, N : 4 m. by B 3148 – Purse Caundle Manor★*AC*,
NE : 5 m. by A 30 – 🚉 Clatcombe 𝒫 814431, N : 1 m.
🛈 Hound St. 𝒫 815341 (summer only).
♦London 128 – Bournemouth 39 – Dorchester 19 – Salisbury 36 – Taunton 31.

🏨 **Eastbury,** Long St., DT9 3BY, 𝒫 813131, Telex 46644, 🌳 – 📺 🛏🚾wc ☎ 🅿 🛴 🔼 AE VISA
⁓
M 8.50/13.50 **t.** and a la carte 🍷 3.00 – **12 rm** ⇌ 34.50/63.00 **t.** – SB (except summer)(weekends
only) 86.00 **st.**

🏨 **Post House** (T.H.F.), Horsecastles Lane, DT9 6BB, W : 1 m. on A 30 𝒫 813191, Telex 46522,
🌳 – 📺 🛏🚾wc ☎ 🛗 🅿 🛴 🔼 AE ⓞ VISA
M 6.95/8.95 **st.** and a la carte 🍷 5.65 – **60 rm** 42.00/52.00 **st.**

🏨 **Half Moon,** Half Moon St., DT9 3LN, 𝒫 812017 – 📺 🛏🚾wc ☎ 🅿 🔼 AE ⓞ VISA ⁓
M (carving rest.) 7.00 **t.** and a la carte – **15 rm**

at Oborne NE : 2 m. by A 30 – ✉ ✆ 0935 Sherborne :

XX **Grange** ⁓ with rm, DT9 4LA, 𝒫 813463, ≼, 🌳 – 📺 🛏🚾wc ☎ 🅿 🔼 VISA ⁓
closed Sunday dinner, Monday, last week August, first week September and 1 to 7 January –
M (dinner only and Sunday lunch) a la carte 9.60/12.70 **t.** 🍷 3.20 – ⇌ 3.00 – **3 rm** 28.00/35.00 **t.**

ALFA-ROMEO, LANCIA Long St. 𝒫 3262   MERCEDES-BENZ Yeovil Rd 𝒫 3350
AUSTIN-ROVER Digby Rd 𝒫 2436

SHERE Surrey 404 S 30 – see Guildford.

SHERIFF HUTTON North Yorks. 402 Q 21 – ✉ York – ✆ 034 77.
♦London 313 – York 10.

🏠 **Rangers House** ⁓, The Park, YO6 1RH, S : 1 ¼ m. off Strensall road 𝒫 397, 🌳 – 🛏🚾wc
🛏🚾wc 🅿. ⁓
closed 8 to 31 January – **6 rm** ⇌ 19.00/42.00 **st.**

434

SHERINGHAM Norfolk 404 X 25 – pop. 6 861 – ECD : Wednesday – ✆ 0263 Cromer.
Envir. : Cromer : SS. Peter and Paul's Church (tower ≼★).
🚉 Station Approach ✆ 824329 (summer only).
♦London 128 – Cromer 4 – ♦Norwich 27.

  ↑ **Beacon,** 1 Nelson Rd, NR26 8BT, ✆ 822019, ⇌ – 🅿 ◪ VISA ⋇
      April-October – **8 rm** ⇌ 12.50/25.00 **st.**

SHIFNAL Salop 402 403 404 M 25 – pop. 6 094 – ECD : Thursday – ✉ ✆ 0952 Telford.
See : St. Andrew's Church★ 12C-16C.
Envir. : Weston Park★ 17C (paintings★★) *AC*, NE : 5 m.
♦London 150 – ♦Birmingham 28 – Shrewsbury 16.

  🏨 Park House, Park St., TF11 9BA, ✆ 460128, ⊐ heated, ⇌ – 📺 ☎ 🅿 ⅍
      19 rm, 1 suite.

AUSTIN-ROVER Chepside ✆ 460412   FORD Park St. ✆ 460631

SHINFIELD Berks. 404 R 29 – see Reading.

SHIPDHAM Norfolk 404 W 26 – pop. 1 974 – ✉ Thetford – ✆ 0362 Dereham.
♦London 102 – East Dereham 5 – ♦Norwich 21 – Watton 6.

  XX **Shipdham Place** ⤳ with rm, Church Close, IP25 7LX, on A 1075 ✆ 820303, ⇌ – ⊟wc ☎
      🅿 ⋇
      closed Sunday to Tuesday January-17 March and 21 to 27 December – **M** (lunch by arrangement
      to residents only) (booking essential)/dinner 18.50 **t.** ⅙ 4.25 – **9 rm** ⇌ 35.00/60.00 **t.**

SHIPLEY West Yorks. 402 O 22 – pop. 28 815 – ECD : Wednesday – ✆ 0274 Bradford.
♦London 216 – Bradford 4 – ♦Leeds 12.

  X **Aagrah,** 27 Westgate, BD18 3QX, ✆ 594660, Indian rest. – ◪ 𝔸𝔼 ⓘ VISA
      closed 23 August and 25 December – **M** (lunch by arrangement)/dinner 9.50 **t.** and a la carte
      5.20/7.60 **t.** ⅙ 2.40.

SHIPSTON-ON-STOUR Warw. 403 404 P 27 – pop. 3 072 – ✆ 0608.
♦London 85 – ♦Birmingham 34 – ♦Oxford 29.

  XX **Old Mill** with rm, Mill St., CV36 4AW, on B 4035 ✆ 61880, ⇌ – ⊟wc 🛉wc 🅿 ◪ 𝔸𝔼 ⓘ
      VISA
      closed 26 and 27 December – **M** *(closed Sunday dinner)* 17.50 **t.** ⅙ 3.00 – **5 rm** ⇌ 22.50/37.50 **t.**
      – SB 52.50/57.50 **t.**

  X **White Bear** with rm, High St., CV36 4AJ, ✆ 61558 – 📺 ⊟wc 🛉wc 🅿 ◪ 𝔸𝔼 ⓘ VISA
      M *(closed Sunday dinner and Bank Holidays)* (bar lunch)/dinner a la carte 8.90/13.35 **t.** ⅙ 2.65
      – **9 rm** ⇌ 25.00/40.00 **t.** – SB 50.00/60.00 **st.**

FORD Church St. ✆ 61425   SUBARU Tredington ✆ 61544

SHIPTON GORGE Dorset – see Bridport.

SHIPTON-UNDER-WYCHWOOD Oxon. 403 404 P 28 – pop. 2 558 – ECD : Wednesday –
✆ 0993.
♦London 81 – ♦Birmingham 50 – Gloucester 37 – ♦Oxford 25.

  🏨 **Shaven Crown,** OX7 6BA, ✆ 830330, « 14C hospice » – 📺 ⊟wc 🅿 ◪ VISA ⋇
      M (bar lunch Monday to Saturday)/dinner a la carte 10.50/15.50 **t.** – **8 rm** ⇌ 22.00/52.00 **t.** –
      SB (except weekends in summer) 58.00/62.00 **st.**

  X **Lamb Inn** with rm, High St., OX7 6DQ, ✆ 830465, ⇌ – ⊟wc 🅿 ◪ 𝔸𝔼 ⓘ VISA ⋇
      M (bar lunch)/dinner 16.25 **t.** ⅙ 3.00 – **5 rm** ⇌ 25.00/37.50 **t.**

PEUGEOT-TALBOT Milton-Under-Wychwood, nr Shipton-Under-Wychwood ✆ 830335

SHOREHAM-BY-SEA West Sussex 404 T 31 – ECD : Wednesday – ✆ 079 17 (4 & 5 fig.) or 0273
(6 fig.).
♦London 58 – ♦Brighton 5 – Worthing 5.

  ↑ Pende-Shore, 416 Upper Shoreham Rd, BN4 5NE, ✆ 2905 – 📺 ⊟wc 🅿
      14 rm.

SHORNE Kent 404 V 29 – pop. 2 565 – ✉ Gravesend – ✆ 047 482.
♦London 27 – Gravesend 4 – Maidstone 12 – Rochester 4.

  🏨 **Inn on the Lake,** DA12 3HB, on A 2 ✆ 3333, Telex 966356, ≼, ⍦, ⇌, park – 📺 ⊟wc ☎
      🅿 ⅍ ◪ 𝔸𝔼 ⓘ VISA ⋇
      M a la carte 12.55/19.55 **st.** ⅙ 4.00 – **78 rm** ⇌ 44.00/60.00 **st.**

SHREWSBURY Salop **402** **403** L 25 – pop. 57 731 – ECD : Thursday – ☎ 0743.

See : Abbey Church★ 11C-14C **D** – St. Mary's Church★ (Jesse Tree window★) **A** – Grope Lane★ 15C.

Envir. : Wroxeter★ (Roman city and baths) *AC*, SE : 6 m. by A 458 and A 5 – Condover Hall★ (15C) *AC*, S : 5 m. by A 49.

⌘ Meole Brace ℰ 64050, S : by A 49.

🗓 The Square ℰ 50761.

♦London 164 – ♦Birmingham 48 – ♦Cardiff 10 – Chester 43 – Derby 67 – Gloucester 93 – ♦Manchester 68 – ♦Stoke-on-Trent 39 – ♦Swansea 124.

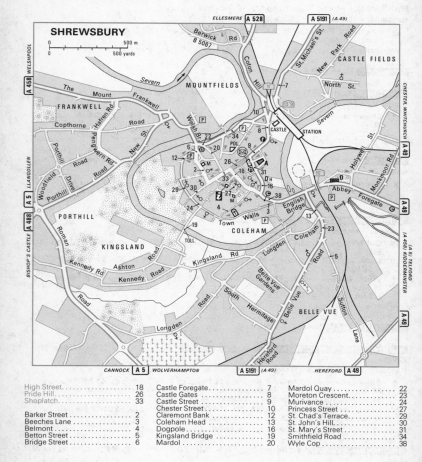

High Street................18	Castle Foregate................7	Mardol Quay................22
Pride Hill................26	Castle Gates................8	Moreton Crescent................23
Shoplatch................33	Castle Street................9	Murivance................24
	Chester Street................10	Princess Street................27
Barker Street................2	Claremont Bank................12	St. Chad's Terrace................29
Beeches Lane................3	Coleham Head................13	St. John's Hill................30
Belmont................4	Dogpole................16	St. Mary's Street................31
Betton Street................5	Kingsland Bridge................19	Smithfield Road................34
Bridge Street................6	Mardol................20	Wyle Cop................38

🏨 **Prince Rupert,** Butcher Row, SY1 1UQ, ℰ 52461, Telex 35100 – 🛗 ▤ rest 📺 ⌷wc ☎ **ℙ**
🛁 ﭏ AE ⓪ *VISA* ✸ **n**
M 7.75/10.00 **t.** and a la carte ⌘ 3.75 – **70 rm** ⟷ 42.00/58.00 **st.**, **4 suites** 58.00/68.00 **st.** – SB (weekends only) 60.00/64.00 **st.**

🏨 **Lion** (T.H.F.), Wyle Cop, SY1 1UY, ℰ 53107 – 🛗 📺 ⌷wc ☎ **ℙ** 🛁 ﭏ AE ⓪ *VISA* **c**
M 4.95/9.75 **st.** and a la carte ⌘ 3.40 – ⟷ 5.65 – **59 rm** 40.00/52.50 **st.**

🏨 **Lord Hill** (De Vere), 131 Abbey Foregate, SY2 6AX, ℰ 52601, Telex 35104 – 📺 ⌷wc ﭏwc
☎ **ℙ** 🛁 ﭏ AE ⓪ *VISA* **e**
M (buffet lunch)/dinner 12.50 **st.** ⌘ 4.50 – **46 rm** ⟷ 26.00/50.00 **st.** – SB (weekends only) 49.00/52.00 **st.**

436

XXX **Antonio's,** Victorian Arcade, Hills Lane, SY1 1PS, ☏ 242244 – AE VISA **o**
closed Sunday dinner, Monday lunch and Bank Holidays – **M** 5.50 **t.** (lunch) and a la carte 10.50/14.55 **t.**

XX **Old Police House,** Castle Court, Castle St, SY1 2BG, ☏ 60668 – VISA **r**
closed Saturday lunch, Sunday, 20 April and 25-26 December – **M** 6.50/12.45 **t.** 2.50.

at Albrighton N : 3 m. on A 528 – ✉ Shrewsbury – ☎ 0939 Bomere Heath :

XX **Albright Hussey,** Broad Oak, SY4 3AF, ☏ 290523, « 16C timbered manor house and gardens » – P. AE VISA
M 8.50/14.00 **st.** and a la carte 13.30/17.95 **st.** 2.50.

at Dorrington S : 7 m. on A 49 – ✉ Shrewsbury – ☎ 074 373 Dorrington :

XX **Country Friends,** SY5 7JD, ☏ 707, – P. AE VISA
closed Monday lunch and Sunday – **M** 9.00 **t.** and a la carte 10.00/14.10 **t.** 2.65.

AUSTIN-ROVER Harlescott ☏ 52288
CITROEN 159 Abbey Foregate ☏ 57711
DAIHATSU Featherbed Lane ☏ 241445
FORD Coton Hill ☏ 3631
LADA Featherbed Lane ☏ 60303
MERCEDES-BENZ Harlescoff ☏ 241191
PEUGEOT-TALBOT Featherbed Lane ☏ 69611
SAAB Westbury Garage ☏ 241 445
VAUXHALL-OPEL Greyfriars ☏ 52321
VOLVO Featherbed Lane ☏ 51251
VW, AUDI English Bridge ☏ 52471

SHURDINGTON Glos. 403 404 N 28 – see Cheltenham.

SIBSON Leics. – see Nuneaton (Warw.).

SIDFORD Devon 403 K 31 – see Sidmouth.

SIDMOUTH Devon 403 K 31 The West Country G. – pop. 10 808 – ECD : Thursday – ☎ 039 55.
Envir. : Seaton, headlands (≤★★), E : 9 m. – Branscombe★, E : 9 m. – Colyton★, E : 10 m.
18 Cotmaton Rd ☏ 3023.
The Esplanade ☏ 6441 (summer only).
♦London 170 – Exeter 14 – Taunton 27 – Weymouth 45.

Victoria, The Esplanade, Peak Hill, EX10 8RY, ☏ 2651, ≤, heated, , , – TV ☎ P. AE VISA.
M 7.75/12.65 **t.** and a la carte – **61 rm** 39.10/96.60 **t.**, **2 suites** 98.90/110.40 **t.**

Riviera, The Esplanade, EX10 8AY, ☏ 5201, ≤ – TV wc wc ☎ . AE
M 7.00/10.00 and a la carte 2.85 – **34 rm** 23.00/68.00.

Salcombe Hill House, Beatlands Rd, EX10 8JQ, ☏ 4697, heated, , – TV wc wc ☎ P. VISA
March-October – **M** 7.00/9.00 **t.** – **32 rm** 18.00/63.00 **t.** – SB (except summer) 44.00/54.00 **st.**

Fortfield, Station Rd, EX10 8NU, ☏ 2403, , – TV wc ☎ P. VISA
M (bar lunch)/dinner 9.00 **t.** and a la carte 2.05 – **52 rm** 22.00/74.00 **t.** – SB (October-16 May) 46.00/56.00 **st.**

Royal Glen, Glen Rd, EX10 8RW, ☏ 3221, « 17C house furnished with many antiques », , – TV wc wc ☎ P. AE VISA
M 5.00/6.00 **t.** and a la carte – **37 rm** 13.75/53.90 **t.** – SB (November-April) 31.25/33.70 **st.**

Littlecourt, Seafield Rd, EX10 8HF, ☏ 5279, heated, – TV wc wc P. VISA
Mid March-mid November – **M** (bar lunch)/dinner 7.50 **t.** 3.50 – **21 rm** 18.00/25.00 **t.** – SB (except summer) 36.00/39.00 **st.**

Abbeydale, Manor Rd, EX10 8RP, ☏ 2060, – TV wc P.
April-October – **M** (bar lunch)/dinner 8.00 **t.** 2.45 – **17 rm** 19.00/48.00 **t.**

Mount Pleasant, Salcombe Rd, EX10 8JA, ☏ 4694, – wc wc P.
Easter-October – **M** (dinner only)(residents only) 7.00 **st.** 3.50 – **15 rm** 16.00/37.00 **t.** – SB (summer only) 36.00/47.00 **st.**

Woodlands, Cotmaton Cross, EX10 8HG, ☏ 3120, – wc wc P
M 3.50/4.75 3.00 – **30 rm** 12.10/37.95 **t.** – SB 33.35/50.60 **st.**

Torbay, Station Rd, EX10 8NW, ☏ 3456 – TV wc wc. VISA
M 5.00/6.50 **t.** and a la carte 2.60 – **28 rm** 10.50/40.75 **t.** – SB (November-April) 27.00/39.00 **st.**

Barrington Villa, Salcombe Rd, EX10 8PU, ☏ 4252, – P
closed mid October-mid December – **9 rm** 12.50/32.30 **st.**

Salcombe Cottage, Hillside Rd, EX10 8JF, ☏ 6829, « 18C thatched cottage », – P
4 rm 15.00/24.00 **st.**

at Sidford N : 2 m. – ✉ ☎ 039 55 Sidmouth :

Applegarth, Church St., EX10 9QP, E : on A 3052 ☏ 3174, « Garden » – TV P. AE VISA
M (bar lunch Monday to Saturday)/dinner 7.50 **t.** and a la carte 2.95 – **6 rm** 22.50/40.00 **t.** – SB (except summer) 44.00/56.00 **st.**

AUSTIN-ROVER Salcombe Rd ☏ 2522
FIAT Crossways, Sidford ☏ 3595

SILCHESTER Hants. 408 404 Q 29 – pop. 1 072 – ⊠ Reading (Berks.) – ✆ 0734.
◆London 62 – Basingstoke 8 – Reading 14 – Winchester 26.

🏨 **Romans** (Best Western) 📎, Little London Rd, RG7 2PN, ℰ 700421, ⤳ heated, 🐎, ✗ – 📺
☎wc ☎ ℗ 🕾. ⚠ Æ ⓞ 𝑽𝑰𝑺𝑨
closed Christmas and New Year – **M** (closed Saturday lunch and Sunday dinner) 9.00/13.00 **st.**
⌖ 3.50 – **25 rm** ⥩ 40.00/58.00 **st.** – SB (weekends only) 55.00/60.00 **st.**

SIMONSBATH Somerset 408 I 30 The West Country G. – ⊠ Minehead – ✆ 064 383 Exford.
◆London 200 – Exeter 40 – Minehead 19 – Taunton 38.

🏨 **Simonsbath House**, TA24 7SH, ℰ 259, ≼, « Tastefully converted 17C country house », 🐎,
squash – 📺 ☎wc ℗. ⚠ Æ ⓞ 𝑽𝑰𝑺𝑨 ⋇
closed 22 December-23 January – **M** (closed lunch to non residents)/dinner 13.00 **t.** – **8 rm**
⥩ 29.00/54.00 **t.**

SITTINGBOURNE Kent 404 W 29 – pop. 35 893 – ECD : Wednesday – ✆ 0795.
◆London 44 – Canterbury 16 – Maidstone 13.

🏨 **Coniston**, 70 London Rd, ME10 1NT, ℰ 23927 – 📺 ☎wc ℗. ⚠ ⚠ Æ ⓞ 𝑽𝑰𝑺𝑨
M 7.15 **st.** and a la carte ⌖ 3.00 – **50 rm** ⥩ 28.00/47.00 **st.**

AUSTIN-ROVER Bapchild ℰ 23085   TALBOT Teynham ℰ 521286
FORD Canterbury Rd ℰ 70711   VAUXHALL-OPEL London Rd. Bapchild ℰ 76222
RENAULT Chalkwell Rd ℰ 76361

SIX MILE BOTTOM Cambs. – see Newmarket (Suffolk).

SKEGNESS Lincs. 402 404 V 24 – pop. 12 645 – ECD : Thursday – ✆ 0754.
🐟 North Shore ℰ 3298.
🎫 Embassy Centre, Grand Parade ℰ 4821.
◆London 145 – Lincoln 41.

🏨 **County,** North Par., PE25 2UB, ℰ 2461, ≼ – 🕮 📺 ☎wc ⅏wc ☎ ℗. ⚠ ⚠ ⓞ 𝑽𝑰𝑺𝑨
M 8.00 **st.** and a la carte ⌖ 4.00 – **44 rm** ⥩ 30.00/48.00 **st.** – SB (except winter) 56.00/70.00 **st.**

🏨 **Vine,** Vine Rd, Seacroft, PE25 3DB, S : 1 ½ m. ℰ 3018, 🐎 – 📺 ☎wc ℗
20 rm

AUSTIN-ROVER Roman Bank ℰ 3671   FORD Wainfleet Rd ℰ 66019
FIAT, ALFA-ROMEO Beresford Av. ℰ 67131   YUGO Clifton Grove ℰ 3589

SKELTON North Yorks. 402 Q 22 – see York.

SKELWITH BRIDGE Cumbria 402 K 20 – see Ambleside.

SKIPTON North Yorks. 402 N 22 – pop. 13 009 – ECD : Tuesday – ✆ 0756.
See : Castle★ (14C) AC.
🐟 Short Lee Lane, off Grassington Rd ℰ 3257, NW : 1 m.
🎫 Victoria Sq. ℰ 2809 (summer only).
◆London 217 – Kendal 45 – ◆Leeds 26 – Preston 36 – York 43.

🏠 **Unicorn** without rest., Devonshire Place, Keighley Rd, BD23 2LP, ℰ 4146 – 📺 ☎wc. Æ 𝑽𝑰𝑺𝑨
10 rm ⥩ 23.00/35.00 **t.**

✗✗ **Oats** with rm, Chapel Hill, BD23 1NL, ℰ 68118 – 📺 ☎wc ⅏wc ☎ ℗. ⚠ Æ ⓞ 𝑽𝑰𝑺𝑨 ⋇
closed 25 and 26 December – **M** 7.75/13.50 **t.** and a la carte – **5 rm** ⥩ 40.00/50.00 **t.**

SLAIDBURN Lancs. 402 M 22 – pop. 332 – ✆ 020 06.
◆London 249 – Burnley 21 – Lancaster 19 – ◆Leeds 48 – Preston 27.

🏠 **Parrock Head Farm** 📎, Near Clitheroe, BB7 3AH, NW : 1 m. ℰ 614, ≼ Bowland Fells, 🐎
– 📺 ☎wc ℗. 🕾
closed mid December-mid February – **M** (dinner only)(residents only) a la carte 5.80/9.75 **st.**
⌖ 2.80 – **8 rm** ⥩ 18.00/40.00 **st.**

SLEAFORD Lincs. 402 404 S 25 – pop. 8 247 – ECD : Thursday – ✆ 0529.
See : St. Denis' Church★ 12C-15C.
🐟 South Rauceby ℰ 052 98 (South Rauceby) 273, W : 1 m. on A 153.
◆London 119 – ◆Leicester 45 – Lincoln 17 – ◆Nottingham 39.

🏛 **Tally Ho Inn,** Aswarby, NG34 8SA, S : 4 ½ m. on A 15 ℰ 052 95 (Culverthorpe) 205, ≼, 🐎 –
📺 ☎wc ⅏wc ℗. ⋇
M (bar lunch)/dinner 4.15/7.55 **t.** – **6 rm** ⥩ 18.00/30.00 **t.**

AUSTIN-ROVER Carre St. ℰ 303034   MAZDA Grantham Rd ℰ 052 98 (Sth. Rauceby) 674
COLT Holdingham ℰ 302545   PEUGEOT-TALBOT Boston Rd ℰ 302518
FORD London Rd ℰ 302921   RENAULT 50 Westgate ℰ 305305

SLOUGH Berks. 404 S 29 – pop. 106 341 – ECD : Wednesday – ☎ 0753.
Envir. : Eton (college★★) S : 2 m.

ਿਸ Farnham Park, Park Rd, Stoke Poges ✆ 028 14 (Farnham Common) 3332, N : 2 m. – ਿਸ Wexham Park, Wexham St. ✆ 028 16 (Fulmer) 3271, N : 2 m.

♦London 29 – ♦Oxford 39 – Reading 19.

　🏨　**Holiday Inn,** Ditton Rd, Langley, SL3 8PT, SE : 2 ½ m. on A 4 ✆ 44244, Telex 848646, ▨, ✎
　　　– 📶 🍽 ▥ ☎ & 🅿. 🍴 🔼 ᴁ ᴀᴇ ⑩ VISA
　　　M 12.50 **t.** and a la carte 🍷 4.95 – 🖵 6.50 – **305 rm** 55.65/72.35, **5 suites** 115.50/172.80 –
　　　SB (weekends only) 66.00/78.00 **st.**

SAAB　Beaconsfield Rd ✆ 028 14 (Farnham Common)　　　VW, AUDI　57 Farnham Rd ✆ 33917
5111　　　　　　　　　　　　　　　　　　　　　　　　　　　　　VW, AUDI-NSU　Colnbrook By-Pass ✆ 682708
VOLVO　Petersfield Av. ✆ 23031

SMETHWICK West Midlands 403 404 O 26 – see Birmingham.

SNAINTON North Yorks. 402 S 21 – pop. 760 – ECD : Wednesday – ✉ ☎ 0723 Scarborough.
♦London 240 – Scarborough 10 – York 29.

　☎　**Coachman Inn,** YO13 9PL, ✆ 85231 – ▥ ⊨wc ਿwc 🅿. 🔼 ᴀᴇ ⑩ VISA
　　　M (bar lunch)/dinner 10.50 **t.** 🍷 3.75 – **12 rm** 🖵 18.00/36.00 **t.** – SB (except summer) 50.00 **st.**

SNEATON North Yorks. 402 S 20 – see Whitby.

SNOWDON (YR WYDDFA) Gwynedd 402 403 H 24.
See : Ascent and ⁂★★★ (1 h 15 mn from Llanberis (Pass★★) by Snowdon Mountain Railway *AC*).
　　Hotels and restaurant see : Beddgelert S : 4 m., *Caernarfon* NW : 9 m.

SOAR MILL COVE Devon – see Salcombe.

SOLIHULL West Midlands 403 404 O 26 – pop. 93 940 – ECD : Wednesday – ☎ 021 Birmingham.
🛈 Central Library, Homer Rd ✆ 705 6789 ext 504/5.

♦London 109 – ♦Birmingham 7 – ♦Coventry 13 – Warwick 13.

　🏨　St. John's Swallow (Swallow), 651 Warwick Rd, B91 1AT, ✆ 705 6777, Telex 339352 – 📶 ▥
　　　⊨wc ☎ 🅿. 🍴
　　　200 rm, 6 suites.

　🏨　**George** (Embassy), The Square, B90 3RH, ✆ 704 1241 – ▥ ⊨wc ☎ 🅿. 🍴. 🔼 ᴀᴇ ⑩ VISA.
　　　✎
　　　M 8.90/10.25 **st.** and a la carte 🍷 3.00 – 🖵 5.00 – **46 rm** 42.00/50.00 **st.** – SB (weekends only)
　　　56.00/60.00 **st.**

　🍴🍴　**Liaison,** 761 Old Lode Lane, B92 8JF, ✆ 743 3993, French rest. – 🔼 ᴀᴇ ⑩ VISA
　　　closed Sunday, Monday, August and 2 weeks at Christmas – **M** (dinner only) a la carte
　　　14.40/17.65 **t.** 🍷 4.25.

AUSTIN-ROVER　Stratford Rd, Shirley ✆ 745 5855　　　FORD　361-369 Stratford Rd ✆ 744 4456
BMW　824 Stratford Rd ✆ 744 4488　　　　　　　　　　HONDA　Station Lane ✆ 056 43 (Lapworth) 2933
DAIHATSU-COLT　Stratford Rd, Hockley Heath ✆　　　PEUGEOT-TALBOT　386 Warwick Rd ✆ 704 1427
056 43 (Lapworth) 2244　　　　　　　　　　　　　　　　RENAULT　270 Stratford Rd, Shirley ✆ 744 1033
DAIMLER-JAGUAR　301 Warwick Rd ✆ 706 2801　　　　VW, AUDI　Stratford Rd, Shirley ✆ 745 5811
FIAT　The Green ✆ 056 44 (Tanworth) 2218

SOMERTON Somerset 403 L 30 – ☎ 0458.
♦London 138 – ♦Bristol 32 – Taunton 17.

　🍴🍴　**Lynch Country House** with rm, Behind Berry, TA11 7PB, ✆ 72316, ≼, « Attractively
　　　converted Regency house », 🔽, 🞕 – ▥ ⊨wc ☎ 🅿. 🔼 ᴀᴇ ⑩ VISA 🍷. ✎
　　　closed 2 weeks January – **M** 10.00 (lunch) and a la carte 11.45/16.25 **t.** 🍷 3.20 – **6 rm**
　　　🖵 35.00/50.00 **t.** – SB 70.00/80.00 **st.**

SONNING-ON-THAMES Berks. 404 R 29 – pop. 1 469 – ECD : Wednesday – ☎ 0734 Reading.
♦London 48 – Reading 4.

　🏨　White Hart, Thames St., RG4 0UT, ✆ 692277, ≼, « Rose gardens on river bank » – ▥ ⊨wc
　　　☎ 🅿. 🍴
　　　25 rm.

　🍴🍴🍴　**French Horn** with rm, Thames St., RG4 0TN, ✆ 692204, ≼ River Thames and gardens – ▥
　　　⊨wc 🅿. 🔼 ᴀᴇ ⑩ VISA. ✎
　　　closed 25-26 December and 1 January – **M** 10.50 **st.** (lunch) and a la carte 19.75/26.25 **st.** 🍷 3.75
　　　– **10 rm** 🖵 50.00/65.00 **st.**

SOURTON Devon 403 H 31 – see Okehampton.

SOUTHAM Glos. 403 404 N 28 – see Cheltenham.

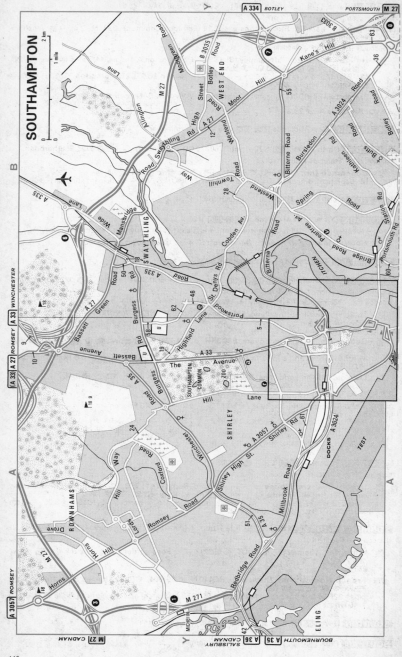

SOUTHAMPTON

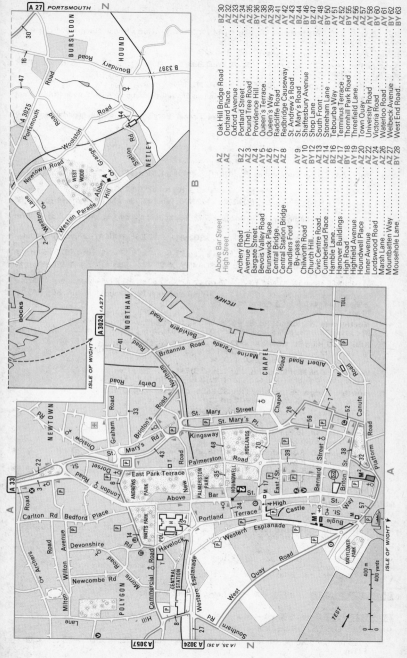

SOUTHAMPTON Hants. **403** **404** P 31 – pop. 211 321 – ECD : Monday and Wednesday – ✆ 0703.

See : Docks★ AY – Tudor House Museum★ (16C) AC AZ **M1** – God's House Tower★ 12C (Museum of Archaelogia) AZ **M2**.

Envir. : Netley (abbey★ ruins 13C) AC, SE : 3 m. BZ **A**.

🕿 Stoneham ✆ 768151, N : 2 m. BY – 🕿, 🕿 West Side Basset Av. ✆ 768732 AY – 🕿 Fleming Park ✆ 0703 (Eastleigh) 612797, N : 6 m. by A 33 AY.

✈ Southampton Airport : ✆ 0703 (Eastleigh) 612341/2, N : 4 m. BY.

🚢 – to America (New York) (Cunard) – to the Isle of Wight : East and West Cowes (Red Funnel Services) 8-18 daily (55 mn to 1 h 10 mn).

🚢 to the Isles of Wight : West Cowes (Red Funnel Services : hydrofoil) Monday/Saturday 14-19 daily : Sunday 15 daily (20 mn).

🛈 Above Bar Precinct ✆ 221106 and 832615.

♦London 87 – ♦Bristol 79 – ♦Plymouth 161.

Plans on preceding pages

🏨 **Polygon** (T.H.F.), Cumberland Pl., SO9 4GD, ✆ 226401, Telex 47175 – 劇 TV ☎ ℗. 🛄 🔺 AE 🅥🅸🆂🅰
    AZ **n**
    M 7.50/10.25 **st.** and a la carte 🍴 3.40 – 🍽 6.00 – **109 rm** 51.00/59.50 **st.**

🏨 **Dolphin** (T.H.F.), 35 High St., SO9 2DS, ✆ 226178, Telex 477735 – 劇 TV ➟wc ☜ ℗. 🛄 🔺
    AE ① 🅥🅸🆂🅰   AZ **i**
    M (bar lunch Saturday and Bank Holidays) 7.25/9.50 **st.** and a la carte 🍴 3.40 – 🍽 5.65 – **72 rm** 42.00/50.00 **st.**

🏨 **Post House** (T.H.F.), Herbert Walker Av., SO1 0HJ, ✆ 228081, Telex 477368, ≼, 🏊 heated –
    劇 TV ➟wc ☎ ℗. 🛄 🔺 AE ① 🅥🅸🆂🅰   AZ **o**
    M (bar lunch Saturday) 6.50/9.50 **st.** and a la carte 🍴 3.40 – 🍽 5.65 – **132 rm** 47.50/57.50 **st.**

🏨 **Southampton Park,** Cumberland Pl., SO9 4NY, ✆ 223467, Telex 47439 – 劇 TV ➟wc ℗.
    🔺 AE ① 🅥🅸🆂🅰   AZ **u**
    M 6.85/9.85 **st.** and a la carte 🍴 3.75 – **75 rm** 🍽 42.50/52.50 **st.** – SB (weekends only) 44.00 **st.**

🏨 Southampton Moat House (Q.M.H.), 119 Highfield Lane, Portswood Junction, SO9 1YQ, ✆
    559555, Telex 47186 – TV ➟wc ☎ ℗. 🛄   BY **e**
    70 rm.

🏠 **Northlands,** Northlands Rd, SO9 3ZW, ✆ 333871 – TV ➟wc 🚿wc ℗. 🔺 🅥🅸🆂🅰 AY **a**
    M (closed Saturday and Sunday) 6.00/15.00 **st.** and a la carte 🍴 5.20 – **22 rm** 🍽 20.00/40.00 **st.**

🏠 **Star,** 26-27 High St., SO9 4ZA, ✆ 226199 – 劇 TV ➟wc 🚿wc ☜ ℗. 🛄 🔺 AE ① 🅥🅸🆂🅰
    M (bar lunch)/dinner a la carte 7.00/11.95 **t.** 🍴 3.75 – **33 rm** 🍽 28.00/49.00 **t.** – SB (except
    September)(weekends only) 39.00/45.00 **st.**   AZ **z**

🏠 **Wessex,** 66-68 Northlands Rd, SO1 2LH, ✆ 31744, ☞ – TV ➟wc 🚿wc ☎ ℗. 🔺 🅥🅸🆂🅰
    M (bar lunch)/dinner 7.00 **t.** and a la carte 🍴 2.50 – **31 rm** 🍽 20.00/38.00 **st.**   AY **r**

↑ **Hunters Lodge,** 25 Landguard Rd, SO1 5DL, ✆ 227919 – TV ℗. 🅥🅸🆂🅰 🍴
    closed 18 December-8 January – **19 rm** 🍽 14.40/26.50 **st.**   AZ **v**

↑ **St. Regulus,** 5 Archers Rd, SO1 2IQ, ✆ 224243, ☞ – TV 🚿wc ℗
    27 rm 🍽 14.75/29.50 **st.**   AZ **x**

↑ **Earley House,** 46 Pear Tree Av., Bitterne, SO2 7JP, ✆ 448117 – ➟wc 🚿wc ℗
    10 rm 🍽 16.00/35.00 **t.**   BY **v**

✗ **La Brasserie,** 33-34 Oxford St., SO1 1DS, ✆ 221046, French rest. – 🔺 AE ① 🅥🅸🆂🅰 AZ **c**
    closed Saturday lunch and Sunday – **M** 8.25/8.80 **st.** and a la carte 🍴 2.95.

✗ **Golden Palace,** 1st Floor, 17 Above Bar St., SO1 0DX, ✆ 226636, Chinese rest. – 🔺 AE ①
    🅥🅸🆂🅰   AZ **e**
    M 2.80/9.90 **t.** and a la carte 7.10/11.90 **t.** 🍴 2.25.

MICHELIN Distribution Centre, Test Lane, SO1 9JX, ✆ 872344 AY

AUSTIN-ROVER - DAIMLER - JAGUAR Marsh Lane
✆ 30911
AUSTIN-ROVER The Causeway ✆ 865021
AUSTIN-ROVER High St., West End ✆ 042 18 (West
End) 3773
AUSTIN-ROVER 102 High Rd ✆ 554346
AUSTIN-ROVER - DAIMLER - JAGUAR, ROLLS
ROYCE The Avenue ✆ 228811
FIAT 115-125 Lodge Rd ✆ 225484

FORD 362-364 Shirley Rd ✆ 775331
FORD Palmerston Rd ✆ 228331
PEUGEOT-TALBOT 21-35 St. Denys Rd ✆ 559533
NISSAN 234 Winchester Rd ✆ 785111
RENAULT Westquay Rd ✆ 39844
VAUXHALL-OPEL Portsmouth Rd, Sholing ✆ 449232
VAUXHALL The Avenue ✆ 226492
VOLVO Millbrook Roundabout ✆ 777616

SOUTHBOROUGH Kent **404** U 30 – see Royal Tunbridge Wells.

SOUTH BRENT Devon **403** I 32 – pop. 2 147 – ECD : Wednesday – ✆ 036 47.

♦London 228 – Exeter 28 – ♦Plymouth 16 – Torquay 17.

🏠 Glazebrook House ⏚, Glazebrook, TQ10 9JE, SW : 1 m. ✆ 3322, ☞, park – TV ➟wc ℗
    12 rm.

SOUTHEND-ON-SEA Essex **404** W 29 – pop. 155 720 – ECD : Wednesday – ✆ 0702.

Envir. : Hadleigh Castle (ruins) ≼★ of Thames *AC*, W : 3 m. – Southend Airport (Historic Aircraft museum) N : 2 m. – ⅂ͤ Belfairs Park, Eastwood Rd, Leigh-on-Sea ℰ 525345.

↗ ℰ 340201/6, N : 2 m. – 🗷 High St. Precinct ℰ 355120 – Civic Centre, Victoria Av. ℰ 355122.

◆London 39 – ◆Cambridge 69 – Croydon 46 – ◆Dover 85.

🏛 **Erlsmere,** 24-32 Pembury Rd, Westcliff-on-Sea, SS0 8DT, ℰ 349025, ⅃ heated – 🆃🆅 ⌂wc
🕮 **ℙ.** 🔼 **VISA.** ⚘
M (bar lunch)/dinner a la carte 5.40/9.40 **t.** 🍷 3.50 – **19 rm** ⊆ 23.00/46.00 **t.**

🏛 **West Park,** 11 Park Rd, Westcliff-on-Sea, SS0 7PQ, ℰ 330729 – 🆃🆅 ⌂wc ⍥wc 🕮 **ℙ.** 🔼
VISA
closed 22 December-1 January – **M** (closed Sunday) (bar lunch)/dinner 6.25 **t.** 🍷 2.75 – **21 rm**
⊆ 20.00/40.00 **st.** – SB (weekends only) 50.00/55.00.

🏛 **Balmoral,** 34-36 Valkyrie Rd, Westcliff-on-Sea, SS0 8BU, ℰ 342947, ⚞ – 🆃🆅 ⌂wc ⍥wc
🕮 **ℙ.** 🔼 **VISA.** ⚘
closed 25 and 26 December – **M** (closed Sunday dinner) (bar lunch)/dinner 6.50 **st.**
and a la carte 🍷 3.50 – **19 rm** ⊆ 24.00/37.00 **st.** – SB (weekends only) 45.75/58.50 **st.**

🏛 **Ilfracombe House,** 11-13 Wilson Rd, SS1 1HG, ℰ 351000 – 🆃🆅 ⌂wc ⍥wc. 🔼 🅰🅴 ⱺ **VISA.**
⚘
M 7.50 **t.** 🍷 2.00 – **12 rm** ⊆ 23.00/35.00 **t.** – SB (except summer)(weekends only) 48.50 **st.**

🏤 **Norfolk,** 32 The Leas, Westcliff-on-Sea, SS0 8JB, ℰ 351069, ⚞ – 🆃🆅 ⌂wc ⍥wc **ℙ.** 🔼
VISA. ⚘
M a la carte 4.25/7.95 **st.** 🍷 2.60 – **14 rm** ⊆ 13.50/35.00 **st.** – SB (October-April) (weekends
only) 25.00/35.00 **st.**

🏠 **Strand,** 165 Eastern Esplanade, SS1 2YB, ℰ 586611 – 🆃🆅 ⍥wc. ⚘
closed January-mid February – **8 rm** ⊆ 10.50/30.00 **s.**

🏠 Arosa, 184 Eastern Esplanade, SS1 3AA, ℰ 585416 – 🆃🆅 ⍥ **ℙ** – **6 rm.**

🏠 **Norman,** 191 Eastern Esplanade, SS1 3AA, ℰ 585212 – 🆃🆅. 🔼 🅰🅴 ⱺ **VISA**
8 rm ⊆ 12.50/23.00 **st.**

XX **Christine's,** 56 The Broadway, Leigh-on-Sea, SS9 1AG, ℰ 76411 – 🔼 🅰🅴 ⱺ **VISA**
closed Tuesday lunch, Sunday dinner, Monday, 31 August-14 September, 5 to 12 January and
Bank Holidays – **M** 8.95/15.95 **t.** 🍷 3.85.

AUSTIN-ROVER Priory Crescent ℰ 67766
FIAT 22 Belle Vue Pl. ℰ 610482
PEUGEOT, TALBOT 139-155 West Rd ℰ 347861
RENAULT 536 London Rd, Westcliff-on-Sea ℰ
344940

ROLLS ROYCE-BENTLEY, MERCEDES-BENZ Sta-
tion Rd, Thorpe Bay ℰ 582233
SAAB 661 London Rd, at Westcliff-on-Sea ℰ 351471
TOYOTA 57 West Rd ℰ 346288
VW, AUDI 2 Comet Way ℰ 526411

SOUTH MIMMS Herts. **404** T 28 – ECD : Thursday – ✉ ✆ 0707 Potters Bar.

◆London 21 – Luton 17.

🏛 **Crest** (Crest), Bignalls Corner, Potters Bar, EN6 3NH, South Mimms Services, junction of A 1
(M), A 6, M 25 on B 197 ℰ 43311, Telex 299162, 🔲 – 🆃🆅 ⌂wc ☎ **ℙ** 🞤. 🔼 🅰🅴 ⱺ **VISA** ⚘
M 9.50/12.00 **st.** and a la carte – ⚞ 5.85 – **120 rm** 54.00/64.00 **st.** – SB (weekends only)
60.00/80.00 **st.**

SOUTH MOLTON Devon **403** I 30 **The West Country G.** – pop. 3 552 – ECD : Wednesday – ✉
✆ 076 95 – 🗷 1 East St. ℰ 4122 and 2378 (summer only).

◆London 210 – Exeter 35 – Taunton 39.

🏛 **Marsh Hall Country House** ⚘ , EX36 3HQ, N : 1 ¼ m. by North Molton road ℰ 2666, ≼,
⚞ – 🆃🆅 ⌂wc ⍥wc 🕮 **ℙ.** 🔼 **VISA.** ⚘
closed 23 to 25 December – **M** 7.65/11.95 **t.** and a la carte 🍷 2.70 – **8 rm** ⊆ 26.95 **t.** –
SB (weekends only) 63.80/72.60 **st.**

XX **Stumbles** with rm, 131-134 East St., EX36 3BU, ℰ 4145 – 🆃🆅 ⌂wc ☎ **ℙ.** 🔼 🅰🅴 ⱺ **VISA**
M a la carte 5.50/11.00 **t.** 🍷 3.20 – **7 rm** ⊆ 17.50/35.00 **t.**

at East Buckland NW : 6 ¼ m. by A 361 – ✉ Barnstaple – ✆ 059 86 Filleigh :

XX **Lower Pitt** ⚘ with rm, EX32 0TD, ℰ 243, ⚞ – ⍥wc **ℙ.** 🔼 **VISA.** ⚘
closed Sunday, Monday, 24-25 December and 1 January – **M** (dinner only) (booking essential)
a la carte 7.30/11.60 **t.** 🍷 3.20 – **3 rm** ⊆ 20.00/40.00 **t.** – SB (weekdays only) 50.00/60.00 **st.**

SOUTH NORMANTON Derbs. **402 403 404** Q 24 – pop. 11 607 (inc. Pinxton) – ECD : Wednesday
– ✆ 0773 Ripley.

◆ London 130 – Derby 17 – ◆ Nottingham 15 – ◆ Sheffield 31.

🏨 **Swallow** (Swallow), Carter Lane East, DE55 2EH, on A 38 ℰ 812000, Telex 377264, 🔲,
▤ rest 🆃🆅 🞤 🞤. 🞤 🔼 🅰🅴 ⱺ **VISA**
M 8.25/11.00 **st.** and a la carte 🍷 3.95 – **123 rm** ⊆ 48.50/60.00 **st.,** **2 suites** 80.00 **st.**

SOUTH PETHERTON Somerset **403** L 31 – pop. 2 235 – ✆ 0460.

◆London 138 – ◆Bristol 41 – Exeter 41 – Taunton 19 – Yeovil 7.5.

XX **Le Tire-Bouchon,** 8 Palmer St., TA13 5DB, ℰ 40272, French rest., ⚞ – **ℙ.** 🔼 **VISA**
closed Sunday to Wednesday and 23 December-31 January – **M** (lunch by arrangement)
9.50/13.00 **st.** 🍷 2.90.

18

SOUTHPORT Merseyside 402 K 23 — pop. 88 596 — ECD : Tuesday — ✆ 0704 — **Envir. :** Rufford Old Hall★ 15C (the Great Hall★★) *AC*, E : 9 m.

🄸 Park Rd ✆ 35286 — 🄸 Hesketh, Cockle Dick's Lane off Cambridge Rd ✆ 36897, N : 1 m. — 🄸 Bradshaws Lane, Ainsdale ✆ 78000, S : 3 m. — 🄳 Cambridge Arcade ✆ 33133 and 40404.

♦London 221 — ♦Liverpool 20 — ♦Manchester 38 — Preston 19.

🏨 **Prince of Wales,** Lord St., PR8 1JS, ✆ 36688, Telex 67415, 🚗 — 📺 ☎ Ⓟ 🄰 🖭 🖭 ⓪ VISA
  M (carving lunch)/dinner 8.75 **t.** and a la carte ⚱ 2.75 — **100 rm** ⊡ 45.00/72.00 **st.** —
  SB 50.00/60.00 **st.**

🏨 **Carlton,** 86-88 Lord St., PR8 1JT, ✆ 35111 — 📳 📺 ⏥wc 🏠wc ☎ Ⓟ 🖭 🖭 VISA
  M a la carte 7.65/13.50 **t.** ⚱ 3.20 — **25 rm** ⊡ 18.00/40.00 **t.** — SB (weekends only) 42.00 **t.**

🏨 **Shelbourne,** 1 Lord St., PR8 2BH, ✆ 41252, 🚗 — 📺 ⏥wc 🏠wc Ⓟ 🖭 🖭 ⓪ VISA 🍽
  M (bar lunch)/dinner 6.50 **st.** and a la carte ⚱ 2.90 — **15 rm** ⊡ 23.00/38.00 **t.** — SB 42.50/44.50 **st.**

🏨 **Bold,** Lord St., PR9 0BE, ✆ 32578 — 📺 ⏥wc 🏠wc ☎ Ⓟ 🖭 🖭
  M 4.90/7.20 **t.** and a la carte ⚱ 2.50 — **24 rm** ⊡ 22.00/39.00 **t.** — SB (weekends only) (except
  Easter and Christmas) 40.00/45.00 **st.**

🏨 **Club House,** 15 Leicester St., PR9 0ER, ✆ 33745 — ⏥wc 🏠wc Ⓟ 🖭 🖭 ⓪ VISA
  M (bar lunch)/dinner 7.95 **t.** ⚱ 1.75 — **13 rm** ⊡ 16.00/32.00 **t.** — SB (weekends only)
  39.50/45.00 **st.**

↑ **Crimond,** 28 Knowsley Rd, PR9 0HN, ✆ 36456, 🔲 — 📺 🏠wc ☎ Ⓟ 🖭 🖭 VISA
  10 rm ⊡ 22.00/38.00 **t.**

XX **Squires,** 78-80 King St., PR8 1LG, ✆ 30046 — 🖭 🖭 ⓪ VISA
  closed Sunday and Bank Holidays — **M** (dinner only) a la carte 12.95/17.65 **t.** ⚱ 2.95.

XX **La Terrasse,** 1st. floor, 180 Lord St., PR9 0QG, ✆ 30995 — 🖭 🖭 ⓪ VISA
  closed Sunday dinner, Monday, Tuesday and first 2 weeks September — **M** (dinner only and
  Sunday lunch)/dinner 9.00 **t.** and a la carte 9.55/11.35 **t.** ⚱ 2.85.

ALFA-ROMEO, LOTUS, SAAB 609 Liverpool Rd ✆
74114
CITROEN Liverpool Rd ✆ 74127
COLT Aughton Rd ✆ 67904
FORD Virginia St. ✆ 31550
LADA Liverpool Rd ✆ 77161

NISSAN 205 Liverpool Rd ✆ 68515
TOYOTA Tulketh St. ✆ 30909
VAUXHALL-OPEL 89-91 Bath St. North ✆ 35535
VOLVO 51 Weld Rd ✆ 66613
VW, AUDI Zetland St. ✆ 31091

SOUTHSEA Hants. 403 404 Q 31 — see Portsmouth and Southsea.

SOUTH SHIELDS Tyne and Wear 401 402 P 19 — pop. 86 488 — ECD : Wednesday — ✆ 091.

🄸 Cleadon Hill ✆ 568942, SE : 3 m. — 🄳 South Foreshore, Sea Rd ✆ 4557411 and 4568841 (summer only).

♦London 284 — ♦Newcastle-upon-Tyne 9.5 — Sunderland 6.

🏨 **Sea,** Sea Rd, NE33 2LD, ✆ 456 6227 — 📺 ⏥wc 🚗 Ⓟ 🖭 🖭 ⓪ VISA
  M 6.60 **st.** and a la carte ⚱ 3.00 — **30 rm** ⊡ 31.50/43.50 **st.** — SB (weekends only) 43.50 **st.**

COLT ✆ 4563166
FORD ✆ 4562271

RENAULT ✆ 4552101

SOUTH WALSHAM Norfolk 404 Y 26 — pop. 543 — ✉ Norwich — ✆ 060 549.

♦London 120 — Great Yarmouth 11 — ♦Norwich 9.

🏨 **South Walsham Hall H. and Country Club** 🏊, South Walsham Rd, NR13 6DQ, ✆ 378,
  Telex 97394, ≼, ⊒ heated, 🐾, 🚗, park, 🍽, squash — 📺 ⏥wc 🏠wc 🚗 Ⓟ 🖭 🖭 ⓪ VISA
  🍽
  closed January — **M** 12.00 **t.** and a la carte ⚱ 4.00 — **19 rm** ⊡ 32.00/45.00 **st.** — SB (weekends
  only) 45.00/60.00 **st.**

SOUTHWELL Notts. 402 404 R 24 — pop. 6 283 — ECD : Thursday — ✆ 0636.

See : Minster★ 12C-13C (Chapter house : foliage carving★★ 13C).

♦London 135 — Lincoln 24 — ♦Nottingham 14 — ♦Sheffield 34.

🏨 **Saracen's Head,** Market Pl., NG25 0HE, ✆ 812701, Group Telex 377201 — 📺 ⏥wc 🚗 Ⓟ
  🄰 🖭 🖭 ⓪ VISA
  M (closed Saturday lunch) 6.95/9.95 **t.** and a la carte ⚱ 3.35 — **27 rm** ⊡ 41.50/66.50 **st.** —
  SB (weekends only) 60.00 **st.**

X **Leo's,** 12 King St., NG25 0EN, ✆ 812119 — 🖭 🖭 ⓪ VISA
  closed Sunday, Monday and Bank Holidays — **M** (dinner only) 16.50 **t.** ⚱ 3.50.

FORD Westgate ✆ 813741

SOUTHWOLD Suffolk 404 Z 27 — pop. 3 756 — ECD : Wednesday — ✆ 0502.

🄵 The Common ✆ 723234, W : ½ m. on A 1095 — 🄳 Town Hall, Market Place ✆ 722366 (summer only).

♦London 108 — Great Yarmouth 24 — ♦Ipswich 35 — ♦Norwich 34.

🏨 **Swan,** Market Pl., IP18 6EG, ✆ 722186, 🚗 — 📳 📺 ⏥wc 🚗 Ⓟ 🄰 — **52 rm.**

🏨 **Crown,** High St., IP18 6DP, ✆ 722275 — 📺 ⏥wc ☎ Ⓟ 🄰 🖭 🖭 VISA
  M 10.00/12.00 **t.** and a la carte — **12 rm** 16.00/32.00 **t.**

🏠 **Pier Avenue,** Station Rd, IP18 6AY, ✆ 722632 — 📺 ⏥wc 🏠wc. 🖭 🖭 VISA
  M 6.00/9.25 **st.** and a la carte ⚱ 3.00 — **13 rm** ⊡ 17.50/42.00 **st.** — SB (October-June) 40.00 **st.**

FORD Bridgefoot Corner ✆ 723170

444

SOUTH WOODHAM FERRERS Essex **404** V 29 – pop. 6 975 – ⊠ ✪ 0245 Chelmsford.
♦London 36 – Chelmsford 12 – Colchester 34 – Southend-on-Sea 13.

🏠 **Oakland,** 2-6 Reeves Way by Merchant St., CM3 5XE, ℘ 322811 – 📺 ⇔wc ☎. ⚠ AE ⓪ **VISA**
M 8.50 t. and a la carte ↓ 1.75 – **33 rm** ⟷ 24.00/34.00 t.

SOUTH ZEAL Devon **403** I 31 The West Country G. – ECD : Thursday – ⊠ ✪ 0837 Okehampton.
♦London 218 – Exeter 17 – ♦Plymouth 36 – Torquay 27.

🏠 **Oxenham Arms,** EX20 2JT, ℘ 840244, « 12C inn », 🐎 – 📺 ⇔wc ☎ P. ⚠ AE ⓪ **VISA**
M 7.50/12.00 t. ↓ 2.40 – **8 rm** ⟷ 22.00/40.00 t. – SB (November-March) 45.00/51.00 **st.**

↑ **Poltimore,** EX20 2PD, S : 1 m. by A 30 ℘ 840209, 🐎 – ⇔wc ♒wc P
7 rm ⟷ 13.00/30.00 **st.**

SOWERBY North Yorks. – see Thirsk.

SPARK BRIDGE Cumbria – see Ulverston.

SPELDHURST Kent **404** U 30 – see Royal Tunbridge Wells.

SPRATTON Northants. **404** R 27 – see Northampton.

SPRIGG'S ALLEY Oxon. – see Chinnor.

SPROTBROUGH South Yorks. **402 403 404** Q 23 – see Doncaster.

STAFFORD Staffs. **402 403 404** N 25 – pop. 60 915 – ECD : Wednesday – ✪ 0785.
See : High House★ 16C – St. Mary's Church (Norman font★) – 🖂 Civic Offices, Riverside ℘ 3181 ext. 216.
♦London 142 – Birmingham 26 – Derby 32 – Shrewsbury 31 – Stoke-on-Trent 17.

🏨 **Tillington Hall** (De Vere), Eccleshall Rd, ST16 1JJ, NW : 1 ½ m. on A 5013 ℘ 53531, Telex
36566 – ▤ 📺 ⇔wc ☎ & P. 🎿 ⚠ AE ⓪ **VISA**
M (closed Saturday lunch) 7.50 **t.** and a la carte ↓ 4.25 – **93 rm** ⟷ 47.00/65.00 **st.** –
SB (weekends only and all of July and August) 57.00/59.00 **st.**

🏠 **Garth,** Moss Pit, ST17 9JD, S : 2 m. on A 449 ℘ 56124 – 📺 ⇔wc 🐎 P. 🎿 ⚠ AE **VISA**
M (buffet lunch Saturday) 4.25/7.50 **t.** and a la carte ↓ 2.85 – **32 rm** ⟷ 23.00/39.50 t. –
SB (weekends only) 46.00/56.00 **st.**

🏠 **Swan,** 46 Greengate St., ST16 2JA, ℘ 58142 – 📺 ⇔wc 🐎 P. 🐾
closed 25 and 26 December – M (grill rest.) a la carte 5.55/11.85 t. ↓ 3.50 – **32 rm**
⟷ 27.50/50.00 t.

🏠 **Vine,** Salter St., ST16 2JU, ℘ 51071 – 📺 P – **26 rm.**

AUSTIN-ROVER-DAIMLER-JAGUAR Lichfield Rd ℘ 51366
BMW Lichfield Rd ℘ 46999
CITROEN Astonfields Rd ℘ 3336
DATSUN Lichfield Rd ℘ 59313
FIAT Milford ℘ 661226
FORD Stone Rd ℘ 51331
LADA Sandon Rd ℘ 45299
MAZDA Derby St. ℘ 55486
PEUGEOT-TALBOT Newport Rd ℘ 51084
RENAULT Wolverhampton Rd ℘ 52118
SAAB Yarlet Bank ℘ 088 97 (Sandon) 248
VAUXHALL-OPEL Walton ℘ 661293
VOLVO Lichfield Rd ℘ 47221

STAINES Surrey **404** S 29 – pop. 51 949 – ECD : Thursday – ✪ 0784.
♦London 26 – Reading 25.

🏨 **Thames Lodge,** Thames St., TW18 4SF, ℘ 64433, Group Telex 8812552, ≤ – ▤ rest 📺
⇔wc ☎ P. 🎿 ⚠ AE ⓪ **VISA**
M (closed Saturday lunch) 9.85 **t.** and a la carte ↓ 3.75 – **47 rm** ⟷ 52.50/65.00 t. – SB (weekends only) 71.50 **st.**

AUSTIN-ROVER 236 Central Trading Estate ℘ 51698   TALBOT Staines Bridge ℘ 55301

STAMFORD Lincs. **402 404** S 26 – pop. 16 127 – ECD : Thursday – ✪ 0780.
See : Burghley House★★ 16C (paintings : Heaven Room★★★) AC.
🏌 Luffenham ℘ 720205, W : 5 m. – 🖂 6 St. Mary's Hill ℘ 64444.
♦London 92 – ♦Leicester 31 – Lincoln 50 – ♦Nottingham 45.

🏨 **The George of Stamford,** 71 St. Martin's, PE9 2LB, ℘ 55171, Telex 32578, « 17C coaching
inn with walled monastic garden » – 📺 ☎ P. 🎿 ⚠ AE ⓪ **VISA**
M a la carte 16.45/20.80 t. ↓ 6.00 – **46 rm** ⟷ 45.00/95.00 t. – **1 suite** 95.00/120.00 t.

🏨 **Lady Anne's,** 37-38 High St., St. Martin's, PE9 2LJ, ℘ 53175, 🐎 – 📺 ⇔wc ♒wc ☎ P.
🎿 ⚠ AE ⓪ **VISA**
M 7.00/9.50 t. and a la carte ↓ 3.50 – **27 rm** ⟷ 29.50/44.00 t. – SB (winter only) (weekends only) 45.00/52.00 **st.**

🏠 **Garden House,** 42 High St., St. Martin's, PE9 2LP, ℘ 63359, 🐎 – 📺 ⇔wc ☎ P. ⚠ **VISA**
M (bar lunch)/dinner 9.50 t. ↓ 2.75 – **21 rm** ⟷ 22.00/55.00 **st.** – SB (except summer)
(weekends only) 45.00/50.00 **st.**

↑ **Welland House,** 19 Broad St., PE9 1PG, ℘ 57028, « 18C town house with antiques » – 🐾
5 rm ⟷ 15.00/42.00 **st.**

XX **Candlesticks** with rm, 1 Church Lane, PE9 2JU, ℰ 64033 – 📺 ⌷wc 🅿. 🔼 𝘝𝘐𝘚𝘈 🍽
M *(closed lunch Tuesday and Saturday and Monday)* 5.50/7.95 ⧆ 3.50 – **4 rm** 20.00/25.00 **t.**

XX **The Courtyard,** 18a Maiden Lane, PE9 2AZ, ℰ 51505 – 🔼 𝖠𝖤 𝘝𝘐𝘚𝘈
closed Sunday dinner and Monday – **M** 7.10/9.95 **t.** and a la carte 11.25/18.00 **t.** ⧆ 4.35.

at Collyweston (Northants.) SW : 3 ¾ m. on A 43 – ✉ Stamford – 💲 078 083 Duddington :

🏠 **Cavalier,** Main St., PE9 3PQ, ℰ 288 – 📺 ⌷wc ⌷wc 🅿. 🔼 ⑩ 𝘝𝘐𝘚𝘈
M 9.00/12.40 **t.** and a la carte ⧆ 2.75 – **7 rm** ⌷ 14.50/32.00 **t.**

AUSTIN-ROVER St. Paul's St. ℰ 52741
FORD Wharf Rd ℰ 55151
PEUGEOT-TALBOT Scotgate ℰ 4003

RENAULT Water St. ℰ 63532
TOYOTA Collyweston ℰ 078 083 (Duddington) 271
VAUXHALL-OPEL West St. ℰ 62571

STANDISH Greater Manchester 🔟🔢🔟🔢 M 23 – pop. 11 504 – ECD : Wednesday – ✉ Wigan – 💲 0257.

♦London 210 – ♦Liverpool 22 – ♦Manchester 21 – Preston 15.

🏛 **Kilhey Court,** Chorley Rd, Worthington, WN1 2XN, E : 1 ¾ m. by B 5239 on A 5106 ℰ 423083, 🌣 – 📺 ⌷wc 🕿 🅿. 🛦. 🔼 𝖠𝖤 ⑩ 𝘝𝘐𝘚𝘈
M 7.50 **t.** (lunch)/dinner a la carte 11.65/22.95 **t.** – **20 rm** ⌷ 35.00/55.00 **t.**

XX **The Beeches** with rm., School Lane, WN6 0TD, on B 5239 ℰ 426432 – 📺 ⌷wc ⌷wc 🅿. 🔼
𝖠𝖤 ⑩ 𝘝𝘐𝘚𝘈 🍽
M 7.00 **st.** and a la carte ⧆ 5.20 – ⌷ 3.25 – **7 rm** 24.00/34.00 **st.**

STANSTEAD ABBOTS Herts. 🔢🔟🔢 U 28 – pop. 1 906 – ✉ Ware – 💲 027 979 Roydon.

♦London 22 – ♦Cambridge 37 – Luton 32 – Ipswich 66.

🏛 **Briggens,** Stanstead Rd, SG12 8LD, E : 2 m. on A 414 ℰ 2416, Telex 817906, ≼, « Arboretum », 🔽 heated, 🛦, 🌣, park, 🎾 – 🎬 📺 🕿 🅿. 🛦. 🔼 𝖠𝖤 ⑩ 𝘝𝘐𝘚𝘈 🍽
M *(closed Sunday lunch)* 9.90/12.15 **t.** and a la carte ⧆ 4.95 – **58 rm** ⌷ 49.50/72.50 **t.** –
SB (weekends only) (except Christmas) 70.00/88.00 **st.**

STANTON HARCOURT Oxon 🔢🔟🔢 🔢🔟🔢 P 28 – pop. 774 – ✉ 💲 0865 Oxford.

♦London 71 – Gloucester 45 – ♦Oxford 13 – Swindon 27.

🏠 **Harcourt Arms,** OX8 1RJ, ℰ 882192 – 📺 ⌷wc 🕿 🅿. 🛦. 🔼 𝖠𝖤 ⑩ 𝘝𝘐𝘚𝘈 🍽
closed Christmas Day – **M** 10.95 **t.** (dinner) and a la carte 10.25/15.00 **t.** ⧆ 2.75 – **16 rm**
⌷ 24.50/44.50 **t.** – SB (weekends only) 50.00 **st.**

STAPLETON Durham 🔢🔟🔢 P 20 – see Darlington.

STEEPLE ASTON Oxon. 🔢🔟🔢 🔢🔟🔢 Q 28 – pop. 1 619 – ECD : Saturday – 💲 0869.

♦London 69 – ♦Coventry 38 – ♦Oxford 10.

🏠 **Hopcroft's Holt,** OX5 3QQ, SW : 1 ¼ m. at junction of A 423 and B 4030 ℰ 40259 – 📺
⌷wc 🕿 🅿. 🛦. 🔼 𝖠𝖤 ⑩ 𝘝𝘐𝘚𝘈
M 8.25/10.00 **t.** and a la carte ⧆ 3.40 – **38 rm** 34.00/54.00 **t.** – SB (weekends only) 56.00 **st.**

X **Red Lion,** South St., OX5 3RY, ℰ 40225 – 🅿. 🔼 𝘝𝘐𝘚𝘈
closed Sunday, Monday and 2 weeks October – **M** (booking essential)(bar lunch)/dinner
11.75 **t.** ⧆ 3.15.

STEVENAGE Herts. 🔢🔟🔢 T 28 – pop. 74 757 – ECD : Monday and Wednesday – 💲 0438.

Envir. : Knebworth House (furniture★) S : 3 m.

🏌 Aston Lane ℰ 043 888 (Shephall) 424 – 🅸 Central Library, Southgate ℰ 69441.

♦London 36 – Bedford 25 – ♦Cambridge 27.

🏛 **Stevenage Moat House** (Q.M.H.), High St., Old Town, SG1 3AZ, ℰ 359111, 🌣 – 📺
⌷wc 🕿 🅿. 🛦. 🔼 𝖠𝖤 ⑩ 𝘝𝘐𝘚𝘈
M 8.25 **st.** and a la carte – **60 rm** ⌷ 37.50/47.50 **st.** – SB (weekends only) 52.50/68.50 **st.**

🏠 Northfield, 15 Hitchin Rd, Old Town, SG1 3BJ, ℰ 314537 – ⌷wc ⌷wc 🅿. 🍽 – **10 rm**.

at Broadwater S : 1 ¾ m. by A 602 on B 197 – ✉ 💲 0438 Stevenage :

🏛 **Roebuck Inn** (T.H.F.), Old London Rd, SG2 8DZ, ℰ 365444, Telex 825505, 🌣 – 📺 ⌷wc 🍽
🅿. 🔼 𝖠𝖤 ⑩ 𝘝𝘐𝘚𝘈
M 8.90/9.95 **st.** and a la carte ⧆ 3.40 – ⌷ 5.65 – **54 rm** 45.00/52.00 **st.**

AUDI, VW Lyton Way ℰ 354691
BMW Hertford Rd, Broadwater ℰ 351565

NISSAN Broadwater Crescent ℰ 315555
VAUXHALL-OPEL 124-6 High St. ℰ 351113

STEYNING West Sussex 🔢🔟🔢 T 31 – pop. 8 318 (inc. Upper Beeding) – ECD : Thursday – 💲 0903.

See : St. Andrew's Church (the nave★ 12C).

♦London 52 – ♦Brighton 12 – Worthing 10.

🏛 **Springwells** without rest., 9 High St., BN4 3GG, ℰ 812446, 🔽 heated, 🌣 – 📺 ⌷wc 🍽 🅿.
🔼 𝖠𝖤 ⑩ 𝘝𝘐𝘚𝘈 🍽
10 rm ⌷ 20.00/45.00 **st.**

STOBOROUGH Dorset – see Wareham.

STOCKBRIDGE Hants. **403 404** P 30 – pop. 524 – ECD : Wednesday – ✪ 0264 Andover.
♦London 75 – Salisbury 14 – Winchester 9.

🏨 **Grosvenor** (Whitbread), High St., SO20 6EU, ✆ 810606, 🚗 – 📺 ➡wc ☎ 🅿. 🔼 AE ⑩ VISA
M 8.50/11.50 **st.** and a la carte – **25 rm** ⛛ 40.00/50.00 **st.** – SB (weekends only) 60.00 **st.**

🏠 **White Hart Inn,** High St., SO20 6HF, ✆ 810475 – 📺 ➡wc 🛋 🅿. 🔼 VISA 🛎
M 8.00/9.50 **st.** and a la carte ⅃ 2.50 – **15 rm** ⛛ 27.50/45.00 **st.**

🏠 **Greyhound Inn,** High St., SO20 6EY, ✆ 810833, ⚲, 🚗 – 📺 ➡wc 🅿. 🔼 VISA 🛎
7 rm ⛛ 24.00/35.00 **st.**

🏠 **Old Three Cups,** High St., SO20 6HB, ✆ 810527, « 15C inn », 🚗 – ➡wc 🅿. 🔼 VISA 🛎
closed 25 December-31 January – **M** (closed Sunday dinner and Monday to non residents)
5.50/6.75 **t.** and a la carte ⅃ 3.50 – **8 rm** ⛛ 16.00/35.00 **t.**

🏠 **Carbery,** Salisbury Hill, SO20 6EZ, on A 30 ✆ 810771, ☐ heated, 🚗 – 🅿. 🛎
closed 2 weeks at Christmas – **11 rm** ⛛ 12.65/23.00 **t.**

XX **Game Larder,** New St., off High St., SO20 6HG, ✆ 810414 – 🔼 AE ⑩ VISA
closed Sunday, Monday, 1 week August and 2 weeks in winter – **M** 8.50 **st.** (lunch)/dinner a la
carte 11.70/16.75 **st.** ⅃ 3.00.

STOCKLAND Devon – see Honiton.

STOCKPORT Greater Manchester **402 403 404** N 23 – pop. 135 489 – ECD : Thursday – ✪ 061
Manchester.

Envir. : Lyme Park★ (16C-18C) *AC*, SE : 4 ½ m.

🏌 Offerton Rd ✆ 427 2001 – 🏌 Goosehouse Green, Romiley ✆ 430 2392, NE : 2 m.

🛈 9 Princes St. ✆ 480 0315.

♦London 201 – ♦Liverpool 42 – ♦Manchester 6 – ♦Sheffield 37 – ♦Stoke-on-Trent 34.

🏨 **Alma Lodge** (Embassy), 149 Buxton Rd, SK2 6EL, on A 6 ✆ 483 4431 – 📺 ➡wc ☎ 🅿. 🛄.
🔼 AE ⑩ VISA
M (carving rest.)(bar lunch Saturday) 7.95/8.50 **st.** and a la carte ⅃ 3.00 – ⛛ 5.00 – **65 rm**
25.00/50.00 **st.**

🏠 **Wycliffe Villa,** 74 Edgeley Rd, Edgeley (via Greek St.), SK3 9NQ, ✆ 477 5395 – 📺 ➡wc
🛋wc 🕿 🅿. 🔼 AE ⑩ VISA 🛎
M (closed Sunday and Bank Holidays) 5.00/10.00 **st.** and a la carte ⅃ 3.00 – **12 rm**
⛛ 26.00/35.00 **st.**

AUSTIN-ROVER 35 Buxton Rd ✆ 480 4244
AUSTIN-ROVER Wellington Rd North ✆ 432 6201
CITROEN Waterloo Rd ✆ 480 4118
COLT School Lane, Heaton Chapel ✆ 432 4790
FIAT Heaton Lane ✆ 480 6661
FORD Oak St., Hazel Grove ✆ 483 9431
FORD Adswood Rd ✆ 480 0211
HONDA, SAAB 31-33 Buxton Rd ✆ 483 6271
MAZDA Wellington Rd North ✆ 442 6466
NISSAN 91 Heaton Moor Rd ✆ 432 9416
PEUGEOT-TALBOT 110 Buxton Rd ✆ 480 0831

RANGE-ROVER, DAIMLER-JAGUAR Town Hall Sq.
✆ 480 7966
RENAULT 596 Didsbury Rd, Heaton Mersey ✆
442 6050
RENAULT 79 Lancashire Hill ✆ 480 7476
SAAB 31-33 Buxton Rd ✆ 483 6271
VAUXHALL-OPEL Wellington Rd South ✆ 480 6146
VAUXHALL-OPEL 398 Wellington Rd North ✆
432 3232
VOLVO Wellington Rd South ✆ 429 7099
VW-AUDI Gt. Portwood St. ✆ 480 1131

STOCKTON-ON-TEES Cleveland **402** P 20 – pop. 86 699 – ECD : Thursday – ✪ 0642.
✈ Tees-side Airport : ✆ 0325 (Darlington) 332811, SW : 6 m.
♦London 251 – ♦ Leeds 61 – ♦ Middlesbrough 4.

🏨 **Swallow** (Swallow), 10 John Walker Sq., TS18 1AQ, ✆ 679721, Telex 587895 – 📶 📺 ☎ ⅊
🅿. 🛄. 🔼 AE ⑩ VISA
M 7.75/11.20 **st.** and a la carte ⅃ 3.25 – **126 rm** ⛛ 49.00/75.00 **st.** – SB (weekends only) 60.00 **st.**

at Eaglescliffe S : 3 ½ m. on A 135 – ✉ ✪ 0642 Stockton-on-Tees :

🏨 **Parkmore** (Best Western), 636 Yarm Rd, TS16 0DH, ✆ 786815, 🔽, 🚗 – 📺 ➡wc 🛋wc ☎
🅿. 🔼 AE ⑩ VISA
M (bar lunch)/dinner 9.45 and a la carte ⅃ 2.95 – **55 rm** ⛛ 27.00/37.00 **t.**, **1 suite** 40.00/50.00 **st.**
– SB (weekends only) 46.00/53.00 **st.**

ALFA-ROMEO Norton Av. ✆ 531127
BMW 45 Norton Rd ✆ 675361
CITROEN Yarm Rd ✆ 780095
FORD Yarm Rd ✆ 675471
LANCIA Billingham Rd ✆ 551542

NISSAN Middleway Mandale Industrial Estate ✆
672617
SAAB, SUBARU Chapel St. ✆ 679781
TOYOTA 336 Norton Rd ✆ 553003
VAUXHALL-OPEL Boathouse Lane ✆ 607804

STOKE BRUERNE Northants. **404** R 27 – pop. 345 – ✉ Towcester – ✪ 0604 Roade.
♦London 70 – ♦Coventry 38 – ♦Leicester 46 – Northampton 7.

X **Butty,** 5 Canalside, ✆ 863654, Italian rest., « Picturesque setting on Grand Union Canal » –
🅿. 🔼 VISA
closed Saturday lunch, Sunday, Monday, 2 weeks summer and 1 week winter – **M** 9.25/
14.95 **st.** and a la carte ⅃ 4.50.

STOKE-ON-TRENT Staffs. **402 403 404** N 24 – pop. 272 446 – ECD : Thursday – ✆ 0782.

See : City Museum and Art Gallery★ Y – Gladstone Pottery Museum★ *AC* V – National Garden Festival U.

Envir. : Little Moreton Hall★★ (16C) *AC*, NW : 8 m. on A 34 U.

🛈 1 Glebe St. ✆ 411222.

♦London 162 – ♦Birmingham 46 – ♦Leicester 59 – ♦Liverpool 58 – ♦Manchester 41 – ♦Sheffield 53.

STOKE-ON-TRENT
NEWCASTLE-UNDER-LYME
BUILT UP AREA

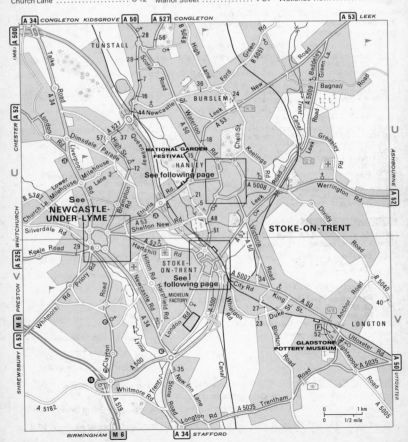

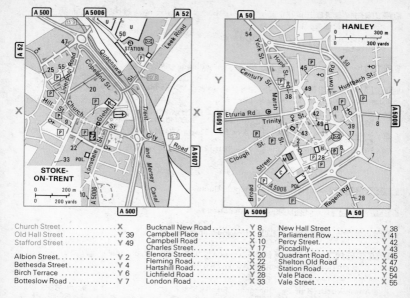

🏨 **North Stafford** (T.H.F.), Station Rd, ST4 2AE, ☎ 48501, Telex 36287 – 🛗 📺 ⇌wc 🛁wc ☎ 🄰
🅿 🌿 🔄 AE ⓪ VISA
X a
M (bar lunch Saturday) 6.95/9.95 **st.** and a la carte ⓘ 2.90 – ⊠ 6.00 – **69 rm** 49.00/60.00 **st.**,
2 suites

↑ **White House,** 94 Stone Rd, Trent Vale, ST4 6SP, S : 2 ¼ m. on A 34 ☎ 642460 – 🅿 🔄 ⅏
closed last week December and first week January – **8 rm** ⊠ 16.75/36.00 **t.**
V e

at Hanley NW : 2 m. by A 5006 – ⊠ ◉ 0782 Stoke-on-Trent :

🏨 **Stakis Grand** (Stakis), 66 Trinity St., ST1 5NB, ☎ 22361 – 🛗 📺 ⇌wc 🕿 🅿 🌿 🔄 AE ⓪
VISA
Y c
M (grill rest.) (bar lunch)/dinner 8.95 **st.** and a la carte ⓘ 3.75 – ⊠ 3.95 – **93 rm** 40.00/51.00 **st.**
– SB 60.00 **st.**

at Basford NW : 1 ¾ m. by A 500 off A 53 – ⊠ ◉ 0782 Stoke-on-Trent :

🏨 **Haydon House,** 5-9 Haydon St., ST4 6JD, ☎ 629311 – 📺 ⇌wc 🛁wc ☎ 🅿 🌿 🔄 AE ⓪
VISA
U a
M 10.00/12.00 **t.** and a la carte – ⊠ 5.00 – **27 rm** 36.00/50.00 **st.**, **4 suites** 65.00/85.00 **st.** –
SB (weekends only) 56.00/77.00 **st.**

MICHELIN Distribution Centre, Unit No. 2, Jamage Road Industrial Estate, Talke Pits, ST7 1QF, ☎
078 16 (Kidsgrove) 71211 by A 34 U

ALFA ROMEO High St., Tunstall ☎ 89226
AUDI, TOYOTA, VW Leek Rd, Hanley ☎ 264888
AUSTIN-ROVER Leek Rd, Endon ☎ 503160
AUSTIN-ROVER Station Rd, Barlaston ☎ 2014
AUSTIN-ROVER Broad St. ☎ 29500
AUSTIN-ROVER King St., Longton ☎ 335533
BMW ☎ 620811
CITROEN Uttoxeter Rd ☎ 312235
DAIHATSU Ashbank ☎ 2426
FIAT Lightwood Rd, Longton ☎ 319212
FORD Clough St. ☎ 29591
FORD King St. ☎ 317381
HONDA Sneyd St., Cobridge ☎ 261593
LADA 292 Waterloo Rd, Cobridge ☎ 22265
LADA Congleton Rd, Biddulph ☎ 512250

MAZDA Moorland Rd ☎ 84215
MERCEDES-BENZ Clough St. ☎ 267872
NISSAN Victoria Rd, Fenton ☎ 416666
PEUGEOT-TALBOT Leek Rd ☎ 24371
RENAULT Werrington Rd, Bucknall ☎ 25406
RENAULT Blue Gates, Biddulph ☎ 514444
SKODA Leek Rd ☎ 261784
SKODA Shelton New Rd ☎ 615106
SUBARU High St., Tunstall ☎ 88997
TOYOTA Leek Rd ☎ 264888
VAUXHALL-OPEL Victoria Rd, Hanley ☎ 271872
VAUXHALL-OPEL Bullocks House Rd ☎ 513952
VAUXHALL-OPEL Lightwood Rd ☎ 310237
VOLVO Duke St. ☎ 334204

STOKE PRIOR Heref. and Worc. – see Leominster.

Ensure that you have up to date **Michelin** maps in your car.

449

STONE Glos. 408 404 M 29 – pop. 667 (inc. Ham) – ✉ Berkeley – ✆ 0454 Falfield.
◆London 130 – ◆Bristol 17 – Gloucester 18.

  ↑   **Elms,** GL13 9JX, on A 38 ✆ 260279 – 🄿
     10 rm ⊑ 12.00/23.00 st.

STONE Heref. and Worc. 408 404 N 26 – see Kidderminster.

STONE Staffs. 402 408 404 N 25 – pop. 12 119 – ECD : Wednesday – ✆ 0785.
◆London 150 – ◆Birmingham 36 – ◆Stoke-on-Trent 9.

  🏛   **Crown,** 38 High St., ST15 8AS, ✆ 813535 – 📺 🛁wc 🚿wc ☎ 🄿 ⚓ 🔊 AE ⓞ VISA
     M 5.25/7.00 t. and a la carte ᐟ 2.75 – **29 rm** ⊑ 31.50/40.00 t.

  🏛   **Stone House,** ST15 0BQ, S : 1 ¼ m. by A 520 on A 34 ✆ 815531, ☞ – 📺 🛁wc 🚿wc ☎ 🄿.
     🔊 AE ⓞ VISA ⚘
     M 5.95/9.25 t. and a la carte ᐟ 2.50 – **22 rm** ⊑ 26.50/38.95 t. – SB (October-March) (weekends
     only) 36.00/53.00 st.

FORD Darlaston Rd ✆ 813332

STON EASTON Somerset – see Farrington Gurney.

STONEHOUSE Glos. 408 404 N 28 – see Stroud.

STONY STRATFORD Bucks. 404 R 27 – see Milton Keynes.

STORRINGTON West Sussex 404 S 31 – pop. 6 915 – ECD : Wednesday – ✆ 090 66.
Envir. : Parham House★ (Elizabethan) *AC*, W : 1 ½ m.
◆London 54 – ◆Brighton 20 – ◆Portsmouth 36.

  🏯   **Abingworth Hall** ⊱, Thakeham Rd, RH20 3EF, N : 1 ¾ m. on B 2139 ✆ 07983 (West
     Chiltington) 3636, Telex 877835, ≼, 🛏 heated, ☞, ⚒ – 📺 ☎ 🄿. ⚓ 🔊 AE ⓞ VISA
     ⚘
     M 16.50 t. (dinner) and a la carte 13.40/20.00 t. ᐟ 3.50 – **22 rm** ⊑ 42.00/78.00 t., **1 suite**
     100.00 t. – SB 80.00/108.00 st.

  🏛   **Little Thakeham** ⊱, Merrywood Lane, Thakeham, RH20 3HE, N : 1 ¾ m. by B 2139 ✆ 4416,
     ≼, « Lutyens house, gardens by Gertrude Jekyll, country house atmosphere », 🛏 heated, ⚒
     – 📺 🛁wc ☎ 🄿. 🔊 AE ⓞ VISA. ⚘
     closed Christmas and New Year – **M** *(closed Monday lunch and Sunday dinner)* (booking
     essential) 15.00/19.50 s. ᐟ 3.50 – **9 rm** ⊑ 60.00/90.00 s.

  XXX   **Manley's,** Manleys Hill, RH20 4BT, ✆ 2331 – 🔊 AE ⓞ VISA
     closed Sunday dinner, Monday, 3 weeks August-September and first week January – **M** a la
     carte 17.20/24.30 s. ᐟ 4.40.

STOURBRIDGE West Midlands 408 404 N 26 – pop. 55 136 – ECD : Thursday – ✆ 0384.
◆London 147 – ◆Birmingham 14 – Wolverhampton 10 – Worcester 21.

     Plan : see Birmingham p.2

  🏨   **Talbot,** High St., DY8 1DW, ✆ 394350 – 📺 🛁wc 🚿wc 🄿
     22 rm   see plan of Birmingham p.2 AU **a**

  ↑   **Limes,** 260 Hagley Rd, Pedmore, DY9 0RW, SE : 1 ½ m. on A 491 ✆ 0562 (Hagley) 882689, ☞
     – 🄿   AU **z**
     10 rm.

     at Belbroughton SE : 7 ½ m. by A 491 on B 4188 – AU – ✉ Stourbridge – ✆ 0562 Bel-
     broughton :

  XXX   **Bell Inn,** Bromsgrove Rd, Bell End, DY9 9XU, E : 1 ½ m. on A 491 ✆ 730232 – 🄿. 🔊 AE ⓞ
     VISA
     closed Saturday lunch, Sunday dinner, Monday, first week January and Bank Holidays –
     M 9.50/19.50 t. and a la carte ᐟ 3.75.

     at Kinver (Staffs.) W : 5 m. by A 458 – AU – ✉ Stourbridge (West Midlands) – ✆ 0384
     Kinver :

  XX   **Berkley's (Piano Room),** High St., DY7 2BR, ✆ 873679 – 🔊 AE ⓞ VISA
     closed Sunday – **M** (dinner only) 16.00 t. ᐟ 2.60.

AUSTIN-ROVER Hagley Rd ✆ 393022
FIAT Clent ✆ 0562 (Belbroughton) 730557
FORD Hagley Rd ✆ 392131
MERCEDES-BENZ, PORSCHE Grange Lane, Lye
✆ 038 482 (Lye) 5575
NISSAN High St ✆ 393231
RENAULT Norton Rd ✆ 396655

TOYOTA 181-183 Bromsgrove Rd, Halesowen ✆ 0562
(Romsley) 710243
VAUXHALL-OPEL The Hayes, Lye ✆ 038 482 (Lye)
3001
VAUXHALL-OPEL Bridgnorth Rd ✆ 394757
VW-AUDI Birmingham St. ✆ 392626

STOURPORT-ON-SEVERN Heref. and Worc. 403 404 N 26 – pop. 17 880 – ECD : Wednesday – 029 93.

Public Library, County Buildings, Worcester St. 2866.

♦London 137 – ♦Birmingham 21 – Worcester 12.

Stourport Moat House (Q.M.H.), 35 Hartlebury Rd, DY13 9LT, E : 1 ¼ m. on B 4193 77333, park, squash – TV wc P. AE VISA
M (bar lunch Saturday) 7.50/8.50 **t.** and a la carte 3.50 – **68 rm** 35.00/46.00 **st.** – SB (weekends only) 50.00 **st.**

Swan, 56 High St., DY13 8BX, 71661 – TV wc wc P. AE VISA
M 6.00/6.50 **s.** and a la carte 3.75 – **32 rm** 27.50/38.00 **st.**

Oakleigh, 17 York St., DY13 9EE, 77568, – TV wc P.
6 rm 16.00/28.00 **st.**

Severn Tandoori, 11 Bridge St., DY13 8UX, 3090, Indian rest. – AE VISA
M 7.00/15.00 **t.** and a la carte 6.25/13.30 **t.** 2.85.

COLT Dunley 3357

STOW-ON-THE-WOLD Glos. 403 404 O 28 – pop. 1 596 – ECD : Wednesday – 0451 Cotswold.

Public Library, St. Edwards Hall 30352 (summer only).

♦London 86 – ♦Birmingham 44 – Gloucester 27 – ♦Oxford 30.

Wyck Hill House, GL54 1HY, S : 2 ¼ m. by A 429 on A 424 31936, Telex 43611, ≤, « Victorian country house », park – TV P. AE VISA
M 8.50/14.50 **t.** and a la carte 2.95 – 5.00 – **16 rm** 65.00/145.00 **t.**, **2 suites** 145.00 **t.** – SB 81.50/90.00 **st.**

Unicorn Crest (Crest), Sheep St., GL54 1HQ, 30257 – TV wc wc P. AE VISA
M (bar lunch Monday to Saturday)/dinner 10.95 **st.** and a la carte – 5.85 – **20 rm** 41.00/51.50 **st.** – SB 64.00/74.00 **st.**

Fosse Manor, Fosse Way, GL54 1JX, S : 1 ¼ m. on A 429 30354, – TV wc wc P. AE VISA
closed 1 week at Christmas – **M** 9.50/10.50 **st.** and a la carte 3.50 – **21 rm** 23.50/60.00 **st.** – SB (except April-November) 45.00/70.00 **st.**

Stow Lodge, The Square, GL54 1AB, 30485, – TV wc P. AE
closed 20 December-mid January – **M** (bar lunch Monday to Saturday)/dinner 8.75 **t.** and a la carte 3.50 – **20 rm** 32.00/55.00 **t.** – SB (November-Easter) (except Christmas) 47.50/55.00 **st.**

Old Stocks, The Square, GL54 1AF, 30666 – wc wc. AE VISA
closed 21 to 30 December – **M** (bar lunch)/dinner 8.50 **t.** – **19 rm** 20.00/40.00 **t.** – SB (November-June) 39.00/44.50 **st.**

King's Arms, The Square, GL54 1AF, 30364 – TV P. AE VISA
closed 25 and 26 December – **M** a la carte 5.50/10.50 **st.** 2.50 – **8 rm** 13.00/26.00 **st.**

Limes, Evesham Rd, GL54 1EJ, 30034, – TV P
5 rm 9.00/27.00 **s.**

at Upper Oddington E : 2 ½ m. by A 436 – Moreton-in-Marsh – 0451 Cotswold :

Horse and Groom, GL56 0XH, 30584 – wc P.
M (bar lunch)/dinner a la carte 7.05/9.00 **t.** 4.50 – **7 rm** 19.00/35.00 **t.** – SB (November-April) 42.00/46.00 **st.**

at Lower Slaughter SW : 3 m. by A 429 – Bourton-on-the-Water – 0451 Cotswold :

Manor, GL54 2HP, 20456, – TV wc P. AE VISA
M 10.00/17.50 **st.** 3.40 – **20 rm** 46.00/75.00 **st.**, **1 suite** 75.00/90.00 **st.** – SB 76.00/86.00 **st.**

at Upper Slaughter SW : 3 ¼ m. by B 4068 – Bourton-on-the-Water – 0451 Cotswold :

Lords of the Manor, GL54 2JD, 20243, « 17C manor house », park – wc P. AE VISA
closed 4 to 19 January – **M** 17.50 **st.** (lunch) and a la carte 14.50/18.05 **st.** 3.25 – 3.25 – **15 rm** 40.00/90.00 **st.** – SB 65.00/85.00 **st.**

at Lower Swell W : 1 ¼ m. on B 4068 – Stow-on-the-Wold – 0451 Cotswold :

Old Farmhouse, GL54 1LF, 30232, – TV wc P. VISA
closed 21 December-28 January – **M** *(closed Monday lunch)* (bar lunch Tuesday to Saturday)/dinner 9.50 **t.** and a la carte 2.65 – **13 rm** 30.00/46.00 **t.** – SB (except Bank Holidays) 45.50/60.00 **st.**

VW Oddington, Moreton-in-Marsh 30422

Pour les , , , nous ne donnons pas le détail de l'installation, ces hôtels possédant, en général, tout le confort.

wc wc

STRATFORD-UPON-AVON Warw. 🅰🅾🅱 🅰🅾🅺 P 27 — pop. 20 941 — ECD : Thursday — 📞 0789.

See : Shakespeare's birthplace★ (16C) *AC*, AB — Hall's Croft★ (16C) *AC*, A B — Anne Hathaway's cottage★ *AC*, W : by Shottery Rd A — Holy Trinity Church★ 14C-15C A.

Envir. : Charlecote Park (castle 16C : interior★) *AC*, NE : 5 m. by B 4086 B — Wilmcote (Mary Arden's House★) (16C) *AC*, NW : 5 m. by A 34 A.

🏌 Tiddington Rd 𝒸 205677, E : by B 4086 B.

🛈 Judith Shakespeare's House, 1 High St. 𝒸 293127.

◆London 96 — ◆Birmingham 23 — ◆Coventry 18 — ◆Oxford 40.

STRATFORD-UPON-AVON

Bridge Street	B 8
Henley Street	A 29
High Street	A 31
Sheep Street	AB 35
Wood Street	A 47

Banbury Road	B 2
Benson Road	B 3
Bridge Foot	B 6
Chapel Lane	A 13
Chapel Street	A 14
Church Street	A 16
Clopton Bridge	B 18
College Lane	A 19
Ely Street	A 22
Evesham Place	A 24
Great William Street	A 25
Greenhill Street	A 27
Guild Street	A 28
Scholars Lane	A 33
Tiddington Road	B 38
Trinity Street	A 40
Warwick Road	B 42
Waterside	B 43
Windsor Street	A 45

Town plans : the names of main shopping streets are indicated in red at the beginning of the list of streets.

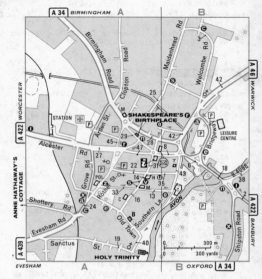

🏨 **Ettington Park** ⑤, Alderminster, CV37 8BS, SE : 6 ¼ m. on A 34 𝒸 740740, Telex 311825, ≼, « Victorian Gothic mansion », ⬛, ⬛, park, ⚒ — 🅿 ☎ 🅿 🏧 🔺 🅰🅴 🔘 𝘝𝘐𝘚𝘈. ⚒
M 15.00/21.50 **t.** and a la carte — ⊆ 7.00 — **49 rm** 65.00/95.00 **st.**, **5 suites** 110.00/135.00 **t.** — SB (weekends only) 125.00 **st.** on A 34 B

🏨 **Moat House International** (Q.M.H.), Bridgefoot, CV37 6YR, 𝒸 67511, Telex 311127, ⚒ — 🔲🔲 🅾 ☎ & 🅿 🏧 🔺 🅰🅴 🔘 𝘝𝘐𝘚𝘈 B e
M 8.50/10.00 **t.** and a la carte ⓘ 4.25 — ⊆ 5.75 — **249 rm** 45.00/62.50 **t.**, **2 suites** 82.00/105.00 **t.** — SB (weekends only) 74.00 **st.**

🏨 **Welcombe** ⑤, Warwick Rd, CV37 0NR, NE : 1 ½ m. on A 46 𝒸 295252, Telex 31347, ≼, « 19C mansion in grounds » 🏌, ⚒, park — 🔲 ☎ 🅿 🏧 🔺 🅰🅴 🔘 𝘝𝘐𝘚𝘈 on A 46 B
closed 29 December-3 January — **M** 11.50/16.50 **st.** and a la carte ⓘ 3.50 — **81 rm** ⊆ 49.00/130.00 **st.** — SB (except Tuesday and Wednesday) 84.50 **st.**

🏨 **Shakespeare** (T.H.F.), Chapel St., CV37 6ER, 𝒸 294771, Telex 311181, « 16C timbered inn » — 🔲🔲 🅿 🏧 🔺 🅰🅴 🔘 𝘝𝘐𝘚𝘈 A v
M 8.50/11.25 **st.** and a la carte ⓘ 3.75 — ⊆ 6.00 — **66 rm** 49.00/69.00 **st.**, **1 suite**.

🏨 **Alveston Manor** (T.H.F.), Clopton Bridge, CV37 7HP, 𝒸 204581, Telex 31324, ⚒ — 🔲 ☎ 🅿 🏧 🔺 🅰🅴 🔘 𝘝𝘐𝘚𝘈 B i
M 8.50/10.50 **st.** and a la carte ⓘ 3.50 — ⊆ 6.50 — **108 rm** 46.00/60.00 **st.**, **3 suites**.

🏨 **White Swan** (T.H.F.), Rother St., CV37 6NH, 𝒸 297022 — 🔲 ⊟wc ⊛ 🅿 🏧 🔺 🅰🅴 🔘 𝘝𝘐𝘚𝘈 A r
M 8.00/9.75 **st.** and a la carte ⓘ 3.40 — ⊆ 5.65 — **35 rm** 43.00/55.00 **st.**

🏨 **Falcon** (Q.M.H.), Chapel St., CV37 6HA, 𝒸 205777, Telex 312522 — 🔲🔲 ⊟wc ☎ 🅿 🏧 🔺 🅰🅴 🔘 𝘝𝘐𝘚𝘈 A s
M 8.50/10.00 **st.** and a la carte ⓘ 3.50 — **73 rm** ⊆ 44.00/79.00 **st.** — SB (except Christmas and New Year) 59.00 **st.**

🏨 **Arden** (Mt. Charlotte), 44 Waterside, CV37 6BA, 𝒸 294949, Telex 311726, ⚒ — 🔲 ⊟wc ⓘⓘwc ☎ 🅿 🏧 B o
59 rm.

🏨 **Swan's Nest** (T.H.F.), Bridgefoot, CV37 7LT, 𝒸 66761 — 🔲 ⊟wc & 🅿 🏧 🔺 🅰🅴 🔘 𝘝𝘐𝘚𝘈 B n
M 7.75/10.25 **st.** and a la carte ⓘ 3.40 — ⊆ 5.65 — **60 rm** 45.00/58.00 **st.**

🏛 **Grosvenor House** (Best Western), 12-14 Warwick Rd, CV37 6YT, ℰ 69213, Telex 311699, 🐾 – 📺 ➖wc 🎇wc 🅿 🔥 🔄 AE ⑩ VISA 🎿
closed 24 to 27 December – **M** 9.00/15.00 t. and a la carte – **57 rm** ⴢ 24.20/56.00 st. – SB 56.50/70.00 st.
B r

🏛 **Dukes,** Payton St., CV37 6UA, ℰ 69300, 🚗 – 📺 ➖wc 🎇wc ☎ 🅿 🔥 VISA
closed Christmas – **M** (closed Sunday lunch to non residents) 9.00/15.00 t. and a la carte ⧊ 2.50 – **17 rm** ⴢ 30.00/60.00 t. – SB (except summer) (weekends only) 57.50/65.00 st.
A o

🏛 **Stratford House,** Sheep St., CV37 6EF, ℰ 68288 – 📺 ➖wc 🎇wc. 🔥 AE ⑩ VISA
closed January – **M** a la carte 5.80/13.00 t. ⧊ 3.00 – **9 rm** ⴢ 35.00/57.00 st. – SB 55.00/60.00 st.
AB u

🏛 **Haytor** 🦢, Avenue Rd, CV37 6UX, ℰ 297799, 🚗 – 📺 ➖wc 🎇wc ⅙ 🅿
15 rm
B c

🏛 **Hylands,** Warwick Rd, CV37 6YW, ℰ 297962 – 📺 🎇wc 🅿 🔥 VISA 🎿
closed Christmas – **M** 5.00/12.00 t. and a la carte ⧊ 2.75 – **16 rm** ⴢ 20.00/46.00 st. – SB 48.00/66.00 st.
B a

↟ **Moonraker House,** 40 Alcester Rd, CV37 9DB, ℰ 67115 – 📺 ➖wc 🎇wc 🅿
18 rm ⴢ 17.00/26.00 st.
A i

↟ **Marlyn,** 3 Chestnut Walk, CV37 6HG, ℰ 293752 – 🎿
closed Christmas – **8 rm** ⴢ 11.95/23.90 st.
A e

↟ **Caterham House,** 58-59 Rother St., CV37 6LT, ℰ 67309 – 🎇wc
13 rm ⴢ 18.00/27.00 st.
A z

↟ **Ashburton,** 27 Evesham Pl., CV37 6HT, ℰ 292444 – 📺 🎇. AE VISA
closed 25 and 26 December – **5 rm** ⴢ 11.50/29.00 t.
A c

↟ **Melita,** 37 Shipston Rd, CV37 7LN, ℰ 292432, 🚗 – 📺 ➖wc 🎇wc 🅿 🎿
closed Christmas-New Year – **12 rm** ⴢ 21.00/36.00 st.
B x

↟ **Hardwick House,** 1 Avenue Rd, CV37 6UY, ℰ 204307 – 📺 🎇wc 🅿 🎿
closed 4 days at Christmas – **12 rm** ⴢ 12.50/33.00 st.
B s

↟ **Stratheden,** 5 Chapel St., CV37 6EP, ℰ 297119 – 📺 ➖wc 🎇wc.
closed February and 23 December-2 January – **10 rm** ⴢ 12.00/35.00 st.
A s

↟ **Virginia Lodge,** 12 Evesham Pl., CV37 6HT, ℰ 292157 – 📺 🅿
closed 22 December-2 January – **8 rm** ⴢ 8.00/16.00.
A x

↟ **Grosvenor Villa,** 9 Evesham Pl., CV37 6HT, ℰ 66192 – 🅿 🎿
8 rm ⴢ 8.00/20.00.
A a

✗✗ **Hussains,** 6a Chapel St., CV37 6PE, ℰ 67506, Indian rest. – ▤. 🔥 AE ⑩ VISA
M 6.50/12.50 t. and a la carte 8.15/9.50 t. ⧊ 4.50.
A s

✗ **Rumours,** 10 Henley St., CV37 6PT, ℰ 204297 – 🔥 AE ⑩ VISA
closed first 2 weeks January – **M** 18.00 t. (dinner) and a la carte 12.00/18.00 t. ⧊ 4.75.
A n

at Ettington SE : 6 ½ m. on A 422 – B – ✉ ✪ 0789 Stratford-upon-Avon :

✗✗✗ **The Chase Country House** 🦢 with rm, Banbury Rd, CV37 7NZ, ℰ 740000, ≼, 🚗, park – 📺 ➖wc ☎ 🅿 🔥 AE ⑩ VISA 🎿
closed 24 December-late January – **M** (closed Saturday lunch and Sunday dinner to non-residents) 16.50 t. and a la carte ⧊ 3.00 – **11 rm** ⴢ 33.00/56.50 t.

at Clifford Chambers SW : 2 m. by A 34 – B – on A 46 – ✉ ✪ 0789 Stratford-upon-Avon :

🏛 **Clifford Manor** 🦢, CV37 8HU, ℰ 292616, « Queen Anne house and walled gardens », 🦢 – 📺 ➖wc ☎ 🅿 🔥 AE ⑩ VISA 🎿
M 15.00/25.00 t. and a la carte ⧊ 2.90 – **8 rm** ⴢ 50.00/80.00 t., **1 suite** 80.00/130.00 t. – SB (except 1 week March and 1 week July) 80.00/95.00 st.

at Wilmcote NW : 4 m. by A 34 – A – ✉ ✪ 0789 Stratford-upon-Avon :

🏛 **Swan House,** The Green, CV37 9XJ, ℰ 67030, 🚗 – 📺 ➖wc 🅿 🔥 AE VISA 🎿
closed 24 to 28 December – **M** (bar lunch)/dinner a la carte 10.30/13.40 t. ⧊ 2.00 – **11 rm** ⴢ 22.00/40.00 st. – SB 48.00/52.00 st.

AUDI, VW Western Rd ℰ 294477
CITROEN 23 Weston Rd ℰ 293577
HYUNDAI, LADA Wellesbourne ℰ 840279
NISSAN Western Rd ℰ 67911

PEUGEOT, TALBOT Alderminster ℰ 078 987 (Alderminster) 331
PEUGEOT, TALBOT Western Rd ℰ 69237
VOLVO Western Rd ℰ 292468

STRATTON Glos. 🔢🔢 O 28 – see Cirencester.

STRATTON ST. MARGARET Wilts. 🔢🔢 O 29 – see Swindon.

STREATLEY Berks. 🔢🔢 Q 29 – pop. 1 055 – ✉ ✪ 0491 Goring.
♦ London 56 – ♦ Oxford 16 – Reading 11.

🏛 **Swan,** High St., RG8 9HR, ℰ 873737, Telex 848259, « ≼ Thameside setting », 🚗 – 📺 ➖wc ☎ 🅿 🔥 VISA 🎿
M 12.50/15.50 t. ⧊ 4.50 – **25 rm** ⴢ 47.50/85.00 t., **1 suite** 110.00/120.00 t. – SB (weekends only) 75.00/90.00 st.

See : The Shoe Museum★ *AC*.

Envir. : at Somerton★, Market Place★, St. Michaels Church★, S : 6 m. – at High Ham (St. Andrews Church★), SW : 8 m.

♦London 138 – ♦Bristol 28 – Taunton 20.

   🏛 **Bear,** 53 High St., BA16 0EF, ✆ 42021 – 📺 ⌷wc ⌷wc ☎ **P** ♨ ⚒ **AE** ① *VISA*
     M 7.25/10.50 t. and a la carte ⌀ 3.40 – **15 rm** ⊐ 30.00/45.00 t.

AUSTIN-ROVER Creeches Lane, Walton ✆ 42735   FORD 189 High St. ✆ 47147

STREETLY West Midlands **403 404** O 26 – see Birmingham.

STRETE Devon – see Dartmouth.

STRETTON Cheshire **402 403 404** M 23 – see Warrington.

STRETTON UNDER FOSSE Warw. **403 404** Q 26 – see Rugby.

STROUD Glos. **403 404** N 28 – pop. 37 791 – ECD : Thursday – ✆ 045 36.

Envir. : Severn Wildfowl Trust★ *AC*, W : 11 m.

🏌 Minchinhampton ✆ 045 383 (Nailsworth) 2642 (Old Course) E : 3 m.

🛈 Council Offices, High St. ✆ 4252.

♦London 113 – ♦Bristol 30 – Gloucester 9.

   🏛 **London,** 30-31 London Rd, GL5 2AJ, ✆ 79992 – 📺 ⌷wc ⌷wc **P** ⚒ ① *VISA*. ⋇
     M *(closed Sunday and Bank Holidays to non residents)* 8.00/12.00 t. and a la carte ⌀ 2.75 –
     10 rm ⊐ 18.00/48.00 – SB (except Bank Holidays) 70.00/85.00 **st.**

   🏠 **Downfield,** 134 Cainscross Rd, GL5 4HN, ✆ 4496 – ⌷wc ⌷wc **P**
     closed 24 December-2 January – **22 rm** ⊐ 12.00/27.00 **st.**

   at Brimscombe SE : 2 ¼ m. on A 419 – ✉ Stroud – ✆ 0453 Brimscombe :

   🏛 **Burleigh Court** ⌂, Burleigh Hill, GL5 2PF, SW : ½ m. off Burleigh Rd ✆ 883804, ≼, ⌷ heated, ⌷ – 📺 ⌷wc ⌷wc ☎ **P** ⚒ **AE** *VISA*. ⋇
     closed 24 to 31 December – **M** 7.95/13.95 t. and a la carte ⌀ 2.50 – **13 rm** ⊐ 37.00/45.60 t. –
     SB (except Bank Holidays) 62.00/72.00 **st.**

   at Rodborough S : ¾ m. by A 46 – ✉ Stroud – ✆ 045 387 Amberley :

   🏛 **Bear of Rodborough,** Rodborough Common, GL5 5DE, E : 1 ½ m. ✆ 3522, Telex 437130, ⌷
     – 📺 ⌷wc ⊕ **P** ♨ ⚒ **AE** ① *VISA*
     M *(closed Saturday lunch)* 12.50 t. and a la carte ⌀ 3.50 – **47 rm** ⊐ 44.00/62.00 t. –
     SB 62.00/70.00 **st.**

   at Amberley S : 3 m. by A 46 – ✉ Stroud – ✆ 045 387 Amberley :

   🏠 **Amberley Inn,** GL5 5AF, ✆ 2565, ⌷ – 📺 ⌷wc ⊕ **P** ⚒ **AE** *VISA*
     M 6.50/10.25 **st.** and a la carte ⌀ 2.90 – **14 rm** ⊐ 34.00/48.00 **st.**

   at Stonehouse W : 2 m. on A 419 – ✉ Stroud – ✆ 045 382 Stonehouse :

   🏛 **Stonehouse Court,** Bristol Rd, GL10 3RA, ✆ 5155, Telex 437244, ⌷, ⌷, park – 📺 ⌷wc
     ⌷wc ☎ **P** ♨ ⚒ **AE** ① *VISA*. ⋇
     closed 26 December-12 January – **M** 8.50 t. (lunch) and a la carte 14.75/16.25 t. ⌀ 2.40 – **23 rm**
     ⊐ 43.00/56.00 t. – SB (weekends only) 62.00 **st.**

ALFA ROMEO Lansdown Rd ✆ 4845
AUSTIN-ROVER Cainscross Rd ✆ 3671
CITROEN London Rd, Bowbridge ✆ 2861
FIAT Stratford Rd ✆ 4007
FORD London Rd ✆ 71341

MAZDA Westward Rd, Ebley ✆ 2000
PEUGEOT-TALBOT Stonehouse ✆ 045 382 (Stonehouse) 2139
RENAULT London Rd ✆ 4203
VAUXHALL-OPEL BEDFORD Westward Rd ✆ 5522

STUBBINGTON Hants. **403 404** Q 31 – pop. 11 531 – ✆ 0329.

♦London 89 – ♦Portsmouth 15 – ♦Southampton 12.

   🏠 **Crofton Manor,** Lychgate Green, off Titchfield Rd, PO14 3NA, ✆ 662014, ⌷ – ⌷wc ☎ **P**
     ⚒ **AE** ① *VISA*
     M *(closed Sunday lunch)* (bar lunch)/dinner a la carte 5.20/12.10 **st.** – **7 rm** ⊐ 23.50/36.00 **st.**

STUCKTON Hants. – see Fordingbridge.

En dehors des établissements désignés par
XXXXX ⋯ ✕,
il existe, dans de nombreux hôtels,
un restaurant de bonne classe.

STUDLAND Dorset 403 404 O 32 The West Country G. – pop. 559 – ECD : Thursday – ⊠ Swanage – ✆ 092 944.

ᵷ Isle of Purbeck ☞ 361.

♦London 130 – Bournemouth 22 – Dorchester 26.

🏛 **Knoll House**, BH19 3AH, ☞ 251, ⤧ heated, 🔟, ᵷ, ☞, park, ⛱ – ▭wc ☎ ℗
April-October – **M** 8.00 **st.** ⓘ 3.00 – **78 rm** ⊊ 28.00/84.00 **st.**

🏛 **Manor House** ♨, Beach Rd, Studland Bay, BH19 3AU, ☞ 288, ≤ Old Harry rocks and Poole
Bay, ☞, park, ⛱ – 📺 ▭wc ▥wc ℗
Easter-October – **M** (bar lunch)/dinner 11.00 **t.** ⓘ 3.50 – **18 rm** ⊊ (dinner included)
32.00/90.00 **t.**

STURMINSTER NEWTON Dorset 403 404 N 31 – pop. 1 781 – ✆ 0258.

♦London 123 – Bournemouth 30 – ♦Bristol 49 – Salisbury 28 – Taunton 41.

XXX **Plumber Manor** ♨ with rm, Hazelbury Bryan Rd, DT10 2AF, SW : 1 ¾ m. ☞ 72507, ≤,
« 18C manor house », ☞, park, ⛱ – 📺 ▭wc ☎ ℗. ◪. ⤧
closed 15 January-28 February – **M** (dinner only) 16.50 **t.** and a la carte 14.00/16.50 **t.** ⓘ 3.00 –
12 rm ⊊ 35.00/65.00 **st.** – SB 68.50/87.00 **st.**

LADA, MAZDA Station Rd ☞ 72155

SUDBURY Derbs. 402 403 404 O 25 – pop. 839 – ⊠ Derby – ✆ 028 372 Marchington.

See : Sudbury Hall** (17C) AC.

♦London 138 – ♦Birmingham 33 – Derby 13 – ♦Stoke-on-Trent 23.

Hotel and restaurant see : Tutbury SE : 6 m., Uttoxeter W : 4 ½ m.

SUDBURY Suffolk 404 W 27 – pop. 17 723 – ECD : Wednesday – ✆ 0787.

ᵻ Public Library, Market Hill ☞ 72092.

♦London 59 – ♦Cambridge 37 – Colchester 15 – ♦Ipswich 21.

🏛 **Mill**, Walnut Tree Lane, CO10 6BD, ☞ 75544, Telex 987623, ≤, ♨ – 📺 ▭wc ☎ ℗. ◪ ☒
⓪ 🆅🆂🅰
M 7.75/9.75 **t.** and a la carte ⓘ 3.70 – **45 rm** ⊊ 35.00/45.00 **t.**

🏨 **Four Swans**, 10 North St., CO10 6RB, ☞ 78103 – 📺 ▭wc ☎ ℗
M 6.00/9.00 **t.** and a la carte ⓘ 2.75 – **17 rm** ⊊ 25.00/40.00 **t.** – SB (weekends only) 54.00 **st.**

↑ **Hill Lodge**, 8 Newton Rd, CO10 6RG, ☞ 77568 – 📺 ▥wc ℗. ⤧
closed 1 week at Christmas – **16 rm** ⊊ 12.00/21.00 **s.**

X **Ford's**, 47 Gainsborough St., CO6 6ET, ☞ 74298, Bistro – 🆅🆂🅰
closed Sunday, 1 week March, 2 weeks August and 1 week after Christmas – **M** (booking
essential) a la carte 4.25/7.90 **t.** ⓘ 1.95.

VAUXHALL-OPEL Cornard Rd ☞ 72301

☞ *Per l'inscrizione nelle sue Guide,*
Michelin non accetta
nè favori, nè denaro !

SUNDERLAND Tyne and Wear 401 402 P 19 – pop. 195 064 – ECD : Wednesday – ✆ 0783.

ᵷ Whitburn, Lizard Lane ☞ 0783 (Whitburn) 292144, N : 2 m. by A 183 A.

ᵻ Crowtree Leisure Centre, Crowtree Rd ☞ 650960 and 650990.

♦London 272 – ♦Leeds 92 – ♦Middlesbrough 29 – ♦Newcastle-upon-Tyne 12.

Plan on next page

🏛 **Seaburn** (Swallow), Queen's Par., SR6 8DB, N : 2 ½ m. on A 183 ☞ 292041, Group Telex
53168, ≤ – 🔟 📺 ▭wc ☎ ℗. ⚙. ◪ ☒ ⓪ 🆅🆂🅰   A c
M (closed Saturday lunch) 6.25/8.95 **st.** and a la carte – ⊊ 5.50 – **82 rm** 41.00/60.00 **st.** –
SB (weekends only) 55.00 **st.**

🏨 **Gelt House**, 23 St. Bedes Terr., SR2 8HS, ☞ 672990 – 📺 ▭wc ▥wc ℗. ◪ 🆅🆂🅰   B a
M (residents only) (lunch by arrangement)/dinner 8.00 **t.** ⓘ 2.90 – **22 rm** ⊊ 18.00/
34.00 **t.**

ALFA-ROMEO, RELIANT ☞ 650281
AUSTIN-ROVER 190 Roker Av. ☞ 656221
AUSTIN-ROVER Allison Rd, West Boldon ☞ 362726
AUSTIN-ROVER Warwick ☞ 210838
BMW Ryhope Rd ☞ 657631
COLT Nth. Bridge St. ☞ 659252

FIAT Durham Rd ☞ 657191
FORD Trimdon St. ☞ 40311
RENAULT, MAZDA High St. West ☞ 40337
TALBOT Newcastle Rd ☞ 488811
VAUXHALL Paley St. ☞ 674 805
VOLVO Nth. Hylton Rd ☞ 491277

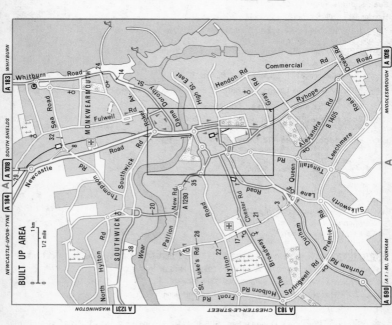

456

SUTTON BENGER Wilts. 📖 **403** **404** N 29 – pop. 839 – ✉ Chippenham – ☎ 0249 Seagry.
♦London 92 – ♦Bristol 26 – Chippenham 4.5 – Swindon 16.

🏨 **Bell House,** High St., SN15 4RH, ℰ 720401, 🐎 – 📺 ⌁wc ☎ 🅿 ♨. 🔼 AE ① VISA
M 6.95 t. (lunch) and a la carte 8.45/14.50 t. ₪ 3.50 – ⌁ 4.95 – **14 rm** 29.50/56.95 t.

SUTTON COLDFIELD West Midlands 📖 **403** **404** O 26 – see Birmingham.

SWAFFHAM Norfolk 📖 **404** W 26 – pop. 4 742 – ECD : Thursday – ☎ 0760.
Envir. : Oxburgh Hall (15C) : Gate house★ AC, SW : 7 ½ m.
♦London 97 – ♦Cambridge 46 – King's Lynn 16 – ♦Norwich 27.

🏨 **George,** Station St., PE37 7LJ, ℰ 21238 – 📺 ⌁wc 🅿 ♨. 🔼 AE ① VISA 🛇
M 6.00/8.50 t. and a la carte – **32 rm** ⌁ 25.00/42.50 t. – SB 54.00/63.00 st.

SWANAGE Dorset 📖 **403** **404** O 32 The West Country G. – pop. 8 411 – ECD : Thursday – ☎ 0929.
See : Site ★ – Durlston Country Park (≼★★) – The Great Globe★.
Envir. : St. Aldhelm's Head★★ (≼★★★), SW : 4 m. by B 3069 – Corfe Castle★★ (≼★★)AC, NW : 6 m.
– Old Harry Rocks★★ (Studland Village - St. Nicholas Church★) N : 4 ½ m. – Studland Beach (≼★),
N : 5 m.

🛈 The White House, Shore Rd ℰ 422885.

♦London 130 – Bournemouth 22 – Dorchester 26 – ♦Southampton 52.

🏨 **Grand,** 12 Burlington Rd, BH19 1LS, ℰ 423353, ≼, 🔲, 🐎 – 📶 ⌁wc �🔥wc ☎ 🅿. 🔼 AE ①
VISA
M a la carte lunch/dinner 10.00 st. ₪ 2.75 – **30 rm** ⌁ 25.00/60.00 st. – SB (except summer and
Bank Holidays) 40.00/60.00 st.

🏨 **The Pines,** Burlington Rd, BH19 1LT, ℰ 425211, ≼, 🐎 – 📶 📺 ⌁wc �🔥wc ☎ 🅿. 🔼 VISA
M 6.75/9.95 t. ₪ 2.55 – **43 rm** ⌁ 23.50/55.00 t. – SB (except summer) 59.00 st.

🛎 **Havenhurst,** 3 Cranborne Rd, BH19 1EA, ℰ 424224 – ⌁wc �🔥wc 🅿. 🛇
March-October – M 5.50 t. **17 rm** ⌁ 14.50/32.00 t.

🛏 **Suncliffe,** 1 Burlington Rd, BH19 1LR, ℰ 423299, 🐎 – �🔥wc 🅿. 🛇
13 rm.

🛏 **Eversden,** 5 Victoria Rd, BH19 1LY, ℰ 423276 – ⌁wc �🔥wc 🅿. 🛇
12 rm ⌁ 9.00/24.00 st.

🛏 **Crowthorne,** 24 Cluny Crescent, BH19 2BT, ℰ 422108 – ⌁wc �🔥wc. 🛇
April-September – **10 rm** ⌁ 10.50/28.00 st.

FORD 281 High St. ℰ 422877

SWANBRIDGE South Glam. 📖 **403** K 29 – see Penarth.

SWANSEA (ABERTAWE) West Glam. 📖 **403** I 29 – pop. 172 433 – ECD : Thursday – ☎ 0792.
Envir. : Cefn Bryn (❄★★★ from the reservoir) W : 12 m. by A 4118 A.
Exc. : Rhosili (site and ≼★★★) W : 18 m. by A 4118 A.
🛈 Morriston ℰ 71079, N : 4 m. by A 48 A.
🛈 Crymlyn Burrows, Jersey Marine ℰ 462403 (summer only) – Singleton St. ℰ 468321 – Ty Croeso, Gloucester
Pl. ℰ 474308 – Oystermouth Sq., The Mumbles ℰ 61302 (summer only).
♦London 191 – ♦Birmingham 136 – ♦Bristol 82 – ♦Cardiff 40 – ♦Liverpool 187 – ♦Stoke-on-Trent 175.

Plan on next page

🏩 **Dragon** (T.H.F.), 39 The Kingsway, SA1 5LS, ℰ 51074, Telex 48309 – 📶 📺 ☎ 🅿. ♨. 🔼 AE
① VISA
               B a
M 6.25/9.95 st. and a la carte ₪ 3.40 – ⌁ 6.00 – **118 rm** 46.00/56.00 st., **1 suite**

🏨 **Ladbroke** (Ladbroke), Phoenix Way, Llansamlet, SA7 9EG, N : 2 ¼ m. by A 4217 A ℰ 790190,
🔲 – 🍽 rest 📺 ⌁wc ☎ & 🅿. ♨. 🔼 AE ① VISA
M 7.95/10.25 t. and a la carte ₪ 3.75 – ⌁ 5.50 – **114 rm** 43.50/52.00 st., **6 suites** 75.00 st. –
SB (weekends only) 63.00/70.00 st.

🏠 **Windsor Lodge,** 15 Mount Pleasant, SA1 6EG, ℰ 42158, « Contemporary decor » – 📺
⌁wc �🔥wc ☎ 🅿. 🔼 AE ① VISA
               B r
closed 25 December – M (lunch by arrangement)/dinner 16.00 t. ₪ 2.50 – **18 rm**
⌁ 23.75/44.00 t. – SB (weekends only) 54.00/70.00 st.

🏠 **Beaumont,** 72-73 Walter Rd, SA1 4QA, ℰ 43956 – 📺 ⌁wc �🔥wc ☎ 🅿. 🔼 AE ① VISA
M (bar lunch)/dinner 12.50 t. ₪ 3.00 – **15 rm** ⌁ 28.00/45.00 t. – SB (weekends only)
58.00/70.00 st.
               A n

🛎 **Alexander,** 3 Sketty Rd, Uplands, SA2 0EU, ℰ 470045 – 📺 ⌁wc �🔥wc 🅿. 🔼 AE ① VISA.
               A c
closed 1 week at Christmas – M (dinner only) 7.00 st. – **7 rm** ⌁ 20.00/32.00 st.

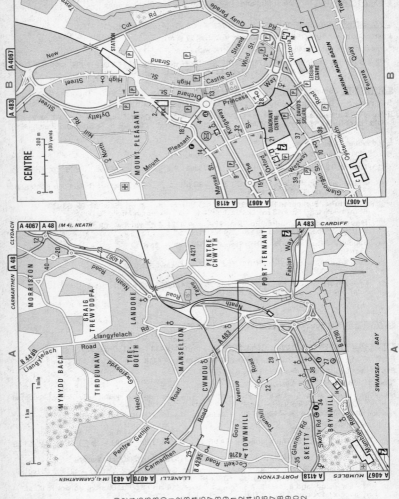

SWANSEA

Zum besseren
Verständnis
der Stadtpläne
lesen Sie bitte
die Zeichenerklärung
auf Seite 43.

458

XX **Oyster Perches**, 45 Uplands Crescent, Uplands, SA2 0NP, ☞ 473173 – 🔳 ⏣ ⓞ 𝑉𝐼𝑆𝐴   A **i**
closed Sunday dinner and second week in February – **M** (lunch by arrangement)/dinner 7.75
and a la carte 7.75/20.95 ‖ 2.00.

X **Jasmine**, 326 Oystermouth Rd, SA1 3UJ, ☞ 52912, Chinese rest. – 🔳 ⏣ ⓞ 𝑉𝐼𝑆𝐴   A **e**
closed 3 days at Christmas – **M** a la carte approx. 12.00.

X **Annie's Bistro**, 56 St. Helens Rd, SA1 4BE, ☞ 55603, Bistro – 🔳 𝑉𝐼𝑆𝐴   A **o**
closed Sunday and Monday – **M** (buffet lunch)/dinner 8.50 **t.** and a la carte 9.20/12.70 **t.**
‖ 3.20.

at Llanrhidian W : 10 ½ m. by A 4118 – A – and B 4271 – ✉ Reynoldston – ☎ 0792
Gower :

🏛 **Fairyhill** ⟡, SA3 1BS, W : 2 ½ m. off B 4295 (Llangennith road) ☞ 390139, « Country house
atmosphere » – �🆃🆅 ⏣wc 🕸wc ☎ 🅿 🔳 ⏣ ⓞ 𝑉𝐼𝑆𝐴
closed 26 December-8 January – **M** *(closed Sunday dinner)* (dinner only and Sunday
lunch)/dinner 14.95 **t.** ‖ 2.50 – **11 rm** ☲ 29.00/59.00 **st.** – SB 49.00/71.00 **st.**

AUSTIN-ROVER - DAIMLER - JAGUAR   511 Carmarthen Rd ☞ 588141
FORD   Garngoch ☞ 893041
HONDA, SAAB   Llangyfelach ☞ 71960
NISSAN   Sway Rd ☞ 75271

PEUGEOT, TALBOT   Neath Rd ☞ 73391
RENAULT   Swansea Ind. Est. ☞ 701801
VAUXHALL   Neath Rd, Morriston ☞ 75101
VW, AUDI-NSU   Gorseinon Rd ☞ 0792 (Gorseinon) 894951

SWAY Hants. 𝟺𝟶𝟹 𝟺𝟶𝟺 P 31 – see Lymington.

SWINDON Wilts. 𝟺𝟶𝟹 𝟺𝟶𝟺 O 29 The West Country G. – pop. 127 348 – ECD : Wednesday –
☎ 0793.

See : Great Western Railway Museum⁎ *AC* – Railway Village Museum⁎ *AC*.

🆅 Bremhill Park, ☞ 782946, E : 4 m. – 🆅 Ogbourne St. George ☞ 067 284 (Ogbourne St. George)
327, S : 7 m. on A 345 – 🆅, 🆅 Broome Manor, Pipers Way ☞ 32403, 2 m. from centre.

🅱 32 The Arcade, David Murray John Building, Brunel Centre ☞ 30328 and 26161 ext. 3056.

♦London 83 – Bournemouth 69 – ♦Bristol 40 – ♦Coventry 66 – ♦Oxford 29 – Reading 40 – ♦Southampton 65.

🏛 **Post House** (T.H.F.), Marlborough Rd, SN3 6AQ, SE : 2 ¾ m. on A 4259 ☞ 24601, Telex
444464, 🔳 – �🆃🆅 ⏣wc 🅿 🅿 🦽 🔳 ⏣ ⓞ 𝑉𝐼𝑆𝐴
M 9.95 **st.** and a la carte ‖ 3.40 – ☲ 5.65 – **103 rm** 49.00/59.00 **st.**

🏛 **Goddard Arms**, 1 High St., Old Town, SN1 3EW, ☞ 692313, Telex 444764 – ▦ rest �🆃🆅
⏣wc 🅿 🅿 🦽 🔳 ⏣ ⓞ 𝑉𝐼𝑆𝐴
M 9.25/9.75 **st.** and a la carte ‖ 3.00 – **65 rm** ☲ 49.50/66.50 **t.** – SB (weekends only) 60.00 **st.**

🏛 **Wiltshire**, Fleming Way, SN1 1TN, ☞ 28282, Telex 444250 – ▯ �🆃🆅 ⏣wc ☎ 🦽 🔳 ⏣ ⓞ
𝑉𝐼𝑆𝐴
M 12.50 **st.** and a la carte ‖ 3.25 – ☲ 5.50 – **85 rm** 48.00/58.00 **st.**

at Blunsdon N : 4 ½ m. on A 419 – ✉ ☎ 0793 Swindon :

🏛 **Blunsdon House** (Best Western), The Ridge, SN2 4AD, ☞ 721701, Telex 444491, ⋞, park –
▯ �🆃🆅 ☎ 🦽 🅿 🦽 🔳 ⏣ ⓞ 𝑉𝐼𝑆𝐴 %
M 6.50/8.00 **st.** and a la carte ‖ 3.20 – **91 rm** ☲ 47.50/62.50 **st.** – SB (except Easter)(weekends
only) 65.00/75.00 **st.**

at Stratton St. Margaret NE : 2 m. on A 420 – ✉ ☎ 0793 Swindon :

🏛 **Crest** (Crest), Oxford Rd, SN3 4TL, NE : 1 ½ m. on A 420 ☞ 822921, Telex 444456 – ▦ rest �🆃🆅
⏣wc ☎ 🦽 🅿 🦽 🔳 ⏣ ⓞ 𝑉𝐼𝑆𝐴
M 9.50/14.50 **st.** and a la carte ‖ 3.50 – ☲ 6.15 – **95 rm** 50.00/71.00 **t.** – SB (weekends only)
70.00/78.00 **st.**

AUSTIN-ROVER, DAIMLER, JAGUAR   Dorkan Way ☞ 612091
BEDFORD, FIAT, VAUXHALL   Drove Rd ☞ 20971
BMW   High St. at Wroughton ☞ 812387

FORD   30 Marlborough Rd ☞ 20002
RENAULT   Elgin Drive ☞ 693841
VAUXHALL   13-21 The Street, Moredon ☞ 23457
VW, AUDI-NSU   Eldene Drive ☞ 31333

SYMONDS YAT Heref. and Worc. 𝟺𝟶𝟹 𝟺𝟶𝟺 M 28 – ✉ Ross-on-Wye – ☎ 0600.

See : Symond's Yat Rock ⋞⋆⋆.

♦London 126 – Gloucester 23 – Hereford 17 – Newport 31.

at Symonds Yat (West) – ✉ Ross-on-Wye – ☎ 0600 Symonds Yat :

↑ **Woodlea** ⟡, HR9 6BL, ☞ 890206, ⅃, ⋞ – 🕸wc 🅿
closed December and January, except Christmas and New Year – **10 rm** ☲ 12.95/26.50 **st.**

TADCASTER North Yorks. 𝟺𝟶𝟸 Q 22 – pop. 5 877 – ECD : Wednesday – ☎ 0937.

♦London 176 – Harrogate 16 – ♦Kingston-upon-Hull 47 – ♦Leeds 16 – York 10.

🏠 **Shann House** without rest., 47 Kirkgate, LS24 9AQ, ☞ 833931 – ⍙ ⏣wc 🕸wc 🅿 🔳 𝑉𝐼𝑆𝐴
8 rm ☲ 17.50/26.00 **st.**

TALKIN Cumbria **401 402** L 19 – see Brampton.

TALLAND BAY Cornwall **403** G 32 – see Looe.

TALSARNAU Gwynedd **402 403** H 25 – see Harlech.

TAL-Y-BONT Gwynedd **402 403** I 24 – see Conwy.

TAL-Y-LLYN Gwynedd **402 403** I 25 – pop. 623 (inc. Corris) – ⌧ Tywyn – ✆ 065 477 Abergynol-wyn.

♦London 224 – Dolgellau 9 – Shrewsbury 60.

🏠 **Minffordd**, LL36 9AJ, NE : 2 ¾ m. by B 4405 on A 487 ✆ 065 473 (Corris) 665, ≤, « Converted 18C farmhouse and inn », 🚗 – ➡wc �📶wc 🕿 🅿. 🔼 ⓪ VISA. 🍴
closed January and February – **M** *(closed Sunday and Monday to non-residents)* (bar lunch residents only)/dinner 10.95 **st.** 🍷 2.50 – **7 rm** 🛏 27.00/42.00 **st.** – SB (except summer) 48.00 **st.**

🏠 **Tynycornel**, LL35 9AJ, on B 4405 ✆ 282, ≤ lake and mountains, 🎣, 🚗 – 📺 ➡wc 🕿 🅿. 🔼 AE ⓪ VISA
closed January and February – **M** a la carte lunch/dinner 10.00 **t.** 🍷 1.60 – **16 rm**.

AUSTIN-ROVER Bolebridge St. ✆ 63535
FORD Upper Gungate ✆ 68411
PEUGEOT-TALBOT Lichfield St. ✆ 61317

RENAULT Watling St. ✆ 892428
VAUXHALL-OPEL Watling St. ✆ 282052
VW-AUDI Coleshill Rd ✆ 288282

TARPORLEY Cheshire **402 403 404** M 24 – ✆ 0829 Kelsall.

♦London 186 – Chester 11 – ♦Manchester 31 – ♦Stoke-on-Trent 27.

🏨 **Willington Hall** 🌳, Willington, CW6 0NB, NW : 3 ½ m. off A 51 ✆ 52321, ≤, « Part Jacobean mansion », 🚗 – 📺 ➡wc 🕿 🅿
10 rm.

TARRANT MONKTON Dorset – see Blandford Forum.

TAUNTON Somerset **403** K 30 The West Country G. – pop. 47 793 – ECD : Thursday – ✆ 0823.

See : Site★★ – St. Mary Magdalene's Church★★ – Museum★ *AC* – St. James Church★ – Hammett St.★ – The Crescent★ – Bath Alley★.

Envir. : Muchelney★★ (Parish Church★★), E : 14 ½ m. – Wellington Monument (≤★★), W : 10 m. – Trull★ Church★, S : 2 m. – Bishops Lydeard★ (Church★), NW : 5 m. – Combe Florey★, NW : 7 m. – Wellington Church★, W : 8 m. – Gaulden Manor★*AC*, NW : 9 m. – Midelney Manor★*AC*, E : 12 m.

🛈 Public Library, Corporation St. ✆ 74785 and 70479.

♦London 168 – Bournemouth 69 – ♦Bristol 50 – Exeter 37 – ♦Plymouth 78 – ♦Southampton 93 – Weymouth 50.

🏯 ✆ **Castle**, Castle Green, TA1 1NF, ✆ 72671, Telex 46488, « Part 12C castle with Norman garden » – ▮ 📺 🏧 🔥 ⚓ 🅿. 🅰. 🔼 AE ⓪ VISA
M 9.75/18.50 **t.** and a la carte 22.95/29.10 **t.** 🍷 3.00 – 🛏 6.95 – **35 rm** 44.00/135.00 **t.**, **1 suite** 225.00 **t.** – SB 95.00 **st.**
Spec. Fillet of red mullet sautéed in butter with a coriander and olive dressing, Beef fillet on a bed of potato with the essence of girolles, A plate of three chocolates served with two sauces.

🏨 **County** (T.H.F.), East St., TA1 3LT, ✆ 87651, Telex 46484 – ▮ 📺 ➡wc 🅿 🅿. 🅰. 🔼 AE ⓪ VISA
M 5.95/9.25 **st.** and a la carte 🍷 3.40 – 🛏 5.65 – **67 rm** 42.00/52.00 **st.**

🏠 **Corner House**, Park St., TA1 4DQ, ✆ 84683 – 📺 ➡wc 🅿. 🔼 AE VISA. 🍴
closed 1 week at Christmas – **M** (lunch by arrangement)/dinner a la carte 9.70/12.65 **t.** –
22 rm 🛏 23.70/44.00 **t.**

at Henlade E : 3 ½ m. on A 358 – ⌧ Taunton – ✆ 0823 Henlade :

🏠 **Falcon**, TA3 5DH, on A 358 ✆ 442502, 🚗 – 📺 ➡wc �📶wc 🕿 🅿. 🔼 VISA. 🍴
closed 1 to 15 January – **M** *(closed Sunday to non-residents)* (bar lunch residents only)/dinner a la carte 7.75/10.75 **st.** 🍷 2.50 – **11 rm** 🛏 31.00/50.00 **st.** – SB (weekends only) 57.75/63.75 **st.**

at Hatch Beauchamp SE : 6 m. on A 358 – ⌧ Taunton – ✆ 0823 Hatch Beauchamp :

XXX **Farthings Country House** 🌳 with rm, TA3 6SG, ✆ 480664, « Tastefully decorated country house », 🚗 – 📺 ➡wc 🅿. 🔼 VISA. 🍴
closed late December-early January – **M** (lunch residents only)/dinner 12.00/16.00 **t.** 🍷 4.00 –
6 rm 🛏 40.00/75.00 **t.** – SB (winter only) 72.00/86.00 **t.**

at Poundisford S : 3 ¾ m. by B 3170 – ⌧ Taunton – ✆ 082 342 Blagdon Hill :

XX **Well House**, Poundisford Park, TA3 7AF, ✆ 566, 🚗 – 🅿. 🔼 AE ⓪ VISA
closed Sunday dinner and Monday – **M** (lunch by arrangement)/dinner 9.50 **t.** 🍷 2.45.

at Rumwell W : 2 ½ m. on A 38 – ⌧ 0823 Taunton :

⌂ **Rumwell Hall**, on A 38 ✆ 75268, 🚗 – ▮ 📺 ➡wc 🅿
11 rm.

460

at Bradford-on-Tone W : 4 m. on A 38 – ✉ Taunton – ✆ 082 346 Bradford-on-Tone :

🏠 Heatherton Grange, Wellington Rd, TA4 1ET, on A 38 ℘ 777 – 📺 🛏wc 🛏wc 🅿
18 rm

AUDI VW   Silver St. ℘ 88371
AUSTIN-ROVER, DAIMLER-JAGUAR   South St. ℘ 88991
FIAT   Priory Av. ℘ 87611

FORD   151-6 East Reach ℘ 85481
LADA, YUGO   16 Kingston Rd ℘ 88288
RENAULT   138 Bridgwater Rd, Bathpool ℘ 412559
SAAB   60 East Reach ℘ 88351

TAVISTOCK Devon 🗺️🅰️🅾️🅱️ H 32 **The West Country G.** – pop. 8 508 – ECD : Wednesday – ✆ 0822.
Envir. : Dartmoor National Park★★ – Lydford★★, Lydford Gorge★★ AC, N : 9 m. – Morwellham★ AC,
W : 4 m. – at Launceston★, Castle★ AC (≤★), St. Mary Magdalene Church★ South Gate★ AC,
NW : 14 m.

🏌️ Down Rd ℘ 2049, SW : 1 m.

🛈 Guildhall, Bedford Sq. ℘ 2938 (summer only).

♦London 239 – Exeter 38 – ♦Plymouth 15.

🏨 **Bedford** (T.H.F.), 1 Plymouth Rd, PL19 8BB, ℘ 3221 – 📺 🛏wc 📶 🅿. 🔒 🔼 🅰️🅴 🆁 VISA
M (bar lunch Monday) 7.50/9.95 **st.** and a la carte 🍷 3.40 – 🍽 5.65 – **32 rm** 40.00/52.00 **st.**

at Gulworthy W : 3 m. on A 390 – ✉ Tavistock – ✆ 0822 Gunnislake :

✕✕ Horn of Plenty 🌿 with rm, PL19 8JD, ℘ 832528, ≤ Tamar Valley and Bodmin Moor, 🌳 – 📺 🛏wc 🛏wc 🅿. 🔼 🅰️🅴 VISA
closed 25 and 26 December – **M** (closed lunch Thursday and Friday) 12.50/25.00 **t.** – 🍽 6.50 –
6 rm

at Mary Tavy N : 4 ½ m. by A 386 – ✉ Tavistock – ✆ 082 281 Mary Tavy :

🏠 **Moorland Hall** 🌿, Brentor Rd, PL19 9PY, ℘ 466, 🌳 – 🛏wc 🛏wc 🅿. 🔼 🅰️🅴 VISA
closed Christmas and New Year – **M** 6.50/9.50 🍷 3.00 – **10 rm** 🍽 18.00/33.00 **st.**

AUSTIN-ROVER   Plymouth Rd ℘ 2301

FORD   122 Plymouth Rd ℘ 3735

TEBAY Cumbria 🗺️🅾️🅱️ M 20 – pop. 594 – ✉ Penrith – ✆ 05874 Orton.
♦London 281 – ♦Carlisle 38 – Kendal 13.

🏠 **Tebay Mountain Lodge,** at Tebay West service area, CA10 3SB, ℘ 351 – 📺 🛏wc 📶 🅿.
🔼 🅰️🅴 🅾️ VISA
M (dinner only) 7.00 **st.** and a la carte 🍷 2.80 – 🍽 4.25 – **30 rm** 29.50/40.50 **st.**

TEDBURN ST. MARY Devon 🗺️🅰️🅾️🅱️ I 31 – pop. 755 – ECD : Thursday – ✉ Exeter – ✆ 064 76.
♦London 209 – Exeter 8.5 – ♦Plymouth 51.

🏛️ **King's Arms Inn,** EX6 6EG, ℘ 224, 🌳 – 📺 🅿. 🔼 🅰️🅴 🅾️ VISA
M (closed Sunday dinner) 6.95 **t.** (lunch) and a la carte 6.70/10.15 **t.** 🍷 2.95 – **7 rm**
🍽 17.50/39.00 **t.**

TEESSIDE AIRPORT Durham 🗺️🅾️🅱️ P 20 – see Darlington.

TEIGNMOUTH Devon 🗺️🅰️🅾️🅱️ J 32 **The West Country G.** – pop. 11 995 – ECD : Thursday – ✆ 062 67.
🛈 The Den, Sea Front ℘ 6271 ext 207/258.

♦London 216 – Exeter 16 – Torquay 8.

🏨 **London,** 24 Bank St., TQ14 8AW, ℘ 6336, 🔥 heated – 📶 📺 🛏wc 🛏wc ☎. 🔼 🅰️🅴 🅾️ VISA
M 5.50/9.00 **t.** and a la carte 🍷 3.00 – **26 rm** 🍽 22.00/46.00 **t.** – SB (except summer and Bank Holidays) 40.00/44.00 **st.**

🏨 **Venn Farm** (Best Western) 🌿, Higher Exeter Rd, TQ14 9PB, off B 3192 ℘ 2196, ≤, 🌳 – 📺 🛏wc 🛏wc 🅿. 🔼 🅰️🅴 VISA 🐾
M (closed Sunday dinner) (bar lunch)/dinner 10.00 **t.** and a la carte 🍷 3.00 – **10 rm**
🍽 30.00/54.00 **t.** – SB (October-March) 50.00/70.00 **st.**

↟ **Belvedere,** 19 Barnpark Rd, TQ14 8PJ, ℘ 4561 – 🛏wc 🅿. 🔼 🐾
13 rm 🍽 10.50/28.00 **st.**

at Shaldon S : 1 m. on A 379 – ✉ Teignmouth – ✆ 0626 Shaldon :

↟ **Glenside,** Ringmore Rd, TQ14 0EP, W : ½ m. on B 3195 ℘ 872448, 🌳 – 📺 🛏wc 🅿. 🔼 VISA
10 rm 🍽 10.00/36.00 **st.**

NISSAN   106 Bitton Park Rd ℘ 2501

461

TELFORD Salop 402 403 404 M 25 – pop. 76 330 – ✪ 0952.

Envir. : Ironbridge Gorge Museum★ (Iron Bridge★★) *AC*, S : 5 m. – Buildwas Abbey★ (ruins 12C) S : 7 m.

◆London 152 – ◆Birmingham 33 – Shrewsbury 12 – ◆Stoke-on-Trent 29.

🏨 **Telford Moat House** (Q.M.H.), Forgegate, Telford Centre, TR3 4NA, 𝒫 506007, Telex 35588, 🔲 – 🕴 📺 🕿 📭. 🔏 🔼 🕭 𝒱𝐼𝒮𝒜
   M *(closed Saturday lunch)* 9.50 **st.** and a la carte 7.55/11.90 **st.** – **98 rm** ⬚ 50.40/61.90 **st.**, **4 suites** 75.00 **st.**

🏨 **Telford Hotel, Golf and Country Club** (Q.M.H.), Great Hay, Sutton Hill, TF7 4DT, S : 4 ½ m. by M 54 (Junction 4) and A 442 𝒫 585642, Telex 35481, ≤, 🔲, 🔽, squash – 📺 ⇌wc 🕿 🕭 📭. 🔏 🔼 𝒱𝐼𝒮𝒜
   M 6.75/8.50 **t.** and a la carte 🍷 3.40 – **58 rm** ⬚ 46.00/56.00 **t.** – SB (weekends only) 55.00 **st.**

🏨 **Buckatree Hall** (Best Western) 🌫, Ercall Lane, The Wrekin, Wellington, TF6 5AL, S : 1 m. off M 54 junction 7 𝒫 614821, ☞, park – 📺 ⇌wc 🕿 🕭 📭. 🔏 🔼 🕭 𝒱𝐼𝒮𝒜
   M 8.05 **t.** and a la carte 10.90/18.00 **t.** 🍷 3.50 – **37 rm** ⬚ 39.50/50.00 **t.**, **1 suite** 60.00 **t.** – SB (weekends only) 54.00 **st.**

🏨 **Charlton Arms** (De Vere), Church St., Wellington, TF1 1DG, 𝒫 51351 – 📺 ⇌wc ☜ 📭. 🔏 **27 rm**.

🏨 **Falcon,** Holyhead Rd, Wellington, TF1 2DD, N : ½ m. off M 54 junction 7 𝒫 55011, ☞ – ⇌wc 🍴wc 📭. 🔼 𝒱𝐼𝒮𝒜
   closed 24 to 26 December – **M** *(closed Sunday dinner)* (bar lunch)/dinner a la carte 6.25/10.15 **t.** 🍷 4.55 – **13 rm** ⬚ 21.50/32.50 **t.**

TEMPLE SOWERBY Cumbria 401 402 M 20 – pop. 341 – ECD : Thursday – ✉ Penrith – ✪ 0930 Kirkby Thore.

◆London 297 – ◆Carlisle 31 – Kendal 38.

🏨 **Temple Sowerby House,** CA10 1RZ, 𝒫 61578, ☞ – 📺 ⇌wc 🕿 🕭 📭. 🔼 𝒱𝐼𝒮𝒜. 🍽
   closed first 2 weeks February and 22 December-3 January – **M** (dinner only) 11.00 **t.** 🍷 2.75 – **12 rm** ⬚ 30.00/50.00 **t.** – SB (except Bank Holidays) 56.00/66.00 **st.**

TENBY (DINBYCH-Y-PYSGOD) Dyfed 403 F 28 – pop. 5 226 – ECD : Wednesday – ✪ 0834.

See : Site★★.

🔽 𝒫 2978.

🅱 Guildhall, The Norton 𝒫 2402 and 3510.

◆London 247 – Carmarthen 27 – Fishguard 36.

🏨 **Imperial** (Best Western), The Paragon, SA70 7HR, 𝒫 3737, ≤ sea and bay – 🕴 📺 ⇌wc 🍴wc 🕿 ⇦ 📭. 🔼 🕭 🕭 𝒱𝐼𝒮𝒜
   M (bar lunch Monday to Saturday)/dinner 12.95 **t.** and a la carte – **46 rm** ⬚ 24.00/80.00 **t.** – SB 50.00/66.00 **st.**

🏨 **Fourcroft,** Croft Terr., SA70 8AP, 𝒫 2886, ≤, 🔼 heated, ☞ – 🕴 📺 ⇌wc 🕿. 🔼 𝒱𝐼𝒮𝒜
   Mid April-mid October – **M** (bar lunch)/dinner 8.50 **st.** 🍷 2.50 – **38 rm** ⬚ 19.00/42.00 **st.** – SB 46.00/50.00 **st.**

🏨 **Harbour Heights,** 11 Croft Terr., SA70 8AP, 𝒫 2132, ≤ – 📺 ⇌wc. 🔼 🕭 🕭 𝒱𝐼𝒮𝒜. 🍽
   M (bar lunch)/dinner 7.50 **st.** 🍷 2.95 – **9 rm** ⬚ 25.00/35.00 **st.** – SB (except June-August) 41.00 **st.**

🏨 **Royal Lion,** 1 High St., SA70 7EX, 𝒫 2127, ≤ – 🕴 📺 ⇌wc – **36 rm**.

🏨 **Buckingham,** Esplanade, SA70 6DU, 𝒫 2622, ≤ – 📺 ⇌wc 🍴wc. 🔼 🕭 🕭 𝒱𝐼𝒮𝒜
   March-October – **M** (bar lunch)/dinner 7.50 **t.** 🍷 2.75 – **21 rm** ⬚ 16.50/38.00 **t.**

↑ **Heywood Lodge,** Heywood Lane, SA70 8BN, 𝒫 2684, ☞ – ⇌wc 📭
   March-October – **13 rm** ⬚ 12.50/30.00 **st.**

TENTERDEN Kent 404 W 30 – pop. 5 698 – ECD : Wednesday – ✪ 058 06.

🅱 Town Hall, High St. 𝒫 3572 (summer only).

◆ London 57 – Folkestone 26 – Hastings 21 – Maidstone 19.

🏨 **White Lion,** High St., TN30 6BD, 𝒫 2921 – ⇌wc 📭. 🔼 🕭 🕭 𝒱𝐼𝒮𝒜
   M 5.25/8.75 **t.** and a la carte 🍷 2.75 – **12 rm** ⬚ 26.00/48.00 **t.** – SB 50.00/60.00 **st.**

↑ **West Cross House,** 2 West Cross, TN30 6JL, 𝒫 2224 – 📭
   March-October – **7 rm** ⬚ 10.00/24.00 **st.**

TERN HILL Salop 402 403 404 M 25 – ✉ Market Drayton – ☎ 063 083.

♦London 161 – ♦Birmingham 44 – Chester 30 – Shrewsbury 16 – ♦Stoke-on-Trent 19.

🏠 **Tern Hill Hall** ⑤, TF9 3PU, SW : ¼ m. on A 53 ℰ 310, ≤, 🐴, – 📺 ⌷wc 🛁 🅿 🔼 ﺎﺩ VISA ⲋ
M *(closed Sunday dinner to non residents)* (bar lunch)/dinner a la carte 7.10/9.90 **st.** ⓵ 2.30 –
10 rm 🖙 22.00/32.00 **st.**

TETBURY Glos. 403 404 N 29 – pop. 4 467 – ECD : Thursday – ☎ 0666.

Envir. : Westonbirt Arboretum★ AC, SW : 3 ½ m.

🏌 Westonbirt 066 66 (Westonbirt) 242, S : 3 m.

🛈 The Old Court House, 63 Long St. ℰ 53552 (summer only).

♦London 113 – ♦Bristol 27 – Gloucester 19 – Swindon 24.

🏨 **Snooty Fox** (Best Western), Market Pl., GL8 8DD, ℰ 52436, Group Telex 449848 – 📺 ☎ 🔼
ﺎﺩ ① VISA ⲋ
M 16.50 **st.** and a la carte ⓵ 4.50 – **12 rm** 🖙 44.60/64.50 **st.** – SB (except Christmas)
63.00/84.00 **st.**

XXX **The Close** with rm, 8 Long St., GL8 8AQ, ℰ 52272, Group Telex 43232, 🐴 – 📺 ⌷wc 🛁wc
☎ 🅿 🔼 ﺎﺩ ① VISA ⲋ
M 7.00/13.75 **st.** and a la carte 17.50/20.00 **st.** – 🖙 4.00 – **12 rm** 34.00/75.00 **st.** –
SB 35.00/45.00 **st.**

at Avening N : 3 m. on B 4014 – ✉ Tetbury – ☎ 045 383 Nailsworth :

XX **Gibbons**, High St., GL8 8NF, ℰ 3070 – 🔼 ﺎﺩ ① VISA
closed lunch Monday and Saturday, Sunday and 2 weeks February – **M** (booking essential)
(lunch by arrangement)/dinner 14.25 **t.**

at Westonbirt SW : 2 ½ m. on A 433 – ✉ Tetbury – ☎ 066 688 Westonbirt :

🏨 **Hare and Hounds** (Best Western), GL8 8QL, ℰ 233, 🐴, park, %, squash – 📺 ⌷wc ☎
🖙 🅿 🛁 🔼 VISA
M 7.75/12.00 **st.** and a la carte ⓵ 3.00 – **27 rm** 🖙 34.00/56.00 **st.** – SB (except late August-early
November) 52.00/64.00 **st.**

at Calcot W : 3 ½ m. on A 4135 – ✉ Tetbury – ☎ 066 689 Leighterton :

🏨 ⊛ **Calcot Manor** ⑤, GL8 8YJ, ℰ 355, ⑆ heated, 🐴 – 📺 ⌷wc ☎ 🅿 🔼 ﺎﺩ ① VISA ⲋ
closed 1 week early January – **M** *(closed Sunday dinner to non-residents)* 12.50/21.00 **st.**
⓵ 2.60 – **10 rm** 🖙 45.00/110.00 **st.** – SB (August and November-March only)(weekdays only)
90.00/130.00 **st.**
Spec. Veal, liver and kidney in puff pastry with port wine sauce and pistachios, Chicken breast with a parcel of
sweet onion and chicken liver mousse, Hot apple and honey souffle with a walnut cream.

VW, AUDI London Rd ℰ 52473

TEWKESBURY Glos. 403 404 N 28 – pop. 9 454 – ECD : Thursday – ☎ 0684.

See : Abbey Church★ 12C-14C.

🛈 Tewkesbury Museum, 64 Barton St. ℰ 295027 (summer only).

♦London 108 – ♦Birmingham 39 – Gloucester 11.

🏨 **Royal Hop Pole** (Crest), Church St., GL20 5RT, ℰ 293236, Telex 437176, 🐴 – 📺 ⌷wc
🛁wc 🖙 🅿 🛁 🔼 🔼
M 7.90/11.50 **t.** and a la carte ⓵ 3.90 – 🖙 6.00 – **29 rm** 46.00/69.00 **t.** – SB 70.00/80.00 **st.**

🏨 **Tewkesbury Park Hotel, Golf and Country Club** ⑤, Lincoln Green Lane, GL20 7DN,
S : 1 ¼ m. by A 38 ℰ 295405, Telex 43563, ≤, 🔼, 🏌, park, squash – 📺 ⌷wc ☎ 🅿 🛁 🔼
ﺎﺩ ① VISA
M *(closed Saturday lunch)* (carving rest.) 7.00/11.00 **st.** and a la carte – **82 rm** 🖙 47.00/59.00 **st.**
– SB (weekends only) 50.00/62.00 **st.**

🏠 **Tudor House**, 51 High St., GL20 5BH, ℰ 297755, « Part Tudor converted town-houses » –
📺 ⌷wc 🛁wc ☎ 🅿 🔼 ﺎﺩ ① VISA ⲋ
M (bar lunch)/dinner 8.25 **t.** and a la carte ⓵ 2.15 – **16 rm** 🖙 25.00/44.00 **t.** – SB (weekends
only) 48.00/52.00 **st.**

at Corse Lawn SW : 6 m. by A 38 and A 438 on B 4211 – ✉ Gloucester – ☎ 045 278 Tirley :

XXX **Corse Lawn House** with rm, GL19 4LZ, ℰ 479, 🐴 – 📺 ⌷wc 🛁 🅿 🔼 ﺎﺩ ① VISA
M 10.50/14.75 **st.** and a la carte 16.50/21.75 **st.** ⓵ 3.00 – **4 rm** 🖙 27.50/42.50 **st.**

AUSTIN-ROVER Gloucester Rd ℰ 293122
FORD Ashchurch Rd ℰ 292398
NISSAN Bredon ℰ 72333

PEUGEOT-TALBOT Bredon Rd ℰ 297575
RENAULT Shuthonger ℰ 298585
TALBOT Bredon Rd ℰ 297575

EUROPE on a single sheet
Michelin map no 920

THAME Oxon. **404** R 28 – pop. 8 300 – ECD : Wednesday – ☎ 084 421.

See : St. Mary's Church★ 13C.

Envir. : Rycote Chapel★ (15C) *AC*, W : 3 ½ m.

🛈 Town Hall ✆ 2834.

◆London 48 – Aylesbury 9 – ◆Oxford 13.

🏨 **Spread Eagle,** 16 Cornmarket, OX9 2BW, ✆ 3661 – 📺 ➡wc ☎ 🅿 🕭 🔼 🗚🖭 ⓞ 𝑽𝑰𝑺𝑨 ⚘
   closed 29 and 30 December – **M** (bar lunch Saturday)/dinner 11.70 **st.** and a la carte ₰ 2.65 –
   ⯐ 3.95 – **26 rm** 39.75/53.00 **st.** – SB (weekends only) 61.00/66.00 **st.**

🏤 **Wellington,** 14 Wellington St., OX9 3BN, ✆ 2682 – 📺 🅿 🔼 🗚🖭 𝑽𝑰𝑺𝑨 ⚘
   M *(closed Sunday dinner)* 10.00/11.00 **st.** and a la carte ₰ 2.75 – **15 rm** ⯐ 19.00/29.00 **st.**

✗ **Thatchers** with rm, 29-30 Lower High St., OX9 2AA, ✆ 2146 – 📺 ➡wc 🛁wc 🅿 🔼 🗚🖭
   M *(closed Sunday)* 12.50 **t.** and a la carte 15.70/19.15 **t.** ₰ 2.95 – **6 rm** ⯐ 34.50/49.50 **st.**

VAUXHALL-OPEL   Park St. ✆ 5566

THAXTED Essex **404** V 28 – pop. 2 177 – ☎ 0371.

◆London 44 – ◆Cambridge 24 – Colchester 31 – Chelmsford 20.

🏠 **Fox and Hounds,** Walden Rd, CM6 2RE, NW : ½ m. on B 184 ✆ 830129 – 📺 🛁wc 🅿 🗚🖭
   𝑽𝑰𝑺𝑨
   M 11.95/14.95 **st.** – **10 rm** ⯐ 29.50/35.00 **st.** – SB (weekends only)(except Christmas) 55.00 **st.**

  at Broxted SW : 3 ¾ m. on B 1051 – ✉ Great Dunmow – ☎ 0279 Bishop's Stortford :

✗✗ **Whitehall** with rm, Church End, CM6 2BZ, ✆ 850603, ≼, « Country house and gardens »,
   ⬥ heated, 🔼 – 📺 ➡wc ☎ 🅿 🔼 🗚🖭 ⚘
   closed 2 to 22 January – **M** *(closed Sunday dinner and Monday to non residents)* 14.50/
   23.50 **t.** ₰ 5.50 – **4 rm** ⯐ 60.00/70.00 **t.** – SB 100.00/110.00 **st.**

THETFORD Norfolk **404** W 26 – pop. 19 591 – ECD : Wednesday – ☎ 0842.

🛈 Ancient House Museum, 21 White Hart St. ✆ 2599.

◆London 83 – ◆Cambridge 32 – Ipswich 33 – King's Lynn 30 – ◆Norwich 29.

🏩 **Bell** (T.H.F.), King St., IP24 2AZ, ✆ 4455, Telex 818868 – 📺 🅿 🕭 🔼 🗚🖭 ⓞ 𝑽𝑰𝑺𝑨
   M 6.95/10.75 **st.** and a la carte ₰ 3.40 – ⯐ 5.65 – **42 rm** 42.00/54.00 **st.**

🏠 **The Historical Thomas Paine** (Best Western), 33 White Hart St., IP24 1AA, ✆ 5631 – 📺
   ➡wc 🛁wc 🖭 🅿 🔼 🗚🖭 ⓞ 𝑽𝑰𝑺𝑨
   M 6.50/9.25 **s.** and a la carte – **14 rm** ⯐ 28.50/40.00 **t.** – SB 48.00/51.00 **st.**

AUSTIN-ROVER   Guildhall St. ✆ 4427

THIRSK North Yorks. **402** P 21 – pop. 7 174 – ECD : Wednesday – ☎ 0845.

See : St. Mary's Church★ (Gothic).

Envir. : Sutton Bank (≼★★) E : 6 m. on A 170.

🛈 Thirsk Museum, 16 Kirkgate ✆ 22755 (summer only).

◆London 227 – ◆Leeds 37 – ◆Middlesbrough 24 – York 24.

🏠 **Golden Fleece** (T.H.F.), Market Pl., YO7 1LL, ✆ 23108 – 📺 ➡wc 🖭 🅿 🔼 🗚🖭 ⓞ 𝑽𝑰𝑺𝑨
   M 5.75/9.50 **st.** and a la carte ₰ 3.40 – ⯐ 5.65 – **22 rm** 42.00/52.00 **st.**

  at Sowerby S : ½ m. – ✉ ☎ 0845 Thirsk :

✗ **Sheppard's Church Farm** with rm, Front St., YO7 1JF, ✆ 23655 – 📺 ➡wc 🅿 🔼 🗚🖭 ⓞ
   𝑽𝑰𝑺𝑨 ⚘
   closed 1 to 10 January – **M** (dinner only and Sunday lunch) 6.25/9.75 **t.** and a la carte
   9.35/17.75 **t.** ₰ 2.65 – **6 rm** ⯐ 16.00/38.00 **t.**

AUSTIN-ROVER   Long St. ✆ 23152   PEUGEOT   Station Rd ✆ 22370

THORNABY-ON-TEES Cleveland **402** Q 20 – pop. 26 319 – ✉ ☎ 0642 Middlesbrough.

◆London 250 – ◆Leeds 62 – ◆Middlesbrough 3 – York 49.

🏩 **Post House** (T.H.F.), Low Lane, Stainton Village, TS17 9LW, SE : 3 ½ m. by A 1045 on A 1044
   ✆ 591213, Telex 58426 – 📺 ➡wc 🖭 🅿 🕭 – **136 rm.**

VAUXHALL   Acklam Rd ✆ 593333

THORNBURY Avon **403** **404** M 29 The West Country G. – pop. 11 948 – ECD : Thursday –
✉ Bristol – ☎ 0454.

◆London 128 – ◆Bristol 12 – Gloucester 23 – Swindon 43.

🏰 **Thornbury Castle** ⯑, Castle St., BS12 1HH, ✆ 418511, Telex 449986, « 16C castle », 🌫,
   park – 📺 🅿 🔼 🗚🖭 ⓞ 𝑽𝑰𝑺𝑨 ⚘
   closed 1 week at Christmas – **M** 13.50 **st.** (lunch)/dinner a la carte 22.25/24.50 **st.** ₰ 3.00
   – ⯐ a la carte approx. 5.00 – **12 rm** 50.00/155.00 **st.**, **1 suite**.

THORNTHWAITE Cumbria **402** K 20 – see Keswick.

THORNTON West Yorks. **402** O 22 – see Bradford.

THORNTON HOUGH Merseyside 402 403 K 24 – ⊠ Wirral – ✆ 051 Liverpool.

♦London 208 – Chester 12 – ♦Liverpool 13.

🏛 **Thornton Hall,** Neston Rd, Wirral, L63 1JF, ℰ 336 3938, Telex 628678, ☞ – TV ⌂wc ☎ ℗.
🅰 AE ⓞ VISA. ⁊
M a la carte 11.60/20.90 **st.** ▯ 2.90 – **38 rm** ☲ 39.00/49.00 **st., 1 suite** 49.00/60.00 **st.**

THORPE Derbs. 402 403 404 O 24 – pop. 227 – ⊠ Ashbourne – ✆ 033 529 Thorpe Cloud.

Envir. : N : Dovedale (valley)★★ – Ashbourne (St. Oswald's Church★ 13C) SE : 3 m.

🎿 at Ashbourne ℰ 0335 (Ashbourne) 42078, SE : 5 m.

♦London 151 – Derby 16 – ♦Sheffield 33 – ♦Stoke-on-Trent 26.

🏛 **Izaak Walton** ⤳, Dovedale, DE6 2AY, W : 1 m. ℰ 261, ≼ Dovedale, ⤳, ☞ – TV ⌂wc ☜ &.
℗. 🅰
33 rm.

🏛 **Peveril of the Peak** (T.H.F.) ⤳, DE6 2AW, ℰ 333, ≼, ☞, ⁊ – TV ⌂wc ☜ ℗. 🅰. 🅰 AE
ⓞ VISA
M 7.50/10.75 **st.** and a la carte ▯ 3.40 – ☲ 5.65 – **41 rm** 42.50/54.00 **st.**

at Wetton (Staffs.) NW : 5 ½ m. by Ilam Rd – ⊠ Ashbourne – ✆ 033 527 Alstonefield :

🏠 **Hallows Grange,** DE6 2AF, ℰ 346 – TV ℗. ⁊
Accommodation April-September only – **M** (booking essential) 6.95/15.00 **st.** ▯ 3.50 – **4 rm**
☲ 26.00/72.00 **st.**

THORPE MANDEVILLE Northants. – see Banbury.

THORPE MARKET Norfolk 404 X 25 – pop. 221 – ⊠ North Walsham – ✆ 026 379 Southrepps.

♦London 130 – ♦Norwich 21.

🏠 **Elderton Lodge** ⤳, NR11 8TZ, S : 1 m. on A 149 ℰ 547, ☞ – TV ⌂wc ℗. 🅰 VISA
M 9.75 **t.** and a la carte ▯ 3.00 – **7 rm** ☲ 16.00/34.00 **t.** – SB (October-April except Bank
Holidays) 46.00/50.00 **st.**

THORPE ST. ANDREW Norfolk 404 Y 26 – see Norwich.

THORVERTON Devon 403 J 31 – ECD : Wednesday – ⊠ ✆ 0392 Exeter.

♦London 200 – Exeter 9 – Taunton 33.

🏯 **Berribridge** ⤳, EX5 5JR, SW : ½ m. ℰ 860259, ☞ – ⌂wc ℗. 🅰 VISA. ⁊
M *(closed Tuesday to non residents)* (dinner only) 18.00 **t.** and a la carte ▯ 3.50 – **4 rm**
☲ 28.00/48.00 **t.**

THREE COCKS (ABERLLYNFI) Powys 403 K 27 – ⊠ Brecon – ✆ 049 74 Glasbury.

♦London 184 – Brecon 11 – Hereford 25 – ♦Swansea 55.

XX **Three Cocks** with rm, LD3 0SL, on A 438 ℰ 215, ☞ – ℗. 🅰 VISA. ⁊
closed January – **M** *(closed Bank Holidays and Sunday lunch except July and August)*
15.00 **st.** and a la carte 12.00/14.70 **st.** ▯ 2.30 – **7 rm** ☲ 18.00/36.00 **st.** – SB (except Bank
Holidays) 58.00 **st.**

THREE MILE STONE Cornwall – see Truro.

THRESHFIELD North Yorks. 402 N 21 – see Grassington.

THURLESTONE Devon 403 I 33 – see Kingsbridge.

TICKTON Humberside – see Beverley.

TILBURY Essex 404 V 29 – pop. 11 430 – ✆ 037 52.

🚢 Shipping connections with the Continent : to USSR (Leningrad) via Norway (Oslo) and
Denmark (Copenhagen) (Baltic Shipping Co.).
🚢 to Gravesend (Sealink) frequent services daily (5 mn).

♦London 24 – Southend-on-Sea 20.

Hotels and restaurants see : London W : 24 m.

TIMPERLEY Greater Manchester 402 ② 403 ③ 404 ⑨ – see Altrincham.

TINTAGEL Cornwall 408 F 32 The West Country G. – pop. 1 566 – ECD : Wednesday except summer – ✆ 0840 Camelford.

See : Arthur's Castle : site★★★ *AC* – Tintagel Church★ – Old Post Office★ *AC*.

Envir. : Delabole Quarry★ *AC*, SE : 4 m. by B 3263 – Camelford★, SE : 6 m. by B 3263 and B 3266.

◆London 264 – Exeter 63 – ◆Plymouth 49 – Truro 41.

  🏠 **Bossiney House,** Bossiney, PL34 0AX, NE : ½ m. on B 3263 ℰ 770240, 🔲, ☞ – ⚌wc ⅏wc 🅿 📭 🆎 ⓞ
    🅽 *VISA*
    Easter-October – **M** (bar lunch)/dinner 8.50 **st.** ₰ 2.30 – **20 rm** ⭤ 23.00/38.00 **st.** –
    SB 43.00/49.00 **st.**

  🕋 **Trewarmett Lodge,** Trewarmett, PL34 0ET, SW : 1 ½ m. on B 3263 ℰ 770460, ≤, ☞ – 🅿
    🅽 *VISA*
    M 4.95/6.50 **st.** and a la carte ₰ 2.80 – **6 rm** ⭤ 12.50/27.00 **st.** – SB 35.00/39.00 **st.**

  🔼 **Old Borough House,** Bossiney, PL34 0AY, NE : ½ m. on B 3263 ℰ 770475 – 🅿 🌿
    4 rm ⭤ 7.50/22.00 **st.**

  ✕ **Mill House Inn** with rm, Trebarwith, PL34 0HD, S : 1 ¼ m. by B 3263 via Treknow ℰ 770200,
    « Former corn mill » – 📺 ⚌wc ⅏wc 🅿 🅽 *VISA*
    M (bar lunch)/dinner a la carte 9.35/14.50 **t.** ₰ 2.45 – **9 rm** ⭤ 16.50/39.00 **t.** – SB (November-
    March) 40.00 **t.**

TINTERN (TYNDYRN) Gwent 403 404 L 28 – pop. 816 – ECD : Wednesday – ✉ Chepstow –
✆ 029 18.

See : Abbey★★ (ruins) *AC*.

🛈 Tintern Abbey ℰ 431 (summer only).

◆London 137 – ◆Bristol 23 – Gloucester 40 – Newport 22.

  🏛 **Beaufort** (Embassy), NP6 6SF, ℰ 777, ☞ – 📺 ⚌wc ⅏wc ☎ 🅿 🔊 🅽 🆎 ⓞ *VISA*
    M (bar lunch)/dinner 9.50 **st.** and a la carte ₰ 2.55 – **24 rm** ⭤ 37.50/53.50 **st.** – SB (weekends
    only) 58.00 **st.**

  🏠 **Royal George,** NP6 6SF, ℰ 205, ☞ – 📺 ⚌wc ☎ 🅿 🅽 🆎 *VISA*
    M (bar lunch)/dinner 6.50 **t.** and a la carte – **15 rm** ⭤ 29.50/43.00 **t.** – SB (weekends only)
    45.25/57.25 **st.**

  🔼 **Parva Farmhouse,** NP6 6SQ, on A 466 ℰ 411 – 🅿
    6 rm ⭤ 14.00/25.00 **st.**

TISBURY Wilts. 403 404 N 30 – pop. 2 254 – ✆ 0747.

◆London 110 – ◆Bristol 47 – Salisbury 14.

  ✕✕ **Garden Room,** 2-3 High St., ℰ 870907 – 🅽 *VISA*
    closed Saturday lunch, Sunday dinner, Monday, 2 weeks February and 1 week October –
    M 7.50/14.00 **t.** ₰ 3.00.

TITCHWELL Norfolk 404 V 25 – pop. 96 – ✉ King's Lynn – ✆ 0485 Brancaster.

◆London 124 – ◆Cambridge 66 – ◆Norwich 41.

  🏠 **Titchwell Manor** (Best Western), PE31 8BB, on A 149 ℰ 210221, ☞ – ⚌wc 🅿 🅽 🆎 ⓞ
    VISA
    M 5.85/9.85 **t.** and a la carte ₰ 3.15 – **10 rm** ⭤ 24.00/50.00 **t.** – SB (except Bank Holidays)
    47.50/58.00 **st.**

TIVERTON Devon 403 J 31 The West Country G. – pop. 14 745 – ECD : Thursday – ✆ 0884.

See : Museum★ *AC*.

Envir. : at Bickleigh★★, Mill Craft Centre and farms★★ *AC*, Castle★ *AC*, S : 4 ½ m. – Knightshayes
Court★ *AC*, N : 2 m. on A 396 – Coldharbour Mill, Uffculme★ *AC*, E : 11 m. by A 373.

🛈 Pheonix Lane ℰ 255827 (summer only).

◆London 190 – Exeter 14 – Taunton 23.

  🏛 **Tiverton,** Blundells Rd, EX16 4DB, E : ½ m. on A 373 ℰ 256120 – ▤ rest 📺 ⚌wc ☜ 🔊 🅿
    🅽 🆎 ⓞ *VISA*
    M 6.50/9.50 **t.** ₰ 3.50 – **29 rm** ⭤ (dinner included) 28.00/54.00 **t.**

  ✕ **Hendersons,** 18 Newport St., EX16 6NL, ℰ 254256 – 🅽 🆎 ⓞ *VISA*
    closed Sunday, Monday, last 3 weeks August and 25 to 29 December – **M** 11.00 **t.** (dinner) and
    a la carte 8.40/14.20 **t.** ₰ 2.85.

  at Oakfordbridge NW : 9 m. on A 396 – ✉ Tiverton – ✆ 039 85 Oakford :

  🕋 **Bark House,** EX16 9HZ, ℰ 236 – 📺 ⚌wc ⅏wc 🅿 🅽 🆎 ⓞ *VISA*
    closed January and February – **M** (lunch residents only)/dinner 10.00 **st.** ₰ 3.50 – ⭤ 3.00 –
    6 rm 13.00/36.00 **st.**

  at Bolham N : 1 ¼ m. on A 396 – ✉ ✆ 0884 Tiverton :

  🏠 **Hartnoll Country House,** EX16 7RA, ℰ 252777, ☞ – 📺 ⚌wc 🅿 🅽 🆎 ⓞ *VISA*
    M (grill rest. only)(bar lunch Monday to Saturday)/dinner 7.50 **t.** and a la carte ₰ 2.75 – **10 rm**
    ⭤ 20.00/35.00 **t.**

CITROEN 31 Leat St. ℰ 252170

TONBRIDGE Kent 404 U 30 – pop. 34 407 – ECD : Wednesday – ✪ 0732.

See : Tonbridge School★ (1553).

Envir. : Ightham Mote★ (Manor House 14C-15C) *AC*, site★ N : 7 m.

🅸🅶 Poult Wood, Higham Lane 🕿 364039, N : 2 m. by A 227.

♦London 33 – ♦Brighton 37 – Hastings 31 – Maidstone 14.

🏨 **Rose and Crown** (T.H.F.), 125 High St., TN9 1DD, 🕿 357966, 🍴 – 📺 ⇔wc ☎ 🅿. 🖧 🔼
　　AE ⓪ VISA
　　M 8.35/9.95 **st.** and a la carte 🕯 3.40 – 🖙 5.65 – **51 rm** 43.00/55.00 **st., 1 suite**.

ALFA-ROMEO, PEUGEOT-TALBOT　Sovereign Way　　RENAULT　London Rd, Hildenborough 🕿 832022
🕿 350288　　　　　　　　　　　　　　　　　VAUXHALL　Waterloo Rd 🕿 354035
AUSTIN-ROVER, DAIMLER-JAGUAR　Cannon Lane　VOLVO　Hildenborough 🕿 832424
🕿 364444　　　　　　　　　　　　　　　　　VW, AUDI-NSU, MERCEDES-BENZ　Vale Rd 🕿
FORD　Avebury Av. 🕿 356301　　　　　　　　355822

TORCROSS Devon 403 J 33 – see Kingsbridge.

TORQUAY Devon 403 J 32 The West Country G. – pop. 54 430 – ECD : Wednesday and Saturday
– ✪ 0803.

See : Kent's Cavern★ *AC* CX A.

Envir. : Cockington★, W : 1 m. AX.

⛴ to Channel Islands : Alderney (Torbay Seaways: Hydrofoil) summer only – to Channel Islands :
St. Peter Port, Guernsey (Torbay Seaways: Hydrofoil) summer only – to Channel Islands :
St. Helier, Jersey (Torbay Seaways: Hydrofoil) summer only.

🄸 Vaughan Parade 🕿 27428.

♦London 223 – Exeter 23 – ♦Plymouth 32.

Plans on following pages

🏨🏨 **Imperial** (T.H.F.), Park Hill Rd, TQ1 2DG, 🕿 24301, Telex 42849, ≤ Torbay, ⅃ heated, 🔼, 🍴,
　　🎾, squash – 🛗 📺 ☎ ⅋ ⇔ 🅿. 🖧. 🔼 AE ⓪ VISA
　　　　　　　　　　　　　　　　　　　　　　　　　　　　CZ a
　　M 11.00/17.00 **st.** and a la carte 🕯 4.50 – 🖙 72.00/124.00 **st., 14 suites**.

🏨🏨 **Palace**, Babbacombe Rd, TQ1 3TG, 🕿 22271, Telex 42606, ⅃ heated, 🔼, 🎾, 🍴, squash
　　– 🛗 📺 ☎ ⇔ 🅿. 🖧. 🔼 AE ⓪ VISA
　　　　　　　　　　　　　　　　　　　　　　　　　　　　CX u
　　M 7.00/13.00 **st.** and a la carte 🕯 3.40 – **141 rm** 🖙 37.00/82.00 **st., 6 suites** 110.00/134.00 **st.** –
　　SB (except Christmas and Bank Holidays) 70.00/76.00 **st.**

🏨🏨 **Grand**, Seafront, TQ2 6NY, 🕿 25234, Telex 42891, ≤, ⅃ heated, 🔼 – 🛗 📺 ☎ ⇔. 🖧. 🔼
　　AE ⓪ VISA
　　　　　　　　　　　　　　　　　　　　　　　　　　　　BZ z
　　M 8.50/13.50 **st.** and a la carte – **110 rm** 🖙 24.00/100.00 **st., 10 suites** 49.00/150.00 **st.** –
　　SB 62.00/114.00 **st.**

🏨 **Livermead House** (Best Western), Sea Front, TQ2 6QJ, 🕿 24361, Telex 42918, ≤, ⅃ heated,
　　🍴, 🎾, squash – 🛗 📺 ⇔wc 🚿wc ☎ 🅿. 🖧. 🔼 AE ⓪ VISA. 🎾
　　　　　　　　　　　　　　　　　　　　　　　　　　　　BZ e
　　M 5.75/9.25 **st.** and a la carte 🕯 3.30 – **69 rm** 🖙 19.50/60.00 **st.** – SB (except Christmas)
　　51.00/69.50 **st.**

🏨 **Livermead Cliff** (Best Western), Sea Front, TQ2 6RQ, 🕿 22881, Telex 42918, ≤, ⅃ heated,
　　🍴, 🎾, squash – 🛗 📺 ⇔wc 🚿wc ☎ 🅿. 🖧. 🔼 AE ⓪ VISA. 🎾
　　　　　　　　　　　　　　　　　　　　　　　　　　　　BX r
　　M 5.75/9.25 **st.** and a la carte 🕯 3.30 – **64 rm** 🖙 19.50/62.00 **st.** – SB (except Christmas)
　　51.00/69.50 **st.**

🏨 **Homers**, Warren Rd, TQ2 5TN, 🕿 213456, ≤ Torbay – 📺 ⇔wc 🚿wc ☎. 🔼 AE ⓪ VISA
　　closed 1 January-12 February – **M** (dinner only) 13.50 **t.** and a la carte 🕯 3.75 – **14 rm**
　　🖙 30.00/60.00 **t., 1 suite** 64.00/80.00 **t.** – SB 50.00/70.00 **st.**
　　　　　　　　　　　　　　　　　　　　　　　　　　　　CZ n

🏨 **Toorak**, Chestnut Av., TQ2 5JS, 🕿 211866, ⅃ heated, 🍴, 🎾 – 📺 ⇔wc ☎ 🅿. 🖧. 🔼 VISA
　　M 5.85/10.45 **st.** 🕯 2.25 – **41 rm** 🖙 31.00/62.00 **st.** – SB (except summer and Bank Holidays)
　　(weekends only) 42.00/54.00 **st.**
　　　　　　　　　　　　　　　　　　　　　　　　　　　　BY v

🏨 **Nepaul**, 27 Croft Rd, TQ2 5UD, 🕿 28457, ≤, 🔼, 🍴, 🎾 – 🛗 📺 ⇔wc 🚿wc ⇔ 🅿. 🔼 AE ⓪
　　VISA
　　　　　　　　　　　　　　　　　　　　　　　　　　　　CY v
　　M 5.95/9.50 **t.** and a la carte 🕯 4.00 – **41 rm** 🖙 23.00/70.00 **t.** – SB (October-May) 40.00/48.00 **st.**

🏨 **Belgrave**, Seafront, Belgrave Rd, TQ2 5HE, 🕿 28566, ⅃ heated, 🍴 – 🛗 📺 ⇔wc ⇔ 🅿.
　　🔼 AE ⓪ VISA
　　　　　　　　　　　　　　　　　　　　　　　　　　　　CZ c
　　M (bar lunch)/dinner 7.50 **t.** – **54 rm** 🖙 21.50/56.00 **t.** – SB (October-May) (weekends only)
　　46.00/54.00 **st.**

🏨 **Kistor**, Belgrave Rd, TQ2 5HF, 🕿 212632, 🔼, 🍴 – 🛗 📺 ⇔wc ☎ 🅿. 🖧. 🔼 AE ⓪ VISA
　　M (buffet lunch Monday to Saturday)/dinner 8.95 **st.** 🕯 2.80 – **52 rm** 🖙 19.00/54.00 **st.** –
　　SB 45.00/58.00 **st.**
　　　　　　　　　　　　　　　　　　　　　　　　　　　　CY r

🏨 **Glenorleigh**, 26 Cleveland Rd, TQ2 5BE, 🕿 22135, ⅃ heated, 🍴 – 🚿wc 🅿. 🎾
　　16 rm 🖙 13.80/20.00 **st.**
　　　　　　　　　　　　　　　　　　　　　　　　　　　　BY n

🏨 **Fairmount House** 🍽, Herbert Rd, Chelston, TQ2 6RW, 🕿 605446, 🍴 – ⇔wc 🚿wc 🅿. AE
　　VISA
　　　　　　　　　　　　　　　　　　　　　　　　　　　　AX a
　　Mid February-mid November – **M** (bar lunch Monday to Saturday)/dinner 7.00 **st.** 🕯 2.80 –
　　7 rm 🖙 12.00/32.00 **t.** – SB (except summer) 41.00 **st.**

🏨 **Brigantine Motor**, 56 Marldon Rd, Shiphay, TQ2 6RW, 🕿 63162, ⅃, 🍴 – 📺 ⇔wc 🚿wc 🅿
　　16 rm.
　　　　　　　　　　　　　　　　　　　　　　　　　　　　AX s

P.T.O. →

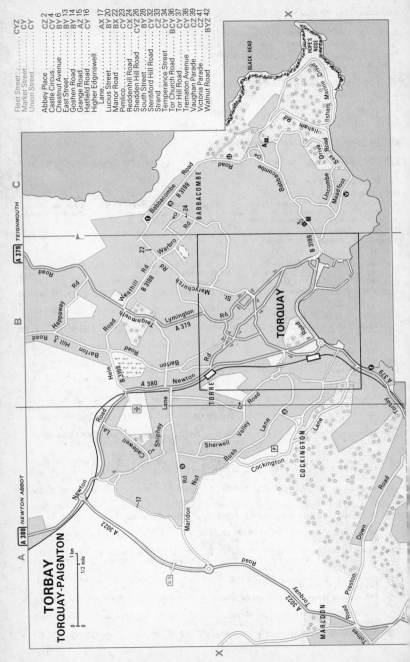

TORBAY
TORQUAY-PAIGNTON

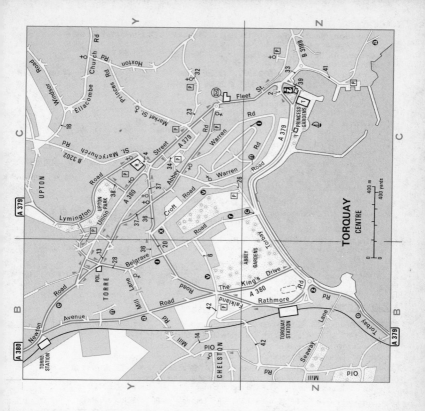

TORQUAY
CENTRE

0 ____ 400 m
0 ____ 400 yards

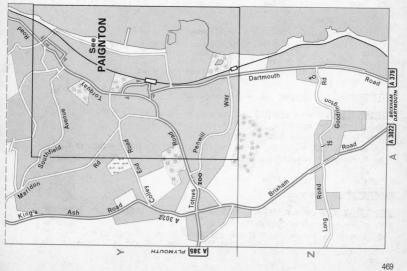

See
PAIGNTON

↑ **Clevedon,** Meadfoot Sea Rd, TQ1 2LQ, ℰ 24260, ⚑ – 📺🚾 ⁿ🚾 🅿 𝑽𝑰𝑺𝑨   CX **v**
  April-October – **14 rm** ⚏ 11.45/32.00 st.

↑ **Cranborne,** 58 Belgrave Rd, TQ2 5HY, ℰ 28046 – 📺 ⌂🚾 ⁿ. ◪ 𝑽𝑰𝑺𝑨, ⅏   BY **i**
  closed December – **14 rm** ⚏ 8.50/26.00 t.

↑ Concorde, 26 Newton Rd, TQ2 5BZ, ℰ 22330, ⌇ heated – 📺 ⌂🚾 ⁿ🚾 🅿 – **22 rm**   BY **e**

↑ **Elmsdale,** 70 Avenue Rd, TQ2 5LF, ℰ 25929 – 🅿. 𝑽𝑰𝑺𝑨   BY **a**
  7 rm ⚏ 8.00/20.00 st.

↑ **Mount Nessing,** St. Lukes Rd North, TQ2 5PD, ℰ 22970 – 🅿. ⅏   CZ **i**
  Easter-October and Christmas – **13 rm** ⚏ 7.50/23.00 t.

XX **Remy's,** 3 Croft Rd, TQ2 5UN, ℰ 22359, French rest. – ◭ 𝑽𝑰𝑺𝑨   CY **x**
  closed Sunday, Monday and first 2 weeks August – **M** (booking essential) (lunch by arrangement)/dinner 11.85 st. ⌕ 3.00.

  at Maidencombe N : 3 ½ m. on A 379 – BX – ✉ ✆ 0803 Torquay :

🏠 **Orestone House** ⌂, Rockhouse Lane, TQ1 4SX, ℰ 38098, ≼, ⌇ heated, ⚑ – 📺 ⌂🚾
  ⁿ🚾 🅿 🅿 ◪ ◭ 𝑽𝑰𝑺𝑨
  closed January and February – **M** (bar lunch)/dinner 9.75 t. and a la carte ⌕ 3.00 – **20 rm**
  ⚏ (dinner included) 29.50/76.00 t. – SB (except summer) 50.00/62.00 st.

  at Babbacombe NE : 1 ½ m. – ✉ ✆ 0803 Torquay :

🏠 **Norcliffe,** 7 Babbacombe Downs Rd, TQ1 3LF, ℰ 38456, ≼, ⚑ – 📺 ⌂🚾 ⁿ 🅿. ◪
  Easter-October – **M** (bar lunch)/dinner 5.50 t. ⌕ 1.50 – **20 rm** ⚏ 9.00/36.00 t. –
  SB 28.00/46.00 st.   CX **r**

XX **Green Mantle,** 135 Babbacombe Rd, TQ1 3SR, ℰ 34292 – ◭ ⑩ 𝑽𝑰𝑺𝑨   CX **a**
  closed Sunday and first 2 weeks November – **M** (dinner only) 14.00 t. and a la carte 11.25/14.00 t.
  ⌕ 2.60.

AUDI, VW Torwood St. ℰ 28635
AUSTIN-ROVER, JAGUAR Lawes Bridge ℰ 62781
CITROEN Walnut Rd ℰ 605858
FORD Lawes Bridge, Newton Rd ℰ 62021

PEUGEOT-TALBOT 141 Newton Rd ℰ 63626
ROLLS ROYCE-BENTLEY, FERRARI, LOTUS, SAAB
Lisburne Sq. ℰ 24321

TOTLAND BAY I.O.W. **403 404** P 31 – see Wight (Isle of).

TOTNES Devon **403** I 32 The West Country G. – pop. 6 133 – ECD : Thursday – ✆ 0803.
See : Site★★ – St. Mary's Church★ – Butterwalk★ – Castle (≼★★★) AC.
🛈 The Plains ℰ 863168 (summer only).
♦London 224 – Exeter 24 – ♦Plymouth 23 – Torquay 9.

↑ Ridgemark, Bridgetown Hill, TQ9 5BH, on A 385 ℰ 862011, ⚑ – 📺 ⁿ🚾 ☎ 🅿 – **7 rm**

XX **Elbow Room,** 6 North St., TQ9 5NZ, ℰ 863480 – ◪ ◭ 𝑽𝑰𝑺𝑨
  closed Sunday and Monday – **M** (carving lunch)/dinner a la carte 7.95/11.95 t.

  at Stoke Gabriel SE : 4 m. by A 385 – ✉ Totnes – ✆ 080 428 Stoke Gabriel :

🏠 **Gabriel Court** ⌂, TQ9 6SF, ℰ 206, ⌇ heated, ⚑, ⅏ – ⌂🚾 ⁿ🚾 🅿 ◪ ◭ ⑩ 𝑽𝑰𝑺𝑨
  closed February – **M** (dinner only and Sunday lunch)/dinner 12.50 st. ⌕ 3.30 – **22 rm**
  ⚏ 22.00/46.00 st.

  at Dartington NW : 2 m. on A 385 – ✉ ✆ 0803 Totnes :

🏠 **Cott Inn,** TQ9 6HE, ℰ 863777, « 14C thatched inn » – 🅿. ◪ ◭ ⑩ 𝑽𝑰𝑺𝑨. ⅏
  M (buffet lunch)/dinner a la carte 9.20/10.50 st. ⌕ 2.50 – **6 rm** ⚏ 18.50/37.00 t. –
  SB (3 October-21 March except Christmas) 60.00 st.

AUSTIN-ROVER Station Rd ℰ 862404
FORD North St. ℰ 862196

VAUXHALL-OPEL The Plains ℰ 862247

TOTON Notts. **402 403 404** Q 25 – see Nottingham.

TOWCESTER Northants. **403 404** R 27 – pop. 5 010 – ✆ 0327.
🛈 Woodlands, Farthingstone ℰ 36291, W : 6 m. M 1 junction 16.
♦London 70 – ♦Birmingham 50 – Northampton 9 – ♦Oxford 36.

🏠 Brave Old Oak, 104 Watling St. East, NN12 7BT, ℰ 50533 – 📺 ⁿ ☜ 🅿 – **12 rm**.

🏠 Saracen's Head, 219 Watling St. West, NN12 7BX, ℰ 50414 – 🅿. ◪ ◭ ⑩ 𝑽𝑰𝑺𝑨
  M 8.25 t. and a la carte ⌕ 2.75 – **12 rm** ⚏ 20.00/30.00 s.

AUSTIN-ROVER Quinbury End ℰ 0327 (Blakesley) 860208

TRALLWNG = Welshpool.

TREBETHERICK Cornwall **403** F 32 – ECD : Wednesday – ✉ Wadebridge – ✆ 020 886.
♦London 286 – Newquay 22 – ♦Plymouth 46 – Truro 32.

🏠 Bodare ⌂, Daymer Bay, PL27 6SA, ℰ 3210, ⚑ – ⌂🚾 ⁿ🚾 🅿. ◪ 𝑽𝑰𝑺𝑨
  20 March-October – **M** (buffet lunch)/dinner 9.50 st. – **17 rm** ⚏ 21.00/42.00 s. – SB (April,
  May and October only) 43.00 s.

TRECASTLE Powys **403** J 28 – ❀ 087 482 Sennybridge.
♦London 183 – Brecon 12.

   🏰 Castle, LD3 8UH, ✆ 354 – 📺 🅿 – **6 rm**.

TREDETHY Cornwall – see Bodmin.

TREFALDWYN = Montgomery.

TREFDRAETH = Newport (Dyfed).

TREFFYNNON = Holywell.

TREFYNWY = Monmouth.

TREGOOSE Cornwall – see St. Columb Major.

TREGREHAN Cornwall **403** F 32 – see St. Austell.

TRESCO Cornwall **403** ㉚ – see Scilly (Isles of).

TREYARNON BAY Cornwall **403** E 32 – see Padstow.

TRING Herts. **404** S 28 – pop. 10 610 – ECD : Wednesday – ❀ 044 282.
See : Church of St. Peter and St. Paul (interior : stone corbels★).
♦London 38 – Aylesbury 7 – Luton 14.

   🏨 **Rose and Crown** (Whitbread), High St., HP23 5AH, ✆ 4071 – 📺 🚻wc ☎ 🅿 🛦 🔼 AE ⓪ *VISA*
       M a la carte 6.65/10.70 **t.** – **28 rm** ⌘ 40.00/48.00 **t.** – SB (weekends only) 52.00/72.00 **st.**

HONDA, RELIANT 110 Western Rd ✆ 4144

TROTTON West Sussex – see Midhurst.

TROUTBECK Cumbria **402** L 20 – see Windermere.

TROUTBECK Cumbria – ✉ Penrith – ❀ 059 683 Threlkeld.
♦London 306 – ♦Carlisle 30 – Kendal 28 – Keswick 9.

   ⤴ **Lane Head Farm**, NW : 1 m. on A 66, CA11 0SY, ✆ 220, ⇗ – 🚻wc 🅿 �
       March-October – **9 rm** ⌘ 13.00/30.00 **st.**

TROWBRIDGE Wilts. **403 404** N 30 The West Country G. – pop. 27 299 – ECD : Wednesday –
❀ 022 14 – **Envir. :** Norton St. Philip (The George Inn★★), W : 6 m. – Steeple Ashton★, The
Green★, E : 7 m. – Edington (St. Mary, St. Catherine and All Saints Church★), SE : 8 m.
♦London 115 – ♦Bristol 27 – ♦Southampton 55 – Swindon 32.

   🏨 **Hilbury Court,** Hilperton Rd, BA14 7JW, ✆ 2949, ⇗ – 📺 🚻wc 🅿 🔼 *VISA*. �
       closed 24 December-1 January – **M** *(closed dinner Friday, Saturday and Sunday)* (bar
       lunch)/dinner 8.00 **t.** ⓰ 3.10 – **12 rm** ⌘ 21.00/34.00 **t.**

TRURO Cornwall **403** E 33 The West Country G. – pop. 17 852 – ECD : Thursday – ❀ 0872.
See : Cornwall County Museum★ *AC* – **Envir. :** Trewithen★★★, NE : 7 ½ m. by A 390 – Trelissick
garden★★, (≼★★) *AC*, S : 8 m. by A 39 and B 3289 – at Probus★ Church Tower★ County Demonstra-
tion Garden★, NE : 8 m. – Feock (Church★), S : 8 ½ m.
🏌 Treliske ✆ 72640, W : 2 m. on A 390 – 🚺 Municipal Building, Boscawen St. ✆ 74555.
♦London 295 – Exeter 87 – Penzance 26 – ♦Plymouth 52.

   🏨 **Royal,** Lemon St., TR1 2QB, ✆ 70345 – 📺 🚻wc ☜ 🅿 🛦 🔼 *VISA*
       closed Christmas – **M** (grill rest. only)(bar lunch Sunday)/dinner 7.50 **st.** and a la carte ⓰ 3.00
       – **34 rm** ⌘ 26.00/43.00 **st.** – SB (weekends only)(except Christmas) 43.50/49.50 **st.**

   🏨 **Brookdale,** Tregolls Rd, TR1 1JZ, ✆ 73513 – 📺 🚻wc 🚻wc ☎ 🅿 🔼 AE ⓪ *VISA*
       closed 1 week at Christmas – **M** (bar lunch)/dinner 10.25 **st.** ⓰ 2.50 – **38 rm** ⌘ 30.45/44.00 **st.**
       – SB (weekends only) 58.00 **st.**

   🏨 **Carlton,** 49 Falmouth Rd, TR1 2HL, ✆ 72450 – 📺 🚻wc 🚻wc 🅿 🔼 *VISA*
       M (bar lunch)/dinner 5.50 **st.** and a la carte ⓰ 2.70 – **24 rm** ⌘ 16.80/31.50 **st.** – SB (weekends
       only) 33.00/37.40 **st.**

   ⤴ **Laniley House** ⬦, Newquay road, nr. Trispen, St. Clement, TR4 9AU, NE : 3 ½ m. by A 390
       off A 3076 ✆ 75201, ⇗ – 📺 🅿 �
       closed Christmas-New Year – **3 rm** ⌘ 12.50/22.00 **s.**

   at Deveron SW : 4 ½ m. by A 39 – ✉ ❀ 0872 Truro :

   ⤴ **Driffold** ⬦, 8 Deveron Lane, TR3 6PA, ✆ 863314, ⇗ – 🚻wc 🅿 �
       7 rm ⌘ 11.50/36.00 **t.**

at Three Mile Stone W : 3 ¼ m. by A 390 – ⊠ ✿ 0872 Truro :

XX **Peacock Cottage** with rm., TR4 9AW, W : ¼ m. ℰ 78479, German rest., ⇗ – **P**. ◪ 🄰🄴 ⑩ *VISA* ⫻
closed lunch Saturday, Sunday and Bank Holidays – **M** 5.00/9.15 **st.** and a la carte 9.50/15.85 **st.**
– **5 rm** ☲ 21.50/35.00 **st.**

AUSTIN-ROVER Lemon Quay ℰ 74321
FORD Lemon Quay ℰ 73933
PEUGEOT-TALBOT Point Mills, Bissoe ℰ 0872
(Devoran) 863073

VAUXHALL Fairmantle St. ℰ 76231
VW, AUDI Three Mile Stone ℰ 79301

TUDWEILIOG Gwynedd 402 403 G 25 – pop. 882 – ⊠ Pwllheli – ✿ 075 887.
♦London 267 – Caernarfon 25.

X **Dive Inn**, LL53 8PB, W : 2 m. by B 4417 ℰ 246, Seafood – **P**
Easter-November and Saturday dinner only in winter – **M** (booking essential) (bar lunch)/dinner
a la carte 9.50/17.00 **t.** ⋀ 3.00.

TUNBRIDGE WELLS Kent 404 U 30 – see Royal Tunbridge Wells.

TURVEY Beds. 404 S 27 – see Bedford.

TUTBURY Staffs. 402 403 404 O 25 – pop. 5 099 (inc. Hatton) – ECD : Wednesday – ⊠ ✿ 0283
Burton-upon-Trent.
♦London 132 – ♦Birmingham 33 – Derby 11 – ♦Stoke-on-Trent 27.

🏛 **Ye Olde Dog and Partridge**, High St., DE13 9LS, ℰ 813030, « Part 15C timbered inn », ⇗
– ⬛ ➪wc ⬛wc ☎ **P**. ◪ 🄰 ⑩ *VISA*
closed 25-26 December and 1 January – **M** 7.50 **t.** (lunch)/dinner a la carte 11.20/17.10 **t.** ⋀ 4.00
– **18 rm** ☲ 40.00/60.00 **t.**

TUXFORD Notts. 402 404 R 24 – pop. 2 547 – ECD : Wednesday – ⊠ Newark – ✿ 0777.
♦London 141 – ♦Leeds 53 – Lincoln 18 – ♦Nottingham 26 – ♦Sheffield 29.

🏛 **Newcastle Arms**, Market Pl., NG22 0LA, ℰ 870208 – ⬛ ➪wc ☞ **P**. ⅍ ◪ 🄰🄴 ⑩ *VISA*
M 8.25/10.25 **st.** and a la carte – ☲ 4.50 – **12 rm** 30.00/40.00 **st.** – SB (weekends only)
45.00/50.00 **st.**

TWEMLOW GREEN Cheshire 402 403 404 N 24 – see Holmes Chapel.

TWO BRIDGES Devon 403 I 32 The West Country G. – ⊠ Yelverton – ✿ 0822 Tavistock.
♦London 226 – Exeter 25 – ♦Plymouth 17.

⌂ **Cherrybrook** ⌖, PL20 6SP, NE : 1 m. on B 3212 ℰ 88260, ≼, ⇗ – ⫻wc **P**
closed Christmas and New Year – **7 rm** ☲ 15.00/32.00 **st.**

TYDDEWI = St. David's.

TYNDYRN = Tintern.

TYNEMOUTH Tyne and Wear 401 402 P 18 – pop. 17 877 – ECD : Wednesday – ✿ 0632 North
Shields (6 fig.) or 091 Tyneside (7 fig.) – **See** : Priory and castle : ruins★ (11C) *AC*.
♦London 290 – ♦Newcastle-upon-Tyne 8 – Sunderland 7.

🏛 **Park**, Grand Par., NE30 4JQ, ℰ 257 1406, ≼ – ⬛ ➪wc ☞ **P**. ⅍ ◪ 🄰🄴 ⑩ *VISA*
closed Christmas, New Year and Bank Holidays – **M** 8.50/9.50 **t.** and a la carte – **31 rm**
☲ 23.00/43.50 **t.** – SB (weekends only) 52.00/54.00 **st.**

VAUXHALL Tynemouth Rd ℰ 570346

UCKFIELD East Sussex 404 U 31 – pop. 10 938 – ECD : Wednesday – ✿ 082 575.
Envir. : Sheffield Park Gardens★★ *AC*, W : 6 m.
♦London 45 – ♦Brighton 17 – Eastbourne 20 – Maidstone 34.

🏰 **Horsted Place** ⌖, Little Horsted, TN22 5TS, S : 2 ½ m. by B 2102 and A 22 on A 26 ℰ 581,
Telex 95548, ≼, « Victorian gothic country house and gardens », ◪, XX – 🕸 ⬛ ⫻ 🕭 **P**. ◪
🄰🄴 ⑩ *VISA*
M (dinner only and Sunday lunch) (lunch by arrangement)/dinner 30.00 **st.** – ☲ 5.00 –,
15 suites 75.00/225.00 **st.**

XX **Sussex Barn**, Ringles Cross, TN22 1HB, N : 1 m. on A 22 ℰ 3827, ⇗ – **P**. ◪ 🄰🄴 ⑩ *VISA*
M 9.75 **t.** (lunch) and a la carte 10.50/31.50 **t.** ⋀ 4.00.

at Framfield SE : 1 ¾ m. on B 2102 – ⊠ Uckfield – ✿ 082 582 Framfield :

X **Coach House**, The Street, TN22 5NL, ℰ 636, ▨ heated – **P**. ◪ 🄰🄴 ⑩ *VISA*
closed Sunday dinner and Monday – **M** 13.25 **t.** ⋀ 3.95.

AUSTIN-ROVER 84-86 High St. ℰ 4255
NISSAN 143-145 High St. ℰ 4722
PEUGEOT-TALBOT Five Ash Down ℰ 082 581 (Bux-ted) 3220

RENAULT Blackboys ℰ 082 582 (Framfield) 317
VAUXHALL-OPEL Maresfield ℰ 2477

ULLSWATER Cumbria 402 L 20 – ✉ Penrith – ☼ 085 36 Pooley Bridge.

See : Lake★.

🛈 Main Car Park, Glenridding ☎ 085 32 (Glenridding) 414 (summer only) – at Pooley Bridge, Eusemere Car Park ☎ 530 (summer only).

◆London 296 – ◆Carlisle 25 – Kendal 31 – Penrith 6.

    at Howtown SW : 4 m. of Pooley Bridge – ✉ Penrith – ☼ 085 36 Pooley Bridge :

🏠 **Howtown** ⧉, CA10 2ND, ☎ 514, ≼, « Tastefully furnished inn », 🐎 – 🅿. ⌖
    April-October – **M** (buffet lunch Monday to Saturday)/dinner 7.50 **t.** – **16 rm** ⚏ (dinner included) 20.00/40.00 **t.**

    at Pooley Bridge on B 5320 – ✉ Penrith – ☼ 085 36 Pooley Bridge :

🏛 **Sharrow Bay Country House** ⧉, CA10 2LZ, S : 2 m. on Howtown Rd ☎ 301, ≼ lake and hills, « Lake-side setting, gardens and tasteful decor » – 📺 ⌷wc ☎ 🅿. ⌖
    March-November – **M** (booking essential) 20.50/28.50 **st.** and a la carte lunch – **30 rm** ⚏ (dinner included) 62.00/174.00 **st.**, **6 suites** 67.00/174.00 **st.**

    at Watermillock on A 592 – ✉ Penrith – ☼ 085 36 Pooley Bridge :

🏰 **Leeming on Ullswater Country House** ⧉, CA11 0JJ, on A 592 ☎ 622, Telex 64111, ≼ lake, hills and gardens, « Elegant installation and gardens », park – ☎ ⅙ 🅿. 🔃 AE ⓪ VISA. ⌖
    Mid March-November – **M** (buffet lunch Monday to Saturday)/dinner 22.50 **t.** ⌂ 3.75 – ⚏ 5.00 – **25 rm** 36.50/86.00 **t.** – SB (March and November) 110.00/120.00 **st.**

🏠 **Old Church** ⧉, CA11 0JN, ☎ 204, ≼ lake and hills, « Lakeside setting », ⤵, 🐎 – ⌷wc 🅿
    3 April-October – **M** (dinner only) 14.50 **st.** ⌂ 4.75 – **11 rm** ⚏ 22.00/54.00 **st.**

ULVERSTON Cumbria 402 K 21 – pop. 11 976 – ECD : Wednesday – ☼ 0229.

Envir. : Furness Abbey★ (ruins 13C-15C) *AC*, SW : 6 ½ m.

🏌 Barrow, Rakesmoor, Hawcoat ☎ 0229 (Barrow-in-Furness) 25444, SW : 7 m. – 🏌 Furness, Walney Island ☎ 0229 (Barrow-in-Furness) 41232 – 🏌 Dunnerholme, Askam-in-Furness ☎ 0229 (Barrow-in-Furness) 62675.

🛈 Coronation Hall, County Sq. ☎ 57120.

◆London 278 – Kendal 25 – Lancaster 36.

🏠 **Lonsdale House,** 15 Daltongate, LA12 7BD, ☎ 52598, 🐎 – 📺 ⌷wc ⌷wc ☎. 🔃 AE ⓪ VISA
    closed 1 week at Christmas – **M** *(closed Sunday)* (dinner only) 8.50 **t.** ⌂ 2.50 – **23 rm** ⚏ 13.80/45.00 **t.**

    at Spark Bridge N : 5 ½ m. by A 590 off A 5092 – ✉ Ulverston – ☼ 0229 85 Lowick Bridge :

🏠 **Bridgefield House** ⧉, LA12 8DA, NW : 1 m. on Nibthwaite Rd ☎ 239, 🐎 – ⌷wc 🅿. 🔃 AE ⓪
    M (dinner only)(booking essential) 15.00 **t.** – **5 rm** ⚏ 15.50/44.00 **t.**

    at Lowick Green NE : 5 m. by A 590 on A 5092 – ✉ Ulverston – ☼ 022 986 Greenodd :

🍴 **Farmers Arms,** LA12 8DT, ☎ 376 – 📺 ⌷wc ⌷wc 🅿. 🔃 AE VISA
    M *(closed Saturday lunch)* 5.25 **t.** (lunch) and a la carte 6.80/10.50 **t.** ⌂ 2.90 – **11 rm** ⚏ 16.00/36.00 **t.**

    at Baycliff S : 5 m. on A 5087 – ✉ Ulverston – ☼ 022 988 Bardsea :

🍴 Fisherman's Arms, Coast Rd, LA12 9RJ, ☎ 387 – 📺 ⌷wc 🅿
    12 rm.

FORD Argyle St. ☎ 53209

UMBERLEIGH Devon 403 I 31 – ☼ 0769 High Bickington.

◆London 215 – Exeter 33 – ◆Plymouth 59 – Taunton 47.

🍴 **Rising Sun,** EX37 9DU, ☎ 60447, ⤵ – ⌷wc 🅿. 🔃 VISA
    March-September and weekends only in winter – **M** (bar lunch)/dinner 9.00 **t.** ⌂ 2.70 – **8 rm** ⚏ 18.00/38.00 **t.** – SB (weekends only) 44.00/48.00 **st.**

UNDERBARROW Cumbria 402 L 21 – see Kendal.

UPLYME Devon 403 L 31 – see Lyme Regis.

UPPER ODDINGTON Glos. – see Stow-on-the-Wold.

UPPER SLAUGHTER Glos. 403 404 O 28 – see Stow-on-the-Wold.

UPPINGHAM Leics. **404** R 26 – pop. 2 761 – ECD : Thursday – ✆ 0572.

Envir. : Kirkby Hall★ (ruins 16 C), SE : 8 m.

♦London 101 – ♦Leicester 19 – Northampton 28 – ♦Nottingham 35.

☎ **Garden,** 16 High St. West, LE15 9QD, ℰ 822352, 屏 – ⊡ ➪wc ♒wc. ◪ *VISA*
M *(closed Sunday dinner to non residents)* (bar lunch)/dinner 8.25 **t.** ▯ 2.75 – **13 rm**
☲ 19.00/32.00 **t.**

✗ **Lake Isle** with rm, 16 High St. East, LE15 9PZ, ℰ 822951, 屏 – ⊡ ➪wc ♒wc ⇐. ◪ 函
① *VISA*
closed Sunday dinner, Monday, 2 weeks February, 2 weeks September-October and Bank
Holidays – **M** 8.50/15.00 **t.** ▯ 2.90 – **5 rm** ☲ 24.00/32.00 **st.**

at Lyddington SE : 2 m. by A 6003 – ⊠ Oakham – ✆ 0572 Uppingham :

🏨 **Marquess of Exeter** ॐ, 52 Main St., LE15 9LT, ℰ 822477 – ⊡ ➪wc ♒wc ☎ ℗ ◪ 函 ①
VISA. ❀
M *(closed Sunday dinner)* 5.50/7.95 **t.** and a la carte ▯ 3.00 – **17 rm** ☲ 34.00/42.00 **t.** –
SB (weekends only) 42.00 **st.**

UPTON ST. LEONARDS Glos. – see Gloucester.

UPTON UPON SEVERN Heref. and Worc. **403** **404** N 27 – pop. 1 537 – ECD : Thursday –
✆ 068 46.

🗓 The Pepperpot, Church St. ℰ 4200.

♦London 116 – Hereford 25 – Stratford-upon-Avon 29 – Worcester 11.

🏨 **White Lion,** High St., WR8 0HJ, ℰ 2551 – ⊡ ➪wc ♒wc ☎ ℗ ◪ 函 *VISA*
M *(closed Christmas Day)* 10.80 **t.** and a la carte ▯ 3.00 – **10 rm** ☲ 32.50/47.50 **t.** –
SB 55.00/63.00 **st.**

⌂ **Pool House,** Hanley Rd, WR8 0PA, NW : ½ m. on B 4211 ℰ 2151, ≤, ⧖, 屏 – ➪wc ♒wc
℗. ◪ 函 *VISA*. ❀
closed Christmas – **9 rm** ☲ 14.00/35.00 **st.**

USK (BRYNBUGA) Gwent **403** L 28 – pop. 1 783 – ECD : Wednesday – ✆ 029 13.

See : Valley★.

🟦 at Pontypool ℰ 049 55 (Pontypool) 3655, W : 7 m.

♦London 144 – ♦Bristol 30 – Gloucester 39 – Newport 10.

🏨 **Glen-yr-Afon House,** Pontypool Rd, NP5 1SY, ℰ 2302, 屏 – ♒wc ℗
M 8.00/10.00 **t.** and a la carte ▯ 3.30 – **15 rm** ☲ 24.15/34.50 **t.** – SB (weekends only)
(September-May) 45.00/71.00 **st.**

at Llangybi S : 2 ½ m. on Llangybi rd – ⊠ Usk – ✆ 063 349 Tredunnock :

🏨 **Cwrt Bleddyn,** NP5 1PG, S : 1 m. ℰ 521, 屏 – ⊡ ➪wc ☎ ℗ 盘. ◪ 函 ① *VISA*. ❀
M 8.95 **t.** (lunch) and a la carte 10.05/15.90 **t.** ▯ 2.95 – **30 rm** ☲ 45.00/85.00 **t.**, **3 suites** 150.00 **t.**
– SB (weekends only) 85.00/125.00 **st.**

UTTOXETER Staffs. **402** **403** **404** O 25 – pop. 10 008 – ECD : Thursday – ✆ 088 93.

Envir. : Alton Towers (gardens★★) *AC* NW : 7 ½ m.

♦London 145 – ♦Birmingham 33 – Derby 19 – Stafford 13 – ♦Stoke-on-Trent 16.

🏨 **White Hart,** Carter St., ST14 8EU, ℰ 2437 – ⊡ ➪wc ♒wc ☎ ℗ ◪ 函 ① *VISA*. ❀
M a la carte 6.05/12.50 **t.** – **28 rm** ☲ 30.00/50.00 **st.** – SB (weekends only) 35.00/55.00 **st.**

FIAT Smithfield Rd ℰ 3838   PEUGEOT-TALBOT Market St. ℰ 2858
FORD, VAUXHALL Derby Rd ℰ 2301

VELINDRE (FELINDRE FARCHOG) Dyfed **403** F 27 – see Newport (Dyfed).

VENN OTTERY Devon **403** K 31 – ⊠ ✆ 040 481 Ottery St. Mary.

♦London 209 – Exeter 11 – Sidmouth 5.

⌂ **Venn Ottery Barton** ॐ, EX11 1RZ, ℰ 2733, ⧖, 屏 – ➪wc ♒wc ℗. ◪ *VISA*
13 rm ☲ 15.00/38.00 **t.**

VENTNOR I.O.W. **403** **404** Q 32 – see Wight (Isle of).

VERYAN Cornwall **403** F 33 The West Country G. – pop. 880 – ⊠ ✆ 0872 Truro.

See : Site★★.

♦London 291 – St. Austell 13 – Truro 13.

🏨 **Nare** ॐ, Carne Beach, TR2 5PF, SW : 1 ¼ m. ℰ 501279, ≤ Carne Bay, ⊿ heated, 屏, ✗ –
➪wc ♒wc ℗. 盘 – **37 rm**

🏨 **Elerkey House,** TR2 5QA, ℰ 501261, 屏 – ➪wc ℗. ◪ *VISA*. ❀
March-October – **M** (bar lunch)/dinner 9.50 **st.** and a la carte ▯ 3.00 – **8 rm** ☲ 15.00/19.00 **st.**

✗ **Treverbyn House,** with rm, Pendower Rd, TR2 5QL, ℰ 501201 – ℗. ❀
March-October – **M** (dinner only) 11.00 ▯ 3.00 – **4 rm** ☲ 15.00/30.00.

at Ruan High Lanes W : 1 ¼ m. on A 3078 – ⊠ ✪ 0872 Truro :

🏠 **Polsue Manor** ⟋, TR2 5LU, ✆ 501270, ≤, ♨, – 🖵 ⊟wc 🅿 🅿. ⚞ VISA
M 8.25/10.45 **t.** and a la carte ⱡ 2.75 – **13 rm** ⌂ 19.00/42.00 **t.** – SB (except July and August) 54.00 **st.**

🏠 **Hundred House,** TR2 5JR, ✆ 501336, ♨ – 🖵 ⊟wc 🅿. ⚞ AE VISA
March-November – **M** (bar lunch)/dinner 11.00 **st.** ⱡ 2.90 – **10 rm** ⌂ 16.00/48.00 **st.** – SB 40.00/58.00 **st.**

WADDESDON Bucks. 404 R 28 – pop. 1 644 – ECD : Thursday – ✪ 029 665.
See : Waddesdon Manor (Rothschild Collection★★★) *AC*.
♦London 52 – Aylesbury 6 – ♦Birmingham 66 – ♦Oxford 25.

Hotels see : Aylesbury E : 5 m.

WADHURST East Sussex 404 U 30 – pop. 3 643 – ECD : Wednesday – ✪ 0580 Ticehurst.
♦ London 44 – Hastings 21 – Maidstone 24 – Royal Tunbridge Wells 6.

🏨 **Spindlewood** ⟋, Wallcrouch, TN5 7JG, SE : 2 ¼ m. on B 2099 ✆ 200430, ≤, ♨, ✻ – 🖵 ⊟wc 🅿 🅿. AE VISA ⚞
closed Christmas – **M** 16.00 **t.** (dinner) and a la carte ⱡ 3.00 – **9 rm** ⌂ 35.00/65.00 **st.** – SB (October-June) 60.00/80.00 **st.**

WAKEFIELD West Yorks. 402 P 22 – pop. 74 764 – ECD : Wednesday – ✪ 0924.
Envir. : Pontefract (castle★ : ruins 12C-13C) *AC*, E : 9 m.

ℹ City of Wakefield, Lupset Park, Horbury Rd ✆ 376214, SW : 1 ¼ m. on A 642 – ℹ Painthorpe House, Painthorpe Lane ✆ 255083, near junction 39 on M 1.
ℹ Town Hall, Wood St. ✆ 370211 ext 7021/2 and 370700 (evenings and weekends).
♦London 188 – Leeds 9 – ♦Manchester 38 – ♦Sheffield 23.

🏨 **Cedar Court,** Denby Dale Rd., Calder Grove, WF4 3QZ, SW : 3 m. on A 636 ✆ 276310, Telex 557647 – 🕻 ⊟ rest 🖵 ☎ 🅿. ⚞. ⚞ AE ⓞ VISA
restricted service Christmas-New Year – **M** 7.95/8.95 **t.** and a la carte ⱡ 3.00 – **100 rm** ⌂ 52.00/62.00 **t.**, **5 suites** 75.00/90.00 **t.** – SB (weekends only) 100.00 **st.**

🏨 **Post House** (T.H.F.), Queen's Drive, Ossett, WF5 9BE, W : 2 ½ m. on A 638 ✆ 276388, Telex 55407 – 🕻 🖵 ☎ 🅿. ⚞ ⚞ AE ⓞ VISA
M *(closed Saturday lunch)* 8.00/9.50 **st.** and a la carte ⱡ 2.75 – ⌂ 5.65 – **96 rm** 48.00/57.00 **st.**

🏨 **Swallow** (Swallow), Queen St., WF1 1JU, ✆ 372111, Telex 557464 – 🕻 🖵 ⊟wc 🅿wc 🅿 ⚞. ⚞ AE ⓞ VISA
M 7.00/10.00 **st.** and a la carte ⱡ 4.00 – **64 rm** ⌂ 40.00/55.00 **st.** – SB 55.00 **st.**

AUSTIN-ROVER Ings Rd ✆ 370100
AUSTIN-ROVER 509 Leeds Rd ✆ 0532 (Leeds) 822254
BMW Ings Rd ✆ 363796
FORD Barnsley Rd ✆ 370551

PEUGEOT-TALBOT Barnsley Rd ✆ 255904
TOYOTA Stanley Rd ✆ 373493
VAUXHALL-OPEL Westgate ✆ 366261
VAUXHALL Ings Rd ✆ 376771
VW-AUDI Ings Rd ✆ 375588

WALBERSWICK Suffolk 404 Y 27 – pop. 435 – ECD : Wednesday – ⊠ ✪ 0502 Southwold.
♦London 106 – Great Yarmouth 28 – ♦Ipswich 33 – ♦Norwich 32.

🏠 **Anchor,** Main St., IP18 6UA, ✆ 722112, ♨ – 🖵 ⊟wc 🅿. ⚞ AE ⓞ VISA
M (bar lunch Monday to Saturday)/dinner 7.70 **t.** ⱡ 3.00 – **14 rm** ⌂ 14.00/36.50 **t.** – SB (November-May) 40.00/42.50 **st.**

WALBERTON West Sussex – see Arundel.

WALL Northumb. 401 402 N 18 – see Hexham.

WALLASEY Merseyside 402 403 K 23 – pop. 62 465 – ✪ 051 Liverpool.
ℹ Warren, Grove Rd ✆ 639 5730.
⊾ to Liverpool (Merseyside Transport) frequent services daily (7-8 mn).
♦ London 226 – Birkenhead 3.5 – ♦ Liverpool 4.

WALLINGFORD Oxon. 403 404 Q 29 – pop. 9 041 – ECD : Wednesday – ✪ 0491.
ℹ 9 St. Martin's St. ✆ 35351 ext. 3810.
♦London 54 – ♦Oxford 12 – Reading 16.

🏨 **Shillingford Bridge,** OX10 8LZ, N : 2 m. on A 329 ✆ 086 732 (Warborough) 8567, Telex 837763, ☟ heated, ✎, – 🖵 ⊟wc 🅿wc 🅿 ☎ 🅿. ⚞ ⚞ AE ⓞ VISA
M 9.00 **t.** and a la carte – **33 rm** ⌂ 37.50/55.00 **t.**

🏨 **George,** 66 High St., OX10 0BS, ✆ 36665 – 🖵 ⊟wc 🅿 ☎ 🅿. ⚞ ⚞ AE ⓞ VISA
M 10.00/10.75 **t.** and a la carte ⱡ 3.25 – ⌂ 5.50 – **39 rm** ⌂ 38.00/52.00 **t.** – SB (weekends only) 64.00 **st.**

✗ **Brown and Boswell,** 28 High St., OX10 0BU, ✆ 34078 – ⚞ ⚞ AE VISA
closed Tuesday lunch, Sunday dinner, Monday, last 2 weeks March and second week October – **M** 4.00/14.00 **t.** and a la carte 12.85/17.00 **t.**

at North Stoke S : 2 ¾ m. by A 4130 and A 4074 on B 4009 – ⊠ ✪ 0491 Wallingford :

🏭 **Springs** ⤳, Wallingford Rd, OX9 6BE, 🕿 36687, Telex 849794, ≼, ⊥ heated, 🛥, 🎾 – 📺 ☎
    🅿. 🛗. 🖭 🖭 ⓞ 𝗩𝗜𝗦𝗔
    M 11.50/18.50 **t.** and a la carte ↥ 3.75 – **34 rm** ⊊ 55.00/96.00 **t.**, **3 suites** 115.00/150.00 **t.** –
    SB (weekends only) (winter only) 95.00/120.00 **st.**

AUSTIN-ROVER 8-10 Watlington Rd, Benson, Nr   FORD 43 High St. 🕿 38424
Wallingford 🕿 38308   PEUGEOT-TALBOT Wood St. 🕿 36017

WALLSEND Tyne and Wear 401 402 P 18 – see Newcastle-upon-Tyne.

WALMLEY West Midlands 403 404 O 26 – see Birmingham.

WALSALL West Midlands 403 404 O 26 – pop. 177 923 – ECD : Thursday – ✪ 0922.
🛇 Calderfields, Aldridge Rd 🕿 32243, N : 1 m. CT.
♦London 126 – ♦Birmingham 9 – ♦Coventry 29 – Shrewsbury 36.

Plan of enlarged area : see Birmingham pp. 2 and 3

🏨 **Crest** (Crest), Birmingham Rd, WS5 3AB, SE : 1 ½ m. on A 34 🕿 33555, Telex 335479 – 🛗
    ▤ rest 📺 ⇌wc ☎ ♿ 🅿. 🛗. 🖭 🖭 𝗩𝗜𝗦𝗔   CT **e**
    M (bar lunch Saturday) 7.65/11.95 **st.** and a la carte – ⊊ 5.95 – **101 rm** 47.50/57.50 **st.** –
    SB (weekends only) 50.00/58.00 **st.**

at Walsall Wood NE : 3 ½ m. on A 461 – CT – ⊠ Walsall – ✪ 0543 Brownhills :

🏨 **Barons Court** (Best Western), Walsall Rd, WS9 9AH, 🕿 376543, Telex 333061 – 🛗 📺
    ⇌wc ☎ ♿. 🛗. 🖭 🖭 ⓞ 𝗩𝗜𝗦𝗔
    M (closed Saturday lunch) 10.00 **t.** and a la carte ↥ 3.20 – **76 rm** ⊊ 37.00/50.00 **t.** –
    SB (weekends only) 54.00/57.00 **st.**

CITROEN Ward St. 🕿 32911   SEAT Wolverhampton Rd 🕿 402000
FORD Wolverhampton St. 🕿 21212   TOYOTA Lichfield Rd, Willenhall 🕿 0922 (Bloxwich)
LADA 152 Green Lane 🕿 645347   493000
PEUGEOT-TALBOT Charlotte St. 🕿 21723   VAUXHALL-OPEL Broadway 🕿 614336
RENAULT Day St. 🕿 613232

WALSGRAVE ON SOWE West Midlands – see Coventry.

WALTON ON THE HILL Surrey – ⊠ ✪ 073 781 Tadworth.
♦London 19 – ♦Brighton 38.

🎮 **Ebenezer Cottage**, 36 Walton St., KT20 7RT, 🕿 3166, « 17C cottage » – 🅿. 🖭 🖭 ⓞ 𝗩𝗜𝗦𝗔
    closed Sunday dinner, Monday and 26 December-1 January – **M** 11.25/14.50 **t.** and a la carte
    15.50/19.90 **t.** ↥ 3.95.

WANSFORD Cambs. 404 S 26 – see Peterborough.

WANTAGE Oxon. 403 404 P 29 – pop. 9 708 – ECD : Thursday – ✪ 023 57.
Envir. : White Horse ≼★.
♦London 75 – ♦Bristol 58 – ♦Oxford 15 – Reading 25.

🏛 **Bear**, Market Pl., OX12 8AB, 🕿 66366, Group Telex 41363 – 🛗 📺 ⇌wc 🚿wc ☎. 🛗 🖭 ⓞ
    𝗩𝗜𝗦𝗔
    M 6.85/9.95 **t.** and a la carte ↥ 2.95 – **34 rm** ⊊ 23.00/54.50 **t.**

🎮 Peking Dynasty, Newbury St., OX12 8BS, 🕿 2517, Chinese rest.

AUSTIN-ROVER Wallingford St. 🕿 3355   VW, AUDI Grove Rd 🕿 65511
SAAB East Hanney 🕿 023 587 (West Hanney) 257

WARE Herts. 404 T 28 – pop. 15 344 – ECD : Thursday – ✪ 0920.
♦London 24 – ♦Cambridge 30 – Luton 22.

🏨 **Ware Moat House** (Q.M.H.), Baldock St., SG12 9DR, N : ½ m. on A 1170 🕿 5011 – 🛗 📺
    ⇌wc 🚿wc ☎. 🛗. 🖭 🖭 ⓞ 𝗩𝗜𝗦𝗔
    M 8.95 **t.** and a la carte – **50 rm** ⊊ 45.00/53.00 **t.**

WAREHAM Dorset 403 404 N 31 The West Country G. – pop. 2 771 – ECD : Wednesday –
✪ 092 95 – See : Site★ – St. Martin's Church★★.
Envir. : Blue Pool★AC, S : 3 m. on A 351 – Smedmore★AC, S : 7 m. by A 351 – Bovington : Tank
Museum★AC, W : 7 m. on A 352 – Lulworth Cove★, SW : 11 m. by A 352.
♦London 123 – Bournemouth 13 – Weymouth 19.

🏨 **Priory** ⤳, Church Green, BH20 4ND, 🕿 2772, « Tastefully renovated part 16C priory with
    gardens », ⤳ – 📺 ⇌wc 🚿wc ☎ 🅿. 🛗 🖭 ⓞ 𝗩𝗜𝗦𝗔. 🎾
    M 11.95/13.50 **t.** and a la carte ↥ 3.75 – **15 rm** ⊊ 85.00/100.00 **t.** – SB (October-April)
    58.00/112.00 **st.**

🏠 **Kemps Country House,** East Stoke, BH20 6AL, W : 2 ¾ m. on A 352 *𝓟* 0929 (Bindon Abbey) 462563, *🚗* – 📺 ⬚wc **P.** 🔌 AE ⓞ *VISA* 🥀
closed 14 December-15 January – **M** 6.00/12.00 **t.** and a la carte – **9 rm** ⪥ 35.00/60.00 **t.** – SB 58.00/65.00 **st.**

🏠 **Worgret Manor,** Worgret Rd, BH20 6AB, W : 1 m. on A 352 *𝓟* 2957, *🚗* – 📺 ⬚wc **P.** 🔌 AE ⓞ *VISA*
closed 25 to 27 December – **M** 5.50/8.75 **t.** and a la carte ⏶ 3.25 – **9 rm** ⪥ 25.00/40.00 **t.** – SB (October-June) 46.00/50.00 **st.**

at Stoborough S : ½ m. on A 351 – ✉ ✆ 092 95 Wareham :

🏛 **Springfield Country,** Grange Rd, BH20 5AL, *𝓟* 2177, ⌇ heated, *🚗*, ⚒ – 📺 ⬚wc ☎ **P.**
🅰 🔌 AE *VISA*
M (bar lunch)/dinner 8.75 **st.** and a la carte ⏶ 2.10 – **30 rm** ⪥ 26.50/62.00 **t.**

WARMINSTER Wilts. **408 404** N 30 The West Country G. – pop. 14 826 – ECD : Wednesday – ✆ 0985.

Envir. : Westbury Hill (White Horse★, ≤★) N : 6 m. – Bratton Castle (≤★★), NE : 6 m.

🆔 Library, Three Horseshoes Mall *𝓟* 218548.

♦London 111 – ♦Bristol 29 – Exeter 74 – ♦Southampton 47.

🏯 **Bishopstrow House** ⑤, Boreham Rd, BA12 9HH, SE : 1 ½ m. on A 36 *𝓟* 212312, ≤, « Tastefully furnished country house », ⌇ heated, 🔲, ⚓, *🚗*, park, ⚒ – 📺 ☎ **P.** 🔌 AE ⓞ *VISA*
M 16.00/21.00 **st.** and a la carte ⏶ 5.50 – ⪥ 6.50 – **25 rm** 53.00/128.00 **st.**, **6 suites** 128.00/200.00 **st.** – SB (October-April) 47.00/125.00 **st.**

🏠 **Old Bell,** 42 Market Pl., BA12 9AN, *𝓟* 216611 – 📺 ⬚wc **P.** 🔌 AE ⓞ *VISA*
M (grill rest. only) a la carte 6.10/10.85 ⏶ 2.50 – **16 rm** ⪥ 25.00/40.00 **t.** – SB (except summer) (weekends only) 38.00 **st.**

✗ **La Petite Cuisine Belge at Vincents,** 60-62 East St., BA12 9BW, *𝓟* 215052 – 🔌 AE ⓞ *VISA*
closed Monday lunch, Good Friday dinner, Sunday, 5 days Christmas and first 2 weeks January – **M** 5.50/13.00 **st.** and a la carte ⏶ 3.75.

at Corton SE : 5 ¼ m. by A 36 and B 3095 – ✉ ✆ 0985 Warminster :

✗ **Dove at Corton,** BA12 0SZ, *𝓟* 50378, *🚗* – 🔌 *VISA*
closed Sunday dinner, Monday except Bank Holidays and 2 weeks mid January – **M** a la carte 8.45/14.25 **st.** ⏶ 2.50.

AUSTIN-ROVER George St. *𝓟* 212808

WARREN ROW Berks – see Knowl Hill.

WARRINGTON Cheshire **402 403 404** M 23 – pop. 81 366 – ECD : Thursday – ✆ 0925.
See : St. Elphin's Church (chancel★ 14C).

🔟🏌 Hill Warren *𝓟* 61775, S : 3 m. – 🔟🏌 Walton Hall, Warrington Rd *𝓟* 630619, S : 2 m. – 🔟🏌 Kelvin Close, Birchwood *𝓟* 0925 (Padgate) 818819.

🆔 80 Sankey St. *𝓟* 36501.

♦London 195 – Chester 20 – ♦Liverpool 18 – ♦Manchester 21 – Preston 28.

🏛 **Patten Arms,** Parker St. (Bank Quay Station), WA1 1LS, *𝓟* 36602 – 📺 ⬚wc ⬚wc 📠 **P.**
🔌 AE ⓞ *VISA*
closed 24 to 27 December – **M** *(closed Saturday lunch and Sunday)* 5.00/6.00 **st.** and a la carte ⏶ 3.25 – **43 rm** ⪥ 35.50/44.50 **st.** – SB (weekends only) 43.00/54.20 **st.**

🏠 **Birchdale** ⑤, Birchdale Rd, Stockton Heath, WA4 5AW, S : 1 ¾ m. by A 49 *𝓟* 63662, *🚗* – **P.**
closed 24 December-2 January – **M** (dinner only) 8.00 **st.** ⏶ 3.00 – **21 rm** ⪥ 18.50/29.00 **st.**

at Grappenhall SE : 2 m. by A 50 – ✉ ✆ 0925 Warrington :

🏛 **Fir Grove,** Knutsford Old Rd, WA4 2LD, *𝓟* 67471, Telex 628117 – 📺 ⬚wc ⬚wc ☎ **P.** 🅰
🔌 AE ⓞ *VISA*
M 8.50 **st.** and a la carte ⏶ 3.10 – **38 rm** ⪥ 32.00/43.00 **st.**

at Stretton S : 3 ½ m. by A 49 on B 5356 – ✉ Warrington – ✆ 092 573 Norcott Brook :

🏠 **Old Vicarage,** Stretton Rd, WA4 4NS, *𝓟* 238, *🚗*, ⚒ – 📶 📺 ⬚wc ⬚wc **P.** 🔌 AE *VISA*
M 7.50/8.50 **st.** ⏶ 3.35 – **36 rm** ⪥ 30.00/41.50 **st.** – SB (weekends only) 70.00/80.00 **st.**

AUSTIN-ROVER Winwick St. *𝓟* 50011
BMW Farrell St. *𝓟* 35987
CITROEN 194-196 Knutsford Rd *𝓟* 68444

FORD Winwick Rd *𝓟* 51111
RENAULT Farrell St. *𝓟* 30448

See : Castle★★ (14C) *AC* Y – St. Mary's Church★ 12C-18C Y **A** – Lord Leycester's Hospital★ Y **B**.

🏇 The Racecourse ⟋ 494316 Y.

🚩 The Court House, Jury St. ⟋ 492212.

♦London 96 – ♦Birmingham 20 – ♦Coventry 11 – ♦Oxford 43.

WARWICK
ROYAL
LEAMINGTON SPA

*Les plans de villes
sont disposés le Nord en haut.*

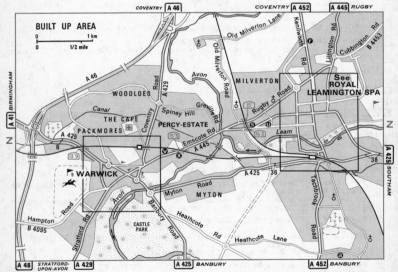

🏨 **Lord Leycester,** 17 Jury St., CV34 4EJ, ⟋ 491481 – 📺 ⌂wc 🛏wc 🅿 ⚓. 🔺 AE Ⓞ VISA
    M a la carte 8.65/11.75 **st**. ⫚ 2.10 – **47 rm** ⯑ 34.00/48.00 **st.** – SB 49.95/54.50 **st.**   Y **n**

🏨 **Woolpack,** 50 Market Pl., CV34 4SD, ⟋ 496191 – 📺 ⌂wc 🛏wc ☎. 🔺 AE Ⓞ VISA 🦮
    closed Christmas Day – **M** (carving rest.) 5.45 **t.** – **30 rm** ⯑ 16.50/31.00.   Y **a**

⌂ **Cambridge Villa,** 20a Emscote Rd, CV34 4PL, ⟋ 491169 – 📺 🛏wc 🅿 VISA
    12 rm ⯑ 12.00/36.00 **s.**   Z **x**

⌂ **Avon,** 7 Emscote Rd, CV34 4PH, ⟋ 491367, 🚗 – 🅿. 🦮
    7 rm ⯑ 9.50/19.00 **st.**   Z **v**

XXX **Westgate Arms** with rm, 3 Old Bowling Green St., CV34 4DD, ℰ 492362, English rest., ☞
– 📺 ⇔wc ☎ 🅿. 🔼 🅰🅴 ⓪ 𝘃𝗜𝗦𝗔 ⇘
                                                   Y **u**
   M 9.50/15.00 **t.** and a la carte ♦ 3.50 – ⇌ 6.50 – **10 rm** 48.50/75.00 **t.** – SB (weekends only)
   97.90 **st.**

XX **Randolph's,** 19-21 Coten End, CV34 4NT, ℰ 491292 – 🔼 𝘃𝗜𝗦𝗔   Y **i**
   closed Sunday and 1 week at Christmas – **M** (dinner only) (booking essential) a la carte
   approx. 16.80 **t.** ♦ 2.85.

XX **Aylesford,** 1 High St., CV34 4AP, ℰ 492799, Italian rest. – 🔼 🅰🅴 ⓪ 𝘃𝗜𝗦𝗔   Y **e**
   closed Monday dinner, Sunday, 1 week at Christmas and Bank Holidays – **M** 9.25 **st.** (lunch)
   and a la carte 10.60/23.05 **st.** ♦ 4.50.

   at Barford S : 4 ½ m. on A 429 – Z – ✉ 🕿 0926 Warwick :

🏠 **Glebe** ⬙, Church St., CV35 8BS, on B 4462 ℰ 624218, ☞ – 📺 ⇔wc 🔐wc ☎ 🅿. 🔼 🅰🅴 ⓪
   𝘃𝗜𝗦𝗔 ⬙
   M 9.50/11.50 **st.** and a la carte ♦ 2.50 – **15 rm** ⇌ 22.50/52.00 **st.** – SB (weekends only) 55.00 **st.**

   at Longbridge SW : 2 m. on A 429 – Z – ✉ 🕿 0926 Warwick :

🏠🏠 **Ladbroke** (Ladbroke), Stratford Rd, CV34 6RE, junction of A 429, A 46 and A 41 ℰ 499555,
   – 📲 📺 ⇔wc ☎ 🅿. ♨ 🔼 🅰🅴 ⓪ 𝘃𝗜𝗦𝗔 ⬙
   M (carving rest.) 9.25 ♦ 3.70 – ⇌ 6.00 – **150 rm** 46.00/66.00 **st.**, **1 suite** 105.00 **st.** –
   SB (weekends only) 66.50 **st.**

FIAT Wharf St. ℰ 496231   VOLVO Nelson Lane ℰ 400642
PORSCHE Birmingham Rd ℰ 491731

WASDALE HEAD Cumbria 🗺️🗺️ K 20 – see Gosforth.

WASHINGBOROUGH Lincs. 🗺️🗺️ 🗺️🗺️ S 24 – see Lincoln.

WASHINGTON Tyne and Wear 🗺️🗺️ 🗺️🗺️ P 19 – pop. 48 856 – ECD : Wednesday – ✉ 🕿 091
Tyneside.

♦London 278 – Durham 13 – ♦Middlesbrough 32 – ♦Newcastle-upon-Tyne 7.

🏠🏠 **George Washington** (Best Western), Stone Cellar Rd, District 12, NE37 1PH, ℰ 417 2626,
   Telex 537143, 🔼, 🔼, squash – 📺 ⇔wc ☎ 🅿. ♨ 🔼 🅰🅴 ⓪ 𝘃𝗜𝗦𝗔
   M (carving rest.) a la carte 12.45/24.20 **st.** ♦ 3.00 – ⇌ 5.85 – **70 rm** 44.00/54.50 **st.** –
   SB (weekends only) 68.00 **st.**

🏠🏠 **Post House** (T.H.F.), Emerson, District 5, NE37 1LB, Junction A 1 (M) and A 195 ℰ 416 2264,
   Telex 537574 – 📲 📺 ⇔wc 📠 🅿. ♨ 🔼 🅰🅴 ⓪ 𝘃𝗜𝗦𝗔
   M 7.50/10.00 **st.** and a la carte ♦ 3.40 – ⇌ 5.65 – **138 rm** 43.00/53.00 **st.**

FORD Parsons Rd ℰ 4167700

WATCHET Somerset 🗺️🗺️ J 30 The West Country G. – pop. 3 055 – ECD : Wednesday – 🕿 0984.
Envir. : Cleeve Abbey★★*AC*, SW : 2 m.
🅱 2 Market St. ℰ 31824.

♦London 180 – ♦Bristol 57 – Taunton 18.

🏠 **Downfield,** 16 St. Decuman's Rd, TA23 0HR, ℰ 31267, ☞ – 📺 ⇔wc 🔐wc 🅿. 🔼 🅰🅴 ⓪
   𝘃𝗜𝗦𝗔
   M a la carte approx. 7.00 **t.** ♦ 2.00 – **6 rm** ⇌ 25.00/30.00 **t.** – SB (except Christmas)
   41.00/57.00 **st.**

WATERGATE BAY Cornwall 🗺️🗺️ E 32 – ✉ Newquay – 🕿 0637 St. Mawgan.

♦London 293 – Newquay 2 – Padstow 8.

🏠 **Tregurrian,** TR8 4AB, ℰ 860280, 🔼 heated – 🔐wc 🅿
   May-September – **M** (bar lunch)/dinner 6.00 **st.** ♦ 2.35 – **28 rm** ⇌ 11.00/40.00 **st.** –
   SB 28.00/48.50 **st.**

WATERHEAD Cumbria 🗺️🗺️ L 20 – see Ambleside.

WATERHOUSES Staffs. 🗺️🗺️ 🗺️🗺️ 🗺️🗺️ O 24 – pop. 1 018 – ✉ Stoke-on-Trent – 🕿 053 86.

♦London 115 – ♦Birmingham 63 – Derby 23 – ♦Manchester 39 – ♦Stoke-on-Trent 17.

XX **Old Beams** with rm, Leek Rd, ST10 3HW, ℰ 254, ☞ – 📺 ⇔wc 🔐wc 🅿. 🔼 🅰🅴 ⓪ 𝘃𝗜𝗦𝗔
   closed Sunday, Monday, first 2 weeks January and first week October – **M** (booking essential)
   8.75 **t.** (lunch) and a la carte 14.65/19.00 **t.** ♦ 3.50 – ⇌ 5.50 – **2 rm** 37.50/52.50 **t.**

WATERINGBURY Kent 🗺️🗺️ V 30 – see Maidstone.

WATERMILLOCK Cumbria 🗺️🗺️ L 20 – see Ullswater.

Plan : see Greater London (North-West)

WATFORD Herts. 404 S 29 – pop. 109 503 – ECD : Wednesday – 🕐 0923.
♦London 21 – Aylesbury 23.

🏨 Ladbroke (Ladbroke), Elton Way, WD2 8HA, Watford By-Pass E : 3 ½ m. on A 41 at junction A 4008 🌮 35881, Telex 923422 – 🔄 📺 🛏wc ☎ 🅿. 🦽 📶 🖭 ① VISA. 💥 BU **e**
155 rm 48.50/58.00 st., **1 suite**.

XX **Flower Drum**, 16 Market St., WD1 7AD, 🌮 26711, Chinese (Szechuan, Peking) rest. – 🖥. 📶 📶 ① VISA AU **a**
closed 24 to 26 December – **M** 6.80/15.50 **t.** and a la carte 🍴 2.80.

HONDA, MERCEDES-BENZ High Rd at Bushey Heath 🌮 01 (London) 950 3311
OPEL 6-10 High Rd at Bushey Heath 🌮 01 (London) 950 6146
PEUGEOT-TALBOT Aldenham 🌮 092 76 (Radlett) 2177

VAUXHALL-OPEL 6-10 High Rd at Bushey Heath 🌮 01 (London) 950 6146
VAUXHALL-OPEL 329 St. Albans Rd 🌮 31716

WATH-IN-NIDDERDALE North Yorks. – see Pateley Bridge.

WATTON Norfolk 404 W 26 – ✉ Thetford – 🕐 0953.
♦London 93 – ♦Cambridge 48 – ♦Norwich 22.

🏨 **Clarence House**, High St., IP25 6AH, 🌮 884252 – 📺 🛏wc. 📶 📶 ① VISA. 💥
M (lunch by arrangement)/dinner 11.50 **t.** 🍴 3.75 – **6 rm** 🛏 24.00/38.00 **st.** – SB (weekends only) 45.00 **st.**

WDIG (GOODWICK) Dyfed – see Fishguard.

WELLAND Heref. and Worc. 403 404 N 27 – see Great Malvern.

WELLINGBOROUGH Northants. 404 R 27 – pop. 38 598 – ECD : Thursday – 🕐 0933.
♦London 73 – ♦Cambridge 43 – ♦Leicester 34 – Northampton 10.

🏨 **Hind** (Q.M.H.), Sheep St., NN8 1BY, 🌮 222827 – 📺 🛏wc ⊜ 🅿. 🦽 📶 📶 ① VISA
M 6.25/8.50 **st.** and a la carte 🍴 2.90 – **32 rm** 🛏 42.00/53.00 **st.** – SB (weekends only) 52.00 **st.**

🏠 **High View**, 156 Midland Rd, NN8 1NG, 🌮 78733 – 📺 🛏wc ☎ 🅿. 📶 📶 ① VISA
15 rm 🛏 17.00/31.00 st.

AUSTIN-ROVER Finedon Rd 🌮 76651
SKODA Talbot Rd 🌮 223924

VAUXHALL-OPEL Oxford St. 🌮 223252

WELLINGTON HEATH Heref. and Worc. – see Ledbury.

WELLS Somerset 403 404 M 30 The West Country G. – pop. 9 252 – ECD : Wednesday – 🕐 0749
– See : Site★★★ – Cathedral★★★ – Vicar's Close★ – Bishop's Palace★*AC* (≤★★ of east end of cathedral).
Envir. : Wookey Hole★★*AC* (Caves ★, Papermill★, Fairground collection ★), NW : 2 m.
📠 East Horrington Rd 🌮 72868 – 🅱 Town Hall, Market Sq. 🌮 72552 and 75987.
♦London 132 – ♦Bristol 20 – ♦Southampton 68 – Taunton 28.

🏨 **Swan** (Best Western), 11 Sadler St., BA5 2RX, 🌮 78877, Telex 449658 – 📺 🛏wc 🛏wc ☎ 🅿. 🦽 📶 📶 ① VISA
M 10.95 **t.** (dinner) and a la carte 7.50/12.00 **t.** 🍴 3.00 – **32 rm** 🛏 35.00/50.00 **t.** – SB (weekends only) 55.00/65.00 **st.**

🏨 **Crown**, Market Pl., BA5 2RP, 🌮 73457 – 📺 🛏wc 🛏wc ☎. 📶 📶 ① VISA
M 7.95/12.95 **t.** and a la carte 🍴 5.95 – **18 rm** 🛏 29.00/42.00 **t.**, **1 suite** 49.00/60.00 **t.** – SB 56.00/64.00 **st.**

🏠 **Star**, 14 High St., BA5 2SQ, 🌮 73055 – 📺 🛏wc. 📶 📶 ① VISA. 💥
M (bar lunch)/dinner 7.95 **t.** and a la carte 🍴 2.50 – **16 rm** 🛏 25.00/35.00 **t.** – SB 43.00/55.00 **st.**

🏡 **White Hart**, Sadler St., BA5 2RR, 🌮 72056 – 📺 🛏wc 🛏wc 🅿. 📶 📶 ① VISA
M 5.75/7.75 **t.** and a la carte 🍴 2.80 – **15 rm** 🛏 21.50/35.50 **t.** – SB 49.00/53.50 **st.**

🏡 **Ancient Gate House**, Sadler St., BA5 2RR, 🌮 72029 – 🛏wc. 📶 📶 ① VISA
M 6.45/7.95 **t.** and a la carte 🍴 2.80 – **10 rm** 🛏 19.00/35.50 **t.** – SB 49.00/53.00 **st.**

at Worth W : 2 ¾ m. by A 371 on B 3139 – 🕐 0749 Wells :

🏡 Worth House, BA5 1LW, 🌮 72041, 🌼 – 🛏wc 🅿. 💥 – **8 rm**.

AUSTIN-ROVER, LAND ROVER Glastonbury Rd 🌮 72626

WELLS-NEXT-THE-SEA Norfolk 404 V 25 – pop. 2 337 – ECD : Thursday – 🕐 0328 Fakenham.
Envir. : Holkam Hall★★ (18C) *AC*, W : 3 m.
♦London 121 – King's Lynn 31 – ♦Norwich 36.

🏠 **Mill House**, Northfield Lane, NR23 1JZ, 🌮 710739, 🌼 – 🅿. 💥
April-November – **7 rm** 🛏 10.50/19.00 **st.**

WELSH HOOK Dyfed – ✉ Haverfordwest – ☎ 0348 Letterston.
♦London 260 – Fishguard 7 – Haverfordwest 10.

   XX **Stone Hall** ⟆ with rm, SA62 5NS, ✆ 840212, « Part 14C manor house with 17C extension »,
    ⇌ – 🅣🅥 ⛴wc ⚏wc ⚠ 🆅🅸🆂🅰 ⚘
    closed 15 to 27 February and 15 to 27 November – **M** (closed Sunday dinner) (lunch by
    arrangement) 10.50 **t.** and a la carte ⅃ 3.00 – **5 rm** ⇌ 19.50/38.00 **t.** – SB (weekends only)
    53.00/58.00 **st.**

WELSHPOOL (TRALLWNG) Powys **402 403** K 26 – pop. 4 869 – ECD : Thursday – ☎ 0938.
🛈 Vicarage Garden Car Park ✆ 2043.
♦London 182 – ♦Birmingham 64 – Chester 45 – Shrewsbury 19.

   🏠 **Royal Oak,** The Cross, SY21 7DG, ✆ 2217 – 🅣🅥 ⛴wc ⚏wc 🅿 ⚠ 🆎 🆅🅸🆂🅰 ⚘
    M a la carte 8.00/10.05 **st.** – **23 rm** ⇌ 17.50/39.00 **st.**

AUSTIN-ROVER Union St. ✆ 3152
FORD Salop Rd ✆ 2391

VAUXHALL-OPEL Newtown Rd ✆ 4444

WELWYN Herts. **404** T 28 – pop. 9 961 (inc. Codicote) – ECD : Wednesday – ☎ 043 871.
♦London 30 – Bedford 31 – ♦Cambridge 32.

   🏨 **Heath Lodge,** Danesbury Park Rd, AL6 9SL, NE : 1 ¼ m. by B 197 ✆ 7064, Telex 827618, 🚗,
    park – 🅣🅥 ⛴wc ⚏wc ⓪ 🆅🅸🆂🅰
    M (closed Saturday lunch) 8.95 **t.** and a la carte ⅃ 3.50 – ⇌ 3.95 – **32 rm** 38.00/55.00 **t.**

COLT 54 Great North Rd ✆ 5911

WELWYN GARDEN CITY Herts. **404** T 28 – pop. 40 665 – ECD : Wednesday – ☎ 0707 Welwyn
Garden.
🛈₈ Panshanger ✆ 33350.
🛈 The Campus ✆ 31212.
♦London 28 – Bedford 34 – ♦Cambridge 34.

   🏨 **Crest** (Crest), Homestead Lane, AL7 4LX, by Cole Green Lane ✆ 324336, Telex 261523, 🚗 –
    🖩 🅣🅥 ⛴wc ⚏wc ⛽ 🅿 ⚠ ⚠ 🆎 ⓪ 🆅🅸🆂🅰
    M (bar lunch Monday to Saturday)/dinner 11.50 **st.** and a la carte ⅃ 3.00 – ⇌ 5.85 – **58 rm**
    47.00/57.00 **st.** – SB (weekends only) 46.00/58.00 **st.**

AUSTIN-ROVER Stanborough Rd ✆ 35131

RENAULT Great North Rd ✆ 070 72 (Hatfield) 64567

WENTBRIDGE West Yorks. **402 404** Q 23 – ✉ ☎ 0977 Pontefract.
♦London 183 – ♦Leeds 19 – ♦Nottingham 55 – ♦Sheffield 28.

   🏨 **Wentbridge House,** Great North Rd, WF8 3JJ, ✆ 620444, 🚗 – 🅣🅥 ⛴wc ⚏wc ☎ 🅿 ⚠
    ⚠ 🆎 🆅🅸🆂🅰 ⚘
    closed Christmas Day – **M** 9.00 **st.** (lunch) and a la carte 15.20/19.20 **st.** ⅃ 4.00 – ⇌ 2.85 –
    20 rm 34.00/47.50 **st.**

    at Barnsdale Bar S : 2 m. on A 1 – ✉ ☎ 0977 Pontefract :

   🏠 **Travelodge** (T.H.F.) without rest., Trunk Rd, WF8 3JB, on A 1 ✆ 620711, Telex 557457 – 🅣🅥
    ⛴wc 🅿 ⚠ 🆎 ⓪ 🆅🅸🆂🅰
    70 rm ⇌ 31.00/42.00 **st.**

WEOBLEY Heref. and Worc. **403** L 27 – pop. 1 080 – ECD : Wednesday – ✉ Hereford – ☎ 0544.
♦London 145 – Brecon 30 – Hereford 12 – Leominster 9.

   🏠 Red Lion, Broad St., HR4 8SE, ✆ 318220 – 🅣🅥 ⛴wc ⚏wc ⛽ 🅿
    7 rm.

WEST BAY Dorset **403** L 31 – see Bridport.

WEST BEXINGTON Dorset – see Bridport.

WEST BRIDGFORD Notts. **403 404** Q 25 – see Nottingham.

WEST BROMWICH West Midlands **403 404** O 26 – see Birmingham.

WESTBURY Wilts. **403 404** N 30 – pop. 9 545 – ✉ ☎ 0373.
♦London 111 – ♦Bristol 32 – Salisbury 25 – Swindon 40.

    at Bratton NE : 2 ½ m. on B 3098 – ✉ Westbury – ☎ 0380 Bratton :

   🍴 **Duke,** Melbourne St., BA13 4RW, ✆ 830242, 🚗 – 🅣🅥 🅿 🆎 🆅🅸🆂🅰 ⚘
    M (closed Sunday dinner) a la carte 4.65/11.30 **t.** ⅃ 2.55 – **5 rm** ⇌ 15.80/20.70 **t.**

WEST CHILTINGTON West Sussex **404** S 31 – pop. 2 044 – ECD : Wednesday and Thursday – ✉ Pulborough – ☎ 079 83.

◆London 50 – ◆Brighton 22 – Worthing 12.

　🏛 **Roundabout** (Best Western), Monkmead Lane, RH20 2PF, S : 1 ¼ m. ℰ 3838, 🚗 – 📺 🖴wc ☎ 🅿. 🍴. 🔼 🖭 *VISA*
　　M 8.90/9.20 **st.** and a la carte ⅃ 3.90 – **21 rm** � 36.75/55.00 **st.** – SB 59.00/69.00 **st.**

WEST CLANDON Surrey – see Guildford.

WEST COKER Somerset **403 404** M 31 – see Yeovil.

WESTERHAM Kent **404** U 30 – pop. 3 392 – ECD : Wednesday – ☎ 0959.
Envir. : Chartwell★ (Sir Winston Churchill's country home, Museum) *AC*, S : 2 m.

◆London 24 – ◆Brighton 45 – Maidstone 22.

　🏛 **Kings Arms,** Market Sq., TN16 1AH, ℰ 62990 – 📺 🖴wc ☎ 🅿. 🔼 🖭 ⓞ *VISA* ⚡
　　M 11.50 **t.** and a la carte – **12 rm** ⊃ districtz 40.00/70.00 **t.**

　XX **Villa Rosa,** Quebec Sq., TN16 1AN, on A 25 ℰ 62139, 🚗 – 🅿. 🔼 🖭 ⓞ *VISA*
　　closed Sunday dinner – **M** a la carte 10.85/15.15 **st.**

AUSTIN-ROVER High St. ℰ 62212　　　　VW, AUDI London Rd ℰ 64333
VW London Rd ℰ 64333

WEST HADDON Northants. **403 404** Q 26 – see Rugby.

WEST HUNTSPILL Somerset **403** L 30 – see Bridgwater.

WEST LULWORTH Dorset **403 404** N 32 – pop. 910 – ECD : Wednesday – ✉ Wareham – ☎ 092 941.
See : Lulworth Cove★.

◆London 129 – Bournemouth 21 – Dorchester 17 – Weymouth 19.

　🏛 **Cromwell House,** Main Rd, BH20 5RJ, ℰ 253, ≤, ⅃, 🚗 – 📺 🖴wc 🖴wc 🅿
　　M (dinner only) 6.50 **st.** ⅃ 2.00 – **14 rm** ⊃ districtz 13.00/32.00 **st.** – SB 36.00/40.00 **st.**

　☎ **Mill House,** BH20 5RQ, ℰ 404, 🚗 – 🖴wc 🖴wc. 🔼 🖭 ⓞ *VISA*
　　M 4.25/7.95 **t.** and a la carte ⅃ 2.85 – **10 rm** ⊃ districtz 12.50/26.00 **t.** – SB (October-June) 34.00/38.00 **st.**

　🏠 **Lulworth,** Main Rd, BH20 5RJ, ℰ 230 – 📺 🖴wc 🖴wc 🅿. 🔼 *VISA* ⚡
　　closed 24 to 26 December – **9 rm** ⊃ districtz 18.00/31.00 **st.**

　🏠 **Gatton House,** Main Rd, BH20 5RU, ℰ 252, 🚗 – 🖴wc 🖴wc 🅿
　　April-October – **8 rm** ⊃ districtz 12.50/31.00 **st.**

WEST MALVERN Heref. and Worc. **403 404** M 27 – see Great Malvern.

WEST MERSEA Essex **404** W 28 – pop. 5 245 – ✉ Colchester – ☎ 0206.
◆ London 58 – Chelmsford 27 – Colchester 9.5.

　XX **Blackwater** with rm, 20-22 Church Rd, CO5 8QH, ℰ 383338 – 📺 🖴wc 🅿. 🔼 🖭. ⚡
　　closed 5 to 21 January – **M** (closed Tuesday lunch and Sunday dinner) 8.55 **t.** (lunch) and a la carte ⅃ 2.90 – **7 rm** ⊃ districtz 18.00/40.00 **t.** – SB (except Sunday and Christmas) 45.00/48.00 **st.**

WESTON Devon **403** K 31 – see Honiton.

WESTONBIRT Glos. **403 404** N 29 – see Tetbury.

WESTON FAVELL Northants. **404** R 27 – see Northampton.

WESTON-ON-THE-GREEN Oxon. **403 404** Q 28 – pop. 479 – ✉ ☎ 0869 Bletchingdon.
◆London 65 – ◆Birmingham 61 – Northampton 33 – ◆Oxford 8.

　🏛 **Weston Manor** (Best Western) ⚡, on A 43, OX6 8QL, ℰ 50621, Telex 83409, ⅃ heated, 🚗, park, ⚡, squash – 📺 🖴wc ☎ 🅿. 🍴. 🔼 🖭 ⓞ *VISA* ⚡
　　M 9.50/12.50 **t.** and a la carte ⅃ 3.65 – **39 rm** ⊃ districtz 47.50/85.00 **t.**, **1 suite** 100.00 **st.** – SB 75.00 **st.**

WESTON-SUPER-MARE Avon **403** K 29 The West Country G. – pop. 60 821 – ECD : Thursday – ☎ 0934.
See : Sea front ≤★★.
⛳ Worlebury ℰ 23214, 2 m. from station BY – ⛳ Uphill Rd North ℰ 21360 AZ.
🛈 Beach Lawns ℰ 26838.
◆London 147 – ◆Bristol 24 – Taunton 32.

482

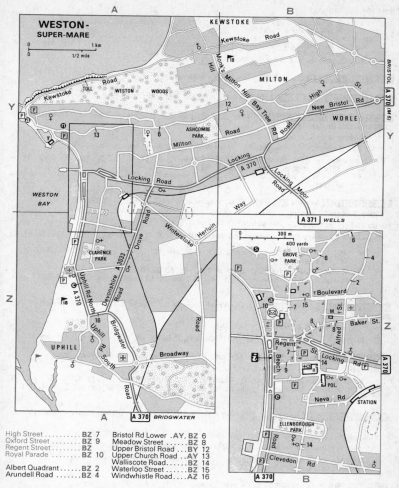

WESTON-SUPER-MARE

Grand Atlantic (T.H.F.), Beach Rd, BS23 1BA, ℰ 26543, ≤, ⌘ heated, ⚓, ✺ – ≉ ℡ ℗. ⚤, 🅰 🆎 ⓪ *VISA*.
M 7.50/9.25 **st.** and a la carte ⌕ 3.40 – ⊡ 5.65 – **77 rm** 39.00/56.00 **st.**
BZ e

Royal Pier, 55-57 Birnbeck Rd, BS23 2EJ, ℰ 26644, ≤ Weston Bay and Bristol Channel – ≉ ℡ ⇌wc ℗. ⚤, 🅰 🆎 ⓪ *VISA*. ✺
M 6.25/10.50 **t.** and a la carte ⌕ 2.70 – **40 rm** ⊡ 26.55/56.00 **t.**, **2 suites** 56.70/65.00 **t.** – SB (weekends only) (November-April) 50.00 **st.**
AY a

Berni Royal, South Par., BS23 1JN, ℰ 23601, ⚓ – ≉ ℡ ⇌wc ⥿wc ☎ ℗. ⚤, 🅰 🆎 ⓪ *VISA*.
M (grill rest. only) a la carte 5.80/11.35 **t.** ⌕ 2.95 – **36 rm** ⊡ 28.00/47.00 **t.** – SB (weekends only) 45.00/51.00 **st.**
BZ a

Queenswood, Victoria Park, BS23 2HZ, ℰ 21759, ≤ – ℡ ⇌wc ⥿wc ☎. 🅰 🆎 ⓪ *VISA*.
M 7.00/9.00 **st.** ⌕ 2.80 – **17 rm** ⊡ 17.50/38.50 **st.** – SB 48.00/52.50 **st.**
BZ s

Beachlands, 17 Uphill Rd North, BS23 4NG, ℰ 21401, ⚓ – ℡ ⇌wc ⥿wc ⟑ ℗. 🅰 🆎 ⓪ *VISA*.
M (bar lunch)/dinner 6.95 **t.** – **18 rm** ⊡ 15.75/34.65 **st.** – SB (October-May) 37.50 **st.**
AZ c

La Petite Auberge with rm, 37 Upper Church Rd, BS23 2DX, ℰ 22351 – ℡ 🅰 🆎 *VISA*
closed Monday lunch, Sunday, 10 to 17 May, 25 October-8 November and 26 to 30 December –
M a la carte 11.50/15.50 **t.** ⌕ 3.00 – **2 rm** ⊡ 14.00/28.00 **t.**
AY n

483

WESTON-SUPER-MARE

AUSTIN-ROVER Alfred St. ☎ 21451
AUSTIN-ROVER 264 Milton Rd ☎ 25707
CITROEN Baker St. ☎ 23995
FORD Winterstoke Rd ☎ 28291
HONDA Bridgwater Rd ☎ 812244
HONDA, SAAB Main Rd ☎ 0934 (Bleadon) 812546

PEUGEOT-TALBOT Broadway ☎ 0934 (Bleadon) 812479
RENAULT Locking Rd ☎ 414007
VAUXHALL-OPEL, BEDFORD Winterstoke Rd ☎ 417886

WESTON TURVILLE Bucks. **404** R 28 – see Aylesbury.

WESTON-UNDER-PENYARD Heref. and Worc. **403** **404** M 28 – see Ross-on-Wye.

WESTON-UNDER-REDCASTLE Salop **402** **403** **404** M 25 – pop. 256 – ⊠ Shrewsbury – ☎ 093 924 Lee Brockhurst.

🛅, 🛅 Hawkstone Park ☎ 611.

♦London 165 – Chester 31 – ♦Birmingham 48 – Shrewsbury 12 – ♦Stoke-on-Trent 25.

🏨 **Hawkstone Park** (Best Western) ॐ, SY4 5UY, ☎ 611, ≼, ☒, 🛅, ➘, ☀, park, ⚒ – ▦ rest 📺 ⌷wc ☏ ৬ ℗ ♨ ◪ ◪ ◉ ◉ ◻
M 5.75/7.95 st. – **59 rm** ⊠ 26.00/52.00 st., **2 suites** 78.00/108.00 st. – SB (January-March) 44.95/49.95 st.

WEST RUNTON Norfolk **404** X 25 – ECD : Wednesday – ⊠ Cromer – ☎ 026 375.

🛅 Links Country Park Hotel ☎ 691.

♦London 135 – King's Lynn 42 – ♦Norwich 24.

🏨 **Links Country Park,** Sandy Lane, NR27 9QH, ☎ 691, 🛅, ☀ – ▯ 📺 ⌷wc ⊡wc ☞ ℗ ◪ ◪ ◻
M 7.95/10.25 st. and a la carte ₰ 3.55 – **34 rm** ⊠ (dinner included) 29.00/84.00 st. – SB 58.00/80.00 st.

XX **Mirabelle,** 7 Station Rd, NR27 9QD, ☎ 396 – ℗ ◪ ◪ ◉ ◻
closed Sunday dinner November-May, Monday and first 2 weeks November – M 8.50/13.50 t. and a la carte 11.50/15.50 t. ₰ 2.80.

WESTWARD HO Devon **403** H 30 The West Country G. – pop. 1 315 – ECD : Tuesday – ⊠ ☎ 023 72 Bideford.

♦London 235 – Bideford 4 – Exeter 47 – ♦Plymouth 62.

🏠 Buckleigh Grange ॐ, Buckleigh Rd, EX39 3PU, ☎ 74468, ☀, ⚒ – ⊡wc ℗ – **11 rm**.

WEST WITTON North Yorks. **402** O 21 – pop. 338 – ⊠ Leyburn – ☎ 0969 Wensleydale.

♦London 241 – Kendal 39 – ♦Leeds 60 – York 53.

🏠 **Wensleydale Heifer,** Main St., DL8 4LS, ☎ 22322 – 📺 ⊡wc ⊡wc ℗ ◪ ◪ ◻
M (bar lunch Monday to Saturday)/dinner 12.95 t. ₰ 3.60 – **20 rm** ⊠ 28.00/42.00 t. – SB (November-May) 58.00 st.

WEST WOODBURN Northumb. **401** **402** N 18 – ECD : Thursday – ⊠ Hexham – ☎ 0660 Bellingham.

🛅 Bellingham ☎ 20446, SW : 4 ½ m.

♦ London 316 – ♦ Carlisle 49 – ♦ Edinburgh 78 – Hawick 35 – ♦ Newcastle-upon-Tyne 35.

🏡 **Bay Horse Inn,** Front St., NE48 2RX, ☎ 70218, ☀ – ℗ ◪ ☖
M 5.00/10.00 st. and a la carte ₰ 2.75 – **4 rm** ⊠ 14.50/26.00 st.

WETHERAL Cumbria **401** **402** L 19 – see Carlisle.

WETHERBY West Yorks. **402** P 22 – pop. 9 467 – ECD : Wednesday – ☎ 0937.
🗓 Council Offices, 24 Westgate ☎ 62706/7.

♦London 208 – Harrogate 8 – ♦Leeds 13 – York 14.

🏨 Ladbroke (Ladbroke), Leeds Rd, LS22 5HE, junction A 58 and A 1 ☎ 63881 – 📺 ⊡wc ☞ ℗
♨ ◪ ◪ ◉ ◻
⊠ 5.50 – **72 rm** 48.50/58.00 st.

XXX **L'Escale,** 16 Bank St., LS22 4NQ, ☎ 63613 – ℗ ◪ ◪ ◉ ◻
closed Sunday dinner, Monday and Bank Holidays – **M** (dinner only and Sunday lunch)/dinner 10.50 st. and a la carte 12.50/16.40 st. ₰ 3.50.

XXX **Linton Spring,** Sicklinghall Rd, LS22 9XX, W : 1 ¾ m. by A 661 ☎ 65353, ☀, park – ℗ ♨
◪ ◪ ◉ ◻
closed Saturday lunch, Sunday dinner, Monday, 26 December and first week January – M 8.95 t. (lunch) and a la carte 12.20/17.30 t. ₰ 3.00.

AUSTIN-ROVER North St. ☎ 62623

WETTON Staffs. – see Thorpe (Derbs.).

♦London 128 – Cromer 7.5 – ♦Norwich 26.

  🏠 Maltings, The Street, NR25 6SY, on A 149 ✆ 275, 🐴 – ⊤ⱱ ⌷wc Ⓟ – **21 rm.**

  XX Gasché's Swiss, The Street, NR25 7SY, on A 149 ✆ 220 – Ⓟ. 🔼 AE ⓞ VISA
    closed Sunday dinner, Monday and Christmas Day – **M** approx. 7.45/15.35 **t.** and a la carte
    🍷 1.80.

          Plan : see Greater London (South-West)

  🏯 **Ship Thistle** (Thistle), Monument Green, High St., KT13 8BQ, ✆ 848364, Telex 894271 – ⊤ⱱ
    ☎ Ⓟ. 🔼 🔼 AE ⓞ VISA. ⅍
                                    by A 3050 AZ
    M 10.50 **t.** and a la carte 🍷 3.50 – **39 rm** 59.00/79.00 **st.**

  XXX **Casa Romana,** 2 Temple Hall, Monument Hill, KT13 8RH, ✆ 43470, Italian rest. – Ⓟ. 🔼 AE
    VISA   by A 3050 AZ
    closed Saturday lunch and Monday – **M** 7.95 **t.** (lunch) and a la carte 11.05/19.50 **t.** 🍷 3.95.

  XX **Colony,** 3 Balfour Rd, KT13 8HE, ✆ 42766, Chinese-Peking rest. – 🔼 AE ⓞ VISA
    M 12.50/15.00 **st.** and a la carte 11.40/17.60 **st.**   by A 317 AZ

  XX Gaylord, 73 Queens Rd, ✆ 42895, Indian rest.   by A 317 AZ

AUSTIN-ROVER Woodham Lane, New Haw ✆
093 23 (Byfleet) 42870
AUSTIN-ROVER 30 Queens Rd ✆ 42233
FIAT, LANCIA Brooklands Rd ✆ 093 23 (Byfleet)
52941
FORD Monument Hill ✆ 46231
MAZDA Spinney Hill, Addlestone ✆ 0784
(Egham) 38581

TOYOTA 51-59 Baker St. ✆ 48247
SAAB Spinney Hill, Addlestone ✆ 093 287 (Otter-
shaw) 3726
VAUXHALL-OPEL New Haw Rd ✆ 53101
VOLVO 168 Oatlands Drive ✆ 54422

Envir. : Chesil Beach** (from Portland* (S : 1 ½ m.) to Abbotsbury) – at Abbotsbury**, NW : 9 m.
by B 3157 Swannery Gardens*AC, Sub Tropical Gardens*AC, St. Catherines Chapel*AC.

⚓ Shipping connections with the Continent : to France (Cherbourg) (Sealink) – to Channel
Islands : St. Peter Port, Guernsey (Sealink) 5-7 weekly (4 h 15 mn day 10 h night) – to Channel
Islands : St. Helier, Jersey (Sealink) 5-7 weekly (6 h 45 mn).

🅑 Pavilion Complex, The Esplanade ✆ 772444 – King's Statue, The Esplanade ✆ 785747 (summer only).

♦London 142 – Bournemouth 35 – ♦Bristol 68 – Exeter 59 – Swindon 94.

  🏠 Streamside, 29 Preston Rd, Overcombe, DT3 6PX, NE : 2 m. on A 353 ✆ 833121, 🐴 – ⊤ⱱ
    ⌷wc 🍴 Ⓟ. 🔼 AE VISA
    M 5.00/8.50 **t.** and a la carte 🍷 3.00 – **15 rm** ⊠ 25.00/39.00 **t.** – SB (except summer) (weekends
    only) 47.50 **st.**

  🏠 Glenburn, 42 Preston Rd, Overcombe, DT3 6PZ, NE : 2 m. on A 353 ✆ 832353 – ⊤ⱱ ⌷wc
    🍴wc. 🔼 VISA. ⅍
    M 6.00/8.00 **t.** and a la carte 🍷 3.00 – **13 rm** ⊠ 22.00/44.00 **t.** – SB (except summer and Bank
    Holidays) 50.00 **st.**

  🏠 Rex, 29 The Esplanade, DT4 8DN, ✆ 773485 – 📶 ⊤ⱱ ⌷wc 🍴wc. 🔼 VISA
    closed 24 to 26 December – **M** (dinner only) 4.95 **t.** and a la carte 🍷 3.00 – **21 rm** ⊠ 20.50/40.00
    – SB 36.00/50.00 **st.**

  ⋔ Sou'West Lodge, Rodwell Rd, DT4 8QT, ✆ 783749 – ⊤ⱱ ⌷wc 🍴wc Ⓟ. ⅍
    9 rm ⊠ 11.00/26.00 **st.**

FORD Dorchester Rd ✆ 782222   PEUGEOT-TALBOT 172 Dorchester Rd ✆ 786311

♦London 233 – ♦Blackpool 32 – Burnley 12 – ♦Manchester 28 – Preston 15.

  🏠 Mytton Fold Farm, Whalley Rd., Langho, BB6 8AB, SW : 1 ¾ m. on A 59 ✆ 48255, 🐴 – ⊤ⱱ
    ⌷wc 🍴wc ☎ & Ⓟ. 🔼 VISA. ⅍
    M 6.25 **t.** (lunch) and a la carte 7.15/13.75 **t.** 🍷 3.00 – **12 rm** ⊠ 23.00/34.00 **t.** – SB (weekends
    only) 44.00 **st.**

  XXX Foxfields, Whalley Rd, Billington, BB6 9HY, SW : 1 ½ m. on A 59 ✆ 2556 – Ⓟ. 🔼 AE ⓞ VISA
    closed Saturday lunch, Monday and Bank Holidays – **M** 9.00 **t.** (lunch) and a la carte
    13.25/18.25 **t.** 🍷 3.75.

♦London 191 – Exeter 36 – Taunton 29.

  🏠 Raleigh Manor ⪜, N : ½ m. on A 396 ✆ 484, ≼, 🐴 – ⌷wc Ⓟ – **7 rm**.

  ⋔ Higherley House ⪜, W : ½ m. on B 3224 ✆ 582, ≼, 🐴 – Ⓟ – **5 rm.**

WHETSTONE Leics. – see Leicester.

WHIMPLE Devon **403** J 31 – see Exeter.

WHIPPINGHAM I.O.W. **403 404** Q 31 – see Wight (Isle of).

WHITBY North Yorks. **402** S 20 – pop. 12 982 – ECD : Wednesday – ✆ 0947.
See : Abbey ruins★ (13C) *AC*, Old St. Mary's Church★ 12C, East Terrace ≼★.
ᵢₛ Low Straggleton ℰ 602768.
🛈 New Quay Rd ℰ 602674.
◆London 257 – ◆Middlesbrough 31 – Scarborough 21 – York 45.

  🏠 **Stakesby Manor,** High Stakesby, YO21 1HL, ℰ 602773, ☂, – 🖵 ⊟wc �𝄖wc 🅿. ⚘
    M (dinner only) 6.95 **t.** and a la carte – **8 rm** ⊊ 19.00/38.00 **t.** – SB (October-April) 37.00 **t.**

  at Sneaton S : 3 m. by A 171 on B 1416 – ✉ ✆ 0947 Whitby :

  🏠 **Sneaton Hall,** YO22 5HP, ℰ 605929, ☂ – 🖵 ⊟wc ᑭwc 🅿. ⓓ
    Easter-October – **M** (dinner only) 10.00 **t.** ≬ 2.75 – **9 rm** ⊊ 17.50/35.00 **t.**

AUSTIN-ROVER 6 Upgang Lane ℰ 603321   RENAULT 18 Silver St. ℰ 602093
FORD Silver St. ℰ 602237   VAUXHALL Argyle Rd ℰ 602898
NISSAN Castle Park ℰ 602841

WHITCHURCH Salop **402 403 404** L 25 – pop. 7 246 – ECD : Wednesday – ✆ 0948.
ᵢₛ Hill Valley, Terrick Rd ℰ 3584, N : 1 m.
🛈 Civic Centre, High St. ℰ 4577.
◆London 171 – ◆Birmingham 54 – Chester 22 – ◆Manchester 43 – Shrewsbury 20.

  🏠 **Redbrook Hunting Lodge,** Wrexham Rd, SY13 3ET, W : 2 ½ m. on A 525 ℰ 094 873 (Red-
    brook Maelor) 204, ☂ – ⊟wc 🅿. 🔂 🆎 ⓓ ⱽᴵˢᴬ ⅏
    M 7.50 **st.** and a la carte ≬ 2.50 – **11 rm** ⊊ 25.00/35.00 **t.** – SB (weekends only) 45.00 **st.**

AUSTIN-ROVER Brownlow St. ℰ 2826   FORD Dodington ℰ 4471
AUSTIN-ROVER, LAND ROVER-RANGE ROVER   RENAULT Wrexham Rd ℰ 2257
Newport Rd ℰ 3333

WHITEBROOK Gwent – see Monmouth.

WHITFIELD Kent **404** X 30 – see Dover.

WHITLAND (HENDY-GWYN) Dyfed **403** G 28 – pop. 1 342 – ECD : Wednesday – ✆ 0994.
🛈 Canolfan Hywel Dda ℰ 240867.
◆London 235 – Carmarthen 15 – Haverfordwest 17.

  🏠 **Waungron Farm** ⬒, SA34 0QX, SW : 1 m. off B 4328 ℰ 240682, ≼, « Converted farm
    buildings », park – 🖵 ⊟wc ᑭwc ⅋. 🅿. ⅏
    M (booking essential) 7.50/8.50 **st.** and a la carte – **14 rm** ⊊ 25.00/32.50 **st.** – SB 45.00/49.50 **st.**

  ↑ Cilpost Farm ⬒, SA34 4RP, N : 1 ¼ m. by North Rd ℰ 240280, ≼, « Working dairy farm », 🔲,
    ☂ – ⊟wc 🅿. ⅏ – **7 rm**

WHITLEY BAY Tyne and Wear **401 402** P 18 – pop. 36 040 – ECD : Wednesday – ✆ 091 Tyneside.
Envir. : Seaton Delaval Hall★ (18C) *AC*, NW : 6 m.
🛈 Central Promenade. ℰ 252 4494 (summer only).
◆London 293 – ◆Newcastle-upon-Tyne 10 – Sunderland 10.

  🏠 **Ambassador,** 38-42 South Par., NE26 2RQ, ℰ 253 1218 – 🖵 ⊟wc ☎ 🅿. 🔂 ⓓ ⱽᴵˢᴬ
    closed Christmas Day – **M** 5.95/8.50 **t.** and a la carte ≬ 3.30 – **28 rm** ⊊ 23.35/38.50 **t.** –
    SB (weekends only) 53.00/61.00 **st.**

AUSTIN-ROVER Cauldwell Lane ℰ 2522231   LADA Fox Hunters Rd ℰ 2528282
CITROEN Claremont Rd ℰ 2525909   VAUXHALL Earsdon Rd, West Monkseaton ℰ
FIAT Claremont Rd ℰ 2523347   2523355
FORD Whitley Rd ℰ 2531221   VW. AUDI Hillheads Rd ℰ 2528225

WHITSTABLE Kent **404** X 29 – pop. 26 227 – ECD : Wednesday – ✆ 0227.
Envir. : Herne Bay : Reculver (church twin towers★ *AC*), E : 8 ½ m.
ᵢₛ Whitstable and Seasalter, Collingwood Rd ℰ 272020, W : off B 2205.
🛈 1 Tankerton Rd ℰ 272233.
◆London 59 – ◆Dover 22 – Maidstone 28 – Margate 19.

  XXX **Giovanni's,** 49-55 Canterbury Rd, CT5 4HH, ℰ 273034, Italian rest. – 🅿. 🔂 🆎 ⓓ ⱽᴵˢᴬ
    closed Monday – **M** 6.50/8.50 **t.** and a la carte ≬ 2.95.

FORD Tankerton Rd ℰ 265613   RENAULT Tower Par. ℰ 261477

WHITTLE-LE-WOODS Lancs. **402** M 23 – see Chorley.

WHITTLESEY Cambs. **404** T 26 – see Peterborough.

♦London 223 – Malton 5 – York 12.

🏛 **Whitwell Hall Country House** ॐ, YO6 7JJ, ℰ 551, ≤, 🔄, 🌳, park, ✕ – 🖵 ⌷wc 🛆wc
⬛ 🅿. ☖ 🔄 🏧 *VISA*.
M (lunch by arrangement) 8.00/16.00 t. ⬧ 3.00 – **20 rm** ☲ 32.00/67.00 t. – SB (November-April)
50.00/65.00 **st.**

WICKHAM Hants. 403 404 Q 31 – pop. 3 485 – ECD : Wednesday – ✆ 0329.

♦London 74 – ♦Portsmouth 12 – ♦Southampton 11 – Winchester 16.

🏛 **Old House,** The Square, PO17 5JG, ℰ 833049, « Tastefully renovated Queen Anne house »,
🌳 – 🖵 ⌷wc ⬛ 🅿. 🔄 🏧 ⓞ *VISA*.
closed 2 weeks Easter, 3 weeks August-September and 10 days at Christmas – **M** *(closed lunch Saturday and Monday and Sunday)* a la carte 13.85/18.50 **st.** – **10 rm** ☲ 46.00/70.00 **st.**

WIDEGATES Cornwall – see Looe.

WIGAN Greater Manchester 402 404 M 23 – pop. 88 725 – ECD : Wednesday – ✆ 0942.

🏌 Haigh Hall Park ℰ 831107, NW : 3 m. – 🏌 Arley Hall, Haigh ℰ 0257 (Standish) 421360, N : 4 m. –
🏌 Pennington Recreation Area, ℰ 672823.

♦London 206 – ♦Liverpool 19 – ♦Manchester 18 – Preston 18.

🏛 Brocket Arms, Mesnes Rd, WN1 2DD, on A 49 ℰ 46283 – 🖵 ⌷wc ☜ 🅿. ☖ ✕
27 rm.

FORD Wallgate ℰ 41393	RENAULT Miry Lane ℰ 39107	
LADA Chapel St., Pemberton ℰ 214028	VAUXHALL-OPEL Warrington Rd ℰ 494848	
NISSAN Crompton St. ℰ 42281	VOLVO Platt Bridge ℰ 866594	
RELIANT Cerrell Post ℰ 214437		

🖙 *There is no paid publicity in this Guide.*

WIGHT (Isle of) 403 404 PQ 31 32 – pop. 118 594.

🛳 from East to West Cowes to Southampton (Red Funnel Services) 8-18 daily (55 mn to 1 h 10 mn) – from Yarmouth to Lymington (Sealink) frequent services daily (30 mn) – from Fishbourne to Portsmouth (Sealink) 15-18 daily (45 mn).

🛥 from West Cowes to Southampton (Red Funnel services : hydrofoil) Monday to Saturday 14-19 daily ; Sunday 15 daily (20 mn) – from Ryde to Southsea (Hovertravel to Southsea Clarence Pier) summer services daily ; winter 8-12 daily (restricted Sundays) (9 mn) – from Ryde to Portsmouth (Sealink to Portsmouth Harbour) frequent services daily (25-30 mn).

Bembridge – pop. 3 470 – ✉ ✆ 0983 Isle of Wight.
Newport 14.

🏛 **Highbury,** Lane End Rd, PO35 5SU, ℰ 872838, 🔄 heated, 🌳 – 🖵 ⌷wc 🛆wc ☜ 🅿. 🔄 🏧
ⓞ *VISA*
closed 24 to 27 December – **M** 5.50/9.50 t. and a la carte ⬧ 2.95 – **9 rm** ☲ 18.50/40.50 **st.** –
SB (November-April) 50.00/55.00 **st.**

🏛 **Elms Country** ॐ, Swaines Rd, PO35 5XS, ℰ 872248, 🌳 – 🖵 ⌷wc 🛆wc ☎ 🅿
March-mid October – **M** (buffet lunch)/dinner 8.50 t. and a la carte ⬧ 3.50 – **12 rm**
☲ 24.00/38.00 t.

PEUGEOT-TALBOT Church Rd ℰ 0983 872121

Chale – pop. 561 – ECD : Thursday – ✉ Ventnor – ✆ 0983 Isle of Wight.
Newport 9.

🏛 **Clarendon,** Newport Rd, PO38 2HA, ℰ 730431, ≤, 🌳 – 🖵 ⌷wc 🛆wc 🅿
M a la carte 4.45/7.60 t. – **13 rm** ☲ 13.00/30.00 – SB 46.00/50.60 **st.**

Cowes – pop. 16 371 – ECD : Wednesday – ✉ ✆ 0983 Isle of Wight.
Envir. : Osborne House★ (19C) *AC*, E : 1 m.
🖪 1 Bath Rd ℰ 291914 (summer only).
Newport 4.

🏛 Holmwood, Egypt Point, 65 Queens Rd, PO30 8BW, ℰ 292508, ≤ – 🖵 ⌷wc 🛆wc ☜ 🅿
19 rm.

🏛 **Fountain,** High St., PO31 7AW, ℰ 292397 – 🖵 ⌷wc ☎. 🔄 🏧 ⓞ *VISA*. ✕
M (bar lunch)/dinner a la carte 7.65/11.35 t. ⬧ 3.50 – **20 rm** ☲ 31.00/42.00 t. – SB (weekends only) 50.00 **st.**

🏛 **Cowes,** 260 Arctic Rd, PO31 7PJ, ℰ 291541, 🔄 – 🖵 ⌷wc 🅿. 🔄 🏧 ⓞ *VISA*
M *(closed Sunday lunch)* 8.00 ⬧ 2.25 – **15 rm** ☲ 22.95/31.00.

✕ **G's,** 10 Bath Rd, PO31 7QN, ℰ 297021 – 🔄 🏧 ⓞ *VISA*
closed Sundays except Bank Holidays, 25 to 27 December, 1 to 3 January and February –
M (lunch by arrangement) a la carte 9.95/15.65 t. ⬧ 4.30.

Freshwater Bay – pop. 5 073 – ECD : Thursday – ⊠ ✪ 0983 Isle of Wight.

🛏 ✆ 752955.

Newport 13.

🏛 **Albion,** Gate Lane, PO40 9RA, ✆ 753631, ≤ – 🖵 ⇔wc ☜ 🅿 🔼 🖪 𝘝𝘐𝘚𝘈
April-October – **M** 6.00/10.00 **st.** 🍷 2.75 – **43 rm** ⇆ 16.00/39.75 **st.** – SB (April, May and October) 58.75 **st.**

⌂ **Blenheim House,** Gate Lane, PO40 9QD, ✆ 752858, ⅀ heated – 🇲wc 🅿 🛇
May-October – **8 rm** ⇆ 13.00/28.00 **st.**

Newport – pop. 19 758 – ECD : Thursday – ⊠ ✪ 0983 Isle of Wight.

Envir. : Shorwell (St. Peter's Church★ 15C) SW : 5 m. – Carisbrooke Castle★★ 12C-16C (keep ≤★) *AC* SW : 1 ½ m.

🛏 St. George's Down, Shide ✆ 525076, SE : 1 m.

🛈 21 High St. ✆ 524343.

🏛 **Bugle** (Whitbread), 117 High St., PO30 1TP, ✆ 522800 – 🖵 ⇔wc ☎ 🅿 🔼 🖪 ⓪ 𝘝𝘐𝘚𝘈
M a la carte 6.45/14.30 **t.** – **26 rm** ⇆ 35.00/45.00 **t.** – SB (weekends only) 56.00 **t.**

AUDI, MERCEDES-BENZ, VW Medina Av. ✆ 523232   SUBARU Blackwater ✆ 523684

Ryde – pop. 19 384 – ECD : Thursday – ⊠ ✪ 0983 Isle of Wight.

🛏 Ryde House Park ✆ 62088.

🛈 Western Gardens, Esplanade ✆ 62905 (summer only).

Newport 7.5.

🏛 **Yelf's** (T.H.F.), Union St., PO33 2LG, ✆ 64062 – 🖵 🖵 ⇔wc ☜ 🔼 🖪 ⓪ 𝘝𝘐𝘚𝘈
M 8.95 **st.** and a la carte 🍷 3.40 – ⇆ 5.65 – **21 rm** 39.00/50.00 **st.**

AUSTIN-ROVER Elmfield ✆ 62717
HONDA Brading Rd ✆ 64166
LANCIA Victoria St. ✆ 63661
SEAT Fishbourne Lane ✆ 0983 (Wootton Bridge) 882465

SKODA Havenstreet ✆ 0983 (Wootton Bridge) 882455
TOYOTA Gorfield Rd ✆ 62281

Seaview – ⊠ ✪ 098 361 Seaview.

🏠 **Seaview,** High St., PO34 5EX, ✆ 2711 – 🖵 ⇔wc 🅿 🔼 🖪 𝘝𝘐𝘚𝘈
M (see **Seaview Rest.** below) **14 rm** ⇆ 18.00/38.00 **t.** – SB (weekends only) 44.00/50.00 **st.**

✗ **Seaview,** (at Seaview H.) High St., PO34 5EX, ✆ 2711 – 🅿 🔼 🖪 𝘝𝘐𝘚𝘈
M 6.95/8.90 **t.** and a la carte 8.95/14.90 **t.** 🍷 2.75.

Shanklin – pop. 8 109 – ECD : Wednesday – ⊠ ✪ 0983 Isle of Wight.

See : Old Village (thatched cottages)★ – The Chine★ *AC*.

Envir. : Brading (Roman Villa : mosaics★ *AC*) N : 3 ½ m.

🛈 67 High St. ✆ 862942.

Newport 9.

🏨 Cliff Tops, 1-5 Park Rd, PO37 6BB, ✆ 863262, ≤, ⅀ heated, ♨ – 🛗 🖵 ☎ 🅿 🔼
98 rm.

🏛 **Hartland,** 41 Victoria Av., PO37 6LT, ✆ 863123, 🗔, ♨ – 🖵 ⇔wc 🇲wc 🅿 🛇
24 rm.

🏛 **Bourne Hall Country** �ります, Luccombe Rd, PO37 6RR, ✆ 862820, ⅀ heated, 🗔, ♨, ✗ – 🖵 ⇔wc ☎ 🅿 🔼 🖪 ⓪ 𝘝𝘐𝘚𝘈 🛇
closed January and December – **M** (bar lunch)/dinner 14.00 **t.** – **25 rm** ⇆ 20.25/53.00 **t.** – SB (except July and August) 40.40/50.40 **st.**

🏠 **Carlton** �ります, Eastcliff Promenade, PO37 6AY, ✆ 862517, ≤, ♨ – 🖵 ⇔wc 🅿 🛇
April-October – **11 rm** ⇆ 16.00/48.00 **st.**

🏠 **Queensmead,** 12 Queens Rd, PO37 6AN, ✆ 862342, ⅀ heated, ♨ – ⇔wc 🇲wc. 𝘝𝘐𝘚𝘈 🛇
April-October – **M** (bar lunch)/dinner 8.50 **st.** 🍷 2.30 – **25 rm** ⇆ 19.00/56.00 **st.** – SB (except summer) 35.00/44.00 **st.**

⌂ **Delphi Cliff,** 7 St. Boniface Cliff Rd, PO37 6ET, ✆ 862179, ≤, ♨ – ⇔wc 🅿 🛇
April-October – **11 rm** ⇆ 10.00/27.00 **st.**

⌂ **Overstrand,** Howard Rd, PO37 6HD, ✆ 862100, ≤, ♨, ✗ – 🖵 ⇔wc 🇲wc 🅿 🔼 🛇
April-September – **15 rm** ⇆ 13.50/37.00 **st.**

✗ **Cottage,** 8 Eastcliff Rd, PO37 6AA, ✆ 862504 – 🔼 𝘝𝘐𝘚𝘈
closed dinner Sunday, Monday except dinner in summer, mid February-mid March and October – **M** (restricted lunch) (booking essential) 5.30 **t.** (lunch) and a la carte 11.10/13.25 **t.**

Totland Bay – pop. 2 316 – ECD : Wednesday – ✉ ☎ 0983 Isle of Wight.
Envir. : Alum Bay (coloured sands★) and the Needles★ SW : 1 m.
Newport 13.

🏨 **Country Garden,** Church Hill, PO39 0ET, on B 3322 ℰ 754521, ≤, ☞ – ⊤⊽ ⇔wc ☜ 🅿. 🖾
🅰🅴 ① 𝚅𝙸𝚂𝙰
M 5.50/8.50 **t.** and a la carte ⁁ 2.50 – **18 rm** ⊊ 22.00/64.00 **t.** – SB (except Christmas)
56.00/64.00 **st.**

🏨 **Nodes Country** ⑤, Alum Bay, Old Road, PO39 0HZ, SW : 1 ½ m. by B 3322 ℰ 752859, ☞
– ⇔wc ��⋔wc 🅿. ⅗
M (bar lunch)/dinner 7.50 **st.** ⁁ 2.50 – **11 rm** ⊊ 15.00/30.00 **t.** – SB (September-May)
36.00/42.00 **st.**

🏨 **Sentry Mead,** Madeira Rd, PO39 0BJ, ℰ 753212, ☞ – ⇔wc 🅿. 🅰🅴
M (bar lunch)/dinner 7.00 **st.** and a la carte ⁁ 2.80 – **13 rm** ⊊ 15.00/50.00 **st.**

⌂ **Littledene Lodge,** Granville Rd, PO39 0AX, ℰ 752411 – ⎾⋔wc 🅿
closed Christmas – **7 rm** ⊊ 10.00/24.00 **st.**

Ventnor – pop. 7 956 – ECD : Wednesday – ✉ ☎ 0983 Isle of Wight.
Envir. : St. Catherine's Point (≤★ from the car-park) W : 5 m.
🖪 34 High St. ℰ 853625 (summer only).
Newport 10.

🏨 **Royal** (T.H.F.), Belgrave Rd, PO38 1JJ, ℰ 852186, ⫟ heated, ☞ – ⧚ ⊤⊽ ⇔wc ☜ 🅿. 🖾 🅰🅴
① 𝚅𝙸𝚂𝙰
M (buffet lunch)/dinner 8.50 **st.** and a la carte ⁁ 3.40 – ⊊ 5.65 – **54 rm** 36.00/50.00 **st.**

🏨 **Ventnor Towers,** 54 Madeira Rd, PO38 1QT, ℰ 852277, ≤, ⫟ heated, ☞, ⅗ – ⊤⊽ ⇔wc
⎾⋔wc ☎ 🅿. 🖾 𝚅𝙸𝚂𝙰
M 6.00/10.00 **st.** and a la carte ⁁ 2.25 – ⊊ 5.00 – **30 rm** 21.50/59.00 **st.** – SB 53.00/59.00 **st.**

⌂ **Madeira Hall** ⑤, Trinity Rd, PO38 1NS, ℰ 852624, ⫟ heated, ☞ – ⊤⊽ ⇔wc ⎾⋔wc 🅿. 🖾
🅰🅴 𝚅𝙸𝚂𝙰
Mid March-October – **12 rm** ⊊ 19.50/46.00 **st.**

⌂ **Channel View,** Hamborough Rd, PO38 1SQ, ℰ 852230, ≤ – ⎾⋔. 🖾 🅰🅴 ①. ⅗
March-October – **14 rm** ⊊ 11.00/28.00 **t.**

at Bonchurch – ✉ ☎ 0983 Isle of Wight :

🏨 **Winterbourne** ⑤, PO38 1RG, ℰ 852535, ≤ gardens and sea, « Country house and gardens »,
⫟ heated – ⊤⊽ ⇔wc ⎾⋔wc 🅿
19 rm.

🏨 **Highfield,** 87 Leeson Rd, Upper Bonchurch, PO38 1PU, on A 3055 ℰ 852800, ≤, ☞ – ⊤⊽
⇔wc ☎ 🅿. 🖾 𝚅𝙸𝚂𝙰
closed November-December – **M** (bar lunch)/dinner 7.30 **st.** ⁁ 3.25 – **12 rm** ⊊ 17.50/35.00 **st.**
– SB (except summer) 84.00/90.00 **st.**

🏨 **Bonchurch Manor** ⑤, Bonchurch Shute, PO38 1NU, ℰ 852868, ≤, 🖾, ☞ – ⊤⊽ ⇔wc
⎾⋔wc 🅿. 🖾 𝚅𝙸𝚂𝙰
closed January-February – **M** (dinner only and Sunday lunch)/dinner 10.00 **st.** ⁁ 3.10 – **11 rm**
⊊ 22.00/44.00 **st.** – SB (except summer) 53.00 **st.**

🏤 **Lake** ⑤, Shore Rd, PO38 1RF, ℰ 852613, ☞ – ⎾⋔wc 🅿
April-October – **M** (bar lunch)/dinner 5.00 **st.** ⁁ 2.75 – **23 rm** ⊊ 10.00/26.00 **t.** –
SB 27.00/30.00 **st.**

⌂ **Horseshoe Bay** ⑤, Shore Rd, PO38 1RN, ℰ 852487, ≤ – ⊤⊽ ⇔wc 🅿. 🖾
Easter-mid October – **7 rm** ⊊ 10.00/27.50 **st.**

⌂ **Under Rock** ⑤, Shore Rd, PO38 1RF, ℰ 852714, « Gardens » – ⊤⊽ 🅿. ⅗
March-October – **7 rm** ⊊ 15.00/30.00 **st.**

at St. Lawrence – ✉ ☎ 0983 Ventnor :

⌂ **Woody Bank,** Undercliff Drive, PO38 1XF, ℰ 852610, ≤, ☞ – ⎾⋔wc 🅿
March-October – **9 rm** ⊊ 16.00/40.00 **t.**

MAZDA Victoria St. ℰ 852650

Whippingham – ✉ ☎ 0983 Isle of Wight.
Newport 3.5.

🏨 **Padmore House** ⑤, Beatrice Av:, PO32 6LP, ℰ 293210, ☞ – ⊤⊽ ⇔wc ⎾⋔ ☎ 🅿. 🖾 🅰🅴 ①
𝚅𝙸𝚂𝙰
closed 25 to 31 December – **M** (closed Saturday lunch) 8.00/11.00 **st.** ⁁ 2.50 – **11 rm**
⊊ 19.75/51.80 **st.** – SB (weekends only) 46.00/50.00 **st.**

AUSTIN-ROVER Mill Rd ℰ 760436

☞ *Michelin puts no plaque or sign*
on the hotels and restaurants mentioned in this Guide.

WILBERFOSS North Yorks. 📟 R 22 – see York.

WILLENHALL West Midlands 🔢 🔢 N 26 – see Coventry.

WILLERBY Humberside 📟 S 22 – see Kingston-upon-Hull.

WILLERSEY Heref. and Worc. 🔢 🔢 O 27 – see Broadway.

WILLERSEY HILL Glos. 🔢 🔢 O 27 – see Broadway (Heref. and Worc.).

WILLINGDON East Sussex 🔢 U 31 – see Eastbourne.

WILLITON Somerset 🔢 K 30 **The West Country** G. – pop. 2 410 – ECD : Saturday – ✉ Taunton – ☎ 0984.

♦London 177 – Minehead 8 – Taunton 16.

   ☎ **Fairfield House,** 51 Long St., TA4 4QY, ✆ 32636 – 🅿. 🄰 AE ⓪ VISA. ✻
       March–November – **M** (dinner only) 8.00 **st.** 🍸 3.00 – **5 rm** ☞ 12.50/21.00 **st.** – SB 32.00/36.00 **st.**

   XX **White House** with rm, 11 Long St., TA4 4QW, ✆ 32306 – 📺 🛏wc 🅿. ✻
       Mid May–October – **M** (dinner only) 17.00 **t.** 🍸 2.25 – **13 rm** ☞ 22.50/45.00 **t.**

AUSTIN-ROVER West Quantoxhead ✆ 32437   PEUGEOT, TALBOT High St. ✆ 32761

WILMCOTE Warw. 🔢 🔢 O 27 – see Stratford-upon-Avon.

WILMINGTON Devon 🔢 K 31 – see Honiton.

WILMINGTON East Sussex 🔢 U 31 – see Eastbourne.

WILMSLOW Cheshire 📟 🔢 🔢 N 24 – pop. 28 827 – ECD : Wednesday – ☎ 0625.

♦London 189 – ♦Liverpool 38 – Manchester 12 – ♦Stoke-on-Trent 27.

   🏨 **Stanneylands** ⤴, Stanneylands Rd, SK9 4EY, N : 1 m. by A 34 ✆ 525225, Telex 666358, « Gardens » – ▤ rest 📺 ☎ ⅗ 🅿. 🄰 🄰 AE ⓪ VISA. ✻
       M *(closed Sunday dinner)* 7.50/18.00 **st.** and a la carte 🍸 2.75 – ☞ 5.50 – **33 rm** 30.00/55.00 **st.** – SB (weekends only) 85.00/125.00 **st.**

   🏨 **Valley Lodge,** Oversley Ford, Altrincham Rd, SK9 4LR, NW : 2 ¾ m. on A 538 ✆ 529201, Telex 666401 – 🛗 📺 🛏wc ☎ 🅿. 🄰 AE ⓪ VISA. ✻
       M 6.75/8.35 **st.** and a la carte 🍸 3.05 – ☞ 4.95 – **105 rm** 38.00/45.00 **st.**

   at Handforth N : 3 m. on A 34 – ✉ Wilmslow :

   🏨 **Belfry,** Stanley Rd, SK9 3LD, ✆ 061 (Manchester) 437 0511, Telex 666358, ☞ – 🛗 📺 ☎ ⅗ 🅿. 🄰 🄰 ⓪ VISA. ✻
       M 9.50/11.50 **st.** and a la carte 🍸 3.25 – ☞ 5.50 – **92 rm** 43.50/53.50 **st.**, **2 suites** 65.00 **st.** – SB (weekends only) 80.00/100.00 **st.**

   🏛 Pinewood, 180 Wilmslow Rd, SK9 3LG, ✆ 0625 (Wilmslow) 529211, ☞ – 🛗 📺 🛏wc ☎ 🅿
       64 rm.

BMW Manchester Rd ✆ 529955   RENAULT Station Rd ✆ 527356
NISSAN Station Rd, Styal ✆ 524145   RENAULT Knutsford Rd ✆ 523669
PORSCHE Green Lane ✆ 526392   VAUXHALL-OPEL Water Lane ✆ 527311

WIMBORNE MINSTER Dorset 🔢 🔢 O 31 **The West Country** G. – pop. 14 193 – ECD : Wednesday – ☎ 0202 Wimborne – **See** : Site★.

🏌 Ashley Wood ✆ 0258 (Blandford) 52253, NW : 8 m. – 🛈 The Quarter Jack, 6 Cook Row, ✆ 886116.

♦London 112 – Bournemouth 10 – Dorchester 23 – Salisbury 27 – ♦Southampton 30.

   🏛 **King's Head** (T.H.F.), The Square, BH21 1JA, ✆ 880101 – 🛗 📺 🛏wc ☎ 🅿. 🄰 🄰 AE ⓪ VISA
       M 5.95/9.95 **st.** and a la carte 🍸 3.40 – ☞ 5.65 – **27 rm** 43.00/55.00 **st.**

   XX **Allendale,** Allendale House, Hanham Rd, BH21 1AS, ✆ 887755 – 🅿. 🄰 AE ⓪ VISA
       closed Sunday dinner and 25-26 December – **M** a la carte 8.85/17.45 **t.** 🍸 3.25.

   XX **Old Town House,** 9 Church St., BH21 1JH, ✆ 888227 – VISA
       closed Sunday dinner and Monday – **M** 7.00/10.00 **st.** and a la carte 10.05/13.80 **st.** 🍸 2.60.

   at Horton N : 6 m. on B 3078 – ✉ Wimborne Minster – ☎ 0258 Witchampton :

   🏠 **Horton Inn,** Cranborne Rd, BH21 5AD, ✆ 840252 – 📺 🛏wc 🅿. 🄰 VISA. ✻
       M *(closed Saturday lunch, Sunday dinner and Monday)* 5.95/10.95 **t.** 🍸 2.95 – **5 rm** ☞ 20.00/40.00.

   at Broadstone S : 3 ¼ m. by A 349 on B 3074 – ✉ Poole – ☎ 0202 Broadstone :

   ⬆ **Fairlight** ⤴, 1 Golf Links Rd, BH18 8BE, ✆ 694316, ☞ – 🛏wc 🅿. 🄰 VISA
       10 rm ☞ 16.00/32.00 **t.**

AUSTIN-ROVER West St. ✆ 882261   VAUXHALL-OPEL Walford Bridge ✆ 884211
FORD Poole Rd ✆ 886211   VOLVO 41 Leigh Rd ✆ 887163

WINCANTON Somerset 403 404 M 30 – pop. 3 613 – ECD : Thursday – ✆ 0963.

🖪 Public Library. 7 Carrington Way ✆ 32173.

◆London 119 – ◆Bristol 37 – Taunton 34 – Yeovil 16.

　🏛　**Holbrook House** ⌂, Holbrook, BA9 8BS, W : 1 ½ m. on A 371, ✆ 32377, ≼, « Country mansion », ⌁ heated, 🐎, park, ✵, squash – 🚻wc 🏻wc 🅿 🖼 AE VISA
closed 31 December – **M** 7.00/9.50 **t.** and a la carte 🛋 2.70 – **20 rm** � 20.00/48.00 **t.** – SB (except Christmas) 40.00/55.00 **st.**

WINCHCOMBE Glos. 403 404 O 28 – pop. 4 822 – ECD : Thursday – ✉ Cheltenham – ✆ 0242.

◆London 100 – ◆Birmingham 42 – Gloucester 15.

　✕　Corner Cupboard, Gloucester St., GL54 5LX, ✆ 602303 – 🅿

WINCHESTER Hants. 403 404 P 30 – pop. 34 127 – ECD : Thursday – ✆ 0962.

See : Cathedral★★★ 11C-13C B – Winchester College★★ 14C B – Pilgrim's Hall★ 14C B E – St. Cross Hospital★ 12C-15C A.

Envir. : Marwell Zoological Park★★ AC, SE : 5 m. on A 333 A.

🖪 The Guildhall, The Broadway ✆ 65406.

◆London 72 – ◆Bristol 76 – ◆Oxford 52 – ◆Southampton 12.

WINCHESTER

High Street . . . . B

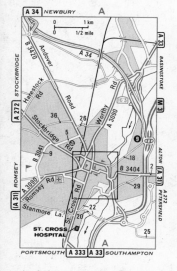

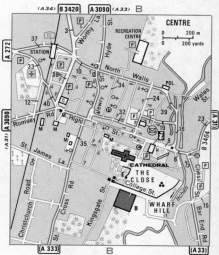

　🏛🏛　**Lainston House** ⌂, Sparsholt, SO21 2LT, NW : 3 ½ m. by A 272 ✆ 63588, Telex 477375, ≼, « 17C manor house », 🐎, park, ✵ – 🆃🆅 ☎ 🔥 🅿 🅰 🖼 AE ① VISA　　by A 272　A
M 14.50/25.00 **t.** and a la carte 🛋 3.75 – ⌁ 6.00 – **32 rm** 48.00/90.00 **t.**, **3 suites** 100.00/125.00 **t.**

　🏛🏛　**Wessex** (T.H.F.), Paternoster Row, SO23 9LQ, ✆ 61611, Telex 47419, ≼ – 🛗 🆃🆅 ☎ 🅿 🅰 🖼 AE VISA
M 9.25/12.50 **st.** and a la carte 🛋 2.95 – ⌁ 6.00 – **94 rm** 52.50/63.50 **st.**, **1 suite**　　B c

　🏛　**Royal**, St. Peter St., SO23 8BS, ✆ 53468, Telex 477071, 🐎 – 🆃🆅 🚻wc ☎ 🅿 🅰　　B n
59 rm.

　🏠　**Chantry Mead**, 22 Bereweeke Rd, SO22 6AJ, ✆ 52767, 🐎 – 🆃🆅 🚻wc 🅿 – **18 rm.**　A a

　✕✕　**Old Chesil Rectory,** 1 Chesil St., SO23 8HU, ✆ 53177, English rest., « 14C restored rectory » – 🖼 AE ① VISA　　B a
closed Sunday dinner and Monday – **M** 6.75 **t.** and a la carte 8.70/14.95 **t.**

ASTON-MARTIN Hursley ℰ 75218
AUSTIN-ROVER Easton Lane, The By-pass ℰ 69182
FORD Bar-End Rd ℰ 62211
VAUXHALL Stockbridge Rd ℰ 63344

TALBOT, CITROEN, PEUGEOT 2-4 St. Cross Rd
  ℰ 61855
VOLVO Kingsworthy ℰ 881414
VW, AUDI St. Cross Rd ℰ 66331

WINDERMERE Cumbria **402** L 20 – pop. 6 835 – ECD : Thursday – ☎ 096 62.

See : Lake★.

Envir. : Kirkstone Pass (on Windermere ≤★) N : 7 m. by A 592 Y.

Cleabarrow ℰ 3123 by A 5074 Z and B 5284.

Victoria St. ℰ 4561.

at Bowness : The Glebe ℰ 2895 (summer only).

♦London 274 – ♦Blackpool 55 – ♦Carlisle 46 – Kendal 10.

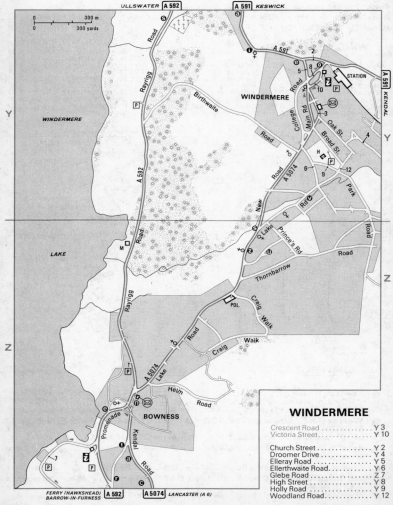

WINDERMERE

Langdale Chase ⊗, LA23 1LW, NW : 3 m. on A 591 ☏ 0966 (Ambleside) 32201, ≤ Lake Windermere and mountains, « Extensive grounds with lake frontage », 🛋, park, ✗ – ▤ rest 📺 ₺ 🅿. 🔟 AE ⓞ VISA   on A 591   Y
M 8.25/15.50 **st.** ₺ 3.40 – **35 rm** ⊠ 30.00/70.00 **st.** – SB (October-April) 60.00/75.00 **st.**

Priory Country House, Rayrigg Rd, LA23 1EX, NW : ¾ m. by A 591 on A 592 ☏ 4377, ≤ Lake Windermere and mountains, 🛋, park – 📺 ⌂wc 🅿. 🔟 AE ⓞ VISA ✗
closed January – **M** (bar lunch Monday to Saturday)/dinner 15.00 **t.** ₺ 4.00 – **15 rm** ⊠ 40.00/70.00 **st.** – SB (October-April) 65.00/70.00 **st.**   by A592   Y

Holbeck Ghyll Country House ⊗, Holbeck Lane, LA23 1LU, NW : 3 ½ m. by A 591 ☏ 0966 (Ambleside) 32375, ≤, « Country house atmosphere », 🛋 – 📺 ⌂wc 🅿. 🔟
March-November – **M** (dinner only) 11.00 **t.** ₺ 2.75 – **11 rm** ⊠ 22.00/46.00 **t.** – SB (November-mid May) 46.00/50.00 **st.**   by A 591   Y

Quarry Garth ⊗, Ambleside Rd, LA23 1LF, NW : 2 m. on A 591 ☏ 3761, 🛋, park – 📺 ⌂wc 🅿
M 6.00/12.00 **st.** and a la carte ₺ 3.50 – **11 rm** ⊠ 15.00/60.00 **st.** – SB 45.00/60.00 **st.**   by A 591   Y

Cedar Manor, Ambleside Rd, LA23 1AX, ☏ 3192, 🛋 – 📺 ⌂wc ⋔wc 🅿. 🔟 VISA   Y i
closed January – **M** (dinner only) 11.50 **t.** ₺ 2.90 – **6 rm** ⊠ 20.00/40.00 **t.** – SB (November-March) 41.00/48.00 **st.**

Glencree, Lake Rd, LA23 2EQ, ☏ 5822 – 📺 ⌂wc ⋔wc 🅿. ✗   Z s
closed mid December-mid February – **M** (dinner only by arrangement) (residents only) 14.00 **st.**
₺ 3.00 – **5 rm** ⊠ 35.00/39.00 **st.**

Rosemount, Lake Rd, LA23 2EQ, ☏ 3739 – ⋔wc 🅿. 🔟 VISA ✗   Z z
closed 14 to 31 December – **8 rm** ⊠ 10.50/24.00 **st.**

Mylne Bridge, Brookside, Lake Rd, LA23 2BX, ☏ 3314 – 📺 ⋔wc 🅿   Y v
March-October – **13 rm** ⊠ 9.00/24.00 **st.**

Ravensworth, Ambleside Rd, LA23 1BA, ☏ 3747 – 📺 ⌂wc ⋔wc 🅿   Y e
13 rm ⊠ 15.50/40.00 **t.**

Braemount House ⊗, Sunny Bank Rd, LA23 2EN, ☏ 5967 – 📺 ⌂wc ⌾ 🅿. 🔟 AE
VISA ✗   Z u
closed January and February – **4 rm** ⊠ 18.00/36.00 **st.**

Willowsmere, Ambleside Rd, LA23 1ES, ☏ 3575, 🛋 – ⌂wc ⋔wc 🅿. 🔟 AE ⓞ VISA
March-mid November – **14 rm** ⊠ 14.50/29.00 **st.**   Y a

Miller Howe with rm, Rayrigg Rd, LA23 1EY, ☏ 2536, ≤ Lake Windermere and mountains,
🛋 – ▤ rest ⌂wc ⋔wc 🅿. 🔟 AE ⓞ
March-December – **M** (dinner only) 20.00 **t.** ₺ 3.75 – **13 rm** ⊠ (dinner included) 75.00/
160.00 **t.**

Roger's, 4 High St., LA23 1AF, ☏ 4954 – 🔟 AE ⓞ VISA   Y o
closed Monday lunch except Bank Holidays, Sunday, 2 weeks February and 25-26 December –
M (booking essential) a la carte 9.50/14.80 **t.** ₺ 2.95.

at Winster SE : 4 ½ m. by A 592 on A 5074 – Z – ⊠ ☺ 09662 Windermere :

Birket Houses ⊗, LA23 3NU, via road to church ☏ 3438, ≤, 🛋, park – 📺 ⌂wc ⌾ 🅿
5 rm.

at Bowness-on-Windermere S : 1 m. – ⊠ ☺ 096 62 Windermere :

Old England (T.H.F.), LA23 3DF, ☏ 2444, Telex 65194, ≤ Lake Windermere and mountains,
🔟 heated, 🛋 – ▤ 📺 ☎ 🅿. 🔟 AE ⓞ VISA   Z e
M 7.50/12.50 **st.** and a la carte ₺ 2.90 – ⊠ 5.65 – **82 rm** 44.00/65.00 **st.**, **2 suites**.

Belsfield (T.H.F.), Kendal Rd, LA23 3EL, ☏ 2448, Telex 65238, ≤ Lake Windermere and
mountains, 🔟, 🛋, ✗ – ▤ 📺 ₺ 🅿. 🔟 🔟 AE ⓞ VISA   Z i
M (buffet lunch Monday to Saturday)/dinner 11.50 **st.** and a la carte ₺ 2.90 – ⊠ 5.65 – **66 rm**
42.50/59.00 **st.**, **6 suites**.

Linthwaite ⊗, Crook Rd, LA23 3JA, S : ¾ m. by A 5074 on B 5284 ☏ 3688, ≤ Belle Isle,
Lake Windermere and mountains, « Extensive grounds and private lake », ⌘, 🛋, park – 📺
⌂wc ⌾ 🅿. ✗   by A 5074
Easter-November – **M** (dinner only) 12.00 **st.** ₺ 2.20 – **11 rm** ⊠ (dinner included) 32.00/64.00 **st.**,
1 suite 68.00 **st.**

Wild Boar (Best Western), Crook Rd, LA23 3NF, SE : 4 m. by A 5074 on B 5284 ☏ 5225, 🛋 –
📺 ⌂wc ⋔wc ☎ 🅿. 🔟 🔟 AE VISA   by A 5074   Z
M 5.00/14.50 **st.** and a la carte ₺ 3.00 – **38 rm** ⊠ 27.00/66.00 **st.** – SB 37.50/45.00 **st.**

Burnside, Kendal Rd, LA23 3EP, ☏ 2211, Telex 65430, ≤, 🛋 – ▤ 📺 ⌂wc ⋔wc ☎ 🅿. 🔟
🔟 VISA   Z c
M (bar lunch)/dinner 8.50 **t.** and a la carte ₺ 3.00 – **45 rm** ⊠ 29.00/60.00 **t.**, **3 suites** 60.00/
80.00 **st.** – SB (winter only) 53.00/60.00 **st.**

Burn How Motel, Back Belsfield Rd, LA23 3HH, ☏ 6226, 🛋 – 📺 ⌂wc 🅿. 🔟 AE ⓞ VISA
                                                                                                                       Z r
closed January-mid February – **M** (bar lunch)/dinner 10.50 **st.** and a la carte ₺ 3.50 – ⊠ 4.50 –
25 rm 25.00/42.00 **st.** – SB (except summer) 42.00/54.00 **st.**

🏠 **Lindeth Fell Country House** ⌕, Kendal Rd, LA23 3JP, S : 1 m. on A 5074 ℰ 3286, ≼ Lake Windermere and mountains, « Country house atmosphere », ⌂, ℱ, park, ℀ – 🅃🆅 – ⌂wc
🚿wc 🅿 🄴 🄰🄴 ⓥ 𝘝𝘐𝘚𝘈 ℀ *by A 5074*
April-October – **M** (bar lunch)/dinner 12.50 **st.** ⌕ 2.70 – **13 rm** ⌣ 25.00/55.00 **st.** – SB (except 21 April-21 May) 59.00/61.50 **st.**

🏠 **Bordriggs** ⌕, Longtail Hill, LA23 3LD, S : 1 m. by A 592 – Z – ℰ 3567, ⊐ heated, ℱ – 🅃🆅
⌂wc 🅿 – **12 rm.**

🏠 **Cranleigh** without rest., Kendal Rd, LA23 3EW, ℰ 3293 – 🅃🆅 ⌂wc 🅿 🄴 🄰🄴 ⓥ 𝘝𝘐𝘚𝘈 ℀
April-October – **9 rm** ⌣ 14.00/32.00 **st.** – SB (except summer) 38.00/44.00 **st.**   Z **a**

↑ **Brooklands,** Ferry View, LA23 3JB, ℰ 2344 – 🚿wc 🅿. ℀   on A 5074   Z
closed January and December – **6 rm** ⌣ (dinner included) 21.50/47.50 **st.**

XXX **Gilpin Lodge Country House** ⌕ with rm, Crook Rd, LA23 3NE, SE : 2 ½ m. by A 5074 on B 5284 ℰ 2295, ≼, ℱ, ℀ – 🅃🆅 ⌂wc 🅿 🄴 🄰🄴 ⓥ 𝘝𝘐𝘚𝘈 ℀ *by A 5074*   Z
closed 3 weeks January – **M** (lunch by arrangement) 10.50/15.50 **t.** ⌕ 3.50 – **6 rm**
⌣ 60.00/80.00 **t.**

XX **Porthole Eating House,** 3 Ash St., LA23 3EB, ℰ 2793 – 🄴 🄰🄴 ⓥ 𝘝𝘐𝘚𝘈   Z **n**
closed Tuesday and mid December-mid February – **M** (dinner only) a la carte 12.25/15.75 **t.**
⌕ 3.30.

at Troutbeck N : 4 m. by A 592 – Y – ✉ Windermere – ☎ 096 63 Ambleside :

🏠 **Mortal Man** ⌕, LA23 1PL, ℰ 3193, ≼, ℱ – ⌂wc 🅿
Mid February-mid November – **M** (bar lunch Monday to Saturday)/dinner 12.00 **st.** ⌕ 3.75 –
12 rm ⌣ (dinner included) 27.50/35.50 **st.**

AUSTIN-ROVER Rayrigg ℰ 2451   PEUGEOT-TALBOT Main Rd ℰ 2441
HONDA Kendal Rd ℰ 2000

WINDSOR Berks. 🄌🄈🄌 S 29 – pop. 30 832 (inc. Eton) – ECD : Wednesday – ☎ 0753.

See : Castle*** (St. George's Chapel***) Z.

Envir. : Eton (College**) N : 1 m. Z – Runnymede (signing of the Magna Carta, 1215, museum) *AC*, SE : 4 m. by A 308 Y.

🛈 Central Station, Thames St. ℰ 852010.

♦London 28 – Reading 19 – ♦Southampton 59.

Plan opposite

🏨 **Oakley Court** ⌕, Windsor Rd, Water Oakley, SL4 5UR, W : 3 m. on A 308 ℰ 0628 (Maidenhead) 74141, Telex 849958, ≼, « Part Gothic mansion on banks of River Thames », ℱ, park –
🅃🆅 ☎ 🅿. ♨. 🄴 🄰🄴 ⓥ 𝘝𝘐𝘚𝘈 ℀ *by A 308*   Y
M 13.00/18.00 **st.** and a la carte ⌕ 7.00 – **92 rm** ⌣ 68.00/139.00 **st.** – SB (except Easter, Christmas and New Year) (weekends only) 99.50 **st.**

🏨 **Castle** (T.H.F.), High St., SL4 1LJ, ℰ 851011, Telex 849220 – ▤ 🅃🆅 ☎ 🅿. ♨. 🄴 🄰🄴 ⓥ 𝘝𝘐𝘚𝘈
M 10.50/13.50 **st.** and a la carte ⌕ 4.25 – ⌣ 6.50 – **85 rm** 56.00/70.00 **st.**, **1 suite**.   Z **c**

🏨 **Wren's Old House**, Thames St., SL4 1PX, ℰ 861354, Telex 847938, ≼, « Former residence of Sir Christopher Wren », ℱ – 🅃🆅 ⌂wc 🚿wc ☎ 🅿. 🄴 🄰🄴 ⓥ 𝘝𝘐𝘚𝘈   Z **v**
M (closed Saturday lunch) 12.50/16.50 **st.** and a la carte ⌕ 5.00 – **39 rm** ⌣ 54.00/78.00 **st.**,
1 suite 90.00/110.00 **st.** – SB (weekends only) 75.00/90.00 **st.**

🏠 **Aurora Garden,** 14 Bolton Av., SL4 3JF, ℰ 868686, ℱ – 🅃🆅 ⌂wc 🚿wc ☎ 🅿. ♨. 🄴 🄰🄴
ⓥ 𝘝𝘐𝘚𝘈   Z **a**
M 8.50/9.50 **st.** and a la carte ⌕ 4.25 – ⌣ 3.50 – **14 rm** 38.00/55.00 **st.** – SB (except Christmas) (weekends only) 59.00/68.00 **st.**

🏠 Ye Harte and Garter, 21 High St., SL4 1LR, ℰ 863426 – ▤ ▤ rest 🅃🆅 ⌂wc 🚿wc ☎ 🅿. 🄴 🄰🄴
ⓥ 𝘝𝘐𝘚𝘈 ℀   Z **e**
closed 25 and 26 December – **M** (grill rest. only) – **50 rm**.

↑ **Fairlight Lodge,** 41 Frances Rd, SL4 3AQ, ℰ 861207 – 🅃🆅 🚿wc 🅿   Z **z**
8 rm ⌣ 17.00/30.00 **st.**

↑ **Trinity,** 18 Trinity Pl., SL4 3AT, ℰ 864186 – 🅃🆅   Z **i**
7 rm ⌣ 12.00/24.00 **st.**

X **La Taverna,** 2 River St., SL4 1QT, ℰ 863020, Italian rest. – ▤. 🄴 🄰🄴 ⓥ 𝘝𝘐𝘚𝘈   Z **n**
closed Sunday and 25-26 December – **M** a la carte 9.80/13.30 **t.** ⌕ 3.00.

at Eton – ✉ ☎ 0753 Windsor :

🏠 **Christopher,** 110 High St., SL4 6AN, ℰ 852359 – 🅃🆅 🚿wc ☎ 🅿. 🄴 🄰🄴 ⓥ 𝘝𝘐𝘚𝘈   Z **u**
M (closed Saturday lunch and Christmas) a la carte 13.85/18.00 **st.** ⌕ 3.25 – ⌣ 3.55 – **21 rm**
31.00/39.00 **s.**

XX **Antico,** 42 High St., SL4 6BD, ℰ 863977, Italian rest. – 🄴 🄰🄴 ⓥ 𝘝𝘐𝘚𝘈   Z **s**
closed Saturday lunch, Sunday and Bank Holidays – **M** a la carte 12.90/18.70 **st.** ⌕ 2.70.

at Eton Wick W : 1 ½ m. on B 3026 – Y – ✉ ☎ 0753 Windsor :

↑ **Elmhurst,** 97 Eton Wick Rd, SL4 6NQ, ℰ 865872, ℱ – 🅃🆅. ℀
7 rm ⌣ 15.00/36.00 **st.**

VAUXHALL-OPEL 72-74 Arthur Rd ℰ 860131

WINDSOR

**North is at the top
on all town plans.**

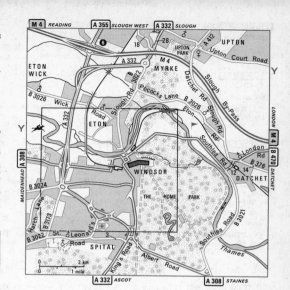

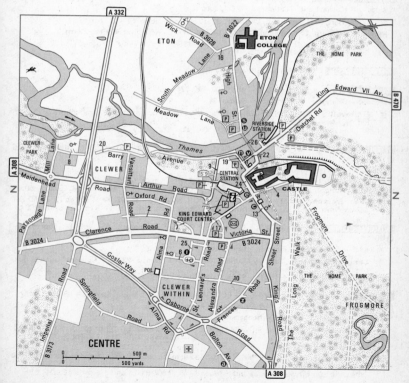

CENTRE

WINKLEIGH Devon **403** I 31 – pop. 1 431 – ✪ 083 783.

♦London 214 – Barnstaple 20 – Exeter 22 – ♦Plymouth 41.

  XX **Kings Arms,** The Square, EX19 8HQ, ℰ 384 – ▤. ◪ AE ⓪ VISA
      closed dinner Sunday to Wednesday and Monday – **M** (booking essential) 5.50/15.50 t. ⌀ 3.20.

WINSFORD Somerset **403** J 30 The West Country G. – pop. 340 – ECD : Thursday – ✉ Minehead – ✪ 064 385.

♦London 194 – Exeter 31 – Minehead 10 – Taunton 32.

  🏠 **Royal Oak Inn,** TA24 7JE, ℰ 232, « Attractive 12C thatched inn » – 📺 ➡wc ☎ Ⓟ. ◪ AE
      ⓪ VISA
      M (bar lunch Monday to Saturday)/dinner 15.00 **st.** and a la carte – **11 rm** ⛁ 35.00/65.00 **st.**

WINSTER Cumbria **402** L 20 – see Windermere.

WINTERBOURNE Avon **403** **404** M 29 – see Bristol.

WISBECH Cambs. **402** **404** U 25 – pop. 22 932 – ECD : Wednesday – ✪ 0945.

Envir. : March (St. Wendreda's Church 15C : the Angel roof★) SW : 10 m. – Long Sutton (St. Mary's Church★ : Gothic) NW : 10 m.

🛈 District Library, Ely Pl. ℰ 583263 and 64009.

♦London 106 – ♦Cambridge 47 – ♦Leicester 62 – ♦Norwich 57.

  🏠 **White Lion,** 5 South Brink, PE13 1JD, ℰ 584813 – 📺 ➡wc ♨wc Ⓟ ☎. ⚐. ◪ AE ⓪ VISA
      (closed Saturday lunch and Sunday dinner) 8.00 **st.** and a la carte ⌀ 3.80 – **18 rm**
      ⛁ 21.00/38.50 **st.**

AUSTIN-ROVER 46 Norwich Rd ℰ 584342   VAUXHALL-OPEL Elm High Rd ℰ 582471
FORD Elm Rd ℰ 582681   VOLVO Sutton Rd ℰ 583082

WITHAM Essex **404** V 28 – pop. 21 875 – ECD : Wednesday – ✪ 0376.

♦London 42 – ♦Cambridge 46 – Chelmsford 9 – Colchester 13.

  🏠 White Hart, 39 Newland St., CM8 2AF, ℰ 512245 – 📺 ➡wc Ⓟ – **13 rm**.

  🏠 Batsford Court, 100 Newland St., CM8 1AH, ℰ 517777 – 📺 ♨wc ☎ Ⓟ – **23 rm**.

AUSTIN-ROVER Newland St. ℰ 513272   NISSAN London Rd ℰ 515575
FORD Colchester Rd ℰ 513496

WITHERSLACK Cumbria – see Grange-over-Sands.

WITHINGTON Glos. **403** **404** O 28 – pop. 500 – ✪ 024 289.

♦London 91 – Gloucester 15 – ♦Oxford 35 – Swindon 24.

  🏠 **Halewell** ⌂, GL54 4BN, ℰ 238, ≤, « Part 15C manor, country house atmosphere », ☐ hea-
      ted, ⚐, ⛳ – 📺 ➡wc ⌖ Ⓟ
      M (dinner only) 12.00 **st.** – **6 rm** ⛁ 35.00/50.00 **st.**

WITHYPOOL Somerset **403** J 30 The West Country G. – pop. 231 – ECD : Thursday – ✉ ✪ 064 383 Exford.

♦London 204 – Exeter 34 – Taunton 36.

  🏠 **Royal Oak Inn,** TA24 7QP, ℰ 236, ⚐ – 📺 ➡wc ♨wc Ⓟ. ◪ AE VISA
      M (bar lunch)/dinner 13.50 **t.** and a la carte ⌀ 2.50 – **8 rm** ⛁ 19.00/44.00 **t.** – SB 29.50/37.50 **st.**

  🏠 **Westerclose Country House** ⌂, TA24 7QR, NW : ¼ m. ℰ 302, ⛲ – ➡wc Ⓟ. ◪ AE VISA
      March-November – **M** (bar lunch)/dinner 9.00 **t.** and a la carte ⌀ 2.40 – **8 rm** ⛁ 15.00/36.00 **t.**

WIVELISCOMBE Somerset **403** K 30 The West Country G. – pop. 1 457 – ECD : Thursday – ✪ 0984.

♦ London 185 – Barnstaple 38 – Exeter 37 – Taunton 14.

  🏠 **Langley House** ⌂, Langley Marsh, TA4 2UF, NW : ½ m. ℰ 23318, « Country house atmos-
      phere », ⛲ – 📺 ➡wc ♨wc Ⓟ. ◪ AE
      M (dinner only) 15.50 **t.** ⌀ 3.30 – **9 rm** ⛁ 18.50/56.00 **t.** – SB 57.50/70.00 **st.**

WOBURN Beds. **404** S 28 – pop. 824 – ECD : Wednesday – ✉ Milton Keynes – ✪ 052 525.

See : Woburn Abbey★★★ (18C) AC, Wild Animal Kingdom★★ AC.

♦London 49 – Bedford 13 – Luton 13 – Northampton 24.

  🏨 **Bedford Arms,** 1 George St., MK17 9PX, ℰ 441, Telex 825205 – 📺 ☎ Ⓟ. ⚐. ◪ AE ⓪ VISA
      M 10.75/12.50 **t.** and a la carte ⌀ 3.25 – ⛁ 5.50 – **55 rm** 46.00/58.00 **t.**, **1 suite** 58.00/85.00 **t.** –
      SB (weekends only) 68.00 **st.**

  XXX **Paris House,** Woburn Park, MK17 9QP, SE : 2 ¼ m. on B 528 ℰ 692, « Reproduction timbered
      house in Park », ⛲ – Ⓟ. ◪ AE ⓪ VISA
      closed Sunday dinner, Monday and February – **M** 13.50/18.00 **t.** and a la carte ⌀ 3.60.

♦London 31 – Guildford 7 – Reading 24.

　🏠　**Northfleet,** Claremont Av., GU22 7SG, ✆ 22971 – 📺 ⇱wc ⇱wc 🕾 **🅿**. ⚒. 🔄 AE ⑩ *VISA*. ✕

　　M *(closed Sunday dinner)* (bar lunch)/dinner 8.50 **t.** ⚬ 3.00 – **22 rm** ⊠ 32.50/45.00 **st.** – SB (weekends only) 67.00 **st.**

WOLF'S CASTLE (CAS-BLAIDD) Dyfed **403** F 28 – ⊠ Haverfordwest – ✆ 043 787 Treffgarne.

♦London 258 – Fishguard 7 – Haverfordwest 8.

　✕✕　**Wolfscastle Country** with rm, SA62 5LZ, on A 40 ✆ 225, ✖, squash – 📺 ⇱wc 🕾 **🅿**. 🔄 AE *VISA*

　　M (bar lunch)/dinner a la carte 8.95/13.80 **t.** ⚬ 2.65 – **15 rm** ⊠ 25.00/38.00 **t.** – SB (October-June)(except Bank Holidays) 45.00/50.00 **st.**

WOLVERHAMPTON West Midlands **402** **403** **404** N 26 – pop. 263 501 – ECD : Thursday – ✆ 0902.

See : St. Peter's Church★ 15C B **A.**

🛆 Oxley Park, Bushbury ✆ 20506, N : 1 ½ m. A – 🛆 Blackhill Wood, Bridgnorth Rd ✆ 892279, S : 5 m. by A 449 A – 🅱 16 Queen's Arcade, Mander Centre ✆ 714571.

♦London 132 – ✦Birmingham 15 – ✦Liverpool 89 – Shrewsbury 30.

Plan of Enlarged Area : see Birmingham pp. 2 and 3

WOLVERHAMPTON

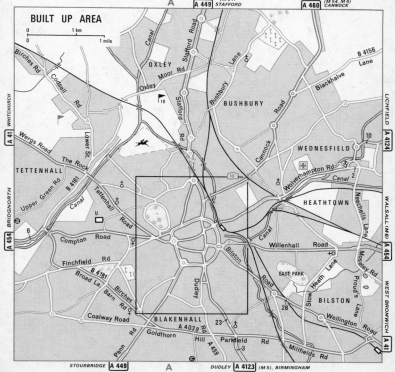

Goldthorn, 126 Penn Rd, WV3 0ER, ℰ 29216, Telex 339516 – 📺 ⌁wc ☎ 🅿 ⚠ 🔌 ᴀᴇ ⓪ 𝘝𝘐𝘚𝘈
M 7.95 **st.** and a la carte ⑃ 2.70 – **82 rm** ⌸ 34.50/36.00 **st.**
B i

Mount (Embassy) ⌂, Mount Rd, Tettenhall Wood, WV6 8HL, W : 2 ½ m. by A 454
ℰ 752055, 🚳 – 🍽 rest 📺 ⌁wc ☎ 🅿 ⚠ 🔌 ᴀᴇ ⓪ 𝘝𝘐𝘚𝘈
A a
M (closed Saturday lunch) 8.40/8.65 **st.** and a la carte ⑃ 3.00 – ⌸ 5.00 – **58 rm** 36.00/50.00 **st.**,
1 suite 60.00/70.00 **st.** – SB (weekends only) 52.00 **st.**

Park Hall (Embassy) ⌂, Park Drive, off Ednam Rd, Goldthorn Park, WV4 5AJ, S : 2 m. by
A 449 ℰ 331121, 🚳 – 📺 ⌁wc ☎ 🅿 ⚠ 🔌 ᴀᴇ ⓪ 𝘝𝘐𝘚𝘈 🍴
A c
M (closed Saturday lunch to non residents) 8.25 **t.** and a la carte ⑃ 3.00 – ⌸ 5.00 – **54 rm**
33.50/40.00 **st.** – SB (weekends only) 48.00/53.00 **st.**

at Pattingham (Salop) W : 6 ¼ m. by A 454 – A – ✉ ☯ 0902 Pattingham :

Patshull Park ⌂, Patshull Park, WV6 7HR, W : 1 ¾ m. by Patshull Rd ℰ 700100, Telex
334849, ≤, ⛳, ⌁, park – 🍽 rest 📺 ⌁wc ☎ 🅿 ⚠ 🔌 ᴀᴇ ⓪ 𝘝𝘐𝘚𝘈
M 6.95/8.95 **t.** – **28 rm** ⌸ 42.50/55.00 **t.**

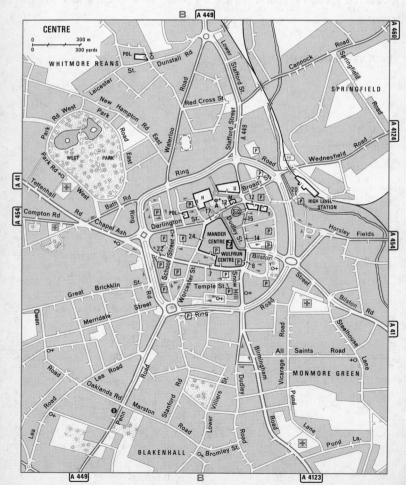

ALFA-ROMEO, CITROEN Merridale Lane 🖉 23295
AUSTIN ROVER-DAIMLER-JAGUAR Stafford St. 🖉 29122
AUSTIN-ROVER Chapel Ash 🖉 26781
AUSTIN-ROVER Wolverhampton Rd, Wednesfield 🖉 731372
BMW, VW, AUDI Rabey St. 🖉 54602
FIAT,LANCIA Warstones Rd 🖉 339104
FORD Bilston Rd 🖉 51515
MAZDA School Rd, Wombourne 🖉 892237

MERCEDES-BENZ Penn Rd 🖉 27897
PEUGEOT-TALBOT Oxford St. Bilston 🖉 42476
RENAULT Bilston Rd 🖉 53111
SKODA, AUSTIN-ROVER Vulcan Rd, Bilston 🖉 402222
TOYOTA Wolverhampton Rd East 🖉 333131
VAUXHALL-OPEL Dudley Rd 🖉 58000
VAUXHALL-OPEL 67-71 Bilston Rd 🖉 52611
VOLVO Parkfield Rd 🖉 333211
VW-AUDI Raby St. 🖉 54602

WOODBRIDGE Suffolk **404** X 27 – pop. 9 697 – ECD : Wednesday – ✆ 0394.

🏌, 🏌 Bromeswell Heath 🖉 382038, E : 2 m.

♦London 81 – Great Yarmouth 45 – ♦Ipswich 8 – ♦Norwich 47.

🏰 **Seckford Hall** 🦢, IP13 6NU, SW : 1 ¼ m. by A 12 🖉 385678, Telex 987446, ≼, « Part Tudor country house », 🦢, ☛, park – 📺 🖭 🅿. 🏂. 🔼 🗛 ⓞ 🆅🆂🅰
closed Christmas Day – **M** 6.95 **st.** (lunch) and a la carte 11.00/21.20 **st.** – **24 rm** ⟷ 39.00/56.00 st. – SB 75.00 st.

🏨 **Crown** (T.H.F.), Thorofare, IP12 1AD, 🖉 4242 – 📺 ☛wc ☎ 🅿. 🔼 🗛 ⓞ 🆅🆂🅰
M (bar lunch)/dinner 15.00 **st.** and a la carte ₰ 3.40 – ⟷ 5.65 – **18 rm** 40.00/52.00 **st.**

AUSTIN-ROVER Melton Rd 🖉 383456   FORD Bawdsey 🖉 039 441 (Shottisham) 1368
FORD 60 Ipswich Rd 🖉 383333

WOODHALL SPA Lincs. **402 404** T 24 – pop. 2 526 – ECD : Wednesday – ✆ 0526.

Envir. : Tattershall Castle★ (15C Keep) *AC*, SE : 3 ½ m.

🏌 🖉 52511.

🅱 Jubilee Park, Stixwould Rd 🖉 52448 (summer only).

♦London 138 – Lincoln 18.

🏨 **Golf,** The Broadway, LN10 6SG, 🖉 53535, 🌲 – 📺 ☛wc 🏐wc ☎ 🅿. 🏂. 🔼 🗛 ⓞ 🆅🆂🅰
M (bar lunch Monday to Saturday)/dinner 8.50 **t.** and a la carte ₰ 2.75 – **51 rm** ⟷ 35.00/45.00 **t.** – SB (weekends only) 53.00/58.00 st.

🏨 **Petwood** 🦢, Stixwould Rd, LN10 6QF, 🖉 52411, 🌲, park – 🍴 📺 ☛wc ☎ 🅿. 🏂. 🔼 🗛 ⓞ 🆅🆂🅰
M (bar lunch)/dinner 9.95 **t.** and a la carte ₰ 2.50 – **30 rm** ⟷ 34.50/54.00 **t.**, **2 suites** 54.00/70.00 **t.** – SB 54.00/64.00 st.

🏠 **Dower House** 🦢, Manor Estate, off Spa Rd, LN10 6PY, 🖉 52588, « Country house atmosphere », 🌲 – ☛wc 🅿. 🔼 🗛 🆅🆂🅰
7 rm ⟷ 23.00/40.00 st.

🏠 **Dunns,** The Broadway, LN10 6XQ, 🖉 52969 – 🅿. 🌾
closed 24 December-7 January – **6 rm** ⟷ 9.00/14.00 **t.**

WOODLANDS Hants. – see Lyndhurst.

WOODSTOCK Oxon. **403 404** P 28 – pop. 3 057 – ECD : Wednesday – ✆ 0993.

See : Blenheim Palace★★★ 18C (park and gardens★★★) *AC*.

Envir. : Rousham (Manor House gardens : statues★) NE : 5 m. – Ditchley Park★ (Renaissance) *AC*, NW : 6 m.

🅱 Library, Hensington Rd 🖉 811038 and 812231.

♦London 65 – Gloucester 47 – ♦Oxford 8.

🏰 **Bear,** Park St., OX7 1SZ, 🖉 811511, Telex 837921, « Part 16C inn » – 📺 ☎ 🅿. 🏂. 🔼 🗛 ⓞ 🆅🆂🅰. 🌾
M (closed Christmas dinner to non residents) 12.50/13.50 **t.** and a la carte ₰ 3.50 – ⟷ 6.50 – **44 rm** 56.80/100.20 **st.**, **4 suites** 118.00 **st.** – SB (except Easter and Christmas) 86.00 **st.**

🏨 **Feathers,** Market St., OX7 1SX, 🖉 812291, Telex 83138, « Tastefully furnished » – 📺 ☛wc 🏐wc ☎. 🏂. 🔼 🗛 ⓞ 🆅🆂🅰
M 11.50/16.50 **t.** and a la carte ₰ 3.50 – **15 rm** ⟷ 40.00/88.00 **t.** – SB (October-April) 85.00/95.00 st.

🏨 **Kings Arms** (Best Western), Market St., OX7 1ST, 🖉 811412 – 📺 ☛wc 🏐wc ☎
10 rm

🏠 **Marlborough Arms** (Best Western), Oxford St., OX7 1TS, 🖉 811227 – 📺 ☛wc 🏐wc ☎ 🅿. 🔼 🗛 ⓞ 🆅🆂🅰
closed 24 to 26 December – **M** 8.00/10.00 **st.** and a la carte ₰ 3.50 – **14 rm** ⟷ 25.00/52.00 **st.** – SB 60.00 **st.**

AUSTIN-ROVER 2 Oxford St. 🖉 811286

WOODY BAY Devon **403** I 30 – see Lynton.

WOOLACOMBE Devon **403** H 30 The West Country G. – pop. 1 171 – ECD : Wednesday – ✆ 0271.

Envir. : Mortehoe** – Morte Point (vantage point ★) – Mortehoe Church ★.

🛈 Hall 70, Beach Rd 🖉 870553 (summer only).

◆London 237 – Barnstaple 15 – Exeter 55.

🏨 **Waters Fall,** Beach Rd, EX34 7AD, 🖉 870365, ≤ Woolacombe Bay, ☞ – 📺wc ℗
March-October and 10 days at Christmas – **M** (dinner only and Sunday lunch)/dinner 7.50 **t.**
🍷 2.50 – **17 rm** 🖙 14.00/39.00 **t.** – SB (except summer) 40.00/45.00 **st.**

🏨 **Little Beach,** The Esplanade, EX34 7DJ, 🖉 870398, ≤ – 📺wc 🛏wc ℗. ☒ VISA
February-October – **M** (bar lunch)/dinner 10.25 **t.** 🍷 2.50 – **10 rm** 🖙 17.00/48.00 **t.** – SB 46.00/62.00 **st.**

🏨 Whin Bay, Bay View Rd, EX34 7DQ, ≤ – 📺 📺wc 🛏wc ℗
18 rm.

at Mortehoe N : ½ m. – ⊠ ✆ 0271 Woolacombe :

🏨 **Watersmeet,** The Esplanade, EX34 7EB, 🖉 870333, ≤, ⤮ heated, ⬦ – 📺 📺wc ☎ ℗. ☒ AE ⓞ VISA
3 April-October – **M** (bar lunch)/dinner 15.00 **st.** 🍷 3.20 – **22 rm** 🖙 (dinner included) 34.50/84.00 **st.**

🏨 **Sunnycliffe,** Chapel Hill, EX34 7EB, 🖉 870597, ≤ – 📺 📺wc 🛏wc ℗. ⬦
closed December and January – **M** (residents only) (bar lunch)/dinner 8.00 **st.** – **8 rm** 🖙 18.00/36.00 **st.** – SB 40.00/42.00 **st.**

↑ **Lundy House,** Chapel Hill, EX34 7DZ, 🖉 870372, ≤, ☞ – 📺wc 🛏wc ℗
closed November-December – **11 rm** 🖙 8.00/25.00 **st.**

WOOLER Northumb. **401 402** N 17 – pop. 1 925 – ECD : Thursday – ✆ 0668.

🛈 Bus Station Car Park, High St. 🖉 81602 (summer only).

◆London 332 – ◆Edinburgh 62 – ◆Newcastle-upon-Tyne 46.

🏨 **Ryecroft,** 28 Ryecroft Way, NE71 6AB, 🖉 81459 – ℗. ☒ VISA
closed 1 to 13 November and 24 to 29 December – **M** (bar lunch Monday to Saturday)/dinner 10.00 **t.** 🍷 3.50 – **11 rm** 🖙 16.50/32.00 **t.** – SB 44.00/50.00 **st.**

🏨 **Tankerville Arms,** 22 Cottage Rd, NE71 6AD, on A 697 🖉 81581, ☞ – 📺wc 🛏wc ℗
M (bar lunch)/dinner 6.50 **st.** and a la carte – **16 rm** 🖙 12.00/28.00 **st.** – SB 22.50 **st.**

FORD Haughead 🖉 81316   RENAULT South Rd 🖉 81472

WOOLVERTON Somerset – see Bath.

☞ *By January 1988 this guide will be out of date.*
Get the new edition.

WORCESTER Heref. and Worc. **403 404** N 27 – pop. 75 466 – ECD : Thursday – ✆ 0905.

See : Cathedral** 13C-15C (crypt** 11C) – The Commandery* (15C) *AC* B.

Envir. : Great Witley : Witley Court (ruins) and the Parish Church of St. Michael and All Saints (Baroque interior**) NW : 12 m. by A 443.

🛈 Guildhall, High St. 🖉 23471.

◆London 124 – ◆Birmingham 26 – ◆Bristol 61 – ◆Cardiff 74.

Plan opposite

🏨 **Giffard** (T.H.F.), High St., WR1 2QR, 🖉 27155, Telex 338869 – 🛗 ▤ 📺 ☎. ♿ ☒ AE ⓞ VISA
r
M (buffet lunch)/dinner 10.50 **st.** and a la carte 🍷 3.40 – 🖙 6.00 – **104 rm** 47.00/58.00 **st.**, **2 suites.**

🏨 Ye Olde Talbot (Whitbread), Friar St., WR1 2NA, 🖉 23573 – ▤ rest 📺 📺wc ☎
e
17 rm.

↑ **Park House,** 12 Droitwich Rd, WR3 7LJ, N : 1 m. on A 38 🖉 21816 – ℗
by A 38
6 rm 🖙 12.50/22.00 **st.**

XX **Brown's,** 24 Quay St., WR1 2JN, 🖉 26263, « Converted corn mill » – ☒ AE VISA
c
closed Saturday lunch and 24 to 31 December – **M** 13.95/17.95 **t.** 🍷 3.50.

MICHELIN Distribution Centre, Blackpole Trading Estate, WR3 8TJ, 🖉 55626 by A 38

ALFA-ROMEO, HONDA Pershore Rd, Stoulton 🖉 840661
BEDFORD, VAUXHALL-OPEL Brook St. 🖉 27781
AUSTIN-ROVER, DAIMLER-JAGUAR Castle St. 🖉 27100
DAIHATSU, LADA Ombersley Rd 🖉 52730 Malvern Rd, Powick 🖉 830361
FORD Bath Rd 🖉 352123
LADA College St. 🖉 27500 28946
MERCEDES-BENZ Cranham Drive 🖉 57219

NISSAN Bransford Rd 🖉 428101
PEUGEOT, TALBOT Bath Rd 🖉 820777
RENAULT St. Martins Gate 🖉 21215
RENAULT The Butts 🖉 24252
SAAB Kempsey 🖉 821132
SKODA Bromsgrove St. 🖉 23532
SUBARU, SEAT Pierpoint St. 🖉 25786
VAUXHALL-OPEL Hallow 🖉 640228
VOLVO Farrier St. 🖉 23338
VW, AUDI Hallow Rd 🖉 640512

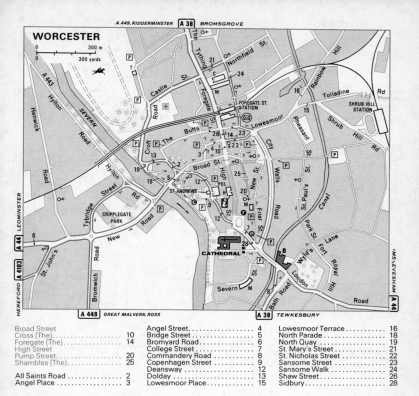

WORCESTER

A 449, KIDDERMINSTER **A 38** BROMSGROVE

scale: 0 — 300 m / 0 — 300 yards

Broad Street	Angel Street	4	Lowesmoor Terrace	16
Cross (The)	10	Bridge Street	5	North Parade	18
Foregate (The)	14	Bromyard Road	6	North Quay	19
High Street		College Street	7	St. Mary's Street	21
Pump Street	20	Commandery Road	8	St. Nicholas Street	22
Shambles (The)	25	Copenhagen Street	9	Sansome Street	23
		Deansway	12	Sansome Walk	24
All Saints Road	2	Dolday	13	Shaw Street	26
Angel Place	3	Lowesmoor Place	15	Sidbury	28

Red Lion	Se il nome di un albergo è stampato in carattere magro, chiedete arrivando le condizioni che vi saranno praticate.

WORFIELD Salop – see Bridgnorth.

WORKINGTON Cumbria **401 402** J 20 – pop. 25 978 – ECD : Thursday – ✆ 0900.
⌖ Branthwaite Rd ✆ 3460 – ⌖ Bankend, Maryport ✆ 090 081 (Maryport) 2605, N : 7 m. on A 596.
♦London 314 – ♦Carlisle 33 – Keswick 21.

🏨 **Westland,** Branthwaite Rd, CA14 4SS, SE : 2 m. by A 596 ✆ 4544, Telex 64229 – 📺 ⇌wc
🛏️wc ⚗ 🅿 🔄. 🅰 🅰🅴 ⓪ 𝘝𝘐𝘚𝘈
M 5.50/9.50 t. and a la carte ↥ 2.40 – **48 rm** ⊇ 20.00/39.00 t. – SB (weekends only) 40.00 **st.**

AUSTIN-ROVER Central Sq. ✆ 2113
FORD Washington St. ✆ 67101

RENAULT Clay Flatts Estate ✆ 4542
TOYOTA ✆ (0946) 830247

WORRALL South Yorks. – see Sheffield.

WORTH Somerset – see Wells.

WORTHING West Sussex **404** S 31 – pop. 90 687 – ECD : Wednesday – ✆ 0903.
Envir. : Shoreham-by-Sea (St. Mary of Haura's Church★ 12C-13C – St. Nichola's Church carved arches★ 12C) E : 5 m. by A 259 BY.
⌖ Worthing Hill Barn, Hill Barn Lane ✆ 37301 BY.
✈ Shoreham Airport : ✆ 079 17 (Shoreham-by-Sea) 2304, E : 4 m. by A 27 BY.
🛈 Town Hall, Chapel Rd ✆ 39999 ext 132/3 – Marine Parade ✆ 210022.
♦London 59 – ♦Brighton 11 – ♦Southampton 50.

WORTHING

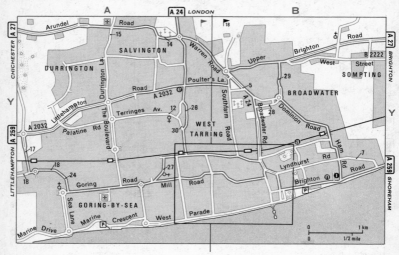

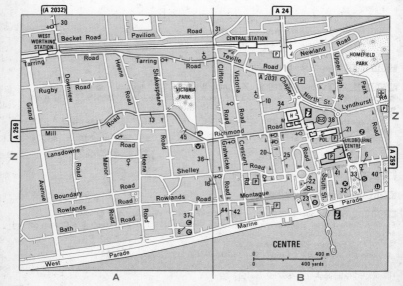

Beach, Marine Par., BN11 3QJ, ℰ 34001, ← – 📶 📺 ☎ Ⓟ. 🏌. 🔼 🆎 ⓞ 𝗩𝗜𝗦𝗔. ✶   AZ **e**
M 7.95/10.25 **t.** and a la carte – **90 rm** ☜ 29.00/52.75 t., **3 suites** 78.75/82.75 t. – SB (weekends only) (October-April except Christmas) 52.75/60.00 **st.**

Chatsworth, Steyne Gdns, BN11 3DU, ℰ 36103, Telex 877046 – 📶 📺 ⌷wc 🔛wc ☎. 🏌.
🔼 🆎 𝗩𝗜𝗦𝗔   BZ **x**
M 7.50/8.75 **t.** and a la carte ⟐ 2.75 – **100 rm** ☜ 29.00/54.00 **st.** – SB (weekends only) (except Bank Holidays) 50.00 **st.**

Eardley, 3-10 Marine Par., BN11 3PW, ℰ 34444, Group Telex 877046, ← – 📶 📺 ⌷wc 🔛wc
☎ Ⓟ. 🏌. 🔼 𝗩𝗜𝗦𝗔   BZ **u**
M (carving lunch) 6.25/7.50 **t.** and a la carte ⟐ 2.70 – **83 rm** ☜ 21.00/52.00 t. – SB (weekends only) (October-April) 45.00/50.00 **st.**

Ardington, Steyne Gdns, BN11 3DZ, ℰ 30451 – 📺 ⌷wc 🔛wc. 🏌. 🔼 🆎 ⓞ 𝗩𝗜𝗦𝗔   BZ **s**
closed 25 December-5 January – **M** 7.50 **t.** (dinner)/lunch a la carte 9.20/12.25 t. ⟐ 3.25 – **60 rm**
☜ 23.00/47.00 **t.** – SB (except summer) (weekends only) 40.00/50.00 **st.**

Beechwood Hall, Wykeham Rd, BN11 4AH, ℰ 32872, ✿ – 📺 ⌷wc Ⓟ. 🏌. 🔼 𝗩𝗜𝗦𝗔
M 5.00/7.25 **t.** and a la carte ⟐ 3.00 – **18 rm** ☜ 25.00/37.00 **t.** – SB (weekends only) 40.00/50.00 **st.**   AZ **a**

Windsor House, 14-20 Windsor Rd, BN11 2LX, ℰ 39655, ✿ – 📺 ⌷wc 🔛wc Ⓟ   BY **i**
✶
M (buffet lunch)/dinner 6.00 **t.** – **28 rm** ☜ 12.50/21.00 **t.** – SB (October-April) 30.00/35.00 **st.**

Wansfell, 49 Chesswood Rd, BN11 2AA, ℰ 30612, ✿ – 📺 ⌷wc 🔛wc Ⓟ. 🔼. ✶   BY **a**
closed Christmas and New Year – **M** 5.50/6.50 t, and a la carte ⟐ 2.40 – **12 rm** ☜ 12.00/34.00 t.

Wolsey, 179-181 Brighton Rd, BN11 2EX, ℰ 36149, ✿ – 📺 🔛wc. 🔼 𝗩𝗜𝗦𝗔   BY **n**
closed Christmas-New Year – **14 rm** ☜ 13.50/32.00 **t.**

Bonchurch, 1 Winchester Rd, BN11 4DJ, ℰ 202492 – 📺 🔛wc Ⓟ. ✶   AZ **v**
8 rm ☜ 9.00/24.00 **st.**

South Dene, 41 Warwick Gdns, BN11 1PF, ℰ 32909 – ✶   BZ **z**
6 rm ☜ 10.00/26.00.

Paragon, 9-10 Brunswick Rd, BN11 3NG, ℰ 33367 – 🔼 🆎 ⓞ 𝗩𝗜𝗦𝗔   AZ **c**
closed Sunday and Bank Holidays – **M** 8.00/10.75 **st.** and a la carte 10.45/15.75 **st.** ⟐ 3.00.

La Gondola, 121 Rectory Rd, BN14 7PH, ℰ 66384, Italian rest.   AY **e**

Grapes, 3 Bath Pl., BN11 3BA, ℰ 32424, Bistro – 🔼 🆎 𝗩𝗜𝗦𝗔   BZ **o**
closed Saturday lunch, Sunday and 25-26 December – **M** 9.60 **t.** (dinner) and a la carte 5.00/10.10 **t.** ⟐ 2.70.

at Findon N : 4 m. by A 24 – AY – ✉ Worthing – ✆ 090 671 Findon :

Findon Manor 🐾, High St., BN14 0TA, ℰ 2733, « Part 16C stone and flint house », ✿ –
📺 ⌷wc ☎ Ⓟ. 🏌. 🔼 🆎 ⓞ 𝗩𝗜𝗦𝗔
closed 25 December-1 January – **M** *(closed Saturday lunch and Sunday dinner)* 8.75 **t.** and a la carte 10.75/13.70 **t.** ⟐ 3.00 – **9 rm** ☜ 36.00/60.00 **t.** – SB (weekends only) 62.00/75.00 **st.**

at East Preston W : 6 ½ m. by A 259 – AY – off B 2225 – ✉ Littlehampton – ✆ 0903 Rustington :

Old Forge, The Street, BN16 1JJ, ℰ 782040, « 17C cottage » – Ⓟ. 🔼 🆎 ⓞ 𝗩𝗜𝗦𝗔
closed Sunday dinner and Monday – **M** 6.45 **t.** (lunch) and a la carte 8.40/20.40 **t.** ⟐ 2.65.

ALFA-ROMEO Lancing ℰ 766981
AUSTIN-ROVER 55 Broadwater Rd ℰ 31111
BMW Angermering ℰ 090 62 (Rushington) 4147
CITROEN 28 Broadwater Rd ℰ 39573
FIAT 123 Upper Brighton Rd ℰ 36065
NISSAN Broadwater Rd ℰ 206091
RENAULT Portland Rd ℰ 200820

SAAB, PEUGEOT-TALBOT St. Lawrence Av. ℰ 207703
SKODA Tarring ℰ 34363
TALBOT Broadwater Rd ℰ 262338
TOYOTA 93 Rowlands Rd ℰ 32571
VAUXHALL-OPEL Goring Rd ℰ 42389
VOLVO 187 Findon Rd ℰ 090 671 (Findon) 3022

WOUGHTON ON THE GREEN Bucks. – see Milton Keynes.

WRAFTON Devon 𝟰𝟬𝟯 H 30 – see Braunton.

WRELTON North Yorks. 𝟰𝟬𝟮 R 21 – see Pickering.

WRENTHAM Suffolk 𝟰𝟬𝟰 Z 26 – pop. 898 – ECD : Wednesday – ✉ Beccles – ✆ 050 275.
◆London 110 – Great Yarmouth 17 – ◆Ipswich 37 – ◆Norwich 26.

Quiggins, 2 High St., NR34 7HB, ℰ 397, « Tasteful decor » – Ⓟ. 🔼 🆎 𝗩𝗜𝗦𝗔
closed Sunday dinner and Monday – **M** (booking essential) 6.50/14.75 t. ⟐ 3.00.

In this guide

a symbol or a character, printed in red or **black**, in **bold** or light type, does not have the same meaning.
Pay particular attention to the explanatory pages (pp. 12 to 19).

WREXHAM (WRECSAM) Clwyd 402 403 L 24 – pop. 39 929 – ECD : Wednesday – ☎ 0978.
See : St. Giles' Church (tower★).
Envir. : Erddig★ (17C-18C) *AC*, SW : 2 m.
🛈 Guildhall Car Park, Town Centre ℰ 357845 (summer only).
◆London 192 – Chester 12 – Shrewsbury 28.

🏨 **Cross Lanes,** Marchwiel, LL13 0TF, SE : 3 ½ m. on A 525 ℰ 780555, 🔄, 🔄, 🐴, park – 📺
🛏wc 🛏wc ☎ 🅿. 🔼 🅰🅴 ⑩ 𝗩𝗜𝗦𝗔
M 7.00/9.00 **st.** and a la carte ⓰ 3.50 – ⊡ 3.50 – **20 rm** 25.00/45.00 **st.** – SB (weekends only)
50.00 **st.**

AUSTIN-ROVER Hightown Rd ℰ 364151	SKODA, HYUNDAI Wrexham Rd ℰ 263438
CITROEN Holt Rd ℰ 356707	TOYOTA Wrexham Rd ℰ 840578
FORD Holt Rd ℰ 351001	VAUXHALL-OPEL, BEDFORD Mold Rd ℰ 263777
NISSAN New Broughton ℰ 757838	VOLVO Hill St. ℰ 262685
RENAULT Regent St. ℰ 356822	VW-AUDI Llay New Rd ℰ 355777

WRIGHTINGTON BAR Lancs. 402 404 L 23 – pop. 3 160 – ⊠ Wigan – ☎ 025 75 Appley Bridge.
◆London 210 – ◆Liverpool 24 – ◆Manchester 30 – Preston 15.

XX **Highmoor,** Highmoor Lane, by Robin Hood Lane, ℰ 2364, « 17C inn » – 🅿. 🔼 🅰🅴 ⑩ 𝗩𝗜𝗦𝗔
closed Sunday dinner, Monday, first week January and last 2 weeks August – **M** a la carte
13.85/18.00 **t.** ⓰ 4.00.

WROTHAM HEATH Kent – pop. 1 669 – ⊠ ☎ 0732 Sevenoaks.
◆London 35 – Maidstone 10.

🏨 **Post House** (T.H.F.), London Rd, TN15 7RS, ℰ 883311, Telex 957309, 🔄, 🐴 – 📺 ☎ 🅿. 🔼.
🔼 🅰🅴 ⑩ 𝗩𝗜𝗦𝗔
M 11.25/13.40 **st.** and a la carte ⓰ 3.40 – ⊡ 5.65 – **119 rm** 53.00/63.00 **st., 2 suites**.

at Ightham W : 2 ½ m. by A 25 on A 227 – ⊠ Sevenoaks – ☎ 0732 Borough Green :

XXX **Town House,** The Street, TN15 9HH, ℰ 884578, « 15C hall », 🐴 – 🅿. 🔼 🅰🅴 ⑩ 𝗩𝗜𝗦𝗔
closed Sunday, Monday, 2 weeks Easter, 2 weeks August-September and 2 weeks Christmas –
M (dinner only)(booking essential) 24.50 **st.** ⓰ 3.90.

WROXHAM Norfolk 404 Y 25 – pop. 2 954 (inc. Hoveton) – ECD : Wednesday – ⊠ Norwich –
☎ 060 53.
◆London 118 – Great Yarmouth 21 – ◆Norwich 7.

🏨 **Wroxham,** Broads Centre, NR12 8AJ, ℰ 2061, ≤ – 📺 🛏wc ☎ 🅿. 🔼 🅰🅴 ⑩ 𝗩𝗜𝗦𝗔
M 5.75/6.75 **t.** and a la carte ⓰ 3.00 – **18 rm** ⊡ 22.00/45.00 **t.** – SB (weekends only)
30.50/51.75 **st.**

WROXTON Oxon. 403 404 P 27 – see Banbury.

WYBOSTON Cambs. – see St. Neots.

WYCH CROSS East Sussex 404 U 30 – see Forest Row.

WYE Kent 404 W 30 – pop. 1 396 – ECD : Wednesday – ⊠ Ashford – ☎ 0233.
◆London 61 – Folkestone 21 – Maidstone 24 – Margate 28.

XX **Wife of Bath,** 4 Upper Bridge St., TN25 5EU, ℰ 812540 – 🅿. 🔼
closed Sunday, Monday and 1 week Christmas – **M** 13.90 **t.** ⓰ 3.95.

at Hassell Street E : 4 ½ m. via Hastingleigh road off Waltham road – ⊠ Ashford –
☎ 023 375 Elmsted :

X **Woodmans Arms Auberge** 🍴 with rm., TN25 5JE, ℰ 250, 🐴 – 📺 🛏wc 🅿
closed last 2 weeks September – **M** (booking essential)(dinner only) 14.50 **st.** ⓰ 2.75 – **3 rm**
⊡ (dinner included) 37.50/60.00 **st.**

AUSTIN-ROVER Bridge St. ℰ 812331	RENAULT Bramble Lane ℰ 812270

WYMONDHAM Norfolk 404 X 26 – pop. 9 088 – ECD : Wednesday – ☎ 0953.
◆London 110 – ◆Cambridge 53 – ◆Norwich 9.

X ❀ **Adlards,** 16 Damgate St., NR18 0BQ, ℰ 603533
closed Sunday and Monday – **M** (dinner only) (booking essential) 17.50 **t.**
Spec. Warm smoked salmon with a tart of quails eggs and white wine shallot sauce, Roast rack of lamb glazed
with rosemary and meaux mustard, Pancake of English plums with cointreau sabayon.

WYNDS POINT Heref. and Worc. 403 404 M 27 – see Great Malvern.

WYRE PIDDLE Heref. and Worc. – see Pershore.

WYTON Cambs. – see Huntingdon.

504

YARCOMBE Devon 403 K 31 – pop. 418 – ✪ 040 486 Upottery.

◆London 157 – Exeter 25 – Taunton 12 – Weymouth 42.

☆ **Yarcombe Inn**, EX14 9BD, ℰ 218 – 📺 ⌂ ⚑ ⚑ AE VISA
M (bar lunch)/dinner a la carte 6.40/12.00 t. ⌂ 2.25 – **5 rm** ⚏ 14.00/34.00 t. – SB (except summer) 38.00/44.00 st.

YARM Cleveland 402 P 20 – pop. 6 360 – ✪ 0642 Middlesbrough.

◆ London 242 – Middlesbrough 8.

🏨 **Crathorne Hall** ⚶, Crathorne, TS15 0AR, S : 3 ½ m. by A 67 ℰ 700398, Telex 587426, « Converted Edwardian mansion house », ⚑, park – 📺 ☎ 🅿 ⚑ ⚑ AE ⓪ VISA ⚶
M (bar lunch Saturday) 7.50/14.50 st. and a la carte – **39 rm** ⚏ 46.00/65.00 st., **3 suites** 85.00 st. – SB (weekends only) 52.00/60.00 st.

YATTENDON Berks. 403 404 Q 29 – pop. 568 – ECD : Saturday – ✉ Newbury – ✪ 0635 Hermitage.

◆London 62 – Newbury 8 – Reading 12.

XXX **Royal Oak** with rm, The Square, RG16 0UF, ℰ 201325, ⚑ – 📺 ⌂wc ☜ 🅿 ⚑ AE VISA
M (closed Sunday dinner and last 2 weeks January) (booking essential) a la carte 16.75/2.50 t. ⌂ 3.80 – **5 rm** ⚏ 40.00/60.00 t. – SB (November-March except Christmas) (weekends only) 80.00 st.

" Short Breaks " (SB)

*Molti alberghi propongono delle condizioni vantaggiose
per un soggiorno di due notti
comprendente la camera, la cena e la prima colazione.*

YELVERTON Devon 403 H 32 – ✪ 0822.

◆London 234 – Exeter 33 – ◆Plymouth 9.

🏨 **Moorland Links** ⚶, PL20 6DA, S : 2 m. on A 386 ℰ 852245, ≤, ⚑, park, ⚘ – 📺 ⌂wc ☎ 🅿 ⚑ ⚑ ⚑ VISA
closed 25 December-2 January – **M** 10.45/15.15 t. – **30 rm** ⚏ 36.00/46.00 t. – SB (weekends only) 63.00 st.

⚘ **Overcombe** ⚶, Horrabridge, PL20 7RN, N : 1 ¼ m. on A 386 ℰ 853501, ≤, ⚑ – 📺 ⌂wc ⚴ 🅿 ⚑ ⓪ VISA
11 rm ⚏ 14.25/31.50 st.

YEOVIL Somerset 403 404 M 31 The West Country G. – pop. 36 114 – ECD : Monday and Thursday – ✪ 0935.

See : St. John the Baptist Church★.

Envir. : Montacute House★★★AC, W : 4 m. on A 3088 – Fleet Air Arm Museum★★AC, NW : 8 m. by A 37 – Long Sutton★ (Church★★), NW : 10 m. – Huish Episcopi : Church Tower★★, NW : 13 m. – Martock : All Saints Church★★, W : 7 m. – Cadbury Castle (≤★★), NE : 11 m. by A 359 – Ham Hill (≤★★) W : 4 m. – Tintinhull House★AC, NW : 5 m.

🏌 Sherborne Rd ℰ 75949.

🛈 Johnson Hall, Hendford ℰ 22884.

◆London 136 – Exeter 48 – ◆Southampton 72 – Taunton 26.

🏨 **Manor Crest** (Crest), Hendford Rd, BA20 1TG, ℰ 23116, Telex 46580, ⚑ – ▤ rest 📺 ⌂wc ⚴ ⚶ ⚑ AE ⓪ VISA
M 9.50/12.50 st. and a la carte ⌂ 4.00 – ⚏ 6.50 – **42 rm** 45.00/56.00 st. – SB (weekends only) 64.00/72.00 st.

⚘ **Preston,** 64 Preston Rd, BA20 2DL, ℰ 74400 – 📺 ⌂wc 🅿 ⚑ VISA ⚶
11 rm ⚏ 12.00/30.00 t.

at Barwick S : 2 m. by A 30 off A 37 – ✉ ✪ 0935 Yeovil :

XX **Little Barwick House** ⚶ with rm, BA22 9TD, ℰ 23902, ≤, ⚑ – 📺 ⌂wc ⌂wc 🅿 ⚑ ⓪ VISA ⚶
closed 25-26 December – **M** (closed Sunday to non-residents) (dinner only) 15.00 st. ⌂ 3.30 – **6 rm** ⚏ 32.00/55.00 st. – SB (October-April) 104.00 st.

at West Coker SW : 3 ½ m. on A 30 – ✉ Yeovil – ✪ 093 586 West Coker :

🏨 **Four Acres**, High St., BA22 9AJ, ℰ 2555, Telex 46666, ⚑ – 📺 ⌂wc ⌂wc ☎ 🅿 ⚑ AE ⓪ VISA
M (closed Sunday dinner to non residents) 10.00 t. and a la carte – **23 rm** ⚏ 35.00/52.00 t. – SB (weekends only) 60.00/65.00 st.

at East Chinnock SW : 5 m. on A 30 – ✉ Yeovil – ✪ 093 586 West Coker :

⚘ **Barrows Country House** ⚶, Weston St., BA22 9EJ, ℰ 2390, ⚑ – 🅿 ⚶
closed 24 December-1 January – **6 rm** ⚏ 9.50/22.00 s.

at Montacute W : 4 m. on A 3088 – ⊠ Yeovil – ⦿ 0935 Martock :

🏠 **Kings Arms,** Bishopston, TA15 6UU, ℰ 822513, 🍴 – 📺 ➡wc ⊕ ℗. 🔼 AE ⓞ VISA. ⁓
10 rm ⊒ 36.00/49.00 t.

XX **Milk House,** 17 The Borough, TA15 6XB, ℰ 823823.

AUSTIN-ROVER, DAIMLER-JAGUAR Market St. ℰ 75242
FORD West Henford ℰ 27421

SAAB 12 Oxford Rd ℰ 26701
VAUXHALL-OPEL Addlewell Lane ℰ 74842

Y-FENNI = Abergavenny.

YORK North Yorks. 🛆🄾🄸 Q 22 – pop. 123 126 – ECD : Monday and Wednesday – ⦿ 0904.
See : Minster★★★ 13C-15C (Chapter House★★★, ⁂★★ from tower, AC, 275 steps) CDY – National Railway Museum★★★ CY – Castle Museum★★ AC DZ M2 – Clifford's Tower★ (13C) AC DYZ B – Art Gallery★ CX M3 – Treasurer's House★ (14C) AC DX E – City Walls★ 14C – The Shambles★ DY.

🏌 Lords Moor Lane, Strensall ℰ 490304, NE : 6 m. by Huntington Rd BY.

🗲 De Grey Rooms, Exhibition Sq. ℰ 21756/7 – York Railway Station, Station Rd ℰ 643700.

◆London 203 – ◆Kingston-upon-Hull 38 – ◆Leeds 26 – ◆Middlesbrough 51 – ◆Nottingham 88 – ◆Sheffield 62.

Plan opposite

🏨🏨 **Royal York,** Station Rd, YO2 2AA, ℰ 53681, Telex 57912, ≼, 🍴 – 🛗 📺 ☎ ℗. 🔼 🔼 AE ⓞ VISA
M 6.50/15.00 t. and a la carte – **126 rm** ⊒ 44.00/95.00 st. – SB 84.00/96.00 st. CY e

Annex : 🏠 Friars Garden, Station Rd, YO2 2AA, ℰ 53681, Telex 57912, 🍴 – 📺 ➡wc 📞 ℗
M (see Royal York H.) – **22 rm**. CY e

🏨🏨 **Middlethorpe Hall** ⁓, Bishopthorpe Rd, YO2 1QP, S : 1 m. ℰ 641241, Telex 57802, ≼, « Tastefully decorated Queen Anne house », 🍴, park – 🛗 📺 ☎ ℗. 🔼 🔼 AE ⓞ VISA. ⁓
M (closed Sunday and Monday) 19.50 **st.** and a la carte ≬ 4.50 **Grill** (dinner only) 19.50 **st.** and a la carte approx 25.00 **st.** ≬ 4.50 – ⊒ 6.00 – **31 rm** 66.00/92.00 **st.**, **5 suites** 125.00/150.00 **st.** – SB (November-April) (except Tuesday, Wednesday and Bank Holidays) 110.00/125.00 **st.** by A 19 BZ

🏨🏨 **Crest** (Crest), Cliffords Tower, 1 Tower St., YO1 1SB, ℰ 648111, Telex 57566 – 🛗 ▦ rest 📺 ☎ ⅙ ℗. 🟰 🔼 AE ⓞ VISA
M 9.50/12.50 t. and a la carte ≬ 4.50 – ⊒ 6.30 – **128 rm** 53.00/63.00 t., **2 suites** 105.00 t. – SB (weekends only) 66.00/78.00 st. DY A

🏨🏨 **Viking** (Q.M.H.), North St., YO1 1JF, ℰ 59822, Telex 57937, ≼ – 🛗 📺 ☎ ℗. 🟰 🔼 AE ⓞ VISA
M (carving lunch)/dinner a la carte 11.75/16.20 **st.** – **186 rm** ⊒ 55.00/80.00 **st.** – SB (weekends only) 72.00 **st.** CY n

🏨🏨 **Judges' Lodging,** 9 Lendal, YO1 2AQ, ℰ 38733, « Tastefully restored 18C Judges'lodgings » – 📺 ℗. AE ⓞ VISA
M (bar lunch)/dinner a la carte 12.50/18.00 ≬ 4.50 – **14 rm** ⊒ 35.00/100.00, **1 suite** 75.00 – SB (autumn and winter) 85.00/125.00 **st.** CY x

🏨 **Mount Royale,** 119 The Mount, YO2 2DA, ℰ 28856, Telex 57414, « Tasteful decor and furnishings », 🔲 heated, 🍴 – 📺 ➡wc ☎ ℗
20 rm. AZ s

🏨 **Post House** (T.H.F.), Tadcaster Rd, YO2 2QF, SW : 1 ¾ m. on A 64 ℰ 707921, Telex 57798, 🍴 – 🛗 📺 ➡wc ➡ ⅙ ℗. 🟰 🔼 AE ⓞ VISA
M 8.20/9.75 **st.** and a la carte ≬ 3.40 – ⊒ 5.65 – **147 rm** 48.00/62.00 **st.** AZ r

🏨 **Ambassador,** 123-125 The Mount, YO2 2DA, ℰ 641316, 🍴 – 🛗 📺 ➡wc ⌘wc ☎ ℗. 🔼 AE ⓞ VISA. ⁓
19 rm ⊒ 28.00/42.00 st. AZ c

🏨 **Hudsons,** 60 Bootham, YO3 7BZ, ℰ 21267 – 📺 ➡wc ⌘wc ☎ ℗. 🔼 AE ⓞ VISA. ⁓ CX a
closed 24 and 25 December – **M** (bar lunch)/dinner 8.50 t. and a la carte ≬ 3.25 – **28 rm** ⊒ 20.00/52.00 t.

🏨 **Dean Court** (Best Western), Duncombe Pl., YO1 2EF, ℰ 25082 – 🛗 📺 ➡wc ☎. 🔼 AE ⓞ VISA. ⁓
M 9.00/14.00 st. ≬ 3.25 – **36 rm** ⊒ 42.00/75.00 st. – SB 41.00 st. CY a

🏨 **Town House,** 98-104 Holgate Rd, YO2 4BB, ℰ 36171, 🍴 – 📺 ➡wc ⌘wc ☎ ℗. 🔼 AE ⓞ VISA
closed 24 December-1 January – **M** (bar lunch)/dinner 7.25 t. and a la carte ≬ 2.60 – **23 rm** ⊒ 17.00/39.00 t. – SB (except summer) 40.00/47.50 st. AZ z

🏨 **Hill,** 60 York Rd, Acomb, YO2 5LW, W : 2 m. by A 59 on B 1224 ℰ 790777, 🍴 – 📺 ➡wc ☎ ℗. 🔼 AE ⓞ VISA. ⁓
closed mid December-mid January – **M** (residents only) (bar lunch)/dinner 11.00 t. ≬ 4.00 – **10 rm** ⊒ 29.00/48.00 t. – SB 49.00/55.00 st. AZ v

🏨 **Cottage,** 3 Clifton Green, YO3 6LH, ℰ 643711 – 📺 ➡wc ⌘wc ☎. 🔼 AE VISA. ⁓ AY v
closed 24 to 26 December – **M** (grill rest. only) (dinner only) – **18 rm** ⊒ 18.00/46.00 st. – SB (except Bank Holidays) 39.00/52.00 st.

YORK

Map of York city centre (detailed inset) with streets including Foss Islands Road, Navigation Rd, Barbican Rd, Cemetery Rd, Huntington Rd, Lowther Street, Haxby Rd, Townend St, Gillygate, Bootham, Clifton, Grosvenor Ter, Burton Stone Lane, MINSTER, Piccadilly, Fishergate, Walmgate, Hope St, Paragon St, Ouse, Bishopthorpe Rd, Nunnery Lane, Nunthorpe Road, Moss St, Scarcroft, Micklegate, Blossom St, Marygate, NATIONAL RAILWAY MUSEUM, STATION.

A 1036, A 1079, A 19, B 1363

400 m / 400 yards

Map of York and surrounding area with: THIRSK A 19, HELMSLEY B 1363, SCARBOROUGH (A 64) A 1036, MALTON, A 1079 (A 166) BRIDLINGTON KINGSTON-UPON-HULL, SELBY A 19, HEWORTH, TANG HALL, HESLINGTON, FULFORD, Fulford Road, Heslington Lane, Hull Rd, Malton Road, Stockton Lane, Tang Hall La., Lawrence St, Wigginton Rd, Huntington Road, Water Lane, CLIFTON, Shipton Rd, Ouse, Bishopthorpe Rd, Tadcaster, LEEDS A 1036, Poppleton Rd, Acomb Rd, Holgate, Water End, ACOMB, Carr Lane, Gale Lane, Beckfield Lane, Boroughbridge Rd, HARROGATE B 1224, WETHERBY A 59.

1 km / 1/2 mile

20

507

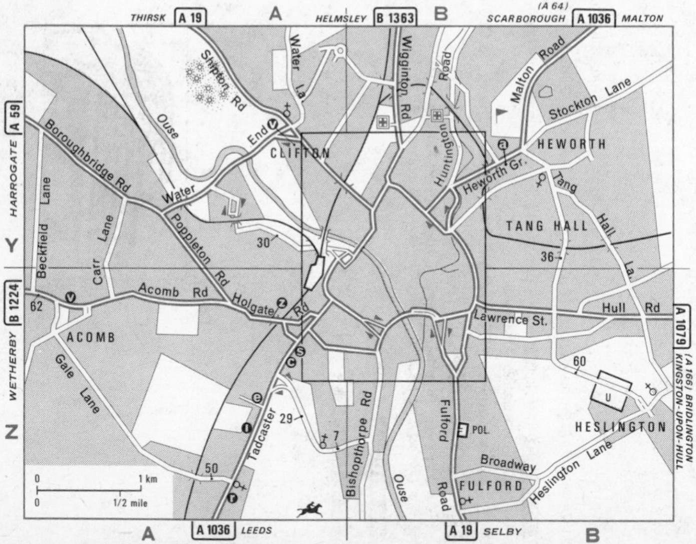

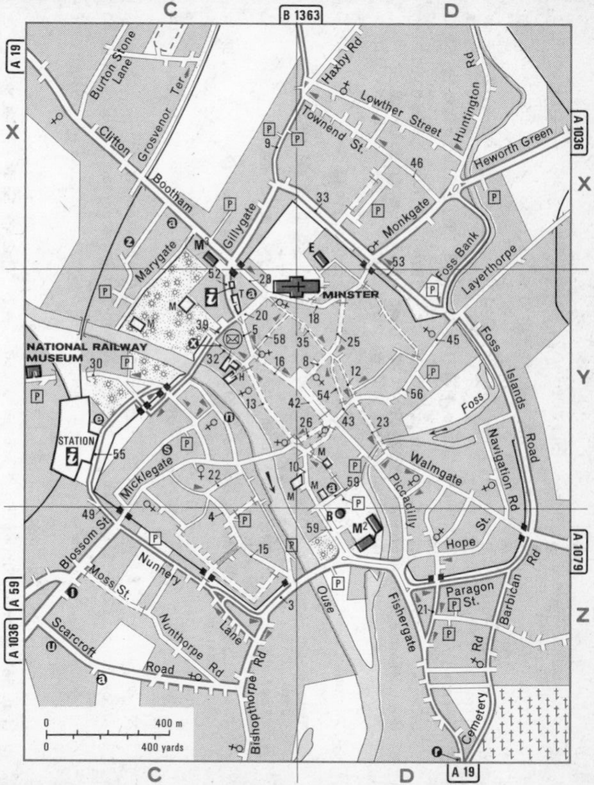

🏨 **Acaster Sheppard,** 63 Blossom St., YO2 2BD, ☎ 643716, Telex 57950 – 📺 🚿wc 🛏 ☎
🚗 🔼 *VISA* 🛎
CZ **i**
closed 25-26 December – **M** (bar lunch)/dinner 7.50 **t.** and a la carte ⌕ 2.50 – **20 rm**
⤶ 20.50/44.00 **t.** – SB 39.00/56.00 **st.**

🏨 **Grasmead House** without rest., 1 Scarcroft Hill, YO2 1DF, ☎ 29996 – 📺 🚿wc. 🔼 *VISA* 🛎
6 rm ⤶ 25.00/38.00 **st.**
CZ **a**

🏨 **Heworth Court,** 76-78 Heworth Green, YO3 7TQ, ☎ 425156 – 📺 🚿wc 🛁wc 🅿 🔼 🆎
⓪ *VISA* 🛎
BY **a**
M 15.50 **t.** and a la carte ⌕ 3.00 – **16 rm** ⤶ 31.00/50.00 **t.** – SB (except Christmas) 28.00/30.00 **st.**

🏨 **Field House,** 2 St. Georges Pl., YO2 2DR, 🌳 – 📺 🛁wc ☎ 🅿 🔼 🆎 *VISA*. 🛎
closed Christmas – **M** (residents only) (dinner only) 9.00 **t.** – **17 rm** ⤶ 19.00/44.00 **t.** –
SB 46.00/58.00 **st.**
AZ **e**

🏠 **Arndale,** 290 Tadcaster Rd, YO2 2ET, ☎ 702424, 🌳 – 📺 🚿wc 🛁wc 🅿. 🛎
AZ **i**
closed Christmas – **8 rm** ⤶ 16.00/38.00 **st.**

🏠 **Priory,** 126 Fulford Rd, YO1 4BE, ☎ 25280, 🌳 – 📺 🛁wc 🅿. 🔼 🆎 ⓪ *VISA*. 🛎
DZ **r**
18 rm ⤶ 16.00/32.00 **st.**

🏠 **Mayfield,** 75 Scarcroft Rd, YO2 1DB, ☎ 54834 – 📺 🚿wc 🛁wc. 🔼 🆎 *VISA*. 🛎
CZ **u**
7 rm ⤶ 18.00/40.00 **st.**

🏠 **Crook Lodge,** 26 St. Mary's, Bootham, YO3 7DD, ☎ 55614 – 📺 🚿wc 🅿
CX **z**
closed January and February – **7 rm** ⤶ 15.50/29.00 **st.**

✕ **Tony's,** 39 Tanner Row, YO1 1JP, ☎ 59622, Greek rest. – 🔼 🆎 *VISA*
CY **s**
closed Saturday lunch, Sunday and 2 weeks February – **M** 8.50 **t.** (dinner) and a la carte
6.80/9.65 **t.** ⌕ 2.25.

at Wilberfoss E : 8 ¼ m. by A 1079 – BZ – ✉ York – ☎ 075 95 Wilberfoss :

✕✕ **Beck Farm,** YO4 5PG, E : 1 ¾ m. by A 1079 on Newton-on-Derwent road ☎ 410, 🌳 – 🅿 🔼
VISA
closed Sunday, February and Bank Holidays – **M** 9.50/17.00 **t.** and a la carte 15.40/18.80 **t.**
⌕ 3.50.

at Skelton NW : 3 m. on A 19 – AY – ✉ ☎ 0904 York :

🏨 **Fairfield Manor,** Shipton Rd, YO3 6XW, ☎ 25621, 🌳 – 📺 ☎ 🅿. 🔼 🆎 ⓪ *VISA*. 🛎
M 6.75/9.25 **t.** ⌕ 3.50 – **25 rm** ⤶ 35.00/85.00 **t.**

ALFA-ROMEO Leeman Rd ☎ 22772
AUSTIN-ROVER, FORD, VAUXHALL-OPEL 117 Long
St. ☎ 0347 (Easingwold) 21694
CITROEN Lowther St. ☎ 22064
COLT Fulford ☎ 33139
FIAT Piccadilly ☎ 34321
FORD Piccadilly ☎ 25371
JAGUAR-DAIMLER Layerthorpe ☎ 58252

LADA Leeman Rd ☎ 59241
NISSAN 21-27 Layerthorpe ☎ 58809
PEUGEOT, TALBOT The Stonebow ☎ 55118
RENAULT Clifton ☎ 58647
TOYOTA 172 Fulford Rd ☎ 52947
VAUXHALL-OPEL Rougier St. ☎ 25444
VAUXHALL-OPEL 100 Layerthorpe ☎ 56671
VOLVO 88-96 Walmgate ☎ 53798

YOXFORD Suffolk 🄌🄌🄌 Y 27 – pop. 690 – ✉ Saxmundham – ☎ 072 877.
◆London 95 – ◆Ipswich 25 – ◆Norwich 55.

🏨 **Satis House,** IP17 3EX, ☎ 418, 🌳 – 📺 🚿wc ☎ 🅿. 🔼 🆎 *VISA*. 🛎
M *(closed Sunday lunch)* (lunch by arrangement)/dinner 12.50 **st.** ⌕ 2.50 – **7 rm**
⤶ 28.50/49.50 **st.** – SB (weekends only) 55.00/61.00 **st.**

✕ **Jacey's,** Blythburgh House, High St., IP17 3EU, ☎ 298 – 🔼 🆎 *VISA*
closed lunch Sunday and Monday – **M** a la carte 10.40/12.20 **t.** ⌕ 2.25.

YR WYDDFA = Snowdon.

YR WYDDGRUG = Mold.

Scotland

Place with at least :

one hotel or restaurant	●	Tongue
one pleasant hotel	🏠 , ✗ with rm	
one quiet, secluded hotel	🍃	
one restaurant with	✿, ✿✿, ✿✿✿, M	
See this town for establishments located in its vicinity	ABERDEEN	

La località possiede come minimo :

una risorsa alberghiera	●	Tongue
un albergo ameno	🏠 , ✗ with rm	
un albergo molto tranquillo, isolato	🍃	
un'ottima tavola con	✿, ✿✿, ✿✿✿, M	
La località raggruppa nel suo testo le risorse dei dintorni	ABERDEEN	

Localité offrant au moins :

une ressource hôtelière	●	Tongue
un hôtel agréable	🏠 , ✗ with rm	
un hôtel très tranquille, isolé	🍃	
une bonne table à	✿, ✿✿, ✿✿✿, M	
Localité groupant dans le texte les ressources de ses environs	ABERDEEN	

Ort mit mindestens :

einem Hotel oder Restaurant	●	Tongue
einem angenehmen Hotel	🏠 , ✗ with rm	
einem sehr ruhigen und abgelegenen Hotel	🍃	
einem Restaurant mit	✿, ✿✿, ✿✿✿, M	
Ort mit Angaben über Hotels und Restaurants in seiner Umgebung	ABERDEEN	

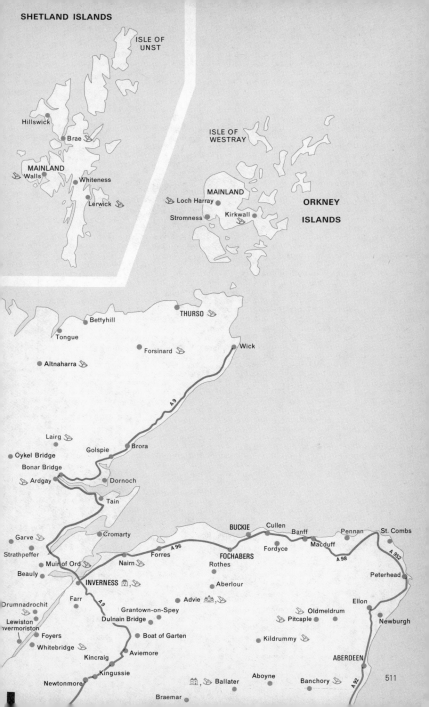

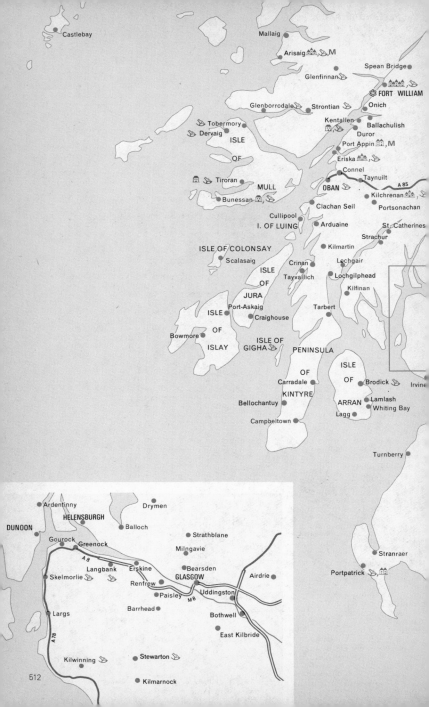

SCOTLAND

Towns

ABERDEEN Aberdeen. (Grampian) **401** N 12 **Scotland G** – pop. 186 757 – ECD : Wednesday and Saturday – ✪ 0224.

See : Old Aberdeen** X – St. Machar's Cathedral** (West front***, heraldic ceiling***) X **A** – Mercat Cross** Y **B** – Art Gallery** Y **M** – King's College Chapel* (Crown spire***, medieval fittings***) X **D** – Brig o'Balgownie* by Don Street X – Maritime Museum* Z **M1** – Provost Skene's House* (Painted ceiling**) Y **E** – Marischal College* Y **U**.

Envir. : Deeside** and Lin O'Dee* Tour of 64 m., W : by A 93 X – Grampian Castles** (Craigievar***) W : 27 m. by A 944 X and B 9119 – Crathes Castle**, SW : 14 m. by A 93 X – Kildrummy*, NW : 36 m. by A 944 X – Castle Fraser* (exterior**) W : 16 m. by A 944 X – Pitmedden Gardens**, N : 16 m. by A 92 X and B 999 – Haddo House*, NW : 26 m. by A 92 X and B 9005.

🅱 King's Links, 19 Golf Rd ℰ 581464 X – 🅱 St. Fittick's Rd, Balnagask ℰ 876407 X.

✈ Aberdeen Airport ℰ 722331 Telex 73120 NW : 7 m. by A 96 X – **Terminal** : Bus Station, Guild St. (adjacent to Railway Station).

🚃 ℰ 582005.

⛴ by P & O Ferries : Orkney & Shetland Services : to Shetland Islands : Lerwick 3 weekly (14 h).

🛈 St. Nicholas House, Broad St. ℰ 632727 – Stonehaven Rd ℰ 873030 (summer only) – Railway Station, Guild St. (summer only).

♦Edinburgh 130 – ♦Dundee 67.

Plan opposite

🏨 **Stakis Tree Tops** (Stakis), 161 Springfield Rd, AB9 2QH, ℰ 313377, Telex 73794 – 🛗 📺 ☎ 🅿 ☕ ⬛ AE ⓞ VISA
X s
M 10.50/15.00 **t.** and a la carte ♨ 3.50 – ⛁ 3.70 – **92 rm** 25.00/63.00 **t.**, **1 suite** 40.00/63.00 **t.** – SB 46.00/74.00 **st.**

🏨 **Caledonian Thistle** (Thistle), 10-14 Union Terr., AB9 1HE, ℰ 640233, Telex 73758 – 🛗 📺 ☎ 🅿 ⬛ AE ⓞ VISA
Z i
M 12.00 **t.** and a la carte ♨ 3.50 – ⛁ 6.25 – **75 rm** 53.00/87.00 **st.**, **2 suites** 85.00/100.00 **st.**

🏨 **Station**, 78 Guild St., AB9 2DN, ℰ 587214, Telex 73161 – 🛗 📺 ☎ 🅿 ⬛ AE ⓞ VISA
closed 24 December-5 January – **M** 9.75 **t.** and a la carte 11.20/16.60 **t.** ♨ 3.00 – ⛁ 5.50 –
Z o
59 rm 27.50/53.00 **t.**, **1 suite** 65.00/75.00 **t.** – SB (weekends only) 49.90/74.90 **st.**

🏨 **Royal**, 1-3 Bath St., AB1 2HY, ℰ 585152 – 🛗 📺 ⬛wc ⬛wc ☎ 🅿 ⬛ AE ⓞ VISA
Z a
M (bar lunch)/dinner 10.00 **t.** and a la carte ♨ 2.80 – **42 rm** 30.00/43.00 **t.**, **1 suite** 60.00 **t.** – SB (weekends only) 58.00 **st.**

🏠 **Cedars**, 339 Great Western Rd, AB1 6NW, ℰ 583225 – 📺 ⬛wc ⬛ 🅿 AE
X e
13 rm ⛁ 16.00/30.00 **st.**

🏠 **Bracklinn**, 348 Great Western Rd, AB1 6LX, ℰ 317060 – 📺 ⬛
X c
6 rm ⛁ 16.50/28.00 **st.**

🏠 **Russell**, 50 St. Swithin St., AB1 6XJ, ℰ 323555 – 🅿 ⬛
Z c
9 rm ⛁ 14.00/24.00 **st.**

XX **Nargile**, 77-79 Skene St., AB1 1QD, ℰ 636093, Turkish rest. – ⬛ AE ⓞ VISA
Y a
closed Sunday and 25 December-5 January – **M** 4.95/14.95 **st.** and a la carte 6.40/16.25 **st.**
♨ 3.20.

XX **Atlantis**, 145 Crown St., AB1 2HR, ℰ 591403, Seafood – 🅿 ⬛ AE ⓞ VISA
Z r
closed Sunday, Christmas and New Year – **M** 4.50 **st.** (lunch) and a la carte 8.50/17.50 **st.**
♨ 3.50.

XX **Aberdeen Rendezvous**, 218-222 George St., AB1 1BS, ℰ 633610, Chinese-Peking rest. –
⬛ AE ⓞ VISA
Y c
M 8.50/14.50 **t.** and a la carte 10.00/14.50 **t.** ♨ 3.80.

X **Poldino's**, 7 Little Belmont St., AB1 1JG, ℰ 647777, Italian rest. – ⬛ AE ⓞ VISA
YZ u
closed Sunday, Christmas Day and New Years Day – **M** a la carte 8.90/13.60 **t.** ♨ 3.20.

at Altens S : 3 m. on A 956 – X – ✉ ✪ 0224 Aberdeen :

🏨 **Skean Dhu Altens** (Mt. Charlotte), Souterhead Rd, AB1 4LE, ℰ 877000, Telex 739631, ⬛ heated – 🛗 🖩 📺 ☎ & 🅿 ☕ ⬛ AE ⓞ VISA
M (buffet lunch Saturday and Sunday) 8.50/9.85 **st.** and a la carte ♨ 3.00 – **221 rm** ⛁ 51.00/59.00 **st.**

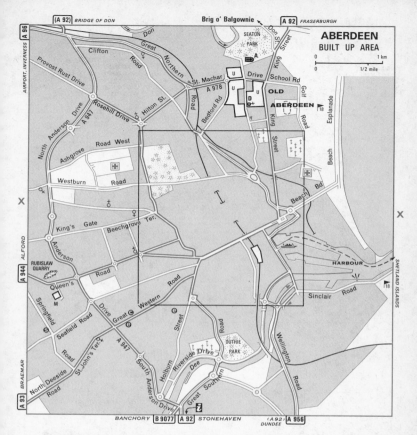

at Banchory-Devenick SW : 4 ½ m. on B 9077 – X – ⊠ ✪ 0224 Aberdeen :

🏛 **Ardoe House** ⟩⟩, South Deeside Rd, AB1 5YP, ℰ 867355, ≼, ⟩, ⟨, park – ☒ ⌂wc 🛏wc ⟨⟩ ℗. 🛁. ⟨ 🆎 ⓪ *VISA*
M 6.20 **st.** and a la carte 14.45/20.95 **st.** ⟨ 3.50 – **20 rm** ⊡ 28.00/60.00 **st.**

at Westhill W : 6 ½ m. by A 944 – X – ⊠ ✪ 0224 Aberdeen :

🏛 **Westhill Inn,** Westhill Drive, AB3 6TT, ℰ 740388, Telex 739925 – ⧈ ☒ ⌂wc 🛏wc ☎ ℗. 🛁. ⟨ 🆎 ⓪ *VISA*
M 6.50/9.50 **st.** and a la carte 11.55/21.65 **st.** ⟨ 3.50 – **52 rm** ⊡ 33.00/49.00 **st.** – SB (weekends only) 45.00/55.00 **st.**

at Bucksburn NW : 4 m. by A 96 – X – on A 947 – ⊠ ✪ 0224 Aberdeen :

🏛 **Bucksburn Moat House** (Q.M.H.), Oldmeldrum Rd, AB2 9LN, ℰ 713911, Telex 73108, ☒, – ⧈ ☒ ℗. 🛁. ⟨ 🆎 ⓪ *VISA*
M 11.00 **st.** and a la carte 11.50/14.00 **st.** and a la carte ⟨ 3.00 – ⊡ 5.50 – **98 rm** 46.00/54.00 **t.**, **1 suite** 95.00 **t.** – SB (weekends only) 56.00 **st.**

at Dyce NW : 5 ½ m. by A 96 – X – on A 947 – ⊠ ✪ 0224 Aberdeen :

🏛 **Holiday Inn,** Riverview Drive, Farburn, AB2 0AZ, ℰ 770011, Telex 739651, ☒, – ⊟ ☒ ☎ ⅋ ℗. 🛁. ⟨ 🆎 ⓪ *VISA*
M 12.95 **t.** and a la carte 13.65/19.45 **t.** ⟨ 4.30 – ⊡ 6.50 – **154 rm** 57.00/68.00, **1 suite** 98.00/151.00 – SB (weekends only) 64.00/88.00 **st.**

at Aberdeen Airport NW : 6 m. by A 96 – X – ⊠ ✪ 0224 Aberdeen :

🏛 **Aberdeen Airport Skean Dhu** (Mt. Charlotte), Argyll Rd, AB2 0DU, ℰ 725252, Telex 739239, ⟩, heated – ☒ ☎ ⅋ ℗. 🛁. ⟨ 🆎 ⓪ *VISA*
M (bar lunch Saturday and Sunday) 8.05/10.00 **st.** ⟨ 3.00 – **148 rm** ⊡ 51.00/59.00 **st.**

515

ABERDEEN

George Street . . . . Y
St. Nicolas Street . . . . Y 30
Union Street . . . . Z

Broad Street . . . . Y 6
Castle Street . . . . Y 7
College Street . . . . Z 9
Craigie Loanings . . . . Y 12
East North Street . . . . Y 16
Great Southern Road . . . . Z 18
Guild Street . . . . Z 19
Justice Street . . . . Y 21
Loch Street . . . . Y 22
Millburn Street . . . . Z 23
Regent Quay . . . . Z 24
Rosemount
  Terrace . . . . Y 25
Rosemount Viaduct . . . . Y 26
St. Andrew Street . . . . Y 28
St. Swithin Street . . . . Z 31
School Hill . . . . YZ 32
South Esplanade West . . . . Z 33
South Mount Street . . . . Y 34
Springbank Terrace . . . . Z 35
Spring Garden . . . . Y 36
Trinity Quay . . . . Z 37
Union Terrace . . . . Z 39
Upperkirkgate . . . . Y 40
Victoria Street . . . . Z 42
Waverley Place . . . . Z 43
Wellington Place . . . . Z 45
Wellington Road . . . . Z 47
Woolmanhill . . . . Y 48

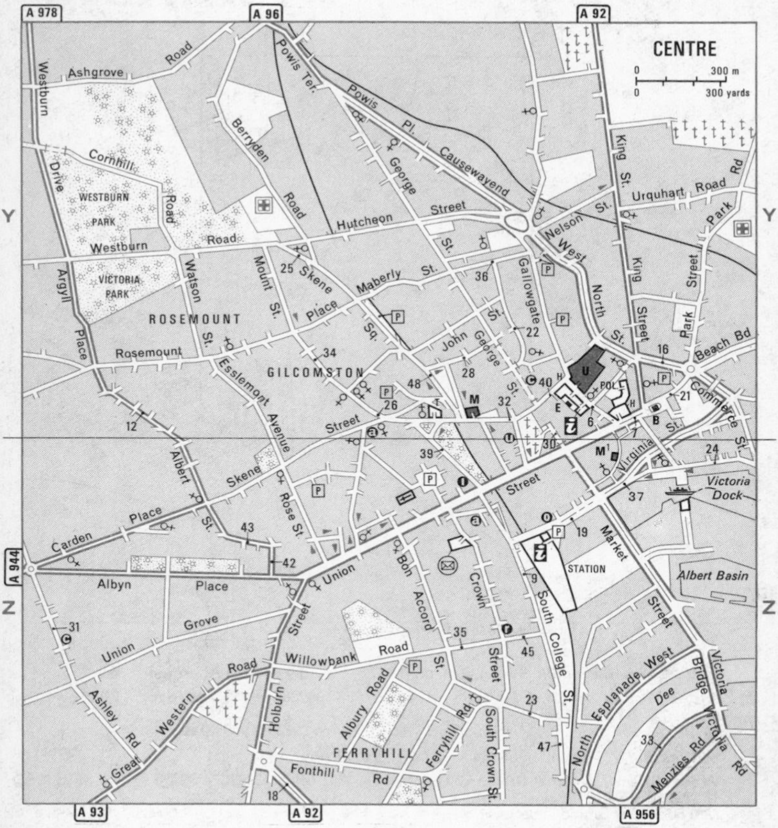

MICHELIN Distribution Centre, Wellington Rd, AB9 2JZ, ☏ **875075 by A 956** X

ALFA-ROMEO 542 Gt Western Rd ☏ 310181
AUSTIN-ROVER 92 Crown St. ☏ 590381
AUSTIN-ROVER, ROLLS ROYCE 19 Justice Mill Lane ☏ 596151
BMW Grey St. ☏ 313355
FIAT 870 Gt Northern Rd ☏ 695573
FORD Menzies Rd ☏ 879024
FORD 29 Union Glen ☏ 589022
LANCIA 3 Whitehall Rd ☏ 641349
MERCEDES-BENZ, FIAT 366 King St. ☏ 634211
NISSAN 78 Powis Terr. ☏ 41313
RENAULT Lang Stracht ☏ 683181
VAUXHALL-OPEL 16 Dee St. ☏ 589216
VW, AUDI 94 Hilton Drive ☏ 43327

ABERDOUR Fife. (Fife) **401** K 15 **Scotland G – pop. 1 460 – ECD : Wednesday –** ☎ **0383.**

See : Site★ – Castle★ – ⛳18 **Dodhead, Burntisland ☏ 0592 (Burntisland) 873247, E : 5 m. on A 92.**

♦**Edinburgh 17 – Dunfermline 7.**

Woodside, 80 High St., KY3 0SW, ☏ **860328** – TV wc wc ☎ P. AE VISA
M 8.00/10.00 **t.** 2.50 – **21 rm** 35.00/49.50 **t.**, **1 suite** 50.00/70.00 **t.** – SB (weekends only) 60.00/80.00 **st.**

ABERFELDY Perth. (Tayside) **401** I 14 Scotland G – pop. 1 477 – ECD : Wednesday – ✆ 0887.

See : Site★.

Envir. : St. Mary's Church (Painted ceiling★) NE : 2 m. by A 827 – Loch Tay★★, SW : 6 m. by A 827.

🛈 District Tourist Association, 8 Dunkeld St. ℘ 20276 (summer only).

◆Edinburgh 76 – ◆Glasgow 73 – ◆Oban 77 – Perth 32.

   🏛 **Guinach House** ⌂, Urlar Rd, PH15 2ET, ℘ 20251, ☞ – 📺
   March-October – **M** 6.50/10.00 **st.** ⌖ 3.70 – **7 rm** ⌷ 18.00/36.00 **st.** – SB (November-February) 24.50 **st.**

   🏯 **Cruachan,** Kenmore St., PH15 2BL, ℘ 20545, ☞ – 📺 ⌷wc 🅿 ⊙
   M (bar lunch)/dinner 9.50 **t.** and a la carte – **9 rm** ⌷ 12.00/32.00 **t.** – SB (October-March) 36.00/40.00 **st.**

   ⌂ **Balnearn,** Crieff Rd, PH15 2BJ, ℘ 20431, ☞ – 🅿
   13 rm ⌷ 10.35/20.70 **t.**

   at Fortingall W : 8 m. by B 846 – ✉ ✆ 088 73 Kenmore :

   ⌂ **Rose Villa** ⌂, PH15 2LL, ℘ 335, ☞ – ⌷wc 🅿
   March-October – **4 rm** ⌷ 18.50/33.00 **st.**

SUBARU, FORD Dunkeld St. ℘ 20254

ABERFOYLE Perth. (Central) **401** G 15 – pop. 546 – ECD : Wednesday – ✉ Stirling – ✆ 087 72.

🛝 Braeval ℘ 493.

🛈 Main St. ℘ 352 (summer only).

◆Edinburgh 56 – ◆Glasgow 27.

   Hotels see : *Callander* NE : 10 ½ m., *Drymen* SW : 11 ½ m.

ABERLADY E. Lothian (Lothian) **401** L 15 – pop. 884 – ECD : Wednesday – ✆ 087 57.

🛝 Kilspindie, ℘ 216.

◆Edinburgh 16 – Haddington 5 – North Berwick 7.5.

   🏯 **Kilspindie House,** Main St., EH32 0RE, ℘ 319 – ⌷wc ⌷wc 🅿 ⚛ 𝘝𝘐𝘚𝘈
   M (bar lunch)/dinner 8.30 **t.** and a la carte ⌖ 3.00 – **12 rm** ⌷ 18.50/36.00 **st.** – SB (October-March) 39.50/52.00 **st.**

   XX **Green Craig House** ⌂ with rm, SW : ¾ m. on A 198, EH32 0PY, ℘ 301, ≼, ☞ – 📺 ⌷wc
   ⌷wc 🅿 ⚛ 𝘝𝘐𝘚𝘈 ⌿
   M *(closed lunch Saturday and Sunday)* 13.50 **t.** ⌖ 3.00 – **8 rm** ⌷ 32.00/54.00 **t.**

ABERLOUR Banff. (Grampian) **401** K 11 – pop. 879 – ECD : Wednesday – ✆ 034 05.

Envir. : Dufftown (Glenfiddich Distillery★) SE : 4 m. by A 941 – Huntly Castle (Heraldic carvings★★★) E : 1 ½ m. by A 941 and A 920.

◆Edinburgh 189 – ◆Aberdeen 59 – ◆Inverness 54.

   🏛 **Dowans,** AB3 9LS, SW : ¾ m. by A 95 ℘ 488, ≼, ⚞, ☞ – ⌷wc 🅿 ⚛ 𝘝𝘐𝘚𝘈
   closed December and January – **M** 4.25/7.50 ⌖ 2.30 – **13 rm** ⌷ 12.00/32.00.

AUSTIN-ROVER, LAND ROVER-RANGE ROVER 15-19 High St. ℘ 505

ABOYNE Aberdeen. (Grampian) **401** L 12 – pop. 1 477 – ECD : Thursday – ✆ 0339.

Envir. : Craigievar Castle★★★ (17C) *AC*, NE : 12 m.

🛝 Formaston Park ℘ 2328, E : end of Village – 🛝 Tarland ℘ 033 981 (Tarland) 413, NW : 5 m.

◆Edinburgh 131 – ◆Aberdeen 30 – ◆Dundee 68.

   🏛 **Birse Lodge** ⌂, Charleston Rd, AB3 5EL, ℘ 2253, ☞ – ⌷wc 🕾 🅿 ⚛ ⊙
   Mid March-mid October – **M** (bar lunch)/dinner 12.00 **t.** ⌖ 3.20 – **16 rm** ⌷ 22.00/44.00 **t.**

AUSTIN-ROVER Main Rd ℘ 2440

ACHILTIBUIE Ross and Cromarty (Highland) **401** D 9 – ✆ 085 482.

◆Edinburgh 243 – ◆Inverness 84 – Ullapool 25.

   🏛 **Summer Isles** ⌂, IV26 2YG, ℘ 282, « ≼ Picturesque setting overlooking Summer Isles », ⚞ – ⌷wc 🅿
   Easter-mid October – **M** (dinner only) 19.00 **st.** – **13 rm** ⌷ 20.00/65.00 **st.**

ACHNASHEEN Ross and Cromarty (Highland) **401** E 11 – ECD : Wednesday – ✆ 044 588.

◆Edinburgh 202 – ◆Inverness 43.

   🏛 **Ledgowan Lodge** (Best Western) ⌂, IV22 2EJ, on A 890 ℘ 252, ≼, ⚞, ☞ – ⌷wc 🅿 ⚛
   ⚛ ⊙ 𝘝𝘐𝘚𝘈
   Easter-mid October – **M** 6.00/15.00 **t.** ⌖ 2.50 – **17 rm** ⌷ 20.00/55.00 **t.** – SB 50.00/70.00 **st.**

ADVIE Moray. (Highland) **401** J 11 – ✉ Grantown-on-Spey – ☎ 080 75.
♦Edinburgh 153 – ♦Inverness 46.

    Tulchan Lodge ⚲, PH26 3PW, on B 9102 ⌨ 200, Telex 75405, ≤ Spey Valley, « Victorian sporting lodge », ⚲, ⚘, park – ☎ ℗. ✄
      Mid April-mid November – **M** 15.00/30.00 t. ⅜ 3.50 – **11 rm** ⚏ 87.00/150.00 t.

AIRDRIE Lanark. (Strathclyde) **401 402** I 16 – pop. 45 320 – ECD : Wednesday – ☎ 023 64.
♦Edinburgh 32 – ♦Glasgow 14 – Motherwell 6.5 – Perth 53.

    🏨 **Staging Post,** 8-10 Anderson St., ML1 1XL, ⌨ 67525 – TV ➡wc ☎ ℗. ⚊ AE ⓞ VISA. ✄
      closed 26 December and 1 January – **M** 5.00 t. and a la carte 7.15/14.05 t. ⅜ 3.05 – **9 rm** ⚏ 24.00/42.00 t.

AIRTH Stirling. (Central) **401** I 15 – pop. 972 – ✉ Falkirk – ☎ 032 483.
♦Edinburgh 30 – Dunfermline 14 – Falkirk 7 – Stirling 8.

    Airth Castle ⚲, FK2 8JF, ⌨ 411, Telex 777975, ≤, « Castle and stables in extensive grounds », ⚲, ⚘, park – TV ☎ ⅙ ℗. ⚊. ✄
      47 rm

ALLOWAY Ayr (Strathclyde) **401 402** G 17 – see Ayr.

ALTENS Aberdeen. (Grampian) – see Aberdeen.

ALTNAHARRA Sutherland (Highland) **401** G 9 – ✉ Lairg – ☎ 054 981.
♦Edinburgh 239 – ♦Inverness 83 – Thurso 61.

    🏨 **Altnaharra** ⚲, IV27 4UE, ⌨ 222, ≤, ⚲, ⚘ – ➡wc ℗. ⚊. ✄
      M (bar lunch)/dinner 12.00 t. ⅜ 1.95 – **20 rm** ⚏ 15.50/25.50 t., **2 suites** 17.50/25.50 t. – SB (wine included) (except mid September-October and March-April) 28.00/35.00 **st.**

ALYTH Perth. (Tayside) **401** K 14 – pop. 2 258 – ECD : Wednesday – ☎ 082 83.
🛇 Pitcrocknie ⌨ 2268, E : 1 ½ m.
♦Edinburgh 63 – ♦Aberdeen 69 – ♦Dundee 16 – Perth 21.

    🏨 **Lands of Loyal** ⚲, Loyal Rd, PH11 8JQ, N : ½ m. by B 954 ⌨ 3151, ≤, « Victorian country house », ⚘, park – ➡wc ☎ ℗. ⚊ VISA
      M 8.50/12.50 **st.** and a la carte ⅜ 3.00 – **10 rm** ⚏ 28.00/50.00 **st.** – SB 70.00/78.00 **st.**

ANSTRUTHER Fife. (Fife) **401** L 15 – pop. 2 865 – ECD : Wednesday – ☎ 0333 - 🛇.
See : Scottish Fisheries Museum★★.
Envir. : The East Neuk★★ (coastline from Crail to St. Monance by A 917) – Kellie Castle★, NW : 7 m. by A 959.
🛇 Marsfield ⌨ 310387.
🛈 Scottish Fisheries Museum, St. Ayles ⌨ 310628.
♦Edinburgh 46 – ♦Dundee 23 – Dunfermline 34.

    🏨 **Craw's Nest,** Bankwell Rd, KY10 3DS, ⌨ 310691, ⚘ – TV ➡wc 🚿wc ☎ ℗. ⚊. ⚊ AE ⓞ VISA. ✄
      M 6.25/10.50 t. and a la carte ⅜ 3.50 – **50 rm** ⚏ 25.00/45.00 t. – SB (weekends only) 49.50/55.00 **st.**

    ✗ **Cellar,** 24 East Green, KY10 3AA, ⌨ 310378, Seafood – ⚊ AE VISA
      closed Monday lunch, Sunday, 1 week May, 1 week November and 24 to 26 December – **M** a la carte 12.70/16.75 t. ⅜ 4.95.

ARBROATH Angus (Tayside) **401** M 14 Scotland G – pop. 23 934 – ECD : Wednesday – ☎ 0241.
See : Site★ – Abbey★ AC.
Envir. : St. Vigeans Museum★ by A 92.
🛇 Elliot ⌨ 72272, S : 1 m.
🛈 Market Pl., ⌨ 72609 and 76680.
♦Edinburgh 72 – ♦Aberdeen 51 – ♦Dundee 16.

    Hotel see : **Montrose** NE : 13 ½ m.

BMW Montrose Rd ⌨ 72919   FORD Millgate ⌨ 73051

ARDENTINNY Argyll. (Strathclyde) **401** F 15 – ECD : Wednesday – ✉ Dunoon – ☎ 036 981.
♦Edinburgh 107 – Dunoon 13 – ♦Glasgow 64 – ♦Oban 71.

    🏨 **Ardentinny** ⚲, PA23 8TR, ⌨ 209, ≤ Loch Long, ⚘ – TV ➡wc 🚿wc ℗. ⚊ AE ⓞ VISA
      closed January-February – **M** 14.00 t. (dinner) and a la carte 6.60/11.35 t. ⅜ 3.25 – **11 rm** ⚏ 24.00/50.00 t. – SB 55.00/64.00 **st.**

ARDEONAIG Perth. (Central) – see Killin.

518

ARDGAY Ross and Cromarty (Highland) **401** G 10 – ✿ 086 32.
♦Edinburgh 205 – ♦Inverness 49 – ♦Wick 77.

⌂ **Croit Mairi** ⟨S⟩, Kincardine Hill, IV24 3DJ, S : 1 ¼ m. off A 9 ⌂ 504, ≼ Dornoch Firth and hills, 🚗 – 🅿. 🅂 🄰🄴 ⓪ 𝘝𝘐𝘚𝘈. 🅂
   closed late October-early November – **5 rm** 🖙 13.00/20.00 st.

ARDROSSAN Ayr. (Strathclyde) **401** **402** F 17 – pop. 11 386 – ECD : Wednesday – ✿ 0294.
🚢 by Caledonian MacBrayne : to the Isle of Arran : Brodick 3-10 daily (55 mn).
♦Edinburgh 75 – ♦Ayr 18 – ♦Glasgow 32.

   Hotels see : **Kilmarnock** SE : 11 ½ m., **Largs** N : 11 ½ m.

ARDUAINE Argyll. (Strathclyde) **401** D 15 – ECD : Wednesday – ✉ Oban – ✿ 085 22 Kilmelford.
♦Edinburgh 142 – ♦Oban 20.

🏨 **Loch Melfort** ⟨S⟩, PA34 4XG, ⌂ 233, ≼ Sound of Jura, 🚗 – 🖵wc 🅿. 🅂
   Mid April-mid October – **M** (bar lunch)/dinner 15.00 **t.** and a la carte ⌂ 4.50 – 🖙 3.00 – **26 rm**
   35.00/60.00 **t.**

ARDVASAR Inverness. (Highland) **401** C 12 – see Skye (Isle of).

ARISAIG Inverness. (Highland) **401** C 13 – ECD : Thursday – ✿ 068 75.
See : Site★ – ≼★ of Sound of Arisaig.
Envir. : Silver Sands of Morar★, N : 6 m. by A 830.
♦Edinburgh 172 – ♦Inverness 102 – ♦Oban 88.

🏨 **Arisaig House** ⟨S⟩, Beasdale, PH39 4NR, SE : 3 ¼ m. on A 830 ⌂ 622, Telex 777279, ≼ Loch
   Nan Uamh and Roshven Mountains, 🚗, park – 🖵 🕾 🅿 𝘝𝘐𝘚𝘈. 🅂
   Easter-October – **M** (booking essential) (restricted lunch residents only)/dinner 20.50 **t.** –
   14 rm 🖙 36.50/115.50 **t.**

⌂ **Arisaig,** PH39 4NH, ⌂ 210, ≼ – 🖵wc 🅿
   March-October – **M** (bar lunch)/dinner 14.00 **st.** ⌂ 3.50 – **13 rm** 🖙 19.00/33.00 **st.**

ARMADALE Inverness. (Highland) **401** C 12 – Shipping Services : see Skye (Isle of).

ARRAN (Isle of) Bute. (Strathclyde) **401** **402** DE 16 17 Scotland G – pop. 4 726.
See : Site★★ – Brodick Castle★★.
🚢 by Caledonian MacBrayne : from Brodick to Ardrossan 3-10 daily (55 mn) – from Lochranza to
Claonaig (Kintyre Peninsula) summer only : 6-8 daily (30 mn).

   Brodick – pop. 884 – ECD : Wednesday – ✉ ✿ 0770 Brodick.
   🏌 ⌂ 2349, ½ m. from Pier.
   🄱 The Pier ⌂ 2401/2140.

⌂ **Auchrannie** ⟨S⟩, KA27 8BZ, ⌂ 2234, 🚗 – 🖵wc 🅿
   Easter-September – **16 rm** 🖙 11.00/26.00 **st.**

   Lagg – ✉ Kilmory – ✿ 077 087 Sliddery.

🏠 **Lagg,** KA27 8PQ, ⌂ 255, 🚗 – 🖵wc 🅿
   March-October – **M** 7.00/12.00 **t.** – **17 rm** 🖙 20.00/40.00 **t.**

   Lamlash – pop. 908 – ECD : Wednesday except summer – ✉ Brodick – ✿ 077 06 Lamlash.
   🏌 ⌂ 296.

⌂ **Glenisle,** Shore Rd, KA27 8LY, ⌂ 258, ≼, 🚗 – 🖵wc 🅿
   April-October – **15 rm** 🖙 8.55/25.00 **t.**

   Whiting Bay – ECD : Wednesday except summer – ✉ Brodick – ✿ 077 07 Whiting Bay.
   🏌.

🏠 **Whiting Bay,** Shore Rd, KA27 8QJ, ⌂ 247, ≼, 🚗, 🎾 – 🖵 🖵wc 🖵wc 🅿. 🅂 𝘝𝘐𝘚𝘈
   Easter-October and Christmas – **M** (bar lunch)/dinner 10.50 **t.** ⌂ 3.00 – **18 rm** 🖙 17.50/40.00 **t.**

🏕 **Cameronia,** Shore Rd, ⌂ 254 – 🅿
   M (bar lunch)/dinner 5.50 **st.** and a la carte ⌂ 2.50 – **6 rm** 🖙 12.00/24.00 **t.** – SB 34.00/36.00 **st.**

AUCHENCAIRN Kirkcudbright. (Dumfries and Galloway) **401** **402** I 19 – ✉ Castle Douglas –
✿ 055 664.
♦Edinburgh 98 – ♦Dumfries 21 – Stranraer 62.

🏨 **Balcary Bay** ⟨S⟩, Balcary, DG7 1QZ, SE : 2 m. by A 711 ⌂ 217, ≼ Auchencairn bay, hills and
   countryside, 🚗 – 🖵wc 🆎 🅿. 🅂 🄰🄴 ⓪ 𝘝𝘐𝘚𝘈
   March-November – **M** a la carte 9.00/18.00 **t.** ⌂ 3.00 – **9 rm** 🖙 18.00/36.00 **s.**

AUCHTERARDER Perth. (Tayside) 📖 I 15 – pop. 2 838 – ECD : Wednesday – ☎ 076 46.
🐟 Orchil Rd ℘ 2804, SW : 1 m. – 🏌, 🏌, 🏌, 🏌 Gleneagles ℘ 3543.
🅱 Crown Wynd, High St., ℘ 3450 (summer only).
◆Edinburgh 55 – ◆Glasgow 45 – Perth 14.

🏨🏨🏨 **Gleneagles**, PH3 1NF, SW : 1 ½ m. by A 9 ℘ 2231, Telex 76105, ≼, « Championship golf courses and extensive leisure facilities », 🏊, 🏌, 🏊, 🎾, park, %, squash – 📳 📺 🕿 🕭 🅟.
🔼, 🄰 🄰🄴 🄾 🆅🅸🆂🅰
M (see also Eagle's Nest rest.) 15.50/20.50 **t.** and a la carte 🦿 5.50 – 🖙 8.50 – **254 rm** 65.00/130.00 **t.**, **20 suites** 215.00/255.00 **t.**

🏨🏨 **Auchterarder House** ⬥, PH3 1DZ, N : 1 ½ m. on B 8062 ℘ 2939, « Scottish Jacobean house », 🌳, park – 📺 🕿 🅟, 🄰 🆅🅸🆂🅰 ⅜
M (booking essential) 19.00/25.00 **t.** 🦿 4.00 – **11 rm** 🖙 40.25/85.00 **t.**

🏨 **Cairn Lodge** ⬥, Orchill Rd, PH3 1LX, ℘ 2634, 🌳 – 📺 ⌁wc 🕿 🅟. 🄰 🄰🄴. ⅜
closed 3 days Christmas and 3 days New Year – **M** 9.00 **t.** (lunch)/dinner a la carte 12.75/18.70 **t.**
🦿 3.50 – **5 rm** 🖙 35.00/50.00 **t.**

🏨 **Collearn House**, PH3 1DF, ℘ 3553, 🌳 – 📺 ⌁wc 🕿 🅟. 🄰 🄰🄴 🄾 🆅🅸🆂🅰
M 10.00 **t.** and a la carte 🦿 3.30 – **8 rm** 🖙 25.00/40.00 **t.** – SB 28.00/35.00 **st.**

XXXX **Eagle's Nest** (at Gleneagles H.), PH3 1NF, SW : 1 ½ m. by A 9 ℘ 2231, Telex 76105, 🌳 – 🖿
🅟 🄰 🄰🄴 🄾 🆅🅸🆂🅰
closed Sunday and mid January-1 March – **M** (dinner only) a la carte 26.45/33.25 **t.** 🦿 4.25.

AUCHTERHOUSE Angus. (Tayside) 📖 K 14 – ✉ Dundee – ☎ 082 626.
◆Edinburgh 69 – ◆Dundee 7 – Perth 24.

XXX **Old Mansion House** ⬥ with rm, DD3 0QN, ℘ 366, ≼, « 15-17C country house », 🏊 heated, 🌳, park, % – 📺 ⌁wc 🕿 🅟. 🄰 🄰🄴 🄾 🆅🅸🆂🅰
closed 25 December-4 January – **M** 10.50 **t.** (lunch) and a la carte 13.30/21.60 **t.** – **6 rm**
🖙 45.00/70.00 **t.**

AUCHTERMUCHTY Fife (Fife) 📖 K 15 – pop. 1 643 – ✉ Cupar – ☎ 0337.
◆Edinburgh 37 – ◆Dundee 22 – Perth 16 – Stirling 33.

X **The Hollies**, 2 Low Rd, KY14 7AU, ℘ 28279 – 🄰 🆅🅸🆂🅰
closed Sunday dinner, Monday and 2 weeks February – **M** (booking essential) 8.95 **t.** and a la carte 14.95/18.75 **t.**

AUCHTERTOOL Fife (Fife) 📖 K 15 – ECD : Wednesday – ✉ ☎ 0592 Kirkcaldy.
◆Edinburgh 23 – ◆Dundee 38 – Dunfermline 8 – Perth 33.

🏨 **Camilla**, KY2 5XW, ℘ 780590 – 📺 ⌁wc 🕿 🅟. 🄰 🄰🄴 🆅🅸🆂🅰
M 5.25/10.00 **st.** and a la carte 🦿 3.75 – **13 rm** 🖙 25.00/36.00 **st.** – SB 50.00 **st.**

AULTBEA Ross and Cromarty (Highland) 📖 D 10 – ECD : Wednesday – ☎ 044 582.
◆Edinburgh 234 – ◆Inverness 79 – Kyle of Lochalsh 80.

🏨 **Aultbea**, IV22 2HX, ℘ 201, ≼ – ⌁wc 🅟. 🄰 🆅🅸🆂🅰
May-October – **M** (bar lunch)/dinner 9.00 **t.** 🦿 2.10 – **8 rm** 🖙 15.00/35.00 **t.**

AVIEMORE Inverness. (Highland) 📖 I 12 **Scotland G** – pop. 1 510 – ECD : Wednesday – Winter Sports – ☎ 0479.
See : Site★.
Envir. : ⁂★★★ from Cairn Gorm (alt. 4 084 ft.) SE : 8 ½ m. by B 970 (chair lift *AC*) – Highland Wildlife Park★, S : by A 9.
🅱 Grampian Rd ℘ 810363.
◆Edinburgh 129 – ◆Inverness 29 – Perth 85.

🏨🏨 **Stakis Coylumbridge Resort** (Stakis), PH22 1QH, SE : 1 ¾ m. by B 970 ℘ 810661, Telex 75272, ≼, 🏊, 🏊, 🌳, 🎾, % – 📺 🕿 🕭 🅟. 🔼. 🄰 🄰🄴 🄾 🆅🅸🆂🅰
M 6.00/10.00 **t.** and a la carte 🦿 3.60 – 🖙 3.90 – **173 rm** 39.50/70.00 **t.**, **4 suites** 80.00/90.00 **t.** – SB (except Easter, Christmas and New Year) 70.00/80.00 **st.**

🏨🏨 **Stakis Strathspey** (Stakis), Aviemore Centre, PH22 1PF, ℘ 810681, Telex 75213, ≼ Cairngorms – 📳 📺 🅟. 🄰 🄰🄴 🄾 🆅🅸🆂🅰 ⅜
M (bar lunch)/dinner 10.00 **st.** 🦿 4.00 – 🖙 3.90 – **89 rm** 35.00/55.00 **st.** – SB (December-February) 56.00/80.00 **st.**

🏨🏨 **Post House** (T.H.F.), Aviemore Centre, PH22 1PJ, ℘ 810771, Telex 75597, ≼ – 📳 📺 ⌁wc 🕭 🕭 🔼. 🄰 🄰🄴 🄾 🆅🅸🆂🅰
M (bar lunch)/dinner 10.50 **st.** and a la carte 🦿 3.40 – 🖙 5.65 – **103 rm** 40.00/54.00 **st.**

🏨🏨 **Badenoch**, Aviemore Centre, PH22 1PH, ℘ 810261, ≼ – 📳 📺 ⌁wc 🕿 🅟. 🄰 🄰🄴 🄾 🆅🅸🆂🅰
M (bar lunch)/dinner 9.00 **st.** and a la carte 🦿 3.00 – **81 rm** 🖙 15.00/45.80 **st.** – SB (except Easter, Christmas and New Year) 32.00/44.00 **st.**

AUSTIN-ROVER   Main Rd ℘ 810492   FORD   115 Grampian Rd ℘ 810232

Envir. : Alloway★ (Burns' Cottage and Museum★) S : 3 m. by B 7024 BZ – Culzean Castle★ (Setting★★★, Oval staircase★★) SW : 14 m. by A 719 BZ.

📷 Belleisle ⚲ 0292 (Alloway) 41258 BZ – 📷 Dalmilling, Westwood Av., Whitletts ⚲ 263893 BZ.

🛈 39 Sandgate ⚲ 284196.

◆Edinburgh 81 – ◆Glasgow 35.

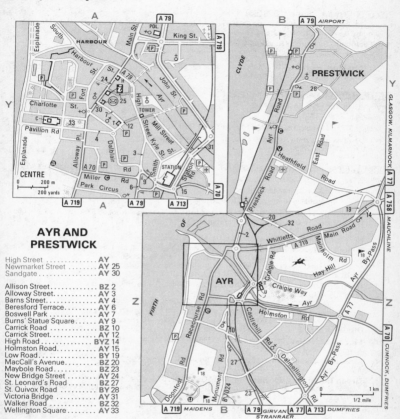

AYR AND PRESTWICK

🏨 **Pickwick,** 19 Racecourse Rd, KA7 2TD, ⚲ 260111 – 📺 ⌂wc 🛁wc ☎ **P.** **VISA**. ⚶ BZ **e**
M 10.00/15.00 t. and a la carte 🍷 2.00 – **15 rm** ⌁ 33.00/52.00 t. – SB (November-March) (weekends only) 40.00 **st.**

🏨 **Marine Court,** 12 Fairfield Rd, KA7 2AR, ⚲ 267461, 🔲 – 📺 ⌂wc 🛁wc ☎ **P.** ⚘ ☒ AE ① **VISA** AY **a**
M 9.50/11.50 t. and a la carte 🍷 2.95 – **29 rm** ⌁ 38.50/55.00 t. – SB 60.00/80.00 **st.**

🏨 **Belleisle House** ⚲, Doonfoot Rd, Belleisle Park, KA7 4DU, S : 1 ½ m. on A 719 ⚲ 42331, ≤ – 📺 ⌂wc 🛁wc ☎ **P.** ⚘ ☒ AE ① **VISA** BZ **u**
M 5.95/10.95 t. and a la carte 🍷 2.75 – **17 rm** ⌁ 31.50/44.00 t. – SB (weekends only) 52.00/60.00 **st.**

🏠 **Clifton,** 19 Miller Rd, KA7 2AX, ⚲ 264521 – 📺 🛁wc **P.** ☒ AE **VISA**. ⚶ AY **c**
11 rm ⌁ 20.00/32.00 **st.**

at Alloway S : 3 m. on A 719 – BZ – ✉ ✆ 0292 Ayr :

🏨 **Balgarth,** 8 Dunure Rd, KA7 4HR, on A 719 ⚲ 42441, 🌺 – 📺 ⌂wc 🛁wc ☎ **P.** ☒ AE ① **VISA**
M 9.95 t. and a la carte 7.65/14.60 t. 🍷 2.75 – **15 rm** ⌁ 18.00/36.00 t.

AYR

ALFA-ROMEO, FIAT Galloway Av. ✆ 260416
AUSTIN-ROVER, DAIMLER-JAGUAR 18 Holmston Rd ✆ 266944
MERCEDES-BENZ Heathfield Industrial Estate ✆ 282727
PEUGEOT-TALBOT Alloway Pl. ✆ 263140

SAAB, SEAT Cambuslea Rd ✆ 266146
TOYOTA 65 Peebles St. ✆ 267606
VAUXHALL 196 Prestwick Rd ✆ 261631
VOLVO Burn's Statue Sq. ✆ 282711
VW, AUDI 24 Dalblair Rd ✆ 269522

AYTON Berwick. (Borders) **401 402** N 16 – ECD : Thursday – ✆ 089 07.
Envir. : Manderston★, SW : 10 m. by B 6355 and A 6105 – Foulden★ S : 4 m. – Eyemouth (Museum★) N : 2 m. by B 6255 – St. Abb's Head★★, N : 5 m. – Fast Castle (Site★★) NW : 7 m. off A 1107.
🔓 at Eyemouth, Gunsgreen House ✆ 0390 (Eyemouth) 50551, N : 3 m. by A 6355.
♦Edinburgh 48 – Berwick-upon-Tweed 8.

🏠   **Red Lion,** High St., TD14 5QP, ✆ 81400 – **P.** 🔼 AE ⓘ 𝘝𝘐𝘚𝘈
M a la carte 7.75/9.55 – **9 rm** � 11.50/21.00 **st.**

BALLACHULISH Argyll. (Highland) **401** E 13 – ECD : Wednesday – ✆ 085 52.
Envir. : Glen Coe★★, E : 6 m. by A 82.
🛈 ✆ 296 (summer only).
♦Edinburgh 117 – ♦Inverness 80 – Kyle of Lochalsh 90 – ♦Oban 38.

🏠   **Lyn Leven,** White St., PA39 4JW, ✆ 392, ≤ – 📺 🗖wc **P.**
8 rm ⊊ 12.00/28.00.

BALLATER Aberdeen. (Grampian) **401** K 12 – pop. 1 051 – ECD : Thursday – ✆ 0338.
🕦₈ ✆ 55567.
🛈 Station Sq. ✆ 55306 (summer only).
♦Edinburgh 111 – ♦Aberdeen 41 – ♦Inverness 70 – Perth 67.

🏨   **Craigendarroch Hotel and Country Club** ≫, Braemar Rd, AB3 5XA, on A 93 ✆ 55858, Telex 739952, ≤ Dee valley and Grampians, 🔲, 🚿, squash – 🍴 📺 ☎ **P.** 🏇 🔼 AE ⓘ 𝘝𝘐𝘚𝘈 ⊱
M 12.50/18.75 **st.** – **23 rm** ⊊ 65.00/80.00 **st.** – SB 58.25 **st.**

🏠   **Tullich Lodge** ≫, AB3 5SB, E : 1 ½ m. on A 93 ✆ 55406, ≤ Dee valley and Grampians, « Country house atmosphere », 🚿 – 🗖wc 🗖wc ☎ **P.** 🔼
Mid March-mid December – **M** (bar lunch) (booking essential)/dinner 16.00 **st.** 🍷 4.50 – **10 rm** ⊊ 42.00/84.00 **st.** – SB 100.00/110.00 **st.**

🏠   **Darroch Learg,** Braemar Rd, AB3 5UX, ✆ 55443, ≤ Dee Valley and Grampians, 🚿 – 📺 🗖wc 🗖wc **P.** 𝘝𝘐𝘚𝘈
February-October – **M** 5.00/10.00 **st.** 🍷 2.00 – **23 rm** ⊊ 18.00/42.00 **st.**

🏠   **Alexandra,** 12 Bridge Sq., AB3 6QJ, ✆ 55376 – 📺 🗖wc **P.** 🔼 AE ⓘ 𝘝𝘐𝘚𝘈
M (bar lunch) /dinner 14.00 **st.** and a la carte 🍷 3.00 – **6 rm** ⊊ 14.00/30.00 **st.** – SB 46.00/56.00 **st.**

🏠   **Moorside House,** 26 Braemar Rd, AB3 5RL, ✆ 55492, 🚿 – 🗖wc **P.** ⊱
March-October – **8 rm** ⊊ 17.00/22.00.

🏠   **Morvada,** Braemar Rd, AB5 3RL, ✆ 55501, 🚿 – 🗖wc **P.** ⊱
May-October – **7 rm** ⊊ 10.00/24.00 **st.**

✗   **Green Inn** with rm, 9 Victoria Rd, AB3 5QQ, ✆ 55701 – 📺 🗖wc. 🔼 𝘝𝘐𝘚𝘈
March-October – **M** (restricted lunch) 7.75/12.45 **t.** and a la carte 7.60/10.10 **t.** – **3 rm** ⊊ –/25.00 **t.**

PEUGEOT Riverside Garage, Aboyne Rd ✆ 85323

BALLOCH Dunbarton (Strathclyde) **401** G 15 – ✆ 038 985 Arden.
Envir. : Loch Lomond★★ – Ben Lomond★★ – Luss N : 9 m. by A 82.
🛈 ✆ 0389 (Alexandria) 53533 (summer only).
♦Edinburgh 62 – ♦Glasgow 18 – Helensburgh 7.

🏨   **Lomond Castle** ≫, Arden, G83 8RB, N : 2 m. on A 82 ✆ 681, ≤, 🔲, 🚿, 🚿, park – 📺 🗖wc ☎ **P.** 🏇 🔼 AE ⓘ 𝘝𝘐𝘚𝘈
M 8.00/11.50 **t.** and a la carte – **21 rm** ⊊ 32.00/65.00 **t.** – SB (except summer)(weekends only) 39.00/59.00 **st.**

BALMACARA Ross and Cromarty (Highland) **401** D 12 – ECD : Wednesday – ✉ Kyle of Lochalsh – ✆ 059 986.
♦Edinburgh 197 – Kyle of Lochalsh 4.5.

🏨   **Balmacara,** IV40 8DH, ✆ 283, ≤ coast and mountains – 🗖wc 🗖wc **P.** 🔼 𝘝𝘐𝘚𝘈
M (bar lunch)/dinner 10.50 **t.** and a la carte 🍷 3.50 – **30 rm** ⊊ 22.50/45.00 **t.**

BANAVIE Inverness. (Highland) **401** E 13 – see Fort William.

522

BANCHORY Kincardine. (Grampian) **401** M 12 – pop. 4 683 – ECD : Thursday – ✆ 033 02.

Envir. : Crathes Castle**, E : 2 m. by A 93 – Craigievar Castle***, N : 17 m. by A 980 – Castle Fraser* (exterior**) N : 14 m. by A 980 and B 977.

☕ Kinneskie ✆ 2365 – 🟢 Torphins ✆ 033 982 (Torphins) 493, NW : 6 m.

🅰 Dee St. Car Park ✆ 2000 (summer only).

♦Edinburgh 118 – ♦Aberdeen 17 – ♦Dundee 55 – ♦Inverness 94.

🏨 **Banchory Lodge** ♨, Dee St., AB3 3HS, ✆ 2625, ≤, « Part 18C house on River Dee », ⊸,
🔲 – 🔲 ⌷wc 🅿 ⚙ 🆎 ⓪ 🆅🆂🅰
closed 12 December-28 January – **M** 7.50/16.50 **st.** and a la carte – **24 rm** ⊑ 30.00/
50.00 **st.**

🏨 **Raemoir House** ♨, AB3 4ED, N : 2 ½ m. on A 980 ✆ 4884, ≤, « 18C mansion with 16C
Ha-House », 🌳, park – 🔲 ⌷wc 🕿 🅿 🆎 ⓪ 🆅🆂🅰
M (bar lunch Monday to Saturday)/dinner 15.50 t. ▯ 3.75 – **22 rm** ⊑ 35.00/60.00 t. –
SB 70.00 **st.**

🏨 **Tor-Na-Coille** ♨, Inchmarlo Rd, AB4 3AB, ✆ 2242, 🌳, park – ▐◎ 🔲 ⌷wc ⋔wc 🕿 🅿 🆎
🆎 ⓪ 🆅🆂🅰
M (bar lunch)/dinner 11.50 t. and a la carte ▯ 3.50 – **23 rm** ⊑ 35.00/50.00 t. – SB (weekends
only) 50.00/70.00 **st.**

AUSTIN-ROVER North Deeside Rd ✆ 2255   RENAULT North Deeside Rd ✆ 2847

BANCHORY-DEVENICK Aberdeen. (Grampian) – see Aberdeen.

*In alta stagione, e soprattutto nelle stazioni turistiche,
e prudente prenotare con un certo anticipo.
Avvertire immediatamente l'albergatore se non potete più
occupare la camera prenotata.
Se scrivete ad un albergo all'estero, allegate alla vostra
lettera un tagliando - risposta internazionale (disponibile presso gli uffici postali)*

BANFF Banff. (Grampian) **401** M 10 Scotland G – pop. 3 843 – ECD : Wednesday – ✆ 026 12.

See : Site* – Duff House* – Mercat Cross*.

☕ Royal Tarlair, Macduff ✆ 0261 (Macduff) 32897.

🅰 Collie Lodge ✆ 2419 (summer only).

♦Edinburgh 177 – ♦Aberdeen 47 – Fraserburgh 26 – ♦Inverness 74.

🏨 **Banff Springs,** Golden Knowes Rd, AB4 2JE, W : ¾ m. on A 98 ✆ 2881, ≤ – 🔲 ⌷wc ⋔wc
🕿 🅿 🆎 🆎 🆎 ⓪ 🆅🆂🅰 🌳 🍴
M (bar lunch)/dinner 10.00 t. and a la carte ▯ 3.80 – **30 rm** ⊑ 27.60/38.00 t., **2 suites** 54.00 **st.**
– SB (weekends only) 44.00/48.00 **st.**

🏠 **County,** 32 High St., AB4 1AE, ✆ 5353, ≤, 🌳 – 🔲 ⌷wc 🕿 🅿 🆎 ⓪
M 5.75/15.50 t. ▯ 3.50 – **7 rm** ⊑ 23.00/48.00 t. – SB 45.00/60.00 **st.**

↟ **Carmelite House,** 40 Low St., AB4 1AY, ✆ 2152 – 🅿
8 rm ⊑ 10.50/23.00 **st.**

AUSTIN-ROVER Castle St. ✆ 2473   FORD Bridge Rd ✆ 2673

BANNISKIRK Caithness (Highland) – see Thurso.

BARRA (Isle of) Inverness. (Outer Hebrides) (Western Isles) **401** X 12 13 – pop. 1 232.

🛫 at North Bay ✆ 041 889 1311.

🚢 by Caledonian MacBrayne : from Castlebay to Oban summer only : 1-2 weekly (5-8 h) – to
Lochboisdale (South Uist) 1-4 weekly (2 h).

🚢 by Western Isles Council : to Vatersay Saturday only (5 mn).

   Castlebay – ✉ ✆ 087 14 Castlebay.
   🅰 ✆ 336 (summer only).

🏨 **Isle of Barra** ♨, Tangusdale Beach, PA80 5XW, NW : 2 m. on A 888 ✆ 383, ≤ sea and
mountains – ⌷wc 🅿 🆎 🆎 ⓪ 🆅🆂🅰
May-October – **M** (bar lunch)/dinner 15.00 **st.** ▯ 2.95 – **36 rm** ⊑ 27.50/45.00 **st.** –
SB 55.00/65.00 **st.**

BARRHEAD Renfrew. (Strathclyde) **401** **402** G 16 – pop. 18 419 – ECD : Tuesday – ✉ ✆ 041
Glasgow.

♦Edinburgh 56 – ♦Ayr 32 – ♦Glasgow 10.

🏠 **Dalmeny Park,** Lochlibo Rd, G78 1LG, SW : ½ m. on A 736 ✆ 881 9211, « Gardens » – 🔲
⋔wc 🕿 🅿 🆎 🆎 ⓪ 🆅🆂🅰 🍴
closed 26 December and 1-2 January – **M** (closed Sunday dinner to non residents)
7.50/11.00 **st.** and a la carte ▯ 3.75 – **18 rm** ⊑ 30.00/48.00 **st.** – SB (weekends only) 66.00/
82.00 **st.**

21

BATHGATE W. Lothian (Lothian) **401** J 16 – pop. 14 429 – ECD : Wednesday – 🕿 0506.

Envir. : Cairnpapple Hill★ (burial cairn★) N : 3 m.

🖪 Edinburgh Rd ♟ 52232.

♦Edinburgh 20 – ♦Glasgow 28.

  🏛 **Golden Circle** (Swallow), Blackburn Rd, EH48 2EL, S : 1 ¾ m. on B 792 ♟ 53771, Telex 72606 – 🔊 📺 🚻wc 🛎wc ⚦ 🅿. 🏊. 🔼 🄰🄴 ⑩ 𝗩𝗜𝗦𝗔
    M 6.25/9.25 **st.** and a la carte ♨ 3.95 – **74 rm** � 37.00/49.00 **st.** – SB 48.00 **st.**

FORD Linlithgow Rd ♟ 56685   VW, AUDI Blackburn Rd ♟ 52948

BEARSDEN Dunbarton. (Strathclyde) **401** G 16 – pop. 27 146 – ECD : Tuesday and Saturday – ✉ 🕿 041 Glasgow.

♦Edinburgh 51 – ♦Glasgow 5.

  ✗ **La Bavarde,** 19 New Kirk Rd, G61 9JS, ♟ 942 2202 – 🔼 🄰🄴 ⑩ 𝗩𝗜𝗦𝗔
    closed Sunday, Monday, last 3 weeks July and 2 weeks Christmas – **M** 5.00/13.50 **t.** and a la carte 9.85/12.70 **t.** ♨ 2.50.

  ✗ **Amritsar Tandoori,** 9 Kirk Rd, G61 3RG, ♟ 942 7710, Indian rest. – 🔼 🄰🄴 ⑩ 𝗩𝗜𝗦𝗔
    closed Sunday lunch, Christmas Day and 1 January – **M** a la carte 7.45/12.00 **t.** ♨ 3.00.

PEUGEOT-TALBOT, VOLVO Bearsden Cross ♟   PORSCHE Maxwell Av. ♟ 943 1155
942 2225

BEATTOCK Dumfries. (Dumfries and Galloway) **401 402** J 18 – ✉ Moffat – 🕿 068 33.

♦Edinburgh 60 – ♦Carlisle 41 – ♦Dumfries 20 – ♦Glasgow 59.

  🏛 **Auchen Castle** 🦢, DG10 9SH, N : 2 m. by A 74 ♟ 407, ≼, 🎣, 🛲, park – 📺 🚻wc 🛎wc 🕿
    🅿. 🔼 🄰🄴 ⑩ 𝗩𝗜𝗦𝗔
    closed 22 December-4 January – **M** (bar lunch)/dinner 11.60 **st.** ♨ 3.05 – **25 rm**
    ⊐ 30.00/45.00 **st.** – SB October-July 45.00/49.00 **st.**

  🏠 **Beattock House,** DG10 9QB, ♟ 403, 🛲 – 🛎wc 🅿. 🄰🄴 𝗩𝗜𝗦𝗔
    M a la carte 5.25/10.00 **t.** ♨ 3.75 – **7 rm** ⊐ 17.50/37.00 **t.**

  ☛ *Pour être inscrit au **guide Michelin***
    - pas de piston,
    - pas de pot-de-vin !

BEAULY Inverness. (Highland) **401** G 11 – pop. 1 135 – ECD : Thursday – 🕿 0463.

♦Edinburgh 69 – ♦Inverness 13 – ♦Wick 25.

  🏠 **Priory,** The Square, IV4 7BX, ♟ 782309 – 📺 🚻wc 🛎wc 🕿. 🔼 🄰🄴 ⑩ 𝗩𝗜𝗦𝗔
    M a la carte 5.40/9.95 **t.** ♨ 3.00 – **12 rm** ⊐ 21.95/39.50 **t.** – SB (weekends only) 37.50/
    47.50 **st.**

SUBARU High St. ♟ 782266

BELLOCHANTUY Argyll. (Strathclyde) **401** C 17 – see Kintyre (Peninsula).

BENBECULA Inverness. (Western Isles) **401** X 11 – see Uist (Isles of).

BETTYHILL Sutherland (Highland) **401** H 8 – ✉ Thurso – 🕿 064 12.

🖪 ♟ 342 (summer only).

♦Edinburgh 225 – ♦Inverness 13 – Thurso 31.

  ☝ **Bettyhill,** KW14 7SS, ♟ 202, ≼, 🎣 – 🛎wc 🅿
    April-October – **M** (bar lunch)/dinner 10.00 **t.** ♨ 4.00 – **22 rm** ⊐ 13.00/29.50 **t.**

BIRSAY Orkney (Orkney Islands) **401** K 6 – see Orkney Islands (Mainland).

BLACKFORD Perth. (Tayside) **401** I 15 – pop. 551 – ECD : Wednesday – ✉ Auchterarder – 🕿 076 482.

♦Edinburgh 53 – ♦Glasgow 44 – Perth 18.

  ☝ **Blackford,** Moray St., PH4 1QF, ♟ 246 – 📺 🚻wc 🛎wc 🅿. 🔼 𝗩𝗜𝗦𝗔
    M (bar meals only) – **4 rm** ⊐ 16.50/28.00 **t.**

BLAIR ATHOLL Perth (Tayside) **401** I 13 – 🕿 079681.

♦Edinburgh 78 – ♦Inverness 78 – Perth 34.

  🏛 Atholl Arms, PH18 5SG, ♟ 205 – 📺 🛎wc 🅿
    30 rm.

BLAIRGOWRIE Perth (Tayside) 🗺️ J 14 – pop. 7 028 – ✆ 0250.

🎁 Wellmeadow ℰ 2960 (2258 when closed)(summer only).

◆Edinburgh 60 – ◆Dundee 19 – Perth 16.

> 🏨 **Kinloch House** ॐ, PH10 6SG, W : 3 m. on A 923 ℰ 025 084 (Essendy) 237, ≼, « Country house atmosphere », 🚗, park – 🛁wc �🛁wc 🅿. 🔺 🄰🄴 ➀
> *closed 10 to 28 December* – **M** (bar lunch)/dinner 12.75 **st.** – **12 rm** 🖙 29.50/48.00 **st.**

> 🏨 **Altamount House** ॐ, Coupar Angus Rd, PH10 6JN, ℰ 3512, 🚗 – 📺 🛁wc ⍰wc 🅿. 🔺 🄰🄴 ➀ 𝚅𝙸𝚂𝙰. ❀
> *closed 4 January-13 February and 9 to 19 October* – **M** *(closed Monday dinner and mid October-Easter to non residents)* (bar lunch Monday to Saturday)/dinner 11.50 **t.** – **7 rm** 🖙 25.00/50.00 **t.**

> 🏨 Rosemount Golf, Golf Course Rd, PH10 6LJ, SE : 1 ¾ m. off A 923 ℰ 2604, 🚗 – ⍰wc ⍰wc 🅿 – **12 rm**.

BLAIRLOGIE Stirling. (Central) – see Stirling.

BOAT OF GARTEN Inverness. (Highland) 🗺️ I 12 – ECD : Thursday – ✆ 047 983.

🏌️ ℰ 282.

🎁 Boat Hotel Car park ℰ 307 (summer only).

◆Edinburgh 133 – ◆Inverness 28 – ◆Perth 89.

> 🏨 **The Boat**, PH24 3BH, ℰ 258, 🚗 – 📺 🛁wc ⍰wc ☎ 🅿. 🔺 🄰🄴 ➀ 𝚅𝙸𝚂𝙰
> *closed 1 November-20 December* – **M** 11.55/12.50 **st.** – **34 rm** 🖙 20.00/40.00 **st.** – SB 52.00/60.00 **st.**

> 🏠 **Moorfield House**, Deshar Rd, PH24 3BN, ℰ 646, 🚗 – ⍰wc 🅿
> *closed 1 November-20 December* – **6 rm** 🖙 12.00/30.00 **t.**

BONAR BRIDGE Sutherland (Highland) 🗺️ G 10 – pop. 533 – ECD : Wednesday – ✆ 086 32 Ardgay.

🏌️ ℰ 577.

🎁 Ardgay ℰ 333 (summer only).

◆Edinburgh 206 – ◆Inverness 50 – ◆Wick 76.

> 🏨 **Bridge**, Dornoch Rd, IV24 3EB, ℰ 204, ≼ – 📺 🛁wc ⍰wc ☎ 🅿. 🔺 🄰🄴 ➀ 𝚅𝙸𝚂𝙰
> **M** (bar lunch)/dinner a la carte 7.10/16.60 **t.** 🍷 2.50 – **16 rm** 🖙 18.00/40.00 **t.** – SB 40.00 **st.**

BONNYRIGG Midlothian (Lothian) 🗺️ 🗺️ K 16 – see Edinburgh.

BOTHWELL Lanark. (Strathclyde) 🗺️ 🗺️ H 16 **Scotland G** – ✆ 0698.
See : Castle★.
Envir. : Blantyre : David Livingstone Centre (Museum★) off A 724.
◆Edinburgh 39 – ◆Glasgow 8.5.

> 🏨 **Silvertrees**, 27 Silverwells Crescent, G71 8DP, ℰ 852311, 🚗 – 📺 🛁wc ☎ 🅿. 🔺 🄰🄴 ➀ 𝚅𝙸𝚂𝙰
> **M** *(closed Sunday dinner)* 7.45/9.50 **t.** and a la carte 🍷 3.70 – **26 rm** 🖙 40.50/44.00 **t.**, **2 suites** 46.00 **t.**

BOWMORE Argyll. (Strathclyde) 🗺️ B 16 – see Islay (Isle of).

BRAE Shetland (Shetland Islands) 🗺️ P 2 – see Shetland Islands (Mainland).

BRAEMAR Aberdeen. (Grampian) 🗺️ J 12 – ECD : Thursday except summer – ✆ 033 83.
Envir. : Lin O' Dee★, W : 7 m.
🏌️ Cluniebank Rd ℰ 618.
🎁 Balnellan Rd ℰ 600 (summer only).
◆Edinburgh 85 – ◆Aberdeen 58 – ◆Dundee 51 – Perth 51.

> 🏠 **Callater Lodge**, 9 Glenshee Rd, AB3 5YQ, ℰ 275, 🚗 – 🅿. 🔺 𝚅𝙸𝚂𝙰
> *closed mid October-26 December* – **9 rm** 🖙 12.00/24.00 **st.**

AUSTIN-ROVER Ballater Rd ℰ 301

BRESSAY (Isle of) Shetland (Shetland Islands) 🗺️ Q 3 – Shipping services : see Shetland Islands.

Pleasant hotels and restaurants
are shown in the Guide by a red sign.
Please send us the names
of any where you have enjoyed your stay.
Your Michelin Guide will be even better.

🏨🏨🏨 ... 🏠

XXXXX ... X

BRIDGE OF ALLAN Stirling. (Central) **401** I 15 – pop. 4 551 – ECD : Wednesday – ☎ 0786.
Envir. : Dollar (Castle Campbell★ (site★★★) E : 12 m. by A 91 – Wallace Monument (፨★★) S : 2 m.
by A 9 – Doune★ (Castle★, Motor Museum★) NW : 7 m. by A 9 and B 824.

ⓖ Sunnylaw ℰ 83233, N : ½ m. off A 9.
♦Edinburgh 21 – ♦Dundee 54 – ♦Glasgow 33.

⌂ **Royal,** 55 Henderson St., FK9 4HG, ℰ 832284, 舞 – 圭 TV ⌂wc ☎ Ⓟ ⚠ ☒ AE ⓪ VISA
M (bar lunch)/dinner 10.00 **st.** ₰ 2.90 – **33 rm** ⊊ 23.00/52.00 **st.** – SB (September-May) 53.95 **st.**

BRIDGE OF CALLY Perth. (Tayside) **401** J 14 – ✉ Blairgowrie – ☎ 025 086.
♦Edinburgh 66 – ♦Dundee 25 – Perth 22.

☎ **Bridge of Cally,** PH10 7JJ, on A 93 ℰ 231, ⌇, 舞 – ⌂wc ⌂wc Ⓟ ☒ ⓪ VISA ⚶
closed November – **M** (bar lunch)/dinner 11.00 **t.** ₰ 2.35 – **9 rm** ⊊ 18.00/32.00 **t.**

BRODICK Bute. (Strathclyde) **401 402** E 17 – see Arran (Isle of).

BRORA Sutherland (Highland) **401** I 9 – pop. 1 728 – ECD : Wednesday – ☎ 0408.
♦Edinburgh 234 – ♦Inverness 78 – ♦Wick 49.

⌂ **Links,** Golf Rd, KW9 6QS, ℰ 21225, ≼ – TV ⌂wc Ⓟ ☒ AE ⓪ VISA
closed January and February – **M** 6.50/12.50 **st.** and a la carte ₰ 2.75 – **26 rm** ⊊ 24.00/55.00 **t.**
– SB 55.00/70.00 **st.**

BROUGHTON Peebles. (Borders) **401 402** J 17 – ECD : Wednesday – ✉ Biggar (Lanark) –
☎ 089 94 – ⓖ Broughton Rd, Biggar ℰ 0899 (Biggar) 20618, W : 6 m.
♦Edinburgh 30 – Moffat 24 – Peebles 12.

⌂ **Greenmantle,** Main St., ML12 6HQ, ℰ 302 – TV ⌂wc Ⓟ ☒ AE ⓪ VISA
M 8.50/9.50 **t.** and a la carte ₰ 3.25 – **6 rm** ⊊ 21.00/38.00 **t.** – SB 40.00 **st.**

BROUGHTY FERRY Angus (Tayside) **401** L 14 – see Dundee.

BUCKIE Banff. (Grampian) **401** L 10 – pop. 7 869 – ECD : Wednesday – ☎ 0542.
ⓖ Buckpool, Barrhill Rd ℰ 32236 – ⓖ Strathlene ℰ 31798, E : ½ m.
♦Edinburgh 195 – ♦Aberdeen 66 – ♦Inverness 56.

☎ **Cluny,** 2 High St., AB5 1AL, ℰ 32922 – TV ⌂wc ⌂wc Ⓟ ☒ AE ⓪ VISA
closed 1 and 2 January – **M** *(closed Monday lunch)* 4.25 **st.** (lunch) and a la carte 5.75/10.75 **t.**
₰ 2.40 – **16 rm** ⊊ 13.50/33.00 **t.** – SB 43.00/55.00 **st.**

at Drybridge S : 2 m. by A 942 – ✉ Drybridge – ☎ 0542 Buckie :

XX **Old Monastery,** AB5 2JB, SW : 2 m. ℰ 32660, ≼, « Former chapel overlooking Spey Bay »
– Ⓟ
closed Sunday, Monday, 3 weeks January, 2 weeks October and 3 days at Christmas –
M a la carte 10.15/12.70 **t.** ₰ 2.70.

VAUXHALL-OPEL Marine Place ℰ 32327

BUCKSBURN Aberdeen. (Grampian) **401** N 12 – see Aberdeen.

BUNCHREW Inverness (Highland) – see Inverness.

BUNESSAN Argyll. (Strathclyde) **401** B 15 – see Mull (Isle of).

BUSBY Lanark. (Strathclyde) **401 402** H 16 – see Glasgow.

BUTE (Isle of) Bute. (Strathclyde) **401 402** E 16 – pop. 7 733.
⛴ by Caledonian MacBrayne : from Rothesay to Wemyss Bay, summer only : 4-13 daily (30 mn)
– from Rhubodach to Colintraive, summer only : frequent services daily (5 mn).
🛈 Rothesay : The Pier ℰ 0700 (Rothesay) 2151.

CAIRNGORM (Mountains) Inverness. (Highland) **401** J 12 Scotland G.
See : ፨★★★ from Cairn Gorm (alt. 4 048 ft.) (chairlift AC).
Hotels see : Aviemore NW, Braemar SE.

CAIRNRYAN Wigtown. (Dumfries and Galloway) **401 402** E 19.
⛴ by Townsend Thoresen : to Larne 4-6 daily (2 to 2 h 30 mn).
♦ Edinburgh 126 – ♦ Ayr 45 – Stranraer 6.5.
Hotel see : Stranraer S : 6 ½ m.

CALLANDER Perth. (Central) 401 H 15 **Scotland G** – pop. 2 286 – ECD : Wednesday except summer – ☎ 0877.

See : Site★.

Envir. : The Trossachs★★★: Loch Katrine★★ – Hilltop Viewpoint (❄★★★) W : 10 m. by A 821 – Inchmahone Priory (Monument★) S : 6 m. by A 81 and B 8034.

🛆 ℰ 30090.

🖪 Leny Rd ℰ 30342 (summer only).

◆Edinburgh 52 – ◆Glasgow 43 – ◆Oban 71 – Perth 41.

🏛 **Roman Camp** ⌂, Main St., FK17 8BG, ℰ 30003, ≼, « 17C hunting lodge in extensive gardens », 🏕, park – 📺 ⊏wc ▥wc ☎ 🅿
Mid March-November – **M** (lunch by arrangement) 12.00/18.50 st. ⓘ 3.75 – **11 rm** ⊆ 38.00/66.00 st., **3 suites** 72.00/75.00 st. – SB (except summer) 70.00/88.00 st.

🏠 **Lubnaig**, Leny Feus, FK17 8AS, ℰ 30376, 🚗 – ▥wc 🅿
Easter-mid November – **M** (dinner only) 10.00 st. ⓘ 2.50 – **10 rm** ⊆ 14.50/35.00 st.

🏠 **Pinewood**, Leny Rd, FK17 8AP, ℰ 30111 – ⊏wc ▥wc 🅿. ⊡ Æ
M (lunch by arrangement)/dinner 9.00 t. ⓘ 2.90 – **16 rm** ⊆ 13.25/29.25 t. – SB 41.20/44.50 st.

🏤 **Bridgend**, Bridgend, FK17 8AA, ℰ 30130, 🚗 – 📺 ⊏wc ▥wc ☎ 🅿. ⊡ Æ ⓞ *VISA*
closed November – **M** (bar lunch)/dinner a la carte 8.20/13.80 t. ⓘ 2.20 – **7 rm** ⊆ 26.00/40.00 t. – SB 60.00 st.

🏠 **Highland House**, 8 South Church St, FK17 8BN, ℰ 30269 – ▥wc
April-October – **10 rm** ⊆ 10.50/23.50 t.

🏠 **Glenorchy**, Leny Rd, FK17 8AL, ℰ 30329 – ⊏wc ▥wc 🅿. *VISA*. ⌧
11 rm ⊆ 12.50/31.00 t.

CAMPBELTOWN Argyll (Strathclyde) 401 D 17 – see Kintyre (Peninsula).

CANNA (Isle of) Inverness. (Highland) 401 A 12 – Shipping Services : see Mallaig.

CANONBIE Dumfries (Dumfries and Galloway) 401 402 L 18 – ☎ 054 15 Canonbie.

◆Edinburgh 80 – ◆Carlisle 15 – ◆Dumfries 34.

XX **Riverside Inn** with rm, DG14 0UX, ℰ 295 – 📺 ⊏wc 🅿. ⊡ *VISA*. ⌧
closed 2 weeks February – **M** (closed Sunday lunch) (booking essential)(bar lunch)/dinner 13.50 t. ⓘ 2.75 – **6 rm** ⊆ 34.00/46.00 t. – SB (November-April) 48.00 st.

CARFRAEMILL Berwick (Borders) 401 402 L 16 – see Lauder.

CARRADALE Argyll. (Strathclyde) 401 D 17 – see Kintyre (Peninsula).

CASTLEBAY Inverness. (Outer Hebrides) (Western Isles) 401 X 13 – see Barra (Isle of).

CASTLE DOUGLAS Kirkcudbright. (Dumfries and Galloway) 401 402 I 19 **Scotland G** – pop. 3 546 – ECD : Thursday – ☎ 0556.

Envir. : Threave Garden★★ and Castle★, SW : 3 m. by A 75.

🛆 ℰ 2801.

🖪 Markethill ℰ 2611 (summer only).

◆Edinburgh 98 – ◆Ayr 49 – ◆Dumfries 18 – Stranraer 57.

🏠 **King's Arms**, St. Andrew St., DG7 1EL, ℰ 2626 – ⊏wc ▥wc 🅿. ⊡ Æ ⓞ *VISA*
M (bar lunch)/dinner 12.00 t. and a la carte ⓘ 3.00 – **14 rm** ⊆ 17.00/43.00 st. – SB 55.00/57.00 st.

AUSTIN-ROVER Morris House ℰ 2560
FORD, LADA Oakwell Rd ℰ 2805

VAUXHALL-OPEL King St. ℰ 2038

CATTERLINE Kincardine (Grampian) 401 N 13 – see Stonehaven.

CLACHAN SEIL Argyll. (Strathclyde) 401 D 15 – ECD : Wednesday – ✉ Oban – ☎ 085 23 Balvicar.

◆Edinburgh 137 – ◆Oban 14.

🏤 **Willowburn** ⌂, Isle of Seil, PA34 4TJ, ℰ 276, ≼ – ▥wc 🅿. ⊡ Æ ⓞ *VISA*
M 7.50 st. and a la carte ⓘ 3.20 – **6 rm** ⊆ 11.00/33.00 st. – SB (October-May) 35.00/45.00 st.

CLAONAIG (Cap) Argyll. (Strathclyde) 401 402 D 16 – Shipping Services : see Kintyre (Peninsula).

CLEISH Fife. (Tayside) 401 J 15 – see Kinross.

CLOSEBURN Dumfries (Dumfries and Galloway) 401 402 I 18 – see Thornhill.

COLINTRAIVE Argyll. (Strathclyde) **401 402** E 16 – ✪ 070 084.

⚓ by Caledonian MacBrayne : to Rhubodach (Isle of Bute) summer only : frequent services daily (5 mn).

♦Edinburgh 127 – ♦Glasgow 81 – ♦Oban 81.

COLL (Isle of) Argyll. (Strathclyde) **401** A 14 – pop. 153.

⚓ by Caledonian MacBrayne : from Arinagour, to Oban summer only : 5-7 weekly (3 h 30 mn) – from Arinagour to Isle of Tiree summer only : 3-4 weekly (1 h).

⚓ by Caledonian MacBrayne : from Arinagour to Tobermory (Isle of Mull) 3 weekly(1 h 20 mn) – from Arinagour to Lochaline May to September 2 weekly (2 h 30 mn).

COLONSAY (Isle of) Argyll. (Strathclyde) **401** B 15 – pop. 132 – ✪ 095 12 Colonsay.

📷₈ 🖉 316.

⚓ by Caledonian MacBrayne : summer only, from Scalasaig to Oban 6 weekly (2 h 30 mn).

Scalasaig – ECD : Wednesday – ✉ ✪ 095 12 Colonsay.

🏠 **Isle of Colonsay** ⛵, PA61 7YP, 🖉 316, ≼, « 18C inn », 🌰 – 🛏wc 🅿. 🔳 🗚 ⓪ **VISA**
M (bar lunch)/dinner 11.50 **st.** ₰ 2.40 – **11 rm** ⚏ 16.50/47.50 **st.** – SB (except mid May-August) 50.00/55.00 **st.**

COLVEND Kircudbright. (Dumfries and Galloway) – ✉ Dalbeattie – ✪ 055 663 Rockcliffe.

♦ Edinburgh 99 – ♦Dumfries 19.

🏠 **Clonyard House,** DG5 4QW, NW : 1 m. on A 710 🖉 372, 🌰 – 📺 🛏wc 🛏wc 🔥 🅿. 🔳 **VISA**
M (bar lunch)/dinner 9.00 **st.** and a la carte ₰ 2.80 – **10 rm** ⚏ 12.00/37.00 **st.** – SB (March-October) 42.00 **st.**

COMRIE Perth. (Tayside) **401** I 14 – pop. 1 406 – ECD : Wednesday – ✪ 0764.

📷₉ Comrie 🖉 70544, E. off A 85.

♦Edinburgh 61 – ♦Glasgow 51 – ♦Oban 70 – Perth 24.

🏠 **Royal,** Melville Sq., PH6 2DN, 🖉 70200, 🌰 – 📺 🛏wc ☎ 🅿. 🔳 🗚 **VISA** ⚜
M 12.50 **t.** (dinner) and a la carte 12.80/18.30 **t.** ₰ 5.75 – **14 rm** ⚏ 19.50/42.00 **t.** – SB (except Easter and Christmas) 63.00 **st.**

🏠 **Comrie,** Drummond St., PH6 2DY, 🖉 70239, – 🛏wc 🛏wc 🅿
April-October – **M** 7.00/10.00 **st.** and a la carte ₰ 2.00 – **12 rm** ⚏ 13.75/37.00 **st.**

CONNEL Argyll. (Strathclyde) **401** D 14 – ECD : Wednesday – ✪ 063 171.

♦Edinburgh 118 – ♦Glasgow 88 – ♦Inverness 113 – ♦Oban 5.

🏠 **Lochnell Arms,** North Connel, PA37 1RF, 🖉 408, ≼, 🌰 – 🛏wc 🅿. 🔳 🗚 ⓪ **VISA**
M 6.00/10.00 **st.** ₰ 2.30 – **11 rm** ⚏ 14.00/32.00 **st.** – SB (October-May) 44.00/46.00 **st.**

🏠 **Ossian's** ⛵, Bonawe Rd, North Connel, PA37 1RB, 🖉 322, ≼, 🌰 – 🛏wc 🅿. 🔳 🗚 ⓪ **VISA**
M 12.00/18.00 **t.** ₰ 2.40 – **14 rm** ⚏ 18.00/38.00 **t.**

CRAIGHOUSE Argyll. (Strathclyde) **401** C 16 – see Jura (Isle of).

CRAIL Fife. (Fife) **401** M 15 – pop. 1 106 – ECD : Wednesday – ✪ 033 35.

See : Site★★ – Old Town★★ – Upper Crail★.

Envir. : The East Neuk★★ (coastline from Crail SW by A 917 to St. Monande).

♦Edinburgh 54 – ♦Dundee 25 – Dunfermline 41.

🏠 Marine, 54 Nethergate South, KY10 3TZ, 🖉 50207, ≼, 🌰 – 🛏
12 rm.

CRIANLARICH Perth (Central) **401** G 16 – ✪ 083 83.

♦Edinburgh 82 – ♦Glasgow 52 – Perth 53.

🏠 **Allt-Chaorain House** ⛵, FK20 8RU, NW : 1 m. on A 82 🖉 283, ≼, 🌰 – 🛏wc 🅿. 🔳 **VISA**
March-October – **9 rm** ⚏ 14.00/32.00 **t.**

CRIEFF Perth. (Tayside) **401** I 14 Scotland G – pop. 5 101 – ECD : Wednesday – ✪ 0764.

See : Site★.

Envir. : Drummond Castle Gardens★ AC, S : 2 m. by A 822 – Tullibardine Chapel★, S : 6 m. by A 822 and A 823 – Strathallan Aero Park★, SE : 6 m. by B 8062 – Upper Strathearn★ (Loch Earn★★) NW : 12 m. by A 85.

📷₈ Perth Rd 🖉 2909 – 📷₉ Peat Rd, Muthill 🖉 3319, S : 3 m. on A 822.

🏁 James Sq. 🖉 2578 (summer only).

♦Edinburgh 60 – ♦Glasgow 50 – ♦Oban 76 – Perth 18.

🏨 **Murraypark** ⹁, Connaught Terr., PH7 3DJ, ℰ 3731, 斧 – ⇔wc ☜ 🅿. 🆎 ⑩ 𝚅𝙸𝚂𝙰
M 8.50/14.50 **t.** and a la carte ⫯ 3.50 – **15 rm** ⨶ 22.00/46.00 **t.**

🏡 **Gwydyr House**, Comrie Rd, PH7 4BP, on A 85 ℰ 3277, ≼, 斧 – 📺 🅿
Easter-October – **M** (bar lunch)/dinner 7.35 **t.** and a la carte ⫯ 2.75 – **10 rm** ⨶ 10.25/23.50 **t.**

⌂ **Leven House**, Comrie Rd, PH7 4BA, on A 85 ℰ 2529, ≼
April-October – **9 rm** ⨶ 10.00/20.00 **t.**

at Sma'Glen NE : 4 m. by A 85 on A 822 – ⊠ ✪ 0764 Crieff :

🏡 **Foulford Inn** ⹁, PH7 3LN, ℰ 2407 – 🅿
closed February – **M** (closed Sunday dinner) 5.00/9.00 **t.** and a la carte ⫯ 3.00 – **11 rm**
⨶ 12.00/28.00 **t.** – SB 35.00/41.00 **st.**

VAUXHALL, SUZUKI Comrie Rd ℰ 2125

CRINAN Argyll. (Strathclyde) 𝟜𝟘𝟙 D 15 – ⊠ Lochgilphead – ✪ 054 683.
See : Site★ – Envir. : Kilmory Knap (Macmillan's Cross★) SW : 14 m.
♦Edinburgh 137 – ♦Glasgow 91 – ♦Oban 36.

🏨 **Crinan,** PA31 8SR, ℰ 235, « ≼ imposing setting, overlooking Loch Crinan and Sound of Jura », 斧 – 🛏 ⇔wc ☜ 🅿. 🔼 𝚅𝙸𝚂𝙰
Mid March-mid October – **M** (closed Tuesday lunch and Monday) (buffet lunch)/dinner 24.50 **t.**
⫯ 3.50 (rest. see also **Lock 16** below) – **22 rm** ⨶ 35.00/75.00.
✕✕ **Lock 16** (at Crinan H.), PA31 8SR, ℰ 235, Seafood, « ≼ imposing setting, overlooking Loch Crinan and Sound of Jura » – 🅿.

CROCKETFORD Kirkcudbright (Dumfries and Galloway) 𝟜𝟘𝟙 𝟜𝟘𝟚 I 18 – ✪ 055 669.
♦Edinburgh 86 – ♦Dumfries 9 – ♦Stranraer 67.

🏨 **Galloway Arms,** DG2 8RA, ℰ 240 – 📺 ⇔wc 🅿. ⑩ 𝚅𝙸𝚂𝙰. ⚡
M 7.00/12.00 **t.** and a la carte ⫯ 3.80 – **11 rm** ⨶ 16.00/40.00 **t.** – SB 48.00/56.00 **st.**

CROMARTY Ross and Cromarty (Highland) 𝟜𝟘𝟙 H 10 – pop. 685 – ECD : Wednesday – ✪ 038 17.
♦Edinburgh 182 – ♦Inverness 26 – ♦Wick 126.

✕ **Le Chardon,** 20 Church St., IU11 8XA, ℰ 471 – 🔼 🆎 𝚅𝙸𝚂𝙰
closed Monday – **M** (lunch by arrangement)/dinner 14.00 **t.**

CROSSFORD Fife. (Fife) – see Dunfermline.

CULLEN Banff. (Grampian) 𝟜𝟘𝟙 L 10 Scotland G – pop. 1 378 – ECD : Wednesday – ✪ 0542.
See : Auld Kirk★ (Sacrament house★, carved panels★).
Envir. : Deskford Church (Sacrament house★) S : 4 m. by B 9018 – Portsoy★ E : 5 ½ m. by A 98.
🏌 The Links ℰ 40685.
🛈 20 Seafield St. ℰ 40757 (summer only).
♦Edinburgh 189 – ♦Aberdeen 59 – Banff 12 – ♦Inverness 61.

🏨 **Seafield Arms,** Seafield St., AB5 2SG, ℰ 40791 – 📺 ⇔wc 🅿. 🔼 🆎 ⑩ 𝚅𝙸𝚂𝙰
M 6.50/10.50 **t.** and a la carte ⫯ 3.50 – **25 rm** ⨶ 21.80/40.00 **t.** – SB 54.00 **st.**

CULLIPOOL Argyll. (Strathclyde) 𝟜𝟘𝟙 D 15 – see Luing (Isle of).

CULLODEN Inverness. (Highland) 𝟜𝟘𝟙 H 11 – see Inverness.

CUPAR Fife. (Fife) 𝟜𝟘𝟙 K 15 – pop. 6 662 – ECD : Thursday – ✪ 0334.
🛈 Fluthers car park ℰ 55555 (summer only).
♦Edinburgh 45 – ♦Dundee 15 – Perth 23.

✕ **Ostler's Close,** 25 Bonnygate, KY15 4BU, ℰ 55574 – 🔼 𝚅𝙸𝚂𝙰
closed Monday lunch, Sunday and 2 weeks February – **M** a la carte 12.50/16.90 **t.**

DALIBURGH Inverness. (Outer Hebrides) (Western Isles) 𝟜𝟘𝟙 X 12 – see Uist (South) (Isles of).

DALRY (ST. JOHN'S TOWN OF) Kirkcudbright. (Dumfries and Galloway) 𝟜𝟘𝟙 𝟜𝟘𝟚 H 18 –
⊠ Castle Douglas – ✪ 064 43.
♦Edinburgh 82 – ♦Dumfries 27 – ♦Glasgow 66 – Stranraer 47.

🏨 **Lochinvar,** Main St., DG7 3UP, ℰ 210 – ⇔wc 🅿. 🔼 🆎 𝚅𝙸𝚂𝙰
M (bar lunch)/dinner 8.50 **st.** and a la carte ⫯ 2.25 – **17 rm** ⨶ 12.50/28.50 **st.** – SB 35.00/
45.00 **st.**

🏨 Milton Park ⹁, DG7 3SR, N : 1 m. by A 713 ℰ 286, ≼, ⹁, 斧, ⚡ – ⇔wc 🅿 – **17 rm**.

DERVAIG Argyll. (Strathclyde) 𝟜𝟘𝟙 B 14 – see Mull (Isle of).

DIRLETON E. Lothian (Lothian) 𝟜𝟘𝟙 𝟜𝟘𝟚 L 15 – see Gullane.

529

DORNIE Ross and Cromarty (Highland) **401** D 12 – ⊠ Kyle of Lochalsh – ✆ 059 985.
◆Edinburgh 212 – ◆Inverness 74 – Kyle of Lochalsh 8.

  🏠 **Loch Duich,** IV40 8DY, ℰ 213, ≼ Eilean Donan Castle and hills, ⟡ – 🅿 , ▣ 𝚅𝙸𝚂𝙰 . ✻
   Easter-October – **M** (bar lunch)/dinner 12.00 **t.** ⬥ 2.35 – **18 rm** ⊂⊃ 17.00/40.00 **t.** –
   SB 25.00/27.00 **st.**

DORNOCH Sutherland. (Highland) **401** H 10 **Scotland G** – pop. 1 006 – ECD : Thursday – ✆ 0862.
See : Site★.

🛇₁₈, ⌐₉ Royal Dornoch, Golf Rd ℰ 810219.

🛈 The Square, ℰ 810400.

◆Edinburgh 219 – ◆Inverness 63 – ◆Wick 65.

  🏨 **Royal Golf** ⚘, Grange Rd, IV25 3LG, ℰ 810283, ≼Dornoch Firth, ⟡ – ▣ ⌐wc ☎ 🅿 . ▣
   🅰🅴 ⓞ 𝚅𝙸𝚂𝙰
   March-October – **M** 5.00/16.00 **st.** ⬥ 4.50 – **35 rm** ⊂⊃ 27.00/64.00 **st.**, **2 suites** 80.00/120.00 **st.**
   – SB 68.00/88.00 **st.**

  🏨 **Dornoch Castle,** Castle St., IV25 3SD, ℰ 810216, « Former bishop's palace, part 16C », ⟡
   – 🛗 ⌐wc ⧉wc 🅿 . ▣ 🅰🅴 𝚅𝙸𝚂𝙰
   20 April-October – **M** 6.00/15.00 **st.** and a la carte – **20 rm** ⊂⊃ 16.00/58.00 **st.** –
   SB 49.50/78.50 **st.**

PEUGEOT St. Gilbert St. ℰ 810255

DOUNE Perth. (Central) **401** H 15 **Scotland G** – pop. 1 020 – ECD : Wednesday – ✆ 0786.
See : Site★ – Castle★.
Envir. : Doune Motor Museum★, NW : 1 m. by A 84.

◆Edinburgh 45 – ◆Glasgow 35 – Perth 33 – Stirling 8.

  🏠 **Woodside,** Stirling Rd, FK16 6AB, on A 84 ℰ 841237, ⟡ – ⌐wc 🅿 . ▣
   M *(closed Sunday dinner to non-residents)* (bar lunch)/dinner 12.00 **t.** and a la carte ⬥ 3.25 –
   14 rm ⊂⊃ 20.00/36.00 **t.**

  ✗ **Broughton's,** Blair Drummond, FK9 4XE, S : 3 m. by A 84 on A 873 ℰ 841897, ⟡ – 🅿 . ▣
   closed Sunday, Monday, 3 weeks in spring and 1 week in autumn – **M** (booking essential)
   (dinner only) 13.50 **t.** ⬥ 3.40.

DRUMNADROCHIT Inverness. (Highland) **401** G 11 – pop. 542 – ⊠ Milton – ✆ 045 62.
Envir. : Loch Ness★★ – Loch Ness Monster Exhibition★.

◆Edinburgh 172 – ◆Inverness 16 – Kyle of Lochalsh 66.

  🏨 **Polmaily House** ⚘, IV3 6XT, W : 2 m. on A 831 ℰ 343, « Country house atmosphere », ⬓,
   ⟡, park, ✳ – ⌐wc 🅿 . ▣ 𝚅𝙸𝚂𝙰 . ✻
   Easter-mid October – **M** (bar lunch, residents only)/dinner a la carte 12.00/15.50 **t.** ⬥ 3.50 –
   9 rm ⊂⊃ 25.00/56.00 **t.**

DRYBRIDGE Banff. (Grampian) – see Buckie.

DRYMEN Stirling. (Central) **401** G 15 – pop. 771 – ECD : Wednesday – ✆ 0360.
Envir. : Loch Lomond★★, W : 3 m.

◆Edinburgh 64 – ◆Glasgow 18 – Stirling 22.

  🏨 **Buchanan Arms,** Main St., G63 0BQ, ℰ 60588, ⟡ – ▣ ⌐wc ☎ & 🅿 . 🎿 . ▣ 🅰🅴 ⓞ 𝚅𝙸𝚂𝙰
   M 6.95/11.75 **t.** and a la carte ⬥ 2.95 – **35 rm** ⊂⊃ 34.00/68.00 **t.** – SB (November-April)
   50.00/100.00 **st.**

DULNAIN BRIDGE Inverness. (Highland) **401** J 12 – ECD : Wednesday – ⊠ Grantown-on-Spey
(Moray Highland) – ✆ 047 985.
◆Edinburgh 140 – ◆Inverness 31 – Perth 96.

  🏠 Muckrach Lodge, PH26 3LY, W : ½ m. on A 938 ℰ 257, ≼, ⟡ – ⌐wc 🅿 . ✻
   9 rm.

  🏠 **Skye of Curr** ⚘, Skye of Curr Rd, PH26 3PA, ℰ 345, ≼, ⟡ – 🅿 . ▣ 🅰🅴 ⓞ 𝚅𝙸𝚂𝙰
   M (bar lunch)/dinner 9.75 **t.** – **8 rm** ⊂⊃ 13.50/30.00 **st.**

DUMFRIES Dumfries. (Dumfries and Galloway) **401** **402** J 18 **Scotland G** – pop. 31 307 – ECD :
Thursday – ✆ 0387.
See : Site★ – Midsteeple★ A A – Lincluden College (Tomb★) by College Street A.
Envir. : Sweetheart Abbey★, S : 8 ¼ m. by A 710 A – Caerlaverock Castle★, SE : 9 m. by B 725 B –
Ruthwell Cross★, SE : 16 m. by B 725 B – Glenkiln (Sculptures★) E : 10 m. by A 75 B – Kippford★,
SW : 18 m. by A 710 or A 711 A – Drumlanrig Castle★★, NW : 18 m. by A 76 A.

🛇₁₈ Lauriston Av. ℰ 3582 A – ⌐₉ Lochmaben ℰ 552, NE : 8 m. by A 709 B.

🛈 Whitesands ℰ 53862 (summer only).

◆Edinburgh 80 – ◆Ayr 59 – ◆Carlisle 34 – ◆Glasgow 79 – ◆Manchester 155 – ◆Newcastle-upon-Tyne 91.

DUMFRIES

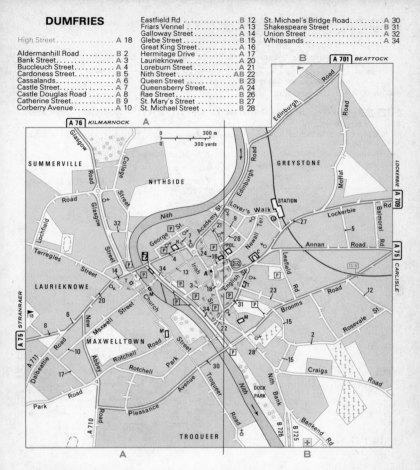

🏛 **Station,** 49 Lovers Walk, DG1 1LT, 🖉 54316, Telex 778654 – |🕭| 📺 🛏wc 🚿wc ☎ 🄿. 🖭 🅰🄴
ⓓ 𝐕𝐈𝐒𝐀
B e
M (bar lunch)/dinner 10.50 **t.** and a la carte ⚕ 3.00 – **30 rm** 🖙 30.00/50.00 **t.** – SB (except Christmas and New Year)(weekends only) 56.00 **st.**

FIAT 123 Whitesands 🖉 64875   VOLVO Annan Rd 🖉 61437
FORD Main Rd 🖉 038771 (Amisfield) 710491
PEUGEOT-TALBOT St. Mary's Industrial Estate 🖉 63076

DUNAIN PARK Inverness. (Highland) – see Inverness.

DUNBAR E. Lothian (Lothian) **401** M 15 **Scotland G** – pop. 5 795 – ECD : Wednesday – ✪ 0368.

See : Tolbooth★ – John Muir's Birthplace★.

Envir. : Museum of Flight★, W : 5 m. by A 1087 and A 1 – Preston Mill★, W : 6 m. by A 1087, A 1 and B 1407 – Tyninghame★, NW : 6 m. by A 1 and A 198 – Tantallon Castle★★, NW : 10 m. by A 1087, A 1 and A 198.

🏌 Winterfield, North Rd 🖉 62280 – 🏌 East Links 🖉 62317, S : ½ m.

🇿 Town House, High St. 🖉 63353.

◆Edinburgh 28 – ◆Newcastle-upon-Tyne 90.

⌂ **Marine,** 7 Marine Rd, EH42 1AR, 🖉 63315
10 rm 🖙 10.00/20.00 **st.**

DUNBLANE Perth. (Central) **401** I 15 **Scotland G** – pop. 6 783 – ECD : Wednesday – 🕾 0786.
See : Site★ – Cathedral★★ – 🛈 Stirling Rd 🖉 824428 (summer only).
♦Edinburgh 42 – ♦Glasgow 33 – Perth 29.

🏛 **Cromlix House** ⟂, Kinbuck, FK15 9JT, N : 3 ¼ m. by A 9 on B 8033 🖉 822125, ≼, « Antique furnishings », ⟂, 🐎, park, ⟂ – 📺 ☎ 🅿. 🔼 AE ⓪ VISA
M 13.50/25.00 **st.** ⚹ 3.75 – **14 rm** ⌂ 55.00/97.50 **st., 5 suites** 97.50/125.00 **st.** – SB (November and January-March)(weekdays only) 140.00/180.00 **st.**

AUSTIN-ROVER Stirling Rd 🖉 823271

DUNDEE Angus (Tayside) **401** L 14 **Scotland G** – pop. 172 294 – ECD : Wednesday – 🕾 0382.
See : The Frigate Unicorn★ Y A.

🛅, 🛅 Caird Park 🖉 453606 off Kingsway Bypass at Mains Loan Z – 🛅 Camperdown Park 🖉 645450, NW : 2 m. by A 923 Z.

✈ Dundee Airport : 🖉 643242, SW : 1 ½ m. Z – 🛈 Nethergate Centre 🖉 27723.
♦Edinburgh 63 – ♦Aberdeen 67 – ♦Glasgow 83.

DUNDEE

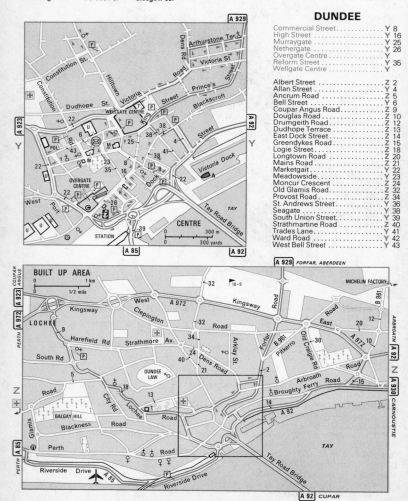

🏛 **Angus Thistle** (Thistle), 101 Marketgait, DD1 1QU, ℰ 26874, Telex 76456 – 🔲 🔳 📺 ⇔wc ☜
🅿 🔥 🔼 🗛 ⓞ *VISA*
                                          Y c
M 7.00/10.50 **t.** and a la carte 🍷 3.00 – ⊆ 6.25 – **58 rm** 40.00/65.00 **st.**, **5 suites** 130.00 **st.** –
SB (weekends only) 62.00 **st.**

🏛 **Invercarse**, 371 Perth Rd, DD2 1PG, W : 2 m. on B 911 ℰ 69231, Telex 76608, 🍴 – 📺 ⇔wc
🍴wc ☜ 🅿 🔥 🔼 🗛 ⓞ *VISA*
                                         Z n
M *(closed Saturday lunch)* 6.15/10.25 **st.** and a la carte 11.40/15.20 **st.** 🍷 2.85 – ⊆ 4.65 – **40 rm**
33.50/47.50 **st.**, **1 suite** 50.00/70.00 **st.** – SB (weekends only) 54.50/55.50 **st.**

🏛 **Queen's**, 160 Nethergate, DD1 4DU, ℰ 22515 – 🔲 📺 ⇔wc ☎ 🅿 🔥 🔼 🗛 ⓞ *VISA*
🍽
                                         Y e
M (bar lunch)/dinner 10.50 **t.** and a la carte 🍷 2.95 – **48 rm** 30.00/78.00 **t.** – SB (weekends only)
46.00/72.00 **st.**

at Broughty Ferry E : 4 ½ m. by A 930 – Z – (Dundee Road) – ⊠ ☼ 0382 Dundee :

🏛 **Tayview** without rest., 71-73 St. Vincent St., DD5 2EZ, ℰ 79438 – ⇔wc. 🔼 *VISA* 🍽
11 rm ⊆ 25.00/45.00 **t.**

at Invergowrie W : 4 ¾ m. by A 85 on A 872 – Z – ⊠ ☼ 0382 Dundee :

🏛 **Swallow** (Swallow), Kingsway West (Dundee Ring Road), DD2 5JT, ℰ 641122, Telex 76694,
🔲 🍴 – 📺 ☎ 🖒 🅿 🔼 🗛 ⓞ *VISA*
M 6.50/12.00 **st.** and a la carte 🍷 3.90 – **69 rm** ⊆ 52.00/65.00 **st.** – SB 60.00 **st.**

ALFA-ROMEO, HONDA Queen St., Broughty Ferry
ℰ 77257
AUSTIN-ROVER 64 Ward Rd ℰ 24013
CITROEN 3 Roseangle ℰ 28483
DAIHATSU, RELIANT 25 Rosebank St. ℰ 25406
FIAT, LADA, LANCIA MacAlpine Rd ℰ 818004
FORD Balfield Rd ℰ 60191

MAZDA 166 Seagate ℰ 25007
RENAULT Riverside Drive ℰ 644401
TOYOTA East Kingsway ℰ 457667
VAUXHALL East Dock St. ℰ 26521
VOLVO Riverside Drive ℰ 643295
VW, AUDI 45-53 Gellatly St. ℰ 24251

DUNDONNELL Ross and Cromarty (Highland) 🗺 E 10 – ⊠ Garve – ☼ 085 483.

◆Edinburgh 215 – ◆ Inverness 59.

🏛 **Dundonnell**, IV23 2QS, ℰ 234, ≤ Dundonnell Valley – 📺 ⇔wc ☎ 🅿 🔼 *VISA*
April-October – **M** (bar lunch)/dinner 11.50 **t.** 🍷 2.95 – **24 rm** ⊆ 21.50/45.00 **t.** –
SB 50.00/66.00 **st.**

DUNFERMLINE Fife. (Fife) 🗺 J 15 Scotland G – pop. 52 105 – ECD : Wednesday – ☼ 0383.

See : Site★ – Abbey★ (Norman nave★★).

Envir. : Culross★★★ (Palace★★ and Study★) E : 7 m. by A 994.

🏌 Canmore, Venturefair ℰ 724969, N : 1 m. – 🏌 Pitreavie, Queensferry Rd ℰ 722591 – 🏌 Saline,
Kinneddar Hill ℰ, 852591, NW : 5 m.

🛈 Glen Bridge Car Park ℰ 720999 (summer only).

◆Edinburgh 16 – ◆ Dundee 48 – Motherwell 39.

🏛 **King Malcolm Thistle** (Thistle), Queensferry Rd, KY11 5DS, S : 1 m. on A 823 ℰ 722611,
Telex 727721 – 🔳 rest 📺 ⇔wc ☎ 🅿 🔥 🔼 🗛 ⓞ *VISA*
M 9.50/13.50 **t.** and a la carte 🍷 3.00 – ⊆ 5.95 – **48 rm** 47.00/60.00 **st.** – SB (weekends only)
56.00 **st.**

at Crossford SW : 1 ¾ m. on A 994 – ⊠ ☼ 0383 Dunfermline :

🏛 **Keavil House** 🍽, Main St., KY12 8NY, ℰ 736258, Telex 728227, 🍴, 🍽 – 📺 ⇔wc 🍴wc ☎
🖒 🅿 🔥 🔼 🗛 *VISA*
M dinner 11.00 **t.** and a la carte 7.50/12.90 **t.** 🍷 2.95 – **32 rm** ⊆ 32.00/50.00 **t.** – SB (weekends
only) 59.00 **st.**

AUSTIN-ROVER 18 Halbeath Rd ℰ 731041
FIAT 128-138 Pittencrieff St. ℰ 722565
PEUGEOT-TALBOT 206 Rumbingwell ℰ 731791

RENAULT Headwell Av. ℰ 721914
TOYOTA Bruce St. ℰ 723675
VAUXHALL 3 Carnock Rd ℰ 721511

DUNKELD Perth. (Tayside) 🗺 J 14 Scotland G – ECD : Thursday – ☼ 035 02.

See : Site★ – Cathedral Street★.

🏌 ℰ 524, N : 1 m. on A 923.

🛈 The Cross ℰ 688 (summer only).

◆Edinburgh 58 – ◆ Aberdeen 88 – ◆ Inverness 98 – Perth 14.

🏛 **Stakis Dunkeld House** (Stakis) 🍽, PH8 0HX, ℰ 771, ≤, « Country house in extensive
grounds on banks of River Tay », 🔲, 🍴, park, 🍽 – 📺 ☎ 🅿 🔼 🗛 ⓞ *VISA*
M 7.00/13.50 **st.** and a la carte 🍷 3.40 – ⊆ 3.90 – **35 rm** 45.00/60.00 **st.**, **1 suite** 95.00 **st.** –
SB 75.00/85.00 **st.**

DUNOON Argyll. (Strathclyde) **401** F 16 − pop. 8 797 − ECD : Wednesday − ✆ 0369.
Cowal, Ardenslate Rd ✆ 2216, NE : boundary.

by Caledonian MacBrayne : from Dunoon Pier to Gourock Railway Pier, summer only : frequent
services daily (20 mn) − by Western Ferries : from Hunters Quay to McInroy's Point, Gourock,
summer only : frequent services daily (20 mn).

Pier Esplanade ✆ 3785.

♦Edinburgh 73 − ♦Glasgow 27 − ♦Oban 77.

    at Kirn N : 1 m. on A 815 − ✉ ✆ 0369 Dunoon :

🏠 **Enmore,** Marine Par., PA23 8HH, ✆ 2230, ≼ Firth of Clyde, ≉, squash − 🛏wc 🛁wc **P.** ⓪
    VISA
    closed December and January − **M** (bar lunch)/dinner 13.00 **st.** ▯ 3.50 − **12 rm** ⌷ 18.00/
    32.00 **st.**

    at Sandbank N : 2 ½ m. on A 815 − ✉ ✆ 0369 Dunoon :

🏠 Firpark, Shore Rd, PA23 8QG, ✆ 6506, ≼ Holy Loch, ≉ − 📺 🛏wc **P**
    6 rm.

AUSTIN-ROVER East Boy Promenade ✆ 3094   RENAULT Shore St., Inverary ✆ 0499 (Inverary) 2271
FORD George St. ✆ 3234

DUNVEGAN Inverness. (Highland) **401** A 11 − see Skye (Isle of).

DUROR Argyll. (Strathclyde) **401** E 14 − ✉ Appin − ✆ 063 174.
♦Edinburgh 125 − Fort William 19 − ♦Oban 31.

🏠 **Stewart** (Best Western) ⑤, Glen Duror, PA38 4BW, ✆ 268, ≼, ≉, park − 📺 🛏wc **P.** 🔲
    AE ⓪ **VISA**
    Mid April-October − **M** (bar lunch)/dinner 12.00 **t.** ▯ 3.50 − **26 rm** ⌷ 29.00/48.00 **t.**

DYCE Aberdeen (Grampian) **401** N 12 − see Aberdeen.

EAST KILBRIDE Lanark. (Strathclyde) **401 402** H 16 − pop. 70 454 − ECD : Wednesday −
✆ 035 52.
♦Edinburgh 46 − ♦Ayr 35 − ♦Glasgow 10.

🏨 **Bruce** (Swallow), Cornwall St., G74 1AF, ✆ 29771, Telex 778428 − ▮ 📺 🛏wc ☎ **P.** 🕭 🔲
    AE ⓪ **VISA**
    M *(closed Sunday lunch)* 6.00/9.00 **st.** and a la carte ▯ 3.70 − **84 rm** ⌷ 43.00/54.00 **st.** −
    SB (weekends only) 45.00/48.00 **st.**

🏨 **Stuart,** 2 Cornwall Way, G74 1JR, ✆ 21161, Telex 778504 − ▮ 📺 🛏wc 🛁wc ☎ ⅙. 🕭 🔲
    AE ⓪ **VISA**
    M 5.50 **st.** (lunch) and a la carte 7.25/12.05 **st.** ▯ 3.25 − **39 rm** ⌷ 35.00/45.00 **st.**

🏠 Crutherland Country House ⑤, Strathaven Rd, G75 0QZ, SE : 2 m. on A 726 ✆ 37633, ⌟, ≉
    − 📺 🛏wc 🛁wc 🕭 **P.** ⌖
    21 rm.

🏠 Torrance, 67 Main St., G74 4LN, ✆ 25241 − 📺 🛏wc 🛁wc ☎ **P**
    26 rm.

EAST LINTON E. Lothian (Lothian) **401** M 16 − pop. 1 190 − ECD : Wednesday − ✆ 0620.
♦Edinburgh 22 − ♦Newcastle-upon-Tyne 96.

🏨 **Harvesters,** Station Rd, EH40 3DP, ✆ 860395, ≉ − 📺 🛏wc **P.** 🔲 **AE** ⓪ **VISA**
    closed Christmas Day and first 2 weeks January − **M** (bar lunch)/dinner a la carte 10.95/13.00 **t.**
    ▯ 4.00 − **10 rm** ⌷ 22.00/50.00 **t.**

EDAY (Isle of) Orkney (Orkney Islands) **401** L 6 − Shipping Services : see Orkney Islands (Mainland : Kirkwall).

EDDLESTON Peebles. (Borders) **401 402** K 16 − see Peebles.

    Gebruik voor uw reizen in Engeland, Schotland, Wales en Ierland :

    − de vijf kaarten nrs. **401**, **402**, **403**, **404** en **405** (schaal 1:400 000)

    − zij vormen een uitstekende aanvulling op deze gids
      omdat de plaatsen die op de kaarten rood onderstreept zijn,
      in deze gids zijn opgenomen.

EDINBURGH Midlothian (Lothian) **401** K 16 Scotland G – pop. 408 822 – **☎** 031.

See : Site★★★ – International Festival★★★ (August) – Castle★★ (Site★★★, ≤★★ ※★★★, Great Hall: hammerbeam roof★★, Palace block: Honours of Scotland★★★) DZ – Abbey and Palace of Holyroodhouse★★ (Plasterwork ceilings★★★) BV – Royal Mile★★ : Gladstone's Land★ EYZ **A**, St. Giles' Cathedral★★ (Crown Spire★★★) EZ, Wax Museum★ EZ **M1** – Canongate Tolbooth★ EY **B** Victoria Street★ EZ **84** – Royal Scottish Museum★★, EZ **M2** – New Town★★ : Charlotte Square★★★ CY **14**, National Museum of Antiquities★★ EY **M3**, The Georgian House★ CY **D** – National Portrait Museum★ EY **M3** Princes Street and Gardens : National Gallery of Scotland★★ DY **M4** – Scott Monument★ EY **F** Calton Hill EY : ※ from Nelson Monument★★★ – Royal Botanic Gardens★★★ AV – Edinburgh Zoo★★ AV – Scottish Agricultural Museum★ by A 90 AV – Craigmillar Castle★ BX.

Envir. : Rosslyn Chapel★★, Apprentice Pillar★★★, S : 7 m. by A 101 BX.

ⓑ Silverknowes, Parkway, ℘ 336 3843 W : 4 m. AV – ⓑ Craigmillar Park, Observatory Rd ℘ 667 2837 BX – ⓑ Carrick Knowe, Glendevon Park ℘ 337 1096, W : 5 m. AX.

✈ ℘ 333 1000, Telex 727615, W : 6 m. by A 8 AV – **Terminal : Waverley Bridge**.

🚗 ℘ 556 1100.

🅿 Waverley Market, 3 Princes St., ℘ 557 2727 – Edinburgh Airport ℘ 333 2167.

♦Glasgow 46 – ♦Newcastle-upon-Tyne 105.

Plans on following pages

🏨🏨 **Caledonian,** Princes St., EH1 2AB, ℘ 225 2433, Telex 72179 – 🛗 📺 ☎ & ℗. 🔥. 🔝 🝙 ⓪ _VISA_. ✳
CY **n**
M (rest. see **Pompadour** below) – ⌧ 7.25 – **254 rm** 70.00/105.00, **7 suites** 175.00/195.00 – SB (weekends only)(October-April) 77.00 **st.**

🏨🏨 **Sheraton,** 1 Festival Square, EH3 9SR, ℘ 229 9131, Telex 72398, 🖼 – 🛗 🛗 📺 ☎ & ℗. 🔥. 🔝 🝙 ⓪ _VISA_. ✳
CDZ **v**
M 30.00 **t.** and a la carte ▯ 4.00 – ⌧ 7.00 – **263 rm** 62.00/100.00 **t.**, **14 suites**.

🏨🏨 **George,** 19-21 George St., EH2 2PB, ℘ 225 1251, Telex 72570 – 🛗 🔲 rest 📺 ☎ & ℗. 🔥. 🝙 ⓪ _VISA_. ✳
195 rm, **2 suites**.
DY **z**

🏨🏨 **Carlton Highland,** 1-29 North Bridge, EH1 1SD, ℘ 556 7277, Telex 727001, 🖼, squash – 🛗 🔲 rest 📺 📺 & . 🔥. 🔝 🝙 ⓪ _VISA_.
EY **s**
M 9.95 **t.** and a la carte ▯ 3.75 – **207 rm** ⌧ 60.00/88.00 **st.**, **4 suites** 175.00 **st.**

🏨🏨 **Roxburghe** (Best Western), 38 Charlotte Sq., EH2 4HG, ℘ 225 3921, Telex 727054 – 🛗 🔲 ☎ ℗. 🔥. 🔝 🝙 ⓪ _VISA_
DY **o**
M 8.50/11.50 **t.** and a la carte 11.90/19.50 **t.** ▯ 3.75 – **76 rm** ⌧ 58.00/98.00 **st.**, **2 suites** 140.00/170.00 **st.** – SB 84.00/92.00 **st.**

🏨🏨 **Ladbroke Dragonara** (Ladbroke), Bells Mills, 69 Belford Rd, EH4 3DG, ℘ 332 2545, Telex 727979 – 🛗 📺 ☎ & ℗. 🔥. 🔝 🝙 ⓪ _VISA_
CY **i**
M 9.75/10.95 **t.** and a la carte ▯ 3.80 – ⌧ 6.25 – **146 rm** 60.50/92.50 **t.**, **3 suites** 137.50 **t.** – SB (weekends only) 72.00 **st.**

🏨🏨 **Royal Scot** (Swallow), 111 Glasgow Rd, EH12 8NF, W : 4 ½ m. on A 8 ℘ 334 9191, Telex 727197, 🖼 – 🛗 📺 ☎ & ℗. 🔥. 🔝 🝙 ⓪ _VISA_
by A 8 AV
M (carving lunch)/dinner 11.05 **st.** and a la carte ▯ 3.95 – **252 rm** ⌧ 57.00/70.00 **st.**, **5 suites** 70.00/80.00 **st.** – SB (weekends only)(October-May) 58.50/70.00 **st.**

🏨 **King James Thistle** (Thistle), 1 Leith St., EH1 3SW, ℘ 556 0111, Telex 727200 – 🛗 🔲 rest 📺 📺wc ☎ ℗. 🔥. 🔝 🝙 ⓪ _VISA_
EY **u**
M 10.00/14.50 **t.** and a la carte ▯ 3.50 – ⌧ 6.50 – **147 rm** 45.00/95.00 **st.**, **5 suites** 100.00 **st.** – SB (weekends only) 82.00 **st.**

🏨 **Howard,** 32-36 Gt. King St., EH3 6QH, ℘ 557 3500, Telex 727887 – 🛗 📺 📺wc 🛁wc ☎ ℗. 🔥. 🔝 🝙 ⓪ _VISA_
DY **s**
closed 25, 26 and 31 December-2 January – **M** (closed lunch Saturday and Sunday) 7.50/15.00 **t.** ▯ 3.50 – **25 rm** ⌧ 40.00/85.00 **t.** – SB (except summer)(weekends only) 66.00/77.00 **st.**

🏨 **Bruntsfield** (Best Western), 69-74 Bruntsfield Pl., EH10 4HH, ℘ 229 1393, Telex 727897 – 🛗 📺 📺wc 🛁wc ☎ ℗. 🔥. 🔝 🝙 _VISA_
DZ **e**
M 14.50 **st.** (dinner) and a la carte 13.70/18.95 **st.** ▯ 3.00 – **54 rm** ⌧ 36.00/65.00 **st.** – SB 54.00/90.00 **st.**

🏨 **Ellersly House,** 4 Ellersly Rd, EH12 6HZ, W : 2 ½ m. by A 8 ℘ 337 6888, Group Telex 76357, 🌳 – 🛗 📺 📺wc ☎ ℗. 🔥. 🔝 🝙 ⓪ _VISA_. ✳
AV **v**
M 11.00 **st.** (dinner) and a la carte ▯ 2.65 – ⌧ 5.00 – **55 rm** 45.00/75.00 **st.** – SB (weekends only) 68.00/76.00 **st.**

🏨 **Crest** (Crest), Queens Ferry Rd, EH4 3HL, NW : 2 m. on A 90 ℘ 332 2442, Telex 72541 – 🛗 📺 📺wc 🛁wc ☎ ℗. 🔥. 🔝 🝙 ⓪ _VISA_
AV **x**
M 8.25/12.25 **st.** and a la carte ▯ 3.75 – ⌧ 6.15 – **118 rm** 52.00/67.00 **st.**, **1 suite** 95.00/110.00 **st.** – SB (weekends only) 64.00/72.00 **st.**

🏨 **Barnton Thistle** (Thistle), 562 Queensferry Rd, EH4 6AS, NW : 4 ¾ m. on A 90 ℘ 339 1144, Telex 727928 – 🛗 📺 📺wc ☎ ℗. 🔥. 🔝 🝙 ⓪ _VISA_. ✳
AV **o**
M 8.50/10.25 **t.** and a la carte ▯ 2.75 – ⌧ 6.25 – **50 rm** 45.00/70.00 **st.**, **2 suites** 80.00 **st.** – SB (weekends only) 68.00 **st.**

🏨 **Post House** (T.H.F.), Corstorphine Rd, EH12 6UA, W : 3 m. on A 8 ℘ 334 8221, Telex 727103, 🖼 – 🛗 📺 📺wc ☎ ℗. 🔥. 🔝 🝙 ⓪ _VISA_. ✳
AV **u**
M 7.95/11.95 **st.** and a la carte ▯ 2.95 – ⌧ 5.65 – **207 rm** 52.00/65.00 **st.**, **1 suite**.

P.T.O. →

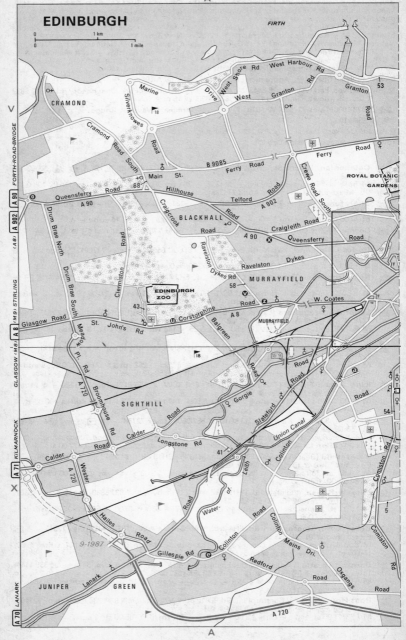

EDINBURGH

0 ____ 1 km
0 ____ 1 mile

FIRTH

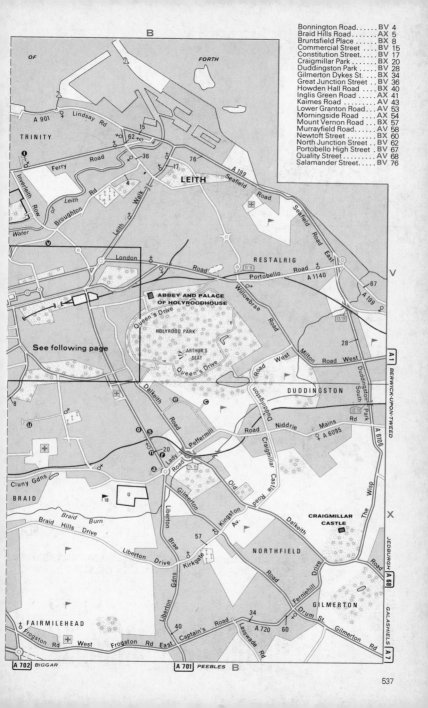

EDINBURGH
CENTRE

538

🏨 **Norton House,** Inglliston, EH28 8LX, W : 9 ¼ m. on A 8 ℰ 333 1275, Telex 727232, 🚗, park – 📺 ⇔wc ☎ 🅿 🦽 🛋 🄰🄴 ⓞ 𝘝𝘐𝘚𝘈
  on A 8 AV
M 7.50/12.75 **st.** and a la carte ≬ 3.75 – **19 rm** ⊆ 52.50/69.50 t.. **2 suites** 115.00 t. –
SB 118.50 **st.**

🏨 **Stakis Grosvenor** (Stakis), Grosvenor St., EH12 5EF, ℰ 226 6001, Telex 72445 – 🛗 📺 ⇔wc 🛁wc ☎ 🦽 🛋 🄰🄴 ⓞ 𝘝𝘐𝘚𝘈
  CZ **a**
M 11.00 **st.** and a la carte ≬ 3.95 – ⊆ 3.95 – **136 rm** 48.00/85.00 – SB 48.00/80.00 **st.**

🏨 **Albany,** 39-43 Albany St., EH1 3QY, ℰ 556 0397, Telex 727079 – 📺 ⇔wc 🛁wc 📠. 🛋 🄰🄴 ⓞ 𝘝𝘐𝘚𝘈
  EY **v**
M *(closed lunch Saturday and Sunday)* a la carte 9.45/15.05 t. ≬ 3.50 – ⊆ 4.95 – **21 rm** 28.00/72.00 t. – SB (October-April) 50.00 st.

🏨 **Old Waverley,** 43 Princes St., EH2 2BY, ℰ 556 4648, Telex 727050 – 🛗 📺 ⇔wc 🛁wc ☎ 🛋 🄰🄴 ⓞ 𝘝𝘐𝘚𝘈
  EY **r**
M (buffet lunch)/dinner 9.75 **st.** and a la carte 8.85/11.85 **st.** ≬ 2.95 – **62 rm** ⊆ 42.00/66.00 **st.** – SB 50.00/80.00 **st.**

🏨 **Hotel de France,** South St. Andrew St., EH2 2AZ, ℰ 556 8774, Telex 727539 – 🛗 📺 ⇔wc ☎ 🛋 🄰🄴 ⓞ 𝘝𝘐𝘚𝘈
  DEY **a**
M 21.50 **st.** and a la carte ≬ 3.75 – **30 rm** ⊆ 49.50/70.00 **st.**

🏨 **Murrayfield,** 18 Corstorphine Rd, EH12 6HN, W : 2 ½ m. on A 8 ℰ 337 1844 – 📺 ⇔wc ☎ 🅿 🛋 🄰🄴 ⓞ 𝘝𝘐𝘚𝘈
  AV **z**
closed New Years Day – **M** (bar lunch)/dinner 8.50 **t.** and a la carte ≬ 2.85 – **36 rm** ⊆ 25.00/45.00 **t.** – SB (except summer)(weekends only) 38.00/50.00 **st.**

🏨 **Kildonan Lodge,** 27 Craigmillar Park, EH16 5PE, ℰ 667 2793 – 📺 🛁wc 🅿 🄰🄴
  BX **r**
M (bar lunch residents only)/dinner a la carte 7.00/10.50 t. ≬ 3.70 – **9 rm** ⊆ 12.50/30.00 t.

🏨 **Iona,** 17 Strathearn Pl., EH9 2AL, ℰ 447 6264 – 📺 🛁 ☎ 🅿 🛋 𝘝𝘐𝘚𝘈
  BX **u**
M 5.00 **t.** (lunch) and a la carte ≬ 3.50 – **21 rm** ⊆ 22.00/46.00 **t.**

🏠 **St. Margarets,** 18 Craigmillar Park, EH16 5PS, ℰ 667 2202 – 📺 🅿
  BX **a**
8 rm ⊆ 15.00/22.00 **s.**

🏠 **Dorstan,** 1 Priestfield Rd, EH16 5HJ, ℰ 667 6721 – 📺 ⇔wc 🛁wc 🅿
  BX **e**
14 rm ⊆ 13.00/35.00 **t.**

🏠 **Buchan,** 3 Coates Gdns, EH12 5LG, ℰ 337 1045 – 📺
  CZ **o**
10 rm ⊆ 12.50/30.00 **st.**

🏠 **International,** 37 Mayfield Gdns, EH9 2BX, ℰ 667 2511 – 📺 ⇔wc 🛁wc
  BX **s**
7 rm ⊆ 13.00/30.00 **st.**

🏠 **Quinton Lodge,** 24 Polwarth Terr., EH11 1NA, ℰ 229 4100, 🚗 – 📺 🅿
  AX **a**
8 rm.

🏠 **Parklands,** 20 Mayfield Gdns, EH9 2BZ, ℰ 667 7184
  BX **o**
6 rm ⊆ 18.00/32.00 **s.**

🏠 **Lomond House,** 9 Zetland Pl., EH5 3HU, ℰ 552 3901 – 🛁wc
  BV **i**
7 rm ⊆ 12.00/30.00 **st.**

🏠 **Glenisla,** 12 Lygon Rd, EH16 5QB, ℰ 667 4098 – 🅿 🛳
  BX **a**
8 rm ⊆ 13.00/24.00 **st.**

🏠 **Galloway,** 22 Dean Park Cres., EH4 1PH, ℰ 332 3672 – ⇔wc
  CY **a**
10 rm ⊆ 12.00/30.00 **t.**

XXXX **Pompadour** (at Caledonian H.), Princes St., EH1 2AB, ℰ 225 2433, Telex 72179 – 🅿 🛋 🄰🄴 ⓞ 𝘝𝘐𝘚𝘈
  CY **n**
closed lunch Saturday and Sunday, 26 December and 1-2 January – **M** 11.50/25.00 **st.** and a la carte 24.50/32.00 **st.** ≬ 4.25.

XXX **Prestonfield House** 🦢 with rm, Priestfield Rd, EH16 5UT, SE : 2 ½ m. off A 68 ℰ 668 3346, Telex 727396, ≼, « Elegant 17C mansion », 🚗, park – 📺 🛁wc ☎ 🛋 🄰🄴 ⓞ 𝘝𝘐𝘚𝘈
  BX **x**
M 11.00/15.90 **t.** and a la carte 17.75/29.75 **t.** ≬ 3.00 – **5 rm** ⊆ 42.50/72.50 **t.**

XXX **Aye,** 80 Queen St., EH2 4NF, ℰ 226 5467, Japanese rest. – 🍽 🛋 🄰🄴 ⓞ 𝘝𝘐𝘚𝘈
  CDY **e**
closed Sunday dinner in winter, Sunday lunch and Monday – **M** 15.00/50.00 **t.** and a la carte.

XX **Cosmo,** 58a North Castle St., EH2 3LU, ℰ 226 6743, Italian rest. – 🛋 🄰🄴
  DY **r**
closed Saturday lunch, Sunday and Monday – **M** a la carte 11.10/17.25 **t.** ≬ 3.30.

XX **Raffaelli,** 10-11 Randolph Pl., EH3 7TA, ℰ 225 6060, Italian rest. – 🛋 🄰🄴 ⓞ 𝘝𝘐𝘚𝘈
  CY **c**
closed Saturday lunch and Sunday – **M** a la carte 9.80/17.60 **t.** ≬ 2.40.

XX **Champany Inn Town,** 2 Bridge Rd, Colinton, EH3 0LF, SW : 4 ½ m. by A 70 on B 701 ℰ 441 2587 – 🛋 🄰🄴 ⓞ 𝘝𝘐𝘚𝘈
  AX **e**
closed Sunday and 24 December-13 January – **M** (grill rest. only) a la carte 9.30/16.85 ≬ 3.75.

XX **Merchants,** 17 Merchant St., EH1 2QD, ℰ 225 4009 – 🛋 🄰🄴 𝘝𝘐𝘚𝘈
  EZ **x**
closed Sunday dinner and Monday – **M** (booking essential) 6.50 **t.** and a la carte 10.75/17.00 **t.** ≬ 2.75.

XX **Martins,** 70 Rose St., North Lane, EH2 3DX, ℰ 225 3106 – 🛋 🄰🄴 ⓞ 𝘝𝘐𝘚𝘈
  DY **n**
closed Saturday lunch, Sunday, Monday, 2 weeks July and 25 December-3 January – **M** 6.50 **t.** (lunch) and a la carte 10.70/18.20 **t.** ≬ 4.50.

P.T.O. →

XX **Shamiana,** 14 Brougham St., Tollcross, EH3 9JH, ✆ 228 2265, Indian rest. – ⊼ AE ⓞ VISA
    DZ **a**
    closed Sunday lunch and 25-26 December – **M** 7.00/14.00 **st.** and a la carte 7.50/12.15 **t.** ◊ 2.50.

XX **L'Auberge,** 56 St. Mary's St., EH1 1SX, ✆ 556 5888, French rest. – ⊼ AE ⓞ VISA
    EYZ **c**
    closed 26 December-1 January – **M** 6.75/19.50 **t.** and a la carte 12.00/25.90 **t.** ◊ 3.20.

XX **Lancer's Brasserie,** 5 Hamilton Pl., Stockbridge, EH3 5BA, ✆ 332 3444, North Indian rest.
    – ⊼ AE VISA
    CY **r**
    M 5.95/9.95 **t.** and a la carte 7.05/10.75 ◊ 2.10.

X **Alp-Horn,** 167 Rose St., EH2 4LS, ✆ 225 4787, Swiss rest. – ⊼
    DY **x**
    closed Sunday, Monday, 3 weeks June-July and 2 weeks at Christmas – **M** a la carte 8.50/12.70 **t.**
    ◊ 3.50.

X **L'Alliance Brasserie,** 7 Merchant St., EH1 2QD, ✆ 225 2002, Bistro
    EZ **a**
    closed Saturday lunch, Sunday, last 2 weeks July and 2 weeks at Christmas – **M** a la carte
    7.00/10.20 **t.** ◊ 3.00.

X Scots, 8-10 Eyre Pl., ✆ 556 1177, Seafood
    BV **v**

X **Verandah,** 17 Dalry Rd, EH11 2BQ, ✆ 337 5828, North Indian rest. – ⊼ AE ⓞ VISA
    CZ **z**
    M 9.95 **t.** and a la carte 7.65/11.15 **t.** ◊ 2.75.

X **Bungalow,** 23 Brougham Pl., EH3 9JV, ✆ 229 1537, Indian rest. – ⊼ AE ⓞ VISA
    DZ **i**
    closed Sunday lunch – **M** 10.00/15.00 **st.** and a la carte 5.60/13.50 **st.** ◊ 3.25.

X **Lune Town,** 38 William St., EH3 7LJ, ✆ 225 9388, Chinese-Cantonese rest. – ⊼ AE ⓞ
    VISA
    CZ **s**
    closed lunch Saturday and Sunday – **M** 6.00/10.00 **t.** and a la carte 10.00 **t.** ◊ 3.50.

X Vito's, 55a Frederick St., EH2 1LH, ✆ 225 5052, Italian rest.
    DY **i**

at Bonnyrigg S : 8 m. by A 7 – BX – on A 6094 – ✉ Bonnyrigg – ☎ 0875 Gorebridge :

🏯 **Dalhousie Castle** ⑤, EH19 3JB, SE : 1 ¼ m. on B 704 ✆ 20153, Telex 72380, ≼, « Converted
    12C castle », park – TV ☎ P. ⚘. ⊼ AE ⓞ VISA. ⅏
    M a la carte 13.20/21.95 **t.** ◊ 3.50 – **24 rm** ⊆ 38.00/89.00 **t.**

ALFA-ROMEO 22 Canning St. ✆ 229 5561	FORD Craighall Rd ✆ 552 5524
AUSTIN-ROVER-DAIMLER-JAGUAR Westfield Av. ✆ 337 3222	FORD Queensferry Rd ✆ 336 2683
	DAIHATSU Westfield Rd ✆ 337 7204
AUSTIN-ROVER Lanark Rd ✆ 443 2936	PORSCHE 300 Colinton Rd ✆ 031 441 6805
AUSTIN-ROVER 70 Slateford Rd ✆ 337 1252	RENAULT 553 Gorgie Rd ✆ 444 1673
CITROEN 13 Lauriston Gardens ✆ 229 4207	TALBOT Lochrin Tollcross ✆ 229 8911
FIAT, LANCIA 8 Glenogle Rd ✆ 556 6404	VOLVO 38 Seafield Rd East ✆ 669 8301
FORD Baileyfield Rd ✆ 669 6261	VOLVO Bankhead ✆ 442 3333
FORD Fountainbridge ✆ 229 3331	VW, AUDI-NSU 454 Gorgie Rd ✆ 346 1661
FORD 12 West Mayfield ✆ 667 1900	VW, AUDI-NSU Marionville Rd ✆ 652 1691

EDZELL Angus (Tayside) 401 M 13 Scotland G – pop. 751 – ECD : Thursday – ☎ 035 64.
Envir. : Castle★ (The Pleasance★★★) W : 1¼ m.

🛆 ✆ 235 – 🛆 at Brechin ✆ 035 62 (Brechin) 2383, S : 5 ½ m.
♦Edinburgh 94 – ♦Aberdeen 36 – ♦Dundee 31.

🏠 **Glenesk,** High St., DD9 7TF, ✆ 319, 🐾, 🐎 – TV ⌷wc ⋔wc ☎ P. ⚘. ⊼ AE ⓞ
    M 10.00/15.00 **st.** and a la carte 8.00/19.50 **t.** ◊ 3.50 – **25 rm** ⊆ 25.00/52.00 **t.**

EGILSAY (Isle of) Orkney (Orkney Islands) 401 L 6 – Shipping Services : see Orkney Islands
(Mainland : Kirkwall).

EIGG (Isle of) Inverness. (Highland) 401 B 13 – Shipping Services : see Mallaig.

ELGIN Moray. (Grampian) 401 K 11 Scotland G – pop. 18 702 – ECD : Wednesday – ☎ 0343.
See : Site★ – Cathedral★ (Chapter House★★).
Envir. : Forres (Sueno's Stone★★) W : 12 ½ m. by A 96.

🛆 Hardhillock, Birnie Rd ✆ 2338, S : 1 m. – 🛆 Hopeman ✆ 830578, N : 7 m.
🇮 17 High St. ✆ 3388 and 2666.
♦Edinburgh 198 – ♦Aberdeen 68 – Fraserburgh 61 – ♦Inverness 39.

🏠 **Mansion House,** The Haugh, IV30 1AW, via Haugh Rd and Murdocks Wynd ✆ 48811, 🐎
    – TV ⌷wc ☎ P. ⊼ AE ⓞ VISA. ⅏
    M 10.00/20.00 **st.** and a la carte ◊ 3.90 – **12 rm** ⊆ 29.50/57.50 **st.** – SB (weekends only)
    54.00/70.00 **st.**

🏠 **Park House,** South St., IV30 1JB, ✆ 7695 – TV ⌷wc ⋔wc ☎ P. ⊼ AE ⓞ VISA
    M 4.60/15.00 **t.** and a la carte ◊ 2.60 – **6 rm** ⊆ 30.00/45.00 **t.**

AUSTIN ROVER-DAIMLER-JAGUAR Station Rd ✆ 48444	NISSAN Borough Briggs Rd ✆ 7473
CITROEN 27 Greyfriars St. ✆ 7416	VAUXHALL-OPEL Edgar Rd ✆ 7688
FORD East Rd ✆ 2176	VW, AUDI Blackfriars Rd ✆ 44977

ELLON Aberdeen. (Grampian) **401** N 11 – pop. 6 304 – ECD : Wednesday – ✆ 0358.
Envir. : Pitmedden Gardens**, SW : 5 m. by A 920 – Haddo House*, NW : 8 m. by 9005.
🛅 McDonald ✆ 20576 – 🅿 Market St. Car Park ✆ 20730 (summer only).
◆Edinburgh 147 – ◆Aberdeen 17 – Fraserburgh 27.

🏨 **Ladbroke Mercury** (Ladbroke), South Rd, AB4 9NP, ✆ 20666, Telex 739200 – 📺 🛏️wc 📞
🅿 🚗 🔄 AE ⓞ VISA
M (bar lunch)/dinner 10.00 **t.** and a la carte 🍴 3.70 – ⚌ 6.00 – **40 rm** 36.00/48.00 **t.** –
SB 63.00 **st.**

ERISKA (Isle of) Argyll. (Strathclyde) **401** D 14 – ✉ Oban – ✆ 063 172 Ledaig.

🏨 **Isle of Eriska** 📖, PA37 1SD, ✆ 371, Telex 777040, ≤ Lismore and mountains, « Country
house atmosphere », 🌲, park, 🎾 – ☎ 👍 🅿 🔄 AE ⓞ
20 February-mid November – **M** (buffet lunch)/dinner 21.00 – **17 rm** ⚌ (dinner included) 94.00/136.00 – SB (20 February-10 April only) 115.00 **t.**

ERSKINE Renfrew. (Strathclyde) **401 402** G 16 – ✆ 041 Glasgow.
◆Edinburgh 55 – ◆Glasgow 9.

🏨 **Crest** (Crest) 📖, Erskine Bridge, PA8 6AN, on A 726 ✆ 812 0123, Telex 777713, ≤, 🌲 – 📶
📶 rest 📺 🔄 🅿 🚗 🔄 AE ⓞ VISA
M 8.95/11.95 **st.** and a la carte 🍴 3.50 – ⚌ 5.95 – **186 rm** 47.50/56.50 **st.**, **2 suites** –
SB (weekends only) 58.00/68.00 **st.**

ESKDALEMUIR Dumfries (Dumfries and Galloway) **401 402** K 18 – ✉ Langholm – ✆ 05416.
◆Edinburgh 71 – ◆Carlisle 33 – ◆Dumfries 28.

🍴 **Hart Manor,** DG13 0QQ, S : ½ m. on B 709 ✆ 217 – 🛏️wc 🅿 VISA
M (closed dinner Sunday and Monday to non residents) (bar lunch)/dinner 12.50 **t.** 🍴 3.00 –
7 rm ⚌ 21.00/41.00 **t.**

ETTRICKBRIDGE Selkirk. (Borders) **401 402** L 17 – see Selkirk.

FALKIRK Stirling. (Central) **401** I 16 – pop. 36 372 – ECD : Wednesday – ✆ 0324.
Envir. : Linlithgow** (Palace** : Gateway*, Fountain**, Great Hall: fireplace**-Old town*,
St. Michael's Church*) E : 8 m. by A 803.
🛅 Grangemouth ✆ 0324 (Polmont) 711500, E : 3 m.
◆Edinburgh 26 – Dunfermline 18 – ◆Glasgow 25 – Motherwell 27 – Perth 43.

🏨 **Stakis Park** (Stakis), Camelon Rd, Arnothill, FK1 5RY, ✆ 28331, Telex 776502 – 📶 📺 🛏️wc
📞 🅿 🚗 🔄 AE ⓞ VISA
M 4.50/15.00 **t.** and a la carte 🍴 3.60 – ⚌ 3.90 – **55 rm** 38.00/48.00 **t.** – SB 42.00/55.00 **st.**

✕ **Pierre's,** 140 Grahams Rd, FK2 7BQ, ✆ 35843, French rest. – 🔄 AE ⓞ VISA
closed Saturday lunch, Sunday, Monday, Christmas Day and 1-2 January – **M** (restricted
lunch) 13.75 **t.** (dinner) and a la carte 8.45/15.20 🍴 2.85.

at Grangemouth NE : 3 m. on A 904 – ✉ ✆ 0324 Grangemouth :

🏨 **Grange Manor,** Glensburgh Rd, FK3 8XJ, SW : 1 m. by A 904 on A 905 ✆ 474836, Telex
777620 – 📺 🛏️wc 🛏️wc ☎ 🅿 🚗 🔄 AE ⓞ VISA 🍽️
M 7.25 **t.** (lunch) and a la carte 10.45/15.00 **t.** 🍴 3.85 – **7 rm** ⚌ 39.00/49.50 **st.** – SB (weekends
only) 50.00 **st.**

at Polmont SE : 3 m. on A 803 – ✉ ✆ 0324 Polmont :

🏨 **Inchyra Grange,** Grange Rd, FK2 0YB, ✆ 711911, Telex 777693, 🌲 – 📺 🛏️wc ☎ 🚗 🅿
🚗 🔄 AE ⓞ VISA
closed 1 to 4 January – **M** 7.00/9.25 **t.** and a la carte 🍴 2.75 – **30 rm** ⚌ 39.50/61.00 **st.** –
SB (weekends only except Christmas and New Year) 48.00/54.00 **st.**

FORD Callendar Rd ✆ 21511
HYUNDAI High Station Rd ✆ 24221
LANCIA Callendar Rd ✆ 24204
MAZDA Main St. ✆ 22584
TOYOTA Lady'smill ✆ 35935
TOYOTA Winchester Av. Denny ✆ 824387
VAUXHALL-OPEL 76-86 Grahams Rd ✆ 21234
VOLVO West End ✆ 23042

FARR Inverness. (Highland) **401** H 11 – ✆ 080 83.
◆Edinburgh 155 – ◆Inverness 10.

✕✕ **Grouse and Trout,** Flichity, IV1 2XE, S : 4 m. by B 851 ✆ 314, ≤, 🌲 – 🅿 🔄 AE ⓞ VISA
M 12.00 **t.** (dinner) and a la carte 9.15/27.70 **t.** 🍴 3.00.

FEOLIN Argyll. (Strathclyde) **401** B 16 – Shipping Services : see Jura (Isle of).

FETLAR (Isle of) Shetland (Shetland Islands) **401** R 2 – Shipping Services : see Shetland Islands.

FIONNPHORT Argyll. (Strathclyde) **401** A 15 – Shipping Services : see Mull (Isle of).

FISHNISH Argyll. (Strathclyde) **401** C 14 – Shipping Services : see Mull (Isle of).

FLOTTA (Isle of) Orkney (Orkney Islands) **401** K 7 – Shipping Services : see Orkney Islands.

FOCHABERS Moray. (Grampian) **401** K 11 **Scotland G** – pop. 1 419 – ECD : Wednesday – ✪ 0343 – ✦Edinburgh 188 – ✦Aberdeen 58 – Fraserburgh 52 – ✦Inverness 48.

  at Tynet NE : 3½ m. on A 98 – ✉ Fochabers – ✪ 054 27 Clochan :

    🏠 **Mill,** AB5 2HJ, on A 98 ℰ 233 – 📺 ⌂wc ⋔wc. ⚑ 🄰🄴 ⓪ 𝖵𝖨𝖲𝖠
    closed 1 and 2 January – **M** *(closed Sunday dinner)* 4.00/9.75 **t.** – **15 rm** ⊆ 19.00/34.00 **t.**

FORDYCE Banffshire (Grampian) **401** L 11 – ✪ 0261 Portsoy.
✦Edinburgh 187 – ✦Aberdeen 57 – ✦Inverness 65.

    ✕✕ **Hawthorne,** AB4 2SL, ℰ 43003 – **P.** ⚑ 🄰🄴 𝖵𝖨𝖲𝖠
    closed Monday and February – **M** (dinner only) a la carte 9.05/13.75 **t.** 🛆 2.90.

FORFAR Angus (Tayside) **401** L 14 – pop. 12 652 – ECD : Thursday – ✪ 0307.
Envir. : Glamis★ (Castle★★, Angus Folk Museum★) SW : 5 ½ m. by A 94 – Meigle Museum★★
(Early Christian Monuments★★) SW : 12 ½ m. by A 94.
🛅 Cunninghill, Arbroath Rd ℰ 2120, E : 1 m. on A 932 – 🄴 The Myre ℰ 67876.
✦Edinburgh 75 – ✦Aberdeen 55 – ✦Dundee 12 – Perth 31.

    🏛 **Benholm** 🐾, 78 Glamis Rd, DD8 1DS, SW : ½ m. on A 94 ℰ 64281, 🌱 – 📺 ⌂wc ⋔wc ☎
    P. – **7 rm.**

    🏠 **Royal,** 31-33 Castle St., DD8 3AE, ℰ 62691 – 📺 ⌂wc ☜ **P.** – **21 rm.**

AUSTIN-ROVER 128 Castle St. ℰ 62542   PEUGEOT-TALBOT Lochside Rd ℰ 62676
FORD Kirriemuir Rd ℰ 62347

FORRES Moray (Grampian) **401** J 11 **Scotland G.** – pop. 8 346 – ECD : Wednesday – ✪ 0309.
✦Edinburgh 165 – ✦Aberdeen 80 – ✦Inverness 27.

    🏠 Ramnee, Victoria Rd, IV36 0BN, ℰ 72410, 🌱 – 📺 ⌂wc ⋔wc **P.** – **20 rm.**

FORSINARD Sutherland (Highland) – ✪ 064 17 Halladale.
✦Edinburgh 271 – Thurso 30 – ✦Wick 51.

    🏠 **Forsinard** 🐾, KW13 6YT, ℰ 221, ≼, 🐾 – ⌂wc ⋔wc 🛆 ⓖ. ⚑ 𝖵𝖨𝖲𝖠
    Easter-October – **M** (booking essential)(bar lunch)/dinner 10.50 **t.** 🛆 2.30 – **10 rm**
    ⊆ 19.00/40.00 **t.**

FORTINGALL Perth (Tayside) **401** H 14 – see Aberfeldy.

FORT WILLIAM Inverness. (Highland) **401** E 13 **Scotland G** – pop. 10 805 – ECD : Wednesday
except summer – ✪ 0397.
See : Site★ – Envir. : Ben Nevis★★, SE : 4 m. – Road to the Isles★★ (Glenfinnan★, Arisaig★ (≼★ of
Sound of Arisaig), Silver Sands of Morar★, Mallaig★) NW : 46 m. by A 830 – Glen Nevis★, SE.
🛅 Torlundy ℰ 4464, N : 3 m. on A 82 – 🄴 ℰ 3781.
✦Edinburgh 133 – ✦Glasgow 104 – ✦Inverness 68 – ✦Oban 50.

    🏰 ✿ **Inverlochy Castle** 🐾, Inverlochy, PH33 6SN, NE : 3 m. on A 82 ℰ 2177, Telex 776229, ≼
    garden, loch and mountains, « Victorian castle in extensive grounds », 🐾, 🌱, park, ✕
    📺 ☎ **P.** ⚑ 𝖵𝖨𝖲𝖠. ✖
    Mid March-mid November – **M** (booking essential) 22.00/29.00 **t.** 🛆 5.00 – **15 rm**
    ⊆ 88.00/120.00 **t.**, **2 suites** 157.00 **t.**
    Spec. Loch Linnhe prawns, Scottish Game (15 August-mid November), Orange souffle.

    🏛 **Ladbroke Mercury** (Ladbroke), Achintore Rd, PH33 6RW, SW : 2 m. on A 82 ℰ 3117, Telex
    778454, ≼ – ⫾ 📺 ⌂wc ☎ **P.** ⚑ 🄰🄴 𝖵𝖨𝖲𝖠
    M (carving rest.) 6.95/10.00 **st.** and a la carte 🛆 4.50 – ⊆ 6.00 – **86 rm** 35.50/55.00 **st.** –
    SB 58.00/72.00 **st.**

    🏠 **Nevis Bank,** Belford Rd, PH33 6BY, ℰ 5721 – 📺 ⌂wc ⋔wc ☎ **P.** ⚑ 🄰🄴 𝖵𝖨𝖲𝖠
    M 5.50/10.95 **t.** and a la carte 🛆 3.25 – **31 rm** ⊆ 25.00/48.00 **t.**, **2 suites** 60.00/80.00 **t.** –
    SB (except Christmas and New Year) 49.50/70.00 **st.**

    ⌂ **Guisachan,** Alma Rd, PH33 6HA, ℰ 3797, ≼ – ⋔wc **P.** ✖
    closed 20 December-5 January – **15 rm** ⊆ 9.00/30.00 **st.**

    ✕✕ **Factor's House** with rm, Torlundy, PH33 6SN, NE : 3 ½ m. on A 82 ℰ 5767, Telex 776229 –
    📺 ⌂wc ☎ **P.** ⚑ 🄰🄴 ⓪ 𝖵𝖨𝖲𝖠. ✖
    Mid March-mid November – **M** *(closed Monday)* (dinner only) 12.50 **t.** 🛆 4.50 – **7 rm**
    ⊆ 35.00/50.00.

  at Banavie N : 3 m. by A 82 and A 830 on B 8004 – ✉ Fort William – ✪ 039 77 Corpach :

    🏠 **Moorings,** PH33 7LY, ℰ 550, ≼, 🌱 – ⌂wc ⋔wc **P.** ⚑ ⓪ 𝖵𝖨𝖲𝖠. ✖
    M (restricted lunch in winter) 12.00/13.00 **st.** and a la carte 🛆 2.50 – **17 rm** ⊆ 19.50/40.00 **st.** –
    SB (except summer) 56.00/62.00 **st.**

AUSTIN-ROVER Gordon Sq. ℰ 2345

FOYERS Inverness. (Highland) **401** G 12 – ✆ 045 63 Gorthleck.

See : Loch Ness★★.

◆Edinburgh 176 – ◆Inverness 18.

🏡 **Foyers,** IV1 2XT, N : ½ m. on B 852 ⌀ 216, ≤ Loch Ness and mountains, ⤢, 🐎 – 🏛 **P**
M 6.00 st. and a la carte ⌀ 2.90 – **9 rm** ☲ 12.00/24.00 st.

GAIRLOCH Ross and Cromarty (Highland) **401** C 10 – ECD : Wednesday except summer –
✆ 0445.

Envir. : Inverewe Gardens★★★, NE : 8 m. by A 832 – Wester Ross★★★ (Gairloch to Ullapool★ via
Loch Maree★★★, Inverewe Gardens★★★, Falls of Measach★ and Loch Broom★★) NE : 56 m. by
A 832 and A 835 – Wester Ross★★★ (Gairloch to Kyle of Lochalsh via Victoria Falls★ Loch Maree★★★,
and Plockton★) S : 102 m. by A 832, A 896 and A 890.

🚉 Gairloch ⌀ 2407, S : 1 m. on A 832 – 🛈 Achtercairn ⌀ 2130.

◆Edinburgh 228 – ◆Inverness 72 – Kyle of Lochalsh 68.

🏨 **Gairloch,** IV21 2BL, ⌀ 2001, ≤ Gair Loch and Isle of Skye, ⤢, ✕ – 📶 �🖇wc 🏛wc **P**. ⤢ 🄰🄴
VISA
April-October – **M** (bar lunch)/dinner 10.00 t. and a la carte ⌀ 3.50 – **51 rm** ☲ 19.00/56.00 t. –
SB (except winter) 42.00/105.00 st.

🏡 **Shieldaig Lodge** ⤢, IV21 2AW, S : 4 m. by A 832 on B 8056 ⌀ 044 583 (Badachro) 250, ≤
Gair Loch, « Former hunting lodge on lochside », ⤢, 🐎, ✕ – �🖇wc **P**. ⤢ **VISA**
April-mid November – **M** (bar lunch)/dinner 9.50 t. – **14 rm** ☲ 27.00/52.00 t.

🏚 **Creag Mor,** Charlestown, IV21 2AH, S : 2 m. on A 832 ⌀ 2068, ⤢ – �🖇wc **P**. ✕
closed mid January-mid February – **M** (bar lunch)/dinner 9.50 st. ⌀ 2.10 – **9 rm**
☲ 16.00/32.00 st.

GALASHIELS Selkirk. (Borders) **401** **402** L 17 – pop. 12 206 – ECD : Wednesday – ✆ 0896.

🚉 Ladhope, ⌀ 3724, NE : ¼ m. – 🚉 Torwoodlee, ⌀ 2260, N : 1 m. on A 7.

🛈 Bank St. ⌀ 55551 (summer only).

◆Edinburgh 34 – ◆Carlisle 61 – ◆Glasgow 71 – ◆Newcastle-upon-Tyne 74.

🏨 **Woodlands House,** Windyknowe Rd, TD1 1RQ, NW : ¾ m. by A 72 and Hall St. ⌀ 4722,
🐎 – 📺 �🖇wc **P**. ⤢ 🄰🄴 ⓞ **VISA**
M (buffet lunch in summer)/dinner 9.75 t. and a la carte ⌀ 2.65 – **9 rm** ☲ 28.50/44.00 t. –
SB 55.00 st.

🏨 **Kingsknowes,** Selkirk Rd, TD1 3HY, SE : 1 ½ m. on A 7 ⌀ 58375, ≤, 🐎, ✕ – 📺 �🖇wc ☎
P. ⤢ 🄰🄴 ⓞ **VISA**
M 9.50 t. and a la carte ⌀ 2.20 – **11 rm** ☲ 30.00/48.00 t. – SB (except summer) 52.00/56.00 st.

GARVE Ross and Cromarty (Highland) **401** F 11 – ECD : Thursday – ✆ 099 74.

◆Edinburgh 184 – ◆Inverness 28 – Wick 130.

🏨 Strathgarve Lodge ⤢, IV23 2PU, N : 2 ¾ m. by A 832 off A 835 ⌀ 204, ≤, ⤢, 🐎, park – 📺
�🖇wc **P** – **14 rm, 1 suite**.

GATEHOUSE OF FLEET Kirkcudbright. (Dumfries and Galloway) **401** **402** H 19 – pop. 894 –
ECD : Thursday – ✆ 055 74 – 🚉.

🛈 Car Park ⌀ 212 (summer only).

◆Edinburgh 113 – ◆Dumfries 33 – Stranraer 42.

🏨 **Cally Palace** ⤢, DG7 2DL, S : 1 ½ m. by A 75 ⌀ 341, ≤, ♨ heated, ⤢, 🐎, park, ✕ – 📶
📺 �🖇wc ☎ 🕭 🐾 **P**. **VISA**
March-October – **M** 5.50/12.50 st. ⌀ 2.50 – **65 rm** ☲ 34.50/69.00 st., **1 suite** – SB (weekends
only) 60.00/75.00 st.

🏨 **Murray Arms** (Best Western), High St., DG7 2HY, ⌀ 207, ⤢, 🐎, ✕ – 📺 �🖇wc ☎ **P**. ⤢
🄰🄴 ⓞ **VISA**
M (bar lunch)/dinner 11.00 st. ⌀ 3.20 – **18 rm** ☲ 25.00/60.00 st., **1 suite** 55.00/60.00 st. –
SB 64.00 st.

GATTONSIDE Roxburgh. (Borders) – see Melrose.

GIFFNOCK Renfrew. (Strathclyde) **401** ⑯ **402** ⑨ – see Glasgow.

GIFFORD E. Lothian (Lothian) **401** L 16 – pop. 665 – ECD : Monday and Wednesday – ✉ Haddington – ✆ 062 081.

◆Edinburgh 20 – Hawick 50.

🏡 **Tweeddale Arms,** High St., EH41 4QU, ⌀ 240 – 📺 �🖇wc ☎ **P**. ⤢ 🄰🄴 **VISA**
M 7.50/10.25 t. and a la carte ⌀ 2.95 – **15 rm** ☲ 29.00/45.00 t. – SB 50.00/60.00 st.

GIGHA (Isle of) Argyll. (Strathclyde) **401** C 16 – pop. 176 – ✆ 058 35.

⛴ by Caledonian MacBrayne : from Ardminish to Tayinloan, summer only : 4-6 daily (20 mn).

🏡 **Gigha** ⤢, PA41 7AD, ⌀ 254, ≤ Sound of Gigha and Kintyre Peninsula, « Tastefully renovated
inn and farmhouse », ⤢, ⌀wc **P**. ⤢ **VISA**
April-October – **M** 6.50/11.50 t. – **9 rm** ☲ 20.00/45.00 t.

GLASGOW Lanark. (Strathclyde) **401 402** H 16 **Scotland** G – pop. 754 586 – ✪ 041.

See : Site★★★ – Burrell Collection★★★ AX **M1** – Cathedral★★★ DYZ – Tolbooth Steeple★ DZ **A** – Hunterian Art Gallery★★ (Whistler Collection★★★, Mackintosh wing★★★) CY **M2** Art Gallery and Museum Kelvingrove★★ CY – City Chambers★ DZ **C** – Glasgow School of Art★ CY **B** – Museum of Transport★★ (Scottish cars★★★, Clyde Room of Ship Models★★★) BX **M3** – Pollok House★ (Spanish paintings★★) AX **D**.

Envir. : Trossachs★★★ N : by A 739 AV and A 81 – Loch Lomond★★, NW : by A 82 AV – Clyde Estuary★ (Dumbarton Castle Site★, Hill House, Helensburgh★) by A 82, AV – Bothwell Castle★ and David Livingstone Centre (Museum★) SE : 9 m. by A 724 BX.

🏌 Linn Park, Simshill Rd ℰ 637 5871, S : 4 m. BX – 🏌 Lethamhill, Cumbernauld Rd ℰ 770 6220 BV – 🏌 Knightswood, Lincoln Av. ℰ 959 2131, W : 4 m. AV.

Access to Oban by helicopter.

✈ Glasgow Airport : ℰ 887 1111, Telex 778219, W : 8 m. by M 8 AV – **Terminal** : Coach service from Glasgow Central and Queen Street main line Railway Stations and from Anderston Cross and Buchanan Bus Stations.

✈ see also Prestwick.

🛈 35-39 St. Vincent Pl. ℰ 227 4880.

◆Edinburgh 46 – ◆Manchester 221.

Plans on following pages

🏨🏨 **Albany** (T.H.F.), Bothwell St., G2 7EN, ℰ 248 2656, Telex 77440, ← – 🛗 🗏 📺 ☎ 🅿 🔩 🔼
ÆΞ ⓪ 𝘝𝘐𝘚𝘈 　　　　　　　　　　　　　　　　　　　　　　　　　　　　　　　　CZ **z**
M 8.00/8.65 **st.** and a la carte ⒧ 3.40 – ⛌ 6.00 – **251 rm** 56.00/67.00 **st.**, **3 suites**.

🏨🏨 **Holiday Inn**, Argyle St., Anderston, G3 8RR, ℰ 226 5577, Telex 776355, 🔲 – 🛗 🗏 📺 ☎ ⅙ 🅿
🔩 **296 rm**, **3 suites**. 　　　　　　　　　　　　　　　　　　　　　　　　　　　CZ **a**

🏨 **One Devonshire Gardens,** 1 Devonshire Gdns, G12 0UX, ℰ 339 20001 – 📺 ☎ 🅿 🔩 🔼
ÆΞ ⓪ 𝘝𝘐𝘚𝘈 　　　　　　　　　　　　　　　　　　　　　　　　　　　　　　　　AV **a**
closed Christmas-New Year – **M** (dinner only and Sunday lunch)/dinner 22.50 **st.** – ⛌ 7.25 –
8 rm 75.00/120.00.

🏨 **Stakis Grosvenor** (Stakis), Grosvenor Terr., Great Western Rd, G12 0TA, ℰ 339 8811, Telex
776247 – 🛗 📺 ☎ 🅿 🔩 🔼 𝘝𝘐𝘚𝘈 　　　　　　　　　　　　　　　　　　　CY **r**
M 8.00/15.00 **t.** and a la carte ⒧ 4.00 – ⛌ 3.90 – **96 rm** 40.00/70.00 **t.**, **2 suites** 90.00/120.00 **t.** –
SB 54.00/68.00 **st.**

🏨 **Hospitality Inn** (Mt. Charlotte), 36 Cambridge St., G3 7DS, ℰ 332 3311, Telex 777334 – 🛗
📺 ☎ ⅙ 🅿 🔩 🔼 ÆΞ ⓪ 𝘝𝘐𝘚𝘈 　　　　　　　　　　　　　　　　　　　　DY **z**
M 5.75/7.50 **st.** and a la carte ⒧ 3.00 – **316 rm** ⛌ 47.50/58.00 **st.**, **3 suites** 100.00 **st.**

🏨 **White House** ⇘ without rest., 12 Cleveden Cres., G12 0PA, ℰ 339 9375 – 📺 ☎ 🔩 🔼
⓪ 𝘝𝘐𝘚𝘈 ⁓ 　　　　　　　　　　　　　　　　　　　　　　　　　　　　　　AV **r**
M (room service only) a la carte approx. 11.85 **t.** ⒧ 2.25 – ⛌ 5.75 – **32 rm** 44.30/55.80 **t.**,
11 suites 63.30/84.50 **t.**

🏨 **Tinto Firs Thistle** (Thistle), 470 Kilmarnock Rd, G43 2BB, ℰ 637 2353, Telex 778329 – 📺
⌸wc 🅿 🔩 🔼 ÆΞ ⓪ 𝘝𝘐𝘚𝘈 ⁓ 　　　　　　　　　　　　　　　　　　　　AX **c**
M 6.50/11.25 **t.** and a la carte ⒧ 3.60 – ⛌ 5.95 – **27 rm** 45.00/65.00 **st.**, **2 suites** 70.00 **st.** –
SB (weekends only) 62.00 **st.**

🏨 **Copthorne,** George Sq., G2 1DS, ℰ 332 6711, Telex 778147 – 🛗 📺 ⌸wc ☎ 🔩 🔼 ÆΞ ⓪
𝘝𝘐𝘚𝘈 　　　　　　　　　　　　　　　　　　　　　　　　　　　　　　　　　DZ **n**
M 10.95 **st.** and a la carte ⒧ 3.45 – ⛌ 4.75 – **143 rm** 40.00/55.00 **st.**, **5 suites** 55.00/80.00 **st.** –
SB (weekends only) 60.00/65.00 **st.**

🏨 **Stakis Pond** (Stakis), 2-4 Shelley Rd, Great Western Rd, G12 2XB, ℰ 334 8161, Telex 776573,
🔲 – 🛗 📺 ⌸wc ☎ 🅿 🔩 🔼 ÆΞ ⓪ 𝘝𝘐𝘚𝘈 　　　　　　　　　　　　　　　AV **i**
M 5.95/8.95 **t.** and a la carte ⒧ 3.50 – ⛌ 3.90 – **133 rm** 42.00/65.00 **t.** – SB 44.00/64.00 **st.**

🏨 **Kelvin Park Lorne,** 923 Sauchiehall St., G3 7TE, ℰ 334 4891, Telex 778935 – 🛗 📺 ⌸wc ☎
🅿 🔩 🔼 ÆΞ ⓪ 𝘝𝘐𝘚𝘈 ⁓ 　　　　　　　　　　　　　　　　　　　　　　　CY **a**
M 7.95/12.50 **t.** and a la carte ⒧ 3.00 – **80 rm** 43.95/53.95 **t.** – SB (weekends only) 49.95/54.95 **st.**

🏨 Stakis Ingram (Stakis), 201 Ingram St., G1 1DQ, ℰ 248 4401, Telex 776470 – 🛗 📺 ⌸wc ☎
🅿 🔩 – **90 rm** 　　　　　　　　　　　　　　　　　　　　　　　　　　　　DZ **c**

🏨 **Bellahouston Swallow** (Swallow), 517 Paisley Rd West, G51 1RW, ℰ 427 3146, Telex
778795 – 🛗 📺 ⌸wc ⑃wc ☎ 🅿 🔩 🔼 ÆΞ ⓪ 𝘝𝘐𝘚𝘈 　　　　　　　　　AX **a**
M (closed lunch Saturday and Sunday) 6.00/9.00 **st.** and a la carte ⒧ 3.95 – **122 rm**
⛌ 46.50/56.00 **st.** – SB (weekends only) 55.00 **st.**

🏨 **Crest** (Crest), 377 Argyle St., G2 8LL, ℰ 248 2355, Telex 779652 – 🛗 📺 ⌸wc ☎ 🔩 🔼 ÆΞ
⓪ 𝘝𝘐𝘚𝘈 ⁓ 　　　　　　　　　　　　　　　　　　　　　　　　　　　　　CZ **x**
M 7.95/11.75 **st.** and a la carte – ⛌ 5.95 – **121 rm** 47.00/59.00 **st.** – SB (weekends only)
58.00/64.00 **st.**

🏨 Newlands, 290 Kilmarnock Rd, G43 2XS, ℰ 632 9171 – 📺 ⌸wc ☎ – **17 rm** 　　AX **n**

🏠 **Dalmeny,** 62 St. Andrews Drive, Nithsdale Cross, Pollokshields, G41 5EZ, ℰ 427 1106 – 📺
⌸wc ⑃wc 🅿 　　　　　　　　　　　　　　　　　　　　　　　　　　　　　AX **o**
10 rm ⛌ 21.50/39.00 **st.**

🏠 **Kirklee,** 11 Kensington Gate, G12 9LG, ℰ 334 5555 – 📺 ⌸wc. ⁓ 　　　　AV **c**
10 rm ⛌ 23.00/34.50 **st.**

GLASGOW
BUILT UP AREA

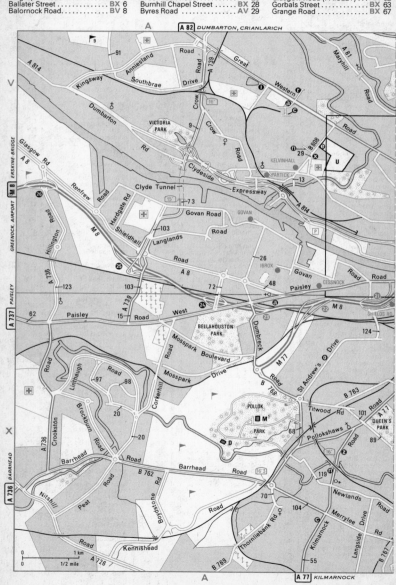

For Street Index see Glasgow p. 6

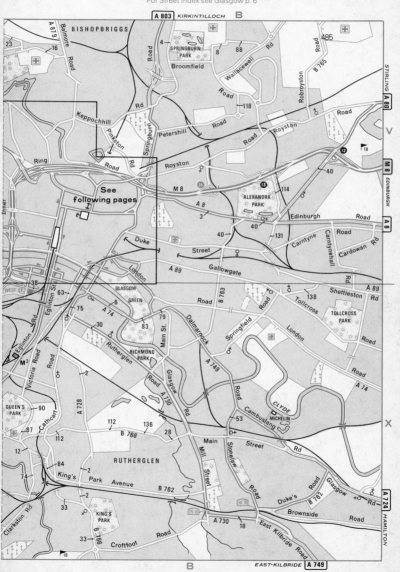

22

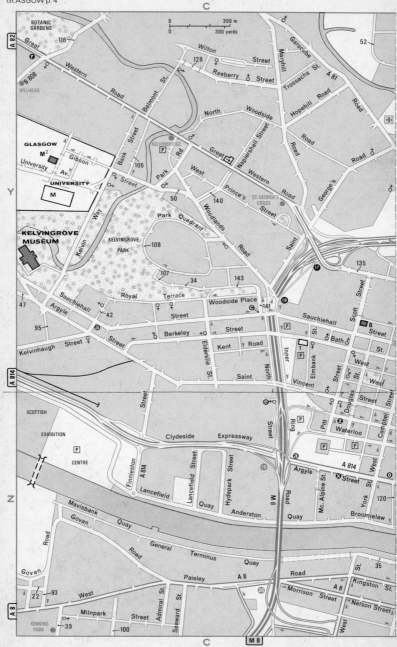

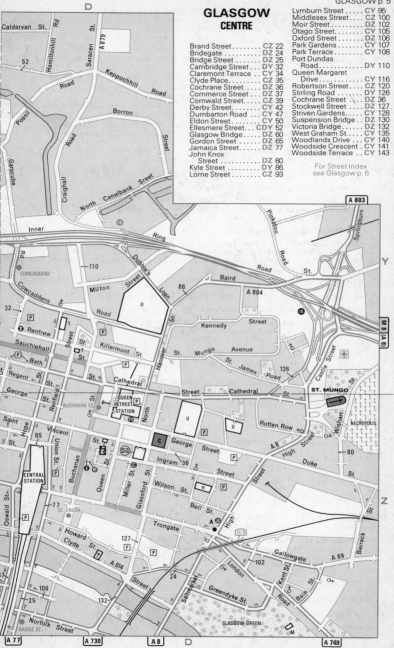

GLASGOW
CENTRE

XXX **Fountain,** 2 Woodside Cres., G3 7UL, ℰ 332 6396 – ◪ 🆑 ⓪ *VISA*   CY **c**
   closed Saturday lunch, Monday dinner, Sunday, 25-26 December and 1-2 January –
   M 9.00/15.00 **t.** and a la carte 13.85/17.75 **t.** ▯ 4.95.

XX **Buttery,** 652 Argyle St., G3 8UF, ℰ 221 8188 – ℗. ◪ 🆑 ⓪ *VISA*   CZ **e**
   closed Saturday lunch, Sunday and Bank Holidays – **M** 11.50 **st.** and a la carte 13.70/21.75 **t.**

XX **Rogano,** 11 Exchange Pl., G1 3AN, ℰ 248 4055, Seafood, « Art deco » – ▤. ◪ 🆑 ⓪ *VISA*   DZ **i**
   closed Sunday and Bank Holidays – **M** a la carte 13.75/22.35 **t.**

XX **Amber Royale,** 336 Argyle St., G2 8LY, ℰ 221 2550, Chinese rest. – ▤. ◪ 🆑 ⓪ *VISA*   CZ **o**
   closed Sunday – **M** 4.50/14.00 **t.** and a la carte 11.00/16.00 **t.** ▯ 3.50.

XX **Colonial,** 25 High St., G1 1LX, ℰ 552 1923 – ◪ 🆑 ⓪ *VISA*   DZ **a**
   *closed Saturday lunch, Monday dinner, Sunday, 17 July-3 August, Christmas, New Year and
   Bank Holidays* – **M** 8.25/17.95 **st.** and a la carte 12.95/19.35 **st.** ▯ 3.60.

X **Poacher's,** Ruthven Lane, off Byres Rd, G12 9BG, ℰ 339 0932 – ℗. ◪ 🆑 ⓪ *VISA*   AV **n**
   closed Sunday, 1-2 January and Bank Holidays – **M** (restricted lunch)/a la carte 9.95/17.00 **t.**
   ▯ 2.90.

X **Le Provençal,** 21 Royal Exchange Sq., G1 3AJ, ℰ 221 0798, French rest. – ◪ 🆑 ⓪ *VISA*   DZ **e**
   closed Sunday – **M** (restricted lunch) a la carte 7.50/15.35 **t.** ▯ 3.75.

X **Ubiquitous Chip,** 12 Ashton Lane, off Byres Rd, G12 8SJ, ℰ 334 5007, Bistro – ◪ 🆑 ⓪   AV **e**
   VISA
   closed Sunday, Christmas Day and 1-2 January – **M** a la carte 6.85/17.70 **t.** ▯ 2.45.

X **Trattoria Sorrento,** 87 Kilmarnock Rd, Shawlands, G41 3YR, ℰ 649 3002, Italian rest.   AX **z**

X **Amber,** 130 Byres Rd, G12 8DQ, ℰ 339 6121, Chinese-Cantonese rest. – ◪ 🆑 ⓪ *VISA*   AV **x**
   M 3.60/12.00 **t.** and a la carte approx. 7.60 **t.** ▯ 3.00.

at Giffnock (Renfrew.) (Strathclyde) S : 5 ¼ m. by A 77 – AX – ✉ 🕿 041 Glasgow :

🏨 **MacDonald Thistle** (Thistle), Eastwood Toll, G46 6RA, at intersection of A 77 and A 726
   ℰ 638 2225, Telex 779138 – 📺 🛏wc 🕿 ℗. ◪ 🆑 ⓪ *VISA*. ⚘
   M 6.95/10.95 **t.** and a la carte ▯ 2.90 – ⎓ 5.95 – **53 rm** 45.00/65.00 **st.** – **4 suites** 70.00 **st.** –
   SB (weekends only) 62.00 **st.**

🏨 **Stakis Redhurst** (Stakis), 77 Eastwoodmains Rd, G46 6QE, ℰ 638 6465 – 📺 🛏wc 📞 ℗.
   ◪ 🆑 ⓪ *VISA*
   M (grill rest. only) a la carte 6.65/9.65 **st.** ▯ 3.10 – ⎓ 3.90 – **19 rm** 42.00/50.00 **st.**

at Busby S : 5 ½ m. by A 727 – AX – on A 726 – ✉ 🕿 041 Glasgow :

🏨 **Busby,** 1 Field Rd, Clarkston, G76 8RX, ℰ 644 2661 – ▤ 📺 🛏wc ▯wc 🕿 ℗. ◪ 🆑 ⓪ *VISA*
   closed 25 December and 1 January – **M** 5.50/6.25 **t.** and a la carte ▯ 3.15 – **14 rm**
   ⎓ 30.00/36.50 **t.** – SB (weekends only) 60.50/75.20 **st.**

at Glasgow Airport (Renfrew.) (Strathclyde) W : 8 m. by M 8 – AV – ✉ 🕿 041 Glasgow :

🏨 **Excelsior** (T.H.F.), Abbotsinch, PA3 2TR, ℰ 887 1212, Telex 777733 – ▤ 📺 🕿 & ℗. ⚘ ◪
   🆑 ⓪ *VISA*
   M 8.95 **st.** and a la carte ▯ 3.40 – ⎓ 6.00 – **290 rm** 52.00/64.00 **st.**, **7 suites**.

MICHELIN Distribution Centre, 60 Cunningham Rd, Rutherglen, G73 1PP, ℰ 647 9516 p. 3 BX

AUSTIN-ROVER 55 Hamilton Rd ℰ 778 8383
AUSTIN-ROVER 215 Queensborough Gdns ℰ
357 1234
AUSTIN-ROVER, MAZDA, TOYOTA 470 Royston Rd
ℰ 552 4718
AUSTIN-ROVER Vineycombe St. ℰ 334 4761
BMW 10 Abbey Drive ℰ 959 1272
FORD 1009 Gallowgate ℰ 554 4321
FORD Temple Industrial Estate, Anniesland ℰ
954 1500
FORD 34 Fenwick Rd ℰ 637 7161
FORD Kilbirnie St. ℰ 423 6644
HONDA Maxwell Rd ℰ 429 4298

NISSAN 77-81 Dumbarton Rd ℰ 334 1241
OPEL-VAUXHALL 10 Holmbank Av. ℰ 649 9321
OPEL-VAUXHALL 712 Edinburgh Rd ℰ 774 2791
PEUGEOT-TALBOT 100 Minerva St. ℰ 248 2345
PORSCHE Maxwell Av. Bearsden ℰ 943 1155
RENAULT 64 Kirkintilloch Rd ℰ 772 6481
SAAB 162 Crow Rd ℰ 334 4661
VAUXHALL-OPEL 640 Pollokshaws Rd ℰ 423 3074
VAUXHALL-OPEL Grand St. ℰ 332 2626
VOLVO 2413-2493 London Rd ℰ 778 8501
VOLVO Bothwell Rd, Hamilton ℰ 728 4100
VW-AUDI Barrhead Rd ℰ 882 4601
VW, AUDI 512 Kilmarnock Rd ℰ 637 2241

▮ **GLENBORRODALE** ▮ Argyll. (Highland) 🔲🔲🔲 C 13 – ✉ Acharacle – 🕿 097 24.
   ◆Edinburgh 151 – ◆Inverness 108 – ◆Oban 72.

🏨 **Glenborrodale Castle** ⬞, Ardnamurchan, PH36 4JP, ℰ 266, ≤ Loch Sunart and gardens,
   « Victorian castle in extensive gardens », park – 📺 🛏wc 🕿 ℗. ◪ 🆑 ⓪ *VISA*
   April-October – **M** (bar lunch)/dinner 12.00 **st.** ▯ 3.60 – **20 rm** ⎓ (dinner included)
   38.50/48.50 **st.**, **1 suite**.

Hotels in categories 🏨🏨🏨 , 🏨🏨🏨 , 🏨🏨 ,
offer every modern comfort and facility -
therefore no particulars are given.

🛏wc ▯wc

🕿

GLENFINNAN Inverness. (Highland) **401** D 13 – ✉ Fort William – ☎ 039 783 Kinlocheil.
See : Site★ – Monument.
♦Edinburgh 150 – ♦Inverness 81 – Kyle of Lochalsh 88 – ♦Oban 67.

🏠 **Glenfinnan House** ⬟, PH37 4LT, ℰ 235, ⪢ Loch Shiel and Ben Nevis, ⬟, 🎋, park – 🚿wc
Ⓟ
Mid April-mid October – **M** (bar lunch)/dinner 11.00 **st.** – **19 rm** � 19.00/45.00 **st.**

🏠 **Stage House,** PH37 4LT, ℰ 246, ⬟ – 🚿wc 🚿wc Ⓟ. ⛳ *VISA*
Mid March-October – **M** (bar lunch)/dinner 10.50 **st.** ⓐ 3.05 – **9 rm** � 20.00/40.00 **st.**

GLENROTHES Fife. (Fife) **401** K 15 – pop. 33 639 – ECD : Tuesday – ☎ 0592.
🏌 Thornton ℰ 771111, S : 3 m. – 🏌 Leslie ℰ 41016, W : 3 m. on A 911.
🅱 Information Kiosk ℰ 754 954.
♦Edinburgh 33 – ♦Dundee 25 – Stirling 36.

🏨 **Stakis Albany** (Stakis), 1 North St., KY7 5NA, ℰ 752292 – ⬗ 📺 ☁wc 🚿wc ☎ Ⓟ. ⛳ ⛳
⛳ ⓘ *VISA*
M (grill rest. only) 9.50 **t.** ⓐ 3.10 – ⊆ 3.90 – **29 rm** 28.75/46.00 **t.**

at Leslie W : 3 m. by A 911 – ✉ Leslie – ☎ 0592 Glenrothes :

🏨 **Balgeddie House** ⬟, Balgeddie Way, KY6 3ET, NE : 1 ¾ m. by A 911 and B 969 via
Formonthills Rd ℰ 742511, ⪢, 🎋 – 📺 ☁wc 🚿wc ☎ Ⓟ. ⛳ ⛳ *VISA*. ⬟
closed 24 December-2 January – **M** a la carte 8.95/17.50 **t.** – ⊆ 5.50 – **18 rm** 38.50/49.50 **st.**

🏠 **Rescobie,** ⬟, Valley Drive, KY6 3BQ, ℰ 742143, 🎋 – 📺 🚿wc Ⓟ. ⛳ ⛳ ⓘ *VISA*
M *(closed lunch Saturday and Sunday)* 5.50/9.50 **t.** and a la carte ⓐ 2.85 – **7 rm** ⊆ 22.00/45.00 **t.**

PEUGEOT-TALBOT North St. ℰ 752262

GLENSHEE Perth. (Tayside) **401** J 13 – see Spittal of Glenshee.

GOLSPIE Sutherland (Highland) **401** I 10 – pop. 1 385 – ECD : Wednesday – ✉ ☎ 040 83.
🏌 ℰ 3266.
♦Edinburgh 228 – ♦Inverness 72 – ♦Wick 54.

🏠 **Golf Links,** Church St., KW10 6TT, ℰ 3408, ⪢, 🎋 – ☁wc 🚿wc Ⓟ. ⛳ ⛳ ⓘ *VISA*
M (booking essential) (bar lunch)/dinner 10.00 **t.** ⓐ 2.25 – **10 rm** ⊆ 16.50/37.00 **t.**

AUSTIN-ROVER Station Rd ℰ 3205   RENAULT Old Bank Rd ℰ 3411

GOUROCK Renfrew. (Strathclyde) **401** F 16 – pop. 11 087 – ECD : Wednesday – ☎ 0475.
⛴ by Caledonian MacBrayne : from Railway Pier to Dunoon Pier, summer only : frequent services
daily (20 mn) – by Western Ferries : from McInroy's Point to Hunters Quay, Dunoon, summer only :
frequent services daily (20 mn).

⛴ by Caledonian MacBrayne : to Kilcreggan, summer only : 4-8 daily (10 mn) – to Helensburgh,
summer only : 3-5 daily (40 mn).

🅱 Information Centre, Municipal Buildings, Shore St., ℰ 31126 (summer only).
♦Edinburgh 71 – ♦Ayr 47 – ♦Glasgow 27.

🏨 **Stakis Gantock** (Stakis), Cloch Rd, PA15 1AR, SW : 2 m. on A 78 ℰ 34671, ⪢ Firth of Clyde
– 📺 ☁wc 🚿wc ☎ Ⓟ. ⛳ ⛳ ⛳ ⓘ *VISA*
M 5.00/8.25 **t.** and a la carte ⓐ 3.60 – ⊆ 3.90 – **63 rm** 39.00/53.00 **t.**

🏠 **Claremont,** 34 Victoria Rd, PA19 1DF, ℰ 31687, ⪢ Firth of Clyde – 📺 Ⓟ
6 rm ⊆ 10.50/21.00 **st.**

FIAT Manor Crescent ℰ 32356

GRAEMSAY (Isle of) Orkney (Orkney Islands) **401** K 7 – Shipping Services : see Orkney Islands.

GRANGEMOUTH Stirling (Central) **401** I 15 – see Falkirk.

GRANTOWN-ON-SPEY Moray. (Highland) **401** J 12 – pop. 1 800 – ECD : Thursday – ☎ 0479.
🏌 ℰ 2079, East town boundary.
🅱 54 High St. ℰ 2773 (summer only).
♦Edinburgh 143 – ♦Inverness 34 – Perth 99.

🏠 **Garth,** The Square, PH26 3HN, ℰ 2836, 🎋 – 📺 ☁wc 🚿wc Ⓟ. ⛳ ⓘ *VISA*
M (bar lunch)/dinner 9.25 **st.** and a la carte ⓐ 2.75 – **17 rm** ⊆ 16.00/31.50 **st.**

🏠 **Dunachton House,** Coppice Court, off Grant Rd, PH26 3LD, ℰ 2098, 🎋 – Ⓟ
closed November – **8 rm** ⊆ 9.25/20.50 **st.**

AUSTIN-ROVER Chapel Rd ℰ 2037   FORD Woodland Service Centre ℰ 2289

GREAT CUMBRAE ISLAND Bute (Strathclyde) **401** **402** F 16 – pop. 1 611 – ☎ 047 553 Millport.
⛴ by Caledonian MacBrayne : from Cumbrae Slip to Largs frequent services daily (10 mn).
⛴ by Caledonian MacBrayne : from Millport to Largs summer only 4-7 daily (30 mn).

GREENLAW Berwick. (Borders) **401 402** M 16 – pop. 608 – ⊠ Duns – ☎ 089 084 Leitholm.
♦ Edinburgh 39 – ♦ Newcastle-upon-Tyne 70.

   🏠 **Purves Hall** ⟋, TD10 6UJ, SE : 4 m. by A 697 ♬ 558, ⯑ heated, 🐎, park, 🎱 – 📺 ⌂wc
      🛏wc 🅿 ◳ *VISA*
      M 9.60 **t.** (dinner) and a la carte 7.15/12.20 **t.** ◳ 3.25 – **7 rm** ⛆ 25.00/48.00 **t.** – SB (weekdays
      only) 50.00/57.50 **st.**

GREENOCK Renfrew. (Strathclyde) **401** F 16 – pop. 58 436 – ECD : Wednesday – ☎ 0475.
🛆 Whinhill, Beith Rd ♬ 210641, S : 2 m.
🅱 Municipal Buildings, 23 Clyde St. ♬ 24400.
♦Edinburgh 70 – ♦Ayr 47 – ♦Glasgow 24 – ♦Oban 98.

   🏠 **Tontine** (Best Western), 6 Ardgowan Sq., PA16 8NG, ♬ 23316 – 📺 ⌂wc ☎ 🅿 ⯑ ◳ ◳
      ◉ *VISA*
      M 5.65/7.50 **st.** and a la carte ◳ 2.75 – **32 rm** ⛆ 27.50/45.00 **st.** – SB (weekends only) 46.00 **st.**

VAUXHALL-OPEL Port Glasgow Rd ♬ 42511   VW, AUDI 60 East Hamilton St. ♬ 83535
VOLVO 46 Campbell St. ♬ 21610 and 23107

GRETNA Dumfries. (Dumfries and Galloway) **401** K 19 – pop. 2 737 – ECD : Wednesday –
☎ 046 13 (3 fig.) or 0461 (5 fig.).
🅱 Annan Rd ♬ 37834 (summer only).
♦Edinburgh 91 – ♦Carlisle 10 – ♦Dumfries 24.

   🏠 **Gretna Chase,** CA6 5JB, S : ¼ m. on B 721 ⊠ Carlisle (Cumbria) ♬ 37517, 🐎 – 📺 ⌂wc
      🛏wc 🅿 ◳ ◳ ◉ *VISA* ◳
      M (bar lunch Monday to Saturday)/dinner a la carte 7.30/10.75 **t.** ◳ 2.00 – **9 rm** ⛆ 25.00/50.00 **t.**
      – SB (weekends only)(November-Easter except Bank Holidays) 55.00/75.00 **st.**

GULLANE E. Lothian (Lothian) **401** L 15 – pop. 2 124 – ECD : Wednesday – ☎ 0620.
Envir. : Dirleton★ (Castle★) E : 2 m. by A 198 – 🛆, 🛆, 🛆 ♬ 843115.
♦Edinburgh 19 – North Berwick 5.

   🏠 **Greywalls** ⟋, Muirfield,Duncur Rd, EH31 2EG, ♬ 842144, ≤ gardens and golf course,
      « Edwardian country house with fine walled gardens », 🎱 – 📺 ⌂wc ☎ 🅿 ◳ ◳ *VISA* ◳
      Mid April-October – **M** 11.50/22.50 **t.** and a la carte ◳ 4.50 – **23 rm** ⛆ 45.00/98.00 **t.**

   ✗ **La Potinière,** Main St., EH31 2AA, ♬ 843214 – 🅿
      closed Saturday lunch, Wednesday, 1 week June, October, 25-26 December and 1-2 January –
      M (lunch only and Saturday dinner) (booking essential) 11.50/16.75 **t.** ◳ 3.50.

   at Dirleton NE : 2 m. by A 198 – ⊠ ☎ 062 085 Dirleton :

   ✗✗ **Open Arms** with rm, EH31 2BG, ♬ 241, 🐎 – 📺 ⌂wc ☎ 🅿 ◳ ◳ ◉ *VISA*
      M 8.00/15.00 **t.** and a la carte 10.35/15.25 **t.** ◳ 4.50 – **7 rm** ⛆ 45.00/75.00 **t.** – SB (except
      summer) 66.00/72.00 **st.**

HADDINGTON E. Lothian (Lothian) **401** L 16 Scotland G – pop. 7 988 – ECD : Thursday –
☎ 062 082 – See : Site★ – High Street★.
Envir. : Gifford★, S : 4 m. by B 8369 – Stenton★, E : 7 m. – Lennoxlove★, S : 1 m.
🛆 Amisfield Park, ♬ 3627.
♦ Edinburgh 17 – Hawick 53 – ♦ Newcastle-upon-Tyne 101.

   ✗✗ **Brown's** with rm, 1 West Rd, EH41 3RD, ♬ 2254, 🐎 – 📺 ⌂wc 🅿 ◳ ◳ *VISA* ◳
      closed 2 weeks October – **M** (dinner only) (booking essential) 14.00 **st.** ◳ 2.80 – **5 rm**
      ⛆ 20.00/44.00 **st.**

HARRIS (Isle of) Inverness. (Outer Hebrides) (Western Isles) **401** Z 10 – pop. 2 137.
See : St. Clement's Church, Rodel (tomb★).
⛴ by Caledonian MacBrayne : from Kyles Scalpay to the Isle of Scalpay : Monday/Saturday
6-12 daily (restricted in winter) (10 mn) – from Tarbert to Uig (Isle of Skye) summer only :
Monday/Saturday 1 daily (2 h) – from Tarbert to Lochmaddy (Isle of Uist) summer only : Monday/
Saturday 5-9 weekly (2 h).

   Scarista – ⊠ ☎ 085 985 Scarista.

   🏠 **Scarista House** ⟋, PA85 3HX, ♬ 238, ≤ beach and mountains, 🐎 – ⌂wc 🅿
      January-September – **M** *(closed Sunday to non-residents)* (dinner only) 16.00 **t.** ◳ 3.00 – **7 rm**
      ⛆ 37.00/54.00 **t.**

   Tarbert – pop. 479 – ECD : Thursday – ⊠ ☎ 0859 Harris.
   🅱 ♬ 2011 (summer only).

   🏠 **Harris,** PA85 3DL, ♬ 2154, ≤, 🐎 – ⌂wc 🛏wc 🅿
      closed mid December-mid January – **M** 6.00/9.50 **t.** ◳ 2.50 – **25 rm** ⛆ 17.00/37.00 **t.** –
      SB (weekends only) 45.60/52.00 **st.**

HAWICK Roxburgh. (Borders) **401 402** L 17 Scotland G – pop. 16 213 – ECD : Tuesday – ☻ 0450.

Envir. : Jedburgh★ (Abbey★★-Mary Queen of Scots House★-Canongate Bridge★) NE : 11 m. by A 698 and B 6358 – Waterloo Monument (🌲★★) NE : 12 m. by A 698, A 68 and B 6400 – Hermitage Castle★, S : 16 m. by B 6399.

🇮🇪 Vertish Hill ☞ 2293, S : 1 ½ m.

🇿 Common Haugh, Car Park ☞ 72547 (summer only).

◆Edinburgh 51 – ◆Ayr 122 – ◆Carlisle 44 – ◆Dumfries 63 – Motherwell 76 – ◆Newcastle-upon-Tyne 62.

   🏠   **Kirklands,** West Stewart Pl., TD9 8BH, ☞ 72263 – 📺 🚻wc 🐎 🅿
        closed 25-26 December and 1 January – **M** (closed Sunday to non-residents) 10.50 **t.** (dinner) and a la carte 9.65/12.45 **t.** 🍶 2.95 – **6 rm** ☞ 25.00/42.00 **t.** – SB (except summer)(weekends only) 44.00/46.00 **st.**

CITROEN, PEUGEOT, TALBOT 61 High St. ☞ 72287   VW, AUDI Commercial Rd ☞ 73211
FORD Earl St. ☞ 73316

HEITON Roxburgh. (Borders) – see Kelso.

HELENSBURGH Dunbarton. (Strathclyde) **401** F 15 – pop. 16 432 – ECD : Wednesday – ☻ 0436.
See : Hill House★.

Envir. : Dunbarton Castle site★, E : 11 m. by A 814 – Loch Lomond★★, NE : 5 m. by B 832.

🛳 to Gourock summer only : 3-5 daily (40 mn).

🇿 Pier Head Car Park, ☞ 2642 (summer only).

◆Edinburgh 68 – ◆Glasgow 22.

   🏨   **Commodore,** 112 West Clyde St., G84 8ES, ☞ 6924, ≼ – 🛗 📺 🚻wc 🕿 🅿. 🏋 🔼 🆎 ⓞ
      🆅🆂🅰
        M 5.00/9.00 **t.** and a la carte – **45 rm** ☞ 37.00/57.00 **t.**, **1 suite** 67.00 **t.** – SB (weekends only except Christmas and New Year) 44.00/48.00 **st.**

   at Rhu NW : 2 m. on A 814 – ✉ ☻ 0436 Rhu :

   🏨   **Rosslea Hall** 🔊, Ferry Rd, G84 8NF, ☞ 820684, ≼, ≉ – 📺 🚻wc 🛁wc 🕿 🅿. 🏋 🔼 🆎
      ⓞ 🆅🆂🅰
        M 5.50/11.50 **t.** and a la carte 🍶 4.00 – **31 rm** ☞ 38.00/55.00 **st.** – SB (weekdays only) 66.00 **st.**

AUSTIN-ROVER 135 East Clyde St. ☞ 3344   TOYOTA 145 East Clyde St. ☞ 2779
RENAULT 103 East Clyde St. ☞ 6021

HILLSWICK Shetland (Shetland Islands) **401** P 2 – see Shetland Islands (Mainland).

HOWGATE Midlothian (Lothian) **401 402** K 16 – ✉ ☻ 0968 Penicuik.
◆Edinburgh 11 – Peebles 11.

   ✗   **Old Howgate Inn,** 7 Wester Howgate, EH26 8QB, ☞ 74244, Smörrebrod – 🅿. 🔼 🆎 ⓞ
      🆅🆂🅰
        closed Christmas Day and New Years Day – **M** a la carte 5.75/11.15 **t.** 🍶 2.40.

HOY (Isle of) Orkney (Orkney Islands) **401** K 7 – see Orkney Islands.

HUMBIE E. Lothian (Lothian) **401 402** L 16 – ☻ 087 533.
◆Edinburgh 17 – ◆Carlisle 83.

   🏰   **Johnstounburn House** (Mt. Charlotte) 🔊, EH36 5PL, S : ¾ m. on A 6137 ☞ 696, ≼, « Part 17C country house », ≉, park – 📺 🕿 🅿. 🔼 🆎 ⓞ 🆅🆂🅰
      M (bar lunch Monday to Saturday)/dinner 16.00 **st.** and a la carte 🍶 3.50 – **20 rm** ☞ 49.50/90.00 **st.** – SB (weekends only) 80.00 **st.**

INCHNADAMPH Sutherland. (Highland) **401** F 9 – ✉ Lairg – ☻ 057 12 Assynt.
◆Edinburgh 239 – ◆Inverness 83.

   🏠   **Inchnadamph** 🔊, IV27 4HL, ☞ 202, ≼ Loch Assynt and mountains, ≉ – 🚻wc 🅿. 🔼 ⓞ
      🆅🆂🅰
        Mid March-October – **M** 5.50/7.50 **st.** 🍶 2.50 – **27 rm** ☞ 19.00/42.00 **t.**

INNERLEITHEN Peebles. (Borders) **401 402** K 17 – pop. 2 463 – ☻ 0896.
Envir. : Traquair House★★, S : 1 m. by A 709.

🇮🇪 ☞ 830951.

◆Edinburgh 30 – Galashiels 12 – ◆Glasgow 59 – Hawick 25.

   ↰   **Tighnuilt House,** Peebles Rd, EH44 6RD, W : ½ m. on A 72 ☞ 830491, ≼, ≉ – 🅿
      April-November – **6 rm** ☞ 8.50/24.00 **s.**

INVERGOWRIE Perth. (Tayside) **401** K 14 – see Dundee.

INVERMORISTON Inverness. (Highland) **401** G 12 – ✪ 0320 Glenmoriston.

See : Loch Ness★★.

◆Edinburgh 168 – ◆Inverness 29 – Kyle of Lochalsh 56.

🏨 **Glenmoriston Arms,** IV3 6YA, ✆ 51206, ␥ – 📺 ⌂wc ▥wc ☎ ℗. 🔼 AE ⓪ VISA
closed 24 December-4 January – **M** (bar lunch)/dinner a la carte 10.70/16.50 **t.** ▯ 3.00 – **8 rm**
⊠ 18.50/40.00 **t.**

INVERNESS Inverness. (Highland) **401** H 11 **Scotland G** – pop. 38 204 – ECD : Wednesday –
✪ 0463.

See : Site★ – Museum and Art Gallery★★ M.

Envir. : Loch Ness★★ by A 82 – Loch Ness Monster Exhibition★ – Cawdor Castle★, E : 14 m. by
A 82, A 96 and B 9090 – Clava Cairns★, E : 10 m. by B 9006 – Culloden Moor, E : 6 m. by B 9006 –
Fortrose (Cathedral Site★) N : 16 m. by B 865, A 9 and A 832.

🏌18 ✆ 231989, S : 1 m. by Culcabock Rd.

✈ Dalcross Airport : ✆ 232471, NE : 8 m. by A 96.

🚗 ✆ 242124.

🅱 23 Church St. ✆ 234353.

◆Edinburgh 156 – ◆Aberdeen 107 – ◆Dundee 134.

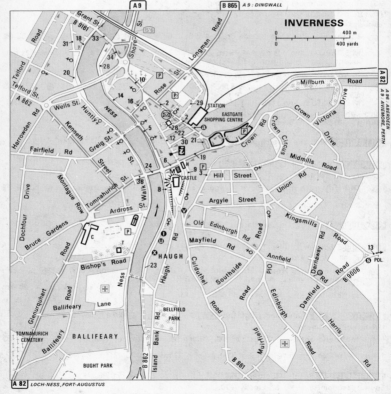

INVERNESS

▲▲ **Kingsmills** (Swallow), Culcabock Rd, IV2 3LP, ℰ 237166, Telex 75566, 🚗, squash – 📺 ☎
🅿 🔼 🆎 *VISA*   s
M 7.00/11.50 **st.** and a la carte 🍴 3.95 – **60 rm** ☲ 46.00/64.00 **st.**, **6 suites** 90.00/125.00 **st.** –
SB (weekends only) 68.00/75.00 **st.**

🏛 **Station**, 16-18 Academy St., IV1 1LG, ℰ 231926 – 📱 📺 ➦wc 🗍wc ☎ 🉐 🔼 🆎 ⓘ *VISA* a
closed 10 days Christmas-New Year – **M** (buffet lunch)/dinner 13.50 **st.** and a la carte 🍴 3.50 –
64 rm ☲ 30.00/68.00 **st.** – SB (October-April) 65.00 **st.**

🏛 **Ladbroke** (Ladbroke), Millburn Rd, IV2 3TR, E : by A 96 at junction A 9 and A 96 ℰ 239666,
Telex 75377 – 📱 📺 ➦wc ☎ 🉐 🔼 🆎 ⓘ *VISA*
M (carving rest.) 6.75/9.75 **t.** and a la carte 🍴 3.75 – ☲ 6.00 – **116 rm** 42.00/58.50 **t.** –
SB (weekends only) 67.50 **st.**

🏛 **Craigmonie** (Best Western), 9 Annfield Rd, IV2 3HX, ℰ 231649 – 📱 📺 ➦wc ☎ 🅿 🔼 🔼
🆎 ⓘ *VISA*   e
M 5.75/12.00 **t.** and a la carte 🍴 3.50 – **30 rm** ☲ 31.00/43.00 **t.** – SB 62.00/75.00 **st.**

🏠 **Glen Mhor**, 9-12 Ness Bank, IV2 4SG, ℰ 234308 – 📺 ➦wc 🗍wc ☎ 🅿 🔼 🆎 ⓘ *VISA*   i
closed 1-2 January – **M** 14.00 **t.** (dinner) and a la carte 🍴 3.50 – **30 rm** ☲ 17.50/60.00 **t.** –
SB (October-April)(weekends only) 46.00/60.00 **st.**

🏠 **Glenmoriston**, 20 Ness Bank, IV3 6YB, ℰ 223777, 🚗 – 📺 ➦wc 🗍wc ☎ 🅿 🔼 🆎 *VISA* 🎇
M *(closed Sunday November-April)* (bar lunch)/dinner 15.00 **t.** and a la carte 🍴 3.40 – **20 rm**
☲ 20.00/45.00 **t.** – SB (weekends only) 49.00/69.00 **st.**   x

⌂ **Felstead**, 18 Ness Bank, IV2 4SF, ℰ 231634 – 🅿
May-September – **8 rm** ☲ 10.00/24.00 **st.**   u

⌂ **Craigside House**, 4 Gordon Terr., IV2 3HD, ℰ 231576, ≼ – 📺 🗍wc. 🎇
Mid March-mid November – **6 rm** ☲ 30.00 **s.**   v

at Culloden E : 3 m. by A 96 – ✉ 🕿 0463 Inverness :

▲▲ **Culloden House** 🐾, IV1 2NZ, ℰ 790461, Telex 75402, ≼, 🚗, park, ✒ – 📺 ☎ 🅿 🔼 🆎 ⓘ
VISA
M a la carte lunch/dinner 21.50 **t.** 🍴 3.15 – **20 rm** ☲ 65.00/130.00 **t.**, **1 suite** – SB (November-
March except Christmas and New Year) 120.00 **st.**

at Dunain Park SW : 2 ½ m. on A 82 – ✉ 🕿 0463 Inverness :

🏠 **Dunain Park** 🐾, IV3 6JN, ℰ 230512, ≼, « Country house and gardens », park – 📺 ➦wc
🅿 🔼 🆎 ⓘ *VISA*
M *(closed Saturday lunch)* 12.00/17.50 **t.** 🍴 3.00 – **8 rm** ☲ 36.00/72.00 **t.** – SB (November-April)
57.00/62.00 **st.**

at Bunchrew W : 3 m. on A 862 – ✉ 🕿 0463 Inverness :

🏛 **Bunchrew House** 🐾, IV3 6TA, ℰ 234917, ≼ Beauly Firth, 🐟, 🚗, park – 📺 ➦wc ☎ 🅿.
🔼 🆎 ⓘ *VISA*
M 9.50/12.50 **st.** 🍴 3.50 – **6 rm** ☲ 45.00/75.00 **st.** – SB 69.00/88.00 **st.**

AUSTIN-ROVER-DAIMLER-JAGUAR, LAND ROVER-
RANGE ROVER, ROLLS ROYCE 66 Harbour Rd ℰ
220011
BMW Harbour Rd ℰ 236566
FIAT, LANCIA 8 Tomnahurich St. ℰ 235777
FORD Harbour Rd ℰ 238001

LADA Harbour Rd ℰ 226226
PEUGEOT, TALBOT Harbour Rd ℰ 231536
RENAULT 16 Telford St. ℰ 222848
VAUXHALL-OPEL 112 Academy St. ℰ 234311
VOLVO Harbour Rd ℰ 230885
VW, AUDI Harbour Rd ℰ 231313

▬ **IONA (Isle of)** Argyll. (Strathclyde) 🔳 A 15 Scotland G – pop. 268 – 🕿 0463.

See : Site★ – Maclean's Cross★ – St. Oran's Chapel★ – St. Martin's Cross★ – Infirmary Museum★.
🚢 by Caledonian MacBrayne : to Fionnphort (Isle of Mull) frequent services daily in summer,
restricted service in winter (5 mn).

▬ **IRVINE** Ayr (Strathclyde) 🔳🔳 F 17 – pop. 32 507 – 🕿 0294.

♦Edinburgh 75 – Ayr 14 – ♦Glasgow 29.

▲▲ **Hospitality Inn** (Mt. Charlotte), Roseholm, Annick Water, KA11 4LD, E : ¾ m. on A 71
ℰ 74272, Telex 777097, « Exotic indoor garden with 🖼 » – 📺 ☎ 🕭 🅿 🔼 🆎 ⓘ *VISA*
M 9.50/15.50 **st.** 🍴 3.00 – **128 rm** ☲ 44.50/57.75 **st.**

▬ **ISLAY (Isle of)** Argyll. (Strathclyde) 🔳 B 16 – pop. 3 997.

✈ Glenegedale Airport : ℰ 0496 (Port Ellen) 2361 – 🚢 by Western Ferries : from Port Askaig
to Feolin (Isle of Jura) Monday/Saturday 10 daily : Sunday 3-4 daily (5 mn) – by Caledonian Mac-
Brayne : from Port Ellen to Kennacraig (Kintyre Peninsula) 1-3 daily (2 h) – from Port Askaig to
Kennacraig (Kintyre Peninsula) Monday/Saturday 1 daily (1 h 45 mn).

🛈 at Bowmore ℰ 049 681 (Bowmore) 254 (summer only).

▬ **Bowmore** – ✉ 🕿 049 681 Bowmore.

🏠 **Lochside**, Shore St., PA43 7LB, ℰ 244, ≼, 🐟 – 📺 ➦wc 🗍 🐾. 🔼 🆎 *VISA*
M (bar lunch)/dinner 10.00 **t.** and a la carte 🍴 2.65 – **7 rm** ☲ 21.00/44.00 **st.**

▬ **Port Askaig** – ECD : Tuesday – ✉ 🕿 049 684 Port Askaig.

🏠 **Port Askaig**, PA46 7RD, ℰ 245, ≼ Sound of Islay and Jura, 🚗 – 📺 ➦wc 🗍wc 🅿
M (bar lunch)/dinner 10.50 **st.** 🍴 3.85 – ☲ 5.00 – **9 rm** 14.00/32.00 **st.**

ISLEORNSAY Inverness. (Highland) **401** C 12 – see Skye (Isle of).

JEDBURGH Roxburgh. (Borders) **401 402** M 17 **Scotland G** – pop. 4 053 – ECD : Thursday – ✆ 0835.

See : Site* – Abbey** – Mary Queen of Scots House* – Canongate Bridge*.

Envir. : Waterloo Monument (⁎⁎**) N : 3 m. by A 68 and B 6400.

♦Edinburgh 48 – ♦Carlisle 54 – ♦Newcastle upon Tyne 57.

⌂ **Ferniehirst Mill Lodge** ⟨⟩, TD8 6PQ, S : 3 m. on A 68 ℰ 63279, park – ⌷wc ⛝wc **P**. ⁎
     April-October – **11 rm** ⟿ 17.50/35.00 t.

JOHN O'GROATS Caithness. (Highland) **401** K 8 – Shipping Services : see Orkney Islands.

JURA (Isle of) Argyll. (Strathclyde) **401** C 15 – pop. 239.

⟱ by Western Ferries : from Feolin to Port Askaig (Isle of Islay) Monday/Saturday 10 daily, Sunday 3-4 daily (5 mn).

  Craighouse – ECD : Tuesday – ✉ ✆ 049 682 Jura.

⌂ **Jura** ⟨⟩, PA60 7XU, ℰ 243, ⟨ Small Isles Bay, ⟨⟩, ⌗ – ⌷wc **P**. **⟨⟩ AE ⓞ VISA**
     M (bar lunch)/dinner 9.50 **st**. ⟨ 2.75 – **18 rm** ⟿ 17.50/39.00 st., **1 suite** 45.00 st.

KELSO Roxburgh. (Borders) **401 402** M 17 **Scotland G** – pop. 5 547 – ECD : Wednesday – ✆ 0573.

See : Site* – Market Square** – ⟨* from Kelso Bridge.

Envir. : Mellerstain*** (ceilings***-Library***) NW : 6 m. by A 6089 – Floors Castle*, NW : 2 m. by A 6089 – Smailholm Tower* (⁎**) NW : 6 m. by A 6089 and B 6397 – Ladykirk (Kirk O'Steil*) NE : 16 m. by A 698, A 697, A 6112 and B 6437 – Flodden Field, NE : 11 m. by A 698 and A 697.

▯₁₈ ℰ 23009.

⛿ Turret House ℰ 23464 (summer only).

♦Edinburgh 44 – Hawick 21 – ♦Newcastle-upon-Tyne 68.

🏨 **Ednam House**, Bridge St., TD5 7HT, ℰ 24168, ⟨, ⌗ – **TV** ⌷wc ⛝wc ☎ **P**. ⟨⟩ **VISA**
     M (bar lunch Monday to Saturday)/dinner 10.50 **t**. – **32 rm** ⟿ 22.00/48.00 t. – SB 48.40/62.40 **st**.

     at Heiton SW : 3 m. by A 698 – ✉ Kelso – ✆ 057 35 Roxburgh :

🏨 **Sunlaws House** ⟨⟩, TD5 8JZ, ℰ 331, ⟨, « Victorian country house », ⟨⟩, ⌗, park, ⁎ –
     TV wc ☎ ⟨ **P**. ⟨⟩ **AE ⓞ VISA**
     M 6.50/14.50 **t**. and a la carte ⟨ 3.50 – **20 rm** ⟿ 35.00/70.00 **t**. – SB (December-March)(except Christmas and New Year) 79.00/83.00 **st**.

AUSTIN-ROVER-JAGUAR Bridge St. ℰ 24345   TALBOT Sheddon Par. Rd ℰ 24488
RENAULT Golf Course Rd ℰ 24720

KENMORE Perth. (Tayside) **401** I 14 – ECD : Thursday except summer – ✉ Aberfeldy – ✆ 088 73.

See : Site*.

Envir. : Loch Tay** – Ben Lawers**, SW : 8 m. by A 827.

▯₁₈ Taymouth Castle ℰ 228.

♦Edinburgh 82 – ♦Dundee 60 – ♦Oban 71 – Perth 38.

🏨 **Kenmore**, PH15 2NU, ℰ 205, ▯₁₈, ⟨⟩, ⌗ – ⫶ **TV** ⌷wc ☎ **P**. ⟨⟩ **AE VISA**. ⁎
     M 12.00 **t**. (dinner) and a la carte ⟨ 3.50 – **38 rm** ⟿ 26.00/58.00 **st**. – SB 35.00/39.00 **st**.

KENNACRAIG Argyll. (Strathclyde) **401** D 16 – Shipping Services : see Kintyre (Peninsula).

KENTALLEN Argyll. (Highland) **401** E 14 – ✉ Kentallen – ✆ 063 174 Duror.

♦Edinburgh 123 – Fort William 17 – ♦Oban 33.

🏠 **Ardsheal House** ⟨⟩, PA38 4BX, SW : ¾ m. by A 828 ℰ 227, ⟨, « Country house in lochside setting », ⌗, park, ⁎ – ⌷wc ⛝wc **P**
     Easter-October – **M** (restricted lunch)/dinner 20.00 **t**. ⟨ 3.50 – **13 rm** ⟿ (dinner included) 65.00/140.00 **t**.

✗ **Holly Tree**, Kentallen Pier, PA38 4BY, ℰ 292, ⟨ Loch Linnhe and mountains – **P**. ⟨⟩ ⓞ
     VISA
     closed Wednesday in April, May and October and 6 January-6 February – **M** *(closed lunch Monday to Wednesday February-Easter, November and December)* 8.00/12.50 **t**. and a la carte 12.10/16.75 **t**.

KILCHOAN Argyll. (Highland) **401** B 13 – ✉ Acharacle – ✆ 097 23.

⟱ by Caledonian MacBrayne : to Tobermory (Isle of Mull) summer only Monday/Saturday 3-6 daily (35 mn).

♦Edinburgh 163 – ♦Inverness 120 – ♦Oban 92.

556

KILCHRENAN Argyll. (Strathclyde) 401 E 14 – ⊠ Taynuilt – ☎ 086 63.

♦Edinburgh 117 – ♦Glasgow 87 – ♦Oban 18.

🏠 **Ardanaiseig** ⊗, PA35 1HE, NE : 4 m. by B 845 ℘ 333, ≤ gardens and Loch Awe, « Country house in extensive informal gardens on Loch Awe », ⊗, park, ✗ – 📺 ☎ 🅿 🖭 🖭 𝑉𝐼𝑆𝐴 ❀
Easter-mid October – **M** (restricted lunch) 11.05/23.00 **st.** ⅊ 4.00 – **14 rm** ⊆ (dinner included) 79.00/196.00 **st.**

🏠 **Taychreggan** ⊗, Lochaweside, PA35 1HQ, SE : 1 ¼ m. ℘ 211, ≤ Loch Awe, « Lochside setting », ⊗, 🍴, park – ⇔wc 🖭 🖭 🖭 𝑉𝐼𝑆𝐴
Mid April-mid October – **M** (buffet lunch)/dinner 13.50 **t.** ⅊ 3.00 – **16 rm** ⊆ 26.50/60.00 **t.**

KILCREGGAN Dunbarton. (Strathclyde) 401 F 16 – Shipping Services : see Gourock.

KILDRUMMY Aberdeen. (Grampian) 401 L 12 Scotland G – ⊠ Alford – ☎ 033 65.

See : Castle★.

Envir. : Craigievar Castle★★★, SE : 13 m. by A 944 and A 980 – Huntly Castle (Heraldic carvings★★) N : 15 m. by A 97.

♦Edinburgh 137 – ♦Aberdeen 35.

🏠 **Kildrummy Castle** (Best Western) ⊗, AB3 8RA, S : 1 ¼ m. on A 97 ℘ 288, ≤ gardens and Kildrummy Castle, « 19C mansion in extensive park », ⊗ – 📺 ⇔wc ☎ 🅿 🖭 🖭 ⓞ 𝑉𝐼𝑆𝐴
closed 4 January-14 March – **M** 9.00/14.50 **t.** and a la carte ⅊ 3.25 – **16 rm** ⊆ 32.00/66.00 **t.**

KILFINAN Argyll. (Strathclyde) 401 E 16 – ☎ 070 082.

♦Edinburgh 124 – ♦Glasgow 78 – ♦Oban 78.

🏠 **Kilfinan** ⊗, Tighnabruaich, PA21 2AP, ℘ 201 – 📺 ⇔wc ☎ 🖭 🖭 ⓞ 𝑉𝐼𝑆𝐴
M (bar lunch)/dinner 13.00 **t.** and a la carte – ⊆ 4.50 – **11 rm** 21.00/29.00 **t.**

KILLIECRANKIE Perth. (Tayside) 401 I 13 – see Pitlochry.

KILLIN Perth. (Central) 401 H 14 – pop. 545 – ECD : Wednesday – ☎ 056 72.

Envir. : Loch Tay★★, Ben Lawers★★, NE : 8 m. by A 827 – Kenmore★, NE : 17 m. by A 827.

🛆 ℘ 312.

🅱 Main St. ℘ 254 (summer only).

♦Edinburgh 72 – ♦Dundee 65 – Perth 43 – ♦Oban 54.

🏠 **Morenish Lodge,** FK21 8TX, NE : 2 ½ m. on A 827 ℘ 258, ≤ Loch Tay and hills, ⊗, ✗ – ⇔wc 🍴wc 🅿 🖭 𝑉𝐼𝑆𝐴.
Mid April-mid October – **M** (bar lunch)/dinner 11.00 **t.** ⅊ 2.50 – **12 rm** ⊆ 22.00/52.00 **t.**

🏠 **Bridge of Lochay,** FK21 8TS, N : ½ m. on A 827 ℘ 272 – ⇔wc 🍴wc 🅿
March-October – **M** 5.25/8.50 **t.** ⅊ 2.75 – **17 rm** ⊆ 13.50/32.00 **t.**

🏠 **Dall Lodge,** Main St., FK21 8TN, N : ¼ m. on A 827 ℘ 217, ⊗ – ⇔wc 🅿
Easter-October – **9 rm** ⊆ 12.50/28.50 **t.**

at Ardeonaig NE : 7 ¼ m. – ⊠ ☎ 056 72 Killin :

🏠 **Ardeonaig** ⊗, South Loch Tayside, FK21 8SU, ℘ 400, Telex 76163, ⊗, 🍴, park – ⇔wc 🍴wc 🅿
April-October – **M** (bar lunch)/dinner 14.50 **st.** and a la carte ⅊ 3.00 – **14 rm** ⊆ 23.50/43.00 **st.**

KILMARNOCK Ayr. (Strathclyde) 401 402 G 17 Scotland G – pop. 51 799 – ECD : Wednesday – ☎ 0563.

See : Dean Castle (Arms and armour collection★-musical instruments★).

🛆 Annanhill, Irvine Rd ℘ 21644, W : 1 m. – 🛆 Caprington, Ayr Rd ℘ 23702.

🅱 62 Bank St., ℘ 39090.

♦Edinburgh 62 – ♦Ayr 13 – ♦Dumfries 58 – ♦Glasgow 22.

🏠 **Howard Park** (Swallow), 136 Glasgow Rd, KA3 1UT, N : 2 m. on B 7038 ℘ 31211, Group Telex 53168 – 🛗 📺 ⇔wc 🕸 🅿 🛆 🖭 🖭 ⓞ 𝑉𝐼𝑆𝐴
M 6.00/8.50 **st.** and a la carte ⅊ 3.95 – **46 rm** ⊆ 38.00/48.00 **st.** – SB (weekends only) 48.00 **st.**

KILMARTIN Argyll. (Strathclyde) 401 D 15 – ⊠ Lochgilphead – ☎ 054 65.

♦Edinburgh 138 – ♦Glasgow 92 – ♦Oban 30.

✗ **Cairn,** by Lochgilphead, PA31 8RQ, ℘ 254 – 🅿 🖭 ⓞ 𝑉𝐼𝑆𝐴
closed Monday to Wednesday November-March – **M** (booking essential) a la carte 5.75/11.20 **t.**

KILNINVER Argyll. (Strathclyde) 401 D 14 – see Oban.

KILWINNING Ayr. (Strathclyde) **401 402** F 17 – pop. 16 196 – ✪ 0294.

◆Edinburgh 77 – ◆Ayr 16 – ◆Glasgow 31.

Montgreenan Mansion House ⌂, Montgreenan Estate, Torranyard, KA13 7QZ, NE : 3 ½ m. by B 785 (Fergushill Rd) ✆ 57733, ≤, « Georgian house in extensive grounds », 🌿, park, ⛳ – **TV** ☎ **P**. ◱ **AE** **VISA** ◱.
M 9.00/17.50 **t.** and a la carte ⓘ 3.50 – **11 rm** ⊇ 40.00/85.00 **t.** – SB (except summer) 74.00/120.00 **st.**

KINCLAVEN Perth. (Tayside) **401** J 14 – ⊠ Stanley – ✪ 025 083 Meikleour.

◆Edinburgh 56 – Perth 12.

Ballathie House ⌂, PH1 4QN, ✆ 268, ≤, « Country house in extensive grounds on banks of River Tay », ⌖, 🌿, park, ⛳ – **TV** ⌷wc **P**. ◱ **AE** **①** **VISA**
March-November – **M** (bar lunch Monday to Saturday)/dinner 13.75 **t.** and a la carte ⓘ 3.50 – **21 rm** ⊇ 29.00/51.00 **t.** – SB (except summer) 65.00/89.00 **st.**

KINCRAIG Inverness. (Highland) **401** I 12 – ECD : Wednesday – ⊠ Kingussie – ✪ 054 04.

◆Edinburgh 119 – ◆Inverness 37 – Perth 75.

Ossian, PH21 1NA, by A 9 ✆ 242, ≤, ⌖, 🌿 – **P**. ◱ **VISA**
Mid February-mid November and Christmas – **M** (bar lunch)/dinner 12.00 **st.** and a la carte ⓘ 3.50 – **6 rm** ⊇ 16.00/31.00 **st.**

KINGUSSIE Inverness. (Highland) **401** H 12 – pop. 1 140 – ECD : Wednesday – ✪ 054 02.

🛆 ✆ 374, ½ m. from town shops off A 9.

🛈 Caledonia Buildings, King St. ✆ 297 (summer only).

◆Edinburgh 117 – ◆Inverness 41 – Perth 73.

Osprey, Ruthven Rd, PH21 1EN, ✆ 510 – ⌷wc **P**. ◱ **AE** **①** **VISA**
closed November and December – **M** (dinner only) 13.00 **t.** – **8 rm** ⊇ 14.00/44.00 **t.** – SB 48.00/65.00 **st.**

The Cross with rm, 25-27 High St., PH21 1HX, ✆ 762 – ⌷wc. ⌖
closed Sunday in winter, Monday, 2 weeks May and 3 weeks December – **M** (dinner only) a la carte 9.75/12.45 **t.** ⓘ 2.00 – **3 rm** ⊇ 12.50/25.00 **t.**

FORD High St. ✆ 631

KINLOCHBERVIE Sutherland (Highland) **401** E 8 – ECD : Wednesday – ⊠ Lairg – ✪ 097 182.

Envir. : Cape Wrath★★★ (⌖★★), SE : 28 ½ m. by B 801 and A 838.

◆Edinburgh 276 – Thurso 93 – Ullapool 61.

Kinlochbervie ⌂, IV27 4RP, ✆ 275, ≤ Loch Inchard and sea – **TV** ⌷wc ☎ **P**. ◱ **AE** **①** **VISA**
restricted service November-Easter – **M** (booking essential) (bar lunch)/dinner 17.95 **t.** ⓘ 3.50 – **14 rm** ⊇ 30.00/70.00 **t.** – SB 60.00/100.00 **st.**

KINLOCHEWE Ross and Cromarty (Highland) **401** E 11 – ⊠ Achnasheen – ✪ 044 584.

Envir. : Loch Maree★★★ and Victoria Falls★, NW : 10 m. by A 832.

◆Edinburgh 208 – ◆Inverness 52.

Kinlochewe, IV22 2PA, ✆ 253, ≤, ⌖, 🌿 – **P**. ◱ **VISA**
April-November – **M** (bar lunch)/dinner 11.50 **t.** ⓘ 3.00 – **10 rm** ⊇ 18.00/38.00 **t.**

KINROSS Kinross. (Tayside) **401** J 15 – pop. 3 493 – ECD : Thursday – ✪ 0577.

🛆 Green Hotel, Beeches Park ✆ 63467 – 🛆 Milnathort ✆ 64069, N : 2 m.

🛈 Turfhills Service Area (off junction 6, M 90) ✆ 63680 (summer only).

◆Edinburgh 28 – Dunfermline 13 – Perth 18 – Stirling 25.

Windlestrae, The Muirs, KY13 7AS, ✆ 63217, 🌿 – **TV** ⌷wc ☎ **P**. ⌖. ◱ **AE** **①** **VISA**
M 11.50/15.00 **t.** and a la carte ⓘ 2.80 – **18 rm** ⊇ 35.00/48.00 **t.** – SB (except July, August and Christmas)(weekends only) 60.00/88.00 **st.**

Green (Best Western), 2 The Muirs, KY13 7AS, ✆ 63467, Telex 76684, « Gardens », ◱, 🛆, ⌖, squash – **TV** ⌷wc ☎ **P**. ⌖. ◱ **AE** **①** **VISA** ⌖. 🌿
M (buffet lunch Monday to Saturday)/dinner 12.00 **t.** and a la carte ⓘ 3.35 – **44 rm** ⊇ 38.00/52.00 **t.** – SB (except Christmas and New Year) 70.00/90.00 **st.**

at Cleish SW : 4 ½ m. by B 996 and B 9097 – ⊠ Kinross – ✪ 057 75 Cleish Hills :

Nivingston House ⌂, KY13 7LS, ✆ 216, ≤, 🌿 – **TV** ⌷wc ⌷wc ☎ **P**. ◱ **AE** **①** **VISA**
M 10.50/16.00 **t.** ⓘ 4.00 – **17 rm** ⊇ 38.50/55.00 **t.** – SB (weekends only) 55.00/72.50 **st.**

FORD High St. ✆ 62424

KINTYRE (Peninsula) Argyll. (Strathclyde) **401** D 16 17 **Scotland G.**

See : Carradale★ – Saddell (grave stones★).

✈ at Campbeltown (Machrihanish Airport) : ☎ 0586 (Campbeltown) 53021.

⛴ by Caledonian MacBrayne : from Claonaig to Lochranza (Isle of Arran) summer only 6-8 daily (30 mn) – from Kennacraig to Port Ellen (Isle of Islay) 1-3 daily (2 h) – from Kennacraig to Port Askaig (Isle of Islay) Monday/Saturday 1 daily (1 h 45 mn).

Bellochantuy – ✉ Campbeltown – ✆ 058 32 Glenbarr.

🏨 **Putechan Lodge**, PA28 6QE, on A 83 ☎ 266, ≤ – 📺 ➡wc **P**. 🔼 ⓪ **VISA**
closed 6 January-1 March – **M** a la carte 9.50/14.05 **t.** ▮ 3.25 – **12 rm** ☲ 19.00/50.00 **t.**

Campbeltown – ECD : Wednesday – ✉ ✆ 0586 Campbeltown.
♦Edinburgh 176.

↑ **Seafield**, Kilkerran Rd, PA28 6JL, ☎ 54385, ☞ – 📺 ➡wc **P**. 🔼 ⒶⒺ ⓪ **VISA**
12 rm ☲ 16.00/34.00 **t.**

Carradale – ECD : Wednesday – ✉ ✆ 058 33 Carradale.
🏌₉ ☎ 624.
♦Edinburgh 164 – ♦Glasgow 121 – ♦Oban 74.

🏨 **Carradale**, PA28 6RY, ≤, ☞, squash – ➡wc **P**. 🔼 **VISA**
April-October – **M** 6.00/12.00 **st.** ▮ 3.75 – **19 rm** ☲ 18.00/36.00 **st.** – SB 50.00/61.00 **st.**

Tarbert – pop. 1 429 – ECD : Wednesday – ✉ ✆ 088 02 Tarbert.
🏌₅ ☎ 565, W : 1 m.
🅱 ☎ 429 (summer only).
♦Edinburgh 139 – ♦Glasgow 96 – ♦Oban 49.

✗ **West Loch** with rm, West Tarbert, PA29 6YF, SW : 1 m. on A 83 ☎ 283, ≤ – **P**. 🔼
closed November – **M** 14.50 **t.** (dinner) a la carte lunch 8.75/11.30 **t.** ▮ 3.75 – **6 rm**
☲ 20.00/31.00 **t.**

Plans de ville : Les rues sont sélectionnées en fonction de leur importance
pour la circulation et le repérage des établissements cités.
Les rues secondaires ne sont qu'amorcées.

KIRKCALDY Fife. (Fife) **401** K 15 **Scotland G** – pop. 46 356 – ECD : Wednesday – ✆ 0592.
🏌 Balwearie ☎ 260370 – 🏌 Dunnikier Park, Dunnikier Way ☎ 261599, North boundary.
🅱 Esplanade ☎ 267775 (summer only).
♦Edinburgh 27 – ♦Dundee 32 – ♦Glasgow 54.

at West Wemyss NE : 4 ½ m. by A 955 – ✉ ✆ 0592 Kirkcaldy :

🏨 **Belvedere**, Coxstool, KY1 4SN, ☎ 54167, ≤ – 📺 ➡wc ☎ **P**. 🔼 **VISA**
M *(closed Sunday to non-residents)* 11.85/13.15 **st.** ▮ 4.20 – **20 rm** ☲ 29.00/45.00 **st.** –
SB 60.00 **st.**

AUSTIN-ROVER 39 Rosslyn St. ☎ 51997
BMW Bennochy Rd ☎ 262191
CITROEN, VAUXHALL-OPEL 24 Victoria Rd ☎ 264755
FORD Forth Av. ☎ 261199

HYUNDAI Meldrum Rd ☎ 200354
SAAB 180-186 St. Clair St. ☎ 52291
VOLVO Wemyssfield ☎ 262141

KIRKCUDBRIGHT Kirkcudbright. (Dumfries and Galloway) **401** **402** H 19 **Scotland G** –
pop. 3 352 – ECD : Thursday – ✆ 0557.
See : Site★.
Envir. : Dundrennan Abbey★, SE : 5 m. by A 711.
🏌 Stirling Cres.
🅱 Harbour Sq. ☎ 30494 (summer only).
♦Edinburgh 108 – ♦ Dumfries 28 – Stranraer 50.

🏨 **Selkirk Arms**, Old High St., DG6 4JG, ☎ 30402, ☞ – ➡wc **P**. 🔼 ⒶⒺ ⓪ **VISA** ✖
M (buffet lunch)/dinner 9.50 **t.** and a la carte ▮ 2.75 – **26 rm** ☲ 17.50/41.00 **t.** – SB (except
Christmas and New Year) 45.00/49.50 **st.**

AUSTIN-ROVER Mews Lane ☎ 30412

KIRKMICHAEL Perth. (Tayside) **401** J 13 – ✉ Blairgowrie – ✆ 025 081 Strathardle.
♦Edinburgh 74 – Perth 30 – Pitlochry 12.

🏨 **Log Cabin** ⬙, Blairgowrie, PH10 7NB, W : 1 m. ☎ 288, ≤, « Scandinavian pine chalet », ➹
– ➡wc 🔼wc ⬚ **P**. 🔼 ⓪ **VISA**
closed mid November-mid December – **M** (bar lunch)/dinner 13.00 **st.** and a la carte ▮ 3.25 –
13 rm ☲ 27.50/55.00 **st.** – SB (except summer) 65.00 **st.**

559

KIRKWALL Orkney (Orkney Islands) **401** L 7 — see Orkney Islands (Mainland).

KIRN Argyll. (Strathclyde) **401 402** F 16 — see Dunoon.

KYLEAKIN Inverness. (Highland) **401** C 12 — Shipping Services : see Skye (Isle of).

KYLE OF LOCHALSH Ross and Cromarty (Highland) **401** C 12 **Scotland G** — pop. 803 — ECD : Thursday — ✆ 0599.

Envir. : Eilean Donan Castle★ (Site★★) E : 8 m. by A 87 — Plockton★, N : 6 m.

� by Caledonian MacBrayne : to Kyleakin (Isle of Skye) frequent services daily (5 mn).

� by Caledonian MacBrayne : to Mallaig summer only 3 weekly (2 h).

🛈 ℰ 4276 (summer only).

◆Edinburgh 204 — ◆ Dundee 182 — ◆Inverness 82 — ◆Oban 125.

🏥 **Lochalsh,** Ferry Rd, IV40 8AF, ℰ 4202, Telex 75318, ≼ Skye Ferry and hills — 🍴 📺 ☎ 🅿 🖾 ÆE ⓪ 𝘝𝘐𝘚𝘈
closed Christmas week — **M** (bar lunch)/dinner 14.50 **st.** and a la carte ᐟ 3.50 — **38 rm** ⟷ 25.00/89.00 **st.** — SB 67.00/97.00 **st.**

FORD   Main Rd ℰ 4329

KYLES SCALPAY Inverness. (Western Isles) (Highland) **401** Z 10 — Shipping Services : see Harris (Isle of).

LAGG Bute. (Strathclyde) — see Arran (Isle of).

LAGGAN Inverness (Highland) **401** H 12 — ✉ Newtonmore — ✆ 052 84.

◆Edinburgh 110 — ◆Inverness 52 — Perth 66.

🏠 **Gaskmore House,** PH20 1BS, E : ¾ m. on A 86 ℰ 250, ≼ — 📺 ⟷wc ᐣᐤwc ☎ 🅿 𝘝𝘐𝘚𝘈
M a la carte 5.85/11.70 **t.** ᐟ 3.25 — **8 rm** ⟷ 19.50/39.00 **t.**

LAIDE Ross and Cromarty (Highland) **401** D 10 — ✉ Achnasheen — ✆ 044 582 Aultbea.

Envir. : Inverewe Gardens★★★, S : 8 m. by A 832.

◆Edinburgh 32 — ◆Inverness 76.

🏠 **Ocean View,** Sand Passage Rd, Sand, IV22 2ND, ℰ 385, ≼ sea and Summer Isles — 🅿

LAIRG Sutherland (Highland) **401** G 9 — pop. 628 — ECD : Wednesday — ✆ 0549.

🛈 ℰ 2160 (summer only).

◆Edinburgh 218 — ◆Inverness 61 — ◆Wick 72.

🏨 **Sutherland Arms,** IV27 4AT, ℰ 2291, ≼, ⤳, ⟷ — ⟷wc 🅿 🖾 ÆE ⓪ 𝘝𝘐𝘚𝘈
April-October — **M** (bar lunch)/dinner 10.50 **t.** ᐟ 3.00 — **24 rm** ⟷ 29.00/54.00 **t.**

🏠 **Achany House** ⚘, IV27 4EB, S : 4 m. on B 864 ℰ 2433, « Georgian mansion with country house atmosphere », ⟷ — ⟷wc 🅿
Easter-October — **M** (bar lunch)/dinner 12.00 **t.** ᐟ 2.50 — **6 rm** ⟷ 24.00/48.00 **t.**

LAMLASH Bute. (Strathclyde) **401** E 17 — see Arran (Isle of).

LANARK Lanark. (Strathclyde) **401 402** I 16 **Scotland G** — pop. 9 673 — ECD : Thursday — ✆ 0555.

See : New Lanark★.

🛈 Horsemarket, Ladyacre Rd ℰ 61661 (summer only) — South Vennel ℰ 2544.

◆Edinburgh 34 — ◆Carlisle 78 — ◆ Glasgow 28.

🏨 **Cartland Bridge,** ML11 9UF, NW : ¾ m. on A 73 ℰ 4426, ⟷ — ⊚ 🅿 🖾 🖾 ÆE ⓪ 𝘝𝘐𝘚𝘈
M 7.00/9.50 **st.** and a la carte — ⟷ 3.00 — **15 rm** 18.00/36.00 **st.**

✕ **Ristorante La Vigna,** 40 Wellgate, ML11 9DT, ℰ 4320, Italian rest. — 🖾 ÆE ⓪ 𝘝𝘐𝘚𝘈
closed Sunday lunch — **M** a la carte 10.30/26.80 **t.** ᐟ 3.35.

CITROEN   30 West Port ℰ 2581   VAUXHALL   St. Leonard St. ℰ 2185

LANGBANK Renfrew. (Strathclyde) **401** G 16 — ECD : Saturday — ✆ 047 554.

◆Edinburgh 63 — ◆ Glasgow 17 — Greenock 7.

🏨 **Gleddoch House** ⚘, PA14 6YE, SE : 1 m. by B 789 ℰ 711, Telex 779801, ≼ Clyde and countryside, « Tastefully furnished », 🖾, ⚘, ⟷, park, squash — 📺 ⟷wc ᐣᐤwc ☎ 🅿 🖾 ⓪ 𝘝𝘐𝘚𝘈
M 9.00/19.50 **t.** and a la carte ᐟ 3.70 — **20 rm** ⟷ 58.00/78.00 **t.**, **1 suite** 98.00 **t.**

LARGS Ayr. (Strathclyde) 401 402 F 16 Scotland G – pop. 9 619 – ECD : Wednesday – ☎ 0475.
See : Skelmorlie Aisle* (Monument* and ceiling*).

⌖₁₈ Irvine Rd ℘ 673594 S : 1 m. – ⌖₁₈ Routenburn, ℘ 673230.

🚢 by Caledonian MacBrayne : to Cumbrae Slip (Great Cumbrae Island) frequent services daily (10 mn).

🚢 by Caledonian MacBrayne : to Millport (Great Cumbrae Island) summer only 4-7 daily (30 mn).

🛈 Promenade ℘ 673765.

♦Edinburgh 76 – ♦Ayr 32 – ♦Glasgow 30.

� **Glen Eldon,** 2 Barr Cres., KA30 8PX, ℘ 673381 – 📺 ⎓wc ⵏⵏwc ℗. ✀
closed mid January-1 March – **M** (bar lunch)/dinner 10.00 **t.** ⵏ 3.40 – **9 rm** ⵑ 17.50/35.00 **t.** – SB (except summer) 40.00 **st.**

⌂ **Haylie,** 108 Irvine Rd, KA30 8EY, ℘ 673207, ≼ Firth of Clyde and Islands, ✿ – ⎓wc ℗. 🆖 🄰🄴 ⓞ 𝘝𝘐𝘚𝘈
8 rm ⵑ 14.50/32.00 **st.**

LAUDER Berwick. (Borders) 401 402 L 16 Scotland G – pop. 799 – ECD : Thursday – ☎ 057 82.
See : Thirlestane Castle (Plasterwork ceilings**).

⌖₅ ℘ 381, W : ½ m.

♦Edinburgh 27 – Hawick 31 – ♦Newcastle-upon-Tyne 78.

☸ **Black Bull,** Market Pl., ℘ 208 – ⎓wc ℗
M 5.00/10.00 **st.** and a la carte ⵏ 3.50 – **14 rm** ⵑ 12.00/36.00 **st.**

at Carfraemill N : 4 m. on A 68 – ✉ Lauder – ☎ 057 85 Oxton :

🏚 **Carfraemill,** TD2 6RA, ℘ 200 – 📺 ⎓wc ☎ ℗. 🄰🄴 𝘝𝘐𝘚𝘈
M 4.50/8.75 **t.** ⵏ 2.00 – **10 rm** ⵑ 16.00/35.00 **st.** – SB 40.00/44.00 **st.**

LERAGS Argyll. (Strathclyde) – see Oban.

LERWICK Shetland (Shetland Islands) 401 Q 3 – see Shetland Islands (Mainland).

LESLIE Fife. (Fife) 401 K 15 – see Glenrothes.

LETHAM Fife. (Fife) 401 K 15 – ✉ Ladybank – ☎ 033 781.

♦Edinburgh 43 – ♦Dundee 16 – Perth 18.

🏛 **Fernie Castle** ⌂, KY7 7RU, NE : ½ m. on A 914 ℘ 381, ✿, park – 📺 ⎓wc ⵏⵏwc ⊛ ℗. 🆖 🄰🄴 ⓞ 𝘝𝘐𝘚𝘈. ✀
closed 5 January-5 March – **M** (lunch by arrangement)/dinner 14.50 **t.** ⵏ 3.00 – **15 rm** ⵑ 35.00/70.00 **t.** – SB 70.00/90.00 **st.**

LEVEN Fife. (Fife) 401 K 15 – pop. 8 596 – ECD : Thursday – ☎ 0333.

⌖₁₈ Leven Links ℘ 26381.

🛈 South St. ℘ 29464.

♦Edinburgh 36 – ♦Dundee 23 – ♦Glasgow 65.

at Lundin Links E : 2 m. on A 915 – ✉ ☎ 0333 Lundin Links :

🏛 **Old Manor,** Leven Rd, KY8 6AJ, ℘ 320368, ≼, ✿ – 📺 ⎓wc ☎ ℗. 🆖 🄰🄴 𝘝𝘐𝘚𝘈. ✀
closed 26 December and 1-2 January – **M** 6.95/12.85 **t.** and a la carte ⵏ 3.00 – **19 rm** ⵑ 34.00/49.00 **t.** – SB (weekends only) 59.00/62.50 **st.**

AUSTIN-ROVER The Promenade ℘ 23449   FIAT Scoonie Rd ℘ 27003

LEWIS (Isle of) Ross and Cromarty (Outer Hebrides) (Western Isles) 401 Z 8 Scotland G.
See : Callanish Standing Stones** – Carloway Broch*.

🚢 by Caledonian MacBrayne : from Stornoway to Ullapool Monday/Saturday 1-2 daily (3 h 30 mn).

Stornoway – pop. 8 660 – ECD : Wednesday – ✉ ☎ 0851 Stornoway.

✈ Stornoway Airport : ℘ 2256 and 2281, Telex 75495, E : 2 ½ m. – **Terminal :** British Airways, Cromwell St.

🛈 Area Tourist Officer, 4 South Beach St. ℘ 3088.

☸ Royal, Cromwell St., PA87 2DG, ℘ 2109 – ✀ – **22 rm.**

AUSTIN-ROVER 11-16 Bayhead St. ℘ 3246   VAUXHALL-OPEL Bayhead St. ℘ 2888
FORD 80 Keith St. ℘ 3225   VW, AUDI Sandwick Rd ℘ 5553

LEWISTON Inverness. (Highland) 401 G 12 – ☎ 045 62 Drumnadrochit.
See : Loch Ness**.

♦Edinburgh 173 – ♦Inverness 17.

☸ **Lewiston Arms,** IV3 6UN, ℘ 225, ✿ – ℗. 𝘝𝘐𝘚𝘈
M (bar lunch)/dinner a la carte 4.90/8.00 **t.** ⵏ 3.25 – **8 rm** ⵑ 12.00/24.00 **t.**

561

LINLITHGOW W. Lothian (Lothian) **401** J 16 – pop. 9 524 – ✪ 050 683 Philipstoun.
◆Edinburgh 19 – Falkirk 9 – ◆Glasgow 35.

XXX **Champany Inn,** Champany, EH49 7LU, NE : 2 m. on A 803 at junction with A 904 ✗ 4532, « Converted horse-mill » – **P.** 🅐 **AE** ⓪ **VISA**
closed Saturday lunch, Sunday and 24 December-13 January – **M** (grill rest.) a la carte 16.50 **t.** 🍷 3.75.

LISMORE (Isle of) Argyll. (Strathclyde) **401** D 14 – pop. 156.
⛴ by Caledonian MacBrayne : from Achnacroish to Oban Monday/Saturday 2-3 daily (1 h).
⛴ to Port Appin Monday/Saturday 5 daily ; Sunday 4 daily (10 mn).
   Hotels see : Oban.

LIVINGSTON Midlothian (Lothian) **401** J 16 – pop. 38 594 – ✪ 0506.
◆Edinburgh 16 – Falkirk 23 – ◆Glasgow 32.

🏨 **Ladbroke** (Ladbroke), Almondview, Almondvale, EH54 6QB, ✗ 31222, 🔟 – 📺 ➙wc ☎ 🅛
P. 🅐 🅐 **AE** ⓪ **VISA**
M (carving rest.) 7.50/12.50 **st.** and a la carte 🍷 4.00 – ⟠ 6.00 – **114 rm** 43.00/55.00 **st.**, **6 suites** 85.00 **st.** – SB 95.00 **st.**

LOCHALINE Argyll. (Highland) **401** C 14.
⛴ by Caledonian MacBrayne : to Fishnish (Isle of Mull) Monday/Saturday 13-17 daily (15 mn).
⛴ by Caledonian MacBrayne : to Tobermory (Isle of Mull) May-September 2 weekly (1 h) – to Arinagour (Isle of Coll) May-September 2 weekly (2 h 30 mn) – to Isle of Tiree (via Coll and Tobermory) May-September 2 weekly (3 h 55 mn) – to Oban May-September 2 weekly (1 h 10 mn).
◆Edinburgh 129 – ◆Inverness 109 – Kyle of Lochalsh 116 – ◆Oban 6.
   Hotels see : Mull (Isle of).

LOCHBOISDALE Inverness. (Western Isles) **401** Y 12 – Shipping Services : see Uist (South) (Isles of).

LOCHCARRON Ross and Cromarty (Highland) **401** D 11 Scotland G – ECD : Thursday – ✪ 052 02.
Envir. : Plockton★ S : 17 m. by A 896 and A 890.
◆Edinburgh 221 – ◆Inverness 65 – Kyle of Lochalsh 23.

🍴 **Lochcarron,** IV54 8YS, ✗ 226, ≤ Loch Carron – ➙wc **P.** 🅐 **VISA**
M *(closed Sunday lunch)* (bar lunch)/dinner 10.00 **t.** and a la carte 🍷 2.00 – **7 rm** ⟠ 15.00/36.00 **t.** – SB 46.00/54.00 **st.**

LOCHEARNHEAD Perth. (Central) **401** H 14 – ECD : Wednesday – ✪ 056 73.
◆Edinburgh 65 – ◆Glasgow 56 – ◆Oban 57 – Perth 36.

🏠 **Mansewood Country House,** FK19 8NS, S : ½ m. on A 84 ✗ 213, 🐎 – ➙wc **P.**
closed January and February – **8 rm** ⟠ 12.50/29.50 **st.**

LOCHGAIR Argyll. (Strathclyde) **401** D 15 – ✪ 0546 Minard.
◆Edinburgh 122 – ◆Glasgow 76 – ◆Oban 46.

🏨 **Lochgair,** PA31 8SA, on A 83 ✗ 86333, 🐟, 🐎 – ➙wc **P.** 🎾
10 April-mid October – **M** 11.00 **t.** and a la carte 🍷 2.70 – **10 rm** ⟠ 13.00/34.00.

LOCHGILPHEAD Argyll. (Strathclyde) **401** D 15 – pop. 2 391 – ECD : Tuesday – ✪ 0546.
🅱 Lochnell St. ✗ 2344 (summer only).
◆Edinburgh 130 – ◆Glasgow 84 – ◆Oban 38.

🏨 **Stag,** Argyll St., PA31 8NE, ✗ 2496 – 📺 ➙wc 🚿wc ☎ 🅐 **VISA**
M (bar lunch)/dinner 4.50 **t.** and a la carte 6.80/11.75 **t.** 🍷 3.30 – **21 rm** ⟠ 15.50/35.00 **t.**

LOCH HARRAY Orkney (Orkney Islands) **401** K 6 – see Orkney Islands (Mainland).

LOCHINVER Sutherland (Highland) **401** E 9 – ECD : Tuesday – ✉ Lairg – ✪ 057 14.
🅱 ✗ 330 (summer only).
◆Edinburgh 251 – ◆Inverness 95 – ◆Wick 105.

🏨 **Culag** (Best Western), IV27 4LQ, ✗ 209, ≤, 🐟, 🐎 – 🛗 ➙wc **P.** 🅐 🅐 **AE** ⓪ **VISA**
May-early October – **M** (bar lunch Monday to Friday)/dinner 13.00 **t.** and a la carte 🍷 3.00 – **43 rm** ⟠ 24.00/60.00 **t.** – SB 70.00 **st.**

🏠 **Ardglas** 🍲, IV27 4LI, ✗ 257, ≤ Loch Inver – **P.**
8 rm ⟠ 8.50/18.00 **st.**

LOCHMADDY Inverness. (Outer Hebrides) (Western Isles) **401** Y 11 – see Uist (North) (Isles of).

LOCHRANZA Bute. (Strathclyde) **401 402** E 16 – Shipping Services : see Arran (Isle of).

LOCKERBIE Dumfries. (Dumfries and Galloway) **401 402** J 18 – pop. 3 545 – ECD : Tuesday – ☎ 057 62.

☐ Corrie Rd ℘ 2463.

◆Edinburgh 74 – ◆Carlisle 27 – ◆Dumfries 13 – ◆Glasgow 73.

🏠 **Lockerbie House** ⬚, Boreland Rd, DG11, N : 1 m. on B 723 ℘ 2610, ≤, park – 📺 ⌂wc
P **☒** **AE** **①** **VISA**
closed 25 to 26 December and 1 January – **M** (bar lunch)/dinner 12.00 **st.** and a la carte ⬙ 3.50
– **26 rm** ⬚ 23.00/46.00 **st.** – SB 32.50 **st.**

🏠 **Dryfesdale** ⬚, Dryfe Rd, DG11 2SF, NW : 1 m. off A 74 ℘ 2427, ≤, 🚗 – 📺 ⌂wc ☎ **P.**
☒ **AE** **①** **VISA**
closed Christmas and New Year – **M** a la carte 9.50/13.05 **t.** ⬙ 3.00 – **11 rm** ⬚ 17.50/
42.00 **t.**

FORD Carlisle Rd ℘ 3240

LOSSIEMOUTH Moray. (Grampian) **401** K 10 – pop. 6 650 – ECD : Thursday – ☎ 034 381.

☐₈, ☐₈ Stotfield Rd, Moray ℘ 2018.

◆Edinburgh 203 – ◆Aberdeen 73 – Fraserburgh 66 – ◆Inverness 44.

🏠 **Stotfield,** Stotfield Rd, IV31 6QS, ℘ 2011 – 📺 ⌂wc ⬚wc ☎ **P.** **☒** **AE** **VISA**
M (restricted lunch) 4.95/13.00 **st.** and a la carte ⬙ 2.50 – **50 rm** ⬚ 24.00/38.00 **st.** –
SB 50.00/76.00 **st.**

LUING (Isle of) Argyll. (Strathclyde) **401** D 15 – pop. 183.

⛴ to Isle of Seil (Strathclyde Regional Council) frequent sailings daily (5 mn).

Cullipool – ✉ Oban – ☎ 085 24 Luing :

✗ **Longhouse Buttery,** PA34 4TX, ℘ 209, ≤, Seafood – **P**
18 May-3 October – **M** *(closed Sunday)* (lunch only) a la carte 4.30/8.50 **t.** ⬙ 3.55.

LUNDIN LINKS Fife. (Fife) **401** L 15 – see Leven.

MACDUFF Banff. (Grampian) **401** M 10 – pop. 3 893 – ECD : Wednesday – ☎ 0261.

☐₈ Royal Tarlair ℘ 32897.

◆ Edinburgh 176 – ◆ Aberdeen 46 – Fraserburgh 24 – ◆ Inverness 76.

🏠 **Fife Arms,** Shore St., AB4 1UB, ℘ 32408, ≤ – 📺 ⌂wc ⬚wc ☎ **☒** **AE** **①** **VISA**
M 4.00/9.00 **st.** and a la carte ⬙ 3.00 – **22 rm** ⬚ 16.00/39.00 **st.** – SB (except summer)
38.00/48.00 **st.**

☎ **Deveron House,** 27-29 Union Rd, AB4 1UD, ℘ 32309 – 📺 ⌂wc ⬚wc **P.** ⬚
17 rm.

MAINLAND Orkney (Orkney Islands) **401** KL 6 – see Orkney Islands.

MAINLAND Shetland (Shetland Islands) **401** PQ 3 – see Shetland Islands.

MALLAIG Inverness. (Highland) **401** C 12 – pop. 998 – ECD : Wednesday – ☎ 0687.

See : Site★.

Envir. : Silver Sands of Morar★, S : by A 830 – Arisaig, S : 9 m. by A 830.

⛴ by Caledonian MacBrayne : to Armadale (Isle of Skye) summer only Monday/Saturday
3-5 daily (30 mn).

⛴ by Caledonian MacBrayne : to Isles of Eigg, Muck, Rhum, Canna, return Mallaig Monday/Satur-
day 2-3 weekly (7 h) – to Kyle of Lochalsh summer only 3 weekly (2 h) – to Armadale (Isle of Skye)
summer only 2 weekly (30 mn).

🛈 Station Buildings ℘ 2170 (summer only).

◆Edinburgh 179 – ◆ Inverness 110 – ◆Oban 96.

☎ **Marine,** 10 Station Rd, PH41 4PY, ℘ 2217 – ⌂wc. **AE** **VISA**
closed Christmas and New Year – **21 rm** ⬚ 14.00/32.00 **st.**

MEIGLE Perth. (Tayside) **401** K 14 – ☎ 082 84.

◆Edinburgh 62 – ◆Dundee 13 – Perth 18.

🏠 **Kings of Kinloch** ⬚, Coupar Angus Rd, PH12 8QX, W : 1 m. on A 94 ℘ 273, ≤, 🚗 – **P.**
☒. ⬚
closed January – **M** 14.50 **t.** (lunch)/dinner a la carte 9.40/13.80 **t.** ⬙ 3.40 – **7 rm** ⬚ 24.00/
45.00 **t.**

MELROSE Roxburgh. (Borders) **401 402** L 17 **Scotland G** – pop. 2 143 – ECD : Thursday – ✪ 089 682.

See : Site★ – Abbey★★ (Decorative sculpture★★★).

Envir. : Gildon Hill North (✳★★★) – Scott's View★★ – Abbotsford★★, W : 4 m. by A 6091 – Dryburgh Abbey★★★ (setting★★★) SE : 4 m. by A 6091.

⏚ Dingleton ✆ 2855, South boundary – 🚩 Priorwood Gdns, near Abbey ✆ 2555 (summer only).

◆Edinburgh 38 – Hawick 19 – ◆Newcastle-upon-Tyne 70.

   🏠 **Burts**, Market Sq., TD6 9PN, ✆ 2285, 🍴 – 📺 ➚wc 🛏wc ☎ 🅿. 🖿 🆎 ⓞ 𝗩𝗜𝗦𝗔
   M 8.25 t. (lunch) and a la carte 9.30/16.25 t. 🍷 3.00 – **21 rm** � 20.00/42.00 t. – SB (November-May) 52.00/56.00 **st.**

   at Gattonside NW : 2 ¼ m. by A 6091 on B 6360 – ✉ ✪ 089 682 Melrose :

   ✗ **Hoebridge Inn**, TD6 9LZ, ✆ 3082 – 🅿. 𝗩𝗜𝗦𝗔
   closed Monday, first 2 weeks April, first 2 weeks October, Christmas Day and New Years Day –
   M (dinner only) a la carte 9.00/13.80 t. 🍷 2.90.

HONDA   Palma Pl. ✆ 2048

MILLPORT Bute. (Strathclyde) **401 402** F 16 – Shipping Services : see Great Cumbrae Island.

MILNGAVIE Dunbarton. (Strathclyde) **401** H 16 – pop. 12 030 – ECD : Tuesday and Saturday – ✉ ✪ 041 Glasgow.

⏚ Dougalston ✆ 956 5750.

◆Edinburgh 53 – ◆Glasgow 7.

   🏨 **Black Bull Thistle** (Thistle), Main St., G62 6BH, ✆ 956 2291, Telex 778323 – 📺 ➚wc 🛏wc
   ☎ 🅿. 🖾. 🖿 🆎 ⓞ 𝗩𝗜𝗦𝗔
   M 4.50/11.00 t. and a la carte 🍷 3.25 – ⊑ 5.95 – **27 rm** 42.00/55.00 **st.**

AUSTIN-ROVER   Main St. ✆ 956 2255   VAUXHALL-OPEL   Glasgow Rd ✆ 956 1126

MOFFAT Dumfries. (Dumfries and Galloway) **401 402** J 17 **Scotland G** – pop. 1 990 – ECD : Wednesday – ✪ 0683.

Envir. : Grey Mare's Tail★★.

🚩 Church Gate ✆ 20620 (summer only).

◆Edinburgh 61 – ◆Dumfries 22 – ◆Carlisle 43 – ◆Glasgow 60.

   🏨 **Ladbroke Mercury Motor Inn** (Ladbroke), Ladyknowe, DG10 9EL, ✆ 20464 – 📺 ➚wc
   ☎ 🅿 🖾. 🖿 🆎 ⓞ 𝗩𝗜𝗦𝗔
   closed 23 to 29 December – **M** (bar lunch)/dinner 9.50 **st.** and a la carte 🍷 3.70 – ⊑ 6.00 –
   51 rm 31.50/47.00 **st.** – SB 66.00/94.00 **st.**

   🏠 **Beechwood Country House** 🦢, up Harthope Pl., off Academy Rd, DG10 9RS, ✆ 20210,
   🍴 – ➚wc 🛏wc 🅿 🖾 𝗩𝗜𝗦𝗔 🍷 🎕
   closed January – **M** (bar lunch)/dinner 12.75 t. 🍷 2.85 – **8 rm** ⊑ 34.00/68.00 t. –
   SB 64.00/68.00 **st.**

   🏠 **Moffat House**, High St., DG10 9HL, ✆ 20039, 🍴 – ➚wc 🛏wc 🅿. 🖿 🆎 ⓞ 𝗩𝗜𝗦𝗔
   March-November, Christmas and New Year – **M** (bar lunch)/dinner a la carte 5.55/9.60 t. 🍷 3.50
   – **14 rm** ⊑ 27.00/42.00 t.

   ⌂ **Hartfell House**, Hartfell Cres., DG10 9AL, ✆ 20153, 🍴 – 🅿
   March-November – **9 rm** ⊑ 10.00/20.00 t.

   ⌂ **Arden House**, High St., DG10 9HG, ✆ 20220 – 🛏wc 🅿
   April-October – **7 rm** ⊑ 8.50/21.00 s.

MONTROSE Angus (Tayside) **401** M 13 **Scotland G** – pop. 12 127 – ECD : Wednesday – ✪ 0674.

Envir. : Brechin (Round Tower★) W : 7 m. by A 935 – Aberlemno Stones★ (summer only) W : 13 m. by A 935 and B 9134 – Glen Esk★ (via Brechin and Edzell) 29 m. by A 935, B 9667, B 966, B 974 and A 937 – Cairn O'Mount Road★ (≤★★) N : 20 m. by A 937 and B 974.

⏚ Medal and Broomfield, East Links Rd ✆ 72634, E : 1 m. off A 92 – 🚩 212 High St ✆ 72000.

◆Edinburgh 92 – ◆Aberdeen 39 – ◆Dundee 29.

   🏨 **Park**, John St., DD10 8RJ, ✆ 73415, Telex 76367, 🍴 – 📺 ➚wc 🛏wc 📺 🅿. 🖾
   59 rm, **1 suite**.

NISSAN   New Wynd ✆ 3606

MUCK (Isle of) Inverness. (Highland) **401** B 13 – Shipping Services : see Mallaig.

MUIR OF ORD Ross and Cromarty (Highland) **401** G 11 – pop. 1 707 – ECD : Thursday – ✪ 0463.

⏚ ✆ 870825 – 🚩 ✆ 870433 and 870525.

◆Edinburgh 169 – ◆Inverness 13 – ◆Wick 123.

   🏨 **Ord House** 🦢, IV6 7UH, off A 832 ✆ 870492, ≤, « Country house atmosphere », 🍴, 🍴,
   park – ➚wc 🅿
   April-October – **M** (bar lunch)/dinner 10.00 t. 🍷 2.75 – **13 rm** ⊑ 18.00/40.00 t.

MULL (Isle of) Argyll. (Strathclyde) **401** C 14 Scotland G – pop. 2 605.

See : Site★ – Calgary Bay★★ – Isle of Iona★ – Torosay Castle (Gardens★-≤★).

⚓ by Caledonian MacBrayne : from Craignure to Oban, summer 4-6 daily, winter Monday/Saturday 1-3 daily (45 mn) – from Fishnish to Lochaline Monday/Saturday 13-17 daily (15 mn).

⚓ by Caledonian MacBrayne : from Fionnphort to Isle of Iona frequent services daily in summer, restricted service in winter (5 mn) – from Tobermory to Kilchoan summer only Monday/Saturday 3-6 daily (35 mn) – from Tobermory to Arinagour (Isle of Coll) 3 weekly (1 h 20 mn) – from Tobermory to Isle of Tiree 1-2 daily (2 h 45 mn) – from Tobermory to Lochaline May-September 2 weekly (1 h) – from Tobermory to Oban 7 weekly (2 h direct).

🛈 48 Main St. at Tobermory ℰ 0688 (Tobermory) 2182.

Bunessan – ECD : Wednesday – ✉ Bunessan – ✆ 068 17 Fionnphort :

🏠 **Ardfenaig House** ⟋, PA67 6DX, W : 3 m. by A 849 ℰ 210, ≤, « Country house atmosphere », 🐎, park – **℗**
May-September – **M** (bar lunch)/dinner 15.00 **st.** ₪ 2.50 – **5 rm** ⚏ (dinner included) 45.00/90.00 **st.**

Dervaig – ✉ Tobermory – ✆ 068 84 Dervaig.

🏠 **Druimnacroish** ⟋, PA75 6QW, SE : 2 m. by B 8073 ℰ 274, ≤ Bellart Glen, « Converted steading », 🐎 – 📺 ⚌wc ₺ **℗**. 🔺 AE ⓪ VISA. ✷
May-October – **M** (dinner only) (booking essential) 15.00 **st.** – **7 rm** ⚏ 37.00/74.00 **st.**

Tiroran – ✉ ✆ 068 15 Tiroran.

🏠 **Tiroran House** ⟋, PA39 6ES, ℰ 232, ≤ Loch Scridain, « Country house atmosphere », 🐎, park – ⚌wc **℗**
May-12 October – **M** (booking essential)(lunch. residents only) 7.00/18.00 **st.** ₪ 2.75 – **9 rm** ⚏ 30.00/88.00 **st.**

Tobermory – pop. 843 – ECD : Wednesday – ✉ ✆ 0688 Tobermory.

🚢 Western Isles ℰ 2381 – 🛈 48 Main St. ℰ 2182 (summer only).

🏠 **Tobermory,** 53 Main St., PA75 6NT, ℰ 2091, ≤
April-October – **M** *(closed Sunday lunch)* (buffet lunch)/dinner 8.00 **t.** (booking essential) ₪ 2.50 – **15 rm** ⚏ 16.00/38.00 **t.**

⌂ **Harbour House,** 59 Main St., PA75 6NT, ℰ 2209, ≤
closed December and January – **9 rm** ⚏ 15.00/35.00 **t.**

NAIRN Nairn. (Highland) **401** I 11 Scotland G – pop. 7 366 – ECD : Wednesday – ✆ 0667.
Envir. : Cawdor Castle★, S : 7 m. by A 9090 – Brodie Castle★, E : 2 m. – Forres (Sueno's Stone★★) E : 11 m. by A 96 and B 9011.

🏌 🏌 Seabank Rd ℰ 52103 – 🏌 Nairn Dunbar, Lochloy Rd ℰ 52741.
🛈 62 King St. ℰ 52753 (summer only).

◆Edinburgh 172 – ◆Aberdeen 91 – ◆Inverness 16.

🏨 **Newton** ⟋, Inverness Rd, IV12 4RX, off A 96 ℰ 53144, ≤, « Country house in extensive grounds », 🐎, park, ✼ – ⅏ 📺 ☎ **℗**. 🔺 🔺 AE ⓪ VISA
M 6.00/11.50 **t.** and a la carte 10.75/17.20 **t.** ₪ 3.30 – **44 rm** ⚏ 23.50/59.00 **t.**, **3 suites** 38.00/75.00 **t.** – SB (weekends only) 48.00/65.00 **st.**

🏨 **Golf View,** Seabank Rd, IV12 4HD, ℰ 52301, ≤, ⤋ heated, 🐎, ✼ – ⅏ 📺 **℗**. 🔺 🔺 AE ⓪ VISA
M 6.50/16.00 **t.** and a la carte ₪ 3.50 – **55 rm** ⚏ 32.00/64.00 **t.**

🏠 **Clifton** ⟋, Viewfield St., IV12 4HW, ℰ 53119, ≤, « Tasteful decor », 🐎 – ⚌wc **℗**. 🔺 AE ⓪ VISA
March-November – **M** (booking essential) a la carte 10.25/14.25 **t.** ₪ 3.50 – **16 rm** ⚏ 34.00/69.00 **t.**

⌂ **Greenlawns,** 13 Seafield St., IV12 4HG, ℰ 52738, 🐎 – 📺 ⚌wc **℗**
8 rm ⚏ 12.50/33.50 **t.**

⌂ **Bruach House,** 35 Seabank Rd, IV12 4EU, ℰ 54194 – ⚌wc **℗**
closed Christmas and New Year – **8 rm** ⚏ 10.00/27.00 **t.**

AUSTIN-ROVER King St. ℰ 52304.   TALBOT Inverness Rd ℰ 52335

NETHERLEY Kincardine (Grampian) **401** N 12 – see Stonehaven.

NEWBURGH Aberdeen. (Grampian) **401** N 12 – ✆ 035 86.
◆Edinburgh 144 – ◆Aberdeen 14 – Fraserburgh 33.

🏠 **Udny Arms,** Main St., AB4 0BL, ℰ 444 – 📺 ⚌wc ₪wc ☎ **℗**. 🔺 AE VISA
M (restricted lunch)/dinner 15.25 **t.** and a la carte ₪ 2.70 – ⚏ 4.00 – **26 rm** 30.00/40.00 **t.** – SB (weekends only) 64.50/68.50 **st.**

🏠 **Foveran House** ⟋, Foveran, AB4 OAP, SW : 1 m. on A 975 ℰ 398, Group Telex 265871, park, ✼ – 📺 ⚌wc ₪wc **℗**. 🔺 AE VISA
M a la carte 5.05/16.95 **t.** – ⚏ 4.00 – **17 rm** 30.00/40.00 **t.** – SB (weekends only) 35.00 **st.**

NEW GALLOWAY Kirkcudbright (Dumfries and Galloway) **401 402** H 18 – pop. 290 – ✪ 064 42.
♦Edinburgh 88 – ♦Ayr 36 – Dumfries 25.

  ↑ **Leamington,** High St., DG7 3RN, ☏ 327
    Easter-October – **9 rm** ⌿ 11.50/27.00 t.

NEW SCONE Perth. (Tayside) **401** J 14 – see Perth.

NEWTONMORE Inverness. (Highland) **401** H 12 – pop. 1 010 – ECD : Wednesday – ✪ 054 03.
☰ Golf Course Rd ☏ 328 – ☐ ☏ 274 (summer only).
♦Edinburgh 113 – ♦Inverness 43 – Perth 69.

  🏠 **Ard-na-Coille,** Kingussie Rd, PH20 1AY, ☏ 214, ≤ – 🛁wc
    April-October and 26 December-4 January – **M** (dinner only) 12.00 t. ▯ 2.50 – **10 rm**
    ⌿ 17.00/65.00 t.

  ↑ **Coig-na-Shee** 🌄, Fort William Rd, PH20 1DG, ☏ 216, 🌳 – ☐
    closed December and January – **6 rm** ⌿ 11.50/25.00 s.

  ✗ **Gables,** Main St., PH20 1DA, ☏ 231 – 🂰 𝑽𝑰𝑺𝑨
    closed November and Wednesday in winter – **M** (bar lunch)(Sunday lunch in winter)/dinner a
    la carte approx. 11.15 t. ▯ 3.25.

NEWTON STEWART Wigtown. (Dumfries and Galloway) **401 402** G 19 – pop. 3 212 – ECD :
Wednesday – ✪ 0671.
Envir. : Galloway Forest Parks★, N – Queen's Way★ (Newton Stewart to New Galloway) 19 m. by
A 712.
☐ Dashwood Sq. ☏ 2431 (summer only).
♦Edinburgh 131 – ♦Dumfries 51 – ♦Glasgow 87 – Stranraer 24.

  🏨 **Kirroughtree** 🌄, DG8 6AN, NE : 1 ½ m. on A 712 ☏ 2141, ≤ woodland and River Cree,
    « Country house and gardens », park – 📺 ☎ ☐. 🌿
    March-mid November – **M** (lunch by arrangement)/dinner 21.00 st. and a la carte – **22 rm**
    ⌿ 36.00/76.00 st. – SB 82.00/93.00 st.

  🏠 **Creebridge House** 🌄, Minnigaff, DG8 6NP, ☏ 2121, 🌳 – 📺 🛁wc ☐. 🂰 𝑽𝑰𝑺𝑨
    Accomodation closed 20 December-6 January – **M** (bar lunch)/dinner 13.50 st. ▯ 2.85 – **17 rm**
    ⌿ 20.00/54.00 st. – SB (except summer)(weekends only) 58.00 st.

  🏠 **Bruce,** 88 Queen St., DG8 6JL, ☏ 2294 – 📺 🛁wc 🐾 ☐. 🂰 🅰🅴 ⓪ 𝑽𝑰𝑺𝑨
    closed December and January – **M** 11.00 st. (dinner) and a la carte ▯ 2.95 – **17 rm**
    ⌿ 22.50/41.00 st. – SB (winter only) 58.00 st.

  🏠 **Crown,** 101 Queen St., DG8 6GW, ☏ 2727 – 🛁wc ☐. 🂰 𝑽𝑰𝑺𝑨
    M (bar lunch)/dinner 10.00 st. and a la carte ▯ 2.70 – **10 rm** ⌿ 13.50/31.00 st. –
    SB 41.00/51.00 st.

VW-AUDI Queen St. ☏ 2112   VOLVO Minnigaff ☏ 3101
RENAULT Duncan Park, Wigtown ☏ 098 84 (Wig-
town) 3287

NEWTON WAMPHRAY Dumfries. (Dumfries and Galloway) **401 402** J 18 – ECD : Wednesday –
✉ Moffat – ✪ 057 64 Johnstone Bridge.
♦Edinburgh 64 – ♦Carlisle 36 – ♦Dumfries 22 – ♦Glasgow 63.

  ☝ **Red House,** DG10 9NF, off A 74 ☏ 214, ≤, 🌳 – ☐. ⓪
    M (residents only)(bar lunch)/dinner 7.50 st. – **6 rm** ⌿ 14.75/29.50 st. – SB 40.00/45.00 st.

NORTH BERWICK E. Lothian (Lothian) **401** L 15 Scotland G – pop. 4 861 – ECD : Thursday –
✪ 0620.
Envir. : Tantallon Castle★★ (Site★★★) E : 3 m. by A 198 – Tyninghame★, S : 6 m. by A 198 – Preston
Mill★, S : 8 m. by A 198 and B 1407 – Museum of Flight★, S : 10 m. by A 198 and B 1407.
☰ New Clubhouse, Beach Rd ☏ 2135 – ☐ Quality St. ☏ 2197.
♦Edinburgh 24 – ♦Newcastle-upon-Tyne 102.

  🏨 **Marine** (T.H.F.), Cromwell Rd, EH39 4LZ, ☏ 2406, ≤, ⟱ heated, 🌳, ✗, squash – ⬦ 📺 ☐.
    🖐. 🂰 🅰🅴 ⓪ 𝑽𝑰𝑺𝑨
    M (buffet lunch)/dinner 12.00 st. ▯ 2.90 – ⌿ 5.65 – **86 rm** 38.00/56.00 st.

  🏠 **Point Garry,** 20 West Bay Rd, EH39 4AW, ☏ 2380, ≤ – 🛁wc 🛁wc ☐. 🂰
    April-October – **M** (bar lunch)/dinner 8.80 t. and a la carte ▯ 2.85 – **15 rm** ⌿ 18.00/40.00 st.

  🏠 **Blenheim House,** 14 Westgate, EH39 4AF, ☏ 2385, ≤, 🌳 – 📺 🛁wc ☐. 𝑽𝑰𝑺𝑨
    M 6.50/9.50 t. and a la carte – **11 rm** ⌿ 19.00/45.00 t.

  🏠 **Nether Abbey,** 20 Dirleton Av., EH39 4BQ, ☏ 2802, 🌳 – 🛁wc 🛁wc ☐. 🂰 𝑽𝑰𝑺𝑨
    M (bar lunch)/dinner 10.50 t. ▯ 3.50 – **15 rm** ⌿ 16.00/31.50 t.

  ↑ **Craigview,** 5 Beach Rd, EH39 4AB, ☏ 2257 – 📺 🛁wc ☐
    6 rm ⌿ 27.00 st.

FORD 52 Dunbar Rd ☏ 2232

NORTH RONALDSAY (Isle of) Orkney (Orkney Islands) **401** M 5 – Shipping Services : see
Orkney Islands (Mainland : Kirkwall).

OBAN Argyll. (Strathclyde) **401** D 14 **Scotland G** – pop. 7 476 – ECD : Thursday – ☉ 0631.

See : Site★.

Envir. : Loch Awe★★ – Inverary★★ (Castle★★-Interior★★★) – Loch Fyne★★ – Bonawe Furnace★ – Cruachan Power Station★ – Auchindrain★ – Crinan★, 83 m. by A 85, A 819, A 83 and A 816 – Sea Life Centre★, N : 11 m. off A 828.

Access to Glasgow by helicopter.

⇤ by Caledonian MacBrayne : to Craignure (Isle of Mull) summer 4-6 daily ; winter Monday/Saturday 1-3 daily (45 mn) – to Castlebay (Isle of Barra) summer only : 1-2 weekly (5 h to 8 h) – to Lochboisdale (South Uist) 3-6 weekly (6 h direct ; 8 h via Castlebay) – to Arinagour (Isle of Coll) summer only : 5-7 weekly (3 h 15 mn to 5 h 45 mn) – to Isle of Tiree 3-4 weekly (4 to 5 h) – to Scalasaig (Isle of Colonsay) summer only : 6 weekly (2 h 30 mn) – to Achnacroish (Isle of Lismore) Monday/Saturday 2-3 daily (1 h).

⇤ to Tobermory (Isle of Mull) 7 weekly (1 h 45 mn to 2 h 15 mn) – to Lochaline May-September 2 weekly (1 h 10 mn).

🛈 Argyll Sq. ✆ 63122.

◆Edinburgh 123 – ◆Dundee 116 – ◆Glasgow 93 – ◆Inverness 118.

🏨 **Alexandra,** Corran Esplanade, PA34 5AA, ✆ 62381, ≤ – ‖🅿 📺 ⇋wc 🅿 🔼 🆎 ⑩ 𝗩𝗜𝗦𝗔
April-October – **M** (bar lunch)/dinner 10.00 **t.** and a la carte ◊ 2.90 – **56 rm** ⌳ 34.00/58.00 **t.**

🏨 Great Western, Corran Esplanade, PA34 5PP, ✆ 63101, Group Telex 778215, ≤ – ‖🅿 📺 ⇋wc
🅿 ⚿
76 rm.

🏠 Soroba House, Soroba Rd, PA34 4SB, S : 1 ¼ m. on A 816 ✆ 62628, ☞, ⚄ – 📺 ⇋wc 🅿
16 rm, 14 suites.

🏠 **Manor House,** Gallanach Rd, PA34 4LS, ✆ 62087, ≤ – ⇋wc ⋔wc 🅿 🔼 ⑩ 𝗩𝗜𝗦𝗔
closed Christmas Day and 1-2 January – **M** (bar lunch)/dinner 17.00 **st.** and a la carte ◊ 3.00 –
11 rm ⌳ 32.00/44.00 **st.**

🏠 Rowan Tree, George St., PA34 5NX, ✆ 62954 – 📺 ⇋wc 🅿 🔼 🆎 ⑩ 𝗩𝗜𝗦𝗔 – **24 rm**
⌳ 25.00/42.00 **t.**

↑ **Corriemar,** Esplanade, PA34 5AQ, ✆ 62476, ≤ – ⋔wc 🅿
Easter-mid October – **15 rm** ⌳ 14.00/33.00 **t.**

at Lerags S : 3 m. by A 816 – ⊠ ☉ 0631 Oban :

↑ **Foxholes** ⚄, PA34 4SE, ✆ 64982, ≤, ☞ – 📺 ⇋wc 🅿
April-October – **7 rm** ⌳ (dinner included) 32.20/64.40 **t.**

at Kilninver SW : 8 m. on A 816 – ⊠ ☉ 085 26 Kilninver :

🏨 **Knipoch,** PA34 4QT, NE : 1 ½ m. on A 816 ✆ 251, ≤, « Tastefully furnished », ☞ – 📺
⇋wc ☞ 🅿 🔼 🆎 ⑩ 𝗩𝗜𝗦𝗔 ⚿
closed January – **M** (bar lunch)/dinner 23.50 **t.** ◊ 3.50 – **19 rm** ⌳ 41.50/83.00 **t.**

AUSTIN-ROVER Airds Pl. ✆ 63173
FORD Soroba Rd ✆ 63061

SUBARU Stevenson St. ✆ 66566
VOLVO, OPEL, BEDFORD Breadalbane Pl. ✆ 63066

OLDMELDRUM Aberdeen. (Grampian) **401** N 11 – pop. 1 343 – ECD : Wednesday – ☉ 065 12.

Envir. : Pitmedden Gardens★★, E : 5 m. by A 920 – Haddo House★, N : 9 m. by B 9170 and B 9005 – Fyvie Castle, N : 8 m. by A 947.

🖙 9 .

◆Edinburgh 148 – ◆Aberdeen 18 – Fraserburgh 30 – ◆Inverness 89.

🏨 **Meldrum House** ⚄, AB5 0AE, N : 1 ½ m. on A 947 ✆ 2294, ≤, « Country house atmosphere », ☞, park – 📺 ⇋wc ⋔wc ☞ 🅿 🆎 ⑩
Mid March-mid December – **M** (lunch by arrangement)/dinner 19.00 **st.** ◊ 3.75 – **11 rm**
⌳ 46.50/75.90 **st.**

RENAULT Station Rd ✆ 2338

ONICH Inverness. (Highland) **401** E 13 – ECD : Saturday except summer – ⊠ Fort William –
☉ 085 53.

◆Edinburgh 123 – ◆Glasgow 93 – ◆Inverness 79 – ◆Oban 39.

🏠 **The Lodge on the Loch,** Creag Dhu, PH33 6RY, on A 82 ✆ 238, ≤ Loch Linnhe and mountains, ☞ – ⇋wc ⋔wc 🅿 🔼 🆎 ⑩ 𝗩𝗜𝗦𝗔
April-October – **M** 7.50/12.00 **st.** and a la carte ◊ 3.20 – **20 rm** ⌳ 15.50/30.50 **st.** –
SB 53.00/78.00 **st.**

🏠 **Onich,** PH33 6RY, on A 82 ✆ 214, ≤ Loch Linnhe and mountains, ☞ – ⇋wc 🅿 🔼 🆎 ⑩
𝗩𝗜𝗦𝗔
M 5.50/9.50 **st.** and a la carte ◊ 3.10 – **24 rm** ⌳ 18.00/51.00 **st.** – SB (except summer) 54.00 **st.**

🏠 **Allt-Nan-Ros,** PH33 6RY, on A 82 ✆ 210, ≤ Loch Linnhe and mountains, ☞ – 📺 ⇋wc
⋔wc ☎ 🅿 🔼 🆎 ⑩ 𝗩𝗜𝗦𝗔
April-October – **M** (bar lunch)/dinner 14.00 **t.** ◊ 3.00 – **19 rm** ⌳ 24.00/61.00 **st.**

↑ **Cuilcheanna House** ⚄, PH33 6SD, ✆ 226, ≤, ☞ – 🅿
Easter-September – **8 rm** ⌳ 16.00/28.00 **t.**

ORKNEY ISLANDS Orkney (Orkney Islands) 🗺 401 KL 6 and 7 Scotland G – pop. 19 040.

🛬 see Mainland : Kirkwall.

🚢 ⚓ see Mainland : Kirkwall and Stromness – by Orkney Islands Shipping Co. : service between Longhope (Isle of Hoy), Lyness (Isle of Hoy), Flotta (Isle of), Houton, Graemsay (Isle of), Stromness and return, daily itinerary varies consult operator.

⚓ by Thomas & Bews : from Burwick (South Ronaldsay) to John O'Groats summer only 2-4 daily (45 mn).

HOY

Old Man of Hoy Scotland G.
See : Old Man of Hoy★★★ (sandstone stack).

MAINLAND

Birsay Scotland G – ✉ ☎ 085 672 Birsay.
See : Brough of Birsay (site★★).

Kirkwall Scotland G – pop. 5 947 – ECD : Wednesday – ✉ ☎ 0856 Kirkwall.
See : Site★ – St. Magnus Cathedral★★★ – Earl's Palace★ – Tankerness House Museum★.
Envir. : Italian Chapel★ – Unston Cairn★ – Ring of Brodgar★ – Corrigall Farm Museum★.
🛆 Grainbank ✆ 2457, W : 1 m.
🛬 Kirkwall Airport : ✆ 2421, Telex 75473, S : 3 ½ m.
⚓ by Orkney Islands Shipping Co. : to Westray via Eday, Stronsay, Sanday and Papa Westray 3 weekly (2 to 6 h) – to North Ronaldsay 1 weekly (2 h 30 mn) – to Wyre via Rousay and Egilsay 1 weekly (1 to 4 h) – to Shapinsay 1-4 daily (25 mn) – by P & O Ferries to Scalloway (Shetland Islands) summer 2 weekly: winter 1 fortnightly (8 h).
🛈 Broad St. ✆ 2856.

🏨 **Kirkwall,** Harbour St., KW15 1LF, ✆ 2232, ≼ – 🛗 📺 ⌂wc 🛁wc ☎. 🅰 🆎 ⓸ VISA
M 5.00/20.00 **st.** and a la carte 🍷 2.80 – **42 rm** ⊆ 20.00/36.00 **st.**

🏠 **Foveran** 🍴, St. Ola, KW15 1SF, SW : 3 m. on A 964 ✆ 2389, ≼ Sea, « Tranquil setting on the banks of Scapa Flow » – ⌂wc 🛁wc 🅿. 🅰 VISA
closed February and October – **M** (closed Sunday) (dinner only) a la carte 7.50/13.00 **t.** 🍷 2.75
– **8 rm** ⊆ 18.50/31.00 **t.**

🏠 Ayre, Ayre Rd, KW15 1QX, ✆ 2197 – ⌂wc 🛁 🅿. 🅰 VISA
⊆ 2.90 – **31 rm** 14.50/33.00 **st.**

🏠 Lynnfield 🍴, Holm Rd, KW15 1BX, S : 1 ¼ m. on A 961 ✆ 2505, 🚗 – 📺 🛁 🅿
7 rm

🏠 **Bellavista,** Carness Rd, KW15 1TB, N : 1 m. via Cromwell Rd ✆ 2306 – 🅿. 🍽
8 rm ⊆ 9.00/18.00 **s.**

COLT, TALBOT Gt Western Rd ✆ 2805   RENAULT Gt Western Rd ✆ 2601
FIAT Junction Rd ✆ 2158   VAUXHALL Burnmouth Rd ✆ 2950
FORD Castle St. ✆ 3212

Loch Harray – ✉ Loch Harray – ☎ 085 677 Harray.

🏠 **Merkister** 🍴, KW17 2LF, ✆ 366, ≼, 🐟, 🚗 – 🛁wc 🅿. 🅰 🆎
Mid April-September – **M** (bar lunch)/dinner 15.00 **t.** and a la carte 🍷 4.50 – **16 rm**
⊆ 18.50/40.00 **t.**

Stromness Scotland G – pop. 1 816 – ECD : Thursday – ✉ ☎ 0856 Stromness.
See : Site★ – Pier Arts Centre (Collection of abstract art★).
Envir. : Old Man of Hoy★★★.
🛆 Ness ✆ 850593.
🚢 by P & O Ferries : Orkney and Shetland Services : to Scrabster Monday/Saturday 1-3 daily (2 h).
⚓ to Moaness (Isle of Hoy) 2-3 daily (25 mn).
🛈 Ferry Terminal Building, Pierhead ✆ 850716 (summer only).

🏠 Stromness, 108 Victoria St., KW16 3AA, ✆ 850298, 🚗 – 🛗 ⌂wc 🛁wc
39 rm

✗ **Hamnavoe,** 35 Graham Pl., ✆ 850606. 🅰 VISA
closed Monday, Tuesday from November-April, first 2 weeks January and last 2 weeks October
– **M** a la carte 3.95/16.25 **t.**

OUT SKERRIES Shetland (Shetland Islands) **401** R 2 – Shipping Services : see Shetland Islands (Mainland : Lerwick).

OYKEL BRIDGE Sutherland. (Highland) **401** F 10 – ⊠ Lairg – ✪ 054 984 Rosehall.

◆Edinburgh 222 – ◆Inverness 66 – Lochinver 33.

   血 **Oykel Bridge** ⌂, IV27 4HE, ✆ 218, ≼, ⬎, ⇌ – ➱wc **P**
      March-September – **M** (bar lunch)/dinner 16.00 **st.** ⌀ 3.45 – **16 rm** ⊑ 25.00/50.00 **st.**

PAISLEY Renfrew. (Strathclyde) **401 402** G 16 **Scotland G** – pop. 84 330 – ECD : Tuesday – ✪ 041 Glasgow.

See : Museum and Art gallery (Paisley Shawl Section★).

▥ Barshaw Park ✆ 889 2908, E : 1 m. of Paisley Cross off A 737.

🛈 Town Hall, Abbey Close, ✆ 889 0711.

◆Edinburgh 53 – ◆Ayr 35 – ◆Glasgow 7.5 – Greenock 17.

   血 Stakis Watermill (Stakis), Lonend, PA1 1SR, ✆ 889 3201 – ⧆ ▥ ➱wc ☜ **P**. ◪ 🅰🄴 ⓞ **VISA**
      51 rm ⊑ 38.00/49.00 **t.**

   血 Rockfield, 125 Renfrew Rd, PA3 4DS, ✆ 889 6182 – ▥ ➱wc ▥wc ☜ **P**
      20 rm

AUSTIN-ROVER 46 New Sneddon St. ✆ 889 7882
AUSTIN-ROVER 92 Glasgow Rd ✆ 889 8526
FIAT 4-8 Lochfield Rd ✆ 884 2281
FORD 37-41 Lonend ✆ 887 0191

HYUNDAI, SUBARU 11-17 Weir St. ✆ 889 6866
PEUGEOT, TALBOT 7 West St. ✆ 889 0011
VAUXHALL-OPEL 69 Espedair St. ✆ 889 5254

PAPA WESTRAY (Isle of) Orkney (Orkney Islands) **401** L 5 – Shipping Services : see Orkney Islands (Mainland : Kirkwall).

PEAT INN Fife. (Fife) **401** L 15 – ⊠ Cupar – ✪ 033 484.

◆Edinburgh 45 – Dundee 21 – Perth 28.

   XXX ✿ **The Peat Inn**, KY15 5LH, ✆ 206 – ⅖ **P**. ◪ 🅰🄴 ⓞ **VISA**
      closed Sunday, Monday, 2 weeks January, 1 week April and 1 week October – **M** (booking essential) 11.00/23.00 **st.** and a la carte 17.20/19.80 **st.** ⌀ 4.00
      Spec. Pigeon breast on a pastry case with wild mushrooms, Loin of lamb in a red wine sauce with cassis and rosemary (Mid September), Almond praline ice-cream in a lacy biscuit cup and a coffee bean sauce.

PEEBLES Peebles. (Borders) **401 402** K 17 – pop. 6 404 – ECD : Wednesday – ✪ 0721.

▥ Kirkland St. ✆ 20197 – ▥ West Linton ✆ 0968 (West Linton) 60589.

🛈 Chambers Institute, High St. ✆ 20138 (summer only).

◆Edinburgh 24 – Hawick 31 – ◆Glasgow 53.

   血血 **Peebles Hydro,** Innerleithen Rd, EH45 8LX, ✆ 20602, Telex 72568, ≼, ◪, ⇌, park, ⚒, squash – ⧆ ▥ ☎ **P**. ⚐. ◪ 🅰🄴 ⓞ **VISA**. ⚘
      M 7.50/11.50 **st.** ⌀ 3.50 – **139 rm** ⊑ 35.50/78.50 **st.**, **3 suites** 75.25/91.00 **st.** – SB 64.50/95.50 **st.**

   血 **Cringletie House** ⌂, EH45 8PL, N : 3 m. on A 703 ✆ 072 13 (Eddleston) 233, ≼, « Country house in extensive grounds », ⇌, park, ⚒ – ⧆ ➱wc **P**
      closed 27 December-February – **M** (restricted lunch Monday to Saturday)/dinner 15.50 **t.** ⌀ 3.50 – **16 rm** ⊑ 22.00/50.00 **t.** – SB (except summer) 63.00/70.00 **st.**

   血 **Park** (Swallow), Innerleithen Rd, EH45 8BA, ✆ 20451, ⇌ – ▥ ➱wc ▥wc ☜ **P**. ◪ 🅰🄴 ⓞ **VISA**
      M 7.50/10.50 **st.** and a la carte ⌀ 3.95 – **28 rm** ⊑ 38.00/56.00 **st.** – SB (except Christmas and New Year) 60.00/70.00 **st.**

   血 **Tontine** (T.H.F.), 39 High St., EH45 8AJ, ✆ 20892 – ▥ ➱wc ☎ **P**. ◪ 🅰🄴 ⓞ **VISA**
      M (bar lunch)/dinner 9.50 **st.** and a la carte ⌀ 3.40 – ⊑ 5.65 – **37 rm** 38.00/48.00 **st.**

   at Eddleston N : 4 ½ m. on A 703 – ⊠ Peebles – ✪ 072 13 Eddleston :

   XX **Horse Shoe Inn**, EH45 8QP, ✆ 225 – **P**. ◪ 🅰🄴 ⓞ **VISA**
      closed 25 December and 1 January – **M** 7.45/12.95 **t.** and a la carte 9.80/17.35 **t.** ⌀ 2.40.

PENNAN Aberdeen (Grampian) **401** N 10 – pop. 92 – ⊠ ✪ 03466 New Aberdour.

◆Edinburgh 181 – ◆Aberdeen 51 – Fraserburgh 12 – ◆Inverness 85.

   ⌂ **Pennan Inn**, 17-19 Main St., AB4 4JB, ✆ 201 – ▥. **VISA**. ⚘
      M *(closed dinner Sunday and Monday)* a la carte 5.20/13.50 **st.** ⌀ 3.50 – **4 rm** ⊑ 17.50/27.50 **st.**

AUSTIN-ROVER Innerleithen Rd ✆ 20627
LANCIA, SUZUKI George St. ✆ 20545

VAUXHALL-OPEL 104 Old Town ✆ 20886

PERTH Perth. (Tayside) **401** J 14 Scotland G – pop. 41 916 – ECD : Wednesday – ✆ 0738.

See : Black Watch Regimental Museum★ Y **M1** – Georgian terraces★ Y – Museum and Art Gallery★ Y **M2** – Branklyn Garden★ by A 85 Z – Kinnoull Hill (≤★) by Bowerswell Road Y.

Envir. : Scone Palace★★, N : 2 m. by A 93 Y – Huntingtower Castle★, NW : 3 m. by A 9 Y – Elcho Castle★, SE : by A 912 Z – Abernethy Round Tower★, SE : 8 m. by A 912 Z and A 913 – Cairnwell (❄★★) N : 40 m. by A 93 Y.

🏌 Craigie Hill, Cherrybank ✆ 24377, West boundary, by A 9 Z.

🛈 The Round House, Marshall Pl. ✆ 22900 and 27108.

◆Edinburgh 44 – ◆Aberdeen 86 – ◆Dundee 22 – Dunfermline 29 – ◆Glasgow 64 – ◆Inverness 112 – ◆Oban 94.

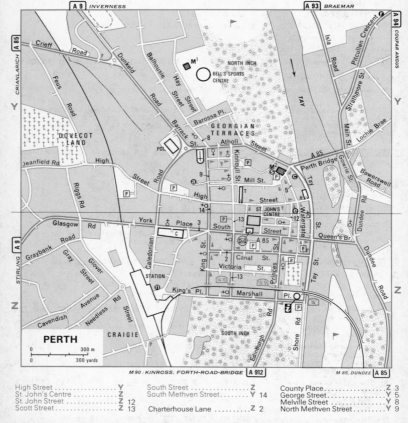

🏨 **Hunting Tower** ⌲, Crieff Rd, PH1 3JT, W : 3 ½ m. on A 85 ✆ 83771, Telex 76204, ≤, ⌖, ☞ – TV ⇌wc ⃦wc ☎ Ⓟ. 🄰. 🄽 🄰🄴 ⓞ VISA on A 85 Y

M 7.50/13.00 **t.** and a la carte ⅋ 3.00 – **15 rm** ⚏ 33.00/48.00 **t.**

🏨 **Royal George** (T.H.F.), Tay St., PH1 5LD, ✆ 24455 – TV ⇌wc ☎ Ⓟ. 🄰. 🄽 🄰🄴 ⓞ VISA Y c

M 7.25/9.50 **st.** and a la carte ⅋ 3.40 – ⚏ 5.65 – **43 rm** 38.00/54.00 **st.**

🏨 **Station,** Leonard St., PH2 8HE, ✆ 24141, Telex 76481, ⌖ – ⴀ TV ⇌wc ☎ Ⓟ. 🄰. 🄽 🄰🄴 ⓞ VISA Z n

M 5.25/7.20 **st.** and a la carte – **70 rm** ⚏ 22.00/42.50 **st., 2 suites.**

🏨 **Stakis City Mills** (Stakis), West Mill St., PH1 5QP, ✆ 28281 – TV ⇌wc ☎ Ⓟ. 🄰. 🄽 🄰 VISA Y a

M 9.25 **st.** (dinner) and a la carte **t.** ⅋ 3.10 – ⚏ 3.90 – **78 rm** 37.00/54.00 **t.**, **1 suite** 60.00/ 80.00 **t.** – SB 48.00/62.00 **st.**

🏠 **Pitcullen,** 17 Pitcullen Cresent, PH2 7HT, NE : ¾ m. on A 94 ✆ 26506 – Ⓟ Y r

closed December and January – **6 rm** ⚏ 9.00/18.00 **st.**

XX **Coach House,** 8 North Port, PH1 5LU, ℰ 27950 – 🖃 VISA 　　　　　Y　s
closed Sunday, Monday, first 2 weeks January and 2 weeks mid July – **M** 8.50/16.50 t.
🍷 3.00.

X **Timothy's,** 24 St. John St., PH1 5SP, ℰ 26641, Smörrebrod – 🖃 　　　　　Y　e
closed Sunday, Monday, Christmas and New Year – **M** a la carte 4.25/7.80 t. 🍷 3.00.

at New Scone NE : 2 ½ m. on A 94 – Y – ⊠ ☺ 0738 Perth :

🏛 **Balcraig House** ≫, E : 1 ½ m. by A 94 ℰ 51123, ≼, 🛲, park, ℀ – 🖵 ⊟wc ☎ 🅿. 🖭 ⓪
VISA. ℀
M (lunch by arrangement)/dinner 21.00 **st.** 🍷 3.50 – **10 rm** � 47.50/85.00 **st.** – SB (except
summer) (weekends only) 99.50 **st.**

🏛 **Murrayshall House** ≫, PH2 7PH, E : 1 ½ m. by A 94 ℰ 51171, ≼, ऻ₈, 🛲, park – 🖵 ⊟wc
⋔wc ☎ 🅿. 🖃 🖭 ⓪ VISA. ℀
M 5.50/10.00 **t.** and a la carte 🍷 2.50 – **20 rm** � 25.00/49.00 **t.** – SB (November-April)
53.00/77.00 **st.**

AUSTIN-ROVER　Dunkeld Rd ℰ 28211
BMW, ROLLS ROYCE　50-56 Leonard St. ℰ 25481
CITROEN　60 South St. ℰ 23335
DATSUN, FIAT, LOTUS, MERCEDES-BENZ, SAAB
172 Dunkeld Rd ℰ 28211

FORD　Riggs Rd ℰ 25121
PEUGEOT-TALBOT　Glenearn Rd ℰ 20811
VAUXHALL　Dunkeld Rd ℰ 26241
VOLVO　Arran Rd, North Muirton ℰ 22156
VW, AUDI　Dunkeld Rd ℰ 25252

PETERHEAD Aberdeen. (Grampian) 🔢 O 11 – pop. 16 804 – ECD : Wednesday – ☺ 0779.

ऻ₈, ऻ₅ Craigewan ℰ 2149.

◆Edinburgh 165 – ◆Aberdeen 35 – Fraserburgh 18.

🏛 **Waterside Inn,** 1 Fraserburgh Rd, AB4 7BN, NW : 2 m. on A 952 ℰ 71121, Telex 739413, 🛲
– 🖵 ⊟wc ☎ 🅿. 🔬. 🖃 🖭 ⓪ VISA
M (gill rest. only) 5.00/12.00 **st.** and a la carte 🍷 3.50 – **120 rm** � 32.50/48.00 **st.** – SB (except
Christmas and New Year) (weekends only) 48.00 **st.**

🏛 Palace, Prince St., AB4 6PL, ℰ 74821 – ▮ 🖵 ⊟wc ☎ 🅿
93 rm.

VAUXHALL-OPEL　West Rd ℰ 72440

PITCAPLE Aberdeen. (Grampian) 🔢 M 12 – ☺ 046 76.

◆Edinburgh 51 – ◆Aberdeen 21.

🏛 **Pittodrie House** ≫, AB5 9HS, SW : 1 ¾ m. off A 96 by Chapel of Garioch Rd ℰ 444, Telex
739935, ≼, « Country house atmosphere », 🛲, park, ℀, squash – 🖵 ⊟wc ⋔wc ☎ ⟺
🅿. 🖃 🖭 VISA
M (bar lunch)/dinner 18.50 **st.** – **12 rm** � 34.00/60.00 **st.** – SB (except summer) (weekends
only) 60.00 **st.**

PITLOCHRY Perth. (Tayside) 🔢 I 13 Scotland G – pop. 2 194 – ECD : Thursday – ☺ 0796.

See : Site★.

Envir. : Blair Castle★★ and Blair Atholl (Falls of Bruar★) NW : 7 m. by A 9 – Queen's View★★, NW :
6 m. by A 9 and B 8019.

ऻ₈ Estates Office ℰ 2117 – ऻ₅ Blair Atholl ℰ 079 681 (Blair Atholl) 407.

🅸 22 Atholl Rd ℰ 2215 and 2751.

◆Edinburgh 71 – ◆Inverness 85 – Perth 27.

🏛 **Atholl Palace** (T.H.F.) ≫, PH16 5LY, ℰ 2400, Telex 76406, ≼, 🛆 heated, 🛲, park, ℀ – ▮
🖵 🅿. 🔬. 🖃 🖭 ⓪ VISA
M (bar lunch)/dinner 10.50 **st.** and a la carte 🍷 3.40 – � 5.65 – **84 rm** 38.00/58.00 **st.**, **9 suites**.

🏛 **Green Park** ≫, Clunie Bridge Rd, PH16 5JY, ℰ 3248, ≼ Loch Faskally and mountains, 🛲 –
🖵 ⊟wc ⋔wc 🅿. ℀
Mid April-October – **M** (bar lunch)/dinner 11.50 **st.** and a la carte 🍷 2.50 – **37 rm**
� 19.50/51.00 **t.** – SB (spring only) 56.00 **st.**

🏛 **Pine Trees** ≫, Strathview Terr., PH16 5QR, ℰ 2121, ≼, 🛲 – 🖵 ⊟wc ⋔wc ⟺ 🅿. 🖃 🖭
⓪ VISA
April-December – **M** 7.50/12.00 **t.** 🍷 2.50 – **24 rm** � 15.00/50.00 **t.**

🏛 **Burnside,** 19 West Moulin Rd, PH16 5EA, on A 924 ℰ 2203, 🛲 – 🖵 ⊟wc ⋔wc 🔬 🅿. 🖭
⓪ VISA. ℀
Late March-October – **M** (bar lunch)/dinner 9.15 **t.** and a la carte 🍷 4.95 – **23 rm**
� 17.40/41.00 **t.**

🏛 **Fisher's,** 75-79 Atholl Rd, PH16 5BN, ℰ 2000, 🛲 – ▮ ⊟wc 🅿. ℀
75 rm.

P.T.O. →

🏛 **Port-an-Eilean** 🏖, Strathtummel, PH16 5RU, NW : 10 m. by A 9 on B 8019 ℰ 088 24 (Tummel Bridge) 233, ≤ Loch Tummel and mountains, « Victorian shooting lodge on banks of Loch Tummel », 🔧, 🍴, park – ⌂wc 🅿.
May-October – **M** (bar lunch)/dinner 9.00 t. 🍷 3.00 – **10 rm** ⊑ 21.00/38.00 t.

🏛 **Castlebeigh** 🏖, 10 Knockard Rd, PH16 5HJ, off A 924 ℰ 2925, 🍴 – ⌂wc 🅿. 🔺 𝑽𝑰𝑺𝑨
May-October – **M** (bar lunch)/dinner 10.50 s. 🍷 3.80 – **18 rm** ⊑ 18.50/39.00 st. – SB (weekends only) 55.00 st.

🏛 **Craigard** 🏖, Strathview Terr., PH16 5AZ, ℰ 2592, ≤, 🍴 – 📺 ⌂wc 🏛wc 🅿. 🔺 𝑽𝑰𝑺𝑨
Mid April-October – **M** 4.00/10.00 t. – **10 rm** ⊑ 15.50/40.00 t.

🏛 **Queen's View** 🏖, Strathtummel, PH16 5NR, NW : 6 ½ m. by A 9 on B 8019 ℰ 3291, ≤ Loch Tummel and mountains, 🔧, 🍴 – ⌂wc 🅿. 🔺 𝔸𝔼 ⓞ 𝑽𝑰𝑺𝑨
Mid March-October – **M** 12.45/10.10 t. and a la carte 🍷 3.50 – **12 rm** ⊑ 16.40/39.30 t.

🏛 **Acarsaid**, 8 Atholl Rd, PH16 5BX, ℰ 2389 – ⌂wc 🏛wc 🅿. 🔺 𝑽𝑰𝑺𝑨 ⚘
Mid April-October – **M** (bar lunch)/dinner 10.50 t. and a la carte 🍷 3.30 – **19 rm** ⊑ 18.50/36.00 t.

🏛 **Birchwood**, 2 East Moulin Rd, PH16 5DW, ℰ 2477, 🍴 – ⌂wc 🏛wc 🅿. 🔺 𝑽𝑰𝑺𝑨. ⚘
closed Christmas and January – **M** 5.00/9.75 t. and a la carte 🍷 1.80 – **16 rm** ⊑ 18.50/41.00 t.

🏠 **Airdaniar**, 160 Atholl Rd, PH16 5AR, ℰ 2266, 🍴 – 📺 🏛wc 🅿
10 rm.

🏠 **Claymore**, 162 Atholl Rd, PH16 5AR, ℰ 2888, 🍴 – 📺 ⌂wc 🏛wc 🅿. 🔺 𝑽𝑰𝑺𝑨
Easter-October – **12 rm** ⊑ 17.00/60.00 t.

🏠 **Moulin**, 11-13 Kirkmichael Rd, PH16 5EW, N : 1 m. on A 924 ℰ 2196, 🍴 – ⌂wc 🅿. 🔺 𝔸𝔼 ⓞ
closed January and February – **M** (bar lunch)/dinner 10.00 t. 🍷 2.45 – **18 rm** ⊑ 16.50/40.00 t. – SB 50.00/55.00 st.

🏠 **Balrobin**, Higher Oakfield, PH16 5HT, ℰ 2901, 🍴 – 🏛wc 🅿
March-October – **8 rm** ⊑ 16.00/39.00 st.

🏠 **Craig Urrard**, 10 Atholl Rd, PH16 5BX, ℰ 2346, 🍴 – 📺 🏛wc 🅿. 🔺 𝔸𝔼 𝑽𝑰𝑺𝑨
12 rm ⊑ 13.50/30.00 t.

at Killiecrankie NW : 3 ¾ m. by A 9 on B 8079 – ✉ Pitlochry – ☎ 079 684 Killiecrankie :

🏛 **Killiecrankie** 🏖, PH16 5LG, ℰ 3220, ≤, 🍴 – ⌂wc 🏛wc 🅿
Easter-October – **M** (bar lunch)/dinner 13.50 t. 🍷 2.35 – **12 rm** ⊑ 17.35/75.40 t.

FORD Pitlochry Garage, Perth Rd ℰ 2316

PLOCKTON Ross and Cromarty (Highland) 𝟰𝟬𝟭 D 11 – pop. 425 – ☎ 059 984.
♦Edinburgh 210 – ♦Inverness 88.

🏛 **Haven**, Innes St., IV52 8TW, ℰ 223, ≤, 🍴 – 📺 ⌂wc 🅿. 🔺 𝑽𝑰𝑺𝑨
closed 21 December-6 February – **M** (bar lunch)/dinner 10.50 t. 🍷 2.50 – **12 rm** ⊑ 19.00/37.00 t.

POLMONT Stirling. (Central) 𝟰𝟬𝟭 𝟰𝟬𝟮 I 16 – see Falkirk.

PORT APPIN Argyll. (Strathclyde) 𝟰𝟬𝟭 D 14 – ECD : Thursday – ☎ 063 173 Appin.
🚢 to Lismore (Isle of) Monday/Saturday 5 daily : Sunday 4 daily (10 mn).
♦Edinburgh 136 – Ballachulish 20 – ♦Oban 24.

🏛 **Airds** 🏖, PA38 4DF, ℰ 236, ≤ Loch Linnhe and hills of Kingairloch, « Former ferry inn on lochside », 🍴 – ⌂wc 🏛wc 🅿. ⚘
Mid March-mid November – **M** (bar lunch)/dinner 20.00 t. 🍷 4.00 – **17 rm** ⊑ (dinner included) 54.00/114.00 t.

PORT ASKAIG Argyll. (Strathclyde) 𝟰𝟬𝟭 B 16 – see Islay (Isle of).

PORTPATRICK Wigtown. (Dumfries and Galloway) 𝟰𝟬𝟭 𝟰𝟬𝟮 E 19 – pop. 595 – ECD : Thursday – ✉ Stranraer – ☎ 077 681.
🏌, 🏌 Dunskey ℰ 81725.
♦Edinburgh 141 – ♦Ayr 60 – ♦Dumfries 80 – Stranraer 9.

🏛 **Knockinaam Lodge** 🏖, DG9 9AD, SE : 3 ¼ m. off A 77 ℰ 471, ≤ garden and sea, 🔧, park – 📺 ⌂wc 🅿 ☎ 🔺 𝔸𝔼 ⓞ 𝑽𝑰𝑺𝑨
Easter-December – **M** 16.75 t. (dinner) and a la carte – **10 rm** ⊑ (dinner included) 50.00/120.00 t.

🏛 **Fernhill**, Heugh Rd, DG9 8TD, ℰ 220, ≤, 🍴 – 📺 ⌂wc 🏛wc 🅿. 🔺 𝔸𝔼 ⓞ 𝑽𝑰𝑺𝑨
closed January and February – **M** 10.00 t. (dinner) and a la carte 🍷 2.75 – **15 rm** ⊑ 20.00/50.00 t. – SB 57.00 st.

🏠 **South Cliff House**, DG9 8LE, ℰ 411, ≤ – 🅿 ⚘
closed January, February and November – **5 rm** ⊑ 11.50/31.00 st.

PORTREE Inverness. (Highland) **401** B 11 – see Skye (Isle of).

PORTSONACHAN Argyll. (Strathclyde) **401** E 14 – ⊠ Dalmally – ✆ 086 63 Kilchrenan.
♦ Edinburgh 109 – ♦ Glasgow 72 – ♦ Oban 31 – Perth 80.

  XX **Portsonachan** ⤶ with rm, Lochaweside, PA33 1BL, ✆ 224, ≤ Loch Awe and Ben Cruachan,
    🦢, 🥓 – ⌂wc. 🔼 VISA
    March-mid November and 23 December-3 January – **M** (buffet lunch)/dinner 13.50 **t.** ⓵ 2.50 –
    18 rm ⥮ 17.50/51.00 – SB (except summer) 45.00/50.00 **st.**

PRESTWICK Ayr. (Strathclyde) **401 402** G 17 – pop. 13 355 – ECD : Wednesday – ✆ 0292.
🛫 ✆ 79822, Telex 77209 – **Terminal : Buchanan Bus Station.**
🛫 see also Glasgow.
🛈 Prestwick Airport ✆ 79822.
♦Edinburgh 78 – ♦Ayr 2 – ♦Glasgow 32.

      Plan of Built up Area : see Ayr

  🏨 **Carlton,** 187 Ayr Rd, KA9 1TP, ✆ 76811 – 📺 ⌂wc ☜ 🅿. 🔼 🄰🄴 ⓞ VISA   BY **v**
    M (bar lunch)/dinner 9.75 **t.** and a la carte ⓵ 3.00 – **37 rm** ⥮ 32.00/49.00 **t.** – SB (weekends
    only) 44.00 **st.**

  ↥ **Kincraig,** 39 Ayr Rd, KA9 1SY, ✆ 79480 – 🅿. 🕅   BY **c**
    6 rm ⥮ 10.00/18.00 **st.**

AUSTIN-ROVER 1 Monkton Rd ✆ 77415   VAUXHALL-OPEL 97-99 Main St. ✆ 70545

RAASAY (Isle of) Inverness. (Highland) **401** B 11 – pop. 182 –see Skye (Isle of).
⇝ by Caledonian MacBrayne : to Sconser (Isle of Skye) Monday/Saturday 3-6 daily (15 mn).

RENFREW Renfrew. (Strathclyde) **401** G 16 – pop. 21 456 – ECD : Wednesday – ✆ 041 Glasgow.
♦Edinburgh 53 – ♦Glasgow 7.

  🏨 **Stakis Normandy** (Stakis), Inchinnan Rd, PA4 9EJ, ✆ 886 4100, Telex 778897 – 🛗 📺
    ⌂wc ☎ ≳ 🅿. ⌂. 🔼 🄰🄴 ⓞ VISA
    M 6.50/11.75 **t.** ⓵ 3.40 – ⥮ 3.90 – **142 rm** 44.00/52.50 **t.** – SB 44.00/46.00 **st.**

  🏨 **Glynhill,** 169 Paisley Rd, PA4 8XB, ✆ 886 5555, Telex 779536 – 📺 ⌂wc ☜ 🅿. ⌂. 🔼 🄰🄴
    ⓞ VISA
    M 6.50/12.00 **t.** and a la carte ⓵ 3.80 – **80 rm** ⥮ 29.00/52.00 **st.** – SB (except Christmas and
    New Year)(weekends only) 52.00 **st.**

PEUGEOT, TALBOT 18-20 Fulbar St. ✆ 886 3354   VAUXHALL-OPEL Porterfield Rd ✆ 886 2777

RHU Dunbarton. (Strathclyde) **401 402** F 15 – see Helensburgh.

RHUBODACH Bute. (Strathclyde) **401 402** E 16 – Shipping Services : see Bute (Isle of).

RHUM (Isle of) Inverness. (Highland) **401** B 13 – Shipping Services : see Mallaig.

ROBERTON Roxburgh. (Borders) **401 402** L 17 – ⊠ Hawick – ✆ 0750 Ettrick Valley.
♦Edinburgh 56 – ♦Carlisle 46 – Hawick 55.

  🕿 **West Buccleuch** ⤶, Ettrick Valley, TD9 7NQ, W : 8 m. on B 711 ✆ 62230, 🔼, 🥓 – 🅿. 🄰🄴
    ⓞ VISA
    M (bar lunch)/dinner 7.95 **t.** ⓵ 2.70 – **7 rm** ⥮ 12.75/27.00 **t.** – SB 35.00/40.00 **st.**

ROCKCLIFFE Kirkcudbright. (Dumfries and Galloway) **401 402** I 19 – ⊠ Dalbeattie – ✆ 055 663.
🛈 Colvend, Sand Hills ✆ 398.
♦Edinburgh 100 – ♦Dumfries 20 – Stranraer 69.

  🏨 **Baron's Craig** ⤶, DG5 4QF, ✆ 225, ≤, 🥓, park – 📺 ⌂wc 🅿. 🔼 VISA
    9 April-11 October – **M** 8.00/15.00 **t.** ⓵ 2.50 – **26 rm** ⥮ 25.00/70.00 **t.** – SB 70.00/96.00 **st.**

ROTHES Moray. (Grampian) **401** K 11 – pop. 1 414 – ECD : Wednesday – ✆ 034 03.
♦Edinburgh 192 – ♦Aberdeen 62 – Fraserburgh 58 – ♦Inverness 49.

  🏨 **Rothes Glen** ⤶, IV33 7AH, N : 3 m. on A 941 ✆ 254, ≤, « Country house atmosphere », 🥓,
    park – 📺 ⌂wc ☎ 🅿. 🔼 🄰🄴 ⓞ VISA
    closed January – **M** 7.80/15.00 **t.** and a la carte ⓵ 5.00 – **16 rm** ⥮ 42.00/60.00 **t.** –
    SB 74.00/95.70 **st.**

ROUSAY (Isle of) Orkney (Orkney Islands) **401** K 6 – Shipping Services : see Orkney Islands
(Mainland : Kirkwall).

ST. ANDREWS Fife. (Fife) **401** L 14 Scotland G – pop. 10 525 – ECD : Thursday – ☎ 0334.

See : Site★★ – Cathedral★ – West Port★.

Envir. : The East Neuk★★ (coastline from Crail to St. Monance) SE : 16 m. by A 917 – Leuchars Parish Church★, NW : 6 m. by A 91 and A 919 – Ceres★ (Fife Folk Museum) W : 9 m. by B 939 – Kellie Castle★, S : 9 m. by B 9131 and B 9171.

☐ Eden Course, ☐ Jubilee Course, ☐ New Course, St. Andrews Links ℘ 73393 – ☐ St. Michaels ℘ 033 483 (Leuchars) 365, N : 5 m.

🛈 South St. ℘ 72021.

♦Edinburgh 51 – ♦Dundee 14 – Stirling 51.

🏨 **Old Course Golf and Country Club,** Old Station Rd, KY16 9SP, ℘ 74371, Telex 76280, ≤ golf courses and sea, ☒ – ᐅ ☐ ☎ ఉ ℗. ᐅ. ᐅ ᐅ ⑩ ᘉᔕᴀ
    M (rest. see **Eden** below) – 9.50/16.50 **st.** and a la carte ᐅ 4.00 – **145 rm** ☲ 44.00/115.00 **st.,**
    5 suites 88.00/155.00 **st.** – SB 170.00/179.00 **st.**

🏨 **Rusacks** (T.H.F.), 16 Pilmour Links, KY16 9JQ, ℘ 74321, ≤ – ᐅ ☐ ☎ ℗. ᐅ ᐅ ⑩ ᘉᔕᴀ
    M (buffet lunch Monday to Saturday)/dinner 17.50 **st.** and a la carte ᐅ 3.40 – **50 rm**
    42.00/70.00 **st.** – SB (October-April)(weekends only) 66.00/88.00 **st.**

🏨 **Rufflets** ⚘, Strathkinness Low Rd, KY16 9TX, W : 1 ½ m. on B 939 ℘ 72594, ≤, « Country house, gardens » – ☐ ⇌wc ℘. ᐅ ᐅ ᘉᔕᴀ. ᐅ
    closed January and February – **M** 6.50/15.00 **t.** and a la carte ᐅ 4.80 – **21 rm** ☲ 36.00/64.00 **t.**
    – SB (November-April except Easter, Christmas and New Year) 69.00/76.00 **st.**

🏨 **St. Andrews Golf,** 40 The Scores, KY16 9AS, ℘ 72611, ≤ – ᐅ ☐ ⇌wc ☎. ᐅ. ᐅ ᐅ ⑩ ᘉᔕᴀ
    M (bar lunch Monday to Saturday)/dinner 13.25 **t.** and a la carte ᐅ 3.75 – **23 rm** ☲ 40.00/64.00 **t.**
    – SB (weekends only)(April-October) 64.00 **st.**

XXX **Eden** (at Old Course Golf and C. C.), Old Station Rd, KY16 9SP, ℘ 74371, Telex 76280 – ℗. ᐅ ᐅ ⑩ ᘉᔕᴀ
    M 9.50 **st.** and a la carte 18.50/26.75 **st.** ᐅ 4.00.

ST. BOSWELLS Roxburgh. (Borders) **401 402** L 17 – pop. 1 086 – ☎ 0835.

Envir. : Dryburgh Abbey★★ (Setting★★★).

☐ ℘ 22359, off A 68 at St. Boswells Green.

♦Edinburgh 39 – ♦ Glasgow 79 – Hawick 17 – ♦Newcastle-upon-Tyne 66.

🏨 **Dryburgh Abbey** ⚘, TD6 0RQ, N : 3 ½ m. by B 6404 on B 6356 ℘ 22261, ≤, ⚲, 🖙, park – ⇌wc ℗. ᐅ. ᐅ ᐅ ⑩ ᘉᔕᴀ
    M (buffet lunch)/dinner 12.50 **t.** ᐅ 3.00 – **28 rm** ☲ 21.50/65.00 **t.** – SB (November-May) 60.00 **st.**

ST. CATHERINES Argyll. (Strathclyde) **401** E 15 – ✉ Cairndow – ☎ 0499 Inveraray.

Envir. : Inveraray★★ (Castle★★-interior★★★) NW : 12 m. by A 815 and A 83 – Auchindrain★, NE : 18 m. by A 815 and A 83 SW.

♦Edinburgh 99 – ♦Glasgow 53 – ♦Oban 53.

↥ **Thistle House,** PA25 8AZ, on A 815 ℘ 2209, ≤, 🖙 – ℗. ❀
    May-October – **6 rm** ☲ 12.50/33.00 **st.**

ST. COMBS Aberdeen. (Grampian) **401** O 11 – pop. 817 – ECD : Wednesday – ✉ Fraserburgh – ☎ 034 65 Inverallochy.

♦Edinburgh 173 – ♦Aberdeen 43 – Fraserburgh 6.

🏨 **Tufted Duck** ⚘, AB4 5YS, ℘ 2481, ≤, 🖙 – ☐ ⇌wc ᐅwc ☎ ℗. ᐅ ᐅ ⑩ ᘉᔕᴀ
    M (lunch by arrangement)/dinner 10.00 **t.** and a la carte ᐅ 3.25 – **18 rm** ☲ 22.00/36.70 – SB (weekends only) 40.70 **st.**

ST. FILLANS Perth. (Tayside) **401** H 14 – ECD : Wednesday – ☎ 076 485.

☐ ℘ 312.

♦Edinburgh 67 – ♦Glasgow 57 – ♦Oban 64 – Perth 30.

🏨 **Four Seasons,** PH6 2NF, ℘ 333, ≤ Loch Earn and mountains, 🖙 – ☐ ⇌wc ℗. ᐅ ᐅ ᐅ
    Easter-October – **M** 8.50/12.50 **t.** and a la carte ᐅ 2.30 – **12 rm** ☲ 26.00/65.00 **st.**

SANDAY (Isle of) Orkney (Orkney Islands) **401** M 6 – Shipping Services : see Orkney Islands (Mainland : Kirkwall).

SANDBANK Argyll. (Strathclyde) **401 402** F 16 – see Dunoon.

SCALASAIG Argyll. (Strathclyde) **401** B 15 – see Colonsay (Isle of).

SCALPAY (Isle of) Inverness. (Highland) **401** A 10 – Shipping Services : see Harris (Isle of).

SCARISTA Inverness. (Outer Hebrides) (Western Isles) – see Harris (Isle of).

SCOURIE Sutherland (Highland) **401** E 8 – ⊠ Lairg – ✆ 0971.
♦Edinburgh 263 – ♦Inverness 107.

🏠 **Scourie** ⬠, IV27 4SX, ℘ 2396, ≤, ⬠ – ⊟wc 🅟, 🔼 ⓪ *VISA*
April-25 October – **M** (bar lunch Monday to Saturday)/dinner 9.00 t. ⬠ 1.90 – **20 rm** ⚏ 22.50/43.50 t. – SB (except summer) 45.00/57.00 **st.**

🏠 **Eddrachilles** ⬠, Badcall Bay, IV27 4TH, S : 2½ m. on A 894 ℘ 2080, ≤ Badcall Bay and islands, 🐴 – ⊟wc 🏠wc 🅟
March-October – **M** (bar lunch)/dinner 6.85 t. and a la carte ⬠ 2.30 – **11 rm** ⚏ 24.00/42.80 t.

SCRABSTER Caithness. (Highland) **401** J 8 – Shipping Services : see Thurso.

SELKIRK Selkirk. (Borders) **401 402** L 17 Scotland G – pop. 5 469 – ✆ 0750.
Envir. : Bowhill★★, W : 3 m. by A 708.
🛅 ℘ 20621, S : 1 m.
🎫 Halliwell's House ℘ 20054 (summer only).
♦Edinburgh 40 – ♦Glasgow 73 – Hawick 11 – ♦Newcastle-upon-Tyne 73.

🏨 **Philipburn House** ⬠, TD5 5LS, W : 1 m. at junction A 707 and A 708 ℘ 20747, 🏊 heated, 🐴 – 📺 ⊟wc 🕿 🅟, 🔼 𝔸𝔼 ⓪ *VISA*. 🎐
closed January – **M** 9.00/14.50 t and a la carte ⬠ 3.25 – **16 rm** ⚏ (dinner included) 33.00/88.00 t. – SB (except July, August, Christmas and New Year) 33.00/88.00 **st.**

at Ettrickbridge SW : 7 m. on B 7009 – ⊠ ✆ 0750 Ettrickbridge :

🏨 **Ettrickshaws** ⬠, TD7 5HW, SW : 1 m. by B 7009 ℘ 52229, ≤, « Attractive setting overlooking Ettrick Water », ⬠, 🐴, park – 📺 ⊟wc 🅟, 🔼 𝔸𝔼 ⓪ *VISA*. 🎐
closed Christmas-mid February – **M** (dinner only) 14.00 t. ⬠ 2.90 – **6 rm** ⚏ (dinner included) 30.00/80.00 t. – SB 54.00/80.00 **st.**

SHAPINSAY (Isle of) Orkney (Orkney Islands) **401** L 6 – Shipping Services : see Orkney Islands (Mainland : Kirkwall).

Wenn Sie an ein Hotel im Ausland schreiben,
fügen Sie Ihrem Brief einen internationalen Antwortschein bei
(im Postamt erhältlich).

SHETLAND ISLANDS Shetland (Shetland Islands) **401** PQ 3 Scotland G – pop. 27 271.
See : Site★ – Up Helly Aa★★ (last Tuesday in January).
✈ see Mainland : Lerwick and Sumburgh.
✈ Unst Airport : at Baltasound ℘ 095 781 (Baltasound) 404/7.

🚢 Shipping connections with the Continent : from Lerwick to Faroe Islands (Thorshavn) (Smyril Line) – to Norway (Bergen) (Smyril Line) – to Iceland (Seydisfjordur via Thorshavn) (Smyril Line) summer only – by P & O Ferries : Orkney and Shetland Services : from Lerwick to Aberdeen 3 weekly (14 h) – by Shetland Islands Council : from Lerwick (Mainland) to Bressay 10-14 daily (10 mn) – from Laxo (Mainland) to Symbister (Isle of Whalsay) 5-7 daily (25 mn) – from Toft (Mainland) to Ulsta (Isle of Yell) 16-20 daily (22 mn) – from Gutcher (Isle of Yell) to Belmont (Isle of Unst) 13-17 daily (restricted on Sunday) (10 mn) – from Gutcher (Isle of Yell) to Oddsta (Isle of Fetlar) 2-3 daily (25 mn) – by P & O Ferries from Scalloway to Kirkwall (Orkney Islands) via Westray (Orkney Islands) summer 2 weekly; winter 1 fortnightly (8 h).

🚢 by J.W. Stout : from Fair Isle to Sumburgh (Gruntness) 2 weekly (2 h 45 mn) – by Shetland Islands Council : from Lerwick (Mainland) to Skerries 2 weekly (3 h).

MAINLAND

Brae – ⊠ ✆ 080 622 Brae.

🏨 **Busta House** ⬠, ZE2 9QN, SW : 1½ m. ℘ 506, ≤, « Part 16C and 18C country house », 🐴 – 📺 ⊟wc 🏠wc 🕿 🅟, 🔼 𝔸𝔼 ⓪ *VISA*
M (bar lunch)/dinner 13.50 t. ⬠ 3.00 – **21 rm** ⚏ 27.00/40.00 t.

Hillswick – ⊠ ✆ 080 623 Hillswick.

🏠 **St. Magnus Bay** ⬠, ZE2 9RW, ℘ 372, ≤, 🐴 – 🏠wc 🕿 🅟, 🔼
M 5.50/8.50 t. and a la carte ⬠ 4.25 – **26 rm** ⚏ 17.00/38.00 t.

Lerwick Scotland G – pop. 7 223 – ECD : Wednesday – ⊠ ✪ 0595 Lerwick.

See : Clickhimin Broch★ – Shetland Croft House Museum★ – Mousa Broch★★★ (island site)
S : 13 m.

☞ Dale ✎ 369, NW : 3 ½ m. on A 970.

✈ Tingwall Airport : ✎ 3535/2024, NW : 6 ½ m. by A 971.

🛈 Market Cross ✎ 3434.

🏨 **Shetland,** Holmsgarth Rd, ZE1 0PW, ✎ 5515, Telex 75432, ≤, 🔲 – 🕸 📺 ⇔wc ☎ ❖ ❷. 🚗.
🕳 ﾒﾓ ⓪ 𝘝𝘐𝘚𝘈
M 7.00/9.50 **st.** and a la carte ⏶ 3.50 – **64 rm** ⊏⊐ 45.00/52.00 **st.** – SB (weekends only)
52.00 **st.**

🏨 Kveldsro House, Greenfield Pl., ZE1 0AN, ✎ 2195 – 📺 ⇔wc ☎ ❷. ⋘
closed Christmas and New Year – **14 rm**.

at Walls – ⊠ ✪ 0595 Walls :

✗ **Burrastow House** ⋙ with rm, ZE2 9PD, SW : 2 ½ m. ✎ 307, ≤, « 18C house overlooking
Vaila Sound », ☛ – 📺 ⇔wc ❷
closed 23 December-6 January – **M** (closed Sunday and Thursday to non residents) (dinner
only) 22.00 **t.** ⏶ 2.70 – **3 rm** ⊏⊐ 27.00/54.00 **st.** – SB (October-April) (weekends only) 63.00 **st.**

AUSTIN-ROVER, LAND ROVER-RANGE ROVER 25   PEUGEOT-TALBOT, RENAULT Great Western Rd
Broad St. ✎ 3003   ✎ 2805

Sumburgh – ⊠ ✪ 0950 Sumburgh.

See : Jarlshof★★ (prehistoric village).

✈ ✎ 60654, Telex 75451.

Whiteness – ⊠ Whiteness – ✪ 059 584 Gott.

☝ Westings, Wormadale, ZE2 9LJ, SE : 2 m. on A 971 ✎ 242, ≤ The Deeps and Islands – 📺
🗆wc ❷. ⋘ – **6 rm**.

Remember the speed limits that apply in the United Kingdom, unless otherwise
signposted.

– 60 mph on single carriageway roads

– 70 mph on dual carriageway roads and motorways

SHIEL BRIDGE Ross and Cromarty (Highland) 🟦🟦🟦 D 12 – ⊠ ✪ 059 981 Glenshiel.

🛈 ✎ 0599 (Glenshiel) 81264 (summer only).

♦Edinburgh 204 – ♦Inverness 66 – Kyle of Lochalsh 16.

🏠 **Kintail Lodge,** IV40 8HL, ✎ 275, ≤ Loch Duich and mountains, ☛ – ⇔wc ❷. 🔲
𝘝𝘐𝘚𝘈
M (bar lunch)/dinner 15.00 **st.** – **11 rm** ⊏⊐ 19.00/58.00 **st.** – SB (November-mid May except
Easter. Christmas and New Year) 40.00/50.00 **st.**

SHIELDAIG Ross and Cromarty (Highland) 🟦🟦🟦 D 11 – ⊠ Strathcarron – ✪ 052 05.

♦Edinburgh 226 – ♦ Inverness 70 – Kyle of Lochalsh 36.

☝ Tigh-An Eilean, Main St., IV54 8XN, ✎ 251, ≤ Shieldaig Islands and Loch – ⇔wc ❷
⋘
13 rm.

SKEABOST Inverness. (Highland) 🟦🟦🟦 B 11 – see Skye (Isle of).

SKELMORLIE Ayr. (Strathclyde) 🟦🟦🟦 F 16 – pop. 1 606 – ECD : Wednesday – ✪ 0475 Wemyss
Bay.

♦Edinburgh 78 – ♦Ayr 39 – ♦Glasgow 32.

🏨 **Manor Park** ⋙, PA17 5HE, S : 2 ¾ m. on A 78 ✎ 520832, ≤ gardens and Firth of Clyde,
« Extensive gardens », park – 📺 ⇔wc 🗆wc ☎ ❷. ⋘
closed 3 January-3 March – **M** 12.50 **t.** (dinner) and a la carte ⏶ 3.00 – **23 rm** ⊏⊐ 32.50/
65.00 **t.**

🏠 **Redcliffe,** 25 Shore Rd, PA17 5EH, on A 78 ✎ 521036, ≤, ☛ – 📺 ⇔wc 🗆wc ☜ ❷. 🔲 ﾒﾓ
⓪
M 10.00/20.00 **t.** and a la carte ⏶ 3.00 – **10 rm** ⊏⊐ 29.50/45.00 **t.** – SB (weekends only)
70.00/90.00 **st.**

SKYE (Isle of) Inverness. (Highland) **401** B 11 and 12 **Scotland G** – pop. 8 139.

See : Site★★ – Cuillin Hills★★★.

🛬 at Broadford : ℰ 047 12 (Broadford) 202.

🚢 by Caledonian MacBrayne : from Kyleakin to Kyle of Lochalsh : frequent services daily (5 mn) – from Armadale to Mallaig summer only 2 weekly (30 mn) – from Uig to Tarbert (Isle of Harris) Monday/Saturday summer only : 5-9 weekly (2 h 30 mn direct - 4 h 45 mn via Lochmaddy) – from Uig to Lochmaddy (North Uist) Monday/Saturday 5-9 weekly (1 h 45 mn direct - 4 h 45 mn via Tarbert) – from Sconser to Isle of Raasay ; Monday/Saturday 3-6 daily (15 mn).

🚢 by Caledonian MacBrayne : from Armadale to Mallaig summer only 2 weekly (30 mn).

Ardvasar **401** C 12 – ⊠ 😊 047 14 Ardvasar

🏛 **Ardvasar,** IV48 8RS, ℰ 223, 🚗 – 🛏wc 🅿. 𝘝𝘐𝘚𝘈
closed January and February – **M** 6.00/15.00 t. ⓘ 3.00 – **12 rm** ⊃ 17.00/40.00 t.

Dunvegan **Scotland G** – ⊠ 😊 047 022 Dunvegan – See : Dunvegan Castle★.

🏠 **Harlosh** ⌂, IV51 5AB, S : 3 m. by A 863 ℰ 367, ≤ Loch Bracadale and Islands, 🌳 – 🛏wc
🅿. 🍴
April-October – **M** (dinner only) 9.00 t. and a la carte ⓘ 3.25 – **7 rm** ⊃ 13.50/30.00 t.

✗ **Three Chimneys,** Colbost, IV51 9SY, ℰ 258 – 🅿. 🔺 𝘝𝘐𝘚𝘈
Easter-October – **M** (closed Sunday lunch) (booking essential) (restricted lunch)/dinner a la carte 7.55/15.40 t.

Isleornsay – ⊠ 😊 047 13 Isleornsay.

🏛 **Kinloch Lodge** ⌂, IV43 8QY, ⊠ Sleat N : 3 ½ m. by A 851 ℰ 333, ≤ Loch Na Dal, « Country house atmosphere », 🌳, 🚗 – 🛏wc 🅿. 🔺 𝘝𝘐𝘚𝘈
closed 10 January-28 February and Christmas – **M** (dinner only) 19.50 t. ⓘ 3.00 – **9 rm** ⊃ 30.00/90.00 t. – SB (November-April) 70.00/90.00 st.

🏛 **Toravaig House** ⌂, IV44 8RJ, ⊠ Sleat, SW : 3 m. on A 851 ℰ 231, 🚗 – 🛏wc ⋔wc 🅿. 𝘈𝘌 ⓞ 𝘝𝘐𝘚𝘈
March-October – **M** (bar lunch)/dinner 12.50 t. ⓘ 3.25 – **10 rm** ⊃ 22.00/48.00 t.

Portree **Scotland G** – pop. 1 533 – ECD : Wednesday – ⊠ 😊 0478 Portree.

See : Site★★ – Skye Croft Museum★, N : 18 m. by A 850 and A 856 – Trotternish Peninsula★★, N : 40 m. by A 850, A 856 and A 855.

🅱 Meall House ℰ 2137.

🏛 **Rosedale,** Beaumont Cres., IV51 9DB, ℰ 2531, ≤ harbour – 🛏wc ⋔wc 🅿
Mid May-September – **M** (bar lunch)/dinner 10.50 t. – **21 rm** ⊃ 19.00/46.00 t.

🏠 **Kings Haven,** 11 Bosville Terr., IV51 9DJ, ℰ 2290 – ⋔wc
April-October – **M** (lunch residents only) 5.00/13.50 st. ⓘ 2.70 – **7 rm** ⊃ 18.50/37.00 t.

AUSTIN-ROVER, FORD Dunvegan Rd ℰ 2554   RENAULT Dunvegan Rd ℰ 2002

Raasay Isle of – ⊠ Kyle of Lochalsh – 😊 047 862 Raasay.

🏛 **Isle of Raasay** ⌂, IV40 8PB, ℰ 222, ≤ Narrows of Raasay and Skye, 🚗 – 📺 🛏wc ⓖ
🅿
April-September – **M** (bar lunch)/dinner 12.00 t. ⓘ 3.60 – **12 rm** ⊃ 18.00/36.00 t. – SB 56.00 st.

Skeabost – ECD : Wednesday – ⊠ 😊 047 032 Skeabost Bridge.

🏛 **Skeabost House** ⌂, IV51 9NP, ℰ 202, ≤ Loch Snizort Beag, « Country house in grounds bordering loch », ᠮ̶ᵧ, 🌳, 🚗, park – 🛏wc 🅿
17 April-17 October – **M** (buffet lunch)/dinner 10.80 t. ⓘ 3.25 – **26 rm** ⊃ 19.00/50.00 t.

Prices	For full details of the prices quoted in the guide, consult p. 16.

SMA'GLEN Perth. (Tayside) **401** I 14 – see Crieff.

SOUTH QUEENSFERRY W. Lothian (Lothian) **401** J 16 **Scotland G** – pop. 7 485 – ECD : Wednesday – 😊 031 Edinburgh – See : Forth Bridges★★.

Envir. : Dalmeny (St. Cuthbert's Church★ – Dalmeny House★) E : 2 m. by B 924 – Hopetoun House★★, W : 2 m. by A 904 – Abercorn Parish Church (Hopetoun Loft★) W : 3 m. by A 904.

◆Edinburgh 9 – Dunfermline 7 – ◆Glasgow 41.

🏛 **Forth Bridges Moat House** (Q.M.H.), EH30 9SF, junction A 90 and Forth Bridge ℰ 331 1199, Telex 727430, ≤ Firth of Forth and Bridges, 🔺, squash – 📺 🛏wc 🅿. 🅿. 🛎. 🔺 𝘈𝘌 ⓞ 𝘝𝘐𝘚𝘈
M (closed Saturday lunch) 7.50/8.75 st. and a la carte ⓘ 3.00 – ⊃ 5.25 – **108 rm** 43.75/54.75 t. – SB (weekends only) 60.00 st.

SPEAN BRIDGE Inverness. (Highland) 401 F 13 – ECD : Thursday – ☎ 039 781.

♦Edinburgh 139 – ♦Inverness 58 – Kyle of Lochalsh 65 – ♦Oban 60 – Perth 95.

- **Letterfinlay Lodge,** PH34 4DZ, N : 7 ½ m. on A 82 ☎ 039 784 (Invergloy) 222, ≤ Loch Lochy and mountains, 🎣, 🛋 – 🛁wc 🚿wc Ⓟ. 🅂 AE ⓓ VISA
  March-November – **M** 7.00/12.00 **st.** 🅱 3.00 – **15 rm** ☕ 15.00/44.00 **st.**
- **Spean Bridge,** PH34 4ES, ☎ 250, 🎣 – 🛁wc Ⓟ. 🅂 AE ⓓ VISA
  M (bar lunch)/dinner 9.50 **st.** 🅱 2.50 – **26 rm** ☕ 17.50/35.00 **st.**

SPITTAL OF GLENSHEE Perth. (Tayside) 401 J 13 – Winter Sports – ✉ Blairgowrie – ☎ 025 085 Glenshee – 🅸 Newton Terr., Blairgowrie ☎ 0250 (Blairgowrie) 2785.

♦Edinburgh 78 – ♦Dundee 37 – Perth 34.

- **Dalmunzie House** 🐎, PH10 7QG, NW : 1 ½ m. ☎ 224, ≤, 🏌9, 🎣, 🛋, park, 🎾 – 🛗 🛁wc Ⓟ. 🅂 AE ⓓ
  January-October – **M** (bar lunch)/dinner 14.50 **t.** 🅱 3.00 – **20 rm** ☕ 19.50/58.00 **t.** – SB 56.00/70.00 **st.**

STEWARTON Ayr. (Strathclyde) 401 402 G 16 – pop. 6 319 – ECD : Wednesday and Saturday – ☎ 0560.

♦Edinburgh 68 – ♦Ayr 21 – ♦Glasgow 22.

- XXX **Chapeltoun House** 🐎 with rm, KA3 3ED, SW : 2 ½ m. by B 769 ☎ 82696, ≤, « Country house in extensive grounds », 🎣, 🛋, park – 📺 🛁wc 🚿wc ☎ Ⓟ. 🅂 AE VISA. 🚭
  closed 25-26 December and first 2 weeks January – **M** (booking essential) 10.50/19.50 **t.** and a la carte 12.70/20.70 **t.** 🅱 3.50 – **6 rm** ☕ 60.00/80.00 **t.**

STIRLING

Dumbarton Road	B 10
Murray Place	B 15
Port Street	B
Thistle Centre	B
Upper Craigs	B 29
Barnton Street	B 2
Borestone Crescent	A 3
Causewayhead Road	A, B 4
Corn Exchange Road	B 5
Cornton Road	A 7
Coxithill Road	A 8
Drummond Place	B 9
Goosecroft Road	B 12
King Street	B 13
Newhouse	A 16
Park Place	A 18
Queen Street	B 20
Randolph Terrace	A 22
St. John Street	B 23
St. Mary's Wynd	B 24
Seaforth Place	B 25
Shirra's Brae Road	A 26
Spittal Street	B 27
Union Street	B 28
Victoria Square	B 30
Weaver Row	A 31

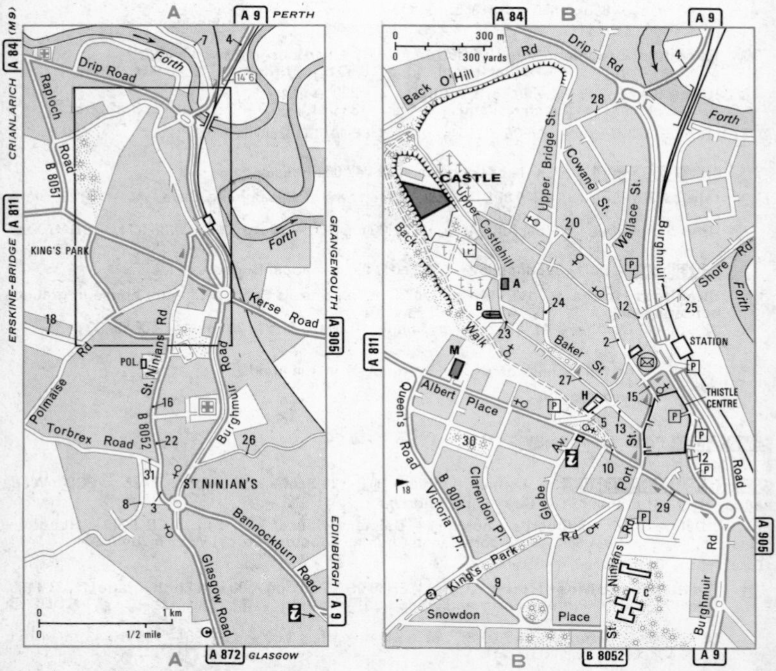

STIRLING Stirling. (Central) 🔢 I 15 Scotland G – pop. 36 640 – ECD : Wednesday – ✆ 0786.

See : Site★★ – Castle★★ (Site★★★-external elevations★★★-Stirling Heads★★★) B – Argyll and Sutherland Highlanders Regimental Museum★ B M – Argyll's Lodging★ (Renaissance decoration★) B A – Church of the Holy Rude★ B B.

Envir. : Wallace Monument (❄★★) N : 2 ½ m. by A 9 A and B 998 – Dunblane★ (Cathedral★★) N : 6 ½ m. by A 9 A – Doune★ (Castle★-Motor Museum★) NW : 8 m. by A 84 A, – A 9 and B 824 – Bannockburn, S : 2 m. by A 9 A.

🏌 Queens Rd ✆ 64098 B – 🏌 Alva Rd, Tillicoultry ✆ 0259 (Tillicoultry) 50741, E : 9 m. by A 9 A.
🚲 ✆ 73085.

🚗 Dumbarton Rd ✆ 75019 – Bannockburn ✆ 815663 (summer only).

♦Edinburgh 37 – Dunfermline 23 – Falkirk 14 – ♦Glasgow 28 52 – Motherwell 30 – ♦Oban 87 – Perth 35.

Plan opposite

🏨 **Park Lodge** without rest., 32 Park Terr., FK8 2JS, ✆ 74862, « Georgian house with period decor », 🌳 – 📺 🛁wc ☎ 🅿 🔊 ⓘ 𝗩𝗜𝗦𝗔 ✄ 　　　　　　　　　B a
9 rm ⚄ 33.00/45.00.

🏨 **King Robert,** Glasgow Rd, FK7 0LJ, ✆ 811666 – 📺 🛁wc ☎ 🅿 🔊 𝖠𝖤 ⓘ 𝗩𝗜𝗦𝗔 ✄ 　　A c
M 8.00/10.00 st. and a la carte ⚄ 3.00 – 20 rm ⚄ 28.00/38.00 st.

at Blairlogie NE : 4 ½ m. by A 9 on A 91 – A – ✉ Stirling – ✆ 0259 Alva :

🏨 **Blairlogie House,** FK9 5QE, ✆ 61441, 🌳 – 🛁wc 🚿wc 🅿 🔊 𝗩𝗜𝗦𝗔
M 7.50/12.50 t. and a la carte ⚄ 3.20 – 7 rm ⚄ 25.00/55.00 t. – SB (weekends only) 45.00/52.50 st.

CITROEN, VAUXHALL-OPEL 119-139 Glasgow Rd　　　FIAT 44 Causeway Head Rd ✆ 62426
✆ 0786 (Bannockburn) 811234　　　　　　　　　　FORD Drip Rd ✆ 70519

STONEHAVEN Kincardine. (Grampian) 🔢 N 13 Scotland G – pop. 7 834 – ECD : Wednesday – ✆ 0569.

Envir. : Dunnottar Castle★★ (site★★★) S : 2 m. by A 92 – Muchalls Castle (plasterwork ceilings★★) N : 5 m. by A 92.

🏌 Cowie ✆ 62124, N : 1 m. on Aberdeen Rd.

🚲 The Square ✆ 62806 (summer only).

♦Edinburgh 114 – ♦Aberdeen 16 – ♦Dundee 51.

at Netherley N : 6 m. on B 979 – ✉ Netherley – ✆ 0569 Stonehaven :

✕✕ **Lairhillock,** AB3 2QS, ✆ 30001 – 🅿 🔊 𝖠𝖤 ⓘ 𝗩𝗜𝗦𝗔
closed 25-26 December and 1-2 January – M 8.75/14.50 t.

at Catterline S : 6 m. by A 92 – ✉ Stonehaven – ✆ 056 95 Catterline :

✕ **Creel Inn,** AB3 2UL, ✆ 254, Seafood – 🅿 🔊 𝖠𝖤
closed Sunday dinner, Monday and January – M (bar lunch)/dinner a la carte 10.80/20.05 t. ⚄ 3.00.

AUSTIN-ROVER 64-74 Barclay St. ✆ 62077　　　　　FORD 110 Barclay St. ✆ 63666

STORNOWAY Ross and Cromarty (Outer Hebrides) (Western Isles) 🔢 A 9 – see Lewis (Isle of).

STRACHUR Argyll. (Strathclyde) 🔢 E 15 – ECD : Wednesday – ✉ Cairndow – ✆ 036 986.

♦Edinburgh 104 – ♦Glasgow 58 – ♦Oban 58.

🏨 **Creggans Inn,** PA27 8BX, on A 815 ✆ 279, ≤ Loch Fyne, 🌳 – 🛁wc 🍴 ⚿ 🅿 🔊 𝖠𝖤 ⓘ 𝗩𝗜𝗦𝗔
M a la carte 6.00/15.00 t. ⚄ 3.80 – 22 rm ⚄ 35.00/65.00 t.

STRANRAER Wigtown. (Dumfries and Galloway) 🔢 🔢 E 19 Scotland G – pop. 10 766 – ECD : Wednesday – ✆ 0776.

Envir. : Logan Botanic Garden★ S : 13 m. by A 77, A 716 and B 7065.

🏌 Creachmore by Stranraer, Leswalt ✆ 87245, SW : 2 m.

🚢 by Sealink : to Larne 4-8 daily (2 h 15 mn) – to Douglas (Isle of Man) by Isle of Man Steam Packet Co., summer only ; 1 weekly (6 h) – to Larne by Townsend Thoresen 4-6 daily (2 h to 2 h 30 mn).

🚲 Port Rodie ✆ 2595 (summer only).

♦Edinburgh 132 – ♦Ayr 51 – ♦Dumfries 75.

🏨 **North West Castle,** Portroddie, DG9 8EH, ✆ 4413, Telex 777088, 🔲 – 🛗 📺 🛁wc ⚿ 🅿 ✄
M (bar lunch)/dinner 10.00 t. and a la carte – 77 rm ⚄ 25.00/45.50 t. – SB 52.00/60.00 st.

AUSTIN-ROVER Leswalt Rd ✆ 3636　　　　　　　VOLVO Hanover Sq. ✆ 3939
COLT ✆ 87634

STRATHBLANE Stirling. (Central) 401 H 16 – pop. 1 933 – ECD : Wednesday – ✉ Glasgow – ☎ 0360 Blanefield.

♦Edinburgh 52 – ♦Glasgow 11 – Stirling 26.

   🏨 **Country Club** ❀, 41 Milngavie Rd, G63 4AH, S : ¾ m. on A 81 ℰ 70491, ❀, park – 📺 ➾wc ⓜwc ☜ ❷. ⚞ ⒶⒺ ⓞ 𝘝𝘐𝘚𝘈
   M 6.50/13.50 t. and a la carte ↓ 4.00 – **10 rm** ⌂ 35.00/45.00 t. – SB (weekends only)(winter only) 60.00/100.00 **st.**

   🏨 **Kirkhouse Inn,** Glasgow Rd, G63 9AA, ℰ 70621 – 📺 ➾wc ➾ ❷. ⚞ ⒶⒺ ⓞ 𝘝𝘐𝘚𝘈
   M 6.95/12.95 t. and a la carte ↓ 4.00 – **17 rm** ⌂ 26.00/46.00 t., **1 suite** 46.00 – SB 55.00/74.00 **st.**

STRATHCONON Ross and Cromarty (Highland) – ✉ Muir of Ord – ☎ 099 77 Strathconon.

♦Edinburgh 184 – ♦Inverness 28.

   🏠 **East Lodge** ❀, IV6 7QQ, W : 11 m. off A 832 ℰ 222, ≤, ⤜, ❀ – 📺 ➾wc ⓜwc ❷. ⚞ ⓞ 𝘝𝘐𝘚𝘈
   M (bar lunch)/dinner 9.50 t. ↓ 2.75 – **10 rm** ⌂ 12.50/31.00 t.

STRATHPEFFER Ross and Cromarty (Highland) 401 G 11 – pop. 1 244 – ECD : Thursday – ☎ 0997.

🛈 Visitors' Centre ℰ 21415 (summer only).

♦ Edinburgh 174 – ♦ Inverness 18.

   🏠 **Holly Lodge,** Golf Course Rd, IV14 9AR, ℰ 21254, ❀ – 📺 ➾wc ⓜwc ❷
   Easter-September – **M** (dinner only) 12.00 t. ↓ 3.00 – **7 rm** ⌂ 25.00/60.00 t.

STRATHY Sutherland (Highland) 401 I 8 – ☎ 064 14.

♦Edinburgh 289 – ♦Inverness 133 – Thurso 21 – Tongue 22.

   Hotel see : Bettyhill SW : 12 m.

STROMNESS Orkney (Orkney Islands) 401 K 7 – see Orkney Islands (Mainland).

STRONSAY (Isle of) Orkney (Orkney Islands) 401 M 6 – Shipping Services : see Orkney Islands (Mainland : Kirkwall).

STRONTIAN Argyll (Highland) 401 D 13 – ✉ ☎ 0967.

♦Edinburgh 139 – Fort William 23 – ♦Oban 66.

   🏠 **Kilcamb Lodge** ❀, PH36 4HY, ℰ 2257, ≤, ⤜, ❀, park – ➾wc ⓜwc ❷. ❀
   March-December – **M** (bar lunch)/dinner 14.50 t. ↓ 4.00 – **10 rm** ⌂ (dinner included) 34.50/69 t.

SUMBURGH Shetland (Shetland Islands) 401 Q 4 – see Shetland Islands (Mainland).

TAIN Ross and Cromarty (Highland) 401 H 10 – pop. 3 428 – ECD : Thursday – ☎ 0862.

🛈 The Clubhouse ℰ 2314.

♦Edinburgh 191 – ♦Inverness 35 – ♦Wick 91.

   🏨 **Royal,** High St., IV19 1AB, ℰ 2013 – 📺 ➾wc ⓜwc ☎ ❷. ⚘ ⚞ ⒶⒺ ⓞ 𝘝𝘐𝘚𝘈
   M 9.75 t. (dinner) and a la carte ↓ 3.10 – **25 rm** ⌂ 20.00/39.00 t.

TOYOTA Knockbreck Rd ℰ 2175

TARBERT Argyll. (Strathclyde) 401 D 16 – see Kintyre (Peninsula).

TARBERT Inverness. (Outer Hebrides) (Western Isles) 401 Z 10 – see Harris (Isle of).

TAYINLOAN Argyll. (Strathclyde) 401 D 16 – Shipping Services : see Gigha (Isle of).

TAYNUILT Argyll. (Strathclyde) 401 E 14 – ECD : Wednesday – ☎ 086 62.

♦Edinburgh 111 – ♦Glasgow 81 – ♦Oban 12.

   🏠 **Polfearn** ❀, PA35 1JQ, N : 1 m. ℰ 251, ≤, ❀ – ➾wc ⓜwc ❷
   M 8.00/10.00 t. ↓ 2.50 – **16 rm** ⌂ 16.00/36.00 t.

TAYVALLICH Argyll. (Strathclyde) 401 D 15 – ✉ Lochgilphead – ☎ 054 67.

♦Edinburgh 141 – ♦Glasgow 95 – ♦Oban 40.

   ✕ **Tayvallich Inn,** by Lochgilphead, PA31 8PR, ℰ 282, ≤ – ❷. ⚞ 𝘝𝘐𝘚𝘈
   April-October and Friday and Saturday in winter – **M** (bar lunch)/dinner a la carte 6.80/12.75 t. ↓ 2.75.

THORNHILL Dumfries. (Dumfries and Galloway) **401** **402** I 18 **Scotland** G – pop. 1 449 – ECD : Thursday – ✪ 0848.

Envir. : Drumlanrig Castle★★, NW : 4 m. by A 76.

☷ ✆ 30546.

✦Edinburgh 64 – ✦Ayr 44 – ✦Dumfries 15 – ✦Glasgow 63.

- 🏨 **Buccleuch and Queensberry,** 112 Drumlanrig St., DG3 5LU, ✆ 30215 – ⌷wc 🅿. ☒ VISA
  M (bar lunch)/dinner 9.00 **st.** and a la carte ↥ 3.00 – **11 rm** ⬚ 19.50/42.00 **st.**

  at Closeburn S : 7 ½ m. by A 76 – ✪ 08484 Thornhill :

- 🏛 **Trigony House,** DG3 5EZ, ✆ 31211, ⟲, ☞ – ⋔wc 🅿
  M (bar lunch)/dinner 7.50 **t.** ↥ 2.60 – **9 rm** ⬚ 14.00/24.00 **t.** – SB (weekends only)(July-February) 40.00 **st.**

THURSO Caithness. (Highland) **401** J 8 **Scotland** G – pop. 8 828 – ECD : Thursday – ✪ 0847.

Envir. : Coast road to Durness via Strathy Point★ (≤★★★) – Torrisdale Bay★ – Ben Loyal★★ – Coldbackie (≤★★) – Ben Hope★ – Loch Eriboll (≤★★★) W : 74 m. by A 836 and A 838.

⚓ by P & O Ferries : Orkney and Shetland Services : from Scrabster to Stromness (Orkney Islands) Monday/Saturday 1-3 daily (2 h).

🛈 Car Park, Riverside ✆ 2371 (summer only).

✦Edinburgh 289 – ✦Inverness 133 – ✦Wick 21.

  at Banniskirk SE : 8 m. by A 882 on A 895 – ✉ ✪ 084 783 Halkirk :

- ⌂ **Banniskirk House** ⌂, KW12 6XA, ✆ 609, ☞, park – 🅿
  April-September (booking essential in winter) – **8 rm** ⬚ 8.50/18.00 **st.**

CITROEN Couper Sq. Riverside ✆ 62778   FORD Mansons Lane ✆ 63101

TIREE (Isle of) Argyll. (Strathclyde) **401** Z 14 – pop. 780.

✈ ✆ 087 92 (Scarinish) 456.

⚓ by Caledonian MacBrayne : to Arinagour (Isle of Coll) summer only : 3-4 weekly (1 h) – to Oban 3-4 weekly (4 h 30 mn-5 h).

⚓ to Tobermory (Isle of Mull) 1-2 daily (2 h 45 mn) – to Lochaline (via Coll and Tobermory) May-September 2 weekly (3 h 55 mn).

TIRORAN Argyll. (Strathclyde) **401** B 14 – see Mull (Isle of).

TOBERMORY Argyll. (Strathclyde) **401** B 14 – see Mull (Isle of).

TONGUE Sutherland (Highland) **401** G 8 – ECD : Saturday – ✉ Lairg – ✪ 080 05.

Envir. : Coast Road east via Coldbackie (≤★★) – Ben Loyal★★ – Torrisdale Bay★ – Strathy Point★ (≤★★★) E : 24 m. by A 836 – Coast road west via Ben Hope★ – Loch Eriboll (≤★★★) – Cape Wrath★★★ (≤★★★) W : 44 m. by A 838.

✦Edinburgh 257 – ✦Inverness 101 – ✦Thurso 43.

- 🏨 **Ben Loyal,** Main St., IV27 4XE, ✆ 216, ≤ – ⌷wc 🅿. ☒ VISA
  closed New Year – **M** (bar lunch)/dinner 9.50 **t.** – **18 rm** ⬚ 21.00/37.00 **t.**

TROON Ayr. (Strathclyde) **401** **402** G 17 – pop. 14 035 – ECD : Wednesday – ✪ 0292.

☷ ✆ 311555.

🛈 Municipal Buildings, South Beach ✆ 315131.

✦Edinburgh 77 – ✦Ayr 7 – ✦Glasgow 31.

- 🏩 **Marine,** 8 Crosbie Rd, KA10 6HE, ✆ 314444, Telex 777595, ≤, ☞ – ▤ 📺 ☎ 🅿. ▨. ☒ ☒ ① VISA
  M 7.50/14.95 **t.** and a la carte ↥ 3.15 – **71 rm** ⬚ 50.00/72.00 **t.**, **6 suites** 84.00/94.00 **t.**

- 🏨 **Piersland House,** 15 Craigend Rd, KA10 6HD, ✆ 314747, ☞ – 📺 ⌷wc ⋔wc ☎ 🅿. ☒ ☒ ① VISA
  M (bar lunch)/dinner 12.50 **t.** and a la carte ↥ 3.00 – **15 rm** ⬚ 36.00/66.00 **t.** – SB (winter only) 60.00 **st.**

- 🏨 **Sun Court,** 19 Crosbie Rd, KA10 6HF, ✆ 312727, ≤, ☞, ✗, squash – 📺 ⌷wc ☜ 🅿. ▨. ☒ ☒ ①
  M 7.50/11.50 **st.** and a la carte ↥ 2.40 – **20 rm** ⬚ 34.00/60.00 **st.** – SB (weekends only) 74.00 **st.**

- 🏛 **Ardneil,** 51 St. Meddans St., KA10 6NU, ✆ 311611 – 📺 ⌷wc 🅿. ✗ – **8 rm**.

- ✗ **Campbell's Kitchen,** 3 South Beach, KA10 6EF, ✆ 314421, Bistro – ☒
  closed Sunday dinner, Monday, 25-26 December and 1-2 January – **M** 8.50/17.50 **t.** and a la carte 12.40/16.20 **t.** ↥ 2.95.

AUSTIN-ROVER Dundonald Rd ✆ 314141   FORD 72-76 Portland St. ✆ 312312
DAIHATSU St. Meddans St. ✆ 312099

TURNBERRY Ayr. (Strathclyde) **401 402** F 18 – ECD : Wednesday – ✉ Girvan – ☎ 065 53.
🏠, 🏠 Turnberry Hotel ✆ 202.

◆Edinburgh 97 – ◆Ayr 15 – ◆Glasgow 51 – Stranraer 36.

🏨 **Turnberry** ⚘, Maidens Rd, on A 719 ✆ 202, Telex 777779, ≤ golf course and bay,
🐟, 🏠, 🍽, 🏊 – 💈 📺 ☎ & ⓟ. 🔥, 🅰🅴 ⑩ 𝘝𝘐𝘚𝘈
closed 1 January-26 February – **M** 12.00/21.50 **st.** and a la carte ╏6.25 – **120 rm**
🛏 60.00/140.00 **st.**, **6 suites** 170.00/255.00 **st.** – SB (November-March) 167.00/202.00 **st.**

TWEEDSMUIR Lanark. (Strathclyde) **401 402** J 17 – ✉ Biggar – ☎ 089 97.

◆Edinburgh 38 – ◆Carlisle 58 – ◆Dumfries 57 – ◆Glasgow 37.

XX **Crook Inn** ⚘ with rm, ML12 6QN, N : 1 m. on A 701 ✆ 272, ≤, ⌘, 🐎 – 🚻wc ⓟ. 🅰🅴 ⑩
M 5.95/12.50 **t.** and a la carte ╏2.65 – **7 rm** 🛏 26.00/44.00 **t.** – SB 60.00/64.00 **st.**

TYNET Moray (Grampian) – see Fochabers.

UDDINGSTON Lanark. (Strathclyde) **401 402** H 16 – pop. 10 681 – ECD : Wednesday – ✉ Glasgow – ☎ 0698.

◆Edinburgh 41 – ◆Glasgow 10.

🏛 **Redstones**, 8-10 Glasgow Rd, G71 7AS, ✆ 813774 – 📺 🚻wc 🍴wc ☎ ⓟ. 🔥 🅰🅴 ⑩ 𝘝𝘐𝘚𝘈
🍽
closed 1 and 2 January – **M** *(closed Sunday)* 5.95/9.50 **t.** and a la carte ╏4.00 – **14 rm**
🛏 35.00/47.00 **t.** – SB (weekends only) 53.00/64.00 **st.**

X Il Buongustaio, 84 Main St., G71 7LR, ✆ 816000, Italian rest.

UIST (Isles of) Inverness. (Western Isles) **401** XY 11 and 12 – pop. 3 677.

⚓ see Benbecula.

🚢 by Caledonian MacBrayne from Lochboisdale : to Oban 3-6 weekly (5 h 30 mn direct ;
7 h 30 mn via Castlebay) – from Lochmaddy to Uig (Isle of Skye) Monday/Saturday 5-9 weekly
(1 h 45 mn direct - 4 h 45 mn via Tarbert) – from Lochmaddy to Tarbert (Isle of Harris) summer
only : Monday/Saturday 5-9 weekly 2 h direct - 4 h 45 mn via Uig.

Benbecula – ✉ Liniclate – ☎ 0870 Benbecula.
🛬 Benbecula Airport : ✆ 2051.

🏛 **Dark Island**, PA88 5PJ, ✆ 2414, ≤ – 🚻wc 🍴wc ⓟ. 🔥 𝘝𝘐𝘚𝘈
M 5.00/10.00 **t.** and dinner a la carte ╏3.00 – **27 rm** 🛏 28.00/60.00 **t.**

Daliburgh (South Uist) – ✉ ☎ 087 84 Lochboisdale.

🏛 **Borrodale**, PA81 5SS, ✆ 444, ≤, ⌘ – 🚻wc 🍴wc ⓟ. 🔥 𝘝𝘐𝘚𝘈
M 5.50/10.50 **st.** ╏2.50 – **13 rm** 🛏 17.50/38.50 **st.**

Lochboisdale (South Uist) – ECD : Thursday – ✉ ☎ 087 84 Lochboisdale.
🛈 ✆ 286 (summer only).

🏛 **Lochboisdale**, PA81 5TH, ✆ 332, ≤ Lochboisdale and harbour, ⌘ – 🚻wc 🍴 ⓟ. 🔥 𝘝𝘐𝘚𝘈
M (bar lunch Monday to Saturday)/dinner 10.50 **t.** and a la carte ╏2.50 – 🛏 2.00 – **20 rm**
18.00/40.00 **t.**

Lochmaddy (North Uist) – ECD : Thursday – ✉ ☎ 087 63 Lochmaddy.
🛈 ✆ 321 (summer only).

🏛 Lochmaddy, PA28 5AA, ✆ 331, ≤ Lochmaddy and islands, ⌘ – ⓟ – **15 rm**.

ULLAPOOL Ross and Cromarty (Highland) **401** E 10 Scotland G – pop. 1 006 – ECD : Tuesday
except summer – ☎ 0854.

See : Site★.

Envir. : Falls of Measach★★ in the Corrieshalloch Gorge★, S : 11 m. by A 835 – Loch Broom★★,
Loch Assynt★★ and Lochinver, N : 37 m. by A 835 and A 837.

🚢 by Caledonian MacBrayne : to Stornoway (Isle of Lewis) Monday/Saturday 1-2 daily
(3 h 30 mn).
🛈 ✆ 2135 (summer only).

◆Edinburgh 215 – ◆Inverness 59.

🏨 **Royal** (Best Western), Garve Rd, IV26 2SY, ✆ 2181, ≤ Loch Broom, ⌘, 🐎, park – 🚻wc
☎ ⓟ. 🔥 🅰🅴 ⑩ 𝘝𝘐𝘚𝘈
closed 24 December-4 January – **M** (bar lunch)/dinner 11.75 **t.** and a la carte ╏3.75 – **57 rm**
🛏 27.00/60.00 **t.**, **1 suite** 70.00/90.00 **t.** – SB (October-April) 42.00/54.00 **st.**

🏨 **Ladbroke Mercury Motor Inn** (Ladbroke), North Rd, IV26 2UD, ✆ 2314, ≤ – 📺 🚻wc
ⓟ. 🔥 🅰🅴 ⑩ 𝘝𝘐𝘚𝘈
April-September – **M** (bar lunch)/dinner 10.50 **t.** and a la carte ╏3.75 – 🛏 6.00 – **60 rm**
33.00/51.00 **t.**

🏛 **Ceilidh Place,** 14 West Argyle St., IV26 2TY, 🌭 2103, « Tasteful decor » – 🛏wc 🅿. 🔊 AE
ⓘ VISA
April-September – **M** (buffet lunch)/dinner a la carte 8.20/14.20 **t.** ⅜ 2.75 – **15 rm**
⌁ 23.00/55.00 **st.**

🏛 **Harbour Lights Motel,** Garve Rd., 🌭 2222, ≤ Loch Broom, � – 🛏wc 🎐wc 🅿 – **22 rm**.

🏠 **Ferry Boat Inn,** Shore St., 🌭 2366, ≤ – **12 rm.**

✗ **Altnaharrie Inn** 🌭 with rm, IV26 2SS, SW : ½ m. via private ferry 🌭 085 483 (Dundonnell) 230, ≤ Loch Broom and Ullapool, « Idyllic setting on bank of Loch Broom », 🐟, � –
🛏wc. 🌺
Easter-mid October – **M** (booking essential) (restricted lunch, residents only)/dinner 25.00 **st.**
⅜ 2.40 – **4 rm** ⌁ 30.00/65.00 **st.**

UNST Shetland (Shetland Islands) 401 R 1 – Shipping Services : see Shetland Islands.

UPHALL W. Lothian (Lothian) 401 J 16 – ECD : Wednesday – ✆ 0506 Broxburn – 📮 🌭 856404.
♦Edinburgh 13 – ♦Glasgow 32.

🏛 **Houstoun House,** EH52 6JS, 🌭 853831, Telex 727148, ≤, « Gardens », park – 📺 ☎ 🅿. 🔊
AE ⓘ VISA
M 10.75/16.25 **st.** ⅜ 3.30 – ⌁ 2.50 – **30 rm** 46.00/78.00 **st.** – SB (weekends only) 63.50/71.50 **st.**

VATERSAY Inverness (Western Isles) 401 X 13 – Shipping Services : see Barra (Isle of).

WALKERBURN Peebles. (Borders) 401 402 K 17 – pop. 713 – ✆ 089 687.
♦Edinburgh 32 – Galashiels 10 – Peebles 8.

🏛 **Tweed Valley** 🌭, Galashiels Rd, EH43 6AA, 🌭 220, ≤, 🐟, � – 📺 🛏wc 🎐wc 🅿. 🔊 AE
ⓘ VISA
M 6.50 **t.** (lunch) and a la carte 8.00/11.65 **t.** ⅜ 3.50 – **16 rm** ⌁ 24.00/54.00 **st.** – SB 57.00/59.50 **st.**

WALLS Shetland (Shetland Islands) 401 P 3 – see Shetland Islands (Mainland).

WEMYSS BAY Renfrew. (Strathclyde) 401 402 F 16 – ECD : Wednesday – ✆ 0475.
⚓ by Caledonian MacBrayne : to Rothesay (Isle of Bute) summer only : 4-13 daily (30 mn).

Hotels see : **Largs** S : 4 ½ m., **Skelmorlie** S : 1 ½ m.

WESTHILL Aberdeen. (Grampian) 401 N 12 – see Aberdeen.

WESTRAY (Isle of) Orkney (Orkney Islands) 401 KL 6 – Shipping Services : see Orkney Islands
(Mainland : Kirkwall).

WEST WEMYSS Fife. (Fife) – see Kirkcaldy.

WHALSAY (Isle of) Shetland (Shetland Islands) 401 R 2 – Shipping Services : see Shetland
Islands.

WHITEBRIDGE Inverness (Highland) 401 G 12 – ✆ 045 63 Gorthleck.
♦Edinburgh 171 – ♦Inverness 23 – Kyle of Lochalsh 67 – ♦Oban 92.

🏛 **Knockie Lodge** 🌭, IV1 2UP, SW : 3 ½ m. by B 862 🌭 276, ≤ Loch Nanlann and mountains,
« Tastefully converted hunting lodge », 🐟, �, park – 🛏wc 🅿. 🔊 AE VISA. 🌺
May-October – **M** (bar lunch)/dinner 15.00 **t.** – **10 rm** ⌁ 30.00/70.00 **t.**

🏛 **Whitebridge,** IV1 2UN, 🌭 226, ≤, 🐟, � – 📺 🛏wc 🎐wc 🅿. 🔊 AE ⓘ VISA
Easter-October – **M** (bar lunch)/dinner 9.00 **t.** – **12 rm** ⌁ 14.25/33.50 **t.**

WHITENESS Shetland (Shetland Islands) 401 Q 3 – see Shetland Islands (Mainland).

WHITING BAY Bute (Strathclyde) 401 402 E 17 – see Arran (Isle of).

WHITHORN (Isle of) Wigtown. (Dumfries and Galloway) 401 402 G 19 **Scotland G** – pop. 989 –
ECD : Wednesday – ✆ 098 85.
Envir. : Priory Museum (Early Christian Crosses★★) NW : 4 m. by A 750.
♦Edinburgh 52 – ♦Ayr 72 – ♦Dumfries 72 – Stranraer 34.

🏛 **Steam Packet,** Harbour Rd, DG8 8LL, 🌭 334 – 📺 🛏wc
M 5.00/10.50 **st.** and a la carte ⅜ 3.00 – **4 rm** ⌁ 15.00/30.00 **t.**

🏠 **Queens Arms,** 22 Main St., DG8 8LF, 🌭 369 – 📺 🛏wc 🅿. AE ⓘ VISA
M (bar lunch)/dinner 10.50 **st.** and a la carte ⅜ 2.75 – **10 rm** ⌁ 14.00/32.00 **st.** – SB (October-
May) 40.00/44.00 **st.**

WICK Caithness. (Highland) 🔢 K 8 **Scotland** G – pop. 7 770 – ECD : Wednesday – 📞 0955.
Envir. : the Hill O'Many Stanes★, S by A 9 – Grey Cairns of Camster★, S by A 9 – Duncansby Head★ and the stacks of Duncansby★★, N : 17 m. by A 9.

🛬 Reiss 🖉 2726, N : 3 m.

✈ 🖉 2215, N : 1 m.

🛈 Caithness Tourist Organisation, Whitechapel Rd off High St. 🖉 2596.

♦Edinburgh 282 – ♦Inverness 126.

🏨 Ladbroke Mercury Motor Inn (Ladbroke), Riverside, KW1 4NL, 🖉 3344 – 📺 🛏wc ☎ 🅿. 🏄 **48 rm**.

DATSUN, VAUXHALL Francis St. 🖉 4123　　　　　　TALBOT George St. 🖉 2321
FORD Francis St. 🖉 2103

WIGTOWN Wigtown. (Dumfries and Galloway) 🔢 G 19 – pop. 1 040 – ECD : Wednesday – ✉ Newton Stewart – 📞 098 886 Mochrum.

♦Edinburgh 137 – ♦Ayr 61 – ♦Dumfries 61 – Stranraer 26.

🏨 **Corsemalzie House** 🦌, DG8 9RL, SW : 6 ½ m. by A 714 on B 7005 🖉 254, « Country house atmosphere », 🦢, 🐎, park – 📺 🛏wc 🗄wc 🅿. 🏄 AE ④ VISA
closed 20 January-6 March – **M** (lunch by arrangement)/dinner 11.50 **t.** and a la carte ↕ 2.90 – **15 rm** 🍽 31.50/53.00 **t.** – SB 53.00/67.00 **st.**

WORMIT Fife. (Fife) 🔢 L 14 – ECD : Wednesday – ✉ 📞 0382 Newport-on-Tay.

♦Edinburgh 53 – ♦Dundee 6 – St. Andrews 12.

🏨 **Sandford Hill** 🦌, DD6 8RG, S : 2 m. at junction of A 914 and B 946 🖉 541802, ≤, 🐎 – 📺 🛏wc ☎ 🅿. 🏄 AE ④ VISA
closed 1 and 2 January – **M** 9.20/12.00 **t.** and a la carte – **15 rm** 🍽 33.00/51.50 **t.** – SB (weekends only) 50.00/60.00 **st.**

WYRE (Isle of) Orkney (Orkney Islands) 🔢 L 6 – Shipping Services : see Orkney Islands (Mainland : Kirkwall).

YELL (Isle of) Shetland (Shetland Islands) 🔢 Q 2 – Shipping Services : see Shetland Islands (Mainland).

Northern Ireland

Place with at least :

one hotel or restaurant	● Londonderry
one pleasant hotel	🏨 , ✕ with rm
one quiet, secluded hotel	🐦
one restaurant with	✿, ✿✿, ✿✿✿, M
See this town for establishments located in its vicinity	BELFAST

Localité offrant au moins :

une ressource hôtelière	● Londonderry
un hôtel agréable	🏨 , ✕ with rm
un hôtel très tranquille, isolé	🐦
une bonne table à	✿, ✿✿, ✿✿✿, M
Localité groupant dans le texte les ressources de ses environs	BELFAST

La località possiede come minimo :

una risorsa alberghiera	● Londonderry
un albergo ameno	🏨 , ✕ with rm
un albergo molto tranquillo, isolato	🐦
un'ottima tavola con	✿, ✿✿, ✿✿✿, M
La località raggruppa nel suo testo le risorse dei dintorni	BELFAST

Ort mit mindestens :

einem Hotel oder Restaurant	● Londonderry
einem angenehmen Hotel	🏨 , ✕ with rm
einem sehr ruhigen und abgelegenen Hotel	🐦
einem Restaurant mit	✿, ✿✿, ✿✿✿, M
Ort mit Angaben über Hotels und Restaurants in seiner Umgebung	BELFAST

586

NORTHERN IRELAND

Towns

See : Road★★★ (A 2) from Larne to Portrush.

ANTRIM (Coast Road) Antrim **405** O 3.
See : Road★★★ (A 2) from Larne to Portrush.

BALLYCASTLE Antrim **405** N 2 – pop. 3 284 – ✪ 026 57.
See : Site★★ – Envir. : Giant's Causeway★★★ (Chaussée des Géants) basalt formation (from the car-park *AC*, ½ h Rtn on foot) NW : 12 m. – White Park Bay★★ NW : 8 ½ m. – Carrick-a-Rede (≼★★ of Rathlin Island) NW : 5 ½ m.
🛆 ♱ 62536 – ▮ Sheskburn House, 7 Mary St. ♱ 62024.
♦Belfast 60 – Ballymena 28 – Larne 40.

  ♤   **Antrim Arms,** 75 Castle St., BT54 6AS, ♱ 62284 – ℗
      M (bar lunch)/dinner a la carte 5.00/11.50 **t.** ▯ 3.00 – **16 rm** ⟑ 13.00/28.00 **t.** – SB 34.00/35.00 **st.**

FORD Sheskburn Garage ♱ 62478   TOYOTA 47-49 Market Sq. ♱ 62733

BALLYGALLEY Antrim **405** O 3 – pop. 424 – ✉ Larne – ✪ 057 483.
♦Belfast 27 – Ballymena 24 – Larne 4.

  🏛   **Ballygally Castle,** 274 Coast Rd, BT40 2QX, ♱ 212, ≼, ♨, ℀ – 📺 ⌂wc ☎ ℗ ◪ Æ ⓪ **VISA**
      M 7.00/11.00 **t.** ▯ 3.25 – **30 rm** ⟑ 25.50/38.00 **t.** – SB (weekends only) 80.00 **st.**

BALLYMENA Antrim **405** N 3 – pop. 28 166 – ✪ 0266.
Envir. : Glen of Glenariff★★★ – Glenariff (or Waterfoot) site★ NE : 19 m.
🛆 Broughshane ♱ 861207, E : 2 m. on A 42 – ▮ 2 Ballymoney Rd ♱ 46043.
♦Belfast 28 – ♦Dundalk 78 – Larne 21 – ♦Londonderry 51 – ♦Omagh 53.

  🏛   **Country House** ⟨⟩, 20 Doagh Rd ✉ Kells, BT42 3LZ, SE : 6 m. by A 36 on B 59 ♱ 891663, ♨ – 📺 ⌂wc ☎ ℗ ◪ ⬛ Æ ⓪ **VISA** ℀
      M 5.95/12.00 **t.** and a la carte 8.25/13.25 **t.** ▯ 3.25 – **13 rm** ⟑ 29.50/39.50 **st.**

  🏛   **Adair Arms,** 1-5 Ballymoney Rd, BT43 5BS, ♱ 3674 – 📺 ⌂wc ☎ ℗ ◪ ⬛ Æ ⓪ **VISA**
      M 6.50/12.00 **t.** and a la carte ▯ 3.50 – **39 rm** ⟑ 29.50/42.00 **t.** – SB (weekends only) 35.00 **st.**

  ✗   **Water Margin,** 8-10 Cully Backey Rd, ♱ 48643, Chinese rest. – ⬛ Æ ⓪ **VISA**
      M a la carte 5.25/15.95 **st.** ▯ 2.50.

ALFA-ROMEO, LOTUS Broadway Av. ♱ 2161   VW, AUDI 1-5 Railway St. ♱ 46014
AUSTIN-ROVER Waveney Av. ♱ 3557

BALLYNAHINCH Down **405** O 4 – pop. 3 721 – ✉ ✪ 0238.
♦Belfast 14 – Downpatrick 10.

  ✗   **Woodlands,** 29 Spa Rd, BT24 8PT, SW : 1 ½ m. by A 24 on B 175 ♱ 562650, ♨ – ℗ ⬛ ⓪
      VISA
      closed Sunday to Wednesday – **M** (dinner only)(booking essential) 13.95 **t.** ▯ 2.60.

BELFAST Antrim **405** O 4 – pop. 329 958 – ✪ 0232.
See : City Hall★★ 1906 BZ – Queen's University★★ 1906 AZ **U** – Ulster Museum★ AZ **M** – Church House★ 1905 BZ **B** – Botanic Gardens (hot houses★) AZ – Bellevue Zoological Gardens (site★, ≼★) *AC*, by A 6 AY.
Envir. : Stormont (Parliament House★ 1932, terrace : vista★★) E : 4 m. by Belmont Rd AZ – The Giant's Ring★ (prehistoric area) S : 5 m. by Malone Rd AZ – Lisburn (Castle gardens ≼★) SW : 8 m. by A 1 AZ.
🛆 Balmoral, Lisburn Rd ♱ 668540 AZ – 🛆 Fortwilliam, Downview Av. ♱ 771770, N : 2 m. AY – 🛆, 🛆 Malone, 240 Upper Malone Rd, Dunmurry ♱ 612695 by A 55 AZ – 🛆 Shandon Park ♱ 794856, E : 3 m. by A 55 AZ.
✈ Belfast Airport : ♱ 229271, NW : 12 m. by M 2 Motorway AY – **Terminal :** Coach service (Ulsterbus Ltd.) from Great Victoria Street Station (40 mn).
⚓ to Liverpool (Belfast Car Ferries) 1 daily (9 h) – to Isle of Man : Douglas (Isle of Man Steam Packet Co.) June-September 1-2 weekly (4 h 30 mn).
▮ River House, 52 High St., BT1 2DS ♱ 246609 – Belfast Airport, Aldergrove ♱ 084 94 (Crumlin) 52103.
♦Dublin 103 – ♦Londonderry 70.

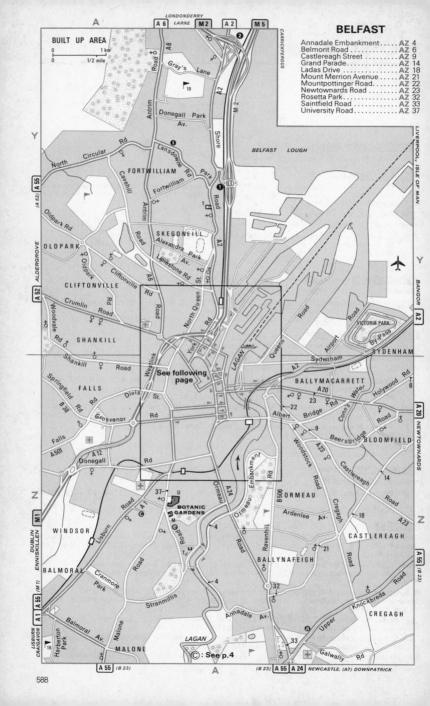

BUILT UP AREA

0 ____ 1 km
0 ____ 1/2 mile

BELFAST LOUGH

LIVERPOOL, ISLE OF MAN

See following page

© : See p.4

BELFAST
CENTRE

589

🏨 **Forum,** Great Victoria St., BT2 7AP, ℰ 245161, Telex 74491, ⇐ – 🛗 📺 ☎ 🅿 🕍 ᴧ 🖭 ⑩ 🆚 ⅏
    BZ **e**
M (carving rest.) 9.50 **t.** and a la carte ⅃ 4.25 – ⇆ 4.75 – **200 rm** 54.50/69.50 **t.**, **8 suites** 109.50 **t.**

🏨 **Stormont,** 587 Upper Newtownards Rd, BT4 3LP, E : 4 ½ m. by A 2 on A 20 ℰ 658621 – 🛗
📺 ᴧ ᴧ 🖭 ⑩ 🆚 ⅏
    on A 20 AZ
closed Christmas Day – **M** 9.00 **t.** and a la carte ⅃ 3.00 – **67 rm** ⇆ 44.00/60.00 **t.**

🏨 **Drumkeen,** Upper Galwally, off Upper Knockbreda Rd, BT8 4TL, SE : 3 m. by A 24 off A 55
ℰ 645321 – 📺 ⌷wc ☎ 🅿 🕍 ᴧ 🖭 🆚 ⅏
    AZ **a**
M 5.75/9.50 **t.** ⅃ 3.00 – **28 rm** ⇆ 35.00/50.00 **t.**

⌂ **Somerton,** 22 Lansdowne Rd, BT15 4DB, ℰ 778717 – 📺
    AY **i**
8 rm.

⌂ **Camera,** 44 Wellington Park, BT9 6DP, ℰ 660026 – ⌷wc. 🆚 ⅏
    AZ **c**
11 rm ⇆ 10.00/28.00 **st.**

✗ **Strand,** 12 Stranmillis Rd, BT9 5AA, ℰ 682266, Bistro – ᴧ 🖭 ⑩ 🆚
    AZ **e**
closed Sunday, 20 April, 12-13 July and 25-26 December – **M** (booking essential) 10.00 **t.** and a la carte 7.30/10.75 **t.** ⅃ 2.45.

at Dunmurry SW : 5 ½ m. on A 1 – AZ – ✉ 🅲 0232 Belfast :

🏨 **Conway** (T.H.F.), Kingsway, BT17 9ES, ℰ 612101, Telex 74281, ⅃ heated, ☞, squash – 🛗
📺 ☎ 🅿 🕍 ᴧ 🖭 ⑩ 🆚
M 6.50/8.50 **st.** and a la carte ⅃ 3.25 – **75 rm** ⇆ 49.50/63.00 **st.**, **1 suite.**

MICHELIN Distribution Centre, 40 Mallusk Road, Newtonabbey, BT38 8PX, ℰ 42616 by N7 AZ

AUSTIN-ROVER Saintfield Rd ℰ 649774
AUSTIN-ROVER 52-80 Shankil Rd ℰ 242456
AUSTIN-ROVER-DAIMLER-JAGUAR 10-18 Adelaide St. ℰ 230566
AUSTIN-ROVER Upper Newtownards Rd, Dundonald ℰ 2651
BEDFORD, OPEL-VAUXHALL 17-29 Ravenhill Rd ℰ 51422
CITROEN 357 Albertbridge Rd ℰ 57575 57766
FORD Lislea Drive ℰ 662231

FORD 397 Upper Newtownards Rd ℰ 654687
FORD 58-82 Antrim Rd ℰ 744744
HYUNDAI 27, Pakenham St., Donegal Pass ℰ 232111
PEUGEOT-TALBOT 226 York St. ℰ 747133
RENAULT Boucher Rd ℰ 681721
SAAB 250-252 Donegall St. ℰ 221019
TOYOTA 39-49 Adelaide St. ℰ 228225
VAUXHALL-OPEL 46 Florenceville Av. ℰ 641350
VAUXHALL-OPEL 83-87 York Rd ℰ 744869
VOLVO 59-75 Ladas Drive ℰ 703666

During the season, particularly in resorts, it is wise to book in advance.
However, if you find you cannot take up a hotel booking you have made,
please let the hotel know immediately.
If you are writing to a hotel abroad enclose an International Reply Coupon
(available from Post Offices.)

BUSHMILLS Antrim **405** M 2 – ✉ Bushmills – 🅲 02657 Derrock.

◆Belfast 57 – Ballycastle 12 – Coleraine 10.

✗ **Auberge de Seneirl** ⌷ with rm, 28 Ballyclough Rd, BT57 8UZ, SW : 3 m. by B 17 on Seneirl Rd ℰ 41536, French rest. – 📺 ⌷wc 🅿 ⅏
closed Saturday lunch, Sunday, Monday and Tuesday except July and August – **M** (dinner only and lunch during July and August) 9.00/15.50 **t.** and a la carte 8.95/12.45 **t.** ⅃ 2.65 – **5 rm** ⇆ 12.50/24.00 **t.**

CARNLOUGH Antrim **405** O 3 – pop. 1 462 – ✉ Ballymena – 🅲 0574.

🖪 Post Office, Harbour Rd ℰ 85210.

◆Belfast 37 – Ballymena 16 – Larne 14.

🏨 **Londonderry Arms,** Harbour Rd, BT44 0EU, ℰ 85255 – 📺 ⌷wc ⌷wc ☎ 🅿 ᴧ 🖭 ⑩ 🆚 ⅏
M 7.45/9.95 **st.** and a la carte ⅃ 2.65 – **12 rm** ⇆ 18.00/32.00 **st.** – SB (weekends only)(except Easter and Christmas) 46.00/48.50 **st.**

CARRICKFERGUS Antrim **405** O 3 – pop. 17 633 – 🅲 096 03.

See : Castle★★ (13C) *AC* – Sea Front★ – St. Nicholas' Church★ 12C-18C.

Envir. : Island Magee Peninsula (Port Muck★, Isle of Muck★, Power Station ⇐★) NE : 9 m.

🖪 35 North Rd ℰ 63713.

🖪 Castle Green ℰ 63604 (summer only).

◆Belfast 10 – Larne 14.

🏨 **Coast Road,** 28 Scotch Quarter, BT38 7DP, ℰ 61021 – 📺 ⌷wc ⌷wc ☎ ⑩ 🆚 ⅏
closed 25 and 26 December – **M** (closed Sunday dinner) (bar lunch)/dinner a la carte 5.95/11.30 **st.** ⅃ 2.75 – **20 rm** ⇆ 17.00/21.00 **st.**

PEUGEOT, TALBOT 72 Belfast Rd ℰ 62299
RENAULT Larne Rd ℰ 63516

CASTLEROCK Londonderry – see Coleraine.

COLERAINE Londonderry **405** L 2 – pop. 15 967 – ✪ 0265.

Envir. : Giant's Causeway★★★ (Chaussée des Géants) basalt formation (from the car-park *AC*, ½ h Rtn on foot) NE : 9 m. – Downhill Castle (Mussenden Temple★ 18C : ≤★★★ *AC*) NW : 7 m. – Portrush (site★, ≤★) N : 6 m. – Dunluce Castle (site★, ≤★) NE : 8 m. – W : Benevenagh Mountain★.

🛆 Castlerock ℰ 026 584 (Castlerock) 314, W : 5 m. – ⌂₈, ⌂₈, ⌂₉ Royal Portrush, Dunluce Rd, Portrush ℰ 0265 (Portrush) 822311.

🛆 Swimming Pool, Main St., Castlerock ℰ 848258 (summer only).

◆Belfast 53 – Ballymena 25 – ◆Londonderry 31 – ◆Omagh 65.

🏠 **Greenhill House** ❦, 24 Greenhill Rd, Aghadowey, BT51 4EU, S : 9 m. by A 29 on B 66 ℰ 026 585 (Aghadowey) 241, ☞ – 🕿wc ❷. 🔼 ❀
March-October – **7 rm** ⊂ 11.50/23.00 st.

❌❌ **MacDuffs** ❦ with rm, Blackheath House, 112 Killeague Rd, Blackhill, S : 8 m. by A 29 on Macosquin road ℰ 026 585 (Aghadowey) 433, « 18C former manse », 🔲, ☞ – 📺 ☐wc 🕿wc ❷. ❀
closed Sunday, Monday, second week January, 2 weeks October-November and 25-26 December – **M** (dinner only) a la carte 8.70/12.30 t. ⒧ 3.00 – **6 rm** ⊂ 20.00/35.00 t.

at Castlerock NW : 6 m. by A 2 off B 119 – ✉ ✪ 0265 Castlerock :

🏠 **Maritima,** 43 Main St., BT51 4RA, ℰ 848388, ≤ – 🕿wc ❷
6 rm ⊂ 11.00/22.00 s.

FORD 80-82 Bushmills Rd ℰ 2361   VAUXHALL-OPEL, BEDFORD Hanover Pl. ℰ 2386

CRAIGAVON Armagh **405** M 4 – pop. 10 195 – ✉ ✪ 0762 Portadown.

Envir. : Ardress House★ 17C (site★, drawing-room plasterwork★★) *AC*, W : 11 m. – Rich Hill (site★, church : scenery★) SW : 9 ½ m.

⌂₈ Turmoyra Lane, Silverwood, Lurgan ℰ 0762 (Lurgan) 6606, NE : 3 m.

◆Belfast 28 – Armagh 13.

🏨 Seagoe, Upper Church Lane, BT53 5QS, ℰ 333076, ☞ – 📺 ☐wc 🕿 ❷. 🛆 ❀
38 rm, 2 suites.

AUSTIN-ROVER 65-79 Avenue Rd ℰ 07622 (Lurgan)   FORD Highfield Rd ℰ 42424
3275

CRAWFORDSBURN Down **405** O 4 – pop. 140 – ✪ 0247 Helen's Bay.

⌂₈ Carnalea, Station Rd ℰ 0247 (Bangor) 465004 – ⌂₈, ⌂₈ Clandeboye, Conlig ℰ 0247 (Bangor) 465767.

◆Belfast 10 – Bangor 3.

🏨 **Old Inn,** 15 Main St., BT19 1JH, ℰ 853255, ☞ – 📺 ☐wc 🕿wc 🕿 ❷. 🔼 🖭 ⓪ 𝗩𝗜𝗦𝗔 ❀
closed 25 December and 1 January – **M** *(closed Sunday lunch)* 6.50/9.00 t. and a la carte – ⊂ 4.50 – **21 rm** 33.00/48.00 t. – SB (weekends only) 73.00/77.00 **st.**

DOWNPATRICK Down **405** O 5 – pop. 8 245 – ✪ 0396.

Envir. : Saul (St. Patrick's Memorial Church : site★, ≤★) NE : 3 m. – Castle Ward 1765 (great hall★) NE : 6 m. – Portaferry : Strangford (site★, Audley's Castle : top ❅★★, 44 steps) NE : 8 m.

⌂₈ Saul Rd ℰ 2152 – ⌂₈ Castle Pl., Ardglass ℰ 0396 (Ardglass) 841219, SE : 7 m.

🚢 to Portaferry, frequent services daily (5 mn).

◆Belfast 22 – Bangor 27.

🏨 **Abbey Lodge,** 38 Belfast Rd, BT30 9AV, NW : 1 m. on A 7 ℰ 4511 – 📺 ☐wc 🕿 ❷. 🛆 🔼 🖭 ⓪ 𝗩𝗜𝗦𝗔 ❀
M 6.00/10.00 t. and a la carte ⒧ 2.75 – **22 rm** ⊂ 17.00/30.00 t.

FIAT, FORD Church St. ℰ 2777

DUNADRY Antrim **405** N 3 – ✪ 084 94 Templepatrick.

Envir. : Antrim (round tower★ 10C) NW : 5 m. – Shane's Castle★ (16C ruins) *AC*, NW : 5 ½ m. (access by miniature railway).

◆Belfast 15 – Larne 18 – ◆Londonderry 56.

🏨 **Dunadry Inn,** 2 Islandreagh Drive, BT41 2HA, ℰ 32474, Telex 747245, ☞ – 📺 🕿 ❷. 🛆 🔼 🖭 ⓪ 𝗩𝗜𝗦𝗔 ❀
closed 24 to 27 December – **M** (buffet lunch) 6.50/12.00 **st.** and a la carte 13.50/16.00 s. ⒧ 3.00 – **64 rm** ⊂ 48.00/58.00 **st.** – SB (weekends only) 42.00/54.00 **st.**

DUNMURRY Antrim **405** N 4 – see Belfast.

ENNISKILLEN Fermanagh **405** J 4 – pop. 10 429 – ✪ 0365.

See : Lough Erne★★★ (Upper and Lower) – On Lower Lough Erne, by boat *AC* : Devenish Island (site★★, monastic ruins : scenery★) and White Island★.

Envir. : Castle Coole★ 18C (site★) E : 1 m. – Florence Court (site★, park★) *AC*, SW : 8 m.

🏌 Castlecoole *℘* 25250.

🛈 Lakeland Visitor Centre, Shore Rd *℘* 23110 and 25050.

◆Belfast 87 – ◆Londonderry 59.

🏨 **Killyhevlin**, Dublin Rd, BT74 6HQ, SE : 1 ¾ m. on A 4 *℘* 23481, ≤, ≉, park – 📺 🗠wc ⓚwc ☎ ❿. ⬛ ⬛ ⴻ ⑩ *VISA*
M a la carte 7.85/13.55 ⬧ 3.00 – **23 rm** 🗠 32.50/55.00 t., **1 suite** 90.00/120.00 t.

🏨 **Royal**, 4 East Bridge St., *℘* 22399 – 📺 ⓚwc. ⬛ *VISA*
M (carving lunch) 6.50/8.50 **st.** and a la carte ⬧ 3.25 – **11 rm** 🗠 17.50/30.00 **st.** – SB 32.50/39.00 **st.**

🏨 **Fort Lodge**, Forthill St., *℘* 23275 – 📺 🗠wc ⓚwc ☎ ❿
12 rm.

⌂ **Willoughby**, 24 Willoughby Pl., BT74 7EX, *℘* 25275 – ❿. ⋇
12 rm 🗠 10.00/18.00 st.

AUSTIN-ROVER Dublin Rd *℘* 23475   VAUXHALL-OPEL Tempo Rd *℘* 24366

GLENGORMLEY Antrim **405** O 3 – ✉ Newtownabbey – ✪ 023 13.

◆Belfast 6 – Larne 15.

🏨 **Chimney Corner**, 630 Antrim Rd, BT36 8RH, NW : 2 m. on A 6 *℘* 44925, Telex 748158, 🏌, ≉, ⋇ – 📺 🗠wc ☎ ❿. ⬛ ⬛ ⬛ ⴻ ⑩ *VISA* ⋇
closed 10 days at Christmas – **M** 6.00/10.00 t. and a la carte ⬧ 3.50 – **63 rm** 🗠 38.00/50.00 t.

XX **Sleepy Hollow**, 15 Kiln Rd, BT36 8SU, N : 2 m. by A 8(M) off B 56 *℘* 44042 – ❿. ⬛ ⴻ ⑩ *VISA*
closed Sunday to Tuesday – **M** (dinner only) 14.75 **st.** ⬧ 2.90.

AUSTIN-ROVER 144 Antrim Rd *℘* (Belfast) 773606   VW-AUDI 45 Mallusk Rd *℘* 7111
RENAULT 612 Antrim Rd *℘* 3496

HILLSBOROUGH Down **405** N 4 – ✪ 0849.

See : Government House★ 18C – the Fort★ 17C.

Envir. : Legananny Dolmen ≤★ S : 16 m.

🏌 68 Eglantine Rd, Lisburn *℘* 023 82 (Lisburn) 2186, S : 3 m.

◆Belfast 13.

🏨 **White Gables**, 14 Dromore Rd, BT26 6HU, *℘* 682755 – 📺 🗠wc ☎ ❿. ⬛ ⬛ ⴻ ⑩ *VISA*. ⋇
M (closed Sunday lunch) 6.00/7.95 **t.** and a la carte ⬧ 3.00 – **25 rm** 🗠 25.00/45.00 t.

TOYOTA 23 Lisburn Rd *℘* 682188

HOLYWOOD Down **405** O 4 – pop. 9 462 – ✪ 023 17.

Envir. : Craigavad : Ulster Folk and Transport Museum★ (Cultra Manor) *AC*, NE : 3 m.

🏌 Nuns Walk, Demesne Rd *℘* 2138.

◆Belfast 5 – Bangor 6.

🏩 **Culloden** ⟡, 142 Bangor Rd, BT18 0EX, E : 1 ½ m. on A 2 *℘* 5223, Telex 74617, ≤, ≉, park, ⋇, squash – ⬛ 📺 ☎ 🕭 ❿. ⬛ ⬛ ⬛ ⴻ ⑩ *VISA*
M 10.00 t. and a la carte – **73 rm** 🗠 58.00/68.00 t., **5 suites** – SB (weekends only) 70.00 **st.**

FIAT 36-38 Shore Rd *℘* 5636

IRVINESTOWN Fermanagh **405** J 4 – pop. 1 827 – ✪ 036 56.

◆Belfast 78 – ◆Dublin 132 – Donegal 27.

🏤 **Mahon's**, Mill St., BT74 9XX, *℘* 21656 – 🗠wc ☎ ❿. ⬛ *VISA*
M 5.00/7.50 t. and a la carte ⬧ 2.80 – **22 rm** 🗠 15.00/30.00 t.

LARNE Antrim **405** O 3 – pop. 18 224 – ✪ 0574.

Exc. : Antrim Coast Road★★★ (A 2) from Larne to Portrush.

🏌 Cairndhu, 192 Coast Rd *℘* 057 483 (Ballygally) 248, N : 4 m. – 🏌 Larne, 54 Ferris Bay Rd, Islandmagee *℘* 0574 (Larne) 82228.

⛴ to Stranraer (Sealink) 4-8 daily (2 h 15 mn) – to Cairnryan (Townsend Thoresen) 4-6 daily (2 h to 2 h 30mn).

🛈 Council Offices, Victoria Rd *℘* 72313 – Car Park, Murrayfield Shopping Centre, Broadway *℘* 72313 (summer only) – Larne Harbour *℘* 70517.

◆Belfast 23 – Ballymena 20.

⌂ **Derrin House**, 2 Prince's Gdns, BT40 1RQ, off Glenarm Rd (A 2) *℘* 73269 – ❿
closed Christmas week – **7 rm** 🗠 9.00/20.00 **st.**

AUSTIN-ROVER Point St. *℘* 2071   FORD 39 Glynn Rd *℘* 5411

LISBURN Antrim 405 N 4 – ✪ 08462.

🔝 68 Eglantine Rd, Lisburn ✆ 023 82 (Lisburn) 2186, S : 3 m.

◆Belfast 11 – ◆Dundalk 41.

　XX　**Hansom Cab,** 35 Railway St., BT28 1XP, ✆ 74652 – 🔄 AE ⓞ VISA
　　　closed 13 to 31 July – **M** (dinner only Wednesday to Saturday and Sunday lunch)
　　　8.00 **t.** and a la carte ⓐ 3.50.

LONDONDERRY Londonderry 405 K 2-3 – pop. 62 697 – ✪ 0504.

See : City Walls★★ 17C – Guildhall★ 1908 – Memorial Hall★.

Envir. : Grianan of Aileach★ (Republic of Ireland) (stone fort) ⚘★★★ NW : 5 m. – Dungiven (priory :
site★) SE : 18 m.

🔝 City of Derry, 49 Victoria Rd, Prehen ✆ 42610.

✈ Eglinton Airport : ✆ 810784, E : 6 m.

🗓 Foyle St. ✆ 267284.

◆Belfast 70 – ◆Dublin 146.

　🏨　**Everglades,** Prehen Rd, BT47 2PA, S : 1 ½ m. on A 5 ✆ 46722, Telex 748005 – 📺 ☎ ♿ Ⓟ.
　　　🔄 🔄 AE ⓞ VISA ⚘
　　　closed 25 and 26 December – **M** 5.00/9.95 **st.** and a la carte ⓐ 3.75 – � 4.25 – **38 rm**
　　　32.50/65.00 **st.**

　🏨　**White Horse Inn,** 68 Clooney Rd, BT47 3PA, NE : 5 ¼ m. on A 2 ✆ 0504 (Campsie) 860606 –
　　　📺 ⌷wc ☎ Ⓟ. 🔄 AE ⓞ VISA ⚘
　　　M a la carte 4.70/11.05 **t.** ⓐ 2.50 – ⊒ 3.25 – **44 rm** 22.00/44.00 **t.**

BEDFORD, VAUXHALL-OPEL Maydown ✆ 860601　　　PEUGEOT, TALBOT Campsie ✆ 860588
FORD 173 Strand Rd ✆ 267613　　　　　　　　　　VW, AUDI 24 Buncrana Rd ✆ 65985

NEWCASTLE Down 405 O 5 – pop. 6 246 – ✪ 039 67.

Envir. : Tollymore Forest Park★ AC, NW : 2 m. by B 180 – Dundrum (castle★ 13C ruins : top ⚘★★,
70 steps) NE : 3 m. – Loughinisland (the 3 churches★ : 1000-1547-1636) NE : 8 m.

Exc. : SW : Mourne Mountains★★ (Slieve Donard★, Silent Valley★, Lough Shannagh★ : reservoir
1948).

🗓 61 Central Promenade ✆ 22222.

◆Belfast 30 – ◆Londonderry 101.

　🏨　**Burrendale,** Castlewellan Rd, BT33 0JZ, N : 1 m. on A 50 ✆ 22599, ☞ – 📺 ⌷wc ☎ Ⓟ.
　　　🔄 ⓞ VISA
　　　M (bar lunch)/dinner 13.50 **t.** – **30 rm** ⊒ 21.00/35.00 **t.**

　🏨　**Enniskeen** ⚘, 98 Bryansford Rd, BT33 0LF, NW : 1 m. ✆ 22392, ≤, ☞, park – 📺 ⌷wc ☜
　　　Ⓟ. 🔄 VISA ⚘
　　　Mid March-early November – **M** 6.75/8.50 **st.** and a la carte ⓐ 2.75 – **12 rm** ⊒ 17.50/35.90 **st.**
　　　– SB (except Bank Holidays) 45.00/51.00 **st.**

TOYOTA 23 Bryansford Village ✆ 22383

NEWRY Down 405 M N 5 – pop. 19 026 – ✪ 0693.

Envir. : Slieve Gullion★★, Ring of Gullion : Ballitemple viewpoint★★, Bernish Rock viewpoint★★, –
Cam Lough★, Killevy Churches (site★) SW : 5 m. – Derrymore House (site★) AC, NW : 2 ½ m. –
Rostrevor (Fairy Glen★) SE : 8 ¾ m. – Carlingford Lough★ SE : 10 m.

🔝 Warrenpoint, Dromore Rd ✆ 069 37 (Warrenpoint) 72219, S : 5 m.

🗓 Arts Centre, Bank Parade ✆ 66232.

◆Belfast 39 – Armagh 20 – ◆Dundalk 13.

PEUGEOT, TALBOT 18 Edward St. ✆ 2877　　　　　RENAULT 49-53 Merchants Quay ✆ 3626

NEWTOWNARDS Down 405 O 4 – pop. 20 531 – ✪ 0247.

Envir. : Scrabo Tower (site★) SW : 1 m. – Mount Stewart Gardens★ AC – Temple of the Winds
≼ ★ AC, SE : 5 ½ m. – Grey Abbey★ (Cistercian ruins 12C) AC, SW : 7 m.

🔝 Kirkistown Castle, 142 Main Rd, Cloughey ✆ to 024 77 (Portavogie) 71233, SE : 25 m. – 🔝 Scrabo,
233 Scrabo Rd ✆ 812355, W : 2 m.

◆Belfast 10 – Bangor 5.

　🏨　**Strangford Arms,** 92 Church St., BT23 4AL, ✆ 814141 – 📺 ⌷wc ☎ Ⓟ. 🔄 🔄 AE ⓞ VISA
　　　⚘
　　　closed 20-21 April and Christmas Day – **M** 8.00/11.50 **t.** and a la carte ⓐ 4.20 – ⊒ 5.00 – **36 rm**
　　　38.00/60.00 **t.**

FORD Regent St. ✆ 812626　　　　　　　　　　　VW, AUDI Portaferry Rd ✆ 815505
VAUXHALL-OPEL Portaferry Rd ✆ 813376

Red Lion	If the name of the hotel is not in bold type, on arrival ask the hotelier his prices.

OMAGH Tyrone **405** K 4 – pop. 14 627 – ✆ 0662.

Envir. : Gortin Glen Forest Park★, Gortin Gap★ (on B 48) NE : 9 m. – Glenelly Valley★ NE : 17 m. by Plumbridge.

🏌 Dublin Rd ✆ 3160 – 🏌 Fintona ✆ 0662 (Fintona) 841480, S : 5 ½ m.

🛈 1 Market St., ✆ 478312.

◆Belfast 68 – ◆Dublin 112 – ◆Dundalk 64 – ◆Londonderry 34 – ◆Sligo 69.

FORD   Derry Rd ✆ 2788
RENAULT   Cookstown Rd ✆ 3451

VW-AUDI, VAUXHALL-OPEL   60 Dublin Rd ✆ 3116

PORTAFERRY Down **405** P 4 – pop. 2 148 – ✆ 024 77.

⛴ to Downpatrick, frequent services daily (5 mn).

◆ Belfast 29 – Bangor 24.

🏨 **Portaferry**, 10 The Strand, BT22 1PE, ✆ 28231, ≼ – ➜wc ♒wc. 🅰🅴 ⓪ 𝖵𝖨𝖲𝖠. ❄
closed Christmas Day – **M** (closed Sunday dinner) 8.00 **t.** and a la carte 🍴 3.15 – **6 rm**
⚎ 16.00/30.00 **t.** – SB 41.25/44.00 **st.**

PORT BALLINTRAE Antrim **405** M 2 – pop. 586 – ✉ ✆ 026 57 Bushmills.

🏌 Portballintrae, Bushmills ✆ 31317, N : 1 m.

🛈 Beach Rd ✆ 31672 (summer only).

◆Belfast 68 – Coleraine 15.

🏨 **Bayview**, 2 Bayhead Rd, BT57 8RZ, ✆ 31453, ≼ – 📺 ➜wc 🕿 🅿. 🅰 𝖵𝖨𝖲𝖠. ❄
M (closed Sunday dinner) 6.40 **st.** and a la carte 🍴 2.00 – **16 rm** ⚎ 21.00/35.00 **st.** –
SB 50.00 **st.**

PORTRUSH Antrim **405** L 2 – pop. 5 114 – ✆ 0265.

🏌, 🏌, 🏌 Royal Portrush, Dunluce Rd, ✆ 822311.

🛈 Town Hall ✆ 823333.

✗✗ **Ramore,** The Harbour, BT56 8BN, ✆ 824313 – 🅿
closed Sunday, Monday and 2 weeks January-February – **M** (booking essential)(dinner only) a
la carte 10.30/15.15 **t.** 🍴 3.00.

PORTSTEWART Londonderry **405** L 2 – pop. 5 312 – ✆ 026 583.

🏌, 🏌 117 Strand Head ✆ 2015, West boundary.

🛈 Town Hall, The Crescent ✆ 2286.

◆Belfast 67 – Coleraine 6.

🏨 **Edgewater**, 88 Strand Rd, BT55 7LZ, ✆ 3314, ≼ – 📺 ➜wc ♒wc 🕿 🅿. 🅰 ⓪ 𝖵𝖨𝖲𝖠. ❄
M 5.50/6.95 **t.** and a la carte 🍴 2.95 – **28 rm** ⚎ 19.50/33.00 **t.** – SB 45.00/60.00 **st.**

SEAFORDE Down **405** O 5 – ✉ Downpatrick – ✆ 0396 87.

◆Belfast 22 – Downpatrick 7 – Newcastle 8.

✗✗ **Nutgrove** ⤳ with rm, Nutgrove Rd, Annadorn, BT30 8QN, E : 3 m. by Seaforde road and
Drumgooland road ✆ 275, « Country house atmosphere », 🌳 – ➜wc 🅿
closed Sunday, Monday and December-March – **M** (unlicensed)(booking essential)(dinner
only) 15.00 **t.** – **2 rm** ⚎ 25.00/40.00 **t.**

STRABANE Tyrone **405** J 3 – pop. 10 340 – ✆ 0504.

🏌 Ballycolman ✆ 882271.

🛈 Lifford Rd ✆ 883735 (summer only).

◆Belfast 87 – Donegal 34 – ◆Dublin 98 – ◆Londonderry 14.

🏨 **Fir Trees**, Melmount Rd, BT82 9JT, ✆ 883003 – 📺 ➜wc ⊛ 🅿. 🅰 🅴 ⓪ 𝖵𝖨𝖲𝖠. ❄
M 7.00/8.95 **st.** and a la carte 🍴 3.50 – **26 rm** ⚎ 22.00/32.00 **st.** – SB (weekends only)
50.00 **st.**

AUSTIN-ROVER   4 Derry Rd ✆ 882334

FORD   132 Melmont Rd ✆ 06626 (Sion Mills) 58275

WARINGSTOWN Armagh **405** N 4 – ✉ ✆ 0762.

◆Belfast 26 – Craigavon 4.

✗✗ Grange, Main St., ✆ 881989, 🌳 – 🅿.

GREEN TOURIST GUIDES

Picturesque scenery, buildings

Attractive routes

Touring programmes

Plans of towns and buildings.

Channel

Islands

Place with at least :		La località possiede come minimo :	
one hotel or restaurant	● Herm	una risorsa alberghiera	● Herm
one pleasant hotel	🏠, ✗ with rm	un albergo ameno	🏠, ✗ with rm
one quiet, secluded hotel	ॐ	un albergo molto tranquillo, isolato	ॐ
one restaurant with	✿,✿✿,✿✿✿, M	un'ottima tavola con	✿,✿✿,✿✿✿, M
See this town for establishments located in its vicinity	GOREY	La località raggruppa nel suo testo le risorse dei dintorni	GOREY

Localité offrant au moins :		Ort mit mindestens :	
une ressource hôtelière	● Herm	einem Hotel oder Restaurant	● Herm
un hôtel agréable	🏠, ✗ with rm	einem angenehmen Hotel	🏠, ✗ with rm
un hôtel très tranquille, isolé	ॐ	einem sehr ruhigen und abgelegenen Hotel	ॐ
une bonne table à	✿,✿✿,✿✿✿, M	einem Restaurant mit	✿,✿✿,✿✿✿, M
Localité groupant dans le texte les ressources de ses environs	GOREY	Ort mit Angaben über Hotels und Restaurants in seiner Umgebung	GOREY

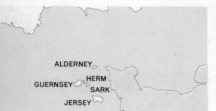

Towns

ALDERNEY **408** Q 33 and **230** ⑨ – pop. 2 068 – ECD : Wednesday – ✿ 048 182.
See : Telegraph Bay★ (cliffs★) – Clonque Bay★ – Braye Bay★.
✈ ⌀ 2711 - Booking Office : Aurigny Air Services ⌀ 2889 Air Ferries ⌀ 2993.

⛴ Shipping connections with the Continent : to France (Saint-Malo) (via Guernsey, Sark and Jersey)(Condor : hydrofoil) summer only – to Torquay (Torbay Seaways : hydrofoil) summer only – to Jersey (St. Helier) (Condor : hydrofoil) 3 weekly summer only (2 h 30 mn) – to Guernsey (St. Peter Port) (Condor : hydrofoil) summer only 3 weekly (45 mn) – to Sark (Condor : hydrofoil) summer only 2 weekly (1 h 30 mn).

🛈 States Office ⌀ 2994.

    St. Anne – ✉ St. Anne – ✿ 048 182 Alderney.
    🛅 ⌀ 2835, E : 1 m.

🏠 Chez André, Victoria St., ⌀ 2777 – 🛁wc. 🎇
   14 rm.

🏠 **Inchalla** 🍴, Le Val, ⌀ 3220, 🌮 – 📺 🛁wc 🅿. 🅰🅴 𝘝𝘐𝘚𝘈. 🎇
   M *(closed Sunday dinner)* (dinner only and Sunday lunch)/dinner 8.50 and a la carte ⬧ 1.70 – ⌇ 2.50 – **11 rm** 14.40/36.30 – SB (October-May) 89.00/98.00 **s.**

XX **Nellie Gray's**, Victoria St., ⌀ 3333 – 🅰🅴 ⓪ 𝘝𝘐𝘚𝘈
   April-October – **M** *(closed Sunday lunch)* (buffet lunch)/dinner a la carte 7.25/13.00 ⬧ 2.40.

X **Georgian House** with rm, Victoria St., ⌀ 2471 – 📺 🛁wc. 🅰🅴 ⓪ 𝘝𝘐𝘚𝘈 🎇
   M a la carte 8.00/14.75 ⬧ 1.95 – **4 rm** ⌇ 16.50/40.00 – SB (October-March) 56.00 **s.**

    Braye – ✉ Braye – ✿ 048 182 Alderney.

X **First and Last**, ⌀ 3162, ≼ Harbour – 🅰🅴 ⓪ 𝘝𝘐𝘚𝘈
   closed Monday – **M** a la carte 11.00/14.50 ⬧ 2.25.

GUERNSEY **408** OP 33 and **230** ⑨ ⑩ – pop. 53 637 – ✿ 0481.
See : Icart Point ≼★★★ – Cobo Bay★★ – Fort Pézéries ≼★★ – Fort Doyle ≼★ – Fort Saumarez ≼★ – Moulin Huet Bay★ – Rocquaine Bay★ – Moye Point (Le Gouffre★).
✈ La Villiaze, Forest ⌀ 37766.

⛴ Shipping connections with the Continent : to France (Saint-Malo) (Condor Shipping Co.) cars only (passengers travel by hydrofoil) summer only – to France (Saint-Malo) (Emeraude Ferries) - to France (Cherbourg)(Sealink) – to Portsmouth (via Jersey)(Sealink) 6-7 weekly (12 h 30 mn) – to Weymouth (Sealink) summer 1-3 daily : winter 6 weekly (4 h 30 mn and 9 h via Jersey) – to Jersey (St. Helier) (Sealink) 1-2 daily (2 h) – to Portsmouth (Channel Island Ferries) 6-7 weekly (10 h).

⛴ Shipping connections with the Continent : to France (Saint-Malo) (Condor : hydrofoil) summer only – to France (Carteret and Cherbourg) (Service Maritime) summer only – to Jersey (St. Helier) (Condor : hydrofoil) 1-4 daily in summer (1 h) – to Alderney (Condor : hydrofoil) summer only 3 weekly (45 mn) – to Herm by Herm Seaway, 7 daily (25 mn), by Trident 8 daily, (1 h) – to Sark (Isle of Sark Shipping Co.) 1-6 daily (40 mn) – to Torquay (Torbay Seaways : hydrofoil) summer only.

🛈 Crown Pier, St. Peter Port ⌀ 23552 – The Airport, La Villiaze ⌀ 37267.

    L'Ancresse – ✿ 0481 Guernsey.
    🛅 ⌀ 45070.

🏠 **Lynton** 🍴, Hacse Lane, ⌀ 45418, 🌮 – 🛁wc 🍴wc 🅿. 𝘝𝘐𝘚𝘈. 🎇
   May-September – **14 rm** ⌇ 17.00/40.00.

    Fermain Bay – ✉ St. Peter Port – ✿ 0481 Guernsey.

🏨 **La Favorita** 🍴, Fermain Lane, ⌀ 35666, 🌮 – 📺 🛁wc 🕿 🅿. 𝘝𝘐𝘚𝘈. 🎇
   March-November – **M** (bar lunch)/dinner 6.00 **s.** and a la carte ⬧ 1.70 – **30 rm** ⌇ 15.00/45.00 **s.** – SB (except summer) 60.00/70.00 **s.**

🏨 **Le Chalet** 🍴, Fermain Lane, ✉ St. Martin, ⌀ 35716, ≼ – 📺 🛁wc 🍴wc 🕿 🅿. 🅰🅴 ⓪ 𝘝𝘐𝘚𝘈
   21 April-19 October – **M** 6.00/7.75 **s.** and a la carte ⬧ 1.75 – **50 rm** ⌇ 18.70/39.40 **s.** – SB (except summer) 40.00/50.00 **s.**

Pembroke Bay – ✉ Vale – ☎ 0481 Guernsey.

St. Peter Port 5.

Pembroke 🐎, ☎ 47573 – TV ⛆wc ☎ P. AE VISA. ✂
M 5.50/7.50 and a la carte 🍷 2.10 – ☕ 3.00 – **14 rm** 19.50/39.00.

St. Martin – pop. 5 842 – ECD : Thursday – ✉ St. Martin – ☎ 0481 Guernsey.

See : Church★ 11C.

St. Peter Port 2.

Green Acres 🐎, Les Hubits, ☎ 35711, 🏊 heated, 🌳 – ▤ rest TV 🛁wc ☎ P. VISA ✂
M (bar lunch)/dinner 7.00 and a la carte 🍷 2.20 – **48 rm** ☕ 32.50/54.00.

Bella Luce, La Fosse, Moulin Huet, ☎ 38764, 🏊 heated, 🌳 – TV 🛁wc ⛆wc P
closed 3 weeks January-February – **M** (bar lunch Monday to Saturday)/dinner 8.50 and a la carte 🍷 2.15 – **31 rm** ☕ 17.00/55.00.

La Trelade, Forest Rd, ☎ 35454, 🏊 heated – 🛗 TV 🛁wc ☎ P. VISA
M (bar lunch)/dinner 7.00 and a la carte 🍷 2.00 – **45 rm** ☕ 14.50/50.00 – SB (November-March) 50.00 **s.**

Windmill, Rue Poudreuse, ☎ 37402, 🏊 heated, 🌳 – TV 🛁wc ⛆wc P. ✂
April-October – **M** 7.00 **s.** 🍷 1.90 – **18 rm** ☕ 19.00/40.00.

La Cloche 🐎, Les Traudes, ☎ 35421, 🏊 heated, 🌳 – TV 🛁wc ⛆wc ☎ P. ✂
March-October – **M** (lunch residents only)/dinner 8.50 🍷 1.90 – **10 rm** ☕ 20.00/46.00.

Wellesley, Sausmarez Rd, ☎ 38028, 🌳 – 🛁wc ⛆wc P. ✂
April-October – **9 rm** ☕ 16.00/32.00.

AUSTIN-ROVER, JAGUAR Ville au Roi ☎ 37661
MAZDA, YUGO Forest Rd ☎ 35753
VOLVO St. Andrews Rd, Bailiffs Cross, St. Martin ☎ 37641

St. Peter Port – pop. 15 587 – ECD : Thursday – ✉ St. Peter Port – ☎ 0481 Guernsey.

See : St. Peter's Church★ 14C Z – **Castle Cornet★ (✻★)** *AC* Z – **Hauteville House (Victor Hugo Museum★ : 5 pearl-embroidered tapestries★★)** *AC* Z – **Victoria Tower : top ✻★★, 100 steps** Y.

Envir. : Les Vauxbelets (Little Chapel★) SW : 2 ½ m. by Mount Durand Z – **Saumarez Park★ W : 2 ½ m. by Grange Rd** Z – **Vale (castle ≤ ★) NW : 4 ½ m. by St. Georges Esplanade** Y.

ℹ Crown Pier ☎ 23552.

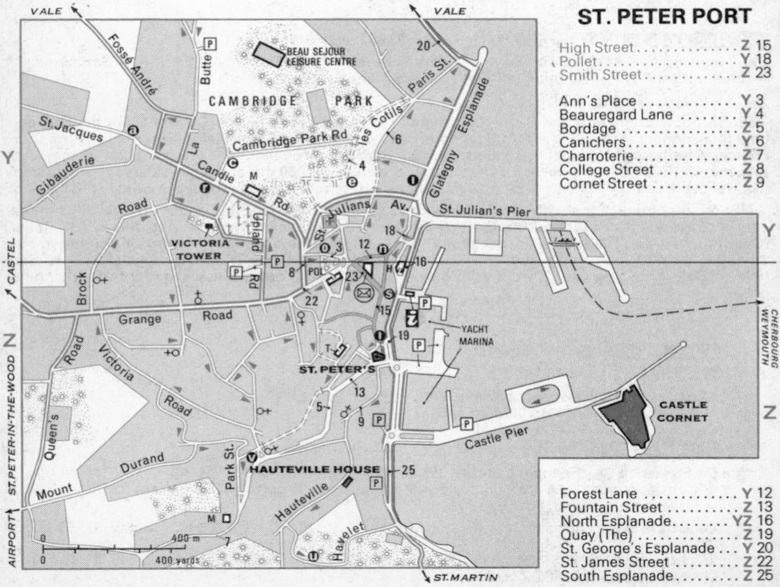

ST. PETER PORT

High Street .... Z 15
Pollet .... Y 18
Smith Street .... Z 23

Ann's Place .... Y 3
Beauregard Lane .... Y 4
Bordage .... Z 5
Canichers .... Y 6
Charroterie .... Z 7
College Street .... Z 8
Cornet Street .... Z 9

Forest Lane .... Y 12
Fountain Street .... Z 13
North Esplanade .... YZ 16
Quay (The) .... Z 19
St. George's Esplanade .... Y 20
St. James Street .... Z 22
South Esplanade .... Z 25

🏨 **St. Pierre Park,** Rohais, by Grange Rd, ℰ 28282, Telex 4191662, ≤, ⬚, ⓕ, ⇔, park, ⸸ – ▤ 📺 ☎ ⅃ ⓟ ⌸ ☒ ⅍ ⓞ 𝘝𝘐𝘚𝘈 ⸸
M a la carte lunch/dinner 11.00 ⓙ 2.25 (see also rest. **Victor Hugo**) – **131 rm** ☱ 32.00/39.25 **s.**, **3 suites** 104.00/118.50 **s.**

🏨 **Duke of Richmond,** Cambridge Park, ℰ 26221, Telex 4191462, ⅃ heated – ▤ ▤ rest 📺 ☎ ⌸ ☒ ⅍ ⓞ 𝘝𝘐𝘚𝘈
M 6.00/9.00 and a la carte ⓙ 2.00 – **74 rm** ☱ 27.50/65.00, **1 suite** 45.00/90.00 – SB (except summer)(weekends only) 50.00/60.00 **s.**

🏨 **Old Government House,** St. Ann's Pl., ℰ 24921, Telex 4191144, ⅃ heated, ⇔ – ▤ 📺 ☎ ⌸ ☒ ⅍ ⓞ 𝘝𝘐𝘚𝘈
M 6.00/8.25 and a la carte ⓙ 2.20 – **73 rm** ☱ 25.00/87.00.

🏨 **Royal,** Glategny Esplanade, ℰ 23921, Telex 4191221, ≤, ⅃ heated, ⇔ – ▤ 📺 ☎ ⓟ ⌸ ☒ ⅍ ⓞ 𝘝𝘐𝘚𝘈 ⸸
M 6.00/7.00 ⓙ 2.00 – **78 rm**.

🏨 **La Collinette,** St. Jacques, ℰ 71033, ⅃ heated, ⇔ – 📺 ⌸wc ☎ ⓟ ☒ ⅍ ⓞ 𝘝𝘐𝘚𝘈 ⸸
M 5.00/6.50 and a la carte ⓙ 2.25 – **22 rm** ☱ 15.00/56.00 **s.**

🏨 **Les Rocquettes,** Les Gravées, ℰ 22146 – 📺 ⌸wc ☎ ⓟ ☒ ⅍ ⓞ 𝘝𝘐𝘚𝘈
closed 20 December-6 January – **M** (bar lunch)/dinner 7.00 **s.** and a la carte 4.50/8.80 **s.** ⓙ 1.80 – **26 rm** ☱ 11.50/40.00 **s.**

🏨 **De Havelet,** Havelet, ℰ 22199, ⇔ – 📺 ⌸wc ☎ ⓟ ☒ ⅍ ⓞ 𝘝𝘐𝘚𝘈
M 6.00/8.00 **s.** and a la carte ⓙ 2.60 – **31 rm** ☱ 23.00/56.50 **s.**

🏨 **Dunchoille,** Guelles Rd, ℰ 22912, ⅃ heated, ⇔ – ⌸wc ▥wc ⓟ ⸸
M (closed Monday to Thursday in winter to non residents) (bar lunch) Monday to Saturday)/dinner 10.00 **s.** and a la carte ⓙ 1.75 – **24 rm** ☱ 13.50/44.00 **s.** – SB (except summer) 30.00/44.00 **s.**

🏨 **Moore's Central,** Le Pollet, ℰ 24452 – ▤ 📺 ⌸wc ☎ ☒ ⅍ ⓞ 𝘝𝘐𝘚𝘈
M a la carte lunch/dinner 6.75 **s.** ⓙ 1.60 – **40 rm** ☱ 15.50/41.00 **s.** – SB 37.00/50.00 **s.**

🏠 **Midhurst House,** Candie Rd, ℰ 24391, ⇔ – 📺 ⌸wc ▥wc ⸸
March-October – **8 rm** ☱ 16.00/32.00 **s.**

XXXX **Victor Hugo** (at St. Pierre Park H.), Rohais, by Grange Rd, ℰ 28282, Telex 4191662 – ⓟ ☒ ⅍ ⓞ 𝘝𝘐𝘚𝘈
closed Saturday lunch and Sunday dinner – **M** 6.50 (lunch) and a la carte 10.45/12.45 ⓙ 2.25.

XXX **La Frégate** ⇘ with rm, Les Côtils, ℰ 24624, ≤ town and harbour, « Country house atmosphere », ⇔ – ▤ rest ⌸wc ☎ ⓟ ☒ ⅍ ⓞ 𝘝𝘐𝘚𝘈
M 7.50/11.50 **s.** and a la carte 8.65/18.00 **s.** ⓙ 2.50 – ☱ 5.00 – **13 rm** 25.00/65.00 **s.**

XX **Le Nautique,** Quay Steps, ℰ 21714, ≤ – ☒ ⅍ ⓞ 𝘝𝘐𝘚𝘈
closed Sunday and first 3 weeks January – **M** a la carte 8.00/11.80 ⓙ 2.30.

XX **La Piazza,** Trinity Sq., ℰ 25085 – ☒ ⅍ 𝘝𝘐𝘚𝘈
closed Sunday and 20 December-20 January – **M** a la carte 7.00/11.50 ⓙ 2.40.

XX **Steak and Stilton,** 23 The Quay, ℰ 23080 – ☒ ⅍ ⓞ 𝘝𝘐𝘚𝘈
closed 5 January-1 February – **M** a la carte 9.85/14.50 **s.** ⓙ 2.65.

ASTON-MARTIN, LANCIA, NISSAN, PEUGEOT-TALBOT, ROLLS ROYCE Rue du Pré ℰ 24261
BMW, MERCEDES-BENZ 16 Glategny Esplanade ℰ 23916
FORD Les Banques ℰ 24774
HONDA Doyle Rd ℰ 24025
RENAULT Upland Rd ℰ 26846

St. Saviour – pop. 2 432 – ✉ St. Saviour – ☎ 0481 Guernsey.
St. Peter Port 4.

🏨 **L'Atlantique,** Perelle Bay, ℰ 64056, ≤, ⅃ heated, ⇔ – 📺 ⌸wc ☎ ⓟ ☒ ⅍ ⓞ 𝘝𝘐𝘚𝘈 ⸸
M (bar lunch)/dinner 7.25 and a la carte ⓙ 2.20 – **21 rm** ☱ 13.50/46.00.

🏨 **La Hougue Fouque Farm,** Route-des-Bas-Courtil, ℰ 64181, ⅃ heated – 📺 ⌸wc ▥wc ☎ ⓟ ☒ 𝘝𝘐𝘚𝘈 ⸸
M 5.75/8.25 and a la carte ⓙ 1.90 – **16 rm** ☱ 30.00/70.00.

🏨 **La Girouette Country House** ⇘, ℰ 63269, ⇔ – 📺 ⌸wc ▥wc ☎ ⓟ ☒ ⅍ 𝘝𝘐𝘚𝘈 ⸸
Mid March-October – **M** (dinner only and Sunday lunch) 6.00/6.50 ⓙ 2.00 – **14 rm** ☱ 14.00/48.50.

Vazon Bay – ✉ Vazon Bay – ☎ 0481 Guernsey

🏨 **Les Embruns,** Route de la Margion, Castel, ℰ 64834, ⅃ heated, ⇔ – 📺 ⌸wc ⓟ
May-September – **M** (dinner only) 8.00 ⓙ 2.00 – **16 rm** ☱ 22.00/44.00.

HERM ISLAND 408 P 33 and 230 ⑩ – pop. 37 – ☎ 0481 Guernsey.
⇔ to Guernsey by Herm Seaway, 6 daily (25 mn) by Trident 8 daily (1 h).
🛈 Administrative Office ℰ 22377.

Herm – ✉ Herm – ☎ 0481 Guernsey.

🏨 **White House** ⇘, ℰ 22159, ≤, ⅃, ⇔, park, ⸸ – ⌸wc ☒ 𝘝𝘐𝘚𝘈 ⸸
April-October – **M** 5.95/7.95 and a la carte ⓙ 2.50 – **30 rm** ☱ (dinner included) 34.00/76.00.

JERSEY **403** OP 33 and **230** ⑪ – pop. 72 970 – ✪ 0534.

See : Devil's Hole★ (site★★) *AC* private access, ¾ h Rtn on foot by a steep road – Grosnez Castle ≼★ – La Hougue Bie Tumulus★ (prehistoric tomb) *AC* – St. Catherine's Bay★ – Fliquet Bay (St. Catherine's Breakwater ≼★★) – Sorel Point ≼★ – Noirmont Point ≼★ – Jersey zoo (site★) *AC*.

✈ States of Jersey Airport ℰ 46111, Telex 4192332.

🚢 Shipping connections with the Continent : to France (Saint-Malo) (Emeraude Ferries) - to France (Cherbourg)(Sealink) – to France (Saint-Malo) (Condor Shipping Co.) cars only (passengers travel by hydrofoil) summer only – to Portsmouth (Sealink) 6-7 weekly (9 h 30 mn) – to Weymouth (Sealink) 1 daily (6 h 45 mn) – to Guernsey (St. Peter Port) (Sealink) 6-7 weekly (2 h 45 mn) – to Portsmouth (Channel Island Ferries) 6-7 weekly (7 h 45 mn).

🚤 Shipping connections with the Continent : to France (Saint-Malo) (Condor : hydrofoil) (Vedettes Blanches, summer only) (Vedettes Armoricaines) – to France (Granville) (Vedettes Armoricaines and Vedettes Vertes Granvillaises) - from Gorey to France (Carteret) (Service Maritime Carteret and Vedettes Blanches et Verts) – from Gorey to France (Portbail) (Service Maritime Carteret) – to Sark (Condor : hydrofoil) summer only Monday/Saturday 1-2 daily (45 mn-1 h 30 mn) – to Guernsey (St. Peter Port) (Condor : hydrofoil) 1-4 daily in summer (1 h) – to Alderney (Condor : hydrofoil) summer 3 weekly (2 h 5 mn) – to Torquay (Torbay Seaways : hydrofoil) summer only.

🛈 Weighbridge, St. Helier ℰ 78000 and 24779.

Bonne Nuit Bay – ✉ St. John – ✪ 0534 Jersey.
St. Helier 6.

🏨 Cheval Roc ⌕, ℰ 62865, ≼ Bonne Nuit Bay, ⊿ heated – 🛏wc 🅿
45 rm.

🏨 **Bonne Nuit,** ℰ 61644, ≼ Bonne Nuit Bay, 🍴 – 🛏wc 🛏wc 🕾 🅿 🔃 🆎 ⑩ *VISA* ✵
April-19 October – **M** (seafood) 6.00 and a la carte 8.20/16.20 ⓖ 1.95 – **30 rm** ⥂ 12.50/60.00 **s.**

Bouley Bay – ✉ Trinity – ✪ 0534 Jersey.
St. Helier 5.

🏨 **Water's Edge** ⌕, ℰ 62777, Group Telex 4191462, ≼ Bouley Bay, ⊿ heated, 🍴 – 🛗 📺 🛏wc 🅿 🔃 🆎 ⑩ *VISA*
Mid April-mid October – **M** 8.80/14.00 **s.** and a la carte ⓖ 2.50 – **56 rm** ⥂ 32.00/117.00.

Corbiere – ✉ St. Brelade – ✪ 0534 Jersey.
St. Helier 8.

✕✕ Sea Crest, with rm, Petit Port, ℰ 42687, ≼, ⊿ heated, 🍴 – 📺 🛏wc 🕾 🅿 ✵
7 rm.

Gorey – ✉ St. Martin – ✪ 0534 Jersey.
See : Mont Orgueil Castle★ (≼★★, paintings★) *AC*.
St. Helier 4.

🏨 **Old Court House,** Gorey Village, ℰ 54444, Telex 4192032, ⊿ heated, 🍴 – 🛗 📺 🛏wc 🕾 🅿 🔃 🆎 ⑩ *VISA* ✵
April-October – **M** 4.50/7.50 **s.** and a la carte ⓖ 2.00 – **58 rm** ⥂ 20.50/70.00.

🏠 **Trafalgar Bay,** Gorey Village, ℰ 53216, Telex 4192349, ⊿ heated, 🍴 – 🛏wc 🅿 🔃 *VISA* ✵
June-September – **M** (bar lunch)/dinner 6.00 ⓖ 2.00 – **35 rm** ⥂ 15.95/37.90.

at Gorey Pier – ✉ St. Martin – ✪ 0534 Jersey :

🏠 **Moorings,** ℰ 53633 – ▤ rest 📺 🛏wc 🛏wc 🕾 🔃 *VISA*
M a la carte 8.75/18.50 **s.** ⓖ 2.50 – **17 rm** ⥂ 23.00/70.00 **s.**

🏠 Seascale, ℰ 54395 – 🛏wc 🛏wc 🕾 🔃 *VISA* ✵
M 4.00/9.00 – **9 rm**.

🏠 **Dolphin,** ℰ 53370 – 📺 🛏wc 🕾 🔃 *VISA*
March-October – **M** 6.00/9.00 **s.** and a la carte ⓖ 2.20 – **17 rm** ⥂ 17.00/42.00 **s.**

La Haule – ✉ St. Brelade – ✪ 0534 Jersey.
St. Helier 5.

🏨 **La Place** ⌕, Route du Coin, by B 25 on B 43 ℰ 44261, Telex 4191462, ⊿ heated – 📺 🅿 🔃 🆎 ⑩ *VISA* ✵
M 7.00/7.50 and a la carte ⓖ 2.50 – **40 rm** ⥂ 22.50/40.00 – SB (November-March except Christmas and New Year) 45.00 **s.**

Portelet Bay – ✉ St. Brelade – ✪ 0534 Jersey.
St. Helier 5.

🏨 **Portelet** ⌕, Route de Vortelet, ℰ 41204, Telex 4192039, ≼, ⊿ heated, 🍴, ✵ – 📺 🅿 🔃 🆎 ⑩ *VISA* ✵
May-11 October – **M** 9.50 – **86 rm** ⥂ 27.00/73.00 **s.**

La Pulente – ⊠ St. Brelade – ☎ 0534 Jersey.
St. Helier 7.

Atlantic ♨, La Moye, ☞ 44101, Telex 4192405, ≤, ⌁ heated, ≈, ℅ – ◨ ⊡ ☎ ❷, ⚒, ⛰
AE ⓪ VISA ⅍
closed January-7 March – **M** 7.50/11.50 and a la carte – **46 rm** ⊊ 38.00/98.00 **s.**

Rozel Bay – ⊠ St. Martin – ☎ 0534 Jersey.
St. Helier 6.

Le Couperon de Rozel, ☞ 62190, ⌁ heated – ⇔wc ❷. ⛰ AE ⓪ VISA ⅍
15 April-mid October – **M** 6.00/10.50 and a la carte ⅃ 2.20 – **32 rm** ⊊ 18.00/70.00 **s.**

St. Aubin – ⊠ St. Aubin – ☎ 0534 Jersey.
St. Helier 4.

Lat Our, High St., ☞ 43770 – ⊡ ⇔wc ⋔wc ❷. ⛰ AE VISA ⅍
closed 1 January-2 March – **M** (dinner only and Sunday lunch)/dinner 8.50 and a la carte
⅃ 1.75 – **21 rm** ⊊ 13.25/44.00 **s.**

Panorama St. Aubin without rest., High St., ☞ 42429, ≤ – ⊡ ⇔wc ⋔wc ❷. ⛰ AE ⓪
VISA ⅍
Mid March-mid December – **16 rm** ⊊ 17.00/38.00.

Portofino, High St., ☞ 42100, Italian rest. – ⛰ VISA
closed Monday and 25-26 December – **M** 3.90/7.95 and a la carte 8.55/14.15 ⅃ 2.10.

Old Court House Inn with rm, St. Aubin's Harbour, ☞ 46433 – ⊡ ⇔wc ☎. ⛰ VISA ⅍
M a la carte 11.00/17.50 **s.** ⅃ 2.10 – **8 rm** ⊊ 25.00/60.00 **s.**, **1 suite** 70.00/90.00 **s.**

St. Brelade's Bay – pop. 8 566 – ⊠ St. Brelade – ☎ 0534 Jersey.
See : Site★.
St. Helier 6.

L'Horizon, ☞ 43101, Telex 4192281, ≤ St. Brelades Bay, ⊠ – ◨ ⊡ ☎ ⅃ ₺, ⚒. ⛰ AE ⓪
VISA ⅍
M 15.00 (lunch)/dinner a la carte ⅃ 2.05 (see also rest. **Star Grill** below) – **104 rm**
⊊ 35.00/121.00 **s.**, **4 suites** 118.00/145.00 **s.**

St. Brelade's Bay, ☞ 46141, ≤, ⌁ heated, ≈, ℅ – ◨ ⊡ ☎ ❷. ⛰ AE ⓪ VISA ⅍
18 April-October – **M** 6.00/10.50 and a la carte ⅃ 2.00 – **80 rm** ⊊ 27.00/59.00.

Chateau Valeuse, rue de la Valeuse, ☞ 43476, ⌁ heated, ≈ – ⇔wc ⋔wc ❷
26 rm.

Star Grill, (at L'Horizon H.), ☞ 43101, Telex 4192281, ≤ St. Brelades Bay – ❷. ⛰ AE ⓪ VISA
M (closed Monday except Bank Holidays) (booking essential) a la carte 16.30 **s.** ⅃ 2.50.

FORD Airport Rd ☞ 43222   VW-AUDI Airport Rd ☞ 41131
DATSUN La Move ☞ 45546

St. Clement – pop. 6 541 – ⊠ St. Clement – ☎ 0534 Jersey.
St. Helier 2.

Shakespeare, Samares, St. Clement's Coast Rd, ☞ 51915 – ⊡ ⇔wc ☎ ❷. ⛰ AE ⓪ VISA
closed February – **M** (bar lunch)/dinner 9.00 and a la carte ⅃ 2.00 – **32 rm** ⊊ 25.00/50.00 **s.**

Ambassadeur, St. Clement's Coast Rd, ☞ 24455, Group Telex 4192296, ≤, ⌁ heated – ◨
⊡ ⇔wc ☎ ⛰ AE ⓪ VISA
closed January-February – **M** 11.00 and a la carte ⅃ 2.25 – **41 rm** ⊊ 14.00/52.00 **s.**

St. Helier – pop. 29 941 – ECD : Thursday and Saturday – ⊠ St. Helier – ☎ 0534 Jersey.
See : Fort Regent ⋇★★★ (Militia Museum) AC z – Elizabeth Castle ⋇★ AC z – Rocher des
Proscrits (au Havre des Pas) z.
🛈 Weighbridge ☞ 78000 and 24779.

Plan on next page

De la Plage, Havre des Pas, ☞ 23474, Telex 4192328, ≤ – ◨ ⊡ ❷. ⛰ AE ⓪ VISA ⅍   Z **s**
Mid April-October – **M** 7.15/9.35 **s.** and a la carte 13.00/16.00 ⅃ 1.75 – **78 rm** ⊊ 25.00/75.00 **s.**

Beaufort, Green St., ☞ 32471, Telex 4192160, ⊠ – ◨ ⊡ ☎ ❷. ⛰ AE ⓪ VISA ⅍   Z **r**
M (bar lunch)/dinner 7.00 and a la carte ⅃ 1.80 – **54 rm** ⊊ 32.00/86.00 **s.**

Pomme d'Or, The Esplanade, ☞ 78644, Telex 4192309 – ◨ ▤ rest ⊡ ⇔wc ☎. ⚒. ⛰
⓪ VISA ⅍   Z **u**
M (buffet lunch)/dinner 9.00 **s.** and a la carte ⅃ 1.85 – **151 rm** ⊊ 30.95/54.80 **s.** – SB (week-ends only) 43.00/53.00 **s.**

Savoy, Rouge Bouillon, ☞ 27521, ⌁ heated – ◨ ⊡ ⇔wc ⋔wc ☎ ❷. ⛰ ⅍   Y **i**
Easter-October – **M** 5.00/7.00 **s.** and a la carte ⅃ 2.20 – **61 rm** ⊊ 16.00/52.00 **s.**

Apollo, 9 St. Saviour's Rd, ☞ 25441, Telex 4192086 – ◨ ⊡ ⇔wc ☎ ❷. ⛰ AE ⓪ VISA ⅍   Z **e**
M 5.50/7.00 and a la carte ⅃ 1.70 – **53 rm** ⊊ 27.00/55.00.

P.T.O. →

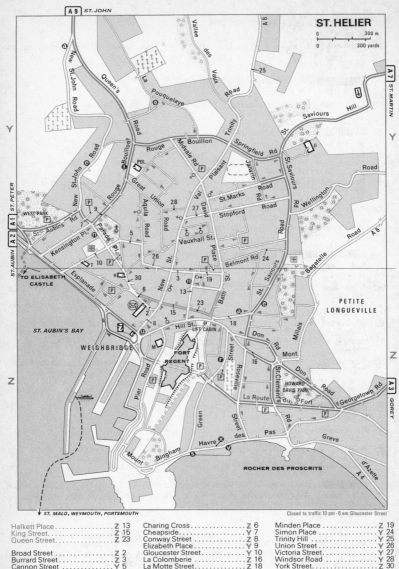

🏠 **Uplands,** St. John's Rd, ℰ 70460, 🏊 heated, 🍴 – 📺 🛏wc 🅿. 🛁　　　　　　**Y** `a`
20 April-20 October – **M** (bar lunch)/dinner 6.00 **s.** ⓘ 1.65 – **28 rm** ⚏ 16.00/32.00 **s.**

🏠 **Mountview,** 46 New St. John's Rd, ℰ 78887, Telex 4192341 – 🚿 📺 🛏wc 🍴wc 🅿. 🖭 VISA　**Y** `e`
Mid March-mid November – **M** a la carte 8.35/12.00 **s.** ⓘ 2.00 – **35 rm** ⚏ 19.00/59.00 **s.**

🏠 Fort d'Auvergne, Havre des Pas, ℰ 73006 – 🚿 🛏wc 🍴wc ☎. VISA　　　　　　　　　**Z** `v`
April-October – **65 rm** ⚏ 12.00/41.00 **s.**

🏠 **Millbrook House** ⚓, Rue de Trachy, W : 1 ¾ m. by A 1 ℰ 33036, 🍴 – 🚿 🛏wc 🍴wc 🅿.　**Y**
🛁 – May-September – **M** (dinner only) 5.00 ⓘ 1.50 – **27 rm** ⚏ 18.00/36.00　　　　by A 1

Closed to traffic 10 pm - 6 am Gloucester Street

↓ ST. MALO, WEYMOUTH, PORTSMOUTH

⌂ **Almorah,** 1 Almorah Cres., La Pouquelaye, ℰ 21648, ⚞ – ⌷wc ℗. ⌘   Y **o**
April-October – **16 rm** ⊡ 13.00/40.00 **s.**

⌂ **Lorraine,** 8 Havre des pas, ℰ 74470 – ⊡ ⍾wc. ◨ 𝘝𝘐𝘚𝘈. ⌘   Z **x**
closed Mid October-January – **9 rm** ⊡ 8.50/25.50 **s.**

XX **La Capannina,** 65-67 Halkett Pl., ℰ 34602, Italian rest. – ◨ AE ① 𝘝𝘐𝘚𝘈   Z **n**
closed Sunday – **M** (booking essential) a la carte 9.90/18.30 **s.**

XX **Mauro's,** 37 La Motte St., ℰ 20147 – ▤. ◨ AE ① 𝘝𝘐𝘚𝘈   Z **a**
closed Sunday, 1 to 21 January and Bank Holidays – **M** 5.50/10.50 and a la carte 9.65/13.80
◊ 1.90.

X La Buca, The Parade, ℰ 34283, Italian rest.   Y **n**

ASTON-MARTIN, ROLLS-ROYCE-BENTLEY, LAND-
ROVER-RANGE-ROVER 33-35 Lamotte St. ℰ 31341
AUSTIN-ROVER Havre des Pas ℰ 33233
CITROEN 50 New St. ℰ 24541

FORD Longueville ℰ 73777
NISSAN 1-2 Victoria St. ℰ 37357
PEUGEOT 17 Esplanade ℰ 33623
TALBOT, LANCIA Victoria St. ℰ 37357

St. Lawrence – pop. 3 845 – ⊠ St. Lawrence – ✆ 0534 Jersey.
See : German Military Underground Hospital★ *AC* Y.
St Helier 3.

🏛 **Little Grove** ⌂, Rue de Haut, by A 11 ℰ 25321, ⌇ heated, ⚞ – ⊡ ☎ ℗. ◨ AE ① 𝘝𝘐𝘚𝘈.
⌘
M 8.50/15.00 and a la carte ◊ 2.10 – **13 rm** ⊡ 59.50/79.00 **s., 2 suites** 103.00/127.00 **s.**

St. Martin – pop. 3 095 – ⊠ St. Martin – ✆ 0534 Jersey.
St. Helier 4.

🏠 **Le Relais de St. Martin,** ℰ 53271, ⌇, ⚞ – ⌷wc ⍾wc ℗. ⌘
April-October – **M** (dinner only) 7.00 – **12 rm** ⊡ 12.00/20.00 **s.**

St. Peter – pop. 3 713 – ⊠ St. Peter – ✆ 0534 Jersey.
Envir. : St. Ouen Manor★ *AC*, NW : 2 m.
St. Helier 5.

🏛 **Mermaid,** Airport Rd, on B 36, ℰ 41255, Telex 4192249, ≼, ⌇ heated, ⚞ – ⊡ ☎ ℗. 🎾
68 rm.

🏛 **Greenhill Country,** Coin Varin, Mont de l'Ecole, on C 112 ℰ 81042, Telex 4192249, ⌇ heated
– ⊡ ⌷wc ⍾wc ℗. ◨ AE ① 𝘝𝘐𝘚𝘈. ⌘
closed mid December-mid February – **M** 4.50/8.00 and a la carte ◊ 1.60 – **18 rm** ⊡ 30.00/82.00.

St. Saviour – pop. 10 910 – ECD : Thursday – ⊠ St. Saviour – ✆ 0534 Jersey.
St. Helier 1.

🏛 **Longueville Manor,** Longueville Rd, on A 3 ℰ 25501, Telex 4192306, ⌇ heated, ⚞, park –
🍴 ▤ rest ⊡ ☎ ℗. ◨ AE ① 𝘝𝘐𝘚𝘈
M 14.50/16.00 and a la carte ◊ 2.25 – **33 rm** ⊡ 44.00/85.00 **s., 1 suite** 145.00/165.00 **s.** –
SB (winter weekends only) 78.00 **s.**

PORSCHE Five Oaks ℰ 26156
RENAULT Bagot Rd ℰ 36471

FIAT, MAZDA Belroyal Corner ℰ 22556

SARK 🄃🄀🄃 P 33 and 🄃🄉🄀 – pop. 560 – ✆ 048 183.
See : La Coupée★★★ (isthmus) – Port du Moulin★★ – Creux Harbour★ – Happy Valley★ – Little
Sark★ – La Seigneurie★ (manor 18C, Residence of the Seigneur of Sark).

⚓ Shipping connections with the Continent : to France (Saint-Malo) (Condor : hydrofoil) summer
only – to Jersey (St. Helier) (Condor : hydrofoil) summer Monday/Saturday 1-2 daily (1 h 15 mn-2 h)
– to Guernsey (St. Peter Port) (Isle of Sark Shipping Co.) 1-8 daily (40 mn) – to Alderney (Condor :
hydrofoil) summer only 2 weekly (1 h 45 mn).

🛈 ℰ 2345.

🏠 **Petit Champ** ⌂, ℰ 2046, ≼ coast, Herm, Jetou and Guernsey, « Country house atmosphere », ⌇ heated, ⚞ – ⌷wc ⍾wc. ◨ AE ① 𝘝𝘐𝘚𝘈. ⌘
Easter-mid October – **M** (booking essential to non-residents) 7.00/9.45 **s.** ◊ 2.00 – **16 rm**
⊡ 16.50/20.00 **s.**

🏠 **Stocks** ⌂, ℰ 2001, ⌇, ⚞ – ⍾wc. AE 𝘝𝘐𝘚𝘈
16 April-7 October – **M** 10.00/12.50 **s.** and a la carte ◊ 2.30 – **23 rm** ⊡ 21.00/55.00 **s.**

XX **Aval du Creux** with rm, Harbour Hill, ℰ 2036, ⚞ – ⊡ ⍾wc. ◨ AE 𝘝𝘐𝘚𝘈
Easter-October – **M** (booking essential) 9.50 (dinner) and a la carte 12.55/16.20 – **13 rm**
⊡ 26.00/52.00.

Michelin road map of GREECE (scale 1:700 000), no 🄈🄈🄀.

Isle
of Man

Place with at least :

one hotel or restaurant ● Douglas
one pleasant hotel 🏨, ✕ with rm
one quiet, secluded hotel 🐦
one restaurant with ❀, ❀❀, ❀❀❀, M
See this town for establishments located in its vicinity

Localité offrant au moins :

une ressource hôtelière ● Douglas
un hôtel agréable 🏨, ✕ with rm
un hôtel très tranquille, isolé 🐦
une bonne table à ❀, ❀❀, ❀❀❀, M
Localité groupant dans le texte les ressources de ses environs

La località possiede come minimo :

una risorsa alberghiera ● Douglas
un albergo ameno 🏨, ✕ with rm
un albergo molto tranquillo, isolato 🐦
un'ottima tavola con ❀, ❀❀, ❀❀❀, M
La località raggruppa nel suo testo le risorse dei dintorni

Ort mit mindestens :

einem Hotel oder Restaurant ● Douglas
einem angenehmen Hotel 🏨, ✕ with rm
einem sehr ruhigen und abgelegenen Hotel 🐦
einem Restaurant mit ❀, ❀❀, ❀❀❀, M
Ort mit Angaben über Hotels und Restaurants in seiner Umgebung

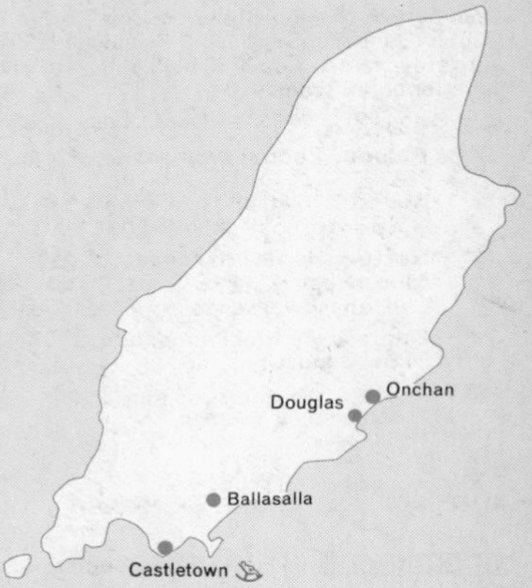

ISLE OF MAN

Towns

BALLASALLA 402 G 21 – ☎ 0624.
Douglas 8.

✕✕ **La Rosette,** Main Rd, ✆ 822940
closed Monday lunch and Sunday – **M** a la carte 6.70/21.05 **t.** 🍷 4.80.

CASTLETOWN 402 G 21 – pop. 3 141 – ECD : Thursday – ☎ 0624.
See : Rushen Castle★★ (13C) *AC* : Keep ☀★ – Port Erin (site★) W : 4 ½ m.
⛳18 Fort Island ✆ 822201, E : 2 m.
ℹ Commissioner's Office, Parliament Sq. ✆ 823518.
Douglas 10.

🏨 Castletown Golf Links 🐦, Fort Island, E : 2 m. ✆ 822201, Telex 627636, ≤ sea and golf links, 🏊 heated, ⛳18, 🎾 – 🛁wc 🚿wc ☎ 🅿 – **65 rm**.

✕ **Bunters,** Parliament Sq., ✆ 824000
closed Sunday – **M** (dinner only) 12.00 **t.** and a la carte 11.15/14.20 **t.** 🍷 3.00.

DOUGLAS **402** G 21 – pop. 19 944 – ECD : Thursday – ☼ 0624.

See : Manx Museum★★ – The Promenades★ – A 18 Road★★ From Douglas to Ramsey.

Envir. : Snaefell ☀★★★ (by electric railway from Laxey) *AC*, NE : 7 m. – Laxey (waterwheel★ : Lady Isabella) NE : 6 m. – St. John's (Tynwald Hill) NW : 8 m. – Peel : Castle★ (ruins 13C-16C) *AC*, NW : 11 ½ m.

🏌 Pulrose Park ✆ 5952, 1 m. from Douglas Pier – 🏌 Howstrake at Onchan ✆ 24299, N : 1 m.

✈ Ronaldsway Airport, ✆ 0624 (Castletown) 823311, SW : 7 m. – **Terminal :** Coach service from Lord St.

⛴ by Isle of Man Steam Packet Co : to Belfast : June-September 1-2 weekly (4 h 30 mn) – to Dublin : June-September 1-3 weekly (4 h 30 mn) – to Fleetwood : July-August, 2 weekly (3 h 15 mn) – to Heysham 1-3 daily (3 h 45 mn) – to Liverpool : summer only 1-2 weekly (3 h) – to Stranraer : summer only 1 weekly (6 h).

🛈 13 Victoria St. ✆ 74323 – Public Library, 10 Elm Tree Rd at Onchan ✆ 22311.

 🏨 **Palace,** Central Promenade, ✆ 74521, Telex 627742, ≼, ⃕, – ▐ TV ⌷wc ☎ 🅿. ◪ AE ⓪ *VISA*
  M 5.50/7.75 **st.** and a la carte ⏣ 3.50 – ⌷ 5.25 – **135 rm** 33.50/55.50 **t.. 2 suites** 95.00/190.00 **t.**
  – SB (weekends only) 48.50 **st.**

 🏨 **Sefton,** Harris Promenade, ✆ 26011, ≼ – ▐ TV ⌷wc ☜ ら 🅿. ◪ AE ⓪ *VISA*. ﹪
  M (carving rest.) 5.50/7.75 **t.** ⏣ 3.50 – **80 rm** ⌷ 22.75/39.50 **t.** – SB (except Easter, summer and
  Christmas)(weekends only) 45.00/78.00 **st.**

 🏨 **Empress,** Central Promenade, ✆ 27211 – ▐ TV ⌷wc ﹏wc ☜. ﹪
  94 rm. 3 suites.

AUSTIN-ROVER Westmoreland Rd ✆ 23481
BMW 41-45 Bucks Rd ✆ 73380
CITROEN Kingswood Grove ✆ 24114
FIAT Station Rd ✆ 832021
FORD Douglas ✆ 73211
MERCEDES-BENZ Douglas Rd ✆ 822884

PEUGEOT-TALBOT, COLT, FIAT Peel Rd ✆ 24519
RENAULT Peel Rd ✆ 73342
SAAB West St. ✆ 813350
TOYOTA Westmoreland Rd ✆ 75556
VAUXHALL-OPEL The Milestone, Peel Rd ✆ 73781
VOLVO New Castletown Rd ✆ 74683

ONCHAN **402** G 21 – ☼ 0624 Douglas.

Douglas 1.5.

 XXX **Boncomptes,** King Edward Rd, ✆ 75626, ≼ – 🅿. ◪ ⓪ *VISA*
  closed Saturday lunch and Sunday – **M** 6.50 **t.** (lunch) and a la carte 11.50/16.10 **t.**

Republic
of Ireland

Prices quoted in this section of the guide are in '' Punts ''

Dans cette partie du guide, les prix sont indiqués en monnaie irlandaise '' Punts ''

In questa parte della guida, i prezzi sono indicati in lire irlandesi '' Punts ''

In diesem Teil des Führers sind die Preise in irländischer Währung '' Punts '' angegeben

Place with at least :

one hotel or restaurant .... ● Longford

one pleasant hotel .... 🏠 , ✗ with rm

one quiet, secluded hotel .... 🐾

one restaurant with .... ✿, ✿✿, ✿✿✿, M

See this town for establishments
located in its vicinity .... SLIGO

Localité offrant au moins :

une ressource hôtelière .... ● Longford

un hôtel agréable .... 🏠 , ✗ with rm

un hôtel très tranquille, isolé .... 🐾

une bonne table à .... ✿, ✿✿, ✿✿✿, M

Localité groupant dans le texte
les ressources de ses environs .... SLIGO

La località possiede come minimo :

una risorsa alberghiera .... ● Longford

un albergo ameno .... 🏠 , ✗ with rm

un albergo molto tranquillo, isolato .... 🐾

un'ottima tavola con .... ✿, ✿✿, ✿✿✿, M

La località raggruppa nel suo testo
le risorse dei dintorni .... SLIGO

Ort mit mindestens :

einem Hotel oder Restaurant .... ● Longford

einem angenehmen Hotel .... 🏠 , ✗ with rm

einem sehr ruhigen und abgelegenen Hotel ..... 🐾

einem Restaurant mit .... ✿, ✿✿, ✿✿✿, M

Ort mit Angaben über Hotels und Restaurants
in seiner Umgebung .... SLIGO

REPUBLIC OF IRELAND

Towns

ABBEYLEIX Laois **405** J 9 – pop. 1 402 – ECD : Wednesday – ✆ 0502 Portlaoise – 🏌.
Envir. : Dunamase Rock (castle★★ 13C-16C ruins), site★★, ✳★★ NE : 13 ½ m.
♦Dublin 64 – Kilkenny 21 – ♦Limerick 65 – ♦Tullamore 30.

  🏩 **Hibernian House,** Lower Main St., ℰ 31252 – 🛏wc. 🔄 *VISA*. ⚘
     M 6.00/10.00 **st.** and a la carte 🍷 4.00 – **13 rm** 🍽 13.00/30.00 **st.**

ACHILL ISLAND Mayo **405** B 5 and 6.
See : Achill Sound★ – The Atlantic Drive★★★ SW : Coast road from Cloghmore to Dooega – Keel :
(the strand★) – Lough Keel★.
🏌 Achill Sound, Westport, in Keel ℰ 43202.
🛈 ℰ Achill Sound 51 (June-August).

      Dugort – ✉ Achill Island – ✆ 098 Westport.
  ↑ **Gray's** 🛏, ℰ 43244, ☞ – 🛏wc 🅿. ⚘
     March-7 October – **15 rm** 🍽 (dinner included) 22.00/44.00 **t.**

ADARE Limerick **405** F 10 – pop. 785 – ✆ 061 Limerick.
See : ≤★ from the bridge of the River Maigue.
🏌 ℰ 94204.
🛈 ℰ 94255 (June-August).
♦Dublin 131 – ♦Killarney 59 – ♦Limerick 10.

  🏨 Dunraven Arms, Main St., ℰ 86209, Telex 70202, ☞ – 🛏wc 🛏wc ☎ 🅿. ⚘
     25 rm.
  🏠 **Woodlands House,** SE : 2 m. by N 21 on Croom Rd ℰ 86118, ☞ – 🛏wc 🛏wc ☎ 🅱 🅿.
     🔄 🆎 ⓞ *VISA*. ⚘
     closed Christmas Day – **M** (dinner only and Sunday lunch)/dinner 10.15 **t.** 🍷 3.50 – **12 rm**
     🍽 17.50/28.00 **st.** – SB 38.00/40.00 **st.**
  XX **Mustard Seed,** Main St., ℰ 86451 – 🔄 *VISA*
     closed Monday in winter, Sunday and Christmas Day – **M** (dinner only) 18.00 **t.**

AHAKISTA Cork **405** D 13 – ✉ ✆ 027 Bantry.
♦Dublin 217 – ♦Cork 63 – ♦Killarney 59.

  XX **Shiro,** ℰ 67030, Japanese rest., ☞ – 🅿
     closed January – **M** (dinner only) 20.00 **st.** 🍷 4.50.

ANNAMOE Wicklow **405** N 8 – ✉ ✆ 0404 Wicklow.
Envir. : Glendalough (ancient monastic city★★ : site★★★, St. Kervin's Church★) and Upper Lake★ in
Glendalough Valley★★★ SW : 5 m.
♦Dublin 29 – Wexford 72.

  XX **Armstrong's Barn,** ℰ 5194, ☞ – 🅿. 🆎 *VISA*
     closed Sunday, Monday and Christmas-Easter – **M** (dinner only) (booking essential) 17.50 **t.**
     🍷 4.50.

ARAN ISLANDS ★★ Galway **405** CD 8.
See : Inishmore Island (Kilronan harbour★).
Access by boat or aeroplane from Galway City or by boat from Kilkieran, or Fisherstreet (Clare).

     Hotels see : Galway.

ARDARA Donegal **405** G 3 – ✆ 075 411.
♦Dublin 188 – Donegal 24 – ♦Londonderry 58.

  ↑ **Bay View House** 🛏, Portnoo Rd, N : ¾ m. ℰ 41145, ≤ Loughros Bay and hills, ☞ – 🛏wc
     🅿. ⚘
     closed Christmas – **7 rm** 🍽 10.00/22.00 **st.**

ARDMORE Waterford 405 I 12 – pop. 318 – ✆ 024 Youghal.
◆Dublin 139 – ◆Cork 34 – ◆Waterford 43.

🏠 **Cliff House,** ℰ 94106, ≤, ≉, – ➾wc 🛁wc 🅟. 🆀 ⓪ 𝖵𝖨𝖲𝖠
22 May-24 September – **M** (bar lunch)/dinner 11.95 **t.** and a la carte 🍴 4.00 – **16 rm**
☲ 14.50/36.00 **t.**

ASHFORD Wicklow 405 N 8 – pop. 536 – ✆ 0404 Wicklow.
◆Dublin 28 – Wicklow 4.

🏠 Cullenmore, NE : 2 m. on N 11 ℰ 4108 – 📺 ➾wc ⊜ ⅙ 🅟. 🛁
13 rm

ATHLONE Westmeath 405 I 7 – pop. 9 444 – ECD : Thursday – ✆ 0902.
Envir. : Clonmacnoise★★ (medieval ruins) SW : 8 m. – N : Lough Ree★.
🖈 17 Church St. ℰ 72866.
◆Dublin 75 – ◆Galway 57 – ◆Limerick 75 – Roscommon 20 – ◆Tullamore 24.

🏨 **Prince of Wales,** Church St., ℰ 72626, Telex 53068 – 📺 ➾wc ⊜ 🅟. 🛁. 🆀 🆀 ⓪ 𝖵𝖨𝖲𝖠
closed 24 to 27 December – **M** 8.00/13.50 **st.** and a la carte – **42 rm** ☲ 23.00/39.00 **st.**

FORD Dublin Rd ℰ 75426

AVOCA Wicklow 405 N 9 – pop. 289 – ✆ 0402 Arklow.
See : Vale of Avoca★ from Arklow to Rathdrum on T 7.
◆Dublin 47 – ◆Waterford 72 – Wexford 55.

🏨 **Vale View,** Kilcashel, N : 1 ¾ m. on T 7 ℰ 5236, ≤, ✾ – 📺 ➾wc ⊜ 🅟. 🆀 🆀 ⓪ 𝖵𝖨𝖲𝖠
M 7.50/12.50 **t.** and a la carte 🍴 3.65 – **10 rm** ☲ 17.50/35.00 **t.** – SB 50.00 **st.**

🏠 Woodenbridge, Vale of Avoca, SW : 1 ½ m. ℰ 5146, ≉ – ➾wc ⊜ 🅟
12 rm.

BALLINA Mayo 405 E 5 – pop. 6 856 – ECD : Thursday – ✆ 096.
Envir. : Rosserk Abbey★ (Franciscan Friary 15C) N : 4 m. – Ballycastle (cliffs★) NW : 3 m. near
Downpatrick Head★ NW : 18 m.
🖈 ℰ 21050, E : 1 m. – 🖈 Belmullet ℰ Belmullet 28.
🖈 ℰ 21544 (July-August).
◆Dublin 150 – ◆Galway 73 – Roscommon 64 – ◆Sligo 37.

🏨 **Downhill,** Sligo Rd, ℰ 21033, Telex 40796, ◳, ≉, squash – 📺 ➾wc 🛁wc ☎ 🅟. 🆀 🆀 ⓪
𝖵𝖨𝖲𝖠. ✾
closed 22 to 26 December – **M** 11.00/18.00 **s.** and a la carte 🍴 9.00 – **54 rm** ☲ 55.00/77.00 **t.** –
SB (except summer)(weekends only) 55.00/66.00 **st.**

🏠 **Mount Falcon Castle** ◿, Foxford Rd, S : 4 m. on Foxford-Ballina road (T 40/N 57)
ℰ 21172, Telex 40899, ≤, « Country house atmosphere », ⌇, park, ✾ – ➾wc 🅟. 🆀 🆀 ⓪
𝖵𝖨𝖲𝖠
closed February-March and Christmas – **M** (lunch by arrangement)/dinner 15.00 **t.** – **10 rm**
☲ 25.00/60.00 **t.**

AUSTIN-ROVER Lord Edward St. ℰ 21037

BALLINASCARTY Cork 405 F 12 – ✉ Clonakilty – ✆ 023 Bandon.
◆Dublin 188 – ◆Cork 27.

🏨 **Ardnavaha House** ◿, SE : 2 m. by L 63 ℰ 49135, ≤, ⌁ heated, ⌇, ≉, park, ✾ – ➾wc
⊜ 🅟. 🆀 🆀 ⓪ 𝖵𝖨𝖲𝖠. ✾
April-mid October – **M** 9.50/14.50 **t.** and a la carte – **36 rm** ☲ 26.00/46.00 **t.** – SB 67.00/75.00 **st.**

BALLINASLOE Galway 405 H 8 – pop. 6 374 – ECD : Thursday – ✆ 0905.
🖈 ℰ 42126.
🖈 ℰ 2332 (July-August).
◆Dublin 91 – ◆Galway 41 – ◆Limerick 66 – Roscommon 36 – ◆Tullamore 34.

🏨 **Hayden's,** Dunlo St., ℰ 42347, Telex 53947, ≉ – 🛗 📺 ➾wc ☎ 🅟. 🆀 🆀 ⓪ 𝖵𝖨𝖲𝖠. ✾
closed 24 to 27 December – **M** 8.50/13.00 **t.** and a la carte – ☲ 3.95 – **53 rm** 15.00/19.00 **t.**

FORD Kilmartins ℰ 42204   RENAULT Brackernagh ℰ 42420
PEUGEOT Dunlo St. ℰ 42290

BALLINDERRY Tipperary 405 H 8 – ✉ ✆ 067 Nenagh.
◆Dublin 111 – ◆Galway 53 – ◆Limerick 41.

🏠 **Gurthalougha House** ◿, W : 1 ¾ m. ℰ 22080, « ≤ Country house on banks of Lough
Derg », ≉, park – ➾wc 🅟
closed Christmas – **7 rm** ☲ 28.00/46.00 **st.**

BALLYBOFEY Donegal 405 I 3 – pop. 2 928 – ECD : Wednesday – ✪ 074 Letterkenny.
🔓 ✆ 31093.
♦Dublin 148 – ♦Londonderry 30 – ♦Sligo 58.

🏨 **Kee's**, Main St., Stranorlar, NE : ½ m. on N 15 ✆ 31018 – 📺 ➘wc ➲ 🄿 🅫 AE VISA
closed 24 to 26 December – **M** 12.50 **t.** (dinner) and a la carte 🍷 3.30 – **26 rm** ☷ 17.00/30.00 **t.**
– SB 42.50/45.00 **st.**

🏨 **Jackson's**, Glenfinn St., ✆ 31021, Telex 42010, ☞ – 📺 ➘wc 🛏wc ☎ 🄿 🅫 AE VISA
closed Christmas Day – **M** 6.50/11.00 **st.** and a la carte 🍷 3.20 – **44 rm** ☷ 17.50/32.00 **st.** –
SB (weekends only) 37.50/39.50 **st.**

BALLYCONNEELY Galway 405 B 7 – ⊠ ✪ 095 Clifden.
♦ Dublin 189 – ♦ Galway 54.

🦢 **Erriseask House** ⏾, ✆ 23553, ⇐ – 🛏wc ➲ 🄿 🅫 VISA ⌖
May-mid September – **M** (bar lunch)/dinner 12.00 **st.** – **11 rm** ☷ 15.00/34.00 **st.** –
SB 49.00/53.00 **st.**

BALLYHACK Wexford – pop. 221 – ⊠ New Ross – ✪ 051 Waterford.
♦Dublin 105 – ♦Waterford 8.5.

✗ **Neptune**, Ballyhack Harbour, ✆ 89284, Seafood – 🅫 AE ① VISA
closed Monday, January and February – **M** 7.90/16.90 **st.** and a la carte 10.80/15.30 **st.** 🍷 4.90.

BALLYHEIGE Kerry 405 C 10 – ✪ 066.
♦ Dublin 187 – ♦ Killarney 33 – ♦ Limerick 67.

🏨 **White Sands**, ✆ 33102 – ➘wc 🛏wc ☎ 🄿 🅫 AE VISA
Easter-September – **M** (buffet lunch)/dinner 15.00 **st.** and a la carte 🍷 4.00 – **26 rm**
☷ 19.00/38.00 **st.** – SB 39.00/46.00 **st.**

BALLYLICKEY Cork 405 D 12 – ⊠ ✪ 027 Bantry.
♦Dublin 216 – ♦Cork 55 – ♦Killarney 45.

🏨 **Sea View House** ⏾, ✆ 50462, ⇐, ☞ – ➘wc 🛏wc ➲ 🄿 🅫 VISA
April-October – **M** (bar lunch Monday to Saturday)/dinner 15.50 **t.** 🍷 5.00 – **10 rm**
☷ 22.50/52.00 **st.** – SB 61.50/68.50 **st.**

🏨 **Green Acre Lodge**, N : 1 m. on N 71 ✆ 50906, ⇐, ☞ – 📺 ➘wc 🛏wc ☎ 🄿 AE ① VISA
⌖
M 9.00/15.00 **st.** and a la carte 🍷 3.25 – **9 rm** ☷ 18.00/36.00 **st.** – SB (November-April) 48.00 **st.**

✗✗ **Ballylickey House** ⏾ with rm, ✆ 50071, ⇐, French rest., ⌕ heated, ⌕, park – ➘wc ➲
🄿 🅫 VISA ⌖
Mid March-mid November – **M** 15.00/17.00 **t.** and a la carte 13.00/18.00 **t.** 🍷 5.50 – ☷ 6.50 –
9 rm 30.00/45.00 **t.**, **2 suites** 60.00 **t.**

BALLYLIFFIN Donegal 405 J 2 – pop. 260 – ⊠ ✪ 077 Buncrana.
Envir. : Carndonagh (Donagh Cross★) SE : 6 m. – Lough Naminn★ S : 6 m.
🔓 Lifford ✆ 19.
♦Dublin 180 – Donegal 83 – ♦Londonderry 35.

🏨 **Strand**, ✆ 76107, ☞ – 📺 ➘wc 🛏wc ☎ 🄿 🅫 VISA ⌖
closed 17 April and 24 to 26 December – **M** 7.00/15.00 **t.** 🍷 3.50 – **12 rm** ☷ 20.00/28.00 **t.** –
SB (weekends only) 46.00/56.00 **st.**

BALLYNAHINCH Galway 405 C 7 – ⊠ Ballinafad – ✪ 095 Clifden.
See : Lake★.
♦Dublin 140 – ♦Galway 41 – Westport 49.

🏨 **Ballynahinch Castle** ⏾, ✆ 21269, Telex 50809, ⇐ Owenmore river and woods, ⌕, ☞,
park, ⌕ – ➘wc ➲ 🄿 🅫 AE ① VISA ⌖
April-October – **M** (lunch by arrangement) 10.55/19.00 **st.** 🍷 4.50 – **20 rm** ☷ 48.00/84.00 **st.**

BALLYVAUGHAN Clare 405 E 8 – ✪ 065 Ennis.
Envir. : SW : Coast road L 54 from Ailladie to Fanore : Burren District (Burren limestone terraces★★)
– Corcomroe Abbey★ (or Abbey of St. Maria de Petra Fertilis : 12C Cistercian ruins) NE : 6 m.
♦Dublin 149 – Ennis 34 – ♦Galway 29.

🏨 **Gregans Castle** ⏾, SW : 3 ¼ m. on T 69 ✆ 77005, Telex 70130, ⇐ Countryside and Galway
Bay, « Attractively furnished », ☞ – ➘wc 🄿 VISA ⌖
Mid March-October – **M** 10.00/17.00 **t.** and a la carte 🍷 4.50 – **16 rm** ☷ 29.00/60.00 **t.**, **1 suite**
70.00/80.00 **t.**

🏨 **Hylands**, ✆ 77037 – ➘wc 🛏wc ☎ 🄿 🅫 ① VISA ⌖
Easter-September – **M** (bar lunch)/dinner 13.00 **t.** 🍷 4.00 – **11 rm** ☷ 19.00/33.00 **t.** –
SB 51.50/58.50 **st.**

BANAGHER Offaly **405** I 8 – pop. 1 378.

See : ≤★ from the bridge of Shannon – Envir. : Clonfert (St. Brendan's Cathedral : west door★ 12C, east windows★ 13C) NW : 4 ½ m. – Birr : Castle Demesne (arboretum★, gardens★, telescope of Lord Rosse) *AC*, SE : 8 m.

◆Dublin 83 – ◆Galway 54 – ◆Limerick 56 – ◆Tullamore 24.

↑ **Brosna Lodge,** Main St., ℰ 51350, 🌫 – ⊟wc 🅿. ⁑
  10 rm 11.00/24.00 st.

BANTEER Cork **405** F 11 – pop. 217 – ✪ 029.

◆Dublin 154 – ◆Cork 34 – ◆Killarney 29 – ◆Limerick 48.

🏛 **Clonmeen House** ⍋, E : 2 m. on Mallow road ℰ 56008, 🎣, 🌫, park – ⊟wc 🅿. ⁑
  15 May-2 October – **M** (lunch by arrangement) 13.00/18.00 t. 🛦 4.50 – ⊊ 3.50 – **12 rm**
  28.00/50.00 t., **5 suites** 64.00/74.00 t.

BANTRY Cork **405** D 12 – pop. 2 862 – ECD : Wednesday – ✪ 027.

See : Bantry Bay★★ – Bantry House (interior★★, ≤★) *AC* – Envir. : Glengarrif (site★★★) NW : 8 m. – NE : Shehy Mountains★★.

🛆 Donemark ℰ 50579, on Glengariff road – 🛈 ℰ 50229 (July-August).

◆Dublin 218 – ◆Cork 57 – ◆Killarney 48.

RENAULT Barrack St. ℰ 50092   VAUXHALL-OPEL The Square ℰ 50023

BARNA Galway **405** E 8 – ✪ 091 Galway.

◆Dublin 135 – ◆Galway 3.

✕ **Ty Ar Mor,** Sea Point, ℰ 92223, ≤, Seafood – 🅿. 🖪 🖭 ⓪ 𝘝𝘐𝘚𝘈
  M (dinner only in winter) 7.00/17.00 st. and a la carte 8.80/16.00 t. 🛦 4.10.

BETTYSTOWN Meath **405** N 6 – ⊠ ✪ 041 Drogheda.

🛈 ℰ 27534.

◆Dublin 28 – Drogheda 6.

✕✕ **Coastguard Inn,** ℰ 27115, ≤ – 🅿. 🖪 🖭 ⓪ 𝘝𝘐𝘚𝘈
  closed Sunday, Monday, Christmas and Bank Holidays – **M** (dinner only) 16.50 t. and a la carte
  15.95/20.25 t. 🛦 4.00.

BIRR Offaly **405** I 8 – pop. 3 679 – ✪ 0509.

🛈 ℰ 206 (June-August).

Athlone 28 – ◆Dublin 87 – Kilkenny 49 – ◆Limerick 49.

🏛 County Arms, Railway Rd, ℰ 20191, 🌫, squash – 📺 ⊟wc ▥wc 🕾 🅿. ⁑ – **17 rm**.

BLARNEY Cork **405** G 11 – pop. 1 980 – ⊠ ✪ 021 Cork.

See : Castle★ 15C (top ⁂★, 112 steps) *AC*.

◆Dublin 167 – ◆Cork 6.

🏛 Blarney, ℰ 85281, 🌫 – 📺 ⊟wc ▥wc 🕾 🕹 🅿. ⌴ – **76 rm**.

BLESSINGTON Wicklow **405** M 8 – pop. 988 – ✪ 045 Naas.

Envir. : Lackan ≤★ SE : 4 ½ m. – SE : Poulaphuca Lake★ (reservoir).

◆Dublin 20.

🏛 **Downshire House,** Main St., ℰ 65199, 🌫, ⁑ – ⊟wc 🕾 🅿. ⁑
  closed 2 weeks Christmas – **M** 8.50/14.50 t. and a la carte 🛦 5.00 – ⊊ 4.40 – **23 rm** 17.00/30.00 t.

BORRIS Carlow **405** L 10 – ✪ 0503 Carlow.

◆Dublin 68 – Kilkenny 16 – ◆Waterford 30.

✕✕ **Step House** with rm, ℰ 73401, 🌫 – ⊟wc. 𝘝𝘐𝘚𝘈
  May-October – **M** *(closed Sunday and Monday)* (dinner only) 16.95 t. and a la carte
  11.90/17.80 t. 🛦 4.00 – **3 rm** ⊊ 16.00/32.00 t.

BOYLE Roscommon **405** H 16 – pop. 1 737 – ✪ 079.

See : Cistercian Abbey★ 12C – Envir. : NE : Lough Key★ – 🛆 Roscommon Rd ℰ 62594.

🛈 ℰ 145 (June-August).

◆Dublin 107 – Ballina 40 – ◆Galway 74 – Roscommon 26 – ◆Sligo 24.

🏛 **Royal,** Bridge St., ℰ 62016 – 📺 ⊟wc ▥wc ☎ 🅿. 🖪 🖭 ⓪ 𝘝𝘐𝘚𝘈
  closed 25 and 26 December – **M** 7.50/12.50 t. and a la carte 🛦 4.20 – **16 rm** ⊊ 23.00/42.00 t. –
  SB (weekends only) 40.00/50.00 st.

🏛 **Forest Park,** Dublin Rd, E : ½ m. on N 4 ℰ 62229, 🌫 – 📺 ⊟wc ☎ 🅿. 🖪 🖭 ⓪ 𝘝𝘐𝘚𝘈. ⁑
  closed 24 to 26 December – **M** 7.50/12.50 st. and a la carte 🛦 5.00 – **12 rm** ⊊ 23.00/45.00 st. –
  SB 55.00/65.00 st.

FORD Elphin St. ℰ 22

BRAY Wicklow **405** N 8 – pop. 22 853 – ECD : Wednesday – ✪ 01 Dublin.

🖪 Woodbrook ✔ 824799, N : 1 m. – 🖪 Ravenswell Rd ✔ 862484 – 🖪 ✔ 867128/9 (July-August).

♦Dublin 13 – Wicklow 20.

  🏨 **Esplanade,** Sea Front, Strand Rd., ✔ 862056 – **P.** 🔼 AE ⓞ VISA ⌘
    closed 20 December-1 January – **M** (closed Sunday dinner) 7.50/11.50 **st.** and a la carte ♦ 4.25
    – **40 rm** ⊊ 12.00/26.00. **t.** – SB (except Christmas) 38.00 **st.**

  XX **Tree of Idleness,** Seafront, ✔ 863498, Greek-Cypriot rest. – 🔼 AE ⓞ VISA
    closed Monday, 17 April, first 3 weeks September and Christmas – **M** (dinner only) 12.50 **t.** and
    a la carte 14.75/19.75 **t.** ♦ 4.50.

BUNRATTY Clare **405** F 9 – ✉ ✪ 061 Limerick.

See : Castle (Great Hall★) AC – Folk Park★ AC.

♦Dublin 129 – Ennis 15 – ♦Limerick 8.

  🏨 **Fitzpatrick's Shannon Shamrock Inn,** ✔ 61177, Telex 26214, 🔄, ☞ – ▤ rest 📺 🛏wc ☎ ₰
    P. 🈀 🔼 AE ⓞ VISA ⌘
    closed Christmas Day – **M** 6.00/14.00 **t.** and a la carte ♦ 4.50 – **104 rm.**

  XX **MacCloskey's,** Bunratty House Mews, ✔ 74082 – **P.** 🔼 AE ⓞ VISA
    closed Sunday and Monday – **M** (dinner only) 19.00 **t.** ♦ 4.80.

CAHER Tipperary **405** I 10 – pop. 2 120 – ECD : Thursday – ✪ 052.

See : Castle★ (12C-15C) the most extensive medieval castle in Ireland.

🖪 Cahir Park, ✔ 41474, S : 1 m. – 🖪 ✔ 41453 (July-August).

♦Dublin 112 – ♦Cork 49 – Kilkenny 41 – ♦Limerick 38 – ♦Waterford 39.

  🏨 **Kilcoran Lodge,** SW : 4 ¾ m. on N 8 ✔ 41288, ☞ – 📺 🛏wc ♨wc ☎ **P.** 🈀 🔼 AE ⓞ
    VISA
    M 7.75/12.50 **t.** and a la carte ♦ 4.00 – **23 rm** ⊊ 20.50/38.00. **t.** – SB 56.25 **st.**

CAHERDANIEL Kerry **405** B 12.

Envir. : Sheehan's Point ≤★★★ W : 5 m. – Staigue Fort★ (prehistoric stone fort : site★, ≤★) AC,
NE : 5 m.

♦Dublin 238 – ♦Killarney 48.

FORD Dublin Rd ✔ 41432

CAPPOQUIN Waterford **405** I 11 – pop. 950 – ✉ Lismore – ✪ 058 Dungarvan.

♦Dublin 136 – ♦Cork 31 – ♦Waterford 40.

  ↖ **Richmond House** ⌲, SE : ½ m. on N 72, ✔ 54278, ☞, park – 🛏wc **P.** 🔼 ⓞ VISA ⌘
    February-October – **9 rm** ⊊ 11.00/24.00 **t.**

CARAGH LAKE Kerry **405** C 11 – ✪ 066 Tralee.

See : Lough Caragh★.

♦Dublin 212 – ♦Killarney 22 – Tralee 25.

  🏨 **Caragh Lodge** ⌲, ✔ 69115, ≤, « Country house atmosphere, fine gardens », ⌇, park, ⌘
    – 🛏wc **P.** 🔼 VISA ⌘
    March-mid October – **M** (dinner only) a la carte 12.00/16.00 **t.** ♦ 5.00 – **10 rm** ⊊ 27.00/50.00 **t.**

  🏨 **Ard-na-Sidhe** ⌲, ✔ 69105, ≤, « Country house atmosphere », ⌇, ☞, park – 🛏wc **P.**
    🔼 VISA ⌘
    May-mid September – **M** (dinner only) 17.00 **st.** ♦ 8.00 – **18 rm** ⊊ 38.00/58.00 **st.**

CARLINGFORD Louth **405** N 5 – pop. 631 – ✪ 042.

♦Dublin 66 – ♦Dundalk 13.

  🏠 **McKevitt's Village,** Market Sq., ✔ 73116 – 📺 🛏wc ♨wc. 🔼 VISA ⌘
    closed 25 to 27 December – **M** 10.00/14.00 **st.** and a la carte ♦ 3.50 – **10 rm** ⊊ 18.00/36.00 **st.**
    – SB (except Bank Holidays) 40.00/48.00 **st.**

  XX **Oscar's,** The Square, ✔ 73162 – **P.** 🔼 ⓞ VISA
    closed Sunday dinner and Monday September-May – **M** 7.50/13.00 **t.** and a la carte
    12.20/16.60 **t.** ♦ 3.50.

CARLOW Carlow **405** L 9 – pop. 11 722 – ECD : Thursday – ✪ 0503.

🖪 Oak Park ✔ 31695 – 🖪 ✔ 31554 (July-August).

♦Dublin 52 – Kilkenny 25 – ♦Tullamore 44 – Wexford 46.

  🏨 **Royal,** 9-13 Dublin St., ✔ 31621 – 📺 🛏wc ☎ **P.** 🔼 AE ⓞ VISA
    closed 25 to 28 December – **M** (grill rest.) 10.50/15.50 **st.** and a la carte ♦ 3.85 – **30 rm**
    ⊊ 25.00/44.00 **st.** – SB (weekends only) 42.50/45.00 **st.**

  🏨 **Carlow Lodge,** Kilkenny Rd, S : 2 m. on N 9 ✔ 42002, ☞ – 📺 🛏wc ☎ **P.** ⌘ – **10 rm.**

CARRICKMACROSS Monaghan 405 L 6 – pop. 1 768 – ECD : Wednesday – ☎ 042.

☞ Nuremore H. ✆ 61438.

◆Dublin 97 – ◆Dundalk 14.

🏨 **Nuremore** ⑤, SE : 1 m. on N 2 ✆ 61438, ≤, ⌧, ☞, ⌇, ☞, park, squash – 📺 🛁wc 🚿wc
☎ 🅿. 🔥 🔼 🆀 🔟 💳. ⌇
closed 24 and 25 December – **M** 8.25/15.95 **st.** and a la carte ⌁ 3.90 – **39 rm** ⌸ 32.75/52.80 **st.**
– SB (weekends only) 76.45 **st.**

CARRICK-ON-SHANNON Leitrim 405 H 6 – pop. 2 037 – ECD : Wednesday – ☎ 078.

☞ ✆ 20157.

🛈 ✆ 20170 (June-September).

◆Dublin 97 – Ballina 50 – Roscommon 26 – ◆Sligo 34.

🏨 **County,** Bridge St., ✆ 20550 – 📺 🛁wc 🚿wc ☜ 🅿. 🔼 🆀 💳 ⌇
M 6.50/11.50 **st.** and a la carte ⌁ 3.75 – **16 rm** ⌸ 16.50/32.00 **st.**

AUSTIN-ROVER Cartober ✆ (078) 20080

CASHEL Tipperary 405 I 10 – pop. 2 436 – ECD : Wednesday – ☎ 062.

See : St. Patrick's Rock★★★ (or Rock of Cashel) : site and ecclesiastical ruins 12C-15C (❄★★) *AC* –
Hore Abbey★ ruins 13C – St. Dominick's Abbey★ ruins 13C.

Envir. : Holycross Abbey★★ (12C) *AC*, N : 9 m.

🛈 Town Hall ✆ 61333.

◆Dublin 101 – ◆Cork 60 – Kilkenny 34 – ◆Limerick 36 – ◆Waterford 44.

🏰 **Cashel Palace** ⑤, Main St., ✆ 61411, Telex 26938, « Former Archbishop's palace, gardens »
– 📺 ☎ 🅿. 🔥 🔼 🆀 🔟 💳 ⌇
M 12.00/26.00 **t.** and a la carte ⌁ 5.00 – ⌸ 7.25 – **20 rm** 59.00/110.00 **t.**

XX **Chez Hans,** Rockside, ✆ 61177, « Converted 19C church » – 🅿
closed Sunday, Monday and January – **M** (dinner only) a la carte 13.50/16.50 **t.** ⌁ 3.75.

DAIHATSU, TALBOT Ladyswell St. ✆ 61155

CASHEL BAY Galway 405 C 7 – ☎ 095 Clifden.

Envir. : SE : Kilkieran Peninsula★★.

◆Dublin 173 – Galway 41.

🏨 **Cashel House** ⑤, ✆ 31001, Telex 50812, ≤, « Country house set in attractive grounds »,
⌇, ☞, ⌇ – 🛁wc 🅿. 🔼 🆀 🔟 💳
March-October – **M** (bar lunch)/dinner 18.50 **t.** and a la carte ⌁ 4.25 – **32 rm** ⌸ 31.50/72.00 **t.**

🏨 **Zetland** ⑤, ✆ 31011, Telex 50853, ≤, ⌇, ☞ – 🛁wc 🅿. 🔼 🆀 🔟 💳
20 April-15 October – **M** (bar lunch)/dinner 17.50 **t.** ⌁ 5.00 – **19 rm** ⌸ 45.00/60.00 **t.** –
SB 75.00/100.00 **st.**

CASTLEBAR Mayo 405 E 6 – pop. 6 409 – ECD : Thursday – ☎ 094.

Envir. : Ballintuber Abbey★ (13C-15C) S : 7 m. – Pontoon (❄★, moraines★) NE : 10 m.

☞ Rocklands ✆ 21649.

🛈 ✆ 21207 (July-August).

◆Dublin 152 – Ballina 25 – ◆Galway 48 – ◆Sligo 54.

🏨 **Breaffy House** (Best Western) ⑤, SE : 2 ¾ m. on T 39 ✆ 22033, Telex 53790, ☞, park – 🛗
📺 🛁wc ☎ 🅿. 🔥 🔼 🆀 🔟 💳
closed Christmas – **M** 8.40/16.25 **st.** ⌁ 4.00 – **40 rm** ⌸ 25.00/46.00 **t.**

CITROEN, TALBOT Breaffy Rd ✆ 21975   RENAULT Spencer St. ✆ 21355

CASTLECONNELL Limerick 405 G 9 – pop. 1 053 – ☎ 061 Limerick.

◆Dublin 111 – ◆Limerick 9.

🏨 **Castle Oaks House** ⑤, ✆ 377666, ≤, ⌇ – 📺 🛁wc ☎ 🅿. 🔥 🔼 🆀 💳. ⌇
M 8.50/17.50 **t.** – **11 rm** ⌸ 28.00/75.00 **t.**

CASTLEDERMOT Kildare 405 L 9 – pop. 805 – ☎ 0503 Carlow.

Envir. : Baltinglass (abbey ruins : scenery★) NE : 7 m.

◆Dublin 44 – Kilkenny 33 – Wexford 54.

XX **Doyle's Schoolhouse** with rm, Main St., ✆ 44282 – 🚿wc 🅿 – **4 rm.**

CAVAN Cavan 405 J 6 – pop. 3 240 – ☎ 049.

🛈 ✆ 31942 (June-September).

◆Dublin 71 – Drogheda 58 – Enniskillen 40.

🏨 **Kilmore,** Dublin Rd, E : 2 m. on N 3 ✆ 32288 – 📺 🛁wc ☎ ⌖ 🅿. 🔥 – **39 rm.**

🏨 **Farnham Arms,** ✆ 32577 – 📺 🛁wc ☎ 🅿 – **30 rm.**

FIAT Dublin Rd ✆ (049) 31188   FORD Farnham St. ✆ (049) 31700

CHARLEVILLE (RATH LUIRC) Cork **405** F 10 – pop. 2 874 – ECD : Thursday – ✪ 061 Limerick.

Envir. : Kilmallock (Dominican Friary ruins 13C, SS. Peter and Paul church 14C : scenery★) NE : 6 m. – Kilfinnane (site★) E : 11 m.

👓 🖉 257.

♦Dublin 138 – ♦Cork 38 – ♦Killarney 57 – ♦Limerick 24.

🏛 **Deerpark,** Limerick Rd, N : ½ m. on N 20 🖉 44573, 🍴 – 📺 ⌂wc 🅫 🄿. 🔽 *VISA*. 🕱
M 5.25/9.50 t. and a la carte 🛭 4.00 – **20 rm** 🖙 17.50/33.00 t.

FORD Limerick Rd 🖉 561

CLIFDEN Galway **405** B 7 – pop. 796 – ECD : Thursday – ✪ 095.

Envir. : E : Connemara★★ : The Twelve Pins★ (mountains), Lough Inagh★ – Cleggan (site★★) NW : 6 m. – Streamstown Bay★ NW : 2 m.

👓 Connemara, Ballyconneely 🖉 Ballyconneely 5, W : 8 m.

🄱 🖉 103 (June-August).

♦Dublin 181 – Ballina 77 – ♦Galway 49.

🏛 **Rock Glen Country House** 🕭, S : 1 ¼ m. by L 102 🖉 21035, 🍴 – ⌂wc ☎ 🄿. 🔽 🄰🄴 ⓞ *VISA*. 🕱
Mid March-October – **M** 10.00/15.00. 🛭 4.00 – **30 rm** 🖙 26.00/50.00 t.

🏛 **Abbeyglen Castle** 🕭, Sky Rd, W : ½ m. 🖉 21070, Telex 50866, ≤, ⤬ heated, 🍴, 🕱 – 📺 ⌂wc 🅫 🄿. 🔽 🄰🄴 ⓞ *VISA*
M 8.00/15.00 t. 🛭 5.00 – 🖙 5.50 – **42 rm** 22.00/50.00 t., **2 suites** 80.00/100.00 t.

🏠 **Ardagh** 🕭, Ballyconneely road, S : 1 ¾ m. on L 102 🖉 21384, ≤ Ardbear Bay, 🔦 – ⌂wc ☎ 🄿. 🔽 🄰🄴 *VISA*. 🕱
April-October – **M** (bar lunch)/dinner 14.00 t. 🛭 4.00 – **20 rm** 🖙 27.00/40.00 t.

🏔 **Clifden Bay,** Main St., 🖉 21167 – ⌂wc. 🔽 🄰🄴 ⓞ *VISA*
May-October – **M** (bar lunch)/dinner 13.00 t. 🛭 4.50 – **38 rm** 🖙 15.00/50.00 t. – SB (except summer) 50.00/70.00 st.

🍴 **Shades,** The Square, 🖉 21215 – 🔽 🄰🄴 ⓞ *VISA*
April-September – **M** *(closed Monday)* (restricted lunch) a la carte 13.85/17.00 t.

CLONMEL Tipperary **405** I 10 – pop. 12 407 – ECD : Thursday – ✪ 052.

See : The Main Guard★ 1674.

Envir. : Ahenny (2 high crosses★) NE : 16 m. – S : Nire Valley★ (≤★★).

👓 Lyreanearla, 🖉 21138.

🄱 🖉 22960 (July-August).

♦Dublin 108 – ♦Cork 59 – Kilkenny 31 – ♦Limerick 48 – ♦Waterford 29.

🏛 **Clonmel Arms,** Sarsfield St., 🖉 21233, Telex 80263 – 🕼 📺 ⌂wc 🍴wc ☎. 🅰. 🔽 🄰🄴 ⓞ *VISA*
M 8.50/13.00 st. and a la carte 🛭 3.75 – 🖙 5.50 – **33 rm** 26.00/50.00 st. – SB (weekends only) 60.00/70.00 st.

AUDI, MAZDA, MERCEDES-BENZ, VW Upper Irish-town 🖉 22199
NISSAN, RENAULT Dungarvon Rd 🖉 22399

RENAULT Thomas St. 🖉 22430
SKODA, TOYOTA Cashel Rd 🖉 21652

CONG Mayo **405** E 7 – pop. 213 – ✪ 092.

See : Ashford Castle (site ★).

Envir. : Ross Abbey★★, Franciscan Friary (tower 🕸★, 80 steps) SE : 9 m.

♦Dublin 160 – Ballina 49 – ♦Galway 28.

🏰 **Ashford Castle** 🕭, 🖉 46003, Telex 53749, ≤ Lough Corrib and countryside, « Tastefully converted castle », 👓, 🔦, 🍴, park, 🕱 – 🕼 📺 ☎ 🄿. 🅰. 🔽 🄰🄴 ⓞ *VISA*. 🕱
M 13.50/27.00 st. and a la carte 21.30/37.10 st. – 🖙 6.00 – **82 rm** 80.00/160.00 t., **9 suites** 200.00/220.00 t.

COOTEHILL Cavan **405** K 5 – pop. 1 554 – ECD : Tuesday – ✪ 049 Cavan.

Envir. : Bellamont Forest★ N : 1 ½ m.

♦Dublin 68 – ♦Dundalk 33.

🏛 White Horse, Market St., 🖉 52124 – ⌂wc 🍴wc 🅫 🄿
30 rm.

Pour vos déplacements en Grande-Bretagne :

– cinq cartes détaillées nᵒˢ **401**, **402**, **403**, **404**, **405** à 1/400 000
– utilisez-les conjointement avec ce guide,
   un souligné rouge signale toutes les localités citées dans ce guide.

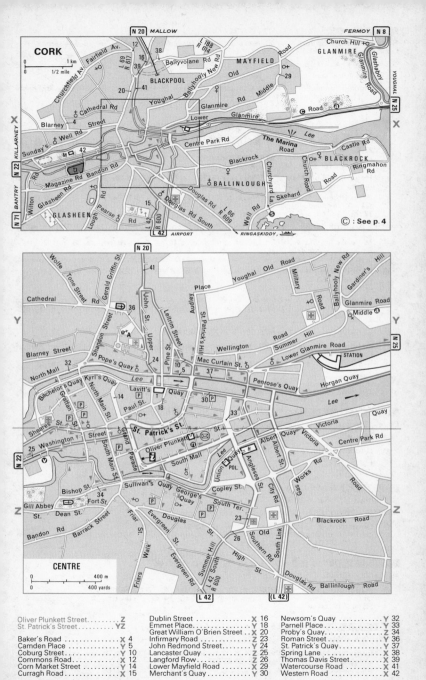

CORK Cork **405** G 12 – pop. 136 344 – ✪ 021.

See : St. Patrick's Street★ YZ – St. Ann's Shandon Church★ 18C (steeple ❄★ AC, 134 steps) Y A –
University College★ 1845 X U – The Marina ⩽★ X.

🛫 Little Island ✆ 353263, E : 5 m. by N 25 X – 🛫 Monkstown ✆ 841225, S : 7 m. by L 66 X.

✈ ✆ 965388, S : 4 m. by L 42 X – Terminal : Bus Station, Parnell Pl.

⛴ Shipping connections with the Continent : to France (Roscoff) (Brittany Ferries) – to France
(Le Havre) (Irish Continental Line).

🛈 Cork City, Tourist House, Grand Parade ✆ 273251 – Cork Airport ✆ 964347 (July-August).

♦Dublin 154.

Plan on preceding page

🏨 **Jury's,** Washington St., ✆ 966377, Telex 766073, ⊐ heated, ☞, squash – 📺 ☎ & ℗. 🍴
🔄 AE ⓞ VISA.   Z v
closed 25-26 December – **M** 9.00/13.00 t. and a la carte ᐧ 4.50 – ⊑ 6.20 – **140 rm** 55.00/100.00 t.
– SB (weekends only) 57.90/65.00 **st.**

🏨 **Imperial,** South Mall, ✆ 965333, Telex 75126 – ⧉ 📺 ☎. 🍴 🔄 AE ⓞ VISA. ✖   Z n
closed 1 week at Christmas – **M** 9.00/16.00 t. and a la carte ᐧ 5.00 – **89 rm** ⊑ 50.00/76.00 t.

🏨 **Silver Springs,** Tivoli, E : 2 ½ m. on N 25 ✆ 507533, Telex 76111, ☞, ✖ – ⧉ 📺 ☎ ℗. 🍴
✖   X c
72 rm

🏨 ❀ **Arbutus Lodge,** Middle Glanmire Rd, Montenotte, ✆ 501237, Telex 75079, ⩽, ☞ –
▤ rest 📺 ⊂wc ▥wc ☎ ℗. AE ⓞ VISA. ✖   Y a
M (closed Sunday) 15.95/20.95 **st.** and a la carte ᐧ 6.25 – **20 rm** ⊑ 38.35/69.30 **st.** –
SB (weekends only) 88.00 **st.**
Spec. Cassolette of fresh prawn tails, Fillet of turbot with sea urchin sauce, Noisettes of venison with elderberries.

🏨 **Lotamore House** without rest., Tivoli, E : 3 ¼ m. on N 25 ✆ 822344, ⩽, ☞, park – 📺 ⊂wc
▥wc ⊛ ℗. 🔄 AE VISA   X a
22 rm ⊑ 20.00/30.00 **st.**

XX **Lovett's,** Churchyard Lane, off Well Rd, Douglas, ✆ 294909 – ℗. 🔄 AE ⓞ VISA   X s
closed Saturday lunch, Sunday and Bank Holidays – **M** 11.00/14.50 **st.** and a la carte
14.20/20.50 **st.** ᐧ 4.75.

at Glounthaune E : 7 m. on N 25 – X – ✉ ✪ 021 Cork :

🏨 **Ashbourne House,** ✆ 353319, « Extensive gardens », ⊐ heated, ✖ – 📺 ⊂wc ▥wc ☎
℗. 🔄 AE ⓞ VISA. ✖
M 8.00/15.00 **st.** ᐧ 4.00 – **26 rm** ⊑ 30.00/46.00 t. – SB (weekends only) 69.00/75.00 **st.**

FIAT   24 Watercourse Rd ✆ 503228   OPEL 26 St. Patricks Quay ✆ 276657
FIAT, LANCIA 11 South Terr. ✆ 507344   RENAULT ✆ 44655
FORD Dennehys Cross ✆ 42846

COURTMACSHERRY Cork **405** F 13 – pop. 231 – ✉ ✪ 023 Bandon.

Envir. : Timoleague (Franciscan Abbey★ 16 C) W : 1 ½ m.

♦Dublin 190 – ♦Cork 29.

🏠 **Courtmacsherry** ➲, ✆ 46198, ⩽, ☞, park, ✖ – ⊂wc ℗. VISA. ✖
Easter-September – **M** (bar lunch Monday to Saturday)/dinner 13.50 t. ᐧ 4.50 – **15 rm**
⊑ 16.50/22.00 t. – SB 60.00/66.00 **st.**

COURTOWN Wexford **405** N 10 – pop. 337 – ✪ 055 Gorey.

🛫 Courtown Harbour ✆ 21533.

♦Dublin 62 – ♦Waterford 59 – Wexford 42.

🏠 **Courtown,** ✆ 25108, ⊠ – ⊂wc ▥wc ℗. 🔄 AE ⓞ VISA. ✖
Easter-October – **M** (bar lunch Monday to Saturday)/dinner 15.00 and a la carte – **28 rm**
⊑ 15.00/38.00 t. – SB 59.00/62.00 st.

CROSSHAVEN Cork **405** H 12 – pop. 1 419 – ✉ ✪ 021 Cork.

♦Dublin 173 – ♦Cork 12.

🏠 **Whispering Pines,** ✆ 831843, ⩽, ➲ – ⊂wc ▥wc ℗. 🔄 AE ⓞ VISA. ✖
closed Christmas – **M** (dinner only) 11.50 **st.** ᐧ 4.50 – **15 rm** ⊑ 18.00/31.00 **st.** –
SB 44.00/48.00 **st.**

CROSSMOLINA Mayo **405** E 5 – pop. 1 335 – ✉ ✪ 096 Ballina.

♦Dublin 108 – ♦Waterford 12.

🏠 **Enniscoe House** ➲, Castlehill, S : 2 m. on L 140 ✆ 31112, ⩽, « Georgian country house,
antiques », ➲, park – ⊂wc ℗. 🔄 AE VISA. ✖
April-October – **M** (dinner only) 16.00 t. ᐧ 4.50 – **7 rm** ⊑ 27.00/60.00 t.

618

DALKEY Dublin 405 N 8 – ✪ 01 Dublin.
♦Dublin 11.

XX **Guinea Pig,** 17-18 Railway Rd, ℰ 859055, Seafood – ⚠ AE ⓞ VISA
closed Sunday, 2 weeks Easter and 1 week August – **M** (dinner only)(booking essential)
16.95 **t.** and a la carte 15.50/28.00 **t.** ⏶ 4.50.

DELGANY Wicklow 405 N 8 – pop. 7 442 (inc. Greystones) – ✉ Bray – ✪ 01 Dublin.
⌷₈ ℰ 874536.
♦Dublin 19.

🏨 **Glenview** ⌂, Glen of the Downs, NW : 2 m. on N 11 by L 164 ℰ 862896, Telex 30638, ≤, 🦅,
park – ⇌wc ⚙ 🅟. 🛁. AE VISA. 🦮
M 11.00/20.00 **t.** ⏶ 6.50 – ⊇ 6.00 – **23 rm** 34.00/52.00 **t.**

DINGLE Kerry 405 B 11 – pop. 1 358 – ECD : Thursday – ✪ 066 Tralee.
See : Dingle Bay★.
Envir. : NE : Conair Pass ⋇★ – Fahan : Belvedere (coast road) ≤★ SW : 7 ½ m. – Kilmakedar
(church★ 12C), Gallarus Oratory★ 8C, NW : 5 m.
🛈 ℰ 51188 (July-August).
♦Dublin 216 – ♦Killarney 51 – ♦Limerick 95.

⌂ **Milltown House** ⌂, W : ¾ m. ℰ 51372, ≤ – ⇌wc 🕮wc 🅟. 🦮
Easter-October – **7 rm** ⊇ 20.00/22.00 **t.**

⌂ **Alpine House,** Mail Rd, ℰ 51250, 🦅 – 🕮wc 🅟. 🦮
March-October – **15 rm** ⊇ 22.00 **t.**

X **Half Door,** John St., ℰ 51600, Seafood – ⚠ AE ⓞ VISA
Mid March-mid November – **M** *(closed Tuesday)* a la carte 10.50/13.25 **st.** ⏶ 5.50.

X **Doyle's Seafood Bar,** 4 John St., ℰ 51174 – ⚠ AE ⓞ VISA
Mid March-mid November – **M** *(closed Sunday)* a la carte 12.05/14.50 **t.** ⏶ 5.00.

DONEGAL Donegal 405 H 4 – pop. 1 956 – ECD : Wednesday – ✪ 073.
See : Franciscan Priory (site★, ≤★).
⌷₈ Murvagh ℰ Ballintra 54, S : 8 m.
🛈 ℰ 21148 (June-August).
♦Dublin 164 – ♦Londonderry 48 – ♦Sligo 40.

🏨 **Hyland Central** (Best Western), The Diamond, ℰ 21027, Telex 40522, 🦅 – 🕴 TV ⇌wc
🕮wc ☎ 🅟. ⚠ AE VISA. 🦮
closed 25 to 27 December – **M** 8.50/14.00 **t.** and a la carte ⏶ 4.50 – **57 rm** ⊇ 26.00/44.00 **t.** –
SB (except July-August)(weekends only) 50.00/60.00 **st.**

at St. Ernan's Island SW : 2 ¼ m. by N 15 – ✉ ✪ 073 Donegal :

🏠 **Ernan Park** ⌂, ℰ 21065, ≤Donegal Bay–, park – TV ⇌wc ☎ 🅟. ⚠ AE ⓞ VISA. 🦮
M (bar lunch)/dinner 12.50 **t.** and a la carte ⏶ 3.50 – **12 rm** ⊇ 17.50/40.00 **t.** – SB 30.00/35.00 **st.**

AUSTIN-ROVER Quay St. ℰ 073 21039   NISSAN Kerrykell ℰ 3
FORD The Glebe ℰ 073 21017   RENAULT ℰ 073 21117

DROGHEDA Louth 405 M 6 – pop. 23 247 – ECD : Wednesday – ✪ 041.
See : St. Lawrence's Gate ★ 13C.
Envir. : Mellifont Abbey★★ (Cistercian ruins 1142) NW : 4 ½ m. – Monasterboice (3 tall crosses★★
10C) NW : 5 ½ m. – Dowth Tumulus ⋇★ W : 4 m. – Duleek (priory★ 12C ruins) SW : 5 m. –
Newgrange Tumulus★ (prehistoric tomb) AC, SW : 7 m.
⌷₈ County Louth, Baltray ℰ 22327, E : 3 m.
🛈 ℰ 7070 (July-August).
♦Dublin 31 – ♦Dundalk 22 – ♦Tullamore 69.

🏨 **Boyne Valley,** SE : 1 ½ m. on N 1 ℰ 37737, 🦅, park – TV ⇌wc 🕮wc ⚙ 🅟. 🛁. ⚠ AE ⓞ
VISA
M 6.80/12.50 **t.** and a la carte ⏶ 3.60 – ⊇ 4.50 – **20 rm** 19.00/35.00 **t.** – SB 50.00/55.00 **st.**

🏠 **Glenside,** Smithstown, SE : 3 m. on N 1 ℰ 29049, 🦅 – TV ⇌wc 🕮wc ☎ 🅟
14 rm.

FIAT, LANCIA North Rd ℰ 37920   NISSAN North Rd ℰ 38566
FORD North Rd ℰ 31106   PEUGEOT Palace St. ℰ 37303

DROICHEAD NUA = Newbridge.

DROMAHAIR Leitrim 405 H 5 – pop. 273 – ✪ 071 Sligo.
♦Dublin 141 – ♦Sligo 8.

🏠 **Drumlease Glebe House** ⌂, NE : 2 ¼ m. ℰ 64141, ≤, « Country house atmosphere », ⅃,
⌇, 🦅 – ⇌wc 🕮wc 🅟. ⚠ AE VISA. 🦮
18 April-17 October – **M** (dinner only)(residents only) 17.50 **t.** ⏶ 5.50 – **8 rm** ⊇ 27.00/58.00 **t.**

DUBLIN

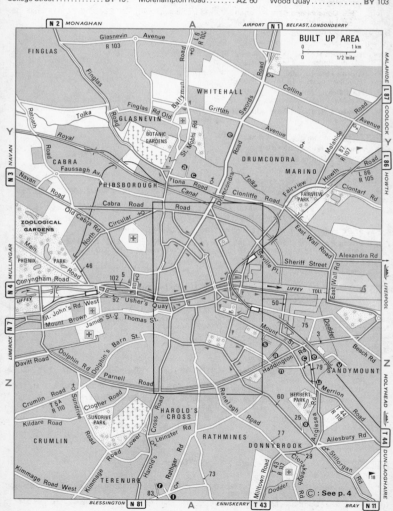

© : See p. 4

See : National Gallery★★★ BY — Castle (State apartments★★★ *AC*) BY — Christ Church Cathedral★★ 12C BY — National Museum (Irish antiquities, Art and Industrial)★★ BY M2 — Trinity College★ (Library★★) BY — National Museum (Zoological Collection)★ BY M1 — Municipal Art Gallery★ BX M3 — O'Connell Street★ (and the General Post Office) BXY — St. Stephen's Green★ BZ — St. Patrick's Cathedral (interior★) BZ — Phoenix Park (Zoological Gardens★) AY.

Envir. : St. Doolagh's Church★ 13C (open Saturday and Sunday, afternoon only) NE : 7 m. by L 87 AY.

🅶 Edmondstown, Rathfarnham ℰ 932461, S : 3 m. by N 81 AZ — 🅶 Elm Park, Nutley House, Dunnybrook ℰ 693438, S : 3 m. AZ — 🅶 Lower Churchtown Rd, Milltown ℰ 977060, S : by T 43 AZ.

✈ ℰ 379900, N : 5 ½ m. by N 1 AY — **Terminal :** Busaras (Central Bus Station) Store St.

⚓ to Liverpool (B & I Line) 2 daily (8 h) — to Holyhead (B & I Line) 1-2 daily (3 h 30 mn) — to the Isle of Man : Douglas (Isle of Man Steam Packet Co.) June-September 1-3 weekly (4 h 30 mn).

🛈 14 Upper O'Connell St. ℰ 747733 — Dublin Airport ℰ 376387 and 375533.

♦Belfast 103 — ♦Cork 154 — ♦Londonderry 146.

Plans on preceding pages

🏨 **Berkeley Court,** Lansdowne Rd, Ballsbridge, ℰ 601711, Telex 30554, ⛶ — 🛗 🍽 rest 📺 ☎ ⟸ 🅿 🏌 🔆 AE ⓞ VISA ✂
AZ **c**
M 14.00/17.00 t. and a la carte — **200 rm** 75.00/95.00 t. — SB (weekends only) 88.00 **st.**

🏨 **Shelbourne (T.H.F.),** 27 St. Stephen's Green, ℰ 766471 — 🛗 📺 ☎ ⟸ 🅿 🏌 🔆 AE ⓞ VISA
M 17.00/19.00 t. and a la carte ⟨ 5.50 — **167 rm, 6 suites.**
BZ **s**

🏨 **Westbury,** Grafton St., ℰ 868109, Telex 91091 — 🛗 🍽 rest 📺 ⚌wc ☎ 🅿 🏌 🔆 AE ⓞ VISA
BY **z**
M 13.00/16.00 t. and a la carte ⟨ 4.10 — ⚏ 6.00 — **146 rm** 70.00/98.00 t., **4 suites** 225.00/275.00 t.

🏨 **Jury's,** Pembroke Rd, Ballsbridge, ℰ 605000, Telex 93723, ⛴ heated, ⛶ — 🛗 📺 ☎ 🔆 🅿 🏌 🔆 AE ⓞ VISA
AZ **c**
M 16.25/17.25 t. and a la carte ⟨ 7.00 — ⚏ 7.00 — **300 rm** 69.50/82.00 t., **4 suites** 150.00/250.00 t.

🏨 **Blooms,** Anglesea St., ℰ 715622, Telex 31688 — 🛗 📺 ☎ 🅿 🔆 AE ⓞ VISA ✂
BY **e**
M 8.00/15.00 **st.** and a la carte ⟨ 4.50 — ⚏ 7.00 — **86 rm** 67.50/115.00 t.

🏨 **Buswells,** 25-26 Molesworth St., ℰ 764013, Telex 90622 — 🛗 📺 ⚌wc ☎ 🏌 ✂
BY **u**
70 rm.

🏨 **Mount Herbert,** Herbert Rd, Ballsbridge, ℰ 684321, Telex 92173, ⛴ — 🛗 📺 ⚌wc ☎ 🔆 🅿 🔆 AE ⓞ VISA
AZ **v**
M 7.50/10.95 t. and a la carte ⟨ 3.90 — **88 rm** ⚏ 15.95/39.90 t. — SB (weekends only) 39.00/55.00 **st.**

🏨 **Skylon** without rest., Upper Drumcondra Rd, N : 2 ½ m. on N 1 ℰ 379121, Group Telex 90790 — 🛗 📺 ⚌wc ☎ 🅿 🏌 ✂
AY **e**
88 rm.

🏨 **Tara Tower,** Merrion Rd, SE : 4 m. on T 44 ℰ 694666 — 🛗 📺 ⚌wc ☎ 🅿 🏌 ✂
on T 44 AZ
83 rm.

🏠 **Ariel House** without rest., 52 Lansdowne Rd, Ballsbridge, ℰ 685512, ⛴ — 📺 ⚌wc ⚌wc ☎ 🅿 ✂
AZ **e**
15 rm ⚏ 25.00/50.00.

🏠 **Maples House,** 79-81 Iona Rd, Glasnevin, ℰ 728382 — ⚌wc ⚊ 🅿 🔆 AE ⓞ VISA ✂ AY **c**
M (closed Saturday lunch and Sunday) a la carte 9.50/15.80 t. ⟨ 3.75 — **20 rm** ⚏ 20.00/38.00 t. — SB (weekends only) 50.00/65.00 **st.**

↑ **Egans House,** 7-9 Iona Park, Glasnevin, ℰ 303611 — 📺 ⚌wc ⚌wc ⚊ 🔆 🅿 VISA AY **a**
⚏ 4.60 — **24 rm** 14.30/30.60 t.

↑ **Kilronan House,** 70 Adelaide Rd, ℰ 755266 — ⚌wc ⚊ ✂ BZ **r**
closed 23 to 30 December — **11 rm** ⚏ 26.00/40.00 t.

↑ **St. Aidan's,** 32 Brighton Rd, Rathgar, ℰ 906178 — 📺 ⚌wc ⚌wc 🅿 🔆 AE ⓞ VISA AZ **r**
12 rm ⚏ 15.00/32.00 t.

↑ **Abrae Court,** 9 Zion Rd, Rathgar, ℰ 979944 — ⚌wc 🅿 ✂ AZ **i**
14 rm.

XXXX **Le Coq Hardi** with rm, 35 Pembroke Rd, ℰ 689070 — 🍽 rest 📺 ⚌wc 🅿 🔆 AE ⓞ VISA ✂
AZ **n**
closed Saturday lunch, Sunday, 2 weeks August, 2 weeks Christmas and Bank Holidays —
M 12.50/22.00 t. and a la carte 15.70/25.50 t. ⟨ 6.00 — **3 rm** ⚏ 155.00 **st.**

XXX **Patrick Guilbaud,** 46 St. James's Pl., St. James' St., off Lower Baggot St., ℰ 764192, French rest. — 🍽 🅿 🔆 AE ⓞ VISA ✂ BZ **n**
closed Saturday lunch, Sunday and Bank Holidays — **M** 11.80/19.50 t. and a la carte.

XXX **Whites on The Green,** 119 St. Stephen's Green, ℰ 751975 — 🍽 🔆 AE ⓞ VISA BZ **a**
closed Saturday lunch, Sunday, 24 to 31 December and Bank Holidays — **M** 9.75/18.00 t. and a la carte 18.00/26.75 t. ⟨ 5.00.

XX **Ernie's,** Mulberry Gdns., ℰ 693300 – 🆎 ⓪ *VISA*   AZ **o**
closed Sunday, Monday, first 2 weeks July and 1 week at Christmas – **M** (dinner only) a la carte 20.25/28.75 **t.** ⅋ 6.25.

XX **Locks,** 1 Windsor Terr., Portobello, ℰ 752025 – 🔃 🆎 ⓪ *VISA*   BZ **u**
closed Saturday lunch, Sunday, 24 December-2 January and Bank Holidays – **M** 10.25 **t.** (lunch) and a la carte 16.50/19.50 **t.** ⅋ 3.90.

XX **Park,** 26 Main St., Blackrock, SE : 4 ½ m. on T 44 ℰ 886177 – 🍽. 🔃 🆎 ⓪ *VISA*   – **M** (booking essential) 7.50/19.50 **t.** ⅋ 5.90.   on T44   AZ
closed Saturday lunch, Sunday, Monday, 3 days at Christmas and Bank Holidays

XX **Lord Edward,** 23 Christchurch Pl., ℰ 752557, Seafood – 🔃 🆎 ⓪ *VISA*   BY **c**
closed Saturday lunch, Sunday and Bank Holidays – **M** 11.95 **t.** (lunch) and a la carte 15.45/24.65 **t.** ⅋ 4.25.

XX **Old Dublin,** 90-91 Francis St., ℰ 751173, Russian-Scandinavian rest. – 🔃 🆎 ⓪ *VISA*   BY **i**
closed Saturday lunch, Sunday and Bank Holidays – **M** 9.50/15.00 **t.**

XX **Bentleys,** 46 Upper Baggot St., ℰ 682760 – 🔃 🆎 ⓪ *VISA*   AZ **a**
closed Saturday lunch, Monday dinner, Sunday, 2 weeks July, 1 week at Christmas and Bank Holidays – **M** a la carte 13.50/18.65 **t.** ⅋ 3.95.

XX **Small Home,** 41-43 Shelbourne Rd, Ballsbridge, ℰ 608087 – 🔃 🆎 ⓪ *VISA*   AZ **u**
closed Saturday lunch, Sunday dinner and Bank Holidays – **M** 8.50/12.50 **t.** and a la carte 12.00/14.50 **t.** ⅋ 4.00.

XX **Imperial,** 12a Wicklow St., ℰ 772580, Chinese rest.   BY **v**

X **Dobbin's,** 15 Stephen's Lane, ℰ 764679, Bistro – 🔃 🆎 ⓪ *VISA*   AZ **s**
closed Saturday lunch, Monday dinner, Sunday and Bank Holidays – **M** a la carte 13.65/22.25 **t.** ⅋ 4.95.

X **Mitchell's Cellars,** 21 Kildare St., ℰ 680367 – 🔃 🆎 ⓪ *VISA*   BZ **x**
closed Saturday June-October, Sunday and Bank Holidays – **M** (lunch only) a la carte 6.65/8.05 **t.** ⅋ 3.95.

X **Cafe de Paris** The Galleria, 6 St. Stephen's Green, ℰ 778499 – 🔃 🆎 ⓪ *VISA*   BY **o**
closed lunch Saturday and Sunday – **M** 12.00/15.00 **st.** and a la carte 10.45/14.45 **st.** ⅋ 2.35.

at Dublin Airport N : 6 ½ m. by N 1 – AY – ✉ 😊 01 Dublin :

🏨 **Dublin International** (T.H.F.), ℰ 379211, Telex 24612 – 📺 ⇌wc ☎ ⅙ 🅿 ♨ 🔃 🆎 ⓪ *VISA*
M 12.75/13.50 **st.** and a la carte ⅋ 4.50 – **195 rm** 60.00/82.00 **st.**

MICHELIN Distribution Centre, 4 Spilmak Pl., Bluebell Industrial Estate, Naas Rd, Dublin 12, ℰ 509096 by N7 AZ

AUSTIN-ROVER, JAGUAR Temple Rd ℰ 885085
AUSTIN-ROVER, NISSAN 48-52 New St. ℰ 780033
AUSTIN-ROVER Northbrook Rd ℰ 970811
AUSTIN-ROVER, JAGUAR, NISSAN Richmond Rd ℰ 379162
BMW, ROLLS-ROYCE-BENTLEY, SUZUKI, VOLVO, LOTUS Townsend St. ℰ 779177
BMW, MITSUBISHI Ballygall Rd East ℰ 342577
BMW, SKODA, TOYOTA Rathgar Av. ℰ 979456
CITROEN, PEUGEOT Buckingham St. ℰ 745821
DAIHATSU ℰ 401393
FIAT, LANCIA Milltown Rd ℰ 698577
FIAT, LANCIA 56 Howth Rd ℰ 332301
FIAT North Rd ℰ 342977
FIAT, LANCIA 84 Prussia St. ℰ 791722
FIAT, LANCIA Herberton Rd ℰ 754216
FORD 172-175 Parnell St. ℰ 747831
FORD Naas Rd ℰ 505721
FORD Stillorgan Rd ℰ 886821
HONDA Upper Rathmines Rd ℰ 971227
HONDA ℰ 806467
MERCEDES-BENZ, TOYOTA 54 Glasnevin Hill ℰ 373771

NISSAN Howth Rd ℰ 314066
NISSAN Bluebell Av. ℰ 507887
NISSAN Merrion Rd ℰ 693911
OPEL Beach Rd ℰ 686011
OPEL 146 Cabra Rd ℰ 301222
OPEL Emmet Rd, Inchicore ℰ 755535
OPEL New Rd ℰ 592438
PEUGEOT, MAZDA Church Pl. ℰ 973999
PEUGEOT-TALBOT, CITROEN 23 Parkgate St. ℰ 710333
RENAULT 232 North Circular Rd, Grangegorman ℰ 300799
RENAULT 19 Conyngnam Rd ℰ 775677
RENAULT 27 Upper Drumcondra Rd ℰ 373706
RENAULT Newlands Cross ℰ 593751
SKODA, TOYOTA Kilbarrack Rd ℰ 322701
TOYOTA Smithfield Market ℰ 721222
VW, AUDI, MAZDA, MERCEDES-BENZ 218-224 North Circular Rd ℰ 792011
VW, AUDI-NSU, MAZDA, MERCEDES-BENZ Ballybough Rd ℰ 723033
VW, AUDI-NSU, MAZDA, MERCEDES-BENZ Harolds Cross Rd ℰ 975757

DUNDALK Louth 🔢🔢🔢 M 5 – pop. 25 663 – ECD : Thursday – 😊 042.

⛳ Blackrock, ℰ 32731, S : 3 m.

🎫 Market Sq. ℰ 35484.

◆Dublin 53 – Drogheda 22.

🏨 **Ballymascanlon House** (Best Western) ♨, N : 3 ½ m. by N 1 ℰ 71124, Group Telex 43735, 🔃, 🌿, park, ✖, squash – 📺 ⇌wc ▥wc ☎ 🅿 ♨ 🔃 🆎 ⓪ *VISA*
closed Christmas Day – **M** 7.50/13.50 **t.** and a la carte ⅋ 3.75 – **36 rm** ⇌ 27.00/50.00 **st.** – SB (weekends only) 52.00/58.00 **st.**

DUNDERRY Meath – see Navan.

DUNFANAGHY Donegal **405** I 2 – pop. 390 – ⊠ ۞ 074 Letterkenny – **Envir.** : Doe Castle★ 16C ruins (site★, ≤ ★) SE : 7 ½ m. – SW : Bloody Foreland Head★ – 🛅 ℘ 074 (Letterkenny) 36208.

◆Dublin 172 – Donegal 54 – ◆Londonderry 43.

🏠 **Arnold's,** Main St., ℘ 36208, ≤, ☞, ※ – ⌂wc **ℙ**. 𝖠𝖤 **①** **VISA**. ※
Easter-October – **M** (bar lunch Monday to Saturday)/dinner 10.50 **t.** – **36 rm** ☲ 24.00/44.00 **t.** – SB 50.00/64.00 **st.**

🏠 **Carrig Rua,** Main St., ℘ 36133, ≤ – ⌂wc **ℙ**. 𝖠𝖤 **VISA**
Easter-September – **M** a la carte lunch/dinner 11.50 **t.** ▯3.75 – **22 rm** ☲ 15.00/35.00 **t.** – SB 48.00/52.00 **st.**

at Port-na-Blagh E : 1 ½ m. on T 72 – ⊠ ۞ 074 Letterkenny :

🏠 **Shandon** ⌂, Marble Hill Strand, NE : 2 ½ m. ℘ 36137, ≤ bay and hills, ☜, ☞, ※ – ▤ ⌂wc ☏ **ℙ** – **55 rm.**

🏠 **Port-na-Blagh,** ℘ 36129, ≤ Sheephaven Bay and harbour, ☜, ☞, ※ – ⌂wc **ℙ**. 𝖠𝖤
Easter-September – **M** 6.00/12.00 **st.** and a la carte ▯3.50 – **56 rm** ☲ 17.50/42.00 **st.** – SB (except summer) 51.00/59.00 **st.**

DUNGARVAN Waterford **405** J 11 – pop. 6 631 – ECD : Thursday – ۞ 058.

🛅 Ballinacourty, ℘ 41605 – **🛈** ℘ 41741 (July-August).

◆Dublin 124 – ◆Cork 48 – ◆Killarney 90 – ◆Waterford 29.

✕ Seanachie, SW : 5 ½ m. by N 25, ℘ 46285 – **ℙ**.

DUN LAOGHAIRE Dublin **405** N 8 – pop. 54 496 – ۞ 01 Dublin.

See : Windsor Terrace ≤★ over Dublin Bay – 🛅 Eglinton Park ℘ 801055.

🚢 to Holyhead (Sealink) 2 daily (3 h 30 mn) – **🛈** St. Michaels Wharf ℘ 805760, 806547 and 806984/5/6.

◆Dublin 9.

DUN LAOGHAIRE

Georges Street
Mulgrave Street
Patrick Street

ⓒ : See p. 4

624

XXX **Mirabeau,** Marine Par., Sandycove, ✆ 809873 – ▨ ▣ ◉ ▩   **x**
closed Saturday lunch, Sunday, Monday, last 2 weeks February and 25 to 28 December –
M (booking essential) 9.50/16.00 **t.** and a la carte 14.75/24.75 **t.** ⌂ 5.00.

XXX **na Mara,** 1 Harbour Rd, ✆ 806767, Seafood – ▨ ▣ ◉ ▩   **i**
closed Sunday, Monday, 1 week Easter and 1 week Christmas – **M** 10.60/14.70 **t.** and a la carte
15.05/24.75 **t.** ⌂ 4.50.

XX **Digby's,** 5 Windsor Terr., ✆ 804600, ≤ – ▨ ▣ ◉ ▩   **a**
closed Saturday lunch, 17 April and 25-26 December – **M** (restricted lunch)/dinner 19.50 **t.**
⌂ 4.60.

X **Trudi's,** 107 Lower George's St., ✆ 805318, Bistro – ▨ ▣ ◉ ▩   **u**
closed Sunday and Monday – **M** (dinner only) a la carte 10.35/14.65 **t.** ⌂ 5.35.

X **Russell's,** 56 Glasthule Rd, Sandycove, ✆ 808878   **e**
closed Sunday – **M** (dinner only) 12.60 **t.** and a la carte 9.80/12.60 **t.** ⌂ 3.50.

HONDA, OPEL Crofton Pl. ✆ 800341   RENAULT Rochestown Av. ✆ 852555
MITSUBISHI, TOYOTA Glasthule Rd ✆ 802991

DUNMORE EAST Waterford ▨▨▨ L 11 – pop. 734 – ✆ 051 Waterford.

◆Dublin 108 – ◆Waterford 11.

X **Ship,** Bayview, ✆ 83141 – ▩
closed Sunday and Monday except July and August – **M** a la carte 9.60/16.00 **t.** ⌂ 4.95.

DURRUS Cork ▨▨▨ D 13 – ✉ – ✆ 027.

◆Dublin 210 – ◆Cork 56 – ◆Killarney 53.

XX **Blairs Cove,** SW : 1 m. on L 56 ✆ 61127, « Converted barn », ☞ – ℗. ▨ ▣ ◉ ▩
*closed lunch Monday to Thursday mid October-Easter, Sunday Easter-October, January and
February* – **M** (dinner only and Sunday lunch)(booking essential)/dinner 18.00 **t.**

EMO Laois ▨▨▨ K 8 – pop. 200 – ✉ ✆ 0502 Portlaoise.

◆Dublin 49 – ◆Limerick 74 – ◆Tullamore 20.

🏠 **Montague,** E : 1 ¾ m. on N 7 ✆ 26154, ☞ – ▥ ⌂wc ☎ & ℗. ⌖. ▨ ▣ ◉ ▩
M 7.50/15.00 **t.** and a la carte ⌂ 3.90 – **75 rm** ⊠ 19.00/75.00 **t.** – SB 56.00/68.00 **st.**

ENNIS Clare ▨▨▨ F 9 – pop. 6 223 – ECD : Thursday – ✆ 065.

See : Franciscan Friary★ (13C ruins).

Envir. : Tulla (site★, ancient church ※ ★★) E : 10 m. – Killone Abbey (site★) S : 4 m. – Dysert
O'Dea (site★) NW : 6 ½ m. – Kilmacduagh monastic ruins★ (site★) NE : 16 ½ m.

🏌 Drumbiggle Rd ✆ 24074 – 🏦 Bank Pl. ✆ 21366.

◆Dublin 142 – ◆Galway 42 – ◆Limerick 22 – Roscommon 92 – ◆Tullamore 93.

🏠 **Old Ground** (T.H.F.), O'Connell St., ✆ 28127, Telex 28103, ☞ – ▥ ⌂wc ☎ ℗. ⌖. ▨ ▣
◉ ▩
M 7.50/15.00 **st.** and a la carte ⌂ 3.75 – **60 rm** 46.00/63.00 **st.**

🏠 **Auburn Lodge,** Galway Rd, N : 1 ½ m. on N 18 ✆ 21247, ☞, squash – ▥ ⌂wc ☎ ℗. ▨
▣ ◉ ▩
closed 22 to 27 December – **M** 7.50/13.00 **t.** and a la carte ⌂ 6.50 – **45 rm** ⊠ 25.00/40.00 **t.** –
SB (weekends only) 44.00/52.00 **st.**

DAIHATSU, TOYOTA, LADA Gort Rd ✆ 21904   ISUZIA Tulla Rd ✆ 22758
FORD Lifford ✆ 21035

ENNISKERRY Wicklow ▨▨▨ N 8 – pop. 1 179 – ✆ 01 Dublin.

See : Site★ – Powerscourt Demesne (gardens★★★, Araucaria Walk★) *AC*.

Envir. : Powerscourt Waterfall★ *AC*, S : 4 m. – Lough Tay★★ SW by T 43, T 61, L 161.

◆Dublin 17 – ◆Waterford 100.

Hotel and restaurant see : Bray SE : 3 ½ m.

FAHAN Donegal ▨▨▨ J 2 – ✉ Lifford – ✆ 077 Buncrana.

🏌 North West, Lisfannon, ✆ Buncrana 12.

◆Dublin 156 – ◆Londonderry 11 – ◆Sligo 95.

XX **St. John's,** ✆ 60289, « Lough-side setting » – ℗. ▨ ▣ ◉ ▩
closed Monday, 17 April, 24-25 December and 2 weeks February-March – **M** (dinner only)
13.50 **t.** and a la carte 13.65/22.05 **t.** ⌂ 3.55.

FEAKLE Clare ▨▨▨ G 9 – pop. 188.

◆Dublin 125 – ◆Galway 36 – ◆Limerick 25.

🏠 **Smyth's Village** ⬦, ✆ 2, ☞, park, ※ – ⌂wc ⌂wc ℗. ※
April-October – **M** (lunch by arrangement)(booking essential) 6.00/8.00 **t.** – **12 rm**
⊠ 11.00/20.00 **t.**

GALWAY Galway **405** E 8 – pop. 37 835 – ECD : Monday – 🕾 091.

See : Lynch's Castle★ 16C.

Envir. : NW : Lough Corrib★★★ – Claregalway (Franciscan Friary★ 13C) NE : 7 m. – Abbeyknockmoy (Cistercian Monastery★ 12C ruins) NE : 18 m. – Tuam (St. Mary's Cathedral : chancel arch★ 12C) NE : 20 m.

🏌 Galway, Salthill ⌕ 23038, W : 3 m.

✈ Carnmore Airport ⌕ 55569, NE : 4 m.

⛴ to Aran Islands: Kilronan (Inishmore), Inishmaan and Inishere (C.I.E) 2-7 weekly.

🛈 Aras Failte, Eyre Sq. ⌕ 63081.

◆Dublin 135 – ◆Limerick 64 – ◆Sligo 90.

🏨 **Great Southern,** Eyre Sq., ⌕ 64041, Telex 50164, 🖿 – 🛗 📺 ☎. 🅐 🔊 AE ⓪ VISA
M 9.00/14.00 **t.** and a la carte ⎸ 4.50 – ⌹ 5.00 – **120 rm** 45.00/70.00 **t.**

🏨 **Ardilaun House,** Taylor's Hill, ⌕ 21433, Telex 50013, ⚘ – 🛗 📺 ⌷wc ☎ 🅿 🅐 🔊 AE ⓪
VISA 🛞
closed 1 week at Christmas – **M** 8.00/15.75 **t.** and a la carte ⎸ 7.50 – **95 rm** ⌹ 27.00/50.00 **t.**,
2 suites 75.00/100.00 **t.**

🏨 Galway Ryan, Dublin Rd, E : 1 ¼ m. on N 6 ⌕ 53181, Telex 50149, ⚘ – 🛗 📺 ⌷wc ☎ 🅿. 🛞
96 rm

↔ **Adare House,** 9 Father Griffin Pl., Lower Salthill, ⌕ 62638 – 🅿. 🛞
10 rm ⌹ 12.00/28.00 **st.**

XX **Casey's Westwood,** Dangan Upper, Newcastle, NW : 1 ¾ m. on N 59 ⌕ 21442 – 🅿. 🔊 AE
VISA
M (restricted lunch) 7.50/13.50 **st.** and a la carte (approx.) 14.80 **t.** ⎸ 4.50.

at Salthill SW : 2 m. – ✉ Salthill – 🕾 091 Galway :

🏨 **Anno Santo,** Threadneedle Rd, ⌕ 22110 – 📺 ⌷wc 🕾 🅿. 🔊 AE ⓪ VISA. 🛞
closed 20 December-1 January – **M** (closed November-February) 6.50/12.50 **st.** and a la carte
– ⌹ 5.20 – **13 rm** 15.80 **st.**

🏨 **Rockbarton Park,** 5-7 Rockbarton Pk., ⌕ 22018 – ⌷wc ⋔wc 🕾 🅿. 🔊 AE ⓪ VISA
closed Christmas week – **M** (closed Sunday) (bar lunch)/dinner 12.00 **t.** and a la carte ⎸ 4.75 –
⌹ 3.95 – **11 rm** 9.00/23.00 **t.**

⚘ **Lochlurgain,** 22 Monksfield, Upper Salthill, ⌕ 22884 – ⌷wc ⋔wc. 🔊 AE VISA. 🛞
14 March-October – **M** (bar lunch)/dinner 13.95 **st.** and a la carte ⎸ 3.95 – **14 rm**
⌹ 16.95/39.95 **st.** – SB 51.95/65.00 **st.**

BMW, NISSAN Headford Rd ⌕ 65296   TOYOTA Bohermore ⌕ 63664
CITROEN, PEUGEOT, SAAB Spanish Par. ⌕ 62167

GARRYVOE Cork **405** H 12 – ✉ Castlemartyr – 🕾 021 Cork.

◆Dublin 161 – ◆Cork 23 – ◆Waterford 62.

🏨 **Garryvoe,** Castlemartyr, ⌕ 646718 – ⌷wc ⋔wc 🕾 🅿. 🔊 AE ⓪ VISA. 🛞
closed Christmas Day – **M** 9.00/15.00 **t.** and a la carte – ⌹ 4.50 – **19 rm** 12.00/26.00 **t.** –
SB 50.00 **st.**

GLENBEIGH Kerry **405** C 17 – pop. 195 – 🕾 066 Tralee.

◆Dublin 200 – ◆Killarney 21 – Tralee 24.

🏨 **Towers,** ⌕ 68212 – ⌷wc 🕾 🅿. 🔊 AE ⓪ VISA
April-October – **M** (bar lunch Monday to Saturday)/dinner 16.00 **t.** ⎸ 5.00 – **22 rm**
⌹ 24.00/44.00 **st.**

GLENDALOUGH Wicklow **405** MN 8 – 🕾 0404.

See : Ancient monastic city★★ (site★★★, St. Kervin's Church★) and Upper Lake★ in Glendalough Valley★★★.

◆Dublin 34 – Wexford 71.

🏨 **Royal,** ⌕ 5135 – ⌷wc 🅿. 🔊 ⓪ VISA. 🛞
Mid March-mid November – **M** 9.00/16.50 **t.** and a la carte ⎸ 5.60 – **13 rm** ⌹ 27.00/46.00 **t.** –
SB 45.00/50.00 **st.**

GLENGARRIFF Cork **405** D 12 – pop. 159 – 🕾 027.

See : Site★★★.

Envir. : S : Garinish Island (20 mn by boat AC) : Italian gardens★ – Martello Tower ⚒★★ AC.

🏌 ⌕ 63150, E : 1 m.

🛈 ⌕ 63084 (July-August).

◆Dublin 224 – ◆Cork 63 – ◆Killarney 37.

🏨 Casey's, ⌕ 63010, ⚘ – ⌷wc 🅿
20 rm.

GLEN OF AHERLOW Tipperary **405** H 10 – ⊠ 🕾 062 Tipperary.

See : Glen of Aherlow★ (statue of Christ the King★★).

♦Dublin 118 – Cahir 6 – Tipperary 9.

🏠 **Glen,** 𝒫 56146, 🚗 – ⇌wc 🛏wc ☎ 🅿. 🔼 🖭 _VISA_. 🎇
M 7.50/13.00 **t.** and a la carte ⓜ 4.20 – **20 rm** ⊑ 20.00/42.00 **t.** – SB (except Christmas) 62.00/68.00 **st.**

GLOUNTHAUNE Cork – see Cork.

GOREY Wexford **405** N 9 – pop. 2 588 – ECD : Wednesday – 🕾 055.

🖪 𝒫 21248 (July-August).

♦Dublin 58 – Waterford 55 – Wexford 38.

XXX **Marlfield House** ⌂ with rm, Courtown Rd, E : 1 m. 𝒫 21124, Telex 80757, ≤, « Regency house and conservatory », 🌳, park – 🖭 ⇌wc 🛏wc 🅿. 🎇
closed 3 days at Christmas – **M** (booking essential) 16.50/18.50 **t.** – **12 rm** ⊑ 75.00/100.00 **t.**

GOUGANE BARRA Cork **405** D 12 – ⊠ 🕾 026 Ballingeary.

See : Lake (site★).

♦Dublin 206 – ♦Cork 45.

🏠 **Gougane Barra** ⌂, 𝒫 47069, ≤ lough and mountains, 🎣 – ⇌wc 🅿. 🔼 ⓞ _VISA_. 🎇
April-September – **M** 12.00 **t.** and a la carte – **28 rm** 17.00/34.00 **t.** – SB 45.10 **st.**

HOWTH Dublin **405** N 7 – ⊠ 🕾 01 Dublin.

See : Howth Summit ≤★★ – Cliff Walk ≤★★ – Harbour★ – St Mary's Abbey★ (ruins 13C, 15C), site★ – Howth Gardens (rhododendrons★, site★, ≤★) AC.

🟦 Deer Park Hotel 𝒫 322624.

♦Dublin 10.

🏠 **Howth Lodge** (Best Western), 𝒫 390288, ≤ – 🖭 ⇌wc 🛏wc ☎ 🅿. 🏄. 🔼 🖭 ⓞ _VISA_. 🎇
closed 24 December-2 January – **M** (closed Saturday lunch and Sunday dinner) (bar lunch Monday to Saturday)/dinner 16.00 **st.** and a la carte ⓜ 4.00 – ⊑ 5.50 – **17 rm** 26.00/46.00 **st.** – SB (weekends only)(April-September) 55.00/64.00 **st.**

XX **King Sitric,** Harbour Rd, East Pier, 𝒫 325235, Seafood – 🔼 🖭 ⓞ _VISA_
closed Saturday lunch, Sunday, 10 days at Easter, 10 days at Christmas and Bank Holidays – **M** approx. 10.00/10.50 **t.** and a la carte ⓜ 5.40.

INISHANNON Cork **405** G 12 – pop. 241 – 🕾 021 Cork.

🟦 Castlebernard, Bandon 𝒫 41111, SW : 5 m.

♦Dublin 175 – ♦Cork 14 – ♦Killarney 46 – Bandon 4.5.

🏠 **Innishannon House** ⌂, S : ¾ m. on L 41 𝒫 775121, Telex 75398, 🎣, 🚗 – 🖭 ⇌wc 🕾 🅿. 🔼 🖭 ⓞ _VISA_
closed 3 days at Christmas – **M** 8.30/14.95 **st.** and a la carte ⓜ 4.75 – **12 rm** ⊑ 28.00/44.00 **st.** – SB 62.00/68.00 **st.**

FIAT, LANCIA 𝒫 023 (Bandon) 41514
FORD 72 Main St. 𝒫 023 (Bandon) 41522

NISSAN, OPEL Irishtown 𝒫 023 (Bandon) 41264
RENAULT Clonakilty Rd 𝒫 023 (Bandon) 41617

KANTURK Cork **405** F 11 – pop. 1 976 – ECD : Wednesday – 🕾 029.

♦Dublin 161 – ♦Cork 33 – ♦Killarney 31 – ♦Limerick 44.

🏠 **Assolas Country House** ⌂, E : 3 ¼ m. by L 38 on L 186 𝒫 50015, ≤, « Country house atmosphere », 🎣, 🚗, park, 🎇 – ⇌wc 🅿. 🎇
Mid April-October – **M** (closed Sunday) (booking essential)(dinner only) 17.00 **t.** ⓜ 4.50 – **10 rm** ⊑ 33.00/60.00 **t.**

AUDI, MAZDA 𝒫 12

KELLS Kilkenny **405** K 10 – pop. 2 623.

See : Augustinian Priory★★ 14C.

Envir. : Kilree's Church (site★, round tower★) S : 2 m.

♦Dublin 86 – Kilkenny 9 – ♦Waterford 23.

Hotels and restaurant see : Kilkenny N : 9 m.

KENMARE Kerry 🗺 D 12 – pop. 1 123 – ECD : Thursday – ☎ 064 Killarney.

Envir. : Kenmare River Valley★★ E : by L 62.

🏌 ℰ 41291.

🛈 ℰ 41233 (July-August).

◆Dublin 210 – ◆Cork 58 – ◆Killarney 20.

🏨 ☼ **Park** ⟐, ℰ 41200, Telex 73905, ≼, « Antiques, paintings », 🌴, park, ℀ – 🛐 ☎ 🕭 🅿. 🔄 🕭 VISA. ℅

Easter-mid November and Christmas-New Year – **M** 13.50/26.95 **t.** and a la carte 🍷 7.50 – **50 rm** ☲ 57.00/136.00 **st.**, **6 suites** 155.00/186.00 **st.**

Spec. Crème de poisson au crabe et melon, Tranche de trois poissons aux deux mousses, Trois cœurs au chocolat.

↟ **Remy's House,** Main St., ℰ 41589 – 🕥 🅕wc ☎. 🔄 🕭 ⑩ VISA

March-October – **5 rm** ☲ 14.00/22.00 **st.**

℀ **Lime Tree,** Shelbourne St., ℰ 41225, « Converted schoolhouse » – 🅿

Easter-31 October – **M** a la carte 13.30/18.80 **t.** 🍷 4.00.

FORD Henry St. ℰ 41166   NISSAN Shelbourne St. ℰ 41355

KILKENNY Kilkenny 🗺 K 10 – pop. 9 466 – ECD : Thursday – ☎ 056.

See : St. Canice's Cathedral★★ 13C – Grace's Castle (Courthouse)★ – Castle (park★, ≼★).

Envir. : Jerpoint Abbey★★ (ruins 12C-15C) SE : 12 m. – Callan (St. Mary's Church★ 13C-15C) SW : 13 m.

🏌 Glendine ℰ 22125, N : 1 m.

🛈 Rose Inn St. ℰ 21755.

◆Dublin 71 – ◆Cork 86 – ◆Killarney 115 – ◆Limerick 69 – ◆Tullamore 52 – ◆Waterford 29.

🏨 Kilkenny, College Rd, ℰ 62000, Telex 80177, 🔄, 🌴, ℀ – 🕥 🛏wc ☎ 🅿. 🛁 – **60 rm**.

🏨 **Newpark,** Castlecomer Rd, N : ¾ m. on N 77 ℰ 22122, Telex 80080, 🌴, ℀ – 🖺 rest 🕥 🛏wc 🅕wc ☎ 🅿. 🛁. 🔄 🕭 ⑩ VISA. ℅

M 8.25/14.85 **t.** and a la carte 🍷 5.25 – ☲ 6.00 – **43 rm** 32.50/47.00 **t.** – SB (except Bank Holiday weekends) 62.00/70.00 **st.**

℀℀ **Lacken House** with rm, Dublin Rd, ℰ 61085, 🌴 – 🅕wc 🅿. 🔄 🕭 ⑩ VISA. ℅

closed Sunday and Monday – **M** (dinner only) 15.00 **t.** and a la carte 10.70/17.25 **t.** 🍷 5.00 – **9 rm** ☲ 14.00/36.00 **t.** – SB 40.00/50.00 **st.**

at Knocktopher S : 13 m. on N 10 – ✉ ☎ 056 Kilkenny :

℀℀ **Knocktopher Abbey,** ℰ 28618, ≼, 🌴 – 🅿. 🔄 🕭 VISA

closed Sunday – **M** (dinner only) 14.50 **t.** and a la carte 14.00/20.25 **t.**

FORD Patrick St. ℰ 21016   RENAULT Irishtown ℰ 21494
OPEL Green St. ℰ 21304

KILLALOE Clare 🗺 G 9 – pop. 1 022 – ECD : Wednesday – ☎ 061.

See : site★ – **Envir. :** N : Lough Derg Coast Road★★ (L 12) to Tuamgraney, Lough Derg★★★ (Holy Island : site★★) – Nenagh : Butler Castle (keep★ 13C) NE : 9 m.

◆Dublin 109 – Ennis 32 – ◆Limerick 13 – ◆Tullamore 58.

🏨 Lakeside, ℰ 76122, ≼, 🐟, 🌴 – 🛏wc ☎ 🅿. 🛁 – **32 rm**.

KILLARNEY Kerry 🗺 D 11 – pop. 7 693 – ECD : Thursday – ☎ 064.

Envir. : SW : Killarney District, Ring of Kerry : Lough Leane★★★, Muckross House (gardens★★★) – Muckross Abbey★ (ruins 13C), Tork Waterfall (Belvedere : ≼★★, 251 steps), Lady's View Belvedere★★ – Gap of Dunloe★★.

🏌, 🏌 Mahoney's Point ℰ 31242, W : 3 m.

🛈 Town Hall ℰ 31633.

◆Dublin 189 – ◆Cork 54 – ◆Limerick 69 – ◆Waterford 112.

🏨 **Europe** ⟐, Fossa, W : 3 ½ m. on T 67 ℰ 31900, Telex 28213, ≼ lake and mountains, 🔄, 🐟, 🌴, park, ℀ – 🖺 🕥 ☎ 🕭 🅿. 🛁. 🔄 🕭 ⑩ VISA. ℅

March-October – **M** 15.00/19.00 **st.** and a la carte 🍷 8.00 – **175 rm** ☲ 48.00/75.00 **st.**, **6 suites** 85.00/125.00 **st.**

🏨 **Great Southern,** ℰ 31262, Telex 26998, 🔄, 🌴, ℀ – 🖺 🕥 ☎ 🕭 🅿. 🛁. 🔄 🕭 ⑩ VISA

closed 2 January-10 March – **M** (buffet lunch)/dinner 13.00 **t.** and a la carte 🍷 4.50 – ☲ 5.00 – **180 rm** 45.00/76.00 **t.**, **2 suites** 106.00/146.00 **t.** – SB 70.00/124.00 **st.**

🏨 **Dunloe Castle** ⟐, Beaufort, W : 6 m. by T 67 ℰ 44111, ≼ Gap of Dunloe, countryside and mountains, 🔄, 🐟, park, ℀ – 🖺 🕥 ☎ 🕭 🅿. 🛁. 🔄 🕭 ⑩ VISA

Mid March-mid October – **M** 15.00/19.00 **st.** and a la carte 🍷 8.00 – **140 rm** ☲ 38.00/75.00 **st.**, **1 suite** 80.00/110.00 **st.**

🏨 **Aghadoe Heights** ⟐, NW : 3 ½ m. by N 22 ℰ 31766, Telex 73942, ≼ countryside, lake and mountains, 🌴, ℀ – 🕥 ☎ 🕭 🅿. 🛁. 🔄 🕭 ⑩ VISA

closed 1 to 20 January and 21 to 31 December – **M** (buffet lunch)/dinner 17.00 **t.** and a la carte 🍷 4.50 – ☲ 6.50 – **60 rm** 30.00/72.00 **t.**, **1 suite** 75.00/115.00 **t.** – SB (weekends only) 63.00/95.00 **st.**

🏨 **Cahernane** 🏛, Muckross Rd, S : 1 m. on N 71 🕿 31895, Telex 28123, ≤, 🐾, 🚗, ※ – 📟wc
🕿 🅿. 🔼 🆎 ⓪ 𝓥𝓘𝓢𝓐
April-October and December – **M** (bar lunch)/dinner 19.75 **st.** and a la carte ▯ 5.00 – **52 rm**
⊐ 38.00/70.00 **st.**

🏨 **Castlerosse** (Best Western) 🏛, W : 2 m. on T 67 🕿 31144, Telex 70010, ≤ lake and mountains, 🐾, 🚗, ※ – 📟wc 🅰️ 🅿. 🔼 🆎 ⓪ 𝓥𝓘𝓢𝓐
April-October – **M** (dinner only and Sunday lunch)/dinner a la carte 12.00/17.00 –
40 rm ⊐ 36.00/52.00 **t.**

🏨 **Royal,** College St., 🕿 31853 – 📺 📟wc 🛁wc 🕿. 🔼. ※
March-October – **M** (bar lunch Monday to Saturday)/dinner 11.00 **t.** ▯ 7.00 – **28 rm** ⊐ 29.00/
45.00 **t.** – SB 55.00/65.00 **st.**

🏤 **Linden House,** New Rd, 🕿 31379 – 📟wc 🛁wc 🅿. ※
closed December and January – **M** *(closed Monday to non residents)* (dinner only) 10.00 **t.**
and a la carte ▯ 4.00 – **11 rm** ⊐ 11.00/20.00 **t.**

🏠 Carriglea Farmhouse 🏛, Muckross Rd, S : 1 ½ m. on N 71 🕿 31116, ≤, 🚗 – 📟wc 🛁wc 🅿.
※
9 rm.

🏠 Gardens, Countess Rd, off Muckross Rd, 🕿 31147, 🚗 – 📟wc 🛁wc 🅿. ※
21 rm.

🏠 **Kathleens Country House,** Madams Height, Tralee Rd, N : 2 m. on N 22 🕿 32810, ≤, 🚗
– 📟wc 🅿. ※
Mid March-October – **10 rm** ⊐ 25.00/35.00 **st.**

🏠 **Loch Lein Farm** 🏛, Fossa, W : 4 m. on T 67 🕿 31260, ≤, 🚗 – 📟wc 🛁wc 🅿. ※
Mid March-October – **12 rm** ⊐ 12.00/25.00 **st.**

🏠 Castle Lodge, Muckross Rd, 🕿 31545 – 🛁wc 🅿.
17 rm.

✕ **Gaby's,** 17 High St., 🕿 32519, Seafood bistro – 🔼 🆎 ⓪ 𝓥𝓘𝓢𝓐
Mid March-November – **M** *(closed Monday lunch and Sunday)* 25.00 **t.** and a la carte
14.80/25.50 **t.** ▯ 5.00.

AUDI, MAZDA, MERCEDES-BENZ, VW Park Rd 🕿   AUSTIN-ROVER, NISSAN Muckross Rd 🕿 31237
31355   FORD New Rd 🕿 31087

KILLINEY Dublin 𝟒𝟎𝟓 N 8 – ⚙ 01 Dublin.

♦Dublin 8 – Bray 4.

🏨 **Fitzpatrick's Castle,** 🕿 851533, 🔼, 🚗, ※, squash – 🛗 📺 🕿 🅿. 🔼 🆎 ⓪ 𝓥𝓘𝓢𝓐
M 7.50/17.00 **t.** and dinner a la carte ▯ 4.25 – ⊐ 6.60 – **96 rm** 39.00/84.50 **t.**, **7 suites**
79.50/139.50 **t.**

🏨 **Court,** Killiney Bay, 🕿 851622, ≤, 🚗 – 🛗 📺 🕿 🅿. 🔼 🆎 𝓥𝓘𝓢𝓐
closed Christmas Day – **M** 8.50/18.00 **t.** and a la carte ▯ 3.80 – ⊐ 5.75 – **36 rm** 46.50/56.50 **t.**

KILLYBEGS Donegal 𝟒𝟎𝟓 G 4 – pop. 1 570.

See : Fishing harbour★ – Carpet factory.

Envir. : NW : Glen Bay★★ – Glencolumbkille (site★★, folk village) NW : 14 m. – Portnoo (site★).

♦Dublin 181 – ♦Londonderry 65 – ♦Sligo 57.

KILTIMAGH Mayo 𝟒𝟎𝟓 F 6 – pop. 1 145 – ECD : Monday – ⚙ 094 Castlebar.

♦Dublin 140 – ♦Sligo 52.

🏠 **Westway,** James St., 🕿 81145 – 📟wc 🅿. 🔼 𝓥𝓘𝓢𝓐
closed 24 December-2 January – **M** *(closed Saturday lunch, Sunday and Bank Holidays)* (bar
lunch)/dinner 13.75 **t.** and a la carte – **13 rm** ⊐ 13.50/30.00 **t.**

KINSALE Cork 𝟒𝟎𝟓 G 12 – pop. 1 765 – ECD : Thursday – ⚙ 021 Cork.

See : St. Multose's Church★ 12C.

🏌 Ringmeanean, Belgooly 🕿 72197.

🚩 🕿 72234 (July-August).

♦Dublin 178 – ♦Cork 17.

🏨 Acton's (T.H.F.), Pier Rd, 🕿 772135, Telex 75443, ≤, 🔼, 🚗 – 🛗 📺 🕿 🅿. 🔼 🆎 ⓪
𝓥𝓘𝓢𝓐
M (bar lunch Monday to Saturday)/dinner 7.50/12.00 **st.** and a la carte ▯ 4.75 – **54 rm**
⊐ 43.00/80.00 **st.** – SB 55.00/75.00 **st.**

🏠 **Old Presbytery,** Cork St., 🕿 772027 – 𝓥𝓘𝓢𝓐. ※
5 rm ⊐ 10.50/21.00 **st.**

P.T.O. →

XX **Billy Mackesy's Bawnleigh House,** N : 5 ½ m. on Old Cork Rd ℰ 771333 – ℗
closed Sunday, Monday, 17 August-3 September and 20 to 31 December – **M** (dinner only)
9.25 **t.** and a la carte.

XX **Blue Haven** with rm, 3 Pearse St., ℰ 772209, Seafood – ⌂wc. ⬛ AE ⓞ VISA. ⅍
closed January and February – **M** a la carte 13.50/21.00 **st.** ⓘ 5.00 – **10 rm** ⌷ 25.00/60.00 **st.** –
SB 68.00/72.00 **st.**

XX **Vintage,** 50 Main St., ℰ 772502 – ⬛ AE ⓞ VISA
closed Sunday, January and February – **M** (dinner only) 20.00 **st.** and a la carte 14.40/17.50 **t.**
ⓘ 6.00.

X Man Friday, Scilly, SE : ½ m. ℰ 772260.

X **Bernards,** Milk Market, ℰ 772233 – ⬛ ⓞ VISA
closed 1 week November and January – **M** (dinner only) a la carte 13.90/18.00 **t.** ⓘ 5.25.

X **Cottage Loft,** Castlepark, SW : 1 ¾ m. by L 42 ℰ 772803, Seafood – ℗. ⬛ VISA
closed Monday – **M** (dinner only and Sunday lunch)/dinner 12.50 **st.** and a la carte ⓘ 5.00.

X **Coyle's,** 23 Lower O'Connell St., ℰ 772664 – ⬛ VISA
closed February – **M** (closed lunch Monday to Saturday) 10.00/15.00 **t.** and a la carte
15.00/19.00 **t.** ⓘ 6.00.

KNOCKTOPHER Kilkenny – see Kilkenny.

LAHINCH Clare 𝟜𝟘𝟝 D 9 – pop. 473 – ✪ 065.
Envir. : Cliffs of Moher★★★ (O'Brien's Tower ⅍★★ N : 1 h Rtn on foot) NW : 5 ½ m.
ᴵ₈, ᴵ₈ ℰ 81003.
◆Dublin 162 – ◆Galway 49 – ◆Limerick 41.

LEENANE Galway 𝟜𝟘𝟝 C 7.
See : ⩽★ on Killary Harbour★.
Exc. : SE : Joyces Country : by road L 100 from Leenane to Clonbur : Lough Nafooey★ – ⅍★ from
the bridge on Lough Mask★★.
◆Dublin 173 – Ballina 56 – ◆Galway 41.

Hotels see : Clifden SW : 19 m.

LETTERFRACK Galway 𝟜𝟘𝟝 C 7 – ✪ 095 Clifden.
Envir. : Kylemore Abbey (site★★) and Kylemore Lake★, E : 4 m. – Renvyle (castle ⩽★) NW : 5 m.
◆Dublin 189 – Ballina 69 – ◆Galway 57.

🏰 **Rosleague Manor** ⌕, W : 1 ½ m. on T 71 ℰ 41101, ⩽ Ballynakill harbour and Tully mountain,
« Country house atmosphere », 🌿, park – ⌂wc ⌂wc ℗. ⬛ VISA. ⅍
Easter-October – **M** (bar lunch)/dinner 16.50 **t.** and a la carte ⓘ 5.00 – **15 rm** ⌷ 37.00/65.00 **t.**
– SB (November-Easter) 90.00/130.00 **st.**

LETTERKENNY Donegal 𝟜𝟘𝟝 I 3 – pop. 6 444 – ECD : Monday – ✪ 074.
See : St. Eunan's Cathedral ⩽★.
Envir. : Grianan of Aileach★ (stone fort) ⅍★★★ NE : 18 m. – Gartan Lake★ NW : 8 ½ m.
ᴵ₈ Barnhill ℰ 21150, NE : 1 m.
🄴 Derry Rd ℰ 21160.
◆Dublin 150 – ◆Londonderry 21 – ◆Sligo 72.

🏠 **Gallagher's,** 100 Upper Main St., ℰ 22066 – �📺 ⌂wc ☎ ℗. ⬛ AE ⓞ VISA. ⅍
closed 25 to 31 December – **M** 7.50/10.50 **st.** and a la carte ⓘ 3.50 – **26 rm** ⌷ 20.00/34.00 **st.** –
SB (weekends only) 42.00/48.00 **st.**

LIMERICK Limerick 𝟜𝟘𝟝 G 9 – pop. 60 736 – ECD : Thursday – ✪ 061.
Envir. : Monasteranenagh Abbey★ (ruins 12C) S : 14 m. by N 20 Z.
ᴵ₈ Ballyclough ℰ 44083, S : 3 m. by N 20 Z.
✈ Shannon Airport : ℰ 061 (Shannon) 61444, Telex 26222, W : 16 m. by N 18 Y – **Terminal** :
Limerick Railway Station.
🄴 The Granary, Michael St. ℰ 317522.
◆Dublin 120 – ◆Cork 58.

Plan opposite

🏨 Limerick Inn, Ennis Rd, NW : 4 m. on N 18 ℰ 51544, Telex 28121, ⬛, ⅍ – ⧓ ▤ rest 📺 ☎ &
℗. ⌖. ⅍   on N 18   Y
156 rm, 4 suites.

🏨 Jury's, Ennis Rd, ℰ 55266, Telex 28266, 🌿 – ▤ rest 📺 ☎ & ℗. ⌖   Y z
96 rm.

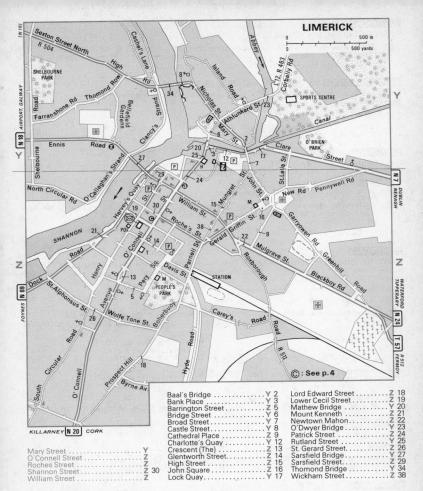

LIMERICK

0   500 m
0   500 yards

© : See p.4

🏨 Two Mile Inn, Ennis Rd, NW : 3 ½ m. on N 18 ℘ 53122, Telex 70157, 🍴 – 📺 🛏️wc 🕿 🕭 🅿️. 🏊 on N 18 Y
125 rm.

🏨 **New Greenhills,** Ennis Rd., NW : 2 ¼ m. on N 18 ℘ 53033, Telex 70246, 🍴 – 📺 🛏️wc 🕿 🅿️. 🏊 🔼 AE ⓪ VISA. ❄️ on N 18 Y
M 8.50/13.50 st. and a la carte ⓘ 5.50 – **55 rm** 🖵 25.50/56.00 st.

🏨 Limerick Ryan, Ennis Rd, NW : 1 ¼ m. on N 18 ℘ 53922, Telex 26920 – 🛗 📺 🛏️wc 🕿 🅿️. 🏊 ❄️ on N 18 Y
184 rm.

🏨 **Royal George,** O'Connell St., ℘ 44566, Telex 26910 – 🛗 📺 🛏️wc 🕿. 🏊 🔼 AE ⓪ VISA Z c
M 8.00/10.50 st. and a la carte ⓘ 4.50 – 🖵 5.00 – **60 rm** 20.00/44.00 t.

🏨 **Cruise's Royal,** 5-7 O'Connell St., ℘ 44977, Telex 70088 – 🛗 📺 🛏️wc 🕿. 🏊 🔼 AE ⓪ VISA. ❄️ Z a
M 8.00/15.00 t. and a la carte ⓘ 5.15 – 🖵 6.00 – **73 rm** 21.00/37.10 t.

AUSTIN-ROVER, SUZUKI, VOLVO Coonagh Cross ℘ 51577
BMW, NISSAN Castle St. ℘ 43133
FORD Lansdowne ℘ 52244

MAZDA, AUDI, MERCEDES-BENZ, PORSCHE, VW Dublin Rd ℘ 46000
MITSUBISHI Raheen ℘ 27277
OPEL, BEDFORD Ennis Rd ℘ 53211

♦Dublin 164 – ♦Galway 51 – ♦Limerick 43.

   🏨 **Liscannor Golf**, ℰ 81186, ⩽ Liscannor harbour, 🚗 – ⊟wc 🕾 🅿. 🔼 AE ⓪ *VISA* ⅋
     April-October – **M** (bar lunch)/dinner 14.00 **st.** and a la carte – **25 rm** ⌷ 26.00/48.00 **t.** –
     SB 60.00/66.00 **st.**

Envir. : Cliffs of Moher★★★ (O'Brien's Tower ⅋★★ N : 1 h Rtn on foot) SW : 8 m.
🖪 ℰ 62 (July-September).
♦Dublin 167 – ♦Galway 39 – ♦Limerick 47.

   🏠 **Sheedy's Spa View**, Sulphir Hill, ℰ 74026, 🚗, ⅋ – ⊟wc 🅿. 🔼 *VISA* ⅋
     15 March-October – **M** (bar lunch)/dinner 15.00 **t.** and a la carte 🍴 7.50 – **11 rm** ⌷ 24.00/35.00 **t.**

See : Castle (site★) – **Envir. :** SE : Blackwater Valley★★ (from Lismore to the mouth, by a scenic
road along the right bank of the River Blackwater).
🛈 ℰ 54026, N : 1 m.
♦Dublin 143 – ♦Cork 37 – ♦Killarney 74 – ♦Waterford 44.

   🏠 **Ballyrafter House** 🦢, N : ¾ m. by T 30 on L 34 ℰ 54002, 🚗, park – ⊟wc 🅿. 🔼 ⓪. ⅋
     Easter-October – **M** (bar lunch)/dinner 11.00 **t.** 🍴 4.50 – **12 rm** ⌷ 16.00/33.00 **t.** – SB (weekends
     only) 53.00/56.00 **st.**

TOYOTA Lismore ℰ 54147

Envir. : SE : Lough Derravaragh★ – Lough Owel★ – Multyfarman (Franciscan College park : Stations
of the Cross★) – Lough Lene★ – Fore (St. Feichin's Church and ruined priory 13C★) – Lough
Ennell★.
🛈 Dublin Rd ℰ 46310 – 🖪 ℰ 6566 (June-August).
♦Dublin 74 – Roscommon 19 – ♦Sligo 57 – ♦Tullamore 47.

   🏨 **Longford Arms**, 24 Main St., ℰ 46296 – 📺 ⊟wc 🛁wc 🕾 🅿. 🎿. 🔼 AE ⓪ *VISA*
     closed 4 days at Christmas – **M** 9.25/13.50 **st.** and a la carte 🍴 3.50 – **51 rm** ⌷ 19.50/39.50 **st.**
     – SB 58.00/76.00 **st.**

FORD Dublin Rd ℰ 46421
MAZDA, VW, AUDI Dublin Rd ℰ 46321
NISSAN Drumlish ℰ 24104

RENAULT Athlone Rd ℰ 46615
TOYOTA Lanesboro ℰ 21159
TOYOTA Athlone Rd ℰ 45621

♦Dublin 81 – ♦Tullamore 54.

   🏡 **Robin Hill** 🦢, ℰ 83121, 🚗 – 🅿
     M *(closed Monday to non-residents)* (dinner only) 10.50 **st.** 🍴 3.30 – **5 rm** ⌷ 10.00/20.00 **st.**

🛈 Lackadove ℰ 41072.
♦Dublin 186 – ♦Cork 25 – ♦Killarney 30.

   🏠 **Castle**, Main St., ℰ 41074 – ⊟wc 🛁wc 🕾. 🔼 ⓪ *VISA*. ⅋
     M 6.00/10.00 **t.** and a la carte 🍴 3.50 – **18 rm** ⌷ 14.00/28.00 **t.**

Envir. : Swords (St. Columba's Church : towers★) W : 2 ½ m. – Lusk (church : round towers★)
NW : 8 m.
🛈 ℰ 451428.
♦Dublin 9 – Drogheda 24.

   XX **Johnny's**, 9 St. James's Terr., ℰ 450314 – 🔼 AE ⓪ *VISA*
     closed Sunday, Monday, 1 week at Easter, September-mid October and 1 week at Christmas –
     M (dinner only) a la carte 14.05/23.20 **t.** 🍴 4.85.

FORD Main St. ℰ 452044

🛈 Balleyellis ℰ 21145, SE : 1 ½ m. from Mallow Bridge.
♦Dublin 149 – ♦Cork 21 – ♦Killarney 40 – ♦Limerick 41.

   🏨 **Longueville House** 🦢, W : 3 ½ m. by N 72 ℰ 47156, Telex 75498, ⩽, « Georgian mansion
     in extensive grounds », 🦢, 🚗, park – ⊟wc 🛁wc 🅿. ⓪ *VISA*. ⅋
     2 April-October – **M** (booking essential) (bar lunch and Sunday dinner, residents only)/
     dinner 18.00 **st.** and a la carte 🍴 5.00 – **17 rm** ⌷ 38.00/71.00 **st.** – SB (weekends only)
     85.00/105.00 **st.**

OPEL Buttevant ℰ 23338

MAYNOOTH Kildare **405** M 7 – pop. 3 388 – ECD : Wednesday – ✪ 01 Dublin.

♦Dublin 15.

XXX **Moyglare Manor** ⤫ with rm, Moyglare, N : 2 m. ℰ 286351, Telex 90358, ≤, « Georgian country house with antique furnishings », ⌖, park – ⇔wc 🅿 ⚡ 🆎 ⓓ 𝗩𝗜𝗦𝗔 ⌕
closed 24 to 26 December – **M** *(closed Saturday lunch)* 12.95/25.00 **t.** and a la carte 14.15/24.20 **t.**
– **11 rm** ⤶ 60.00/90.00 **t.**

MOUNTSHANNON Clare **405** G 9.

♦ Dublin 129 – ♦ Galway 45 – ♦ Limerick 30.

☈ Mountshannon, Main St., ℰ 62, ⌖ – ⋔wc – **11 rm**.

MOVILLE Donegal **405** K 2 – pop. 1 252 – ✪ 077.

♦Dublin 165 – ♦Londonderry 19.

🏠 **McNamara's,** ℰ 82010 – ⇔wc ⋔wc. 𝗩𝗜𝗦𝗔
closed Christmas Day and Boxing Day – **M** (bar lunch)/dinner 7.00/12.00 **st.** and a la carte ⓘ 4.20 – **13 rm** ⤶ 16.50/30.00 **st.** – SB 50.00 **st.**

MOYARD Galway **405** C 7 – ✪ 095 Clifden.

♦Dublin 187 – ♦Galway 55.

🏠 Crocnaraw Country House ⤫, ℰ 41068, ≤, ⟟, ⌖ – ⇔wc 🅿. ⌕ – **10 rm**.

MOYCULLEN Galway **405** E 9 – pop. 228 – ✉ Rosscahill – ✪ 091 Galway.

♦Dublin 139 – ♦Galway 7.

☈ **Knockferry Lodge** ⤫, Knockferry (on Lough Corrib), NE : 6 ½ m. ℰ 80122, ⟟ – ⇔wc 🅿.
🆎 ⓓ 𝗩𝗜𝗦𝗔 ⌕
Easter-October – **M** (booking essential)(bar lunch)/dinner 11.50 **t.** – **12 rm** ⤶ 15.50/29.00 **t.**

XX **Drimcong House,** NW : 1 m. on N 59 ℰ 85115, « 17C estate house », ⌖ – 🅿. ⚡ 🆎 ⓓ
𝗩𝗜𝗦𝗔
closed Sunday, Monday, January and February – **M** (booking essential)(dinner only) 14.95 **st.**
and a la carte 18.50/24.50 **t.** ⓘ 4.50.

MULLINGAR Westmeath **405** JK 7 – pop. 7 854 – ✪ 044 – Envir. : N : Lough Derravaragah★ – Lough Owel★ – Multyfarman (Franciscan College park: Stations of the Cross★ – NE : Lough Lene★ – Fore (St. Feichin's Church and ruined priory 13C★) – S : Lough Ennell.

🅩 Dublin Road ℰ 48650.

♦ Dublin 49 – ♦ Drogheda 36.

🏠 **Greville Arms,** Pearse St., ℰ 48563, Telex 91880 – 📺 ⇔wc ⋔wc ☎ 🅿. ⚞ ⚡ ⓓ 𝗩𝗜𝗦𝗔 ⌕
M 5.75/12.00 **st.** and a la carte ⓘ 3.95 – **28 rm** ⤶ 20.00/39.50 **st.** – SB (weekends only) 49.90 **st.**

FIAT, LANCIA Dublin Rd ℰ (044) 48806   FORD Harbour St. ℰ (044) 48403

NAAS Kildare **405** M 8 – pop. 8 345 – ✪ 045.

♦Dublin 19 – Kilkenny 50.

🏠 Town House, Limerick Rd, ℰ 79226 – 📺 ⇔wc ⋔wc ☎ 🅿 – **11 rm**.

NAVAN Meath **405** L 7 – pop. 4 124 – ECD : Thursday – ✪ 046.

Envir. : Bective Abbey★ (12C ruins) S : 3 m.

🅟 Royal Tara, Bellinter Park ℰ 25244.

♦Dublin 30 – Drogheda 16 – ♦Dundalk 34.

at Dunderry SW : 5 ½ m. by N 51 on L 23 – ✉ ✪ 046 Navan :

XXX ✿ **Dunderry Lodge,** W : ¾ m. ℰ 31671, « Converted farm buildings » – 🅿. ⚡ 🆎 ⓓ 𝗩𝗜𝗦𝗔
closed Saturday lunch, Sunday, Monday, 15 to 22 April and 20 December-10 February –
M (booking essential) 9.00/15.00 **t.** and a la carte 18.50/22.00 **t.** ⓘ 6.00
Spec. Terrine of two fish, sauce verte, Supreme of pigeon Empress Eugenie, Magret of wild duck with a confit of pears (September-January).

PEUGEOT-TALBOT Castlemartin ℰ 21949   TOYOTA Kells Rd ℰ 21336
RENAULT Cannon Row ℰ 21312   VW-AUDI, MERCEDES-BENZ Dublin Rd ℰ 21212

NEWBAWN Wexford **405** L 10 – see New Ross.

NEWBRIDGE (DROICHEAD NUA) Kildare **405** L 8 – pop. 5 780 – ECD : Tuesday – ✪ 045 Naas.

Envir. : Kildare (St. Brigid's Cathedral★ 13C-19C and round tower★ 9C-10C) SW : 5 m. – Tully (National Stud★, Japanese gardens★ *AC*) SW : 6 m. via Kildare – Old Kilcullen (site★, ⌖★) – 🅟 Cill-Dara, ℰ 045 (Kildare) 21433, Kildare Town, SW : 5 m. – 🅟 Curragh ℰ 045 (Curragh) 41238, S : 3 m.

♦Dublin 28 – Kilkenny 57 – ♦Tullamore 36.

🏨 **Keadeen,** Ballymany, SW : 1 m. on N 7 ℰ 31666, ⌖ – 📺 ⚐ ⚞ 🅿. ⚞ ⌕
M 14.00/17.00 **st.** and a la carte ⓘ 5.00 – **37 rm** ⤶ 40.00/100.00 **st.**, **1 suite** 100.00/120.00 **st.**

FIAT Moorefield ℰ 31725

NEWMARKET-ON-FERGUS Clare **405** F 7 – pop. 1 348 – ✪ 061 Shannon.

♦Dublin 136 – Ennis 8 – ♦Limerick 15.

🏛 **Dromoland Castle** ⌖, NW : 1 ½ m. on N 18 𝒫 71144, Telex 26854, ≼, « Converted castle », 🏊, ⌖, park, ⌖ – 📺 ☎ 🅿 🏾 🚗 AE ⑩ VISA ⌖
April-October – **M** 15.00/25.00 t. 🍴 6.50 – ⌖ 9.50 – **77 rm** 95.00/125.00 t.

NEWPORT Mayo **405** D 6 – pop. 470 – ✪ 098.

See : St. Patrick's Church★, modern Irish-Romanesque style (site★).

Envir. : Burrishoole Abbey (site★) NW : 2 m.

♦Dublin 164 – Ballina 37 – ♦Galway 60.

🏛 **Newport House** ⌖, 𝒫 41222, Telex 53740, « Country house atmosphere, antiques », ⌖, ⌖, park – 📺wc 📺wc 🅿, AE ⑩ VISA ⌖
19 March-September – **M** (buffet lunch)/dinner 21.00 **st.** and a la carte 🍴 4.00 – **20 rm** ⌖ 37.00/62.00 **st.**

NEW ROSS Wexford **405** L 10 – pop. 5 386 – ECD : Wednesday – ✪ 051.

Envir. : St. Mullins Monastery (site★) N : 9 m. – John F. Kennedy Memorial Park★ 1968 (arboretum, ≼★) S : 7 ½ m. – SW : River Barrow Valley★.

🏌 Tinneranny 𝒫 21433.

🛈 𝒫 21857 (July-August).

♦Dublin 88 – Kilkenny 27 – ♦Waterford 15 – Wexford 23.

🏛 **Five Counties,** SE : ½ m. on N 25 𝒫 21703, Telex 80577, park – 📺 📺wc 📺wc ☎ 🅿, 🚗 AE ⑩ VISA ⌖
M 9.00/15.00 t. and a la carte 🍴 4.25 – **35 rm** ⌖ 27.00/60.00 t. – SB 50.00/60.00 **st.**

⌂ **Inishross House,** 96 Mary St., 𝒫 21335 – 🅿. ⌖
6 rm ⌖ 9.00/18.00 **st.**

at Newbawn E : 8 m. by N 25 and L 160 – ✉ ✪ 051 New Ross :

XX **Cedar Lodge** with rm, Carrigbyrne, N : 1 ½ m. on N 25 𝒫 28386 – 📺 📺wc ☜ 🅿. 🚗 AE
VISA
closed mid January-mid February – **M** 12.00/17.75 **st.** and a la carte – **13 rm** ⌖ 35.00/45.00 t. – SB 75.00 **st.**

FIAT, LANCIA Rosebercon 𝒫 21122   FORD Waterford Rd 𝒫 21403

OUGHTERARD Galway **405** E 7 – pop. 748 – ✪ 091 Galway.

See : The northern scenic road (cul-de-sac) ≼★★ on Lough Corrib★★★.

Envir. : Aughnanure Castle★ (16C) SE : 3 m. – Leckavrea Mountain★ NW : 13 m. – Gortmore (≼★★ S : on Kilkieran Bay, ≼★ NW : on the Twelve Pins) SW : 16 m.

🏌 Gurteeva 𝒫 82131.

♦Dublin 149 – ♦Galway 17.

🏛 **Currarevagh House** ⌖, NW : 4 m. 𝒫 82313, ≼, « Country house atmosphere », ⌖, ⌖, park, ⌖ – 📺wc 📺wc 🅿. ⌖
15 April-3 October – **M** *(closed lunch to non residents)* (booking essential) 6.70/13.75 t. 🍴 3.75 – **15 rm** ⌖ 27.50/55.00 t.

🏛 **Sweeney's Oughterard House** ⌖, W : ½ m. on T 71 𝒫 82207, ⌖ – 🛗 📺wc ☎ 🅿. 🚗 AE ⑩ VISA
closed 4 days at Christmas – **M** a la carte 14.70/23.00 t. 🍴 4.50 – **20 rm** ⌖ 31.00/72.00 t.

PARKNASILLA Kerry **405** C 12 – ✪ 064 Sneem.

🏌 Parknasilla 𝒫 45122.

♦Dublin 224 – ♦Cork 72 – ♦Killarney 34.

🏛 **Parknasilla Great Southern** ⌖, 𝒫 45122, Group Telex 73899, ≼ Kenmare river, bay and mountains, 🏊, 🏌, ⌖, ⌖, park, ⌖ – 📺 ☎ 🅿 🏾 🚗 AE ⑩ VISA ⌖
16 April-October and Christmas – **M** 12.00/19.00 t. and a la carte 🍴 5.75 – ⌖ 6.00 – **57 rm** 59.00/87.00 t., **1 suite** 74.00 t. – SB 108.00/138.00 **st.**

PORTLAOISE Laois **405** K 8 – pop. 4 049 – ✪ 0502.

🏌 Heath 𝒫 26533, E : 4 m.

🛈 𝒫 21178 (July-August).

♦ Dublin 54 – Kilkenny 31 – ♦Limerick 67.

🏛 **Killeshin,** Dublin Rd, E : 1 m. on N 7 𝒫 21663, Telex 60036 – 📺 📺wc 📺wc 🅿 🏾 🚗 AE ⑩ VISA ⌖
M 6.95/12.95 t. and a la carte 🍴 4.50 – **44 rm** ⌖ 25.00/42.00 t.

PORT NA BLAGH Donegal **405** I 2 – see Dunfanaghy.

RAPHOE Donegal **405** J 3 – pop. 1 070 – ✪ 074.

Envir. : Beltany Stone Circle★ (site★) from the road 10 mn on foot, S : 2 m.

♦Dublin 139 – Donegal 29 – ♦Londonderry 20 – ♦Sligo 69.

  🏠 **Central,** The Diamond, ℰ 45126 – �🗄wc. ⅏
  closed 23 to 30 December – **M** *(closed lunch Sunday and Bank Holidays)* 6.50/8.50 **st.**
  and a la carte – **9 rm** ⇌ 13.50/25.00 **st.**

RATH LUIRC = Charleville.

RATHMULLAN Donegal **405** J 2 – pop. 584 – ⊠ ✪ 074 Letterkenny.

Envir. : Mulroy Bay ★★ NW : 8 m. – Fanad Head ≤★ N : 20 m.

🏌 Otway, Saltpans ℰ Rathmullen 58319.

♦Dublin 165 – ♦Londonderry 36 – ♦Sligo 87.

  🏛 **Rathmullan House** ⅍, N : ½ m. on R 247 ℰ 58188, ≤ Lough Swilly and hills, « Country
  house atmosphere, gardens », ⅍, ⽊, park, ⅍ – �🗄wc ⅏wc 🅟 🅿 ☒ 🆎 𝗩𝗜𝗦𝗔. ⅏
  Easter-October – **M** (restricted lunch) 9.00/15.00 **t.** 🛢 4.00 – **20 rm** ⇌ 17.50/60.00 **t.** –
  SB 74.25/89.10 **st.**

  🏠 **Fort Royal** ⅍, N : 1 m. off R 247 ℰ 58100, ≤ Lough Swilly, 🏌, ⽊, park, ⅍, squash –
  ⅏wc 🅿 🅟 🆎 ⓞ 𝗩𝗜𝗦𝗔
  Mid April-September – **M** (bar lunch)/dinner 13.50 **st.** 🛢 4.00 – **20 rm** ⇌ 32.00/60.00 **st.** –
  SB 65.00/75.00 **st.**

RATHNEW Wicklow **405** N 8 – pop. 1 366 – ⊠ ✪ 0404 Wicklow.

♦Dublin 31 – ♦Waterford 82 – Wexford 65.

  🏛 **Tinakilly House** ⅍, ℰ 69274, ≤, « Victorian country house », ⽊, park – 📺 ⅏wc ☎ 🅿.
  🆎 𝗩𝗜𝗦𝗔. ⅏
  closed January – **M** 10.00/17.95 **t.** 🛢 5.00 – **14 rm** ⇌ 50.00/70.00 **t.**

  🏠 **Hunter's,** N : ¾ m. on L 29 ℰ 4106, « Converted 18C inn with garden » – ⅏wc 🅿. 🅿 🆎
  ⓞ 𝗩𝗜𝗦𝗔. ⅏
  M 10.00/16.00 **t.** 🛢 4.25 – **17 rm** ⇌ 22.50/45.00 **t.**

REDCASTLE Donegal **405** K 2 – ⊠ ✪ Moville.

♦Dublin 162 – ♦Londonderry 17.

  🏛 Redcastle, ℰ 243, ≤, 🏌, ⅍, park, ⅍, squash – 📺 ⅏wc ☜ 🅿. ⅏ – **14 rm**.

RENVYLE Galway **405** C 7 – ⊠ Connemara – ✪ 095 Clifden.

♦ Dublin 196 – ♦ Galway 61.

  🏛 **Renvyle House** ⅍, ℰ 43434, Telex 50896, ≤ Atlantic Ocean, ⤱ heated, 🏌, ⅍, ⽊, park,
  ⅍ – ⅏wc ☎ 🅿. 🅿 🆎 ⓞ 𝗩𝗜𝗦𝗔
  Mid April-30 November and Christmas-New Year – **M** 8.50/13.90 **t.** 🛢 3.90 – **70 rm**
  ⇌ 35.50/46.00 **t.**, **1 suite** 50.00/80.00 **t.**

RIVERSTOWN Sligo **405** G 5 – pop. 262 – ✪ 071 Sligo.

♦Dublin 123 – ♦Sligo 13.

  🏠 **Coopershill** ⅍, ℰ 65108, ≤, ⽊, park – ⅏wc 🅿. 🆎 𝗩𝗜𝗦𝗔. ⅏
  Easter-September – **M** (dinner only) 15.00 – **5 rm** ⇌ 23.00/50.00.

ROSAPENNA Donegal **405** I 2 – ✪ 074 Letterkenny.

♦ Dublin 216 – Donegal 52 – ♦ Londonderry 47.

  🏛 **Rosapenna Golf** (Best Western), Downings, ℰ 55301, ≤, 🏌, ⅍ – ⅏wc ☜ 🅿. 🅿 🆎 ⓞ
  𝗩𝗜𝗦𝗔
  March-October – **M** (bar lunch)/dinner 14.50 **t.** 🛢 4.50 – **40 rm** ⇌ 22.00/48.50 **t.** –
  SB 60.00/73.50 **st.**

ROSCREA Tipperary **405** I 9 – ✪ 0505.

♦Dublin 75 – ♦Limerick 45.

  🏠 **Racket Hall,** Dublin Rd, E : 1 ¾ m. on N 7 ℰ 21748, ⽊ – ⅏wc ⅏wc ☜ 🅿. 🅿 🆎 ⓞ 𝗩𝗜𝗦𝗔.
  ⅏
  closed 25 and 26 December – **M** 7.00/12.50 **st.** and a la carte 🛢 4.75 – ⇌ 4.50 – **10 rm**
  20.00/35.00 **st.**

ROSSES POINT Sligo **405** G 5 – see Sligo.

Do not use yesterday's maps for today's journey.

ROSSLARE Wexford **405** M 11 – pop. 779 – ✪ 053.
⌗ ℰ 32113.

♦Dublin 104 – ♦Waterford 50 – Wexford 12.

🏨 **Kelly's Strand,** Strand Rd, ℰ 32114, ⌇ heated, 🔲, 🚗, ✻, squash – 🔋 📺 ☎ 🅿. 🎿
closed 6 December-20 February – **M** 9.00/15.90 t. 🛆 8.30 – **93 rm** ⌇ 37.50/54.00 t.

🏨 Casey's Cedars, Strand Rd, ℰ 32124, Telex 80237, 🚗 – 📺 ⌷wc ☎ 🛆 🅿. 🎿 🎿 – **34 rm**.

✗ **Le Gourmet,** Strand Rd, ℰ 32157, French rest.
Mid June-mid September – **M** (lunch by arrangement) 13.50 **st.** and a la carte 12.40/14.80 **t.**
🛆 6.00.

ROSSLARE HARBOUR Wexford **405** N 11 – pop. 777 – ✪ 053 Wexford.
🚢 Shipping connections with the Continent : to France (Cherbourg), (Le Havre) (Irish Continental Line) – to Fishguard (Sealink) 1-4 daily (3 h 30 mn) – to Pembroke (B & I Line) (4 h 15 mn).
🛈 ℰ 33232.

♦Dublin 105 – ♦Waterford 51 – Wexford 13.

🏨 **Rosslare,** ℰ 33110, Telex 80772, ≼, squash – 📺 ⌷wc ☎ 🅿. 🔼 🆎 _VISA_
closed Christmas Day – **M** 9.50/13.50 st. and a la carte 🛆 4.20 – ⌇ 3.50 – **25 rm** 12.50/50.00 st.
– SB 46.00/58.00 **st.**

🏨 **Tuskar House,** St. Martins Rd, ℰ 33363, ≼, 🚗 – ⌷wc ☎ 🅿. 🔼 🆎 ⓞ _VISA_. 🎿
M (bar lunch)/dinner 12.95 **st.** and a la carte 🛆 3.95 – **20 rm** ⌇ 18.00/36.00 – SB 49.00/69.00 **st.**

ROSSNOWLAGH Donegal **405** H 4 – ✪ 072 Bundoran.

♦Dublin 157 – Donegal 9 – ♦Sligo 33.

🏨 **Sand House** 🦢, ℰ 51777, Telex 40460, ≼ bay, beach and mountains, 🐟, ✻ – 🅿. 🔼 🆎 ⓞ _VISA_. 🎿
Easter-September – **M** (approx) 8.50/16.50 **t.** and a la carte – **40 rm** ⌇ 25.00/65.00 **t.**

ST ERNAN'S ISLAND Donegal – see Donegal.

SALTHILL Galway **405** E 8 – see Galway.

SCHULL (SKULL) Cork **405** D 13 – pop. 502 – ✪ 028 Skibbereen.
Envir. : E : Roaringwater Bay★.

♦Dublin 226 – ♦Cork 65 – ♦Killarney 64.

✗ **Ard-na-Greine Inn** 🦢 with rm, SW : 1 ¾ m. by L 57 ℰ 28181, 🚗 – ⌷wc ⌷wc 🅿. 🆎 ⓞ _VISA_. 🎿
Easter-October – **M** (booking essential) (bar lunch)/dinner 16.50 **t.** 🛆 5.00 – **7 rm**
⌇ 37.00/56.00 **t.**

✗ Courtyard, Main St., ℰ 28209.

SCOTSTOWN Monaghan **405** K 5 – pop. 286 – ⊠ Clones – ✪ 047 Monaghan.

♦Dublin 85 – ♦Dundalk 37 – Donaghan 5.

🏨 **Hilton Park** 🦢, N : 1 m. ℰ 56007, ≼ woodland and lake, « 18C mansion house in extensive grounds », 🖇, 🐟, 🚗, park – ⌷wc – ⌷wc 🅿.
Easter-September – **M** (dinner only)(residents only) 17.50 **t.** 🛆 4.00 – **5 rm** ⌇ 27.50/80.00 **t.** –
SB (weekdays only) 96.00/122.10 **st.**

SHANAGARRY Cork **405** H 12 – ⊠ ✪ 021 Cork.

♦Dublin 163 – ♦Cork 25 – ♦Waterford 64.

✗✗ **Ballymaloe House** 🦢 with rm, NW : 1 ¾ m. on L 35 ℰ 652531, Telex 75208, ≼, « Country house atmosphere », ⌇ heated, 🚗, park, ✻ – ⌷wc ⌷wc ☎ 🛆 🅿. 🔼 🆎 ⓞ _VISA_. 🎿
closed 24 to 26 December – **M** (buffet lunch)/dinner 19.00 **t.** 🛆 5.00 – ⌇ 4.50 – **31 rm**
28.50/60.00 **t.** – SB (November-February) 67.00 **st.**

SHANNON AIRPORT Clare **405** F 9 – ✪ 061 Limerick.
⌗ ℰ Shannon 61020 – ✈ ℰ 61444, Telex 26222 – **Terminal :** Limerick Railway Station ℰ 42433.
🛈 ℰ 61664 and 61604.

♦Dublin 136 – Ennis 16 – ♦Limerick 15.

🏨 **Shannon International,** ℰ 61122, Telex 24018 – 📺 ⌷wc ☎ 🅿. 🔼 🆎 ⓞ _VISA_. 🎿
April-October – **M** (buffet lunch)/dinner 16.00 **t.** and a la carte 🛆 5.50 – ⌇ 6.00 – **120 rm**
41.00/60.00 **t.**

SKERRIES Dublin **405** N 7 – pop. 5 793 – ✪ 01 Dublin.

♦Dublin 19 – Drogheda 15.

🏠 Pier House, Harbour Rd, ℰ 491708, ≼ – ⌷wc ⌷wc – **11 rm**.

✗ **Red Bank,** 7 Church St., ℰ 491005, Seafood – 🔼 🆎 ⓞ _VISA_
closed Sunday, Monday, last week October and November – **M** (dinner only) 14.50 **t.** and a la carte 17.25/19.25 **t.** 🛆 4.35.

SKIBBEREEN Cork 405 E 13 – pop. 2 130 – ☎ 028.

🛈 Town Hall ☎ 21766.

♦Dublin 205 – ♦Cork 51 – ♦Killarney 68.

  XX **Mill House,** Rineen, E : 5 m. by L 60 on Union Hall road ☎ 36299, ☞ – P. 🖽 🖭 ⑩ VISA
      closed Monday, January, February and November – **M** (dinner only)(booking essential) 14.50 **t.**
      ⌂ 4.00.

SKULL = Schull.

SLANE Meath 405 M 6 – pop. 690 – ☎ 041 Drogheda.

See : Hill of Slane (site★, ≼★).

♦Dublin 42 – Drogheda 8 – ♦Dundalk 26.

  XX **Slane Castle,** W : 1 m. on N 51 ☎ 24207 – P. 🖽 🖭 ⑩ VISA
      closed Monday, Tuesday and January-mid March – **M** (dinner only and Sunday lunch) 13.50 **t.**
      and a la carte 14.60/22.85 **t.** ⌂ 3.90.

SLIEVERUE Waterford – see Waterford.

SLIGO Sligo 405 G 5 – pop. 17 232 – ☎ 071.

See : Sligo Abbey★ (13C ruins) – Court House★ – Envir. : E : Lough Gill★★★ (Innisfree★) Park's Castle (site★★), Lough Colgagh★★, Drumcliff (High Cross) ≼★ on Benbulbin Moutains N : 4 m. – Glencar Lough★ NE : 6 m. – Carrowmore (Megalithic cemetery★) SW : 2 m.

🛅 Strandhill ☎ 68188, W : 8 m. – 🛈 Aras Reddan, Temple St. ☎ 61201.

♦Dublin 133 – ♦Belfast 126 – ♦Dundalk 106 – ♦Londonderry 86.

  🏨 Sligo Park, Pearse Rd, S : 1 m. on N 4 ☎ 60291, ☞ – TV & P. 🏄 – **60 rm**.
  🏨 **Ballincar House** ⑤, Rosses Point Rd, NW : 2 ½ m. on R 291 ☎ 5362, ≼, ☞, ℀, squash –
      TV ⌂wc ⌂wc P. 🖽 🖭 VISA. ℀
      closed 23 December-20 January – **M** 7.00/14.50 **t.** and a la carte ⌂ 4.00 – **20 rm** ⫼ 20.00/40.00 **t.**
      – SB (October-April) 48.00 **st.**

    at Strandhill W : 7 m. on L 132 – ✉ ☎ 071 Sligo :

  XX **Knockmuldowney** ⑤ with rm, ☎ 68122, ☞ – TV ⌂wc ☎ P. 🖽 🖭 ⑩ VISA. ℀
      March-October – **M** (bar lunch residents only)/dinner 11.50 **t.** and a la carte ⌂ 4.00 – **6 rm**
      ⫼ 30.00/50.00 **t.**

    at Rosses Point NW : 5 m. on R 291 – ✉ ☎ 071 Sligo :

  XX Reveries, ☎ 77371, ≼ Mount Knocknarae, Sligo Bay and Oyster Island.
  X **Moorings,** ☎ 77112, Seafood – P. 🖽 🖭 ⑩ VISA
      closed Sunday and 2 weeks at Christmas – **M** (dinner only and bar lunch May-September)/dinner a la carte 12.00/26.00 **t.** ⌂ 3.90.

AUSTIN-ROVER Bridge St. ☎ 2091
FIAT, LANCIA Ballinode ☎ 2188

FORD Bundoran Rd ☎ 2610
VW Ballisodare ☎ 67291

SPIDDLE Galway 405 E 8 – ☎ 091 Galway.

♦Dublin 143 – ♦Galway 11.

  🏠 **Bridge House,** Main St., ☎ 83118, ☞ – ⌂wc ⌂wc P. 🖽 VISA. ℀
      closed 2 weeks at Christmas – **M** 10.00/17.00 **t.** and a la carte ⌂ 4.75 – **14 rm** ⫼ 18.00/45.00 **t.**
      – SB 50.00/60.00 **st.**
  🏠 **Park Lodge,** E : 1 ¾ m. on L 100 ☎ 83159, ≼ – ⌂wc ⌂wc P. 🖽 🖭 ⑩ VISA. ℀
      May-October – **M** (bar lunch)/dinner 13.00 **t.** ⌂ 3.75 – **23 rm** ⫼ 26.00/44.00 **t.**

STRANDHILL Sligo 405 G 5 – see Sligo.

TEMPLEGLENTAN Limerick 405 E 10 – ☎ 069 Newcastle West.

♦Dublin 154 – ♦Killarney 36 – ♦Limerick 33.

  🏠 Devon Inn, on N 21 ☎ 62811, ☞ – TV ⌂wc ⌂wc ☎ P. ℀ – **18 rm**.

THURLES Tipperary 405 I 9 – pop. 7 352 – ☎ 0504.

See : Catholic Cathedral (interior)★.

🛅 Turtula ☎ 21983.

♦Dublin 93 – Kilkenny 29 – ♦Limerick 39.

  🏠 **Hayes,** Liberty Sq., ☎ 22122 – ⌂wc P. 🏄 🖽 VISA
      closed 25 and 26 December – **M** 8.50/13.00 **t.** and a la carte – **36 rm** ⫼ 26.00/52.00 **t.**

TIMOLEAGUE Cork 405 F 13 – pop. 259 – ✉ ☎ 023 Bandon.

♦Dublin 182 – ♦Cork 28.

  X **Racing Demon,** E : 1 m. off L 42 ☎ 46468, ≼ – P. 🖭 ⑩ VISA
      closed Monday and October-mid March – **M** (dinner only) 13.50 **t.** ⌂ 3.75.

TIPPERARY Tipperary 405 H 10 – pop. 4 984 – ECD : Wednesday – ✆ 062.
Envir. : S : Glen of Aherlow★ (statue of Christ the King ≤★★).
🛏 Rathanny 🖉 51119, S : 1 m.
◆Dublin 113 – ◆Cork 57 – ◆Limerick 24 – ◆Waterford 53.

　⋔　**Ach-na-Sheen House,** Waterford Rd, 🖉 51298 – ▭wc 🄿. 𝗩𝗜𝗦𝗔
　　　closed 21 December-5 January – **13 rm** ⊊ 11.50/26.00 **st.**

TRALEE Kerry 405 C 11 – pop. 16 495 – ECD : Wednesday – ✆ 066.
🛏 Mount Hawke 🖉 51150 – 🎭 Aras Siamsa, Godfrey Pl. 🖉 21288.
◆Dublin 185 – ◆Killarney 20 – ◆Limerick 64.

　🏨　**Ballygarry House,** SE : 1 ½ m. on N 21 🖉 21233, 🛲 – 📺 ▭wc 🎜wc ☎ 🄿 – **16 rm.**
　🏨　**Brandon,** Princes Quay, 🖉 23333, Group Telex 73130 – 🛗 📺 ▭wc ☎ 🄿. 🚗 𝗡𝗔 𝗔𝗘 ⓪ 𝗩𝗜𝗦𝗔
　　　⍟
　　　closed 1 week at Christmas – **M** 7.25/12.50 **st.** and a la carte ▯ 4.50 – **160 rm** ⊊ 32.25/64.00 **st.**
　🍴　**Ocean Billow,** 29 Castle St., 🖉 21377, Seafood – 𝗩𝗜𝗦𝗔
　　　closed 1 week at Christmas – **M** *(closed Monday, Saturday lunch and Sunday)* 11.80/16.95 **st.**
　　　▯ 4.00.

FIAT Ashe St. 🖉 21124　　　　　　　　　　　　　　TOYOTA Denny St. 🖉 21688
FORD Edward St. 🖉 21555　　　　　　　　　　　　VW The Market and Rock St. 🖉 21193

TRIM Meath 405 L 7 – pop. 2 144 – ECD : Thursday – ✆ 046 – 🛏 🖉 31463, SW : 2 ½ m.
◆Dublin 28 – Drogheda 25 – ◆Dundalk 43.

　🏨　**Wellington Court,** Summerhill Rd, 🖉 31516 – 📺 ▭wc 🄿. 𝗡𝗔 𝗔𝗘 ⓪.
　　　M (bar lunch Monday to Saturday)/dinner 12.00 **t.** and a la carte ▯ 3.50 – **18 rm** ⊊ 17.60/27.60 **t.**

TYRELLSPASS Westmeath 405 J 7 – pop. 307 – ✆ 044 Mullingar.
◆Dublin 51 – ◆Tullamore 13.

　🕌　**Village,** 🖉 23171 – ▭wc 🎜wc 🄿. 𝗡𝗔 𝗔𝗘 ⓪ 𝗩𝗜𝗦𝗔. ⍟
　　　closed 25 to 27 December – **M** *(closed Sunday dinner October-June)* (bar lunch Monday to
　　　Saturday)/dinner 15.00 **t.** and a la carte ▯ 5.25 – **10 rm** ⊊ 15.50/31.00 **t.**

VIRGINIA Cavan 405 K 6 – pop. 657 – ✆ 049 Cavan.
Envir. : Kells : St. Columba's House★ 9C – St. Columba's Church : old tower★ 1783 – Churchyard
(high crosses★) SE : 11 m. – 🛏 🖉 35.
◆Dublin 52 – ◆Dundalk 59 – Roscommon 56 – ◆Tullamore 59.

　🏨　**Park** ⌂, 🖉 47235, ≤, 🛏, 🔾, 🛲, park, ⍟ – ▭wc 🎜wc ☎ 🄿. 𝗡𝗔 𝗔𝗘 ⓪ 𝗩𝗜𝗦𝗔.
　　　closed January – **M** 8.00/13.50 **st.** and a la carte – **22 rm** ⊊ 17.50/27.00 **st.**

WATERFORD Waterford 405 K 11 – pop. 38 473 – ✆ 051.
See : Franciscan ruins of the French Church★ 13C-16C (Grey Friars Street).
🛏 Newrath 🖉 74182 – 🎭 41 The Quay 🖉 75788.
◆Dublin 96 – ◆Cork 73 – ◆Limerick 77.

　🏩　**Granville,** Meagher Quay, 🖉 55111, Telex 80188 – 🛗 📺 ☎. 🚗 𝗡𝗔 𝗔𝗘 ⓪ 𝗩𝗜𝗦𝗔. ⍟
　　　closed 25 and 26 December – **M** 7.75/13.50 **st.** and a la carte ▯ 4.95 – **66 rm** ⊊ 30.00/61.00 **st.**
　🏨　**Tower,** The Mall, 🖉 75801, Telex 80699 – 🛗 📺 ▭wc ☎. 🚗 𝗡𝗔 𝗔𝗘 ⓪ 𝗩𝗜𝗦𝗔
　　　M 8.00/13.00 **st.** and a la carte ▯ 4.00 – **82 rm** ⊊ 25.00/32.00 **st.** – SB (weekends only) 64.00 **st.**

　　at Slieverue N : 2 m. on N 25 – ✉ ✆ 051 Waterford :

　⋔　**Diamond Hill,** SW : ½ m. on N 25 🖉 32855, 🛲 – 🎜wc 🄿. 𝗩𝗜𝗦𝗔. ⍟
　　　closed 24 December-1 January – **10 rm** ⊊ 14.00/28.00 **st.**

NISSAN, RENAULT 3 Michael St. 🖉 76181　　　　　TOYOTA William St. 🖉 74037
OPEL, BEDFORD Catherine St. 🖉 74988

WATERVILLE Kerry 405 B 12 – pop. 478 – ✆ 0667 – Envir. : Sheehan's Point ≤★★★ S : 6 m. –
Remains of Carhan House (birthplace of Daniel O'Connell) N : 11 m. – Ballinskelligs (Augustinian
Monastery ≤★) W : 9 m.
◆Dublin 238 – ◆Killarney 48.

　🏫　**Waterville Lake** ⌂, 🖉 4133, Telex 73806, ≤ Lough Currane, Atlantic and Countryside, ⌂,
　　　🛏, 🔾, 🛲, ⍟ – 🛗 🔾 🄿. 🚗 𝗡𝗔 𝗔𝗘 ⓪ 𝗩𝗜𝗦𝗔. ⍟
　　　16 April-10 October – **M** 8.50/18.00 **st.** and a la carte ▯ 5.00 – **84 rm** ⊊ 44.50/73.00 **st.**, **8 suites**
　　　123.00 **st.** – SB 97.00 **st.**
　🏨　**Butler Arms,** 🖉 4144, Group Telex 73826, 🔾, 🛲, ⍟ – ▭wc 🎜wc ☎ 🄿. 𝗡𝗔 𝗔𝗘 ⓪ 𝗩𝗜𝗦𝗔. ⍟
　　　16 April-12 October – **M** (bar lunch)/dinner 16.50 **st.** and a la carte ▯ 5.00 – **29 rm**
　　　⊊ 27.00/46.00 **st.** – SB 73.00/78.00 **st.**
　⋔　Sunset House, 🖉 4258 – 🄿 – **8 rm.**
　🍴　**Huntsman** with rm, 🖉 4124, ≤, Seafood – 📺 ▭wc 🎜wc 🄿. 𝗡𝗔 𝗔𝗘 ⓪ 𝗩𝗜𝗦𝗔. ⍟
　　　10 March-October – **M** 10.50/16.00 **t.** and a la carte 11.25/19.00 **t.** ▯ 4.00 – **4 rm**
　　　⊊ 16.00/22.00 **st.**

WESTPORT Mayo **405** D 6 – pop. 3 378 – ECD : Wednesday – ✪ 098 Newport.

See : Westport House★ *AC*.

Envir. : Croagh Patrick Mountain★ (statue of St. Patrick ≼★, pilgrimage) SW : 6 m. – Roonah Quay ≼★ on Clare Island W : 15 m.

🛅 Carrowholly ✆ 547.

🛈 The Mall ✆ 098 (Newport) 25711.

♦Dublin 163 – ♦Galway 50 – ♦Sligo 65.

XX **Ardmore,** The Quay, W : ½ m. on T 39 ✆ 25994, ≼ – **P.** 🖭 🖼 ① *VISA*
closed Sunday, 12 to 26 February, first 2 weeks November and 24 to 26 December – **M** (dinner only and bar lunch June-September) a la carte 9.50/13.50 **t.** ⚱ 4.00.

WEXFORD Wexford **405** M 10 – pop. 11 417 – ECD : Thursday – ✪ 053.

Envir. : Johnstown Castle (the park-arboretum★) SW : 4 m.

🛅 Mulgannon ✆ 42238, SE : 1 m.

🛈 Crescent Quay ✆ 23111.

♦Dublin 88 – Kilkenny 49 – ♦Waterford 38.

🏨 **Talbot,** Trinity St., ✆ 22566, Telex 80658, 🔲, squash – 🅱 🖭 🛏wc ☎ **P.** 🖾 🖭 🖼 ① *VISA*. ✖
M 9.00/15.00 **t.** and a la carte ⚱ 4.10 – ⌧ 6.00 – **103 rm** 30.50/53.00 **t.** – SB (winter only) (weekends only) 60.00/70.00 **st.**

🏨 **Ferrycarrig** ⏇, Ferrycarrig Bridge, NW : 2 ¾ m. on N 11 ✆ 22999, Telex 80147, ≼, ☞, ✖ – 🖭 🛏wc ☎ **P.** 🖾 🖭 ① *VISA*
M (bar lunch Monday to Saturday)/dinner 15.00 **t.** and a la carte – ⌧ 4.95 – **38 rm** 23.10/45.00 **t.** – SB 50.00/65.25 **st.**

🏨 **Whites** (Best Western), George's St., ✆ 22311, Telex 80630 – 🅱 🖭 🛏wc ☎ **P.** 🖾 🖭 🖭 ① *VISA*. ✖
closed Christmas Day – **M** (bar lunch)/dinner 13.50 **st.** and a la carte ⚱ 6.00 – **66 rm** ⌧ 32.00/48.00 **st.** – SB (weekends only)(October-May) 68.00 **st.**

🏨 **Whitford House,** New Line Rd, SW : 2 m. on L 159 ✆ 43444, 🔲, ☞ – 🖭 🛏wc 🛏wc ☎ **P.** *VISA*. ✖
closed 20 December-6 January – **M** (bar lunch)/dinner 12.50 **st.** and a la carte ⚱ 4.00 – **20 rm** ⌧ 18.85/36.00 **st.** – SB 50.00/55.00 **st.**

BEDFORD, OPEL Ferrybank ✆ 22107
FORD Ferrybank ✆ 23329
MITSUBISHI, VOLVO, SUZUKI ✆ 22998

SUBARU Redmond Rd ✆ 23133
TOYOTA Carriglawn, Newtown Rd ✆ 23788
VW-AUDI Drinagh ✆ 22377

WICKLOW Wicklow **405** N 9 – pop. 5 178 – ECD : Thursday – ✪ 0404.

Envir. : Ashford (Mount Usher or Walpole's Gardens★) *AC*, NW : 4 m.

🛅 Blainroe ✆ 3168, S : 3 ½ m.

🛈 ✆ 2904.

♦Dublin 33 – ♦Waterford 84 – Wexford 67.

XX **Old Rectory** with rm, ✆ 67048, ☞ – 🛏wc 🕿 **P.** ✖
16 April-27 October – **M** (booking essential)(dinner only) 18.50 **st.** and a la carte ⚱ 6.50 – **5 rm** ⌧ 27.00/54.00 **st.** – SB 80.00/84.00 **st.**

FIAT Bollarney ✆ 2212
FORD Whitegates ✆ 2331

VW, AUDI-NSU, MAZDA The Glebe ✆ 2126

YOUGHAL Cork **405** I 12 – pop. 5 870 – ECD : Wednesday – ✪ 024.

See : St. Mary's Collegiate Church★ 13C.

Envir. : Ardmore (site★, round tower★ 10C, cathedral ruins★ 12C, ≼★) E : 5 ½ m.

🛅 Knockaverry ✆ 92787.

🛈 ✆ 2390 (July-August).

♦Dublin 146 – ♦Cork 30 – ♦Waterford 47.

X **Aherne's Seafood Bar,** 163 North Main St., ✆ 92424 – **P.** 🖭 🖭 ① *VISA*
closed Sunday lunch, Monday except dinner July and August and 4 days at Christmas – **M** 7.50 **t.** (lunch) and a la carte 12.55/18.00 **t.** ⚱ 4.00.

RENAULT North Abbey ✆ 2019

MAJOR HOTEL GROUPS

Abbreviations used in the Guide and central reservation telephone numbers

PRINCIPALES CHAINES HOTELIÈRES

Abréviations utilisées dans nos textes et centraux téléphoniques de réservation

PRINCIPALI CATENE ALBERGHIERE

Abbreviazioni utilizzate nei nostri testi e centrali telefoniche di prenotazione

DIE WICHTIGSTEN HOTELKETTEN

Im Führer benutzte Abkürzungen der Hotel-ketten und ihre Zentralen für telefonische Reservierung

BEST WESTERN HOTELS.....	BEST WESTERN	01 (London) 541 0033
		041 (Glasgow) 204 1794
CREST HOTELS LTD	CREST	01 (London) 236 3242
DE VERE HOTELS PLC.....	DE VERE	0925 (Warrington) 35471
EMBASSY HOTELS	EMBASSY	01 (London) 581 3466
GREENALL WHITLEY HOTELS	GREENALL WHITLEY	0925 (Warrington) 35471
INTER-CONTINENTAL HOTELS LTD.....	INTER-CON	01 (London) 491 7181
LADBROKE HOTELS	LADBROKE	01 (London) 734 6000
MOUNT CHARLOTTE HOTELS LTD	MT. CHARLOTTE	0532 (Leeds) 444866
NORFOLK CAPITAL HOTELS LTD	NORFOLK CAP.	01 (London) 589 7000
QUEENS MOAT HOUSES PLC	Q.M.H.	0423 (Harrogate) 526444
		0789 (Stratford upon Avon) 298677
		0932 (Walton upon Thames) 231010
RANK HOTELS LTD	RANK	01 (London) 262 2893
STAKIS HOTELS	STAKIS	041 (Glasgow) 332 4343 and 01 (London) 222 4081
SWALLOW HOTELS PLC	SWALLOW	0783 (Sunderland) 294666
THISTLE HOTELS LTD	THISTLE	01 (London) 937 8033
TRUSTHOUSE FORTE (U.K.) LTD	T.H.F.	01 (London) 567 3444
WHITBREAD COACHING INNS	WHITBREAD	0582 (Luton) 454646

TRAFFIC SIGNS
A few important signs

SIGNALISATION ROUTIÈRE
Quelques signaux routiers importants

SEGNALETICA STRADALE
Alcuni segnali importanti

VERKEHRSZEICHEN
Die wichtigsten Straßenverkehrszeichen

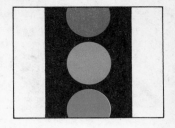

Please note : The maximum speed limits in Great Britain are 70 mph (112 km/h) on motorways and dual carriageways and 60 mph (96 km/h) on all other roads, except where a lower speed limit is indicated.

N.B. N'oubliez pas qu'il existe des limitations de vitesse en Grande-Bretagne : 70 mph (112 km/h) sur routes à chaussée séparée et autoroutes, 60 mph (96 km/h) sur autres routes, sauf indication d'une vitesse inférieure.

N.B. In Gran Bretagna esistono dei limiti di velocità : 70 mph (112 km/h) sulle strade a doppia carreggiata e autostrade, 60 mph (96 km/h) sulle altre strade, salvo che sia indicata una velocità inferiore.

Zur Beachtung : In Großbritannien gelten folgende Geschwindigkeitsbegrenzungen : 70 mph (112 km/h) auf Autobahnen und Straßen mit getrennten Fahrbahnen, 60 mph (96 km/h) auf allen anderen Straßen, wenn keine niedrigere Geschwindigkeit angezeigt ist.

Warning signs — Signaux d'avertissement
Segnali di avvertimento — Warnzeichen

T junction
Jonction avec autre route
Confluenza con altra strada
Straßeneinmündung

Right-hand lane closed
Voie de droite barrée
Corsia di destra sbarrata
Rechte Fahrbahn gesperrt

Roundabout
Sens giratoire
Senso rotatorio
Kreisverkehr

Quayside or river bank
Débouché sur un quai ou une berge
Banchina o argine senza sponda
Ufer

Dual carriageway ends
Fin de chaussée à deux voies
Fine di doppia carreggiata
Ende der zweispurigen Fahrbahn

Two-way traffic crosses one-way road
Voie à deux sens croisant voie à sens unique
Strada a due sensi che incrocia una strada a senso unico
Straße mit Gegenverkehr kreuzt Einbahnstraße

Change to opposite carriageway
Déviation sur chaussée opposée
Deviazione sulla carreggiata opposta
Überleitung auf Gegenfahrbahn

Level crossing with automatic half barriers ahead
Passage à niveau automatique
Passaggio a livello automatico con semi-barriere
Bahnübergang mit automatischen Halbschranken

Distance to give way sign ahead
Cédez le passage à 50 yards
Dare la precedenza a 50 iarde
Vorfahrt gewähren in 50 yards Entfernung

Height limit
Hauteur limitée (en pieds et pouces)
Altezza limitata (piedi e pollici)
Maximale Höhe (in Fuß und Zoll)

Ralentir maintenant
Rallentare subito
Geschwindigkeit verringern

Opening or swing bridge
Pont mobile
Ponte mobile
Bewegliche Brücke

641

Signs giving orders

Signaux de prescriptions absolues
Segnali di prescrizione (di divieto o d'obbligo)
Gebots- und Verbotszeichen

National speed limit applies
Fin de limitation de vitesse
Fine di limitazione di velocità
Ende der Geschwindigkeitsbeschränkung

School crossing patrol
Sortie d'école
Uscita di scolari
Achtung Schule

No stopping (« clearway »)

Arrêt interdit

Fermata vietata

Halteverbot

All vehicles prohibited
(plate gives details)
Circulation interdite à tous véhicules
(plaque donnant détails)
Divieto di transito a tutti i veicoli (la
placca sottostante fornisce dei dettagli)
Verkehrsverbot für Fahrzeuge aller Art
(näherer Hinweis auf Zusatzschild)

Give priority to vehicles from opposite
direction
Priorité aux véhicules venant de face
Dare la precedenza ai veicoli che proven-
gono dal senso opposto
Dem Gegenverkehr Vorrang gewähren

Voie à stationnement réglementé

Sosta regolamentata

Fahrbahn mit zeitlich begrenzter
Parkerlaubnis

Width limit
Largeur limitée (en pieds et pouces)
Larghezza limitata (piedi e pollici)
Breite begrenzt (in Fuß und Zoll)

Plate below sign at end of restriction
Fin d'interdiction
Fine del divieto posta sotto il segnale
Ende einer Beschränkung

Information signs

Signaux de simple indication
Segnali di indicazione
Hinweiszeichen

One-way street
Rue à sens unique
Via a senso unico
Einbahnstraße

No through road
Voie sans issue
Strada senza uscita
Sackgasse

Accès à une chaussée à deux voies
Accesso ad una carreggiata a due corsie
Zufahrt zu einer zweispurigen Fahrbahn

Ring road
Voie de contournement
Strada di circonvallazione
Ringstraße

Warning signs on rural motorways

Signaux d'avertissement sur autoroutes
Segnali di avvertimento su autostrade
Warnzeichen auf Autobahnen

Maximum advised speed
Vitesse maximum conseillée
Velocità massima consigliata
Empfohlene Höchstgeschwindigkeit

1 Lane closed
1 voie barrée
1 Corsia sbarrata
1 Fahrstreifen gesperrt

Count-down markers at exit from
motorway (or primary route if green-backed)
Balises situées sur autoroute ou route principale
(fond vert) et annonçant une sortie
Segnali su autostrada o strade principali (fondo
verde) annuncianti un'uscita
Hinweise auf Abfahrten an Autobahnen und
Hauptverkehrsstraßen (Grünengrund)

End of restriction

Route libre

Strada libera

Straße frei

Direction to service area, with fuel, parking, cafeteria and restaurant facilities.

Indication d'aire de service avec carburant, parc à voitures, cafeteria et restaurant.

Indicazione di area di servizio con carburante, parcheggio, bar e ristorante

Hinweis auf Tankstelle, Parkplatz, Cafeteria und Restaurant

Warning signs on urban motorways
Signaux d'avertissement sur autoroutes urbaines
Segnali di avvertimento su autostrade urbane
Warnzeichen auf Stadtautobahnen

_1_    _2_    _3_

The insets show (flashing amber lights) (1) advised maximum speed, (2) lane to be used; (3) (flashing red lights), you must stop.

L'ensemble de ces panneaux indique : (1) la vitesse maximale conseillée, (2) la voie à utiliser (signaux lumineux jaunes) ; (3) l'arrêt obligatoire (signaux lumineux rouges).

L'insieme di questi segnali indica : (1) la velocità massima consigliata, (2) la corsia da imboccare (segnali luminosi gialli) ; (3) la fermata obbligatoria (segnali luminosi rossi).

Diese Schilder (mit blinkenden Ampeln) weisen hin auf : 1. die empfohlene Höchstgeschwindigkeit, 2. die zu befahrende Fahrbahn (gelbes Licht) und 3. Halt (rotes Licht).

In town — En ville
In città — in der Stadt

SIGNALISATION SHOWN ON OR ALONG KERBS

SIGNALISATION MATÉRIALISÉE SUR OU AU LONG DES TROTTOIRS

SEGNALI TRACCIATI SOPRA O LUNGO I MARCIAPIEDI

ZEICHEN AUF ODER AN GEHWEGEN

OTHER ROAD SIGNS

AUTRES PANNEAUX

ALTRI CARTELLI INDICATORI

ZUSÄTZLICHE VERKEHRSZEICHEN

No waiting during every working day
Stationnement interdit tous les jours ouvrables
Sosta vietata nei giorni feriali con indicazioni complementari
Parkverbot an Werktagen

Stationnement interdit de 8 h 30 à 18 h 30 du lundi au samedi
Sosta vietata da lunedì a sabato dalle 8,30 alle 18,30
Parkverbot Montag bis Samstag von 8.30 bis 18.30 Uhr

No loading or unloading during every working day

Livraisons interdites tous les jours ouvrables

Carico e scarico vietato nei giorni feriali con indicazioni complementari

Be- und Entladen verboten an allen Werktagen

Livraisons interdites de 8 h 30 à 18 h 30 du lundi au samedi
Carico e scarico vietato da lunedi a sabato dalle 8,30 alle 18,30
Be- und Entladen verboten von Montag bis Samstag von 8.30 bis 18.30 Uhr

No waiting during every working day and additional times as indicated
Stationnement interdit tous les jours ouvrables plus autres périodes indiquées sur panneaux
Divieto di sosta tutti i giorni feriali e negli altri periodi indicati sul cartello
Parkverbot an Werktagen und den auf Zusatzschildern angegebenen Zeiten

At any time

Stationnement interdit en permanence

Divieto permanente di sosta

Parkverbot zu jeder Zeit

No loading or unloading during every working day and additional times as indicated
Livraisons interdites tous les jours ouvrables plus autres périodes indiquées sur panneaux
Divieto di carico e scarico tutti i giorni feriali e negli altri periodi indicati sul cartello
Be- und Entladen verboten an Werktagen und den auf Zusatzschildern angegebenen Zeiten

No loading at any time

Livraisons interdites en permanence

Divieto permanente di carico e scarico

Be- und Entladeverbot zu jeder Zeit

No waiting during any other periods
Stationnement interdit à toute autre période
Sosta vietata in determinate ore
Parkverbot zu bestimmten Zeiten

Waiting Limited 8 am-6 pm 20 minutes in any hour

Stationnement limité à 20 mn de 8 h à 18 h
Sosta limitata a 20 mn dalle 8 alle 18
Höchstparkdauer 20 Min. in der Zeit von 8.00 bis 18.00 Uhr

No loading or unloading during any other periods

Livraisons interdites à toute autre période

Divieto di carico e scarico in determinate ore

Be- und Entladeverbot zu bestimmten Zeiten

No loading Mon-Fri 8.00-9.30 am 4.30-6.30 pm

Livraisons interdites du lundi au vendredi de 8 h à 9 h 30 et de 16 h 30 à 18 h 30
Carico e scarico vietato da lunedi a venerdi dalle 8 alle 9,30 e dalle 16,30 alle 18,30
Be- und Entladeverbot Montag bis Freitag von 8.00 bis 9.30 und von 16.30 bis 18.30 Uhr

Remember : speed limit in Great Britain 70 mph and in Eire 60 mph.

Direction signs on the road network
Panneaux de direction sur le réseau routier
Cartelli direzionali sulla rete stradale
Richtungsschilder auf den Straßen

Motorways and A (M) class roads
Sur autoroutes et routes classées A (M)
Sulle autostrade e strade classificate A (M)
Autobahn M und Schnellstraße A (M)

Primary routes

Apart from motorways, « Primary routes » provide the major road network linking towns of local and national traffic importance

Sur grands itinéraires routiers « Primary routes »

En complément du système autoroutier, les grands itinéraires constituent un réseau de routes recommandées reliant les villes selon leur importance dans le trafic national

Sui principali itinerari stradali (Primary routes)

I principali itinerari, unitamente alle autostrade, costituiscono una rete di strade consigliate che collegano le città secondo la loro importanza nel traffico nazionale

Empfohlene Fernverkehrsstraßen (Primary routes)

Sie bilden ein überregionales Straßennetz, das verkehrswichtige Orte verbindet ; sie ergänzen das Autobahnnetz

Other A class roads
Sur autres routes classées A
Sulle altre strade classificate A
Andere Straße der Kategorie A

B class roads
Sur routes classées B
Sulle strade classificate B
Straße der Kategorie B

Unclassified roads — Local direction sign
Sur routes non classées — Signalisation locale
Sulle strade non classificate — Segnaletica locale
Nicht klassifizierte Straßen — Örtliche Richtungsschilder

ADDRESSES OF SHIPPING COMPANIES AND THEIR PRINCIPAL AGENTS

ADRESSES DES COMPAGNIES DE NAVIGATION ET DE LEURS PRINCIPALES AGENCES

INDIRIZZI DELLE COMPAGNIE DI NAVIGAZIONE E DELLE LORO PRINCIPALI AGENZIE

ADRESSEN DER SCHIFFAHRTSGESELLSCHAFTEN UND IHRER WICHTIGSTEN AGENTUREN

BALTIC SHIPPING CO.

5 Mezhevoi Canal, Leningrad L35, USSR.

Agents : C.T.C. Lines (UK), 1-3 Lower Regent St., London, SW1Y 4NN, ✆ (01) 930 5833, Telex 917193.

Scannautic A/C, C.G. Hambrose Pl. 5, Oslo 1, ✆ 421051, Telex 76146.

Baltic Shipping Co, 35 Hertzen St., Leningrad 190000, U.S.S.R. ✆ 315.89.86, Telex 551.

Transtours, 49 Avenue de l'Opéra, 75067 Paris, France, ✆ (1) 42 61 58 28, Telex 230732.

BELFAST CAR FERRIES

47 Donegal Quay, Belfast, BTI 3ED, ✆ (0237) 226800, 220364, Telex 74268.

Agent : Langton Docks, Bootle, Merseyside, L20 1BY, ✆ (051) 922 6234.

B & I LINE

16 Westmoreland St., Dublin 2, Eire, ✆ 724711, Telex 25651.

Agents : 155 Regent St., London, W1R 7FD, ✆ (01) 734 4681, Telex 23523.

42 Grand Par., Cork, Eire, ✆ (021) 273024, Telex 26137.

Reliance House, Water St., Liverpool, L2 8TP, ✆ (051) 227 3131, Telex 627839.

BRITISH RAIL see SEALINK and HOVERSPEED

BRITTANY FERRIES

BAI Brittany Ferries, Gare Maritime Roscoff, Port du Bloscon 29211, France, ✆ 98 61 22 11, Telex 940360.

Agents : Millbay Docks, Plymouth, PL1 3EW, Devon, ✆ (0752) 21321, Telex 45380.

The Brittany Centre, Wharf Rd, Portsmouth, PO2 8RU, Hampshire. ✆ (0705) 827701, Telex 86878.

Gare Maritime, 35400 St-Malo, France, ✆ 99 56 68 40, Telex 740426.

Tourist House, 42 Grand Parade, Cork, Eire, ✆ (021) 507666, Telex 75088.

Modesto Pineiro & Co., 27 Paseo de Pereda, Santander, Spain, ✆ (042) 214500, Telex 35913.

CALEDONIAN MACBRAYNE LTD.

Ferry Terminal, Gourock, PA19 1QP, Renfrewshire, Scotland, ✆ (0475) 34531, Telex 779318.

CHANNEL ISLAND FERRIES

Norman House, Albert Johnson Quay, Portsmouth, PO2 7AE, ✆ (0705) 864431, Telex 869393.

Agents : Wharf Rd, Portsmouth, PO2 8RU, ✆ (0705) 819416.

New North Quay, St. Helier, Jersey, Channel Islands, ✆ (0534) 38300.

Piquet House, St. Peter Port, Guernsey, Channel Islands, ✆ (0481) 711111.

COMMODORE SHIPPING SERVICES AND CONDOR LTD.

Commodore House, Bulwer Av., St. Sampsons, Guernsey, Channel Islands, ✆ (0481) 46841, Telex 4191289.

Agents : Commodore Travel Ltd., 28 Conway St., St. Helier, Jersey, Channel Islands, ✆ (0534) 71263, Telex 419 2079.

Condor Ltd., Morvan Fils, 2 Place du Poids du Roi, 35402 St. Malo, France, ✆ 99 56 42 29, Telex 950486.

CUNARD LINE LTD.

South Western House, Canute Rd, Southampton, Hampshire, SO9 1ZA, ✆ (0703) 229933, Telex 477577.

Agents : 30a Pall Mall, London SW1Y 5LS, ✆ (01) 491 3930, Telex 295483.
555 Fifth Av., New York, NY 10017, USA, ✆ (212) 880 7500, Telex 220436.
American Express Co. Inc., 11 rue Scribe, Paris 75009, France, ✆ (1) 42 66 09 99, Telex 210718.

DFDS SEAWAYS

Sankt Annae Plads 30, DK-1295 Copenhagen K, Denmark, ✆ (01) 11 22 55, Telex 19416.
DFDS Seaways, Scandinavia House, Parkeston Quay, Harwich, CO12 4QG, ✆ (0255) 554681, Telex 987542.

Agents : DFDS Seaways Tyne Commission Quay, North Shields, NE29 6EE, Tyne and Wear, ✆ (091) 257 5655, Telex 537285.
DFDS, Skandiahamnen, PO BOX 8895, S-40272 Goteborg, 8 Sweden, ✆ (031) 54 03 00.
A/S Danske-Batene, Karl Johansgate 1, Oslo 1, Norway, ✆ (02) 429350, Telex 18129.
Skandiahamnen, P.O. Box 8895, S-40272 Gothenburg 8, Sweden, ✆ (031) 54 03 00, Telex 20688.
DFDS, Jessenstrasse 4, 2000 Hamburg 50, West Germany, ✆ (040) 389030, Telex 2161759.

EMERAUDE FERRIES

Agents : Emeraude Ferries, Albert Quay, St. Helier, Jersey, Channel Islands, ✆ (0534) 74458, Telex 4192311 SEACAR.
Emeraude Ferries, Victoria Pier, St. Peter Port, Guernsey, ✆ (0481) 711414, Telex 4191571.
Gare Maritime du Naye, 35400 St-Malo, France, ✆ 99 81 61 46, Telex 950271.

FRED OLSEN LINES

11 Conduit St., London W1R 0LS, ✆ (01) 491 3760, Telex 263670.

Agent : Fred Olsen, Hamilton House, Foster Rd, Parkeston, Harwich, Essex CO12 4Q4, ✆ (0255) 508444.

FRED OLSEN LINES KDS

Fergeterminaten, P.O. Box 82, N 4601 Kristiansand, Norway, ✆ (042) 26500, Telex 21969.

Agent : Fred Olsen Lines, 11 Conduit St., London W1R OLS, ✆ 491 3760, Telex 263670.

HERM SEAWAY

Guernseybus Ltd., Picquet House, St. Peter Port, Guernsey, Channel Islands, ✆ (0481) 24677.

HOVERSPEED

Maybrook House, Queens Gardens, Dover, Kent CT17 9UQ, ✆ (0304) 216205, Telex 96323.
Agents : International Hoverport, Boulogne, France, ✆ 21 30 27 26, Telex 110008.
International Hoverport, Calais, France, ✆ 21 96 65 70, Telex 810856.

HOVERTRAVEL LTD.

Quay Road, Ryde, Isle of Wight, P033 2HB.

Agent : Clarence Pier, Southsea, Portsmouth, PO5 3AD, Hampshire, ✆ (0705) 829988.

IRISH CONTINENTAL LINE LTD.

19/21 Aston Quay, Dublin 2, Eire, ✆ (01) 774331, Telex 30355.

Agent : Transport et Voyages, 8 Rue Auber, 75441 Paris, Cedex 09, ✆ (1) 42 66 91 91, Telex 042210696.

ISLE OF MAN STEAM PACKET CO. LTD.

P.O. Box 5, Imperial Buildings, Douglas, Isle of Man, ✆ (0624) 23344, Telex 629414.

Agents : W.E. Williames & Co. Ltd., 35/39 Middlepath St., Belfast, Northern Ireland, ✆ (0232) 55411, Telex 747166.
B & I Line, 16 Westmoreland St., Dublin 2, Eire ✆ (01) 724711, Telex 002725651.
Queens Terr., Fleetwood, Lancashire, ✆ (039 17) 6263 (summer), ✆ 0624 (Douglas I.O.M.) 23344 (winter).
Sea Terminal, Heysham, Lancashire, LA3 2XF, ✆ (0524) 53802.
Sealink (Scotland and Northorn Ireland), Sea Terminal, Stranraer, Wigtownshire DG9 8EJ, ✆ (0776) 2262, Telex 778125.

ISLE OF SARK SHIPPING CO. LTD.

White Rock, St. Peter Port, Guernsey, Channel Islands, ✆ (0481) 24059, Telex 419 1549.

ISLES OF SCILLY STEAMSHIP CO. LTD.

Hugh Town, St. Mary's, Isles of Scilly, TR21 OLJ, ✆ 0720 (Scillonia) 22357/8.
Agent : 16 Quay St., Penzance, TR18 4BD, Cornwall, ✆ (0736) 62009/64013.

LUNDY CO.

Lundy, Bristol Channel, via Bideford, Devon, EX39 2LY, ✆ 0271 (Woolacombe) 870870.

MERSEYSIDE PASSENGER TRANSPORT EXECUTIVE

24, Hatton Garden, Liverpool L3 2AN, Merseyside, ✆ (051) 227 5181.

NORFOLK LINE BV

Kranenburgweg 211, 2583 ER Scheveningen, Netherlands, ✆ (070) 527400, Telex 31515.

Agent : Atlas House, Southgates Rd, Great Yarmouth, Norfolk NR30 3LN, ✆ (0493) 856133, Telex 97449.

NORTH SEA FERRIES LTD.

Noordzee Veerdiensten, Beneluxhaven, Europoort, P.O. Box 1123, 3180 AC Rozenburg Z.H., Netherlands, ✆ (01819) 62077, Telex 29571.

Agents : King George Dock, Hedon Rd, Hull, HU9 5QA, Humberside, ✆ (0482) 795141, Telex 592349.

Leopold II Dam (Havendam) B8380, Zeebrugge, Belgium, ✆ (050) 543430, Telex 81469.

NORWAY LINE

Postboks 4004, N5015 Bergen-Dreggen, Norway, ✆ 05-325969, Telex 40425 NLINE.

Agent : Tyne Commission Quay, North Shields, NE29 6EA, ✆ (0632) 585555, Telex 537275.

OLAU-LINE (UK) LTD.

Sheerness, Kent, ME12 1SN, ✆ (0795) 666666 and 663355, Telex 965605.

Agents : Olau-Line Terminal, Buitenhaven, Postbus 231, Vlissingen, Netherlands, ✆ (01184) 88000, Telex 37817.

ORKNEY ISLANDS SHIPPING CO. LTD.

4 Ayre Road, Kirkwall, Orkney Islands, Scotland, ✆ (0856) 2044.

ORWELL & HARWICH NAVIGATION CO. LTD.

The Quay, Harwich, Essex, ✆ (0255) 502004.

P & O FERRIES : ORKNEY & SHETLAND SERVICES

P.O. Box 5, P & O Ferry Terminal, Jamieson's Quay, Aberdeen, AB9 8DL, Scotland, ✆ (0224) 572615, Telex 73344.

Agents : Terminal Building, Scrabster, Caithness, KW14 7UJ, Scotland, ✆ (0847) 62052.
Harbour Street, Kirkwall, Orkney Islands, KW15 1LE, Scotland, ✆ (0856) 3330, Telex 75296.
Holmsgarth Terminal, Lerwick, Shetland Islands, ZE1 0PW, Scotland, ✆ (0595) 5252, Telex 75294.
Terminal Bldg., Stromness, Orkney Islands, KW16 3AA, Scotland, ✆ (0856) 850 655, Telex 75221.

RED FUNNEL SERVICES

12 Bugle St., Southampton, SO9 4LJ, Hampshire, ✆ (0703) 226211.

Agents : Fountain Pier, West Cowes, Isle of Wight, ✆ (0983) 292101 (car ferry) and 292704 (Hydrofoil).

THE SALLY LINE LTD

54 Harbour Parade, Ramsgate, Kent, CT11 8LN ✆ (0843) 595522, Telex 96389.

Agents : 81 Piccadilly, London W1, ✆ (01) 409 0536 and 858 1127, Telex 291860.
Sally Viking Line, Dunkerque Port-Ouest, 59279 Loon Plage, France, ✆ 28 68 43 44, Telex 820329 SALLY F.

SEALINK U.K. LTD.

Sealink UK Ltd., 163/203 Eversholt St., London, NW1 1BG, ✆ (01) 387 1234, Telex 269295 BRSLIN G.
SNCF, 88 Rue Saint-Lazare, 75436 Paris Cedex 09, France.
RTM Belgian Maritime Transport Authority, 30 Rue Belliard, B.1040 Brussels, Belgium, ✆ 230 0180, Telex 23851.
Zeeland Steamship Co., Hook of Holland, Netherlands.

Agents : Sealink UK Ltd., Southern House, Lord Warden Square, Dover, CT17 9DH, Kent, ✆ (0304) 203203 Ext. 3187, Telex 96139.
Sealink UK Ltd., Fishguard Harbour, Dyfed, Wales, SA64 0BX, ✆ (0348) 872881, Telex 48167.
Sealink UK Ltd., Car Ferry Booking Office, Lymington Pier, Lymington, Hampshire, SO4 8ZE, ✆ (0590) 73301.
Sealink UK Ltd., Newhaven Harbour, East Sussex, BN9 0BG, ✆ (0273) 514131, Telex 87151.
Sealink UK Ltd., Channel Islands Services, Norman House, Continental Ferry Terminal, Portsmouth, Hampshire, PO2 7AE, ✆ (0705) 811315, Telex 86636.
Sealink UK Ltd., Isle of Wight Ferry Services, P.O. Box 59, Portsmouth, Hampshire, PO1 2XB, ✆ (0705) 827744, Telex 86440.

Sealink UK Ltd., Car Ferry Office, The Slipway, Fishbourne Lane, Cowes, Isle of Wight, PO33 4EU, ☎ (0983) 882432.

Sealink UK Ltd., Weymouth Quay, Weymouth, Dorset, DT4 8DY, ☎ (030 57) 86363, Telex 41245.

Sealink UK Ltd., Car Ferry Office, The Slipway Quay Street, Yarmouth, Isle of Wight, PO41 0PB, ☎ (0983) 760213.

Sealink (Scotland and Northern Ireland) Ltd., Stranraer Harbour, Dumfries and Galloway, DG9 8EJ, ☎ (0776) 2262, Telex 778125.

Sealink UK Ltd., The Jetty, St Peter Port, Guernsey, Channel Islands, ☎ (0481) 24742, Telex 4191249.

Sealink UK Ltd., 7 Wests Centre, Bath St., St Helier, Jersey, Channel Islands, ☎ (0534) 77122, Telex 4192262.

Sealink UK Ltd., 15 Westmoreland St., Dublin 2, Eire, ☎ 714455, Telex 30847.

Sealink UK Ltd, Dun Laoghaire Harbour Dun Laoghaire, Dublin, ☎ (01) 801905, Telex 30319.

British Rail, Rosslare Harbour, Country Wexford, ☎ (053) 33115, Telex 28389.

Manager British Rail, Montergade 5, DK 1116 Kobenhavn K, Denmark, ☎ 12 64 60, Telex 15370.

Armement Naval SNCF, Gare Maritime BP 27, F-62201 Boulogne-sur-Mer, France, ☎ 21 30 25 11, Telex 110908.

Armement Naval SNCF, Terminal TNM, Gare Maritime, F-62100 Calais, France, ☎ 21 96 70 70, Telex 130086.

Agence Maritime Tellier, Gare Maritime, F-50100 Cherbourg, France, ☎ 33 53 24 27, Telex 170684.

Armement Naval SNCF, Gare Maritime BP 85, F-76203 Dieppe, France, ☎ 35 82 24 87, Telex 770924.

Manager British Rail, Neue Mainzer Strasse 22, D-6000 Frankfurt/Main, Germany, ☎ 23.23.81, Telex 416421.

Manager British Rail, Via Pirelli 11, 20124 Milan, Italy, ☎ 655 2297, Telex 310412.

Manager British Rail, Leidseplein 5, Amsterdam, Netherlands, ☎ 234 133, Telex 13395.

Manager British Rail, Centralbahnplatz 9, 4002 Basel, Switzerland, ☎ 23 14 04, Telex 62739.

SERVICE MARITIME CARTERET-JERSEY

BP 15, 50270 Barneville-Carteret, France, ☎ 33 53 87 21, Telex 170477.

Agent : CNTM Ltd., Gorey, Jersey, Channel Islands, ☎ (0534) 53737.

SHETLAND ISLANDS COUNCIL

Grantfield, Lerwick, Shetland, ZE1 ONT, ☎ (0595) 2024, Telex 75218.

SMYRIL LINE

P.O. Box 370, Jonas Broncksgoeta 25, 3800 Thorshavn, Faroe Islands, ☎ (042) 15900, Telex 81296.

Agents : P & O Ferries, Orkney & Shetland Services, P.O. Box 5, P & O Ferry Terminal, Aberdeen, AB9 8DL, Scotland, ☎ (0224) 572615, Telex 73344.

Ferdaskrivistofa Rikisins, Skogarhlid 6, Reykjavik, Iceland, ☎ (91) 25855, Telex 2049.

Smyril Line (Norge) Englegarden, Nyebryggen 5000 Bergen ☎ (05) 320970, Telex 42109.

THOMAS & BEWS FERRIES

Ferry Office, John O'Groats, Caithness, Scotland, ☎ (095 581) 353 (summer).

Windieknap, Brough, Thurso, Caithness, Scotland, ☎ (084 785) 619 (winter).

TORBAY SEAWAY

Beacon Quay, Torquay, Devon, ☎ (0803) 214397, Telex 42500.

TOWNSEND THORESEN

Agents : 127 Regent Street, London, W1R 8LB, ☎ (01) 734 4431, Telex 23802.

Main Reservation Centre, Enterprise Hse., Channel View Rd Dover, CT17 9TJ, Kent, ☎ (0304) 223000 Reservations : ☎ 203388, Telex 965104, Reservations : 96200.

Continental Ferry Port, Mile End, Portsmouth Hants, ☎ (0705) 827677 and 755521.

European House, The Docks, Felixstowe, IP11 8TB, Suffolk, ☎ (0394) 604802.

Cairnryan, Stranraer, Wigtownshire, Scotland, ☎ (058 12) 276 and 277.

Larne Harbour, Larne, Co. Antrim, Northern Ireland, ☎ (0574) 74321, Telex 74528.

Car Ferry Terminal, Doverlaan 7, B-8380 Zeebrugge, Belgium, ☎ (050) 54.50.50, Telex 81306.

Terminal Car Ferry, 62226 Calais Cedex, France, ☎ 21 97 21 21, Telex 120878.

9 Place de la Madeleine, 75008 Paris, France, ☎ 42 66 40 17, Telex 210679.

Gare Maritime, 50101 Cherbourg, France, ☎ 33 44 20 13, Telex 1707656.

Quai de Southampton, 76600 Le Havre, France, ☎ 35 21 36 50, Telex 190757.

Leidsestraat 32, Amsterdam, Netherlands, ☎ (020) 223832, Telex 14601.

VEDETTES ARMORICAINES

Gare Maritime de la Bourse, B.P. 180, 35049 St-Malo, France, ☎ 99 56 48 88, T NAVIPAX.

Agents : Vedettes Armoricaines, Albert Pier, St. Helier, Jersey, ☎ 20361, Telex 4192131 NAVIEX.

Boutins Travel Bureau, Library Pl., St. Helier, Jersey, ☎ 21532/3/4, Telex 4192149.

12 rue Georges-Clemenceau, B.P. 24, 50400 Granville, France, ☎ 33 50 77 45, Telex 170449 F.

VEDETTES BLANCHES

Les Vedettes Blanches, Gare Maritime, 35400 St-Malo, France, ☎ 99

Agent : Vedettes Blanches, 17 Seaton Pl., St. Helier, Jersey 4192311 EMFJER.

VEDETTES VERTES GRANVILLAISES

1-3 rue Le Campion, 50400 Granville, France, ☎ 33 50 16 36, Tel

Agent : Marine Management Ltd., Albert Quay, St. Helier 4192311 SEACAR.

WESTERN FERRIES (ARGYLL) LTD.

16 Woodside Crescent, Glasgow, Scotland, G3 7UT, ☎ BUILT.

Agent : Hunters Quay, Dunoon, Argyll, Scotland, ☎ (

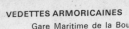

MAIN ROAD MAP

Great Britain
Ireland

Grande-Bretagne
Irlande

1 in : 16 miles – 1/1 000 000

MICHELIN

PNEU MICHELIN, 46, Av. de Breteuil 75341 PARIS CEDEX 07

MANUFACTURE FRANÇAISE DES PNEUMATIQ

Société en commandite par actions au capital de 700 000 000 de
Place des Carmes-Déchaux - 63 Clermont-Ferrand (France)
R.C.S. Clermont-Fd B 855 200 507
© Michelin et Cie, Propriétaires-Éditeurs 1987
Dépôt légal 2-87 — ISBN 2.06.006.577-1

Printed in France – 12-86-72

Photocomposition : S.C.I.A., La Chapelle d'Armentières - Impression : TARDY QUERCY, Bourges n° 13312